UNIVERSITY CASEBOOK SERIES

EDITORIAL BOARD

ROBERT C. CLARK
DIRECTING EDITOR
Distinguished Service Professor and Austin Wakeman Scott
Professor of Law and Former Dean of the Law School
Harvard University

DANIEL A. FARBER
Sho Sato Professor of Law and Director, Environmental Law Program
University of California at Berkeley

SAMUEL ISSACHAROFF
Bonnie and Richard Reiss Professor of Constitutional Law
New York University

HERMA HILL KAY
Barbara Nachtrieb Armstrong Professor of Law and
Former Dean of the School of Law
University of California at Berkeley

SAUL LEVMORE
William B. Graham Distinguished Service Professor of Law and
Former Dean of the Law School
University of Chicago

THOMAS W. MERRILL
Charles Evans Hughes Professor of Law
Columbia University

ROBERT L. RABIN
A. Calder Mackay Professor of Law
Stanford University

CAROL M. ROSE
Gordon Bradford Tweedy Professor Emeritus of Law and Organization
and Professorial Lecturer in Law
Yale University
Lohse Chair in Water and Natural Resources
University of Arizona

CASES AND MATERIALS

FUNDAMENTALS OF CORPORATE TAXATION

EIGHTH EDITION

by

STEPHEN SCHWARZ
Professor of Law Emeritus
University of California, Hastings College of the Law

DANIEL J. LATHROPE
Distinguished E.L. Professor of Law
University of San Francisco School of Law

FOUNDATION PRESS
2012

THOMSON REUTERS™

This publication was created to provide you with accurate and authoritative information concerning the subject matter covered; however, this publication was not necessarily prepared by persons licensed to practice law in a particular jurisdiction. The publisher is not engaged in rendering legal or other professional advice and this publication is not a substitute for the advice of an attorney. If you require legal or other expert advice, you should seek the services of a competent attorney or other professional.

Nothing contained herein is intended or written to be used for the purposes of 1) avoiding penalties imposed under the federal Internal Revenue Code, or 2) promoting, marketing or recommending to another party any transaction or matter addressed herein.

© 1985, 1987, 1991, 1997, 2002 FOUNDATION PRESS
© 2005, 2008 By THOMSON REUTERS/FOUNDATION PRESS
© 2012 By THOMSON REUTERS/FOUNDATION PRESS

     1 New York Plaza, 34th Floor
     New York, NY 10004
     Phone Toll Free 1–877–888–1330
     Fax 646–424–5201
     foundation–press.com
Printed in the United States of America

ISBN 978–1–60930–068–5

Mat #41188379

To our families

PREFACE

The useful life of this new edition of *Fundamentals of Corporate Taxation* will include its 30th anniversary. The unrelenting pace of change during these three decades has contributed to the reputation of tax textbooks as one of the world's most perishable commodities. This became clear shortly after publication of the First Edition when enactment of the Tax Reform Act of 1986 profoundly affected the tax planning agenda for C corporations and their shareholders. Since then, we have seen frequent changes in the individual tax rates, massive regulations projects, periodic tinkering with a patchwork quilt of anti-abuse provisions, an assault on corporate tax shelters, and gradual widening of the eligibility gates for S corporations. The scope and complexity of all these developments have validated our mission way back when to craft a rich mix of materials to help students learn the "fundamentals" of corporate tax, which has long been regarded as one of the most demanding courses in the law school curriculum.

The constant barrage of legislation and regulations, followed by a more recent quiet period of political gridlock and the accompanying uncertainty about tax rates and prospects for "reform," present a continuing challenge to teachers, students and casebook authors. Throughout all the twists and turns, we have strived to provide a teaching text, not a treatise, that is adaptable to different levels of coverage and up-to-date. Although more detail has become unavoidable with each new edition, we once again pause at the outset to remind ourselves and others of the importance of teaching the "fundamentals" of corporate tax by the problem method. As we said in the Preface to the First Edition:

> * * * [I]n our collective experience, we have been troubled by a common denominator in the many fine corporate tax casebooks and texts: their sheer bulk. In this book and a previously published companion volume, Fundamentals of Partnership Taxation, we attempt to chart a different course by bringing the "fundamentals" philosophy to the teaching of taxation of the business enterprise. * * * [T]he fundamentals approach involves selectivity of subject matter, emphasis on basic concepts, avoidance of esoteric detail and realistic depth of coverage. To those ends, this volume is the product of self restraint—although perhaps not enough. At times, we opted for over inclusion to accommodate the varied teaching biases and favorite cases and topics of experienced instructors (including ourselves). We have continued, however, to select and edit cases with care. Lengthy citations, obscure questions and meanderings into minutia have been avoided. Throughout the book, we have made an effort to remember what it was like when we studied corporate tax; this volume is designed as a

teaching book, not the definitive treatise. And so, of course, we expect students to do the reading!

We also believe that the most effective way to teach and learn tax fundamentals is by the problem method. This book thus contains a comprehensive yet manageable set of problems to accompany every major topic. The problems are designed to help students decipher the statute and apply it in a wide variety of alternative fact situations. Some are "building block" problems with specific answers. We are mindful, however, of the tendency to become preoccupied with technical trivia and have also included some more sophisticated (and realistic) problems with a planning orientation.

The primary sources in any tax course are the Code and Regulations. But the statute frequently is unintelligible when read out of context. To provide a foundation of understanding, this book includes extensive explanatory text to accompany the problems and a selection of cases, rulings, legislative history and other materials. The goal of the text is not merely to paraphrase the Code. In addition to describing the *workings* of the statute, we have attempted to explain *why* it works the way it does. If presented as a purely mechanical exercise, the problem method can degenerate into a mindless series of computations, leaving one without insights into the function of the statute, the relationship between sections and the broad principles governing the taxation of corporations and shareholders. By first explaining the "why" as well as the "how," we hope that even the computational problems will serve as launching pads for the discussion of more important policy and planning issues.

This edition incorporates a number of developments occurring over the past four years, including codification of the economic substance doctrine, significant new final and proposed regulations affecting reorganizations and corporate divisions, and the continuing policy debate about reform of the corporate income tax. And this edition is more than just an update. Concerned that each new detail and the authors' voracious appetites were causing the book to gain too much weight, we revisited each chapter with the goal of clearing out unnecessary clutter. To that end, some cases and notes were edited, and dated or redundant materials were removed, giving us room to add a few new problems. Although the Eighth Edition still may have too much detail for some (and not enough for others), we are pleased to report that it is 23 pages shorter than its predecessor–no small feat considering the long-winded proclivities of the legal and academic professions.

Turning to organization and emphasis, the Eighth Edition retains the pedagogically proven "cradle to grave" organization. Chapter 1 provides an introduction to business enterprise taxation, offering perspective on the influential policies that have shaped Subchapter C and analyzing the impact of changes occurring over the past several decades. Chapter 1 also surveys the corporate regular and alternative minimum taxes and highlights (with some new excerpts) contemporary policy issues, including proposals to "integrate" the corporate and individual income taxes or reform the corporate income tax. It also anticipates, as do later chapters, how the tax stakes would be affected if rates should change in the future, as they are scheduled to do in 2013.

Chapters 2 and 3, which examine corporate formations and capital structure, set the stage for a study of Subchapter C's double tax regime and the bias in favor of debt that has helped taxpayers avoid its full impact. Chapter 3 includes updated coverage of hybrid instruments and adds a more recent case illustrating how courts deal with the distinction between debt and equity.

Chapters 4 through 6 cover operating distributions, stock redemptions, and stock dividends (including Section 306 stock). For a brief time after passage of the Tax Reform Act of 1986, these chapters lost much of their vitality because ordinary income and capital gains were taxed at the same rate. Then, as many predicted, a meaningful capital gains rate preference was restored, breathing new life into these operational chapters and validating our decision to retain textual discussion and problems even when the stakes were low. And then with the decision—not yet permanent—to tax qualified dividends and long-term capital gains at the same reduced rate, it was deja vu all over again. The historical agenda was to avoid dividend treatment and "bail out" corporate earnings at capital gains rates, but since 2003 the major advantage of a capital gains bailout is recovery of basis. As we await the fate of the "Bush tax cuts" and the outcome, if any, of the long-promised "fundamental tax reform" (and the 2012 elections), this is yet another "transitional" edition that does its best to discuss the planning implications in the midst of the current unstable landscape. As a hedge, some traditional materials have been retained, just in case Congress leads us back to earlier times. It will be up to instructors to decide how much emphasis to give to characterization issues in view of the altered stakes in corporate-shareholder transactions.

Complete liquidations and taxable acquisitions are addressed in Chapters 7 and 8. The discussion of taxable stock acquisitions offers selective coverage of Section 338 without getting too bogged down in arcane minutia. Chapters 9 through 12 cover the still vibrant topics of tax-free reorganizations and divisions, including the rules and limitations affecting carryovers of corporate tax attributes. These materials incorporate recent regulations projects on a variety of topics. Chapter 9 has been revised to include a more efficient set of problems on acquisitive reorganizations to illustrate the doctrinal rules in a transactional setting that we hope will be more interesting to students and teachers. With this edition, the carryover rules and limitations are now joined in one chapter.

Chapter 13, covering affiliated corporations, was extensively updated and revised in an earlier edition. Many instructors will not have time to cover this material. For those who wish students to achieve literacy, not mastery, this chapter offers what we hope is a coherent primer on the intricacies of multiple tax benefits, Section 482 allocations, and consolidated groups.

Chapter 14, which is devoted to anti-abuse rules, begins with a new section on codification of the economic substance doctrine, including a short problem. Some instructors may prefer to assign this material earlier, and it is designed as a self-standing overview for those who do. The remainder of the chapter examines the accumulated earnings and personal holding company penalty taxes. These taxes were not repealed, but their significance is diminished almost to the vanishing point whenever most dividends and long-term capital gains are taxed at the same rate. Although these materials remain intact and ready to spring back into action at a moment's notice (and that may be necessary in 2013), they have become more of a historical relic under the rate regime in effect through the end of 2012 and are not worthy of extensive coverage except in tax history seminars.

Part Three (Chapter 15) is devoted to S corporations, which remain a popular alternative for businesses whose structure can accommodate to a simpler pass-through taxing regime. Similar surveys of Subchapter S are included in our companion volume, *Fundamentals of Partnership Taxation*, and in *Fundamentals of Business Enterprise Taxation*, an alternative text for a combined course on corporate and partnership tax. Tax professors continue to debate whether S corporations are best covered in corporate tax, a course on pass-through entities, or a combined business enterprise taxation course offering. Our books accommodate any of these approaches.

Turning to matters of style, we assume that the text will be assigned with the most recent edition of the Code and Regulations. Suggested assignments to these sources are provided for each topic. Instructors should review these assignments carefully, editing when necessary to ensure that they are consistent with the desired coverage. Deletions from cases and other authorities have been made freely, with asterisks used to denote substantive omissions, but citations and internal cross references in excerpted materials have been deleted without so indicating. Editorial additions are in brackets. Footnotes to the original text are numbered consecutively within each section, and many footnotes have been deleted from cases without renumbering those that remain. The text is current through April 1, 2012.

The authors extend special thanks to Professor Bruce McGovern for his constructive suggestions and invaluable assistance in updating several chapters on an earlier edition when he was an LL.M student at the University of Florida College of Law. We remain indebted to many former students who assisted on prior editions, particularly: Ted Brooks, Mitch Salamon, Ray Kawasaki, Terri Murray, Jim Potratz, Jeff Anthony, Garo Kalfayan, Steve Vogelsang, Julie Divola, Joe Bartlett, Marilyn Cleveland, Chris Detzel, and Jeffrey Essner.

SUMMARY OF CONTENTS

TABLE OF CONTENTS

TABLE OF INTERNAL REVENUE CODE SECTIONS

TABLE OF TREASURY REGULATIONS

TABLE OF REVENUE RULINGS

TABLE OF MISCELLANEOUS RULINGS

TABLE OF CASES

Principal cases are in bold type. Non-principal cases are in roman type. References are to Pages.

TABLE OF AUTHORITIES

CASES AND MATERIALS

FUNDAMENTALS OF CORPORATE TAXATION

PART ONE

INTRODUCTION

CHAPTER 1

An Overview of the Taxation of Corporations and Shareholders

A. Introduction

1. Taxation of Business Entities

Since the time when the British Crown begrudgingly recognized collective profit-seeking enterprises, the artificial legal entity known as the "corporation" has served as a principal vehicle for conducting business in a capitalist economic system. Legal advisors to the earliest American corporations spent much of their time defining the relationship between the corporation and the state and developing hoary doctrines to regulate corporate governance and control. It was not until late in the 19th century that the genteel world of corporate law was jolted by the emergence of the income tax as a principal government revenue raising device. The life of the corporate lawyer would never be the same again. From the ill-fated Income Tax of 1894, which at the time was viewed as a Socialist plot because it imposed a two percent tax on individual and corporate net income,[1] to the Payne–Aldrich Tariff Act of 1909, which imposed a modest one percent tax on corporate net income over $5,000,[2] to the Sixteenth Amendment and beyond, the income tax gradually came to influence how corporations conducted their affairs. It is now well acknowledged, though often lamented, that taxes have invaded virtually every aspect of American business life. They shape and often twist management decisions and generally are an unpleasant distraction to those who would prefer to devote their full resources to the pursuit of profit.

The decision to superimpose an income tax on a system that recognized artificial entities as separate from their owners raised a fundamental structural question. The dilemma confronting the architects of the federal income tax was whether to treat corporations, partnerships, trusts and other vehicles for conducting business as separate taxable entities or as an aggregate of the underlying owners.

Since the earliest income tax acts, a corporation has been treated as a distinct taxable entity, separate and apart from its shareholders. Once that policy decision was made, a host of additional questions followed. What

---

1. See Bittker & Lokken, Federal Income Taxation of Income, Estates and Gifts ¶ 1.1.2; see also Pollock v. Farmers' Loan & Trust Co., 157 U.S. 429, 15 S.Ct. 673 (1895).

2. See Bittker & Eustice, Federal Income Taxation of Corporations and Shareholders ¶ 1.01.

rates should be applied to corporate income? Should they resemble the graduated rates applicable to individuals or is a flat rate more appropriate? How should the tax system treat transactions between a corporation and its shareholders? If a corporation already has been taxed on its earnings, should those earnings be taxed again when they are distributed to the shareholders? If so, is it appropriate to give the corporation a deduction for the amount of the distribution? In short, must corporate income be taxed twice—once when earned by the corporation and again, after distribution to the shareholders?[3]

The answers will unfold throughout this text. But it serves no purpose to hide the ball on the most fundamental question. Congress, having decided to treat the corporation as a separate taxpaying entity, went on to craft a double tax regime. A tax is imposed annually, at the rates set forth in Section 11, on the taxable income of a corporation. That income is taxed again when a corporation distributes dividends to its shareholders. Those dividends are not deductible by the distributing corporation but are taxed to its shareholders at rates that vary depending on whether the shareholder is an individual, a corporation, or a tax-exempt entity such as a charity or retirement fund.[4] Because the corporation is treated as a separate taxable entity, transactions between corporations and their shareholders are taxable events. The tax consequences of these transactions and other major changes and adjustments in a corporation are governed by Subchapter C (Sections 301 to 385) of the Internal Revenue Code of 1986, a challenging and fascinating body of law that is the principal subject of this book. Corporations subject to the double tax regime also draw their identity (and monogram) from Subchapter C. Collectively, the Code refers to them as "C corporations."[5]

Congress made a markedly different policy decision in the case of partnerships, which are treated by Subchapter K of the Code as pass-through entities that do not pay federal income tax. Instead, partners include their respective shares of partnership income, deductions, losses and other items when determining their tax liability.[6] Ongoing adjustments to the basis of a partner's interest in the partnership ensure that income and losses are not taxed (or deducted) twice.[7] Partnerships are treated as entities, however, for purposes of selecting a taxable year, computing and characterizing partnership income, filing information returns, making elections, undergoing audits by the Internal Revenue Service and in several substantive contexts, such as formation and termination, transactions between partners and partnerships, and sales of partnership interests.[8] The

---

3. See, e.g., McLure, Must Corporate Income Be Taxed Twice? (1979).

4. Until 2013, dividends received by noncorporate shareholders are taxed at the same preferential rates as long-term capital gains. I.R.C. § 1(h)(11). For corporate shareholders, some relief from a potential triple tax is provided by a 70, 80 or 100 percent dividends received deduction under Section 243. See Section B1 of this chapter, infra.

Tax-exempt shareholders are generally not taxed on dividends they receive.

5. I.R.C. § 1361(a)(2).

6. I.R.C. § 701.

7. I.R.C. § 705.

8. I.R.C. §§ 721; 707; 741. See generally, Schwarz & Lathrope, Cases and Materials on Fundamentals of Partnership Taxation (9th ed. 2012).

principal features of a pass-through tax regime are: (1) income generated by the business is taxed only once to the beneficial owners of the enterprise, whether or not they receive current distributions, and (2) losses pass through to the owners and, subject to various timing limitations,[9] may be deducted against income from other sources. More recently, the tax benefits of the partnership pass-through system have been extended to limited liability companies, an increasingly popular form of legal entity.[10]

The double tax regime generally applicable to corporations and the pass-through system governing partnerships and limited liability companies represent the Code's two fundamental alternatives for taxing business enterprises. To level the playing field and respond to the special problems of unique industries, Congress occasionally has deviated from these two basic models. Thus, to minimize the role of taxes on the choice of form for smaller businesses, some closely held corporations may elect under Subchapter S to be treated as conduits if they satisfy a strict set of eligibility requirements.[11] Conversely, to preclude widely held businesses from disincorporating to escape the double tax regime of Subchapter C, most "publicly traded" partnerships are treated as corporations for tax purposes.[12] Other types of hybrid entities qualify for pass-through treatment if they satisfy requirements designed to limit the nature of their business operations,[13] and corporations in certain discrete industries are governed by specialized taxing regimes.[14] Despite these departures from the norm, the central question remains—shall business profits be subjected to one or two levels of tax? The debate on this question continues to rage and will arise repeatedly throughout the text.

2.   INFLUENTIAL POLICIES

Four broad tax policy decisions have shaped the development of Subchapter C and contributed to its corpulent physique. The interrelationship of these policies influences taxpayer behavior regarding the type of entity in which to conduct a business enterprise, capital structure and financing of corporate activities, dividend and compensation policy, estate planning and a myriad of other tax and business planning decisions. During the recent past, the policies underlying Subchapter C have been in a state of disequilibrium as Congress periodically tinkers with the tax rates as part of the highly politicized tax legislative process. An overview of the past and

---

9. See I.R.C. §§ 704(d); 465; 469.

10. See Section C2b of this chapter, infra.

11. These are known as "S corporations." I.R.C. § 1361(a)(1). The Code imposes no limit on the value of an S corporation, but eligibility for Subchapter S status is restricted to corporations having not more than 100 shareholders or more than one class of stock. See Section 1B4 of this chapter and Chapter 15, infra.

12. See I.R.C. § 7704 and Section C2b of this chapter, infra.

13. See e.g., Subchapter M, governing regulated investment companies (mutual funds) and real estate investment trusts.

14. See, e.g., Subchapter L (Insurance Companies), Subchapter H (banks and trust companies), and Subchapter F (tax-exempt organizations and cooperatives).

current synergy of these influential policies and how they affect choice of business entity decisions is appropriate before moving on.

The Double Tax. The concept at the heart of Subchapter C is the double taxation of corporate income. In many situations, of course, the double tax is more theoretical than real. Corporations have been adept at minimizing their taxable income by taking advantage of self-help strategies to be revealed later in the text and by utilizing numerous tax preferences scattered throughout the Code to provide an incentive for various activities. Many large publicly traded corporations are taxed at effective rates well below the statutory maximum, and many large shareholders, such as wealthy charities and qualified retirement funds, do not pay taxes on the dividends they receive.

The decision to treat corporations as separate taxable entities, distinct from their shareholders, is controversial.[1] Some of the debate is about the incidence of the corporate tax—whether it is borne by shareholders, employees, corporate managers, consumers of the company's goods and services, or investors in general.[2] Critics also point to the adverse impact of the tax on the allocation of economic resources; its complexity; the disadvantages it places on U.S. companies in the global economy; and many other evils, including three distinct biases: (1) against corporate as opposed to noncorporate investment (because only corporate capital is subject to a second tax); (2) in favor of debt financing for businesses organized as C corporations (because corporations can deduct the interest they pay on debt but not dividends to holders of equity capital); and (3) in favor of retention of earnings at the corporate level as opposed to distribution of dividends.[3]

If a double tax is accepted as the appropriate corporate taxing model, the discussion then turns to the "integrity" of the corporate-level tax. For example, should the corporate income tax apply not only to operating profits but also to distributions of appreciated property and sales in connection with corporate liquidations? The outcome of this controversy will unfold as these and other transactions are studied later in this text. For now, it is sufficient to observe that the defenders of the corporate income tax largely prevailed on these questions. The results were a

---

1. See generally Shaviro, Decoding the Corporate Tax (2009).

2. See, e.g., Harberger, "The Incidence of the Corporation Income tax," 70 J.Pol.Econ. 215 (1962); Klein, "The Incidence of the Corporation Income Tax: A Lawyer's View of a Problem in Economics," 65 Wisc.L. Rev. 576 (1965). Many economists have given up on this question, concluding that they are unable to ascertain who bears the burden of the corporate tax. See generally Break, "The Incidence and Economic Effects of Taxation," in The Economics of Public Finance (Brookings 1974).

3. See generally American Law Institute, Federal Income Tax Project—Subchapter C 341–355 (1982). Commentators also point to the "compensating biases" in the individual income tax, such as the rate structure, preferential capital gains rates, and the ability of individuals to obtain a stepped-up basis in appreciated property acquired from a decedent. See Zolt, "Corporate Tax After the Tax Reform Act of 1986: A State of Disequilibrium," 66 N.C.L. Rev. 839 (1988).

strengthened double tax regime, an increase in the tax costs of operating a profitable business as a C corporation, and greater pressure on techniques to reduce these costs. More recently, the pendulum has shifted in the other direction, most notably with the reduction in the tax rate on dividends that has been in effect since 2003 but is scheduled to expire at the end of 2012.[4] The enactment of various business tax incentives to stimulate economic growth, some of which are temporary, also has softened the impact of the corporate income tax for those industries targeted for tax relief.[5]

The desire to avoid the double tax on corporate profits while obtaining limited liability for all the owners of a business has fueled the emergence of new legal forms, such as the limited liability company. Entities similar to the LLC have long been used in other countries. Examples include the Latin American *limitada* and the German *Gesellschaft mit beschrankter Haftung* ("GmbH").[6] The origins of the LLC in the United States can be traced to the search by foreign investors in the oil and gas industry for a U.S. business entity that would combine limited liability protection for all owners with one level of taxation. Because nonresident aliens may not own stock in an S corporation, the investors' objectives could not be met using the corporate form. So they began lobbying state legislatures, and by the late 1970's Wyoming had enacted the first domestic limited liability company statute.[7] LLCs were not practically viable, however, until the Internal Revenue Service ruled, first privately and then in a 1989 published ruling, that a Wyoming LLC would be treated as a partnership rather than a corporation for tax purposes.[8]

The explosive growth of the LLC as a "best of all worlds" legal form breathed new life into the business enterprise tax policy debate. Consider the following questions. Why does the Internal Revenue Code have two separate pass-through tax regimes for closely held business enterprises, one (Subchapter K) for partnerships and LLCs and the other (Subchapter S) for certain corporations, each with different qualification standards and operative provisions?[9] If a single pass-through regime were adopted, would Subchapter K be preferable to Subchapter S, or would some combination of the two be the best approach?[10] Why are C corporations singled out for a

---

4. Beginning in 2003 and continuing at least through 2012, most dividends received by noncorporate shareholders are taxed at the same 15 maximum rate as long-term capital gains. I.R.C. § 1(h)(11)(A). See Chapter 4A2, infra.

5. See, e.g., I.R.C. § 199, providing a special tax deduction for income attributable to domestic production activities.

6. See Carney, "Limited Liability Companies: Origins and Antecedents," 66 U.Colo. L.Rev. 855 (1995).

7. See Hamill, "The Limited Liability Company: A Catalyst Exposing The Corporate Integration Question," 95 Mich. L. Rev. 393, 399 (1996), for a history of LLC's rise

from obscurity to its current position as a mainstream form of business entity.

8. Rev. Rul. 88–76, 1988–2 C.B. 360. See Section C1 of this chapter, infra.

9. See Lokken, "Taxation of Private Business Firms: Imagining a Future Without Subchapter K," 4 Fla. Tax Rev. 249 (1999); Schwidetzky, "Is it Time to Give the S Corporation a Proper Burial?", 15 Va. Tax Rev. 591 (1996); Rands, "Passthrough Entities and Their Unprincipled Differences Under Federal Tax Law," 49 SMU L. Rev. 15 (1995).

10. See Eustice, "Subchapter S Corporations and Partnerships: A Search for the Passthrough Paradigm," 39 Tax L. Rev. 345

double tax regime? Is it because they enjoy limited liability under state law? Presumably not, because LLCs are not subject to Subchapter C. Does the rise of the LLC undermine the policy underlying the double tax and threaten to destroy the corporate tax base? Would it make more sense to limit Subchapter C to large corporations (based on revenues) or publicly traded entities? Or should there be a single one-tier tax regime for all business income without regard to the organizational form?[11] The remaining chapters provide an opportunity to reconsider these issues as you study the Code's two corporate tax regimes in greater depth.

Tax Rates on Ordinary Income: Corporate and Individual. For C corporations with significant taxable income, the corporate income tax is essentially a 34 or 35 percent flat rate tax with no preferential rate for long-term capital gains.[12] Corporations with smaller amounts of income, however, can take advantage of lower rates (15 and 25 percent) on their first $75,000 of taxable income.[13] Individuals pay tax at graduated rates beginning at 10 percent of taxable income and peaking at a nominal rate of 35 percent.[14] And profits of C corporations are potentially taxed both at the corporate and shareholder levels when they are distributed as dividends or when the shareholders sell their stock.

As this book went to press in early 2012, federal income tax rates were in flux, with deficit reduction and tax reform high on the political agenda but trapped in partisan gridlock. For 2012, the top individual rate is 35 percent but it is scheduled to increase to 39.6 percent in 2013 unless Congress and the President agree to extend what have become known as the Bush tax cuts. For some high-income taxpayers, the marginal rate in 2013 may be even higher if, as also scheduled, the disallowance of some itemized deductions and phase-out of personal exemptions are restored.[15] The outlook for dividends and capital gains also is uncertain. Beginning in 2003 and continuing at least until the end of 2012, most dividends received by noncorporate shareholders were taxed at the same preferential 15 percent rate as long-term capital gains.[16] In 2013, the generally applicable capital gains rate is set to increase to 20 percent, dividends once again will be taxed as ordinary income, and a new 3.8 percent Medicare contributions tax on unearned income of high-income taxpayers takes effect. Other variables that may affect the overall tax burden include the corporate and individual alternative minimum taxes; proposals targeted to raises taxes on "high income" taxpayers; a long list of corporate tax benefits, ranging from

(1989); August, "Benefits and Burdens of Subchapter S in a Check-the-Box World," 4 Fla. Tax Rev. 287 (1999).

11. See, e.g., Yin, "The Future Taxation of Private Business Firms," 4 Fla. Tax Rev. 141 (1999); Klein & Zolt, "Business Form, Limited Liability, and Tax Regimes: Lurching Toward a Coherent Outcome," 66 Colo.L.Rev. 1001 (1995).

12. I.R.C. §§ 11; 1201(a).

13. I.R.C. 11(b). Certain corporations with major shareholders who render personal services, such as professional corporations of lawyers, accountants, architects, and the like, are not entitled to the lower marginal corporate rates. I.R.C. §§ 11(b)(2); 448(d)(2).

14. I.R.C. § 1.

15. See I.R.C. §§ 68, 151(d)(3).

16. I.R.C. § 1(h)(11).

accelerated depreciation to targeted subsidies for particular industries, that lower the effective corporate tax rate; employment taxes imposed on owners who also perform services for the business; and the impact of state and local taxes.

The relationships among the tax rates also have been influential, particularly on the choice of legal entity in which to conduct a business or investment activity. At one time, when the maximum individual tax rate on ordinary income peaked at 70 percent or higher and the top corporate rate was 46 percent, C corporations served as an attractive refuge from the steeper individual rates. This rate differential prompted privately held firms to conduct their business and investment activities as C corporations rather than pass-through entities, such as partnerships, because their income was taxed at lower rates and could remain in corporate solution to compound at tax-preferred rates until the business was sold or liquidated. In the meantime, shareholders who wished to withdraw earnings utilized tax efficient strategies to avoid the sting of the double tax. For example, owner-employees of a C corporation typically have distributed profits in the form of salary and fringe benefits that are tax-deductible by the corporation and, in the case of many fringe benefits, excludable by the owner-employee. Shareholders also can loan funds or lease property to a C corporation and withdraw earnings in the form of tax-deductible interest or rent. For many C corporations engaged in active business activities, these traditional strategies to mitigate the impact of the double tax have withstood the test of time. The most recent data indicates that in 2008, nearly 53 percent of all C corporations filing returns reported no taxable income, and only 30 percent of C corporations had any corporate tax liability after tax credits were taken into account.[17]

To be sure, the Service had weapons to combat the self-help tax strategies. Payments of salary or interest could be attacked as unreasonable compensation or disguised dividends but usually these arguments were reserved for the most egregious cases. Congress also enacted penalty taxes to patrol against excessive accumulations or avoidance of the individual progressive rates.[18] With foresight and good planning, however, an active business that paid reasonable compensation and justified any accumulations of earnings on the basis of reasonable business judgment could avoid constructive dividends and the corporate penalty taxes with relative ease.

Along with the tax rates, several other key policy variables have influenced taxpayer behavior. When individuals and C corporations are subject to the same top rate and dividends and long-term capital gains are both taxed at relatively low rates, the incentive for C corporations to accumulate rather than distribute earnings is much less compelling than when corporations enjoyed a significant tax rate advantage over individuals. This rate parity, together with the prospect of two levels of tax when a

17. Statistics of Income—2008, Returns of Active Corporations, Other than Forms 1120S, 1120–REIT, and 1120–RIC, Table 22.

18. See I.R.C. § 531 et seq. (accumulated earnings tax); § 541 (personal holding company tax).

C corporation is sold, provides a greater incentive to use a pass-through entity instead of a C corporation, particularly if the business intends to distribute its earnings currently, does not have owners who work for the firm, or holds assets that are likely to appreciate in value over a relatively short time horizon. It would be rare, for example, for a venture investing in real estate or financial assets for current income or capital appreciation (or both) to operate as a C corporation because the costs of doing so would be prohibitive in light of the double tax. In some cases, however, C corporations still offer tax savings, especially for businesses able to pay out most of their earnings as compensation to their high-income owners.

Preferential Capital Gains Rates. The policy decision to tax long-term capital gains at substantially lower rates than ordinary income is another feature of the tax system that historically eased the tax burden of conducting a business as a C corporation. Rather than paying dividends, tax advisors devised techniques to "bail out" earnings at capital gains rates. A "bailout" is a distribution of earnings in a transaction, such as a redemption of stock, that qualifies as a "sale or exchange," enabling the shareholder to recover all or part of her stock basis and to benefit from preferential capital gain treatment on any realized gain. In some cases, such as where the shareholder has died and the basis of her stock has been stepped up to its date-of-death value, the bailout may be accomplished tax-free.[19] Over the years, Congress responded with complex anti-bailout provisions to ensure that distributions resembling dividends would be taxed as ordinary income.[20]

When dividends and capital gains are taxed at the same preferential rates, the traditional incentive for a bailout just about disappears. Under that type of rate structure, the tax goal of a bailout would not be to convert dividend income to capital gain but rather to enable shareholders to recover all or part of the basis in their stock. But if capital gains are taxed at a much lower rate than dividends, as could happen beginning in 2013, a bailout would reassume its role as a strategy to reduce the double tax on C corporations and their shareholders and make many of the topics covered in this course much more compelling.

Nonrecognition. Under the realization principle, gains and losses are not taxable until they are realized in a sale, exchange or other event that makes the gain or loss "real" and more easily measurable. The nonrecognition concept assumes that certain realization events should not be impeded by the imposition of a tax. Transactions that qualify for nonrecognition treatment may go forward on a tax-free basis on the theory that they are mere changes in form which result in a continuity of investment. To ensure that any realized gain or loss is merely deferred rather than eliminated, the typical nonrecognition provision includes corollary rules providing for transferred and exchanged bases and tacked holding periods.[21] The nonrec-

---

19. See I.R.C. § 1014.

20. See, e.g., I.R.C. §§ 302; 304; 306.

21. See, e.g., I.R.C. § 1031, which provides for nonrecognition on certain like-kind exchanges.

ognition principle pervades Subchapter C, affecting transactions ranging from the simple corporate formation to complex mergers and acquisitions.

The opportunity to qualify a corporate transaction for nonrecognition has assumed even greater importance with the strengthening of the corporate tax. A corporation must pay tax on the appreciation in its assets on a sale or distribution in connection with a complete liquidation.[22] Standing in sharp contrast are acquisitions known as tax-free reorganizations, which ordinarily are free of tax to all the parties, albeit with the trade-off of transferred bases and a carryover of other tax attributes. Taxpayers are thus encouraged to structure sales of a corporate business to come within an applicable nonrecognition provision in order to avoid (or at least defer) tax at the corporate and shareholder levels.

Perspective. In the first edition of this book, published in 1985, we observed that "[t]he corporate tax system previewed here is not engraved in stone," and predicted that "change is in the air, and tax lawyers and students must be prepared, often at a moment's notice, to discard old concepts and master new ones."[23] Before the ink was dry, Congress enacted the historic Tax Reform Act of 1986. Subsequent developments, most recently the significant (but still not permanent) rate reduction for qualified dividends, have contributed to an unstable tax environment—and frequent revisions of tax textbooks.

And so, once again, as in every prior edition, we ask—what of the future? In the previous edition, we observed that the spirited debate over Subchapter C appears to have subsided. That is no longer true. Corporate tax reform has returned to center stage to play a starring role in a vibrant tax policy debate, but the outcome is uncertain. As always, tax lawyers (and students) must be nimble and prepared, often with little notice, to discard (or relearn) old concepts and master new ones. Today's law may be tomorrow's history. To assist in that aspect of the learning process and provide perspective, policy materials have been interspersed throughout the text. Later in this chapter, for example, students are invited to consider the pros and cons of "integration" of the corporate and individual taxes and other corporate tax reform options.[24] Additional proposals emanating from Congress, the Treasury Department, the American Law Institute, and commentators are considered later in the text in connection with the specific issues and trouble spots to which they relate.

3.   THE COMMON LAW OF CORPORATE TAXATION

Although the study of corporate taxation principally involves the application of complex statutes to particular transactions, the Code is not the only analytical tool. In scrutinizing taxpayer behavior, the courts at an

---

22.   See Chapter 7B2, infra. Certain taxable acquisitions of stock will continue to trigger only shareholder-level gain but the bases of the acquired corporation's assets will transfer to the purchaser.

23.   Lind, Schwarz, Lathrope & Rosenberg, Cases and Materials on Fundamentals of Corporate Taxation 3–4 (1st ed. 1985).

24.   See Section E of this chapter, infra.

early date went beyond the literal statutory language and began to formulate a set of doctrines that have become the "common law" of federal taxation. Some of these principles, such as the assignment of income doctrine, were encountered in the basic income tax course. Unlike the Code, which often provides bright-line rules for solving problems, the judicial doctrines are imprecise. The very vagueness of these pronouncements, however, has contributed to their influence. When the system is working, they loom large in the tax advisor's conscience and serve to thwart aggressive schemes that literally comply with the statute but are incompatible with its intended purpose.[1] This introductory survey is intended to preview some of the reasoning that lies at the heart of this tax jurisprudence.

Viewed most broadly, the judicial doctrines ask a simple question that is central to almost every transaction studied in this text. Have the taxpayers actually done what they, and their documents, represent, or are the economic realities of the transaction—and the attendant tax consequences—other than what the taxpayers purport them to be? The tests used to resolve this question bear many labels which are often used interchangeably. What follows is a summary of the terminology that will soon become familiar.

Sham Transaction Doctrine. If a transaction is a "sham," it will not be respected for tax purposes. A "sham" is best defined as a transaction that never actually occurred but is represented by the taxpayer to have transpired—with favorable tax consequences of course.[2] One court has colorfully described a sham as an "attempt by a taxpayer to ward off tax blows with paper armor,"[3] in a purported transaction that "gives off an unmistakably hollow sound when it is tapped."[4]

Because a "sham" often connotes near fraudulent behavior, the courts tend to reserve this doctrine in its purest form for the more egregious cases. But the pejorative term also is used to describe the kinds of transactions that are challenged under the related economic substance doctrine. In one typically overlapping formulation, the Fourth Circuit articulated the following two-part test to define a sham:[5]

> To treat a transaction as a sham, the court must find that the taxpayer was motivated by no business purpose other than obtain-

1. See generally Bittker & Lokken, Federal Taxation of Income, Estates and Gifts ¶ 4.3.1.

2. See, e.g., Knetsch v. United States, 364 U.S. 361, 81 S.Ct. 132 (1960).

3. Waterman Steamship Corp. v. Commissioner, 430 F.2d 1185 (5th Cir.1970), cert. denied, 401 U.S. 939, 91 S.Ct. 936 (1971).

4. Id. at 1196, quoting United States v. General Geophysical Co., 296 F.2d 86, 89 (5th Cir.1961), cert. denied, 369 U.S. 849, 82 S.Ct. 932 (1962).

5. Rice's Toyota World, Inc. v. Commissioner, 752 F.2d 89, 91 (4th Cir.1985). See also Winn–Dixie Stores, Inc. v. Commissioner, 254 F.3d 1313 (11th Cir. 2001); Kirchman v. Commissioner, 862 F.2d 1486 (11th Cir. 1989). For cases where courts have declined to characterize a questionable transaction as a sham, see Compaq v. Commissioner, 277 F.3d 778 (5th Cir.2001); IES Industries, Inc. v. United States, 253 F.3d 350 (8th Cir.2001).

ing tax benefits in entering the transaction, and that the transaction has no economic substance because no reasonable possibility of a profit exists.

Economic Substance Doctrine. The economic substance doctrine is one of the IRS's principal weapons in its assault on abusive tax shelters. Its essence is that claimed tax benefits should be denied if the transactions that give rise to them lack economic substance apart from tax considerations even if the purported activity actually occurred. Most courts have been receptive to the doctrine, but they disagree over its proper formulation.[6] Some apply a conjunctive two-part test requiring a taxpayer first to establish the presence of economic substance (an objective inquiry) and then a business purpose (a subjective test).[7] Others use a narrower disjunctive approach that respects a transaction if it has either a business purpose or economic substance.[8] Still others treat economic substance and business purpose as "precise factors" to consider rather than a rigid test.[9] The courts also disagree regarding the type of non-tax economic benefit that a taxpayer must establish to demonstrate economic substance.[10]

After many years of controversy, Congress finally codified the economic substance doctrine to clarify how and when that doctrine should be applied and to sharpen its bite with a strict penalty regime.[11] This new and as yet untested statutory weapon, and the corporate tax shelters that prompted its enactment, are discussed in Chapter 14, along with several other corporate tax anti-avoidance rules.

Substance Over Form. The form of a transaction frequently is determinative of its tax consequences. Since the early days of the income tax, however, the courts have been willing to go beyond the formal papers and evaluate the "substance" of a transaction. A familiar example is the proper classification of a business arrangement as a sale or a lease.[12] The docu-

---

6. For a hostile view, see Coltec Industries v. United States, 62 Fed. Cl. 716, 752–756 (2004), where the court held that the economic substance doctrine was unconstitutional because it violated separation of powers principles. This outlier decision was reversed on appeal by the Federal Circuit, which described the trial court's decision as "untenable" and upheld the doctrine as a permissible tool of construction that allowed courts to look beyond the literal language of a statute if a strict construction would violate legislative intent. Coltec Industries v. United States, 454 F.3d 1340, 1352 (Fed. Cir. 2006), cert. denied, 549 U.S. 1206, 127 S.Ct. 1261 (2007).

7. See, e.g., Pasternak v. Commissioner, 990 F.2d 893, 898 (6th Cir. 1993).

8. Black & Decker Corp. v. United States, 436 F.3d 431 (4th Cir. 2006); Rice's Toyota World v. Commissioner, supra note 5.

9. See, e.g., ACM Partnership v. Commissioner, 157 F.3d 231 (3d Cir. 1998), cert. denied, 526 U.S. 1017, 119 S.Ct. 1251 (1999); Sacks v. Commissioner, 69 F.3d 982, 985 (9th Cir. 1995).

10. One widely used formulation requires an objective determination of whether a "reasonable possibility of profit" exists or, put differently, finds no economic substance if there is no reasonable expectation of a pretax profit for the transaction under scrutiny. See, e,g,. Dow Chemical Co. v. United States, 435 F.3d 594 (6th Cir. 2006); Rice's Toyota World v. Commissioner, supra note 5.

11. I.R.C. § 7701(*o*). See Chapter 14B, infra.

12. See, e.g., Frank Lyon Co. v. United States, 435 U.S. 561, 98 S.Ct. 1291 (1978).

ments used by the taxpayer may use one label, but the courts are not inhibited from examining the arrangement and restructuring it for tax purposes to comport with the economic realities.

The tension between form and substance will be evident throughout the chapters that follow. Is a corporate instrument "debt," as the taxpayer contends, or "equity," as the Service usually will assert? Is a payment to a shareholder-employee really "compensation" or is it a disguised dividend? Who, in substance, made a sale of corporate assets—the corporation or its shareholders? It is impossible to generalize as to when and how this doctrine will be applied. Individual cases turn on the particular facts and the court's attitude toward tax avoidance.

Despite the influence of this doctrine over time, some courts have shown reluctance to accept attempts by the Service to restructure legitimate transactions to reach a result that will produce more revenue. The Tax Court, for example, has been wary of extending the judicial doctrines where Congress has mandated that particular results shall flow from a given form and the taxpayers have carefully structured an otherwise legitimate transaction to comply with the statutory requirements.[13]

Business Purpose. The business purpose doctrine is conceptually linked to the sham and substance-versus-form tests. A transaction motivated by a business purpose usually is compared to one that has no substance, purpose or utility apart from tax avoidance. As originally formulated by Judge Learned Hand,[14] the business purpose doctrine was applied to deny tax-free status to a transaction that would not have been consummated but for the tax savings that would result if its form were respected. The doctrine took hold and has become an independent requirement for tax recognition of many transactions.[15]

Step Transaction Doctrine. When courts apply the step transaction doctrine, they combine (or "step") formally distinct transactions to determine the tax treatment of the single integrated series of events. The doctrine frequently is applied in conjunction with the other judicial tests.

The courts disagree on the standard to be employed in applying the step transaction doctrine. Some require a binding legal commitment to complete all the steps from the outset before combining them, while others require only a "mutual interdependence" of steps or a preconceived intent to reach a particular end result.[16]

---

13. See, e.g., Esmark, Inc. v. Commissioner, 90 T.C. 171 (1988), affirmed, 886 F.2d 1318 (7th Cir.1989). See also United Parcel Service of America, Inc. v. Commissioner, 254 F.3d 1014 (11th Cir.2001), rev'g 78 T.C.M. (CCH) 262 (1999).

14. See Helvering v. Gregory, 69 F.2d 809 (2d Cir.1934).

15. See, e.g., Reg. § 1.355–2(b), requiring a corporate business purpose to qualify as

a tax-free corporate division under Section 355; Reg. § 1.701–2(a), providing that business purpose is implicit in the intent of Subchapter K.

16. This doctrine is analyzed in some detail in connection with corporate liquidations and corporate reorganizations. See, e.g., Commissioner v. Court Holding Co., infra p. 324.

The meaning and scope of all this common law tax jurisprudence has befuddled (and yet challenged) tax advisors for decades. Our modest goal here is to identify the principal terminology and give fair warning that literal compliance with the Code may not be enough for a transaction to pass muster. Students should not expect to master a precise or consistent explanation of the judicial doctrines. It will be enough to develop a sense of smell for the kinds of cases in which the doctrines might be invoked.

B. THE CORPORATION AS A SEPARATE TAXABLE ENTITY

1. THE CORPORATE INCOME TAX

Code: §§ 11(a), (b)(1) & (2); 63(a). Skim §§ 199(a), (b), (c); 243(a); 1201(a); 1211(a); 1212(a)(1).

Students are often surprised to learn that a study of corporate taxation devotes very little time to the determination of a corporation's tax liability. The reason is that the concepts used in making that determination already should have been mastered in the basic federal income tax course. Those same broad principles—gross income, deductions, assignment of income, timing and characterization—apply in computing the taxable income of a C corporation, and we only need to pause briefly to discuss the rate structure and a few other special rules applicable to C corporations.

Rates. A C corporation, like an individual, is a separate taxable entity for federal income tax purposes. The corporation selects its own taxable year and method of accounting, computes its taxable income under applicable principles of the tax law and otherwise is generally treated like any other taxable person. The corporate rates are found in Section 11, which provides a limited number of brackets for lower income corporations but becomes an essentially flat rate tax for more profitable companies. The maximum corporate rate is 35 percent on a corporation's taxable income in excess of $10,000,000.[1] For corporate income under $10,000,000 the rates are as follows:[2]

Taxable Income	Rate
$0 to $50,000	15%
$50,001 to $75,000	25%
$75,001 to $10,000,000	34%

The simple schedule above is modified, however, to prevent the most profitable corporations from enjoying the benefits of the lower graduated rates. Section 11(b) imposes an additional five percent tax on taxable income in excess of $100,000 up to a maximum increase of $11,750, which is the amount of tax savings from the lower rates on the first $75,000 of taxable income. This rate "bubble" in effect creates a 39 percent marginal bracket on taxable income between $100,000 and $335,000. In addition,

1. I.R.C. § 11(b).   **2.** Id.

corporations with taxable income in excess of $15,000,000 must increase their tax by the lesser of three percent of the excess, or $100,000. As a result of this second (double?) bubble, corporations with taxable income over $18,333,333 are taxed at a flat 35 percent rate on all their income.

To prevent doctors, lawyers, entertainers and other incorporated service providers from taking advantage of the lower marginal corporate rates, Section 11(b)(2) denies the benefit of those rates to any "qualified personal service corporation" as defined in Section 448(d)(2). Incorporated service businesses are thus subject to a 35 percent flat rate tax on all their taxable income. In general, a "qualified personal service corporation" is a corporation substantially engaged in the performance of services in the fields of health, law, engineering, architecture, accounting, actuarial science, performing arts, or consulting, if substantially all of the corporation's stock is held (directly or indirectly) by employees performing services for the corporation, retired employees, or the estates of employees or retirees.[3]

Determination of Taxable Income. Section 63(a) defines taxable income as "gross income minus the deductions allowed by this chapter." In the case of a corporation, this amount generally is determined by applying the same principles and Code sections applicable to individuals. A few differences, primarily attributable to the distinct status of the corporation as an artificial business entity, are worth mentioning.

First, because a corporation has no "personal" expenses, it is not entitled to any personal or dependency exemptions and, unlike an individual, it receives no standard deduction. Corporations thus are not concerned with distinguishing between "above-the-line" deductions allowable in reaching adjusted gross income and "below-the-line" itemized deductions or in applying the Section 67 two percent of adjusted gross income floor to "miscellaneous itemized deductions" or the Section 68 overall limitation on itemized deductions.

In addition, most of the personal deductions allowed to individuals are not available to corporations. For example, a corporation is not entitled to a medical expense deduction under Section 213 or a spousal support deduction under Section 215. Moreover, Section 212, which allows a deduction for certain expenses incurred for the production of income or maintenance of income-producing property or for tax advice, is expressly applicable only to individuals. Corporations need not worry however, because virtually all of their ordinary expenses in the pursuit of profit are deductible under Section 162.

On the other hand, certain *limitations* on the deductibility of personal expenses of individuals do not apply to corporations. For example, Section 165(c), which limits the deductibility of nonbusiness losses; Section 166(d), which characterizes nonbusiness bad debts as short-term capital losses; and Section 183(a), which limits deductions for activities not motivated by profit, are among a number of restrictive sections that do not apply to C

---

3. I.R.C. § 448(d)(2).

corporations. This is because it is generally assumed that all of a corporation's activities are motivated by the pursuit of profit.[4]

By virtue of their unique status, corporations are entitled to one important deduction not available to individuals. To prevent multiple taxation as earnings wend their way through a chain of corporations, corporate shareholders generally are entitled to deduct 70 percent (or, in some cases, 80 or 100 percent) of the dividends they receive from other corporations. The effect of the 70 percent dividends received deduction is that corporations are subject to tax at a maximum rate of 10.5 percent on dividends—an amount derived by applying the top 35 percent corporate rate to the 30 percent includable portion of the dividends.

The remaining differences in the treatment of corporations and individuals are the result of a conscious legislative choice to treat them differently. For example, the percentage limitation on corporate charitable deductions is 10 percent of taxable income as compared to an overall 50 percent limit on individual charitable contributions.[5] The at-risk limitations in Section 465 and the passive loss limitations in Section 469, which are aimed at tax shelter activities of individual taxpayers, generally do not apply to C corporations.[6] And publicly traded corporations may not deduct more than $1 million per year for otherwise reasonable compensation paid to certain high-level corporate executives.[7]

Another significant difference relates to the treatment of corporate capital losses. Corporations may deduct capital losses only to the extent of capital gains during the taxable year. Although the excess may not be applied against ordinary income, it may be carried back for three years and carried forward for five years. By contrast, individuals are permitted to deduct capital losses to the extent of capital gains, and up to $3,000 of excess losses may be deducted against ordinary income. Unused capital losses may be carried forward indefinitely by an individual taxpayer.[8]

Deduction for Domestic Production Activities. The stated maximum corporate income tax rate of 35 percent was reduced by approximately 3 percent in 2010 when the Section 199 deduction for domestic production activities was fully phased in.[9] This generous tax benefit was the centerpiece of the American Jobs Creation Act of 2004, which repealed a long-standing export subsidy ruled illegal by the World Trade Organization.[10] To

---

4. Certain payments made by a corporation to or on behalf of its shareholders may be nondeductible because they are in fact dividends, but their disallowance is the result of the classification of the payments as constructive dividends rather than the "personal" nature of the payments. See Chapter 4E, infra.

5. I.R.C. § 170(b)(2).

6. I.R.C. §§ 465(a)(1); 469(a)(2)(B), (j)(1).

7. I.R.C. § 162(m). This limitation only applies to the chief executive officer and the

four other most highly compensated executives. I.R.C. § 162(m)(3). Various types of commissions and performance-based compensation are exempt. I.R.C. § 162(m)(4). Tax advisors have been adept at designing compensation plans to avoid the impact of this provision.

8. I.R.C. §§ 1211, 1212.

9. I.R.C. § 199.

10. Another generous provision added by the 2004 legislation created a one-year amnesty for companies to repatriate profits earned outside the United States at a reduced compensate for the lost tax break and stimulate the creation of new jobs in the United States, Congress added the Section 199 deduction, which permits U.S. taxpayers engaged in certain domestic production activities to deduct 9 percent of the lesser of their taxable income or "qualified production activities income."[11] The deduction is allowed for purposes of both the regular and alternative minimum taxes and is available to individuals, trusts, partnerships and S corporations as well as domestic C corporations.[12]

Section 199 is a typically complex provision littered with definitions and special rules. In keeping with the "fundamentals" philosophy of the text, the following discussion is limited to a few highlights. "Qualified production activities income," the base on which the deduction is determined, equals a taxpayer's "domestic production gross receipts" reduced by the sum of: (1) the cost of goods sold allocable to those receipts, (2) other allocable expenses, and (3) a ratable portion of other not directly allocable deductions and losses.[13] The key term that unlocks the gate to the deduction is "domestic production gross receipts," which are gross receipts derived from various "production" activities within the United States. "Production" is much broader than just "manufacturing." It includes farming, equipment leasing, licensing of software and films (but not if the film is "pornographic"), construction, production of electricity, natural gas and drinking water, and even some service businesses such as engineering or architecture.[14] As a result, many companies that did not benefit from the repealed export subsidy will qualify for the new deduction.

The statute draws some fine lines in determining what activities qualify for the deduction. Income from the sale of food and beverages prepared by the taxpayer at a retail establishment, such as a restaurant or facility selling take-out food items, does not qualify,[15] but profits from processing food (e.g., from an in-store bakery in a supermarket) are eligible for the tax break.[16] As explained in the legislative history, "the gross receipts of a meat packing establishment" qualify but "the activities of a master chef who creates a venison sausage for his or her restaurant menu" do not.[17] U.S. companies that roast coffee beans and use them to brew coffee for sale qualify for the deduction on the roasting but not the brewing activity.[18] The Service has been delegated the authority to provide additional guidance through regulations.

---

tax rate of 5.25 percent. I.R.C. § 965(a). Technology and pharmaceutical companies with large amount of overseas cash especially benefited from this "tax holiday."

11. I.R.C. § 199(a). The deduction cannot exceed 50 percent of "W–2 wages" (defined as wages and certain elective deferrals, such as contributions to Section 401(k) plans) paid by the taxpayer as an employer during the taxable year. I.R.C. § 199(b).

12. I.R.C. §§ 199(d)(1), (6).

13. I.R.C. § 199(c)(1).

14. I.R.C. § 199(c)(4).

15. I.R.C. § 199(c)(4)(B).

16. H.R. Rep. No. 108–755, 108th Cong., 2d Sess. 13 (2004).

17. Id. at 12.

18. Id. at 13.

The Section 199 deduction was intended to stimulate the creation of new jobs within the United States. It has become clear that deciphering the intricacies of this new deduction will boost the gross receipts of law and accounting firms, but the definition of "domestic production" does not yet extend to the services provided by tax advisers.

Taxable Year and Accounting Method. Most C corporations have the flexibility to adopt either a calendar year or a fiscal year as their annual accounting period.[19] Certain "personal service corporations" must use a calendar year, however, unless they can show a business purpose for using a fiscal year.[20] For this purpose, a "personal service corporation" is one whose principal activity is the performance of personal services that are substantially performed by "employee-owners" who collectively own more than 10 percent (by value) of the corporation's stock.[21] This generally forces most personal service corporations to use a calendar year, subject to an exception in Section 444 which permits them to elect to adopt or change to a fiscal year with a "deferral period" of not more than three months.[22] As a result, a personal service corporation that otherwise would be required to use a calendar year may elect a taxable year ending September 30, October 31 or November 30. To prevent any tax savings that might result from the use of a fiscal year, personal service corporations making a Section 444 election must make certain minimum distributions (e.g., primarily of compensation) to employee-owners during the portion of the employee's fiscal year that ends on December 31.[23] If these minimum distribution requirements are not met, the electing corporation must defer certain otherwise currently deductible payments (e.g., compensation) to employee-owners.[24] A personal service corporation that establishes a business purpose for a fiscal year is not required to make a Section 444 election and is not subject to these distribution requirements and deduction limitations.[25]

In general, C corporations are required to use the accrual method of accounting.[26] Exemptions are provided for corporations engaged in the farming business, "qualified personal service corporations"[27] and any other

19. See generally I.R.C. § 441. A fiscal year is any period of 12 months ending on the last day of any month other than December. I.R.C. § 441(e).

20. I.R.C. § 441(i)(1). Deferral of income to shareholders is not treated as a business purpose. Id.

21. I.R.C. §§ 269A(b)(1); 441(i)(2). An employee-owner is defined as any employee who owns, on any day during the taxable year, any of the outstanding stock of the corporation after applying certain attribution rules. I.R.C. § 269A(b)(2), as modified by I.R.C. § 441(i)(2).

22. I.R.C. § 444(b)(2). The "deferral period" of a taxable year is the number of months between the beginning of the taxable year elected and the close of the required

taxable year that ends within the taxable year elected.

23. See generally I.R.C. § 280H.

24. I.R.C. § 280H(a), (b), (c).

25. I.R.S. Notice 88–10, 1988–1 C.B. 478.

26. I.R.C. § 448(a).

27. This is the same category of corporations that is deprived of the lower graduated rates in Section 11. Substantially all of the activities of the corporation must involve the performance of services in the fields of health, law, engineering, accounting, architecture, actuarial science, performing arts, or consulting, and substantially all of the stock must be held by employees, their estates or their heirs. I.R.C. § 448(d)(2).

corporation whose average annual gross receipts for a three-year measuring period preceding the taxable year do not exceed $5 million.[28]

In addition to these general accounting rules, Section 267 regulates certain transactions between corporations and their shareholders to prevent the acceleration of losses on related party transactions and to preclude timing advantages when the corporation and its owner-employees use different methods of accounting. For example, Section 267(a)(1) provides that losses from sales or exchanges of property between an individual shareholder and a more-than–50 percent-owned corporation may not be deducted.[29] The forced matching rules in Section 267(a)(2) prevent an accrual method corporation from accruing and deducting compensation paid to a cash method owner-employee in the year when the services are performed but deferring payment until the following taxable year to provide the employee with a timing advantage. When an owner-employee owns, directly or indirectly, more than 50 percent of the payor corporation, the corporation's deduction is deferred until such time as the owner-employee includes the amount in income.[30]

Credits. Like any taxpayer engaged in business or investment activities, a corporation is entitled to several valuable tax credits. The most significant is the foreign tax credit, which is available to corporations with income from foreign sources.[31] Others include the rehabilitation and energy credits,[32] the work opportunity credit,[33] and the credit for research expenditures.[34]

2. THE CORPORATE ALTERNATIVE MINIMUM TAX

Code: §§ 55(a), (b)(1)(B) & (2), (c)(1), (d)(2) & (3)(A), (e)(1); 56(a)(1)(A), (c)(1), (g)(1), (2), (3), (4)(A)–(C)(ii), (6); 57(a)(5)(A), (6). Skim § 53.

C Corporations also are potentially subject to the alternative minimum tax ("AMT"), which is designed "to ensure that no taxpayer with substantial economic income can avoid significant tax liability by using exclusions, deductions and credits."[1] The AMT generally can be described as a flat rate tax which is imposed on a broader income base than the taxable income yardstick used for the regular corporate tax. But that deceptively simple description only begins to explain a complex statutory scheme that takes

28. I.R.C. § 448(b).

29. The loss disallowance applies to transactions between related parties as defined in Section 267(b). A corporation and its more-than-50–percent (measured by value) shareholders are considered related. I.R.C. § 267(b)(2). Percentage ownership is determined after application of attribution rules in Section 267(c).

30. I.R.C. § 267(a)(2). This section also may apply to payments of interest and other deductible expenses. In the case of personal service corporations, the corporation and *any* owner-employee (regardless of the percentage

ownership) are treated as related parties for purposes of the forced matching rules in Section 267. Id.

31. I.R.C. § 27.

32. I.R.C. §§ 46–48.

33. I.R.C. § 51.

34. I.R.C. § 41.

1. S. Rep. No. 99–313, 99th Cong., 2d Sess. 518 (1986). See generally Lathrope, The Alternative Minimum Tax—Compliance and Planning with Analysis.

many twists and turns before reaching "alternative minimum taxable income," the base that Congress believed was a truer measure of a corporation's economic results.

The corporate AMT is payable only to the extent that it exceeds a corporation's regular tax liability.[2] The AMT generally is 20 percent of the amount by which a corporation's alternative minimum taxable income, as defined in Section 55(b)(2), exceeds a $40,000 exemption amount.[3] "Alternative minimum taxable income" ("AMTI") is the corporation's taxable income, increased by various tax preference items and adjusted to eliminate certain timing benefits (e.g., accelerated cost recovery) that are available under the regular tax.[4] Certain "small" corporations are exempt from the corporate AMT. To qualify for this exemption for a taxable year, a corporation's average annual gross receipts must be $7.5 million or less for all preceding three-taxable-year periods (taking into account only taxable years beginning after 1993).[5] In its first year of existence, a corporation is exempt from the AMT regardless of its gross receipts.[6]

Section 56 lists the principal adjustments made in arriving at a corporation's alternative minimum taxable income.[7] Many are narrow and beyond the scope of this text, but a few adjustments will be familiar to students who have completed the basic income tax course. For example, depreciation on tangible personal property eligible for the 200 percent declining balance method under the regular tax is limited to the 150 percent declining balance method for AMT purposes.[8] A special net operating loss, known as the "alternative minimum tax net operating loss," also must be used in computing alternative minimum taxable income.[9]

In extending the AMT concept to corporations, Congress was responding to several highly publicized cases of corporations that reported significant operating profits in their financial statements to shareholders but paid minimal amounts of corporate income tax.[10] In an effort to improve

---

2. I.R.C. § 55(a).

3. I.R.C. § 55(b), (d)(2). The $40,000 exemption amount is phased out at the rate of 25 cents for each dollar that a corporation's alternative minimum taxable income exceeds $150,000. I.R.C. § 55(d)(3)(A). The exemption is thus fully phased out when a corporation's alternative minimum taxable income reaches $310,000.

4. I.R.C. § 55(b)(2).

5. I.R.C. § 55(e)(1)(A). The $7.5 million limit is reduced to $5 million for the first three-taxable-year period taken into account. I.R.C. § 55(e)(1)(B).

6. I.R.C. § 55(e)(1)(C).

7. Certain specialized adjustments in Section 58 also must be made. I.R.C. § 55(b)(2)(A).

8. I.R.C. § 56(a)(1)(A)(ii). For property placed in service after 1986 but before 1999, AMT depreciation also must be computed using the longer class lives prescribed by the alternative depreciation system of Section 168(g). I.R.C. § 56(a)(1)(A)(i).

9. In general, the AMT net operating loss must be computed in a manner consistent with the adjustments and preferences in the alternative minimum tax scheme. The special net operating loss may not offset more than 90 percent of a corporation's alternative minimum taxable income, determined without the net operating loss deduction. I.R.C. § 56(a)(4), (d). Net operating losses carried back from taxable years ending in 2001 or 2002 and carryforwards of net operating losses to those years are not subject to the 90 percent limitation. I.R.C. § 56(d)(1)(A)(ii).

10. See, e.g., Citizens for Tax Justice, "Corporate Taxpayers and Corporate Freeloaders," 29 Tax Notes 947 (Dec. 2, 1985).

perceptions, Section 56(g) requires an upward AMTI adjustment equal to 75 percent of the amount by which "adjusted current earnings" ("ACE") exceed AMTI determined without regard to this adjustment or AMT net operating losses ("pre-ACE AMTI").[11] The purpose of the ACE adjustment is to reach an even more accurate measure of a corporation's economic performance. ACE is determined by starting with pre-ACE AMTI and making several additional adjustments.[12]

Understanding the final round of ACE adjustments requires a brief introduction to the concept of "earnings and profits." The principal function of earnings and profits is to determine whether distributions paid by C corporations to their shareholders are dividends or a return of capital.[13] The computation of earnings and profits begins with taxable income and requires a number of adjustments which are designed to provide a truer measure of the corporation's economic performance. Consequently, certain amounts that were excluded from gross income for purposes of computing pre-ACE AMTI but that are taken into account in determining a corporation's "earnings and profits" must be included in determining ACE. An example is tax-exempt municipal bond interest, which increases a corporation's wealth but (except for interest on certain private activity bonds) is not included in the AMT base. Similarly, items that are disallowed as deductions in computing earnings and profits are added back for ACE purposes. An example is the 70 percent dividends received deduction for corporate shareholders.[14]

Once ACE is determined, the final step is to increase pre-ACE AMTI by 75 percent of the excess of ACE over pre-ACE AMTI.[15] After this orgy of adjustments, one wonders why Congress did not simply adopt ACE (or earnings and profits, for that matter) as the base for the corporate AMT. The answer presumably is political compromise, a force that has complicated the tax system in general and the alternative minimum tax in particular.

The determination of AMTI requires one more step. Once the required Section 56 adjustments are made, a corporation must increase taxable income by the amount of certain tax preference items, most of which are very specialized. Some of the more familiar preferences included in Section 57(a) are: (1) the excess of percentage depletion over cost depletion; (2) excess intangible drilling costs; and (3) tax-exempt interest on certain private activity bonds issued after August 7, 1986.

A limited number of credits may be applied against a corporation's

11. A negative adjustment also is allowed—i.e., pre-ACE AMTI may be reduced by 75 percent of the excess of pre-ACE AMTI over ACE. I.R.C. § 56(g)(2).

12. I.R.C. § 56(g)(3).

13. See I.R.C. §§ 301; 316; and Chapter 4, infra.

14. See I.R.C. § 243(a). An exception is provided for deductions that qualify for a 100 or 80 percent dividends received deduction, provided that the dividends are paid from earnings that were taxable to the payor. I.R.C. § 56(g)(4)(C)(ii).

15. As noted earlier, if pre-ACE AMTI exceeds ACE, then pre-ACE AMTI is decreased by the difference. See note 11, supra.

alternative minimum tax liability.[16] In addition, a minimum tax credit is allowed against a corporation's *regular* tax liability. The minimum credit was enacted in recognition of the fact that many of the alternative minimum tax adjustments and items of tax preference reflect deferral of tax liability rather than permanent tax avoidance. An adjustment thus is required so that taxpayers do not lose these benefits altogether.[17] In general, Section 53(a) allows a corporation's alternative minimum tax to be credited against regular tax liability (reduced by certain other credits) in later years.[18] The minimum tax credit may be carried over until it is fully used, but it cannot be used as a credit against the alternative minimum tax.[19]

Not surprisingly, the corporate AMT is unpopular in the business community, which has placed complete repeal of this tax high on its wish list of proposed legislation. Advocates of tax simplification also have recommended a phase-out and eventual repeal of both the individual and corporate AMT.[20] Although these proposals have broad support in Congress, the revenue loss from AMT repeal would be substantial, and the best guess is that the AMT will remain part of the corporate tax landscape unless and until it can be given a proper burial as part of a comprehensive overall of the federal tax system.

3.   MULTIPLE CORPORATIONS

Code: Skim §§ 1501; 1502; 1503; 1504(a), (b); 1551; 1561; 1563.

Because corporations are easier to create than individuals, multiple corporations might be used to save taxes. For example, if Sole Shareholder owns a corporation that generates $1,000,000 of net income annually, he might be tempted to divide the enterprise into 20 separate companies, each with an annual income of $50,000 and each therefore taxed at a maximum rate of only 15 percent. This income-splitting ploy is precluded by Section 1561, which denies certain multiple tax benefits to a "controlled group of corporations."[1] Generally speaking, corporations are a controlled group if they constitute either a "parent-subsidiary controlled group" or a "brother-sister controlled group" under ownership tests in Section 1563.

The Code also contains provisions which permit an "affiliated group of corporations" to elect to consolidate its results for purposes of tax reporting.[2] In broad outline, the effect of a consolidated return election is to treat

---

16.   See I.R.C. § 38(c) (regular investment tax credit); § 59(a) (alternative minimum tax foreign tax credit).

17.   S. Rep. No. 99–313, supra note 1, at 521.

18.   I.R.C. § 53(a), (b), (d)(1)(B).

19.   I.R.C. § 53(c).

20.   See, e.g., Staff of the Joint Committee on Taxation, Study of the Overall State of the Federal Tax System and Recommendations for Simplification, vol. II, pp. 2–23 (JCS–3–01, April 2001).

1.   Section 1551 limits controlled groups to one use of the lower rates in Section 11(b). The entire group's income must be combined for purposes of applying Section 11. See Chapter 13, infra.

2.   I.R.C. §§ 1501–1504.

the affiliated group as a single corporate entity for tax purposes. The consolidated return rules are covered in more detail in Chapter 13, and selected issues involving consolidated returns are raised in the context of various transactions discussed later in this book. The ownership test applied to determine whether corporations are affiliated, however, is used in several provisions of Subchapter C[3] and is worth a brief glance at this early juncture. Section 1504(a)(2) employs an 80 percent of voting power and value standard to test corporate ownership of another corporation. That standard is met if a corporation possesses at least 80 percent of the total voting power of the stock in another corporation and has at least 80 percent of the total value of the stock of such corporation. For purposes of this test, certain nonconvertible, nonvoting preferred stock is disregarded.[4]

4.   THE S CORPORATION ALTERNATIVE

In General. As previewed earlier, Subchapter C's strengthened double tax regime has created an incentive for closely held businesses to select a legal form that qualifies for pass-through tax treatment. For businesses that require the corporate form for nontax reasons,[1] Subchapter S of the Code provides a relatively simple but not always available means to achieve this goal. Enacted to reduce the tax influences on the choice of entity decision, Subchapter S permits the shareholders of a "small business corporation" to elect to be taxed under a conduit approach similar to the taxation of partnerships. Subchapter S's role as an alternative to the two-tier system applicable to C corporations merits a brief introduction to its provisions.[2]

The principal obstacle to making an S election are the eligibility requirements found in the Code's definition of "small business corporation" in Section 1361. In general, a corporation may make an S election only if it has not more than 100 shareholders who must be individuals other than nonresident aliens, estates or certain trusts,[3] and an S corporation may not have more than one class of stock.[4]

The income of an S corporation generally is subject to a single, shareholder-level tax.[5] The income, losses, deductions and credits of an S corporation pass through to its shareholders, but the character of those items is determined at the corporate level.[6] Basis and distribution rules are

---

3. See, e.g., I.R.C. §§ 332(b)(1); 336(e)(1); 338(d)(3).

4. I.R.C. § 1504(a)(4).

1. For businesses that do not require the corporate form but desire limited liability for all their owners, the limited liability company is emerging as an entity of choice. See Section C2b of this chapter, infra.

2. For detailed coverage of S corporations, see Chapter 15, infra.

3. I.R.C. § 1361(b)(1)(A), (B), (C). Members of a "family," broadly defined, may elect to be treated as one shareholder for purposes of this requirement. I.R.C. § 1361(c)(1).

4. I.R.C. § 1361(b)(1)(D).

5. But see I.R.C. §§ 1374 and 1375, which impose a corporate-level tax on certain S corporations that previously were C corporations.

6. I.R.C. § 1366(a), (b).

designed to assure that the shareholders may receive previously taxed income without paying additional tax.[7]

Even though S corporations and their shareholders are taxed under a special regime, S corporations remain "corporations" for purposes of Subchapter C.[8] Thus, the two corporate subchapters often operate in tandem when an S corporation engages in transactions, such as distributions of appreciated property, stock redemptions and liquidations, that are subject to Subchapter C.[9]

Contrary to predictions of their demise, S corporations have shown surprising vitality. In 1997, for the first time, a majority of corporate tax returns were filed by S corporations,[10] and the popularity of S corporations has continued to increase. Between 2000 and 2008, there was a 42 percent increase in returns filed by S corporations and, by 2008, S corporations accounted for 69 percent of the 5.8 million corporate tax returns filed.[11]

S Corporations vs. Partnerships and LLCs. When a pass-through tax regime is the desired alternative for tax purposes, the owners of the business must choose among three legal forms: S corporations, partnerships, or limited liability companies. The ownership and capital structure restrictions imposed on S corporations may require use of a partnership or LLC, such as when the number of shareholders exceeds the S corporation limit or there is a need to issue two or more classes of stock. In addition, Subchapter K is much more flexible than Subchapter S. To accommodate different types of owners, partnerships and LLCs may make special allocations of partnership income and deduction items, while shareholders of an S corporation must include corporate income and loss on a pro rata share basis.[12] Thus, partners may agree to share certain income or deductions disproportionately, and the agreement will be respected for tax purposes if it reflects their economic business deal. In most cases, partnerships and LLCs (but not S corporations) also can distribute appreciated property in kind without immediate recognition of taxable gain.

Unlike S corporation shareholders, partners may increase the basis of their partnership interests by their allocable share of entity-level debts.[13] That additional "basis credit" may be important for maximizing the ability to deduct losses realized by the enterprise—e.g., in ventures that own leveraged real estate—or avoiding gain on distributions.[14] For these and other reasons, the conventional wisdom is that Subchapter K is more taxpayer-friendly than Subchapter S. In fact, much of the popularity of the

7. I.R.C. §§ 1367(a); 1368(a), (b).

8. I.R.C. § 1371(a)(1).

9. See Chapter 15G, infra.

10. Treubert & Janquet, "Corporation Income Tax Returns, 1998," 21 SOI Bulletin 66, 67 (2001).

11. See IRS Statistics of Income Integrated Business Data (Table 1: Selected data on businesses 1980–2008).

12. Compare I.R.C. § 704(b)(2) with I.R.C. § 1366(a).

13. See I.R.C. §§ 722; 752(a).

14. See I.R.C. §§ 704(d); 731(a)(1); 1366(d)(1); 1368(b).

LLC is attributable to the fact that they offer limited liability to all investors combined with the more flexible partnership tax regime.

In other situations, however, the goals of business owners may be better achieved with an S corporation, such as where there are only a few owners and the flexibility of Subchapter K is not necessary. Many entrepreneurs prefer to conduct their business as a state law corporation instead of a partnership or limited liability company because they (or their advisors) are more comfortable with the corporate governance structure. Subchapter S provides these owners with a relatively simple pass-through tax regime. As discussed below, S corporations also are often used by service providers to minimize their exposure to employment taxes.

On the other hand, S corporations are not a viable choice for a business with foreign investors, who are not permissible S corporation shareholders, and institutional investors (e.g., tax-exempt pension funds and charitable organizations) are discouraged by the tax system from investing in any type of active business that is operated as a pass-through entity.[15] Venture capital funds, which provide a large source of capital for start-up companies, appear to be more comfortable using the familiar C corporation capitalized with several classes of stock, a structure not available in an S corporation.[16]

Employment Tax Considerations. As previewed above, where a principal owner of a business also is a service provider, employment taxes can be an influential factor in selecting the S corporation over other available legal forms. Employment taxes are imposed in addition to income taxes on employee wages[17] and on net earnings from self-employment.[18] A self-employed individual, such as a sole proprietor or a general partner (general partners are not treated as employees of the partnership for which they render services), must pay a 12.4 percent Social Security tax on self-employment income up to a wage base ($110,100 in 2012)[19] and an additional 2.9 percent Medicare tax on all income from self-employment.[20]

---

15. Stripped of detail, pension funds and other tax-exempt organizations are potentially subject to the "unrelated business income tax" on income passing through from an operating business conducted as a partnership or S corporation, but they are generally not taxable on income from "portfolio" investments, such as dividends and interest received from an equity or debt interest in a C corporation. See generally I.R.C. §§ 511 et seq.

16. See Bankman, "The Structure of Silicon Valley Start-ups," 42 UCLA L. Rev. 1737 (1994), which observes that venture capitalists are foregoing valuable tax benefits (e.g., current deductibility of start-up losses) by using C corporations rather than a business form eligible for pass-through tax treatment. See also Fleischer, "The Rational Exu-berance of Structuring Venture Capital Start-ups," 57 Tax L. Rev. 137 (2003).

17. One-half the employment tax on wages is paid by the employee through withholding and the other half is paid by the employer, which may deduct the tax as a business expense.

18. I.R.C. § 1401.

19. I.R.C. § 1402(a). The rate was dropped to 10.4 percent in 2011 and 2012 to provide an economic stimulus. Self-employed taxpayers may take an above-the-line deduction for one-half of self-employment tax paid. I.R.C. § 164(f).

20. Beginning in 2013, the Medicare tax rate increases to 3.8 percent for taxpayers with self-employment income above certain thresholds. I.R.C. § 3101(b)(2).

S corporations are often used by service providers to avoid the un-capped Medicare portion of employment taxes. Assume, for example, that Trial Lawyer, a single taxpayer, has $500,000 of net earnings from self-employment and no other earned income. If she conducts her practice as a sole proprietor, her self-employment tax will consist of 12.4 percent on self-employment income up to the applicable wage base and 2.9 percent on the entire $500,000 ($14,500).[21] Assume Trial Lawyer incorporates her practice using an S corporation which nets the same $500,000, pays the lawyer a salary of $150,000, and either retains the $350,000 balance or distributes it as a dividend. Some tax advisors take the position that as long as the compensation paid by the S corporation to a shareholder-employee is within a reasonable range, the Medicare tax can be avoided on that shareholder's remaining portion of S corporation income.[22] If this is correct, Trial Lawyer would save $10,150 in 2012 (the 2.9 percent Medicare tax on $350,000) and even more in 2013 and beyond. Whether or not the S corporation employment tax avoidance gambit should succeed is debatable, although anecdotal evidence suggests that it is widely used and often goes unchallenged.[23]

PROBLEM

Boots, Inc. is a "C" corporation engaged in the shoe manufacturing business. It also holds a small portfolio of securities. Boots is a calendar year, accrual method taxpayer with two equal shareholders, Emil and Betty, who are unrelated cash method taxpayers. Use the rates in § 11 to determine Boots, Inc.'s tax liability, and assume for convenience that Emil and Betty each are taxable at a combined federal and state flat rate of 40% on ordinary income and a combined flat rate of 20% on qualified dividends and long-term capital gains. During the current year, Boots has the following income and expense items and makes no distributions to its shareholders:

Income:	
Gross profit—sale of inventory	$2,600,000
Capital gains	200,000
Municipal bond interest (not private activity bond)	10,000
Expenses and Losses:	
Operating Expenses (includes § 199 deduction)	800,000
ACRS depreciation (5–year property; $4,000,000 cost; all placed in service in current year)	800,000
Capital losses	220,000

21. In 2013 and thereafter, the Medicare tax for a single taxpayer on $500,000 of self-employment income would be $17,200—2.9 percent on the first $200,000 and 3.8 percent on the $300,000 that exceeds the $200,000 high-income threshold for single taxpayers.

22. In egregious cases, such as where little or no compensation is paid and the S corporation distributes a large dividend to its sole owner, the Service likely will reclassify all or part of the dividend as wages for employment tax purposes. See Chapter 11H, infra.

23. See Tax Gap: Actions Needed to Address Noncompliance with S Corporation Tax Rules (U.S. Government Accountability Office, GAO–10–195, Dec. 2009). Legislation to close this loophole has been proposed but not yet enacted.

(a) Determine Boots, Inc.'s taxable income and its regular tax liability for the current year.

(b) What result in (a), above, if Boots distributes $330,000 each to Emil and Betty as qualified dividends?

(c) What result in (a), above, if instead of paying dividends Boots pays Emil and Betty salaries of $500,000 each? What other strategies could Emil and Betty employ to reduce the impact of the corporate "double tax"? In general, what are the risks of these strategies. See, e.g., §§ 79; 105(a), (b); 106; 119; 162(a)(3); 163; 267; 1363(a); 1366(a)(1), (c).

C. CORPORATE CLASSIFICATION

1. IN GENERAL

Code: § 7701(a)(3).

The classification of a business relationship may have profound tax consequences. Entities classified as C corporations are subject to the double tax regime of Subchapter C, while the tax treatment of partnerships is governed by the single tax pass-through regime of Subchapter K. The classification area has a rich and textured history, as the stakes have changed in response to shifting tax incentives to utilize one form of business entity over another. After decades of strife, much confusion, and reams of boilerplate classification opinion letters issued by high-priced counsel, there is good news. The Internal Revenue Service has simplified this topic considerably (and shortened your reading assignment) by adopting a classification system that as a practical matter permits a closely held unincorporated business to elect its taxing regime.

For tax purposes, Section 7701 defines a corporation to include "associations, joint-stock companies, and insurance companies." Thus, if an entity is an unincorporated "association," it will be classified as a corporation. The longstanding, now repealed classification regulations did not define the term "association." Instead, they listed six characteristics ordinarily found in a "pure" corporation: (1) associates (i.e., two or more persons joining together in shared control and ownership of the venture); (2) an objective to carry on business and divide the gains therefrom; (3) continuity of life (a corporation continues in existence despite the death or withdrawal of one or more shareholders); (4) centralization of management (i.e., management responsibility is vested in directors and is not exercised directly by the shareholders); (5) limited liability (shareholders are not personally liable for corporate debts); and (6) free transferability of interests (i.e., shareholders may dispose of their shares).[1] The regulations then explained that "an organization will be treated as an association if the corporate characteris-

---

1. Reg. § 301.7701–2(a)(1) (pre–1997).

tics are such that the organization more nearly resembles a corporation than a partnership or trust."[2] Under those regulations, characteristics common to corporations and partnerships (associates and a business objective) were disregarded in classifying an entity as an association or a partnership. The remaining characteristics (continuity of life, centralized management, limited liability, and free transferability of interests) were then weighted equally and an organization was classified as an association only if it had three of the remaining corporate characteristics.[3]

The "old" (now-repealed) regulations were issued at a time when professional service providers (e.g., doctors and lawyers), forbidden from incorporating under state law, attempted to form entities that qualified as "associations" taxable as corporations. Their tax planning agenda was to qualify for tax advantages, such as qualified retirement plans and tax-free fringe benefits, that were then available to corporations and their employees but not to partnerships and partners.[4] The Treasury's mission was to make it more difficult for unincorporated entities to qualify as corporations for federal tax purposes, but its efforts were undercut by the subsequent willingness of state legislators to permit the formation of professional corporations.[5]

One result of this early fray was that the old regulations reflected an anti-association, pro-partnership bias. This redounded to the benefit of high-income taxpayers seeking to shelter their compensation, dividends, or interest income with losses from strategically structured investment activities in real estate and other tax-favored industries. Limited partnerships became the vehicle of choice for these "tax shelters" because they permitted losses to pass through to investors, allowed the partners to maximize those losses by including their share of partnership debt in the basis of their partnership interests, and provided protection for the limited partners against personal liability for debts of the enterprise. These goals could not be achieved in a C or S corporation. The Service's effort to convince the courts that limited partnerships should be classified as "associations" was unsuccessful.[6] Even after tax shelters were derailed by the enactment of the passive loss rules and other restrictions, the Service continued to issue stringent guidelines for limited partnerships seeking a favorable classification ruling.[7] Most tax advisors bypassed the ruling process, and the well informed easily were able to structure a limited partnership that would avoid "association" classification.

2. Id.

3. Reg. § 1.7701–2(a) (pre–1997).

4. United States v. Kintner, 216 F.2d 418 (9th Cir.1954). Cf. Morrissey v. Commissioner, 296 U.S. 344, 56 S.Ct. 289 (1935). Virtually all of the advantages of corporate classification in the retirement plan context have been eliminated.

5. See, e.g., West's Ann. Cal. Corp. Code §§ 13400–13410; Maryland Code, Corporations and Associations, Title 5, Subtitle 1 (2010); West's Florida Statutes Annotated, ch. 621.

6. See Larson v. Commissioner, 66 T.C. 159 (1976).

7. See, e.g., Rev. Proc. 89–12, 1989–1 C.B. 798; Rev. Proc. 91–13, 1991–1 C.B. 477.

In the 1980s, limited liability companies (LLCs) emerged on the scene and quickly became touted as the "best of all worlds" alternative for conducting a closely held business. An LLC is an unincorporated entity in which the owners, called "members," have limited liability for the enterprise's debts and claims even if they participate in management. Members of an LLC have great flexibility in structuring the governance of their venture through the LLC's "operating agreement." The Internal Revenue Service gave a major boost to the LLC movement by classifying a Wyoming LLC as a partnership for federal tax purposes.[8] That ruling was followed by others making it clear that an LLC could be structured as either an association or a partnership depending on the flexibility provided by state law and the desires of the members.[9] LLCs are now authorized in every state, and virtually all states permit single-member LLCs.[10]

2.   CORPORATIONS VS. PARTNERSHIPS

a.   "CHECK–THE–BOX" REGULATIONS

Code: § 7701(a)(3).

Regulations: §§ 301.7701–1(a)(1) & (2); –2(a), (b)(1)–(3), (c)(1) & (2); –3(a), (b)(1).

The "old" classification regulations were based on the traditional state-law differences between a pure corporation and other types of organizations, such as partnerships.[1] State law developments, however, largely blurred the classic distinctions between corporations and the unincorporated forms for doing business. For example, the increasingly popular LLC offers all its investors (including those involved in management) limited liability for obligations of the venture—a characteristic traditionally available only in a corporation—along with classification as a partnership for federal tax purposes.

The Service eventually concluded that the state law differences between corporations and partnerships had narrowed to such a degree that the venerable corporate resemblance test for classifying unincorporated entities should be abandoned in favor of a simpler classification regime that is generally elective.[2] To that end, the regulations have discarded the four-factor classification system, which was de facto elective for individuals with skilled tax advisors, and replaced it with a "check-the-box" system in which most new unincorporated entities automatically will be classified as part-

8. Rev. Rul. 88–76, 1988–2 C.B. 360.

9. See Rev. Rul. 93–38, 1993–1 C.B. 233, where LLCs formed under the Delaware statute were classified as an association or a partnership depending on the terms of the LLC agreement.

10. Bishop & Kleinberger, Limited Liability Companies: Tax and Business Law ¶ 1.04 [3][d].

1. Reg. § 301.7701–2(a)(1) (pre–1997).

2. Preamble to Final Regulations on Simplification of Entity Classification Rules, 61 Fed. Reg. 66584 (Dec. 18, 1986). The elective regime became effective as of January 1, 1997. Reg. § 301.7701–1(f).

nerships for federal tax purposes unless the entity elects to be an association taxable as a C corporation.

General Classification Rules. The regulations only apply to entities that are treated for federal tax purposes as being separate from their owners.[3] If an organization recognized as a separate entity for federal tax purposes is not a trust, it is a "business entity" under the regulations.[4] Certain business entities are automatically classified as corporations.[5] Most importantly, a business entity organized under a federal or state statute that refers to the entity as "incorporated" or as a "corporation," "body corporate," or "body politic," is treated as a corporation for federal tax purposes,[6] as are other business entities taxable as corporations under other Code provisions, such as publicly traded partnerships which are treated as corporations under Section 7704.[7]

Under the regulations, a noncorporate business entity (an "eligible entity") with at least two members is classified as a partnership unless an election is made for the entity to be classified as an association. Thus, partnership status is the default classification for unincorporated entities with two or more members.[8]

Single–Owner Organizations. The regulations treat a noncorporate business entity that has a single owner as a "tax nothing." A single-owner entity is disregarded for tax purposes and treated as an extension of its owner unless the entity elects to be classified as an association and thus taxed as a C corporation.[9] Consequently, if no such election is made, the entity is treated for federal tax purposes as if it were a sole proprietorship (if owned by an individual), or a branch or division (if owned by another business entity, such as a C corporation)[10] This rule is particularly useful in the vast majority of states which permit single-member LLCs.

Foreign Organizations. The regulations list certain business entities formed in specific jurisdictions (e.g., a public limited company formed in Hong Kong) that will be automatically classified as a corporation.[11] In the absence of a contrary election, other foreign entities are classified as: (1) a partnership if the entity has two or more members and at least one member does not have limited liability, (2) an association if all members have limited liability, or (3) disregarded as an entity separate from its owner if the entity has a single owner that does not have limited liability.[12]

3. See Reg. § 301.7701–1(a).

4. Reg. § 301.7701–2(a).

5. Reg. § 301.7701–2(b)(1) through (8).

6. Reg. § 301.7701–2(b)(1).

7. Reg. § 301.7701–2(b)(7). See Section C2b of this chapter, infra, for a discussion of publicly traded partnerships.

8. Reg. §§ 301.7701–2(c)(1), 301.7701–3(a), 301.7701–3(b)(1)(i).

9. Reg. §§ 301.7701–2(c)(2), 301.7701–3(a), 301.7701–3(b)(1)(ii).

10. Reg. § 301.7701–2(a). See Miller, "The Strange Materialization of the Tax Nothing," 87 Tax Notes 685 (May 5, 2000).

11. Reg. § 301.7701–2(b)(8).

12. Reg. § 301.7701–3(b)(2)(i). Limited liability generally exists if the member has no personal liability for the debts of or claims against the entity by reason of being a member. Reg. § 301.7701–3(b)(2)(ii).

Existing Entities. Under the "check-the-box" system, an existing business entity generally retains the same classification that it claimed under the prior regulations unless it elects otherwise. An exception is provided for an entity with a single owner that claimed to be a partnership under the earlier regulations but which is disregarded as an entity separate from its owner under the current version.[13]

Election. A classification election under the regulations may be designated as effective up to 75 days before or twelve months after the election is filed.[14] The election generally must be signed either by (1) each member of the electing entity, including prior members affected by a retroactive election, or (2) by an officer, manager, or member authorized to make the election.[15] If an entity makes a classification election, a new classification election generally cannot be made for 60 months, unless the Service allows such an election and more than 50 percent of the ownership interests in the entity are owned by persons that did not own any interests when the first election was made.[16]

Change in Number of Members of an Entity. The regulations provide that the classification of an eligible entity as an association generally is not affected by any change in the numbers of members of the entity.[17] But if an eligible entity (such as a limited liability company) is classified as a partnership and its membership is reduced to one member, it becomes a disregarded entity.[18] A single-member disregarded entity also is classified as a partnership if it gains more than one member.[19]

Elective Changes in Classification. The regulations also prescribe the tax consequences when an entity makes a valid election to change its tax classification. If a partnership elects to be reclassified as an association, it is deemed to contribute all of its assets and liabilities to the association for stock and then to liquidate by distributing the stock to its partners.[20] If an association elects to be classified as a partnership, it is deemed to liquidate by distributing all of its assets and liabilities to its shareholders who then contribute the assets and liabilities to a newly formed partnership.[21] If an association with one owner elects to be classified as a disregarded entity, it is deemed to liquidate by distributing all of its assets and liabilities to the single owner.[22] Finally, if a disregarded entity elects to be classified as an association, the owner is deemed to contribute all of the assets and liabilities of the entity to the association for stock in the association.[23]

---

13. Reg. § 301.7701–3(b)(3).

14. Reg. § 301.7701–3(c)(1)(iii).

15. Reg. § 301.7701–3(c)(2).

16. Reg. § 301.7701–3(c)(1)(iv).

17. Reg. § 301.7701–3(f)(1).

18. Reg. § 301.7701–3(f)(2).

19. Id.

20. Reg. § 301.7701–3(g)(1)(i).

21. Reg. § 301.7701–3(g)(1)(ii).

22. Reg. § 301.7701–3(g)(1)(iii). If an association is deemed to liquidate under Section 332 (relating to complete liquidations of certain corporate subsidiaries), the election to change classification is considered to be the adoption of a plan of liquidation. Reg. § 301.7701–3(g)(2)(ii).

23. Reg. § 301.7701–3(g)(1)(iv).

The tax treatment of a change in classification is determined under all relevant provisions of the Internal Revenue Code and general principles of tax law, including the step transaction doctrine.[24] An election to change the classification of an eligible entity is treated as occurring at the start of the day for which the election is effective.[25]

b.   PUBLICLY TRADED PARTNERSHIPS

Code: § 7704.

For a brief time after enactment of the Tax Reform Act of 1986, the publicly traded partnership ("PTP") surfaced as a refuge from the costly double tax regime of Subchapter C. Unlike an S corporation, a PTP could have an unlimited number of shareholders. It could register its limited partnership interests, known as "units," with the Securities and Exchange Commission, and the units were freely tradable on a securities exchange or in the over-the-counter market. A profitable PTP thus avoided the corporate income tax and passed through its income to noncorporate limited partners at the lower individual rates.

Alarmed at the proliferation of PTPs and the potential erosion of the corporate tax base, Congress responded by enacting Section 7704, which classifies certain PTPs as corporations for tax purposes. As defined, a "publicly traded partnership" is any partnership whose interests are: (1) traded on an established securities market, or (2) readily tradable on a secondary market (or its substantial equivalent).[26] The regulations generally provide that an interest is "readily tradable" if "taking into account all of the facts and circumstances, the partners are readily able to buy, sell, or exchange their partnership interests in a manner that is comparable, economically, to trading on an established securities market."[27]

An important exception from reclassification is provided for partnerships if 90 percent or more of their gross income consists of certain passive-type income items (e.g., interest, dividends, real property rents, gains from the sale of real property and income and gains from certain natural resources activities).[28] These excepted PTPs continue to be treated as pass-through entities for federal tax purposes. The scope of this narrow escape hatch came under scrutiny after several large private investment firms "went public" in 2007 using a PTP structure under which they offered publicly traded units representing limited partnership interests. One of the largest IPO transactions involved The Blackstone Group, a global asset firm with approximately $88.4 billion under management. In addition to providing advisory services, Blackstone manages a variety of investment pools, including private equity and venture capital funds, real estate

---

24. Reg. § 301.7701–3(g)(2).

25. Reg. § 301.7701–3(g)(3)(i). Transactions deemed to occur as a result of the election are treated as occurring immediately before the close of the day before the election is effective. Id.

26. I.R.C. § 7704(b).

27. Reg. § 1.7704–1(c)(1).

28. I.R.C. § 7704(c).

partnerships, and hedge funds. Before it went public, Blackstone easily qualified for pass-through tax treatment, and it sought to continue avoiding the corporate-level tax as a public company by employing the PTP structure and qualifying for the passive income exception even though the bulk of its profits are derived from an active money management business.[29]

In response to news reports about the lavish compensation and expensive birthday party of Blackstone's CEO and critical commentary about financial service firm IPOs, legislation was introduced providing generally that the Section 7704(c) exception will not apply in the case of a PTP that directly or indirectly derives income from investment adviser or related asset management services. The stated goal of the proposed legislation was to preserve the integrity of the corporate tax base for firms that seek access to public markets and to curtail any special treatment for the lucrative asset management business.

Although this proposal enjoyed bipartisan support when it was introduced, it failed to gain traction and did not become law. It thus remains "on the shelf" and ready to be resuscitated if and when Congress decides to reconsider the issue.[30]

3. CORPORATIONS VS. TRUSTS

Regulations: § 301.7701–4(a), (b).

Trusts, like corporations, may be taxpaying entities, but the income taxation of trusts differs from the taxation of corporations in several important respects. First, a corporation is taxed on its profits as they are earned under the relatively flat rates in Section 11. If it later distributes the remaining after-tax earnings as dividends, the shareholders are subject to a second tax. But there is no double tax on trust income. Under the complex rules of Subchapter J, trust income currently distributed to beneficiaries is generally not taxed to the trust. Rather, the income is taxed to the recipient beneficiaries to the extent of the trust's "distributable net income." If, however, trust income is accumulated, it is taxed to the trust when earned under the rates in Section 1(e) but normally not taxed again when distributed to the beneficiaries. Also, through 2012, dividends are generally taxable to noncorporate shareholders at the 15 percent maximum long-term capital gains rate but, unless the preferential rate on qualified dividends is extended or made permanent, dividends will be taxable at ordinary income tax rates beginning in 2013. Tax rates on dividends do not depend on the character of the corporation's earnings. By contrast, trust income retains its tax character in the hands of the beneficiaries.

The regulations distinguish between "ordinary trusts" created to take title to property for the purpose of protecting and conserving it for the

---

29. For press coverage of this transaction, see Anderson, "Blackstone Founders Prepare to Count Their Billions," N.Y. Times, June 12, 2007, at C1.

30. The proposal has resurfaced in the debate about the deficit and tax reform. See Sullivan, "Economic Analysis: What the Debt Limit Debate Teaches Us About Tax Reforms," 132 Tax Notes 215 (July 18, 2010).

beneficiaries, and "business" or "commercial" trusts which are created to carry on a business for profit. An ordinary trust is classified as a "trust" and taxed under Subchapter J.[1] A business trust, on the other hand, is a business entity that is classified under the check-the-box regulations.[2] Because a business trust is an unincorporated entity, it will be classified as a partnership for federal tax purposes if it has two or more members and does not make an election to be classified as a corporation.[3]

D.   Recognition of the Corporate Entity

The premise underlying Subchapter C is that a corporation is an entity separate and apart from its shareholders. In addition to questions of classification, issues have arisen over the years as to whether an entity organized as a corporation under state law should be respected as such for tax purposes. These cases often involve corporations that are formed to avoid state usury laws or to act as nontaxable agents of a related partnership. The case below is the Supreme Court's most recent pronouncement on this issue.

Commissioner v. Bollinger

Supreme Court of the United States, 1988.
485 U.S. 340, 108 S.Ct. 1173.

■ Justice Scalia delivered the opinion of the Court.

Petitioner the Commissioner of Internal Revenue challenges a decision by the United States Court of Appeals for the Sixth Circuit holding that a corporation which held record title to real property as agent for the corporation's shareholders was not the owner of the property for purposes of federal income taxation. 807 F.2d 65 (1986). We granted certiorari, 482 U.S. 913, 107 S.Ct. 3183, 96 L.Ed.2d 672 (1987), to resolve a conflict in the courts of appeals over the tax treatment of corporations purporting to be agents for their shareholders. * * *

I.

Respondent Jesse C. Bollinger, Jr., developed, either individually or in partnership with some or all of the other respondents, eight apartment complexes in Lexington, Kentucky. (For convenience we will refer to all the ventures as "partnerships.") Bollinger initiated development of the first apartment complex, Creekside North Apartments, in 1968. The Massachusetts Mutual Life Insurance Company agreed to provide permanent financing by lending $1,075,000 to "the corporate nominee of Jesse C. Bollinger, Jr." at an annual interest rate of eight percent, secured by a mortgage on the property and a personal guaranty from Bollinger. The loan commit-

---

1. Reg. § 301.7701–4(a).

2. Reg. § 301.7701–4(b).

3. Reg. § 301.7701–2(c)(1); –3(a), (b)(1)

(i).

ment was structured in this fashion because Kentucky's usury law at the time limited the annual interest rate for noncorporate borrowers to seven percent. Ky.Rev.Stat. §§ 360.010, 360.025 (1972). Lenders willing to provide money only at higher rates required the nominal debtor and record title holder of mortgaged property to be a corporate nominee of the true owner and borrower. On October 14, 1968, Bollinger incorporated Creekside, Inc., under the laws of Kentucky; he was the only stockholder. The next day, Bollinger and Creekside, Inc., entered into a written agreement which provided that the corporation would hold title to the apartment complex as Bollinger's agent for the sole purpose of securing financing, and would convey, assign, or encumber the property and disburse the proceeds thereof only as directed by Bollinger; that Creekside, Inc., had no obligation to maintain the property or assume any liability by reason of the execution of promissory notes or otherwise; and that Bollinger would indemnify and hold the corporation harmless from any liability it might sustain as his agent and nominee.

Having secured the commitment for permanent financing, Bollinger, acting through Creekside, Inc., borrowed the construction funds for the apartment complex from Citizens Fidelity Bank and Trust Company. Creekside, Inc., executed all necessary loan documents including the promissory note and mortgage, and transferred all loan proceeds to Bollinger's individual construction account. Bollinger acted as general contractor for the construction, hired the necessary employees, and paid the expenses out of the construction account. When construction was completed, Bollinger obtained, again through Creekside, Inc., permanent financing from Massachusetts Mutual Life in accordance with the earlier loan commitment. These loan proceeds were used to pay off the Citizens Fidelity construction loan. Bollinger hired a resident manager to rent the apartments, execute leases with tenants, collect and deposit the rents, and maintain operating records. The manager deposited all rental receipts into, and paid all operating expenses from, an operating account, which was first opened in the name of Creekside, Inc., but was later changed to "Creekside Apartments, a partnership." The operation of Creekside North Apartments generated losses for the taxable years 1969, 1971, 1972, 1973, and 1974, and ordinary income for the years 1970, 1975, 1976, and 1977. Throughout, the income and losses were reported by Bollinger on his individual income tax returns.

Following a substantially identical pattern, seven other apartment complexes were developed by respondents through seven separate partnerships. For each venture, a partnership executed a nominee agreement with Creekside, Inc., to obtain financing. (For one of the ventures, a different Kentucky corporation, Cloisters, Inc., in which Bollinger had a 50 percent interest, acted as the borrower and titleholder. For convenience, we will refer to both Creekside and Cloisters as "the corporation.") The corporation transferred the construction loan proceeds to the partnership's construction account, and the partnership hired a construction supervisor who oversaw construction. Upon completion of construction, each partnership actively managed its apartment complex, depositing all rental receipts into, and paying all expenses from, a separate partnership account for each apartment complex. The corporation had no assets, liabilities, employees, or bank accounts. In every case, the lenders regarded the partnership as the owner of the apartments and were aware that the corporation was acting as agent of the partnership in holding record title. The partnerships reported the income and losses generated by the apartment complexes on their partnership tax returns, and respondents reported their distributive share of the partnership income and losses on their individual tax returns.

The Commissioner of Internal Revenue disallowed the losses reported by respondents, on the ground that the standards set out in National Carbide Corp. v. Commissioner, 336 U.S. 422, 69 S.Ct. 726, 93 L.Ed. 779 (1949), were not met. The Commissioner contended that *National Carbide* required a corporation to have an arm's-length relationship with its shareholders before it could be recognized as their agent. Although not all respondents were shareholders of the corporation, the Commissioner took the position that the funds the partnerships disbursed to pay expenses should be deemed contributions to the corporation's capital, thereby making all respondents constructive stockholders. Since, in the Commissioner's view, the corporation rather than its shareholders owned the real estate, any losses sustained by the ventures were attributable to the corporation and not respondents. Respondents sought a redetermination in the United States Tax Court. The Tax Court held that the corporations were the agents of the partnerships and should be disregarded for tax purposes. On appeal, the United States Court of Appeals for the Sixth Circuit affirmed. 807 F.2d 65 (1986). We granted the Commissioner's petition for certiorari.

II.

For federal income tax purposes, gain or loss from the sale or use of property is attributable to the owner of the property. * * * The problem we face here is that two different taxpayers can plausibly be regarded as the owner. Neither the Internal Revenue Code nor the regulations promulgated by the Secretary of the Treasury provide significant guidance as to which should be selected. It is common ground between the parties, however, that if a corporation holds title to property as agent for a partnership, then for tax purposes the partnership and not the corporation is the owner. Given agreement on that premise, one would suppose that there would be agreement upon the conclusion as well. For each of respondents' apartment complexes, an agency agreement expressly provided that the corporation would "hold such property as nominee and agent for" the partnership, and that the partnership would have sole control of and responsibility for the apartment complex. The partnership in each instance was identified as the principal and owner of the property during financing, construction, and operation. The lenders, contractors, managers, employees, and tenants—all who had contact with the development—knew that the corporation was merely the agent of the partnership, if they knew of the existence of the corporation at all. In each instance the relationship between the corporation and the partnership was, in both form and substance, an agency with the partnership as principal.

The Commissioner contends, however, that the normal indicia of agency cannot suffice for tax purposes when, as here, the alleged principals are the controlling shareholders of the alleged agent corporation. That, it asserts, would undermine the principle of Moline Properties v. Commissioner, 319 U.S. 436, 63 S.Ct. 1132, 87 L.Ed. 1499 (1943), which held that a corporation is a separate taxable entity even if it has only one shareholder who exercises total control over its affairs. Obviously, *Moline's* separate-entity principle would be significantly compromised if shareholders of closely held corporations could, by clothing the corporation with some attributes of agency with respect to particular assets, leave themselves free at the end of the tax year to make a claim—perhaps even a good-faith claim—of either agent or owner status, depending upon which choice turns out to minimize their tax liability. The Commissioner does not have the resources to audit and litigate the many cases in which agency status could be thought debatable. Hence, the Commissioner argues, in this shareholder context he can reasonably demand that the taxpayer meet a prophylactically clear test of agency.

We agree with that principle, but the question remains whether the test the Commissioner proposes is appropriate. The parties have debated at length the significance of our opinion in National Carbide Corp. v. Commissioner, supra. In that case, three corporations that were wholly owned subsidiaries of another corporation agreed to operate their production plants as "agents" for the parent, transferring to it all profits except for a nominal sum. The subsidiaries reported as gross income only this sum, but the Commissioner concluded that they should be taxed on the entirety of the profits because they were not really agents. We agreed, reasoning first, that the mere fact of the parent's control over the subsidiaries did not establish the existence of an agency, since such control is typical of all shareholder-corporation relationships, id., 336 U.S. at 429–434, 69 S.Ct., at 730–732; and second, that the agreements to pay the parent all profits above a nominal amount were not determinative since income must be taxed to those who actually earn it without regard to anticipatory assignment, id., at 435–436, 69 S.Ct., at 733–734. We acknowledged, however, that there was such a thing as "a true corporate agent ... of [an] owner-principal," id., at 437, 69 S.Ct., at 734, and proceeded to set forth four indicia and two requirements of such status, the sum of which has become known in the lore of federal income tax law as the "six *National Carbide* factors":

> "[1] Whether the corporation operates in the name and for the account of the principal, [2] binds the principal by its actions, [3] transmits money received to the principal, and [4] whether receipt of income is attributable to the services of employees of the principal and to assets belonging to the principal are some of the relevant considerations in determining whether a true agency exists. [5] If the corporation is a true agent, its relations with its principal must not be dependent upon the fact that it is owned by the principal, if such is the case. [6] Its business purpose must be

the carrying on of the normal duties of an agent." Id., at 437, 69 S.Ct., at 734 (footnotes omitted).

We readily discerned that these factors led to a conclusion of nonagency in *National Carbide* itself. There each subsidiary had represented to its customers that it (not the parent) was the company manufacturing and selling its products; each had sought to shield the parent from service of legal process; and the operations had used thousands of the subsidiaries' employees and nearly $20 million worth of property and equipment listed as assets on the subsidiaries' books. Id., at 425, 434, 438, and n. 21, 69 S.Ct., at 728, 732–733, 734, and n. 21.

The Commissioner contends that the last two *National Carbide* factors are not satisfied in the present case. To take the last first: The Commissioner argues that here the corporation's business purpose with respect to the property at issue was not "the carrying on of the normal duties of an agent," since it was acting not as the agent but rather as the owner of the property for purposes of Kentucky's usury laws. We do not agree. It assuredly was not acting as the owner in fact, since respondents represented themselves as the principals to all parties concerned with the loans. Indeed, it was the lenders themselves who required the use of a corporate nominee. Nor does it make any sense to adopt a contrary-to-fact legal presumption that the corporation was the principal, imposing a federal tax sanction for the apparent evasion of Kentucky's usury law. To begin with, the Commissioner has not established that these transactions were an evasion. Respondents assert without contradiction that use of agency arrangements in order to permit higher interest was common practice, and it is by no means clear that the practice violated the spirit of the Kentucky law, much less its letter. It might well be thought that the borrower does not generally require usury protection in a transaction sophisticated enough to employ a corporate agent—assuredly not the normal *modus operandi* of the loan shark. That the statute positively envisioned corporate nominees is suggested by a provision which forbids charging the higher corporate interest rates "to a corporation, the principal asset of which shall be the ownership of a one (1) or two (2) family dwelling." Ky.Rev.Stat. § 360.025(2) (1987)—which would seem to prevent use of the nominee device for ordinary home-mortgage loans. In any event, even if the transaction did run afoul of the usury law, Kentucky, like most States, regards only the lender as the usurer, and the borrower as the victim. See Ky.Rev.Stat. § 360.020 (1987) (lender liable to borrower for civil penalty), § 360.990 (lender guilty of misdemeanor). Since the Kentucky statute imposed no penalties upon the borrower for allowing himself to be victimized, nor treated him as *in pari delictu,* but to the contrary enabled him to pay back the principal without any interest, and to sue for double the amount of interest already paid (plus attorney's fees), see Ky.Rev.Stat. § 360.020 (1972), the United States would hardly be vindicating Kentucky law by depriving the usury victim of tax advantages he would otherwise enjoy. In sum, we see no basis in either fact or policy for holding that the corporation was the principal because of the nature of its participation in the loans.

Of more general importance is the Commissioner's contention that the arrangements here violate the fifth *National Carbide* factor—that the corporate agent's "relations with its principal must not be dependent upon the fact that it is owned by the principal." The Commissioner asserts that this cannot be satisfied unless the corporate agent and its shareholder principal have an "arm's-length relationship" that includes the payment of a fee for agency services. The meaning of *National Carbide*'s fifth factor is, at the risk of understatement, not entirely clear. Ultimately, the relations between a corporate agent and its owner-principal are *always* dependent upon the fact of ownership, in that the owner can cause the relations to be altered or terminated at any time. Plainly that is not what was meant, since on that interpretation all subsidiary-parent agencies would be invalid for tax purposes, a position which the *National Carbide* opinion specifically disavowed. We think the fifth *National Carbide* factor—so much more abstract than the others—was no more and no less than a generalized statement of the concern, expressed earlier in our own discussion, that the separate-entity doctrine of *Moline* not be subverted.

In any case, we decline to parse the text of *National Carbide* as though that were itself the governing statute. As noted earlier, it is uncontested that the law attributes tax consequences of property held by a genuine agent to the principal; and we agree that it is reasonable for the Commissioner to demand unequivocal evidence of genuineness in the corporation-shareholder context, in order to prevent evasion of *Moline*. We see no basis, however, for holding that unequivocal evidence can only consist of the rigid requirements (arm's-length dealing plus agency fee) that the Commissioner suggests. Neither of those is demanded by the law of agency, which permits agents to be unpaid family members, friends, or associates. See Restatement (Second) of Agency §§ 16, 21, 22 (1958). It seems to us that the genuineness of the agency relationship is adequately assured, and tax-avoiding manipulation adequately avoided, when the fact that the corporation is acting as agent for its shareholders with respect to a particular asset is set forth in a written agreement at the time the asset is acquired, the corporation functions as agent and not principal with respect to the asset for all purposes, and the corporation is held out as the agent and not principal in all dealings with third parties relating to the asset. Since these requirements were met here, the judgment of the Court of Appeals is

Affirmed.

■ JUSTICE KENNEDY took no part in the consideration or decision of this case.

E. TAX POLICY ISSUES

1. CORPORATE INTEGRATION

The double tax on corporate profits has always been controversial. Economists and corporate finance theorists contend that it creates economic distortions and is inequitable, especially when compared to the pass-through treatment available to businesses that operate as partnerships, limited liability companies, or S corporations. Calls frequently have been made for "integration" of the individual and corporate income taxes into a single comprehensive system,[1] and the federal income tax began to move in that direction, albeit temporarily, by reducing the burden of the double tax with the introduction in 2003 of a preferential 15 percent rate on qualified dividends received by noncorporate shareholders.[2] The scheduled expiration of this crude but simple form of corporate tax relief has reignited the policy debate.

Although many developed countries have adopted an integration model to tax business income,[3] the conventional wisdom is that a fully integrated system in the United States is not a realistic option in the near term. A separate tax on corporations is a politically popular way to raise revenue. Proponents of the classic double tax system have argued that the concentration of economic power represented by the earnings of at least public companies is an appropriate object of a tax system that purports to be built on principles of fairness and ability to pay. Many closely held businesses are able to avoid the double tax by operating as partnerships, LLCs, or S corporations. Even if they do not qualify for pass-through treatment, most well-advised closely held C corporations engage in "self-help" integration techniques (such as payments of deductible compensation or interest) to avoid the sting of the corporate tax. Moreover, a large of amount of the taxable income of publicly traded corporation is only taxed once, at the corporate level, because of the significant concentration of stock held by tax-exempt pension funds and charitable endowments.

Despite these practical and political realities, proponents of integration continue to argue that the corporate income tax increases the cost of capital for U.S. corporations. It is said to be an indirect tax on shareholders rather than a cost of doing business that is passed on to consumers. So viewed, the tax violates notions of vertical equity (by uniformly taxing income earned indirectly by dissimilarly situated shareholders) and horizontal equity (because income earned through a C corporation is taxed more heavily than the same item of income earned through a proprietorship, S corporation or partnership).[4] Free-market economists contend that integration would encourage corporate earnings to be more freely distributed to shareholders, who then could decide whether to reinvest in the business instead of leaving that reinvestment decision to corporate managers.

1. See, e.g., McLure, "Integration of the Personal and Corporate Income Taxes: The Missing Element in Recent Tax Reform Proposals," 88 Harv.L.Rev. 532 (1975); Canellos, "Corporate Tax Integration: By Design or By Default?" in Corporate Tax Reform: A Report of the Invitational Conference on Subchapter C 129 (Am. Bar Ass'n Section on Taxation; N.Y. State Bar Ass'n Tax Section, 1988); Graetz & Warren, "Integration of Corporate and Individual Income Taxes: An Introduction," 84 Tax Notes 1767 (Sept. 27, 1999).

2. See Chapter 4A2, infra.

3. Among the countries with fully or partially integrated business taxation regimes are Canada, Germany, France, Australia, Italy, and the United Kingdom.

4. See Canellos, supra note 1, at 130–131.

With corporate tax reform again moving to the front burner in the tax policy conversation, it is worth pausing to consider how such a taxing regime that eliminates separate corporate and shareholder levels of taxation might be implemented. The potential integration models fall into two broad categories. The first, referred to as "full" or "complete" integration, would eliminate the corporate income tax and apply a pass-through taxing system to C corporations and their shareholders. A leading alternative is "partial" integration, which typically contemplates different types of tax relief for dividends paid by a corporation. Variations include giving shareholders a tax credit equal to a percentage of dividends paid or allowing shareholders to exclude from gross income a portion of dividends received during the year. Alternatively, the corporation could be permitted to deduct some or all of the dividends it pays its shareholders. The excerpts below survey the major integration prototypes.

Excerpt From Canellos, "Tax Integration by Design or by Default?"

Reprinted in Corporate Tax Reform: A Report of the Invitational Conference on Subchapter C 132–35 (American Bar Association, Section of Taxation; New York State Bar Association, Tax Section, 1988.)*

Formal Means for Achieving Integration

If it is determined that there should be some formal integration of corporate and shareholder taxation, the next issue is to choose among the range of techniques for achieving such integration. These techniques differ in terms of whether (1) double taxation is mitigated with respect to both retained and distributed assets; and (2) the actual taxpayer on corporate earnings is the corporation or the shareholder.

The purest form of integration is referred to as full or complete integration, and in effect represents the system of tax applicable to partnerships and S corporations. Under full integration, corporate earnings are attributed on some basis to shareholders who pay tax on them whether or not distributed. In turn, corporate losses flow through to shareholders for deduction by them subject to applicable restrictions on such flow through (such as basis rules, at risk rules, and the new passive loss limitations). The mechanics of existing full integration schemes differ. Thus, in the case of S corporations, the "entity" nature of the corporation predominates more than in the case of partnerships, which under Subchapter K are more often viewed as aggregates. As an example, the basis of corporate assets is generally not affected by sales of the S corporation's stock, whereas Section 754 allows for such an adjustment in the case of sales of partnership interests.

* Reprinted by permission of Peter C. Canellos; American Bar Association; and New York State Bar Association. Copyright © American Bar Association, 1988. All Rights Reserved.

A scheme of complete integration was recommended in the 1977 Treasury Department study entitled "Blueprints for Basic Tax Reform." Under that system, the holder of corporate shares on the first day of the corporation's taxable year would be attributed all the earnings of the corporation for the taxable year. His basis would be increased by any allocated earnings, and would be decreased by distributions and losses. Where shares were sold during the taxable year, the seller would not be taxed on the current year's income, nor would he have any basis increase in respect of such income. Given the premise of "Blueprints" that capital gain and ordinary income would be taxed alike, the exclusion of current year's income was fully offset by the failure to increase basis for current year's income.

"Blueprints" dealt at length with the administrative difficulties of a fully integrated scheme. Thus, the problem of taxing shareholders on amounts not received was to be ameliorated through a system of corporate remittance of a "withholding" tax. This tax was to be considered paid on behalf of shareholders. The audit adjustment problem was to be solved by having the adjustment treated as an income or deduction item attributed to those persons holding shares on the first day of the year in which the adjustment was made. Despite these efforts to grapple with the problems of full integration, "Blueprints" never got off the drawing board. In this respect, it shares the fate of all other schemes for applying a full integration system to corporations in general. In this connection, full integration systems were considered and rejected by Canada and Germany for reasons of theory as well as practicality.

A second system of integration provides for a deemed paid credit for shareholders receiving distributions. The corporation is the initial taxpayer. In essence, tax paid by the corporation on distributed earnings would be attributed to shareholders. Distributions would be "grossed up" and the shareholder would apply the attributed tax as a credit against his tax on the "grossed up" dividend. In effect, this system taxes the shareholder in much the same way in which United States domestic corporations are taxed on distributions from foreign subsidiaries. The credit system has been adopted in many foreign countries and represents the generally prevailing corporate integration system.

The credit system raises a number of serious issues. First, there is the issue whether credit should be allowed only for corporate taxes actually paid. If so, integration has the effect of cutting back on corporate tax preferences such as investment tax credits, as well as possibly eliminating the benefit of foreign tax credits. Second, there is the issue whether tax should be paid by the corporation in connection with distributions (the advance corporation tax in the United Kingdom being an example). Such a tax payment assures that the Treasury will receive tax equal to the credit claimed by shareholders and represents in effect a corporate minimum tax applicable even if preferences would otherwise reduce the effective rate of corporate "mainstream" tax below the rate of attributed credit. A third significant issue is whether the credit should be made available to foreign shareholders in domestic corporations. Such credit has generally not been provided to foreign shareholders in the absence of tax treaties. Indeed, a major advantage of the credit system is the leverage which it provides to the taxing jurisdiction in negotiating favorable treaties with other countries.

A third system of integration reduces the corporate tax on distributed profits. This can be achieved by either a dividends-paid deduction or a split-rate system which taxes distributed earnings at a lower rate than retained earnings. The split-rate system had been used in Germany prior to Germany's adoption of the credit system. A dividends-paid deduction had been recommended in the 1984 Treasury Department Tax Reform Proposals, as well as the House version of the 1986 Act. This system of integration relieves corporate tax on distributed earnings at the corporate level rather than offsetting the second tax otherwise payable by shareholders. It raises some of the same issues discussed above in the case of the credit system. In addition, it raises other serious concerns. First, unless measures are taken to alter this result, a dividends-paid deduction or split-rate system has the effect of allowing corporate earnings to pass untaxed to shareholders who are not taxpayers (e.g., tax-exempt organizations and foreign shareholders). The Treasury Department's tax reform proposals would have sought to recapture some of the tax lost as the result of distributions to foreign shareholders by imposing a special withholding tax on dividends qualifying for the dividends-paid deduction. It acknowledged, however, that such a withholding tax would violate most existing tax treaties.

A final system for achieving integration with respect to distributed earnings is to exclude such distributions from the recipient's income.* This system would permit a shareholder to exclude from income dividends paid from a "previously taxed income" account. Issues raised by this system of integration include whether a selling shareholder should receive a basis increase for undistributed, previously-taxed income allocated to his account; and the allocation of distributions among the categories of previously-taxed income, pre-integration earnings, and earnings accumulated after integration which had not been previously taxed (for example, because of corporate tax preferences).

As this short summary demonstrates, difficult issues must be considered and dealt with in determining which, if any, path to express integration should be taken. Typically, the integration scheme which is adopted is tailored to meet the needs of the particular taxing jurisdiction—its historic tax system, the nature of its capital markets, the role of inward and outward international investment, and other factors. Where integration was adopted, it followed a long period of scholarly analysis and political input. Much of that work has already been undertaken in the United States. Despite these efforts, however, we are no closer to formal integration than we were in the sixties. Indeed, the 1986 Act has gone in the

* An analysis of this approach is contained in Peel, A Proposal for Eliminating Double Taxation of Corporate Dividends, 39 Tax Lawyer 1 (1985).

opposite direction by increasing the relative burden of corporate as compared with individual income taxes.

Excerpt From Joint Committee on Taxation, Present Law and Background Relating to Selected Business Tax Issues

(JCX–41–06), September 19, 2006.

IV. CORPORATE INTEGRATION

A. Background and Issues

The present law structure of a separate entity level tax on corporate income has long been recognized to create a variety of economic distortions. The two levels of tax on corporate form income (entity and individual level), as compared to the single individual level tax imposed on pass-through entities (S-corps, partnerships, LLCs), create a bias against the corporate form of organization; this in turn limits investors' access to publicly traded equity investment, which may impose a particular burden to smaller investors who are less likely to have significant access to equity investments in pass-through entities. To the extent that the two levels of tax impose a higher level of tax on investment generally, the incentive to save is reduced. The resulting increase in the cost of capital needed to finance new investment will lead to lower capital formation, thereby reducing future output and productivity. An additional distortion resulting from the present law corporate income tax rules is the incentive to finance new investments from debt rather than equity on account of the deductibility of interest payments on debt but no comparable deduction for dividends paid on equity.[39] Over-reliance on debt financing can increase bankruptcy risk. Finally, there may be incentives created for the retention of earnings in the corporation, which may lead to distortions in the allocation of capital to the extent that corporations with current earnings have less favorable investment opportunities than would their shareholders.[40] In addition, present law results in considerable complexity and tax planning as taxpay-

---

39. Some investors, however, may prefer equity to debt. * * *

40. The two-tier tax on dividend distributions can make it more desirable for a corporation to use retained earnings rather than new equity for its investments. Shareholders can find such earnings retention attractive (subject to the accumulated earnings tax and personal holding company rules * * *) if the shareholder expects to defer tax on capital gains for a substantial period or to hold stock until death (so that appreciation can be passed to his heirs free of individual income tax).

There also may be an incentive under present law to retain earnings if the corporation's effective tax rate on reinvestment is lower than the shareholder tax rate on distributed earnings. By contrast, if the shareholder's tax rate is significantly lower than the corporation's effective tax rate—for example, if the shareholder is a tax-exempt entity or is entitled to a corporate dividends-received deduction or to the lower rates on dividends to individuals, or if the distribution can be structured as a stock buyback eligible for capital gains rates and basis recovery—there may be a tax incentive to distribute earnings or a reduced incentive to retain earnings.

ers seek to structure the most tax-favorable form of doing business and providing returns to investors.

At the same time, proposals to eliminate separate corporate and shareholder levels of taxation (referred to as "corporate integration") involve significant policy decisions and can also produce considerable complexity. Under present law, although the Code provides rules for imposing separate tax at the corporate and at the shareholder level, this does not always result in actual payment of two levels of tax. In some cases, the amounts that are distributed to shareholders may have borne less than a full tax at the corporate level due to the operation of various deductions, deferrals, or other provisions that have reduced or eliminated corporate level tax. Also, in some cases, shareholders are tax-exempt, or the rate of tax the shareholder may pay is reduced due to capital gains treatment, the lower rates for dividends of individuals, the dividends-received deduction for corporations, step-up in basis of stock at death, or other provisions. Thus, under present law, the combined individual and corporate tax rates on corporate earnings that are distributed to shareholders may not be as great as two full levels of tax, and may be less than a single full level of tax. If a decision were made to increase corporate integration, policy decisions would need to be made regarding those situations in which at least one level of tax should be collected and at which level (corporate or shareholder) it should be collected. Complexity would be involved in co-ordinating the tax results at the entity and individual levels.

As one example, consider a corporation whose earnings are subject to little or no tax due to tax incentives or preferences for particular types of investment or business activities. Under present law, earnings of such a corporation distributed to taxable investors, or gains of such investors from retained earnings, may still be taxed to the investors at the "second level" of tax. In considering a form of corporate integration, decisions would have be made whether to collect at least one full level of tax or whether to pass through the tax benefits to investors. If the latter decision is made, issues may still arise regarding the appropriate investors to receive the benefit and how to treat situations where shares have changed hands between the time of the tax benefited activities and the time of the distribution. Present law rules for partnerships contain elaborate rules that attempt to prevent the misallocation of certain tax benefits to partners.

As another example, consider a corporation that conducts a business activity and that has tax-exempt shareholders. Under present law, the income from the business activity is taxed at the corporate level although the tax-exempt shareholders are not taxed on dividend income or capital gain from their investment. Under present law, the single-level-of-tax regimes do collect a business income tax from business activities, even when there are tax-exempt investors. Thus, if the tax-exempt corporate shareholders of C corporation conducting a business were instead equity owners of a partnership or of an S corporation that conducted the same business, they would be subject to unrelated business income tax on their share of partnership or S corporation income from such business, whether or not distributed. In considering a form of corporate integration, a decision would have to be made whether to continue the present law approach that the presence of tax-exempt equity investors does not exempt business income from tax.[41]

Foreign investment situations also present issues relating to the adoption and design of an integrated system. As one example, under present law, the U.S. collects a corporate level tax on U.S. corporate income and a withholding tax on dividend distributions to foreign shareholders.[42] Integration proposals that would unilaterally reduce the tax on dividends to foreign investors or provide refundable credits for any U.S. corporate tax paid could raise issues if foreign countries do not provide similar benefits to U.S investors.

B.   Integration Approaches

A number of methods could be used to achieve full or partial integration, each of which has associated policy and administrative considerations.[43]

One form, known as "full" integration, involves passing through all items of corporate income and deduction to shareholders, including the pass-through of items of a publicly-traded corporation. This approach would tax investors currently on their share of corporate income even if such income is not distributed to them. Full integration is considered to involve administrative difficulties in determining a shareholder's appropriate share of income, especially when stock changes hands during a corporate taxable year.

Other forms of integration include reduction of the corporate tax on distributed or retained corporate earnings, or of the individual tax on distributed earnings or on capital gains attributable to undistributed earnings. Complexity can arise, however, if it is desired to design a system that will assure the collection of one level of tax, because of the necessity for mechanisms that assure that the amounts exempted at either the shareholder or corporate level in fact are taxed at the other level.

The principal approaches to integration usually discussed involve forms of dividend relief and thereby apply only to distributed earnings. One approach would give relief by allowing the corporation or shareholders to

---

41. Because present law does not impose tax on interest payments to tax-exempt investors paid by partnerships or S corporations engaged in business activity, there is an incentive for tax-exempt investors to hold debt rather than equity of business conducted in such pass-through forms under present law. In considering approaches to integration, consideration may be given to whether to continue this type of difference in the treatment of debt and equity when imposing only a single level of tax.

42. However, interest paid to foreign shareholders is generally not taxed by the U.S.

43. For a more extensive discussion of the background and issues relating to integration, see Michael J. Graetz and Alvin C. Warren, Jr., Integration of the U.S. Corporate and Individual Income Taxes (Tax Analysts, 1998); Joint Committee on Taxation, Federal Income Tax Aspects of Corporate Financial Structures, JCS–1–89 (January 18, 1989).

deduct or exclude a portion of dividends. Another approach provides a credit to shareholders for taxes paid by the corporation. In 1992, the Treasury Department published a report containing a prototype for a form of dividend relief through exclusion of previously taxed dividends from shareholder income.[44] In 1993, the American Law Institute published a proposal involving a credit system based on the model used by a number of other countries.[45] Other proposals relating to approaching a single level of tax on business income are discussed in the 2005 Report of the President's Advisory Panel on Tax Reform.[46]

In 2003, the President's budget proposals to the Congress contained a dividend relief proposal that attempted to provide relief to shareholders of corporations on dividends attributable to previously taxed income of the corporation and also to provide a basis adjustment in a shareholder's stock for undistributed previously taxed income allocated to such stock.[47] Subsequently, The Jobs Growth and Tax Relief Act of 2003, following a dividend relief approach, temporarily reduced and conformed (but did not eliminate) the tax rates on dividends and capital gains, through the end of 2008. The Tax Increase Prevention and Reconciliation Act of 2005 extended this rate structure though 2010 [and it later was extended again through 2012. Ed.].

As noted previously, a determination whether to adopt a particular form of integration involves significant policy determinations. Among the policy decisions are whether to pass through any corporate business level tax benefits to individual investors; how to treat income attributable to tax-exempt investors; how to treat international transactions; and how to treat existing corporate equity investments. Some decisions may be more easily implemented if the basic form of relief is structured as a dividend exclusion at either the corporate or shareholder level. Other issues may be more readily addressed by giving shareholders a credit for their share of the corporate tax when they receive dividends.

---

44. U.S. Department of the Treasury, Integration of the Individual and Corporate Tax Systems, Taxing Business Income Once (1992). This study also considered alternative integration prototypes. One was a "shareholder allocation" prototype that would tax both distributed and retained earnings at the shareholder's tax rate. Another was a "Comprehensive Business Income Tax" prototype that would, in effect, extend a dividend exclusion system to payments of interest, and deny interest deductions, in order to equalize the treatment of debt and equity; and that would tax corporate and noncorporate businesses in the same manner. (See introduction to the study at p.15). This study and a general introduction on corporate integration can be found reprinted in Graetz and Warren, *op. cit., supra.*

45. Alvin C. Warren, Jr., Integration of Individual and Corporate Income Taxes (American Law Institute, 1993). This study and a general introduction on corporate integration can be found reprinted in Graetz and Warren, *op.cit., supra.*

46. The President's Advisory Panel on Tax Reform; Simple, Fair and Pro–Growth: Proposals to Fix American's Tax System (November 2005), Chapters 7, 8 and 9 (discussing a proposal for a business tax reform while retaining some individual tax on investment returns, and also including discussions of value added and sales taxes as alternatives to an income tax).

47. Department of the Treasury, General Explanations of the Administration's Fiscal Year 2004 Revenue Proposals, February 2003.

In addition, a system imposing only one level of tax would not necessarily be simpler than present law. For example, the rules for taxing income of partnerships (which is subject to tax only at the partner level) are quite complex. Similarly, those integration approaches that provide dividend relief and that also seek to collect at least one level of tax can involve complexity. This can result from the need to provide rules that track whether income has borne one level of tax when earned at the corporate entity level (or instead has enjoyed tax benefits that reduce or eliminate the corporate level tax), and whether the particular type of shareholder to which the income is distributed would otherwise generally pay tax on the distribution, absent integration relief.

NOTE

After a flurry of activity in the early and mid–1990s, the integration debate went back into hibernation. Historically, the business community has not embraced the concept of integration, preferring instead to work within the existing system with its many opportunities to reduce or eliminate the corporate income tax. Corporate lobbyists continue to focus their attention on expanding corporate tax preferences (such as accelerated depreciation, research and development incentives, and targeted tax credits) and repealing the corporate alternative minimum tax. Some commentators have suggested that corporate managers view integration as a threat to their power base because it would force them to act more as stewards of shareholders interests.[4] It seemed more and more likely that integration would remain a topic for occasional academic discourse rather than a viable political reality.

And then, surprising the skeptics, President George W. Bush revived the debate in early 2003 with a bold proposal that became the controversial centerpiece of his economic stimulus package. The original proposal provided for a 100 percent exclusion for all dividends paid out of income previously taxed at the corporate level. The excerpt below is from a Treasury Department press release explaining the proposal and providing an overview of some of the details. Keep in mind that the description of "current law" is as it was prior to individual taxpayer rate reductions (known as the "Bush tax cuts") enacted in 2003.

Description of President's Dividend Exclusion Proposal

U.S. Dept. of the Treasury, Jan. 21, 2003.

Eliminate the Double Taxation of Corporate Earnings

Current Law

Income earned by a corporation is taxed at the corporate level, generally at the rate of 35 percent. If the corporation distributes earnings to

---

4. See, e.g., Arlen & Weiss, "A Political Theory of Corporate Taxation," 105 Yale L.   J. 325 (1995).

shareholders in the form of dividends, the income generally is taxed a second time at the shareholder level (at rates as high as 38.6 percent). If a corporation instead retains its earnings, the value of corporate stock will reflect the retained earnings. When shareholders sell their stock, that additional value will be taxed as capital gains (generally at a maximum rate of 20 percent for long-term capital gains). The combined rate of tax on corporate income can be as high as 60 percent, far in excess of rates of tax imposed on other types of income.

Reasons for Change

The double taxation of corporate profits creates significant economic distortions.

- First, double taxation creates a bias in favor of debt as compared to equity, because payments of interest by the corporation are deductible while returns on equity in the form of dividends and retained earnings are not. Excessive debt increases the risks of bankruptcy during economic downturns.

- Second, double taxation of corporate profits creates a bias in favor of unincorporated entities (such as partnerships and limited liability companies), which are not subject to the double tax.

- Third, because dividends are taxed at a higher rate than are capital gains, double taxation of corporate profits encourages a corporation to retain its earnings rather than distribute them in the form of dividends. This lessens the pressure on corporate managers to undertake only the most productive investments because corporate investments funded by retained earnings may receive less scrutiny than investments funded by outside equity or debt financing.

- Fourth, double taxation encourages corporations to engage in transactions such as share repurchases rather than to pay dividends because share repurchase permit the corporation to distribute earnings at reduced capital gains tax rates.

- Fifth, double taxation increases incentives for corporations to engage in transactions for the sole purpose of minimizing their tax liability.

By eliminating double taxation, the proposal will reduce tax-induced distortions that, in the current tax system, encourage firms to use debt rather than equity finance and to adopt noncorporate rather than corporate structures. Because shareholders will be exempt from tax only on distributions of previously taxed corporate income, the proposal will reduce incentives for certain types of corporate tax planning. In addition, the proposal will enhance corporate governance by eliminating the current bias against the payment of dividends. Dividends can provide evidence of a corporation's underlying financial health and enable investors to evaluate more readily a corporation's financial condition. This, in turn, increases the accountability of corporate management to its investors.

Proposal

Overview

The proposal would integrate the corporate and individual income taxes so that corporate earnings generally will be taxed once and only once. Under the proposal, public and private corporations would be permitted to distribute nontaxable dividends to their shareholders to the extent that those dividends are paid out of income previously taxed at the corporate level. The proposal generally would be effective for distributions made on or after January 1, 2003, with respect to corporate earnings after 2000.

To calculate the amount that can be distributed to its shareholders without further tax, a corporation will compute an excludable dividend amount (EDA) for each year. The EDA reflects income of the corporation that has been fully taxed. Thus, for example, a corporation with $100 of income that pays $35 of U.S. income taxes will have an EDA of $65 that can be distributed as excludable dividends.

If an amount would be a dividend under current law, it will be treated as an excludable dividend to the extent of EDA. Excludable dividends will not be taxed to shareholders. If a corporation's distributions during a calendar year exceed its EDA, only a proportionate amount of each distribution will be treated as an excludable dividend. Ordering rules are provided below for distributions that exceed EDA.

The capital gains tax on the sale of stock will be retained. Without further change, this would create an incentive for corporations to distribute previously taxed income as excludable dividends rather than retaining earnings for future investment. This is because excludable dividends would not be taxed to the shareholders but capital gains that represent retained earnings would be taxed to the shareholders when they sell their shares.

To ensure that distributions and retentions of previously taxed earnings are treated similarly, shareholders will be permitted to increase their basis in their shares to reflect that the retained earnings have already been taxed at the corporate level. As an alternative to distributing excludable dividends, corporations generally may allocate throughout the year all or a portion of the EDA to provide these basis increases. The basis increases will not be taxable. The effect of the basis increases will be to reduce the capital gains realized when shareholders sell their stock to the extent that the sales price reflects the corporation's retained, previously taxed earnings.

NOTE

The Bush Administration's proposal received a mixed response from Congress and the business community. Opponents argued that it was too complex, favored the wealthy without providing any immediate economic stimulus, and contributed to the federal budget deficit. Tax-privileged sectors, such as issuers of municipal bonds, banks, insurance companies, and real estate investment trusts, were concerned that their existing tax preferences would be undermined. Tax-exempt shareholders, such as pension funds and charitable foundations, as well as companies that were losing money or able to shelter their income from the corporate income tax, had little to gain from the proposal.

Supporters argued that eliminating the double tax on corporate earnings was a long overdue correction to a flawed system that encouraged excessive corporate debt, discouraged the payment of dividends and, in so doing, contributed to a misallocation of capital by favoring retained earnings over cash payouts. Some proponents predicted that a full dividend exclusion would make corporate managers more accountable to shareholders and increase shareholder confidence in the credibility of corporate earnings reports.

It became clear as the debate raged that the Bush dividend exclusion proposal would not be enacted because of its complexity and revenue effect. The ultimate compromise—a 15 percent maximum rate on both qualified dividends and most long-term capital gains—took a small step toward integrating the corporate and individual income taxes. Notably, dividends qualify for the reduced rate whether or not they are paid out of income previously taxed at the corporate level. Some of the details are discussed in Chapter 4. These reduced rates, however, expire at the end of 2012 unless Congress and the President agree to extend or make them permanent.

2.   OTHER CORPORATE TAX REFORM OPTIONS

Even though corporate integration is the norm in many developed countries and enjoys wide support from academics, adoption of any of the integration models in the United States would be a radical step that is unlikely to be taken during the remaining life expectancy of the current co-authors of this text. But a more traditional approach to corporate tax reform is within the realm of possibility and an active dialogue is in progress, at least for political posturing purposes. The recent discussion has emphasized three broad avenues for reform: (1) lowering the statutory corporate rates to make U.S. companies more competitive in the global economy; (2) broadening the tax base; and (3) changing and simplifying the rules on how U.S. companies with foreign active business income are taxed.[1]

In his 2011 State of the Union address, President Obama included a call for corporate tax reform that would lower rates without increasing the deficit and eliminate enough corporate tax breaks to make the package revenue-neutral. Few if any specifics were provided, but examples of "tax expenditures" that would need to be curtailed are accelerated depreciation for plant and equipment, tax credits for research, taxpayer-friendly provisions benefitting the oil and gas industry and many more. A somewhat more specific model was proposed by the National Commission on Fiscal Responsibility and Reform, a Presidentially-appointed bipartisan panel

---

1. For an entire book on this topic, see   (2009).
Shaviro, Decoding the U.S. Corporate Tax

chaired by Allen Simpson and Erskine Bowles. The Commission issued a report outlining a broad six-part blueprint of tax and deficit reduction options in December 2010.[2] Calling the Internal Revenue Code "broken" and in urgent need of comprehensive reform, the Simpson–Bowles Commission crisply summarized an emerging consensus with regard to the corporate tax:[3]

> The corporate income tax * * * hurts America's ability to compete. On the one hand, statutory rates in the U.S. are significantly higher than the average for industrialized countries (even as revenue collection is low), and our method of taxing foreign income is outside the norm. The U.S. is one of the only industrialized countries with a hybrid system of taxing active foreign-source income. The current system puts U.S. corporations at a competitive disadvantage against their foreign competitors. * * *

> Tax reform should lower tax rates, reduce the deficit, simplify the tax code, reduce the tax gap, and make America the best place to start a business and create jobs. Rather than tinker around the edges of the existing tax code, the Commission proposes fundamental and comprehensive tax reform that achieves these basic goals [the goals were lower rates, a broader base, less spending through the tax code, deficit reduction, and maintaining or increasing progressivity in the tax code. Ed.]

The Commission recommended replacing the current corporate tax rate structure with a single rate between 23 and 29 percent and eliminating all "special subsidies" for businesses. Among the most prominent "tax expenditures" targeted for repeal were accelerated cost recovery methods, various tax benefits for the oil and gas industry, the deduction for domestic production activities, numerous business tax credits, and the ability to use last in-first out inventory accounting.[4]

There is actually some bipartisan sentiment for lowering corporate tax rates, but the devil is in the details. Some Republican legislators agree that the statutory corporate tax rates, which are among the highest in the world, should be reduced to stimulate economic growth. But they are less enthusiastic about eliminating corporate tax breaks, arguing that most were enacted to stimulate deserving industries. President Obama appears to agree that corporate income tax rates should be reduced in exchange for a broader base, but at the same time he continues to support use of the tax system to stimulate certain types of economic activity, such as clean energy, research, education and jobs. The business community is divided. Some sectors would welcome a corporate tax rate reduction even if it means fewer deductions and credits. Others, especially businesses that can reduce their effective tax rates by using targeted tax breaks, are less enthusiastic.

---

2. The Moment of Truth, Report of the National Commission on Fiscal Responsibility and Reform (December 2010), available at http://www.fiscalcommission/gov/sites/fiscal commission.gov/files/documents/TheMoment ofTruth12_1_2010.pdf.

3. Id. at 28.

4. Id. at 29.

Owners of businesses operating as pass-through entities (such as partnerships, LLCs and S corporations) are concerned because they would not benefit from a lower corporate income tax rate and yet lose valuable tax breaks.

Further complicating the task is the treatment of U.S. multinational corporations—a topic well beyond the scope of this text. Suffice it to note that any corporate tax overhaul would require lawmakers to confront the complex issue of how and when U.S. multinational corporations are taxed on the active business income they earn abroad. Most other industrialized countries use a "territorial" system, taxing corporations only on income earned within their borders irrespective of the residence of the taxpayer. The United States, however, taxes worldwide income, generally deferring taxation of most active business income earned abroad until it is repatriated and using the foreign tax credit to prevent double taxation. The Simpson–Bowles Commission recommended a move toward a territorial system to bring the U.S. more in line with its international trading partners, but its report did not delve into the many devilish details, including anti-avoidance and transition rules.

For now, all the talk about corporate tax reform is part of a broader political conversation about deficits, taxes and the economy. Although the Obama administration has promised that a comprehensive plan is "coming soon," corporate tax reform was not seriously discussed as part of the deficit reduction negotiations that broke down in 2011. As this text went to press in early 2012, the Treasury Department finally issued its "framework" for business tax reform,[5] which contained five major elements: (1) reducing the statutory corporate rate from 35 to 28 percent while eliminating "loopholes and subsidies" to reduce distortions that hurt productivity and growth; (2) adding tax incentives (loopholes and subsidies?) to strengthen American manufacturing and innovation; (3) strengthening the international tax system, including establishing a new minimum tax on foreign earnings, to encourage domestic investment; (4) simplifying and cutting taxes for "small businesses;" and (5) not adding a "dime to the deficit" by ensuring that business tax reform was revenue neutral. The conversation is sure to continue, but enactment of any meaningful tax reform must await the outcome of the 2012 elections. Even then, a real consensus for a tax reform package where there are both winners and losers will be difficult to achieve without a change in the political environment.

5. The President's Framework of Business Tax Reform: A Joint Report by the White House and the Department of the Treasury (Feb. 2012).

PART TWO

TAXATION OF C CORPORATIONS

CHAPTER 2

FORMATION OF A CORPORATION

A. INTRODUCTION TO SECTION 351

Code: §§ 351(a), (c), (d)(1)–(2); 358(a), (b)(1); 362(a), (e); 368(c); 1032(a); 1223(1), (2); 1245(b)(3).

Regulations: §§ 1.351–1(a), (b); 1.358–1(a), –2(b)(2); 1.362–1(a); 1.1032–1(a), (d).

Policy of Section 351. In order to commence business operations, a corporation needs assets. It normally acquires these assets—known as the initial "capital" of a corporation—by issuing shares of stock in exchange for cash or other property, or by borrowing. When a corporation raises its equity capital by issuing stock solely for cash, the tax consequences are routine: the shareholder simply has made a cash purchase and takes a cost basis in the shares acquired.[1] If the corporation issues stock for property other than cash, the exchange would be a taxable event without a special provision of the Code. The shareholder would recognize gain or loss equal to the difference between the fair market value of the stock received and the adjusted basis of the property transferred to the corporation.[2] The exchange also might be taxable to the corporation. Its gain—more theoretical than real—would be the excess of the fair market value of the cash and property received over the corporation's zero basis in the newly issued shares.

A simple example illustrates the possibilities. Assume that A decides to form Venture, Inc. by transferring appreciated property with a value of $100 and a basis of $10 in exchange for Venture stock with a value of $100. A would realize $90 of gain and, in theory, Venture might be said to realize $100 of gain by issuing its stock. If both parties were taxed on this simple transaction, however, corporate formations would be severely impeded. To remove these tax obstacles, Congress long ago decided that routine incorporations should be tax free to the shareholders and the corporation. At the shareholder level, Section 351(a) provides that no gain or loss shall be recognized if property is transferred to a corporation by one or more persons solely in exchange for its stock if the transferor or transferors of property are in "control" of the corporation "immediately after the exchange." Section 351 applies both to transfers to newly formed and preexisting corporations provided that the transferors of property have "control" immediately after the exchange. At the corporate level, Section 1032(a) provides that a corporation shall not recognize gain or loss on the

---

1. I.R.C. § 1012.　　　　**2.** I.R.C. § 1001(a).

receipt of money or other property in exchange for its stock (including treasury stock).[3] These general rules are accompanied by special basis provisions and are subject to several exceptions, all of which will be discussed as this chapter unfolds.

The policy of Section 351 is one familiar to nonrecognition provisions. The transfer of appreciated or depreciated property to a corporation controlled by the transferor is viewed as a mere change in the form of a shareholder's investment. Consider, for example, the sole proprietor who decides to incorporate an ongoing business. The proprietor clearly *realizes* gain in a theoretical sense when the assets of the business are exchanged for all of the new corporation's stock. But he has neither "cashed out" nor appreciably changed the nature of his investment. He owns and operates the same business with the same assets, only now in corporate solution. Incorporation does not seem to be the appropriate occasion to impose a tax if the transferred assets have appreciated or to allow a deductible loss if the assets have decreased in value.

This policy is more difficult to defend in the case of a minority shareholder. Consider a taxpayer who exchanges appreciated land with a basis of $40 and a fair market value of $100 for a ten percent stock interest in a newly formed corporation with a total net worth of $1,000. As a result of the exchange, the taxpayer's continuing interest in the land has been significantly reduced, and he now owns a ten percent interest in a variety of other assets. Presumably, the exchange should be taxable and he should recognize $60 of gain. Similarly, if two or more unrelated taxpayers join together and transfer various assets to a new corporation in exchange for its stock, they arguably have changed the form of their investment; each now owns a part of several assets in corporate solution rather than all of the assets previously owned directly. Despite these arguments, Congress chose not to make such fine distinctions, perhaps because its primary goal in enacting Section 351 was to facilitate a wide variety of corporate formations. Section 351 thus is broad enough to embrace transfers of property by a group of previously unrelated persons—provided, of course, that the specific statutory requirements set forth below have been met.[4]

Basic Requirements. The three major requirements to qualify for nonrecognition of gain or loss under Section 351 are as follows:

(1) One or more persons (including individuals, corporations, partnerships and other entities) must transfer "property" to the corporation;

(2) The transfer must be solely in exchange for stock of the corporation; and

(3) The transferor or transferors, as a group, must be in "control" of the corporation "immediately after the exchange."

---

3. See Reg. § 1.1032–1(a).

4. But see I.R.C. § 351(e)(1), which disallows nonrecognition in the case of a "transfer of property to an investment company." This provision is intended to preclude a group of taxpayers from achieving a tax-free diversification of their investment portfolios through an exchange with a newly formed investment company. See Reg. § 1.351–1(c) for the details.

"Control" for this purpose is defined by Section 368(c) as "the ownership of stock possessing at least 80 percent of the total combined voting power of all classes of stock entitled to vote and at least 80 percent of the total number of shares of all other classes of stock of the corporation." These requirements are not as simple as they may first appear. Section 351 contains several statutory terms of art, each of which has raised issues over the years. Before studying the requirements in detail, however, it is necessary to complete the basic statutory scheme by turning to the corollary rules on basis and holding period.

Shareholder Basis and Holding Period. If Section 351 applies to a transfer, any gain or loss realized by the shareholder is not currently recognized. The policy of nonrecognition requires the preservation of these tax attributes to prevent total forgiveness of the unrecognized gain or forfeiture of any unrecognized loss. This goal is achieved by Section 358(a)(1), which provides that the basis of the stock ("nonrecognition property") received in a Section 351 exchange shall be the same as the basis of the property transferred by the shareholder to the corporation—an "exchanged basis" in the jargon of the Code.[5] Returning to the introductory example, if A transfers property to Venture, Inc. with a basis of $10 and a fair market value of $100 for stock with a value of $100 in a transaction governed by Section 351, A's basis in the stock will be $10. Assuming no decrease in the value of the stock, the $90 of gain that went unrecognized on the exchange will be recognized if and when A sells the stock.[6]

In keeping with this policy, Section 1223(1) provides that where a transferor receives property with an exchanged basis, such as stock in a Section 351 exchange, the holding period of that property is determined by including the period during which he held the transferred property if the transferred property is a capital asset or a Section 1231 asset; if it is not, the transferor's holding period begins on the date of the exchange.

Tax Consequences to Transferee Corporation. On the corporate side, Section 1032 provides that a corporation does not recognize gain or loss when it issues stock in exchange for money or property. Moreover, a corporation that receives property in exchange for its stock in a Section 351 exchange steps into the shoes of the transferor. Section 362(a) generally prescribes a "transferred basis"[7]—i.e., the corporation's basis in any property received in a Section 351 exchange is the same as the transferor's basis, thus preserving the gain or loss inherent in the asset for later recognition by the corporation. And Section 1223(2) provides that if property has a transferred (also known as a carryover) basis to the corporation, the transferor's holding period likewise will carry over.

---

5. I.R.C. § 7701(a)(44).

6. If a shareholder dies without selling the stock, however, his basis will be stepped up (or down) to its fair market value on the date of his death (or six months thereafter, if the alternate valuation date is elected for federal estate tax purposes). I.R.C. § 1014(a).

This would be the case, of course, if the shareholder had simply continued to hold the transferred assets out of corporate solution and thus is not inconsistent with the policy of Section 358.

7. I.R.C. § 7701(a)(43).

Limitations on Transfer of Built-in Losses. When controlling shareholders transfer noncash assets to a corporation in a Section 351 exchange, the economic gain or loss inherent in those assets is reflected in both the transferor's stock basis and the transferee corporation's basis in the assets. This potential for duplication of the same economic gain or loss has been a longstanding feature of the Section 351 nonrecognition scheme. When Congress discovered that some U.S. corporations were exploiting these rules by deducting the same losses twice, it did what came naturally and enacted yet another statutory watchdog to limit the recognition of losses. In so doing, it not only curtailed a potentially abusive tax shelter but also adversely affected many other transactions that may not be motivated by tax avoidance.

If property with a net built-in loss is transferred to a corporation in a Section 351 transaction or as a contribution to capital, the transferee corporation's aggregate adjusted basis of such property is limited to the fair market value of the transferred property immediately after the transfer.[8] This limitation is applied on a transferor-by-transferor basis rather than to an aggregated group of transferors.[9] Transferred property has a "net built-in loss" when the aggregate adjusted basis of the property exceeds its fair market value.[10] Any gain recognized by a transferor that increases the transferee corporation's basis in the transferred property is taken into account in determining whether the transferred property has a "net built-in loss" in the transferee's hands.[11]

If multiple properties are transferred in the same transaction, some with built-in gains and others with built-in losses, the basis limitation only applies when there is a *net* built-in loss.[12] If more than one property with a built-in loss is transferred, the aggregate reduction in basis is allocated among the properties in proportion to their respective built-in losses immediately before the transaction.[13] Alternatively, the shareholder and the corporation may jointly elect to reduce the shareholder's basis in the stock that it receives to its fair market value.[14] The amount of basis reduction resulting from this election may not be any larger than what is necessary to eliminate the duplication of loss in the transferred assets. Thus, the amount of any stock basis reduction equals the amount of asset

---

8. I.R.C. § 362(e)(2).

9. Prop. Reg. § 1.362–4(b)(2).

10. Prop. Reg. § 1.362–4(b)(4)(ii), –4(d) Example 6.

11. Prop. Reg. § 1.362–4(b)(4)(ii), –4(d) Example 6.

12. I.R.C. § 362(e)(2)(A)(ii). Similar basis limitation rules apply to transactions where there is an "importation of a net built-in loss," such as a transfer of loss property to a domestic corporation by a person not subject to U.S. tax. See I.R.C. § 362(e)(1). The non-importation rule is designed to prevent the shifting of losses from transferors who

are not subject to U.S. tax, such as a foreign person or a domestic tax-exempt entity, to transferees who are taxable and can use the loss. In overlap situations where a transaction is subject to both loss limitation rules, Section 362(e)(2) can apply to the portion of the transaction not described in Section 362(e)(1). Prop. Reg. §§ 1.362–4(b)(3); 1.362–4(d) Example 7.

13. I.R.C. § 362(e)(2)(B); Prop. Reg. § 1.362–4(b)(1).

14. I.R.C. § 362(e)(2)(C).

basis reduction that would have been required under Section 362(e)(2) if the election had not been made.[15] If the election is made, the assets continue to have a built-in loss in the hands of the transferee corporation, but the loss will not be duplicated on the disposition of the shareholder's stock.

More to Come. All these basis rules are subject to modifications to be discussed later in this chapter,[16] and both Sections 358 and 362 apply to a variety of corporate transactions other than Section 351. For the moment, however, it is best to ignore these distractions and focus on the policy of continuity of tax characteristics that is an essential corollary to the nonrecognition principle of Section 351.

PROBLEM

A, B, C, D and E, all individuals, form X Corporation to engage in a manufacturing business. X issues 100 shares of common stock. A transfers $25,000 cash for 25 shares; B transfers inventory with a value of $10,000 and a basis of $5,000 for 10 shares; C transfers unimproved land with a value of $20,000 and a basis of $25,000 for 20 shares; D transfers equipment with a basis of $5,000 and a value of $25,000 (prior depreciation taken was $20,000) for 25 shares; and E transfers a $20,000 (face amount and value) installment note for 20 shares. E received the note in exchange for land with a $2,000 basis that he sold last year. The note is payable over a five-year period, beginning in two years, at $4,000 per year plus market rate interest.

(a) What are the tax consequences (gain or loss recognized, basis and holding period in the stock received) to each of the transferors? As to E, see I.R.C. § 453B(a); Reg. § 1.453–9(c)(2).

(b) What are the tax consequences (gain recognized, basis and holding period in each of the assets received) to X Corporation?

(c) Assume all the same facts except that C transfers two parcels of unimproved land (Parcel #1 and Parcel #2), each with a value of $10,000. C's basis in Parcel #1 is $15,000 and C's basis in Parcel #2 is $8,000. What result to C and X Corporation?

(d) There was $5,000 of gain inherent in the inventory transferred by B. If X Corporation later sells the inventory for $10,000, and B sells his stock for $10,000, how many times will that $5,000 of gain be taxed? Is there any justification for this result?

B.   REQUIREMENTS FOR NONRECOGNITION OF GAIN OR LOSS UNDER SECTION 351

The introductory problem illustrates that a tax-free exchange is easily accomplished if a group of individuals forms a corporation by transferring

---

15.   Prop. Reg. § 1.362–4(c)(3).   **16.**   See Section C1 of this chapter, infra.

property solely in exchange for common stock. But variations abound in the world of corporate formations, and the desires of the parties for a more complex transaction may conflict with the policy of nonrecognition. This section explores the requirements of Section 351 in more depth and shows that it often is possible, through careful planning, to reconcile these competing objectives.

1.   "CONTROL" IMMEDIATELY AFTER THE EXCHANGE

Code: §§ 351(a); 368(c).

Regulations: § 1.351–1(a)(1).

Section 351 applies only if the transferors of property, as a group, "control" the corporation immediately after the exchange. For this purpose, "control" is defined by Section 368(c) as: (1) the ownership of at least 80 percent of the total combined voting power of all classes of stock entitled to vote, and (2) at least 80 percent of the total number of shares of all other classes of stock. The dual standard apparently was designed to ensure that the requisite control would not exist unless the transferors owned more than 80 percent of both the voting power and the total value of the corporation. Both prongs of the "control" test raise potentially thorny definitional questions—e.g., what is "stock entitled to vote?"; how is "voting power" determined? But these questions seldom arise in practice either because the routine corporate formation involves only one class of voting common stock or the transferors of property collectively emerge from the exchange owning 100 percent of all classes of stock.

The requisite control must be obtained by one or more transferors of "property" who act in concert under a single integrated plan. There is no limit on the number of transferors, and some may receive voting stock while others receive nonvoting stock. If the corporation issues more than one class of nonvoting stock, the Service requires that the transferor group must own at least 80 percent of *each* class.[1]

To be part of an integrated plan, the transfers need not be simultaneous. It is sufficient if the rights of the parties are "previously defined" and the agreement proceeds with an "expedition consistent with orderly procedure."[2] More important than timing is whether the transfers are mutually interdependent steps in the formation and carrying on of the business. Thus, it is possible for transfers separated by less than an hour to be considered separately for purposes of the control requirement or for transfers several years apart to be treated as part of an integrated plan.[3]

Finally, the transferors of property must be in control "immediately after the exchange." Momentary control will not suffice if the holdings of the transferor group fall below the required 80 percent as a result of

---

1. Rev.Rul. 59–259, 1959–2 C.B. 115.

2. Reg. § 1.351–1(a)(1).

3. Compare Henricksen v. Braicks, 137 F.2d 632 (9th Cir.1943), with Commissioner v. Ashland Oil & Refining Co., 99 F.2d 588 (6th Cir.1938).

dispositions of stock in a taxable transaction pursuant to a binding agreement or a prearranged plan.[4] But a voluntary disposition of stock, particularly in a donative setting, should not break control even if the original transferor of property parts with the shares moments after the incorporation exchange.[5]

As illustrated by the case below, the courts have taken a practical approach to this much-litigated issue, focusing less on timing and more on the previously defined rights and obligations of the parties.

Intermountain Lumber Co. v. Commissioner

United States Tax Court, 1976.
65 T.C. 1025.

■ WILES, JUDGE: * * *

[From 1948 until March, 1964, Dee Shook owned a sawmill in Montana, where Milo Wilson had logs processed into rough lumber for a fee. The rough lumber was processed into finished lumber at a separate plant jointly owned by Shook and Wilson. In March, 1964, the sawmill was damaged by fire. Shook and Wilson wanted to replace it with a larger facility, but Shook was financially unable to do so. Shook convinced Wilson to personally coguarantee a $200,000 loan to provide financing and, in return, Wilson insisted on becoming an equal shareholder with Shook in the rebuilt sawmill enterprise.

On May 28, 1964, Shook, Wilson and two other individuals incorporated S & W Sawmill, Inc. ("S & W"). Minutes of the first meeting of shareholders on July 7, 1964, recited in part that "Mr. Shook informed the meeting that a separate agreement was being prepared between he and Mr. Wilson providing for the sale of one-half of his stock to Mr. Wilson." Several days later, Shook transferred his sawmill site to S & W in exchange for 364 shares of S & W common stock. The company also issued one share to each of its four incorporators. No other stock was issued. On the same day, Shook and Wilson entered into "An Agreement for Sale and Purchase of Stock" under which Wilson was to purchase 182 shares of Shook's stock for $500 per share, plus annual interest, to be paid in installments. As each principal payment on the purchase price was made, a proportionate number of shares of stock were to be transferred on the corporate records and delivered to Wilson. A certificate for the 182 shares was placed in escrow. Shook also executed an irrevocable proxy granting Wilson voting rights in the 182 shares.

On August 19, 1964, S & W borrowed $200,000 from an outside lender, in part upon the personal guarantees of Shook and Wilson. On July 1, 1967, the taxpayer in this case, Intermountain Lumber Co. (referred to in the

---

4. See American Bantam Car Co. v. Commissioner, 11 T.C. 397 (1948), affirmed per curiam, 177 F.2d 513 (3d Cir.1949), cert. denied, 339 U.S. 920, 70 S.Ct. 622 (1950).

5. See D'Angelo Associates, Inc. v. Commissioner, 70 T.C. 121 (1978); Stanton v. United States, 512 F.2d 13 (3d Cir.1975).

opinion as "petitioner"), acquired all the outstanding S & W stock from Shook and Wilson. S & W became a wholly owned subsidiary of Intermountain, and the companies filed consolidated tax returns for the years involved in this controversy.

The specific question before the Tax Court related to the tax basis of S & W's assets for purposes of depreciation claimed on the Intermountain Lumber group's consolidated return. In a role reversal, the Service contended that the transfer of assets to S & W was tax-free under Section 351, requiring S & W to take a transferred basis in the assets under Section 362. In support of a higher cost basis, the taxpayer argued that the incorporation did not qualify under Section 351 because Mr. Shook did not have control immediately after the exchange. Ed.]

OPINION

Section 351 provides, in part, that no gain shall be recognized if property is transferred to a corporation by one or more persons solely in exchange for stock or securities ["or securities" was deleted from the statute in 1989. Ed.] in such corporation and immediately after the exchange such person or persons are in control of the corporation. "Control" is defined for this purpose in section 368(c) as ownership of stock possessing at least 80 percent of the total combined voting power of all classes of stock entitled to vote and at least 80 percent of the total number of shares of all other classes of stock of the corporation.

In this case, respondent is in the unusual posture of arguing that a transfer to a corporation in return for stock was nontaxable under section 351, and Intermountain is in the equally unusual posture of arguing that the transfer was taxable because section 351 was inapplicable. The explanation is simply that Intermountain purchased all stock of the corporation, S & W, from its incorporators, and that Intermountain and S & W have filed consolidated income tax returns for years in issue. Accordingly, if section 351 was applicable to the incorporators when S & W was formed, S & W and Intermountain must depreciate the assets of S & W on their consolidated returns on the incorporators' basis. Sec. 362(a). If section 351 was inapplicable, and the transfer of assets to S & W was accordingly to be treated as a sale, S & W and Intermountain could base depreciation on those returns on the fair market value of those assets at the time of incorporation, which was higher than the incorporators' cost and which would accordingly provide larger depreciation deductions. Secs. 167(g), 1011, and 1012.

Petitioner thus maintains that the transfer to S & W of all of S & W's property at the time of incorporation by the primary incorporator, one Dee Shook, was a taxable sale. It asserts that section 351 was inapplicable because an agreement for sale required Shook, as part of the incorporation transaction, to sell almost half of the S & W shares outstanding to one Milo Wilson over a period of time, thereby depriving Shook of the requisite percentage of stock necessary for "control" of S & W immediately after the exchange.

Respondent, on the other hand, maintains that the agreement between Shook and Wilson did not deprive Shook of ownership of the shares immediately after the exchange, as the stock purchase agreement merely gave Wilson an option to purchase the shares. Shook accordingly was in "control" of the corporation and the exchange was thus nontaxable under section 351.

Respondent has abandoned on brief his contention that Wilson was a transferor of property and therefore a person to also be counted for purposes of control under section 351. Respondent is correct in doing so, since Wilson did not transfer any property to S & W upon its initial formation in July of 1964. Wilson's agreement to transfer cash for corporate stock in March of 1965 cannot be considered part of the same transaction.

Since Wilson was not a transferor of property and therefore cannot be counted for control under section 351, William A. James, 53 T.C. 63, 69 (1969), we must determine if Shook alone owned the requisite percentage of shares for control. This determination depends upon whether, under all facts and circumstances surrounding the agreement for sale of 182 shares between Shook and Wilson, ownership of those shares was in Shook or Wilson.

A determination of "ownership," as that term is used in section 368(c) and for purposes of control under section 351, depends upon the obligations and freedom of action of the transferee with respect to the stock when he acquired it from the corporation. Such traditional ownership attributes as legal title, voting rights, and possession of stock certificates are not conclusive. If the transferee, as part of the transaction by which the shares were acquired, has irrevocably foregone or relinquished at that time the legal right to determine whether to keep the shares, ownership in such shares is lacking for purposes of section 351. By contrast, if there are no restrictions upon freedom of action at the time he acquired the shares, it is immaterial how soon thereafter the transferee elects to dispose of his stock or whether such disposition is in accord with a preconceived plan not amounting to a binding obligation. * * *

After considering the entire record, we have concluded that Shook and Wilson intended to consummate a sale of the S & W stock, that they never doubted that the sale would be completed, that the sale was an integral part of the incorporation transaction, and that they considered themselves to be coowners of S & W upon execution of the stock purchase agreement in 1964. These conclusions are supported by minutes of the first stockholders meeting on July 7, 1964, at which Shook characterized the agreement for sale as a "sale"; minutes of a special meeting on July 15, 1964, at which Shook stated Wilson was to "purchase" half of Shook's stock; the "Agreement for Sale and Purchase of Stock" itself, dated July 15, 1964, which is drawn as an installment sale and which provides for payment of interest on unpaid principal; Wilson's deduction of interest expenses in connection with the agreement for sale, which would be inconsistent with an option; the S & W loan agreement, in which Shook and Wilson held themselves out as the "principal stockholders" of S & W and in which S & W covenanted to equally insure Shook and Wilson for $100,000; the March 1965 stock purchase agreement with S & W, which indicated that Shook and Wilson "*are* to remain *equal*" (emphasis added) shareholders in S & W; the letter of May 1967 from Shook and Wilson to Intermountain, which indicated that Wilson owed Shook the principal balance due on the shares as an unpaid obligation; and all surrounding facts and circumstances leading to corporate formation and execution of the above documents. Inconsistent and self-serving testimony of Shook and Wilson regarding their intent and understanding of the documents in evidence is unpersuasive in view of the record as a whole to alter interpretation of the transaction as a sale of stock by Shook to Wilson.

We accordingly cannot accept respondent's contention that the substance varied from the form of this transaction, which was, of course, labeled a "sale." The parties executed an "option" agreement on the same day that the "agreement for sale" was executed, and we have no doubt that they could and indeed did correctly distinguish between a sale and an option.

The agreement for sale's forfeiture clause, which provided that Wilson forfeited the right to purchase a proportionate number of shares for which timely principal payments were not made, did not convert it into an option agreement. Furthermore, the agreement for sale made no provision for forgiving interest payments on the remaining principal due should principal payments not be made on earlier dates; indeed, it specifically provided that "Interest payment must always be kept current before any delivery of stock is to be made resulting from a payment of principal."

We thus believe that Shook, as part of the same transaction by which the shares were acquired (indeed, the agreement for sale was executed before the sawmill was deeded to S & W), had relinquished when he acquired those shares the legal right to determine whether to keep them. Shook was under an obligation, upon receipt of the shares, to transfer the stock as he received Wilson's principal payments. * * * We note also that the agreement for sale gave Wilson the right to prepay principal and receive all 182 shares at any time in advance. Shook therefore did not own, within the meaning of section 368(c), the requisite percentage of stock immediately after the exchange to control the corporation as required for nontaxable treatment under section 351.

We note also that the basic premise of section 351 is to avoid recognition of gain or loss resulting from transfer of property to a corporation which works a change of form only. See Bittker & Eustice, Federal Income Taxation of Corporations and Shareholders, par. 3.01, p. 3–4 (3d ed. 1971). Accordingly, if the transferor sells his stock as part of the same transaction, the transaction is taxable because there has been more than a mere change in form. * * * In this case, the transferor agreed to sell and did sell 50 percent of the stock to be received, placed the certificates in the possession of an escrow agent, and granted a binding proxy to the purchaser to vote the stock being sold. Far more than a mere change in form was effected.

We accordingly hold for petitioner.

NOTE

The Service has taken a pragmatic (some might say "nuanced") view of the issue in *Intermountain Lumber* when the subsequent disposition of stock, even though pursuant to a prearranged binding commitment, is not taxable. Revenue Ruling 2003–51[1] involved a plan by two corporations, referred to here as X Co. and Y Co., to consolidate certain businesses in a holding company structure. To accomplish that goal, X Co. transferred $40 of business assets to a wholly owned subsidiary, X Sub Co., for X Sub Co. stock (the first transfer). Then, pursuant to a preexisting agreement, X Co. transferred its X Sub Co. stock to Y Sub Co., a subsidiary of Y Co., for stock of Y Sub Co. (the second transfer). At the same time as the second transfer, Y Co. also contributed $30 of cash to Y Sub Co. for additional stock (the third transfer). Finally, Y Sub Co. transferred its own business assets and the $30 it got from Y Co. to X Sub Co. (the fourth transfer). When the dust settled, X Co. and Y Co. owned 40 percent and 60 percent, respectively, of Y Sub Co. and Y Sub Co. owned 100 percent of X Sub Co. The issue in the ruling was the tax results of the first transfer. X Co. clearly would have qualified for nonrecognition of gain under Section 351 on the first transfer but for its preexisting obligation to also make the second transfer. In holding that the first transfer satisfied the "control immediately after the exchange requirement," Revenue Ruling 2003–51 distinguishes between prearranged dispositions of stock that are taxable and those that are nontaxable:

> Treating a transfer of property that is followed by ... *a prearranged sale of the stock* received as a transfer described in § 351 is not consistent with Congress' intent in enacting § 351 to facilitate rearrangement of the transferor's interest in its property. Treating a transfer of property that is followed by *a nontaxable disposition of the stock* received as a transfer described in § 351 is not necessarily inconsistent with the purposes of § 351. Accordingly, the control requirement may be satisfied in such a case, even if the stock received is transferred pursuant to a binding commitment in place upon the transfer of the property in exchange for the stock. (Emphasis added.)

Revenue Ruling 2003–51 also notes that its result is supported by the fact that the transaction could have been rearranged to more directly qualify for nonrecognition under Section 351. For example, X Co. could have contributed the business assets directly to Y Sub Co. for Y Sub Co. stock at the same time as Y Co. contributed the $30 of cash to the subsidiary. Those transfers would have been protected by Section 351. Y Sub Co. could have then transferred its assets to a newly formed X Sub Co. in a second tax-free Section 351 exchange. Thus, Revenue Ruling 2003–51

---

1. 2003–1 C.B. 938.

concludes that treating X Co.'s first transfer as within Section 351 is not inconsistent with the purposes of that section.

PROBLEM

Consider whether the following transactions qualify under Section 351:

(a) A and B are unrelated individuals. A forms Newco, Inc. on January 2 of the current year by transferring a capital asset with a basis of $10,000 and a value of $50,000 for all 50 shares of Newco common stock. On March 2, in an unrelated transaction, B transfers a capital asset with a basis of $1,000 and a value of $10,000 for 10 shares of Newco nonvoting preferred stock (that is not nonqualified preferred stock).

(b) Same as (a), above, except the transfers by A and B were part of a single integrated plan.

(c) Same as (b), above, except A transferred 25 of her 50 shares to her daughter, D, as a gift on March 5 (three days after B's transfer). What if A's gift to D were on January 5?

(d) Same as (b), above, except that two months after B's transfer, A sold 15 shares to E pursuant to a preexisting oral understanding, without which Newco would not have been formed.

2. TRANSFERS OF "PROPERTY" AND SERVICES

Regulations: § 1.351–1(a)(1), (2).

If the transferors of "property" must have control immediately after the exchange, the question then becomes: what is "property?" Although the term is not specifically defined for purposes of Section 351, it has been broadly construed to include cash, capital assets, inventory, accounts receivable, patents, and, in certain circumstances, other intangible assets such as nonexclusive licenses and industrial know-how.[1]

Section 351(d)(1) specifically provides, however, that stock issued for services shall not be considered as issued in return for property.[2] This rule makes good sense in the case of a promoter of the enterprise or even the company lawyer, each of whom contributes no capital but still receives stock in exchange for services rendered to the corporation. Inasmuch as the stock is compensation for those services, the tax consequences are properly determined under Sections 61 and 83.

Apart from realizing ordinary income, a person who receives stock solely in exchange for services may cause the other parties to the incorporation to recognize gain or loss. The pure service provider is not considered a transferor of property and may not be counted as part of the control

---

1. See, e.g., E.I. Du Pont de Nemours & Co. v. United States, 471 F.2d 1211 (Ct.Cl. 1973); Rev.Rul. 64–56, 1964–1 C.B. 133 (industrial know-how); Rev.Rul. 69–357, 1969–1 C.B. 101 (money is "property").

2. See also Reg. § 1.351–1(a)(1)(i).

group for purposes of qualifying the exchange under Section 351. But if a person receives stock in exchange for both property and services, *all* that shareholder's stock is counted toward the 80 percent control requirement.[3]

These rules offer some tempting opportunities for the tax planner. Assume, for example, that Promoter and Investor join forces to form a new corporation. In exchange for his services, Promoter receives 25 percent of the corporation's common stock. In exchange for $500,000 of highly appreciated property, Investor receives the other 75 percent. Investor, as the only transferor of property, does not have control and thus must recognize gain on the transaction unless Promoter somehow can qualify as a transferor of property—a status easily achieved, perhaps, by the mere transfer of $100 in cash.

Life is not so simple in the world of Subchapter C. To prevent such facile maneuvering around the control requirement, the regulations provide that the stock will not be treated as having been issued for property if the primary purpose of the transfer is to qualify the exchanges of the other property transferors for nonrecognition and if the stock issued to the nominal transferor is "of relatively small value" in comparison to the value of the stock already owned or to be received for services by the transferor.[4] In other words, the accommodation transfer gambit fails if the value of the property transferred is *de minimis* relative to the stock received for services. This regulation has been interpreted generously by the Service in Revenue Procedure 77–37,[5] which provides that property transferred "will not be considered to be of relatively small value * * * if the fair market value of the property transferred is equal to, or in excess of, 10 percent of the fair market value of the stock already owned (or to be received for services) by * * * [the transferor]."

3. SOLELY FOR "STOCK"

Code: Skim § 351(g).

The final requirement for nonrecognition is that the transfers of property be made "solely" in exchange for "stock" of the controlled corporation. "Stock" generally means an equity investment in the company, and in this context the term has presented relatively few definitional problems. It does not include stock rights or warrants.[1] At one time, Section 351(a) applied to transfers of property solely in exchange for both stock and corporate debt securities, but the term "securities" eventually was deleted. A "security" was construed by the courts as a relatively long-term debt obligation (e.g., a bond or debenture) which provided the holder with a continuing degree of participation in corporate affairs, albeit as a

---

3. Reg. § 1.351–1(a)(1)(ii), –1(a)(2) Example (3).

4. Reg. § 1.351–1(a)(1)(ii). See also Estate of Kamborian v. Commissioner, 469 F.2d 219 (1st Cir.1972).

5. 1977–2 C.B. 568, § 3.07.

1. Reg. § 1.351–1(a)(1), last sentence.

creditor.[2] After the amendment, debt securities received in a Section 351 transaction, along with all forms of nonsecurity debt (e.g., a short-term note), are treated as boot, leaving only stock to qualify as nonrecognition property.

Certain preferred stock with debt-like characteristics, labelled by Section 351(g)(2) as "nonqualified preferred stock," is treated as "other property," known in tax jargon as "boot", rather than stock for purposes of Sections 351 and 356 (relating to recognition of gain or loss on certain otherwise tax-free corporate acquisitions). "Nonqualified preferred stock" is generally defined as preferred stock[3] with any of the following characteristics: (1) the stockholder has the right to require the issuing corporation or a "related person"[4] to redeem or purchase the stock, (2) the issuer or a related person is required to redeem or purchase the stock, (3) the issuer or a related person has the right to redeem or purchase the stock and, as of the issue date, it is more likely than not that such right will be exercised, or (4) the dividend rate on such stock varies in whole or in part with reference to interest rates, commodity prices, or similar indices.[5] The first three of these categories apply only if the right or obligation with respect to the redemption or purchase of the stock may be exercised within the 20–year period beginning on the issue date of the stock, and such right or obligation is not subject to a contingency which, as of the issue date, makes remote the likelihood of the redemption or purchase.[6]

The effect of Section 351(g) is to treat debt-like preferred stock as boot, resulting in potential recognition of gain (but generally not loss) to the recipient under Section 351(b). A taxpayer is allowed to recognize a loss, however, if only nonqualified preferred stock is received in an exchange.[7] The legislative history indicates that nonqualified preferred stock still will be treated as "stock" for all other purposes until the Treasury provides otherwise in prospective regulations issued under the authority of Section 351(g)(4).[8] This hybrid status as boot for gain recognition purposes but stock for other purposes is more significant in connection with tax-free acquisitive reorganizations, which are covered later in the text.[9]

PROBLEM

Nate Network ("Nate") developed an idea for a new social media venture. He would like to form a start-up company, raise $150,000 of

2. Camp Wolters Enterprises, Inc. v. Commissioner, 22 T.C. 737 (1954), affirmed, 230 F.2d 555 (5th Cir.1956), cert. denied, 352 U.S. 826, 77 S.Ct. 39 (1956).

3. For this purpose, "preferred stock" is stock which is limited and preferred as to dividends and does not participate in corporate growth to any significant extent. I.R.C. § 351(g)(3)(A).

4. Persons are "related" if they bear any of the relationships described in Sections 267(b) or 707(b), such as family members,

controlling shareholders or partners, a corporate affiliate, etc. I.R.C. § 351(g)(3)(B).

5. I.R.C. § 351(g)(2)(A).

6. I.R.C. § 351(g)(2)(B).

7. I.R.C. § 351(g)(1)(B).

8. Staff of Joint Committee on Taxation, General Explanation of Tax Legislation Enacted in 1997, 105th Cong., 1st Sess. 210 (1997).

9. See Chapter 9, infra.

additional capital and hire an experienced person to manage the business. He has located Venturer, who is willing to invest $150,000 cash and Manager, who has agreed to serve as chief operating officer if the terms are right.

The parties have decided to join forces and form Newco Network, Inc. ("Newco") as a "C" corporation. Nate will transfer tangible assets and intellectual property with an aggregate basis of $50,000 and an agreed fair market value of $200,000 (do not be concerned with the character of the individual assets for this problem); Venturer will contribute $150,000 cash; and Manager will enter into a five-year employment contract. Nate would like effective control of the business; Venturer is interested in a guaranteed preferred return on his investment but also wants to share in the growth of the company; and Manager wants to be fairly compensated (she believes her services are worth approximately $80,000 per year) and receive stock in the company, but she can not afford to make a substantial cash investment. All the parties wish to avoid adverse tax consequences.

Consider the following alternative proposals and evaluate whether they meet the tax and non-tax objectives of the parties:

(a) In exchange for their respective contributions, Nate will receive 200 shares and Venturer will receive 150 shares of Newco stock. Manager will agree to a salary of $40,000 per year for five years and will receive 150 shares of Newco common stock upon the incorporation. (Assume that the value of the stock is $1,000 per share.)

(b) Same as (a), above, except Manager will receive compensation of $80,000 per year and will pay $150,000 for her Newco stock. Any difference if Manager, unable to raise the cash, gave Newco her unsecured $150,000 promissory note, at market rate interest, payable in five equal installments, in exchange for her 150 shares?

(c) Same as (a), above, except Manager will pay $1,000 for her 150 shares and the incorporation documents specify that she is receiving those shares in exchange for her cash contribution rather than for future services.

(d) Same as (c), above, except Manager will pay $20,000 cash rather than $1,000.

(e) Same as (d), above, except Manager will receive only 20 shares of stock without restrictions; the other 130 shares may not be sold by Manager for five years and will revert back to the corporation if Manager should cease to be an employee of the company during the five-year period. See I.R.C. § 83. Would you advise Manager to make a § 83(b) election in this situation? What other information would you need?

(f) In general, is there another approach to structuring the formation of Newco that would harmonize the goals of the founders? Consider the use of two classes of stock.

C. TREATMENT OF BOOT

1. IN GENERAL

Code: §§ 351(b); 358(a), (b)(1); 362(a). Skim § 351(g).

Regulations: §§ 1.351–2(a); 1.358–1, –2; 1.362–1.

Proposed Regulations: § 1.351–2(b).

In the introductory section of this chapter, a simple example illustrated the need for Section 351. Recall that A decided to form Venture, Inc. by transferring appreciated property with a value of $100 and a basis of $10 in exchange for Venture stock with a value of $100. Without a special provision of the Code, A would have recognized a $90 gain on the exchange. But since A received solely stock and owned 100 percent of Venture, the transaction qualified for nonrecognition under Section 351. To preserve the gain that went unrecognized, A took a $10 exchanged basis in the Venture stock under Section 358, and Venture took a $10 transferred basis in the contributed assets under Section 362. If A had received more than one class of stock, the transaction still would have qualified under Section 351, and A would have been required to allocate his aggregate exchanged basis of $10 among the various classes of stock received in proportion to their relative fair market values.[1]

But suppose that A, perhaps motivated by the tax advantages of corporate debt,[2] capitalizes Venture, Inc. with the same $100 asset by taking back common stock with a value of $80 and a corporate note with a value of $20. The transaction fails to qualify under Section 351(a) because A, although clearly in "control" of Venture, has not exchanged his $100 asset "solely" in exchange for stock. A's position is not unlike the real estate investor who, desiring a tax-free like-kind exchange, trades his highly appreciated $500,000 building in exchange for other real estate with a value of $450,000 and $50,000 of cash to even out the deal. The question for both A and the real estate investor becomes: should the receipt of this "boot" require full recognition of their realized gain, or should there be a statutory middle ground?

In the corporate setting, this question is answered by Section 351(b). It provides that if an exchange otherwise would have qualified under Section 351(a) but for the fact that the transferor received "other property or money" in addition to stock, then the transferor's realized gain (if any) must be recognized to the extent of the cash plus the fair market value of the other property received. Translated more concisely, Section 351(b) provides that any gain realized by a transferor on an otherwise qualified Section 351(a) exchange must be recognized only to the extent of the boot received. The gain is characterized by reference to the character of the

---

1. Reg. § 1.358–2(b)(2).   **2.** See Chapter 3A, infra.

assets transferred, taking into account the impact of the recapture of depreciation provisions.[3] Despite the presence of boot, however, no *loss* may be recognized under Section 351(b).[4]

In the example where A receives $80 of stock and a $20 corporate note in exchange for his $100 asset with a $10 basis, Section 351(b) will require A to recognize $20 of his $90 realized gain.[5] This makes sense, of course, because to the extent that A has transferred his asset in exchange for property other than stock, he has changed not merely the form of his investment but the substance as well. To that extent, nonrecognition treatment is inappropriate.

As noted earlier, if a shareholder transfers property in a tax-free Section 351(a) transaction, the unrecognized gain on the transfer will be preserved through an exchanged basis in the transferor's stock and again through a transferred basis in the corporation's assets. But if a shareholder recognizes some gain as a result of the receipt of boot, not all of his realized gain must be accounted for at a later time. To avoid this potential double recognition of gain, the shareholder may increase his basis in the stock, securities and other property received by an amount equal to the gain recognized on the transfer.[6] This higher basis will result in less gain (or more loss) if and when the shareholder later sells the property received from the corporation.

The shareholder's basis in the "nonrecognition property" (i.e., stock) received from the corporation thus equals the basis in the property transferred to the corporation, decreased by the fair market value of any other property and the amount of cash received, and increased by the gain recognized on the transfer. The boot takes a fair market value basis. Since any gain recognized by the shareholder is attributable to the boot, and since his continuing investment is represented by the nonrecognition property, the unrecognized gain inherent in the property transferred to the corporation logically should now be preserved in the nonrecognition property. These goals are achieved by assigning the boot a fair market value basis and allocating the remaining basis to the nonrecognition property.[7]

Applying these rules to our previous example, if A received $80 of Venture, Inc. stock and a $20 note in exchange for his $100 asset with a basis of $10, his recognized gain would be $20—the fair market value of the

---

3. See I.R.C. §§ 1245(b)(3); 1250(d)(3). Also relevant is I.R.C. § 1239, which characterizes the recognized gain on the transfer of depreciable property to a corporation as ordinary income if the transferor and certain related parties own more than 50 percent of the value of the transferee corporation's stock.

4. See also I.R.C. § 267(a)(1), disallowing losses on sales or exchanges between related taxpayers, including an individual and a corporation more than 50 percent in value of which is owned by the individual (actually or through attribution rules).

5. This example only addresses the *amount* of A's gain. The *timing* of gain triggered by the receipt of installment boot is considered in Section C2 of the chapter, infra.

6. I.R.C. § 358(a)(1)(B)(ii).

7. I.R.C. § 358(a)(2).

boot. A's basis in the note would be $20, its fair market value. A's basis in the stock would be determined as follows:

Basis of Asset Transferred	$ 10
Less: Fair Market Value of Note Received	(20)
Plus: Gain Recognized	20
Basis of Stock	$ 10

The arithmetic makes sense. Remember that the value of the Venture stock was $80. By assigning the stock a $10 basis, Section 358 preserves the $70 of realized gain that went unrecognized on the partially tax-free exchange. There is no more gain to be preserved, so it is logical to give the boot a fair market value basis.[8]

At the corporate level, Section 362(a) provides that the corporation's basis in the property received on a Section 351 exchange is the same as the transferor's basis, increased by any gain recognized on the exchange. This rule ensures that any gain or loss not recognized by the shareholder will be reflected in the corporation's basis in the transferred assets. Returning one last time to the example, since A recognized $20 of gain on the exchange, Venture's basis in the transferred asset would be $30 (a $10 transferred basis in A's hands plus $20 gain recognized).

If a transferor exchanges several assets in exchange for stock and boot, the transaction becomes more complex. For purposes of determining the gain recognized (and, if relevant, the character of that gain), it becomes necessary to allocate the boot among the transferred assets. Similar allocations are required to determine the basis of the assets in the hands of the corporation. Although these questions rarely arise in the routine corporate formation, they have titillated tax commentators and caused unnecessary anguish to students of corporate tax.[9] The ruling below is the Service's attempt at an orderly resolution of this problem.

Revenue Ruling 68–55

1968–1 Cum.Bull. 140.

Advice has been requested as to the correct method of determining the amount and character of the gain to be recognized by Corporation X under section 351(b) of the Internal Revenue Code of 1954 under the circumstances described below.

Corporation Y was organized by X and A, an individual who owned no stock in X. A transferred 20x dollars to Y in exchange for stock of Y having a fair market value of 20x dollars and X transferred to Y three separate assets and received in exchange stock of Y having a fair market value of 100x dollars plus cash of 10x dollars.

---

8. As before, this example only addresses the amount of gain recognized under Section 351(b) and the resulting basis consequences.

9. For the seminal article on boot allocation, see Rabinovitz, "Allocating Boot in Section 351 Exchanges," 24 Tax L.Rev. 337 (1969).

In accordance with the facts set forth in the table below if X had sold at fair market value each of the three assets it transferred to Y, the result would have been as follows:

	Asset I	**Asset II**	**Asset III**
Character of asset	Capital asset held more than 6 months.	Capital asset held not more than 6 months.	Section 1245 property.
Fair market value	$22x	$33x	$55x
Adjusted basis	40x	20x	25x
Gain (loss)	($18x)	$13x	$30x
Character of gain or loss	Long-term capital loss.	Short-term capital gain.	Ordinary income.

The facts in the instant case disclose that with respect to the section 1245 property the depreciation subject to recapture exceeds the amount of gain that would be recognized on a sale at fair market value. Therefore, all of such gain would be treated as ordinary income under section 1245(a)(1) of the Code.

Under section 351(a) of the Code, no gain or loss is recognized if property is transferred to a corporation solely in exchange for its stock and immediately after the exchange the transferor is in control of the corporation. If section 351(a) of the Code would apply to an exchange but for the fact that there is received, in addition to the property permitted to be received without recognition of gain, other property or money, then under section 351(b) of the Code gain (if any) to the recipient will be recognized, but in an amount not in excess of the sum of such money and the fair market value of such other property received, and no loss to the recipient will be recognized.

The first question presented is how to determine the amount of gain to be recognized under section 351(b) of the Code. The general rule is that each asset transferred must be considered to have been separately exchanged. See the authorities cited in Revenue Ruling 67–192, C.B. 1967–2 C.B. 140, and in Revenue Ruling 68–23, which hold that there is no netting of gains and losses for purposes of applying sections 367 and 356(c) of the Code. Thus, for purposes of making computations under section 351(b) of the Code, it is not proper to total the bases of the various assets transferred and to subtract this total from the fair market value of the total consideration received in the exchange. Moreover, any treatment other than an asset-by-asset approach would have the effect of allowing losses that are specifically disallowed by section 351(b)(2) of the Code.

The second question presented is how, for purposes of making computations under section 351(b) of the Code, to allocate the cash and stock received to the amount realized as to each asset transferred in the exchange. The asset-by-asset approach for computing the amount of gain realized in the exchange requires that for this purpose the fair market value of each category of consideration received must be separately allocated to the transferred assets in proportion to the relative fair market values of the transferred assets. See section 1.1245–4(c)(1) of the Income Tax Regulations which, for the same reasons, requires that for purposes of computing the amount of gain to which section 1245 of the Code applies each category of consideration received must be allocated to the properties transferred in proportion to their relative fair market values.

Accordingly, the amount and character of the gain recognized in the exchange should be computed as follows:

	Total	Asset I	Asset II	Asset III
Fair market value of asset transferred	$110x	$22x	$33x	$55x
Percent of total fair market value		20%	30%	50%
Fair market value of Y stock received in exchange	$100x	$20x	$30x	$50x
Cash received in exchange	10x	2x	3x	5x
Amount realized	$110x	$22x	$33x	$55x
Adjusted basis		40x	20x	25x
Gain (loss) realized		($18x)	$13x	$30x

Under section 351(b)(2) of the Code the loss of 18x dollars realized on the exchange of Asset Number I is not recognized. Such loss may not be used to offset the gains realized on the exchanges of the other assets. Under section 351(b)(1) of the Code, the gain of 13x dollars realized on the exchange of Asset Number II will be recognized as short-term capital gain in the amount of 3x dollars, the amount of cash received. Under sections 351(b)(1) and 1245(b)(3) of the Code, the gain of 30x dollars realized on the exchange of Asset Number III will be recognized as ordinary income in the amount of 5x dollars, the amount of cash received.

NOTE

Overall understanding of Section 351 may be enhanced by an analysis of the additional results to the shareholder ("X") and the corporation ("Y") in the transaction described in Revenue Ruling 68–55. X's basis in the Y stock received will be an exchanged basis ($40 from Asset I, plus $20 from Asset II, plus $25 from Asset III = $85), increased by its total gain recognized on the transfer ($3 on Asset II, plus $5 on Asset III = $8) and decreased by the fair market value of the boot (including cash) received ($10) for a total basis of $83 ($85 + $8 − 10).

The next question is X's holding period for the stock. X received stock worth $100 together with $10 cash for assets with a value of $110 (Asset I $22, Asset II $33, Asset III $55). Thus, it could be said that $^{22}/_{110}$ of the stock was received in exchange for Asset I, $^{33}/_{110}$ was received in exchange for Asset II, and $^{55}/_{110}$ was received in exchange for Asset III. In that event, each share could be considered to have a split holding period allocated in proportion to the fair market value of the transferred assets. This approach was adopted by the Service in Revenue Ruling 85–164.[1] In so ruling, the Service rejected an alternative approach, under which some shares would take a tacked holding period and other shares a holding period commencing as of the date of the exchange. The latter approach would permit a shareholder selling a portion of his holdings to designate shares with the longer holding period.

The next step is a determination of Y's basis in the assets received. In the ruling, Y's basis in those assets will be their adjusted bases in X's hands ($40 for Asset I, plus $20 for Asset II, plus $25 for Asset III) increased by the gain recognized to X (zero on Asset I, plus $3 on Asset II, plus $5 on Asset III) for a total of $93 ($40 + $20 + $25 + $3 + $5). Nothing in the Code, regulations or rulings explains how this basis is allocated among the assets. The underlying premise of Section 362, however, is that any gain or loss which is realized but not recognized by the transferor on the Section 351 transfer will be recognized by the corporation on a later sale. This concept is carried out by giving each separate asset its original transferred basis and then increasing the basis by the amount of gain recognized by the transferor on that asset.[2] On the facts in Revenue Ruling 68–55, Y's basis in Asset I would be $40 (transferred basis) since no gain or loss was recognized on that asset. If Y sells Asset I for its $22 fair market value, it then will recognize the $18 loss realized but not recognized by the transferor. Y's basis in Asset II would be $23 (transferred basis of $20 increased by the $3 of gain recognized on Asset II). Of the $13 of realized gain on Asset II, $3 already has been recognized, and Y will recognize the $10 additional gain if it sells that asset for its fair market value of $33. Finally, Asset III will take a basis of $30 (transferred basis of $25, increased by $5 gain recognized) so that if Y sold the asset for its fair market value of $55, it will recognize the $25 additional realized gain that was not recognized by X.

2.   TIMING OF SECTION 351(b) GAIN

Proposed Regulations: § 1.453–1(f)(1)(iii), –(f)(3)(i), (ii), (iii) Example (1).

The preceding discussion concerned the amount of gain recognized by a transferor who receives boot in a Section 351 transaction. What about the timing of that gain? If the boot is cash or other corporate property, the transferor recognizes any Section 351(b) gain immediately upon receipt of the boot. But gain is more typically recognized when a shareholder transfers appreciated property in exchange for a mixture of stock and corporate debt instruments.[1] In that event, the question becomes—*when* must that gain be recognized? And if the gain may be deferred, what is the resulting impact on the shareholder's basis in her stock under Section 358 and the corporation's basis in its assets under Section 362? The answers lie in the relationship between Section 351 and the installment sale rules in Section 453.

---

1. 1985–2 C.B. 117.

2. See, e.g., P.A. Birren & Son v. Commissioner, 116 F.2d 718 (7th Cir.1940).

1. For the tax incentives to capitalize a corporation with debt, see Chapter 3A, infra.

For many years, it was not clear whether a shareholder could defer the reporting of Section 351 gain triggered by the receipt of corporate debt obligations. The Code resolves this question in an analogous context by permitting deferral of gain for installment boot received in a Section 1031 like-kind exchange and certain other corporate nonrecognition transactions.[2] In proposed regulations, issued in 1984 but still not made final, the Treasury extended this rule to allow a transferor who receives installment boot in a Section 351(b) transaction to defer gain until payments are received on the corporate debt.[3] These regulations also permit a transferor to immediately increase the basis in any nonrecognition property received (e.g., stock) by the transferor's total potential recognized gain, but they delay the corporation's corresponding Section 362(a) basis increase in its assets until the transferor actually recognizes gain on the installment method.[4]

The operation of the proposed regulations is best illustrated by an example. In a conventional installment sale (i.e., a deferred payment sale not made in conjunction with a nonrecognition provision), Section 453 directs the seller to construct a fraction by dividing the realized gain (known in Section 453 parlance as the "gross profit") by the total principal payments to be received on the sale ("total contract price").[5] The seller then applies the fraction to each payment received to determine the gain recognized in the year of sale and as installment payments are later received. Adopting the facts of our continuing example, assume A sells his appreciated asset ("Gainacre"), which has an adjusted basis of $10 and a fair market value of $100, for $80 cash and a $20 note with market rate interest and principal payable in equal installments over the next five years. A's realized gain is $90. A's total payments received will be $100: $80 in the year of sale and $20 in subsequent years. Under the installment method, $^{90}/_{100}$, or 90 percent, of each payment received must be reported as taxable gain.

Now assume that A transfers Gainacre to Venture, Inc., in exchange for 80 shares of Venture stock (worth $80), and a $20 Venture five-year note. A again realizes $90 of gain but recognizes that gain only to the extent of the $20 boot received. For timing purposes, the regulations divide the exchange into two separate transactions: a Section 351(a) nonrecognition exchange to the extent of the stock received by the transferor and an installment sale to the extent of the boot received. The basis of the transferred property is first allocated to the nonrecognition transaction. The regulations implement this bifurcation approach as follows:[6]

---

2. I.R.C. § 453(f)(6).

3. Prop.Reg. § 1.453–1(f)(3)(ii). Any gain attributable to recapture of depreciation or dispositions of dealer property cannot be deferred. I.R.C. § 453(i), (*l*).

4. Prop. Reg. § 1.453–1(f)(3)(ii).

5. I.R.C. § 453(c). For purposes of this and subsequent examples, assume that the property sold is unencumbered and is otherwise eligible for installment sale treatment.

6. Prop.Reg. § 1.453–1(f)(1)(iii); – 1(f)(3)(ii).

1. A's basis in Gainacre ($10) is first allocated to the Venture stock ("nonrecognition property")[7] received in the exchange in an amount up to the fair market value of that property. The entire $10 of basis is thus allocated to the $80 of Venture stock received by A.

2. If the transferor's basis in the transferred property exceeds the fair market value of the nonrecognition property received, that "excess basis" is then allocated to the installment portion of the transaction. There is no excess basis to allocate in this example because the Gainacre basis ($10) does not exceed the value of the nonrecognition property (stock worth $80).

3. Section 453 is then applied to the installment portion of the transaction. For this purpose, the "selling price" is the sum of the face value of the installment obligation ($20 here) and the fair market value of any other boot (none here). Where, as here, there are no liabilities, the total contract price is the same as the selling price ($20). The gross profit is the selling price less any "excess basis" allocated to the installment obligation ($20–0 = $20). A's gross profit ratio is thus $^{20}\!/\!_{20}$, or 100%. To determine his recognized gain, A applies that percentage to any boot received in the year of sale and to payments as they are received on the installment note. A thus recognizes no gain in the year of the exchange; his entire $20 "boot" gain is recognized as the note is paid off over the next five years. Note that the gross profit ratio is normally 100% if the boot received is less than the realized gain.[8]

For purposes of determining a shareholder's basis in the nonrecognition property received in a Section 351/453 transaction, the regulations treat the shareholder as electing out of the installment method.[9] Returning to the example, A's basis in his Venture stock under Section 358 is $10, determined as follows: $10 (A's basis in Gainacre) decreased by $20 (total boot received by A) and increased by $20 (the entire gain A would have recognized if he reported all his gain in the year of sale).

Determining the corporation's basis in the transferred property is more complicated. Adopting what one commentator has called a "rollercoaster basis" approach,[10] the regulations provide that the corporation's

---

7. The proposed regulations refer to nonrecognition property as "permitted property." Prop.Reg. § 1.453–1(f)(1)(i).

8. If the boot exceeds the transferor's realized gain, then some of the basis of the transferred property must be allocated to the installment portion of the transaction. For example, assume the same transaction, except A's basis in Gainacre is $90 and his realized gain is thus only $10. Although A receives $20 of boot, his recognized gain is limited to $10 under Section 351(b). The proposed regulations again direct A to allocate his basis in Gainacre ($90) to the Venture

stock received but only up to the fair market value of that "nonrecognition property" ($80 here). The $10 "excess basis" is allocated to the installment sale, resulting in a gross profit of $10 ($20 selling price less $10 excess basis) and a gross profit ratio of ½. A thus must report ½ of each payment received on the note as taxable gain.

9. Prop.Reg. § 1.453–1(f)(3)(ii).

10. See Bogdanski, "Closely Held Corporations: Section 351 and Installment 'Boot,'" 11 J.Corp.Tax'n 268 (1984).

basis in the transferred property is the same as the transferor's basis increased by the gain recognized only if, as and when that gain is actually recognized. In the example, Venture initially takes a transferred basis of $10 in Gainacre, and that basis gradually is increased by $20 as Venture pays off the note and A recognizes his deferred gain on the installment method.[11] Query whether this rollercoaster basis approach is appropriate, considering that Venture in effect has incurred a liability in connection with its acquisition of Gainacre. If the teachings of the *Crane* case are followed, it would seem that Venture should be permitted to increase its basis by the full $20 liability notwithstanding that A may defer his boot gain over five years. An immediate step-up in basis of the transferred property would be particularly appealing to the corporation when the property is depreciable real estate with no lurking recapture gain.

PROBLEM

A, B and C form X Corporation by transferring the following assets, each of which has been held long-term:

Transferor	Asset	Adj. Basis	F.M.V.
A	Equipment (all § 1245 gain)	$15,000	$22,000
B	Inventory	7,000	20,000
	Land	13,000	10,000
C	Land	20,000	50,000

In exchange, A receives 15 shares of X common stock (value—$15,000), $2,000 cash and 100 shares of X preferred stock (value—$5,000), B receives 15 shares of X common stock (value—$15,000) and $15,000 cash, and C receives 10 shares of X common stock (value—$10,000), $5,000 cash and X's note for $35,000, payable in two years. None of the transferors is a "dealer" in real estate. Assume that the preferred stock issued to A is not "nonqualified preferred stock."

(a) What are the tax consequences (gain or loss realized and recognized, basis and holding period) of the transfers described above to each shareholder and to X Corporation?

(b) What result to C in (a), above, if instead of land, C transferred depreciable equipment with the same adjusted basis and fair market value as the land and an original cost to C of $50,000? See § 453(i).

D. ASSUMPTION OF LIABILITIES

Code: §§ 357(a)–(c); 358(d). Skim § 357(d).

Regulations: §§ 1.357–1, –2; 1.358–3.

Many corporate formations involve the transfer of encumbered property or the assumption of liabilities by the transferee corporation. In most

---

11. Id. Suppose Venture sells Gainacre prior to the due date of the note. Should Venture recognize a loss when the note is eventually paid off? See Prop. Reg. § 1.453–1(f)(3)(iii) Example (1).

circumstances, a taxpayer who is relieved of a debt in connection with the disposition of property must include the debt relief in the amount realized even if the debt is nonrecourse. This is the teaching of the celebrated *Crane* case,[1] and the Supreme Court took a similar approach nine years earlier in United States v. Hendler.[2] Interpreting the corporate reorganization provisions, the Court held in *Hendler* that the assumption and subsequent payment of the transferor's liabilities by a transferee corporation constituted boot to the transferor. If that rule applied to a corporate formation, however, many incorporations of a going business would become taxable events to the extent of the liabilities assumed, and the policy of Section 351 would be seriously frustrated.

To prevent this result, Congress promptly responded to *Hendler* by enacting the statutory predecessor of Section 357. Section 357(a) now provides that the assumption of a liability[3] by a transferee corporation in a Section 351 exchange (and several other transactions to be studied later) will neither constitute boot nor prevent the exchange from qualifying under Section 351. Rather than treating the debt relief as boot, the Code postpones the recognition of any gain attributable to the transferred liabilities. This deferral is accomplished by Section 358(d), which reduces the basis in the stock received in the exchange by treating the relieved liabilities as "money received" by the transferor for purposes of determining the shareholder's basis.

Section 357 is subject to two exceptions. The first (Section 357(b)) prevents abuse and the second (Section 357(c)) avoids the tax taboo of a negative basis. Under the Section 357(b) "tax avoidance" exception, the assumption of a liability is treated as boot if the taxpayer's "principal purpose" in transferring the liability was the avoidance of federal income taxes or was not a bona fide business purpose. This essentially factual determination is made after "taking into consideration the nature of the liability and the circumstances in the light of which the arrangement for the assumption or acquisition was made."[4] If an improper purpose exists,

---

1. Crane v. Commissioner, 331 U.S. 1, 67 S.Ct. 1047 (1947).

2. 303 U.S. 564, 58 S.Ct. 655 (1938).

3. A recourse liability is treated as "assumed" if, based on all the facts and circumstances, the transferee has agreed to, and is expected to, satisfy the liability (or a portion of it), whether or not the transferor has been relieved of the liability. I.R.C. § 357(d)(1)(A). A nonrecourse liability is generally treated as having been assumed by any transferee who takes an asset subject to the liability. I.R.C. § 357(d)(1)(B). If a nonrecourse liability also is secured by other assets not transferred to

the corporation, the amount treated as assumed must be reduced by the lesser of the portion of the liability that the owner of the other assets has agreed to and is expected to satisfy, or the fair market value of those other assets. I.R.C. § 357(d)(2).

4. I.R.C. § 357(b)(1). In evaluating whether the business purpose is bona fide, the regulations require both the transferor and the corporation to demonstrate a "*corporate* business reason" (emphasis added) for the assumption of the liabilities when they report a Section 351 transaction on their all the relieved liabilities, not merely the evil debts, are treated as boot.[5] Section 357(b) was designed to prevent taxpayers from transferring personal obligations to a newly formed corporation or from achieving a "bail out without boot" by borrowing against property on the eve of incorporation and then transferring the encumbered asset to the corporation. Perhaps because the rule is more draconian than necessary, it has been sparingly applied. Section 357(b) is accompanied by an odd burden of proof rule providing that in "any suit" where the taxpayer has the burden of proving the absence of an improper purpose, that burden shall not be met unless the taxpayer "sustains such burden by the clear preponderance of the evidence."[6]

The purpose of the second exception is more technical. Section 357(c) provides that if the sum of the liabilities assumed by the corporation exceed the aggregate adjusted bases of the properties transferred by a particular transferor,[7] the excess shall be considered as gain from the sale or exchange of the property. According to the regulations, the character of the Section 357(c) gain is determined by allocating the gain among the transferred assets in proportion to their respective fair market values.[8] A simple illustration explains the need for Section 357(c). Assume our friend, A, forms Venture, Inc. by transferring a building with an adjusted basis of $30, a fair market value of $100 and an outstanding mortgage of $55. In exchange, Venture issues common stock with a value of $45 and takes the building subject to the $55 mortgage. If Section 357(a) applied, without more, A would recognize no gain on the exchange, but pause to consider his basis in the stock under Section 358. It would be $30 (the basis of the building), less $55 (the liability, treated as boot for basis purposes under Section 358(d)), or a *minus* $25. Although tax scholars have debated the issue, the Code abhors a negative basis.[9] Section 357(c) conveniently avoids that taboo by requiring A to recognize $25 gain (the excess of the $55 liability over his $30 adjusted basis). A's basis then becomes zero, and the Code is not further complicated by the mysteries of algebra.

Section 357(c) is itself subject to an exception. Under general tax principles, a taxpayer who is relieved of a liability that would be deductible if paid directly by the taxpayer does not recognize gain if the debt is discharged because any potential income would be offset by a corresponding deduction upon payment.[10] For example, a lender's discharge of a borrow-

---

income tax returns. Reg. § 1.351–3(a)(6), – 3(b)(7).

5.   Reg. § 1.357–1(c).

6.   I.R.C. § 357(b)(2). This standard adds little to the normal burden of proof imposed in tax litigation and has largely been ignored by the courts.

7.   Section 357(c) is applied on a transferor-by-transferor basis. Rev.Rul. 66–142, 1966–1 C.B. 66.

8.   Reg. § 1.357–2(b). As the problems illustrate, this approach can be anomalous insofar as it requires an allocation of gain (for characterization purposes) to an asset with no realized gain.

9.   For a contrary view on the viability of a negative basis, see Cooper, "Negative Basis," 75 Harv.L.Rev. 1352 (1962).

10.   See I.R.C. § 108(e)(2), which provides that no income shall be realized from the discharge of indebtedness to the extent er's $1,000 interest expense on a home mortgage is economically equivalent to the lender's transfer of $1,000 cash to the borrower (gross income) and a retransfer of $1,000 cash as interest by the borrower to the lender (offsetting deduction). Taken together, these transactions should not result in any net income to the borrower.[11] In keeping with this approach, Section 357(c)(3) excludes from the term "liabilities," for purposes of determining the excess of liabilities over basis, any obligation that would give rise to a deduction if it had been paid by the transferor[12] or which would be described in Section 736(a).[13] These same types of obligations also are not treated as "liabilities" for purposes of determining the basis of the stock received by the transferor under Section 358.[14]

The origin of this exception is best understood by looking back to the difficulties encountered by cash basis proprietors who incorporated a going business prior to the enactment of Section 357(c)(3). Consider the plight of Accountant ("A"), a cash basis taxpayer whose sole proprietorship consisted of the following assets and liabilities:

Assets	Adj. Basis	F.M.V.
Cash	$100	$100
Accounts Receivable	0	200
Equipment	50	250
	$150	$550
Liabilities		
Accounts payable		$400

Assume A incorporates his business by transferring all the assets to Newco in exchange for $150 of Newco stock and Newco's assumption of the

the payment of the liability would have given rise to a deduction.

11. Cf. I.R.C. § 7872. The example assumes that the interest is deductible "qualified residence interest" under Section 163(h).

12. Excepted from this exception are obligations which, when incurred, resulted in the creation of, or an increase in, the basis of any property—e.g., obligations to pay for small tools purchased on credit. I.R.C. § 357(c)(3)(B). To illustrate, assume cash method Proprietor ("P") buys $100 of small tools on credit, promising to pay the seller in two months. Pending payment of the obligation, P has a $100 basis in the tools (P's cost). One month later, P transfers the tools and the related obligation to a new corporation in a Section 351 transaction. The obligation is appropriately treated as a "liability" for purposes of Section 357(c)—but not to worry because the amount of that liability is offset by P's basis in the transferred tools. In comparison, contingent liabilities that have not yet given rise to a capital expenditure (and thus have not created or increased ba-

sis) are not included in determining the amount of liabilities assumed by the transferee. See Rev. Rul. 95–74, infra, p. 103.

13. Section 736(a) applies to payments made to a retiring partner or to a deceased partner's successor in interest in liquidation of that partner's interest in the partnership. Section 736(a) payments, like accounts payable of a cash basis taxpayer, have the effect of reducing gross income when paid and thus are appropriately excluded from "liabilities" for purposes of Section 357(c) and 358(d).

14. I.R.C. § 358(d)(2). But see I.R.C. § 358(h), a specialized anti-abuse rule, which generally provides that if, after application of the general Section 358 basis rule, the transferor's basis of stock received in a Section 351 transaction exceeds its fair market value, that basis must be stepped down (but not below fair market value) by the amount of any liabilities not taken into account under Section 358(d) (e.g., "deductible" or contingent liabilities that do not result in a basis reduction) and assumed by another person as part of the exchange.

$400 accounts payable. If the payables are "liabilities" for purposes of Section 357(c)(1), A recognizes $250 gain—the excess of the $400 liabilities assumed by Newco over the $150 aggregate adjusted basis of the assets transferred to the corporation. A's adjusted basis in the Newco stock would be zero.[15]

The harshness of this result becomes apparent when it is compared to an economically equivalent transaction. Suppose, for example, that A had retained the payables, transferred the $550 in assets to Newco in exchange for $150 of Newco stock and $400 cash and then used the cash to pay his creditors. Although A would recognize $400 gain under Section 351(b), that gain would be offset by the $400 deduction that A would receive on payment of the payables. Alternatively, A could have avoided any gain simply by retaining sufficient assets to pay the deductible accounts payable.

As these examples illustrate, the inclusion of accounts payable as "liabilities" for purposes of Section 357(c) often caused cash basis taxpayers to recognize more gain by having their obligations assumed than they would have recognized if they received equivalent cash boot or withheld sufficient assets to pay the liabilities. Several courts attempted to cure this anomaly by excluding certain deductible liabilities from the scope of Section 357(c), but the cases lacked a uniform rationale.[16] To resolve these ambiguities and halt the litigation, Congress amended Sections 357(c) and 358(d) to provide that deductible obligations no longer would be considered "liabilities" for these limited purposes. Congress also indicated that this exception was not intended to affect either the transferee corporation's tax treatment of the excluded liabilities or the definition of liabilities for any other provision of the Code, including Sections 357(a) and 357(b).[17]

If all else fails, a transferor can avoid recognizing Section 357(c) gain simply by contributing additional cash to the corporation in an amount equal to the excess of assumed liabilities over the aggregate adjusted basis of the other contributed assets. A more intriguing question is whether a cash poor transferor can eliminate the gain by remaining personally liable on the assumed debts or by transferring a personal note to the corporation for the Section 357(c) excess. The courts are confused by these questions, as evidenced by the *Peracchi* case and the Note following.

15. A's basis is derived as follows: $150 (basis in assets transferred by A) minus $400 (liabilities assumed by Newco, treated as "money received" for basis purposes) plus $250 (gain recognized by A). I.R.C. § 358(a)(1), (d)(1).

16. See Focht v. Commissioner, 68 T.C. 223 (1977) ("liability" under Sections 357(c) and 358(d) limited to obligations which, if transferred, cause gain recognition under *Crane* case); Thatcher v. Commissioner, 61 T.C. 28 (1973), reversed in part and affirmed in part 533 F.2d 1114 (9th Cir.1976) (analyze transaction as "ordinary exchange" and give transferor constructive deduction for accounts payable discharged by corporation in same year as transfer to the extent of the lesser of accounts receivable or Section 357(c) gain); Bongiovanni v. Commissioner, 470 F.2d 921 (2d Cir.1972) (Section 357(c) only applies to "tax liabilities"—i.e., liens, mortgages, etc.).

17. Staff of Joint Committee on Taxation, General Explanation of the Revenue Act of 1978, 96th Cong., 1st Sess. 219–220 (1979).

Peracchi v. Commissioner

United States Court of Appeals, Ninth Circuit, 1998.
143 F.3d 487.

■ KOZINSKI, CIRCUIT JUDGE:

We must unscramble a Rubik's Cube of corporate tax law to determine the basis of a note contributed by a taxpayer to his wholly-owned corporation.

The Transaction

The taxpayer, Donald Peracchi, needed to contribute additional capital to his closely-held corporation (NAC) to comply with Nevada's minimum premium-to-asset ratio for insurance companies. Peracchi contributed two parcels of real estate. The parcels were encumbered with liabilities which together exceeded Peracchi's total basis in the properties by more than half a million dollars. As we discuss in detail below, under section 357(c), contributing property with liabilities in excess of basis can trigger immediate recognition of gain in the amount of the excess. In an effort to avoid this, Peracchi also executed a promissory note, promising to pay NAC $1,060,000 over a term of ten years at 11% interest. Peracchi maintains that the note has a basis equal to its face amount, thereby making his total basis in the property contributed greater than the total liabilities. If this is so, he will have extracted himself from the quicksand of section 357(c) and owe no immediate tax on the transfer of property to NAC. The IRS, though, maintains that (1) the note is not genuine indebtedness and should be treated as an unenforceable gift; and (2) even if the note is genuine, it does not increase Peracchi's basis in the property contributed.

The parties are not splitting hairs: Peracchi claims the basis of the note is $1,060,000, its face value, while the IRS argues that the note has a basis of zero. If Peracchi is right, he pays no immediate tax on the half a million dollars by which the debts on the land he contributed exceed his basis in the land; if the IRS is right, the note becomes irrelevant for tax purposes and Peracchi must recognize an immediate gain on the half million. The fact that the IRS and Peracchi are so far apart suggests they are looking at the transaction through different colored lenses. To figure out whether Peracchi's lens is rose-tinted or clear, it is useful to take a guided tour of sections 351 and 357 and the tax law principles undergirding them.

Into the Lobster Pot: Section 351[2]

The Code tries to make organizing a corporation pain-free from a tax point of view. A capital contribution is, in tax lingo, a "nonrecognition" event: A shareholder can generally contribute capital without recognizing

---

2. "Decisions to embrace the corporate form of organization should be carefully considered, since a corporation is like a lobster pot: easy to enter, difficult to live in, and painful to get out of." Boris I. Bittker & James S. Eustice, Federal Income Taxation of Corporations and Shareholders ¶ 2.01[3] (6th ed.1997) (footnotes omitted) (hereinafter Bittker & Eustice).

gain on the exchange.[3] It's merely a change in the form of ownership, like moving a billfold from one pocket to another. See I.R.C. § 351. So long as the shareholders contributing the property remain in control of the corporation after the exchange, section 351 applies: It doesn't matter if the capital contribution occurs at the creation of the corporation or if—as here—the company is already up and running. The baseline is that Peracchi may contribute property to NAC without recognizing gain on the exchange.

Gain Deferral: Section 358(a)

Peracchi contributed capital to NAC in the form of real property and a promissory note. Corporations may be funded with any kind of asset, such as equipment, real estate, intellectual property, contracts, leaseholds, securities or letters of credit. The tax consequences can get a little complicated because a shareholder's basis in the property contributed often differs from its fair market value. The general rule is that an asset's basis is equal to its "cost." See I.R.C. § 1012. But when a shareholder like Peracchi contributes property to a corporation in a nonrecognition transaction, a cost basis does not preserve the unrecognized gain. Rather than take a basis equal to the fair market value of the property exchanged, the shareholder must substitute the basis of that property for what would otherwise be the cost basis of the stock. This preserves the gain for recognition at a later day: The gain is built into the shareholder's new basis in the stock, and he will recognize income when he disposes of the stock.

The fact that gain is deferred rather than extinguished doesn't diminish the importance of questions relating to basis and the timing of recognition. In tax, as in comedy, timing matters. Most taxpayers would much prefer to pay tax on contributed property years later—when they sell their stock—rather than when they contribute the property. Thus what Peracchi is seeking here is gain deferral: He wants the gain to be recognized only when he disposes of some or all of his stock.

Continuity of Investment: Boot and Section 351(b)

Continuity of investment is the cornerstone of nonrecognition under section 351. Nonrecognition assumes that a capital contribution amounts to nothing more than a nominal change in the form of ownership; in substance the shareholder's investment in the property continues. But a capital contribution can sometimes allow a shareholder to partially termi-

---

3. The income tax often operates as a tax on transactions. Regardless of when a taxpayer realizes accretions to his economic wealth, income is usually recognized when a measuring event occurs, such as receipt of a paycheck or the "sale or exchange" of property. But the Code exempts certain sales and exchanges from recognition, such as when a sale is involuntary, or merely a change in the form of ownership, or otherwise warrants nonrecognition. See generally Boris I. Bittker & Lawrence Lokken, Federal Taxation of In-come, Estates and Gifts ¶ 44.1.1 (2d ed. 1990) ("The Code contains numerous nonrecognition provisions covering a wide range of transactions that have little in common except that they have elicited a legislative judgment that the taxpayer's realized gain or loss should not be taxed or deducted when the exchange or other event occurs.") Congress has not deemed the organization of a corporation an appropriate event for recognition of income.

nate his investment in an asset or group of assets. For example, when a shareholder receives cash or other property in addition to stock, receipt of that property reflects a partial termination of investment in the business. The shareholder may invest that money in a wholly unrelated business, or spend it just like any other form of personal income. To the extent a section 351 transaction resembles an ordinary sale, the nonrecognition rationale falls apart.

Thus the central exception to nonrecognition for section 351 transactions comes into play when the taxpayer receives "boot"—money or property other than stock in the corporation—in exchange for the property contributed. See I.R.C. § 351(b). Boot is recognized as taxable income because it represents a partial cashing out. It's as if the taxpayer contributed part of the property to the corporation in exchange for stock, and sold part of the property for cash. Only the part exchanged for stock represents a continuation of investment; the part sold for cash is properly recognized as yielding income, just as if the taxpayer had sold the property to a third party.

Peracchi did not receive boot in return for the property he contributed. But that doesn't end the inquiry: We must consider whether Peracchi has cashed out in some other way which would warrant treating part of the transaction as taxable boot.

Assumption of Liabilities: Section 357(a)

The property Peracchi contributed to NAC was encumbered by liabilities. Contribution of leveraged property makes things trickier from a tax perspective. When a shareholder contributes property encumbered by debt, the corporation usually assumes the debt. And the Code normally treats discharging a liability the same as receiving money: The taxpayer improves his economic position by the same amount either way. See I.R.C. § 61(a)(12). NAC's assumption of the liabilities attached to Peracchi's property therefore could theoretically be viewed as the receipt of money, which would be taxable boot. See United States v. Hendler, 303 U.S. 564, 58 S.Ct. 655, 82 L.Ed. 1018 (1938).

The Code takes a different tack. Requiring shareholders like Peracchi to recognize gain any time a corporation assumes a liability in connection with a capital contribution would greatly diminish the nonrecognition benefit section 351 is meant to confer. Section 357(a) thus takes a lenient view of the assumption of liability: A shareholder engaging in a section 351 transaction does not have to treat the assumption of liability as boot, even if the corporation assumes his obligation to pay. See I.R.C. § 357(a).

This nonrecognition does not mean that the potential gain disappears. Once again, the basis provisions kick in to reflect the transfer of gain from the shareholder to the corporation: The shareholder's substitute basis in the stock received is decreased by the amount of the liability assumed by the corporation. See I.R.C. § 358(d), (a). The adjustment preserves the gain for recognition when the shareholder sells his stock in the company, since his taxable gain will be the difference between the (new lower) basis and the sale price of the stock.

Sasquatch and The Negative Basis Problem: Section 357(c)

Highly leveraged property presents a peculiar problem in the section 351 context. Suppose a shareholder organizes a corporation and contributes as its only asset a building with a basis of $50, a fair market value of $100, and mortgage debt of $90. Section 351 says that the shareholder does not recognize any gain on the transaction. Under section 351 the shareholder takes a substitute basis of $50 in the stock, then adjusts it downward under section 357 by $90 to reflect the assumption of liability. This leaves him with a basis of minus $40. A negative basis properly preserves the gain built into the property: If the shareholder turns around and sells the stock the next day for $10 (the difference between the fair market value and the debt), he would face $50 in gain, the same amount as if he sold the property without first encasing it in a corporate shell.[8]

But skeptics say that negative basis, like Bigfoot, doesn't exist. Compare Easson v. Commissioner, 33 T.C. 963, 970, 1960 WL 1347 (1960) (there's no such thing as a negative basis) with Easson v. Commissioner, 294 F.2d 653, 657–58 (9th Cir.1961) (yes, Virginia, there is a negative basis). Basis normally operates as a cost recovery system: Depreciation deductions reduce basis, and when basis hits zero, the property cannot be depreciated farther. At a more basic level, it seems incongruous to attribute a negative value to a figure that normally represents one's investment in an asset. Some commentators nevertheless argue that when basis operates merely to measure potential gain (as it does here), allowing negative basis may be perfectly appropriate and consistent with the tax policy underlying nonrecognition transactions. See, e.g., J. Clifton Fleming, Jr., The Highly Avoidable Section 357(c): A Case Study in Traps for the Unwary and Some Positive Thoughts About Negative Basis, 16 J. Corp. L. 1, 27–30 (1990). Whatever the merits of this debate, it seems that section 357(c) was enacted to eliminate the possibility of negative basis. See George Cooper, Negative Basis, 75 Harv. L.Rev. 1352, 1360 (1962).

Section 357(c) prevents negative basis by forcing a shareholder to recognize gain to the extent liabilities exceed basis. Thus, if a shareholder contributes a building with a basis of $50 and liabilities of $90, he does not receive stock with a basis of minus $40. Instead, he takes a basis of zero and must recognize a $40 gain.

Peracchi sought to contribute two parcels of real property to NAC in a section 351 transaction. Standing alone the contribution would have run afoul of section 357(c): The property he wanted to contribute had liabilities

---

8. If the taxpayer sells the property outright, his amount realized includes the full amount of the mortgage debt, see Crane v. Commissioner, 331 U.S. 1, 14, 67 S.Ct. 1047, 91 L.Ed. 1301 (1947), and the result is as follows: Amount realized ($10 cash + $90 debt) – $50 Basis = $50 gain.

in excess of basis, and Peracchi would have had to recognize gain to the extent of the excess, or $566,807 * * *.[10]

The Grift: Boosting Basis with a Promissory Note

Peracchi tried to dig himself out of this tax hole by contributing a personal note with a face amount of $1,060,000 along with the real property. Peracchi maintains that the note has a basis in his hands equal to its face value. If he's right, we must add the basis of the note to the basis of the real property. Taken together, the aggregate basis in the property contributed would exceed the aggregate liabilities [including the note at face value, the aggregate basis of the contributed properties would be $2,041,406 and would exceed the $1,548,213 of aggregate liabilities, Eds.].

Under Peracchi's theory, then, the aggregate liabilities no longer exceed the aggregate basis, and section 357(c) no longer triggers any gain. The government argues, however, that the note has a zero basis. If so, the note would not affect the tax consequences of the transaction, and Peracchi's $566,807 in gain would be taxable immediately.[11]

Are Promises Truly Free?

Which brings us (phew!) to the issue before us: Does Peracchi's note have a basis in Peracchi's hands for purposes of section 357(c)?[12] The language of the Code gives us little to work with. The logical place to start is with the definition of basis. Section 1012 provides that "[t]he basis of property shall be the cost of such property. . . ." But "cost" is nowhere defined. What does it cost Peracchi to write the note and contribute it to his corporation? The IRS argues tersely that the "taxpayers in the instant case incurred no cost in issuing their own note to NAC, so their basis in the note was zero." * * * See Alderman v. Commissioner, 55 T.C. 662, 665 (1971); Rev. Rul. 68–629, 1968–2 C.B. 154, 155.[13] Building on this premise,

---

10. Peracchi remained personally liable on the debts encumbering the property transferred to NAC. NAC took the property subject to the debts, however, which is enough to trigger gain under the plain language of section 357(c). See Owen v. Commissioner, 881 F.2d 832, 835–36 (9th Cir.1989).

11. The government does not dispute that the note and the two parcels of real estate were contributed as part of the same transaction for purposes of section 351. Their bases must therefore be aggregated for purposes of section 357(c).

12. Peracchi owned all the voting stock of NAC both before and after the exchange, so the control requirement of section 351 is satisfied. Peracchi received no boot (such as cash or securities) which would qualify as "money or other property" and trigger recognition under 351(b) alone. Peracchi did not receive any stock in return for the property contributed, so it could be argued that the exchange was not "solely in exchange for stock" as required by section 351. Courts have consistently recognized, however, that issuing stock in this situation would be a meaningless gesture: Because Peracchi is the sole shareholder of NAC, issuing additional stock would not affect his economic position relative to other shareholders. See, e.g., Jackson v. Commissioner, 708 F.2d 1402, 1405 (9th Cir.1983).

13. We would face a different case had the Treasury promulgated a regulation interpreting section 357(c). A revenue ruling is entitled to some deference as the stated litigating position of the agency which enforces the tax code, but not nearly as much as a regulation. Ruling 68–629 offers no rationale, let alone a reasonable one, for its holding that it costs a taxpayer nothing to write a promissory note, and thus deserves little weight.

the IRS makes Peracchi out to be a grifter: He holds an unenforceable promise to pay himself money, since the corporation will not collect on it unless he says so.

It's true that all Peracchi did was make out a promise to pay on a piece of paper, mark it in the corporate minutes and enter it on the corporate books. It is also true that nothing will cause the corporation to enforce the note against Peracchi so long as Peracchi remains in control. But the IRS ignores the possibility that NAC may go bankrupt, an event that would suddenly make the note highly significant. Peracchi and NAC are separated by the corporate form, and this gossamer curtain makes a difference in the shell game of C Corp organization and reorganization. Contributing the note puts a million dollar nut within the corporate shell, exposing Peracchi to the cruel nutcracker of corporate creditors in the event NAC goes bankrupt. And it does so to the tune of $1,060,000, the full face amount of the note. Without the note, no matter how deeply the corporation went into debt, creditors could not reach Peracchi's personal assets. With the note on the books, however, creditors can reach into Peracchi's pocket by enforcing the note as an unliquidated asset of the corporation.

The key to solving this puzzle, then, is to ask whether bankruptcy is significant enough a contingency to confer substantial economic effect on this transaction. If the risk of bankruptcy is important enough to be recognized, Peracchi should get basis in the note: He will have increased his exposure to the risks of the business—and thus his economic investment in NAC—by $1,060,000. If bankruptcy is so remote that there is no realistic possibility it will ever occur, we can ignore the potential economic effect of the note as speculative and treat it as merely an unenforceable promise to contribute capital in the future.

When the question is posed this way, the answer is clear. Peracchi's obligation on the note was not conditioned on NAC's remaining solvent. It represents a new and substantial increase in Peracchi's investment in the corporation.[14] The Code seems to recognize that economic exposure of the shareholder is the ultimate measuring rod of a shareholder's investment. Cf. I.R.C. § 465 (at-risk rules for partnership investments). Peracchi therefore is entitled to a step-up in basis to the extent he will be subjected to economic loss if the underlying investment turns unprofitable. Cf. HGA Cinema Trust v. Commissioner, 950 F.2d 1357, 1363 (7th Cir.1991) (examining effect of bankruptcy to determine whether long-term note contributed by partner could be included in basis). See also Treas. Reg. § 1.704–1(b)(2)(ii)(c)(1) (recognizing economic effect of promissory note contributed by partner for purposes of partner's obligation to restore deficit capital account).

---

14. We confine our holding to a case such as this where the note is contributed to an operating business which is subject to a non-trivial risk of bankruptcy or receivership. NAC is not, for example, a shell corporation or a passive investment company; Peracchi got into this mess in the first place because NAC was in financial trouble and needed more assets to meet Nevada's minimum premium-to-asset ratio for insurance companies.

The economics of the transaction also support Peracchi's view of the matter. The transaction here does not differ substantively from others that would certainly give Peracchi a boost in basis. For example, Peracchi could have borrowed $1 million from a bank and contributed the cash to NAC along with the properties. Because cash has a basis equal to face value, Peracchi would not have faced any section 357(c) gain. NAC could then have purchased the note from the bank for $1 million which, assuming the bank's original assessment of Peracchi's creditworthiness was accurate, would be the fair market value of the note. In the end the corporation would hold a million dollar note from Peracchi—just like it does now—and Peracchi would face no section 357(c) gain.[15] The only economic difference between the transaction just described and the transaction Peracchi actually engaged in is the additional costs that would accompany getting a loan from the bank. Peracchi incurs a "cost" of $1 million when he promises to pay the note to the bank; the cost is not diminished here by the fact that the transferor controls the initial transferee. The experts seem to agree: "Section 357(c) can be avoided by a transfer of enough cash to eliminate any excess of liabilities over basis; and since a note given by a solvent obligor in purchasing property is routinely treated as the equivalent of cash in determining the basis of the property, it seems reasonable to give it the same treatment in determining the basis of the property transferred in a s 351 exchange." Bittker & Eustice ¶ 3.06[4][b].

We are aware of the mischief that can result when taxpayers are permitted to calculate basis in excess of their true economic investment. See Commissioner v. Tufts, 461 U.S. 300, 103 S.Ct. 1826, 75 L.Ed.2d 863 (1983). For two reasons, however, we do not believe our holding will have such pernicious effects. First, and most significantly, by increasing the taxpayer's personal exposure, the contribution of a valid, unconditional promissory note has substantial economic effects which reflect his true economic investment in the enterprise. The main problem with attributing basis to nonrecourse debt financing is that the tax benefits enjoyed as a result of increased basis do not reflect the true economic risk. Here

---

15. In a similar vein, Peracchi could have first swapped promissory notes with a third party. Assuming the bona fides of each note, Peracchi would take a cost basis in the third party note equal to the face value of the note he gave up. Peracchi could then contribute the third party note to NAC, and (thanks to the added basis) avoid any section 357(c) gain. NAC could then close the circle by giving the third party note back to the third party in exchange for Peracchi's note, leaving Peracchi and NAC in exactly the same position they occupy now. The IRS might attack these maneuvers as step transactions, but that would beg the question: Does the contribution of a shareholder's note to his wholly-owned corporation have any real economic effect, or is it just so much window dressing? If the debt has real economic effect, it shouldn't matter how the shareholder structures the transaction. The only substantive difference between the avoidance techniques just discussed—swapping notes or borrowing from a third party—and the case here is the valuation role implicitly performed by the third party. A bank would not give Peracchi the face value of the note unless his credit warranted it, while we have no assurance that NAC wouldn't do so. We readily acknowledge that our assumptions fall apart if the shareholder isn't creditworthy. Here, the government has stipulated that Peracchi's net worth far exceeds the value of the note, so creditworthiness is not at issue. But we limit our holding to cases where the note is in fact worth approximately its face value.

Peracchi will have to pay the full amount of the note with after-tax dollars if NAC's economic situation heads south. Second, the tax treatment of nonrecourse debt primarily creates problems in the partnership context, where the entity's loss deductions (resulting from depreciation based on basis inflated above and beyond the taxpayer's true economic investment) can be passed through to the taxpayer. It is the pass-through of losses that makes artificial increases in equity interests of particular concern. See, e.g., Levy v. Commissioner, 732 F.2d 1435, 1437 (9th Cir.1984). We don't have to tread quite so lightly in the C Corp context, since a C Corp doesn't funnel losses to the shareholder.[16]

We find further support for Peracchi's view by looking at the alternative: What would happen if the note had a zero basis? The IRS points out that the basis of the note in the hands of the corporation is the same as it was in the hands of the taxpayer. Accordingly, if the note has a zero basis for Peracchi, so too for NAC. See I.R.C. § 362(a).[17] But what happens if NAC—perhaps facing the threat of an involuntary petition for bankruptcy—turns around and sells Peracchi's note to a third party for its fair market value? According to the IRS's theory, NAC would take a carryover basis of zero in the note and would have to recognize $1,060,000 in phantom gain on the subsequent exchange, even though the note did not appreciate in value one bit. That can't be the right result.

Accordingly, we hold that Peracchi has a basis of $1,060,000 in the note he wrote to NAC. The aggregate basis exceeds the liabilities of the properties transferred to NAC under section 351, and Peracchi need not recognize any section 357(c) gain.

Genuine Indebtedness or Sham?

The Tax Court never reached the issue of Peracchi's basis in the note. Instead, it ruled for the Commissioner on the ground that the note is not genuine indebtedness. The court emphasized two facts which it believed supported the view that the note is a sham: (1) NAC's decision whether to collect on the note is wholly controlled by Peracchi and (2) Peracchi missed the first two years of payments, yet NAC did not accelerate the debt. These facts certainly do suggest that Peracchi paid imperfect attention to his

16. Our holding therefore does not extend to the partnership or S Corp context.

17. But see Lessinger v. Commissioner, 872 F.2d 519 (2d Cir.1989). In Lessinger, the Second Circuit analyzed a similar transaction. It agreed with the IRS's (faulty) premise that the note had a zero basis in the taxpayer's hands. But then, brushing aside the language of section 362(a), the court concluded that the note had a basis in the corporation's hands equal to its face value. The court held that this was enough to dispel any section 357(c) gain to the taxpayer, proving that two wrongs sometimes do add up to a right. We agree with the IRS that Lessinger's approach is untenable. Section 357(c) contemplates measuring basis of the property contributed in the hands of the taxpayer, not the corporation. Section 357 appears in the midst of the Code sections dealing with the effect of capital contributions on the shareholder; sections 361 et seq., on the other hand, deal with the effect on a corporation, and section 362 defines the basis of property contributed in the hands of the corporation. Because we hold that the note has a face value basis to the shareholder for purposes of section 357(c), however, we reach the same result as Lessinger.

obligations under the note, as frequently happens when debtor and creditor are under common control. But we believe the proper way to approach the genuine indebtedness question is to look at the face of the note and consider whether Peracchi's legal obligation is illusory. And it is not. First, the note's bona fides are adequate: The IRS has stipulated that Peracchi is creditworthy and likely to have the funds to pay the note; the note bears a market rate of interest commensurate with his creditworthiness; the note has a fixed term. Second, the IRS does not argue that the value of the note is anything other than its face value; nothing in the record suggests NAC couldn't borrow against the note to raise cash. Lastly, the note is fully transferable and enforceable by third parties, such as hostile creditors. On the basis of these facts we hold that the note is an ordinary, negotiable, recourse obligation which must be treated as genuine debt for tax purposes. See Sacks v. Commissioner, 69 F.3d 982, 989 (9th Cir.1995).

The IRS argues that the note is nevertheless a sham because it was executed simply to avoid tax. Tax avoidance is a valid concern in this context; section 357(a) does provide the opportunity for a bailout transaction of sorts. For example, a taxpayer with an unencumbered building he wants to sell could take out a nonrecourse mortgage, pocket the proceeds, and contribute the property to a newly organized corporation. Although the gain would be preserved for later recognition, the taxpayer would have partially cashed out his economic investment in the property: By taking out a nonrecourse mortgage, the economic risk of loss would be transferred to the lender. Section 357(b) addresses this sort of bailout by requiring the recognition of gain if the transaction lacks a business purpose.

Peracchi's capital contribution is not a bailout. Peracchi contributed the buildings to NAC because the company needed additional capital, and the contribution of the note was part of that transaction. The IRS, in fact, stipulated that the contribution had a business purpose. Bailout potential exists regardless of whether the taxpayer contributes a note along with the property; section 357(b), not 357(c), is the sword the Service must use to attack bailout transactions.

Is the note a gift?

The IRS also offers a more refined version of the sham transaction argument: The note was really a gift to NAC because Peracchi did not receive any consideration from the exchange. The IRS admits that the tax deferral resulting from avoiding section 357(c) gain is a benefit to Peracchi. It argues, nonetheless, that this is not enough to make the bargain enforceable because it works no detriment to NAC. This argument would classify all contributions of capital as gifts. A corporation never gives up anything explicitly when it accepts a capital contribution. Instead, the corporation implicitly promises to put the money to good use, and its directors and officers undertake the fiduciary duty to generate the highest possible return on the investment. The contribution of the note was no more a gift than the contribution of $1 million in cash to the corporation would have been; it does not reflect the ''detached and disinterested generosity'' which characterizes a gift for purposes of federal income taxation. See Commissioner v. Duberstein, 363 U.S. 278, 285, 80 S.Ct. 1190, 4 L.Ed.2d 1218 (1960).

The Aftermath

We take a final look at the result to make sure we have not placed our stamp of approval on some sort of exotic tax shelter. We hold that Peracchi is entitled to a step up in basis for the face value of the note, just as if he contributed cash to the corporation. See I.R.C. § 358. If Peracchi does in fact keep his promise and pay off the note with after tax dollars, the tax result is perfectly appropriate: NAC receives cash, and the increase in basis Peracchi took for the original contribution is justified. Peracchi has less potential gain, but he paid for it in real dollars.

But what if, as the IRS fears, NAC never does enforce the note? If NAC goes bankrupt, the note will be an asset of the estate enforceable for the benefit of creditors, and Peracchi will eventually be forced to pay in after tax dollars. Peracchi will undoubtedly have worked the deferral mechanism of section 351 to his advantage, but this is not inappropriate where the taxpayer is on the hook in both form and substance for enough cash to offset the excess of liabilities over basis. By increasing his personal exposure to the creditors of NAC, Peracchi has increased his economic investment in the corporation, and a corresponding increase in basis is wholly justified.[20]

Conclusion

We hold that Peracchi has a basis of $1,060,000 in the note, its face value. As such, the aggregate liabilities of the property contributed to NAC do not exceed its basis, and Peracchi does not recognize any § 357(c) gain. The decision of the Tax Court is REVERSED. The case is remanded for entry of judgment in favor of Peracchi.

■ FERNANDEZ, CIRCUIT JUDGE, DISSENTING:

Is there something that a taxpayer, who has borrowed hundreds of thousands of dollars more than his basis in his property, can do to avoid taxation when he transfers the property? Yes, says Peracchi, because by using a very clever argument he can avoid the strictures of 26 U.S.C. § 357(c). He need only make a promise to pay by giving a ''good,'' though unsecured, promissory note to his corporation when he transfers the property to it. That is true even though the property remains subject to the encumbrances. How can that be? Well, by preparing a promissory note the taxpayer simply creates basis without cost to himself. * * * Thus he can extract a large part of the value of the property, pocket the funds, use

20. What happens if NAC does not go bankrupt, but merely writes off the note instead? Peracchi would then face discharge of indebtedness income to the tune of $1,060,000. This would put Peracchi in a worse position than when he started, since discharge of indebtedness is normally treated as ordinary income. Peracchi, having increased his basis in the stock of the corporation by $1,060,000 would receive a capital loss (or less capital gain) to that extent. But the shift in character of the income will normally work to the disadvantage of a taxpayer in Peracchi's situation.

them, divest himself of the property, and pay the tax another day, if ever at all.

But as with all magical solutions, the taxpayer must know the proper incantations and make the correct movements. He cannot just transfer the property to the corporation and promise, or be obligated, to pay off the encumbrances. That would not change the fact that the property was still subject to those encumbrances. According to Peracchi, the thaumaturgy that will save him from taxes proceeds in two simple steps. He must first prepare a ritualistic writing—an unsecured promissory note in an amount equal to or more than the excess of the encumbrances over the basis. He must then give that writing to his corporation. That is all.[1] But is not that just a "promise to pay," which "does not represent the paying out or reduction of assets?" Don E. Williams Co. v. Commissioner, 429 U.S. 569, 583, 97 S.Ct. 850, 858, 51 L.Ed.2d 48 (1977). Never mind, he says. He has nonetheless increased the total basis of the property transferred and avoided the tax. I understand the temptation to embrace that argument, but I see no real support for it in the law.

Peracchi says a lot about economic realities. I see nothing real about that maneuver. I see, rather, a bit of sortilege that would have made Merlin envious. The taxpayer has created something—basis—out of nothing.

Thus, I respectfully dissent.

NOTE

An Alternative Rationale. As noted in Judge Kozinski's opinion in *Peracchi*, the Second Circuit reached a similar result in Lessinger v. Commissioner,[1] but its rationale was different. The Second Circuit concluded that a shareholder's basis in his own note equals its face amount because, necessarily, the note's basis to the corporation was face value. While it may lead to an equitable result, this backwards reasoning is not supported by the Code. The following excerpt from a commentary on *Lessinger* illustrates the court's faulty logic:[2]

> Before turning to the court's application of Section 357(c) to the note—a genuinely intriguing question—one should clear the air about the general question of the basis on which Section 357(c) must be focusing. To say that this is the corporation's basis in the transferred assets is preposterous. If nothing else, such a reading will in many cases be circular. Section 362(a) gives the corporation

---

1. What is even better, he need not even make payments on the note until after the IRS catches up with him. I, by the way, am dubious about the proposition that the Tax Court clearly erred when it held that the note was not even a genuine indebtedness.

1. 872 F.2d 519 (2d Cir.1989).

2. Bogdanski, "Shareholder Debt, Corporate Debt: Lessons from *Leavitt* and *Les-*

singer," 16 J.Corp.Tax'n 348, 352–53 (1990). For a competing view, see Quiring, "Section 357(c) and the Elusive Basis of the Issuer's Note," 57 Tax Law. 97 (2003), and for the rebuttal, see Bogdanski, "Section 358 and *Crane*—A Reply to My Critics," 57 Tax Law. 905 (2004).

a carryover basis in the assets received from the shareholder, increased by any gain recognized by the shareholder on the exchange. The classic instance of recognized gain on a Section 351 exchange is under Section 357(c); thus, one cannot determine a corporation's basis in its assets without first determining the shareholder's gain under Section 357(c). To declare, as the Second Circuit did, that the amount of the gain generally turns on the corporation's basis in its assets leads to an endless circle.

To illustrate, assume a shareholder transfers to a corporation, Blackacre, in which the shareholder has a basis of $30,000, subject to a mortgage of $40,000. To determine the gain under Section 357(c) under the appellate decision in *Lessinger,* one would have to first determine the corporation's basis under Section 362(a). Under the latter section, however, the corporation's basis must reflect the gain under Section 357(c), and thus, one must compute the shareholder's gain in order to determine the corporation's basis. Perhaps the court meant that one should determine the corporation's basis without regard to the debt, or that Section 357(c) looks at different bases depending on whether a shareholder note or hard assets are being transferred, but these are even more thoroughly incredible stretches of the Code language.

Perhaps the Second Circuit was trying to say that Mr. Lessinger should receive "basis credit" for his own note because of his future obligation to transfer cash to the corporation or its creditors. In other contexts, a taxpayer's acceptance of even a nonrecourse liability on the acquisition of property gives rise to a cost basis that includes the amount of the future obligation.[3] If Mr. Lessinger's liability were genuine and enforceable by the corporation's creditors, as the court concluded, he arguably is as much entitled to basis credit as is the purchaser of property financed with nonrecourse debt.

Effect of Shareholder's Continuing Personal Liability. The courts historically have been less sympathetic on a closely related question: whether a shareholder's continuing personal liability on debts transferred to a corporation in a Section 351 transaction causes those debts to be excluded for purposes of Section 357(c). The Tax Court has consistently rejected the notion that transferred liabilities are excluded from the Section 357(c) arithmetic if the transferring shareholder remains personally liable for the debt.[4] The Ninth Circuit once appeared to disagree but later had a change of heart. In Jackson v. Commissioner,[5] that court held that Section 357(c) did not apply on an incorporation of a partnership where the taxpayer's share of the partnership's liabilities exceeded his adjusted basis in the

---

3. Parker v. Delaney, 186 F.2d 455 (1st Cir.1950). Cf. Crane v. Commissioner, 331 U.S. 1, 67 S.Ct. 1047 (1947); Commissioner v. Tufts, 461 U.S. 300, 103 S.Ct. 1826 (1983).

4. See, e.g., Smith v. Commissioner, 84 T.C. 889 (1985), affirmed, 805 F.2d 1073

(D.C.Cir.1986); Rosen v. Commissioner, 62 T.C. 11 (1974), affirmed in unpublished opinion, 515 F.2d 507 (3d Cir.1975).

5. 708 F.2d 1402 (9th Cir.1983).

transferred partnership interest but the taxpayer remained personally liable on the debts. On these facts, the court reasoned that the corporation had not assumed any liabilities and thus the taxpayer did not have any Section 357(c) gain. This result was criticized by courts and commentators,[6] but it is consistent with the Second Circuit's reasoning in *Lessinger* that taxpayers enjoy no economic benefit (and thus no taxable gain) for the excess of transferred liabilities over basis when they retain genuine personal liability on the debts. In a later case, the Ninth Circuit upheld the Tax Court's finding of Section 357(c) gain on a transfer of encumbered equipment to a controlled corporation where the liabilities exceeded the taxpayer's basis even though the transferor had guaranteed the liabilities and remained personally liable following the transfer.[7] Although the court purported to distinguish its earlier *Jackson* holding as not involving property subject to debt, the two decisions are difficult to reconcile.

In a more recent case,[8] the taxpayers, in connection with the incorporation of their family farming business, contributed assets subject to liabilities that exceeded the aggregate adjusted basis of the transferred assets. The taxpayers remained liable as guarantors on the debts. The Seventh Circuit, affirming the Tax Court, held that the taxpayers recognized Section 357(c) gain on the incorporation and, in so holding, followed the line of cases strictly interpreting the statute. Citing *Peracchi* and *Lessinger*, the taxpayers contended that a strict reading of Section 357(c) was based on "outdated precedent" and urged the court to exercise its equitable power to craft a judicial exception to the plain language of the statute. Both the Tax Court and Seventh Circuit declined the invitation to do so and distinguished the pro-taxpayer cases on the ground that personal guaranties of corporate debt are not the same as incurring debt to the corporation. The court reasoned that a guaranty is not an economic outlay but merely a promise to pay in the future if certain events should occur.

The uneasy relationship between owner debt, entity debt and basis is raised in many settings. Similar conceptual questions will resurface with varying results in other contexts involving C and S corporations.[9]

Determination of Amount of Liability Assumed. Section 357(d) attempts to clarify the amount and effect of liability assumptions under Section 357 and several other provisions covered later in the text. A recourse liability is treated as having been "assumed" if, based on all the facts and circumstances, the transferee has agreed to and is expected to

---

6. See, e.g., Estate of Juden v. Commissioner, 865 F.2d 960, 962 (8th Cir.1989); Bogdanski, "Of Debt, Discharge, and Discord": Jackson v. Commissioner, 10 J.Corp.Tax'n 357 (1984).

7. Owen v. Commissioner, 881 F.2d 832 (9th Cir.1989), cert. denied, 493 U.S. 1070, 110 S.Ct. 1113 (1990).

8. Seggerman Farms, Inc. v. Commissioner, 308 F.3d 803 (7th Cir. 2002).

9. See, e.g., Section 3B, infra (treatment of shareholder guaranteed debt for purposes of characterizing debt and equity in C corporation's capital structure); Chapter 15D, infra (treatment of shareholder debt and S corporation debt guaranteed by shareholders in determining basis of S corporation stock under Section 1366); I.R.C. § 752 (allocation of liabilities in determining partner's basis in partnership interest and for other purposes).

satisfy the liability, whether or not the transferor has been relieved of it.[10] Nonrecourse liabilities generally are treated as having been assumed by a transferee who takes an asset subject to the liability, except the amount is reduced by the lesser of: (1) the amount of such liability which an owner of other assets not transferred to the transferee and also subject to such liability has agreed with the transferee to, and is expected to, satisfy, or (2) the fair market value of those other assets.[11] The purpose of this convoluted exception is to prevent double counting the same liability for basis adjustment purposes.

Section 357(d) was enacted to eliminate a corporate tax shelter that exploited ambiguities in the interpretation of the phrase "transferred subject to a liability" in an earlier version of Section 357.[12] Most of the abusive transactions were used by domestic corporations to overstate the basis of encumbered assets received in transfers from foreign affiliates that were indifferent to any potential Section 357(c) gain triggered by the transfer because they were not subject to U.S. tax. If the plan succeeded, the domestic corporation would benefit from excessive depreciation deductions, tax losses, or reduced gain on a future sale of the asset.[13]

Fortunately, the confusing language in Section 357(d) rarely affects most simple incorporations. But it raises some questions (and offers planning opportunities) that could arise in a purely domestic, non-abusive setting. For example, recourse debt is treated as assumed only if the transferee has agreed and is expected to satisfy it. As one commentator has asked, "expected by whom"—the transferee, the transferor, or both?[14] Without such an agreement and expectation, a liability would not be treated as "assumed," perhaps eliminating a Section 357(c) problem that otherwise might have existed. A similar factual inquiry may be required with nonrecourse debt, which generally is treated as "assumed" unless a third party has pledged other assets as collateral and "has agreed to, and is expected to, satisfy" the obligation.

As for planning, it has been suggested that Section 357(c) problems could be avoided, at least with respect to recourse debt, if a shareholder who transfers encumbered property to a controlled corporation enters into an agreement with the corporation providing that the shareholder will satisfy the debt. In that event, the debt would not be treated as "assumed"

---

10. I.R.C. § 357(d)(1)(A). Where more than one person agrees to satisfy a liability, only one of them would be "expected" to satisfy it.

11. I.R.C. § 357(d)(2). See also I.R.C. § 362(d), which limits the basis of property in the hands of the transferee to effectuate a similar policy against double counting.

12. See Staff of Joint Committee on Taxation, Description of Revenue Provisions Contained in the President's Fiscal Year 2000 Budget Proposal 197, JCS–1–99, 106th Cong., 1st Sess. (1999).

13. See Department of Treasury, White Paper, "The Problem of Corporate Tax Shelters: Discussion, Analysis and Legislative Proposals," App. A (July 1, 1999).

14. Bogdanski, "Section 357(d)—Old Can, New Worms," 27 J. Corp. Tax'n 17, 22–23 (2000). See also Banks–Golub, "Recent Amendments to Code Sec. 357: Congress Responds to 'Artificial Basis Creation,'" 78 Taxes 19 (2000).

under Section 357(d), and neither Section 357(a) nor Section 357(c) would apply to the transfer.[15] This strategy would be an alternative to contributing a note to the corporation in the amount of the potential Section 357(c) gain.

PROBLEMS

1. A organized X Corporation by transferring the following: inventory with a basis of $20,000 and a fair market value of $10,000 and unimproved land held for several years with a basis of $20,000, a fair market value of $40,000 and subject to a recourse debt of $30,000. In return, A received 20 shares of X stock (fair market value, $20,000) and X took the land subject to the debt.

(a) Assuming no application of Section 357(b), how much gain, if any, does A recognize and what is A's basis and holding period in the stock?

(b) What result in (a), above, if the basis of the land were only $5,000?

(c) In (b), above, what is the character of A's recognized gain under Reg. § 1.357–2(b)? Does this result make sense? How else might the character of A's gain be determined?

(d) In (b), above, what is X Corporation's basis in the properties received from A?

(e) What might A have done to avoid the recognition of gain in (b), above?

2. B organized Y Corporation and transferred a building with a basis of $100,000 and a fair market value of $400,000. The building was subject to a first mortgage of $80,000 which was incurred two years ago for valid business reasons. Two weeks before the incorporation of Y, B borrowed $10,000 for personal purposes and secured the loan with a second mortgage on the building. In exchange for the building, Y Corporation will issue $310,000 of Y common stock to B and will take the building subject to the mortgages.

(a) What are the tax consequences to B on the transfer of the building to Y Corporation?

(b) What result if B did not borrow the additional $10,000 and, instead, Y Corporation borrowed $10,000 from a bank and gave B $310,000 of Y common stock, $10,000 cash and will take the building subject to the $80,000 first mortgage?

(c) Is the difference in results between (a) and (b), above, justified?

15. See Bogdanski, supra note 14, at 26–28. In dicta, the Tax Court in Seggerman Farms, Inc. v. Commissioner, 81 T.C.M. 1543 (2001), aff'd 308 F.3d 803 (7th Cir. 2002), indicated that remaining personally liable for the transferred debt and providing a personal guarantee would not be sufficient to satisfy Section 357(d)(1)(A).

(d) When might there be legitimate business reasons for a corporation assuming a transferor's debt or taking property subject to debt?

E. INCORPORATION OF A GOING BUSINESS

The preceding sections were designed to illustrate the basic requirements and exceptions for qualifying as a tax-free incorporation. For pedagogical reasons, the problems have involved relatively isolated fact patterns, and it has been assumed that the Code and regulations will provide an answer to virtually every question. When a going business is incorporated, however, matters may become more complex. The mix of assets transferred by a sole proprietorship or partnership may include "ordinary income" property, such as accounts receivable and inventory, and the corporation may assume accounts payable, contingent liabilities, and supplies the cost of which was deducted by the transferor prior to the incorporation. Questions arise as to the proper taxpayer to report the receivables and to deduct the payables. In addition, these items potentially raise a broad issue that will recur throughout our study of Subchapter C: to what extent must a nonrecognition provision yield to judicially created "common law" principles of taxation or to more general provisions of the Code?

This section examines the special problems raised by midstream transfers and, in so doing, provides an opportunity to review some concepts introduced earlier in the chapter.

Hempt Brothers, Inc. v. United States

United States Court of Appeals, Third Circuit, 1974.
490 F.2d 1172, cert. denied 419 U.S. 826, 95 S.Ct. 44 (1974).

■ ALDISERT, CIRCUIT JUDGE.

[A cash method partnership transferred all its assets, including $662,820 in zero basis accounts receivable, to a newly formed corporation in exchange for all the corporation's stock. Because the exchange qualified under Section 351, the Service contended that the partnership's zero basis in the receivables carried over to the corporation under Section 362, causing the corporation to realize income upon their collection. In an odd reversal of roles, because the statute of limitations had run on earlier years, the corporation contended that the receivables were not "property" within the meaning of Section 351 and that their transfer to the corporation was an assignment of income by the partnership, subjecting the partners to tax when the receivables were transferred or collected and providing the corporation with a cost (i.e., fair market value) basis and no income upon collection. The Court thus was required to address the relationship between Section 351 and the assignment of income doctrine.]

I.

Taxpayer argues here, as it did in the district court, that because the term "property" as used in Section 351 does not embrace accounts receivable, the Commissioner lacked statutory authority to apply principles associated with Section 351. The district court properly rejected the legal interpretation urged by the taxpayer.

The definition of Section 351 "property" has been extensively treated by the Court of Claims in E.I. Du Pont de Nemours and Co. v. United States, 471 F.2d 1211, 1218–1219 (Ct.Cl.1973), describing the transfer of a non-exclusive license to make, use and sell area herbicides under French patents:

> Unless there is some special reason intrinsic to * * * [Section 351] * * * the general word "property" has a broad reach in tax law. * * * For section 351, in particular, courts have advocated a generous definition of "property," * * * and it has been suggested in one capital gains case that nonexclusive licenses can be viewed as property though not as capital assets. * * *

We see no adequate reason for refusing to follow these leads.

We fail to perceive any special reason why a restrictive meaning should be applied to accounts receivables so as to exclude them from the general meaning of "property." Receivables possess the usual capabilities and attributes associated with jurisprudential concepts of property law. They may be identified, valued, and transferred. Moreover, their role in an ongoing business must be viewed in the context of Section 351 application. The presence of accounts receivable is a normal, rather than an exceptional accoutrement of the type of business included by Congress in the transfer to a corporate form. They are "commonly thought of in the commercial world as a positive business asset." As aptly put by the district court: "There is a compelling reason to construe 'property' to include * * * [accounts receivable]: a new corporation needs working capital, and accounts receivable can be an important source of liquidity." Hempt Bros., Inc. v. United States, supra, at 1176. In any event, this court had no difficulty in characterizing a sale of receivables as "property" within the purview of the "no gain or loss" provision of Section 337 as a "qualified sale of property within a 12–month period." Citizens' Acceptance Corp. v. United States, 462 F.2d 751, 756 (3d Cir.1972).

The taxpayer next makes a strenuous argument that "[t]he government is seeking to tax the wrong person."[4] It contends that the assignment of income doctrine as developed by the Supreme Court applies to a Section 351 transfer of accounts receivable so that the transferor, not the transferee-corporation, bears the corresponding tax liability. It argues that the assignment of income doctrine dictates that where the right to receive

---

4. We put aside the pragmatic consideration that the transferee-corporate taxpayer raises the argument that the partnership should be taxed at a time when the statute of limitations has presumably run against the transferor partners, who ostensibly are the stockholders of the new corporation.

income is transferred to another person in a transaction not giving rise to tax at the time of transfer, the transferor is taxed on the income when it is collected by the transferee; that the only requirement for its application is a transfer of a right to receive ordinary income; and that since the transferred accounts receivable are a present right to future income, the sole requirement for the application of the doctrine is squarely met. In essence, this is a contention that the nonrecognition provision of Section 351 is in conflict with the assignment of income doctrine and that Section 351 should be subordinated thereto. Taxpayer relies on the seminal case of Lucas v. Earl, 280 U.S. 538, 50 S.Ct. 16, 74 L.Ed. 600 (1929), and its progeny for support of its proposition that the application of the doctrine is mandated whenever one transfers a right to receive ordinary income.

On its part, the government concedes that a taxpayer may sell for value a claim to income otherwise his own and he will be taxable upon the proceeds of the sale. Such was the case in Commissioner v. P.G. Lake, Inc., 356 U.S. 260, 78 S.Ct. 691, 2 L.Ed.2d 743 (1958), in which the taxpayer-corporation assigned its oil payment right to its president in consideration for his cancellation of a $600,000 loan. Viewing the oil payment right as a right to receive future income, the Court applied the reasoning of the assignment of income doctrine, normally applicable to a gratuitous assignment, and held that the consideration received by the taxpayer-corporation was taxable as ordinary income since it essentially was a substitute for that which would otherwise be received at a future time as ordinary income.

Turning to the facts of this case, we note that here there was the transfer of accounts receivable from the partnership to the corporation pursuant to Section 351. We view these accounts receivable as a present right to receive future income. In consideration of the transfer of this right, the members of the partnership received stock—a valid consideration. The consideration, therefore, was essentially a substitute for that which would otherwise be received at a future time as ordinary income to the cash basis partnership. Consequently, the holding in *Lake* would normally apply, and income would ordinarily be realized, and thereby taxable, by the cash basis partnership-transferor at the time of receipt of the stock.

But the terms and purpose of Section 351 have to be reckoned with. By its explicit terms Section 351 expresses the Congressional intent that transfers of property for stock or securities will not result in recognition. It therefore becomes apparent that this case vividly illustrates how Section 351 sometimes comes into conflict with another provision of the Internal Revenue Code or a judicial doctrine, and requires a determination of which of two conflicting doctrines will control.

As we must, when we try to reconcile conflicting doctrines in the revenue law, we endeavor to ascertain a controlling Congressional mandate. Section 351 has been described as a deliberate attempt by Congress to facilitate the incorporation of ongoing businesses and to eliminate any technical constructions which are economically unsound.

Appellant-taxpayer seems to recognize this and argues that application of the *Lake* rationale when accounts receivable are transferred would not create any undue hardship to an incorporating taxpayer. "All a taxpayer [transferor] need do is withhold the earned income items and collect them, transferring the net proceeds to the Corporation. Indeed * * * the transferor should retain both accounts receivable and accounts payable to avoid income recognition at the time of transfer and to have sufficient funds with which to pay accounts payable. Where the taxpayer [transferor] is on the cash method of accounting [as here], the deduction of the accounts payable would be applied against the income generated by the accounts receivable."

While we cannot fault the general principle "that income be taxed to him who earns it," to adopt taxpayer's argument would be to hamper the incorporation of ongoing businesses; additionally it would impose technical constructions which are economically and practically unsound. None of the cases cited by taxpayer, including *Lake* itself, persuades us otherwise. In *Lake* the Court was required to decide whether the proceeds from the assignment of the oil payment right were taxable as ordinary income or as long term capital gains. Observing that the provision for long term capital gains treatment "has always been narrowly construed so as to protect the revenue against artful devices," 356 U.S. at 265, 78 S.Ct. at 694, the Court predicated its holding upon an emphatic distinction between a conversion of a capital investment—"income-producing property"—and an assignment of income *per se*. "The substance of what was assigned was the right to receive future income. The substance of what was received was the present value of income which the recipient would otherwise obtain in the future." Ibid., at 266, 78 S.Ct. at 695. A Section 351 issue was not presented in *Lake*. Therefore the case does not control in weighing the conflict between the general rule of assignment of income and the Congressional purpose of nonrecognition upon the incorporation of an ongoing business.

We are persuaded that, on balance, the teachings of *Lake* must give way in this case to the broad Congressional interest in facilitating the incorporation of ongoing businesses. As desirable as it is to afford symmetry in revenue law, we do not intend to promulgate a hard and fast rule. We believe that the problems posed by the clash of conflicting internal revenue doctrines are more properly determined by the circumstances of each case. Here we are influenced by the fact that the subject of the assignment was accounts receivable for partnership's goods and services sold in the regular course of business, that the change of business form from partnership to corporation had a basic business purpose and was not designed for the purpose of deliberate tax avoidance, and by the conviction that the totality of circumstances here presented fit the mold of the Congressional intent to give nonrecognition to a transfer of a total business from a non-corporate to a corporate form.

But this too must be said. Even though Section 351(a) immunizes the transferor from immediate tax consequences, Section 358 retains for the transferors a potential income tax liability to be realized and recognized upon a subsequent sale or exchange of the stock certificates received. As to the transferee-corporation, the tax basis of the receivables will be governed by Section 362.

* * *

Revenue Ruling 95–74

1995–2 Cum.Bull. 36.

ISSUES

(1) Are the liabilities assumed by S in the § 351 exchange described below liabilities for purposes of §§ 357(c)(1) and 358(d)?

(2) Once assumed by S, how will the liabilities in the § 351 exchange described below be treated?

FACTS

Corporation P is an accrual basis, calendar-year corporation engaged in various ongoing businesses, one of which includes the operation of a manufacturing plant (the Manufacturing Business). The plant is located on land purchased by P many years before. The land was not contaminated by any hazardous waste when P purchased it. However, as a result of plant operations, certain environmental liabilities, such as potential soil and groundwater remediation, are now associated with the land.

In Year 1, for bona fide business purposes, P engages in an exchange to which § 351 of the Internal Revenue Code applies by transferring substantially all of the assets associated with the Manufacturing Business, including the manufacturing plant and the land on which the plant is located, to a newly formed corporation, S, in exchange for all of the stock of S and for S's assumption of the liabilities associated with the Manufacturing Business, including the environmental liabilities associated with the land. P has no plan or intention to dispose of (or have S issue) any S stock. S is an accrual basis, calendar-year taxpayer.

P did not undertake any environmental remediation efforts in connection with the land transferred to S before the transfer and did not deduct or capitalize any amount with respect to the contingent environmental liabilities associated with the transferred land.

In Year 3, S undertakes soil and groundwater remediation efforts relating to the land transferred in the § 351 exchange and incurs costs (within the meaning of the economic performance rules of § 461(h)) as a result of those remediation efforts. Of the total amount of costs incurred, a portion would have constituted ordinary and necessary business expenses that are deductible under § 162 and the remaining portion would have constituted capital expenditures under § 263 if there had not been a § 351 exchange and the costs for remediation efforts had been incurred by P.
* * *

LAW AND ANALYSIS

Issue 1: * * * The legislative history of § 351 indicates that Congress viewed an incorporation as a mere change in the form of the underlying business and enacted § 351 to facilitate such business adjustments generally by allowing taxpayers to incorporate businesses without recognizing gain. * * * Section 357(c)(1), however, provides that the transferor recognizes gain to the extent that the amount of liabilities transferred exceeds the aggregate basis of the assets transferred.

A number of cases concerning cash basis taxpayers were litigated in the 1970s with respect to the definition of "liabilities" for purposes of § 357(c)(1), with sometimes conflicting analyses and results. * * * In response to this litigation, Congress enacted § 357(c)(3) to address the concern that the inclusion in the § 357(c)(1) determination of certain deductible liabilities resulted in "unforeseen and unintended tax difficulties for certain cash basis taxpayers who incorporate a going business." S.Rep. No. 1263, 95th Cong., 2d Sess. 184–85 (1978), 1978–3 C.B. 482–83.

Congress concluded that including in the § 357(c)(1) determination liabilities that have not yet been taken into account by the transferor results in an overstatement of liabilities of, and potential inappropriate gain recognition to, the transferor because the transferor has not received the corresponding deduction or other corresponding tax benefit. Id. To prevent this result, Congress enacted § 357(c)(3)(A) to exclude certain deductible liabilities from the scope of § 357(c), as long as the liabilities had not resulted in the creation of, or an increase in, the basis of any property (as provided in s 357(c)(3)(B)). * * *

While § 357(c)(3) explicitly addresses liabilities that give rise to deductible items, the same principle applies to liabilities that give rise to capital expenditures as well. Including in the § 357(c)(1) determination those liabilities that have not yet given rise to capital expenditures (and thus have not yet created or increased basis) with respect to the property of the transferor prior to the transfer also would result in an overstatement of liabilities. Thus, such liabilities also appropriately are excluded in determining liabilities for purposes of § 357(c)(1). * * *

In this case, the contingent environmental liabilities assumed by S had not yet been taken into account by P prior to the transfer (and therefore had neither given rise to deductions for P nor resulted in the creation of, or increase in, basis in any property of P). As a result, the contingent environmental liabilities are not included in determining whether the amount of the liabilities assumed by S exceeds the adjusted basis of the property transferred by P pursuant to § 357(c)(1).

Due to the parallel constructions and interrelated function and mechanics of §§ 357 and 358, liabilities that are not included in the determination under § 357(c)(1) also are not included in the § 358 determination of the transferor's basis in the stock received in the § 351 exchange. * * * Therefore, the contingent environmental liabilities assumed by S are not treated as money received by P under § 358 for purposes of determining P's basis in the stock of S received in the exchange.

Issue 2: In Holdcroft Transp. Co. v. Commissioner, 153 F.2d 323 (8th Cir.1946), the Court of Appeals for the Eighth Circuit held that, after a transfer pursuant to the predecessor to § 351, the payments by a transferee corporation were not deductible even though the transferor partnership would have been entitled to deductions for the payments had the partnership actually made the payments. The court stated generally that the expense of settling claims or liabilities of a predecessor entity did not arise as an operating expense or loss of the business of the transferee but was a part of the cost of acquiring the predecessor's property, and the fact that the claims were contingent and unliquidated at the time of the acquisition was not of controlling consequence.

In Rev. Rul. 80–198, 1980–2 C.B. 113, an individual transferred all of the assets and liabilities of a sole proprietorship, which included accounts payable and accounts receivable, to a new corporation in exchange for all of its stock. The revenue ruling holds, subject to certain limitations, that the transfer qualifies as an exchange within the meaning of § 351(a) and that the transferee corporation will report in its income the accounts receivable as collected and will be allowed deductions under § 162 for the payments it makes to satisfy the accounts payable. In reaching these holdings, the revenue ruling makes reference to the specific congressional intent of § 351(a) to facilitate the incorporation of an ongoing business by making the incorporation tax free. The ruling states that this intent would be equally frustrated if either the transferor were taxed on the transfer of the accounts receivable or the transferee were not allowed a deduction for payment of the accounts payable. * * *

The present case is analogous to the situation in Rev. Rul. 80–198. For business reasons, P transferred in a § 351 exchange substantially all of the assets and liabilities associated with the Manufacturing Business to S, in exchange for all of its stock, and P intends to remain in control of S. The costs S incurs to remediate the land would have been deductible in part and capitalized in part had P continued the Manufacturing Business and incurred those costs to remediate the land. The congressional intent to facilitate necessary business readjustments would be frustrated by not according to S the ability to deduct or capitalize the expenses of the ongoing business.

Therefore, on these facts, the Internal Revenue Service will not follow the decision in Holdcroft Transp. Co. v. Commissioner, 153 F.2d 323 (8th Cir.1946). Accordingly, the contingent environmental liabilities assumed from P are deductible as business expenses under § 162 or are capitalized under § 263, as appropriate, by S under S's method of accounting (determined as if S has owned the land for the period and in the same manner as it was owned by P).

HOLDINGS

(1) The liabilities assumed by S in the § 351 exchange described above are not liabilities for purposes of § 357(c)(1) and § 358(d) because the

liabilities had not yet been taken into account by P prior to the transfer (and therefore had neither given rise to deductions for P nor resulted in the creation of, or increase in, basis in any property of P).

(2) The liabilities assumed by S in the § 351 exchange described above are deductible by S as business expenses under § 162 or are capital expenditures under § 263, as appropriate, under S's method of accounting (determined as if S has owned the land for the period and in the same manner as it was owned by P).

LIMITATIONS

The holdings described above are subject to § 482 and other applicable sections of the Code and principles of law, including the limitations discussed in Rev. Rul. 80–198, 1980–2 C.B. 113 (limiting the scope of the revenue ruling to transactions that do not have a tax avoidance purpose). * * *

NOTE

Receivables and Payables. When there is a valid business purpose for the transfer of receivables and payables on the incorporation of a going business, the Service's position is that the transferee corporation (and not the transferor) must report the receivables in income as they are collected and deduct the payables when they are paid.[1] This position is consistent with the Government's position in *Hempt Brothers* that the assignment of income doctrine normally will not override Section 351. But to prevent abuse in situations where receivables are accumulated or payables prepaid in anticipation of the incorporation, the Service has noted the following limitations:[2]

Section 351 of the Code does not apply to a transfer of accounts receivable which constitute an assignment of an income right in a case such as Brown v. Commissioner, 40 B.T.A. 565 (1939), aff'd 115 F.2d 337 (2d Cir.1940). In *Brown,* an attorney transferred to a corporation, in which he was the sole owner, a one-half interest in a claim for legal services performed by the attorney and his law partner. In exchange, the attorney received additional stock of the corporation. The claim represented the corporation's only asset. Subsequent to the receipt by the corporation of the proceeds of the claim, the attorney gave all of the stock of the corporation to his wife. The United States Court of Appeals for the Second Circuit found that the transfer of the claim for the fee to the corporation had no purpose other than to avoid taxes and held that in such a case the intervention of the corporation would not prevent the attorney from being liable for the tax on the income which resulted from services under the assignment of

1. Rev.Rul. 80–198, 1980–2 C.B. 113. See also Rev.Rul. 95–74, p. 103 supra.

2. Id.

income rule of Lucas v. Earl, 281 U.S. 111, 50 S.Ct. 241 (1930). Accordingly, in a case of a transfer to a controlled corporation of an account receivable in respect of services rendered where there is a tax avoidance purpose for the transaction (which might be evidenced by the corporation not conducting an ongoing business), the Internal Revenue Service will continue to apply assignment of income principles and require that the transferor of such a receivable include it in income when received by the transferee corporation.

Likewise, it may be appropriate in certain situations to allocate income, deductions, credits, or allowances to the transferor or transferee under section 482 of the Code when the timing of the incorporation improperly separates income from related expenses. See Rooney v. United States, 305 F.2d 681 (9th Cir.1962), where a farming operation was incorporated in a transaction described in section 351(a) after the expenses of the crop had been incurred but before the crop had been sold and income realized. The transferor's tax return contained all of the expenses but none of the farming income to which the expenses related. The United States Court of Appeals for the Ninth Circuit held that the expenses could be allocated under section 482 to the corporation, to be matched with the income to which the expenses related. Similar adjustments may be appropriate where some assets, liabilities, or both, are retained by the transferor and such retention results in the income of the transferor, transferee, or both, not being clearly reflected.

Tax Benefit Rule. Even when a transferor contributes Section 351 "property" to a controlled corporation, a problem may arise if the transferor deducted the cost of that property prior to the transfer. Under the tax benefit rule, if an amount has been deducted and a later event occurs that is fundamentally inconsistent with the premise on which the deduction was initially based, the earlier deduction must be effectively "cancelled out" by the recognition of income equal to the amount previously deducted.[3] For example, a taxpayer who pays $1,000 for minor office supplies to be used in his business would deduct that amount when paid on the assumption that those supplies soon would be exhausted. If that taxpayer later incorporates before the supplies are used and receives $1,000 of stock in the exchange, an event has occurred that is inconsistent with the presumption upon which the earlier deduction was based. But recognition of $1,000 of current income on the transfer of the supplies to a controlled corporation in exchange for its stock is also inconsistent with Section 351.

Whether or not the tax benefit rule overrides Section 351 has been unsettled for many years but the importance of the issues appears to have diminished. In Nash v. United States,[4] an accrual method taxpayer transferred accounts receivable to a newly formed corporation in exchange for

3. See Bittker & Lokken, Federal Taxation of Income, Estates and Gifts ¶ 5.7.1.

4. 398 U.S. 1, 90 S.Ct. 1550 (1970). See also Rev.Rul. 78–280, 1978–2 C.B. 139.

stock. The taxpayer already had included the receivables in income and also had deducted a reserve for bad debts. Applying the tax benefit rule, the Service argued that the taxpayer should be taxed on an amount equal to the previously deducted bad debt reserve because the taxpayer's presumption that some of those debts would turn bad while held in his business had proved erroneous. Although the debts still might become worthless, that event would occur only when they were held by the new corporation—a separate business. The Supreme Court held that the net amount the taxpayer had included in his income as a result of the receivables (i.e., the excess of all accrued receivables over the deducted reserve for bad debts) equalled the value of the stock received for the receivables, so that the earlier deduction for the reserve for bad debts was not inappropriate and did not generate income under the tax benefit rule.

The specific fact pattern addressed in *Nash* is no longer important because accrual method taxpayers are now generally precluded from deducting a reserve for bad debts. Moreover, in a subsequent case, the Supreme Court held that the tax benefit rule applies whenever a later unforeseen event is "fundamentally inconsistent" with the premise underlying a taxpayer's earlier deduction.[5] This broader holding suggests that the Court might uphold application of the tax benefit rule in another factual setting involving a transfer to a newly formed corporation. On the other hand, the Code specifically provides that the depreciation recapture provisions, which are grounded on tax benefit rule principles, do not override Section 351.[6]

PROBLEM

Architect, a cash basis taxpayer, has been conducting a business as a sole proprietorship for several years. Architect decides to incorporate, and on July 1 of the current year he forms Design, Inc. a C corporation, to which he transfers the following assets:

Asset	A.B.	F.M.V.
Accounts Receivable	$ 0	$ 60,000
Supplies	0	20,000
Unimproved Land	60,000	120,000
Total	$ 60,000	$200,000

The land was subject to contingent environmental liabilities that Architect had not taken into account (i.e., had not deducted or capitalized) for tax purposes at the time of the incorporation. The supplies were acquired nine months ago and their cost was immediately deducted by Architect as an ordinary and necessary business expense.

In exchange, Architect receives 100 shares of Design common stock with a fair market value of $100,000. In addition, Design assumes $70,000

---

5. Hillsboro Nat'l Bank v. Commissioner, 460 U.S. 370, 103 S.Ct. 1134 (1983).

6. See, e.g., I.R.C. § 1245(b)(3).

of accounts payable to trade creditors of Architect's sole proprietorship and a $30,000 bank loan incurred by Architect two years ago for valid business reasons, and it assumed the environmental liabilities associated with the land.

Design elects to become a cash method, calendar year taxpayer. During the remainder of the current year, it pays $30,000 of the accounts payable and collects $40,000 of the accounts receivable transferred by Architect. In the following taxable year, Design paid $20,000 in environmental remediation expenses that qualified for a current deduction under Section 162 when paid or accrued.

(a) What are the tax consequences (gain or loss recognized, basis and holding period) of the incorporation to Architect and Design, Inc.?

(b) Who will be taxable upon collection of the accounts receivable: Architect, Design or both?

(c) When Design pays the accounts payable assumed from Architect and incurs the environmental remediation costs, may it properly deduct these expenses?

(d) Assume that Architect is in the highest marginal individual tax bracket and Design, Inc. anticipates no significant taxable income for the current year. What result if Architect decides to pay (and deduct) personally all the accounts payable and transfers the accounts receivable to the corporation?

(e) Would your answers be any different if Architect had been an accrual method taxpayer?

(f) Is Design, Inc. limited in its choice of accounting method (i.e., cash or accrual) or taxable year? See §§ 441; 448.

F. COLLATERAL ISSUES

1. CONTRIBUTIONS TO CAPITAL

Code: §§ 118(a); 362(a)(2), (c).

Regulations: § 1.118–1.

When a shareholder transfers property to a corporation and does not receive stock or other consideration in exchange, the transaction is a contribution to capital. Although Section 351 does not apply to capital contributions, the contributing shareholder does not recognize gain or loss on a contribution of property other than cash to a corporation. Instead, the shareholder may increase the basis in her stock by the amount of cash and the adjusted basis of any contributed property.[1] Contributions to capital by shareholders also are excludable from the gross income of the transferee corporation.[2] The corporation's basis in property received as a nontaxable shareholder contribution to capital is the same as the transferor's basis.[3]

---

1. Reg. § 1.118–1.

2. I.R.C. § 118(a). Contributions to capital by a nonshareholder (e.g., a transfer of

If a sole shareholder transfers property to a corporation, or if all shareholders transfer property in the same proportion as their holdings, the issuance of new stock has no economic significance. After some waffling on the issue,[4] the courts now agree that issuance of stock in these circumstances would be "a meaningless gesture" and consequently have held that such transfers are constructive Section 351 exchanges.[5]

Majority shareholders of a financially distressed corporation may surrender some of their stock back to the company in order to improve its credit rating. The proper tax treatment of a voluntary non-pro rata contribution of stock perplexed the courts for many years, as taxpayers sought to immediately deduct their basis in the surrendered shares as an ordinary loss while the Service contended that the surrender was akin to a contribution to capital. In Commissioner v. Fink,[6] the Supreme Court resolved the question by holding that controlling shareholders do not realize a deductible ordinary loss when they surrender part of their stock without receiving cash or property in return and retain voting control of the corporation. The Court analogized this type of transaction to a shareholder's voluntary forgiveness of a corporate debt owed to the shareholder, which is treated as a contribution to capital. Basis in the shares surrendered may be reallocated to stock retained by the shareholder.

2. INTENTIONAL AVOIDANCE OF SECTION 351

Section 351 is not an elective provision. It applies whenever its requirements are met. Historically, some taxpayers attempted to avoid Section 351 in order to recognize a loss[1] or to step-up the basis of an asset after recognizing a gain to increase the transferee corporation's cost recovery deductions.[2] When long-term capital gains enjoy a significant tax rate preference, taxpayers have also found it advantageous to freeze appreciation as capital gain on an asset that was about to be converted into "ordinary income" property—e.g., land held for investment that the taxpayer intended to subdivide. In these cases, the tax savings achieved by

property by a municipality to encourage the corporation to build a facility within the city limits) also are excludable. Reg. § 1.118–1.

3. I.R.C. § 362(a)(2). This rule parallels Section 362(a)(1), which provides that the corporation takes a transferred basis in property received in a Section 351 exchange. For the corporation's basis in property contributed by a nonshareholder, see I.R.C. § 362(c).

4. See, e.g., Abegg v. Commissioner, 429 F.2d 1209 (2d Cir.1970), cert. denied, 400 U.S. 1008, 91 S.Ct. 566 (1971).

5. See, e.g., Peracchi v. Commissioner, supra p. 84. As *Peracchi* illustrates, applying Section 351 to contributions to capital by a

sole shareholder may be significant insofar as it triggers the application of other Code sections, such as Section 357, to the transaction.

6. 483 U.S. 89, 107 S.Ct. 2729 (1987).

1. Recognition of losses in this manner on a sale between a controlling (more than 50 percent) shareholder and a corporation would be limited by Section 267.

2. But see I.R.C. § 1239, which characterizes gain on sales of property between related taxpayers (e.g., a corporation and a more–than–50–percent shareholder) as ordinary income if the property is depreciable in the hands of the transferee.

converting ordinary income into capital gain outweighed the disadvantage of accelerating recognition of part of the gain.

Planning to avoid Section 351 may present as great a challenge as satisfying its requirements. As illustrated by the *Intermountain Lumber* case earlier in the chapter,[3] one potentially successful avoidance strategy is to break control after the exchange by a prearranged disposition of more than 20 percent of the stock. Another possibility is to structure an incorporation transfer as a taxable "sale" rather than a tax-free Section 351 exchange.[4]

To illustrate the sale technique, assume Investor owns undeveloped land with an adjusted basis of $50,000 and a fair market value of $300,000. Investor intends to subdivide the land and sell home sites at an aggregate sales price of $500,000. If he developed the land as an individual, Investor would recognize $450,000 of ordinary income.[5] But with long-term capital gains taxed at a significantly lower rate than ordinary income, Investor may benefit by selling the land to a controlled corporation for $300,000 of corporate installment obligations. He would recognize $250,000 of predevelopment capital gain on the sale, the corporation would take a $300,000 stepped-up basis in the land, and the future ordinary income would be limited to $200,000.

The sale strategy was successful in Bradshaw v. United States,[6] where the taxpayer transferred 40 acres of Georgia land in which he had a basis of $8,500 to a new corporation in exchange for $250,000 of unsecured corporate installment notes. The corporation's only other capital was a $4,500 automobile transferred on the same day in exchange for common stock. The court treated the transfer of land as a sale and permitted the taxpayer to report his gain on the installment method.[7] In so doing, the court rejected the Service's claim that the notes were really stock even though it conceded that the corporation was thinly capitalized. A contrary result was reached in Burr Oaks Corp. v. Commissioner,[8] where three taxpayers transferred land to a corporation in exchange for two-year notes with a face amount of $330,000. The corporation's only equity capital was $4,500. The court held that the transfer was a nontaxable Section 351 exchange rather than a sale because the notes, payment of which was dependent on the profitability of an undercapitalized corporation, were really preferred stock.

---

3. See p. 62, supra.

4. See generally Bittker & Eustice, Federal Income Taxation of Corporations and Shareholders ¶ 3.14.

5. For convenience, assume no upward adjustments to basis during the subdivision phase.

6. 683 F.2d 365 (Ct.Cl.1982).

7. The deferral of gain achieved by the taxpayer in *Bradshaw* is foreclosed under current law. Because a shareholder and his wholly owned corporation are "related parties," a later sale of the land by the corporation will accelerate recognition of any gain that otherwise would be deferred on the shareholder's installment sale to the corporation. I.R.C. § 453(e), (f)(1).

8. 365 F.2d 24 (7th Cir.1966), cert. denied, 385 U.S. 1007, 87 S.Ct. 713 (1967). See also Aqualane Shores, Inc. v. Commissioner, 269 F.2d 116 (5th Cir.1959).

In the last analysis, resolution of the "Section 351 vs. sale" issue turns on the facts in each case and the court's inclination to reclassify what the taxpayer labels "debt" into what the Service believes to be "equity."[9]

3. Organizational and Start-Up Expenses

Code: §§ 195; 212(3); 248.

Regulations: § 1.248–1(b).

A corporation incurs a variety of expenses in connection with its incorporation. Corporations may elect to deduct currently up to $5,000 of these "organizational expenditures" in the taxable year in which they begin business, but this $5,000 maximum current deduction is reduced by the amount by which total organizational expenditures exceed $50,000.[1] Organizational expenditures that are not currently deductible must be amortized over the 180–month period beginning with the month in which the corporation begins business.[2] A similar rule is provided for "start-up expenditures,"[3] which generally are amounts the corporation incurs after formation but before beginning business operations.

"Organizational expenditures" are defined as expenditures which are: (1) incident to the creation of the corporation, (2) chargeable to capital account, and (3) of a character which, if expended to create a corporation having a limited life, would be amortizable over that life.[4] Examples include legal fees for drafting the corporate charter and bylaws, fees paid to the state of incorporation, and necessary accounting services.[5] Specifically excluded are the costs of issuing or selling stock and expenditures connected with the transfer of assets to the corporation, presumably because such expenses do not create an asset that is exhausted over the life of the corporation.[6] "Start-up expenditures" are amounts that the corporation could have deducted currently as trade or business expenses if they had been incurred in an ongoing business. Pure capital expenditures, such as costs of acquiring a particular asset, are neither organizational nor start-up expenditures and must be capitalized and added to the basis of the asset.

Whether or not they are borne by the corporation, certain items are considered as expenses of the shareholders and, as such, they may neither be deducted nor amortized by the corporation. For example, expenses connected with the acquisition of stock (e.g., appraisal fees) must be capitalized and added to the shareholder's basis in the stock.[7]

9. See Chapter 3B, infra.

1. I.R.C. § 248(a)(1).

2. I.R.C. § 248(a)(2).

3. I.R.C. § 195(b).

4. I.R.C. § 248(b).

5. Reg. § 1.248–1(b)(2).

6. Reg. § 1.248–1(b)(3)(i). See S.Rep. No. 1622, 83d Cong.2d Sess. 224.

7. See Woodward v. Commissioner, 397 U.S. 572, 90 S.Ct. 1302 (1970); United States v. Hilton Hotels Corp., 397 U.S. 580, 90 S.Ct. 1307 (1970).

PROBLEM

A currently conducts a computer software manufacturing business as a sole proprietorship. With the assistance of B, a wealthy investor, A plans to incorporate and then expand the business. A will contribute the assets and liabilities of her proprietorship and B will invest enough cash to give him a 49 percent interest in the corporation. After numerous appraisals, lengthy negotiations and considerable expense, A and B have agreed that the net worth of A's proprietorship is $510,000. B thus will contribute $490,000 cash for his 49 percent interest.

To what extent do the following expenses incurred in connection with the incorporation constitute organizational expenditures that are either currently deductible or amortizable under Section 248:

(a) $3,000 in fees paid by A for appraisals of her proprietorship for purposes of the negotiations with B.

(b) Is there any difference in (a), above, if the appraisal fees are paid by the corporation?

(c) Legal fees paid by the corporation for the following services:

   (i)   drafting the articles of incorporation, by laws and minutes of the first meeting of directors and shareholders;
   (ii) preparation of deeds and bills of sale transferring A's assets to the corporation;
   (iii) application for a permit from the state commissioner of corporations to issue the stock and other legal research relating to exempting the stock from registration under federal securities laws;
   (iv) preparation of a request for a Section 351 ruling from the Internal Revenue Service;
   (v)   drafting a buy-sell agreement providing for the repurchase of shares by the corporation in the event A or B dies or becomes incapacitated.

(d) Same as (c), above, except the legal fees were all paid by A.

CHAPTER 3

CAPITAL STRUCTURE

A. INTRODUCTION

The organizers of a business venture face a major decision in planning the capital structure of their company. The simplest method of raising corporate capital is by issuing stock in exchange for contributions of money, property or services. Stock—known as "equity" in corporate finance parlance—may be common or preferred, and either type may be issued in various classes with different rights and priorities as to voting, dividends, liquidations, convertibility, and the like. A corporation also may raise capital by borrowing, either from the same insider group that owns the company's stock or from banks and other outside lenders. Corporate debt typically is evidenced by a variety of instruments including bonds, notes, convertible debentures, and more exotic hybrid securities designed by Wall Street's financial architects. Although both shareholders and creditors contribute capital, their relationship to the corporation is markedly different. As one early case put it, a shareholder is "an adventurer in the corporate business," taking risk and profit from success, while a creditor, "in compensation for not sharing the profits, is to be paid independently of the risk of success, and gets a right to dip into capital when the payment date arrives."[1]

To some extent, decisions concerning the proper mix of debt and equity are made without regard to tax considerations. Most businesses rely on both short and long-term debt to finance their operations. Quite apart from taxes, traditional corporate finance theorists believed that debt financing contributed to a higher rate of investment return. This conventional wisdom did not go unchallenged. In their well known writings on corporate finance, Professors Modigliani and Miller took the view that, assuming away taxes and other factors, the value of a corporation is unrelated to the amount of debt used in its capital structure.[2] On the other hand, excessive debt has its pitfalls, and CFOs of fiscally conservative public companies may be reluctant to risk insolvency or a shaky credit rating by loading the corporate balance sheet with liabilities.[3] In short, many factors other than taxes affect corporate financing decisions.

1. Commissioner v. O.P.P. Holding Corp., 76 F.2d 11, 12 (2d Cir.1935).

2. For a general discussion of the debate, Klein, Coffee & Partnoy, Business Organization and Finance, Legal and Economic Principles 352–385 (11th ed. 2010).

3. The statement in the text is belied by the surge of debt financing that accompanied the corporate mergers and restructurings of the 1980's and the significant increases in corporate debt in 2001 and beyond. See, e.g., Zuckerman, "Climb of Corporate Debt

Although the tax system may not always drive financing behavior, it profoundly influences the capital structure of both publicly traded and closely held C corporations. Consider the decision facing A and B, who each plan to invest $100,000 on the formation of closely held Newco, Inc. At first glance, it might seem that issuing any Newco debt to A and B would be a needless exercise. If the investors agree on their respective contributions and the allocation of ownership and voting power, what difference does it make whether they hold stock, bonds or notes? The answer is often found in the Internal Revenue Code, which distinguishes between debt and equity for tax purposes, tipping the scales in favor of issuing a healthy dose of debt. This tax bias toward debt financing is influential both at the time of formation and on later occasions in a corporation's life cycle.

The principal advantage of issuing debt as opposed to equity is avoidance of the "double tax." Even though most dividends now qualify for a preferential tax rate (at least until that rate expires in 2013 unless it is extended or made permanent), they still are includible in a shareholder's income and are not deductible by the corporation. The earnings represented by these dividends are thus taxed at both the corporate and shareholder levels.[4] But interest paid on corporate debt, while also includible in the recipient's income, is deductible by the corporation.[5] Assuming the owners of the business desire an ongoing return on their investment before a sale, there is an incentive to distribute earnings with tax-deductible dollars.[6]

Several other features of the tax law reflect a bias in favor of debt over equity. The repayment of principal on a corporate debt is a tax-free return of capital to the lender. If the amount repaid exceeds the lender's basis in the debt, the difference generally is treated as a capital gain under Section 1271. In contrast, when a corporation redeems (i.e., buys back) stock from a shareholder—a transaction quite similar to the repayment of a debt—the entire amount received may be taxed as a dividend if the shareholder or related persons continue to own stock in the corporation.[7]

The issuance of debt at the time of incorporation also may provide a defense against subsequent imposition of the accumulated earnings tax.[8] The obligation to repay a debt at maturity may qualify as a "reasonable business need," justifying an accumulation of corporate earnings,[9] while

Trips Analysts' Alarm," Wall St. Journal, Dec. 31, 2001, at C1 (reporting that U.S. corporations were incurring debt at record levels as of the end of 2001). The tax system continues to provide incentives for C corporations to engage in debt-financed acquisitions and stock repurchases.

4. The dividends received deduction provides some additional tax relief for corporate shareholders. See I.R.C. § 243 and Chapter 4A, infra.

5. I.R.C. § 163(a).

6. But see Andrews, "Tax Neutrality Between Equity Capital and Debt," 30 Wayne L.Rev. 1057 (1984), suggesting that this traditional "simple view" is inadequate because it fails to recognize the opportunity for corporations to raise equity capital by accumulating earnings—a process that redounds to the benefit of shareholders without subjecting them to tax until the earnings are distributed or the shares are sold.

7. I.R.C. § 302. See Chapter 5C, infra.

8. I.R.C. § 531 et seq. See Chapter 14B, supra.

9. Reg. § 1.537–2(b)(3). Repayment of debt owed to shareholders, however, may be subjected to greater scrutiny. See Smoot the same type of accumulation for a redemption of stock normally is not regarded as reasonable for purposes of the accumulated earnings tax.[10]

The choice between debt and equity has significant tax ramifications in many other contexts. For example, the classification of a corporate investment may have an impact on whether transfers of property to a corporation qualify for nonrecognition under Section 351. Complete nonrecognition of gain or loss is available only when the contributing taxpayer receives solely stock. Conversely, taxpayers who wish to recognize gain on the transfer of property to a controlled corporation may attempt to accomplish their objective by taking back boot in the form of installment debt obligations.[11] That goal will be thwarted if the notes are reclassified as stock. Classification of an interest in a corporation also may control the character of a loss if the investment becomes worthless.[12]

The tax distinctions between debt and equity have fueled an ongoing policy debate. The relationship between the favorable tax treatment of debt and the explosive growth in debt-financed corporate acquisitions have captured the public's attention for several decades. But Congress to date has declined to embrace a comprehensive legislative solution to the problems of excessive debt. Instead, it has been content to enact narrowly targeted provisions aimed at isolated abuses that are seen as threats to the integrity of the corporate income tax. The excerpt below from a Congressional study on the income tax aspects of corporate financial structures, which predates the reduced tax rate on qualified dividends, offers some general insights into the debt vs. equity policy debate.

Excerpt From Joint Committee on Taxation, Federal Income Tax Aspects of Corporate Financial Structures

101st Cong., 1st Sess. pp. 53–58 (Jan. 18, 1989).

A.   Tax Advantage of Debt Versus Equity

The total effect of the tax system on the incentives for corporations to use debt or equity depends on the interaction between the tax treatment at the shareholder and corporate levels.

The case of no income taxes.—In a simple world without taxes or additional costs in times of financial distress, economic theory suggests that the value of a corporation, as measured by the total value of the outstanding debt and equity, would be unchanged by the degree of leverage of the firm. This conclusion explicitly recognizes that debt issued by the corporation represents an ownership right to future income of the corporation in a fashion similar to that of equity. In this simple world there would be no

Sand & Gravel Corp. v. Commissioner, 241 F.2d 197 (4th Cir.1957), cert. denied 354 U.S. 922, 77 S.Ct. 1383 (1957).

10.   See, e.g., Bittker & Eustice, Federal Income Taxation of Corporations and Shareholders ¶ 7.07.

11.   See Chapter 2F2, infra.

12.   See Section D of this chapter, infra.

advantage to debt or to equity and the debt-equity ratio of the firm would not affect the cost of financing investment.

Effect of corporate income tax

Tax advantages

Taxes greatly complicate this analysis. Since the interest expense on debt is deductible for computing the corporate income tax while the return to equity is not, the tax at the corporate level provides a strong incentive for debt rather than equity finance.

Table IV–A.—Effect of Debt Financing on Returns to Equity Investment

Item	All-equity corporation	50–percent debt-financed corporation
Beginning Balance Sheet:		
Total assets	$1,000	$1,000
Debt...............................	0	500
Shareholders' equity	1,000	500
Income Statement:		
Operating income....................	150	150
Interest expense	0	50
Taxable income.....................	150	100
Income tax	51	34
Income after corporate tax	99	66
Return on Equity [1] (percent)..........	9.9	13.2

The advantages of debt financing can be illustrated by comparing two corporations with $1,000 of assets that are identical except for financial structure: the first is entirely equity financed; while the second is 50–percent debt financed. Both corporations earn $150 of operating income. The all-equity corporation pays $51 in corporate tax [this and later examples assume a 34 percent corporate income tax rate, Ed.] and retains or distributes $99 of after-tax income ($150 less $51). Thus, as shown in Table IV–A, the return on equity is 9.9 percent ($99 divided by $1,000).

The leveraged corporation is financed by $500 of debt and $500 of stock. If the interest rate is 10 percent, then interest expense is $50 (10 percent times $500). Taxable income is $100 after deducting interest expense. The leveraged corporation is liable for $34 in corporate tax (34 percent times $100) and distributes or retains $66 of after-tax income ($100 less $34). Consequently, the return on equity is 13.2 percent ($66 divided by $500). Thus, as shown in Table IV–A, increasing the debt ratio from zero to 50 percent increases the rate of return on equity from 9.9 to 13.2 percent.

This arithmetic demonstrates that a leveraged corporation can generate a higher return on equity (net of corporate income tax) than an

1. Return on equity is computed as income after corporate tax divided by beginning shareholders' equity.

unleveraged company or, equivalently, that an unleveraged company needs to earn a higher profit before corporate tax to provide investors the same return net of corporate tax as could be obtained with an unleveraged company. More generally, the return on equity rises with increasing debt capitalization so long as the interest rate is less than the pre-tax rate of return on corporate assets. This suggests that the Code creates an incentive to raise the debt-equity ratio to the point where the corporate income tax (or outstanding equity) is eliminated.

Costs of financial distress

With higher levels of debt the possibility of financial distress increases, as do the expected costs to the firm which occur with such distress. These additional costs include such items as the increase in the costs of debt funds; constraints on credit, expenditure or operating decisions; and the direct costs of being in bankruptcy. These expected costs of financial distress may, at sufficiently high debt-equity ratios, offset the corporate tax advantage to additional debt finance.

Effect of shareholder income tax

The above analysis focuses solely on the effect of interest deductibility at the corporate level. Shareholder-level income taxation may offset to some degree the corporate tax incentive for corporate debt relative to equity.

Shareholder treatment of debt and equity

The conclusion that debt is tax favored relative to equity remains unchanged if interest on corporate debt and returns on equity are taxed at the same effective rate to investors. In this case, the returns to investors on both debt and equity are reduced proportionally by the income tax; the advantage to debt presented by corporate tax deductibility remains. One noteworthy exception exists if the marginal investments on both debt and equity are effectively tax-exempt. Given the previously documented importance of tax-exempt pension funds in the bond and equity markets, this case may be of some importance.

Shareholder level tax treatment of equity

In general, returns to shareholders and debtholders are not taxed the same. Although dividends, like interest income, are taxed currently, equity income in other forms may reduce the effective investor-level tax on equity below that on debt. First, the firm may retain earnings and not pay dividends currently. In general, the accumulation of earnings by the firm will cause the value of the firm's shares to rise. Rather than being taxed currently on corporate earnings, a shareholder will be able to defer the taxation on the value of the retained earnings reflected in the price of the stock until the shareholder sells the stock. Thus, even though the tax rates on interest, dividends, and capital gains are the same [the tax rates were the same for a few years after the Tax Reform Act of 1986; under current law, interest is taxable as ordinary income while long-term capital gains and qualified dividends are taxed at preferential rates, Ed.], the ability to defer the tax on returns from equity reduces the effective rate of individual tax on equity investment below that on income from interest on corporate debt.

Other aspects of capital gain taxation serve to reduce further the individual income tax on equity. Since tax on capital gain is normally triggered after a voluntary recognition event (e.g., the sale of stock), the taxpayer can time the realization of capital gain income when the effective rate of tax is low. The rate of tax could be low if the taxpayer is in a low or zero tax bracket because other income is abnormally low, if other capital losses shelter the capital gain, or if changes in the tax law cause the statutory rate on capital gains to be low. Perhaps most important, the step up in the adjusted tax basis of the stock upon the death of the shareholder may permit the shareholder's heirs to avoid tax completely on capital gains. For all these reasons, the effective rate of tax on undistributed earnings may be already quite low.

Corporations can distribute their earnings to owners of equity in forms that generally result in less tax to shareholders than do dividend distributions. Share repurchases have become an important method of distributing corporate earnings to equity holders. When employed by large publicly traded firms, repurchases of the corporation's own shares permit the shareholders to treat the distribution as a sale of stock (i.e., to obtain capital gain treatment, and recover the basis in the stock without tax). The remaining shareholders may benefit because they have rights to a larger fraction of the firm and may see a corresponding increase in the value of their shares. Thus, less individual tax will generally be imposed on a $100 repurchase of stock than on $100 of dividends. In addition, share repurchases allow shareholders to choose whether to receive corporate distributions by choosing whether to sell or retain shares, so as to minimize tax liability.

Acquisitions of the stock of one corporation for cash or property of another corporation provides a similar method for distributing corporate earnings out of corporate solution with less shareholder tax than through a dividend. The target shareholders generally treat the acquisition as a sale and recover their basis free of tax. For purposes of analyzing the individual tax effect of corporate earnings disbursements, this transaction can be thought of as equivalent to a stock merger of the target with the acquiror followed by the repurchase of the target shareholders' shares by the resulting merged firm. The result is similar to the case of a share repurchase in that cash is distributed to shareholders with less than the full dividend tax, except that two firms are involved instead of one.

Since dividends typically are subject to more tax than other methods for providing returns to shareholders, the puzzle of why firms pay dividends remains. Because dividends are paid at the discretion of the firm, it appears that firms cause their shareholders to pay more tax on equity income than is strictly necessary. Until a better understanding of corporate distribution policy exists, the role of dividend taxation on equity financing decisions remain uncertain.

To summarize, although the current taxation of dividends to investors is clearly significant, there are numerous reasons why the overall individual tax on equity investments may be less than that on interest income from debt. Since the effective shareholder tax on returns from equity may be less than that on debt holdings, the shareholder tax may offset some or all of the advantage to debt at the corporate level.

Interaction of corporate and shareholder taxation

With shareholders in different income tax brackets, high tax rate taxpayers will tend to concentrate their wealth in the form of equity and low tax rate taxpayers will tend to concentrate their wealth in the form of debt. The distribution of wealth among investors with different marginal tax rates affects the demand for investments in the form of debt or equity. The interaction between the demand of investors, and the supply provided by corporations, determines the aggregate amount of corporate debt and equity in the economy.

At some aggregate mix between debt and equity, the difference in the investor-level tax on income from equity and debt may be sufficient to offset completely, at the margin, the apparent advantage of debt at the corporate level. Even if the difference in investor tax treatment of debt and equity is not sufficient to offset completely the corporate tax advantage, the advantage to debt may be less than the corporate-level tax treatment alone would provide.

* * *

Implications for policy

The analysis above suggests that any policy change designed to reduce the tax incentive for debt must consider the interaction of both corporate and shareholder taxes. For example, proposals to change the income tax rates for individuals or corporations will change the incentive for corporate debt. Likewise, proposals to change the tax treatment of tax-exempt entities may alter the aggregate mix and distribution of debt and equity.

In addition, proposals to reduce the bias toward debt over equity, for example, by reducing the total tax on dividends, must confront the somewhat voluntary nature of the dividend tax. Since the payment of dividends by corporations generally is discretionary and other means exist for providing value to shareholders with less tax, corporations can affect the level of shareholder level tax incurred. Until a better understanding of the determinants of corporate distribution behavior exists, the total impact of policies designed to reduce the bias between debt and equity are uncertain.

* * *

NOTE

The traditional tax bias for debt over equity has been weakened as long as qualified dividends are taxed at the same preferential rate as long-term capital gains. The Bush Administration's original proposal to allow a 100 percent shareholder-level exclusion for dividends paid from previously taxed corporate earnings would have largely eliminated the bias and profoundly altered the stakes for future capital structure decisions.

The 15 percent rate on qualified dividends, if it becomes permanent,[1] would be a major step toward neutralizing the debt vs. equity distinction. As long as dividends are taxed at preferential rates, equity investments will be more attractive to taxable investors. Not all shareholders pay taxes, however—e.g., tax-exempt pension funds and charities—and corporations still benefit from the ability to deduct interest paid on corporate debt. It thus seems premature to relegate the discussion of capital structure in this chapter to the recycling bin.

B.   DEBT VS. EQUITY

1.   COMMON LAW STANDARDS

Taxpayers have considerable flexibility to structure corporate instruments as debt or equity. In view of the sharply disparate tax treatment of debt and equity, it is hardly surprising that the Service may be unwilling to accept the taxpayer's label as controlling.[1] Form would be elevated over substance if every piece of paper embossed with a corporate seal and bearing the label "debt" were treated as such for tax purposes. To prevent tax avoidance through the use of excessive debt, the Service may recast a purported debt obligation as equity. The tax consequences of a recharacterization can be extremely unpleasant. An interest payment becomes a dividend and the corporation loses its deduction. If and when the note is repaid, the "creditor" finds himself in the role of shareholder, and the "loan repayment" may turn into a taxable dividend instead of a tax-free return of capital.

It is one thing to list the advantages of debt and identify the unfortunate ramifications of reclassification. It is quite another to describe with any precision the process employed by the courts and the Service to determine whether a particular instrument is debt or equity. The case law first approaches the issue by describing a spectrum. At one end is equity, a risk investment with the potential to share in corporate profits. At the other end is debt, evidenced by the corporation's unconditional promise to pay back the contributed funds, with market rate interest, at a fixed maturity date. A pure equity investor—the shareholder—has voting rights and upside potential. A pure debt holder—the creditor—is an outsider with no prospect of sharing in the growth of the enterprise. Many classification controversies involve "hybrid securities" having features common to both

---

1. Unless extended, the preferential rate will expire at the end of 2012.

1. The characterization of an instrument at its issuance is binding on the issuer, but not the Service. I.R.C. § 385(c)(1). A holder of an instrument generally is bound by the issuer's characterization unless the holder discloses an inconsistent position on a tax return. I.R.C. § 385(c)(2).

debt and equity, and the courts must decide whether these instruments falling in the middle of the spectrum are closer to one end or the other.

Any process that looks at something decidedly gray and tries to determine whether it more closely resembles black or white is bound to be frustrating. And so it is here. The litigated cases are legion and the court decisions have been aptly vilified as a "jungle"[2] and a "viper's tangle."[3] The issue is murky because classification of an obligation as debt or equity traditionally is treated as a question of fact to be resolved by applying vague standards that require the weighing of many factors.[4] In a manner reminiscent of the approach to determining whether an asset is "held primarily for sale to customers," the courts have spewed forth laundry lists of "factors," but it is difficult to discern which are controlling in a given case. Exhaustive research leaves one with the firm conviction that the courts are applying an amorphous and highly unsatisfactory "smell test."

Synthesizing the decisional morass is a perilous enterprise, but the principal factors enunciated by the courts over the years may be summarized as follows:[5]

Form of the Obligation. Labels are hardly controlling, but the decisions provide some guidance for a corporation that wishes to avoid reclassification of debt as equity. At a minimum, debt instruments should bear the usual indicia of debt—an unconditional promise to pay; a specific term; remedies for a default; and a stated, reasonable rate of interest, payable in all events.[6] Equity characteristics should be avoided. For example, the likelihood of reclassification is far greater with a hybrid instrument that makes payment of interest contingent on earnings or provides the holder with voting rights.[7]

The Debt/Equity Ratio. The debt/equity ratio of a corporation is the ratio of the company's liabilities to the shareholders' equity. The ratio has long been used as a tool to determine whether a corporation is thinly capitalized. Thin capitalization, in turn, creates a substantial risk that what purports to be debt will be reclassified as equity on the theory that no rational creditor would lend money to a corporation with such nominal equity.

---

2. Commissioner v. Union Mutual Insurance Co. of Providence, 386 F.2d 974, 978 (1st Cir.1967).

3. Bittker & Eustice, Federal Income Taxation of Corporations and Shareholders ¶ 4.04 (4th ed. 1979).

4. For this reason, the Service ordinarily declines to issue advance rulings on the classification on an instrument as debt or equity. Rev. Proc. 2012–3, § 4.02(1), 2012–1 I.R.B. 118. The courts are divided over whether the debt vs. equity question is one of fact or law, or a mixed question of fact and law. See Indmar Products Co., Inc. v. Commissioner, infra p. 124.

5. See generally Plumb, "The Federal Income Tax Significance of Corporate Debt: A Critical Analysis and a Proposal," 26 Tax L.Rev. 369 (1971), a classic article that somehow manages to survey the landscape with only 1,591 footnotes. For a more recent summary, see Hariton, "Essay: Distinguishing Between Equity and Debt in the New Financial Environment," 49 Tax L. Rev. 499 (1994).

6. See Wood Preserving Corp. v. United States, 347 F.2d 117, 119 (4th Cir.1965).

7. See Fellinger v. United States, 363 F.2d 826 (6th Cir.1966).

The trouble with this attempt at quantification is that the cases are inconsistent as to what constitutes an excessive debt/equity ratio. For example, depending on all the other factors, a debt/equity ratio of 3–to–1, which most would regard as conservative, has been held to be excessive,[8] while ratios of 50–to–1 and higher have been held to be acceptable.[9] Some cases apply different norms for different industries,[10] others ignore the ratio entirely,[11] and some evaluate the ratio in the context of the overall growth prospects of the business.[12]

And how is the debt/equity ratio to be computed? Consider some of the basic questions on which there has been disagreement. Is debt limited to shareholder debt or does it include debts to outsiders?[13] Does outside debt include accounts payable to trade creditors or only long-term liabilities? What about shareholder guaranteed debt?[14] In determining "equity," are assets taken into account at their book value (i.e., adjusted basis) or fair market value?[15] The differences in approach can be considerable.

Intent. Some cases have turned on the "intent" of the parties to create a debtor-creditor relationship.[16] "Intent" presumably is not gleaned by a subjective inquiry; it would be meaningless to place the corporate insiders on the witness stand and ask whether they "intended" to be shareholders or creditors. The more reasoned decisions measure "intent" by objective criteria such as the lender's reasonable expectation of repayment, evaluated in light of the financial condition of the company, and the corporation's

8. See Schnitzer v. Commissioner, 13 T.C. 43 (1949).

9. See Bradshaw v. United States, 231 Ct.Cl. 144, 683 F.2d 365, 367–68 (1982) (50–to–1 ratio not fatal because corporation was likely to and did in fact pay off debts when due); Baker Commodities, Inc. v. Commissioner, 48 T.C. 374 (1967), affirmed, 415 F.2d 519 (9th Cir.1969), cert. denied, 397 U.S. 988, 90 S.Ct. 1117 (1970) (692–to–1 ratio is acceptable because cash flow and earning power of business could cover payments).

10. Compare Tomlinson v. 1661 Corp., 377 F.2d 291 (5th Cir.1967) (improved real estate; debt traditionally high) with John Lizak, Inc. v. Commissioner, 28 T.C.M. 804 (1969) (construction business less able to carry heavy debt burden).

11. See Gooding Amusement Co. v. Commissioner, 23 T.C. 408, 419 (1954), affirmed, 236 F.2d 159 (6th Cir.1956), cert. denied, 352 U.S. 1031, 77 S.Ct. 595 (1957).

12. See, e.g., Delta Plastics, Inc. v. Commissioner, 85 T.C.M. 940 (2003) (26–to–1 ratio was acceptable because likely success of business would reduce ratio to 4–to–1 within three years).

13. Compare Ambassador Apartments, Inc. v. Commissioner, 50 T.C. 236, 245

(1968), affirmed, 406 F.2d 288 (2d Cir.1969) (consider outside debt) with P.M. Finance Corp. v. Commissioner, 302 F.2d 786, 788 (3d Cir.1962) (consider only shareholder debt).

14. Compare Murphy Logging Co. v. United States, 378 F.2d 222 (9th Cir.1967) (disregard shareholder guaranteed debt) with Plantation Patterns, Inc. v. Commissioner, 462 F.2d 712 (5th Cir.1972), cert. denied, 409 U.S. 1076, 93 S.Ct. 683 (1972) (shareholder guaranteed debt recharacterized as equity contribution by guarantor.)

15. See Nye v. Commissioner, 50 T.C. 203, 216 (1968). In Bauer v. Commissioner, 748 F.2d 1365 (9th Cir.1984), the court computed stockholders' equity by adding together paid-in capital and retained earnings and arrived at outside debt/equity ratios for different years ranging from approximately 2 to 1 to 8 to 1. The Tax Court had determined a ratio for one year of approximately 92 to 1 by limiting shareholders' equity to initial paid-in capital.

16. See Gooding Amusement Co. v. Commissioner, 236 F.2d 159 (6th Cir.1956), cert. denied, 352 U.S. 1031, 77 S.Ct. 595 (1957).

ability to pay principal and interest.[17] Hindsight also plays a role. For example, if the corporation consistently fails to pay interest or repay debts when they are due, its claim to debtor status may be highly questionable.[18]

Proportionality. In a closely held setting, debt held by the shareholders in the same proportion as their stock holdings normally raises the eyebrows of the Service.[19] The rationale is that if debt is held in roughly the same proportion as stock, the "creditors" have no economic incentive to act like creditors by setting or enforcing the terms of the so-called liability. The unanswered question is whether proportionality, without other negative factors, is sufficient in itself to convert the obligation into stock.[20]

Subordination. If a corporation has borrowed from both shareholders and outside sources, the independent creditors frequently will require that the shareholder debt be subordinated to the claims of general creditors. Although subordination of inside debt would appear to be inevitable if significant unsecured outside financing is desired, some courts have regarded it as the smoking pistol.[21] Once again, however, it is difficult to advise a client with any certainty that subordination is fatal per se. The economic realities of closely held corporate life would suggest that it should not be determinative, but it grows in importance when combined with other negative factors such as thin capitalization, proportionality, and failure to pay any dividends.[22]

This distillation of factors barely scratches the surface. The *Indmar Products* case, which follows, provides an illustration of one court's approach to the problem.

Indmar Products Co., Inc. v. Commissioner

United States Court of Appeals, Sixth Circuit, 2006.
444 F.3d 771.

■ McKeague, Circuit Judge.

Indmar Products Co., Inc. ("Indmar") appeals the decision of the Tax Court to disallow interest deductions the company claimed for tax years 1998–2000, and to assess accuracy-related tax penalties for those years. The interest deductions relate to a number of advances made to Indmar by its

17. Indmar Products Co., Inc. v. Commissioner, supra note 5; Fin Hay Realty Co. v. United States, 398 F.2d 694 (3d Cir.1968); Gilbert v. Commissioner, 248 F.2d 399 (2d Cir.1957).

18. See Slappey Drive Industrial Park v. United States, 561 F.2d 572, 582 (5th Cir.1977); Estate of Mixon v. United States, 464 F.2d 394, 409 (5th Cir.1972).

19. See Charter Wire, Inc. v. United States, 309 F.2d 878, 880 (7th Cir.1962), cert. denied, 372 U.S. 965, 83 S.Ct. 1090 (1963).

20. For a negative view, see Harlan v. United States, 409 F.2d 904, 909 (5th Cir. 1969) (proportionality may be considered but has no significant importance).

21. See P.M. Finance Corp. v. Commissioner, 302 F.2d 786, 789–90 (3d Cir.1962); R.C. Owen Co. v. Commissioner, 23 T.C.M. 673, 676 (1964), affirmed, 351 F.2d 410 (6th Cir.1965), cert. denied, 382 U.S. 967, 86 S.Ct. 1272 (1966).

22. See Tyler v. Tomlinson, 414 F.2d 844 (5th Cir.1969).

majority stockholders over several years. Indmar argued at trial that the advances were legitimate loans made to the company, and thus it could properly deduct the interest payments made on these advances under 26 U.S.C. § 163(a). The Tax Court, following the position taken by the Commissioner of Internal Revenue (the "Commissioner"), disagreed, concluding that the advances were equity contributions and therefore the company could not deduct any purported interest payments on these advances. The court imposed penalties on Indmar based on the deductions. * * *

Upon review of the record, we conclude that the Tax Court clearly erred in finding the advances were equity. The Tax Court failed to consider several factors used by this court for determining whether advances are debt or equity, ignored relevant evidence, and drew several unsupported inferences from its factual findings. We reverse and find that the stockholder advances were bona fide debt.

I. BACKGROUND

A. Stockholder Advances to Indmar

Indmar, a Tennessee corporation, is a marine engine manufacturer. In 1973, Richard Rowe, Sr., and Marty Hoffman owned equal shares of Indmar. In 1987, after Hoffman passed away, Richard and his wife, Donna Rowe, together owned 74.44% of Indmar, with their children and children's spouses owning the rest. By all accounts, Indmar has been a successful company. From 1986 to 2000, Indmar's sales and costs-of-goods sold increased from $5m and $3.9m to $45m and $37.7m, respectively. In addition, Indmar's working capital (current assets minus current liabilities) increased from $471,386 to $3.8m. During this period, Indmar did not declare or pay formal dividends.

Since the 1970s, Indmar's stockholders have advanced funds to it, receiving a 10% annual return in exchange. Hoffman started the practice in the 1970s. Beginning in 1987, the Rowes (as well as their children) began to make advancements on a periodic basis. Indmar treated all of the advances as loans from stockholders in the corporate books and records, and made monthly payments calculated at 10% of the advanced funds. Indmar reported the payments as interest expense deductions on its federal income tax returns. Consistent with Indmar's reporting, the Rowes reported the payments as interest income on their individual income tax returns.

The parties did not initially document the advances with notes or other instruments. Beginning in 1993, the parties executed notes covering all of the advances at issue. Specifically, Indmar executed a promissory note in 1993 with Donna Rowe for $201,400 (i.e., her outstanding balance). The note was payable on demand and freely transferable, had no maturity date or monthly payment schedule, and had a fixed interest rate of 10%. In 1995, Indmar executed a similar promissory note with Richard Rowe for $605,681 (i.e., his outstanding balance). In 1998, when the outstanding transfers totaled $1,222,133, Indmar executed two line of credit agreements with the Rowes for $1m and $750,000. The line of credit agreements provided that the balances were payable on demand and the notes were freely transferable. In addition, the agreements provided a stated interest rate of 10% and had no maturity date or monthly payment schedule. None of the advances were secured.

Repayments of the advances were paid on demand, based on the needs of the stockholders, and not subject to set or predetermined due dates. The record indicates that between 1987 and 2000, the total advance balances ranged from $634,000 to $1.7m, and Indmar made purported interest payments between $45,000 and $174,000 each year.

The parties structured the advances as demand loans to give the Rowes flexibility as creditors. Moreover, as demand loans, the advances were treated by the Rowes as short-term debt under Tennessee law, thereby excepting interest payments from a 6% state tax on dividends and interest on long-term debts. * * * Indmar, however, reported the advances as long-term liabilities on its financial statements to avoid violating loan agreements with First Tennessee Bank ("FTB"), its primary creditor, who required a minimum ratio of current assets to current liabilities.

In order to reconcile the treatment and execution of the advances as demand loans versus listing them as long-term debt in its financial reports, Indmar received waivers from the Rowes agreeing to forego repayment on the notes for at least 12 months. From 1989 to 2000, the notes to Indmar's financial statements disclosed that "The stockholders have agreed not to demand payment within the next year," and in 1992 and 1993, the Rowes signed written agreements stating that they would not demand repayment of the advances. Indmar did all of this under the direction of its accountant.

Despite the annual waivers, the Rowes demanded and received numerous partial repayments of the advances. Specifically, in 1994 and 1995, Richard Rowe demanded repayment of $15,000 and $650,000, respectively, to pay his taxes and purchase a new home. He also demanded repayment of $84,948, $80,000, $25,000, and $70,221 from 1997–2000 to pay litigation expenses, boat repairs, and tax expenses. Donna Rowe demanded repayment of $180,000 in 1998 for boat repairs. The Rowes made additional advances in 1997 and 1998 of $500,000 and $300,000, respectively. The balance of notes payable to stockholders on December 31, 2000, totaled $1,166,912.

As Indmar was a successful, profitable company, numerous banks sought to lend money to it. FTB worked hard to retain Indmar's business, made funds immediately available upon request, and was willing to lend Indmar 100% of the stockholder advances.

In its loan agreements with Indmar, FTB required the company to subordinate all transfers, including stockholder advances, to FTB's loans. FTB did not strictly enforce the subordination provision, however, as Indmar repaid—with FTB's knowledge—some of the stockholder advancements at the same time FTB loans remained outstanding. As an example, when Richard demanded repayment of $650,000 to purchase a new home, Indmar borrowed the entire amount from FTB at 7.5% (the prime lending rate was 8.75%). Indmar secured the loan with inventory, accounts and general intangibles, equipment, and the personal guarantee of the Rowes. Richard Moody, the FTB lending officer who worked with Indmar on the loan, testified that he knew Indmar used the proceeds to repay Richard. Indmar had loans outstanding with FTB at the time.

As stipulated by the parties, the prime lending rate ranged from a low of 6% to a high of 10.5% between 1987–1998. In 1997, Indmar and FTB executed a promissory note for $1m that was modified in 1998. The interest rate on the note (7.85%) was below the prime lending rate. Indmar also had a collateralized line of credit with FTB. Similar to the stockholder advances, the bank line of credit was used for short-term working capital. FTB charged the following rates for the secured line of credit [from 1995 to 2000, the rates ranged from 8 to 9.5 percent. Ed.]:

B.   Claimed Deductions at Issue

On its tax returns for 1998–2000, Indmar claimed deductions for the purported interest payments paid on the stockholder advances. The Commissioner issued a notice of deficiency. Indmar filed a petition in the Tax Court challenging the Commissioner's decision. After trial, the Tax Court concluded that the advances did not constitute genuine indebtedness and thus the payments to the stockholders were not deductible. The Tax Court calculated a total tax deficiency of $123,735 and assessed $24,747 in penalties. Indmar timely appealed.

II.   LEGAL ANALYSIS

A.   Determining Whether Advance Is Debt or Equity.

* * * The basic question before us is whether the advances made to the company by the stockholders were loans or equity contributions. Under 26 U.S.C. § 163(a), a taxpayer may take a tax deduction for "all interest paid or accrued ... on indebtedness." There is no similar deduction for dividends paid on equity investments. Thus, if the advances were loans, the 10% payments made by Indmar to the Rowes were "interest" payments, and Indmar could deduct these payments. If, on the other hand, the advances were equity contributions, the 10% payments were constructive dividends, and thus were not deductible.

Over the years, courts have grappled with this seemingly simple question in a wide array of legal and factual contexts. The distinction between debt and equity arises in other areas of federal tax law, see, e.g., Roth Steel Tube Co. v. Comm'r, 800 F.2d 625, 629–30 (6th Cir.1986) (addressing the issue in the context of the deductibility of advances as bad debt under 26 U.S.C. § 166(a)(1)), as well as bankruptcy law * * * The Second Circuit set out the "classic" definition of debt in Gilbert v. Commissioner: "an unqualified obligation to pay a sum certain at a reasonably close fixed maturity date along with a fixed percentage in interest payable regardless of the debtor's income or lack thereof." 248 F.2d 399, 402 (2d Cir.1957). "While some variation from this formula is not fatal to the taxpayer's effort to have the advance treated as a debt for tax purposes, ...

too great a variation will of course preclude such treatment." Id. at 402–03. The question becomes, then, what is "too great a variation"?

To determine whether an advance to a company is debt or equity, courts consider "whether the objective facts establish an intention to create an unconditional obligation to repay the advances." * * * In doing so, courts look not only to the form of the transaction, but, more importantly, to its economic substance. See, e.g., Fin Hay Realty Co. v. United States, 398 F.2d 694, 697 (3d Cir.1968) ("The various factors . . . are only aids in answering the ultimate question whether the investment, analyzed in terms of its economic reality, constitutes risk capital entirely subject to the fortunes of the corporate venture or represents a strict debtor-creditor relationship."); Byerlite Corp. v. Williams, 286 F.2d 285, 291 (6th Cir.1960) ("In all cases, the prevailing consideration is that artifice must not be exalted over reality, whether to the advantage of the taxpayer, or to the government.").

The circuit courts have not settled on a single approach to the debt/equity question. We elucidated our approach in *Roth Steel,* setting out eleven non-exclusive factors for courts to consider:

> (1) the names given to the instruments, if any, evidencing the indebtedness; (2) the presence or absence of a fixed maturity date and schedule of payments; (3) the presence or absence of a fixed rate of interest and interest payments; (4) the source of repayments; (5) the adequacy or inadequacy of capitalization; (6) the identity of interest between the creditor and the stockholder; (7) the security, if any, for the advances; (8) the corporation's ability to obtain financing from outside lending institutions; (9) the extent to which the advances were subordinated to the claims of outside creditors; (10) the extent to which the advances were used to acquire capital assets; and (11) the presence or absence of a sinking fund to provide repayments.

800 F.2d at 630. No single factor is controlling; the weight to be given a factor (if any) necessarily depends on the particular circumstances of each case. * * *

B.   Standard of Review

We review the Tax Court's factual findings for "clear error" and its application of law de novo. * * * The circuits are split on whether the debt/equity question is one of fact or law, or a mixed question of fact and law. * * * Earlier panels of this court have held that the question is one of fact. * * * Accordingly, we review the Tax Court's findings for clear error.

With these principles in mind, we now turn to the Tax Court's decision in this case.

C.   *Roth Steel* Factors

After discussing some, but not all, of the *Roth Steel* factors, the Tax Court concluded that the Rowes' advances were equity contributions.

Specifically, it found the following factors weighed in favor of equity: (i) Indmar did not pay any formal dividends (although this is not one of the Roth Steel factors); (ii) there was no fixed maturity date or obligation to repay; (iii) repayment came from corporate profits and would not be paid if there were not sufficient profits; (iv) advances were unsecured; (v) there was no sinking fund; and (vi) at the time advances were made, there was no unconditional and legal obligation to repay. The court found that several factors weighed in favor of debt: (i) Indmar reported the advances on its federal income tax returns as interest expenses; (ii) external financing was available; (iii) Indmar was adequately capitalized; (iv) the advances were not subordinated to all creditors; and (v) the Rowes did not make the advances in proportion to their respective equity holdings. The court concluded that the factors favoring equity certainly outweigh those favoring debt. * * * As explained below, we find that the Tax Court clearly erred in concluding that the advances were equity contributions rather than bona fide debt. The Tax Court failed to consider several Roth Steel factors. It also did not address in its analysis certain uncontroverted testimony and evidence upon which the parties stipulated. Consideration of all of the record evidence in this case leaves us "with the definite and firm conviction that a mistake has been committed." Holmes, 184 F.3d at 543.

1.   Fixed Rate of Interest and Interest Payments

The first factor to which we look is whether or not a fixed rate of interest and fixed interest payments accompanied the advances. * * * The absence of a fixed interest rate and regular payments indicates equity; conversely, the presence of both evidences debt. * * * In its findings of fact, the Tax Court determined that the advances were made with a 10% annual return rate. The court also found that Indmar made regular monthly interest payments on all of the advances.The fixed rate of interest and regular interest payments indicate that the advances were bona fide debt. In its analysis, however, the Tax Court took a different view. Rather than analyzing these facts within the Roth Steel framework (i.e., as objective indicia of debt or equity), the Tax Court focused instead on why the Rowes made the advancements: it concluded that the Rowes "characterized the cash transfers as debt because they wanted to receive a 10–percent return on their investment and minimize estate taxes." * * * Yet, neither of these intentions is inconsistent with characterizing the advances as loans.

For tax purposes, it is generally more important to focus on "what was done," than "why it was done." United States v. Hertwig, 398 F.2d 452, 455 (5th Cir.1968). "In applying the law to the facts of this case, . . . it is 'clear that the objective factors . . . are decisive in cases of this type.' " Raymond, 511 F.2d at 191 (quoting Austin Village, 432 F.2d at 745). It is largely unremarkable that the Rowes wanted to receive a return from their advances. Most, if not all, creditors (as well as equity investors) intend to profit from their investments. Bordo Prods. Co. v. United States, 201 Ct.Cl. 482, 476 F.2d 1312, 1322 (1973). As long as the interest rate is in line with the risks involved, a healthy return on investment can evidence debt.

Of course, "[e]xcessively high rates would . . . raise the possibility that a distribution of corporate profits was being disguised as debt. Were such the purpose of an exorbitant interest rate, the instrument involved would probably not qualify as debt in form." Scriptomatic, Inc. v. United States, 555 F.2d 364, 370 n. 7 (3d Cir.1977) (citing William T. Plumb, Jr., The Fed. Income Tax Significance of Corporate Debt: A Critical Analysis & A Proposal, 26 Tax L.Rev. 369, 439–40 (1971)). The Tax Court found that the 10% rate exceeded the federal prime interest rate during most of the period at issue, as well as the rate charged by FTB on several of its loans to Indmar.

The record indicates that the 10% rate was not an "exorbitant interest rate" under the circumstances. Indmar had a collateralized line of credit with FTB, which, similar to the stockholder advances, was available for short-term working capital. The rate charged by FTB for the line of credit ranged between 8%–9.5%, a rate not much below the fixed rate of 10% charged by the Rowes. The rate differential makes financial sense when considering the differences in security—the FTB line of credit was secured while the Rowes' advances were not.[2]

As for the Rowes' desire to minimize their estate taxes, this also offers little to the analysis. "Tax avoidance is entirely legal and legitimate. Any taxpayer 'may so arrange his affairs that his taxes shall be as low as possible; he is not bound to choose that pattern which will best pay the Treasury; there is not even a patriotic duty to increase one's taxes.' " * * * The desire to avoid or minimize taxes is not itself directly relevant to the question whether a purported loan is instead an equity investment. Rather, such a desire is only tangentially relevant, by acting as a flag to the Commissioner and courts to look closely at the transaction for any objective indicia of debt.

Far from proving the Commissioner's position, the existence and consistent payment of a fixed, reasonable interest rate strongly supports the inference that the advances were bona fide loans.

2.   Written Instruments of the Indebtedness

"The absence of notes or other instruments of indebtedness is a strong indication that the advances were capital contributions and not loans." * * * In its analysis, the Tax Court found that Indmar "failed to establish that, at the time the transfers were made, it had the requisite unconditional and legal obligation to repay the Rowes (e.g., the transfers were not documented)." * * *

The Tax Court focused on only half the story. For years 1987–1992, the Rowes did make advancements without executing any notes or other

---

2. The government took pains during trial to show that Indmar could have received a lower interest rate from FTB than its stockholders. Had the 10% rate been exorbitant, this would have been a useful line of inquiry. Under the circumstances here, the rate was not exorbitant, and whether Indmar could have received a better rate through FTB is of no import. To show bona fide debt, a taxpayer does not need to prove that it received the financially optimal rate, just a commercially reasonable one.

instruments. Beginning in 1993, and for all the tax years at issue in this case, the parties executed notes of loans and lines of credit covering all of the advances at issue, as the Tax Court noted in its findings of fact. Yet, in its analysis of the Roth Steel factors, the Tax Court was silent as to the subsequent execution of notes. After-the-fact consolidation of prior advances into a single note can indicate that the advances were debt rather than equity contributions. * * * The Tax Court erred by focusing on the initial lack of documentation without addressing the subsequent history of executed notes.

3.   Fixed Maturity Date and Schedule of Payments

"The absence of a fixed maturity date and a fixed obligation to repay indicates that the advances were capital contributions and not loans." * * * Based on the Rowes' waivers, the Tax Court concluded that there was no fixed maturity date or fixed obligation to repay. While correct, we find that this factor carries little weight in the final analysis. The parties structured the advances as demand loans, which had ascertainable (although not fixed) maturity dates, controlled by the Rowes. * * * Furthermore, the temporary waiver of payment does not convert debt into equity "since [the stockholders] still expected to be repaid." * * * Where advances are documented by demand notes with a fixed rate of interest and regular interest payments, the lack of a maturity date and schedule of payments does not strongly favor equity. To give any significant weight to this factor would create a virtual per se rule against the use of demand notes by stockholders, even though "[m]uch commercial debt is evidenced by demand notes." * * *

4.   The Source of Repayments

"An expectation of repayment solely from corporate earnings is not indicative of bona fide debt regardless of its reasonableness." * * * Repayment can generally come from "only four possible sources . . .: (1) liquidation of assets, (2) profits from the business, (3) cash flow, and (4) refinancing with another lender." * * * The Tax Court found that the "source of repayments" factor favored equity. It relied upon Richard Rowe's testimony that Indmar was expected to make a profit and that repayment "has to come from corporate profits or else the company couldn't pay for it." * * * The full colloquy from the testimony, however, is more equivocal:

Q.   . . . [A]t the time that you made these advances, were you anticipating that the repayment was going to come from corporate profits?

A.   Yes, sir. It has to come from corporate profits or else the company couldn't pay for it. Unless it made profit—and I have always believed from the first day we started, that we were going to be profitable.

Q.   Was it your understanding and intent, at the time you made these advances, that if the company was not, in fact, profitable, you would not be repaid?

A. I had no intentions of not being repaid, sir.

Q. Why is that?

A. I believe it's me. It's my personality.

Q. Is that because you intended to make a profit?

A. Yes, sir.

There are at least two plausible ways to read this testimony. One can read it the way the Tax Court apparently did—Rowe's testimony was, at best, contradictory: repayment must come from profits, but he had no intention of not being repaid, regardless of the company's fortunes. Given the apparent contradiction, one should focus on the statement against Indmar's interest: Rowe admitted that repayment of the advances "has to come from corporate profits or else the company couldn't pay for it." If repayment "has" to come from profits, then this would imply that repayment was tied to the company's fortunes, suggesting the advances were equity contributions.

Another way to read the testimony, however, is that Rowe, as a small businessman and unsecured creditor, believed that full repayment of all of Indmar's debt required a thriving, successful business, which, ultimately, required profits. In other words, struggling companies near or at bankruptcy do not repay their debts, at least not dollar for dollar. Under this reading, his testimony is consistent with debt. * * *

If there was no other evidence to support one view or the other, we could not say that the Tax Court's reading was clearly erroneous. Credibility determinations are left to the fact finder, and our review on appeal is strictly limited. The "Tax Court 'is not bound to accept testimony at face value even when it is uncontroverted if it is improbable, unreasonable or questionable.' " Lovell & Hart, Inc. v. Comm'r, 456 F.2d 145, 148 (6th Cir.1972) (quoting Comm'r v. Smith, 285 F.2d 91, 96 (5th Cir.1960)). On the other hand, the Tax Court cannot ignore relevant evidence in making its factual findings and any inferences from those findings.

Here, there is undisputed testimony by Rowe and the FTB lending officer, corroborated by stipulated evidence in the record, that clearly weighs in favor of debt on this factor. Indmar repaid a significant portion of the unpaid advances—$650,000—not from profits but by taking on additional debt from FTB. While the interest rate on the FTB loan was lower than 10%, Indmar had to secure the bank loan with inventory, accounts and general intangibles, equipment, and personal guarantees. Thus, Indmar repaid a significant portion of the unsecured stockholder advancements by taking on secured debt from a bank, rather than by taking the funds directly from earnings. This is important evidence that the parties had no expectation that Indmar would repay the advances "solely" from earnings. The Tax Court did not discuss or even cite this evidence in its Roth Steel analysis.

5. The Extent to Which the Advances Were Used to Acquire Capital Assets

Nor did the Tax Court address whether Indmar used the advances for working capital or capital expenditures. "Use of advances to meet the daily operating needs of the corporation, rather than to purchase capital assets, is indicative of bona fide indebtedness." * * * Richard Rowe testified that Indmar always went to a bank for funds to buy capital equipment. He also testified that all of the advances he made to Indmar were used for working capital, as opposed to capital equipment. This is uncontroverted testimony. The government points, however, to Rowe's testimony that he advanced funds even when Indmar did not "need" the funds, and argues that this somehow cuts against his testimony that the advances were used as working capital.The government's argument is unpersuasive. We do not find that Rowe's testimony on this subject was "improbable, unreasonable or questionable," especially in the absence of the Tax Court addressing this factor in its analysis.[5] A review of Indmar's financial statements shows that it used all of the funds it received in various ways, including working capital and capital equipment expenditures. Thus, Indmar used the advances it received from the Rowes, even if not immediately upon receipt— i.e., Indmar identified a "need" for the advances at some point. There is nothing specific in the record, including Indmar's financial statements, that suggests the advances went to purchase capital equipment as opposed to being used for working capital. Accordingly, the government's supposition does not counter Rowe's testimony, and this factor squarely supports a finding of debt.

6. Sinking Fund

"The failure to establish a sinking fund for repayment is evidence that the advances were capital contributions rather than loans." Id. The Tax Court was correct to point out that the lack of a sinking fund favors equity. This factor does not, however, deserve significant weight under the circumstances. First, a sinking fund (as a type of reserve) is a form of security for debt, and the Tax Court also counted the general absence of security for the stockholder advances as favoring equity. Second, the presence or absence of a sinking fund is an important consideration when looking at advances made to highly leveraged firms. In that case, the risk of repayment will likely be high on any unsecured loans, so any commercially reasonable lender would require a sinking fund or some other form of security for repayment. Where a company has sound capitalization with outside creditors ready to loan it money (as here), there is less need for a sinking fund. * * *.

---

5. As the Tax Court did not address this factor, it made no credibility determinations with respect to Richard Rowe's testimony relating to the use of the advancements. At one point in its decision the Tax Court did find that Rowe's testimony was "contradicto-ry, inconsistent, and unconvincing" and that the parties "manipulated facts," but this was in specific reference to its discussion about the inconsistent treatment of the advances as demand debt and long-term debt.

7.   The Remaining *Roth Steel* Factors

On the remaining *Roth Steel* factors, the Tax Court determined that one favored equity (lack of security for the advances) and four favored debt (the company had sufficient external financing available to it; the company was adequately capitalized; the advances were not subordinated to all creditors; and the Rowes did not make the advances in proportion to their respective equity holdings). These findings are well-supported in the record.

8.   Failure to Pay Dividends

The Tax Court included in its discussion of *Roth Steel* a factor not actually cited in that case—Indmar's failure to pay dividends. In support, the Tax Court cited our decision in Jaques v. Commissioner. The relevance of Jaques to this case is questionable. That case involved the withdrawal of funds by a controlling stockholder from his closely-held corporation. The stockholder argued that the withdrawal itself was a loan. We rejected the argument, relying in part on the fact that the corporation had never issued a formal dividend, and thus the withdrawal could have been a disguised dividend. Jaques, 935 F.2d at 107–08. The situation here is the exact opposite—the stockholders were advancing money to the corporation (not from), and it is the nature of those advances that we must determine.

Had the Rowes charged Indmar an exorbitant interest rate, the lack of any formal dividends might have been relevant to showing that the payments were not interest payments, but disguised dividends. As this was not the case, see supra Section II.C.1, we do not address further the relevance, if any, of the lack of dividend payments to the debt/equity question presented here.

D.   The Tax Court Committed Clear Error

To summarize, eight of the eleven Roth Steel factors favor debt. The three remaining factors suggest the advances were equity, but, as we explained above, two of the factors—the absence of a fixed maturity date and schedule of payments and the absence of a sinking fund—deserve little weight under the facts of this case. Moreover, the non-Roth Steel factor relied upon by the Tax Court—Indmar's failure to pay dividends—has questionable relevance to our inquiry. The only factor weighing in favor of equity with any real significance—the lack of security—does not outweigh all of the other factors in favor of debt.

Accordingly, the trial evidence, when reviewed as a whole, conclusively shows that the Rowes' advances to Indmar were bona fide loans. The Tax Court committed clear error in finding otherwise.

III.   CONCLUSION

For the foregoing reasons, we reverse the Tax Court's determination that the stockholders' advances were equity contributions. We find that the advances exhibited clear, objective indicia of bona fide debt. Accordingly, we also reverse the Tax Court's assessment of accuracy-related penalties.

■ ROGERS, CIRCUIT JUDGE, concurring.

I concur fully in the majority opinion. I write separately to explain why the legal, non-factual components of the tax court's analysis are properly examined on appeal without deference to the tax court, notwithstanding the overall "clearly erroneous" standard that our court has stated to be applicable to the determination of whether a particular transaction is debt or equity. [Judge Rogers went on to discuss the conflicting precedents on the standard of review and concluded that, when the underlying facts are not in dispute, an appellate court should not apply the clearly erroneous standard to the debt vs. equity issue, which is a mixed question of fact and law. Ed.] Applying "clearly erroneous" deference to lower court legal determinations, no matter how hidden or embedded such determinations are in overall determinations that are partly or even largely factual, is fundamentally at odds with the rule of law.[1]

■ MOORE, CIRCUIT JUDGE, dissenting.

[Judge Moore's dissent, which supported application of the clearly erroneous standard of review, has been omitted. Ed.]

2. HYBRID INSTRUMENTS

The types of financial instruments available to investors have proliferated. As one commentator has described the reality of today's world of corporate finance, "[i]n exchange for capital, corporations can offer investors any set of rights that can be described by words, subject to any conceivable set of qualifications, and in consideration of any conceivable set of offsetting obligations."[1]

The flexibility afforded corporate issuers has contributed to an array of exotic products that seek "best of both worlds" treatment—i.e., debt for tax purposes and equity for regulatory, financial rating, and accounting purposes. These hybrid instruments have been created and marketed by large financial institutions and Wall Street law firms who have advised corporate issuers that they may deduct the "interest" paid on the purported debt while treating the instruments as equity for financial statement or regulatory purposes. The excerpt below, from a study by the Joint Committee on Taxation on the tax treatment of business debt, surveys some of the incentives to create hybrid instruments.

1. Indeed, commentators have expressed concern that there is no predictable legal distinction between loans to a business and equity investment, and that the unpredictability of this legal distinction is partially caused by the issue being "treated as one of fact to be resolved by applying vague standards...." See Stephen A. Lind, Stephen Schwarz, Daniel J. Lathrope & Joshua D. Rosenberg, Fundamentals of Business Enterprise Taxation 474 (3d ed.2005). These authors note, "Exhaustive research leaves one with the firm conviction that the courts are applying an amorphous and highly unsatisfactory 'smell test.'" Id.

1. Hariton, "Distinguishing Between Equity and Debt in the New Financial Environment," 49 Tax L.Rev. 499, 501 (1994).

Excerpt From Joint Committee on Taxation, Present Law and Background Relating to the Tax Treatment of Business Debt*

July 11, 2011 (JCX–41–11), 80–85.

3.   Incentives to create hybrid instruments

In general

Taxpayers have significant flexibility to create economically similar instruments and categorize them as debt or equity. In general, instruments are not bifurcated into part debt and part equity, and the categorization as one type of instrument or the other applies across the board for all tax purposes. Taxpayers may have incentives to create instruments with hybrid features, that is, having features of both debt and equity, either solely for Federal income tax purposes, or because of additional benefits that may occur if the instrument is classified in a different manner for other purposes such as financial reporting, regulatory capital, or foreign tax purposes.

For example, issuers may seek to structure an instrument offering many of the attributes of equity while still providing an interest deduction. Some investors may seek debt-like protections while allowing for the possibility of sharing in the earnings or appreciation of a business. [If] instruments characterized as debt for tax purposes contain significant equity like features, the economic risks of high leverage might be mitigated. For example, a debt instrument having a long term that permits deferral of cash interest or principal payments, or an instrument that allows final payment of interest or principal (or both) in an amount of issuer stock rather than cash, may provide some cushion against an issuer's default and bankruptcy. Similarly, debt instruments held by a shareholder of the issuer could be perceived by third parties as equity-like to the extent the debt-holding stockholders are less likely to exercise their rights as creditors and drive a troubled issuer into bankruptcy. Such shareholders might instead voluntarily cancel or restructure their debt to avoid bankruptcy and preserve the potential for the corporation to improve its performance and ultimately increase their overall return through their return to equity.

To the extent debt provides interest deductions but also some flexibility against causing bankruptcy and lacks covenants that inhibit operations, it might be viewed in the marketplace as creating a less risky capital structure than other, more restrictive debt.

* * *

Corporate interest deductions on certain hybrid instruments

A corporation may issue debt that is convertible to corporate equity. Such an instrument could be viewed as part debt and part equity, with the amount paid to the corporation being attributable in part to the fixed

---

* Some footnotes have been omitted, and others have been renumbered.

interest debt instrument, and in part to the conversion feature. Treasury regulations and rulings provide inconsistent results for similar types of instruments, depending upon how the conversion feature is structured. If an instrument is simply convertible into stock of the issuer or related party, the amount of the interest deduction that is considered the economic equivalent of a payment on the amount attributable to conversion features is denied.

Under an IRS ruling,[1] if the instrument is not automatically convertible at a specific price, but rather is convertible only if one or more contingencies is satisfied (e.g., only if corporate earnings or share prices change by a specified threshold amount), then the rules for determining the market comparable for interest deduction purposes allow the instrument to be treated as if it did not have a conversion feature, thus allowing more interest to be deducted in advance of actual payment. Depending on the point at which the fixed conversion price is set compared to the conditions of the contingency, the two instruments could be economically very similar. The IRS has solicited comments on whether the approach allowing deductible interest to be determined as if there were no contingency should be extended beyond contingent convertible bonds. Commentators have expressed different views and have noted other inconsistencies in the treatment of potentially similar instruments that offer a debt holder the opportunity to participate in corporate growth or appreciation. The inconsistencies in treatment may allow taxpayers to select the treatment most favorable by proper structuring of the investment.

A corporation also may issue debt that is under certain circumstances payable in corporate equity. Section 163(l) denies interest deductions for such instruments. The IRS has ruled that certain hybrid instruments are not within the scope of this denial.[2]

Advantages when debt instruments for tax is treated as equity or part equity for financial accounting, rating agency or regulatory purposes

Federal income tax is not the only context in which classification of an instrument as debt or equity has significance. And because classification rules applicable in different contexts vary, taxpayers have designed hybrid instruments to achieve different, advantageous results under the different rules. Examples of other contexts include rules under U.S. GAAP determining the treatment of instruments for financial accounting purposes, bank regulatory rules determining whether an instrument qualifies as equity capital for purposes of bank capital requirements and the rules of various rating agencies considering how an instrument is treated for purposes of financial tests in assigning credit ratings to issuers. Although the treatment of an instrument for non-tax purposes is a factor in the Federal income tax classification analysis, it is not determinative.

Trust preferred securities[3] are an example of a hybrid securities instrument developed, and adapted over time, to be classified differently for

---

1. Rev. Rul. 2002–3.

2. See, e.g., Rev. Rul. 2003–97, 2003–34 I.R.B. 380.

3. The term "trust preferred securities" as used in this pamphlet is a generic term for various, but similar, financial prodtax, financial accounting, regulatory or rating agency purposes. Trust preferred securities are an instrument used to raise capital involving the creation of an additional entity to stand between the corporation raising the funds and the investors in the instrument.[4] For example, a corporation interested in raising capital could issue debt or preferred stock directly to investors. As an alternative, in the case of trust preferred securities, a corporate issuer forms a passthrough entity by contributing capital in exchange for a common equity interest. The passthrough entity then sells preferred equity interests to investors. The passthrough entity then lends the money it received from the corporation (as a capital contribution) and the investors (in exchange for the preferred equity interests) back to the corporation. As a result, the corporation has funds raised from investors, and has an obligation to make payments on indebtedness to the newly created passthrough entity. Payments on the corporation—passthrough entity indebtedness are typically designed to match the payments required on the passthrough entity-investor preferred securities. In other words, the passthrough entity operates as a conduit to receive payments of interest from the corporation, which it pays on to its preferred interest holders.

Prior to changes in the financial accounting rules in 2003, the simplified structure described above allowed the corporation interest deductions on amounts paid through to the investors for Federal tax purposes without treating the arrangement as a liability for financial accounting purposes. For Federal income tax purposes, the debt between the corporate issuer and the passthrough entity was designed to qualify as debt. Similarly, the terms of the preferred interests issued to investors was designed to qualify as debt for Federal income tax purposes even if treated as issued by the corporate issuer directly. Under U.S. GAAP rules, the passthrough entity was consolidated with the corporate issuer, with the effect that the loan between the corporate issuer and the passthrough entity (which would be treated as a liability for GAAP) was ignored for financial accounting purposes, and the preferred securities were treated as issued directly by the corporation. These preferred securities were designed to qualify as equity for GAAP purposes.

In 2003, U.S. GAAP rules were revised to require that trust preferred securities be reflected as a liability for financial accounting purposes. However, the trust preferred security structure has also involved benefits for credit rating purposes. Very generally, rating agencies such as Moody's Investor services and Standard and Poor's may assign a credit rating to certain company instruments. These agencies are concerned primarily with a company's ability to make payments on an instrument as required,

---

ucts including monthly income preference shares (MIPS), trust originated preferred securities (TOPrS), quarterly income preference shares (QUIPS), trust preferred securities (TruPS), and more recent variants such as enhanced capital advantaged preferred securities (ECAPS) and Enhanced TruPS (ETruPS).

4. The additional entity can be a foreign limited liability company, a domestic partnership or state law trust. Different structures have used different entities for a variety of non-tax reasons over time including compliance with securities laws, transaction costs and investor convenience.

without default. An important component of such an analysis is the composition of the issuer's capital structure, and the degree of flexibility a company has in periods of impaired cash flow. For example, Moody's Investor Services' rules have granted partial "equity credit" to hybrid instruments that allow, like trust preferred securities, for the deferral of periodic payments. In effect, giving "equity credit" for hybrid instruments could make such instruments more attractive to issuers than other financing alternatives, especially if such credit improved the company's credit rating.

In addition to credit rating benefits, for an issuer of trust preferred securities that is a bank holding company, such securities were designed to count as Tier 1 regulatory capital. Very generally, under U.S. bank regulatory capital requirements, banks are required to hold some minimum level of capital (e.g., three percent of total assets) and satisfy a minimum risk-based capital ratio (e.g., a ratio of total capital to total risk-weighted assets of eight percent). These requirements are generally designed to insure banks hold capital sufficient to absorb potential losses. Debt issued directly by a bank could give rise to tax deductible interest payments, but would not qualify as capital for regulatory purposes. Preferred stock issued directly by the bank could count as equity capital, but generally would not give rise to interest deductions. For certain banks, specifically, bank holding companies regulated by the Federal Reserve Board, trust preferred securities meeting certain requirements counted as Tier 1 capital. For banks other than bank holding companies, trust preferred securities did not count as Tier 1 capital. Section 171(b) of the Dodd–Frank Wall Street Reform and Protection Act generally phases out the treatment of trust preferred securities as Tier 1 capital for most large bank and thrift holding companies.

* * *

3. SECTION 385

Code: § 385.

Background. Many years ago, Congress concluded that a determined effort was needed to alleviate the uncertainties flowing from the debt/equity case law, especially in light of "the increasing use of debt for corporate acquisition purposes."[1] Frustrated in its attempt to draft precise definitions, Congress delegated the chore to the executive branch by enacting Section 385, which authorizes the Treasury to promulgate such regulations "as may be necessary or appropriate" to determine for all tax purposes whether an interest in a corporation is to be treated as stock or debt. Section 385(b) requires the regulations to set forth "factors" to be taken into account in determining whether a debtor-creditor relationship exists and specifies the following factors which may (but need not) be included in the regulations:

---

1. S.Rep. No. 91–552, 91st Cong., 1st Sess. 511 (1969), reprinted in 1969–3 C.B. 423, 511. See also H.R.Rep. No. 91–413, 91st Cong., 1st Sess. 265 (1969), reprinted in 1969–3 C.B. 200, 265.

1. Form—i.e., whether the instrument is evidenced by a written, unconditional promise to pay a sum certain on demand or on a specific date in return for an adequate consideration and bears a fixed interest rate.

2. Subordination to any indebtedness of the corporation.

3. The debt/equity ratio.

4. Convertibility into stock.

5. Proportionality—i.e., the relationship between holdings of stock in the corporation and holdings of the purported debt interest being scrutinized.

The Regulations Project. Section 385 was hailed by leading commentators as "perhaps the most important and potentially far-reaching corporate provision added by the Tax Reform Act of 1969,"[2] and the literature was replete with predictions as to the content of the regulations.[3] In March, 1980, 11 years after Section 385 was enacted, the Treasury issued a lengthy, detailed and controversial set of proposed regulations.[4] "Final" regulations were promulgated in December, 1980,[5] followed by amendments and effective date extensions, but all versions of the regulations were withdrawn in 1983[6] and the project has since been abandoned.

Although a detailed examination of the now long defunct regulations would not be productive, some features are noteworthy if only because they represented a concentrated attempt to bring order out of the chaos. For example, the regulations[7] distinguished straight debt from hybrid instruments, appropriately relegating hybrid securities to second class status. A "hybrid" was defined as an instrument convertible into stock or providing for any contingent payment to the holder.[8] In virtually all cases, hybrids would have been treated as preferred stock for tax purposes, at least if they were not held by independent creditors.[9] Straight debt—defined as anything other than a hybrid instrument[10]—still had a fighting chance of avoiding reclassification if certain other requirements were met.

The concept of proportionality played a central role in the regulatory scheme because "it generally makes little economic difference (aside from tax consequences) whether proportionate shareholder advances are made as debt or equity * * *."[11] Elaborate definitions of proportionality were pro-

---

2. Bittker & Eustice, Federal Income Taxation of Corporations and Shareholders, ¶ 4.05 (3rd ed. 1971).

3. Id. at 4–16 to 4–19. See also Recommendations as to Federal Tax Distinction between Corporate Stock and Indebtedness, N.Y. State Bar Association Tax Section Committee on Reorganization Problems, 25 Tax Lawyer 57 (1971).

4. 45 Fed.Reg. 18957 (1980).

5. T.D. 7747 (filed Dec. 29, 1980), 45 Fed.Reg. 86438 (Dec. 31, 1980), known as the "December 29" regulations.

6. T.D. 7920, 48 Fed.Reg. 31054 (July 6, 1983).

7. Unless otherwise indicated, citations which follow are to the December 30, 1981 version of the regulations.

8. Prop.Reg. § 1.385–3(d).

9. Prop.Reg. § 1.385–0(c)(2).

10. Prop.Reg. § 1.385–3(e).

11. T.D. 7747, 45 Fed.Reg. 86438, 86440 (Explanation of Changes), reprinted in 1981–1 C.B. 143.

vided, and special scrutiny was required for instruments held in substantial proportion to equity investments.[12]

Another contribution of the regulations was their precise definition of two debt/equity ratios—"outside" (which took into account *all* liabilities, including those to independent creditors) and "inside" (considering only shareholder debt).[13] Corollary rules provided that assets were to be reflected at adjusted basis rather than fair market value and trade liabilities were to be disregarded.[14] The debt/equity ratio was used to determine whether a corporation's debt was "excessive". A debt was excessive if the instrument's terms and conditions, viewed in combination with the corporation's financial structure, would not have been satisfactory to a bank or other financial institution making ordinary commercial loans.[15] It was not excessive, however, if the outside debt/equity ratio did not exceed 10–to–1 and the inside debt/equity ratio did not exceed 3–to–1.[16] Thus, even proportionate straight debt issued for cash would not be reclassified if it fell within this safe harbor from "excessive debt" and bore a "reasonable" (within specified ranges) interest rate. Variations on these themes abounded.

The regulations were withdrawn because lobbyists convinced the Treasury that they would have a negative impact on particular industries and on small businesses generally.[17] Although some of the regulatory themes ultimately may be adopted by the courts, the Treasury is unlikely to initiate the mobilization that would be required to resurrect this project.

Bifurcation of Instruments. Despite the Treasury's lack of success in implementing the goals of Section 385, Congress has not given up hope. Section 385 was amended to allow (but not require) the Treasury to classify an interest having significant debt and equity characteristics as "in part stock and in part indebtedness."[18] According to the legislative history, bifurcation may be appropriate where a debt instrument provides for payments that are dependent to a significant extent on corporate performance, such as through "equity kickers" (i.e., provisions in a debt instrument that provide the holder with an equity interest in certain circumstances), contingent interest (which is dependent on corporate performance), significant deferral of payment, subordination, or an interest rate high enough to suggest a significant risk of default.[19]

---

12. Prop.Reg. § 1.385–6. In general, proportional straight debt instruments were treated as debt only if issued to "independent creditors" or if they were marketable instruments issued by a public company; otherwise they generally were reclassified as equity unless they were: (a) issued for cash or, if issued for property, the stated annual interest rate was "reasonable," and (b) the corporation did not have "excessive debt" at the time the instrument was issued. Prop.Reg. § 1.385–6(a)(3), (e), (g).

13. Prop.Reg. § 1.385–6(g)(4).

14. Prop.Reg. § 1.385–6(h).

15. Prop.Reg. § 1.385–6(f)(2).

16. Prop.Reg. § 1.385–6(g)(3).

17. See, e.g., Levin & Bowen, "The Section 385 Regulations Regarding Debt Versus Equity: Is the Cure Worse than the Malady?" 35 Tax Lawyer 1 (1981).

18. I.R.C. § 385(a). This regulatory authority may be exercised on a prospective basis only.

19. H.Rep. No. 101–247, 101st Cong., 1st Sess. 1236 (1989).

If the Treasury ever accepts this Congressional challenge, several options could be considered. One approach would disallow interest deductions in excess of a specified rate of return to investors on the theory that a higher than normal risk is tantamount to an equity investment. For example, the regulations might specify a reference rate (such as the rate on comparable-term Treasury obligations) that is relatively risk-free and permit interest paid up to that rate to be deductible but deny a deduction for the additional "risk" element because it is more akin to a dividend. Under this type of broad disallowance approach, a corporation that issued a 20–year $100,000 unsecured debt instrument paying 14 percent interest (14,000 per year) at a time when comparable Treasury bonds were yielding 10 percent would be permitted to deduct only $10,000 per year as interest and the remaining $4,000 per year would be a nondeductible dividend.[20]

Another option is to limit bifurcation to instruments that provide for a combination of a fixed return and an additional return based on earnings. The regulations might treat the fixed return as interest while classifying the performance-based component as a nondeductible dividend. A closely related alternative, which finds isolated support in the case law, would be to divide one instrument into separate components—i.e., one part as debt and another as equity.[21]

Obligation of Consistency. Section 385(c) provides that a corporate issuer's characterization of an instrument as debt or equity at the time of issuance shall be binding on the issuer and all holders of the interest—but not binding, of course, on the Service. This rule of consistency does not apply, however, to holders who disclose on their tax return that they are treating the interest in a manner inconsistent with the issuer's characterization.

The Future. Perhaps in the 22d century, when the Section 385 regulations are reissued, we will know the Treasury's thinking on these questions.

PROBLEMS

1. Aristocrat, Baker and Chef have formed Chez Guevara, Inc. ("Chez") to operate a gourmet restaurant and bakery previously operated by Chef as a sole proprietorship. Aristocrat will contribute $80,000 cash, Baker will contribute a building with a fair market value of $80,000 and an adjusted basis of $20,000, and Chef will contribute $40,000 cash and the goodwill from his proprietorship with an agreed value of $40,000 and has a zero

---

20. In narrowly targeted situations, Congress began moving in this direction with the legislation enacted in 1989. See, e.g., I.R.C. §§ 163(e)(5), (i). Query whether any broader approach would discriminate against start-up companies or firms engaged in high-risk businesses?

21. Two courts have used this approach with respect to hybrid instruments. See Richmond, Fredericksburg and Potomac R.R. v. Commissioner, 528 F.2d 917 (4th Cir.1975); Farley Realty Corp. v. Commissioner, 279 F.2d 701 (2d Cir.1960). In most other cases, the courts have applied an all-or-nothing approach.

basis. In return, each of the parties will receive 100 shares of Chez common stock, the only class outstanding.

Chez requires at least $1,800,000 of additional capital in order to renovate the building, acquire new equipment and provide working capital. It has negotiated a $900,000 loan from Friendly National Bank on the following terms: interest will be payable at two points above the prime rate, determined semi-annually, with principal due in ten years and the loan will be secured by a mortgage on the renovated restaurant building.

Evaluate the following alternative proposals for raising the additional $900,000 needed to commence business, focusing on the possibility that the Service will reclassify corporate debt instruments as equity:

(a) Aristocrat, Baker and Chef each will loan Chez $300,000, and each will take back a $300,000 five-year corporate note with variable interest payable at one point below the prime rate, determined annually.

(b) Same as (a), above except that each of the parties will take back $300,000 of 10% 20–year subordinated income debentures; interest will be payable only out of the net profits of the business.

(c) Same as (a), above, except that the $900,000 loan from Friendly National Bank will be unsecured but personally guaranteed by Aristocrat, Baker and Chef, who will be jointly and severally liable.

(d) Aristocrat will loan the entire $900,000, taking back a $900,000 corporate note with terms identical to those described in (a), above.

(e) Same as (d), above, except that commencing two years after the incorporation, Chez ceases to pay interest on the notes because of a severe cash flow problem.

2. In view of the confused state of the law, how should a tax advisor plan the capital structure of a corporation to avoid the risk of reclassification of debt as equity. From the standpoint of the tax advisor, is the vagueness of the law in this area preferable to more detailed "bright line" rules in the Code or regulations? Which approach is preferable as a matter of policy?

C. CHARACTER OF GAIN OR LOSS ON CORPORATE INVESTMENT

Code: §§ 165(g)(1), (2); 166(a), (d), (e); 1244(a)–(c). Skim §§ 1045; 1202.

Regulations: §§ 1.165–5(a)–(c); 1.166–5; 1.1244(a)–1(a), (b).

Since equity and debt securities held by investors are usually capital assets, gain or loss on the sale of stock, bonds and other debt instruments generally is a capital gain or loss.[1] As discussed below, the Code also

---

1. In some cases, where the original issue discount and market discount rules apply, all or part of the gain on the sale or maturity of a debt instrument may be ordinary income. See generally I.R.C. §§ 1271–1275.

includes a few special characterization rules, some to stimulate investment and others to clarify the tax treatment of transactions that technically do not constitute a "sale or exchange."

Gain on Sale of Qualified Small Business Stock. To encourage long-term investment in small start-up companies, Section 1202 generally permits noncorporate shareholders to exclude from gross income 50 percent of the gain from a sale or exchange of "qualified small business stock" held for more than five years.[2] The exclusion is available for up to $10 million of recognized gain per qualifying corporation.[3] Seven percent of the amount excluded from gross income under Section 1202 is treated as a tax preference item for purposes of the alternative minimum tax.[4] To qualify its stock for this tax benefit, the issuer must have aggregate gross assets of $50 million or less (including the proceeds of the newly issued stock) at the time the stock is issued[5] and must meet certain active trade or business requirements.[6]

That's the good news. The bad news is that long-term capital gain from the sale of qualified small business stock—known as "Section 1202 gain"—is taxed at a maximum rate of 28 percent.[7] As a result, the maximum effective rate on a sale of qualified small business stock, after taking into account the 50 percent exclusion, is 14 percent, which is not much better than the generally applicable 15 percent maximum rate.[8]

Another tax benefit is provided by Section 1045, which allows noncorporate shareholders to elect to defer otherwise taxable gain from a sale of qualified small business stock held for more than six months by rolling over the proceeds into new qualified small business stock within 60 days of the sale.

Worthless Securities. Even the most optimistic taxpayers who embark on a business venture are well advised to anticipate the tax consequences if their endeavor should result in a loss. Sole proprietors, partners (including members of limited liability companies) and shareholders in an S corporation may deduct the losses from their business operations as they are incurred if they materially participate in the activity.[9] But shareholders or creditors of a C corporation normally must be content to recognize a capital

2. I.R.C. § 1202(a)(1). To qualify, the shareholder must be an original issuee of the stock.

3. I.R.C. § 1202(b)(1). In some cases involving larger investors, higher limits may apply.

4. I.R.C. § 57(a)(7). To stimulate the economy, Congress increased the exclusion to as much as 100 percent for purposes of both the regular and alternative minimum taxes, but as this book went to press in early 2012 these temporary increases had expired. The Obama administration has proposed to make the 100 percent exclusion permanent and

would eliminate the excluded portion of the gain as an AMT preference.

5. I.R.C. § 1202(c)(1), (d).

6. I.R.C. § 1202(c)(2), (e).

7. I.R.C. § 1(h)(4), (7).

8. When Section 1202 was first enacted, the rate differential was six percent. If the proposal to increase the exclusion to 100 percent for regular and alternative minimum tax purposes is accepted, a meaningful differential would be restored.

9. See generally I.R.C. § 469 for limitations on the timing of losses incurred in a passive activity.

loss at the time their investment is sold or becomes worthless. If a loss results from the worthlessness of stock or debt evidenced by a "security" which is a capital asset, the calamity is treated as a hypothetical sale or exchange on the last day of the taxable year in which the loss is incurred.[10]

Debts Not Evidenced by a Security. For noncorporate lenders, the tax consequences of losses sustained on a debt not evidenced by a security are governed by the bad debt deduction rules in Section 166. Business bad debts are ordinary losses, while nonbusiness bad debts are artificially treated as short-term capital losses.[11] When a shareholder who is also an employee loans money to a closely held corporation and later is not repaid, an issue arises over whether the loan was made as an investment or in a trade or business carried on by the taxpayer. The loss almost always is treated as a nonbusiness bad debt on the theory that the dominant motivation for making the loan was to protect the taxpayer's investment in the corporation rather than his employment relationship.[12]

Section 1244 Stock. As discussed above, it is virtually impossible for shareholders to avoid nonbusiness bad debt treatment if they sustain a loss in their creditor capacity. Whatever their roles, corporate insiders generally are regarded as investors.[13] These rules place corporate investors who suffer losses at a tax disadvantage relative to those who conduct their affairs through other business vehicles. In the case of a small business, this dichotomy makes little sense and may prove to be particularly unfair to those who are forced into the C corporation form for nontax reasons. In the same legislation that produced the earliest version of Subchapter S, Congress provided some limited relief by enacting Section 1244 in order to "encourage the flow of new funds into small business" by placing small business shareholders on more of a par with proprietors and partners.[14] If certain detailed statutory requirements are met, an individual shareholder may (within limits) treat a loss from the sale, exchange or worthlessness of "Section 1244 stock" as an ordinary loss even if it might otherwise have been treated as a capital loss.

Because Section 1244 was designed to stimulate investment in small businesses, only individual taxpayers and partnerships (but not trusts and estates) who were original issuees of the stock are eligible for ordinary loss treatment.[15] Donees, heirs and other transferees of the original investor will continue to be limited to capital loss treatment under Section 165.

---

10. See I.R.C. §§ 165(g)(1), (g)(2).

11. I.R.C. § 166(a), (d).

12. United States v. Generes, 405 U.S. 93, 92 S.Ct. 827 (1972).

13. See, e.g., Benak v. Commissioner, 77 T.C. 1213 (1981); but see Bowers v. Commissioner, 716 F.2d 1047 (4th Cir.1983).

14. H.R.Rep. No. 2198, 85th Cong., 1st Sess. (1958), reprinted in 1959–2 C.B. 709, 711.

15. I.R.C. § 1244(a). A partner qualifies for a Section 1244 ordinary loss only if he was a partner when the partnership acquired the stock. Reg. § 1.1244(a)–1(b)(2). The regulations also provide that ordinary loss treatment is not available to a partner who has received the stock in a distribution from the partnership. Reg. § 1.1244(a)–1(b). Unlike a partnership, an S corporation is not eligible for ordinary loss treatment under Section 1244. Rath v. Commissioner, 101 T.C. 196 (1993).

Section 1244 stock may be either common or preferred stock that has been issued for money or property.[16] Stock issued for services thus does not qualify.[17] To prevent the benefits of Section 1244 from extending beyond the small business community, its reach is limited to stock of a "small business corporation," a status achieved if the aggregate amount of money and other property received by the corporation for stock, as a contribution to capital and as paid-in surplus does not exceed $1,000,000.[18] This determination is made at the time the stock is issued, but the $1,000,000 cap includes both amounts received for the newly issued stock and any stock previously issued by the corporation.[19]

Qualification under Section 1244 when the stock is issued does not automatically guarantee that an ordinary loss will be allowed when a loss is realized. Section 1244(c)(1)(C) also requires that, for the five taxable years ending before the year in which the loss was sustained, the corporation must have derived more than 50 percent of its aggregate gross receipts from sources other than passive investment income items (royalties, rents, dividends, interest, annuities and sales or exchanges of stock or securities). The requirement is designed to preclude ordinary loss treatment to shareholders of corporations engaged primarily in investment rather than active business activities. If these investment losses had been incurred directly, the taxpayer would have been limited to capital loss treatment and the corporate form should not facilitate an end run around this limitation. If the loss is sustained before the corporation has a five-year measuring period, then the gross receipts test is applied by substituting the taxable years ending before the date of the loss in which the corporation was in existence.[20]

The aggregate amount that may be treated by the taxpayer as an ordinary loss for any one taxable year may not exceed $50,000 or, in the case of married couple filing a joint return, $100,000.[21] In the case of partnerships, the limit is determined separately as to each partner.[22]

Section 1244 is a "no lose" provision in the sense that nothing is lost by passing a corporate resolution declaring that an equity interest is being issued as Section 1244 stock even if the stock ultimately fails to qualify. Although there is no longer a requirement for a formal plan, it generally is regarded as good practice to include a reference to Section 1244 in the corporate resolution approving the issuance of stock in a qualifying corporation, if only to remind the shareholders that ordinary loss treatment is available if that unhappy event should later occur.

16. I.R.C. § 1244(c)(1)(B).

17. Reg. § 1.1244(c)–1(d).

18. I.R.C. § 1244(c)(3).

19. Id. See also Reg. § 1.1244(c)–2(b). If the capital receipts exceed $1,000,000, the corporation may designate certain shares as Section 1244 stock provided that the amounts received for such designated stock do not exceed $1,000,000 less amounts received for stock or as capital contributions in prior years.

20. I.R.C. § 1244(c)(2)(A).

21. I.R.C. § 1244(b).

22. Reg. § 1.1244(b)–1(a).

PROBLEM

High Technologies, Inc. ("Hi–Tech") is a small semiconductor company owned and operated by Thelma High and Allen Woody. Thelma and Allen formed Hi–Tech three years ago by each contributing $400,000 in exchange for 50 percent of the corporation's common stock. Hi–Tech has been planning a major expansion of its manufacturing facility and has decided to seek outside financing. It recently approached Jennifer Leech about the possibility of her investing $200,000 in Hi–Tech.

After investigating the corporation's financial position, Jennifer has decided to make the investment. Her objectives are to obtain maximum security while at the same time participating in Hi–Tech's potential growth. Jennifer also is concerned about the rapid change in computer technology and would like to plan for the most favorable tax consequences in the unfortunate event that her investment in Hi–Tech becomes worthless. Consider to what extent Jennifer will realize her economic and tax goals if, in the alternative, her investment takes the following forms:

(a) A $200,000 unregistered five-year Hi–Tech note bearing market rate interest.

(b) A $200,000 Hi–Tech registered bond bearing market rate interest.

(c) A $190,000 Hi–Tech registered bond bearing market rate interest and warrants to purchase Hi–Tech common stock at a favorable price.

(d) $200,000 of Hi–Tech common stock.

(e) $200,000 of Hi–Tech convertible preferred stock.

(f) Same as (d), above, except that Thelma and Allen originally capitalized Hi–Tech by each contributing $500,000.

(g) Same as (d), above, except that Jennifer plans to give the Hi–Tech common stock to her son, Peter, as a wedding gift.

(h) Same as (d), above, except that Jennifer and her son, Peter, will purchase the Hi–Tech common stock through Leech Associates, a venture capital partnership.

CHAPTER 4

NONLIQUIDATING DISTRIBUTIONS

A. INTRODUCTION

1. DIVIDENDS: IN GENERAL

Code: §§ 243(a), (b)(1); 301(a), (c); 316(a); 317(a).

Regulations: §§ 1.301–1(c); 1.316–1(a)(1)–(2).

It was once said that a corporation derives no greater pleasure than through making distributions to its shareholders. As one court observed, "like the 'life-rendering pelican,' [a corporation] feeds its shareholders upon dividends."[1] In the case of a close corporation, however, this colorful marine analogy does not always capture reality. Closely held companies, influenced by the federal tax law, typically resist paying dividends and expend considerable energy to avoid the sting of the double tax. Many public companies retain profits for internal expansion, to finance acquisitions, or to repurchase their own stock.[2] But if an enterprise is successful, the pressure may mount to distribute earnings to the shareholders, and distributions often occur in connection with major changes in a corporation's capital structure, such as liquidations, mergers and recapitalizations. At that point, it becomes necessary to classify the distribution as a taxable dividend, a nontaxable return of capital, or as gain from a sale of the shareholder's stock. Simple as the task may seem, drawing these lines has been a central issue in the taxation of corporations and shareholders. Not surprisingly, the statutory scheme is complex and sometimes even illogical.

Distributions come in many forms. A corporation may distribute its own stock or debt obligations; redeem (i.e., repurchase) stock from its shareholders by distributing cash or property; or distribute its net assets in liquidation of the entire business. The tax consequences of these and other more complex transactions are considered in later chapters.[3] This chapter lays a foundation by examining the corporate and shareholder level tax treatment of nonliquidating (or "operating") distributions of cash or property—distributions commonly referred to as "dividends." We are about to learn, however, that not all distributions classified as dividends under state law or designated as such in the corporate minutes are dividends for federal tax purposes.

1. Commissioner v. First State Bank of Stratford, 168 F.2d 1004, 1009 (5th Cir.1948), cert. denied, 335 U.S. 867, 69 S.Ct. 137 (1948).

2. For an expanded discussion of the influence of federal tax law on corporate dividend policy, see Section A3 of this chapter, infra.

3. See Chapters 5–7, infra.

Determining the tax consequences of a nonliquidating distribution requires an excursion through several sections of the Code. Section 301 governs the amount and classification to corporate and noncorporate share-holders of distributions of "property" made by a C corporation with respect to its stock.[4] Under Section 301(c)(1), distributions that are "dividends" within the meaning of Section 316 must be included in gross income.[5] In order to prevent multiple taxation, corporate shareholders may deduct 70 percent (or sometimes 80 or 100 percent) of the dividends they receive.[6] Most dividends received by noncorporate shareholders are taxed at prefer-ential long-term capital gains rates.[7] Distributions that are not dividends are first treated as a recovery of the shareholder's basis in his stock, and any excess over basis is treated as gain from the sale or exchange of the stock.[8]

Section 316(a) defines a "dividend" as any distribution of property made by a corporation to its shareholders out of (1) earnings and profits accumulated after February 28, 1913 ("accumulated earnings and profits") or (2) earnings and profits of the current taxable year ("current earnings and profits"). "Earnings and profits," a term of art to be examined in more detail below, is a concept that attempts to distinguish distributions of corporate profits from returns of capital. Section 316(a) also includes two irrebuttable presumptions: every distribution is deemed to be made out of earnings and profits to the extent that they exist and is deemed to be made from the most recently accumulated earnings and profits.

In testing for dividend status, the regulations look first to current earnings and profits, determined as of the close of the taxable year in which the distribution is made.[9] A distribution out of current earnings and profits is thus a taxable dividend even if the corporation has a historical deficit. This seemingly harsh rule was enacted many years ago as a relief measure to permit corporations with deficits to pay dividends and thus avoid an undistributed profits tax then in effect. Although the tax was later re-pealed, the "nimble dividend" rule survived without any Congressional

---

4. Distributions to shareholders in their other capacities (e.g., employee, credi-tor, lessor) are thus not embraced by Section 301. "Property" is deemed to include money and other corporate assets but not stock in the distributing corporation or rights to ac-quire stock. I.R.C. § 317(a).

5. See also I.R.C. § 61(a)(7).

6. I.R.C. § 243(a), (b)(1), (c). See Chap-ter 1B1 supra. Potential abuses of the divi-dends received deduction are policed by an assortment of Code provisions. See Section F of this chapter, infra.

7. I.R.C. § 1(h)(11), which will expire at the end of 2012 unless extended or made permanent. See Section A2 of this chapter, infra.

8. I.R.C. § 301(c)(2), (3). The rules in the text apply to distributions by C corpora-tions that do not file a consolidated return. Distributions received by one member of a consolidated group from another member generally are tax-free, but the distributee must reduce its basis in the stock of the payor by the amount of the distribution. See Reg. § 1.1502–13(f)(2)(ii) and Chapter 13B, supra. Distributions by S corporations gener-ally are tax-free to the extent of the share-holder's basis, and any excess is treated as gain from a sale of the S corporation stock. § 1368(b). See Chapter 15E, infra.

9. Reg. § 1.316–1(a)(1).

explanation of why it was still necessary.[10] The rule at least simplifies the inquiry because it is rare for a company to make distributions during a period when it is operating at a loss. Only when distributions exceed current earnings and profits must reference be made to the historical track record of the corporation.

The dual focus in Section 316 on current and accumulated earnings and profits may produce anomalous results because dividend status is determined by reference to the corporation's overall financial success rather than the gain or loss realized by a particular shareholder. To be sure, most dividends represent an increase in the shareholder's wealth rather than a return of capital, but this is not inevitable under the current scheme. For example, the existence of accumulated earnings and profits will cause a distribution to be classified as a dividend even if those profits were earned before the shareholder acquired his stock.

To illustrate, assume that Shareholder forms Corporation with initial paid-in capital of $110. During its first year of operation, Corporation earns $20 and distributes $30 to Shareholder. The distribution consists of a $20 dividend (out of current earnings and profits) and a $10 return of capital, and Shareholder reduces his stock basis by $10 to $100. In year two, assume Corporation earns $50 and makes no distributions, ending the year with $50 of accumulated earnings and profits. At the beginning of year three, Buyer (an individual) acquires all the stock of Corporation for $150, and Shareholder realizes a $50 long-term capital gain. Assume further that Corporation, now wholly owned by Buyer, suffers a $10 loss in year three, causing its accumulated earnings and profits account to decrease to $40. If Corporation breaks even in year four but distributes $30, Buyer is taxed on the entire distribution because it is made from accumulated earnings and profits. But in substance Buyer has received merely a return of capital. After all, he paid $150 for the stock, and the company has since lost $10 while distributing $30 to Buyer, who is understandably surprised to realize $30 of ordinary income even though the value of his investment has declined.

In an academically tidy world, the curious result illustrated above should not occur. Instead, the tax treatment of distributions should depend on the gain or loss realized by the shareholder rather than the corporation's financial track record over time. Ideally, Shareholder should be taxed at ordinary income rates to the extent that the gain on a sale of his stock is attributable to undistributed corporate earnings while he was a shareholder. It then would be unnecessary to tax those earnings again when they are distributed to Buyer, who logically should be treated as receiving a return of capital rather than a $30 dividend.

In the early days of the income tax, taxpayers in Buyer's position argued that distributions out of preacquisition earnings should not be

---

10. See Bittker & Eustice, Federal Income Taxation of Corporations and Share- holders ¶ 8.02[3].

taxable since they did not represent any real gain to the shareholder. The Supreme Court put this argument to rest, reasoning:[11]

> Dividends are the appropriate fruit of stock ownership, are commonly reckoned as income, and are expended as such by the stockholder without regard to whether they are declared from the most recent earnings, or from a surplus accumulated from the earnings of the past, or are based upon the increased value of the property of the corporation. The stockholder is, in the ordinary case, a different entity from the corporation, and Congress was at liberty to treat the dividends as coming to him *ab extra,* and as constituting a part of his income when they came to hand.

Despite its conceptual flaws, the present approach is defensible on practical grounds. Since shares in publicly held corporations are traded daily, it would be difficult to determine precisely the corporation's earnings during the period that any particular shareholder held his stock. The current scheme at least ensures that earnings will be taxed to some shareholder, even if that shareholder may not be the theoretically correct one. Moreover, the presumption that distributions are made out of a corporation's earnings and profits to the extent they exist often eliminates the chore of tracing the source of a distribution and considerably simplifies the system.

2. QUALIFIED DIVIDENDS

Code: § 1(h)(11).

For most of our tax history, dividends have been taxed as ordinary income. Relief from multiple taxation is provided to corporate shareholders by the Section 243 dividends received deduction. From time to time, individual shareholders also have received very modest relief from double taxation, most often in the form of a limited dividend exclusion that ranged from $50 to $400 before it was repealed in 1986.

As previewed in Chapter 1,[1] President George W. Bush made eliminating double taxation of corporate earnings a centerpiece of economic stimulus legislation introduced in early 2003. The eventual compromise was a "temporary" rate reduction on certain "qualified dividend income" received by noncorporate shareholders. Effective for eligible dividends received from January 1, 2003 through December 31, 2012, the maximum rate on qualified dividend income is reduced to 15 percent for taxpayers whose ordinary income otherwise would be taxed at higher rates, and to 0 percent for lower-income taxpayers whose ordinary income otherwise would be taxed in the 10 or 15 percent marginal brackets. Technically, these preferential rates have been implemented by including "qualified dividend income" within the definition of "net capital gain" in Section 1(h), which provides for the maximum rate on long-term capital gains for noncorporate

11. Lynch v. Hornby, 247 U.S. 339, 343, 38 S.Ct. 543, 545 (1918).

1. See p. 48, supra.

taxpayers.[2] The dividend rate reduction applies for both the regular tax and the individual alternative minimum tax.

To be eligible for the reduced rates, a dividend must be received from a domestic corporation or a foreign corporation that meets certain criteria.[3] Unlike President Bush's original proposal, a qualified dividend need not be derived from earnings that were taxed at the corporate level. But some income items that are labelled "dividends" do not qualify for the rate reduction. Familiar examples are credit union and money market fund dividends, "dividends" paid on hybrid corporate instruments (e.g., certain types of preferred stock that are treated as debt by the issuing corporation), and payments in lieu of dividends on stock that has loaned as part of a short sale transaction.[4] Corporate payors must identify which dividends are "qualified" on the Form 1099's that they send at the end of the year, but shareholders are responsible for determining if they comply with the holding period requirements discussed below.

To prevent arbitrage opportunities on short-term trades, the common stock with respect to which the dividend was paid must have been held by the taxpayer for more than 60 days in the 121–day period beginning 60 days before the stock's ex-dividend date.[5] The ex-dividend date is the first date on which a share with respect to which a dividend has been declared is sold without the buyer being entitled to the dividend.[6] Without this rule, a taxpayer could acquire stock shortly before becoming entitled to a dividend, sell the stock at a capital loss that could offset short-term capital gain or up to $3,000 of ordinary income if the taxpayer has no capital gains, but still pay tax on the dividend at the preferential rate. Several other rules have been included to prevent opportunistic exploitation of the rate reduction.[7]

The preferential rates on long-term capital gains, including qualified dividends, are scheduled to expire for taxable years beginning after December 31, 2012. If Congress does not take further action, the top capital gains rate would go back up to 20 percent and dividends once again would be taxed as ordinary income at marginal rates peaking at 39.6 percent. The Obama administration once proposed to maintain the zero and 15 percent tax rates on qualified dividends and long-term capital gains for married filing jointly taxpayers with incomes up to $250,000 and single taxpayers with incomes up to $200,000 but increase the rate to 20 percent for higher-income taxpayers. In 2012, however, the administration changed course

---

2. I.R.C. § 1(h)(11)(A). Although qualified dividends are treated as net capital gain for rate reduction purposes, they are still ordinary income and may not be offset by capital losses without being subject to the $3,000 limitation in Section 1211(b).

3. I.R.C. § 1(h)(11)(B)(ii).

4. I.R.C. § 1(h)(11)(B)(ii).

5. I.R.C. § 1(h)(11)(B)(iii), which imports, with some modifications, similar holding period limitations on the corporate dividends received deduction and requires a longer holding period (91 days during the 181–day period beginning 90 days before the ex-dividend date) for dividends paid with respect to preferred stock. See I.R.C § 246 and Section F2 of this chapter, infra.

6. Under stock exchange rules, the ex-dividend date is typically three days before the date on which shareholders of record are entitled to receive a declared dividend.

7. See, e.g., I.R.C. § 1(h)(11)(D)(ii).

and proposed to let the reduced rates on qualified dividends expire as scheduled and again tax dividends received by high-income taxpayers as ordinary income.[8]

3.   ECONOMIC IMPACT OF DIVIDEND RATE REDUCTIONS

Factors Influencing Corporate Dividend Policy. The distribution policies of closely held C corporations are often motivated by the goal of getting corporate profits to the shareholders at the lowest tax cost. For that reason, closely held companies typically have resisted paying dividends, preferring instead to distribute earnings in the form of tax-deductible salary, interest or rent, or to engage in transactions (such as redemptions) where shareholders can bail out earnings at capital gains rates.[1] Dividend policies of publicly traded corporations vary widely. Most "old economy" companies adhere to the tradition of paying quarterly dividends, increasing them at regular intervals and rarely reducing their payouts unless the company is in serious financial difficulty. Many "new economy" companies, such as those in the technology sector, opt not to pay dividends, hoping instead to reward investors with increased share prices.

What is it that motivates public companies to pay dividends and to what extent do the tax laws influence corporate dividend policy? These questions have stimulated a lively theoretical debate.[2] One view is that companies pay dividends to serve as a signal to the financial markets of a their profitability and future expectations[3], enhancing shareholder value through their positive impact on the price of the stock. Beginning in the 1980s, however, and continuing through 2003, dividends became less fashionable. In explaining this decline, some corporate finance theorists explained that, apart from taxes and transaction costs, shareholders benefit more when a corporation deploys its available cash for business expansion, acquisition of other companies, or repurchases of its own stock. Under this theory, shareholders should be indifferent to a corporation's dividend policy because they reap the same benefit when the stock price increases to reflect undistributed earnings and they are free to generate "homemade dividends" by strategically timed sales of stock.[4] Throughout this debate, there also has been much discussion of the different interests of corporate managers and shareholders, and the potential "agency costs" when managers use retained earnings to make suboptimal investments or simply hoard

---

8. General Explanation of the Administration's Fiscal Year 2013 Revenue Proposals 71 (Dept. of the Treasury, Feb. 2012).

1. See Chapters 1D & 3A, supra; Section E of this chapter, infra; and Chapter 5, infra.

2. See generally Hamilton & Booth, Business Basics for Law Students: Essential Concepts and Applications § 12.11 (4th ed. 2006); Klein, Coffee & Partnoy, Business Organization and Finance 395 et seq. (11th ed. 2010). For a historical perspective, see Bank, "Is Double Taxation a Scapegoat for Declining Dividends? Evidence from History," 56 Tax L. Rev. 463 (2003).

3. Hamilton, supra note 2, at § 12.12.

4. See, e.g., Modigliani & Miller, "Dividend Policy, Growth, and the Valuation of Shares," 34 J. of Bus. 411 (1961), for an early articulation of the "dividend irrelevance" theory. See also Shaviro, Decoding the U.S. Corporate Tax 73–88 (2009).

cash.[5] Encouraging dividends is said to counteract this form of managerial empire building and imposes a measure of discipline. Returning the money to investors in the form of dividends, so the argument goes, allows capital to be redirected more efficiently and promotes economic growth.[6]

Impact of Taxes on Dividend Payout. The dividend rate reductions introduced in 2003 provided an opportunity for economists to revisit the impact of taxes on corporate dividend policy. The traditional view is that the "double tax" on corporate profits lowers a shareholder's return on investment and encourages corporations to hoard cash, locking in huge stockpiles of capital that could be reinvested more efficiently if it were distributed and redeployed by shareholders. It follows from this thesis that lower tax rates will lead to higher dividends and new investments by the shareholders who receive them. Others contend that dividend tax cuts do not cause corporations to increase their payouts because their many institutional shareholders, such as pension funds and large charities, don't pay taxes. These contrarians also argue that since most new investments are made by corporations from retained earnings, dividend tax rate reductions are not an effective investment stimulus.

Some evidence to date suggests that the dividend tax cuts did influence corporate behavior and contribute to at least a short-term increase in payouts by public companies. A dramatic early example was Microsoft Corporation's decision to distribute $32 billion as an extraordinary dividend at the end of 2004, use another $30 billion to repurchase stock over the next four years, and raise its modest quarterly dividend.[7] More generally, several studies revealed that dividends rose sharply in the years following the rate reductions.[8] The percentage of public companies paying dividends began to increase in 2003 for the first time in more than two decades; many firms that had been paying regular dividends raised their payouts significantly after the tax cut; and a few companies such as Microsoft paid special one-time dividends.[9] A report issued by Standard and Poors at the end of 2004 supports the view that the combination of tax cuts and shareholder pressure contributed to a surge in dividend payments.[10] In the first 19 months after the dividend tax cut was enacted, companies in the S & P 500 announced 421 dividend increases, with 24 companies paying dividends for the first time.[11] By mid–2004, regular dividend payments by public companies increased by approximately 20 percent and increases continued

5. See, e.g., Easterbrook, "Two Agency–Cost Explanations of Dividends," 74 Am. Econ. Rev. 650 (1984).

6. See Moore & Kerpen, "Show Me the Money! Dividend Payouts after the Bush Tax Cut" (Cato Institute, Oct. 11, 2004).

7. Guth & Thurm, Microsoft to Dole Out its Cash Hoard, Wall St. Journal, July 21, 2004, at A1.

8. Chetty & Saez, "Do Dividend Payments Respond to Taxes? Preliminary Evidence from the 2003 Tax Cut," (NBER Working Paper 10572), available at www.nber.org/papers/w10572.

9. Id.

10. Opdyke, "Tax Cut, Shareholder Pressure Stoke Surge in Stock Dividends," Wall St. Journal, Jan. 18, 2005, at A1.

11. Id.

through 2005, when dividend payments set a record of $203 billion, 12.4 percent more than 2004.[12]

Broader Economic Effects of Rate Reductions. The economic stimulus effects of the Bush tax cuts also have been debated, with the usual suspects taking predictable political positions. In arguing for extension of the rate reductions, a 2006 Treasury Department report concluded that the lower rates promoted economic growth by increasing capital in the corporate sector and taking a significant step toward removing taxes from important economic decisions. As proof, the Treasury cited a 40 percent increase in the S & P 500 index between the time the President Bush's dividend proposal was first announced and early 2006. Other positive indicators included growth in real gross domestic product and in employment.[13] The counterpoint response from liberal think tanks was that the dividend tax cuts were not principal contributors to the short-term economic recovery and did not have much value in the long run. They argue that a modest economic recovery was expected even without tax cuts because of other factors such as a low interest rate environment and healthy corporate profits,[14] and the severe economic downturn that began in 2008 offers some evidence that any stimulative effect of the Bush tax cuts was short-lived.

In the last analysis, whether or not the dividend rate cuts will be made permanent or allowed to expire is a political question that will be heavily influenced by the outcome of the 2012 elections (unknown and unpredictable as this edition goes to press), the pressure to reduce the federal deficit, and the health of the general economy. Stay tuned.

B.   EARNINGS AND PROFITS

Code: § 312(a), (c), (f)(1), (k)(1)–(3); 316(a). Skim § 312(n).

Regulations: § 1.312–6(a), (b), (d) (first sentence), 1.312–7(b)(1) (first sentence).

The Code makes it clear that distributions are dividends only to the extent that they come from the corporation's earnings and profits, but it curiously does not take the extra step and actually define earnings and profits. Section 312 describes the effects of certain transactions on earnings and profits, and the accompanying regulations provide ample elaboration, but a precise definition of the term is nowhere to be found in the Code or regulations.[1] The function of the earnings and profits concept, however, is

---

12. See U.S. Dept. of the Treasury, Investing in America's Future: Report of the Department of the Treasury on the Economic Effects of Cutting Dividend and Capital Gains Taxes in 2003 ("2006 Treasury Study"), at 8 (March 14, 2006).

13. 2006 Treasury Study, supra note 12, at 2–3.

14. See, e.g., Aron–Dine & Friedman, The Capital Gain and Dividend Tax Cuts and

the Economy, Center on Budget and Policy Priorities (March 27, 2006); Aron–Dine, The Effects of the Capital Gains and Dividend Tax Cuts on The Economy and Revenues, Center on Budget and Policy Priorities (July 12, 2007).

1. For a history of the earnings and profits concept, see Rudick, " 'Dividends' and clear: it is a measuring device used to determine the extent to which a distribution is made from a corporation's economic income as opposed to its taxable income or paid-in capital.

The meaning of earnings and profits, which is a phrase peculiar to the tax law, has evolved over the years. It is roughly analogous (but not identical) to the accounting concept of retained earnings (sometimes called "earned surplus") in that neither amount includes initial paid-in capital or subsequent contributions to capital. The primary difference is that retained earnings are decreased by stock distributions and contingency reserves. If earnings and profits were similarly reduced, a company could avoid ever making a taxable distribution simply by ensuring that its distributions were preceded by nontaxable stock dividends or the establishment of reserves for contingencies. Earnings and profits also are not identical to taxable income. The earnings and profits account is intended to measure the economic performance of the corporation. In contrast, taxable income does not provide a true financial picture because that concept is cluttered with a host of policy incentives and relief provisions that bear little or no relationship to the corporation's capacity to pay dividends.

Although earnings and profits can be determined by making adjustments to either retained earnings or taxable income, the traditional approach is to start with a corporation's taxable income and make adjustments that fall into the four broad categories discussed below. In general, the same accounting method used by the corporation to determine its taxable income is employed in determining earnings and profits.[2]

1. *Certain items excluded from taxable income must be added back.* Items that represent true financial gain but are exempt from tax, such as municipal bond interest, life insurance proceeds and federal tax refunds and otherwise excludable discharge of indebtedness income (unless coupled with a basis reduction under Section 1017) are included in earnings and profits.[3] Contributions to capital and gains that are realized but not recognized for tax purposes (e.g., like-kind exchanges, Section 351 transfers, involuntary conversions under Section 1033) are not added back in computing earnings and profits.[4]

2. *Certain items deductible in determining taxable income must be added back.* Certain deductions and benefits allowed in computing taxable income which do not reflect a real decrease in corporate wealth are not permitted or are restricted in determining earnings and profits. For example, a deductible item that involves no actual expenditure, such as the Section 243 dividends received deduction, must be added back to taxable income in determining earnings and profits. Similarly, the depletion allow-

'Earnings or Profits' Under the Income Tax Law: Corporate Non–Liquidating Distributions," 89 U.Pa.L.Rev. 865 (1941).

2. Reg. § 1.312–6(a).

3. Reg. § 1.312–6(b). In the case of life insurance, the Service has ruled that earnings and profits are increased by the proceeds collected less the aggregate premiums paid by the corporation. Rev.Rul. 54–230, 1954–1 C.B. 114. For discharge of indebtedness income, see I.R.C. § 312(*l*)(1).

4. I.R.C. § 312(f)(1).

ance must be based on the corporation's cost of a depletable asset even if the corporation deducts percentage depletion in computing taxable income.[5]

3. *Certain nondeductible items must be subtracted.* Some items not allowed as deductions in computing taxable income in fact represent actual expenditures that diminish a corporation's capacity to pay dividends. These items reduce earnings and profits. For example, federal income taxes paid during the year by a cash method corporation will reduce earnings and profits,[6] as will losses and expenses disallowed under provisions such as Sections 265 (expenses allocable to tax-exempt income), 267 (losses between related taxpayers) and 274 (travel and entertainment expenses) and charitable contributions in excess of the ten percent corporate limitation. In addition, net operating losses and capital losses in excess of capital gains reduce earnings and profits in the year they are incurred. In order to avoid a double tax benefit, they may not be carried back or forward in determining earnings and profits.

4. *Certain timing adjustments must be made.* Finally, a variety of adjustments are required to override timing rules that allow corporations to artificially defer income or accelerate deductions in computing taxable income.[7] For example, a corporation may not use the generally applicable accelerated cost recovery system (ACRS) of Section 168 in determining earnings and profits. Instead, the cost of depreciable property must be recovered in computing earnings and profits under the alternative depreciation system, which employs the straight line method using specially prescribed and generally longer recovery periods than ACRS.[8] The corporation thus must increase its taxable income by the excess accelerated depreciation allowed for tax purposes.[9] Similarly, if the corporation has elected to expense the cost of eligible property under Section 179, it must amortize that expense ratably over five years in determining earnings and profits.[10] Additional earnings and profits timing rules require a corporation to capitalize otherwise amortizable construction period interest and taxes and to amortize normally deductible mineral exploration costs and intangible drilling expenses over extended time periods.[11]

---

5. Reg. § 1.312–6(c).

6. Rev.Rul. 70–609, 1970–2 C.B. 78; Webb v. Commissioner, 572 F.2d 135 (5th Cir.1978). A few courts, however, have permitted a cash method corporation to reduce its earnings and profits in the year to which the federal taxes relate even though the taxes have not yet been paid. See e.g., Drybrough v. Commissioner, 238 F.2d 735 (6th Cir.1956).

7. See generally I.R.C. § 312(n). To prevent abuse of the dividends received deduction, the Section 312(n) adjustments do not apply to distributions to any 20 percent or more corporate shareholders. I.R.C. § 301(e). The effect of this rule is to reduce earnings and profits only in determining the amount of any dividend to major corporate

shareholders. See Section F5 of this chapter, infra.

8. I.R.C. §§ 312(k)(3)(A); 168(g)(2).

9. The adjusted basis of the property determined under this special provision also is used in determining the impact of a sale or other disposition of property on earnings and profits. I.R.C. § 312(f)(1). In virtually all cases, this rule will cause corporations to have different bases in property for purposes of determining taxable income and earnings and profits.

10. I.R.C. § 312(k)(3)(B).

11. I.R.C. § 312(n)(1), (2).

On the income side, realized gains that are deferred for taxable income purposes under the installment sale method of Section 453 or by the completed contract method of accounting must be currently included in earnings and profits.[12] Moreover, for earnings and profits purposes, gains on the sale of inventory must be reported under the standard first-in-first-out (FIFO) method rather than the last-in-first-out (LIFO) method.[13]

It should be apparent by now that earnings and profits is simply a tax accounting concept designed to better measure a corporation's true financial results. It is an artificial "account" created by the Code—not an actual bank account or liquid fund set aside by the corporation for the payment of dividends. There is no statute of limitations on earnings and profits issues, and a corporation sometimes will face the onerous task of reconstructing many years of financial history in order to determine the tax consequences of a current distribution.[14]

PROBLEM

X Corporation is a cash method, calendar year taxpayer. During the current year, X has the following income and expenses:

Gross profits from sales	$20,000
Salaries paid to employees	10,250
Tax-exempt interest received	3,000
Dividends received from IBM	5,000
Depreciation (X purchased 5–year property in the current year for $14,000; assume the property has a 7–year class life; no § 179 election was made and X elected not to take the special depreciation allowance in § 168(k))	2,800
LTCG on a sale of stock	2,500
LTCL on a sale of stock	5,000
LTCL carryover from prior years	1,000
Estimated federal income taxes paid	800

Determine X's taxable income for the current year and its current earnings and profits.

C. DISTRIBUTIONS OF CASH

Code: §§ 301(a), (b), (c); 312(a); 316(a).

Regulations: §§ 1.301–1(a), (b); 1.316–2(a)–(c).

The taxation of cash distributions by a corporation with respect to its stock is relatively straightforward. The amount of the distribution is simply

---

12. I.R.C. § 312(n)(5), (6).

13. I.R.C. § 312(n)(4).

14. Because it usually is an inherently factual question, the Service will not issue a ruling on the amount of a corporation's earnings and profits. Rev.Proc. 2012–3, § 3.01(37), 2012–1 C.B. 116.

the amount of money received by the shareholder.[1] That amount is taxable as a dividend to the extent of the distributing corporation's current or accumulated earnings and profits.[2] Amounts distributed in excess of available earnings and profits are first applied against and reduce the basis of the shareholder's stock and, to the extent that they exceed the shareholder's basis, they are treated as gain from the sale or exchange of the stock.[3] The distributing corporation generally is permitted to reduce its earnings and profits by the amount of money distributed, except that earnings and profits may be reduced as a result of a distribution only to the extent they exist.[4] Thus, while a deficit in earnings and profits may result from corporate operations, a deficit may not be created or increased by a distribution.[5]

When there are insufficient current earnings and profits available to cover all cash distributions made during the year, earnings and profits must be allocated to the distributions in order to determine dividend status under the following rules:[6]

(1) First, current earnings and profits, determined as of the end of the year, are prorated among the distributions by using the following formula:[7]

$$\frac{\text{Current E \& P}}{\text{allocated to distribution}} = \frac{\text{Amount of}}{\text{distribution}} \times \frac{\text{Total current E \& P}}{\text{Total distributions}}$$

(2) Next, accumulated earnings and profits are allocated chronologically to distributions (i.e., on a first-come, first-served basis).[8]

(3) If the corporation has a current loss but has accumulated earnings and profits from prior years, it will be necessary to determine the amount of accumulated earnings and profits available on the date of distribution. Unless the loss can be earmarked to a particular period, the current deficit is prorated to the date of the distribution.[9]

Revenue Ruling 74–164, below, and the problem which follows test your ability to understand and apply these principles.

Revenue Ruling 74–164

1974–1 Cum.Bull. 74.

Advice has been requested concerning the taxable status of corporate distributions under the circumstances described below.

---

1. The same rule applies to corporate and noncorporate distributees. I.R.C. § 301(b).

2. I.R.C. §§ 301(c)(1); 316(a).

3. I.R.C. § 301(c)(2), (3).

4. I.R.C. § 312(a).

5. Id.

6. This allocation method is significant only if there is a change in shareholder interests during the year or on a non pro rata distribution.

7. Reg. § 1.316–2(b), (c) Example.

8. Id.

9. Reg. § 1.316–2(b).

X corporation and *Y* corporation each using the calendar year for Federal income tax purposes made distributions of $15,000 to their respective shareholders on July 1, 1971, and made no other distributions to their shareholders during the taxable year. The distributions were taxable as provided by section 301(c) of the Internal Revenue Code of 1954.

Situation 1.

At the beginning of its taxable year 1971, *X* corporation had earnings and profits accumulated after February 28, 1913, of $40,000. It had an operating loss for the period January 1, 1971 through June 30, 1971, of $50,000 but had earnings and profits for the entire year 1971 of $5,000.

Situation 2.

At the beginning of its taxable year 1971, *Y* corporation had a deficit in earnings and profits accumulated after February 28, 1913, of $60,000. Its net profits for the period January 1, 1971 through June 30, 1971, were $75,000 but its earnings and profits for the entire taxable year 1971 were only $5,000.

Situation 3.

Assume the same facts as in *Situation* 1 except that *X* had a deficit in earnings and profits of $5,000 for the entire taxable year 1971.

Situation 4.

Assume the same facts as in *Situation* 1 except that *X* had a deficit in earnings and profits of $55,000 for the entire taxable year 1971.

Section 301(a) and 301(c) of the Code provides, in part, that: (1) the portion of a distribution of property made by a corporation to a shareholder with respect to its stock which is a dividend (as defined in section 316), shall be included in the shareholder's gross income; (2) the portion of the distribution which is not a dividend shall be applied against and reduce the adjusted basis of the stock; and (3) the portion which is not a dividend to the extent that it exceeds the adjusted basis of the stock and is not out of increase in value accrued before March 1, 1913, shall be treated as gain from the sale or exchange of property.

Section 316(a) of the Code provides that the term "dividend" means any distribution of property made by a corporation to its shareholders out of its earnings and profits accumulated after February 28, 1913, or out of its earnings and profits of the taxable year computed as of the close of the taxable year without diminution by reason of any distribution made during the year, and *without regard to the amount of earnings and profits at the time the distribution was made.*

Section 1.316–2(a) of the Income Tax Regulations provides, in part, that in determining the source of a distribution, consideration should be given first, to the earnings and profits of the taxable year; and second, to the earnings and profits accumulated since February 28, 1913, only in the case where, and to the extent that, the distributions made during the taxable year are not regarded as out of the earnings and profits of that year.

Applying the foregoing principles, in *Situation* 1, the earnings and profits of *X* corporation for the taxable year 1971 of $5,000 and the earnings and profits accumulated since February 28, 1913, and prior to the taxable year 1971, of $40,000 were applicable to the distribution paid by it on July 1, 1971. Thus, $5,000 of the distribution of $15,000 was paid from the earnings and profits of the taxable year 1971 and the balance of $10,000 was paid from the earnings and profits accumulated since February 28, 1913. Therefore, the entire distribution of $15,000 was a dividend within the meaning of section 316 of the Code.

In *Situation* 2 the earnings and profits of *Y* corporation for the taxable year 1971 of $5,000 were applicable to the distribution paid by *Y* corporation on July 1, 1971. *Y* corporation had no earnings and profits accumulated after February 28, 1913, available at the time of the distribution. Thus, only $5,000 of the distribution by *Y* corporation of $15,000 was a dividend within the meaning of section 316 of the Code. The balance of such distribution, $10,000 which was not a dividend, applied against and reduced the adjusted basis of the stock in the hands of the shareholders, and to the extent that it exceeded the adjusted basis of the stock was gain from the sale or exchange of property.

In the case of a deficit in earnings and profits for the taxable year in which distributions are made, the taxable status of distributions is dependent upon the amount of earnings and profits accumulated since February 28, 1913, and available at the dates of distribution. In determining the amount of such earnings and profits, section 1.316–2(b) of the regulations provides, in effect, that the deficit in earnings and profits of the taxable year will be prorated to the dates of distribution.

Applying the foregoing to Situations 3 and 4 the distribution paid by *X* corporation on July 1, 1971, in each situation was a dividend within the meaning of section 316 of the Code to the extent indicated as follows:

Situation #3

Accumulated Earnings and Profits (E & P) 1/1	$ 40,000
E & P deficit for entire taxable year ($5,000) Prorate to date of distribution 7/1 (½ of $5,000)	(2,500)
E & P available 7/1	$ 37,500
Distribution 7/1 ($15,000)	(15,000) taxable as a dividend
E & P deficit from 7/1–12/31	(2,500)
Accumulated E & P balance 12/31	$ 20,000

Situation #4

Accumulated E & P 1/1	$ 40,000
E & P deficit for entire taxable year ($55,000) Prorate to date of distribution 7/1 (½ of $55,000)	(27,500)

E & P available 7/1	$ 12,500
Distribution 7/1 ($15,000)	(12,500) taxable as a dividend
E & P deficit from 7/1–12/31	(27,500)
Accumulated E & P balance 12/31	$(27,500)

NOTE

Earmarking E & P Deficits. Situations 3 and 4 of Revenue Ruling 74–164 do not consider the possibility of earmarking the entire 1971 deficit (i.e., $5,000 in Situation 3 and $55,000 in Situation 4) to the first half of the year. Under the regulations,[1] if those deficits were sustained in the first half of 1971, the full deficit (not just one-half) would reduce the accumulated earnings and profits available to characterize the July 1 distribution as a dividend. This would not affect the result in Situation 3 but it would change Situation 4, where there would be no dividend.

Return of Capital Distributions and Multiple Tax Lots. The tax treatment of return of capital distributions from C corporations to shareholders who hold multiple "tax lots" of stock has never been crystal clear. If a distribution is not a dividend, Section 301(c)(2) first requires a reduction of stock basis and, once basis is reduced to zero, Section 301(c)(3) treats the remainder of the distribution as gain from the sale of the stock (usually capital gain). If a shareholder has more than one block of stock and the blocks have different per-share bases, the question has been whether the shareholder recovers his aggregate basis before recognizing gain, or whether the distribution must be allocated pro rata to each share of stock. If an allocation is required, the possibility arises that a shareholder will recognize gain on low basis shares even though the basis of the high basis shares has not been fully recovered.

Proposed regulations would answer this question by requiring the nondividend portion of a distribution to be allocated pro rata, on a share-by-share basis, to reduce the adjusted basis of each block of stock held by the shareholder within the class of stock upon which the distribution is made. To illustrate, assume A owns all 100 shares of X Corp. common stock (the only class outstanding); 25 shares (Block 1) were acquired on Date 1 for $25 and 75 shares (Block 2) were acquired on Date 2 for $175. At a time when X Corp. has E & P of $100, it distributes $300 cash to A. Under the proposed regulations, A is treated as receiving $75 (25%) of the distribution with respect to Block 1 and $225 (75%) with respect to Block 2. On Block 1, A has a $25 dividend, a $25 basis reduction, and $25 of gain. On Block 2, A has a $75 dividend, a $150 basis reduction, and $25 of remaining basis in the 75 shares.[2]

PROBLEM

Ann owns all of the common stock (the only class outstanding) of Pelican Corporation. Prior to the transactions below and as a result of a

---

1. Reg. § 1.316–2(b).   **2.** Prop. Reg. § 1.301–2(a) Example.

§ 351 transfer, Ann has a $10,000 basis in her Pelican stock. What results to Ann and Pelican in each of the following alternative situations?

(a) In year one Pelican has $5,000 of current and no accumulated earnings and profits and it distributes $17,500 to Ann?

(b) Pelican has a $15,000 accumulated deficit in its earnings and profits at the beginning of year two. In year two Pelican has $10,000 of current earnings and profits and it distributes $10,000 to Ann.

(c) Pelican has $10,000 of accumulated earnings and profits at the beginning of year two and $4,000 of current earnings and profits in year two. On July 1 of year two, Ann sells half of her Pelican stock to Baker Corporation for $15,000. On April 1 of year two, Pelican distributes $10,000 to Ann, and on October 1 of year 2, Pelican distributes $5,000 to Ann and $5,000 to Baker.

(d) Same as (c), above, except that Pelican has a $10,000 deficit in earnings and profits in year 2 as a result of its business operations.

D.   DISTRIBUTIONS OF PROPERTY

1.   CONSEQUENCES TO THE DISTRIBUTING CORPORATION

a.   BACKGROUND: THE *GENERAL UTILITIES* DOCTRINE

Under the double tax regime of Subchapter C, profits from the sale of appreciated corporate property are taxed twice—first to the corporation when it sells the property and again to the shareholders when the sales proceeds are distributed as dividends. What if a corporation *distributes* appreciated property to its shareholders? The shareholders, of course, receive a taxable dividend to the extent the distribution is out of current or accumulated earnings and profits. Should the distributing corporation also recognize gain—just as if it had sold the property for its fair market value? Or is the corporation entitled to nonrecognition of gain because the property was distributed rather than sold? Does the answer depend on the shareholder's basis in the distributed property? If tax relief is appropriate, should nonliquidating distributions be treated less favorably than liquidating distributions? And what about distributions of loss property? Simple as they may seem, these are among the most controversial questions ever spawned by Subchapter C. The answers will come gradually. The coverage in this chapter is limited to nonliquidating distributions. To set the stage, we begin with a brief history of the rise and fall of what became known as the *General Utilities* doctrine.

In General Utilities & Operating Co. v. Helvering,[1] the Supreme Court first considered the corporate-level tax consequences of a nonliquidating distribution of appreciated property by a corporation to its shareholders.

---

1.   296 U.S. 200, 56 S.Ct. 185 (1935).

The facts were straightforward. General Utilities Corporation had located a buyer for corporate property with a value of $1,000,000 and an adjusted basis of $2,000. Hoping to escape the large corporate-level tax that would be imposed on a sale by the corporation, General Utilities distributed the property to its shareholders with an "understanding" (but not a legal commitment) that they would sell the targeted property to the prospective buyer. Four days later, the shareholders sold the property to the buyer on the same terms negotiated by the corporation. The Service contended that the distribution was a taxable event at the corporate level.

By the time the controversy reached the Supreme Court, the government's principal argument was based on the premise that General Utilities had created an indebtedness to its shareholders by declaring a dividend. It went on to contend that using appreciated property to discharge that indebtedness was a taxable event. Apparently confining its decision to these narrow grounds, the Court held that the corporation recognized no gain because the distribution was not a "sale" and the corporation did not discharge indebtedness with appreciated assets.[2] Despite this limited holding, it long was assumed that *General Utilities* stood for the broader proposition that a distributing corporation does not recognize gain or loss when it makes a distribution in kind with respect to its stock.[3]

The result in *General Utilities* raised fundamental policy questions that went to the heart of the double tax regime. The decision created a significant and arguably unwarranted tax distinction between a distribution in kind of appreciated property and a sale of that same property by the corporation followed by a distribution of the proceeds to the shareholders. In the case of a sale at the corporate level, the corporation recognizes gain and correspondingly must increase its earnings and profits. On distribution of the sale proceeds, the shareholders also are taxed to the extent of the corporation's earnings and profits. Under *General Utilities*, however, the corporation could distribute the same asset to the shareholders without recognizing gain. Although the shareholders were taxable on the distribution, but the asset appreciation escaped tax at the corporate level, and a noncorporate shareholder took the asset with a fair market value basis.[4] This simple comparison demonstrates that the tax treatment of distributions in kind is critical to the integrity of the double tax regime. Because

---

2. The government also argued that the subsequent sale by the shareholders of the assets could be attributed to the corporation, but the Court declined to consider that question since it had not been raised below. Ten years later, in Commissioner v. Court Holding Co., 324 U.S. 331, 65 S.Ct. 707 (1945), the government successfully advanced the attribution argument in the context of a liquidating distribution. See Chapter 7B2, infra. In *General Utilities,* the government alternatively contended that a distribution of appreciated property by a corporation in and of itself constitutes a realization event, but the Court did not address this argument. See Bittker & Eustice, Federal Income Taxation of Corporations and Shareholders ¶ 8.20[2] n. 313.

3. See, e.g., Commissioner v. Godley's Estate, 213 F.2d 529, 531 (3d Cir.1954), cert. denied 348 U.S. 862, 75 S.Ct. 86 (1954). Even before the 1954 Code, however, the *General Utilities* nonrecognition rule was subject to judicially-created exceptions, such as the assignment of income doctrine. See S.Rep. No. 1622, 83rd Cong., 2d Sess. 247 (1954).

4. I.R.C. § 301(d).

the *General Utilities* doctrine was incompatible with the double tax, it was criticized by commentators.[5]

Despite these deficiencies, Congress codified *General Utilities* in the 1954 Code by enacting Section 311(a)(2), which provides that a corporation generally does not recognize gain or loss on a nonliquidating distribution of property.[6] This nonrecognition rule was never absolute. Over the years, the courts applied "common law" doctrines, such as assignment of income[7] and the tax benefit rule,[8] and substance over form,[9] to override Section 311(a) and attribute income back to the corporation. Congress also chipped away at the doctrine with various specialized statutory exceptions until 1986, when it repealed *General Utilities* in the context of both nonliquidating and liquidating distributions of appreciated property.[10]

b.   CORPORATE GAIN OR LOSS

Code: § 311.

Although the nonrecognition rule in Section 311(a)(2) remains in the Code, Section 311(b) stands that rule on its head for nonliquidating distributions of appreciated property. If a corporation distributes appreciated property (other than its own obligations) in a nonliquidating distribution, it must recognize gain in an amount equal to the excess of the fair market value of the property over its adjusted basis. If the distributed property is subject to a liability or if the distributee shareholder assumes a liability in connection with the distribution, the fair market value of the distributed property is treated as not less than the amount of the liability.[11] The deceptive "general" rule of Section 311(a)(2) still applies, however, to disallow recognition of loss on a distribution of property that has declined in value. The objective of this statutory regime is to strengthen the corporate income tax by ensuring that appreciated property may not leave corporate solution and take a stepped-up basis in the hands of the distributee shareholder without the imposition of a corporate-level tax on the appreciation.[12]

---

5. See, e.g., Blum, "Taxing Transfers of Incorporated Business: A Proposal for Improvement," 52 Taxes 516 (1974); Raum, "Dividends in Kind: Their Tax Aspects," 63 Harv.L.Rev. 593 (1950).

6. Prior to 1987, Section 336 provided a similar nonrecognition rule for liquidating distributions. See Chapter 7B2, infra.

7. See, e.g., Commissioner v. First State Bank of Stratford, 168 F.2d 1004 (5th Cir. 1948), cert. denied, 335 U.S. 867, 69 S.Ct. 137 (1948).

8. Cf. Hillsboro National Bank v. Commissioner, 460 U.S. 370, 103 S.Ct. 1134 (1983).

9. Bush Brothers & Co. v. Commissioner, 668 F.2d 252 (6th Cir.1982); Waltham Netoco Theatres, Inc. v. Commissioner, 401 F.2d 333 (1st Cir.1968). But see Anderson v. Commissioner, 92 T.C. 138 (1989).

10. See also Chapter 7B2, infra.

11. I.R.C. § 311(b)(2), incorporating the rule for liquidating distributions in I.R.C. § 336(b).

12. Cf. S.Rep.No. 98–169, 98th Cong., 2d Sess. 177 (1984); H.R.Rep.No. 99–426, 99th Cong., 1st Sess. 282 (1985).

The *General Utilities* doctrine thus no longer applies to nonliquidating distributions of appreciated property. A later chapter examines the repeal of the doctrine in the area of complete liquidations.[13] Despite what appears to be parallel treatment, some differences between the treatment of liquidating and nonliquidating distributions persist, raising lingering policy issues. For example, a distributing corporation generally may recognize a loss on a liquidating distribution of property with a built-in loss.[14] Should nonliquidating distributions be treated similarly? Is the "general" loss disallowance rule in Section 311(a)(2) an indefensible trap for the uninformed? In considering these questions, one should keep in mind that the double tax regime is not universally accepted, and some commentators once argued that relief through limited *General Utilities* type exceptions would be appropriate.[15]

c.   EFFECT ON THE DISTRIBUTING CORPORATION'S EARNINGS AND PROFITS

Code: § 312(a)(3), (b), (c), (f)(1).

Regulations: § 1.312–3.

Nonliquidating distributions of property have several effects upon the earnings and profits of the distributing corporation. Gain recognized by the corporation on the distribution naturally increases current earnings and profits.[16] Following a property distribution, the distributing corporation may reduce accumulated earnings and profits (to the extent thereof) under Section 312(a)(3) by the adjusted basis of the distributed property. On a distribution of appreciated property (other than a corporation's own debt obligations), this rule is modified by Section 312(b)(2), which provides that the earnings and profits reduction rule in Section 312(a)(3) is applied by substituting the fair market value of the property for its adjusted basis. This special rule logically allows a corporation distributing appreciated property to make a downward adjustment to accumulated earnings and profits in an amount equal to the full fair market value of the property. The net result of these earnings and profits adjustments—the first relating to the gain recognized on the distribution and the second relating to the effect of the distribution itself—is the same as if the corporation had sold the property (increasing current earnings and profits by the gain recognized) and then distributed cash equal to the fair market value of the property (decreasing accumulated earnings and profits by that amount).

---

13. See Chapter 7B2, infra.

14. I.R.C. § 336(a), (d).

15. Compare Thompson, "An Analysis of the Proposal to Repeal General Utilities with an Escape Hatch," 31 Tax Notes 1121 (June 16, 1986) with Yin, "General Utilities Repeal: Is Tax Reform Really Going to Pass it By?" 31 Tax Notes 1111 (June 16, 1986).

16. I.R.C. § 312(b)(1), (f)(1). For this purpose and for purposes of determining gain recognized, the adjusted basis of any property is its adjusted basis for purposes of computing earnings and profits. I.R.C. § 312(b), flush language. For example, tangible property depreciated for tax purposes under the accelerated cost recovery system must be depreciated for "E & P" purposes under the § 168(g)(2) alternative depreciation system and thus may have a different "E & P" adjusted basis.

Section 312(c) cryptically adds that "proper adjustment" shall be made for liabilities either assumed by the shareholder or to which the property is subject. Section 1.312–3 of the regulations provides that the "proper adjustment" is a reduction in the Section 312(a)(3) charge to earnings and profits for liabilities assumed or to which the property is subject. This adjustment thus *decreases* the charge to earnings and profits and properly reflects the fact that relief from the liability is an economic benefit to the distributing corporation.

d. DISTRIBUTIONS OF A CORPORATION'S OWN OBLIGATIONS

Code: §§ 311(a), (b)(1); 312(a)(2).

Regulations: § 1.301–1(d)(1)(ii).

By virtue of the parenthetical in Section 311(b)(1)(A), "(other than an obligation of such corporation)", the general gain recognition rule does not apply to distributions by a corporation of its own debt obligations. Consequently, the eroded Section 311(a) continues to govern this situation. At the shareholder level, both the amount of the distribution and the distributee shareholder's basis are equal to the fair market value of the obligation.[17] The distributing corporation's earnings and profits are reduced by the principal amount of the obligation or, in the case of an obligation having original issue discount, by its issue price.[18]

2. CONSEQUENCES TO THE SHAREHOLDERS

Code: §§ 301(a), (b), (c), (d).

The rules governing the shareholder level tax consequences of property distributions are essentially the same as those for cash distributions. The amount of the distribution is the fair market value of the distributed property, reduced by any liabilities assumed by the shareholder or to which the property is subject;[1] that amount is taxed under the now familiar principles in Section 301(c). The shareholder's basis in the distributed property is its fair market value as of the date of the distribution.[2]

PROBLEM

Zane, an individual, owns all of the outstanding common stock in Sturdley Utilities Corporation. Zane purchased his Sturdley stock seven years ago and his basis is $8,000. At the beginning of the current year, Sturdley had $25,000 of accumulated earnings and profits and no current earnings and profits. Determine the tax consequences to Zane and Sturdley in each of the following alternative situations:

17. Reg. §§ 1.301–1(d)(1)(ii), –1(h)(2)(i).

18. I.R.C. § 312(a)(2).

1. I.R.C. § 301(b). The fair market value of the distributed property is determined as of the date of distribution. I.R.C. § 301(b)(3).

2. I.R.C. § 301(d).

(a) Sturdley distributes inventory ($20,000 fair market value; $11,000 basis) to Zane.

(b) Same as (a), above, except that, before the distribution, Sturdley has no current or accumulated earnings and profits.

(c) Sturdley distributes land ($20,000 fair market value; $11,000 basis) which it has used in its business. Zane takes the land subject to a $16,000 mortgage.

(d) Assume Sturdley has $15,000 of current earnings and profits (in addition to $25,000 of accumulated earnings and profits) and it distributes to Zane land ($20,000 fair market value; $30,000 basis) which it held as an investment. Compare the result if Sturdley first sold the land and then distributed the proceeds.

(e) Assume again that Sturdley has $25,000 of accumulated earnings and profits at the beginning of the current year. Sturdley distributes machinery used in its business ($10,000 fair market value, zero adjusted basis for taxable income purposes, and $2,000 adjusted basis for earnings and profits purposes). The machinery is five-year property and has a seven-year class life, was purchased by Sturdley for $14,000 on July 1 of year one (no § 179 election was made), and the distribution is made on January 1 of year seven. See I.R.C. §§ 168(g)(2), 312(k)(3); Reg. § 1.312–15(d).

E.   CONSTRUCTIVE DISTRIBUTIONS

Code: Skim § 7872(a), (c)(1)(C).

Regulations: § 1.301–1(j).

Historically, dividend distributions often combined the worst of all possible worlds from a tax standpoint: they were fully taxable to noncorporate shareholders at the highest ordinary income rates but were not deductible by the distributing corporation. To avoid the double tax, closely held C corporations have attempted to distribute earnings in a form that may be deductible at the corporate level. Notable examples include a corporation's payment of: (1) excessive compensation to shareholders or their relatives;[1] (2) expenses paid for the personal benefit of shareholders (e.g., travel or entertainment, legal expenses);[2] (3) excessive rent for corporate use of shareholder property;[3] and (4) interest on shareholder debt that in substance represents equity.[4] If these payments are not what they purport to be—i.e., if they are not *really* salary, rent or interest, etc., or if

---

1. For the legal standards used in making this determination, see, e.g., Menard, Inc. v. Commissioner, 560 F.3d 620 (7th Cir. 2009), and compare Charles McCandless Tile Service v. United States, 191 Ct.Cl. 108, 422 F.2d 1336 (1970) with Elliotts, Inc. v. Commissioner, 716 F.2d 1241 (9th Cir.1983).

2. See, e.g., Ashby v. Commissioner, 50 T.C. 409 (1968); Hood v. Commissioner, 115 T.C. 172 (2000).

3. See, e.g., International Artists, Ltd. v. Commissioner, 55 T.C. 94 (1970).

4. See Chapter 3, supra.

they are primarily for the personal benefit of shareholders—they risk being reclassified by the Service as a constructive dividend. In that event, the corporate level deduction will be disallowed. Other disguised dividend strategies include labeling what in reality is a distribution as a loan to the shareholder,[5] bargain sales or rentals of corporate property to shareholders[6] and interest free loans.[7]

The constructive dividend area has produced many entertaining controversies involving blatant attempts by taxpayers to milk their corporations while avoiding the double tax. The prototype transaction involves a direct payment or receipt of an economic benefit by the shareholder, and resolution of the issue requires an evaluation of all the facts and circumstances, applying broad standards such as "reasonable compensation;" "shareholder benefit vs. corporate benefit" and "intent."[8] The case below illustrates a typical fact pattern. It is followed by a Note discussing the changing stakes now that most dividends are taxed at a preferential rate.

Nicholls, North, Buse Co. v. Commissioner

Tax Court of the United States, 1971.
56 T.C. 1225.

[Nicholls, North, Buse Co. ("Nicholls") was a Wisconsin corporation in the food-brokerage and food-packing businesses. All of the Nicholls voting common stock was owned by Herbert and Charlotte Resenhoeft, who were married. Herbert served as president and a director of the corporation. Nicholls nonvoting common stock was owned by Herbert, Charlotte and their two sons, Robert and James. James was also an employee of Nicholls.

Herbert Resenhoeft previously had personally owned two boats: *Pea Picker I* and *Pea Picker II*. In 1964, Nicholls acquired a new 52–foot yacht—*Pea Picker III*—at a total cost of $68,290. Nicholls' Board of Directors unanimously approved the purchase of *Pea Picker III* and provided in a corporate resolution that "any expenses incurred in the personal use of the boat are to be borne by H.A. Resenhoeft and an accurate log is to be kept of all business use." During 1964, $1,144.72 was charged to Herbert for personal use of *Pea Picker III*.

Both Robert and James were free to operate *Pea Picker III*, without special permission. Herbert was unable to operate the yacht and had little technical knowledge about yachting. James was the principal operator of *Pea Picker III* and was the family boating enthusiast. In fact, James negotiated Nicholls' purchase of the yacht. During 1964, the use of *Pea Picker III* included personal use by James.

---

5. See, e.g., Williams v. Commissioner, 627 F.2d 1032 (10th Cir.1980).

6. See, e.g., Honigman v. Commissioner, 466 F.2d 69 (6th Cir.1972).

7. Compare Zager v. Commissioner, 72 T.C. 1009 (1979) with I.R.C. § 7872. See also Rountree Cotton Co. v. Commissioner, 113

T.C. 422 (1999), aff'd by order, 12 Fed.Appx. 641 (10th Cir.2001).

8. See generally, Bittker & Eustice, Federal Income Taxation of Corporations and Shareholders ¶ 8.05.

In its original notice of deficiency to Herbert, the Service took the position that he was taxable on $68,878.72, the purchase price for the yacht plus yacht expenses for the year. Later, the Service alternatively argued that Herbert was taxable on a dividend equal to the fair rental value of *Pea Picker III*. Ed.]

The issues with regard to individual petitioner Resenhoeft resolve themselves down to the following: (a) Was there a constructive dividend; (b) may the use of the yacht by James, a stockholder in his own right, be imputed to his father who was in control of the corporation to make the father the recipient of the constructive dividend; and (c) is the measure of the dividend the purchase price of the craft plus actual operating expenses or is the fair rental value of the use of the yacht during the period in question the appropriate measure?

(a) It is well established that any expenditure made by a corporation for the personal benefit of its stockholders, or the making available of corporate-owned facilities to stockholders for their personal benefit, may result in the receipt by the stockholders of a constructive dividend. * * * Upon consideration of all the evidence, including the possible instances of unrecorded personal use, we conclude that *Pea Picker III* was used for business purposes 25 percent and for personal purposes 75 percent of the time in 1964.

(b) Since we have found that there was personal use constituting under some circumstances a dividend, the next question is, to whom was the benefit directed? Resenhoeft has established by convincing evidence that he was not interested in the yacht for his own personal pleasure as a boating enthusiast. He had little knowledge of the workings of such craft, could not operate them himself, and played no direct part in the purchase of *Pea Picker III* or the sale of her predecessor. However, to the extent that he was present on an occasion of personal use, he received a benefit and an argument that others benefited as well is of no avail here. * * * He shared in the friendships and joined in the social activity on board on those occasions.

The question remains, however, whether James' personal use of *Pea Picker III* on occasions when Resenhoeft was not present may nevertheless be attributed to Resenhoeft. The essential elements underlying the taxation of assigned income to the assignor were set down in Helvering v. Horst, 311 U.S. 112 (1940). The Court stated in that case that: "The power to dispose of income is the equivalent of 'ownership' of it and the exercise of that power to procure the payment of income to another is the 'enjoyment' and hence the 'realization' of the income by him who exercises it." In this case Resenhoeft personally owned well over 50 percent of all voting stock and together with his wife owned all of it, and in addition was the president of the company and on the board of directors. It is manifestly clear that it was Resenhoeft's decision that the corporation acquire *Pea Picker III*. Resenhoeft's decision to allow the use of the boat by his sons as they desired and without direct control over either the circumstances of use or the maintenance of appropriate supportive documentation must be given particular emphasis. There is no indication here that information regarding the actual use of the boat, or the type of records maintained, was being kept from Resenhoeft or that he had no way of learning the truth. * * *

The principle of assignment was applied to constructive dividends in Byers v. Commissioner, 199 F.2d 273 (C.A.8, 1952), certiorari denied 345 U.S. 907 (1953). See also Commissioner v. Makransky, 321 F.2d 598 (C.A.3, 1963). We remain unpersuaded that Resenhoeft's purpose in agreeing to the acquisition of a large pleasure craft was only to benefit the corporation. This is particularly so in light of his prior personal ownership of *Pea Picker I* and *II* which were available for the use and benefit of his sons. Once it is understood that Resenhoeft was in complete control of the events, the fact that James, the principle user of the boat for noncorporate purposes, was a mature adult and a shareholder in his own right becomes irrelevant.

(c) Although we have determined that there was a dividend, and that the dividend must be attributed to Resenhoeft, we have yet to ascertain the amount of the dividend. Two standards have been used on different occasions, the first being the initial cost of the facility and the second, the approximate rental value for the period at issue. The standard to be chosen rests on the facts and circumstances of the event rather than on which year (the initial year of purchase or a subsequent year) happens to be before the Court, as was argued by respondent in his briefs. In *Louis Greenspon, supra*, the Court held that continued corporate ownership of farm equipment used by the petitioner shareholder prevented the assessment of a constructive dividend based on the purchase price of the equipment. No determination of a dividend was made based on the rental value since respondent failed to raise that issue. Our holding in *Greenspon* that ownership of the asset is a principal factor has not been altered by subsequent cases involving the year an asset was acquired. Although in some cases subsequent to *Greenspon* we have determined the amount of the dividend to be the acquisition cost, in those cases the evidence clearly pointed to shareholder ownership, * * * or the location of title could not be determined and therefore was presumptively in the shareholder. * * * These cases have not been followed when the title was clearly with the corporation. * * *

In this case, ownership continued to rest with Nicholls. The bill of sale was made in Nicholls' name, Nicholls' principal creditor was informed of the purchase and the yacht's intended devotion to corporate purposes, a license to operate short-wave radio equipment installed on *Pea Picker III* was acquired in the corporate name, registration by U.S. Customs was attempted in the corporate name, registration and licensing was received from the State of Wisconsin in the corporate name, and sales tax was paid by the corporation although a significant savings would have resulted by treating this as a purchase by Resenhoeft. Although a listing in the Lake Michigan Yachting Association catalogue showed James as the owner of the *Pea Picker III*, the association provided no means for noting corporate ownership, and registration in whatever name offered values significant to the corporation as well as to James. Therefore we hold that petitioner has not received a constructive dividend equivalent to the cost of acquisition of *Pea Picker III.*

The issue yet remaining is whether there is another more appropriate measure of the constructive dividend, a dividend which we have already decided Resenhoeft received.

Respondent's alternative theory is that the fair rental value of *Pea Picker III* for the period of use in 1964 is the measure of the dividend received; furthermore, respondent argues that the testimony of the captain in charge of delivering *Pea Picker III* from Florida corroborates the minimum rental value alleged in respondent's amended answer. The amended answer alleged that the fair value was not less than Nicholls' combined depreciation and operating expenses, $4,578.86, of which $1,144.72 concededly was included as income by Resenhoeft at the time he filed his 1964 return. Since we have already determined that Resenhoeft should be charged with 75 percent of the total value of the use of the yacht rather than 100 percent as argued by respondent, the remaining amount actually in dispute is $2,289.42. * * *

Ordinarily, respondent's alternative allegation would be determinative since petitioner has offered no evidence showing that determination to be in error. However, since the theory of a dividend based on rental value comprises a separate issue, involving distinct factual questions, and was raised by the Commissioner for the first time in his amended answer, the rental value suggested by the Commissioner may not be given the presumption it would otherwise be due * * *. Upon Considering all evidence, including the rental value of similar craft used in dissimilar water, we hold that the full rental value of *Pea Picker III* for the period following the shakedown cruise and ending with the final storage of the boat was $4,000. Resenhoeft gained personal benefit and therefore received a constructive dividend from his own use and the use of the craft by his sons equaling 75 percent of the above rental value; of that amount he has voluntarily recognized income to the extent of $1,144.72. We have no reason to believe Nicholls' earnings and profits were insufficient for the payment of a taxable dividend of the amount determined above.

* * *

NOTE

The reduced tax rate on qualified dividends has changed the stakes and planning agenda in some traditional scenarios. The distinction between compensation and a constructive dividend provides a good illustration. Compensation continues to be taxable at the highest ordinary income rates and is subject to employment taxes equal to 12.4 percent of the social security wage base (ignoring the temporary two percent payroll tax rate reduction in effect for 2011 and 2012) of $110,100 (in 2012) and a 2.9 percent medicare tax on all wages while dividends are taxed at a maximum rate of 15 percent and are not subject to employment taxes. But compensation and the employer's share of employment taxes are deductible while dividends are not.

Under the "old arithmetic," with wages and dividends taxed at the same ordinary income rate, it almost always was advantageous to classify distributions to shareholder-employees as compensation rather than a dividend so that the corporation could deduct the payment. Under current law, however, as long as dividends are taxable at no more than 15 percent, there are situations where the aggregate amount of federal taxes is lower if payments are classified as dividends rather than compensation. Important variables are the corporate and individual tax rates and the impact of employment taxes.[1]

To illustrate, consider first the following simple example in a world where wages are not subject to employment taxes, and all income of C corporations and individuals is taxed at a 35 percent rate except for dividends, which are taxed at 15 percent. Assume that X Corporation has $100,000 of earnings to distribute to A, its only employee and shareholder, and is evaluating whether to classify the distribution as a dividend or compensation. The overall tax results are as follows:

	Compensation	Dividend
X's Taxable Income Before Payment to A	$100,000	$100,000
Corporate Income Tax	0	35,000
Payment to A	100,000	65,000
A's Income Tax	35,000	9,750
Net Amount to A	65,000	55,250

The traditional incentive to classify the distribution as compensation remains in this example, despite the lower tax rate on dividends, because of the continuing negative effect of the double tax when a C corporation taxable at the highest marginal rate (35 percent) pays dividends.

Now assume the same facts, except reflect the reality that A is subject to employment taxes of 12.4 percent on the first $110,100[2] of wages and 2.9 percent on all wages, with half of these taxes paid by X Corp. (which can deduct them) and half by A. Assuming that X Corp. has $100,000 available to pay to A before any corporate-level income or employment taxes, the tax results are as follows:

---

1. For more extended analysis of these issues and other variables, see Feld, "Dividends Reconsidered," 101 Tax Notes 1117 (Dec. 1, 2003); Jewett, "Characterization of Income: Compensation vs. Dividends," 103 Tax Notes 1501 (June 21, 2004).

2. This is the wage base in effect for 2012, which is used throughout this discus-

	Compensation[3]	Dividend
X's Taxable Income Before		
Payment to A	$100,000	$100,000
Employment Taxes (X's share)	7,106	0
Corporate Income Tax	0	35,000
Payment to A	92,894	65,000
Employment Taxes (A's share)	7,106	0
A's Income Tax	32,512	9,750
Net Amount to A	53,276	55,250

When employment taxes are taken into account, there is a slight overall advantage to dividend classification. As A's compensation rises, however, the benefit of dividend classification will diminish because the 12.4 percent social security tax is only imposed on the first $110,100 of wages. With larger distributions, the traditional bias toward compensation persists because of the negative impact of the double tax.

The incentives also change if the corporation or the shareholder pays tax at lower marginal rates. If the corporation's taxable income falls within the lower rate brackets in Section 11, that reduces the amount of double tax paid and favors a dividend. Alternatively, if the shareholder pays tax on ordinary income at lower rates, that will favor compensation because the relative tax advantage for dividends will not be as great.

F.   ANTI-AVOIDANCE LIMITATIONS ON THE DIVIDENDS RECEIVED DEDUCTION

1.   IN GENERAL

Code: §§ 243(a)(1), (3), (c); 246(a)(1), (b)(1), (c); 246A; 1059(a), (b), (c), (d), (e)(1). Skim §§ 243(b)(1); 1059(e)(2), (3), (f).

Dividends received by corporate shareholders are treated more generously for tax purposes than dividends received by individuals. If corporate shareholders were taxed in full on the dividends they receive, corporate profits would be subjected to a minimum of three levels of taxation—once when earned, a second time when received as dividends by the corporate shareholder, and again when distributed to the ultimate noncorporate shareholder. To alleviate this multiple taxation, Section 243 generally permits corporate shareholders to deduct 70 percent of dividends received from other corporations. The deduction is increased to 80 percent if the corporate shareholder owns 20 percent or more (by vote or value) of the distributing corporation[1] and to 100 percent for certain "qualifying" divi-

sion.

3.   These computations assume that X has $100,000 available for payment of wages to A before X pays the employer's share of employment taxes (6.2 percent of the first $110,100 of wages plus 1.45% of all wages).

A's wages were determined using the following formula: wages ("W") = $100,000 − .0765W.

1.   I.R.C. § 243(c).

dends if the payor and recipient corporations are members of the same affiliated group.[2] As a result, a maximum of only 30 percent of dividends received by corporate shareholders are subject to tax, for a maximum effective rate of 10.5 percent.[3] The availability of this deduction has inspired tax advisors to devise techniques to take advantage of the lower effective rate on dividends received by corporate shareholders. This section examines ongoing Congressional efforts to curtail some of these abuses.

2. SPECIAL HOLDING PERIOD REQUIREMENTS

The dividends received deduction may motivate corporate shareholders to convert capital gain (taxable at the 35 percent maximum corporate rate) to tax sheltered dividend income (taxable at a maximum rate of 10.5 percent). Assume, for example, that Converter Corporation acquires 100 shares of Distributor, Inc. for $5,250 shortly before the stock goes "ex-dividend."[4] Converter holds the stock, collects a $250 dividend, includes only 30% ($75) in income, and then sells the stock for its post-dividend value of $5,000, claiming a short-term capital loss of $250 which is available to offset other capital gains normally taxable at 35 percent. Without any patrolling mechanism, this maneuver enables a corporate shareholder to convert short-term gain into 70 percent sheltered income.

An earlier version of Section 246(c) attempted to close this loophole by denying any dividends received deduction unless the stock was held for more than 15 days (90 days for certain preferred stock), but corporations concocted methods to diminish the risk of loss during this brief 15–day holding period. Congress responded by increasing the holding period in Section 246(c) to more than 45 days during the 91–day period beginning on the date which is 45 days before the stock goes ex-dividend.[5] In the case of certain preferred stock, the required holding period is 90 days during the 181–day period beginning on the date which is 90 days before the ex-dividend date.[6] The 45 or 90–day period is tolled whenever the corporate shareholder diminishes its risk of loss with respect to the stock in any one of several specified manners.[7] As a result, a corporation is not entitled to

---

2. I.R.C. § 243(a)(3). The term "affiliated group" is generally defined by reference to the rules governing affiliated corporations that file consolidated tax returns. I.R.C. § 243(b)(2). A simple example would be a corporate parent and an 80 percent or more subsidiary. See I.R.C. § 1504(a). A "qualifying dividend" must be paid from earnings and profits accumulated with the payor and recipient corporations are members of the same affiliated group. I.R.C. § 243(b)(1).

3. The 10.5 percent effective rate is derived by multiplying the 30 percent includible portion of the dividends by the 35 percent maximum corporate rate.

4. The "ex-dividend" date is the first date that a buyer of the stock with respect to which a dividend has been declared is not entitled to receive the dividend.

5. I.R.C. § 246(c)(1)(A). For purposes of counting the number of days, the date of disposition but not the date of acquisition is included. I.R.C. § 246(c)(3).

6. I.R.C. § 246(c)(2).

7. I.R.C. § 246(c)(4). See Reg. § 1.246–5.

the dividends received deduction unless it is willing to hold the stock and incur a genuine market risk for the requisite period of time.

3.   EXTRAORDINARY DIVIDENDS: BASIS REDUCTION

If the dividend to be received is extraordinarily large in relation to the price of the stock, a corporate shareholder may incur a minimal risk of loss even if it holds the stock for more than 45 days. This opportunity was illustrated by a dramatic example of a tax-motivated "dividend stripping" transaction described in a Congressional committee report:[8]

> Chrysler's cumulative preferred stock sells at $36 per share shortly before Chrysler is scheduled to distribute $11.69 per share of back dividends. Corporation X has a short-term capital gain of $1 million, on which it will owe tax of $460,000 [the example uses the pre–1987 46 percent corporate rate.] It buys 85,000 shares of Chrysler preferred for $3,060,000 and holds it for 91 days. When the stock goes ex-dividend, the price drops to $24.31 per share. Assume corporation X eventually sells the stock for $24.31. Corporation X has a capital loss of $11.69 per share, or $993,650, which reduces the tax on its capital gain to $2,921, or by $457,079. It receives a dividend of $993,650, of which 85 percent [now 70 percent.], or $844,603 is excluded. The tax on the rest of the dividend is $68,562. Thus, the transaction saves $457,079 of capital gain tax at a price of $68,562 of dividend tax, a net gain of $388,517. This gain is likely to exceed, by far, whatever economic consequences result from fluctuations in the market value of Chrysler preferred during the 91–day mandatory holding period.

To deter this opportunity for tax arbitrage, Congress enacted Section 1059, which provides that a corporate shareholder receiving an "extraordinary dividend" must reduce its basis in the underlying stock (but not below zero) by the amount of the nontaxed (i.e., deductible) portion of the dividend if the corporation has not held the stock for more than two years before the "dividend announcement date"—i.e., the earliest date when the distributing corporation declares, announces or agrees to the amount or payment of the dividend.[9]

To fully understand the workings of Section 1059, some definitions are in order. An "extraordinary dividend" is defined in terms of the size of the dividend in relation to the shareholder's adjusted basis in the underlying stock. A dividend is extraordinary if it exceeds certain threshold percentages—five percent of the shareholder's adjusted basis in the case of most preferred stock and ten percent of the adjusted basis in the case of any

8. Joint Committee on Taxation, Tax Shelter Proposals and Other Tax–Motivated Transactions, 98th Cong., 2d Sess. 39–40 (1984).

9. I.R.C. § 1059(a)(1), (d)(5). A distribution that otherwise would constitute an extraordinary dividend will not be considered as such if the shareholder has held the stock during the entire existence of the corporation or any predecessor corporation. I.R.C. § 1059(d)(6).

other stock.[10] To prevent easy avoidance of these percentage tests, all dividends received by a shareholder with respect to any shares of stock which have ex-dividend dates within the same period of 85 consecutive days are combined and treated as one dividend.[11] Under an alternate test, a taxpayer may elect to determine the status of a dividend as extraordinary by reference to the fair market value (rather than the adjusted basis) of the stock as of the day before the ex-dividend date.[12] This election could be beneficial if the stock had appreciated substantially from the time when it was acquired by the shareholder.

The basis reduction required by Section 1059 is only for the "nontaxed portion" of an extraordinary dividend. The "nontaxed portion" is the total amount of the dividend reduced by the taxable portion—i.e., the portion of the dividend includible in gross income after application of the dividends received deduction.[13] The basis reduction generally occurs immediately before any sale or disposition of the stock.[14] If the nontaxed portion of an extraordinary dividend exceeds the shareholder's adjusted basis in the stock, any excess is treated as gain from the sale or exchange of property in the taxable year in which the extraordinary dividend is received.[15]

The general definition of "extraordinary dividend" is broadened in two special situations. Section 1059(e)(1) provides that any amount treated as a Section 301 distribution to a corporate shareholder shall be an extraordinary dividend, irrespective of the shareholder's holding period in the stock or the size of the distribution, if it is a distribution in redemption of stock which is: (1) part of a partial liquidation of the redeeming corporation[16], or (2) is non pro rata as to all shareholders.[17] In addition, a corporate shareholder will recognize immediate gain with respect to any redemption treated as a dividend (in whole or in part) when the nontaxed portion of the dividend exceeds the basis of the shares surrendered if the redemption is treated as a dividend because of the holding of options that are treated as constructively owned by the shareholder under Section 318.[18] This rather obscure provision was enacted in response to a few highly publicized

---

10. I.R.C. § 1059(c)(1), (2).

11. I.R.C. § 1059(c)(3)(A). In addition, all dividends received with respect to a share of stock which have ex-dividend dates during the same period of 365 consecutive days are treated as extraordinary if the aggregate of such dividends exceeds 20 percent of the basis in such stock. I.R.C. § 1059(c)(3)(B). These rules are extended to include dividends received with respect to shares of stock having a substituted basis. I.R.C. § 1059(c)(3)(C).

12. I.R.C. § 1059(c)(4). This option is available only if the taxpayer establishes the fair market value of the stock to the satisfaction of the Commissioner.

13. I.R.C. § 1059(b).

14. I.R.C. § 1059(d)(1)(A). Section 1059(d)(1)(B) provides that in testing for an extraordinary dividend under Section 1059(c)(1), any reduction in basis required by reason of a prior distribution is treated as occurring at the beginning of the ex-dividend date for such distribution.

15. I.R.C. § 1059(a)(2). This treatment avoids the tax taboo of a negative basis. Cf. I.R.C. § 357(c) and Chapter 2D, supra.

16. "Partial liquidation" is defined for this purpose under the tests in Section 302(e). See Chapter 5D, infra.

17. The tax consequences of stock redemptions are covered in Chapter 5, infra.

18. I.R.C. § 1059(e)(1)(A)(iii).

transactions where corporate taxpayers sought to structure sales of stock as "dividend" redemptions in order to shelter their gain through the dividends received deduction.

Two other special rules carve out liberalizing exceptions. First, certain distributions between an affiliated group of corporations that qualify for the 100 percent dividends received deduction under Section 243(b)(1) are not treated as extraordinary dividends.[19] Second, special relief is provided for "qualified preferred dividends," which are defined as dividends payable with respect to any share of stock which provides for fixed preferred dividends payable not less than annually and was not acquired with dividends in arrears.[20] A "qualified preferred dividend" is not treated as an extraordinary dividend if the dividends received by the shareholder during the period it owned the stock do not exceed an annualized rate of 15 percent of the lower of (a) the shareholder's adjusted basis or (b) the liquidation preference of the stock, and the stock is held by the shareholder for over five years.[21] The theory for this complex exception is that, unlike the typical extraordinary dividend, a qualified preferred dividend offers no potential for effectively purchasing a dividend that accrued prior to the date on which the stock was acquired.

4. DEBT-FINANCED PORTFOLIO STOCK

Corporate shareholders also exploited the dividends received deduction by borrowing funds to acquire dividend paying stock. For example, assume Leverage Corporation borrows $10,000 at 10 percent interest to purchase $10,000 of stock that will pay dividends at an 8 percent annual return ($800 per year). Leverage fully deducts the $1,000 interest expense against ordinary income but only $240 of the $800 dividend received would be taxable if the 70 percent dividends received deduction is available. The deduction thus turns this otherwise uneconomic transaction into a profitable low risk arbitrage maneuver. The interest deduction results in an annual tax savings of $350 ($1,000 × 35%) while the tax owed on the dividends would be $84 if the corporation were in the maximum 35 percent bracket. For an annual outlay of $1,000 in interest and $84 in tax, Leverage receives $800 in income and a tax savings of $350, for a $66 after-tax benefit.

Section 246A precludes this strategy by reducing Leverage's dividends received deduction to the extent the dividends are attributable to "debt-financed portfolio stock." A similar policy is reflected in Section 265(a)(2), which denies a deduction for interest incurred to purchase or carry tax-exempt municipal bonds. Thus, if the "portfolio stock" is entirely debt-financed, Section 246A denies any dividends received deduction. If it is debt-financed in some lesser percentage, then that same percentage of the

---

19. I.R.C. § 1059(e)(2).

20. I.R.C. § 1059(e)(3)(C)(i).

21. I.R.C. § 1059(e)(3)(A), (B). If all these requirements are met except for the five year holding period, the exclusion from extraordinary dividend treatment is more limited. I.R.C. § 1059(e)(3)(A)(ii).

dividends received deduction is denied.[22] In all events, however, the reduction in the dividends received deduction may not exceed the amount of any interest deduction allocable to the dividend (i.e., to the borrowed funds directly attributable to the stock).[23]

Stock is "debt-financed" if it is "portfolio stock" that is encumbered by "portfolio indebtedness" during a "base period" prescribed in the statute.[24] "Portfolio stock" is defined as any stock of a corporation unless the corporate shareholder owns either: (1) 50 percent of the total voting power and value of the corporation or (2) at least 20 percent of the total voting power and value and five or fewer corporate shareholders own at least 50 percent of the voting power and value, excluding preferred stock.[25] "Portfolio indebtedness" means any indebtedness directly attributable to the investment in the portfolio stock.[26] This means that the stock must have been purchased with borrowed funds or that the borrowing must be directly traceable to the acquisition, such as where the stock was pledged as security for a subsequently incurred debt in a case where the corporation reasonably could have been expected to sell the stock rather than incur the indebtedness.[27]

To illustrate, assume that Leverage Corporation acquires 100 shares of publicly traded X Corp. stock for $10,000, paying $6,000 cash from corporate funds and borrowing the $4,000 balance. X Corp. pays Leverage an annual dividend of $1,000. The stock is debt-financed to the extent of $4,000. The percentage of debt-financing is thus 40 percent (the "average portfolio indebtedness," as defined by Section 246A(d)). Under the convoluted formula in Section 246A(a), Leverage subtracts 40 percent from 100 percent and then multiplies the result (60 percent here) by the usual 70 percent dividends received deduction percentage, to reach 42 percent. That lower figure is substituted for 70 percent in determining Leverage's Section 243 deduction. When Leverage receives its $1,000 dividend, it may deduct only $420 (rather than the usual $700).

5.   SECTION 301(e)

The adjustments to earnings and profits required by Sections 312(k) and 312(n) for depreciation and other timing items frequently result in an increase to a corporation's earnings and profits[28] and may cause earnings and profits to exceed the corporation's taxable income. For example, a corporation that reports a gain on the installment method may not defer the gain for purposes of determining its earnings and profits.[29] The in-

22.   I.R.C. § 246A(a), (d).
23.   I.R.C. § 246A(e).
24.   I.R.C. § 246A(c)(1), (d)(4).
25.   I.R.C. § 246A(c)(2), (4).
26.   I.R.C. § 246A(d)(3)(A).
27.   H.R.Rep. No. 98–432, 98th Cong., 2d Sess. 1181 (1984).

28.   The purpose of these adjustments is to ensure that a corporation's earnings and profits more accurately reflect its true economic performance. See Section B of this chapter, supra.

29.   I.R.C. § 312(n)(5).

crease in earnings and profits resulting from these adjustments often ensures that a distribution will be fully taxable as a dividend to noncorporate shareholders. Because of the dividends received deduction, this may prove to be a bonanza to a corporate shareholder. The following example from the legislative history illustrates one type of abuse that concerned Congress:[30]

> For example, assume that P Corporation owns 100 percent of the stock of X Corporation, that P's basis in such stock is $200, that P and X file separate income tax returns, and that X has no current or accumulated earnings and profits. Assume further that X sells an asset for a $1,000 installment note, realizing an $800 gain. Finally, assume that X borrows $500 secured by the installment note and distributes the $500 to P. Under [Section 312(n)], absent a special rule, X Corporation's earnings and profits would be increased by the amount of gain on the installment sale, and P would treat the $500 distribution as a dividend. Thus P would include the $500 in income but would likely qualify for a 100–percent dividends received deduction. If P later sold its X stock for $200 (the value of that stock if it is assumed that X will ultimately have a $300 tax liability, in present value terms, on account of the installment sale), it would not recognize gain or loss on the sale. As a result, P would have realized an overall profit of $500.

Section 301(e) prevents the result illustrated above by providing that the adjustments required by Sections 312(k) and 312(n) shall not be made for purposes of determining the taxable income of (and the adjusted basis of stock held by) any "20 percent corporate shareholder."[31] A 20 percent corporate shareholder is any corporation entitled to a dividends received deduction with respect to a distribution that owns, directly or through the Section 318 attribution rules, either (1) stock in the distributing corporation possessing at least 20 percent of the total combined voting power, or (2) at least 20 percent of the total value of all of the distributing corporation's stock, except nonvoting preferred stock.[32]

The general effect of Section 301(e) is to reduce the distributing corporation's earnings and profits in determining the tax consequences of distributions to 20 percent corporate shareholders. This reduction, in turn, may cause a distribution to be treated as a return of capital coupled with a reduction in the basis of the distributing corporation's stock. Without Section 301(e), the same distribution likely would have been a tax-free dividend with no basis reduction. Thus, applying Section 301(e) to the earlier example, X Corporation will have no earnings and profits for purposes of determining the tax consequences of a distribution to P Corporation. In the absence of earnings and profits, $200 of the distribu-

---

30. Staff of the Joint Committee on Taxation, General Explanation of the Revenue Provisions of the Deficit Reduction Act of 1984 (hereinafter "1984 Act General Explanation"), 98th Cong., 2d Sess. 183 (1984).

31. I.R.C. § 301(e)(1).

32. I.R.C. § 301(e)(2).

tion by X to P will be a return of capital under Section 301(c)(2), and $300 will be taxed to P as gain from the sale or exchange of its X stock under Section 301(c)(3). P's basis in its X stock will be reduced to zero and it will recognize a $200 gain on the later sale of the stock.[33]

PROBLEM

On June 1, Publicly Held Corporation's common stock is selling for $15 per share. On that date, Publicly Held declares a dividend of $1 per share, payable on June 12 to shareholders of record as of June 8. Investor Corporation purchases 1,000 shares of Publicly Held common stock for $15,000 on June 3 (two days before the June 5 ex-dividend date), collects a $1,000 dividend on June 12 and sells the stock for $14,000 on June 15.

(a) What are the tax consequences to Investor Corporation?

(b) What result in (a), above, if Investor sold the stock on December 1, instead of June 15?

(c) What result in (b), above, if Publicly Held had paid a second $1 per share dividend on August 15, and the ex-dividend date was August 5?

(d) What result in (c), above, if the August dividend is $2 per share but Investor holds the Publicly Held stock for 25 months before selling it?

(e) What result if Investor purchased the Publicly Held stock by borrowing $15,000, secured by the stock, and Investor paid $1,200 interest during the year and received $1,000 of dividends?

(f) What result in (e), above, if Investor had borrowed only $7,500 of the $15,000 used to buy the stock and paid $600 interest during the year?

G. USE OF DIVIDENDS IN BOOTSTRAP SALES

TSN Liquidating Corp. v. United States

United States Court of Appeals, Fifth Circuit, 1980.
624 F.2d 1328.

■ RANDALL, CIRCUIT JUDGE:

This case presents the question whether assets distributed to a corporation by its subsidiary, immediately prior to the sale by such corporation of all the capital stock of such subsidiary, should be treated, for federal income tax purposes, as a dividend or, as the district court held, as part of the consideration received from the sale of such capital stock. We hold that on the facts of this case, the assets so distributed constituted a dividend and we reverse the judgment of the district court.

---

33. 1984 Act General Explanation, supra note 30, at 183.

In 1969, TSN Liquidating Corporation, Inc. ("TSN"), which was then named "Texas State Network, Inc.," owned over 90% of the capital stock of Community Life Insurance Company ("CLIC"), an insurance company chartered under the laws of the State of Maine. In early 1969, negotiations began for the purchase of CLIC by Union Mutual Life Insurance Company ("Union Mutual"). On May 5, 1969, TSN and the other CLIC stockholders entered into an Agreement of Stock Purchase (the "Stock Purchase Agreement") with Union Mutual for the sale of the capital stock of CLIC to Union Mutual. The Stock Purchase Agreement provided that there would be no material adverse change in the business or assets of CLIC prior to the closing "except that as of closing certain shares and capital notes as provided in Section '4.(i).' above will not be a part of the assets of [CLIC]." Since the purchase price of the capital stock of CLIC under the Stock Purchase Agreement was based primarily on the book value (or, in some instances, market value) of those assets owned by CLIC on the closing date, the purchase price would be automatically reduced by the elimination of such shares and notes from the assets of CLIC. On May 14, 1969, as contemplated by the Stock Purchase Agreement, the Board of Directors of CLIC declared a dividend in kind, payable to stockholders of record as of May 19, 1969, consisting primarily of capital stock in small, public companies traded infrequently and in small quantities in the over-the-counter market. On May 20, 1969, the closing was held and Union Mutual purchased substantially all the outstanding capital stock of CLIC, including the shares held by TSN. The final purchase price paid by Union Mutual to the selling stockholders of CLIC was $823,822, of which TSN's share was $747,436. Union Mutual thereupon contributed to the capital of CLIC $1,120,000 in municipal bonds and purchased from CLIC additional capital stock of CLIC for $824,598 in cash paid to CLIC.

In its income tax return for the fiscal year ended July 31, 1969, TSN reported its receipt of assets from CLIC as a dividend and claimed the 85% dividends received deduction available to corporate stockholders pursuant to § 243(a)(1) of the Internal Revenue Code of 1954. TSN also reported its gain on the sale of the capital stock of CLIC on the installment method pursuant to § 453 of the Code. [Under current law, installment sale treatment would not be allowed if the CLIC stock were publicly traded. I.R.C. § 453(k)(2). Ed.] On audit, the Internal Revenue Service treated the distribution of the assets from CLIC to TSN as having been an integral part of the sale by TSN of capital stock of CLIC to Union Mutual, added its estimate ($1,677,082) of the fair market value of the assets received by TSN to the cash ($747,436) received by TSN on the sale, and disallowed the use by TSN of the installment method for reporting the gain on the sale of the capital stock of CLIC since aggregating the fair market value of the distributed assets and the cash resulted in more than 30% of the proceeds from the sale being received in the year of sale. TSN paid the additional tax due as a result of such treatment by the Internal Revenue Service, filed a claim for a refund and subsequently instituted this action against the Internal Revenue Service.

The district court made the following findings of fact in part II of its opinion:

> With regard to the negotiations between CLIC and Union Mutual in early 1969, the Court finds that Union Mutual was interested in purchasing CLIC and proposed a formula for valuing the assets, liabilities, and insurance in force, which, together with an additional amount, would be the price paid for the CLIC stock.
>
> The investment portfolio of CLIC was heavily oriented toward equity investments in closely held over-the-counter securities. At least in the mind of CLIC's officers, the makeup of CLIC's investment portfolio was affecting its ability to obtain licenses in various states. As early as the Spring of 1968, the management and principal stockholders of CLIC had begun to seek a solution to the investment portfolio problem. The Court finds, however, that CLIC had never formulated a definite plan on how to solve its investment portfolio problem.
>
> Union Mutual did not like CLIC's investment portfolio but considered bonds to be more in keeping with insurance industry responsibilities. The management of CLIC regarded the Union Mutual offer as a good one, and tried without success to get Union Mutual to take the entire investment portfolio.
>
> Accordingly, the [Stock Purchase Agreement] required CLIC to dispose some of the investment portfolio assets. Thus, the price that would be paid for the CLIC stock was based upon a formula which valued the assets after excluding certain stocks.
>
> * * *
>
> Plaintiff's disposition of the undesirable over-the-counter stock was necessitated by its sale arrangements with Union Mutual. Plaintiff had no definite plans prior to its negotiations with Union Mutual as to how to get rid of the undesirable stock, when it was to get rid of the undesirable stock, or even that it would definitely get rid of the undesirable stock. Accordingly, the Court finds that the dividend in kind of 14 May 1969 was part and parcel of the purchase agreement with Union Mutual.

TSN Liquidating Corp. v. United States, 77–2 U.S.Tax Cas. ¶ 9741 at 88,523 (N.D.Tex.1977). In part III of its opinion, the district court made the following additional findings:

> Union Mutual was interested in purchasing the stock of an approximately $2 million corporation in order that that corporation might be licensed to do business in other states. As of 30 April 1969, CLIC had assets of $2,115,138. On 14 May 1969, CLIC declared a dividend valued at approximately $1.8 million. As a result of this dividend, CLIC was left with assets totaling approximately $300,000. The final purchase price paid by Union Mutual to the selling shareholders of CLIC was $823,822. In addition,

Union Mutual contributed $1,120,000 of municipal bonds to the capital of CLIC and purchased additional shares of stock of CLIC for $824,598. Thus, subsequent to closing on 20 May 1969, CLIC was worth $2,400,000. Thus, CLIC was worth $2 million when the [Stock Purchase Agreement] was signed on 5 May 1969 and worth over $2 million immediately after closing.

There was no business purpose served in this case by the dividend declared by CLIC prior to the sale of all its stock to Union Mutual. It is evident that the dividend benefitted the shareholders of CLIC and not CLIC itself. There was no benefit or business purpose in CLIC's declaration of the dividend separate and apart from the sale. The Court finds that the dividend would not, and could not, have been made without the sale.

* * *

What actually happened in the period 5 through 20 May 1969 was that the stockholders received $1.8 million in virtually tax-free stocks, as well as over $800,000 in cash, for a total of approximately $2.6 million. This was certainly a fair price for a corporation valued at the time of sale at $2,115,138, and reflects a premium paid for good will and policies in force, as well as the fact that CLIC was an existing business with licenses in eight or nine states. Hence, a $2 million corporation was sold for $2.6 million including the dividend and the cash.

After noting the time-honored principle that the incidence of taxation is to be determined by the substance of the transaction rather than by its form and the related principle that the transaction is generally to be viewed as a whole and not to be separated into its component parts, the district court held:

The distribution of assets to [TSN] from its subsidiary, CLIC, immediately prior to [TSN's] disposition of its entire stock interest in CLIC should be treated as a part of the gain from the sale of the stock. Thus, the Court concludes that the in-kind distribution of 14 May 1969 to the stockholders of CLIC is taxable to [TSN] as gain from the sale of its stock. The alleged dividend was merely intented [sic] to be part of the purchase price paid by Union Mutual to CLIC for its stock.

The district court relied for its holding primarily on the cases of Waterman Steamship Corp. v. Commissioner, 430 F.2d 1185 (5th Cir.1970), cert. denied, 401 U.S. 939, 91 S.Ct. 936, 28 L.Ed.2d 219 (1971), and Basic, Inc. v. United States, 549 F.2d 740 (Ct.Cl.1977), all discussed infra.

On appeal, TSN argues that the cases relied upon by the district court are exceptions to what TSN characterizes as the established rule, namely, that assets removed from a corporation by a dividend made in contemplation of a sale of the stock of that corporation, when those assets are in good faith to be retained by the selling stockholders and not thereafter transferred to the buyer, are taxable as a dividend and not as a part of the price paid for the stock for the reason that, in economic reality and in substance, the selling stockholders did not sell and the buyer did not purchase or pay for the excluded assets. The principal cases cited by TSN for its position are Gilmore v. Commissioner, 25 T.C. 1321 (1956), Coffey v. Commissioner, 14 T.C. 1410 (1950), and Rosenbloom Finance Corp. v. Commissioner, 24 B.T.A. 763 (1931). According to TSN, the controlling distinction between the *Coffey* line of cases relied upon by TSN and the *Waterman* line of cases relied upon by the district court is whether the buyer negotiated to acquire and pay for the stock, exclusive of the assets distributed out as a dividend, on the one hand, or whether the buyer negotiated to acquire and pay for the stock, including the assets which were then the subject of a sham distribution designed to evade taxes, on the other hand. In the former case, according to TSN, there is a taxable dividend; in the latter case there is not.

We begin by noting that the district court was certainly correct in its position that the substance of the transaction controls over the form and that the transaction should be viewed as a whole, rather than being separated into its parts. Further, having reviewed the record, we are of the view that the operative facts found so carefully by the district court are entirely accurate (except for the valuation of the distributed assets, as to which we express no opinion). We differ with the district court only in the legal characterization of those facts and in the conclusion to be drawn therefrom. We agree with TSN that this case is controlled by the *Coffey, Gilmore* and *Rosenbloom* cases rather than by the *Waterman* and *Basic* cases relied upon by the district court.

In *Coffey,* the principal case relied upon by TSN, the taxpayers owned the stock of Smith Brothers Refinery Co., Inc. and were negotiating for the sale of such stock. Representatives of the purchasers and representatives of the sellers examined and discussed the various assets owned by Smith Brothers Refinery Co., Inc., and the liabilities of the company, with a view to reaching an agreement upon the fair market value of the stock. During these negotiations, the representatives of the purchasers and of the sellers could not agree upon the value of certain assets (including a contingent receivable referred to as the Cabot payment). The representatives of the purchasers informed the representatives of the sellers that the sellers could withdraw those assets from the assets of the company and that they would buy the stock without those assets being a part of the sale, thereby eliminating the necessity for arriving at a valuation of those assets in determining the value of the stock on a net worth basis. The contract of sale provided that the unwanted assets would be distributed by the corporation as a dividend prior to the sale of the stock. The selling stockholders contended before the tax court, as the Internal Revenue Service does in the case before this court, that the Cabot payment distributed to them as a dividend in kind was "part of the consideration for stock sold and that any profit resulting from its receipt by them is taxable as a capital gain." The tax court rejected that contention because it was contrary to the substance of the transaction:

We do not agree with petitioners that they received the Cabot payment as part of the consideration for the sale of their stock. The purchasers did not agree to buy their stock and then turn over to them $190,000 and the Cabot payment in consideration therefor. From the testimony above set forth it is apparent that they were not interested in the Cabot payment, did not want it included in the assets of the corporation at the time they acquired its stock, and negotiated with petitioners to acquire stock of a corporation whose assets did not include the unwanted Cabot payment. * * * They received $190,000 for their stock. Under the contract of sale, they did not sell or part with their interest in the Cabot contract. It was expressly reserved by them and was a distribution they received as stockholders by virtue of the reservation.

Coffey, 14 T.C. at 1417, 1418. The tax court held the distribution to be a dividend. [The court then discussed two other cases reaching the same conclusion on similar facts. Ed.] * * *

The Internal Revenue Service states that it does not disagree with the holdings in *Coffey, Gilmore* and *Rosenbloom,* but it takes the position that they do not apply in the circumstances of this case. The Internal Revenue Service focuses on the receipt by the selling stockholders of CLIC of investment assets, followed immediately by an infusion by Union Mutual of a like amount of investment assets into CLIC, and says that the reinfusion of assets brings the case before the court within the "conduit rationale" of *Waterman.* In *Waterman,* Waterman Steamship Corporation ("Waterman") was the owner of all the outstanding capital stock of Pan–Atlantic Steamship Corporation ("Pan–Atlantic") and Gulf Florida Terminal Company, Incorporated ("Gulf Florida"). Malcolm P. McLean made an offer to Waterman to purchase all the outstanding capital stock of Pan–Atlantic and Gulf Florida for $3,500,000. Since Waterman's tax basis for the stock of the subsidiaries totaled $700,000, a sale of the capital stock of the subsidiaries for $3,500,000 would have produced a taxable gain of approximately $2,800,000. Because the treasury regulations on consolidated returns provided that the dividends received from an affiliated corporation are exempt from tax, a sale of capital stock of the subsidiaries for $700,000, after a dividend payment to Waterman by the subsidiaries of $2,800,000, would, at least in theory, have produced no taxable gain. The Board of Directors of Waterman rejected McLean's offer, but authorized Waterman's president to submit a counter proposal providing for the sale of all the capital stock in the subsidiaries for $700,000, but only after the subsidiaries paid dividends to Waterman in the aggregate amount of $2,800,000. As finally consummated, the dividends and the sale of the capital stock of the subsidiaries took the following form:

(1) Pan–Atlantic gave a promissory note to Waterman for $2,800,000 payable in 30 days as a "dividend."

(2) One hour later, Waterman agreed to sell all of the capital stock of Pan–Atlantic and Gulf Florida for $700,000.

(3) Thirty minutes later, after the closing of the sale of the capital stock of the subsidiaries had occurred, Pan–Atlantic held a special meeting of its new Board of Directors, and the Board authorized Pan–Atlantic to borrow $2,800,000 from McLean and a corporation controlled by McLean. Those funds were used by Pan–Atlantic promptly to pay off the $2,800,000 note to Waterman (which was not yet due).

In its tax return for the fiscal year involved, Waterman eliminated from income the $2,800,000 received as a dividend from Pan–Atlantic and reported $700,000 as the sales price of the capital stock of the two subsidiaries. Since Waterman's tax basis for the stock was the same as the sales price therefor, no taxable gain was realized on the sale. On audit, the Internal Revenue Service took the position that Waterman had realized a long-term capital gain of $2,800,000 on the sale of the capital stock of the subsidiaries and increased its taxable income accordingly. On appeal from a judgment by the tax court in favor of the taxpayer, the Internal Revenue Service contended that the rules applicable to situations where a regular dividend has been declared are not applicable when the parties contemplate that a purported dividend is to be inextricably tied to the purchase price and where, as was the case before the court, the amount of the dividend is not a true distribution of corporate profits. The Internal Revenue Service argued that the funds were supplied by the buyer of the stock, with the corporation acting as a mere conduit for passing the payment through to the seller. This court agreed with the Internal Revenue Service:

> The so-called dividend and sale were one transaction. The note was but one transitory step in a total, pre-arranged plan to sell the stock. We hold that in substance Pan–Atlantic neither declared nor paid a dividend to Waterman, but rather acted as a mere conduit for the payment of the purchase price to Waterman.

Waterman, 430 F.2d at 1192. The opinion of this court began with this sentence:

> This case involves another attempt by a taxpayer to ward off tax blows with paper armor.

Id. at 1185. The opinion stressed the sham, tax motivated aspects of the transaction:

> Here, McLean originally offered Waterman $3,500,000 for the stock of Pan–Atlantic and Gulf Florida. Waterman recognized that since its basis for tax purposes in the stock was $700,180, a taxable gain of approximately $2,800,000 would result from the sale. It declined the original offer and proposed to cast the sale of the stock in a two step transaction. Waterman proposed to McLean that it would sell the stock of the two subsidiaries for $700,180 after it had extracted $2,800,000 of the subsidiaries' earnings and profits. It is undisputed that Waterman intended to sell the two subsidiaries for the original offering price—with $2,800,000 of the amount disguised as a dividend which would be eliminated from

income under Section 1502. Waterman also intended that none of
the assets owned by the subsidiaries would be removed prior to the
sale. Although the distribution was cast in the form of a dividend,
the distribution was to be financed by McLean with payment being
made to Waterman through Pan–Atlantic. To inject substance into
the form of the transaction, Pan–Atlantic issued its note to Waterman before the closing agreement was signed. The creation of a
valid indebtedness however, cannot change the true nature of the
transaction. * * *

* * *

The form of the transaction used by the parties is relatively
unimportant, for the true substance and effect of their agreement
was that McLean would pay $3,500,000 for all of the assets, rights
and liabilities represented by the stock of Pan–Atlantic and Gulf
Florida.

Id. at 1194–95. This court concluded its opinion in *Waterman* by cautioning
against "giving force to 'a purported [dividend] which gives off an unmistakably hollow sound when it is tapped.' " Id. at 1196 (quoting United
States v. General Geophysical Co., 296 F.2d 86, 89 (5th Cir.1961), cert.
denied, 369 U.S. 849, 82 S.Ct. 932, 8 L.Ed.2d 8 (1962)). A final footnote to
the opinion stated that the decision should not be interpreted as standing
for the proposition that a corporation which is contemplating a sale of its
subsidiary's stock could not under any circumstances distribute its subsidiaries' profits prior to the sale without having such distribution deemed
part of the purchase price. Id. at 1196 n. 21.

In summary, in *Waterman,* the substance of the transaction, and the
way in which it was originally negotiated, was that the purchaser would
pay $3,500,000 of its money to the seller in exchange for all the stock of the
two subsidiaries and none of the assets of those subsidiaries was to be
removed and retained by the sellers. In the case before the court, the
district court found that Union Mutual did not want and would not pay for
the assets of CLIC which were distributed to TSN and the other stockholders of CLIC. Those assets were retained by the selling stockholders. The
fact that bonds and cash were reinfused into CLIC after the closing, in lieu
of the unwanted capital stock of small, publicly held corporations, does not
convert this case from a *Coffey* situation, in which admittedly unwanted
assets were distributed by the corporation to its stockholders and retained
by them, into a *Waterman* situation, in which the distribution of assets was
clearly a sham, designed solely to achieve a tax free distribution of assets
ultimately funded by the purchaser. Indeed, the Internal Revenue Service
does not argue, in the case before the court, that the transaction was in any
respect a sham. Instead, the Service would have us hold that the mere
infusion of assets into the acquired company after the closing, assets which
are markedly different in kind from the assets that were distributed prior
to the closing, should result in the disallowance of dividend treatment for
the distribution of the unwanted assets, and the Service cites *Waterman* as
authority for that proposition. We view the sham aspect—the hollow

sound—of the transaction described in *Waterman* as one of the critical aspects of that decision, and we decline to extend the *Waterman* rule to a case which admittedly does not involve a sham and which, in other important respects, is factually different from *Waterman*.

The Internal Revenue Service also cites *Basic* as authority for the disallowance of dividend treatment for the distribution of the unwanted assets in this case. * * * [The court distinguished the Court of Claims decision in *Basic* on the ground that the asset distributed as a pre-sale dividend in *Basic* was promptly transferred to the buyer while in this case the distributed assets were retained by the target corporation's shareholders. Ed.]

As additional support for its position, the court in *Basic* focused on the absence of a business purpose, viewed from the standpoint of Falls, for the payment of a dividend of a valuable corporate asset, i.e., the capital stock of Carbon, by Falls to Basic. The district court, in the case before this court, applied the same test to the payment of the dividend of the unwanted assets by CLIC to TSN, the controlling stockholder of CLIC, and found that, strictly from the standpoint of CLIC, the dividend was lacking in business purpose and, indeed, could not have taken place apart from the sale and the subsequent infusion of investment assets into CLIC by Union Mutual. However, it seems to us to be inconsistent to take the position that substance must control over form and that a transaction must be viewed as a whole, rather than in parts, and at the same time to state that the business purpose of one participant in a multi-party transaction (particularly where the participant is a corporation controlled by the taxpayer and is not itself a party to the sale transaction) is to be viewed in isolation from the over-all business purpose for the entire transaction. We agree that the transaction must be viewed as a whole and we accept the district court's finding of fact that the dividend of the unwanted assets was "part and parcel of the purchase arrangement with Union Mutual," motivated specifically by Union Mutual's unwillingness to take and pay for such assets. That being the case, we decline to focus on the business purpose of one participant in the transaction—a corporation controlled by the taxpayer—and instead find that the business purpose for the transaction as a whole, viewed from the standpoint of the taxpayer, controls. The facts found by the district court clearly demonstrate a business purpose for the presale dividend of the unwanted assets which fully explains that dividend. We note that there is no suggestion in the district court's opinion of any tax avoidance motivation on the part of the taxpayer TSN. The fact that the dividend may have had incidental tax benefit to the taxpayer, without more, does not necessitate the disallowance of dividend treatment.

Having concluded that the pre-sale distribution by CLIC to its stockholders (including TSN) of assets which Union Mutual did not want, would not pay for and did not ultimately receive is a dividend for tax purposes, and not part of the purchase price of the capital stock of CLIC, we reverse the judgment of the district court and remand for proceedings consistent with this opinion.

Reversed and remanded.

NOTE

Life is not as simple today as it was when the successful tax plan in *TSN Liquidating* was concocted. Several additional provisions of the Code now must be considered in evaluating the continuing viability of a pre-sale distribution of unwanted assets by a corporate shareholder.

As noted earlier,[1] Section 301(e) requires, solely for purposes of computing the amount of any taxable dividend income to a 20 percent or more corporate shareholder and the shareholder's basis in the stock of the distributing corporation, that the distributing corporation's earnings and profits must be determined without regard to the special adjustments in Sections 312(k) and 312(n). Section 301(e), however, will not necessarily impair the technique used in *TSN Liquidating;* it merely limits the utility of pre-acquisition dividend strips to situations where the distributing corporation has substantial earnings and profits before the required earnings and profits timing adjustments.

A more serious impediment is the possibility of a downward adjustment in the basis of the corporate shareholder's stock as a result of the pre-sale dividend. If TSN had been required to reduce the basis in its CLIC stock by the amount of the dividends received deduction that it was allowed on the distribution, the transaction would have lost its allure. A basis reduction would have placed TSN in the position of trading a dollar of dividend income for a dollar of gain on the subsequent sale of its CLIC stock. Since corporations do not enjoy a capital gains preference, they usually are indifferent to the distinction between ordinary income and capital gain.[2] Does current law cause TSN to suffer a basis reduction as a result of the pre-sale dividend? The answer is no unless the distribution is subject to Section 1059. That section requires a basis reduction for the amount of any "extraordinary dividend" which was not taxed to a corporate shareholder because of the dividends received deduction where the stock has not been held for more than two years before the announcement of the dividend.[3] Because of its size (roughly $1.67 million, according to the facts of the case), the dividend to TSN appears to be "extraordinary" under the tests in Section 1059(c). But TSN nonetheless could have avoided any basis reduction if it had held its CLIC stock for more than two years before the dividend was announced.

One final obstacle must be mentioned in the interests of full disclosure. If TSN and CLIC were affiliated corporations and elected to file a consolidated tax return,[4] TSN would have been required to reduce its basis in the

---

1.   See Section F5 of this chapter, supra.

2.   Other tax attributes, however, might cause TSN to prefer one or the other type of income. For example, if TSN had unused capital losses, it might prefer capital gains on the sale to fully taxable dividend income.

3.   I.R.C. § 1059(a). See Section F3 of this chapter, supra.

4.   See Chapter 13, supra.

CLIC stock as a result of the dividend. The consolidated return regulations, which treat an "affiliated group" as a single taxpaying entity, logically eliminate intracorporate dividends from the consolidated group's joint gross income.[5] The dividend is considered a mere reshuffling of profits within a single taxpayer which should not generate additional income. The regulations also provide that a parent's basis in the stock of a subsidiary is generally reduced by the full amount of any excluded intercompany dividend.[6] It follows that the strategy employed in *TSN Liquidating* has no appeal in the context of a consolidated group.

Despite these technical hurdles, a pre-sale dividend is still viable if the selling parent corporation has held the stock of a subsidiary for more than two years and the corporations do not file a consolidated return. The Tax Court's decision in Litton Industries, Inc. v. Commissioner[7] illustrates the importance of form and timing to the success of this technique. The issue in *Litton* was whether a $30 million dividend, paid to Litton by a wholly owned subsidiary in the form of a negotiable promissory note five months prior to Litton's sale of the subsidiary's stock to Nestle Corporation, was truly a dividend rather than part of the proceeds received by Litton on the sale of the stock. The promissory note was later satisfied by Nestle at the same time that it purchased the stock. Dividend treatment was preferable to Litton because of the shelter provided by what was then an 85 percent dividends received deduction.

Distinguishing Waterman Steamship Corp. v. Commissioner[8] (discussed in *TSN Liquidating* at pages 186–189 of the text, supra), the Tax Court held that the payment was a dividend. Favorable (and distinguishing) factors were: (1) unlike *Waterman Steamship,* the dividend and subsequent sale in *Litton* were substantially separated in time (over five months in *Litton* was better than the few hours in *Waterman*); (2) at the time the dividend was declared, no formal action had been taken by the parent to initiate a sale to Nestle and "[t]here was no definite purchaser waiting in the wings with the terms and conditions of sale already agreed upon;"[9] and (3) as in *TSN Liquidating,* the overall transaction was not a sham because a business purpose was served by the dividend. In rejecting the Service's contention that the dividend and subsequent sale of the subsidiary should be treated as one transaction for tax purposes, the court reasoned:[10]

> The term "dividend" is defined in section 316(a) as a distribution by a corporation to its shareholders out of earnings and profits. The parties have stipulated that Stouffer had earnings and profits exceeding $30 million at the time the dividend was declared. This Court has recognized that a dividend may be paid by a note. T.R. Miller Mill Co. v. Commissioner, 37 B.T.A. 43, 49 (1938), affd. 102 F.2d 599 (5th Cir.1939). Based on these criteria, the $30 million distribution by Stouffer would clearly constitute a

5.   Reg. § 1.1502–13(f)(2)(ii).

6.   Reg. § 1.1502–32(b)(2), (3)(v).

7.   89 T.C. 1086 (1987).

8.   430 F.2d 1185 (5th Cir.1970).

9.   89 T.C. at 1099.

10.   Id. at 1099–1100.

dividend if the sale of Stouffer had not occurred. We are not persuaded that the subsequent sale of Stouffer to Nestle changes that result merely because it was more advantageous to Litton from a tax perspective.

It is well established that a taxpayer is entitled to structure his affairs and transactions in order to minimize his taxes. This proposition does not give a taxpayer carte blanche to set up a transaction in any form which will avoid tax consequences, regardless of whether the transaction has substance. Gregory v. Helvering, 293 U.S. 465 (1935). A variety of factors present here preclude a finding of sham or subterfuge. Although the record in this case clearly shows that Litton intended at the time the dividend was declared to sell Stouffer, no formal action had been taken and no announcement had been made. There was no definite purchaser waiting in the wings with the terms and conditions of sale already agreed upon. At that time, Litton had not even decided upon the form of sale of Stouffer. Nothing in the record here suggests that there was any prearranged sale agreement, formal or informal, at the time the dividend was declared.

Petitioner further supports its argument that the transaction was not a sham by pointing out Litton's legitimate business purposes in declaring the dividend. Although the code and case law do not require a dividend to have a business purpose, it is a factor to be considered in determining whether the overall transaction was a sham. T.S.N. Liquidating Corp. v. United States, 624 F.2d 1328 (5th Cir.1980). Petitioner argues that the distribution allowed Litton to maximize the gross after-tax amount it could receive from its investment in Stouffer. From the viewpoint of a private purchaser of Stouffer, it is difficult to see how the declaration of a dividend would improve the value of the stock since creating a liability in the form of a promissory note for $30 million would reduce the value of Stouffer by approximately that amount. However, since Litton was considering disposing of all or part of Stouffer through a public or private offering, the payment of a dividend by a promissory note prior to any sale had two advantages. First, Litton hoped to avoid materially diminishing the market value of the Stouffer stock. At that time, one of the factors considered in valuing a stock, and in determining the market value of a stock was the "multiple of earnings" criterion. Payment of the dividend by issuance of a promissory note would not substantially alter Stouffer's earnings. Since many investors were relatively unsophisticated, Litton may have been quite right that it could increase its investment in Stouffer by at least some portion of the $30 million dividend. Second, by declaring a dividend and paying it by a promissory note prior to an anticipated public offering, Litton could avoid sharing the earnings with future additional shareholders while not diminishing to the full extent of the pro rata dividend, the amount received for the stock. Whether Litton could have come out ahead after Stouffer paid the promissory note is at this point merely speculation about a public offering which never occurred. The point, however, is that Litton hoped to achieve some business purpose, and not just tax benefits, in structuring the transaction as it did.

Under these facts, where the dividend was declared 6 months prior to the sale of Stouffer, where the sale was not prearranged, and since Stouffer had earnings and profits exceeding $30 million at the time the dividend was declared, we cannot conclude that the distribution was merely a device designed to give the appearance of a dividend to a part of the sales proceeds. In this case, the form and substance of the transaction coincide; it was not a transaction entered into solely for tax reasons, and it should be recognized as structured by petitioner.

PROBLEM

Strap Corporation is the sole shareholder of X, Inc. Strap and X do not file a consolidated return, and Strap has held its X stock for more than two years. Strap has a $150,000 basis in its X stock. Boot is a prospective buyer and is willing to purchase all of the X stock, but he is unable to pay the $500,000 price demanded by Strap even though he believes it to be fair. X has $100,000 cash on hand and an ample supply of earnings and profits. To solve these problems, the parties have agreed on the following plan: Strap Corporation will cause X, Inc. to distribute $100,000 to it as a dividend. Promptly thereafter, Strap will sell its X stock to Boot for $400,000. What are the tax consequences of this plan? What if Strap were an individual rather than a corporation?

CHAPTER 5

REDEMPTIONS AND PARTIAL LIQUIDATIONS

A. INTRODUCTION

Code: §§ 302; 317(b).

Proposed Regulations: § 1.302–5(a)(1) & (3), –5(b)(4)(i).

The Logic of Section 302. Shareholders generally recognize a capital gain or loss on the sale of all or part of their stock. Assume, for example, that A purchased 100 shares of X Corporation stock two years ago for $1,000. If A sells 50 of those shares to B, an unrelated outsider, for $750, he will recognize a $250 long-term capital gain. But what if A made the same sale to the corporation? Should that transaction, known as a redemption, also generate a $250 long-term capital gain? We need more facts to answer the question. If A is one of several X shareholders and owns a small percentage of the corporation's stock, a sale of stock to the corporation may be similar (for tax purposes) to a sale to B. But if X has few shareholders and ample earnings and profits and A is a major shareholder, the transaction begins to resemble a dividend.

To illustrate, assume that A's 100 shares constitute all of X Corporation's outstanding stock. In that event, A's "sale" of 50 shares to the corporation in exchange for $750 cash is indistinguishable from a nonliquidating distribution of $750. Although A has surrendered a stock certificate for 50 shares, his proportionate interest in the corporation remains unchanged. When the smoke clears, A continues to control all corporate decisions and he remains the sole shareholder, entitled to 100 percent of X's net assets upon a liquidation. Yet without altering his interest in the business, A has extracted $750 from the corporate coffers. This is the essence of a dividend! But if the "sale" to X were respected, A would be permitted to use a proportionate amount of his stock basis ($500) to offset an equivalent amount of income, and any resulting gain will be taxed at capital gains rates. If A were permitted to avoid dividend characterization with such ease, proportionate redemption programs by shareholders of closely held corporations quickly would become a national sport whenever dividends are taxed at higher rates than capital gains or shareholders have a substantial basis in their stock.

These simple examples identify the fundamental problem in determining the shareholder level tax consequences of a redemption. A line must be drawn between redemptions having the effect of a dividend—that is, transactions that enable shareholders to withdraw cash or other property while leaving their proportionate interest intact—and redemptions that resemble sales because they result in a meaningful reduction in the shareholder's proportionate interest. In the now distant past, the Code had only one vague standard to resolve this question. A redemption was treated as an operating distribution and taxed as a dividend to the extent of the corporation's current and accumulated earnings and profits unless it was not "essentially equivalent to a taxable dividend."[1] Cases were resolved by looking to all the facts and circumstances, including the corporation's "business purpose" and the "net effect" of the transaction.[2]

The enactment of Section 302 introduced a commendable degree of certainty in an area where predictions had been precarious. Section 302(a) provides that a redemption will be treated as an "exchange" if it satisfies one of four statutory tests in Section 302(b). "Exchange" status means that the shareholder generally will recognize capital gain or loss to the extent of the difference between the amount of the distribution and the shareholder's basis in the redeemed stock. A redemption falling outside of Section 302(b) is treated under Section 302(d) as a "distribution to which Section 301 applies." Under the rules studied in the preceding chapter, the distribution will be a dividend to the extent of the corporation's current and accumulated earnings and profits, then a return of capital to the extent of the shareholder's basis in the redeemed stock, and finally gain from the sale or exchange of the stock to the extent of any balance.

Section 302(b) is thus the nerve center for determining the shareholder-level tax consequences of a redemption and the principal focus of this chapter. Three of the five statutory tests (Sections 302(b)(1)–(3)) examine whether there has been a sufficient reduction in the shareholder's ownership interest in the corporation to justify treating the redemption as an exchange. To obtain a more accurate measure, the shareholder's interest before and after the redemption is determined after application of the constructive ownership rules in Section 318.[3] Section 302(b)(4) shifts the focus to the corporate level and provides exchange treatment for any distribution that qualifies as a "partial liquidation" under Section 302(e) because it involves a genuine contraction of the distributing corporation's business. Finally, Section 302(b)(5) provides that redemptions by a mutual fund or real estate investment trust generally will be treated as an exchange.

Basis Consequences. If a redemption is treated as a sale, the basis of the redeemed stock is taken into account in determining the shareholder's gain or loss. If a redemption is treated as a dividend, the regulations

---

1. Internal Revenue Code of 1939, § 115(g).

2. See Bittker & Eustice, Federal Income Taxation of Corporations and Shareholders ¶ 9.01. Another line of authority treated a redemption as not "essentially equivalent to a taxable dividend" if it involved a contraction in the corporation's business activities. This test focused on events at the corporate rather than the shareholder level and gave birth to the tax concept known as a "partial liquidation." The remnants of this concept are considered in Section F of this chapter, infra.

3. I.R.C. § 302(c)(1).

historically have provided that the shareholder's basis in the redeemed stock does not disappear but may be added to the basis of the shareholder's retained stock. If the shareholder no longer owns any stock after the redemption, the basis of the redeemed stock may be added to the basis of stock held by family members or entities whose stock was attributed to the redeemed shareholder under Section 318. The regulations have never been specific about how this basis shift should be allocated when there is more than one related shareholder.[4]

In 2009, the Service issued proposed regulations that, when finalized, will change these straightforward basis rules. The regulations are intended to combat abusive corporate tax shelter transactions (well beyond the scope of our coverage) that exploit the current rule by shifting basis from a foreign shareholder not subject to U.S. tax to a related U.S. taxpayer who then can utilize the additional basis to increase loss or reduce taxable gain.[5] They provide that when an amount received in a redemption is treated as a Section 301 distribution and less than all of the shares of a single class held by the shareholder are redeemed, any portion of the distribution that is not a dividend shall be applied to reduce the adjusted basis of each share held by the redeemed shareholder. This reduction is pro rata, share-by-share to all shares in the class of stock being redeemed, not just to the shares actually surrendered in the redemption.[6] And there's more, but it goes beyond the scope of sensible coverage in this chapter. The goal of the proposed regulations is to treat a dividend equivalent redemption similarly to a Section 301 distribution where no shares are surrendered.[7]

As for basis recovery on dividend equivalent redemptions where the redeemed shareholder surrenders all of its shares in a single class—the teaser often referred to as the "mystery of the disappearing basis"—the proposed regulations prevent a redeemed shareholder from transferring any unrecovered basis to another class of stock or to shares held by a related taxpayer. To prevent basis shifting, they require the unrecovered basis to remain with the redeemed shareholder by treating it as a loss on the disposition of the redeemed stock that must be deferred until the "inclusion date." The "inclusion date" is the date when the conditions for exchange treatment under Sections 302(b)(1), (2) or (3) are met, assuming the facts and circumstances existing at the end of that date had existed immediately after the redemption or, alternatively, when all shares of the issuing corporation (or its successor) become worthless within the meaning of Section 165(g).[8]

An example may help. Assume A owns 250 shares (25 percent) of X Corp. common stock (the only class outstanding) with a $40,000 adjusted basis. A receives $25,000 in redemption of all her shares. X has $100,000 of

4. Reg. § 1.302–2(c), providing for "proper adjustment of the remaining stock."

5. See Notice 2001–45, 2001–33 I.R.B. 129.

6. Prop. Reg. § 1.302–5(a)(1). This is preferable to limiting basis recovery to the shares actually surrendered in the redemption.

7. For an example, see Prop. Reg. § 1.302–5(e) Example 1.

8. Prop. Reg. § 1.302–5(b)(4).

accumulated and no current E & P. Assume further that the distribution is a dividend equivalent redemption because, as will become clear later in this chapter, the remaining X shares are attributed to A from family members or entities related to A. A has a $25,000 dividend. The proposed regulations treat A's $40,000 unrecovered stock basis as a deferred loss that may not be taken into account for tax purposes until the "inclusion date.". Assume that three years later, the remaining X shareholders sell their stock to a buyer unrelated to them or A. If that sale had occurred immediately after A's redemption, she A would have completely terminated her interest in X Corp. and qualified for exchange treatment under Section 302(b)(3). As a result, the date of the stock sale by the shareholders related to A is the "inclusion date," releasing A's $40,000 deferred loss, the character of which is determined as of the time of the redemption.[9] The regulations provide special inclusion date rules for corporate shareholders,[10] and the IRS is still thinking about how these rules should apply to partnerships, trusts and S corporations.

Tax Consequences to Distributing Corporation. Whether a redemption is treated as an exchange or a Section 301 distribution at the shareholder level, the tax consequences to the distributing corporation of a distribution of property in a redemption are governed by Section 311. The distributing corporation recognizes gain on a distribution of appreciated property, but it may not recognize loss on a distribution of property that has declined in value.[11]

Changing Stakes. The tax stakes on a redemption have changed considerably over the years. They are influenced by several variables, such as the type of shareholder (individual or corporate), the shareholder's basis in the redeemed stock, and the applicable tax rates for dividends and capital gains. For most of our tax history, noncorporate shareholders preferred a redemption to be treated as a sale of stock resulting in recovery of the shareholder's basis and recognition of more lightly taxed capital gain. Corporate shareholders prefer dividend treatment because they can shelter most of the distribution if they qualify for the dividends received deduction or completely exclude dividends received from other members of an affiliated group of corporations that file a consolidated tax return.

The introduction of a 15 percent maximum rate on qualified dividends altered the stakes for individual shareholders. As long as the dividend and long-term capital gains rates remain the same, the major advantage to treating a redemption as an exchange is the shareholder's ability to recover the basis of the redeemed stock in determining gain or loss. In some cases, this still provides an incentive to qualify a redemption as an exchange, but not as much as when exchange treatment offered both recovery of basis and

---

9.   Prop. Reg. § 1.302–5(d)(1). See also Prop. Reg. § 1.302–5(e) Example 4 (the example is more complicated than it needs to be; a simpler illustration of the inclusion date would have been preferable).

10.   Reg. § 1.302–5(b)(4)(ii).

11.   I.R.C. § 311(a), (b). For the details and the effect of a redemption on the distributing corporation's earnings and profits, see Section E of this chapter, infra.

a significant capital gains rate preference (as compared to dividends) and hardly at all where a noncorporate shareholder's stock basis is nominal. In special situations, such as where a shareholder has excess capital losses that will offset capital gains but not qualified dividends, on a deferred payment redemption where installment sale reporting under Section 453 would benefit the shareholder, or for foreign shareholders who may incur a withholding tax on U.S. dividends but not on capital gains, exchange treatment also will be preferable.

The Nontax Context. Redemptions are used to accomplish a variety of corporate and shareholder planning objectives. In the case of closely held corporations, a redemption may be the vehicle for a shift of corporate control or for the buyout of a dissatisfied or deceased shareholder. Stock redemptions by publicly traded companies also have become increasingly common transactions for corporations with spare cash that they prefer to distribute rather than reinvest in the business.[12] Keep these contexts in mind in studying the somewhat mechanical aspects of Section 302 at the beginning of this chapter. Later sections explore some of the planning opportunities provided by Section 302.

B.   CONSTRUCTIVE OWNERSHIP OF STOCK

Code: §§ 302(c)(1); 318.

Regulations: § 1.318–1(a), (b), –2, –3(a), (b), –4.

Any system that purports to measure the change in a shareholder's proportionate interest in a corporation would be ineffective if it failed to consider the holdings of closely related shareholders. Returning to our introductory example, assume that A and his daughter, D, each own 50 of the 100 outstanding shares of X Corporation and A sells 30 of his shares to the corporation for $450. A's actual percentage ownership drops from 50 percent (50 out of 100 shares) to 29 percent (20 out of 70 shares). Has he substantially reduced his proportionate interest? Looking only to A's *actual* ownership, the reduction is substantial, but the remaining shares are owned by a close relative. With appropriate skepticism, the drafters of the Code concluded that in determining stock ownership for purposes of the Section 302(b) tests for exchange treatment, an individual taxpayer or entity should be considered as owning stock owned by certain family members and related entities under elaborate attribution rules set forth in Section 318.[1]

Section 318 is one of several sets of constructive ownership rules in the Internal Revenue Code[2] and applies only when it is expressly made applica-

---

12. See Chapter 8F2, infra, which discusses the tax and nontax motivations for stock repurchases by public companies.

1. I.R.C. § 302(c)(1).

2. Other constructive ownership provisions include Sections 267(c), 341(e)(8), and 544.

ble by another provision of the Code.[3] Its principal role is in the redemption area, where it treats a taxpayer as "owning" stock that is actually owned by various related parties. The attribution rules in Section 318 fall into the following four categories.

1. *Family Attribution.* An individual is considered as owning stock owned by his spouse, children, grandchildren and parents. Siblings and in-laws are not part of the "family" for this purpose, and there is no attribution from a grandparent to a grandchild.[4]

2. *Entity to Beneficiary Attribution.* Stock owned by or for a partnership or estate is considered as owned by the partners or beneficiaries in proportion to their beneficial interests.[5] A person ceases to be a "beneficiary" of an estate for this purpose when she receives all property to which she is entitled (e.g., a specific bequest) and the possibility that she must return the property to satisfy claims is remote.[6] Stock owned by a trust (other than a qualified employees' trust) is considered as owned by the beneficiaries in proportion to their actuarial interests in the trust. In the case of grantor trusts, stock is considered owned by the grantor or other person who is taxable on the trust income.[7] Stock owned by a corporation is considered owned proportionately (comparing the value of the shareholder's stock to the value of all stock) by a shareholder who owns, directly or through the attribution rules, 50 percent or more in value of that corporation's stock.[8]

3. *Beneficiary to Entity Attribution.* Stock owned by partners or beneficiaries of an estate is considered as owned by the partnership or estate.[9] All stock owned by a trust beneficiary is attributed to the trust except where the beneficiary's interest is "remote" and "contingent." Grantor trusts are considered to own stock owned by the grantor or other person taxable on the income of the trust.[10] All the stock owned by a 50 percent or more shareholder of a corporation is attributed to the corporation.[11]

4. *Option Attribution.* A person holding an option to acquire stock is considered as owning that stock.[12]

These general rules are supplemented by a set of "operating rules" in Section 318(a)(5), which generally authorize chain attribution (e.g., parent

---

3. Section 318(b) contains a partial list of cross references to sections applying Section 318.

4. I.R.C. § 318(a)(1). Cf. I.R.C. § 318(a)(5)(B).

5. I.R.C. § 318(a)(2)(A).

6. Reg. § 1.318–3(a).

7. I.R.C. § 318(a)(2)(B).

8. I.R.C. § 318(a)(2)(C).

9. I.R.C. § 318(a)(3)(A).

10. I.R.C. § 318(a)(3)(B). Contingent interests are considered remote if the actuarial value of the interest is 5 percent or less of

the value of the trust property, assuming the trustee exercises maximum discretion in favor of the beneficiary.

11. I.R.C. § 318(a)(3)(C).

12. I.R.C. § 318(a)(4). "Options" have been interpreted to include warrants and convertible debentures. Rev.Rul. 68–601, 1968–2 C.B. 124. Even options that are exercisable after the lapse of a fixed period of time are considered as options from the time they are granted. Rev.Rul. 89–64, 1989–1 C.B. 91.

to child to child's trust) except that there can be no double family attribution (e.g., no attribution from parent to child to child's spouse) or "sidewise" attribution (e.g., stock attributed to an entity from a partner, beneficiary or shareholder may not be reattributed from that entity to another partner, beneficiary or shareholder).[13] In addition, option attribution takes precedence over family attribution where both apply.[14] For Section 318 purposes, an S corporation is treated as a partnership, and S corporation shareholders are treated like partners.[15]

The problems below test your ability to apply the attribution rules in some typical factual contexts.

PROBLEMS

1. Wham Corporation has 100 shares of common stock outstanding. Twenty-five shares are owned by Grandfather, 20 shares are owned by Mother (Grandfather's Daughter), 15 shares are owned by Mother's Daughter, 10 shares are owned by Mother's adopted Son, and the remaining 30 shares are owned by Grandmother's estate, of which Mother is a 50% beneficiary. One of Mother's cousins is the other beneficiary of the estate. Mother also has an option to purchase 5 of Son's shares. How much Wham stock do Grandfather, Mother's Daughter and Grandmother's estate own after application of § 318?

2. All the 100 shares of Xerxes Corporation are owned by Partnership, in which A, B, C and D (all unrelated to each other) are equal partners. W, A's wife, owns all of the 100 shares of Yancy Corporation.

  (a) How many shares, if any, of Xerxes Corporation are owned by A, W and M (W's mother)?

  (b) How many shares, if any, of Xerxes are owned by Yancy? Would Yancy constructively own any shares of Xerxes if W owned only 10 percent of Yancy?

  (c) How many shares, if any, of Yancy are owned by Partnership, B, C, D and Xerxes?

C. REDEMPTIONS TESTED AT THE SHAREHOLDER LEVEL

1. SUBSTANTIALLY DISPROPORTIONATE REDEMPTIONS

Code: § 302(b)(2).

Regulations: § 1.302–3.

---

13. I.R.C. § 318(a)(5)(A), (B), (C).

14. I.R.C. § 318(a)(5)(D).

15. I.R.C. § 318(a)(5)(E). This rule applies for purposes of attributing stock to and from the S corporation, but not for determining constructive ownership of stock in the S corporation. Id.

The virtue of Section 302(b)(2) is its certainty. If a shareholder's reduction in voting stock as a result of a redemption satisfies three mechanical requirements, the redemption will be treated as an exchange. To qualify as "substantially disproportionate," a redemption must satisfy the following requirements:

1. Immediately after the redemption, the shareholder must own (actually and constructively) less than 50 percent of the total combined voting power of all classes of stock entitled to vote,[1]

2. The percentage of total outstanding voting stock owned by the shareholder immediately after the redemption must be less than 80 percent of the percentage of total voting stock owned by the shareholder immediately before the redemption,[2] and

3. The shareholder's percentage ownership of common stock (whether voting or nonvoting) after the redemption also must be less than 80 percent of the percentage of common stock owned before the redemption.[3] If there is more than one class of common stock, the 80 percent test is applied by reference to fair market value.[4]

The attribution rules of Section 318 are applicable in measuring stock ownership for purposes of all these percentage tests.

To illustrate, assume Redeemer owns 60 percent of the common stock of a corporation which has only one class of stock outstanding. A redemption which reduces Redeemer's stock interest to a percentage below 48 percent would satisfy Section 302(b)(2). Below that level, Redeemer would own less than 50 percent of the corporation's total combined voting power, and his percentage of voting stock after the redemption (below 48 percent) would be less than 80 percent of his percentage of voting stock before the redemption (60 percent).

The regulations elaborate on the operation of Section 302(b)(2). Stock with voting rights only upon the happening of a specific event (e.g., a default in a payment of dividends on preferred stock) is not considered voting stock until the event occurs.[5] A redemption of solely nonvoting stock

---

1. I.R.C. § 302(b)(2)(B).

2. I.R.C. § 302(b)(2)(C). This requirement may be expressed by the following formula:

$$\frac{\text{Voting shares owned after redemption}}{\text{Total voting shares outstanding after redemption}} \text{ must be less than: } .80 \times \frac{\text{Voting shares owned before redemption}}{\text{Total voting shares outstanding before redemption}}$$

3. I.R.C. § 302(b)(2)(C).

4. The common stock cutback test is applied on an aggregate rather than a class-by-class basis. Thus, if a shareholder's aggregate reduction in all classes of common stock (measured by value) meets the percentage tests in Section 302(b)(2)(C), the redemption will be treated as an exchange even if the shareholder continues to own 100 percent of one class of outstanding common stock. Rev. Rul. 87–88, 1987–2 C.B. 81.

5. Reg. § 1.302–3(a).

will never satisfy Section 302(b)(2) because there will not be a sufficient reduction in the shareholder's interest in voting stock. But if a redemption qualifies as substantially disproportionate under Section 302(b)(2), a simultaneous redemption of nonvoting preferred stock (which is not Section 306 stock)[6] will be treated as an exchange.[7] The Service also has ruled that a redemption of voting preferred stock from a shareholder owning no common stock (either directly or by way of attribution) may qualify under Section 302(b)(2), even though the shareholder can not satisfy the 80 percent test relating to common stock.[8]

The substantially disproportionate redemption safe harbor does not apply to any redemption made pursuant to a plan which has the purpose or effect of a series of redemptions that, taken together, result in a distribution that is not substantially disproportionate with respect to the shareholder.[9] This statutory application of the step transaction doctrine is the subject of the ruling that follows.

Revenue Ruling 85–14

1985–1 Cum.Bull. 83.

ISSUE

Should qualification under section 302(b)(2) of the Internal Revenue Code of a redemption of one shareholder be measured immediately after that redemption, or after a second redemption of another shareholder that followed soon after the first redemption, under the following facts?

FACTS

X, a corporation founded by *A*, is engaged in an ongoing business. As of January 1, 1983, *X*'s sole class of stock, voting common stock, was held by *A, B, C,* and *D,* who are unrelated to each other. *A* owned 1,466 shares, *B* owned 210 shares, *C* owned 200 shares, and *D* owned 155 shares of *X* stock. *A* was president and *B* was vice-president of *X*.

X has a repurchase agreement with all *X* shareholders, except *A*. This agreement provides that if any such shareholder ceases to be actively connected with the business operations of *X*, such shareholder must promptly tender to *X* the then-held *X* shares for an amount equal to the book value of such stock. *X* has a reciprocal obligation to purchase such shares at book value within 6 months of such shareholder's ceasing to be actively connected with *X*'s business operations.

On January 1, 1983, *B* informed *A* of *B*'s intention to resign as of March 22, 1983. Based on this information, *A* caused *X* to adopt a plan of redemption and to redeem 902 shares of *A*'s *X* stock, on March 15, 1983, for

---

6. See Chapter 6C, infra.

7. Reg. § 1.302–3(a).

8. Rev.Rul. 81–41, 1981–1 C.B. 121.

9. I.R.C. § 302(b)(2)(D).

which A received $700x$ dollars. Thus, A then held 564 shares of the 1129 shares (49.96 percent) of the X stock still outstanding, temporarily yielding majority control over the affairs of X until B ceased to be a shareholder. On March 22, 1983, B resigned from X and, in accordance with the X stock purchase agreement, X redeemed for cash all of B's shares within the next 6 months, thus leaving 919 shares of X stock outstanding, restoring majority control to A.

LAW AND ANALYSIS

Section 302(a) of the Code provides that if a corporation redeems its stock and if one of the paragraphs of subsection (b) applies, then such redemption will be treated as a distribution in part or full payment in exchange for the stock.

Section 302(b)(2) of the Code provides that a redemption will be treated as an exchange pursuant to section 302(a) if the redemption is substantially disproportionate with respect to the shareholder, but that this paragraph will not apply unless immediately after the redemption the shareholder owns less than 50 percent of the total combined voting power of all classes of stock entitled to vote.

Under section 302(b)(2)(C) of the Code, one of the requirements for the distribution to be substantially disproportionate is that the ratio that the voting stock of the corporation owned by the shareholder immediately after the redemption bears to all the voting stock of the corporation at such time, is less than 80 percent of the ratio that the voting stock of the corporation owned by the shareholder immediately before the redemption bears to all the voting stock of the corporation at such time.

Section 302(b)(2)(D) of the Code, in dealing with a series of redemptions, provides that section 302(b)(2) is not applicable to any redemption made pursuant to a plan the purpose or effect of which is a series of redemptions resulting in a distribution which (in the aggregate) is not substantially disproportionate with respect to the shareholder.

The percentage provisions contained in sections 302(b)(2)(B) and 302(b)(2)(C) of the Code provide "safe harbor" exchange treatment. Examined separately, the transaction that occurred on March 15, 1983, would qualify as a substantially disproportionate redemption because (i) A's ownership of X's voting stock immediately after the redemption was less than 50 percent of the total combined voting power of all the X stock and (ii) A's ownership of X's voting stock was reduced from 72.18 percent to 49.96 percent, which meets the 80 percent requirement of section 302(b)(2)(C). However, if A's redemption is considered to be part of a section 302(b)(2)(D) series of redemptions which included X's redemption of B's shares, then A's redemption would not constitute a substantially disproportionate redemption because (i) A's ownership of X's voting stock after the redemptions exceeded 50 percent of the total combined voting power of X and (ii) A's ownership of X's voting stock after the redemptions was reduced from 72.18 percent to 61.37 percent, which does not meet the 80 percent requirement of section 302(b)(2)(C).

Section 1.302–3(a) of the Income Tax Regulations states that whether or not a plan described in section 302(b)(2)(D) of the Code exists will be determined from all the facts and circumstances.

In the present situation, although A and B had no joint plan, arrangement, or agreement for a series of redemptions, the redemption of A's shares was causally related to the redemption of B's shares in that A saw an apparent opportunity to secure exchange treatment under section 302(b)(2) of the Code by temporarily yielding majority control over the affairs of X.

Nothing in section 302(b)(2)(D) of the Code or in the legislative history of this section * * * indicates that the existence of a plan depends upon an agreement between two or more shareholders. Thus, a "plan" for purposes of section 302(b)(2)(D) need be nothing more than a design by a single redeemed shareholder to arrange a redemption as part of a sequence of events that ultimately restores to such shareholder the control that was apparently reduced in the redemption.

Under the facts and circumstances here, section 302(b)(2)(D) of the Code requires that the redemptions of A and B be considered in the aggregate. Accordingly, A's redemption meets neither the 50 percent limitation of section 302(b)(2)(B) nor the 80 percent test of section 302(b)(2)(C). Thus, the redemption of A's shares was not substantially disproportionate within the meaning of section 302(b)(2).

HOLDING

Under the facts of this ruling, qualification under section 302(b)(2) of the Code of A's redemption should not be measured immediately after that redemption, but, instead, should be measured after B's redemption that followed soon after A's redemption.

PROBLEMS

1. Y Corporation has 100 shares of common stock and 200 shares of nonvoting preferred stock outstanding. Alice owns 80 shares of Y common stock and 100 shares of its preferred stock. Cathy owns the remaining 20 shares of Y common and 100 shares of Y preferred stock. Alice and Cathy are not related. In each of the following alternative situations, determine whether the redemption satisfies the requirements of § 302(b)(2):

   (a) On January 15, Y Corporation redeems 75 of Alice's preferred shares.

   (b) Same as (a), above, except that Y also redeems 60 shares of Alice's common stock.

   (c) Same as (a), above, except that Y also redeems 70 shares of Alice's common stock.

   (d) What difference would it make in (c), above, if, on December 1 of the same year, Y redeems 10 shares of Cathy's common stock?

2. Z Corporation has 100 shares of voting common stock and 200 shares of nonvoting common stock outstanding. Every share of Z common stock has a fair market value of $100. Don owns 60 shares of Z voting common stock and 100 shares of Z nonvoting common stock. Jerry owns all of the remaining Z stock. Don and Jerry are not related to one another. If Z redeems 30 of Don's voting common shares, will the redemption qualify for exchange treatment under § 302(b)(2)?

2.   COMPLETE TERMINATION OF A SHAREHOLDER'S INTEREST

a.   WAIVER OF FAMILY ATTRIBUTION

Code: § 302(b)(3), (c).

Regulations: § 1.302–4.

The theory of the substantially disproportionate safe harbor is that exchange rather than dividend treatment is appropriate when a distribution in redemption causes a significant reduction in the shareholder's interest in the corporation's voting stock. This policy applies with even greater force in the case of a complete termination of a shareholder's interest, which qualifies for exchange treatment under Section 302(b)(3). For shareholders of a closely held family corporation, however, the attribution rules present a substantial roadblock to a complete termination. Even if all of the stock of a retiring shareholder is redeemed, she will continue to be treated as a 100 percent owner if her children or other related parties hold the remaining shares.

To provide relief where the redeemed shareholder is willing to cut the corporate cord, Section 302(c)(2) eases the path toward a complete termination by waiving the family attribution rules if certain conditions are met. This attribution amnesty is a useful planning tool for shareholders of family corporations, permitting a shareholder to achieve a complete termination even though the remaining shares are held by close relatives. The waiver applies, however, only to *family* attribution; the entity and option attribution rules remain fully applicable.

Waiver of the family attribution rules is available only if immediately after the distribution the redeemed shareholder retains no "interest" in the corporation (other than as a creditor). The ban extends to interests as an officer, director or employee. Section 302(c)(2)(A) also includes a "ten year look forward" rule, under which the shareholder may not retain or acquire (other than by bequest or inheritance) any of the forbidden interests in the corporation "other than an interest as a creditor."[1] To prevent anticipatory bailouts, Section 302(c)(2)(B) provides a "ten year look back"

---

1. This rule is enforced by requiring the redeemed shareholder to file a form with his tax return in which the shareholder agrees to notify the Service of any acquisition of a forbidden interest within ten years from the redemption and to retain such records as may be necessary to permit enforcement of this rule by the Service. The normal three year statute of limitations is extended to one year after the shareholder gives notice of acquisition of a forbidden interest in order to permit the Service to make a retroactive assessment of a deficiency. I.R.C. § 302(c)(2)(A).

rule, under which the family attribution rules may not be waived if during the ten years preceding the redemption either: (1) the redeemed shareholder acquired any of the redeemed stock from a "Section 318" relative or (2) any such close relative acquired stock from the redeemed shareholder. Neither of these exceptions applies, however, if "tax avoidance" was not one of the principal purposes of the otherwise tainted transfer.

The materials that follow illustrate how the Service and the courts have interpreted these intricate requirements.

Lynch v. Commissioner

United States Court of Appeals, Ninth Circuit, 1986.
801 F.2d 1176.

■ CYNTHIA HOLCOMB HALL, CIRCUIT JUDGE:

The Commissioner of the Internal Revenue Service (Commissioner) petitions for review of a Tax Court decision holding that a corporate redemption of a taxpayer's stock was a sale or exchange subject to capital gains treatment. The Commissioner argues that the taxpayer held a prohibited interest in the corporation after the redemption and therefore the transaction should be characterized as a dividend distribution taxable as ordinary income. We agree with the Commissioner and reverse the Tax Court.

I

Taxpayers, William and Mima Lynch, formed the W.M. Lynch Co. on April 1, 1960. The corporation issued all of its outstanding stock to William Lynch (taxpayer). The taxpayer specialized in leasing cast-in-place concrete pipe machines. He owned the machines individually but leased them to the corporation which in turn subleased the equipment to independent contractors.

On December 17, 1975 the taxpayer sold 50 shares of the corporation's stock to his son, Gilbert Lynch (Gilbert), for $17,170. Gilbert paid for the stock with a $16,000 check given to him by the taxpayer and $1,170 from his own savings. The taxpayer and his wife also resigned as directors and officers of the corporation on the same day.

On December 31, 1975 the corporation redeemed all 2300 shares of the taxpayer's stock. In exchange for his stock, the taxpayer received $17,900 of property and a promissory note for $771,920. Gilbert, as the sole remaining shareholder, pledged his 50 shares as a guarantee for the note. In the event that the corporation defaulted on any of the note payments, the taxpayer would have the right to vote or sell Gilbert's 50 shares.

In the years immediately preceding the redemption, Gilbert had assumed greater managerial responsibility in the corporation. He wished, however, to retain the taxpayer's technical expertise with cast-in-place concrete pipe machines. On the date of the redemption, the taxpayer also entered into a consulting agreement with the corporation. The consulting agreement provided the taxpayer with payments of $500 per month for five years, plus reimbursement for business related travel, entertainment, and automobile expenses.[2] In February 1977, the corporation and the taxpayer mutually agreed to reduce the monthly payments to $250. The corporation never withheld payroll taxes from payments made to the taxpayer.

After the redemption, the taxpayer shared his former office with Gilbert. The taxpayer came to the office daily for approximately one year; thereafter his appearances dwindled to about once or twice per week. When the corporation moved to a new building in 1979, the taxpayer received a private office.

In addition to the consulting agreement, the taxpayer had other ties to the corporation. He remained covered by the corporation's group medical insurance policy until 1980. When his coverage ended, the taxpayer had received the benefit of $4,487.54 in premiums paid by the corporation. He was also covered by a medical reimbursement plan, created the day of the redemption, which provided a maximum annual payment of $1,000 per member. Payments to the taxpayer under the plan totaled $96.05.

II

We must decide whether the redemption of the taxpayer's stock in this case is taxable as a dividend distribution under 26 U.S.C. § 301 or as long-term capital gain under 26 U.S.C. § 302(a). Section 302(a) provides that a corporate distribution of property in redemption of a shareholder's stock is treated as a sale or exchange of such stock if the redemption falls within one of four categories described in section 302(b). If the redemption falls outside of these categories, then it is treated as a dividend distribution under section 301 to the extent of the corporation's earnings and profits.[4]

Section 302(b)(3) provides that a shareholder is entitled to sale or exchange treatment if the corporation redeems all of the shareholder's stock. In order to determine whether there is a complete redemption for purposes of section 302(b)(3), the family attribution rules of section 318(a) must be applied unless the requirements of section 302(c)(2) are satisfied. Here, if the family attribution rules apply, the taxpayer will be deemed to own constructively the 50 shares held by Gilbert (100% of the corporation's stock) and the transaction would not qualify as a complete redemption within the meaning of section 302(b)(3).

Section 302(c)(2)(A) states in relevant part:

In the case of a distribution described in subsection (b)(3), [the family attribution rules in] section 318(a)(1) shall not apply if—

2. The corporation leased or purchased a pickup truck for the taxpayer's use in 1977. If someone at the corporation needed the truck, the taxpayer would make it available to him.

4. On the date of the redemption, W.M. Lynch Co. had accumulated earnings and profits of $315,863, and had never paid a dividend.

> (i) immediately after the distribution the distributee has no interest in the corporation (including an interest as officer, director, or employee), other than an interest as a creditor * * *.

The Commissioner argues that in every case the performance of post-redemption services is a prohibited interest under section 302(c)(2)(A)(i), regardless of whether the taxpayer is an officer, director, employee, or independent contractor.

The Tax Court rejected the Commissioner's argument, finding that the services rendered by the taxpayer did not amount to a prohibited interest in the corporation. In reaching this conclusion, the Tax Court relied on a test derived from Lewis v. Commissioner, 47 T.C. 129, 136 (1966) (Simpson, J., concurring):

> Immediately after the enactment of the 1954 Code, it was recognized that section 302(c)(2)(A)(i) did not prohibit office holding per se, but was concerned with a retained financial stake in the corporation, such as a profit-sharing plan, or in the creation of an ostensible sale that really changed nothing so far as corporate management was concerned. Thus, in determining whether a prohibited interest has been retained under section 302(c)(2)(A)(i), we must look to whether the former stockholder has either retained a financial stake in the corporation or continued to control the corporation and benefit by its operations. In particular, where the interest retained is not that of an officer, director, or employee, we must examine the facts and circumstances to determine whether a prohibited interest has been retained under section 302(c)(2)(A)(i).

Lynch v. Commissioner, 83 T.C. 597, 605 (1984) (citations omitted).

After citing the "control or financial stake" standard, the Tax Court engaged in a two-step analysis. First, the court concluded that the taxpayer was an independent contractor rather than an employee because the corporation had no right under the consulting agreement to control his actions.[5] Second, the court undertook a "facts and circumstances" analysis to determine whether the taxpayer had a financial stake in the corporation or managerial control after the redemption. Because the consulting agreement was not linked to the future profitability of the corporation, the court found that the taxpayer had no financial stake. The court also found no evidence that the taxpayer exerted control over the corporation. Thus, the Tax Court determined that the taxpayer held no interest prohibited by section 302(c)(2)(A)(i).

---

5. Finding that the taxpayer was not an employee obviated the need to decide whether the parenthetical language in section 302(c)(2)(A)(i) prohibited employment relationships per se. See Seda v. Commissioner, 82 T.C. 484, 488 (1984) (court stated that "section 302(c)(2)(A)(i) may not prohibit the retention of all employment relationships").

III

* * *

We reject the Tax Court's interpretation of section 302(c)(2)(A)(i). An individualized determination of whether a taxpayer has retained a financial stake or continued to control the corporation after the redemption is inconsistent with Congress' desire to bring a measure of certainty to the tax consequences of a corporate redemption. We hold that a taxpayer who provides post-redemption services, either as an employee or an independent contractor, holds a prohibited interest in the corporation because he is not a creditor.

The legislative history of section 302 states that Congress intended to provide "definite standards in order to provide certainty in specific instances." S.Rep. No. 1622, 83d Cong., 2d Sess. 233, reprinted in 1954 U.S.Code Cong. & Ad.News 4017, 4621, 4870. "In lieu of a factual inquiry in every case, [section 302] is intended to prescribe specific conditions from which the taxpayer may ascertain whether a given redemption" will qualify as a sale or be treated as a dividend distribution. H.R.Rep.No. 1337, 83d Cong.2d Sess. 35, reprinted in 1954 U.S.Cong. & Ad.News 4017, 4210. The facts and circumstances approach created by the Tax Court undermines the ability of taxpayers to execute a redemption and know the tax consequences with certainty.

The taxpayer's claim that the Senate rejected the mechanical operation of the House's version of section 302 is misleading. The Senate did reject the House bill because the "definitive conditions" were "unnecessarily restrictive." S.Rep.No.1622, 83d Cong., 2d Sess. 44, reprinted in 1954 U.S.Code Cong. & Ad.News 4621, 4675. However, the Senate's response was to add paragraph (b)(1) to section 302, which reestablished the flexible, but notoriously vague, "not essentially equivalent to a dividend" test. This test provided that all payments from a corporation that were not essentially equivalent to a dividend should be taxed as capital gains. The confusion that stemmed from a case-by-case inquiry into "dividend equivalence" prompted the Congress to enact definite standards for the safe harbors in section 302(b)(2) and (b)(3). The Tax Court's refusal to recognize that section 302(c)(2)(A)(i) prohibits *all* noncreditor interests in the corporation creates the same uncertainty as the "dividend equivalence" test.

The problem with the Tax Court's approach is apparent when this case is compared with Seda v. Commissioner, 82 T.C. 484 (1984). In *Seda*, a former shareholder, at his son's insistence, continued working for the corporation for two years after the redemption. He received a salary of $1,000 per month. The Tax Court refused to hold that section 302(c)(2)(A)(i) prohibits the retention of employment relations per se, despite the unequivocal language in the statute.[6] Id. at 488. Instead, the court applied the facts and circumstances approach to determine whether

6. Eight of the seventeen Tax Court judges who reviewed *Seda* concurred in the result but would have classified all officer, director, or employee relationships as prohibited interests under section 302(c)(2)(A)(i).

the former shareholder retained a financial stake or continued to control the corporation. The Tax Court found that the monthly payments of $1,000 constituted a financial stake in the corporation. Id. This result is at odds with the holding in *Lynch* that payments of $500 per month do *not* constitute a financial stake in the corporation. Compare Lynch, 83 T.C. at 606–07 with Seda, 82 T.C. at 488. The court also found in *Seda* no evidence that the former shareholder had ceased to manage the corporation. 82 T.C. at 488. Again, this finding is contrary to the holding in *Lynch* that the taxpayer exercised no control over the corporation after the redemption, even though he worked daily for a year and shared his old office with his son. Compare Lynch, 83 T.C. at 607 with Seda, 82 T.C. at 488. *Seda* and *Lynch* thus vividly demonstrate the perils of making an ad hoc determination of "control" or "financial stake."

A recent Tax Court opinion further illustrates the imprecision of the facts and circumstances approach. In Cerone v. Commissioner, 87 T.C. 1 (1986), a father and son owned all the shares of a corporation formed to operate their restaurant. The corporation agreed to redeem all of the father's shares in order to resolve certain disagreements between the father and son concerning the management of the business. However, the father remained an employee of the corporation for at least five years after the redemption, drawing a salary of $14,400 for the first three years and less thereafter. The father claimed that he was entitled to capital gains treatment on the redemption because he had terminated his interest in the corporation within the meaning of section 302(b)(3).

Even on the facts of *Cerone,* the Tax Court refused to find that the father held a prohibited employment interest per se. * * * Instead, the Tax Court engaged in a lengthy analysis, citing both *Seda* and *Lynch*. The court proclaimed that *Lynch* reaffirmed the rationale of *Seda,* even though *Lynch* involved an independent contractor rather than an employee. After comparing the facts of *Seda* and *Cerone,* the Tax Court eventually concluded that the father in *Cerone* held a financial stake in the corporation because he had drawn a salary that was $2,400 per year more than the taxpayer in *Seda* and had been employed by the corporation for a longer period after the redemption. *Cerone,* slip op. at 53. However, the Tax Court was still concerned that prohibited interest in *Seda* might have been based on the finding in that case that the taxpayer had both a financial stake *and* continued control of the corporation. The Tax Court, citing *Lynch,* held that the "test is whether he retained a financial stake *or* continued to control the corporation." * * * Thus, the Tax Court found that the father in *Cerone* held a prohibited interest because he had a financial stake as defined by *Seda*.

Although the Tax Court reached the correct result in *Cerone,* its approach undermines the definite contours of the safe harbor Congress intended to create with sections 302(b)(3) and 302(c)(2)(A)(i). Whether a taxpayer has a financial stake according to the Tax Court seems to depend on two factors, length of employment and the amount of salary. Length of employment after the redemption is irrelevant because Congress wanted taxpayers to know whether they were entitled to capital gains treatment on the date their shares were redeemed. * * * As for the amount of annual salary, the Tax Court's present benchmark appears to be the $12,000 figure in *Seda*. Salary at or above this level will be deemed to be a financial stake in the enterprise, though the $6,000 annual payments in this case were held not to be a financial stake. There is no support in the legislative history of section 302 for the idea that Congress meant only to prohibit service contracts of a certain worth, and taxpayers should not be left to speculate as to what income level will give rise to a financial stake.

In this case, the taxpayer points to the fact that the taxpayers in *Seda* and *Cerone* were employees, while he was an independent contractor. On appeal, the Commissioner concedes the taxpayer's independent contractor status. We fail to see, however, any meaningful way to distinguish *Seda* and *Cerone* from *Lynch* by differentiating between employees and independent contractors. All of the taxpayers performed services for their corporations following the redemption. To hold that only the employee taxpayers held a prohibited interest would elevate form over substance. The parenthetical language in section 302(c)(2)(A)(i) merely provides a subset of prohibited interests from the universe of such interests, and in no way limits us from finding that an independent contractor retains a prohibited interest. Furthermore, the Tax Court has in effect come to ignore the parenthetical language. If employment relationships are not prohibited interests per se, then the taxpayer's status as an employee or independent contractor is irrelevant. What really matters under the Tax Court's approach is how the taxpayer fares under a facts and circumstances review of whether he has a financial stake in the corporation or managerial control.[7] Tax planners are left to guess where along the continuum of monthly payments from $500 to $1000 capital gains treatment ends and ordinary income tax begins.

Our holding today that taxpayers who provide post-redemption services have a prohibited interest under section 302(c)(2)(A)(i) is inconsistent with the Tax Court's decision in Estate of Lennard v. Commissioner, 61 T.C. 554 (1974). That case held that a former shareholder who, as an independent contractor, provided post-redemption accounting services for a corporation did not have a prohibited interest. The Tax Court found that "Congress did not intend to include independent contractors possessing no financial stake

---

7. The Tax Court's focus on managerial control or a financial stake originated with Judge Simpson's concurrence in *Lewis*, 47 T.C. at 136–38. His interpretation of section 302(c)(2)(A) is supported by Bittker, Stock Redemptions and Partial Liquidations Under the Internal Revenue Code of 1954, 9 Stan. L.Rev. 13, 33 n. 72 (1956). Professor Bittker argues that Congress' goal was to ensure that taxpayers who transferred only ostensible control or maintained a financial stake in the corporation did not receive the benefit of capital gains treatment. He is no doubt correct. However, the means selected by Congress to achieve this goal do not allow for an individualized determination of control and financial stakes. Instead, section 302(c)(2)(A)(i) operates mechanically: the taxpayer must sever all but a creditor's interest to avoid the family attribution rules and thereby receive capital gains treatment. Nowhere in the legislative history of section 302(c) does Congress intimate that courts may use a flexible facts and circumstances test to determine the existence of managerial control or a financial stake.

in the corporation among those who are considered as retaining an interest in the corporation for purposes of the attribution waiver rules." Id. at 561. We disagree. In the context of *Lennard,* the Tax Court appears to be using financial stake in the sense of having an equity interest or some other claim linked to the future profit of the corporation. Yet, in cases such as *Seda* and *Cerone,* the Tax Court has found that fixed salaries of $12,000 and $14,400, respectively, constitute a financial stake. Fees for accounting services could easily exceed these amounts, and it would be irrational to argue that the definition of financial stake varies depending on whether the taxpayer is an employee or an independent contractor. In order to avoid these inconsistencies, we conclude that those who provide post-redemption services, whether as independent contractors or employees, hold an interest prohibited by section 302(c)(2)(A)(i) because they are more than merely creditors.

In addition, both the Tax Court and the Commissioner have agreed that taxpayers who enter into management consulting contracts after the redemption possess prohibited interests. Chertkof v. Commissioner, 72 T.C. 1113, 1124–25 (1979), *aff'd,* 649 F.2d 264 (4th Cir.1981); Rev.Ruling 70–104, 1970–1 C.B. 66 (1970). Taxpayers who provide such services are, of course, independent contractors. However, unlike the Commissioner's opinion in Rev. Ruling 70–104 that all management consulting agreements are prohibited interests, the Tax Court applies the financial stake or managerial control test. In *Chertkof,* the court found that because the services provided under the contract "went to the essence" of the corporation's existence, the taxpayer had not effectively ceded control. 72 T.C. at 1124. Here, the Tax Court distinguished *Chertkof* on the ground that the taxpayer did not retain control of the corporation, but instead provided only limited consulting services. *Lynch,* 83 T.C. at 608. We believe that any attempt to define prohibited interests based on the level of control leads to the same difficulties inherent in making a case-by-case determination of what constitutes a financial stake.[8]

IV

Our decision today comports with the plain language of section 302 and its legislative history. See Gardner & Randall, Distributions in Redemption of Stock: Changing Definitions for a Termination of Interest, 8 J. Corp. Tax'n 240, 247–48 (1981); Marusic, The Prohibited Interest of I.R.C. Section 302(c)(2)(A)(i) After Seda and Lynch, 65 Neb.L.Rev. 486, 502, 518–19 (1986); Rose, The Prohibited Interest of Section 302(c)(2)(A), 36 Tax L.Rev. 131, 145–49 (1981). Taxpayers who wish to receive capital gains treatment upon the redemption of their shares must completely sever all

---

8. Determining the existence of control is particularly difficult in the context of a family-held corporation. The exercise of control often will not be obvious because a parent may influence a child, and hence corporate decisionmaking, in myriad ways. Our rule that the provision of services is a prohib-ited interest eliminates the need to make a speculative inquiry into whether the parent still controls the corporation after the redemption. Of course, no rule could or should prohibit post-redemption parent-child communication concerning the management of the corporation.

noncreditor interests in the corporation.[9] We hold that the taxpayer, as an independent contractor, held such a noncreditor interest, and so cannot find shelter in the safe harbor of section 302(c)(2)(A)(i). Accordingly, the family attribution rules of section 318 apply and the taxpayer fails to qualify for a complete redemption under section 302(b)(3). The payments from the corporation in redemption of the taxpayer's shares must be characterized as a dividend distribution taxable as ordinary income under section 301.

Reversed.

Revenue Ruling 59–119

1959–1 Cum.Bull. 68.

A stock redemption agreement between the corporation and the instant shareholder provides that a total of 350x dollars will be paid to such shareholder for all his stock interest in the corporation, 100x dollars to be paid on the closing date and 250x dollars to be paid by the corporation within eight years, payable in quarter-annual installments. The corporation executed an installment judgment note to the shareholder and the judgment note and shares of stock of the corporation to be redeemed are retained by an escrow holder as security for installment payments due. In the event the installment and interest payments are in default, then pursuant to the agreement the escrow holder, upon notice from the taxpayer, may sell the stock of the corporation held by him at public or private sale to satisfy such obligations, however, in no event will the taxpayer become the purchaser of said stock at such sale.

The stock redemption agreement also states that so long as the corporation owes funds to such shareholder it will not, without first receiving the written consent of the shareholder, declare dividends; pay salaries in excess of a certain amount to officers; sell its assets except in the ordinary course of business; or engage in a reorganization, recapitalization, merger, consolidation or liquidation.

Because of the substantial sums due the shareholder, because he plans to reside permanently in another state and will be far removed from the base of operations of the corporation, and pursuant to the advice of persons

---

9. Our definition of a prohibited interest still leaves an open question as to the permissible scope of a creditor's interest under section 302(c)(2)(A)(i). See, e.g., Treas. Reg. § 1.302–4(d) (a creditor's claim must not be subordinate to the claims of general creditors or in any other sense proprietary, i.e., principal payments or interest rates must not be contingent on the earnings of the corporation).

The taxpayer argues that some creditor relationships might result in an "opportunity

to influence" as great or greater than any officer, director, or employee relationship. He cites Rev.Ruling 77–467, 1977–2 C.B. 92 which concluded that a taxpayer who leased real property to a corporation, after the corporation redeemed his shares, held a creditor's interest under section 302(c)(2)(A)(i). While the taxpayer here may be correct in his assessment of a creditor's "opportunity to influence" a corporation, he overlooks the fact that Congress specifically allowed the right to retain such an interest.

skilled in creditor protection matters, he considers it advisable to have a member of the law firm representing him serve on the board of directors of the corporation. Therefore, the instant shareholder and the remaining shareholders, all related, entered into a second agreement whereby a nominee of his law firm will serve on the board of directors as long as the corporation is indebted to the shareholder. Such nominee will be paid x dollars by the corporation for each meeting he attends and such additional sums as determined in the sole discretion of the instant shareholder for other services which may be reasonably necessary to determine that his interests as a creditor are being protected in accordance with the agreements.

The sole purpose of this arrangement is to protect the shareholder as a creditor by determining that the aforementioned conditions are being met rather than running the risk of having to engage in extended litigation at some future date if it is then determined that the conditions of the stock redemption agreement were violated.

* * *

According to the agreement in question, the remaining shareholders and the instant shareholder will appoint, indirectly through the law firm representing such shareholder, a member of that law firm to serve on the board of directors of the corporation. Such a nominee director will be acting solely on the taxpayer's behalf and, therefore, will in effect be his agent. The fact that the nominee director will receive remuneration for his service from someone other than the taxpayer does not make him any less the taxpayer's agent, for the source of remuneration to an agent is only one factor to be considered in determining whether an agency exists between two parties. Such an appointment of an agent to the board of directors is contrary to the condition prescribed in section 302(c)(2) of the Code. For the purposes of section 302(c)(2), it is immaterial whether an interest in the corporation is asserted directly or through an agent.

The fact that the director is a "limited" director in that his only duty will be to determine whether the conditions set forth in the stock redemption agreement are being observed is not material, for section 302(c)(2) of the Code does not make any exception for such directors. Furthermore, that section of the Code does not make an exception for a director whose power is limited because he is a minority member of a board.

In view of the foregoing, it is held that the agreement between the instant shareholder and the remaining shareholders of the corporation, under which a nominee is appointed to serve on the board of directors of the corporation, violates the condition prescribed in section 302(c)(2)(A)(i) of the Code. Accordingly, in the event of such an agreement, the redemption of the taxpayer's stock of the corporation shall be treated as a distribution of property to which section 301 of the Code applies.

However, if the taxpayer-shareholder designates a representative of his law firm to attend the board of director's meetings of the corporation solely for the purposes of determining whether the provisions of the agreement described above have been complied with, and not in the capacity of a director, officer or employee, or advisor, such action will not adversely affect section 302(c)(2) of the Code.

Revenue Ruling 77–293

1977–2 Cum.Bull. 91.

Corporation X had 120 shares of common stock outstanding, all of which were owned by A, its president. A's son, B, had been employed by X for many years as its vice-president and general assistant to the president. Realizing that the future successful operation of X required a thorough knowledge of its operation, products lines, and customer needs, A had trained and supervised B in all phases of the business so that upon A's retirement B would be able to assume responsibility for managing the business.

As part of A's plan to retire from the business and to give ownership of the business to B, A gave 60 shares of X stock to B as a gift, and not as consideration for past, present, or future services. Shortly thereafter, A resigned and B assumed the position of chairman of the board and president of X. X redeemed the remaining 60 shares of stock owned by A in exchange for property. Immediately after the redemption, A was not an officer, director, or employee of X and no longer had any interest in X. A's gift of stock to B was for the purpose of giving B complete ownership and control of X. The earnings and profits of X exceeded the amount of the distribution in redemption of the X stock.

* * *

In the instant case, neither section 302(b)(1) of the Code nor section 302(b)(2) applies since A, through the constructive ownership rules of section 318(a), owned 100 percent of the stock of X both before and after the redemption. Therefore, there was no meaningful reduction under section 302(b)(1) or a substantially disproportionate reduction under section 302(b)(2) of A's stock ownership.

Section 302(c)(2)(A) of the Code provides that for purposes of section 302(b)(3), 318(a)(1) will not apply if (i) immediately after the distribution the distributee has no interest in the corporation (including an interest as an officer, director, or employee), other than an interest as a creditor, (ii) the distributee does not acquire any such interest (other than stock acquired by bequest or inheritance) within ten years from the date of such distribution, and (iii) the distributee files an agreement to notify the district director of any acquisition of any such interest in the corporation. However, pursuant to section 302(c)(2)(B)(ii), the provisions of section 302(c)(2)(A) are not applicable if any person owns (at the time of the distribution) stock the ownership of which is attributable to the distributee under section 318(a) and such person acquired any stock in the corporation, directly or indirectly, from the distributee within the ten-year period ending on the date of the distribution, unless such stock so acquired from the distributee is redeemed in the same transaction. However, section 302(c)(2)(B)(ii) will not apply if the disposition by the distributee did not have as one of its principal purposes the avoidance of Federal income tax.

The structure and legislative history of section 302 of the Code make it clear that the purpose of section 302(c)(2)(B) is not to prevent the reduction of capital gains through gifts of appreciated stock prior to the redemption of the remaining stock of the transferor, but to prevent the withdrawal of earnings at capital gains rates by a shareholder of a family controlled corporation who seeks continued control and/or economic interest in the corporation through the stock given to a related person or the stock he retains. Application of this provision thus prevents a taxpayer from bailing out earnings by transferring part of the taxpayer's stock to such a related person and then qualifying the redemption of either the taxpayer's stock or the transferee's stock as a complete termination of interest by virtue of the division of ownership thus created and the availability of the attribution waiver provisions.

Tax avoidance within the meaning of section 302(c)(2)(B) of the Code would occur, for example, if a taxpayer transfers stock of a corporation to a spouse in contemplation of the redemption of the remaining stock of the corporation and terminates all direct interest in the corporation in compliance with section 302(c)(2)(A), but with the intention of retaining effective control of the corporation indirectly through the stock held by the spouse. Another example, which would generally constitute tax avoidance within the meaning of this provision, is the transfer by a taxpayer of part of the stock of a corporation to a spouse in contemplation of the subsequent redemption of the transferred stock from the spouse. * * *

Whether one of the principal purposes of an acquisition or disposition of stock is tax avoidance within the meaning of section 302(c)(2)(B) of the Code can be determined only by an analysis of all of the facts and circumstances of a particular situation. Here, the gift of X stock by A was to B who is active and knowledgeable in the affairs of the business of X and who intends to control and manage the corporation in the future. The gift of stock was intended solely for the purpose of enabling A to retire while leaving the business to B. Therefore, the avoidance of Federal income tax will not be deemed to have been one of the principal purposes of the gift of stock from A to B, notwithstanding the reduction of the capital gains tax payable by A as a result of the gift of appreciated stock prior to the redemption.

Accordingly, if A files the agreement specified in section 302(c)(2)(A)(iii) of the Code, the redemption by X of its stock from A qualifies as a termination of interest under section 302(b)(3).

Rev.Rul. 57–387, 1957–2 C.B. 225, is modified to the extent that it contains implications to the contrary concerning the reduction of the capital gains tax.

NOTE

Ten–Year–Look–Forward Rule. The prohibition on retaining or acquiring any post-redemption "interest" (other than as a creditor or by bequest or inheritance) in the corporation is one of the major hurdles to utilizing Section 302(c)(2).[1] Until the Ninth Circuit's decision in *Lynch*, however, the courts often rejected the Service's strict view that *any* performances of services, with or without compensation, constitutes a forbidden corporate interest.[2]

The results are mixed in the many other factual contexts arising under the ten-year look-forward rule. The Service has ruled that a prohibited interest is obtained if the redeemed shareholder becomes a custodian under the Uniform Gifts to Minors Act or a voting trustee of corporate stock during the restricted ten year period.[3] But if the shareholder becomes executor of a deceased shareholder's estate and can vote the stock held by the estate, the protection of Section 302(c)(2) is still available by virtue of the exception for stock acquired by bequest or inheritance.[4] In Revenue Ruling 72–380,[5] the Service ruled that since a redeemed shareholder may reacquire a direct stock interest by bequest or inheritance, it was reasonable to permit "acquisition under identical circumstances of the significantly lesser interest embodied in the * * * right of an executor to vote stock in an estate * * *."[6] In Revenue Ruling 79–334[7] the same reasoning was applied to an appointment by will of a previously redeemed shareholder as a trustee of a trust. The ruling concludes that a redeemed shareholder may waive family attribution even though, as trustee, he can vote stock of the corporation in which he once had an interest.

Deferred Payment Redemptions. In the area of deferred payment redemptions, the Service and the courts have disagreed over what constitutes a complete termination of a shareholder's interest or the acquisition of a forbidden proprietary interest for purposes of the waiver of family attribution exception. The regulations provide that to be considered a creditor, the rights of the redeemed shareholder must not be greater than necessary to enforce the claim. An obligation may be treated as proprietary if it is subordinated to claims of general creditors, if payments of principal depend upon corporate earnings, or if the interest rate fluctuates with the corporation's success.[8] Acquisition of corporate property as a result of enforcement

---

1. See generally Rose, "The Prohibited Interest of Section 302(c)(2)(A)," 36 Tax L.Rev. 131 (1981).

2. Compare Rev.Rul. 56–556, 1956–2 C.B. 177 and Rev.Rul. 59–119, 1959–1 C.B. 68 with Estate of Lennard v. Commissioner, 61 T.C. 554 (1974), nonacq. 1978–2 C.B. 1, and Lewis v. Commissioner, 47 T.C. 129 (1966).

3. Rev.Rul. 81–233, 1981–2 C.B. 83; Rev.Rul. 71–426, 1971–2 C.B. 173.

4. I.R.C. § 302(c)(2)(A)(ii).

5. 1972–2 C.B. 201.

6. An executor who also becomes an officer of the corporation acquires a prohibited interest and loses Section 302(c)(2)'s protection. Rev.Rul. 75–2, 1975–1 C.B. 99.

7. 1979–2 C.B. 127.

8. Reg. § 1.302–4(d). A shareholder's ability to defer gain on a credit redemption under the installment method is a separate issue. First, the redemption must be treated as an exchange rather than a dividend. In addition, Section 453(k)(2)(A) denies use of the installment method for sales of stock or of rights as a creditor does not run afoul of Section 302(c)(2) unless the redeemed shareholder acquires stock in the corporation, its parent corporation, or a subsidiary.[9]

The standards applied by the courts to credit redemptions are not as rigid. In Dunn v. Commissioner,[10] a redemption agreement provided for postponement of principal and interest payments on corporate notes given in payment for the shareholder's stock if such payments would violate financial requirements in the corporation's franchise agreement with General Motors. The court concluded that the postponement provision did not require the notes to be classified as equity or give the shareholder an interest in the corporation other than as a creditor. In Estate of Lennard v. Commissioner,[11] the court found that a subordinated demand note, which was paid approximately three months after issuance, did not represent a proprietary interest in the corporation.

The Service has specific guidelines for granting a favorable ruling under Section 302. For example, it ordinarily will not rule on the tax consequences of a redemption of stock for notes when the note payment period extends beyond 15 years.[12] Nor will a ruling be issued under Section 302(b) if the shareholder's stock is held in escrow or as security for payments on corporate notes given as consideration for the redeemed stock because of the possibility that the stock may be returned to the shareholder as a result of a default by the corporation.[13]

Once again, however, the courts have been far more lenient. For example, in Lisle v. Commissioner[14] the Tax Court found a Section 302(b)(3) complete termination where the redeemed shareholders were to be paid for their stock over a 20 year period, the shareholders retained their voting rights pursuant to a security agreement, the stock was held in escrow and could be returned to the shareholders and the shareholders continued to serve as corporate directors and officers. The court concluded that the shareholders were directors and officers in name only and that, based upon the facts present in the case, the security provisions were not inconsistent with a finding that the transaction qualified as a complete redemption.

Other Post–Redemption Interests. The Service will permit a redeemed shareholder to lease property to the corporation on an arms length basis provided that the rental payments are not dependent on corporate earnings or subordinated to the claims of the corporation's general creditors.[15]

---

securities which are traded on an established securities market. This provision thus limits the tax advantage of deferral on a credit redemption to redemptions of stock in closely held corporations.

9. Reg. § 1.302–4(e).

10. 615 F.2d 578 (2d Cir.1980).

11. Note 2, supra.

12. Rev.Proc. 2012–3, § 4.01(20), 2012–1 I.R.B. 119.

13. Id. at § 3.01(31), 2012–1 I.R.B. 115.

14. 35 T.C.M. 627 (1976). The issue in *Lisle* was whether there was a complete termination of the shareholder's interest. The case did not involve a waiver of family attribution issue.

15. Rev.Rul. 77–467, 1977–2 C.B. 92.

Retention of Multiple Interests. A shareholder of a closely held corporation often will retain several different types of interests after a redemption. This raises the question of whether, in determining if the shareholder has retained a prohibited financial stake, we look to each separate economic relationship, or to the totality of continuing interests? In Hurst v. Commissioner,[16] the Tax Court rejected the Service's argument that multiple interests taken together can constitute a prohibited interest and concluded that each interest must be analyzed separately. The taxpayers in *Hurst* were a husband and wife who owned stock in two corporations ("A" and "B").[17] Mr. and Mrs. Hurst each were stockholders of A but only Mr. Hurst owned stock of B. To implement retirement and succession planning, they first sold their A stock to B. B then redeemed 90 percent of Mr. Hurst's B stock, and he sold the remaining 10 percent to his son and two unrelated parties. Both the redemption and sale provided for a 15–year payment term and the corporation's payment obligation was secured by the redeemed or sold B stock. The Hursts continued to own B's corporate headquarters, which they leased back to B; and Mrs. Hurst (remember, she was not a B shareholder) continued as a B employee. All the various agreements (stock purchase, redemption, lease, and employment contract) were cross-collateralized by Mr. Hurst's B stock.

The principal issue was whether the redemption of Mr. Hurst's B stock qualified as a complete termination under Section 302(b)(3) after application of the waiver of family attribution rules in Section 302(c). The Tax Court rejected the Service's arguments that the "total number of related obligations resulting from the transaction gave the [taxpayers] a prohibited interest" that was tantamount to a financial stake in the company's continued success. It held that Mr. Hurst did not retain any prohibited interests by virtue of the 15–year promissory notes (they were not tied to the corporation's financial performance, and using the stock as collateral was consistent with common practice), the lease (it had a fixed rent that was reasonable), or his wife's employment agreement (she owned no B stock, her compensation was not related to the corporation's financial performance, and there was no evidence that she was acting as a surrogate manager for her husband).

Although it involved taxable years before the effective date of the dividend rate reduction, *Hurst* is a good example of why, even apart from basis recovery, characterization still can matter under the current rate regime. Redemptions of closely held stock in the typical "family business" setting are frequently funded with installment notes. If the redemption is treated as an exchange under Section 302, installment sale reporting under Section 453 is available, but there is immediate gain recognition if the distribution is a dividend.

---

16. 124 T.C. 16 (2005).

17. The corporations were S corporations that formerly had been C corporations and, because they had accumulated earnings and profits from their C corporation days, the dividend vs. exchange issue was significant for tax purposes. See Chapter 15G, infra.

b. WAIVER OF ATTRIBUTION BY ENTITIES

Section 302(c)(2) only permits waiver of the *family* attribution rules and requires the "distributee" to file an agreement promising to notify the Service of the acquisition of a forbidden interest within the ten year period following the redemption. What if the redeemed shareholder is a trust, estate or other entity that completely terminates its *actual* interest in the corporation but continues to own shares attributed to a beneficiary from a related family member which then are reattributed from the beneficiary to the entity?[1] May the entity waive family attribution or is the waiver opportunity limited to individual shareholders?

At one time, the Service contended that only individuals could waive family attribution.[2] The Tax Court disagreed, however, holding that an estate or trust that completely terminated its actual interest in a redemption could waive family attribution from a family member to a beneficiary.[3] One appellate court, rejecting what it called a "crabbed reading" of the Code, even held that an entity could waive attribution from a beneficiary to the entity.[4] The problem with these decisions was that they did not prevent the beneficiary from acquiring an interest in the corporation during the ten years after the redemption or require an agreement from the beneficiary to notify the Service if such a forbidden interest were acquired.

Technical as it may seem, this issue was of considerable interest to shareholders of closely held corporations and their estate planners. The Service's rigid position often was an impediment to a redemption of the stock of an estate or trust where family members of the beneficiaries continued to own shares of the company. In the midst of continuing litigation, Congress enacted a special rule for waiver by entities, incorporating appropriate safeguards to preclude the beneficiaries from reacquiring an interest.[5] The Joint Committee on Taxation explained the rule as follows:[6]

> The Act permits an entity to waive the family attribution
> rules if those through whom ownership is attributed to the entity

1. For example, assume Mother's Estate, of which Father is the sole beneficiary, owns 50 of the 100 outstanding shares of X Corporation stock. The other 50 shares are owned by Child. If X redeems Estate's 50 shares, Estate continues to constructively own Child's 50 shares, which are attributed from Child to Father via family attribution and then reattributed from Father to Estate. May Estate break the family attribution chain in order to qualify the redemption as a complete termination?

2. Rev.Rul. 59–233, 1959–2 C.B. 106, Rev.Rul. 68–388, 1968–2 C.B. 122.

3. See Crawford v. Commissioner, 59 T.C. 830 (1973); Johnson Trust v. Commissioner, 71 T.C. 941 (1979); but see Metzger

Trust v. Commissioner, 76 T.C. 42 (1981), affirmed, 693 F.2d 459 (5th Cir.1982).

4. Rickey v. United States, 592 F.2d 1251 (5th Cir.1979). This remarkable example of "flexible" statutory construction was sharply criticized. See Andrews, "Comment: Estate Waiver of the Estate–Beneficiary Attribution Rules in Nonliquidating Redemptions Under Section 302 and Related Matters: The *Rickey* Case in the Fifth Circuit," 35 Tax L.Rev. 147 (1979).

5. I.R.C. § 302(c)(2)(C).

6. Staff of Joint Committee on Taxation, General Explanation of the Tax Equity and Fiscal Responsibility Act of 1982, 98th Cong.2d Sess. 146–47 (1982).

join in the waiver. Thus, a trust and its beneficiaries may waive family attribution to the beneficiaries if, after the redemption, neither the trust nor the beneficiaries hold an interest in the corporation, do not acquire such an interest within the 10–year period, and join in the agreement to notify the IRS of any acquisition. The entity and beneficiaries are jointly and severally liable in the event of an acquisition by any of them within the 10–year period and the statute of limitations remains open to assess any deficiency. The tax increase is a deficiency in the entity's tax but may be asserted as a deficiency against any beneficiary liable under the rules. Congress intended that the tax will be collected from a beneficiary only when it cannot be assessed against or collected from the entity, such as when the entity no longer exists or has insufficient funds. Further, it was intended that the tax will be assessed and collected from the beneficiary whose acquisition causes the deficiency before it is asserted against any other beneficiary.

Under the Act, only family attribution under Section 318(a)(1) may be waived by an entity and its beneficiaries. The waiver rules are not extended to waivers of attribution to and from entities and their beneficiaries (secs. 318(a)(2) and 318(a)(3)). The Act thus is intended to overrule Rickey v. United States, 592 F.2d 1251 (5th Cir.1979). Congress intended that the Act should not be construed to provide any inference as to whether the *Rickey* decision adopts a proper construction of prior law. Nor was any inference intended as to whether the other cases extending the waiver rules for family attribution to entities adopt a proper construction of prior law.

Certain anti-avoidance rules applicable where the redeemed stock was acquired by the distributee from a related party or a related party at the time of the redemption owns stock acquired from the distributee are extended to the entity and affected beneficiaries.

PROBLEMS

1. Randall Corporation is owned by John, John's daughter Alison and Alison's son Chuck. John owns 100 shares of Randall stock, Alison owns 50 shares and Chuck owns 25 shares. Consider whether the following redemptions (in year one) qualify as an exchange under 302(b)(3):

(a) Randall redeems Alison's entire 50 shares for cash.

(b) Same as (a), above, except that Alison fails to file the agreement required in § 302(c)(2)(A)(iii)? What is the purpose of this requirement?

(c) Same as (a), above, except the price paid for Alison's shares is contingent upon Randall's future profits?

(d) Randall redeems 20 of Alison's shares for cash on January 1 of year one and the remaining 30 shares for cash on January 1 of year two.

(e) Same as (a), above, except Alison remains as a director of Randall?

(f) Same as (a), above, except that, two years after the redemption, Randall forms a new subsidiary and Alison becomes an employee of the subsidiary?

(g) Same as (a), above, except that two years after the redemption Chuck dies and leaves his Randall shares to Alison?

2. The B & B Windshield Wiper Corporation ("B & B") was organized ten years ago by Betty and Billy, who are wife and husband. Betty and Billy formed B & B by transferring cash and other property to the corporation in exchange for 150 shares of the corporation's common stock. Betty and Billy own B & B's manufacturing plant and lease the plant to the corporation for an annual rental fee. B & B has been very successful and has a large amount of accumulated earnings and profits.

Five years ago, Betty and Billy's youngest Son, Junior, began working for B & B as a clerk in the domestic subcompact wiper division. Junior's managerial talents were quickly recognized and he has risen rapidly in B & B's corporate structure. Today, Junior is B & B's Vice President in charge of operations and has overall responsibility for production at B & B's manufacturing plant.

Shortly after Junior came to B & B, his parents agreed that he would eventually take over control and management of the company. Betty and Billy have now decided that the time has come to retire. To implement this decision, their accountant has suggested the following plan:

(1) Betty and Billy will give 30 of their 150 B & B shares to Junior to provide him with an ownership interest in the corporation.

(2) B & B will redeem Betty and Billy's remaining 120 shares for $50,000 plus a $400,000 B & B note paying market rate interest. The note will be payable monthly over a 20–year term and will be secured by an interest in the corporation's assets. Additionally, B & B will agree to restrict dividend payments, limit new indebtedness, and refrain from taking certain extraordinary corporate action (e.g., merger or liquidation) during the term of the note.

(3) Betty and Billy will continue to lease the manufacturing plant to B & B under a lease which has a rent escalation clause dependent upon the consumer price index. They also will grant B & B a five year option to purchase the plant at its appraised fair market value.

(a) Will Betty and Billy's redemption be classified as an exchange under Section 302(a)?

(b) Suppose Betty establishes a management consulting firm after leaving B & B. What would be the tax impact on the redemption if B & B hired Betty's firm to perform an analysis of its proposed entry into the Australian windshield wiper market?

3. Cinelab Corporation has 100 shares of common stock outstanding. John owns 50 shares and Mary, John's sister, owns 30 shares. The other 20 shares are owned by the Estate of Sam; Sam was John and Mary's father. Their mother, Bella, is the sole beneficiary of the estate. Consider the tax consequences of the following redemptions of Cinelab stock:

(a) Cinelab redeems Estate's 20 shares.

(b) Same as (a), above, except that Bella is the residuary beneficiary of the estate and John and Mary each receive specific legacies.

(c) Same as (a), above, except that John and Mary are the residuary beneficiaries of the estate.

(d) Same as (a), above, except the 20 shares were owned and redeemed from a trust established under Sam's will providing income to Bella for her life and the remainder to Nancy, another child of Sam and Bella. The life estate and remainder have equal actuarial values.

(e) Any change in the result in (d), above, if Nancy acquires stock in Cinelab three years after the redemption by the trust?

3.   REDEMPTIONS NOT ESSENTIALLY EQUIVALENT TO A DIVIDEND

Code: § 302(b)(1).

Regulations: § 1.302–2.

United States v. Davis

Supreme Court of the United States, 1970.
397 U.S. 301, 90 S.Ct. 1041, rehearing denied, 397 U.S. 1071, 90 S.Ct. 1495 (1970).

■ MR. JUSTICE MARSHALL delivered the opinion of the Court.

In 1945, taxpayer and E.B. Bradley organized a corporation. In exchange for property transferred to the new company, Bradley received 500 shares of common stock, and taxpayer and his wife similarly each received 250 such shares. Shortly thereafter, taxpayer made an additional contribution to the corporation, purchasing 1,000 shares of preferred stock at a par value of $25 per share.

The purpose of this latter transaction was to increase the company's working capital and thereby to qualify for a loan previously negotiated through the Reconstruction Finance Corporation. It was understood that the corporation would redeem the preferred stock when the RFC loan had been repaid. Although in the interim taxpayer bought Bradley's 500 shares and divided them between his son and daughter, the total capitalization of the company remained the same until 1963. That year, after the loan was fully repaid and in accordance with the original understanding, the company redeemed taxpayer's preferred stock.

In his 1963 personal income tax return taxpayer did not report the $25,000 received by him upon the redemption of his preferred stock as income. Rather, taxpayer considered the redemption as a sale of his preferred stock to the company—a capital gains transaction under § 302 of the Internal Revenue Code of 1954 resulting in no tax since taxpayer's basis in the stock equaled the amount he received for it. The Commissioner of Internal Revenue, however, did not approve this tax treatment. According to the Commissioner, the redemption of taxpayer's stock was essentially equivalent to a dividend and was thus taxable as ordinary income under §§ 301 and 316 of the Code. Taxpayer paid the resulting deficiency and brought this suit for a refund. The District Court ruled in his favor, 274 F.Supp. 466 (M.D.Tenn.1967), and on appeal the Court of Appeals affirmed. 408 F.2d 1139 (C.A.6th Cir.1969).

The Court of Appeals held that the $25,000 received by taxpayer was "not essentially equivalent to a dividend" within the meaning of that phrase in § 302(b)(1) of the Code because the redemption was the final step in a course of action that had a legitimate business (as opposed to a tax avoidance) purpose. That holding represents only one of a variety of treatments accorded similar transactions under § 302(b)(1) in the circuit courts of appeals. We granted certiorari, 396 U.S. 815 (1969), in order to resolve this recurring tax question involving stock redemptions by closely held corporations. We reverse.

I

The Internal Revenue Code of 1954 provides generally in §§ 301 and 316 for the tax treatment of distributions by a corporation to its shareholders; under those provisions, a distribution is includable in a taxpayer's gross income as a dividend out of earnings and profits to the extent such earnings exist. There are exceptions to the application of these general provisions, however, and among them are those found in § 302 involving certain distributions for redeemed stock. The basic question in this case is whether the $25,000 distribution by the corporation to taxpayer falls under that section—more specifically, whether its legitimate business motivation qualifies the distribution under § 302(b)(1) of the Code. Preliminarily, however, we must consider the relationship between § 302(b)(1) and the rules regarding the attribution of stock ownership found in § 318(a) of the Code.

Under subsection (a) of § 302, a distribution is treated as "payment in exchange for the stock," thus qualifying for capital gains rather than ordinary income treatment, if the conditions contained in any one of the four paragraphs of subsection (b) are met. In addition to paragraph (1)'s "not essentially equivalent to a dividend" test, capital gains treatment is available where (2) the taxpayer's voting strength is substantially diminished, [or] (3) his interest in the company is completely terminated. * * * [T]axpayer admits that paragraphs (2) and (3) do not apply. Moreover, taxpayer agrees that for the purposes of §§ 302(b)(2) and (3) the attribution rules of § 318(a) apply and he is considered to own the 750 outstanding shares of common stock held by his wife and children in addition to the 250 shares in his own name.

Taxpayer, however, argues that the attribution rules do not apply in considering whether a distribution is essentially equivalent to a dividend under § 302(b)(1). According to taxpayer, he should thus be considered to own only 25 percent of the corporation's common stock, and the distribution would then qualify under § 302(b)(1) since it was not pro rata or proportionate to his stock interest, the fundamental test of dividend equivalency. See Treas.Reg. 1.302–2(b). However, the plain language of the statute compels rejection of the argument. In subsection (c) of § 302, the attribution rules are made specifically applicable "in determining the ownership of stock for purposes of this section." Applying this language, both courts below held that § 318(a) applies to all of § 302, including § 302(b)(1)—a view in accord with the decisions of the other courts of appeals, a longstanding treasury regulation,[6] and the opinion of the leading commentators.[7]

Against this weight of authority, taxpayer argues that the result under paragraph (1) should be different because there is no explicit reference to stock ownership as there is in paragraphs (2) and (3). Neither that fact, however, nor the purpose and history of § 302(b)(1) support taxpayer's argument. The attribution rules—designed to provide a clear answer to what would otherwise be a difficult tax question—formed part of the tax bill that was subsequently enacted as the 1954 Code. As is discussed further, infra, the bill as passed by the House of Representatives contained no provision comparable to § 302(b)(1). When that provision was added in the Senate, no purpose was evidenced to restrict the applicability of § 318(a). Rather, the attribution rules continued to be made specifically applicable to the entire section, and we believe that Congress intended that they be taken into account wherever ownership of stock was relevant.

Indeed, it was necessary that the attribution rules apply to § 302(b)(1) unless they were to be effectively eliminated from consideration with regard to §§ 302(b)(2) and (3) also. For if a transaction failed to qualify under one of those sections solely because of the attribution rules, it would according to taxpayer's argument nonetheless qualify under § 302(b)(1). We cannot agree that Congress intended so to nullify its explicit directive. We conclude, therefore, that the attribution rules of § 318(a) do apply; and, for the purposes of deciding whether a distribution is "not essentially equivalent to a dividend" under § 302(b)(1), taxpayer must be deemed the owner of all 1,000 shares of the company's common stock.

II

After application of the stock ownership attribution rules, this case viewed most simply involves a sole stockholder who causes part of his shares to be redeemed by the corporation. We conclude that such a redemption is always "essentially equivalent to a dividend" within the

---

6. See Treas.Reg. 1.302–2(b).

7. See B. Bittker & J. Eustice, Federal Income Taxation of Corporations and Shareholders 292 n. 32 (2d ed. 1966).

meaning of that phrase in § 302(b)(1)[8] and therefore do not reach the Government's alternative argument that in any event the distribution should not on the facts of this case qualify for capital gains treatment.[9]

The predecessor of § 302(b)(1) came into the tax law as § 201(d) of the Revenue Act of 1921, 42 Stat. 228:

> "A stock dividend shall not be subject to tax but if after the distribution of any such dividend the corporation proceeds to cancel or redeem its stock at such time and in such manner as to make the distribution and cancellation or redemption essentially equivalent to the distribution of a taxable dividend, the amount received in redemption or cancellation of the stock shall be treated as a taxable dividend * * *."

Enacted in response to this Court's decision that pro rata stock dividends do not constitute taxable income, Eisner v. Macomber, 252 U.S. 189 (1920), the provision had the obvious purpose of preventing a corporation from avoiding dividend tax treatment by distributing earnings to its shareholders in two transactions—a pro rata stock dividend followed by a pro rata redemption—that would have the same economic consequences as a simple dividend. Congress, however, soon recognized that even without a prior stock dividend essentially the same result could be effected whereby any corporation, "especially one which has only a few stockholders, might be able to make a distribution to its stockholders which would have the same effect as a taxable dividend." H.R.Rep. No. 1, 69th Cong., 1st Sess., 5. In order to cover this situation, the law was amended to apply "(whether or not such stock was issued as a stock dividend)" whenever a distribution in redemption of stock was made "at such time and in such manner" that it was essentially equivalent to a taxable dividend. Revenue Act of 1926, § 201(g), 44 Stat. 11.

This provision of the 1926 Act was carried forward in each subsequent revenue act and finally became § 115(g)(1) of the Internal Revenue Code of 1939. Unfortunately, however, the policies encompassed within the general language of § 115(g)(1) and its predecessors were not clear, and there resulted much confusion in the tax law. At first, courts assumed that the provision was aimed at tax avoidance schemes and sought only to determine whether such a scheme existed. * * * Although later the emphasis changed and the focus was more on the effect of the distribution, many courts continued to find that distributions otherwise like a dividend were not "essentially equivalent" if, for example, they were motivated by a sufficiently strong nontax business purpose. See cases cited n. 2, supra.

---

8. Of course, this just means that a distribution in redemption to a sole shareholder will be treated under the general provisions of § 301, and it will only be taxed as a dividend under § 316 to the extent that there are earnings and profits.

9. The Government argues that even if business purpose were relevant under § 302(b)(1), the business purpose present here related only to the original investment and not at all to the necessity for redemption. Under either view, taxpayer does not lose his basis in the preferred stock. Under Treas. Reg. 1.302–2(c) that basis is applied to taxpayer's common stock.

There was general disagreement, however, about what would qualify as such a purpose, and the result was a case-by-case determination with each case decided "on the basis of the particular facts of the transaction in question." Bains v. United States, 289 F.2d 644, 646, 153 Ct.Cl. 599, 603 (1961).

By the time of the general revision resulting in the Internal Revenue Code of 1954, the draftsmen were faced with what has aptly been described as "the morass created by the decisions." Ballenger v. United States, 301 F.2d 192, 196 (C.A.4th Cir.1962). In an effort to eliminate "the considerable confusion which exists in this area" and thereby to facilitate tax planning, H.R.Rep. No. 1337, 83d Cong., 2d Sess., 35, the authors of the new Code sought to provide objective tests to govern the tax consequences of stock redemptions. Thus, the tax bill passed by the House of Representatives contained no "essentially equivalent" language. Rather, it provided for "safe harbors" where capital gains treatment would be accorded to corporate redemptions that met the conditions now found in §§ 302(b)(2) and (3) of the Code.

It was in the Senate Finance Committee's consideration of the tax bill that § 302(b)(1) was added, and Congress thereby provided that capital gains treatment should be available "if the redemption is not essentially equivalent to a dividend." Taxpayer argues that the purpose was to continue "existing law," and there is support in the legislative history that § 302(b)(1) reverted "in part" or "in general" to the "essentially equivalent" provision of § 115(g)(1) of the 1939 Code. According to the Government, even under the old law it would have been improper for the Court of Appeals to rely on "a business purpose for the redemption" and "an absence of the proscribed tax avoidance purpose to bail out dividends at favorable tax rates." * * * However, we need not decide that question, for we find from the history of the 1954 revisions and the purpose of § 302(b)(1) that Congress intended more than merely to re-enact the prior law.

In explaining the reason for adding the "essentially equivalent" test, the Senate Committee stated that the House provisions "appeared unnecessarily restrictive, particularly, in the case of redemptions of preferred stock which might be called by the corporation without the shareholder having any control over when the redemption may take place." S.Rep. No. 1622, 83d Cong., 2d Sess., 44. This explanation gives no indication that the purpose behind the redemption should affect the result. Rather, in its more detailed technical evaluation of § 302(b)(1), the Senate Committee reported as follows:

> "The test intended to be incorporated in the interpretation of paragraph (1) is in general that currently employed under section 115(g)(1) of the 1939 Code. Your committee further intends that in applying this test for the future * * * the inquiry will be devoted solely to the question of whether or not the transaction by its nature may properly be characterized as a sale of stock by the redeeming shareholder to the corporation. For this purpose the

presence or absence of earnings and profits of the corporation is not material. Example: X, the sole shareholder of a corporation having no earnings or profits causes the corporation to redeem half of its stock. Paragraph (1) does not apply to such redemption notwithstanding the absence of earnings and profits." S.Rep. No. 1622, supra, at 234.

The intended scope of § 302(b)(1) as revealed by this legislative history is certainly not free from doubt. However, we agree with the Government that by making the sole inquiry relevant for the future the narrow one whether the redemption could be characterized as a sale, Congress was apparently rejecting past court decisions that had also considered factors indicating the presence or absence of a tax-avoidance motive. At least that is the implication of the example given. Congress clearly mandated that pro rata distributions be treated under the general rules laid down in §§ 301 and 316 rather than under § 302, and nothing suggests that there should be a different result if there were a "business purpose" for the redemption. Indeed, just the opposite inference must be drawn since there would not likely be a tax-avoidance purpose in a situation where there were no earnings or profits. We conclude that the Court of Appeals was therefore wrong in looking for a business purpose and considering it in deciding whether the redemption was equivalent to a dividend. Rather, we agree with the Court of Appeals for the Second Circuit that "the business purpose of a transaction is irrelevant in determining dividend equivalence" under § 302(b)(1). Hasbrook v. United States, 343 F.2d 811, 814 (1965).

Taxpayer strongly argues that to treat the redemption involved here as essentially equivalent to a dividend is to elevate form over substance. Thus, taxpayer argues, had he not bought Bradley's shares or had he made a subordinated loan to the company instead of buying preferred stock, he could have gotten back his $25,000 with favorable tax treatment. However, the difference between form and substance in the tax law is largely problematical, and taxpayer's complaints have little to do with whether a business purpose is relevant under § 302(b)(1). It was clearly proper for Congress to treat distributions generally as taxable dividends when made out of earnings and profits and then to prevent avoidance of that result without regard to motivation where the distribution is in exchange for redeemed stock.

We conclude that that is what Congress did when enacting § 302(b)(1). If a corporation distributes property as a simple dividend, the effect is to transfer the property from the company to its shareholders without a change in the relative economic interests or rights of the stockholders. Where a redemption has that same effect, it cannot be said to have satisfied the "not essentially equivalent to a dividend" requirement of § 302(b)(1). Rather, to qualify for preferred treatment under that section, a redemption must result in a meaningful reduction of the shareholder's proportionate interest in the corporation. Clearly, taxpayer here, who (after application of the attribution rules) was the sole shareholder of the corporation both before and after the redemption, did not qualify under this test. The decision of the Court of Appeals must therefore be reversed and the case remanded to the District Court for dismissal of the complaint.

It is so ordered.

■ MR. JUSTICE DOUGLAS, with whom THE CHIEF JUSTICE and MR. JUSTICE BRENNAN concur, dissenting.

I agree with the District Court, 274 F.Supp. 466, and with the Court of Appeals, 408 F.2d 1139, that respondent's contribution of working capital in the amount of $25,000 in exchange for 1,000 shares of preferred stock with a par value of $25 was made in order for the corporation to obtain a loan from the RFC and that the preferred stock was to be redeemed when the loan was repaid. For the reasons stated by the two lower courts, this redemption was not "essentially equivalent to a dividend," for the bona fide business purpose of the redemption belies the payment of a dividend. As stated by the Court of Appeals:

> "Although closely-held corporations call for close scrutiny under the tax law, we will not, under the facts and circumstances of this case, allow mechanical attribution rules to transform a legitimate corporate transaction into a tax avoidance scheme." 408 F.2d, at 1143–1144.

When the Court holds it was a dividend, it effectively cancels § 302(b)(1) from the Code. This result is not a matter of conjecture, for the Court says that in the case of closely held or one-man corporations a redemption of stock is "always" equivalent to a dividend. I would leave such revision to the Congress.

Revenue Ruling 85–106

1985–2 Cum.Bull. 116.

ISSUE

Is a redemption of nonvoting preferred stock not essentially equivalent to a dividend within the meaning of section 302(b)(1) of the Internal Revenue Code when there is no reduction in the percentage of voting and nonvoting common stock owned by the redeemed shareholder, and when the redeemed shareholder continues to have an undiminished opportunity to act in concert with other shareholders as a control group, under the circumstances described below?

FACTS

Corporation X had outstanding three classes of stock consisting of 100 shares of voting common stock, 100 shares of nonvoting common stock, and 50 shares of nonvoting 9 percent cumulative preferred stock. The fair market value of each share of common stock was approximately half the fair market value of each share of preferred stock. The voting common stock was held as follows:

Shareholders	Shares
A	19
B	19
C	18
Minority shareholders	44
Total	100

None of the minority shareholders owned more than five shares. None of the holders of the voting common stock were related within the meaning of section 318(a) of the Code. The combined voting power of *A, B,* and *C* was sufficient to elect a majority of the board of directors of *X*.

The nonvoting common stock and the preferred stock were held (directly and indirectly) in approximately the same proportions as the common stock. *C* held no nonvoting common stock or preferred stock directly, but was the sole remaining beneficiary of a trust, *T*, which owned 18 percent of both the nonvoting common stock and the preferred stock.

The trustees of *T* decided that it would be in the best interests of that trust if most of the *X* preferred stock held by *T* could be converted into cash. After negotiation, *X* redeemed six shares of preferred stock for its fair market value of $6x$ dollars. Following this redemption, *T* continued to hold three shares of preferred stock, and 18 percent of the nonvoting common stock. Under section 318(a)(3)(B) of the Code, *T* is also considered to own the voting common stock owned by its sole beneficiary, *C*.

LAW AND ANALYSIS

Section 302(a) of the Code provides, in part, that if a corporation redeems its stock, and if section 302(b)(1), (2), (3), or (4) applies, such redemption will be treated as a distribution in part or full payment in exchange for the stock.

* * *

The lack of any reduction in *T*'s 18 percent vote prevented this redemption from qualifying under section 302(b)(2) of the Code, and the lack of complete termination of interest prevented it from qualifying under section 302(b)(3). The question remains whether the redemption should be considered not essentially equivalent to a dividend so as to qualify under section 302(b)(1). Under section 1.302–2(b) of the Income Tax Regulations, this determination depends upon the facts and circumstances of each case.

In United States v. Davis, 397 U.S. 301 (1970), 1970–1 C.B. 62, the Supreme Court of the United States held that in order to qualify under section 302(b)(1) of the Code, a redemption must result in a meaningful reduction of the shareholder's proportionate interest in the corporation, and that, for this purpose, the attribution rules of section 318 apply.

In determining whether a reduction in interest is "meaningful", the rights inherent in a shareholder's interest must be examined. The three elements of a shareholder's interest that are generally considered most significant are: (1) the right to vote and thereby exercise control; (2) the right to participate in current earnings and accumulated surplus; and (3) the right to share in net assets on liquidation. Rev.Rul. 81–289, 1981–2 C.B. 82.

In applying the above principles, it is significant that (as a result of section 318(a)(3)(B) of the Code) the redemption did not reduce T's percentage of the vote in X. It is true that T reduced its percentage interest in current earnings, accumulated surplus, and net assets upon liquidation, and reduced the fair market value of its ownership in X. However, when the redeemed shareholder has a voting interest (either directly or by attribution), a reduction in voting power is a key factor in determining the applicability of section 302(b)(1) of the Code.

It is also true that T was not the largest shareholder. A and B each held slightly larger voting interests, and larger interests measured by fair market value. T, however, was not in the position of a minority shareholder isolated from corporate management and control. Compare Rev.Rul. 75–512, where the majority of the redeeming corporation's voting stock was held by a shareholder unrelated (within the meaning of section 318(a)) to the redeemed trust. Also compare Rev.Rul. 76–385, 1976–2 C.B. 92, where the redeemed shareholder's total interest was *de minimis*.

In the present situation, a significant aspect of T's failure to reduce voting power is the fact that the redemption leaves unchanged T's potential (by attribution from C) for participating in a control group by acting in concert with A and B. Compare Rev.Rul. 76–364, 1976–2 C.B. 91, where a reduction in voting interest was found meaningful in itself when it caused the redeemed shareholder to give up a potential for control by acting in concert with one other shareholder. In addition, the Tax Court has indicated significance for this factor of potential group control (*Johnson Trust*, at 947). See also Bloch v. United States, 261 F.Supp. 597, 611–612 (S.D.Tex. 1966), aff'd per curiam, 386 F.2d 839 (5th Cir.1967), where, in finding that "the distributions in question were essentially equivalent to a dividend," the court noted that there was no change in the redeemed shareholder's potential for exercising control "by aligning himself with one or more of the other stockholders."

Although there was a reduction of T's economic interest in X, such reduction was not sufficiently large to result in a meaningful reduction of T's interest. The absence of any reduction of T's voting interest in X (through C) and T's potential (through C) for control group participation are compelling factors in this situation.

In Himmel v. Commissioner, 338 F.2d 815 (2d Cir.1964), dealing with a similar question, a decision was reached permitting the applicability of section 302(b)(1) of the Code. That case, however, was decided prior to the decision of the Supreme Court in *Davis*. Thus, *Himmel* fails to reflect the development in the law represented by the *Davis* limitation on section 302(b)(1) applicability where there is no meaningful reduction of the shareholder's proportionate interest in the corporation. Thus, pursuant to *Davis*, it is proper to view *Himmel* as incorrect to the extent it conflicts with the position contained in this revenue ruling.

HOLDING

The redemption of nonvoting preferred stock held by T does not qualify as a redemption under section 302(b)(1) of the Code, under the facts of this ruling when there is no reduction in the percentage of voting and nonvoting common stock owned by T, and when T continues to have an undiminished opportunity to act in concert with other shareholders as a control group. Since the redemption does not otherwise qualify under section 302(b), it is not a distribution in part or full payment for the stock under section 302(a). Consequently, under section 302(d), the redemption will be treated as a distribution of property to which section 301 applies.

NOTE

The Meaningful Reduction Standard. In interpreting the "meaningful reduction" standard of *Davis*, the Service's rulings have considered the effect of the redemption on the redeemed shareholder's voting power, rights to participate in current and future corporate earnings, and rights to share in net assets on liquidation.[1] As illustrated by Revenue Ruling 85–106, if the shareholder has a voting interest, the key factor in measuring dividend equivalence is the reduction in the shareholder's voting power as opposed to other important economic rights. Whether such a reduction is "meaningful" is essentially a question of fact, but some guidelines have emerged from published rulings. For example, in Revenue Ruling 75–502,[2] the Service ruled that a shareholder's reduction of voting common stock ownership from 57 percent to 50 percent was meaningful where the remaining stock was held by a single unrelated shareholder. The ruling also states that a lesser reduction would not have qualified under Section 302(b)(1) because the shareholder would have continued to have "dominant voting rights."[3]

Turning to minority shareholders, the Service held in Revenue Ruling 75–512[4] that a reduction of common stock ownership from 30 percent to 24.3 percent—a near-miss under the substantially disproportionate redemption safe harbor—was meaningful because the redeemed shareholder experienced a reduction in three significant rights: voting, earnings, and assets on liquidation. A reduction in common stock ownership from 27 percent to 22 percent also was held to be meaningful where the remaining shares were owned by three unrelated shareholders because the redeemed shareholder lost the ability to control the corporation in concert with only one other shareholder.[5]

The Section 302 regulations also focus upon the effect of the redemption upon the shareholder's control of corporate affairs. Thus, pro rata redemptions of a corporation's single class of stock do not qualify for exchange treatment, and the redemption of all of one class of stock also

1. See, e.g., Rev. Rul. 81–289, 1981–2 C.B. 82.

2. 1975–2 C.B. 111.

3. Id.

4. 1975–2 C.B. 112.

5. Rev. Rul. 76–364, 1976–2 C.B. 91.

fails if all outstanding classes of stock are held proportionately.[6] Any redemption of stock from a shareholder owning only nonvoting preferred stock, however, is not essentially equivalent a dividend since the shareholder does not have control over whether the redemption occurs.[7] The Service also has ruled that a redemption of publicly traded common stock that reduces a shareholder's interest from .0001118 percent to .0001081 percent qualifies for exchange treatment since such a shareholder cannot exercise control over corporate affairs.[8] The same reasoning should apply to redemptions by closely held companies of stock held by minority shareholders who reduce their percentage interests, even if the reduction is slight. But a pro rata redemption of stock in a publicly traded corporation will not satisfy the "meaningful reduction" standard even if the shareholder owns only small noncontrolling interest in the corporation.[9]

Suppose that under state law a simple majority of a corporation's outstanding shares can control day-to-day corporate activities through the board of directors but extraordinary corporate action, such as a merger or liquidation, requires approval by two-thirds of the shares. Should a redemption in which a shareholder loses control of extraordinary corporate action but retains control of routine matters (e.g. a reduction to 60% voting control) qualify for exchange treatment under Section 302(b)(1)? In Wright v. United States,[10] the Eighth Circuit determined that such a redemption is not essentially equivalent to a dividend because of the loss of two-thirds control of the corporation. In Revenue Ruling 78–401,[11] the Service takes a more restrictive view of the application of Section 302(b)(1) to these facts. The ruling concludes that if extraordinary corporate action is not "imminent," the retention of day-to-day control of corporate activities is a "predominant factor" and the redemption does not result in a meaningful reduction in the shareholder's interest. It is unclear what position the Service would take if a merger or similar corporate transaction were contemplated or what evidence would substantiate the likelihood of corporate action.

Family Discord. One of the more titillating issues to arise under Section 302(b)(1) involves whether the Section 318(a)(1) family attribution rules should be ignored when there is evidence of family discord between the redeemed shareholder and related continuing shareholders. A typical factual context in which this "family fight" question arises is well illustrated in the following introduction to a leading Tax Court decision:[12]

6. Reg. § 1.302–2(b).

7. Reg. § 1.302–2(a). In Rev.Rul. 77–426, 1977–2 C.B. 87, a redemption of five percent of the outstanding preferred stock from a shareholder owning all of the preferred stock (and only preferred stock) qualified for exchange treatment under Section 302(b)(1).

8. Rev.Rul. 76–385, 1976–2 C.B. 92.

9. Rev.Rul. 81–289, 1981–2 C.B. 82.

10. 482 F.2d 600 (8th Cir.1973).

11. 1978–2 C.B. 127.

12. Cerone v. Commissioner, 87 T.C. 1 (1986). See also the colorful introduction to the Fifth Circuit's opinion in David Metzger Trust v. Commissioner, 693 F.2d 459 (5th Cir.1982) ("We decide today a story driven by tensions as old as Genesis but told in the modern lexicon of the tax law. It is the story of David who built a business and left it in

Petitioner Michael N. Cerone * * * and his son Michael L. Cerone * * * owned and operated the Stockade Cafe * * * each owning 50 percent of the stock of the corporation. The father and son had a volatile relationship and frequently disagreed over management decisions. Over the years their disagreements became more serious, and finally they decided one of them should buy the other's interest in the business. Petitioner did not think he could run the business alone, so it was decided that the corporation would redeem all of his stock. After the redemption, petitioner worked at the Stockade Cafe for several years, but he did not exercise any control over the corporation. This case involves the tax treatment of the payments or distributions petitioner received for his stock.

If the family attribution rules applied to the above fact pattern, the redemption of the father's 50 percent stock interest would not qualify under Section 302(b)(1) because he continued to own 100 percent of the company through attribution from his son. If the attribution chain could be broken, however, the father's reduction of his interest from 50 percent to zero would be "meaningful" and the redemption would qualify for exchange treatment under Section 302(b)(1) even if he failed to meet the specific requirements for waiver of family attribution under Section 302(c).[13]

After its victory in United States v. Davis, the Service consistently rejected attempts by taxpayers to break the chain of family attribution by proving family hostility.[14] Most courts to consider the question agree that the attribution rules apply without regard to family squabbles. Although the First Circuit once held that family discord might "negate the presumption" of the attribution rules,[15] the Tax Court and the Fifth Circuit have refused to allow family discord to nullify the attribution rules in applying Section 302(b)(1).[16]

More recently, the Tax Court has suggested that family discord may be relevant in testing for dividend equivalency under Section 302(b)(1) *after* the attribution rules have been applied. In Cerone v. Commissioner,[17] the court summarized its view of the proper role of family hostility:[18]

the charge of his eldest son Jacob to be shared with Jacob's two sisters Catherine and Cecilia, of their alienation and resulting quarrel with the tax collectors.")

13. See Section C2 of this chapter, supra. Mr. Cerone was unable to waive family attribution under Section 302(c) because he retained a prohibited employment relationship with the corporation after the redemption. 87 T.C. at 29–33.

14. See, e.g., Rev.Rul. 80–26, 1980–1 C.B. 66.

15. Haft Trust v. Commissioner, 510 F.2d 43 (1st Cir.1975), vacating and remanding 61 T.C. 398 (1973).

16. Cerone v. Commissioner, supra note 12; Metzger Trust v. Commissioner, 76 T.C. 42 (1981), affirmed, 693 F.2d 459 (5th Cir.1982), cert. denied, 463 U.S. 1207, 103 S.Ct. 3537 (1983); Haft Trust v. Commissioner, 61 T.C. 398 (1973), vacated and remanded, 510 F.2d 43 (1st Cir.1975).

17. Supra note 12.

18. 87 T.C. at 22. See also Henry T. Patterson Trust v. United States, 729 F.2d 1089 (6th Cir.1984) (percentage reduction

Although we [have] rejected the * * * argument that family discord could preclude application of the attribution rules, we nonetheless noted that family discord does have a role, albeit a limited one, in testing for dividend equivalence under section 302(b)(1). We reasoned that under *United States v. Davis,* supra, the proper analysis is as follows: First, the attribution rules are plainly and straightforwardly applied. Second, a determination is made whether there has been a reduction in the stockholder's proportionate interest in the corporation. If not, the inquiry ends because, if there is no change in the stockholder's interest, dividend equivalency results. If there has been a reduction, then all the facts and circumstances must be examined to see if the reduction was meaningful under *United States v. Davis,* supra. It is at this point, *and only then,* that family hostility becomes an appropriate factor for consideration. * * *.

PROBLEMS

1. Z Corporation has 100 shares of common stock outstanding, owned by A (28 shares), B (25 shares), C (23 shares) and D (24 shares.) Unless otherwise indicated, assume the shareholders are not related. In each of the following alternative situations, determine whether the redemption is not essentially equivalent to a dividend under § 302(b)(1):

(a) Z redeems 7 shares from A.

(b) Z redeems 5 shares from A, and A and D are mother and daughter.

(c) Z redeems 5 shares from A, and A and B are mother and daughter.

(d) Same as (c), above, except that A has not spoken to B since B married "outside her faith."

2. Y Corporation has 100 shares of common stock and 100 shares of nonvoting preferred stock outstanding. The preferred stock is not convertible into Y common stock and is not Section 306 stock (i.e., not stock treated specially in § 306 because of its tax avoidance potential). The Y common and preferred stock are owned by the following unrelated shareholders:

Shareholder	Common Shares	Preferred Shares
A	40	0
B	20	55
C	25	10
D	15	15
E	0	20

Will the following alternative redemptions qualify for exchange treatment under § 302(b)?

from 97 to 93 percent, after applying attribution rules, is meaningful under *Davis* in view   of hostility.)

(a) Y redeems 5 preferred shares from E.

(b) Y redeems all of its outstanding preferred stock.

3. Suppose an individual shareholder owns ten shares of common stock of X Corporation with a basis of $15,000. What happens to the shareholder's basis if five shares are redeemed in a transaction which is properly classified as a dividend? What if all ten shares are redeemed in a transaction which is properly classified as a dividend because a § 302(c)(2) waiver of family attribution is unavailable?

D. REDEMPTIONS TESTED AT THE CORPORATE LEVEL: PARTIAL LIQUIDATIONS

Code: § 302(b)(4), (e).

Section 302(b)(4) provides exchange treatment for redemptions of stock held by noncorporate shareholders if the distribution qualifies as a "partial liquidation." Under Section 302(e)(1), a distribution is treated as in partial liquidation if it is pursuant to a plan, occurs within the taxable year in which the plan is adopted or the succeeding taxable year, and is "not essentially equivalent to a dividend." Although the "not essentially equivalent to a dividend" standard mirrors the language in Section 302(b)(1), the two provisions have a very different focus. For partial liquidation purposes, dividend equivalency is determined at the corporate rather than the shareholder level. Thus, while a pro rata redemption could never escape dividend classification under Section 302(b)(1), any redemption that results in a genuine contraction of the corporation's business may qualify for exchange treatment as a partial liquidation if the distribution is made to a shareholder other than a C corporation. The legislative history of the predecessor of Section 302(e) explains the corporate contraction standard:[1]

> The general language of the proposed draft would include within the definition of a partial liquidation the type of cases involving the contraction of the corporate business. Such as for example, cases which hold that if the entire floor of a factory is destroyed by fire, the insurance proceeds received may be distributed pro rata to the shareholders without the imposition of a tax at the rates applicable to the distribution of a dividend, if the corporation no longer continues its operations to the same extent maintained by the destroyed facility. Voluntary bona fide contraction of the corporate business may of course also qualify to the same extent as under existing law. In addition to the general definition of what constitutes a partial liquidation, your committee's bill provides a rule to indicate one type of distribution that will in any event constitute a partial liquidation. Under this rule, if a corporation is engaged in two or more active businesses which

---

1. S.Rep. No. 1622, 83d Cong., 2d Sess. 49 (1954). See Imler v. Commissioner, 11 T.C. 836 (1948) (the "contraction-by-fire" case referred to in the Senate Report).

has [sic] been carried on for at least 5 years, it may distribute the assets of either one of the businesses in kind, or the proceeds of their sale.

The amorphous corporate contraction doctrine is a perilous yardstick for the tax planner.[2] Recognizing the need for greater certainty, Congress has provided a safe harbor in Section 302(e)(2), which assures partial liquidation status if the distribution consists of the assets of a "qualified trade or business" or is attributable to the termination of such a trade or business, and immediately after the distribution the corporation continues to conduct another qualified trade or business. To be "qualified," a trade or business must have been actively conducted throughout the five-year period ending on the date of the distribution and must not have been acquired by the distributing corporation in a taxable transaction during that period.[3] The active trade or business that the corporation continues to conduct must have a similar five-year business history. The "active" business requirement is designed to patrol against the accumulation of earnings in the form of investment assets, such as real estate or securities, followed by prompt bailout distributions masquerading as corporate contractions.[4]

A distribution may qualify as a partial liquidation even if the shareholders do not actually surrender any stock.[5] If the other requirements of either the general corporate contraction doctrine or the statutory safe harbor are met, the transaction will be treated as a constructive redemption of stock.[6]

Distributions to corporate shareholders do not qualify for partial liquidation treatment even if all the other statutory requirements are met.[7] For purposes of determining whether a shareholder is corporate or noncorporate, stock held by a partnership, estate, or trust (but not an S corporation) is treated as if held proportionately by the partners or beneficiaries.[8] S corporations are thus treated as corporate shareholders and do not qualify for exchange treatment on a partial liquidation under Section 302(b)(4).

At first glance, it might seem that C corporation shareholders would welcome their eviction from the partial liquidation safe harbor because distributions that otherwise would give rise to taxable capital gain would become dividends sheltered by the dividends received deduction. But Congress was not acting in a spirit of generosity. Rather, it was attempting to

2. For the Service's ruling policy on whether a distribution qualifies as a corporate contraction, see Rev.Proc. 2012–3, § 4.01(21), 2012–1 I.R.B. 119 (ordinarily no ruling unless distribution results in a 20 percent or greater reduction in gross revenue, net fair market value of assets, and employees).

3. I.R.C. § 302(e)(3).

4. For the definition of an active trade or business, see Reg. § 1.355–3(b), (c), which govern corporate divisions under Section 355. See Chapter 10B, infra.

5. Fowler Hosiery Co. v. Commissioner, 301 F.2d 394 (7th Cir.1962); Rev.Rul. 90–13, 1990–1 C.B. 65.

6. See Rev.Rul. 77–245, 1977–2 C.B. 105, for the method of computing the tax consequences of a partial liquidation.

7. I.R.C. § 302(b)(4).

8. I.R.C. § 302(e)(5).

put an end to several widely publicized acquisition techniques that used the partial liquidation as a vehicle for obtaining the best of all tax worlds: a stepped-up basis for selected assets of the acquired corporation along with the preservation of favorable tax attributes (e.g., earnings and profits deficits, loss and credit carryovers, etc.)—all at little or no tax cost.[9]

Congress inflicted further punishment on corporate shareholders when it enacted restrictions to prevent abuse of the dividends received deduction.[10] Any amount treated as a dividend to a corporate shareholder under Section 301 is an "extraordinary dividend" under Section 1059 if it is a distribution in redemption of stock which is part of a partial liquidation of the redeeming corporation, regardless of the shareholder's holding period or the size of the distribution.[11] As a result, a corporate shareholder that receives a dividend in a transaction treated as a partial liquidation must reduce its basis in the stock of the redeeming corporation by the portion of the dividend that was not taxed because of the dividends received deduction.[12]

Revenue Ruling 79–184

1979–1 Cum.Bull. 143.

Advice has been requested whether the sale by a parent corporation of all the stock of a wholly owned subsidiary and the distribution of the sales proceeds by the parent to its shareholders qualifies as a distribution in partial liquidation within the meaning of section 346(a)(2) of the Internal Revenue Code of 1954 [now Section 302(e). Ed.].

Corporation P owned all of the single class of outstanding stock of Corporation S for many years, during which time each had been engaged in the active conduct of a trade or business.

Pursuant to a plan, P sold all of the stock of S to an unrelated party for cash and distributed the proceeds of the sale pro rata to its shareholders in redemption of part of their P stock.

Section [302(e)(1)] of the Code provides, in part, that a distribution will be treated as a partial liquidation of a corporation if it is not essentially equivalent to a dividend, is in redemption of a part of the stock of the corporation pursuant to a plan, and occurs within the taxable year in which the plan is adopted or within the succeeding taxable year. Section 1.346–1(a)(2) of the Income Tax Regulations provides that a distribution resulting from a genuine contraction of the corporate business is an example of a

---

9. See, e.g., Henderson, "Federal Tax Techniques for Asset Redeployment Transactions," 37 Tax L.Rev. 325 (1982); Ginsburg, "Taxing Corporate Acquisitions," 38 Tax L.Rev. 171 (1983).

10. See Chapter 4F, supra.

11. I.R.C. § 1059(e)(1).

12. I.R.C. § 1059(a), (b). If the non-taxed portion of the dividend exceeds the shareholder's basis in the redeemed stock, the excess is treated as gain from a sale or exchange of the stock. I.R.C. § 1059(a)(2).

distribution that will qualify as a partial liquidation under section [302(e)(1)].

Generally, for purposes of section [302(e)] of the Code, the business that is terminated or contracted must be operated directly by the corporation making the distribution. See *H.L. Morgenstern*, 56 T.C. 44 (1971). However, Rev.Rul. 75–223, 1975–1 C.B. 109, provides that when a parent corporation liquidates a wholly owned subsidiary and distributes the subsidiary's assets, or the proceeds from the sale of those assets, to its shareholders, the fact that the distributions were attributable to assets used by the subsidiary rather than directly by the parent will not prevent the distribution from qualifying as a "genuine contraction of the corporate business" to the parent within the meaning of section 1.346–1(a)(2) of the regulations. The basis for this holding is that under section 381 a parent corporation that liquidates a subsidiary under section 332 (when section 334(b)(1) applies) inherits attributes (for example, earnings and profits) of the liquidated subsidiary so that after the liquidation of the subsidiary the parent is viewed as if it had always operated the business of the liquidated subsidiary.

However, when a parent corporation distributes the stock of its subsidiary, as in *Situation 3* of Rev.Rul. 75–223, section 381 of the Code does not apply to integrate the past business results of the subsidiary with those of the parent. Therefore, distribution by the parent of subsidiary's stock does not result in the parent corporation taking into account the past operations of the subsidiary. Thus, there is no analogy between a distribution of stock of the subsidiary and a distribution of the assets of a liquidated subsidiary or the proceeds of a sale of such assets. A distribution of the stock of the subsidiary under such circumstances is a corporate separation, governed by section 355, and not a corporate contraction.

Similarly, as in the present case, where *P* sells all of the stock of its wholly owned subsidiary, *S,* and distributes the proceeds to its shareholders, there is no basis for attributing the business activities of *S* to *P*. It is well established that a corporation is a legal entity separate and distinct from its shareholders. New Colonial Ice Co. v. Helvering, 292 U.S. 435 (1934), XIII–1 C.B. 194 (1934); Moline Properties, Inc. v. Commissioner, 319 U.S. 436 (1943), 1943 C.B. 1011. Although the assets of *P* are reduced by the subsequent distribution of the sale proceeds, the sale by *P* of the *S* stock is not in and of itself sufficient to effect a contraction of the business operations of *P* within the contemplation of section 346(a)(2) of the Code. Rather, the overall transaction has the economic significance of the sale of an investment and distribution of the proceeds.

Accordingly, the distribution by *P* to its shareholders of the proceeds of the sale of the *S* stock does not qualify as a distribution in partial liquidation within the meaning of section [302(e)(1)] of the Code, and the distribution will be treated as a distribution by *P* of property taxable to the *P* shareholders under section 301 by reason of section 302(d). See section 1.302–2(b) of the regulations, which provides that all distributions in pro rata redemption of a part of the stock of a corporation generally will be treated as distributions under section 301 if the corporation has only one class of stock outstanding.

PROBLEM

Alpha Corporation operates a book publishing business ("Books") and a bar exam review course ("Cram") as divisions (i.e., not as separately incorporated entities). Alpha's single class of common stock outstanding is owned in equal shares by Michael, Pamela (Michael's wife) and Iris Corporation. Neither Michael nor Pamela owns any stock in Iris. Alpha also owns all of the stock of Beta Corporation, a separately incorporated company which is engaged in the beta processing business, and it directly owns a diversified securities portfolio.

What are the shareholder level tax consequences of the following alternative transactions:

(a) Alpha has operated Books and Cram for more than five years and it distributes the assets of Books to its three equal shareholders in redemption of 50 shares from each shareholder. Any different result if the redemption is made without an actual surrender of shares?

(b) Is there a different result in (a), above, if Alpha had purchased Books three years ago for cash? If so, why should that matter? What if Alpha acquired Books three years ago in a tax-free reorganization?

(c) What if all the assets of Books were destroyed by fire and Alpha distributes one-half of the insurance proceeds equally to its three shareholders in redemption of an appropriate number of shares of stock and retains the remaining proceeds to carry on its book publishing business on a somewhat smaller scale?

(d) Same as (a), above, except that Alpha distributes the assets of Books to Michael in redemption of all of his stock.

(e) Same as (a), above except that Alpha distributes the assets of Books to Iris in redemption of all of its Alpha stock.

(f) Alpha distributes the securities portfolio to its three equal shareholders in redemption of 20 shares from each shareholder.

(g) Alpha sells all of its Beta stock and distributes the proceeds pro rata to the shareholders in redemption of 20 shares from each.

(h) Same as (g), above, except that Alpha liquidates Beta and then distributes the assets of Beta's business, which Beta has operated for more than five years.

E.   CONSEQUENCES TO THE DISTRIBUTING CORPORATION

1.   DISTRIBUTIONS OF APPRECIATED PROPERTY IN REDEMPTION

Code: § 311.

In the preceding chapter, the story of the decline of the *General Utilities* doctrine began to unfold.[1] The assault on *General Utilities* in the

---

1.   See Chapter 4D1, supra.

redemption setting gained momentum when Congress discovered that several insurance companies were redeeming large amounts of their own stock by distributing appreciated securities while avoiding recognition of gain at the corporate level.[2] Congress curtailed this abuse by requiring a corporation to recognize gain on a distribution of appreciated property in a redemption as if the property had been sold for its fair market value. Partial liquidation distributions, however, continued to qualify for nonrecognition at the corporate level, and numerous exceptions demonstrated that Congress was not yet ready to give *General Utilities* a proper burial.[3]

Corporate takeover specialists were quick to exploit these remaining vestiges of the *General Utilities* doctrine. Through carefully orchestrated transactions, they sought to convert a direct sale of property by a corporation, normally a taxable event to the seller, into a tax-free distribution.[4] After several of these schemes were publicized, Congress responded by further narrowing the opportunity for nonrecognition on nonliquidating distributions of appreciated property in redemption. The final demise of *General Utilities* in the redemption context came with the Tax Reform Act of 1986. In adopting Section 311(b), which also applies to nonliquidating distributions, Congress repealed all the remaining exceptions that had provided for nonrecognition of gain to the distributing corporation. As a result, a corporation distributing property in redemption of stock (including a partial liquidation) always recognizes gain but may not recognize loss.

2.   EFFECT ON EARNINGS AND PROFITS

Code: § 312(n)(7).

The effect of a stock redemption on the distributing corporation's earnings and profits initially depends upon the tax consequences of the redemption at the shareholder level. If the redemption is treated as a distribution to which Section 301 applies, the distributing corporation adjusts its earnings and profits in the same manner as on other nonliquidating distributions—i.e., earnings and profits are decreased by the amount of cash and the principal amount of any obligations, and by the greater of the adjusted basis or the fair market value of any property distributed.[1] In addition, the corporation always recognizes gain and correspondingly increases its current earnings and profits on a distribution of appreciated property, and it reduces current earnings and profits by any taxes paid on that gain.[2]

---

2.   See S.Rep. No. 91–552, 91st Cong., 1st Sess. 279, reprinted in 1969–3 C.B. 423, 600.

3.   See I.R.C. § 311(d)(2) (pre–1982).

4.   See Henderson, "Federal Tax Techniques for Asset Redeployment Transac-

tions," 37 Tax L.Rev. 325 (1982). The Service's attack or this strategy was rejected in Esmark, Inc. v. Commissioner, 90 T.C. 171 (1988), aff'd, 886 F.2d 1318 (7th Cir.1989).

1.   I.R.C. § 312(a), (b).

2.   I.R.C. § 311(b); 312(b).

If a redemption (including a partial liquidation) is treated as an exchange to the redeemed shareholder, the effect on earnings and profits is more complex. In that situation, Section 312(n)(7) provides that the part of the distribution in redemption that is properly chargeable to earnings and profits shall be an amount which does not exceed the ratable share of the corporation's accumulated earnings and profits attributable to the redeemed stock. Congress also expressed its intention that earnings and profits never would be reduced by more than the amount of the redemption.[3]

To illustrate the operation of this rule, assume that X Corporation has 1,000 shares of common stock outstanding, and that A and B each acquire 500 of these shares at issuance at a price of $20 per share. Assume further that X is a profitable business that holds $100,000 of net assets, consisting of $50,000 cash and $50,000 of appreciated real property, and X has $50,000 of accumulated earnings and profits. If X distributes $50,000 cash to A in redemption of A's 500 shares, Section 312(n)(7) reduces X's earnings and profits by $25,000—the ratable share of X's $50,000 earnings and profits attributable to A's 50 percent stock interest that was redeemed. The remaining $25,000 of the distribution is charged to X's capital account and, after the redemption, X has $25,000 of remaining accumulated earnings and profits. The following excerpt from the legislative history of the Tax Reform Act of 1984 explains the operation of this rule in the case of a corporation with a more complex capital structure:[4]

> If a corporation has more than one class of stock outstanding, its earnings and profits generally should be allocated among the different classes in determining the amount by which a redemption of all or a part of one class of stock reduces earnings and profits. However, earnings and profits generally should not be allocated to preferred stock which is not convertible and which does not participate to any significant extent in corporate growth. Therefore, a redemption of such preferred stock should result in a reduction of the capital account only, unless the distribution includes dividend arrearages, which will reduce earnings and profits.
>
> Similarly, priorities legally required as between different classes of stock should be taken into account in allocating earnings and profits between classes. For example, assume that corporation X has 1,000 shares of class A common stock and 1,000 shares of class B common stock. Both classes are $10 par value stock and were issued at the same time at a price of $20. The class A common has a preference as to dividends and liquidating distributions in a 2:1 ratio to the class B common, and only the class B common has voting rights. Assume further that Corporation X holds net assets worth $210,000 and has current and accumulated

3. S.Rep. No. 98–169, 98th Cong., 2d Sess. 202 (1984).

4. Staff of Joint Committee on Taxation, General Explanation of the Tax Reform Act of 1984, 98th Cong., 2d Sess. 181 (1984).

earnings and profits of $120,000. If X distributes $140,000 in cash in redemption of all of the class A common, earnings and profits should be reduced by $80,000 and capital account by $60,000.

As illustrated by Revenue Ruling 74–338, which follows, matters become even more complicated when a corporation has both current and accumulated earnings and profits, and in the same year the corporation makes ordinary Section 301 distributions and also repurchases some of its stock in a redemption that qualifies as an exchange to the shareholder under Section 302(a).

Revenue Ruling 74–338

1974–2 Cum. Bull. 101.

Advice has been requested concerning the method of determining the pro rata portion of the total earnings and profits of a corporation attributable to the shares redeemed under the circumstances described below.

Situation 1.

M, a domestic corporation, files its Federal income tax returns on the basis of a calendar year. On July 1, 1973, *M* corporation redeemed for cash, 25 percent of its outstanding common stock in a transaction that qualified as a distribution in redemption of its stock under section 302(a) of the Internal Revenue Code of 1954. As of January 1, 1973, *M* corporation had earnings and profits accumulated after February 28, 1913, of $2,000. For the taxable year 1973, *M* had earnings and profits (current earnings) of $12,000. On June 1 and August 31, 1973, *M* corporation made ordinary distributions of $1,000 and $4,000, respectively, to its shareholders with respect to its stock.

Situation 2.

Assume the same facts as in *Situation 1* except that *M* corporation had current earnings of only $2,000.

Section 316 of the Code defines a dividend as follows:

(a) General Rule.—For purposes of this subtitle, the term "dividend" means any distribution of property made by a corporation to its shareholders—

(1) out of its earnings and profits accumulated after February 28, 1913, or

(2) out of its earnings and profits of the taxable year (computed as of the close of the taxable year without diminution by reason of any distributions made during the taxable year), without regard to the amount of the earnings and profits at the time the distribution was made.

Except as otherwise provided in this subtitle, every distribution is made out of earnings and profits to the extent thereof, and from the most recently accumulated earnings and profits. To the extent that any distribution is, under any provision of this subchapter, treated as a distribution of property to which section 301 applies, such distribution shall be treated as a distribution of property for purposes of this subsection.

Section 1.316–1(a)(1) of the Income Tax Regulations provides, in part, that the earnings and profits of the taxable year shall be computed as of the close of such year, without diminution by reason of any distributions made during the taxable year. For the purpose of determining whether a distribution constitutes a dividend, it is unnecessary to ascertain the amount of the earnings and profits accumulated since February 28, 1913, if the earnings and profits of the taxable year are equal to or in excess of the total amount of the distributions made within such year.

Section 1.316–2(b) of the regulations provides, in part, that if the earnings and profits of the taxable year (computed as of the close of the year without diminution by reason of any distributions made during the year and without regard to the amount of earnings and profits at the time of the distribution) are sufficient in amount to cover all the distributions made during that year, then each distribution is a taxable dividend. See section 1.316–1. If the distributions made during the taxable year consist only of money and exceed the earnings and profits of such year, then that proportion of each distribution which the total of the earnings and profits of the year bears to the total distributions made during the year shall be regarded as out of the earnings and profits of that year. The portion of each such distribution which is not regarded as out of earnings and profits of the taxable year shall be considered a taxable dividend to the extent of the earnings and profits accumulated since February 28, 1913, and available on the date of the distribution. In any case in which it is necessary to determine the amount of earnings and profits accumulated since February 28, 1913, and the actual earnings and profits to the date of a distribution within any taxable year cannot be shown, the earnings and profits for the year in which the distribution was made shall be prorated to the date of the distribution not counting the date on which the distribution was made.

When the amount of ordinary distributions made during a taxable year is greater than the current earnings the amount of any distribution which is made from current earnings and the amount, if any, which is made from accumulated earnings and profits must be determined under the rules provided in section 1.316–2(b) of the regulations.

When a corporation makes a distribution in redemption of its common stock under section 312(e) of the Code, the part of such distribution which is properly chargeable to capital account is not treated as a distribution of earnings and profits. The charge to earnings and profits is the pro rata portion of the total earnings and profits thereof attributable to the shares redeemed regardless of the actual amount of the distribution. See Rev. Rul. 70–531, 1970–2 C.B. 76. However, when both ordinary distributions and redemption distributions are made during the same taxable year, ordinary distributions take priority over redemption distributions as to current earnings and profits. See Rev. Rul. 74–339, [1974–2 C.B. 103].

The application of the foregoing rules to the described factual situations is as follows:

Situation 1:

Step 1. Determine the amount of current earnings available for distributions.

Ordinary distributions of $5,000 ($1,000 + $4,000) are charged against current earnings of $12,000.

The remainder of current earnings ($7,000) is available for other distributions.

Step 2. Determine the total earnings and profits available for distributions made during the taxable year 1973.

Accumulated earnings and profits at January 1, 1973	$2,000

Add—

Remainder of current earnings pro rated as of July 1, 1973, the date of the redemption of common stock (6/12 × $7,000)	$3,500
Total accumulated earnings and profits available at July 1, 1973	$5,500
Pro rata portion of the above attributable to the shares redeemed (25 percent × $5,500)	$1,375
Earnings and profits available for future distributions ($2,000 + $7,000 − $1,375)	$7,625

Situation 2:

Step 1. Determine the pro rata portion of each ordinary distribution made during the taxable year 1973 which is chargeable to the $2,000 of current earnings.

	Portion paid from current earnings
Distribution made on July 1, 1973 ($1,000 × 2,000/5,000)	$400
Distribution made on August 31, 1973 ($4,000 × 2,000/5,000)	$1,600
Total current earnings pro rated	$2,000

Step 2.   Determine the amount of each distribution, if any, chargeable in chronological order to accumulated earnings and profits.

Accumulated earnings and profits at January 1, 1973	$2,000
June 1, 1973. Charge – excess of ordinary distributions over the amount allocated to current earnings and profits ($1,000 – 400)	600
Remainder	$1,400
July 1, 1973. Charge – pro rata portion of total earnings and profits attributable to the shares redeemed (25 percent x $1,400)	350
August 31, 1973. Charge – the excess of ordinary distributions over the amount allocated to current earnings ($4,000 – 1,600 = $2,400) limited to the amount of accumulated earnings and profits available	$1,050

Summary
Situation 1.

Date of Distribution	Amount charged to current earnings	Amount charged to accumulated earnings and profits	Total charged to earnings and profits
June 1, 1973.	$1,000	—	$1,000
July 1, 1973.	—	1,375	1,375
August 31, 1973.	4,000	—	4,000
Totals.	$5,000	$1,375	$6,375
Situation 2.			
June 1, 1973.	$400	$600	$1,000
July 1, 1973.	—	350	350
August 31, 1973.	1,600	1,050	2,650
Totals.	$2,000	$2,000	$4,000

PROBLEM

X Corporation has 200 shares of common stock outstanding. A and B, who are unrelated, each acquired 100 shares of X upon their issuance at a price of $1,000 per share, and they each thus have an adjusted basis of $100,000 in their X stock. At the beginning of the current year, X has $100,000 of accumulated earnings and profits and X has $100,000 of current earnings and profits from operations (after taxes) during the year. What are the tax consequences to X if on July 1 it distributes $250,000 cash in redemption of A's shares in a redemption that qualifies as an exchange under Section 302(a).

3.   STOCK REACQUISITION EXPENSES

Code: § 162(k).

Amounts paid to acquire stock generally must be capitalized as part of the stock's basis.[1] The capitalization requirement applies to the original purchase price of the stock as well as to acquisition expenses, such as brokerage commissions and legal fees.[2] Some older authority held, however, that expenses incurred by a corporation to repurchase its stock, in limited circumstances, might be ordinary and necessary expenses deductible under Section 162.[3] In the midst of the frenzy of hostile corporate takeovers in the 1980's, Congress became concerned that corporate expenditures incurred to fend off unwanted corporate suitors by purchasing their shares— so-called "greenmail" payments—were being characterized as deductible business expenses.[4] Section 162(k)(1) was enacted to make it clear that all expenditures by a corporation incurred in purchasing its own stock, whether representing amounts paid for the stock, a premium paid in excess of the stock's value, or expenses connected with the purchase, are nondeductible, nonamortizable capital expenditures.[5] Section 162(k)(2) contains exceptions for interest payments deductible under Section 163, and several more specialized situations. In 1996, Congress broadened the scope of Section 162(k)(1) by extending its application to any "reacquisition" of stock regardless of whether the transaction is technically treated as a redemption under Subchapter C.

One difficult interpretive problem under the Section 162(k) disallowance rule revolves around the question of what amounts are paid to shareholders "in connection with" a redemption of stock. The legislative history states that while the phrase "in connection with" is to be construed broadly, it is not intended to deny a deduction for "otherwise deductible amounts paid in a transaction which has no nexus with the redemption other than being proximate in time or arising out of the same circumstances."[6] The Conference Report goes on to expand upon this standard:[7]

> For example, if a corporation redeems a departing employee's stock and makes a payment to the employee in discharge of the corporation's obligations under an employment contract, the payment in discharge of the contractual obligation is not subject to disallowance under this provision. Payments in discharge of other types of contractual obligations, in settlement of litigation, or pursuant to other actual or potential legal obligations or rights, may also be outside the intended scope of the provision to the extent it is clearly established that the payment does not represent consideration for the stock or expenses related to its acquisition, and is not a payment that is a fundamental part of a "standstill" or similar agreement.

1.   I.R.C. §§ 263(a), 1012.

2.   Reg. § 1.263(a)–2(c), (e). See Woodward v. Commissioner, 397 U.S. 572, 90 S.Ct. 1302 (1970); United States v. Hilton Hotels Corp., 397 U.S. 580, 90 S.Ct. 1307 (1970).

3.   Five Star Manufacturing Co. v. Commissioner, 355 F.2d 724 (5th Cir.1966).

4.   S.Rep. No. 99–313, 99th Cong., 2d Sess. 223 (1986).

5.   Id.

6.   H.R.Rep. No. 841, 99th Cong., 2d Sess. II—168 (1986).

7.   Id. at II—168–69.

The conferees anticipate that, where a transaction is not directly related to a redemption but is proximate in time, the Internal Revenue Service will scrutinize the transaction to determine whether the amount purportedly paid in the transaction is reasonable. Thus, even where the parties have countervailing tax interests, the parties' stated allocation of the total consideration between the redemption and the unrelated transaction will be respected only if it is supported by all the facts and circumstances.

However, the conferees intend that agreements to refrain from purchasing stock of a corporation or other similar types of "standstill" agreements in all events will be considered related to any redemption of the payee's stock. Accordingly, payments pursuant to such agreements are nondeductible under this provision provided there is an actual purchase of all or part of the payee's stock. The conferees intend no inference regarding the deductibility of payments under standstill or similar agreements that are unrelated to any redemption of stock owned by the payee.

The most controversial interpretive issue to arise since the enactment of Section 162(k) involved the deductibility of loan fees and related expenses incurred by corporations that have engaged in leveraged stock repurchase transactions. The courts disagreed on the scope of the disallowance rule in this setting. The Ninth Circuit upheld the deductibility of various fees incurred to finance a stock redemption in a case where a public corporation sought to amortize $4 million in loan fees incurred in connection with a leveraged buyout designed to enable the company to go private.[8] The court reasoned that Section 162(k) did not extend to financing costs because the borrowing was a transaction separate from the redemption. In so holding, the court rejected the Service's view that the disallowance rule extended to all costs (other than interest expense, which is specifically excepted by statute) directly or indirectly related to a stock redemption, including financing fees. The Tax Court took a contrary view, holding that fees paid to an investment banking firm to obtain loans to finance a stock repurchase as part of a leveraged buyout were not deductible because they were incurred "in connection with redemption of stock."[9] Congress eventually interceded, settling the controversy with a "technical correction" that amended Section 162(k) to make it clear that amounts properly allocable to indebtedness on which interest is deductible may be amortized over the term of the loan even if the debt is incurred by a corporation to repurchase its stock.[10]

8. In re Kroy (Europe) Ltd., 27 F.3d 367 (9th Cir.1994).

9. Fort Howard Corp. v. Commissioner, 103 T.C. 345 (1994).

10. I.R.C. § 162(k)(2)(ii).

F.   REDEMPTION PLANNING TECHNIQUES

1.   BOOTSTRAP ACQUISITIONS

Revenue Ruling 75–447

1975–2 Cum.Bull. 113.

Advice has been requested as to the Federal income tax consequences, in the situations described below, of the redemption by a corporation of part of its stock.

Situation 1

Corporation *X* had outstanding 100 shares of voting common stock of which *A* and *B* each owned 50 shares. In order to bring *C* into the business with an equal stock interest, and pursuant to an integrated plan, *A* and *B* caused *X* to issue, at fair market value, 25 new shares of voting common stock to *C*. Immediately thereafter, as part of the same plan, *A* and *B* caused *X* to redeem 25 shares of *X* voting common stock from each of them. Neither *A, B,* nor *C* owned any stock of *X* indirectly under section 318 of the Internal Revenue Code of 1954.

Situation 2

Corporation *X* had outstanding 100 shares of voting common stock of which *A* and *B* each owned 50 shares. In order to bring *C* into the business with an equal stock interest, and pursuant to an integrated plan, *A* and *B* each sold 15 shares of *X* voting common stock to *C* at fair market value and then caused *X* to redeem five shares from both *A* and *B*. Neither *A, B,* nor *C* owned any stock of *X* indirectly under section 318 of the Code.

Section 302(b)(2) of the Code states that section 302(a), which provides for treating a redemption of stock as a distribution in part or full payment in exchange for the stock, will apply if the distribution is substantially disproportionate with respect to the shareholder. * * *

In Zenz v. Quinlivan, 213 F.2d 914 (6th Cir.1954), a sole shareholder of a corporation, desiring to dispose of her entire interest therein, sold part of her stock to a competitor and shortly thereafter sold the remainder of her stock to the corporation for an amount of cash and property approximately equal to its earned surplus. The Government contended that the redemption was a dividend on the grounds that the result was the same as if the steps had been reversed, that is, as if the stock had been redeemed first and the sale of stock to the competitor had followed. The United States Court of Appeals rejected the Government's contention and held that the purchase of the stock by the corporation (when coupled with the sale of stock to the competitor) was not a dividend to the selling shareholder and that the proceeds should be treated as payment for the stock surrendered under the provisions of the Internal Revenue Code of 1939.

Rev.Rul. 55–745, 1955–2 C.B. 223, states that in situations similar to that in *Zenz,* the amount received by the shareholder from the corporation will be treated as received in payment for the stock surrendered under section 302(a) of the Code since the transaction when viewed as a whole results in the shareholder terminating his interest in the corporation within the meaning of section 302(b)(3).

In determining whether the "substantially disproportionate" provisions of section 302(b)(2) of the Code have been satisfied in *Situation 1* and in *Situation 2,* it is proper to rely upon the holding in *Zenz* that the sequence in which the events (that is, the redemption and sale) occur is irrelevant as long as both events are clearly part of an overall plan. Therefore, in situations where the redemption is accompanied by an issuance of new stock (as in *Situation 1*), or a sale of stock (as in *Situation 2*), and both steps (the sale, or issuance, of stock, as the case may be, and the redemption) are clearly part of an integrated plan to reduce a shareholder's interest, effect will be given only to the overall result for purposes of section 302(b)(2) and the sequence in which the events occur will be disregarded.

Since the *Zenz* holding requires that effect be given only to the overall result and proscribes the fragmenting of the whole transaction into its component parts, the computation of the voting stock of the corporation owned by the shareholder *immediately before* the redemption for purposes of section 302(b)(2)(C)(ii) of the Code should be made before any part of the transaction occurs. Likewise, the computation of the voting stock of the corporation owned by the shareholder *immediately after* the redemption for purposes of section 302(b)(2)(C)(i) should be made after the whole transaction is consummated. Making the immediately before and the immediately after computations in this manner properly reflects the extent to which the shareholder involved in each situation actually reduces his stock holdings as a result of the whole transaction.

Therefore, for purposes of the computations required by section 302(b)(2)(C) of the Code, A and B, in *Situation 1,* will each be viewed as having owned 50 percent (50/100 shares) of X before the transaction and 33⅓ percent (25/75 shares) immediately thereafter. In *Situation 2,* A and B will each be viewed as having owned 50 percent (50/100 shares) of X before the transaction and 33⅓ percent (30/90 shares) immediately thereafter. Furthermore, in each situation, the result would be the same if the redemption had preceded the issuance, or sale, of stock.

Accordingly, in both *Situations 1* and *2,* the requirements of section 302(b)(2) of the Code are satisfied. Therefore, the amounts distributed to A and B in both situations are distributions in full payment in exchange for the stock redeemed pursuant to section 302(a).

NOTE

The classic bootstrap acquisition is a transaction where the buyer purchases all or part of the stock of the target corporation in conjunction with a redemption of some of the selling shareholder's stock. In Zenz v. Quinlivan,[1] which is discussed in Revenue Ruling 75–447, the sole shareholder of a corporation sold part of her stock for cash and, three weeks later, the corporation redeemed her remaining shares. The combined sale and redemption structure was used because the buyer wanted to minimize future dividend exposure by reducing the corporation's earnings and profits. The seller's agenda was to be taxed on both the sale and redemption at then favorable capital gains rates and avoid dividend treatment on the redemption.

The Service argued that the redemption would have been a dividend to the target's shareholder if the distribution had preceded the sale and should not be treated any differently where the parties orchestrated a different order of events. The Sixth Circuit disagreed. Finding that the taxpayer intended from the outset to terminate her entire interest in the corporation, it held that the redemption qualified as an exchange rather than a dividend. The Service subsequently acquiesced to the result in *Zenz* and extended its reasoning to substantially disproportionate redemptions in Revenue Ruling 75–447.

In the case of a noncorporate shareholder, *Zenz* and its progeny have far less significance as long as qualified dividends are taxed at preferential capital gains rates. In a combined sale and redemption transaction, a noncorporate seller ordinarily will suffer no tax disadvantage if the distribution in redemption is characterized as a dividend. The distinction still matters, however, to corporate shareholders. As discussed in Chapter 4,[2] corporate sellers who are seeking to extract liquid assets prior to a sale of stock normally prefer a pre-sale dividend for two reasons: (1) the availability of the dividends received deduction, and (2) corporate capital gains are not taxed at preferential rates.

PROBLEM

Strap is the sole shareholder of Target Corporation. Boot is a prospective buyer and is willing to purchase all of the Target stock, but Boot is unable to pay the $500,000 price demanded by Strap even though he believes it to be fair. Target has more than $100,000 of accumulated earnings and profits and $100,000 cash on hand. Should Strap and Boot structure Boot's acquisition of Target along the lines of the *Zenz* case? Is there a better alternative? What additional facts would you like to know? (Compare to *TSN Liquidating* and the problem on page 193, supra.)

2.   BUY-SELL AGREEMENTS

a.   IN GENERAL

Code: §§ 101(a), 264(a)(1); skim § 2703.

---

1. 213 F.2d 914 (6th Cir. 1954).   **2.** See Chapter 4G, supra.

Closely held corporations frequently use buy-sell stock purchase agreements to ensure continuity of the business, to satisfy economic and tax goals when a shareholder dies or retires, and to resolve shareholder disputes. There are two basic forms of buy-sell agreements. Under a "cross-purchase" agreement, the departing shareholder or the shareholder's estate sells stock to the continuing shareholders. Under the more commonly employed "entity-purchase" agreement, the corporation redeems the departing shareholder's stock, funding the redemption with available cash, borrowed funds, an installment note, or the proceeds of a corporate-owned life insurance policy. The obligation to buy (or sell) may be mandatory or optional, as the parties agree, and is triggered by certain events specified in the agreement. The most common trigger event is a shareholder's death. Other typical trigger events are retirement or disability.

Buy-sell provisions frequently are part of a more comprehensive shareholders' agreement that includes restrictions on the transfer of stock, rights of first refusal to the corporation in the event a shareholder wishes to sell, and provisions to determine the value of any stock purchased pursuant to the agreement. Some primitive agreements set the price based on "book value," an accounting concept that often bears little or no relationship to the economic value of the company. More sophisticated agreements will use a formula based on earnings or provide for an appraisal mechanism on the occurrence of a trigger event.

A goal of many buy-sell agreements for closely-held family businesses is to establish the federal estate tax valuation of the stock upon a shareholder's death. A decedent's gross estate generally includes all property held by the decedent, valued either at the date of death or six months thereafter (the alternate valuation date).[1] In the case of unlisted stock, which cannot be valued by market quotations, fair market value is determined by taking into account a variety of factors, including the corporation's net worth, its earnings history and dividend-paying capacity, and the value of stock of publicly traded companies in the same line of business.[2] If stock is subject to an option or contract to purchase, such as a buy-sell agreement, the regulations provide that the agreement will establish the value if it represents a bona fide business arrangement and is not a device to pass the stock to the natural objects of the decedent's bounty for less than adequate and full consideration.[3] But if the decedent was free to dispose of the stock during his lifetime without price restrictions, "little weight" is given to the price set at death by the option or contract.[4] The courts agree that maintaining control of a closely held business constitutes a bona fide

1. I.R.C. §§ 2031; 2032.

2. I.R.C. § 2031(b); Reg. § 20.2031–2(f)(2). See also Rev. Rul. 59–60, 1959–1 C.B. 237.

3. Reg. § 20.2031–2(h). For the buy-sell agreement price to be binding, the decedent's estate must be obligated to sell the decedent's stock; the buyer either must be obligated to buy the decedent's interest or have an option to do so; and the price specified must have been fair at the time the agreement was made. Id.

4. Id.

business purpose but they require a separate examination of whether a restriction or option constitutes a "testamentary device."[5]

For buy-sell agreements entered into or substantially modified after October 8, 1990, Congress has added some statutory restrictions on the valuation of property subject to an option or contract to purchase. Section 2703(a) provides that the value of any property for estate, gift and generation-skipping tax purposes shall be determined without regard to (1) any option, agreement or other right to acquire or use property at a price less than the fair market value of the property, disregarding the option agreement or right, or (2) any restriction on the right to sell or use such property. Under this general rule, the effect of a buy-sell agreement on valuation would be disregarded. Section 2703(b), however, provides an exception for any option, agreement, right or restriction which satisfies the standards of the regulations (bona fide business arrangement and not a testamentary device) and has terms "comparable to similar arrangements entered into by persons in an arm's length transaction." In adding this comparability standard, Congress intended the taxpayer to show that the agreement was one that could have been obtained in an arm's length bargain with an unrelated party, considering such factors as the term of the agreement, the present value of the affected property, and its expected value at the time of exercise.[6] In noting that this standard would not be met "by showing isolated comparables but requires a demonstration of the general practice of unrelated parties," the Senate Finance Committee stated that expert testimony—e.g., by an appraiser familiar with the industry—would be evidence of such general practice.[7]

Drafters of buy-sell agreements still have some flexibility in their use of valuation methodologies. For example, the legislative history of Section 2703 states that a buy-sell agreement should not be disregarded merely because its terms differ from those used by another similarly situated company.[8] Noting that general business practice may recognize more than one valuation methodology, even within the same industry, the conferees went on to state that "[i]n such situations, one of several generally accepted methodologies may satisfy the standard contained in the conference agreement."[9]

Section 2703 has not resulted in the demise of buy-sell agreements to fix estate tax valuation. It merely places a greater premium on an evidentiary showing that the arrangement is bona fide and not merely a tax-avoidance device to transfer a family business to the next generation for less than adequate and full consideration.

As developed in the next section of the text, buy-sell agreements also may raise constructive dividend issues if they are not properly structured

---

5. See, e.g., St. Louis County Bank v. United States, 674 F.2d 1207 (8th Cir.1982).

6. Senate Finance Committee Explanation of Revenue Provisions, 1991 Budget Reconciliation Bill (Oct. 13, 1990), 101st Cong., 2d Sess. 68 (1990).

7. Id. See also Reg. § 25.2703–1.

8. H.Rep. No. 101–964, 101st Cong., 2d Sess. 157 (1990).

9. Id. See also Reg. § 25.2703–1(b)(4).

and implemented. With most dividends now taxed at 15 percent, these issues may or may not be important depending on other variables, such as the shareholder's stock basis, the need for capital gains to absorb otherwise unavailable capital losses, and the shareholder's other tax characteristics.

b. CONSTRUCTIVE DIVIDEND ISSUES

Revenue Ruling 69–608

1969–2 Cum.Bull. 42.

Advice has been requested as to the treatment for Federal income tax purposes of the redemption by a corporation of a retiring shareholder's stock where the remaining shareholder of the corporation has entered into a contract to purchase such stock.

Where the stock of a corporation is held by a small group of people, it is often considered necessary to the continuity of the corporation to have the individuals enter into agreements among themselves to provide for the disposition of the stock of the corporation in the event of the resignation, death, or incapacity of one of them. Such agreements are generally reciprocal among the shareholders and usually provide that on the resignation, death, or incapacity of one of the principal shareholders, the remaining shareholders will purchase his stock. Frequently such agreements are assigned to the corporation by the remaining shareholder and the corporation actually redeems its stock from the retiring shareholder.

Where a corporation redeems stock from a retiring shareholder, the fact that the corporation in purchasing the shares satisfies the continuing shareholder's executory contractual obligation to purchase the redeemed shares does not result in a distribution to the continuing shareholder provided that the continuing shareholder is not subject to an existing primary and unconditional obligation to perform the contract and that the corporation pays no more than fair market value for the stock redeemed.

On the other hand, if the continuing shareholder, at the time of the assignment to the corporation of his contract to purchase the retiring shareholder's stock, is subject to an unconditional obligation to purchase the retiring shareholder's stock, the satisfaction by the corporation of his obligation results in a constructive distribution to him. The constructive distribution is taxable as a distribution under section 301 of the Internal Revenue Code of 1954.

If the continuing shareholder assigns his stock purchase contract to the redeeming corporation prior to the time when he incurs a primary and unconditional obligation to pay for the shares of stock, no distribution to him will result. If, on the other hand, the assignment takes place after the time when the continuing shareholder is so obligated, a distribution to him will result. While a pre-existing obligation to perform in the future is a necessary element in establishing a distribution in this type of case, it is not until the obligor's duty to perform becomes unconditional that it can be said a primary and unconditional obligation arises.

The application of the above principles may be illustrated by the situations described below.

Situation 1

A and B are unrelated individuals who own all of the outstanding stock of corporation X. A and B enter into an agreement that provides in the event B leaves the employ of X, he will sell his X stock to A at a price fixed by the agreement. The agreement provides that within a specified number of days of B's offer to sell, A will purchase at the price fixed by the agreement all of the X stock owned by B. B terminates his employment and tenders the X stock to A. Instead of purchasing the stock himself in accordance with the terms of the agreement, A causes X to assume the contract and to redeem its stock held by B. In this case, A had a primary and unconditional obligation to perform his contract with B at the time the contract was assigned to X. Therefore, the redemption by X of its stock held by B will result in a constructive distribution to A. See William J. and Georgia K. Sullivan v. United States of America, 244 F.Supp. 605 (1965), affirmed, 363 F.2d 724 (1966), certiorari denied, 387 U.S. 905, 87 S.Ct. 1683 (1967), rehearing denied, 388 U.S. 924, 87 S.Ct. 2104 (1967).

Situation 2

A and B are unrelated individuals who own all of the outstanding stock of corporation X. An agreement between them provides unconditionally that within ninety days of the death of either A or B, the survivor will purchase the decedent's stock of X from his estate. Following the death of B, A causes X to assume the contract and redeem the stock from B's estate.

The assignment of the contract to X followed by the redemption by X of the stock owned by B's estate will result in a constructive distribution to A because immediately on the death of B, A had a primary and unconditional obligation to perform the contract.

Situation 3

All of the stock of X corporation was owned by a trust that was to terminate in 1968. Individuals A and B were the beneficiaries of the trust. Since B was the trustee of the trust, he had exclusive management authority over X through his control of the board of directors. In 1966, A paid to B the sum of 25x dollars and promised to pay an additional 20x dollars to B in 1969 for B's interest in the corpus and accumulations of the trust plus B's agreement to resign immediately as supervisor of the trust and release his control over the management of the corporation. The actual transfer of the stock held in trust was to take place on termination of the trust in 1968. In 1969, X reimbursed A for the 25x dollars previously paid to B, paid 20x dollars to B, and received the X stock held by B.

For all practical purposes, A became the owner of B's shares in 1966. Although naked legal title to the shares could not be transferred until the trust terminated in 1968, B did transfer all of his beneficial and equitable ownership of the X stock to A in exchange for an immediate payment by A of 25x dollars and an unconditional promise to pay an additional 20x dollars upon termination of the trust. The payment by X of 20x dollars to B and

25x dollars to *A* in 1969 constituted a constructive distribution to *A* in the amount of 45x dollars. See Schalk Chemical Company v. Commissioner, 32 T.C. 879 (1959), affirmed 304 F.2d 48 (1962).

Situation 4

A and *B* owned all of the outstanding stock of *X* corporation. *A* and *B* entered into a contract under which, if *B* desired to sell his *X* stock, *A* agreed to purchase the stock or to cause such stock to be purchased. If *B* chose to sell his *X* stock to any person other than *A,* he could do so at any time. In accordance with the terms of the contract, *A* caused *X* to redeem all of *B*'s stock in *X*.

At the time of the redemption, *B* was free to sell his stock to *A* or to any other person, and *A* had no unconditional obligation to purchase the stock and no fixed liability to pay for the stock. Accordingly, the redemption by *X* did not result in a constructive distribution to *A*. See S.K. Ames, Inc. v. Commissioner, 46 B.T.A. 1020 (1942), acquiescence, C.B. 1942–1, 1.

Situation 5

A and *B* owned all of the outstanding stock of *X* corporation. An agreement between *A* and *B* provided that upon the death of either, *X* will redeem all of the *X* stock owned by the decedent at the time of his death. In the event that *X* does not redeem the shares from the estate, the agreement provided that the surviving shareholder would purchase the unredeemed shares from the decedent's estate. *B* died and, in accordance with the agreement, *X* redeemed all of the shares owned by his estate.

In this case *A* was only secondarily liable under the agreement between *A* and *B*. Since *A* was not primarily obligated to purchase the *X* stock from the estate of *B*, he received no constructive distribution when *X* redeemed the stock.

Situation 6

B owned all of the outstanding stock of *X* corporation. *A* and *B* entered into an agreement under which *A* was to purchase all of the *X* stock from *B*. *A* did not contemplate purchasing the *X* stock in his own name. Therefore, the contract between *A* and *B* specifically provided that it could be assigned by *A* to a corporation and that, if the corporation agreed to be bound by the terms, *A* would be released from the contract.

A organized *Y* corporation and assigned the stock purchase contract to it. *Y* borrowed funds and purchased all of the *X* stock from *B* pursuant to the agreement. Subsequently *Y* was merged into *X* and *X* assumed the liabilities that *Y* incurred in connection with the purchase of the *X* stock and subsequently satisfied these liabilities.

The purchase by *Y* of the stock of *X* did not result in a constructive distribution to *A*. Since *A* did not contemplate purchasing the *X* stock in his own name, he provided in the contract that it could be assigned to a corporation prior to the closing date. *A* chose this latter alternative and assigned the contract to *Y*. *A* was not personally subject to an unconditional obligation to purchase the *X* stock from *B*. See Arthur J. Kobacker and

Sara Jo Kobacker, et al. v. Commissioner, 37 T.C. 882 (1962), acquiescence, C.B. 1964 2, 6. Compare Ray Edenfield v. Commissioner, 19 T.C. 13 (1952), acquiescence, C.B. 1953–1, 4.

Situation 7

A and B owned all of the outstanding stock of X corporation. An agreement between the shareholders provided that upon the death of either, the survivor would purchase the decedent's shares from his estate at a price provided in the agreement. Subsequently, the agreement was rescinded and a new agreement entered into which provided that upon the death of either A or B, X would redeem all of the decedent's shares of X stock from his estate.

The cancellation of the original contract between the parties in favor of the new contract did not result in a constructive distribution to either A or B. At the time X agreed to purchase the stock pursuant to the terms of the new agreement, neither A nor B had an unconditional obligation to purchase shares of X stock. The subsequent redemption of the stock from the estate of either pursuant to the terms of the new agreement will not constitute a constructive distribution to the surviving shareholder.

PROBLEM

A, B and C, who are unrelated, each own 1,000 shares of common stock (the only class outstanding) of X Corporation with a fair market value of $400 per share. X has $600,000 of accumulated and no current earnings and profits. A and C each have a $50,000 adjusted basis in their X stock. B, who recently received her stock as an inheritance, has a $400,000 adjusted basis. B wishes to retire and dispose of her stock.

What are the tax consequences of the following alternative transactions:

(a) Pursuant to a cross-purchase buy-sell agreement, B sells 500 shares each to A and C for $200,000 each.

(b) Pursuant to an entity-purchase buy-sell agreement, X redeems all of B's stock for $400,000.

(c) Same as (a), above, except the agreement required A and C to buy B's stock over ten years, with appropriate interest, but they did not have sufficient funds to make the payments so they caused X to make them on their behalf.

(d) A and C had options to buy B's stock when B retired but they were short of funds and allowed X to redeem the stock instead.

(e) The parties previously entered into a cross-purchase agreement under which they agreed that the two surviving shareholders would purchase the X stock owned by the estate of the first shareholder to die. X purchased a life insurance policy on the life of each shareholder and paid the annual premiums. X is the beneficiary under the policies. B died this year, and X used the proceeds from the policy on B's life to completely redeem the stock held by B's estate.

c. REDEMPTIONS INCIDENT TO DIVORCE

Regulations: § 1.1041–2(a), (b), (c), (d).

Arnes v. United States

United States Court of Appeals, Ninth Circuit, 1992.
981 F.2d 456.

■ HUG, CIRCUIT JUDGE:

The issue in this case is whether a taxpayer must recognize for income tax purposes the gain that she realized when, pursuant to a divorce settlement, a corporation redeemed her half of the stock in the corporation, the remaining stock of which was owned by her former husband. The district court, ruling on cross-motions for summary judgment, held that Section 1041 of the Internal Revenue Code of 1986 (I.R.C.) relieved the taxpayer of having to recognize the gain, and awarded the taxpayer a refund of $53,053 for 1988. * * * We affirm.

I.

Joann Arnes, the Taxpayer–Appellee, married John Arnes in 1970. In 1980, they formed a corporation, "Moriah," to operate a McDonald's franchise in Ellensburg, Washington. That corporation issued 5,000 shares of stock in the joint names of John Arnes and Joann Arnes. In 1987, the couple agreed to divorce. McDonald's Corporation required 100% ownership of the equity and profits by the owner/operator, and informed John Arnes that there should be no joint ownership of the restaurant after the divorce.

Joann and John Arnes entered into an agreement to have their corporation redeem Joann Arnes' 50 percent interest in the outstanding stock for $450,000. The corporation would pay that money to Joann Arnes by forgiving a debt of approximately $110,000 that she owed the corporation, by making two payments of $25,000 to her during 1988, and by paying the remainder of approximately $290,000 to her in monthly installments over ten years beginning in February 1988. The agreement was incorporated into the decree of dissolution of the marriage, dated January 7, 1988. Joann Arnes surrendered her 2,500 shares to the corporation on December 31, 1987, and the corporation cancelled her stock certificate on May 4, 1988, then issuing another 2,500 shares to John Arnes.

On her federal income tax return for 1988, Joann Arnes reported that she sold her stock in Moriah on January 2, 1988, for a price of $450,000, and that her basis was $2,500, resulting in a profit of $447,500. She received $178,042 in 1988 as part of the sales price. Using an installment method, she treated $177,045 as long-term capital gain and the remainder as recovery of a portion of her basis.

On December 27, 1989, she filed a timely claim for refund of $53,053 for 1988 on the ground that she was not required to recognize any gain on the transfer of her stock because the transfer was made pursuant to a divorce instrument. The IRS did not allow the claim for refund, and Joann Arnes initiated this suit.

The district court found that the redemption of Joann Arnes' stock in Moriah was required by a divorce instrument, and that John Arnes had benefitted from the transaction because it was part of the marital property settlement, which limited future community property claims that Joann Arnes might have brought against him. The court, in applying the IRS regulations, found that, although Joann transferred her stock directly to Moriah, the transfer was made on behalf of John and should have been treated as having been made to John. Therefore, the transfer qualified for nonrecognition of gain pursuant to the I.R.C. exemption for transfers made to spouses or former spouses incident to a divorce settlement. See 26 U.S.C. § 1041 (1988). Summary judgment was granted in favor of Joann Arnes.

The Government appeals. Meanwhile, in order to insure that the capital gain will be taxed, the Government has asserted a protective income tax deficiency against John Arnes, who has contested the deficiency by filing a petition with the Tax Court. His case is pending but not before this court. The Government maintains that, although Joann Arnes is the appropriate party to be taxed for the gain, John Arnes should be taxed if the district court's ruling is upheld. If neither John nor Joann is taxed, the $450,000 used to redeem Joann's appreciated stock apparently will be taken out of the corporation tax-free.

* * *

III.

The Government contends that the gain resulting from Moriah's redemption of Joann Arnes' stock does not qualify for exemption under section 1041, which is limited to transfers made directly to one's spouse or former spouse, or transfers made into trust for that person. Joann Arnes' transfer to Moriah, the Government contends, is outside the scope of the exemption. Joann Arnes contends that her transfer of stock to Moriah should be considered a transfer to John, resulting in a benefit to John, and absolving her of the obligation to bear the burden of any resulting tax.

* * *

The purpose of [Section 1041] is to defer the tax consequences of transfers between spouses or former spouses. See H.R.Rep. No. 432, Pt. II, 98th Cong., 2d Sess. 1491 (1984), reprinted in 1984 U.S.Code Cong. & Admin.News 697, 1134 ("a husband and wife are a single economic unit"). Property received in such a transfer is excluded from the recipient's gross income. The recipient's basis is then equal to the transferor's basis. 26 U.S.C. § 1041(b)(2)(1988). Later, when the recipient transfers the property to a third party, the gain or loss must be recognized.

After section 1041 was enacted, the Treasury Department published a temporary regulation to implement the statute. Temp. Treas. Reg. § 1.1041–1T (1992). The regulation explains that in certain cases a transfer of property to a third party "on behalf of" a spouse or former spouse should be treated as a transfer to the spouse or former spouse. Id. at Q–9, A–9. One example supplied in the regulation is the case where the transfer to the third party is required by a divorce or separation instrument. Such a transfer of property will be treated as made directly to the nontransferring spouse (or former spouse) and the nontransferring spouse will be treated as immediately transferring the property to the third party. The deemed transfer from the nontransferring spouse (or former spouse) to the third party is not a transaction that qualifies for nonrecognition of gain under section 1041. Temp.Treas.Reg. § 1.1041–1T, A–9 (1992).

The example suggests that the tax consequences of any gain or loss arising from the transaction would fall upon the nontransferring spouse for whose benefit the transfer was made, rather than upon the transferring spouse. Consistent with the policy of the statute, which is to defer recognition until the property is conveyed to a party outside the marital unit, the regulation seems to provide for shifting the tax burden from one spouse to the other, where appropriate.

Thus, a transfer by a spouse to a third party can be treated as a transfer to the other spouse when it is "on behalf of" the other spouse. Whether the redemption of Joann's stock can be construed as a transfer to John, pursuant to the regulation example in A–9, depends upon the meaning of "on behalf of." The district court interpreted the regulation as meaning that a transfer was made "on behalf of" John Arnes if he received a benefit from the transfer. The court then concluded that John did receive a benefit, because the transfer was part of the marital property agreement which settled any future community property claims that Joann Arnes could have asserted against John.

Although no case is directly on point, many tax cases concern transfers made on behalf of other persons. Generally, a transfer is considered to have been made "on behalf of" someone if it satisfied an obligation or a liability of that person. If an employer pays an employee's income tax, that payment is income to the employee. See Old Colony Trust Co. v. Commissioner, 279 U.S. 716, 729–31, 49 S.Ct. 499, 504, 73 L.Ed. 918 (1929). If a corporation assumes a shareholder's bank note in exchange for stock, the shareholder receives a taxable constructive dividend. Schroeder v. Commissioner, 831 F.2d 856, 859 (9th Cir.1987).

In *Schroeder*, the taxpayer borrowed money from a bank to buy stock in the corporation. The corporation later redeemed part of that stock, assumed the taxpayer's bank note, and forgave a debt owed by the taxpayer to the corporation. At the time that the taxpayer borrowed the money from the bank, he owned no part of the corporation and had no authority to act on behalf of the corporation. See id. at 859–60 & n. 7. The taxpayer had the primary obligation to repay the loan, and the corporation's assumption of the loan relieved the taxpayer of that obligation. We held that the redemption of Schroeder's stock was a taxable constructive dividend. Id. at 859.

The Government argues that the Arnes stock transfer is more properly analogized to Holsey v. Commissioner, 258 F.2d 865 (3d Cir.1958), where the Third Circuit held that a shareholder who owned fifty percent of the stock in a corporation did not receive a taxable benefit when the corporation redeemed the other fifty percent of the stock. The court found that the redemption "did not discharge any obligation of [the taxpayer] and did not benefit him in any direct sense," although the result was that the shareholder gained control of the company. Id. at 868.

John Arnes had an obligation to Joann Arnes that was relieved by Moriah's payment to Joann. That obligation was based in their divorce property settlement, which called for the redemption of Joann's stock. Although John and Joann were the sole stockholders in Moriah, the obligation to purchase Joann's stock was John's, not Moriah's. Furthermore, John personally guaranteed Moriah's note to Joann. Under Washington law, Joann could sue John for payment without suing Moriah. See Wash.Rev.Code Ann. § 62A.3–416(1) (West 1979). Thus, John was liable, with Moriah, for the payments due Joann.

We hold that Joann's transfer to Moriah did relieve John of an obligation, and therefore constituted a benefit to John. Joann's transfer of stock should be treated as a constructive transfer to John, who then transferred the stock to Moriah. The $450,000 was paid to Joann by Moriah on behalf of John. The transfer of $450,000 from the corporate treasury need not escape taxation, if we hold, as we do, that Joann is not required to recognize any gain on the transfer of her stock, because it is subject to section 1041. The tax result for Joann is the same as if she had conveyed the property directly to John.

The Government argues that because Joann transferred her stock to the corporation, rather than to John, the exception in section 1041 should not apply. The corporation cancelled Joann's stock and agreed to pay Joann $450,000. As a result, no asset with a carryover basis exists. John received an additional 2,500 shares from the corporation after Joann's shares were cancelled, but he did not carry over Joann's basis, because the transfer was not made directly to him. Under this literal application of the statute, Joann's gain, from the appreciation of the stock, would not be recognized by John if he were to dispose of his stock. Although John became the sole owner of the corporation as a result of the transfer, the net worth of the corporation was depleted, because the corporation incurred the debt of $450,000 to Joann. As the Government puts it, before the stock redemption, John owned half of a corporation worth $900,000; after the redemption, he owned all of a corporation worth $450,000. John has realized no gain; the value of his stock is still in the corporation, and the redemption did not increase the value of John's stock. In contrast, Joann received cash (and debt forgiveness) for her transfer of stock.

We reject the Government's application of the statute. The regulations, particularly as explained by Question and Answer 9, in Temp. Treas. Reg.

§ 1.1041–1T, demonstrate that the statute is meant to apply to situations such as this one, where a transfer is made on behalf of one's former spouse.

Finally, the Government points to one other example in the Temporary Treasury Regulations interpreting section 1041. Question 2 describes a situation in which a corporation wholly owned by one spouse sells property to the other spouse. That sale is not subject to the exemption rule of section 1041. See Temp. Treas. Reg. § 1.1041–1T(a), Q–2, A–2, ex. 3 (1992). The example does not apply to the Arnes transaction because Moriah was owned one-half each by John and Joann.

The judgment of the district court is AFFIRMED.

NOTE

Tax Consequences to Nontransferor Spouse. The Ninth Circuit found that the disposition of Mrs. Arnes' stock was not a redemption but rather a sale to Mr. Arnes in a tax-free transaction under Section 1041. What then are the tax consequences to Mr. Arnes, who was not a party to the case? Assuming that Moriah was a C corporation with sufficient earnings and profits, Mr. Arnes would appear to have a $450,000 constructive dividend (taxable, under current law, at a maximum rate of 15 percent but with no recovery of basis) under the Ninth Circuit's characterization of the transaction. But appearances can be deceiving. Mr. Arnes took his controversy to the Tax Court, which held in a reviewed decision that he did not have a constructive dividend because he was not primarily and unconditionally obligated to acquire his wife's stock.[1] The court supported its decision with the following example from Revenue Ruling 69–608:[2]

> A and B owned all the outstanding stock of X corporation. An agreement between A and B provided that upon the death of either, X will redeem all the X stock owned by the decedent at the time of death. In the event that X does not redeem the shares from the estate, the agreement provided that the surviving shareholder would purchase the unredeemed shares from the decedent's estate. B died and, in accordance with the agreement, X redeemed all of the shares owned by his estate.

> In this case A was only secondarily liable under the agreement between A and B. Since A was not primarily obligated to purchase the X stock from the estate of B he received no constructive distribution when X redeemed the stock.

1. Arnes v. Commissioner, 102 T.C. 522 (1994). See also Blatt v. Commissioner, 102 T.C. 77 (1994) (wife taxable on redemption; no Section 1041 transfer because redemption did not satisfy any legal obligation of husband and wife was not acting "on behalf of" husband at time of acquisition);

Hayes v. Commissioner, 101 T.C. 593 (1993) (redemption of wife's stock was a constructive dividend to husband where husband had a primary and unconditional obligation to purchase that stock; no Section 1041 issue before the court).

2. See supra p. 254.

As a result, neither Mr. nor Mrs. Arnes was taxable on the transaction— the dreaded "whipsaw" result that the Service was trying to avoid.

Which result was more favorable overall for the taxpayers—the Ninth Circuit's or the Tax Court's? Remember that it is usually desirable in a marital dissolution setting for the parties to plan to reduce their overall tax liability. In a concurring opinion in *Arnes*, Tax Court Judge Beghe offered this observation:[3]

> Hewing to the bright line rules of Rev. Rul. 69–608 * * * in the marital dissolution context will reduce the tax costs of divorce for the owners of small businesses held and operated in corporate form. If the shareholder spouses can negotiate their separation agreement with the assurance that the redemption will be tax free to the remaining shareholder and a capital gain transaction to the terminating shareholder, the overall tax costs will ordinarily be less than if the terminating spouse qualifies for nonrecognition under Section 1041, but the remaining spouse suffers a dividend tax. This will leave a bigger pie to be divided in setting the consideration for the share to be redeemed.

Confusion in the Courts: Inconsistent Standards. The Ninth Circuit held that Mrs. Arnes was not taxable under Section 1041 because her transfer was "on behalf of" her husband within the meaning of the Section 1041 regulations. But the Tax Court held that Mr. Arnes did not have a constructive dividend because the corporation did not satisfy his "primary and unconditional" obligation to acquire his wife's stock. So neither spouse was taxed and the Service was whipsawed because different standards were applied to the transferor and nontransferor spouse to determine the tax consequences of the same transaction.

The Tax Court has revisited this issue, but its multiple and conflicting opinions in Read v. Commissioner[4] only added to the confusion. The fact pattern in *Read* was fairly typical. Prior to their marital dissolution, Mr. and Mrs. Read owned virtually all the stock of Mulberry Motor Parts, Inc. ("MMP"), a C corporation. Mrs. Read ("W") agreed to sell her MMP stock to Mr. Read ("H") for cash and a promissory note bearing market rate interest unless H elected to cause MMP or its separate employee stock ownership plan to buy the stock on the same terms. H elected to have MMP redeem W's stock. Although W reported the interest paid by MMP on the promissory note as income, neither W nor H reported any taxable gain on the redemption. Fearing a whipsaw, the Service issued deficiency notices to both parties. But it ultimately aligned itself with W by arguing in the Tax Court that H had received a constructive dividend from MMP in the full amount of the principal and interest payments received by W.

The Tax Court majority viewed the central issue to be whether W's transfer of MMP stock to MMP was made "on behalf of H" so that W was

---

3. 102 T.C. at 541.

4. 114 T.C. 14 (2000).

entitled to nonrecognition of gain under the Section 1041 regulations.[5] W argued that the regulations squarely applied to her situation, while H, seeking to avoid a constructive dividend, relied on established case law in arguing that he should not be taxed because he never had a "primary and unconditional obligation" to purchase W's stock.

The Tax Court majority sided with W, holding for the first time that application of the venerable "primary and unconditional" standard to the nontransferor spouse was inappropriate in divorce-related redemptions. Instead, the majority based its decision on the Section 1041 regulations in holding that W's transfer of MMP stock to MMP was a transfer made "on behalf of" H. The court found that H's election to have MMP redeem W's stock caused W to be acting as H's representative in connection with the redemption. In light of these holdings, the majority sustained the deficiencies asserted against H, noting that H had "indicated" that he would be taxable if the court found that W was entitled to nonrecognition under Section 1041. Because it found H's "indication" as tantamount to a concession, the Tax Court majority offered no analysis of the proper standard to be applied to the nonredeeming spouse. As discussed earlier in this Note, however, the Tax Court previously had applied the "primary and unconditional" standard in holding that a nontransferor spouse does not invariably receive a constructive dividend in a divorce-related redemption.

Nine judges joined the majority opinion in *Read*; six of the nine wrote a concurring opinion with more extensive analysis of the unfavorable tax consequences to H. Seven judges dissented in four separate opinions. Despite differences in emphasis, the essence of the dissents was that the majority should not have discarded the "primary and unconditional" standard in the divorce setting.

Regulations to the Rescue. Reacting to the confusion in the courts, the Service amended the Section 1041 regulations to provide greater certainty in determining the tax consequences of divorce-related redemptions. Unlike the Tax Court majority in *Read*, the regulations seek to harmonize the well recognized "primary and unconditional obligation" standard for constructive dividends with the policy of Section 1041.

The threshold question posed by the regulations is whether a divorce-related redemption results in a constructive distribution to the nontransferor spouse under applicable tax law. For this purpose, "applicable tax law" means the primary and unconditional obligation standard.[6] If the redemption does result in a constructive distribution, the redeemed stock is deemed to have been transferred by the transferor spouse to the nontransferor spouse in a tax-free Section 1041 transaction (provided the requirements of Section 1041 are otherwise met), and then retransferred by the nontransferor spouse to the redeeming corporation.[7] The tax conse-

---

5.   See Reg. § 1.1041–1T(c), Q & A–9.

6.   Reg. § 1.1041–2(a), (d) Examples 1 & 3.

7.   Reg. § 1.1041–2(a)(2), –2(b)(2).

quences of the deemed redemption are then determined under Section 302.[8] As a result, the transferor spouse has no gain or loss on the deemed transfer of stock to the nontransferor spouse, and the nontransferor spouse most likely has a constructive dividend.[9]

If the redemption does not result in a constructive distribution—e.g., because it does not satisfy a primary and unconditional obligation of the nontransferor spouse—the regulations respect the form of the transaction.[10] That means that the corporation is treated as having redeemed stock directly from the transferor spouse in a transaction in which the nontransferor spouse is not a party. As a result, Section 1041 does not apply, the transferor spouse's tax treatment is determined under Section 302 (likely a capital gain), and the nontransferor spouse is not taxed.[11]

The regulations provide a "special rule" permitting spouses to depart from "applicable tax law" and treat a divorce-related redemption as either taxable to the transferor spouse (even if it would have been a constructive dividend to the nontransferor spouse under applicable tax law) or as a constructive distribution to the nontransferor spouse and a tax-free Section 1041 transfer to the transferor spouse (even in the absence of a primary and unconditional obligation).[12] This rule is consistent with the general policy allowing the parties to a divorce to negotiate and ultimately determine the tax consequences of divorce-related transactions (e.g., spousal and child support payments, property transfers, dependency exemptions) as long as they treat the transactions consistently. To utilize the special rule, the parties must memorialize their intent in a written agreement prior to the date on which the nontransferor spouse files his or her first timely filed federal income tax return for the year that includes the date of the stock redemption but no later than the due date of the return (including extensions).[13]

If the regulations had applied to the redemption in the *Arnes* case and the parties had not elected to utilize the special rule, which spouse would have been taxed?

Planning. In light of these permissive regulations, how should the parties plan a divorce-related redemption? For example, how should a redemption be structured if the parties wish to minimize their overall joint tax liability and preserve more dollars for the family? What is the best advice to a transferor or nontransferor spouse who wishes to avoid tax on the redemption? In what circumstances would the parties wish to invoke the "special rule?" Is it still possible, either through separate or joint planning, to structure a redemption so that neither spouse is taxed? Do the

---

8. Reg. § 1.1041–2(b)(2).

9. Whether or not the constructive distribution is a dividend depends on whether the corporation has earnings and profits and whether any of the tests for exchange treatment in Section 302 are met (unlikely in the typical fact pattern).

10. Reg. § 1.1041–2(a)(1).

11. Reg. § 1.1041–2(b)(1).

12. Reg. § 1.1041–2(c).

13. Reg. § 1.1041–2(c)(3).

regulations eliminate all legal controversies over the proper tax treatment of divorce-related redemptions?

PROBLEM

H and W, a married couple on the verge of divorce, each own 50 of the 100 outstanding shares of common stock (the only class outstanding) of Family Corp. ("F"), which has a total value of $1 million and $500,000 of accumulated earnings and profits. H and W each have a $100,000 basis in their F stock. H and W have agreed that on the effective date of their divorce, H will own all the stock of F and W will receive $500,000 for her 50 shares. Consider the tax consequences of the following proposals to meet these goals:

(a) H buys W's stock for $500,000 cash.

(b) H and W agree that F will redeem W's stock for $500,000 cash.

(c) How would you advise each of the parties to structure the transaction?

3.   CHARITABLE CONTRIBUTION AND REDEMPTION

Grove v. Commissioner
United States Court of Appeals, Second Circuit, 1973.
490 F.2d 241.

■ KAUFMAN, CHIEF JUDGE:

We are called upon, once again, to wrestle with the tangled web that is the Internal Revenue Code and decipher the often intricate and ingenious strategies devised by taxpayers to minimize their tax burdens. We undertake this effort mindful that taxpayer ingenuity, although channelled into an effort to reduce or eliminate the incidence of taxation, is ground for neither legal nor moral opprobrium. As Learned Hand so eloquently stated, "any one may so arrange his affairs that his taxes shall be as low as possible: he is not bound to choose that pattern which will best pay the Treasury: there is not even a patriotic duty to increase one's taxes * * *." Helvering v. Gregory, 69 F.2d 809, 810 (2d Cir.1934), aff'd 293 U.S. 465, 55 S.Ct. 266, 79 L.Ed. 596 (1935).

* * *

I.

A full recitation of the undisputed facts underlying this controversy will aid in placing the legal issues raised on appeal in their proper context.

Philip Grove received an engineering degree in 1924 from Rensselaer Polytechnic Institute, a private, tax-exempt educational institution. During the Depression, he founded what is now Grove Shepherd Wilson & Kruge, Inc. and at all times since has controlled a majority of its shares. The balance of the Corporation's shares, with the exception of those held by

RPI, are owned by officers and employees of the Corporation or their relatives.

The Corporation's business is building airfields, highways, tunnels, canals, and other similar heavy construction projects in both the United States and foreign countries. These projects usually involve the investment of large sums of money over an extended period of time and involve a high degree of risk. Since, in this industry, contract payments normally are made only after specified levels of progress are achieved, a firm must always commit substantial amounts of its own funds, whether borrowed or internally generated, to a project. Moreover, a company can determine an acceptable contract price based only on its best estimate of the cost to complete the project. A bad "guess" or unforeseen contingency may require a firm to complete a project while incurring a loss. Not surprisingly, the mortality rate in this industry is high. To protect against such adverse developments, successful firms seek to maintain liquidity by holding ample cash or other assets easily converted to cash. One method of conserving cash, adopted by the Corporation, is to retain all earnings and refrain from paying dividends.

As we have noted, RPI, like all universities and colleges, pursued its alumni with a wide variety of contribution plans. One plan employed "life income funds," and its terms were simple. An alumnus would make a gift of securities to RPI and retain a life interest in the income from the donated securities. Whatever dividends and interest were paid during the donor's life would belong to the donor, while any capital appreciation would inure to RPI. Upon the death of the donor, RPI would obtain full title to the securities.

In 1954, Dr. Livingston Houston, RPI's president, suggested to Grove that he make a gift under the "life income funds" plan. Grove explained that his only significant holdings were shares of his own corporation, but expressed a willingness to donate some of these shares under the plan, with certain qualifications. The Corporation, he stated, could not agree to any obligation or understanding to redeem shares held by RPI. This condition, of course, stemmed from a fear that RPI might seek redemption at a time when the Corporation was hard pressed for cash, which, as we have noted, was an asset crucial to a company in the heavy construction business. Moreover, since Grove at that time was unsure of RPI's money-management qualifications, he further conditioned his gift on a requirement that if RPI disposed of the shares, any proceeds would be invested and managed by an established professional firm.

RPI found these terms acceptable and on December 30, 1954, Grove made an initial gift of 200 shares, valued at $25,560. A letter accompanying the donation set forth the conditions we have recited. Moreover, in addition to retaining an interest in the income from the gift for his life, Grove specified that in the event he should predecease his wife Harriet, she would receive the income until her death.

On the same day, the Corporation and RPI signed a minority shareholder agreement. RPI agreed not to "sell, transfer, give, pledge or hypothecate, or in any way dispose of the whole or any part of the common stock of the Corporation now or hereafter owned * * * until [RPI] shall have first offered the Corporation the opportunity to purchase said shares upon the terms and conditions hereinafter provided." The redemption price was established at book value of the shares as noted on the Corporation's most recent certified financial statement prior to the offer. Pursuant to the contract, the Corporation was "entitled (but not obligated) to purchase all or any part of the shares of stock so offered." If the Corporation did not exercise its option to purchase within sixty days, RPI could transfer the shares to any other party and the Corporation's right of first refusal would not subsequently attach to such transferred shares.[3]

The 1954 gift was the first in a series of annual contributions to RPI by Grove. From 1954 to 1968, Grove donated to RPI between 165 and 250 shares of the Corporation each year, reaching a cumulative total of 2,652 shares, subject to terms substantially similar to those noted earlier.

Generally, RPI offered donated shares to the Corporation for redemption, between one and two years after they were donated by Grove. The transactions followed a similar pattern. On each occasion, the Finance Committee of RPI's Board of Trustees first authorized the sale of specific shares of the Corporation. RPI's treasurer or controller would then write to Sidney Houck, the Corporation's treasurer, informing him of RPI's desire to dispose of the shares. Upon receipt of this letter, Houck would call a special meeting of the Corporation's board of directors to consider whether or not to exercise the Corporation's right of first refusal. The Board would adopt a resolution authorizing redemption and Houck would so inform RPI's financial officer, enclosing a company check for the amount due. By return mail, RPI would forward the appropriate stock certificate to the Corporation for cancellation.

At the time of the first redemption, in December, 1955, RPI opened an investment account at the Albany, New York, office of Merrill Lynch, Pierce, Fenner & Beane ("Merrill Lynch"). The account was captioned "Rensselaer Polytechnic Institute (Philip H. Grove Fund) Account." In accordance with Grove's wishes concerning the management of disposition proceeds, RPI authorized Merrill Lynch to act directly upon investment recommendations made by Scudder, Stevens, & Clark, Grove's personal investment adviser. RPI deposited the proceeds of each redemption transaction into this account which, pursuant to Scudder, Stevens & Clark's instructions, were generally invested in securities of large corporations whose shares traded on organized stock exchanges. Merrill Lynch paid the income from these investments to RPI on a monthly basis. RPI, in turn, made quarterly remittances to Grove, accompanied by an analysis of all account transactions.

3. Other minority shareholders of the Corporation signed similar agreements, which, in effect put in writing the Corporation's practice of redeeming, when financial conditions permitted, any minority-owner shares offered to it, for example, by a departing employee or a deceased employee's widow.

On his personal income tax return for 1963, Grove reported as taxable income dividends of $4,939.28 and interest of $2,535.73 paid to him by RPI from the Merrill Lynch account. For 1964, Grove reported $6,096.05 in dividends and $3,540.81 in interest. The Commissioner, however, assessed deficiencies in Grove's taxable income for these years, asserting that Grove "realized additional dividends in the amounts of $29,000 and $25,800 in 1963 and 1964, respectively, as the result of the redemption of stock by Grove Shepherd Wilson & Kruge, Inc." Accordingly, the Commissioner increased Grove's taxable income by these amounts and demanded payment of additional taxes—in excess of $13,000 for each year. Grove refused to pay and petitioned the Tax Court for a redetermination of his tax liability. The Court, concluding that Grove had made a bona fide gift to RPI, ruled in favor of the taxpayer and the Commissioner appealed.

II.

The Commissioner's view of this case is relatively simple. In essence, we are urged to disregard the actual form of the Grove–RPI–Corporation donations and redemptions and to rewrite the actual events so that Grove's tax liability is seen in a wholly different light. Support for this position, it is argued, flows from the Supreme Court's decision in Commissioner of Internal Revenue v. Court Holding Co., 324 U.S. 331, 65 S.Ct. 707, 89 L.Ed. 981 (1945), which, in language familiar to law students, cautions that "[t]he incidence of taxation depends upon the substance of a transaction * * *. To permit the true nature of a transaction to be disguised by mere formalisms, which exist solely to alter tax liabilities, would seriously impair the effective administration of the tax policies of Congress." Id. at 334, 65 S.Ct. at 708. In an effort to bring the instant case within this language, the Commissioner insists that whatever the appearance of the transactions here under consideration, their "true nature" is quite different. He maintains that Grove, with the cooperation of RPI, withdrew substantial funds from the Corporation and manipulated them in a manner designed to produce income for his benefit. In the Commissioner's view, the transaction is properly characterized as a redemption by the Corporation of Grove's, not RIP's shares, followed by a cash gift to RPI by Grove. This result, it is said, more accurately reflects "economic reality."

The Commissioner's motives for insisting upon this formulation are easily understood once its tax consequences are examined. Although Grove reported taxable dividends and interest received from the Merrill Lynch account on his 1963 and 1964 tax returns, amounts paid by the Corporation to redeem the donated shares from RPI were not taxed upon distribution. If, however, the transactions are viewed in the manner suggested by the Commissioner, the redemption proceeds would be taxable as income to Grove. Moreover, because the redemptions did not in substance alter Grove's relationship to the Corporation—he continued throughout to control a majority of the outstanding shares—the entire proceeds would be taxed as a dividend payment at high, progressive ordinary-income rates, rather than as a sale of shares, at the fixed, and relatively low, capital gains rate. See, 26 U.S.C. § 302; United States v. Davis, 397 U.S. 301, 90 S.Ct. 1041, 25 L.Ed.2d 323 (1970).

Clearly, then, the stakes involved are high. We do not quarrel with the maxim that substance must prevail over form, but this proposition marks the beginning, not the end, of our inquiry. The court in Sheppard v. United States, 361 F.2d 972, 176 Ct.Cl. 244 (1966) perceptively remarked that "all such 'maxims' should rather be called 'minims' since they convey a minimum of information with a maximum of pretense." Id. at 977 n. 9. Each case requires detailed consideration of its unique facts. Here, our aim is to determine whether Grove's gifts of the Corporation's shares to RPI prior to redemption should be given independent significance or whether they should be regarded as meaningless intervening steps in a single, integrated transaction designed to avoid tax liability by the use of mere formalisms.

The guideposts for our analysis are well marked by earlier judicial encounters with this problem. "The law with respect to gifts of appreciated property is well established. A gift of appreciated property does not result in income to the donor so long as he gives the property away absolutely and parts with title thereto before the property gives rise to income by way of sale." Carrington v. Commissioner of Internal Revenue, 476 F.2d 704, 708 (5th Cir.1973), quoting Humacid Co., 42 T.C. 894, 913 (1964). As noted below by the Tax Court, the Commissioner here "does not contend that the gifts of stock by [Grove] to RPI in 1961 and 1962 were sham transactions, or that they were not completed gifts when made." If Grove made a valid, binding, and irrevocable gift of the Corporation's shares to RPI, it would be the purest fiction to treat the redemption proceeds as having actually been received by Grove. The Tax Court concluded that the gift was complete and irrevocable when made. The Commissioner conceded as much and we so find.[9]

It is argued, however, that notwithstanding the conceded validity of the gifts, other circumstances establish that Grove employed RPI merely as a convenient conduit for withdrawing funds from the Corporation for his personal use without incurring tax liability. The Commissioner would have us infer from the systematic nature of the gift-redemption cycle that Grove and RPI reached a mutually beneficial understanding: RPI would permit Grove to use its tax-exempt status to drain funds from the Corporation in return for a donation of a future interest in such funds.

We are not persuaded by this argument and the totality of the facts and circumstances lead us to a contrary conclusion. Grove testified before the Tax Court concerning the circumstances of these gifts. The court, based on the evidence and the witnesses' credibility, specifically found that

---

9. The Commissioner might have argued that at least that portion of the redemption proceeds allocable to Grove's retained life income interest was taxable as a dividend. He chose not to do so and the Tax Court "express[ed] no opinion upon the question, if it were properly presented, whether petition- er derived taxable income upon the redemption of stock to the extent of the life estate which he retained * * *." Since the Commissioner has bypassed this aspect, it would be inappropriate in our discussions of the gifts to attach any special significance to the retained life interest feature.

"[t]here was no informal agreement between [Grove] and RPI that RPI would offer the stock in question to the corporation for redemption or that, if offered, the corporation would redeem it." Findings of fact by the Tax Court, like those of the district court, are binding upon us unless they are clearly erroneous, 26 U.S.C. § 7482(a); Rule 52, F.R.Civ.P., and "the rule * * * applies also to factual inferences [drawn] from undisputed basic facts." Commissioner of Internal Revenue v. Duberstein, 363 U.S. 278, 291, 80 S.Ct. 1190, 1200, 4 L.Ed.2d 1218 (1960). It cannot seriously be contended that the Tax Court's findings here are "clearly erroneous" and no tax liability can be predicated upon a nonexistent agreement between Grove and RPI or by a fictional one created by the Commissioner.

Grove, of course, owned a substantial majority of the Corporation's shares. His vote alone was sufficient to insure redemption of any shares offered by RPI. But such considerations, without more, are insufficient to permit the Commissioner to ride roughshod over the actual understanding found by the Tax Court to exist between the donor and the donee. Behrend v. United States (4th Cir.1972), 73–1 USTC ¶ 9123, is particularly instructive. There, two brothers donated preferred shares of a corporation jointly controlled by them to a charitable foundation over which they also exercised control. The preferred shares were subsequently redeemed from the foundation by the corporation and the Commissioner sought to tax the redemption as a corporate dividend payment to the brothers. The court, in denying liability, concluded that although "it was understood that the corporation would at intervals take up the preferred according to its financial ability * * *, this factor did not convert into a constructive dividend the proceeds of the redemption * * * [because] the gifts were absolutely perfected before the corporation redeemed the stock." Id.

Nothing in the December, 1954, minority shareholder agreement between the Corporation and RPI serves as a basis for disturbing the conclusion of the Tax Court. Although the Corporation desired a right of first refusal on minority shares—understandably so, in order to reduce the possibility of unrelated, outside ownership interests—it assumed no obligation to redeem any shares so offered. In the absence of such an obligation, the Commissioner's contention that Grove's initial donation was only the first step in a prearranged series of transactions is little more than wishful thinking grounded in a shaky foundation. * * *

We are not so naive as to believe that tax considerations played no role in Grove's planning. But foresight and planning do not transform a nontaxable event into one that is taxable. Were we to adopt the Commissioner's view, we would be required to recast two actual transactions—a gift by Grove to RPI and a redemption from RPI by the Corporation—into two completely fictional transactions—a redemption from Grove by the Corporation and a gift by Grove to RPI. Based upon the facts as found by the Tax Court, we can discover no basis for elevating the Commissioner's "form" over that employed by the taxpayer in good faith. "Useful as the step transaction doctrine may be in the interpretation of equivocal contracts and ambiguous events, it cannot generate events which never took place just so an additional tax liability might be asserted." Sheppard v. United States, supra, at 978. In the absence of any supporting facts in the record we are unable to adopt the Commissioner's view; to do so would be to engage in a process of decision that is arbitrary, capricious and ultimately destructive of traditional notions of judicial review. We decline to embark on such a course.

Accordingly, the judgment of the Tax Court is affirmed.

■ OAKES, CIRCUIT JUDGE (dissenting):

Review of the tax consequences of a business transaction requires consideration of the economic realities of the entire transaction. See Gregory v. Helvering, 293 U.S. 465, 55 S.Ct. 266, 79 L.Ed. 596 (1935); South Bay Corp. v. Commissioner of Internal Revenue, 345 F.2d 698, 703, 705 (2d Cir.1965). Whether a transaction should be viewed as two or more steps or as one integrated transaction may result in entirely different tax consequences. * * *

Here, as I see it, the form of the transaction was two-step: a gift of stock followed by a redemption of the stock by the donor controlled corporation. The substance of the transaction, however, was a payment out of corporate earnings and profits to a charity designated by the donor who retained a life interest in the gift.

The factors which distinguish the RPI–Grove transactions from other charitable donations of securities and which persuade me to treat this as an integrated transaction are two: first, the gifts made by the Groves were of stock in a closed corporation that was inevitably redeemed annually; second, by virtue of retaining a life income from the reinvested proceeds and by retaining a measure of control over how those proceeds should be reinvested (by designating the investment adviser who was also the Groves' personal adviser), the Groves were able to achieve a bail-out from their non-dividend-paying closed corporation.

* * *

The majority opinion relies heavily on two cases which I believe are readily distinguishable from the situation here. One is Carrington v. Commissioner of Internal Revenue, 476 F.2d 704 (5th Cir.1973), relied on for the proposition that "[a] gift of appreciated property does not result in income to the donor so long as he gives the property away absolutely and parts with title before the property gives rise to income by way of sale." Here the Groves did not part with all interest in the construction company stock. The reservation of a life interest in the stock (or its reinvested proceeds), when coupled with taxpayer's right, however indirect, to direct the manner in which proceeds would be invested, gave the Groves a very great continuing interest and control, a fact of not inconsiderable tax significance. Cf. Corliss v. Bowers, 281 U.S. 376, 378, 50 S.Ct. 336, 74 L.Ed. 916 (1930) (Holmes, J.) ("taxation is not so much concerned with the refinements of title as it is with actual command over the property taxed. * * * "). More importantly, Carrington involved only one contribution of stock and one redemption; there was no pattern of redemption of stock as was clearly established here at least by the time of the tax years in question.

In Behrend v. United States, CCH 1973 Stand.Fed.Tax Rep. ¶ 9123 (4th Cir.1972), also relied upon by the majority, the proceeds of the redemption were used wholly for the benefit of the charitable foundation which was the recipient of the stock; there was no life estate reserved for the personal benefit of the donors. See 1973 Stand.Fed.Tax Rep. ¶ 9123 at 80,067 ("[P]redominant force" in Behrend decision is "indisputable fact" that the taxpayers therein "did not participate whatsoever in the beneficence of the foundation").

Thus, I believe that when, as here, the nature and conditions of the charitable gift and the pattern of donor-charity behavior are such as to make it for all practical purposes inevitable that the stock given will be offered for redemption and accepted by the closely held corporation, resulting in providing the equivalent of a safe pension fund for the donor stockholders, then the transaction must be treated as a distribution of dividends under §§ 301(a), 301(c) and 316(a) of the Internal Revenue Code of 1954. The majority opinion refers to an "absence of any supporting facts in the record" for the Commissioner's position, but omits to rely upon the one most important fact on which the case should turn: the pattern of redemption over years of giving. I accordingly dissent.

NOTE

The *Grove* case illustrates an effective charitable giving technique for the shareholders of a closely held corporation with the financial capacity to repurchase its stock. After losing several similar cases, the Service stopped challenging "charitable bailouts," announcing in Revenue Ruling 78–197[1] that a charitable contribution of stock followed by a redemption would be treated as a dividend to the donor only if the donee is legally bound or can be compelled by the corporation to surrender the shares for redemption.[2] Although they may not be legally obligated to do so, most charities will be highly motivated to offer the shares for redemption in order to convert the stock into a more liquid and diversified investment.

One desirable aspect of the transaction in *Grove* was Mr. Grove's ability to retain a life income interest in a diversified portfolio managed by his personal investment advisor. This format is no longer available to the philanthropic shareholder unless certain additional requirements are met. In general, a donor who wishes to retain a life income interest in contributed property will not qualify for charitable income and gift tax deductions

---

1. 1978–1 C.B. 83.

2. See also Palmer v. Commissioner, 62 T.C. 684 (1974), affirmed on another issue, 523 F.2d 1308 (8th Cir.1975), where the gift was made to a private foundation controlled by the taxpayer. The Service, however, may continue to challenge transactions where the donated property is later reacquired by the donor, or where the charity uses the redemption proceeds to acquire other property from the donor, pursuant to an informal prearranged understanding. See Blake v. Commissioner, 697 F.2d 473 (2d Cir.1982).

unless the gift is made to a qualified charitable remainder annuity trust or unitrust or a pooled income fund.[3]

PROBLEMS

Philanthropist ("P") owns 25,000 shares of Family Corporation. The fair market value of P's Family stock is $2,500,000 ($100 per share); P's basis is $25,000 ($1 per share). Family has 100,000 shares of common stock (its only class) outstanding; the remaining shares are owned by P's spouse and children. Family has ample accumulated earnings and profits. The Family bylaws require all shareholders to grant the corporation a right of first refusal to buy their stock at fair market value before the shares are offered for sale to an outsider, but the corporation is not required to redeem the stock.

On the occasion of his 25th college reunion, P wishes to make a $100,000 contribution to State University ("SU"). Consider the tax consequences of the following alternative plans:

(a) Family Corporation distributes $100,000 to P in redemption of 1,000 shares of stock. P then contributes $100,000 to SU.

(b) P contributes 1,000 shares of Family stock to SU. Two months later, pursuant to an oral understanding, Family distributes $100,000 to SU in redemption of its 1,000 shares. SU was not legally obligated to surrender the shares for redemption.

(c) Same as (b), above, except that P contributes 250 shares of Family stock to SU in each of the four years following his reunion. (Assume that the value of the stock was $100 per share throughout this period.) Two months after each contribution, Family distributes $25,000 to SU in redemption of the 250 shares.

G.   REDEMPTIONS THROUGH RELATED CORPORATIONS

Code: § 304(a); (b)(1), (2), (3)(A) & (B); (c).

Regulations: § 1.304–2(a), (c) Examples (1) & (3), –3(a).

Proposed Regulations: § 1.304–2(a), –2(c) Examples 1 & 2.

Section 304 is an intricate statutory watchdog designed to prevent an end run around Sections 301 and 302. Despite its complexity, the basic purpose of Section 304—to prevent controlling shareholders from claiming basis recovery and capital gain treatment on transactions that result in a "bailout" of corporate earnings without a significant reduction in control—can be illustrated by a simple example. Assume that Shareholder A owns all of the common stock (the only class outstanding) of X Corporation and Y Corporation, and both corporations have ample earnings and profits. Having read the *Davis* case, A knows that a redemption of either her X or Y

---

3. See I.R.C. §§ 170(f)(2), (3); 664; 2522(c)(2).

stock will result in a dividend and no recovery of basis. But what if A sells some of her X shares to Y or vice versa? Because this is a "sale" rather than a redemption or a distribution, A hopes to extract cash while enjoying exchange treatment, but in substance A's "sale" is indistinguishable from a dividend. Section 304 ensures this result by requiring shareholder sales involving "brother-sister" and "parent-subsidiary" corporations to satisfy one of the tests in Section 302 in order to qualify for capital gain status and recovery of basis.

Section 304 is another area where the tax stakes are less significant as long as dividends and long-term capital gains are taxed at the same preferential rates. As with conventional redemptions and other transactions to be studied later in this text, the importance of dividend classification will depend on variables such as the basis of the stock and the type of shareholder (individual vs. corporate) involved.

Brother–Sister Acquisitions. Section 304(a)(1) applies when one or more persons who are in "control" of each of two corporations transfer stock of one corporation (the "issuing corporation") to the other (the "acquiring corporation") in exchange for cash or other property.[1] "Control" for this purpose is defined as at least 50 percent ownership of either the corporate voting power or of the total value of all classes of stock.[2] In determining control, the Section 318 attribution rules are applicable with certain modifications relating to shareholder-corporation attribution.[3] In the case of a corporation with more than one class of stock, the value prong of the "control" test is applied to the aggregate value of all classes of stock, not class-by-class.[4] Thus, a shareholder who owns 50 percent or more of the value of all the corporation's stock has "control" even if that shareholder owns less than 50 percent of a particular class.

If Section 304(a)(1) applies, Congress devised an intricate method to test the "sale" for dividend equivalence. Returning to the example, when A sells X Corporation stock to Y Corporation for cash, A is treated as having received a distribution of cash in redemption of Y stock (Y being the "acquiring corporation").[5] This hypothetical redemption is then tested under Section 302(b) to determine whether A may treat the transaction as an exchange. Dividend equivalence is determined by reference to A's stock ownership of X (the "issuing corporation"—i.e., the company whose stock is sold) before and after the transaction.[6]

---

1. For this purpose, "property" does not include stock of the acquiring corporation. I.R.C. § 317(a). See Bhada v. Commissioner, 892 F.2d 39 (6th Cir.1989).

2. I.R.C. § 304(c)(1).

3. I.R.C. § 304(c)(3).

4. Rev. Rul. 89–57, 1989–1 C.B. 90.

5. Prop. Reg. § 1.302–2(a)(1).

6. I.R.C. § 304(b)(1); Prop. Reg. § 1.304–2(a)(2). Once again, modified Section

318 corporation-to-shareholder (and vice versa) attribution rules apply in measuring the effect of this hypothetical transaction on A's interest in X. Id. To the extent that Y's purchase of X stock from A for cash is characterized as a distribution to which Section 301 applies, A is treated as having transferred the X stock to Y (the acquiring corporation) in exchange for Y stock in a tax-free Section 351(a) transaction, and then Y is treated as having redeemed (from A) the Y stock that it hypothetically issued in the Section 351 ex-

In the example, A owned 100 percent of the X stock before the sale to Y. After the sale, A continued to own 100 percent of the stock directly and constructively by virtue of her ownership of Y. Because the sale does not reduce A's interest in X (the "issuing corporation"), it fails to satisfy any of the Section 302(b) tests for exchange treatment and thus is treated as a Section 301 distribution from Y to A. Section 304(b)(2) requires the distribution to be treated as a dividend received by A from Y (the "acquiring corporation") to the extent of Y's earnings and profits and then from X to the extent of its earnings and profits. Thus, the earnings and profits of both corporations are available to characterize the distribution to A as a dividend.[7]

Parent–Subsidiary Acquisitions. Section 304(a)(2) applies similar principles when a controlled subsidiary acquires stock of its parent from a shareholder of the parent in return for property. The parent-subsidiary relationship is defined by the same 50 percent "control" test described above.[8] The "property" used to make the acquisition is treated as a distribution in redemption of the parent's stock for purposes of testing dividend equivalency under Section 302.[9] If the redemption fails to qualify as an exchange and thus is treated as a Section 301 distribution, the amount and source of any dividend is first determined by reference to the earnings and profits of the acquiring (subsidiary) corporation and then, if necessary, by the earnings and profits of the issuing (parent) corporation.[10] If the constructive redemption is treated as an exchange, the selling shareholders recognize gain or loss under normal tax principles.

If a transaction is both a brother-sister and a parent-subsidiary acquisition, the parent-subsidiary rules take precedence.[11] But because the attribution rules transform most actual brother and sister corporations into a constructive parent and subsidiary, the regulations provide that an actual brother-sister relationship takes precedence over a constructive parent-subsidiary affiliation, causing Section 304(a)(1) to govern acquisitions by related nonsubsidiary corporations.[12]

Collateral Tax Consequences. In the basic Section 304(a)(1) brother-sister acquisition example above, where the amount paid by Y for A's X stock is treated as a Section 301 distribution, A is deemed to have transferred the X stock to Y in exchange for Y stock in a hypothetical Section 351(a) exchange, and Y is treated as having redeemed the Y stock it hypothetically issued in that exchange. Y thus takes a transferred basis from A in the X stock under Section 362, and A's basis in the Y stock received in the hypothetical Section 351 exchange is equal to A's basis in

change. I.R.C. § 304(a)(1). If the distribution is treated as an exchange under Section 302(a), Y is treated as purchasing the stock of X. See S. Rep. No. 99–313, 99th Cong., 2d Sess. 1048 (1986); Prop. Reg. § 1.304–2(a)(5). These deemed transactions are relevant in determining the basis consequences to the parties. See infra pp. 276–277.

7. I.R.C. § 304(b)(2).

8. I.R.C. § 304(c)(1).

9. I.R.C. § 304(b)(1).

10. I.R.C. § 304(b)(2).

11. I.R.C. § 304(a)(1).

12. Reg. § 1.304–2(c) Example (1).

the X stock that A actually transferred to X.[13] A's basis in the Y stock is decreased on the subsequent deemed redemption of Y stock only if part of the distribution is applied against the Y stock's basis under Section 301(c)(2).[14] To the extent the distribution is a dividend, the reduction in earnings and profits logically should follow the ordering rules in Section 304(b)(2)—i.e., first reduce the acquiring corporation's earnings and profits insofar as they are the source of the dividend and then, if necessary, reduce the issuing corporation's earnings and profits.

If Section 304(a)(1) applies and A's sale of X Corporation stock to Y Corporation is treated as an exchange under Section 302(a), Y is treated as having acquired the X stock by purchase and it thus takes a cost basis under Section 1012, and A's original basis in his Y stock remains unchanged. The theory, based on various fictional transactions (i.e., A is deemed to receive Y stock in exchange for X stock and then Y is deemed to redeem that Y stock from A for cash or other property) is that A "sold" Y stock (to Y) with a basis equal to the basis of the X stock actually transferred by A to Y. As in any actual sale or exchange, the basis of the (hypothetical) Y stock "sold" by A is fully recovered in determining gain or loss on the sale, and thus A's basis in her remaining Y stock is the same as it was before the transaction.[15]

In the brother-sister scenario where the redemption is treated as an exchange, any reduction of earnings and profits is limited by Section 312(n)(7) to an amount not in excess of the redeemed stock's ratable share of earnings and profits.[16] The more difficult question is *which* corporation's earnings and profits? The Code and regulations are silent on this technical teaser. Possibilities include the acquiring corporation's (the transaction is treated as a constructive redemption of acquiring corporation stock and the distributed "property" comes from that entity), the issuing corporation's (the redemption is tested by reference to its stock), neither (the transaction is simply a purchase, not a reduction of either corporation's wealth), or both (pro rata?).[17] One defensible answer is that the required reduction should be made first to the acquiring corporation's earnings and profits and, if necessary, then to the issuing corporation's earnings and profits.

In a parent-subsidiary acquisition, if the constructive redemption of the parent's stock is treated as a dividend, the selling shareholder's basis in the parent stock transferred to the subsidiary is added to the basis in the shareholder's remaining parent stock.[18] The subsidiary takes a cost basis in

---

13. I.R.C. § 304(a)(1); Prop. Reg. § 1.304–2(a)(3), –2(c) Example 2. Reg. § 1.304–2(c) Example (1) reaches the same result using a different approach based on the statute before it was amended in 1997.

14. For those with an interest in the intricate details, see Prop. Reg. § 1.304–2(c) Example 2.

15. Prop. Reg. § 1.304–2(c) Example 1. Reg. § 1.304–2(c) Example 3 reaches the same result using the approach that preceded

statutory amendments to Section 304 in 1997.

16. See Section E2 of this chapter, supra.

17. See Bittker & Eustice, Federal Income Taxation of Corporations and Shareholders ¶ 9.24[4].

18. Reg. § 1.304–3(a).

the parent stock that it acquires.[19] Tracking Section 304(b)(2), it is logical to first reduce the acquiring subsidiary's earnings and profits to the extent they are the source of the dividend and then move on, if necessary, to reduce the parent's earnings and profits. If the redemption is treated as an exchange, the selling shareholder recovers his basis in the transferred parent stock and recognizes capital gain or loss under normal tax principles. The subsidiary takes a cost basis in the acquired parent stock. If the constructive redemption is treated as an exchange, Section 312(n)(7) again should apply, but it is unclear which corporation's earnings and profits are reduced, leaving taxpayers to apply any reasonable approach.

Coordination with Section 351. Enactment of an intricate statute such as Section 304 inevitably whets the appetite of tax lawyers. Consider the sole shareholder of a profitable company with a desire for cash and a distaste for dividends at a time when dividends were taxed at much higher rates than capital gains. Assume that the shareholder borrows against his stock for valid business reasons and then contributes the stock to a newly formed holding company in exchange for the holding company's stock plus its assumption of the shareholder's liability. Or assume that the shareholder transferred all the stock of the operating company to a wholly owned holding company in exchange for additional stock of the holding company plus cash. Are the tax consequences of these transactions determined under Section 351? Or should they be governed by Section 304? Initially, the courts disagreed on which provision should control in these overlap situations.[20]

In an effort to strengthen the anti-bailout objectives of Subchapter C, Congress settled the overlap issue by providing that Section 304 generally will take precedence.[21] The Joint Committee on Taxation explained the amendment as follows:[22]

> The Act extends the anti-bailout rules of sections 304 * * * to the use of corporations, including holding companies, formed or availed of to avoid such rules. Such rules are made applicable to a transaction that otherwise qualifies as a tax-free incorporation under section 351.

> Section 351 generally will not apply to transactions described in section 304. Thus, section 351, if otherwise applicable, will generally apply only to the extent such transaction consists of an exchange of stock for stock in the acquiring corporation. However, section 304 will not apply to debt incurred to acquire the stock of

---

19. Cf. Rev.Rul. 80–189, 1980–2 C.B. 106; Broadview Lumber Co. v. United States, 561 F.2d 698 (7th Cir.1977).

20. Compare Gunther v. Commissioner, 92 T.C. 39 (1989), affirmed, 909 F.2d 291 (7th Cir.1990); Commissioner v. Haserot, 355 F.2d 200 (6th Cir.1965) and Haserot v. Commissioner, 46 T.C. 864 (1966), affirmed sub nom. Commissioner v. Stickney, 399 F.2d 828

(6th Cir.1968) with Coates Trust v. Commissioner, 480 F.2d 468 (9th Cir.1973), cert. denied, 414 U.S. 1045, 94 S.Ct. 551 (1973).

21. I.R.C. § 304(b)(3).

22. Staff of Joint Committee on Taxation, General Explanation of Tax Equity and Fiscal Responsibility Act of 1982, 98th Cong., 2d Sess. 142–43 (1982).

an operating company and assumed by a controlled corporation acquiring the stock since assumption of such debt is an alternative to a debt-financed direct acquisition by the acquiring company. This exception for acquisition indebtedness applies to an extension, renewal, or refinancing of such indebtedness. The provisions of section 357 (other than sec. 357(b)) and Section 358 apply to such acquisition indebtedness provided they would be applicable to such transaction without regard to section 304. In applying these rules, indebtedness includes debt to which the stock is subject as well as debt assumed by the acquiring company.

* * *

This rule, like several other anti-bailout measures in Subchapter C, is much less significant as long as dividends and long-term capital gains are taxed at the same low rate.

Niedermeyer v. Commissioner

United States Tax Court, 1974.
62 T.C. 280, affirmed per curiam 535 F.2d 500 (9th Cir.1976), cert. denied 429 U.S. 1000, 97 S.Ct. 528 (1976).

■ STERRETT, JUDGE: * * *

[In 1966, the taxpayers, Bernard and Tessie Niedermeyer, owned 22.58% of the common stock of American Timber & Trading Co., Inc. ("AT & T"). They also owned 125 of the 2,136 outstanding shares of AT & T preferred stock. Two of the taxpayers' sons, Bernard, Jr. and Walter, owned 67.91% of the common stock of AT & T.

Lents Industries ("Lents") was another corporation controlled by the Niedermeyer family. In 1966, the taxpayers and their sons, Bernard, Jr. and Walter, did not own any stock of Lents, but three other sons (Ed, Linus and Thomas) each owned 22⅛% of the Lents common stock.

On September 8, 1966, the taxpayers sold their AT & T stock to Lents for $174,975.12, but they retained all their preferred stock until December 28, 1966, when they contributed the preferred to a family foundation. After this contribution, the taxpayers ceased to have any interest in AT & T. Since the time of their sale of AT & T common stock, neither of the taxpayers was an officer, director or employee of the company.

The Niedermeyer family had long been active in the business of manufacturing special wood products in Oregon. During 1963, a family dispute arose between Bernard, Jr. and his brothers, Ed, Linus and Thomas. The brothers had been partners in Niedermeyer–Martin Co., another wood product enterprise, but the dispute caused the partnership to incorporate. During the mid–1960's, Bernard, Jr., as controlling shareholder of AT & T, refused to allow AT & T to do any business with Niedermeyer–Martin Co., which became a competitor. The acquisition by Lents of the taxpayers' common stock in AT & T was part of an effort by Ed, Linus and Thomas Niedermeyer to gain control of AT & T.

On their joint federal income tax return for 1966, the taxpayers reported a long-term capital gain of $168,321.58 on the sale of their AT & T common stock to Lents. The Commissioner determined that the entire proceeds of the sale were taxable as ordinary income because the transaction was covered by Section 304(a) and was essentially equivalent to a dividend. Ed.]

OPINION

The ultimate question to be decided in this case is whether petitioners realized a capital gain or received a dividend on the sale of their AT & T common stock to Lents in 1966. The resolution of this question depends on whether the sale in question was a redemption through the use of a related corporation under the provisions of section 304(a)(1) and, if so, whether the distribution by Lents to petitioners is to be treated as in exchange for the redeemed stock under the provisions of section 302(a) or as of property to which section 301 applies.

Section 304(a)(1) provides, in pertinent part, that, if one or more persons are in "control" of each of two corporations and if one of those corporations acquires stock in the other corporation from the person or persons in control, then the transaction shall be treated as a distribution in redemption for purposes of section 302. Section 304(c)(1) defines the term "control" as "the ownership of stock possessing at least 50 percent of the total combined voting power of all classes of stock entitled to vote, or at least 50 percent of the total value of shares of all classes of stock." Section 304(c)[(3)] then states that the constructive ownership of stock rules contained in section 318(a) shall apply for the purpose of determining "control," except that the 50–percent limitations of sections 318(a)(2)(C) and 318(a)(3)(C) shall be disregarded for such purpose.

It is clear that by its terms section 304(a)(1) applies to the factual situation of this case. Prior to the transaction here in question, petitioners, husband and wife, together actually owned 1,083.117 shares out of the 4,803.083 outstanding shares of AT & T common stock, its only class of stock entitled to vote. Two of petitioners' sons owned 3,263.072 shares. Thus a total of 4,346.189 shares, or 90.49 percent, of the outstanding voting stock of AT & T was actually or constructively owned by petitioners. Three of petitioners' other sons owned 48 out of 72 shares, or 67 percent, of the outstanding stock of Lents, the ownership of such stock being constructively attributable to petitioners. Consequently, under section 304(c)(1), either petitioner, or both, are regarded as the person or persons in control of both AT & T and Lents prior to the transaction in question. Accordingly, under section 304(a)(1) the transaction in which Lents acquired petitioners' AT & T common stock must be treated as a redemption. The fact that neither petitioner actually owned stock in the acquiring corporation is of no concern here. * * *

Petitioners object to the applicability of section 304 on the ground that the attribution rules of section 318(a) should not be applied in this case. They base this position upon what they term the "bad blood" exception to the attribution rules as applied in Estate of Arthur H. Squier, 35 T.C. 950 (1961). In *Squier,* a case under section 302 involving the question of whether a distribution was essentially equivalent to a dividend, this Court decided that, based in part on a "sharp cleavage" between the executor of the taxpayer estate and members of the Squier family, and notwithstanding the attribution rules, the redemption in fact resulted in a crucial reduction of the estate's control over the corporation. The Court held that the distribution there was not essentially equivalent to a dividend and implicit in this conclusion was the belief that the attribution rules were not conclusive in all events in determining whether there had been a significant change of control which would allow the conclusion that the distribution was not essentially equivalent to a dividend. We note that in Robin Haft Trust, 61 T.C. 398 (1973), this Court decided that, in light of United States v. Davis, 397 U.S. 301 (1970), the rationale of *Squier* was no longer applicable to section 302(b)(1).

Besides here, as was not the case with *Squier,* no evidence was adduced to show that there were any disputes or cleavage between petitioners and any of their sons. The falling out was apparently between petitioners' sons. Apparently, petitioners would have us infer from the disagreements between Bernard E. Niedermeyer, Jr., majority shareholder of AT & T, and three other of their sons, who together were majority shareholders of Lents, that petitioners did not in fact control either corporation. We are unwilling to make this assumption and consequently petitioners' argument fails on its facts.

Moreover, we are of the opinion that the "control" test of sections 304(a)(1) and 304(c) requires that the attribution rules be applied in every case. Congress expressly indicated that the attribution rules of section 318 are to be applied in determining "control" for section 304 purposes. Section 304(c)(2) states that "Section 318(a)(relating to the constructive ownership of stock) *shall* apply for purposes of determining control under paragraph (1)." (Emphasis supplied.) Under section 304(c)(1) "control" is defined only as the ownership (either actually or constructively) of certain amounts of stock. Through the use of precise rules of attribution Congress intended to remove the uncertainties existing under prior law, which had no specific statutory guidance for constructive ownership of stock in the area of corporate distributions and adjustments, in the administration of the provisions where attribution was deemed appropriate. H.Rept. No. 1337, to accompany H.R. 8300 (Pub.L. No. 591), 83d Cong., 2d Sess., p. A96 (1954). See also *Coyle v. United States,* supra at 490. We think the attribution rules require, through their employment in section 304, that petitioners be treated as in actual control of both AT & T and Lents, notwithstanding any "bad blood" between petitioners' sons.

Petitioners assert that even though the sale is to be treated as a distribution in redemption of Lents' stock under section 304(a)(1), they are entitled to treat the distribution as in full payment in exchange for their stock under section 302(a) by meeting one of the tests contained in section 302(b). The determination under section 302(b) is to be made by reference to the issuing corporation's stock, here the AT & T stock, except that the 50–percent limitations of sections 318(a)(2)(C) and 318(a)(3)(C) are to be disregarded in applying the attribution rules of section 318(a). Sec. 304(b)(1).

Section 302(b) sets forth certain conditions under which a redemption of stock shall be treated as an exchange. If none of those conditions are met, section 302(d) provides that the distribution will then be treated as one to which section 301 applies. Petitioners do not contend that section 302(b)(2) or 302(b)(4) is applicable but they argue that the transaction in question meets the test of either section 302(b)(1) or 302(b)(3).

The test of section 302(b)(1) requires that the redemption be "not essentially equivalent to a dividend." To meet the test of nondividend equivalency the redemption must, after application of the attribution rules of section 318(a) to the stock ownership interests as they existed both before and after the redemption, result in "a meaningful reduction of the shareholder's proportionate interest in the corporation." *United States v. Davis,* supra at 313. In resolution of the question of dividend equivalency, the fact that the transaction in issue may have had a bona fide business purpose is no longer relevant. *United States v. Davis,* supra at 312. Furthermore, the applicability of the attribution rules in section 302(b)(1) is not affected by any "bad blood" between petitioners' sons. *Robin Haft Trust,* supra at 402–403.

As stated above, prior to the redemption petitioners owned, either actually or constructively, 90.49 percent of the outstanding common stock of AT & T. After the redemption, petitioners actually owned no AT & T common stock, although they did own 125 shares out of 2,136 outstanding shares of that corporation's preferred stock. However, petitioners constructively owned 82.96 percent of the outstanding common stock of AT & T comprised as follows: 3,055.221 shares actually owned by their son Bernard E. Niedermeyer, Jr., 207.851 shares actually owned by their son Walter E. Niedermeyer, and 67 percent of the 1,083.117 shares, or 725.688 shares, actually owned by Lents and constructively owned by their sons E. C., L. J., and T.J. Niedermeyer. Sec. 318(a)(5)(A). We do not think a reduction in ownership of the AT & T common stock from 90.49 percent to 82.96 percent constitutes a meaningful reduction of petitioners' proportionate interest in AT & T in the instant case. See Friend v. United States, 345 F.2d 761, 764 (C.A.1, 1965); Stanley F. Grabowski Trust, 58 T.C. 650, 659 (1972); *Fehrs Finance Co.,* supra at 185–186. With such a small change in a high percentage interest, petitioners' control and ownership of AT & T is essentially unaltered and cannot be considered to have undergone a meaningful reduction. An 82.96–percent interest clearly is sufficient to dominate and control the policies of the corporation.

Petitioners next assert, under several theories, that they terminated their interest in AT & T as contemplated in section 302(b)(3). The test provided therein allows the redemption to be treated as an exchange "if the redemption is in complete redemption of all of the stock of the corporation owned by the shareholder." Unless the conditions of section 302(c)(2) are satisfied to exempt petitioners from application of the family attribution rules of section 318(a)(1), these rules apply in their entirety in determining whether there has been a redemption of petitioners' complete stock interest in AT & T.

Petitioners sold all their AT & T common stock to Lents on September 8, 1966, and contributed all their AT & T preferred stock to the Niedermeyer Foundation on December 28, 1966. On September 24, 1968, petitioners filed an amended return for the calendar year 1966 to which was attached the agreement called for in section 302(c)(2)(A)(iii).

It is clear that, if they are to meet the requirements of the test of section 302(b)(3), petitioners must show that they completely terminated their stock interest in AT & T and in so doing they must be able to effect a waiver of the family attribution rules of section 318(a)(1) through use of section 302(c)(2).

While section 1.302–4(b), Income Tax Regs., states that the agreement specified in section 302(c)(2)(A)(iii) must be attached to a return timely filed for the year in which the distribution occurs, several cases have held that some delay in filing the agreement does not vitiate it, and we find those cases to be applicable here where petitioners filed the agreement upon discovering their inadvertent failure to do so earlier. United States v. G.W. Van Keppel, 321 F.2d 717 (C.A.10, 1963); Georgie S. Cary, 41 T.C. 214 (1963).

However, the fact that a proper agreement was filed alone does not effect a waiver of the family attribution rules unless the other requirements of section 302(c)(2) are satisfied. The only other requirement in question here is that petitioners must have had no interest in AT & T, other than an interest as a creditor, immediately after the distribution referred to in section 302(b)(3). In the instant case, however, petitioners retained their 125 shares of AT & T preferred stock, at least until December 28, 1966, after the redemption of all their AT & T common stock on September 8, 1966.

Petitioners contend that ownership of these 125 shares of AT & T preferred stock until December 28, 1966, does not prevent application of the exemption provided in section 302(c)(2) and consequently qualification under section 302(b)(3) as having completely terminated their stock interest in AT & T. Petitioners make the following arguments to show that the AT & T preferred stock retained until December 28, 1966, was not the retention of an interest other than that of a creditor and implicitly was not the retention of a stock interest in AT & T: (1) The preferred stock was actually debt; (2) a de minimis rule should be applied; (3) the relinquishment of their preferred stock interest in AT & T on December 28, 1966, was "immediately after" the sale of their AT & T common stock on September 8, 1966; and (4) at the time of the sale of their AT & T common stock they intended to donate their AT & T preferred stock to charity before the year's end.

While citing no cases in their support, petitioners first argue here that the characteristics of the AT & T preferred stock are those commonly associated with debt instruments. We do not agree. A number of factors have been considered in resolution of this question of fact, see O.H. Kruse Grain & Milling v. Commissioner, 279 F.2d 123, 125–126 (C.A.9, 1960), affirming a Memorandum Opinion of this Court; Wilbur Security Co., 31 T.C. 938, 948 (1959), affd. 279 F.2d 657 (C.A.9, 1960); however, we see no useful purpose in reciting all the factors but will confine discussion herein only to those we think relevant.

While it is true that the preferred stockholders had no right to participate in the management of the corporation, such fact is not so uncharacteristic of preferred stock rights as to be conclusive, standing alone, of the question at hand. John Kelley Co. v. Commissioner, 326 U.S. 521, 530 (1946). We think that the following facts are indicative of the equity flavor of the preferred stock: There was no unconditional obligation to pay a principal sum certain on or before a fixed maturity date; the timing of preferred "dividends" was discretionary with the corporate directors; upon liquidation the preferred stockholders would be paid "from the money and/or property available for distribution to shareholders," which indicates to us that the preferred stock was subordinated in priority to the general creditors; AT & T's articles of amendment to the articles of incorporation used the terms "dividends," "preferred stock," and "shareholders" with reference to the instruments in question; and the preferred stock was created during a reorganization by a transfer of earned surplus to AT & T's capital account.

We think petitioners' second argument attempting to interject a de minimis rule allowing the retention of some small stock interest while qualifying under section 302(b)(3) is wholly without merit. Section 302(b)(3) clearly requires no less than a complete termination of all petitioners' stock interest in the corporation.

Petitioners next assert that they had no interest in AT & T "immediately after the distribution," as the phrase is used in section 302(c)(2)(A)(i), because the December 28, 1966, contribution should be considered to have occurred immediately after the September 8, 1966, redemption. We assume petitioners believe that if they satisfy this requirement of having no interest "immediately after" the redemption, they will also satisfy the requirement in section 302(b)(3) of having completely terminated their stock interest in AT & T. While we express no opinion on petitioners' apparent belief, we think the words "immediately after" must be given their ordinary meaning and that consequently December 28 cannot be considered "immediately after" September 8. Cf. Commissioner v. Brown, 380 U.S. 563, 570–571 (1965).

Petitioners' final argument to satisfy the requirements of sections 302(b)(3) and 302(c)(2)(A)(i) is that, at the time of the transfer of their AT & T common stock to Lents, they intended to donate their remaining AT & T preferred stock to charity by the end of 1966. Petitioners did in fact contribute their 125 shares of AT & T preferred stock to the Niedermeyer Foundation on December 28, 1966.

While petitioners' contention in this regard is not entirely clear, their argument appears to be that the September 8, 1966, transfer was but one step in a plan to terminate completely their interest in AT & T, the final step in such plan being their December 28, 1966, contribution of their remaining preferred stock. The only case cited by petitioners, Arthur D. McDonald, 52 T.C. 82 (1969), involved the question of whether a plan, calling for the redemption of that taxpayer's E & M preferred stock which was followed by a reorganization in which the taxpayer exchanged his E & M common stock for Borden stock, resulted in a distribution with respect to the preferred stock, which was essentially equivalent to a dividend under section 302(b)(1). The Court concluded that, after completion of the plan, the taxpayer's direct interest in E & M was terminated and consequently the redemption was not essentially equivalent to a dividend. Petitioners have not urged, and we consider it wise since the attribution rules would frustrate them, that their intention to donate the AT & T preferred stock by year's end shows that the redemption comes within the provisions of section 302(b)(1). Rather, they apparently contend that their intentions to donate the AT & T preferred stock constituted a plan to terminate their interest in AT & T which, with use of section 302(c)(2)(A), satisfies the requirements of section 302(b)(3).

Where redemptions were executed pursuant to a plan to terminate one's interest in a corporation, it has been held that dividend equivalency may be avoided where the individual redemptions are component parts of a single sale or exchange of an entire stock interest. In Re Lukens' Estate, 246 F.2d 403 (C.A.3, 1957), reversing 26 T.C. 900 (1956); Jackson Howell, 26 T.C. 846 (1956), affd. 247 F.2d 156 (C.A.9, 1957); Carter Tiffany, 16 T.C. 1443 (1951).[4] Where there is a plan which is comprised of several steps, one involving the redemption of stock that results in a complete termination of the taxpayer's interest in a corporation, section 302(b)(3) may apply. Otis P. Leleux, 54 T.C. 408 (1970); Estate of Oscar L. Mathis, 47 T.C. 248 (1966). However, the redemption must occur as part of a plan which is firm and fixed and in which the steps are clearly integrated. *Otis P. Leleux,* supra at 418.

We regard the evidence presented on petitioners' behalf as too insubstantial to prove the existence of such a plan. Petitioner Bernard E. Niedermeyer's self-serving statement during the trial that at the time of transfer of the AT & T common stock on September 28, 1966, he intended to donate the AT & T preferred stock to charity by year's end, and

---

4. The cited cases were decided under the "essentially equivalent to the distribution of a taxable dividend" standard of sec. 115(g)(1), I.R.C. 1939. Sec. 29.115–9, Regs. 111, provided that "a cancellation or redemption by a corporation of all of the stock of a particular shareholder, so that the shareholder ceases to be interested in the affairs of the corporation, does not effect a distribution of a taxable dividend." Under present law, sec. 302(b)(1) would now appear applicable if completion of the plan results in a meaningful reduction in the taxpayer's proportionate interest in the corporation.

petitioners' prior history of contributions do not establish to us a firm and fixed plan in which all the steps are clearly integrated.

The plan certainly was not in writing and there was no evidence of communication of petitioners' asserted donative intention to the charity or to anyone. One of petitioners' sons testified that Lents acquired petitioners' AT & T common stock in an attempt to gain control of AT & T. However, no mention at all was made by this son of any desire on petitioners' part to terminate their total interest in AT & T. Petitioners could easily have changed their minds with regard to any intent to donate the preferred stock. Clearly petitioners' decision to donate the preferred stock has not been shown to be in any way fixed or binding. * * * We note that *Arthur D. McDonald,* supra, cited by petitioners, involved a written plan which was fixed as to its terms and apparently binding. By the above discussion we do not mean to indicate that all such plans need to be in writing, absolutely binding, or communicated to others, but we do think that the above-mentioned factors, all of which are lacking here, tend to show a plan which is fixed and firm.

Since petitioners have not established that the redemption is to be treated as an exchange under section 302(a), the proceeds are to be treated as a distribution of property to which section 301 applies and as a dividend as determined by the respondent.

Decision will be entered for the respondent.

PROBLEMS

1. The *Niedermeyer* case is a good example of a tax planning blunder. It illustrates the need for sensitivity to provisions such as § 304. In reading the case, make sure you can answer the following questions:

(a) Why did § 304 apply to the sale by the taxpayers of their AT & T common stock to Lents?

(b) Given that § 304 applies, how do you test the "redemption" to determine if the taxpayers have a dividend?

(c) Why were the taxpayers unable to waive family attribution and qualify for "sale" treatment under § 302(b)(3)?

(d) How could they have avoided this unfortunate result?

2. Bail Corporation and Out Corporation each have 100 shares of common stock outstanding. Claude owns 80 shares of Bail stock (with a basis of $40,000, or $500 per share) and 60 shares of Out stock (with a basis of $9,000, or $150 per share.) The remaining Bail and Out shares are owned by one individual who is not related to Claude. Bail has no current or accumulated earnings and profits. Out has no current and $5,000 of accumulated earnings and profits. Determine the tax consequences to the various parties in each of the following alternative transactions:

(a) Claude sells 20 of his Out shares, in which he has a $3,000 adjusted basis, to Bail for $4,000.

(b) Claude sells all of his Out shares to Bail for $12,000.

(c) Same as (a), above, except that Claude receives $3,000 and one share of Bail stock (fair market value—$1,000) for his 20 Out shares.

(d) Same as (a), above, except that Claude receives one share of Bail stock (fair market value—$1,000) and Bail takes the 20 Out shares subject to a $3,000 liability that Claude incurred to buy the 20 shares of Out stock.

3. Is Section 304 still necessary?

H. REDEMPTIONS TO PAY DEATH TAXES

Code: § 303(a), (b)(1)–(3), (c). Skim § 6166.

When a shareholder of a closely held corporation dies, it sometimes is necessary to liquidate all or part of the decedent's stock to raise cash to pay death taxes and other expenses. If the shares are not readily marketable and the family as a whole does not want to lose control, a redemption may be an important component of the decedent's estate plan. Because the basis of the stock normally will have been stepped-up to its fair market value at the decedent's death,[1] a redemption qualifying for exchange treatment can be accomplished virtually tax-free—a once-in-a-lifetime opportunity for a painless withdrawal of corporate earnings.

Section 303, one of several income and estate tax provisions offering relief for owners of closely held businesses,[2] makes it possible to avoid dividend treatment and achieve full recovery of basis on a redemption even if the transaction does not come within one of the Section 302(b) tests. If several detailed requirements are met, distributions in redemption are treated as a sale or exchange rather than a dividend up to the sum of federal and state death taxes and allowable funeral and administrative expenses.[3] Curiously, however, the estate is not required to use (or even need) the redemption proceeds to pay taxes and expenses.

To qualify under Section 303, the value of the redeemed stock must be included in determining the decedent's gross estate for federal estate tax purposes.[4] The other principal requirements relate to the relationship of the decedent's holdings in the corporation to his total gross estate and the timing of the distribution.

Relationship of Stock to Decedent's Estate. Congress concluded that income tax relief was justified only when a decedent's holdings in the

---

1. I.R.C. § 1014(a).

2. E.g., I.R.C. §§ 302(c)(2) (waiver of family attribution when testing redemptions), 2032A (estate tax valuation of certain real property), 6166 (extension of time to pay estate tax). Section 303 contains no "closely held" business requirement, but the vast majority of Section 303 redemptions involve close corporations.

3. I.R.C. § 303(a).

4. Id.

corporation represented a substantial portion of his gross estate. Section 303(b)(2) requires that the value of all the stock of the distributing corporation included in the decedent's gross estate must exceed 35 percent of the total gross estate less certain expenses deductible for federal estate tax purposes. A special rule permits the stock of two or more corporations to be aggregated for purposes of this 35 percent test if 20 percent or more in value of each such corporation's total outstanding stock is included in the gross estate. For purposes of the 20 percent requirement, stock held by the decedent's surviving spouse as community property, or held with the decedent prior to death in joint tenancy, tenancy-by-the-entirety, or tenancy-in-common, is treated as if it were included in determining the value of the decedent's gross estate.[5] If a decedent's holdings are close to the 35 percent mark, it may be desirable to engage in various lifetime and post-mortem maneuvers to ensure that Section 303 will be available.

Timing of the Redemption. Section 303 applies only to amounts distributed within a reasonable time after the decedent's death. The redemption must occur within 90 days after the expiration of the three year assessment period for federal estate taxes.[6] If the estate becomes embroiled in a controversy with the Service and files a petition for redetermination of estate tax with the Tax Court, the period is extended to 60 days after the Tax Court's decision becomes final.[7] A further extension is provided if the estate is eligible and elects to pay estate taxes in installments over the extended period (up to 15 years) provided by Section 6166.[8] But if the redemption occurs more than four years after death, the amount that can qualify for Section 303 treatment is limited to the lesser of unpaid death taxes and administrative expenses immediately before the distribution or death taxes and expenses actually paid during the one year period beginning on the date of distribution.[9]

Eligible Shareholders. Although Section 303 is most commonly used by the decedent's estate, other shareholder-beneficiaries sometimes are eligible for its benefits if their interest "is reduced directly (or through a binding obligation to contribute) by any payment" of death taxes or administrative expenses.[10] In the normal case where the decedent's will provides that taxes and expenses are payable out of the residuary estate, specific legatees of stock (including a spouse receiving a bequest eligible for the unlimited marital deduction) are not eligible to use Section 303.

Distributions of Appreciated Property. The most likely asset for a Section 303 redemption is cash, but a corporation that distributes appreciated property to redeem its shares must recognize gain under the now familiar rule in Section 311(b).

---

5. I.R.C. § 303(b)(2)(B).

6. I.R.C. § 303(b)(1)(A). See I.R.C. § 6501(a).

7. I.R.C. § 303(b)(1)(B).

8. I.R.C. § 303(b)(1)(C).

9. I.R.C. § 303(b)(4).

10. I.R.C. § 303(b)(3).

PROBLEMS

George died last year and his gross estate is $6,000,000. George's estate expects to incur a total of $300,000 of death taxes and allowable deductions for expenses and losses under §§ 2053 and 2054. George's gross estate includes stock in X Corporation (fair market value—$600,000) and Y Corporation (fair market value—$1,200,000). The fair market value of all of the outstanding X and Y stock is $4,200,000 and $4,800,000, respectively. George's wife, Adele, also owns $600,000 of X stock. (She and George held a total of $1,200,000 of X stock as tenants-in-common during his life.)

If Y Corporation redeems shares from George's estate, will the redemption qualify for exchange treatment under § 303?

CHAPTER 6

STOCK DIVIDENDS AND SECTION 306 STOCK

A. INTRODUCTION

Code: Skim §§ 305; 306; 317(a).

It should be evident by now that Subchapter C has been the backdrop for a continuing cops and robbers saga. The goals of the robbers are clear enough, even if their methods may be a bit obscure. When they ran out of ideas to avoid the double tax, the robbers historically shifted their focus to bailing out corporate earnings at the least tax cost. The cops were quick to respond, but they sometimes lacked direction and even were known to engage in isolated acts of police brutality. Nowhere does this drama have a richer history than in the area of stock dividends and Section 306 stock. But for many of these skirmishes, the operative word may now be "history," at least as long as dividends and long-term capital gains are taxed at the same preferential rate.

The evolving plot is best appreciated by first putting the underlying transactions into perspective. A stock dividend is simply a distribution of stock (or rights to acquire stock)[1] by a corporation to some or all of its shareholders. If the distributed stock is of the same class as the shareholder's underlying holdings, a stock dividend is similar to what is known as a "stock split." The only difference is that a stock dividend requires the corporation to transfer an appropriate amount from retained earnings to paid-in capital while a stock split merely increases the number of outstanding shares without any adjustment to the corporate capital account.[2] A stock dividend, however, need not be of the same class of stock as the shareholder's existing interest in the corporation. Preferred stock may be distributed with respect to common or vice versa, and more complex capital structures present the opportunity for countless variations.

1. I.R.C. § 305(d)(1) defines the term "stock" to include rights to acquire such stock.

2. Apart from the financial accounting distinctions, the line of demarcation between a stock dividend and a stock split usually is drawn by the relationship of the number of shares distributed to the previously outstanding shares. To better inform shareholders, the rules of the New York Stock Exchange provide that a distribution of less than 25 percent of the shares outstanding prior to the distribution will be a stock dividend. Larger distributions (e.g., distributions of one share for each share held) are labelled splits. New York Stock Exchange Company Manual, § 703.02.

Stock dividends accomplish a variety of business objectives. Some public companies periodically pay small "common on common" stock dividends instead of cash ostensibly to provide their shareholders with some tangible evidence of their interest in corporate earnings while allowing the corporation to retain cash for use in the business. Although these distributions may have an incidental impact on the price of the stock, they are more of a shareholder public relations gesture than an event of any financial consequence. Stock splits often are prompted by a desire to increase the number of outstanding shares and thus reduce the price per share in an attempt to increase the marketability (and market value) of the stock on a listed exchange.

The business objectives may be different in the case of a closely held corporation. In that setting, stock distributions frequently are a vehicle to shift corporate control.[3] To illustrate, assume that all the outstanding stock of Family Corporation is owned by Mrs. Older and has a fair market value of $1,000 per share. Mr. Younger, Older's son, has been employed by Family for several years and Older expects to gradually shift control of the business to Younger. Older's plan faces several obstacles. Gifts of Family common stock to Younger may not be desirable because Older is unwilling to part with that much wealth or the gift tax liability may be prohibitive. Younger also may not be able to afford a significant purchase of stock from his mother because the current price of Family common stock is too high.

As an alternative, Family might distribute a new class of preferred stock to Older. The preferred stock could be structured with dividend rights and a liquidation preference so that its value absorbs most of the net worth of the company, leaving the common stock with only nominal value. The distribution of preferred stock to Older will be tax-free[4] and, since the value of the common stock will be substantially reduced, Older more easily may shift control to Younger through gifts or even sales of common stock.[5]

The tax consequences of the stock distribution to Older in our example are governed by Section 305, which remains significant in the current tax rate environment. Section 305(a) generally provides that gross income does not include a distribution of stock by a corporation to its shareholders with respect to its stock. This exclusion, however, is subject to various exceptions, the most important of which are found in Section 305(b). Consequently, the applicability of the Section 305(b) exceptions is the critical inquiry in analyzing the tax consequences of a stock distribution. These exceptions are examined more closely in the next section of this chapter. It is sufficient for now to note that the preferred stock distribution to Older is

---

3. A recapitalization frequently is an alternative method for making adjustments to the corporation's capital structure. In certain situations, a recapitalization may provide more favorable income tax results. See Chapter 11, infra.

4. I.R.C. § 305(a). The preferred stock, however, would be Section 306 stock assuming Family has earnings and profits. See Section C of this chapter, infra.

5. But see I.R.C. §§ 2701 et seq., which limits the estate planning advantages of this strategy.

not a taxable stock dividend. What do you suppose is the rationale for that result?

Lest we forget the cops and robbers saga, there is one other aspect of the previous example to consider. Recall that Older owns 100 percent of the outstanding Family common stock, and Family makes a tax-free distribution of a new class of preferred stock to Older. Assume further that Family has ample earnings and profits. If Older retained her common stock rather than giving it to her son, the preferred stock distribution historically provided her with an opportunity for tax avoidance. She could sell the preferred stock to Facilitator for cash and, after a short period of time, the corporation could redeem the preferred stock, paying Facilitator an appropriate premium for the shares. When the dust settled, this series of transactions had virtually the same economic effect as a cash distribution by Family to Older: Older has cash in hand, Family's corporate treasury has been depleted, and Older still owned 100 percent of the company. But the tax consequences appeared to be dramatically different. Rather than being stuck with a taxable dividend, Older hoped to enjoy "sale" treatment on the disposition of the preferred stock to Facilitator. A sale enabled Older to recover her basis in the preferred stock and to recognize a long-term capital gain to the extent the amount realized on the sale exceeded her basis.[6] A closer examination reveals that this potential loophole (is it still?) was closed by Section 306, which was the legislative response to Older's tax avoidance plan—the so-called "preferred stock bailout." In our simple example, the preferred stock will bear the taint of "Section 306 Stock," and Section 306(a)(1) will characterize Older's amount realized on the sale to Facilitator as ordinary (dividend?) income.[7] The last section of this chapter explores the details of Section 306 and evaluates its continuing significance.

B.   Taxation of Stock Dividends Under Section 305

Code: §§ 305(a), (b), (c), (d); 307; 312(d)(1)(B), (f)(2); 1223(4).

Regulations: §§ 1.305–1; –2; –3(a), (b), (c); (e) Examples (1), (2), (3), (4), (8), (10) and (11); –4; –5(a); –6; –7(a); 1.307–1.

The current scheme for taxing stock distributions is a distant cousin of statutes fashioned during the infancy of the income tax and is the product of a checkered legislative history. The Revenue Act of 1916 provided that a "stock dividend shall be considered income, to the amount of its cash

---

6. This assumes that Older had a long-term holding period in the Family common stock, which could be tacked in determining the holding period of the preferred. I.R.C. § 1223(5).

7. I.R.C. § 306(a)(1)(A), (c)(1)(A). Prior to the enactment of Section 306 as part of the 1954 Code, the Service argued that in sub-stance these transactions were equivalent to a cash distribution. The argument met with sporadic success. Compare Chamberlin v. Commissioner, 207 F.2d 462 (1953), cert. denied, 347 U.S. 918, 74 S.Ct. 516 (1954), with Rosenberg v. Commissioner, 36 T.C. 716 (1961).

value."[1] In 1920, the Supreme Court considered the constitutionality of this provision in Eisner v. Macomber.[2] Mrs. Macomber, a common shareholder of a corporation with no other class of stock outstanding, received a proportionate distribution of additional common stock. The Supreme Court held that the distribution was not taxable because it did not constitute "income" within the meaning of the 16th Amendment to the Constitution. Although the Court's constitutional commentary has been discredited,[3] the result in *Macomber* is eminently logical and has been codified in Section 305(a). Whatever reshuffling may occur in the corporation's capital account, a common-on-common stock dividend does little more than crowd the shareholder's safe deposit box (or brokerage account) with additional stock certificates or book entry shares evidencing the same ownership interest held before the distribution.

An obedient Congress swiftly responded to the Supreme Court's interpretation of the 16th Amendment with a primitive declaration that stock dividends "shall not be subject to tax."[4] The stock dividend terrain remained calm until the Supreme Court generated a minor tremor in 1936 with its decision in Koshland v. Helvering.[5] Corinne Koshland, a shareholder who owned cumulative nonvoting preferred stock, received a distribution of voting common stock. She subsequently disposed of her preferred stock and asserted that she was entitled to use the stock's full cost basis in determining her gain. Since the prior common stock distribution was received tax-free, the Service contended that a proportionate amount of Mrs. Koshland's basis in her preferred shares should be allocated to the common, thereby increasing the gain on the disposition of her preferred stock. The Supreme Court agreed with the shareholder's contention and in the course of its opinion shed additional light on the meaning of Eisner v. Macomber:[6]

> Although *Eisner v. Macomber* affected only the taxation of dividends declared in the same stock as that presently held by the taxpayer, the Treasury gave the decision a broader interpretation which Congress followed in the Act of 1921. Soon after the passage of that Act, this court pointed out the distinction between a stock dividend which worked no change in the corporate entity, the same interest in the same corporation being represented after the distribution by more shares of precisely the same character, and such a dividend where there had either been changes of corporate identity or a change in the nature of the shares issued as dividends

---

1. Revenue Act of 1916, § 2(a). In Towne v. Eisner, 245 U.S. 418, 38 S.Ct. 158 (1918), the Supreme Court concluded that a stock dividend was not "income" or "dividends" under the Revenue Act of 1913.

2. 252 U.S. 189, 40 S.Ct. 189 (1920).

3. See Bittker & Eustice, Federal Income Taxation of Corporations and Shareholders ¶ 8.40[1].

4. Revenue Act of 1921, § 201(d).

5. 298 U.S. 441, 56 S.Ct. 767 (1936).

6. 298 U.S. at 445–46, 56 S.Ct. at 769–70. In Helvering v. Gowran, 302 U.S. 238, 58 S.Ct. 154 (1937), the Court held that a shareholder took a zero basis in preferred shares received as a nontaxable distribution on common stock.

whereby the proportional interest of the stockholder after the distribution was essentially different from his former interest. Nevertheless the successive statutes and Treasury regulations respecting taxation of stock dividends remained unaltered. We give great weight to an administrative interpretation long and consistently followed, particularly when the Congress, presumably with that construction in mind, has reenacted the statute without change. The question here, however, is not merely of our adopting the administrative construction but whether it should be adopted if in effect it converts an income tax into a capital levy.

We are dealing solely with an income tax act. Under our decisions the payment of a dividend of new common shares, conferring no different rights or interests than did the old—the new certificates, plus the old, representing the same proportionate interest in the net assets of the corporation as did the old—does not constitute the receipt of income by the stockholder. On the other hand, where a stock dividend gives the stockholder an interest different from that which his former stock holdings represented he receives income. The latter type of dividend is taxable as income under the Sixteenth Amendment. Whether Congress has taxed it as of the time of its receipt, is immaterial for present purposes.

Koshland at least educated Congress on the subtleties of taxing stock dividends, but the legislators were not yet up to the task of devising a precise statutory solution. Instead, they tossed the ball back into the judiciary's court by providing in the Revenue Act of 1936 that a distribution of stock or rights to acquire stock was not to be treated as a dividend to the extent it did "not constitute income to the shareholder within the meaning of the Sixteenth Amendment to the Constitution."[7] The Supreme Court declined the invitation to reconsider *Eisner v. Macomber,* preferring to develop a "proportionate interest test," under which a stock dividend was taxable if it increased a shareholder's proportionate interest in the corporation.[8]

It was back to the drawing board, however, with the enactment of the Internal Revenue Code of 1954. Seeking a simple approach, Congress enacted the predecessor of current Section 305, largely as an expression of dissatisfaction with the proportionate interest test. A far more elaborate system was adopted in the Tax Reform Act of 1969. The following excerpt

---

7. Revenue Act of 1936, § 115(f)(1). This test was carried over to the 1939 Code.

8. See the legislative history in the text at pp. 295–296, infra. See also Helvering v. Sprouse, 318 U.S. 604, 63 S.Ct. 791 (1943), where the Supreme Court decided that a pro rata distribution of nonvoting common stock to a shareholder owning voting common stock was nontaxable because it did not change the proportionate interests of the shareholders, and Strassburger v. Commissioner, 318 U.S. 604, 63 S.Ct. 791 (1943), where the Court held that a distribution of cumulative nonvoting preferred stock to the corporation's sole shareholder was not taxable because "[b]oth before and after the event he owned exactly the same interest in the net value of the corporation as before." Id. at 607, 63 S.Ct. at 792.

of legislative history describes the 1954 Code provisions and explains the 1969 amendments.

Excerpt From Senate Finance Committee Report on Tax Reform Act of 1969

S.Rep. No. 91–552, 91st Cong., 1st Sess. 150–54 (1969).

Present law.—In its simplest form, a stock dividend is commonly thought of as a mere readjustment of the stockholder's interest, and not as income. For example, if a corporation with only common stock outstanding issues more common stock as a dividend, no basic change is made in the position of the corporation and its stockholders. No corporate assets are paid out, and the distribution merely gives each stockholder more pieces of paper to represent the same interest in the corporation.

On the other hand, stock dividends may also be used in a way that alters the interests of the stockholders. For example, if a corporation with only common stock outstanding declares a dividend payable at the election of each stockholder, either in additional common stock or in cash, the stockholder who receives a stock dividend is in the same position as if he received a taxable cash dividend and purchased additional stock with the proceeds. His interest in the corporation is increased relative to the interests of stockholders who took dividends in cash.

Present law (sec. 305(a)) provides that if a corporation pays a dividend to its shareholders in its own stock (or in rights to acquire its stock), the shareholders are not required to include the value of the dividend in income. There are two exceptions to this general rule. First, stock dividends paid in discharge of preference dividends for the current or immediately preceding taxable year are taxable. Second, a stock dividend is taxable if any shareholder may elect to receive his dividend in cash or other property instead of stock.

These provisions were enacted as part of the Internal Revenue Code of 1954. Before 1954 the taxability of stock dividends was determined under the "proportionate interest test," which developed out of a series of Supreme Court cases, beginning with Eisner v. Macomber, 252 U.S. 189 (1920) [T.D. 3010, C.B. 3, 25]. In these cases the Court held, in general, that a stock dividend was taxable if it increased any shareholder's proportionate interest in the corporation. The lower courts often had difficulty in applying the test as formulated in these cases, particularly where unusual corporate capital structures were involved.

Soon after the proportionate interest test was eliminated in the 1954 Code, corporations began to develop methods by which shareholders could, in effect, be given a choice between receiving cash dividends or increasing their proportionate interests in the corporation in much the same way as if they had received cash dividends and reinvested them in the corporation. The earliest of these methods involves dividing the common stock of the corporation into two classes, A and B. The two classes share equally in earnings and profits and in assets on liquidation. The only difference is that the class A stock pays only stock dividends and class B stock pays only cash dividends. The market value of the stock dividends paid on the class A stock is equated annually to the cash dividends paid on the class B stock. Class A stock may be converted into class B stock at any time. The stockholders can choose, either when the classes are established, when they purchase new stock, or through the convertibility option whether to own class A stock or class B stock.

In 1956, the Treasury Department issued proposed regulations which treated such arrangements as taxable (under sec. 305(b)(2)) as distributions subject to an election by the stockholder to receive cash instead of stock. In recent years, however, increasingly complex and sophisticated variations of this basic arrangement have been created. In some of these arrangements, the proportionate interest of one class of shareholders is increased even though no actual distribution of stock is made. This effect may be achieved, for example, by paying cash dividends on common stock and increasing by a corresponding amount the ratio at which convertible preferred stock or convertible debentures may be converted into common stock. Another method of achieving this result is a systematic periodic redemption plan, under which a small percentage, such as 5 percent, of each shareholder's stock may be redeemed annually at his election. Shareholders who do not choose to have their stock redeemed automatically increase their proportionate interest in the corporation.

On January 10, 1969, the Internal Revenue Service issued final regulations under which a number of methods of achieving the effect of a cash dividend to some shareholders and a corresponding increase in the proportionate interest of other shareholders are brought under the exceptions in section 305(b), with the result that shareholders who receive increases in proportionate interest are treated as receiving taxable distributions.

General reasons for change.—The final regulations * * * do not cover all of the arrangements by which cash dividends can be paid to some shareholders and other shareholders can be given corresponding increases in proportionate interest. For example, the periodic redemption plan described above is not covered by the regulations, and the committee believes it is not covered by the present statutory language (of sec. 305(b)(2)).

Methods have also been devised to give preferred stockholders the equivalent of dividends on preferred stock which are not taxable as such under present law. For example, a corporation may issue preferred stock for $100 per share which pays no dividends, but which may be redeemed in 20 years for $200. The effect is the same as if the corporation distributed preferred stock equal to 5 percent of the original stock each year during the 20–year period in lieu of cash dividends. The committee believes that dividends paid on preferred stock should be taxed whether they are received in cash or in another form, such as stock, rights to receive stock, or rights to receive an increased amount on redemption. Moreover, the committee believes that dividends on preferred stock should be taxed to the recipients whether they are attributable to the current or immediately preceding taxable year or to earlier taxable years.

Explanation of provisions.—The bill continues (in sec. 305(b)(1)) the provision of present law that a stock dividend is taxable if it is payable at the election of any shareholder in property instead of stock.

The bill provides (in sec. 305(b)(2)) that if there is a distribution or series of distributions of stock which has the result of the receipt of cash or other property by some shareholders and an increase in the proportionate interests of other shareholders in the assets or earnings and profits of the corporation, the shareholders receiving stock are to be taxable (under sec. 301).

For example, if a corporation has two classes of common stock, one paying regular cash dividends and the other paying corresponding stock dividends (whether in common or preferred stock), the stock dividends are to be taxable.

On the other hand, if a corporation has a single class of common stock and a class of preferred stock which pays cash dividends and is not convertible, and it distributes a pro rata common stock dividend with respect to its common stock, the stock distribution is not taxable because the distribution does not have the result of increasing the proportionate interests of any of the stockholders.

In determining whether there is a disproportionate distribution, any security convertible into stock or any right to acquire stock is to be treated as outstanding stock. For example, if a corporation has common stock and convertible debentures outstanding, and it pays interest on the convertible debentures and stock dividends on the common stock, there is a disproportionate distribution, and the stock dividends are to be taxable (under section 301). In addition, in determining whether there is a disproportionate distribution with respect to a shareholder, each class of stock is to be considered separately.

The committee has added two provisions to the House bill (secs. 305(b)(3) and (4)) which carry out more explicitly the intention of the House with regard to distributions of common and preferred stock on common stock, and stock distributions on preferred stock. The first of these provides that if a distribution or series of distributions has the result of the receipt of preferred stock by some common shareholders and the receipt of common stock by other common shareholders, all of the shareholders are taxable (under sec. 301) on the receipt of the stock.

The second of the provisions added by the committee (sec. 305(b)(4)) provides that distributions of stock with respect to preferred stock are taxable (under sec. 301). This provision applies to all distributions on preferred stock except increases in the conversion ratio of convertible preferred stock made solely to take account of stock dividends or stock splits with respect to the stock into which the convertible stock is convertible.

The bill provides (in section 305(b)(5)) that a distribution of convertible preferred stock is taxable (under sec. 301) unless it is established to the satisfaction of the Secretary or his delegate that it will not have the result of a disproportionate distribution described above. For example, if a corporation makes a pro rata distribution on its common stock of preferred stock convertible into common stock at a price slightly higher than the market price of the common stock on the date of distribution, and the period during which the stock must be converted is 4 months, it is likely that a distribution would have the result of a disproportionate distribution. Those stockholders who wish to increase their interests in the corporation would convert their stock into common stock at the end of the 4–month period, and those stockholders who wish to receive cash would sell their stock or have it redeemed. On the other hand, if the stock were convertible for a period of 20 years from the date of issuance, there would be a likelihood that substantially all of the stock would be converted into common stock, and there would be no change in the proportionate interest of the common shareholders.

The bill provides (in sec. 305(c)) that under regulations prescribed by the Secretary or his delegate, a change in conversion ratio, a change in redemption price, a difference between redemption price and issue price, a redemption treated as a section 301 distribution, or any transaction (including a recapitalization) having a similar effect on the interest of any shareholder is to be treated as a distribution with respect to each shareholder whose proportionate interest is thereby increased. The purpose of this provision is to give the Secretary authority to deal with transactions that have the effect of distributions, but in which stock is not actually distributed.

The proportionate interest of a shareholder can be increased not only by the payment of a stock dividend not paid to other shareholders, but by such methods as increasing the ratio at which his stock, convertible securities, or rights to stock may be converted into other stock, by decreasing the ratio at which other stock, convertible securities, or rights to stock can be converted into stock of the class he owns, or by the periodic redemption of stock owned by other shareholders. It is not clear under present law to what extent increases of this kind would be considered distributions of stock or rights to stock. In order to eliminate uncertainty, the committee has authorized the Secretary or his delegate to prescribe regulations governing the extent to which such transactions shall be treated as taxable distributions.

For example, if a corporation has a single class of common stock which pays no dividends and a class of preferred stock which pays regular cash dividends, and which is convertible into the common stock at a conversion ratio that decreases each year to adjust for the payment of the cash dividends on the preferred stock, it is anticipated that the regulations will provide in appropriate circumstances that the holders of the common stock will be treated as receiving stock in a disproportionate distribution (under sec. 305(b)(2)).

It is anticipated that the regulations will establish rules for determining when and to what extent the automatic increase in proportionate interest accruing to stockholders as a result of redemptions under periodic redemption plan are to be treated as taxable distributions. A periodic redemption plan may exist, for example, where a corporation agrees to redeem a small percentage of each common shareholder's stock annually at the election of the shareholder. The shareholders whose stock is redeemed receive cash, and the shareholders whose stock is not redeemed receive an automatic increase in their proportionate interests. However, the committee does not intend that this regulatory authority is to be used to bring isolated redemptions of stock under the disproportionate distribution rule (of sec. 305(b)(2)). For example, a 30 percent stockholder would not be treated as receiving a constructive dividend because a 70 percent stockholder causes a corporation to redeem 15 percent of its stock from him.

Revenue Ruling 78–60

1978–1 Cum. Bull. 81.

Advice has been requested whether under section 302(a) of the Internal Revenue Code of 1954 the stock redemptions described below qualified for exchange treatment, and whether under section 305(b)(2) and (c) the shareholders who experienced increases in their proportionate interests in the redeeming corporation as a result of the stock redemptions will be treated as having received distributions of property to which section 301 applies.

Corporation Z has only one class of stock outstanding. The Z common stock is held by 24 shareholders, all of whom are descendants, or spouses of descendants, of the founder of Z.

In 1975, when Z had 6,000 shares of common stock outstanding, the board of directors of Z adopted a plan of annual redemption to provide a means for its shareholders to sell their stock. The plan provides that Z will annually redeem up to 40 shares to its outstanding stock at a price established annually by the Z board of directors. Each shareholder of Z is entitled to cause Z to redeem two-thirds of one percent of the shareholder's stock each year. If some shareholders choose not to participate fully in the plan during any year, the other shareholders can cause Z to redeem more than two-thirds of one percent of their stock, up to the maximum of 40 shares.

Pursuant to the plan of annual redemption, Z redeemed 40 shares of its stock in 1976. Eight shareholders participated in the redemptions. The following table shows the ownership interests of the Z shareholders before and after the 1976 redemptions. [The table has been omitted. It shows that none of the 24 shareholders owned 13 percent or more of the corporation's stock before or after the redemption and, after the redemption, each shareholder's actual and constructive ownership was at least 97 percent of its ownership prior to the redemption. Ed.]

Issue 1

Section 302(a) of the Code provides that if a corporation redeems its stock, and if section 302(b)(1), (2) or (3) applies, the redemption will be treated as a distribution in part or full payment in exchange for the stock.

Section 302(b)(1) of the Code provides that section 302(a) will apply if the redemption is not essentially equivalent to a dividend. Section 302(b)(2) provides that section 302(a) will apply if the redemption is substantially disproportionate with respect to the shareholder unless the redemption is made pursuant to a plan the purpose or effect of which, in the aggregate, is not substantially disproportionate with respect to the shareholder. Section 302(b)(3) provides that section 302(a) will apply if all of the stock of the corporation owned by the shareholder is redeemed. Section 318(a) contains rules of constructive stock ownership to be applied to those provisions of subchapter C to which they are expressly made applicable. Section 302(c)(1) provides, with an exception not relevant here, that the constructive ownership rules of section 318(a) apply in determining the ownership of stock for purposes of section 302.

Section 302(d) of the Code provides that a stock redemption to which section 302(a) does not apply will be treated as a distribution of property to which section 301 applies.

None of the redemptions here qualified under section 302(b)(3) of the Code because all of the shareholders who participated in the redemptions continue to own stock of Z. Moreover, none of the redemptions qualified under section 302(b)(2) because none of the shareholders who participated in the redemptions experienced a reduction in interest of more than 20 percent, as section 302(b)(2)(C) requires. Therefore, the first question is whether the redemptions were "not essentially equivalent to a dividend" within the meaning of section 302(b)(1).

Section 1.302–2(b) of the regulations provides that the question whether a distribution in redemption of stock is not essentially equivalent to a dividend under section 302(b)(1) of the Code depends on the facts and circumstances.

In United States v. Davis, 397 U.S. 301 (1970), rehearing denied, 397 U.S. 1071 (1970), 1970–1 C.B. 62, the Supreme Court of the United States said that for a redemption to qualify as not essentially equivalent to a dividend under section 302(b)(1) of the Code, the redemption must result in a meaningful reduction of the shareholder's proportionate interest in the corporation. The Court held that the business purpose of the redemption is irrelevant to this determination and that the ownership attribution rules of section 318(a) apply.

Several of the shareholders of Z experienced reductions in their proportionate interests in Z (taking into account constructive stock ownership under section 318 of the Code) as a result of the 1976 redemptions. If their reductions were "meaningful," they are entitled to exchange treatment for their redemptions under section 302(a). Whether the reductions in proportionate interests were 'meaningful' depends on the facts and circumstances.

In this case, an important fact is that the 1976 redemptions were not isolated occurrences but were undertaken pursuant to an ongoing plan for Z to redeem 40 shares of its stock each year. None of the reductions in proportionate interest experienced by Z shareholders as a result of the 1976 redemptions was "meaningful" because the reductions were small and each shareholder has the power to recover the lost interest by electing not to participate in the redemption plan in later years.

Accordingly, none of the 1976 redemptions qualified for exchange treatment under section 302(a) of the Code. All of the redemptions are to be treated as distributions of property to which section 301 applies.

Issue 2

Section 305(b)(2) of the Code provides that section 301 will apply to a distribution by a corporation of its stock if the distribution, or a series of distributions that includes the distribution, has the result of the receipt of property by some shareholders, and increases in the proportionate interests of other shareholders in the assets or earnings and profits of the corporation.

Section 305(c) of the Code authorizes regulations under which a redemption treated as a section 301 distribution will be treated as a section 301 distribution to any shareholder whose proportionate interest in the earnings and profits or assets of the corporation is increased by the redemption.

Section 1.305–7(a) of the Income Tax Regulations provides that a redemption treated as a section 301 distribution will generally be treated as a distribution to which sections 305(b)(2) and 301 of the Code apply if the proportionate interest of any shareholder in the earnings and profits or assets of the corporation deemed to have made the stock distribution is increased by the redemption, and the distribution has the result described in section 305(b)(2). The distribution is to be deemed made to any shareholder whose interest in the earnings and profits or assets of the distributing corporation is increased by the redemption.

Section 1.305–3(b)(3) of the regulations provides that for a distribution of property to meet the requirements of section 305(b)(2) of the Code, the distribution must be made to a shareholder in the capacity as a shareholder and must be a distribution to which section 301 [or one of several other specified sections] applies. A distribution of property incident to an isolated redemption will not cause section 305(b)(2) to apply even though the redemption distribution is treated as a section 301 distribution.

Section 305 of the Code does not make the constructive stock ownership rules of section 318(a) applicable to its provisions.

The 16 shareholders of Z who did not tender any stock for redemption in 1976 experienced increases in their proportionate interests of the earnings and profits and assets of Z (without taking into account constructive stock ownership under section 318 of the Code) as a result of the redemptions. Shareholders B and X, who surrendered small amounts of their stock for redemption in 1976, also experienced increases in their proportionate interests. The 1976 redemptions were not isolated but were undertaken pursuant to an ongoing plan of annual stock redemptions. Finally, the 1976 redemptions are to be treated as distributions of property to which section 301 of the Code applies.

Accordingly, *B, X* and the 16 shareholders of *Z* who did not participate in the 1976 redemptions are deemed to have received stock distributions to which sections 305(b)(2) and 301 of the Code apply. See examples (8) and (9) of section 1.305–3(e) of the regulations for a method of computing the amounts of the deemed distributions.

NOTE

Collateral Tax Consequences. The collateral tax consequences of a stock distribution (e.g., basis, holding period, and effect on earnings and profits) depend upon whether or not the distribution is taxable to the shareholders. Taxable distributions are governed by the rules in Section 301. The amount of the distribution is the fair market value of the stock.[1] The shareholder takes a fair market value basis in the distributed stock, and his holding period runs from the date of the distribution.[2] The distributing corporation recognizes no gain or loss under Section 311(a)(1), and it may reduce its earnings and profits by the fair market value of the distributed stock.[3]

If a stock distribution is nontaxable under Section 305(a), the shareholder must allocate the basis in the stock held prior to the distribution between the old and new stock in proportion to the relative fair market values of each on the date of distribution,[4] and the holding period of the old shares may be tacked on in determining the holding period of the distributed stock.[5] The distributing corporation recognizes no gain or loss on the distribution of its stock[6], and it may not reduce its earnings and profits.[7]

Stock Rights Distributions. Section 305 also governs distributions of stock rights (sometimes called warrants). Public companies occasionally issue rights to acquire additional stock at a favorable price as a means of raising equity capital.[8] Like stock dividends generally, rights distributions are not taxable unless they come within one of the Section 305(b) exceptions.[9] In the case of a nontaxable rights distribution, Section 307(a) generally requires an allocation of basis between the underlying stock and the rights in proportion to their relative fair market values on the date of

1. Reg. § 1.305–1(b)(1). This rule also applies to corporate shareholders. Reg. § 1.301–1(d)(1)(ii). In the case of noncorporate shareholders, taxable stock dividends may be "qualified" and eligible for the preferential rates under Section 1(h)(11) if they are extended beyond 2012.

2. Reg. § 1.301–1(h).

3. Reg. § 1.312–1(d).

4. I.R.C. § 307(a); Reg. § 1.307–1.

5. I.R.C. § 1223(4).

6. I.R.C. § 311(a)(1).

7. I.R.C. § 312(d)(1)(B).

8. See, e.g., Rev.Rul. 72–71, 1972–1 C.B. 99, which is the Service's ruling on a complex rights offering by American Telephone and Telegraph Co.

9. See I.R.C. § 305(d)(1), which treats rights as "stock" for purposes of Section 305.

the distribution.[10] In most cases, however, such an allocation is unnecessary because of an administrative convenience exception in Section 307(b), which provides that the rights shall take a zero basis if their fair market value is less than 15 percent of the value of the stock with respect to which they were distributed. Taxpayers with time on their hands (or the incentive to make an allocation) may elect to use the allocation method prescribed in Section 307(a).[11] Taxable rights distributions are treated as Section 301 distributions; as such, their value (if any) is a dividend to the extent of the distributing corporation's earnings and profits.

PROBLEMS

1. Hill Corporation is organized with two classes of voting common stock: Class A and Class B. Shares in each class of stock have an equal right to Hill's assets and earnings and profits. Frank owns 100 shares of Class A stock, and Fay and Joyce each own 50 shares of Class B stock.

Assuming that Hill Corporation has ample earnings and profits, determine whether the following distributions are taxable under § 301 or excludable under § 305(a):

   (a) A pro rata distribution of nonconvertible preferred stock to both classes of shareholders.

   (b) A pro rata distribution of Class A stock on Class A and Class B on Class B. The Class B shareholders also are given the option to take cash in lieu of additional Class B shares. Joyce exercises this option.

   (c) A pro rata distribution of Class A stock on Class A and a cash distribution on Class B.

   (d) Assume that Class B is a class of nonconvertible preferred stock which pays regular cash dividends and Hill distributes Class B stock to the Class A shareholder.

   (e) Same as (d), above, except that Hill distributes a class of nonconvertible preferred stock which has rights to assets and earnings and profits subordinate to those of the existing Class B stock (i.e., "junior" nonconvertible preferred stock) to the Class A shareholder.

   (f) Assume that Hill has only one class of common stock outstanding and also has issued a series of 10 percent debentures convertible into common stock at the rate of one share of common stock for each $1,000 debenture. Hill makes an annual interest payment to the debenture holders and one month later distributes a "common

---

10. But the regulations permit this allocation only if the rights are exercised (in which event the basis allocated to the rights is added to the cost of the new stock acquired) or sold. If the rights simply lapse, the shareholder recognizes no loss but the basis returns to the underlying stock. Reg. § 1.307–1(a).

11. I.R.C. § 307(b)(2).

on common" stock dividend to the common shareholders without adjusting the conversion ratio on the debentures.

(g) Same as (f), above, except that the debentures are convertible preferred stock. The corporation declares a one-for-one split on the common stock (i.e., each shareholder receives one new share of common stock for each old share) and the conversion ratio of the preferred is doubled.

(h) Assume again that Class A and Class B are both classes of voting common stock. Hill makes a pro rata distribution of Class A on Class A and a distribution of newly issued shares of nonconvertible preferred stock on Class B.

(i) Same as (h), above, except that the preferred stock which is distributed is convertible into Class B stock over 20 years at Class B's market price on the day of the distribution.

2. Z Corporation has one class of common stock outstanding held by unrelated individuals A (500 shares), B (300 shares), and C (200 shares). Will § 305(c) create any tax problems if Z agrees to redeem annually 50 shares of stock at the election of each shareholder, and A makes such an election for two consecutive years?

C. SECTION 306 STOCK

1. THE PREFERRED STOCK BAILOUT

As previewed earlier in this chapter, Section 306 is one of several provisions in Subchapter C that are much less significant as long as dividends and long-term capital gains of noncorporate taxpayers are taxed at the same preferential rates. The specific target of Section 306 was the preferred stock bailout, a device used by shareholders in the "good old days" to withdraw corporate earnings at very favorable capital gains rates. In the classic transaction, a profitable C corporation would make a tax-free distribution of preferred stock to its common shareholders, who then sold the preferred stock to an accommodating investor (often a lightly-taxed insurance company) and reported long-term capital gain on the sale. The investor collected dividends on the preferred stock and, a few years later, the corporation redeemed the preferred stock from the investor. The net effect was the receipt of cash by the shareholders on the sale of the preferred stock and, after the redemption from the investor, there would be no reduction of their proportionate interest in the corporation.

In Chamberlin v. Commissioner,[1] the Service contended that the preferred stock dividend was taxable as ordinary income on these facts. The Sixth Circuit disagreed, using language dear to the hearts of taxpayers ("[t]he general principle is well settled that a taxpayer has the legal right to decrease the amount of what otherwise would be his taxes, or altogether avoid them, by means which the law permits"). The court found that the buyer of the preferred stock (the "investor") made a bona fide investment,

---

1. 207 F.2d 462 (6th Cir. 1953), cert.   denied, 347 U.S. 918, 74 S.Ct. 516 (1954).

the preferred stock dividend was legally paid, the subsequent redemption was a distribution to the investor (not the common shareholders), and nothing in the statute permitted the common shareholders' gain on the sale of the preferred stock to be taxed as ordinary income.

The *Chamberlin* case was decided under the 1939 Code. Left unchecked, the court's endorsement of the preferred stock bailout would have encouraged other closely held corporations to engage in similar profitable end runs around the distribution rules. Although the result in *Chamberlin* possibly would have been overturned in subsequent litigation, the Treasury wisely sought a prompt legislative solution. The central issue facing the drafters of the 1954 Code was whether to attack the bailout by taxing all "preferred on common" stock dividends or to defer the punishment until the shareholder disposed of stock with bailout potential.

Common shareholders who receive a proportionate preferred stock dividend have not increased their interest in the corporation. They simply have a tax opportunity which they may choose to forego for nontax reasons. For example, there may be valid business reasons (e.g., a shift of control from older to younger generation shareholders) for a preferred stock dividend. Recognizing these and other nontax objectives served by preferred stock dividends, Congress concluded that the *receipt* of the dividend was not the appropriate occasion for punitive action.[2] Instead, it chose to label stock with bailout potential as "Section 306 stock" and to require a shareholder to report ordinary income rather than capital gain when Section 306 stock is sold or redeemed. In the case of a sale, the ordinary income amount is generally determined by the amount that would have been a dividend at the time of the stock distribution if cash rather than stock had been distributed.[3] In the case of a redemption, the ordinary income amount is determined at the time of the cash distribution.[4] Other operational and planning aspects of Section 306 are examined below.

Whenever dividends and long-term capital gains are taxed at the same low rate, the advantages to be achieved from a bailout of corporate earnings at "capital gains rates" have diminished considerably. As with redemptions and a few other classic bailout transactions to be studied later, the only remaining tax advantages to noncorporate shareholders of a sale of stock rather than a dividend are recovery of stock basis and, in special situations, the ability to offset capital gains (but not qualified dividends) with capital losses. Section 306 nonetheless remains in the Code, in semi-hibernation until the distinction between dividends and capital gains is restored to its former glory, or until Congress decides that it is no longer necessary.

2.   THE OPERATION OF SECTION 306

a.   SECTION 306 STOCK DEFINED

Code: § 306(c)–(e).

---

2.   S.Rep. No. 1622, 83rd Cong., 2d Sess. 46 (1954).

3.   I.R.C. § 306(a)(1).

4.   I.R.C. § 306(a)(2). See Section C2b of this chapter, infra.

Regulations: §§ 1.306–3(a)–(c), (e).

The definition of Section 306 stock is consistent with the original anti-bailout objectives of the statute. The principal category is stock distributed to a shareholder as a tax-free stock dividend under Section 305(a)—other than "common on common."[1] Ordinarily, this is preferred stock distributed to common shareholders by a corporation with earnings and profits. As the *Chamberlin* case illustrates, preferred stock is the primary vehicle for a bailout because it can be sold without diminishing the shareholder's control or right to share in future corporate growth. "Common" stock is excepted because it lacks bailout potential; it may not be sold without diminishing the shareholder's control and interest in corporate growth.[2]

Although the Service has not defined "common stock" for Section 306 purposes, its published rulings focus on whether a sale of the stock would cause a reduction of the shareholder's equity position in the company. The fundamental inquiry is thus whether the stock has a realistic and unrestricted opportunity to participate in the growth of corporate equity.[3] If stock has either a limited right to dividends or to assets upon liquidation, it is not "common" stock for Section 306 purposes.[4] But voting common stock that is subject to the issuing corporation's first refusal right to purchase the stock at net book value whenever a shareholder wishes to make a transfer is common stock because, upon a transfer, the shareholder will part with some or all of his interest in the future growth of the corporation vis a vis other shareholders.[5]

Congress also concluded that a tax-free stock dividend issued by a corporation with no current or accumulated earnings and profits for the year of the distribution has limited bailout potential. If cash instead of stock had been distributed, the shareholder would not have realized ordinary income whenever the distributing corporation has no earnings and profits. Consequently, Section 306 stock does not include stock which would not have been treated as a dividend at the time of distribution if cash had been distributed in lieu of the stock.[6]

To prevent an easy purge of the taint, Section 306 stock includes stock with a transferred or substituted basis.[7] This category encompasses stock received as a gift which takes a Section 1015 transferred basis, or stock received in exchange for Section 306 stock in a tax-free Section 351 transaction.[8] But the exorcist prevails when stock passes from a decedent and thus qualifies for a date-of-death basis under Section 1014. In that

---

1. I.R.C. § 306(c)(1)(A).

2. See Walter, " 'Preferred Stock' and 'Common Stock': The Meaning of the Terms and the Importance of the Distinction for Tax Purposes," 5 J.Corp.Tax'n 211 (1978).

3. See, e.g., Rev.Rul. 75–222, 1975–1 C.B. 105; Rev.Rul. 79–163, 1979–1 C.B. 131.

4. Rev. Rul. 79–163, supra note 3.

5. Rev. Rul. 76–386, 1976–2 C.B. 95; see also Rev. Rul. 81–91, 1981–1 C.B. 123.

6. I.R.C. § 306(c)(2).

7. I.R.C. § 306(c)(1)(C).

8. In this situation, the old Section 306 stock remains tainted in the hands of the corporation, and the newly issued stock, whatever its class, also is Section 306 stock by virtue of its substituted basis under Section 358. See Rev.Rul. 77–108, 1977–1 C.B. 86.

event, the Section 306 taint is buried along with the decedent and her old basis.

An important but more specialized category is stock (which is not common stock) received in a tax-free corporate reorganization or division when the effect of the transaction is substantially the same as the receipt of a stock dividend or when the stock is received in exchange for Section 306 stock. For example, preferred stock received by the shareholders of the target (i.e., acquired) corporation in a tax-free merger may be a prime candidate for Section 306 classification. This aspect of Section 306 is considered in a later chapter.[9]

The final category of Section 306 stock was added by Congress to thwart the use of a holding company to bail out earnings. Assume, for example, that Schemer holds only common stock in Profitable Co. Finding that Section 306 presents a substantial roadblock to a bailout, Schemer organizes Holding Co., exchanging her Profitable common stock for newly issued Holding common and preferred stock in a tax-free Section 351 transaction. At one time, the Holding preferred stock would not have been Section 306 stock because Holding had no earnings and profits at the time of its incorporation. This offered shareholders the very bailout opportunity that Congress was trying to prevent! Schemer could sell the Holding preferred stock to an institutional investor, recovering her basis and realizing a capital gain, and the stock later could be redeemed by the corporation—all without losing any of her control or share in the growth of Profitable.

Section 306(c)(3) blocks this maneuver by characterizing the preferred stock of Holding Co. (i.e., preferred stock acquired in a Section 351 exchange) as Section 306 stock if the receipt of money instead of the stock would have been treated as a dividend to any extent. Of course, Holding Co. has no earnings and profits so that a distribution of cash would not have been a dividend. To make the statute achieve its objective, Section 306(c)(3)(A) borrows the rules of Section 304 (relating to redemptions through the use of affiliated corporations). In our example, the Holding Co. preferred would be Section 306 stock if Profitable Co. has any current or accumulated earnings and profits. This is because a cash payment by Holding Co. for the Profitable common stock would have resulted in a dividend to Schemer under Section 304(a)(1). In effect, this means that we look to the earnings and profits of the original corporation (Profitable Co.) in determining whether the receipt of cash would have been a dividend.[10]

---

9. See Chapter 11, infra.

10. In testing for the effect of a dividend, the Section 318 attribution rules apply without regard to the 50 percent limitation in Sections 318(a)(2)(C) and 318(a)(3)(C). I.R.C. § 306(c)(4).

b. DISPOSITIONS OF SECTION 306 STOCK

Code: § 306(a).

Regulations: § 1.306–1.

The tax consequences of a disposition of Section 306 stock vary depending on whether the stock is sold or redeemed. On a sale of Section 306 stock, the amount realized is treated as dividend income to the extent of the stock's "ratable share" of the amount that would have been a dividend if the corporation had distributed cash in an amount equal to the fair market value of the stock at the time of the distribution.[11] This rule requires the shareholder to look back to the time of distribution and determine to what extent a cash distribution would have emanated from the corporation's current or accumulated earnings and profits at that time.[12] The balance, if any, of the amount realized is treated as a reduction of the basis of the Section 306 stock, and any excess is treated as gain from the sale or exchange of the stock.[13] Although the ordinary income amount is treated as a dividend received from the corporation to allow noncorporate shareholder to qualify for the preferred rates under Section 1(h), it is not clear if corporate shareholders are eligible for the Section 243 dividends received deduction, or whether the corporation is entitled to reduce its earnings and profits when Section 306 stock is sold.[14] No loss may be recognized if the shareholder's adjusted basis in the stock exceeds the amount realized, and any unrecovered basis must be allocated back to the stock with respect to which the Section 306 stock was distributed.[15]

A shareholder who receives a nontaxable stock dividend of Section 306 stock that later is redeemed by the corporation has used two steps to achieve what could have been accomplished in a single transaction: the withdrawal of cash from the corporation. To reflect that reality and treat the transactions as a single event, Section 306(a)(2) provides that the amount realized on a redemption of Section 306 stock is treated as a

---

11. I.R.C. §§ 306(a)(1)(A), (a)(1)(D).

12. I.R.C. § 306(a)(1)(A). This provision also applies to other nonredemption "dispositions" such as certain pledges of Section 306 stock where the pledgee can only look to the stock as security (an unlikely scenario), but it does not apply to charitable contributions of Section 306 stock. Reg. § 1.306–1(b)(1); Rev.Rul. 57–328, 1957–2 C.B. 229. For charitable deduction purposes, however, a taxpayer who contributes appreciated Section 306 stock to a qualified donee must reduce the fair market value of the donated stock by the amount that would not have been long-term capital gain if the stock had been sold rather than donated. See I.R.C. § 170(e)(1)(A); Pescosolido v. Commissioner, 91 T.C. 52 (1988). It appears that the treatment of Section 306(a)(1) ordinary income as a dividend and thus, if "qualified," part of "adjusted net capital gain" under Section 1(h)(11), does not permit a donor

shareholder from escaping the reduction rule in Section 170 because the gain technically is not "long-term capital gain." Perhaps the Treasury will specify otherwise if and when it issues regulations under the authority of Section 306(a)(1)(D).

13. I.R.C. § 306(a)(1)(B).

14. Section 306(a)(1)(D) provides that any amount treated as ordinary income on a sale of Section 306 stock shall be treated as a dividend "[f]or purposes of section 1(h)(11) and such other provisions as the Secretary shall specify * * *." As of early 2005, the Treasury had not yet "specified" and, until it does, it appears that corporate shareholders may not claim the dividends received deduction, and no earnings and profit reduction is authorized on a sale of Section 306 stock.

15. I.R.C. § 306(a)(1)(C); Reg. § 1.306–1(b)(2) Example (3).

Section 301 distribution, taxable as a dividend (likely a qualified dividend) to the extent of the current or accumulated earnings and profits in the year of redemption.[16] The balance of the distribution, if any, is treated as a reduction of basis and then capital gain under the rules generally applicable to nonliquidating distributions.[17]

c. DISPOSITIONS EXEMPT FROM SECTION 306

Code: § 306(b).

Regulations: § 1.306–2.

Section 306 is aimed only at bailouts, and not every disposition of Section 306 stock presents that opportunity. For example, a shareholder who sells her entire interest in a corporation (including her Section 306 stock) is not withdrawing corporate earnings while preserving control. She is engaging in a transaction that easily could have qualified for capital gain treatment irrespective of any prior stock dividend. Section 306(b)(1) thus provides that the punitive general rule of Section 306(a) shall not apply to nonredemption dispositions if the shareholder completely terminates her interest in the corporation and does not dispose of the stock to a related person within the Section 318 attribution rules.[18] A similar exception is provided for redemptions of Section 306 stock that result in a complete termination of the shareholder's interest under Section 302(b)(3) or qualify as a partial liquidation under Section 302(b)(4).[19]

Other exempt dispositions include: (1) redemptions of Section 306 stock in a complete liquidation;[20] (2) dispositions that are treated as nonrecognition transactions, such as tax-free Section 351 transfers, contributions to capital and the like;[21] and (3) distributions coupled with subsequent dispositions or redemptions of Section 306 stock if the taxpayer satisfies the Service that either: (a) the distribution and subsequent disposition or redemption, or (b) in the case of a prior or simultaneous disposition of the underlying common stock, just the disposition or redemption, was not made pursuant to a plan having tax avoidance as one of its principal purposes.[22]

Although Section 306 is aimed primarily at closely held companies, the Service's hard line position is that holders of Section 306 stock issued by public companies are not automatically entitled to relief under the "no tax avoidance" exception in Section 306(b)(4).[23] The "no tax avoidance" exception is explored in the *Fireoved* case, which follows.

---

16. I.R.C. § 306(a)(2).

17. See I.R.C. § 301(c)(2), (3).

18. For purposes of determining whether there has been a complete termination, the Section 318 attribution rules apply. I.R.C. § 306(b)(1)(A)(iii).

19. I.R.C. § 306(b)(1)(B).

20. I.R.C. § 306(b)(2).

21. I.R.C. § 306(b)(3).

22. I.R.C. § 306(b)(4).

23. Rev. Rul. 89–63, 1989–1 C.B. 90, revoking Rev. Rul. 56–116, 1956–1 C.B. 164.

Fireoved v. United States

United States Court of Appeals, Third Circuit, 1972.
462 F.2d 1281.

■ ADAMS, CIRCUIT JUDGE.

This appeal calls into question the application of section 306 of the Internal Revenue Code of 1954 and the "first in-first out rule" to a redemption of preferred stock in a corporation by plaintiff, one of its principal shareholders. In particular we are asked to decide whether the transaction here had "as one of its principal purposes the avoidance of Federal income tax," whether a prior sale of a portion of the underlying common stock immunized a like proportion of the section 306 stock from treatment as a noncapital asset, and whether another block of the redeemed stock should be considered to represent stock not subject to section 306.

I.   Factual Background

On November 24, 1948, Fireoved and Company, Inc. was incorporated for the purpose of printing and selling business forms. At their first meeting, the incorporators elected Eugene Fireoved, his wife, Marie, the plaintiffs, and a nephew, Robert L. Fireoved, as directors of the corporation. Subsequently, the directors elected Eugene Fireoved as President and Treasurer and Marie Fireoved as Secretary. The corporation had authorized capital stock of 500 shares of $100 par value non-voting, non-cumulative preferred stock and 100 shares of $1 par value voting common stock. On December 31, 1948, in consideration for $100 cash, the corporation issued Eugene Fireoved 100 shares of common stock; for $500 cash, it issued him five shares of preferred stock; and in payment for automotive equipment and furniture and fixtures, valued at $6,000, it issued him an additional 60 shares of preferred stock.

In 1954, when Mr. Fireoved learned that his nephew, Robert, was planning to leave the business, he began discussions with Karl Edelmayer and Kenneth Craver concerning the possibility of combining his business with their partnership, Girard Business Forms, that had been printing and selling business forms for some time prior to 1954. Messrs. Fireoved, Edelmayer and Craver agreed that voting control of the new enterprise should be divided equally among the three of them. Because Mr. Fireoved's contribution to capital would be approximately $60,000 whereas the partnership could contribute only $30,000, it was decided that preferred stock should be issued to Mr. Fireoved to compensate for the disparity. In furtherance of this plan, the directors and shareholders of Fireoved and Company, in late 1954 and early 1955, held several meetings at which the following corporate changes were accomplished: The name of the company was changed to Girard Business Forms; the authorized common stock was increased from 100 to 300 shares and the authorized preferred stock was increased to 1000 shares; Mr. Fireoved exchanged his 100 shares of common and 65 shares of preferred stock for equal amounts of the new stock; an agreement of purchase was authorized by which the company would buy all the assets of the Edelmayer–Craver partnership in return for 200 shares of common and 298 shares of preferred stock; and Mr. Fireoved was issued 535 shares of the new preferred stock as a dividend[6] on his 100 shares of common stock, thereby bringing his total holding of preferred stock to 600 shares to indicate his $60,000 capital contribution compared to the $29,800 contributed by the former partnership.

As the business progressed, Mr. Edelmayer demanded more control of the company. In response, Mr. Fireoved and Mr. Craver each sold 24 shares of common stock in the corporation to him on February 28, 1958.

On April 30, 1959, the company redeemed 451 of Mr. Fireoved's 600 shares of preferred stock at $105 per share, resulting in net proceeds to him of $47,355.[7] The gain from this transaction was reported by Mr. and Mrs. Fireoved on their joint return for the year 1959 as a long term capital gain. Subsequently, the Commissioner of Internal Revenue (Commissioner) assessed a deficiency against the Fireoveds of $15,337.13 based on the Commissioner's view that the proceeds from the redemption of the 451 shares of preferred stock should have been reported as ordinary income and the tax paid at that rate based on section 306. Mr. and Mrs. Fireoved paid the assessment on March 14, 1963, but on March 10, 1965, filed a claim for a refund with the Commissioner.

After the Commissioner disallowed the refund claim on March 8, 1966, the Fireoveds instituted the present action against the United States on August 4, 1967 seeking a refund of the $15,337.13 plus interest on the ground that the transaction came within an exception to section 306, and that they were therefore entitled to report the income as a long term capital gain. The case was tried to the court without a jury on stipulated facts. It is from the district court's determination, 318 F.Supp. 133, on October 29, 1970, that $8,885.50 should be refunded to the taxpayers that both parties appeal.

II.   *Background of Section 306*

Because we are the first court of appeals asked to decide questions of law pursuant to section 306, it is appropriate that we first examine the circumstances that led to the inclusion in 1954 of this section in the Code.

Generally, a taxpayer will benefit monetarily if he is able to report income as a long term capital gain rather than as ordinary income. Under normal circumstances a cash dividend from a corporation constitutes ordinary income to the shareholder receiving such money. Therefore, it would be to the advantage of a shareholder if a method could be devised by which the money could be distributed to him, that would otherwise be paid out as cash dividends, in a form that would permit the shareholder to report such income as a long term capital gain.

---

6. At the time Mr. Fireoved received his stock dividend, the company had accumulated earnings and profits of $52,993.06.

7. In 1959, the company had accumulated earnings and profits of $48,235.

A temporarily successful plan for converting ordinary income to long term capital gain is described by the facts of Chamberlin v. C.I.R., 207 F.2d 462 (6th Cir.1953). * * *

The legislative reaction to the Chamberlin decision was almost immediate, resulting in the addition of section 306 to the 1954 Code, in order to prevent shareholders from obtaining the tax advantage of such bail-outs when such shareholders retain their ownership interests in the company.

* * *

Based on the history of section 306 and its plain meaning evidenced by the provisions, it is not disputed that the 535 shares of preferred stock issued to Mr. Fireoved as a stock dividend in 1954 were section 306 stock. Additionally, it is clear that in 1959, when the company redeemed 451 shares of Mr. Fireoved's preferred stock, the general provisions of section 306 aside from the exceptions—would require that any amount realized by Mr. Fireoved be taxed at ordinary income rates rather than long term capital gain rates, because the company had earnings at that time of $48,235 more than the $47,355 required to redeem the stock at $105 per share.

Thus, the questions to be decided on this appeal are (1) whether certain of the exceptions to section 306 apply to permit the Fireoveds' reporting their gain as a long term capital gain, and (2) whether 65 of the 451 shares redeemed are not section 306 stock because of the first in-first out rule of Treasury Regulation § 1.1012–1(c) [the court's analysis and holding on the second issue has been omitted. Ed.].

III. Was the distribution of the stock dividend "in pursuance of a plan having as one of its principal purposes avoidance of Federal income tax?"

Mr. Fireoved asserts that the entire transaction should fall within the exception established by section 306(b)(4)(A), which provides: "If it is established to the satisfaction of the Secretary or his delegate * * * that the distribution, and the disposition or redemption * * * was not in pursuance of a plan having as one of its principal purposes the avoidance of Federal income tax," then the general rule of section 306(a) will not apply.

As a threshold point on this issue, the Government maintains that because Mr. Fireoved never attempted to obtain a ruling from the "Secretary or his delegate" the redemption should be covered by section 306(a), and the district court should not have reached the question whether the exception applied to Mr. Fireoved. Mr. Fireoved urges that the district court had the power to consider the matter de novo, even without a request by the taxpayer to the Secretary or his delegate. Because the ultimate result we reach would not be altered by whichever of these two courses we choose, we do not resolve this potentially complex procedural problem.[10]

---

10. For the same reason, we do not decide this issue in Part II, infra.

The district court, based on the assumption that it had the power to decide the question, found that although one of the purposes involved in the issuance of the preferred stock dividend may have been business related, another principal purpose was the avoidance of Federal income tax.

Mr. Fireoved's analysis of the facts presented in the stipulations would reach the conclusion that the sole purpose of the stock dividend was business related. He relies heavily on that portion of the stipulation which describes why the decision was made to combine his business with the Edelmayer–Craver partnership: "The partnership could provide the additional manpower which the expected departure of Robert L. Fireoved from the Corporation would require. Additionally, the partnership needed additional working capital which the Corporation had and could provide." Based primarily on the latter sentence, Mr. Fireoved asserts that the district court had no choice but to find that the transaction was business related and that it therefore had no avoidance incentive.

In making this argument, however, Mr. Fireoved overlooks the plain import of the language of section 306(b)(4). Whether the section requires the decision to be made by the Secretary or the district court, it is clear that "one of [the] principal purposes" of the stock dividend was not for "the avoidance of Federal income tax." The stipulation demonstrates no more than that the reorganized company required more capital than could be supplied by the partnership alone. The stipulation is completely in harmony with the following fact situation: After the partnership was combined with the corporation, the business required the $30,000 contributed by the partnership and all of the $60,000 Mr. Fireoved had in the corporation. Mr. Fireoved decided to take the stock dividend rather than to distribute the cash to himself as a dividend, and then to make a loan to the corporation of the necessary money because if he took the cash, he would subject himself to taxation at ordinary income rates. Therefore "one of the principal purposes" of the stock dividend would be for "the avoidance of Federal income tax."

In a situation such as the one presented in this case, where the facts necessary to determine the motives for the issuance of a stock dividend are peculiarly within the control of the taxpayer, it is reasonable to require the taxpayer to come forward with the facts that would relieve him of his liability. Here the stipulation was equivocal in determining the purpose of the dividend and is quite compatible with the thought that "one of the principal purposes" was motivated by "tax avoidance." We hold then that the district court did not err in refusing to apply the exception created by section 306(b)(4)(A).[11]

11. It is important to note that apparently both Mr. Fireoved, in prosecuting this action for a refund, and the Government, in its defense, assumed that if the distribution and redemption of the preferred stock were not controlled by § 306(a), the gain would be subject to taxation as a long term capital gain. This is not necessarily the case at all. Whether or not § 306 governs the transaction, it nonetheless involves a redemption of stock by a corporation to which § 302 could apply. Under the tests set out in § 302(b)— the relevant one of which appears to be § 302(b)(1)—Mr. Fireoved, who had the bur-

*IV.   Did the prior sale by Mr. Fireoved of 24% of his underlying common
stock immunize such portion of the section 306 stock he redeemed in
1959?*

The district court construed section 306(b)(4)(B) to mean that any time
a taxpayer in Mr. Fireoved's position sells any portion of his underlying
common stock and later sells or redeems his section 306 stock, an equivalent proportion of the section 306 stock redeemed will not be subject to the
provisions of section 306(a). The Government has appealed from this
portion of the district court's order and urges that we reverse it, based on
the history and purpose of section 306 and the particular facts here.

The stipulations indicate that, "On February 28, 1958, Fireoved and
Craver each sold 24 shares of common stock in the corporation to Edelmayer," and that appropriate stock certificates were issued. From this fact, Mr.
Fireoved reasons that his sale of 24 of his 100 shares of common stock was
undertaken solely for the business purpose of satisfying Mr. Edelmayer's
desire for more control of the corporation, and therefore he should be given
the benefit of section 306(b)(4)(B). In addition, Mr. Fireoved contends that
the disposition of his section 306 stock was related to a business purpose
because he used part of the proceeds to pay off a $20,000 loan that the
company had made to him.

Mr. Fireoved has the same burden here of showing a lack of a tax
avoidance purpose that he had in section III supra. It is clear from the
limited facts set forth in the stipulations that he has not established that
the disposition of 24% of the 535 shares of the section 306 preferred stock
he owned "was not in pursuance of a plan having as one of its principal
purposes the avoidance of federal income tax."[12] More important, however,
is that an examination of the relevant legislative history indicates that
Congress did not intend to give capital gains treatment to a portion of the
preferred stock redeemed on the facts presented here.

It is apparent from the reaction evinced by Congress to the Chamberlin
case, supra, that by enacting section 306 Congress was particularly concerned with the tax advantages available to persons who controlled corporations and who could, without sacrificing their control, convert ordinary

den of proof, may well have been unable to
show that the redemption was not "essentially equivalent to a dividend." United States v.
Davis, 397 U.S. 301, 90 S.Ct. 1041, 25
L.Ed.2d 323 (1970). We hold, however, that it
is now too late for the Government to raise
this issue.

12.   Consistent with Mr. Fireoved's sale
of 24 shares of common stock in 1958 could
have been his knowledge that one year later
he would be selling his section 306 stock and
a desire on his part to avoid taxation at
ordinary income rates. As noted later in the
opinion, the sale of just 24 shares was enough
so that he retained effective control—in the

form of veto power—over the corporation.
Moreover, the fact that Mr. Fireoved needed
$20,000 of the proceeds to pay off a loan to
the corporation would not meet his burden.
The proceeds of the redemption totaled
$47,355. Thus, although $20,000 of the redemption may not have been to avoid taxes,
we can ascribe no purpose other than tax
avoidance to the receipt of the additional
$27,355. Therefore, since one of the principal
purposes of the redemption of 451 shares of
preferred stock was "the avoidance of Federal income tax," Mr. Fireoved may not take
advantage of § 306(b)(4)(B) for any part of
the redemption.

income to long term capital gains by the device of the preferred stock bail-out. The illustration given in the Senate Report which accompanied section 306(b)(4)(B) is helpful in determining the sort of transactions meant to be exempted by section 306(a):

> Thus if a shareholder received a distribution of 100 shares of section 306 stock on his holdings of 100 shares of voting common stock in a corporation and sells his voting common stock before he disposes of his section 306 stock, the subsequent disposition of his section 306 stock would not ordinarily be considered a tax avoidance disposition since he has previously parted with the stock which allows him to participate in the ownership of the business. However, variations of the above example may give rise to tax avoidance possibilities which are not within the exception of subparagraph (B). Thus if a corporation has only one class of common stock outstanding and it issues stock under circumstances that characterize it as section 306 stock, a subsequent issue of a different Class of common having greater voting rights than the original common will not permit a simultaneous disposition of the section 306 stock together with the original common to escape the rules of subsection (a) of section 306.

Thus, it is reasonable to assume that Congress realized the general lack of a tax avoidance purpose when a person sells all of his control in a corporation and then either simultaneously or subsequently disposes of his section 306 stock. However, when only a portion of the underlying common stock is sold, and the taxpayer retains essentially all the control he had previously, it would be unrealistic to conclude that Congress meant to give that taxpayer the advantage of section 306(b)(4)(B) when he ultimately sells his section 306 stock. Cf. United States v. Davis, 397 U.S. 301, 90 S.Ct. 1041, 25 L.Ed.2d 323 (1970).

Shortly after Fireoved's corporation had been combined with the Edelmayer–Craver partnership, significant changes to the by-laws were made. The by-laws provided that corporate action could be taken only with the unanimous consent of all the directors. In addition, the by-laws provided that they could be amended either by a vote of 76% of the outstanding common shares or a unanimous vote of the directors. When the businesses were combined in late 1954, each of the directors held ⅓ of the voting stock, thereby necessitating a unanimous vote for amendment to the by-laws. After Messrs. Fireoved and Craver each sold 24 shares of common stock to Mr. Edelmayer, Mr. Fireoved held 25⅓% of the common (voting) stock, Mr. Craver 25⅓% and Mr. Edelmayer 49⅓%. It is crucial to note that the by-laws provided for a unanimous vote for corporate action, and after the common stock transfer, the by-laws were capable of amendment only by a unanimous vote because no two shareholders could vote more than 74⅔% of the common stock and 76% of the common stock was necessary for amendment. Thus, although Mr. Fireoved did sell a portion of his voting stock prior to his disposition of the section 306 stock, he retained as much control in the corporation following the sale of his common stock

as he had prior to the sale. Under these circumstances it is not consonant
with the history of the legislation to conclude that Congress intended such
a sale of underlying common stock to exempt the proceeds of the disposition of section 306 stock from treatment as ordinary income. Accordingly,
the district court erred when it held that any of the preferred shares Mr.
Fireoved redeemed were not subject to section 306(a) by virtue of section
306(b)(4)(B).[14]

* * *

PROBLEMS

1. In year one, Argonaut Corporation distributed nonconvertible nonvoting preferred stock worth $1,000 to each of its two unrelated equal common
shareholders, Jason and Vera. The Argonaut common stock owned by each
of the shareholders had a basis of $2,000 prior to the distribution and a
value of $3,000 immediately after the distribution. At the time of the
distribution, Argonaut had $2,000 of earnings and profits. In year three,
Argonaut had $3,000 of earnings and profits.

(a) What are the tax consequences to Jason, Vera and Argonaut of the
distribution of preferred stock in year one?

(b) What results to Vera and Argonaut if Vera sells her preferred stock
to Carl, an unrelated party, for $1,000 in year three?

(c) Same as (b), above, except that Vera sells her preferred stock to
Carl for $1,750?

(d) Same as (b), above, except that Argonaut had no earnings and
profits at the time of the distribution of the preferred stock?

(e) What results if Jason gives his preferred stock to his grandson,
Claude, and Claude later sells the stock for $1,000? What if Jason
dies and bequeaths his preferred stock to Claude?

(f) What result if Jason contributes his preferred stock to a public
charity?

(g) What results to Jason and Argonaut if in year three the corporation redeems half of Jason's common stock for $5,000 and all of his
preferred stock for $1,500?

(h) Same as (g), above, except the corporate bylaws require unanimous
shareholder agreement for corporate action, and the bylaws may be
amended only with the concurrence of more than 75 percent of the
shareholders.

(i) Same as (g), above, except that Argonaut has no accumulated or
current earnings and profits in year three.

14. It is important to note that our
decision relates only to the facts of this case.
We express no view on the situation in which
less than all the voting shares are sold but
enough are disposed of to relinquish effective
control prior to or simultaneous with the sale
of section 306 stock.

2. Zapco Corporation has 100 shares of common stock outstanding all of which are owned by Sam Shifty. Zapco has an ample supply of current and accumulated earnings and profits.

(a) If Sam forms Holding Co. by transferring 50 Zapco shares in exchange for 100 shares of Holding common stock and 100 shares of Holding preferred stock, will any of the Holding shares be Section 306 stock?

(b) What result if Zapco were owned equally (50 shares each) by Sam Shifty and Selma Zap, who is unrelated to Sam, and the two shareholders form Holding Co. by transferring all their Zapco stock with Sam taking back 100 shares of Holding Co. common stock and Selma taking back 50 shares of Holding Co. preferred stock and 50 shares of Holding Co. common stock?

CHAPTER 7

COMPLETE LIQUIDATIONS

A. INTRODUCTION

We have been present at the creation of a corporation and nurtured the corporate entity as it engaged in distributions, redemptions, partial liquidations and maneuvers to mitigate the double tax. This chapter shifts the focus to the end of a C corporation's life cycle.

A few definitions are in order to set the stage. The Code does not define "complete liquidation," but the regulations provide that liquidation status exists for tax purposes "when the corporation ceases to be a going concern and its activities are merely for the purpose of winding up its affairs, paying its debts, and distributing any remaining balance to its shareholders."[1] Legal dissolution under state law is not required for the liquidation to be complete, and a transaction will be treated as a liquidation even if the corporation retains a nominal amount of assets to pay any remaining debts and preserve its legal existence.[2]

Liquidations often are preceded by a sale of substantially all of a corporation's assets and a distribution of the sales proceeds to the shareholders in exchange for their stock. Alternatively, the buyer of a corporate business may acquire all the stock of the target company and either keep the old corporation alive or cause it to be liquidated. But liquidations do not necessarily involve sales. The corporation simply may distribute its assets in kind to the shareholders, who either may sell the assets or continue to operate the business outside of corporate solution. Or a parent corporation may wish to rearrange its holdings by liquidating or selling the stock of a subsidiary.

All these transactions raise challenging tax issues at the shareholder and corporate levels. Historically, individual shareholders have hoped to emerge from a complete liquidation or the sale of a profitable corporate business by realizing a capital gain on their stock and, on an installment sale, by deferring recognition of the gain until cash payments are received. At the corporate level, the goals generally have been to avoid recognition of gain on a distribution or sale of assets while providing the shareholders (in a liquidation) or the purchaser (in an acquisition) with a fair market value basis in the distributed or acquired assets. At one time, most of these objectives could be met with careful planning, but liquidations became far

---

1. Reg. § 1.332–2(c). This regulation technically applies only to the liquidation of a subsidiary, but it has long been assumed to apply also to ordinary liquidations.

2. See, e.g., Rev.Rul. 54–518, 1954–2 C.B. 142.

more expensive after the Tax Reform Act of 1986. This chapter surveys the current landscape, considering first the general shareholder and corporate level tax consequences of complete liquidations and then turning to the special problems raised on the liquidation of a subsidiary. Later chapters will consider the closely related topic of taxable acquisitions of corporate assets or stock, tax-free acquisition techniques known as corporate reorganizations, and the carryover of tax attributes following an acquisition.[3]

B.   COMPLETE LIQUIDATIONS UNDER SECTION 331

1.   CONSEQUENCES TO THE SHAREHOLDERS

Code: §§ 331; 334(a); 346(a); 453(h)(1)(A)–(B).

Regulations: §§ 1.331–1(a), (b), (e); 1.453–11(a)(1), (2)(i), (3), –11(d).

The complete liquidation of a corporation presents an opportunity to revisit several policy issues that recur throughout the study of Subchapter C. Consider the appropriate tax consequences to Owner, a sole shareholder of X Corporation, who desires to liquidate X and continue to operate its business as a proprietorship. Assume that X has been profitable and has ample earnings and profits at the time of its liquidation. From Owner's standpoint, should the liquidation be treated as: (1) a nonrecognition transaction akin to an incorporation, (2) a dividend distribution, (3) an exchange of the stock for the distributed assets or (4) some combination of the above?

If Owner continues to operate the business as a sole proprietorship, the liquidation results in a mere change in the form of his investment. Since Congress granted nonrecognition treatment to Owner when he transferred the business into corporate solution, is it not also appropriate to treat the transfer of those assets back into Owner's hands as a tax-free event? This analogy has a superficial appeal but Congress has never seriously considered it except in very limited situations.[1] Nonrecognition is inconsistent with the double tax regime of Subchapter C because it would facilitate the tax-free bailout of earnings and profits. Moreover, many complete liquidations involve the sale of a business followed by a distribution of the cash proceeds to the shareholders. Cash distributions do not lend themselves to a nonrecognition regime because it is impossible to assign money the substituted basis that would be necessary to preserve the shareholder's gain for recognition at a later time. Similarly, any attempt to preserve the liquidated corporation's earnings and profits in the hands of its former shareholders would be cumbersome and inconsistent with the termination of the corporation.

A stronger case can be made for treating a liquidating distribution as a dividend to the extent of the corporation's remaining earnings and profits.

---

3. See Chapters 8, 9, and 12, infra.

1. See, e.g., I.R.C. § 332, discussed in Section C of this chapter, infra.

Because earnings and profits disappear on a complete liquidation, this is the last chance to tax a shareholder's withdrawal of corporate profits as ordinary income. By triggering the distribution rules of Sections 301 and 316, this approach would focus on the source of the liquidating distribution rather than the shareholder's relationship to his investment. Dividend treatment, however, is inconsistent with Section 302, which treats a distribution in redemption as an exchange if the shareholder completely terminates or substantially reduces his interest in the corporation. Why should a complete termination of the interests of all the shareholders be treated any less favorably? Moreover, if liquidating distributions were treated as dividends to the extent of the corporation's earnings and profits, a shareholder's stock basis might never be recovered.

The redemption analogy suggests a third approach, which would treat a complete liquidation as a sale of stock by the shareholder. This solution is imperfect, if only because it ignores the disappearance of the earnings and profits account, a clean sweep that does not occur on a sale of stock. But after a period of waffling,[2] Congress opted to treat liquidations as exchanges, an approach that permits shareholders to avoid the dividend sting and be taxed at capital gains rates. Congress concluded that the dividend threat was "preventing liquidation of many corporations" because of the high tax cost it imposed and therefore was generating only minimal revenue.[3] It regarded exchange treatment as "consistent with the entire theory of the [Code]" and as "the only method * * * which can be easily administered."[4]

The Congressional policy is codified in Section 331(a), which provides that amounts received by a shareholder in complete liquidation are treated as full payment in exchange for the shareholder's stock. The vast majority of shareholders hold their stock as a capital asset and thus will recognize capital gain or loss in an amount equal to the difference between (1) the money and the fair market value of the property received and (2) the shareholder's adjusted basis in the stock surrendered. Section 334(a) provides that the shareholder's basis in property distributed by a corporation in a complete liquidation that is taxable at the shareholder level shall be the fair market value of the property at the time of the distribution.

Computation of a shareholder's gain or loss on a complete liquidation is ordinarily a straightforward affair. The shareholder's amount realized is the money and the fair market value of all other property received from the liquidating corporation. If a shareholder assumes corporate liabilities or receives property subject to a liability in a liquidating distribution, the amount realized is limited to the value of the property received, net of

---

2. Liquidations were first treated as exchanges in the Revenue Act of 1924. Congress changed its mind briefly from 1934 to 1936 and then reinstated the present system.

3. H.R.Rep. No. 2475, 74th Cong., 2d Sess. (1936), reprinted in 1939–1 (Part 2) C.B. 667, 674.

4. S.Rep. No. 368, 68th Cong., 1st Sess. (1924), reprinted in 1939–1 (Part 2) C.B. 266, 274.

liabilities. In keeping with the principles of the *Crane* case, however, it is assumed that the distributee shareholder will pay the liabilities and he thus obtains a full fair market value basis in the property under Section 334(a).

Shareholders who hold several blocks of stock with different bases and acquisition dates must compute their gain or loss separately for each block rather than on an aggregate basis.[5] This method generally makes a difference, however, only when some shares are held long-term and others short-term; otherwise, the tax consequences will be identical whether the shareholder uses a share-by-share or an aggregate approach.[6]

The timing of a shareholder's gain or loss on a complete liquidation raises thornier questions. A liquidating corporation often is unable to distribute all of its property at one time or within the same taxable year. Recognizing these practical constraints, Section 346(a) defines a complete liquidation to include a series of distributions occurring over a period of time if they are all pursuant to a plan of complete liquidation. Shareholders normally prefer to treat these "creeping complete" liquidations as open transactions so they can defer reporting any gain until the amounts received exceed their stock basis.[7] This cost recovery approach has been sanctioned by the Service in the liquidation context[8] even though it would appear to be foreclosed by Section 453, which requires ratable basis recovery as payments are received even in cases where the selling price cannot be readily ascertained.[9] Since liquidating distributions are treated as payments in exchange for the shareholders' stock, Section 453 technically seems to apply and, if so, shareholders wishing to defer their gain should be required to use the installment method, allocating each distribution between recovery of basis and taxable gain.[10] But taxpayers who wish to use

---

5. Reg. § 1.331–1(e). For example, assume that Shareholder ("S") holds 60 shares of X, Inc. stock long-term with a $30,000 basis and 40 shares short-term with a $50,000 basis. If S receives $100,000 in complete liquidation of X, he must allocate the amount realized ratably between the two blocks as follows:

Long-Term 60 shares		Short–Term 40 shares	
A.R.	$60,000	A.R.	$40,000
A.B.	30,000	A.B.	50,000
LTCG	$30,000	STCL	$10,000

6. For the problems of valuation of the liquidating distribution and handling contingent claims, see Bittker & Eustice, Federal Income Taxation of Corporations & Shareholders ¶ 10.03[2].

7. See, e.g., Burnet v. Logan, 283 U.S. 404, 51 S.Ct. 550 (1931). Cf. I.R.C. § 453(d) (installment method applies unless taxpayer elects out of Section 453).

8. Rev.Rul. 68–348, 1968–2 C.B. 141, amplified by Rev.Rul. 85–48, 1985–1 C.B. 126.

9. See I.R.C. § 453(j)(2); Reg. § 15A.453–1(c).

10. Cf. Reg. § 1.453–11(d), which appears to support the position taken in the text but only when the liquidating corporation distributes an installment obligation described in Section 453(h). See infra notes 11–13 and accompanying text. Installment sale reporting is not available if the stock of the liquidating corporation is publicly traded. See I.R.C. § 453(k)(2). If open transaction reporting is still generally available to liquidating distributions, this restriction should not apply when a shareholder of a public company receives a series of distributions straddling two or more taxable years. See also I.R.C. § 453(d), which permits a taxpayer to "elect out" of installment sale treatment. In the case of a liquidation, an election out would require the shareholder to report his entire the cost recovery approach are not likely to be challenged in light of the Service's longstanding position in published rulings.

A different issue is presented when a liquidating corporation sells certain assets for installment obligations and then distributes the obligations in complete liquidation. In that situation, shareholders who receive the installment obligations may be able to defer part of their Section 331(a) gain on the liquidation by using the installment method of reporting under Section 453. Installment sale reporting is accomplished by treating the shareholders' receipt of payments on the distributed installment obligations as if they were received in exchange for the shareholder's stock.[11] To qualify for this treatment, the obligations must have been acquired by the corporation in respect of a sale or exchange of property during the 12–month period beginning on the date a plan of complete liquidation is adopted and the liquidation must be completed within that 12–month period.[12] Installment obligations arising from the sale of inventory or other "dealer" property by the corporation are eligible for installment sale treatment in the hands of the distributee shareholders only if the obligation resulted from a bulk sale—i.e., the sale was to one person in one transaction and involves substantially all of the property attributable to a trade or business of the corporation.[13] Installment sale reporting is not available, however, if the stock of the liquidating corporation is publicly traded,[14] or if the shareholder elects out of Section 453.[15]

PROBLEM

A owns 100 shares of Humdrum Corporation which he purchased several years ago for $10,000. Humdrum has $12,000 of accumulated earnings and profits. What are the tax consequences to A on the liquidation of Humdrum Corporation in the following alternative situations:

(a) Humdrum distributes $20,000 to A in exchange for his stock?

(b) What result in (a), above, if A receives $10,000 in the current year (year one) and $10,000 in year two? Would there be any problem if

gain in the year of the first distribution except, perhaps, where the value of future distributions is unascertainable. See Reg. § 15A.453–1(d).

11. I.R.C. § 453(h)(1)(A); Reg. § 1.453–11. A shareholder who receives liquidating distributions that include installment obligations in more than one taxable year must reasonably estimate the gain attributable to distributions received in each taxable year based on the best available information and allocate his stock basis pro rata over all payments to be received. When the exact amount of gain is subsequently determined, any adjustment is made in the taxable year in which that determination is made. Alternatively, the shareholder may file an amended return for the earlier year. I.R.C. § 453(h)(2); Reg. § 1.453–11(d).

12. Id. See Reg. § 1.453–11(c).

13. I.R.C. § 453(h)(1)(B); Reg. § 1.453–11(c)(4).

14. I.R.C. § 453(k)(2); Reg. § 1.453–11(a)(2)(i). But if a nonpublicly traded liquidating corporation distributes an installment obligation arising from a corporate-level sale of publicly traded stock, the obligation generally qualifies for installment sale reporting under Section 453(h). Reg. § 1.453–11(c)(2).

15. I.R.C. § 453(d).

Humdrum does not adopt a formal plan of complete liquidation in year one?

(c) Humdrum distributes $8,000 cash and an installment obligation with a face and fair market value of $12,000, payable $1,000 per year for 12 years with market rate interest. The installment obligation was received by Humdrum two months ago, after the adoption of the plan of liquidation, on the sale of a capital asset. Would the result be different if Humdrum's stock were publicly traded? See I.R.C. § 453(k).

(d) Same as (c), above, except the installment obligation was received two years ago and no payments have yet been made.

(e) What result in (a), above, if two years later, A is required to pay a $5,000 judgment against Humdrum in his capacity as transferee of the corporation? Compare this with the result if the judgment had been rendered and paid by the corporation prior to the liquidation. See Arrowsmith v. Commissioner, 344 U.S. 6, 73 S.Ct. 71 (1952).

2.   CONSEQUENCES TO THE LIQUIDATING CORPORATION

Code: § 336(a), (b), (c), (d). Skim § 267(a)(1), (b), (c).

It should come as no surprise at this juncture that Subchapter C requires property distributions by corporations to their shareholders to be analyzed at both the corporate and shareholder levels. Earlier chapters have chronicled the gradual erosion of the *General Utilities*[1] doctrine, under which a corporation generally did not recognize gain on nonliquidating distributions of appreciated property. We have seen that recognition of gain (but not loss) is now the statutory norm in the nonliquidation setting.[2] Should the same rules apply to liquidating distributions and sales of assets by a liquidating corporation? Once again, a brief historical interlude is appropriate before considering the current answers to what was once a debated question.

a.   BACKGROUND

Although the *General Utilities* case involved a distribution of appreciated property by an ongoing business, the doctrine also applied to liquidating distributions. Until the enactment of the 1986 Code, a corporation generally did not recognize gain or loss on the distribution of property in complete liquidation.[3] Prior to the 1954 Code, however, sales of assets by a liquidating corporation were fully taxable.

1. General Utilities & Operating Co. v. Helvering, 296 U.S. 200, 56 S.Ct. 185 (1935); see Chapters 4D1 and 5E1, supra.

2. I.R.C. § 311(a), (b).

3. I.R.C. § 336(a) (pre–1987). This general nonrecognition rule was subject to various exceptions, such as the statutory recapture of depreciation provisions and the judicially created tax benefit rule and assignment of income doctrine. See, e.g., Hillsboro National Bank v. Commissioner, 460 U.S. 370, 103 S.Ct. 1134 (1983).

To illustrate the disparate tax treatment of liquidating distributions and sales under the pre–1954 regime, assume that A is the sole shareholder of Target Corporation ("T") and has a $100,000 basis in her T stock. T's only asset is a parcel of undeveloped land ("Gainacre") with a fair market value of $400,000 and a zero adjusted basis. Purchaser ("P") wishes to acquire Gainacre for $400,000 cash. If T distributed Gainacre to A in complete liquidation, it recognized no gain under the *General Utilities* doctrine, and A took Gainacre with a $400,000 fair market value basis. On a sale of Gainacre to P for $400,000 following the liquidation, A thus would recognize no gain. If, instead, T had sold Gainacre directly to P, it would have recognized $400,000 gain under the pre–1954 regime. In either case, A recognized gain on the liquidation of T, measured by the difference between the amount of the distribution and her $100,000 adjusted basis in the T stock.

The different tax results of these economically equivalent transactions prompted savvy taxpayers to "postpone" sales of corporate assets until after a liquidation in order to avoid a corporate-level tax. The ignorant did what came naturally—and often was a practical necessity for large corporations with many assets and shareholders—by selling assets at the corporate level prior to the liquidation. With such high tax stakes, the courts were called upon to determine who *in substance* made the sale—an inquiry that engendered some anomalous results, as evidenced by the two Supreme Court decisions that follow.

Commissioner v. Court Holding Co.

Supreme Court of the United States, 1945.
324 U.S. 331, 65 S.Ct. 707.

■ MR. JUSTICE BLACK delivered the opinion of the Court.

An apartment house, which was the sole asset of the respondent corporation, was transferred in the form of a liquidating dividend to the corporation's two shareholders. They in turn formally conveyed it to a purchaser who had originally negotiated for the purchase from the corporation. The question is whether the Circuit Court of Appeals properly reversed the Tax Court's conclusion that the corporation was taxable under § 22 of the Internal Revenue Code for the gain which accrued from the sale. The answer depends upon whether the findings of the Tax Court that the whole transaction showed a sale by the corporation rather than by the stockholders were final and binding upon the Circuit Court of Appeals.

It is unnecessary to set out in detail the evidence introduced before the Tax Court or its findings. Despite conflicting evidence, the following findings of the Tax Court are supported by the record:

The respondent corporation was organized in 1934 solely to buy and hold the apartment building which was the only property ever owned by it. All of its outstanding stock was owned by Minnie Miller and her husband. Between October 1, 1939 and February, 1940, while the corporation still had legal title to the property, negotiations for its sale took place. These negotiations were between the corporation and the lessees of the property, together with a sister and brother-in-law. An oral agreement was reached as to the terms and conditions of sale, and on February 22, 1940, the parties met to reduce the agreement to writing. The purchaser was then advised by the corporation's attorney that the sale could not be consummated because it would result in the imposition of a large income tax on the corporation. The next day, the corporation declared a "liquidating dividend," which involved complete liquidation of its assets, and surrender of all outstanding stock. Mrs. Miller and her husband surrendered their stock, and the building was deeded to them. A sale contract was then drawn, naming the Millers individually as vendors, and the lessees' sister as vendee, which embodied substantially the same terms and conditions previously agreed upon. One thousand dollars, which a month and a half earlier had been paid to the corporation by the lessees, was applied in part payment of the purchase price. Three days later, the property was conveyed to the lessees' sister.

The Tax Court concluded from these facts that, despite the declaration of a "liquidating dividend" followed by the transfers of legal title, the corporation had not abandoned the sales negotiations; that these were mere formalities designed "to make the transaction appear to be other than what it was" in order to avoid tax liability. The Circuit Court of Appeals drawing different inferences from the record, held that the corporation had "called off" the sale, and treated the stockholders' sale as unrelated to the prior negotiations.

There was evidence to support the findings of the Tax Court, and its findings must therefore be accepted by the courts. Dobson v. Commissioner, 320 U.S. 489; Commissioner v. Heininger, 320 U.S. 467; Commissioner v. Scottish American Investment Co., 323 U.S. 119. On the basis of these findings, the Tax Court was justified in attributing the gain from the sale to respondent corporation. The incidence of taxation depends upon the substance of a transaction. The tax consequences which arise from gains from a sale of property are not finally to be determined solely by the means employed to transfer legal title. Rather, the transaction must be viewed as a whole, and each step, from the commencement of negotiations to the consummation of the sale, is relevant. A sale by one person cannot be transformed for tax purposes into a sale by another by using the latter as a conduit through which to pass title. To permit the true nature of a transaction to be disguised by mere formalisms, which exist solely to alter tax liabilities, would seriously impair the effective administration of the tax policies of Congress.

It is urged that respondent corporation never executed a written agreement, and that an oral agreement to sell land cannot be enforced in Florida because of the Statute of Frauds, Comp.Gen.Laws of Florida, 1927, vol. 3, § 5779. But the fact that respondent corporation itself never executed a written contract is unimportant, since the Tax Court found from the facts of the entire transaction that the executed sale was in substance the sale of the corporation. The decision of the Circuit Court of Appeals is reversed, and that of the Tax Court affirmed.

It is so ordered.

United States v. Cumberland Public Service Co.

Supreme Court of the United States, 1950.
338 U.S. 451, 70 S.Ct. 280.

■ Mr. Justice Black delivered the opinion of the Court.

A corporation selling its physical properties is taxed on capital gains resulting from the sale. There is no corporate tax, however, on distribution of assets in kind to shareholders as part of a genuine liquidation. The respondent corporation transferred property to its shareholders as a liquidating dividend in kind. The shareholders transferred it to a purchaser. The question is whether, despite contrary findings by the Court of Claims, this record requires a holding that the transaction was in fact a sale by the corporation subjecting the corporation to a capital gains tax.

Details of the transaction are as follows. The respondent, a closely held corporation, was long engaged in the business of generating and distributing electric power in three Kentucky counties. In 1936 a local cooperative began to distribute Tennessee Valley Authority power in the area served by respondent. It soon became obvious that respondent's Diesel-generated power could not compete with TVA power, which respondent had been unable to obtain. Respondent's shareholders, realizing that the corporation must get out of the power business unless it obtained TVA power, accordingly offered to sell all the corporate stock to the cooperative, which was receiving such power. The cooperative refused to buy the stock, but countered with an offer to buy from the corporation its transmission and distribution equipment. The corporation rejected the offer because it would have been compelled to pay a heavy capital gains tax. At the same time the shareholders, desiring to save payment of the corporate capital gains tax, offered to acquire the transmission and distribution equipment and then sell to the cooperative. The cooperative accepted. The corporation transferred the transmission and distribution systems to its shareholders in partial liquidation. The remaining assets were sold and the corporation dissolved. The shareholders then executed the previously contemplated sale to the cooperative.

Upon this sale by the shareholders, the Commissioner assessed and collected a $17,000 tax from the corporation on the theory that the shareholders had been used as a mere conduit for effectuating what was really a corporate sale. Respondent corporation brought this action to recover the amount of the tax. The Court of Claims found that the method by which the stockholders disposed of the properties was avowedly chosen in order to reduce taxes, but that the liquidation and dissolution genuinely ended the corporation's activities and existence. The court also found that at no time did the corporation plan to make the sale itself. Accordingly it found as a fact that the sale was made by the shareholders rather than the corporation, and entered judgment for respondent. One judge dissented, believing that our opinion in Commissioner v. Court Holding Co., 324 U.S. 331, required a finding that the sale had been made by the corporation. Certiorari was granted, 338 U.S. 846, to clear up doubts arising out of the *Court Holding Co.* case.

Our *Court Holding Co.* decision rested on findings of fact by the Tax Court that a sale had been made and gains realized by the taxpayer corporation. There the corporation had negotiated for sale of its assets and had reached an oral agreement of sale. When the tax consequences of the corporate sale were belatedly recognized, the corporation purported to "call off" the sale at the last minute and distributed the physical properties in kind to the stockholders. They promptly conveyed these properties to the same persons who had negotiated with the corporation. The terms of purchase were substantially those of the previous oral agreement. One thousand dollars already paid to the corporation was applied as part payment of the purchase price. The Tax Court found that the corporation never really abandoned its sales negotiations, that it never did dissolve, and that the sole purpose of the so-called liquidation was to disguise a corporate sale through use of mere formalisms in order to avoid tax liability. The Circuit Court of Appeals took a different view of the evidence. In this Court the Government contended that whether a liquidation distribution was genuine or merely a sham was traditionally a question of fact. We agreed with this contention, and reinstated the Tax Court's findings and judgment. Discussing the evidence which supported the findings of fact, we went on to say that "the incidence of taxation depends upon the substance of a transaction" regardless of "mere formalisms," and that taxes on a corporate sale cannot be avoided by using the shareholders as a "conduit through which to pass title."

This language does not mean that a corporation can be taxed even when the sale has been made by its stockholders following a genuine liquidation and dissolution.[3] While the distinction between sales by a corporation as compared with distribution in kind followed by shareholder sales may be particularly shadowy and artificial when the corporation is closely held, Congress has chosen to recognize such a distinction for tax purposes. The corporate tax is thus aimed primarily at the profits of a going concern. This is true despite the fact that gains realized from corporate sales are taxed, perhaps to prevent tax evasions, even where the cash proceeds are at once distributed in liquidation.[4] But Congress has

3. What we said in the *Court Holding Co.* case was an approval of the action of the Tax Court in looking beyond the papers executed by the corporation and shareholders in order to determine whether the sale there had actually been made by the corporation. We were but emphasizing the established principle that in resolving such questions as who made a sale, fact-finding tribunals in tax cases can consider motives, intent, and conduct in addition to what appears in written instruments used by parties to control rights as among themselves. See, e.g., Helvering v. Clifford, 309 U.S. 331, 335–337; Commissioner of Internal Revenue v. Tower, 327 U.S. 280.

4. It has also been held that where corporate liquidations are effected through trusimposed no tax on liquidating distributions in kind or on dissolution, whatever may be the motive for such liquidation. Consequently, a corporation may liquidate or dissolve without subjecting itself to the corporate gains tax, even though a primary motive is to avoid the burden of corporate taxation.

Here, on the basis of adequate subsidiary findings, the Court of Claims has found that the sale in question was made by the stockholders rather than the corporation. The Government's argument that the shareholders acted as a mere "conduit" for a sale by respondent corporation must fall before this finding. The subsidiary finding that a major motive of the shareholders was to reduce taxes does not bar this conclusion. Whatever the motive and however relevant it may be in determining whether the transaction was real or a sham, sales of physical properties by shareholders following a genuine liquidation distribution cannot be attributed to the corporation for tax purposes.

The oddities in tax consequences that emerge from the tax provisions here controlling appear to be inherent in the present tax pattern. For a corporation is taxed if it sells all its physical properties and distributes the cash proceeds as liquidating dividends, yet is not taxed if that property is distributed in kind and is then sold by the shareholders. In both instances the interest of the shareholders in the business has been transferred to the purchaser. Again, if these stockholders had succeeded in their original effort to sell all their stock, their interest would have been transferred to the purchasers just as effectively. Yet on such a transaction the corporation would have realized no taxable gain.

Congress having determined that different tax consequences shall flow from different methods by which the shareholders of a closely held corporation may dispose of corporate property, we accept its mandate. It is for the trial court, upon consideration of an entire transaction, to determine the factual category in which a particular transaction belongs. Here as in the *Court Holding Co.* case we accept the ultimate findings of fact of the trial tribunal. Accordingly the judgment of the Court of Claims is

Affirmed.

■ MR. JUSTICE DOUGLAS took no part in the consideration or decision of this case.

NOTE

The difficulties faced by the courts in reconciling the results in *Court Holding* and *Cumberland* influenced Congress to extend the *General Utilities* doctrine to liquidating sales. Under the 1954 Code version of Section 337, a corporation generally did not recognize gain or loss on a sale of property pursuant to a plan of complete liquidation except for recapture of

tees or agents, gains from sales are taxable to the corporation as though it were a going concern. See, e.g., First National Bank v. United States, 10 Cir., 86 F.2d 938, 941; Treas.Reg. 103, § 19.22(a)–21.

depreciation and a few other items.[1] Aptly named the "anti-*Court Holding*" provision, former Section 337 usually ensured that the tax consequences of liquidating sales and distributions were the same regardless of the form of the transaction. In either case, the corporation generally did not recognize gain or loss, while the buyer (or distributee shareholder) took a fair market value basis in the acquired or distributed assets. As a result, the principal tax cost of a complete liquidation or taxable disposition of assets by a liquidating corporation was the capital gain recognized at the shareholder level.

Shortly after this extension of the *General Utilities* doctrine, reformers began calling for its repeal.[2] Imposing a tax at the shareholder level, they argued, did not justify exempting a liquidating corporation from tax on the disposition of its appreciated property. Until the 1980's, however, support for repeal was limited to the academic community and a handful of principled practitioners. "The General," it was said, had the loyal backing of the troops—battalions of legislators and their business constituents who looked askance at the double tax.[3] One justification for retaining the *General Utilities* doctrine was that it provided relief from the double taxation of corporate earnings by partially integrating the corporate and individual taxes.[4] More specialized pleaders focused on the adverse impact of the double tax on the "largely inflationary gains" on long-held assets of small "Mom and Pop" businesses.[5]

Despite these arguments, the movement for legislative reform gained momentum in the 1980's.[6] Eventually, the House of Representatives included *General Utilities* repeal, along with a permanent exception for certain closely held corporations, in its version of the 1986 tax reform legislation.[7] The House Ways and Means Committee report summarized the rationale for repeal in the liquidation setting:[8]

> The committee believes that the *General Utilities* rule, even in the more limited form in which it exists today, produces many

1. I.R.C. § 337 (pre–1987).

2. See, e.g., Lewis, "A Proposed New Treatment for Corporate Distributions and Sales in Liquidations," 86th Cong., 1st Sess., House Committee on Ways and Means, 3 Tax Revision Compendium 1643 (1959).

3. We are indebted to the late Professor Walter Blum for the military analogy. See Blum, "Behind the *General Utilities* Doctrine, or Why Does the General Have So Much Support from the Troops," 62 Taxes 292 (1984).

4. See, e.g., Nolan, "Taxing Corporate Distributions of Appreciated Property: Repeal of the *General Utilities* Doctrine and Relief Measures," 22 San Diego L.Rev. 97 (1985).

5. See, e.g., "Reform of Corporate Taxation," Hearing before the Committee on Finance, United States Senate, 98th Cong., 1st

Sess. 148, 151, 153–157, 174–176, 185, 268–270 (Oct. 24, 1983).

6. See Staff of the Senate Finance Committee, The Subchapter C Revision Act of 1985: A Final Report Prepared by the Staff, 99th Cong., 1st Sess. 6–8, 42–44, 52–54, 59–68 (S.Prt. 99–47, 1985), recommending repeal of the *General Utilities* doctrine except for liquidating distributions or sales of certain long-held (over five years) assets by closely held corporations with under $2 million in assets.

7. H.R. 3838, 99th Cong., 1st Sess. (1985), §§ 331–335.

8. H.R.Rep. No. 99–426, 99th Cong., 1st Sess. 281 (1985).

incongruities and inequities in the tax system. First, the rule may create significant distortions in business behavior. Economically, a liquidating distribution is indistinguishable from a nonliquidating distribution; yet the Code provides a substantial preference for the former. A corporation acquiring the assets of a liquidating corporation is able to obtain a basis in assets equal to their fair market value, although the transferor recognizes no gain (other than possibly recapture amounts) on the sale. The tax benefits may make the assets more valuable in the hands of the transferee than in the hands of the present owner. The effect may be to induce corporations with substantial appreciated assets to liquidate and transfer their assets to other corporations for tax reasons, when economic considerations might indicate a different course of action. Accordingly, the *General Utilities* rule may be responsible, at least in part, for the dramatic increase in corporate mergers and acquisitions in recent years. The committee believes that the Code should not artificially encourage corporate liquidations and acquisitions, and believes that repeal of the *General Utilities* rule is a major step towards that goal.

Second, the *General Utilities* rule tends to undermine the corporate income tax. Under normally applicable tax principles, nonrecognition of gain is available only if the transferee takes a carryover basis in the transferred property, thus assuring that a tax will eventually be collected on the appreciation. Where the *General Utilities* rule applies, assets generally are permitted to leave corporate solution and to take a stepped-up basis in the hands of the transferee without the imposition of a corporate-level tax. Thus, the effect of the rule is to grant a permanent exemption from the corporate income tax.

The Senate had originally included *General Utilities* repeal in its version of the 1986 bill, but that provision was later dropped, reportedly because of concerns over its adverse impact on corporate entrepreneurs. In reconciling the two bills, the Conference Committee adopted the House's approach. To the surprise of even the tax reformers, the conferees went beyond the earlier proposals by eliminating any permanent exceptions for closely held corporations and providing only limited transitional relief. The General, so it seemed, had been deserted by the troops once the battle went behind closed doors. Against that background we turn to the current corporate-level tax treatment of liquidating distributions and sales.

b.   LIQUIDATING DISTRIBUTIONS AND SALES

The current version of Section 336(a) is the reverse of its 1954 Code predecessor. The general rule requires a liquidating corporation to recognize gain or loss on the distribution of property in complete liquidation as if the property were sold to the distributee at its fair market value. If the distributed property is subject to a liability or the distributee shareholder assumes a liability in connection with the distribution, the fair market value of the property is treated as being not less than the amount of the liability.[1] In strengthening the double tax regime of Subchapter C, Congress greatly increased the tax cost of a complete liquidation. Whenever a corporation makes a liquidating distribution of appreciated property, gain generally will be recognized at the corporate level and the distribution also will be a taxable event to the shareholders.[2]

Once Congress required a liquidating corporation to recognize gain or loss on liquidating distributions, it took the next logical step by conforming the tax treatment of liquidating sales. With the repeal of former Section 337, a corporation generally must recognize gain or loss on any sale of its assets pursuant to a complete liquidation plan.[3]

c. LIMITATIONS ON RECOGNITION OF LOSS

The general rule in Section 336(a) differs in one important respect from the rules in Section 311 governing nonliquidating distributions. It allows the distributing corporation to recognize loss as well as gain. Moreover, although Section 267 disallows losses on sales of property by a corporation to a "related" party (e.g., a controlling shareholder), it does not disallow them on liquidating distributions to related parties.[4] This license to recognize corporate-level losses quickly rattled the Congressional nervous system. To prevent taxpayers from recognizing losses "in inappropriate situations" or inflating the amount of loss actually sustained on a liquidation, the Tax Reform Act of 1986 added the two separate limitations in Section 336(d).[5]

Distributions to Related Persons. Section 336(d)(1) partially reinstates the policy of Section 267 by providing that no loss shall be recognized by a liquidating corporation on the distribution of property to a Section 267 related person if either: (1) the distribution is not pro rata among the shareholders, or (2) the distributed property was acquired by the liquidating corporation in a Section 351 transaction or as a contribution to capital within the five-year period ending on the date of the distribution. These restrictions thus initially focus on the recipient of the loss property. For this purpose, related persons usually will be shareholders who own directly, or through the Section 267 attribution rules, more than 50 percent in value of the stock of the distributing corporation.[6]

---

1. I.R.C. § 336(b). Cf. I.R.C. § 7701(g); Commissioner v. Tufts, 461 U.S. 300, 103 S.Ct. 1826 (1983), rehearing denied, 463 U.S. 1215, 103 S.Ct. 3555 (1983).

2. The general rule is subject to two exceptions. Nonrecognition of gain or loss is preserved for: (1) distributions in complete liquidation of a controlled—i.e., 80 percent—subsidiary (I.R.C. § 337, see Section C2 of this chapter, infra), and (2) distributions in certain tax-free reorganizations (I.R.C. § 336(c), see Chapter 9C2, infra).

3. A corporation that sells or distributes stock in an 80 percent or more subsidiary may elect under Section 336(e), however, to treat the sale as a disposition of the subsidiary's assets and ignore any gain or loss on the sale or distribution of the stock. See also I.R.C. § 338(h)(10) and Chapter 8C3, infra.

4. I.R.C. § 267(a)(1).

5. See H.R.Rep. No. 99–841, 99th Cong., 2d Sess. II–200 (1986).

6. I.R.C. § 267(b)(2), (c).

Neither the statute nor the legislative history explains when a distribution is "not pro rata" among the shareholders. Congress presumably intended to single out situations where a majority shareholder receives an interest in loss property that is disproportionate to his stock interest in the corporation.[7] The legislative history provides scant illumination of the rationale for this rule. The conferees merely expressed an intent to restrict the ability of taxpayers to recognize losses in "inappropriate situations."[8] Perhaps Congress believed that it was necessary to apply the loss disallowance policy of Section 267 to liquidating distributions where the parties exercised a measure of control by targeting distributions of loss property to majority shareholders—but at the same time concluded that pro rata liquidating distributions were less likely to be motivated by tax avoidance.[9]

The rationale for limiting losses on distributions of recently contributed property to a related party is easier to discern—or at least it was before Congress imposed limitations on the transfer of built-in losses in Section 351 transactions.[10] Before the enactment of Section 362(e)(2), taxpayers could duplicate a single economic loss for tax purposes by transferring property with a built-in loss to a corporation in a Section 351 transaction or as a contribution to capital. For example, assume Sole Shareholder ("Sole") transferred Lossacre (adjusted basis—$1,000; fair market value—$500) to her wholly owned X Corporation ("X") in exchange for $500 of X stock in a Section 351 nonrecognition transaction. Under prior law, Sole took a $1,000 exchanged basis in her new X stock,[11] and X took Lossacre with a $1,000 transferred basis.[12] Assume further that, three years later, when Lossacre had the same basis and value, X liquidated, distributing Lossacre and its other assets to Sole. Without an "outbound" limitation, both Sole Shareholder and the corporation would recognize a $500 loss on the liquidation—two losses for the price of none considering that, when the smoke cleared, Sole still owned Lossacre.[13] The same technique was effective for controlling shareholders who owned less than 100 percent of the corporation if on liquidation they received their pro rata share of each corporate asset.[14]

---

7. For example, assume X Corporation has a net worth of $1,000 and is owned 75% by A and 25% by five unrelated shareholders. X distributes Lossacre (value—$750; basis $1,000) to A and $250 cash to the other shareholders. Since Lossacre was not distributed to the shareholders in proportion to their respective stock interests, the distribution is not pro rata and X may not recognize its $250 loss.

8. H.R.Rep. No. 99–841, supra note 5, at II–200.

9. Even if the distribution is pro rata, however, losses may be disallowed if the asset distributed to a related person is "disqualified property" within the meaning of Section

336(d)(1)(B). See text accompanying notes 15–16, infra.

10. See I.R.C. § 362(e)(2) and Chapter 2A, infra.

11. I.R.C. § 358(a).

12. I.R.C. § 362(a).

13. Of course, Sole will now hold Lossacre with a stepped-down fair market value basis of $500, but she will have benefitted from two losses without ever having disposed of the property.

14. As noted previously, corporate-level losses on non pro rata ("bullet") distributions to controlling shareholders are disallowed under Section 336(d)(1)(A)(i).

Section 336(d)(1)(A)(ii) attacks this form of "stuffing" with a rule that extends Section 267 principles to pro rata liquidating distributions of "disqualified property" to a related person. "Disqualified property" is defined as any property acquired by the liquidating corporation during the five-year period preceding the distribution in a Section 351 transaction or as a contribution to capital.[15] Section 362(e)(2), however, now imposes a similar limitation on duplication of losses in "inbound" transfers of built-in losses in Section 351 transactions. Applying that limitation to the above example, Sole would still take a $1,000 exchanged basis in her X stock, but X's basis in Lossacre would be limited to its $500 fair market value at the time it was transferred to X. As a result, on its liquidation three years later, X would have no recognized loss and Section 336(d) would not apply.

In its haste to adopt an inbound loss limitation rule, Congress may not have paused to ask whether the outbound limitations in Section 336(d)(1) should be modified. One answer that may explain the continuing existence of Section 336(d)(1) is that it does not exclusively target *duplication* of losses. It also applies to liquidating distributions of loss property to related persons that are not pro rata or are of "disqualified property," even if the loss was realized while the property was held by the corporation. Although the policy for such a limitation is difficult to defend in the context of a complete liquidation, the Code often limits losses when property is transferred between corporations and shareholders as well as in other related party transactions.[16]

Losses With Tax Avoidance Purpose. Section 336(d)(2) prevents the duplication of *precontribution* built-in losses even on certain distributions to minority shareholders. This limitation applies only if the distributing corporation acquired property in a Section 351 transaction or as a contribution to capital as part of a plan the principal purpose of which was to recognize loss by the corporation on a liquidating sale, exchange or distribution of the property. In that event, Section 336(d)(2) limits the corporation's deductible loss to the amount that accrued after the corporation acquired the property. Precontribution losses are disallowed by a basis step-down rule which requires the corporation to reduce its basis (but not below zero) in the affected property by the amount of built-in loss in the property at the time it was acquired by the corporation.[17]

Section 336(d)(2) is reinforced by a provision that treats any contribution of property after the date that is two years before the adoption of the plan of liquidation as part of a forbidden plan to recognize loss, except as

---

15. I.R.C. § 336(d)(1)(B). The term also includes any property the adjusted basis of which is determined in whole or in part by reference to the adjusted basis of property acquired in a Section 351 transaction or as a contribution to capital—e.g., like-kind property received in a Section 1031 transaction in exchange for property acquired by the corporation in a Section 351 transaction. Id.

16. See, e.g., I.R.C. § 351(b)(2) (no loss on transfers to controlled corporations even if transferor receives boot); § 267(a)(1) (disallowance of losses in related party transactions); § 1015(a) (donee's basis for loss reduced for gifts of built-in loss property).

17. The built-in loss is the excess of the adjusted basis of the property immediately after its acquisition over its fair market value at that time. I.R.C. § 336(d)(2)(A).

the Treasury may provide in regulations.[18] Congress provided extensive guidance on the operation of this two-year presumption and the escape hatches that it expects to be included in future regulations. For example, although a contribution made more than two years prior to the adoption of a liquidation plan might be made with a prohibited purpose, the Conference Report states that in those circumstances the basis step-down rule in Section 336(d)(2) would apply only "in the most rare and unusual cases."[19] The legislative history also directed the Treasury to issue regulations generally providing that even contributions of property within the period covered by the presumption should be disregarded "*unless* there is no clear and substantial relationship between the contributed property and the conduct of the corporation's current or future business enterprises."[20] A "clear and substantial relationship" generally would include a requirement of a corporate business purpose for placing the property in the particular corporation to which it was contributed as compared to retaining the property outside that corporation.[21] If the contributed property has a built-in loss at the time of contribution that is "significant" relative to the built-in corporate gain at that time, "special scrutiny of the business purpose would be appropriate."[22]

Section 362(e)(2), which was studied in Chapter 2 in connection with corporate formations, effectively disallows most precontribution losses by stepping down the basis of built-in loss property when it is transferred to a corporation in a Section 351 transaction. This anti-avoidance rule greatly reduces the role of Section 336(d)(2). But there still are situations where the Section 362(e)(2) "inbound" rule does not step down the basis of built-in loss property and Section 336(d)(2) will apply—e.g., where the corporation holds some properties with built-in losses that are subject to Section 336(d)(2) but the inbound stepdown rule does not apply because the aggregate basis of all properties transferred by a transferor in a Section 351 transaction does not exceed their aggregate fair market value. Query, however, whether the section 336(d)(2) loss limitation rule is still necessary in this situation? Perhaps the best explanation is traditional Congressional paranoia regarding abuse of tax losses.

In short, Section 336(d)(2) still may operate to prevent recognition of a loss but only in very limited circumstances. We must wait and see if Congress decides to revisit these questions but doubt that this technical teaser is a high priority item.

Overlap Situations. If both Section 336(d)(1) and Section 336(d)(2) apply to the same transaction, the harsher rule in Section 336(d)(1) (which

---

18. I.R.C. § 336(d)(2)(B)(ii).

19. H.R.Rep. No. 99–841, supra note 5, at 200. See also Staff of the Joint Committee on Taxation, General Explanation of the Tax Reform Act of 1986 ("1986 Act General Explanation"), 100th Cong., 1st Sess. 343 (1987).

20. H.R.Rep. No. 99–841, supra note 5, at II–201.

21. 1986 Act General Explanation, supra note 19, at 343.

22. Id.

disallows the entire loss rather than just the precontribution built-in loss) takes precedence.[23]

PROBLEM

All the outstanding stock of X Corporation is owned by Ivan (60 shares) and Flo (40 shares), who are unrelated. X has no liabilities and the following assets:

Asset	Adj. Basis	F.M.V.
Gainacre	$100,000	$400,000
Lossacre	800,000	400,000
Cash	200,000	200,000

Unless otherwise indicated, assume that Gainacre and Lossacre each asset have been held by X for more than five years.

On January 1 of the current year, X adopted a plan of complete liquidation. What are the tax consequences to X on the distribution of its assets pursuant to the liquidation plan in each of the following alternatives?

(a) X distributes each of its assets to Ivan and Flo as tenants-in-common in proportion to their stock interests (i.e., Ivan takes a 60% interest and Flo a 40% interest in each asset).

(b) Same as (a), above, except X distributes Lossacre and the cash to Ivan and Gainacre to Flo.

(c) Same as (b), above, except X distributes Gainacre and the cash to Ivan and Lossacre to Flo.

(d) Same as (a), above, except X acquired Lossacre as a contribution to capital four years ago, and X was not required to reduce its basis under § 362(e). Is the result different if Lossacre had a value of $1,000,000 and a basis of $800,000 at the time it was contributed to the corporation?

(e) What result on the distributions in (c), above (i.e., Gainacre and cash to Ivan, Lossacre to Flo) if Lossacre, which had no relationship to X's business operations, was transferred to X by Ivan and Flo in a § 351 transaction 18 months prior to the adoption of the liquidation plan, when Lossacre had a fair market value of $700,000 and an adjusted basis of $800,000? Assume, alternatively, that § 362(e)(2) did and did not apply to the contribution of Lossacre to X.

(f) Now assume that Ivan and Flo own 80% and 20%, respectively, of X, which was formed with Ivan contributing Gainacre and Lossacre (same adjusted basis and fair market values as in introductory facts above) and Flo contributing $200,000 cash. Assume further that

23. 1986 Act General Explanation, supra note 19, at 342, n. 86.

Lossacre is § 336(d)(1) "disqualified property," § 362(e)(2) applied to Ivan's contributions to X but § 336(d)(2) does not apply to the liquidating distribution of Lossacre because there was no "plan" for X to recognize loss on that property. Pursuant to a liquidation plan, X distributes each of the assets to the two the shareholders in proportion to their stock interests.

(g) Same as (f), above, except assume that § 362(e)(2) applied to Ivan's contributions to X and § 336(d)(2) applies to Lossacre because there was a "plan" by X to recognize loss in that property.

C.   LIQUIDATION OF A SUBSIDIARY

1.   CONSEQUENCES TO THE SHAREHOLDERS

Code: §§ 332; 334(b)(1); 1223(1).

Regulations: §§ 1.332–1, –2, –5.

Nonrecognition treatment is inappropriate on an ordinary complete liquidation because it would permit individual shareholders to achieve a tax-free bailout as they watch the corporation's earnings and profits account disappear from the scene. Different policy considerations come into play when a parent corporation liquidates a controlled subsidiary. Since the assets of the subsidiary remain in corporate solution, the liquidation is a mere change in form that should not be impeded by the imposition of a tax. The subsidiary's tax attributes, including its earnings and profits, can be inherited by the parent without administrative burdens. Moreover, the subsidiary could have paid tax-free dividends to the parent under Section 243 or the consolidated return rules. All these factors, together with a desire to encourage the simplification of corporate structures, influenced Congress to adopt a nonrecognition scheme by enacting the statutory predecessor of Section 332.

Section 332 provides that a parent corporation recognizes no gain or loss on the receipt of property in complete liquidation of an 80 percent or more subsidiary if certain conditions are met. In that event, the parent takes the distributed assets with a transferred basis under Section 334(b)(1)[1] and inherits the subsidiary's earnings and profits and other tax attributes under Section 381(a)(1).[2]

---

1. If the liquidating subsidiary is not subject to U.S. tax with respect to the distributed property (e.g., because it is a foreign corporation) and the distributee parent is subject to U.S. tax (e.g., it is a domestic corporation), the distributee's aggregate adjusted basis of the distributed property, if it otherwise would exceed its fair market value, must be limited to the lesser fair market value. I.R.C. § 334(b)(1)(B). The purpose of this limitation is to prevent importation of tax losses into the U.S. tax system through the liquidation of a foreign subsidiary. See Chapter 2A, supra, for a similar rule for incorporation transactions.

2. The parent's basis in the stock of a subsidiary is not taken into account in determining the tax consequences of a Section 332 liquidation and disappears from the scene. This creates the possibility that the parent may be deprived of a loss on its investment in

To qualify under Section 332, the subsidiary must distribute property to its parent in complete cancellation or redemption of its stock pursuant to a plan of liquidation, and the liquidation must meet two formal requirements, one relating to control and the other to timing.

Control. Under Section 332(b)(1), the parent must own at least 80 percent of the total voting power of the stock of the subsidiary and 80 percent of the total value of all outstanding stock of the subsidiary from the date of adoption of the plan of complete liquidation and at all times thereafter until the parent receives the final distribution.[3] This condition normally is not a problem if the subsidiary is wholly owned, but any significant minority ownership creates a risk that the transaction will run afoul of the control requirement. Indeed, a parent corporation sometimes is motivated to intentionally violate the 80 percent tests in order to avoid Section 332 and recognize a loss on its stock in the subsidiary.[4] Conversely, an aspiring parent that does not meet the control test may seek to qualify a liquidation under Section 332 by acquiring more stock of the subsidiary or causing the subsidiary to redeem stock held by minority shareholders shortly before the liquidation. As illustrated by the *Riggs* case, below, this strategy may trigger a controversy with the Service over when the liquidation plan was adopted.

Timing. Section 332 includes two timing alternatives. "One-shot" liquidations qualify if the subsidiary distributes all of its assets within one taxable year[5] even if it is not the same year in which the liquidation plan is adopted.[6] Where the distributions span more than one taxable year, the plan must provide that the subsidiary will transfer all of its property within three years after the close of the taxable year in which the first distribution is made.[7] Failure to meet the deadline will cause the liquidation to be retroactively disqualified.[8]

Minority Shareholders. Nonrecognition under Section 332 is only granted to the controlling parent corporation. It is not available to minority

---

the subsidiary even though it must inherit a low carryover basis in its assets.

3. The stock ownership requirements are derived from Section 1504(a)(2), which sets forth rules for determining whether a corporation is a member of an "affiliated group." For purposes of the stock ownership requirement, most nonconvertible preferred stock is disregarded. I.R.C. § 1504(a)(4). Reg. § 1.332–2(a), which states that the test is whether the parent owns at least 80 percent of the subsidiary's total combined voting power and 80 percent of all other classes of stock (except nonvoting stock limited and preferred as to dividends), does not reflect legislative changes to Section 332(b)(1).

4. See Commissioner v. Day & Zimmermann, Inc., 151 F.2d 517 (3d Cir.1945).

5. I.R.C. § 332(b)(2); Reg. § 1.332–3. In this situation, the adoption by the shareholders of the resolution authorizing the distributions in liquidation is considered an adoption of a "plan" of liquidation even though it may not specify the time for completing the transfers.

6. Rev.Rul. 71–326, 1971–2 C.B. 177.

7. I.R.C. § 332(b)(3); Reg. § 1.332–4.

8. Id. To allow the Service to assert deficiencies for the early distributions in the event of a retroactive disqualification, the parent is required to file a waiver of the normal three year statute of limitations and may be asked to post a bond in order to protect the Commissioner's ability to collect past due taxes.

shareholders, who must determine their gain or loss in the normal manner under Section 331(a) unless the liquidation also qualifies as a tax-free reorganization—a rare situation that will be explored in a later chapter.[9]

George L. Riggs, Inc. v. Commissioner

United States Tax Court, 1975.
64 T.C. 474.

■ DRENNEN, JUDGE: Respondent determined a deficiency in petitioner's income tax for the taxable year ended March 31, 1969, in the amount of $589,882.28.

The sole issue for determination is whether the plan of liquidation of Riggs–Young Corp., a subsidiary of the petitioner, was adopted subsequent to the time when petitioner owned at least 80 percent of the outstanding stock of Riggs–Young, thereby rendering section 332, I.R.C. 1954, applicable to the liquidation so that the gain to petitioner thereon is not to be recognized.

FINDINGS OF FACT

[George L. Riggs, Inc., referred to throughout the opinion as "petitioner," was a holding company which as of December, 1967, owned approximately 35.6 percent (2,432 out of 6,840 shares) of the nonvoting preferred stock and 72.13 percent (8,047 out of 11,156 shares) of the common stock of The Standard Electric Time Co. ("Standard"). Standard owned 90 percent of the outstanding stock of a Delaware subsidiary and 99.5 percent of a California subsidiary. The corporations were in the business of manufacturing and marketing electric clocks and signal devices. Standard was the manufacturing arm of the business, and the two subsidiaries handled marketing.

On December 13, 1967, Frances Riggs–Young, the president of Standard and controlling shareholder of petitioner, notified all of Standard's shareholders that the company and its subsidiaries would be seeking approval for a sale of substantially all of the operating assets of the companies. In connection with the sale, Standard changed its name to Riggs–Young Corporation. The sales were consummated on December 29, 1967. In February, 1968, Riggs–Young (formerly Standard) redeemed all of its preferred stock. On April 17, 1968, the directors of Riggs–Young approved the liquidation of the Delaware and California subsidiaries, and authorized Riggs–Young to offer to redeem common stock from all of its shareholders with the exception of petitioner and Frances Riggs–Young. The stated purpose of this tender offer was to eliminate the minority shareholders and provide them with the opportunity to receive cash for their stock. The Tax Court also found that counsel to petitioner and the related subsidiaries "recognized the desirability of petitioner's owning 80 percent of the common stock of Riggs–Young (1) to permit the filing of

---

9. Reg. § 1.332–5. See Chapter 9B1, infra.

consolidated returns, and (2) to permit the possible further liquidation of Riggs–Young under section 332 of the Code to simplify the corporate structure." 64 T.C. at 480. The letter informing shareholders of the redemption offer stated that "If this offer is accepted by substantially all of the stockholders to whom it is directed, the Directors will consider liquidation and final dissolution of the Corporation." 64 T.C. at 479.

At the time of its redemption offer, petitioner owned 72.13 percent of Riggs–Young's common stock. The remaining shares were owned by members of the Riggs family, related trusts and a small group of unrelated minority shareholders.

The tender offer was made on April 26, 1968 and expired on May 28, 1968. During this period, owners of 2,738 shares of common stock tendered their shares for redemption. As a result of these redemptions, petitioner owned at least 80 percent of Riggs–Young's common stock on May 9, 1968, and its ownership increased to 95.6 percent by May 28. On June 20, 1968, the directors and shareholders of Riggs–Young approved a plan of complete liquidation and dissolution of the corporation. Between June and December, 1968, when the liquidation was completed, Riggs–Young made distributions to petitioner in excess of $2.2 million.

Petitioner realized a gain of $2,168,975 from the liquidation of Riggs–Young, representing the difference between the liquidating distributions and petitioner's $42,465 basis in its Riggs–Young stock. The gain was reported on petitioner's tax return but not recognized under the authority of Section 332. Ed.]

OPINION

The only question for decision is whether petitioner owned at least 80 percent of the outstanding stock of its subsidiary, Riggs–Young Corp., at the time Riggs–Young Corp. adopted a plan of liquidation within the meaning of section 332, I.R.C. 1954, so that the gain realized by petitioner on the liquidation of Riggs–Young is not to be recognized by virtue of that section. The vital question is when did Riggs–Young adopt a plan of liquidation within the meaning of section 332.

Respondent argues that the plan of liquidation was adopted on December 27, 1967, when about 90 percent of the stock of Riggs–Young (then Standard) was voted in favor of selling substantially all of the assets of Riggs–Young and its two subsidiaries, Delaware and California, to SET; or not later than about April 17, 1968, when the board of directors of Riggs–Young voted to liquidate Delaware and California and to make an offer to purchase all of the common stock of Riggs–Young then outstanding with the exception of the stock owned by petitioner and Frances Riggs–Young.[2]

On the other hand petitioner contends that the plan of liquidation of Riggs–Young was first adopted when it was formally adopted by vote of the

---

2. Respondent specifically does not rely on the "end-result" or "step-transaction" theory in this case. * * *

stockholders on June 20, 1968, or at the earliest when counsel for petitioner recommended to petitioner in the early days of June 1968 that it liquidate Riggs–Young. Petitioner also contends that section 332 is an elective section and a taxpayer, by taking appropriate steps, can render that section applicable or inapplicable.

The parties are in agreement that by May 9, 1968, petitioner was the owner of at least 80 percent of the outstanding stock of Riggs–Young.

Section 332(a) of the Code provides as a general rule: "No gain or loss shall be recognized on the receipt by a corporation of property distributed in complete liquidation of another corporation." Subsection (b) of section 332 establishes certain requirements which must be satisfied before subsection (a) becomes applicable. The only requirement of subsection (b) which is in issue in this case is whether petitioner, which received property from Riggs–Young in liquidation, was, on the date of the adoption of the plan of liquidation, the owner of at least 80 percent of the stock of Riggs–Young, the liquidating corporation.

Nowhere in the pertinent statute is the phrase "the date of the adoption of the plan of liquidation" defined. However, in attempting to define this phrase for purposes of the provision of [1954 Code] section 337, the regulations of the Commissioner provide:

> Ordinarily the date of the adoption of a plan of complete liquidation by a corporation is the date of adoption by the shareholders of the resolution authorizing the distribution of all the assets of the corporation (other than those retained to meet claims) in redemption of all of its stock. * * * [Sec. 1.337–2(b), Income Tax Regs.; accord, Virginia Ice & Freezing Corp., 30 T.C. 1251 (1958).]

The date of this shareholder resolution should ordinarily be considered the date of the adoption of the plan of liquidation for purposes of section 332. See sec. 332(b)(2).

This Court has noted, in interpreting section 112(b)(6), I.R.C. 1939 (the predecessor of section 332, I.R.C. 1954), that although the adoption of the plan of liquidation "need not be evidenced by formal action of the corporation or the stockholders. * * * even an informal adoption of the plan to liquidate presupposes some kind of definitive determination to achieve dissolution." Distributors Finance Corp., 20 T.C. 768, 784 (1953). The mere general intention to liquidate is not the adoption of a plan of liquidation. City Bank of Washington, 38 T.C. 713 (1962).

Based on the evidence introduced in the case at bar, we must conclude that a plan for the liquidation of Riggs–Young had not been adopted prior to the critical date of May 9, 1968.

Respondent, in an effort to show that the plan of liquidation of Riggs–Young was informally adopted on December 27, 1967, or no later than April 1968, alludes to actions and statements made in connection therewith taken between December 1967 and June 1968. Petitioner offered the testimony of persons involved in those actions to explain what the parties had in mind in taking those actions and making the statements which cast a quite different light on the reasons therefor. This testimony was creditable and not shaken by cross-examination. In light of such evidence, we cannot agree with respondent's inference that these actions constituted an informal adoption of a plan of liquidation of Riggs–Young prior to May 9, 1968.

Respondent argues that the letter dated December 13, 1967, sent to the common shareholders of Standard (Riggs–Young) notifying them of the proposed sale of its assets and that the corporation was contemplating an offer to purchase the common shares held by all shareholders other than petitioner if the sale was approved, clearly indicates that the shareholders at the meeting on December 27, 1967, intended to approve not only the sale of the assets, but also the liquidation of Standard (Riggs–Young).

We believe this infers too much. As petitioner points out, the use of the word "contemplated" shows the acquisition of the common stock of the minority shareholders was merely a possibility about which a final decision had not been made. In any event, from the possibility of a tender offer to the minority shareholders, we cannot conclude, ipso facto, that a plan for the liquidation had been adopted. Petitioner explained that the possibility of this tender offer was made known to the shareholders in order to avoid any possible disclosure problem with the securities law and to apprise the shareholders, from a fairness standpoint, of eventual possibilities resulting from the sale. This explanation is reasonable.

Respondent next points to the fact that on February 23, 1968, all of the 6,840 shares of preferred stock of Riggs–Young were called for redemption as additional evidence that a definite decision to liquidate the corporation had been made. We believe petitioner adequately explained that this redemption was based on sound business reasons. The preferred stock had a par value of $25 per share and a cumulative dividend of 8 percent. This stock was subject to redemption at the option of Riggs–Young upon payment of the par value and any accumulated dividend. The testimony of Norman Vester, a director of Riggs–Young and president of Security National Bank which was cotrustee of Riggs Trust, and Roger Stokey, the attorney for petitioner, Riggs–Young, and Frances Riggs–Young, reveal that the redemption of the preferred stock was motivated by the desire to eliminate the excessive burden of a cumulative dividend of 8 percent and to reduce the number of shareholders with whom Riggs–Young and National Security Bank, as cotrustee of the majority shareholder, would have to deal. Both Vester and Stokey testified that as of January 19, 1968, the date the board of directors of Riggs–Young voted to redeem the preferred stock, no decision had been made to liquidate the corporation, and, therefore, no plan had been adopted.

Respondent next claims that a letter dated April 23, 1968, from Stokey to Scott C. Jordan categorically shows that a plan to liquidate Riggs–Young had been adopted prior to the date of the letter. Stokey's letter was in response to a letter from Jordan on behalf of Frances Riggs–Young inquiring whether she could participate in the tender offer that was about to be made to the minority shareholders of Riggs–Young. In his letter, Stokey said that Frances Riggs–Young might run some tax risks if she accepted a tender offer by Riggs–Young, apparently basing this statement on his belief that the amount she received from a tender offer might be taxed to her at ordinary income rates. As a result of this potential risk, Stokey stated in the letter: "Accordingly, we are arranging for her to receive her money in a liquidation."

Respondent perceives this statement by Stokey as a clear indication that a plan of liquidation of Riggs–Young had been adopted by a definite decision by April 23, 1963. We cannot so conclude. Stokey testified that "we," referred to as arranging the liquidation, meant Stokey and another member of his law firm, William Gorham. This letter merely shows that the attorneys involved in these transactions were contemplating the possibility of a liquidation of Riggs–Young. It in no way proves that the directors or shareholders of the corporation had made a definite decision or informally adopted a plan of liquidation.

Finally, respondent views the letter dated April 26, 1968, drafted by Frances Riggs–Young as president of Riggs–Young, which contained the tender offer to the common shareholders, other than petitioner and Frances Riggs–Young, as an additional indication of a prior adoption of a plan to liquidate. In this letter, Frances Riggs–Young did state that if substantially all of the shareholders accepted the offer, the directors of the corporation would consider liquidation and final dissolution of Riggs–Young.

Stokey testified that Gorham and he inserted, in this April 26 letter, the reference to the possible consideration of liquidating Riggs–Young. He also candidly admitted that he had undoubtedly discussed the possibility of liquidation of Riggs–Young at some prior point with Frances Riggs–Young, but hastened to add that he neither recommended liquidation at this time nor did she direct steps be taken to liquidate. Further, Stokey testified that he would never have recommended liquidation of Riggs–Young if petitioner had failed to achieve the 80–percent ownership.

Petitioner contends that the tender offer to the minority shareholders was made solely for business considerations and not with an eye toward the eventual liquidation of Riggs–Young. Vester and Stokey both testified that since the assets of Riggs–Young had been exchanged for cash, the primary purpose of the tender offer was to eliminate minority shareholders who might have different investment objectives for this cash than the majority shareholder. The bank, as trustee of Riggs, did not want to have to deal with a large group of minority shareholders. Furthermore, Stokey testified that Frances Riggs–Young desired to have the minority shareholders, many of whom were former employees of Standard, receive cash for their stock rather than have them remain locked in as minority shareholders of a personal holding company.

Stokey testified that another objective of the tender offer was to increase petitioner's ownership of Riggs–Young to 80 percent thereby enabling them to file a consolidated return. According to petitioner, the ultimate liquidation of Riggs–Young was not motivated by tax considerations and the sole advantage to be achieved from the liquidation was the simplification of petitioner's corporate structure. Petitioner alleges that Riggs–Young could have been kept in existence without any tax disadvantage. In fact the liquidation of Riggs–Young actually resulted in a tax disadvantage to Frances Riggs–Young personally since she had to pay capital gains tax on her share of the liquidation proceeds. She was a wealthy woman in her seventies and not in need of these funds and could have left this money in corporate solution until her death to enable it to receive a stepped-up basis for the beneficiaries of her estate.

We believe petitioner's explanations of why the actions were taken and the statements were made are true and that the considerations mentioned were taken into account in making the decisions that followed. While the motives enumerated by petitioner do not directly negate the notion that a liquidation may have been contemplated, discussed, or even intended prior to May 9, 1968, they do serve to sufficiently undermine the conclusions drawn by respondent from the actions and statements to offset any presumptions that respondent's inferences are correct. Without more concrete evidence than we have before us, we cannot agree with respondent that a plan of liquidation of Riggs–Young was adopted within the meaning of section 332 prior to May 9, 1968. Lacking such a finding, we believe the date on which the resolution to liquidate was actually adopted by the shareholders should be controlling.

The very most that can be gleaned from the evidence favorable to respondent's contention is that there may have been a general intent on the part of petitioner's advisers somewhere along the line prior to May 9, 1968, to liquidate Riggs–Young when and if petitioner achieved 80–percent ownership of Riggs–Young stock as a result of the tender offer. However, the formation of a conditional general intention to liquidate in the future is not the adoption of a plan of liquidation. *City Bank of Washington,* supra.

A mere intent by a taxpayer-corporation to liquidate a subsidiary prior to meeting the 80–percent requirement of section 332 should not be tantamount to the adoption of a plan of liquidation for the subsidiary at the point in time when that intent is formulated or manifested. Such a result would thwart the congressional intent of section 332 and prior judicial interpretations of this section and its predecessor.

The predecessor of section 332, I.R.C. 1954, was section 112(b)(6), first enacted in 1935. The purpose of section 112(b)(6) was to encourage the simplification of corporation structures and allow the tax-free liquidation of a subsidiary. * * *

* * *

Based on legislative history of [Section 112(b)(6) of the 1939 Code] and prior judicial decisions, we conclude that section 332 is elective in the sense that with advance planning and properly structured transactions, a corporation should be able to render section 332 applicable or inapplicable. The Commissioner in his regulations has conceded corporations this power in a seemingly analogous situation. See sec. 1.337–2(b), Income Tax Regs.

Such power of planning presupposes some right to forethought and the accompanying intent to achieve the desired goal. It would be a logical inconsistency equivalent to a "Catch–22" to say that a corporation has the power to control the application of this section, but that once the corporation formulates the intent to do so (assuming that at or subsequent to the time the intent was formed, it owned less than the required 80 percent but enough stock to cause the liquidation of the subsidiary), it has adopted a plan of liquidation and has precluded itself from the section.

A basic tenet of our tax laws is that a taxpayer has the legal right to decrease or altogether avoid his taxes by means which the law permits. Gregory v. Helvering, 293 U.S. 465 (1935); Daniel D. Palmer, 62 T.C. 684 (1974). At most, petitioner did no more than follow this prerogative.

The shareholders of Riggs–Young formally adopted the plan of liquidation of the corporation on June 20, 1968. Stokey testified that based on the records contained in his office diary, he did not discuss definite liquidation of the corporation with the corporate officers prior to June 4, 5, or 6, 1968. He concluded that he recommended liquidation on either the 4th or 5th of June 1968, and that a definite decision to liquidate was probably made on June 6, 1968. The testimony of Vester corroborates these statements of Stokey. We recognize that the adoption of a plan of liquidation need not be evidenced by formal action of the corporation or shareholders, *Distributors Finance Corp.,* supra. In this case, however, we find on the evidence that the plan of liquidation was adopted when the formal action was taken on June 20, 1968. Furthermore, even if it can be said that a plan of liquidation was adopted when Stokey first recommended it to the management, see *Distributors Finance Corp.,* supra, this occurred in June 1968 and would satisfy the requirements of section 332.

Respondent has cited and relied on Rev.Rul. 70–106, 1970–1 C.B. 70, as supportive of his position. This Court is not bound by a revenue ruling. Andrew A. Sandor, 62 T.C. 469 (1974). In addition, we find the facts of this case are greatly dissimilar to those contained in the ruling. The ruling assumes a prior agreement between the minority and majority shareholders concerning the redemption of the minority stockholders' stock. The ruling concludes that the liquidation plan was adopted when this agreement was reached. In the case at bar, there is no evidence of an agreement between the minority and majority shareholders prior to the tender offer. *Madison Square Garden Corp.,* supra at 624 n. 4. Since this revenue ruling is inapplicable, proper judicial restraint dictates that we do not comment on the validity or invalidity of the ruling as limited to the facts contained therein. Ronald C. Packard, 63 T.C. 621 (1975).

Decision will be entered for the petitioner. Reviewed by the Court.

2. CONSEQUENCES TO THE LIQUIDATING SUBSIDIARY

Code: §§ 336(d)(3); 337(a), (b)(1), (c), (d). Skim §§ 381(a)(1), (c)(2), (3); 453B(d); 1245(b)(3); 1250(d)(3).

Regulations: § 1.332–7.

Distributions of Property. A liquidating corporation generally recognizes gain or loss on distributions of property in a complete liquidation.[1] A major exception to this general rule is contained in Section 337,[2] which provides that a liquidating subsidiary does not recognize gain or loss on distributions of property to its parent[3] in a complete liquidation to which Section 332 applies. A nonrecognition rule makes sense in this context because the subsidiary's tax attributes, including the built-in gain or loss in its assets, can be preserved in the hands of the parent. Section 334(b)(1) implements this policy by providing that the parent takes a transferred basis in property received from a subsidiary in a Section 332 liquidation. In keeping with this carryover of tax attributes theme, the depreciation recapture provisions do not override Section 337,[4] and recapture potential continues to lurk in the distributed property through the definition of "recomputed basis" in Section 1245 and "additional depreciation" in Section 1250.[5] A liquidating subsidiary likewise does not recognize gain or loss on the distribution of installment obligations if Section 332 applies,[6] and the parent will take a transferred basis in the obligations under Section 334(b)(1).

Distributions to Minority Shareholders. The nonrecognition rule in Section 337(a) is limited to distributions of property by a liquidating subsidiary to "the 80–percent distributee"—i.e., the parent corporation. Distributions to minority shareholders are treated in the same manner as a distribution in a nonliquidating redemption. Accordingly, the distributing corporation will recognize gain but not loss. Recognition of gain is appropriate because minority shareholders do not inherit any built-in gain in the distributed property through a transferred basis but instead take a fair market value basis under Section 334(a). Distributions of loss property are another matter. In order to prevent a controlled subsidiary from recognizing losses (but not gains) by "bullet" distributions of loss property to minority shareholders, Section 336(d)(3) provides that no loss shall be recognized to a subsidiary on a distribution of property to minority shareholders in a Section 332 liquidation.

Transfer of Property to Satisfy Indebtedness of Subsidiary to Parent. Section 337 applies only to liquidating *distributions.* If a subsidiary is indebted to its parent, a transfer of property to satisfy the debt normally would be a taxable event rather than a nontaxable distribution governed by Section 337(a), causing the subsidiary to recognize gain or loss and the parent to take a fair market value basis in the distributed property. The

---

1. I.R.C. § 336(a).

2. This "new" Section 337 is not to be confused with its 1954 Code counterpart, "old" Section 337, which provided for nonrecognition of gain or loss on certain liquidating sales. Old timers wish Congress had avoided confusion by retiring former Section 337's number and placing it on a monument in "old" Yankee Stadium.

3. Section 337(a) refers to the parent as "the 80–percent distributee," which is defined in Section 337(c) as a corporation that meets the 80 percent stock ownership requirements specified in Section 332(b).

4. I.R.C. §§ 1245(b)(3); 1250(d)(3).

5. I.R.C. §§ 1245(a)(2); 1250(b)(1), (3).

6. I.R.C. § 453B(d)(1).

disparate treatment of distributions in complete liquidation and transfers of property to satisfy intercorporate indebtedness might tempt a subsidiary to distribute appreciated property as part of the liquidation while simultaneously using loss property to extinguish any indebtedness to the parent. Section 337(b)(1) prevents this ploy by providing that any transfer of property in satisfaction of a subsidiary's debt to its parent shall be treated as a distribution, subjecting the transfer to the general nonrecognition rule of Section 337(a). As a necessary corollary, Section 334(b)(1) provides that the parent takes a transferred basis in the distributed property.

Distributions to Tax–Exempt and Foreign Parents. Ever vigilant, Congress was concerned that taxpayers might turn the deferral provided by Section 337 into a permanent exemption from the corporate-level tax. Consider the following possibility. A and B, the sole shareholders of highly appreciated X Corporation, wish to sell the business and avoid at least one level of tax. They sell all their stock to tax-exempt Charity, Inc. and recognize gain on the sale or, if they are philanthropic, they could donate the stock to Charity and take a charitable deduction. Charity now owns 100 percent of the X stock but it does not wish to operate the business. Charity wishes to liquidate X in a tax-free transaction at both the corporate and shareholder levels under Sections 332 and 337(a). Although Charity must take a transferred basis in the property distributed by X, no tax ever would be collected on the subsequent sale of those assets because Charity is exempt from tax.

This technique might have been vulnerable under the step transaction and other judicial doctrines, but Congress decided to attack it from within the Code. Section 337(b)(2) thus provides that the general corporate-level nonrecognition rule for liquidations of a subsidiary shall not apply where the parent is a tax-exempt organization. Nonrecognition is restored, however, if the distributed property is used by the tax-exempt parent in an "unrelated trade or business" immediately after the distribution.[7] In that event, there is no loophole to plug because the tax-exempt organization is subject to tax on its unrelated business income.[8] A similar rule requires recognition of corporate-level gain in the case of a liquidating distribution to a parent that is a foreign corporation, except as the Treasury may provide in regulations. The legislative history indicates that the regulations should permit nonrecognition if the appreciation on the distributed property is not being removed from the U.S.'s taxing jurisdiction prior to recognition.[9] In both situations where the subsidiary recognizes gain or loss, the parent takes a fair market value basis in the distributed assets.[10]

7. Exempt organizations may be taxable on income from an "unrelated business"—i.e., a regularly carried on trade or business activity that is not substantially related to the organization's exempt purposes. See I.R.C. §§ 511 et seq.

8. If the tax-exempt parent later disposes of the distributed property or ceases to use it in an unrelated trade or business, any gain not recognized on the earlier liquidation becomes taxable as unrelated business income. I.R.C. § 337(b)(2)(B)(ii).

9. H.R.Rep. No. 99–841, 99th Cong., 2d Sess. II–202 (1986).

10. I.R.C. § 334(b)(1)(A).

PROBLEMS

1.   P, Inc. ("P") owns 90 percent of the outstanding stock of S, Inc. ("S"). Individual ("I") owns the remaining 10 percent of S. P's basis in its S stock is $3,000. I's basis in his S stock is $200. S has accumulated earnings and profits of $2,000 and the following assets:

Asset	Adjusted Basis	Fair Market Value
Land	$3,000	$8,000
Equipment	2,500	1,000
Inventory	100	1,000

S wishes to liquidate and distribute all of its assets to its shareholders. What are the tax consequences to P, S and I in the following alternative situations?

(a) S distributes the inventory to I and the other assets to P.

(b) S distributes the equipment to I and the other assets to P. How might S improve this result?

(c) What result in (b), above, if P's basis in its S stock were $30,000 and S had a $30,000 basis in the land?

(d) Is (c), above, a situation where P might wish to avoid the application of § 332? Why? How might this be accomplished? Consider in this regard the § 332 qualification requirements and how a parent might assure that they are not met.

2.   Child Corporation has 100 shares of common stock outstanding. Mother Corporation owns 75 shares (basis—$1,000) and Uncle, an individual who recently inherited his stock, owns 25 shares (basis—$3,000). Child has no earnings and profits, a $10,000 net operating loss carryover and the following assets (all held long-term):

Asset	Adjusted Basis	Fair Market Value
Cash	$2,000	$2,000
Installment Note	1,000	4,000
Land	100	1,000
Equipment (all § 1245 gain)	100	1,000
Total	$3,200	$8,000

What are the tax consequences in the following alternative situations, disregarding the impact of any tax paid by Child as a result of its liquidating distributions?

(a) Child adopts a plan of complete liquidation and distributes $2,000 cash to Uncle and all its remaining assets to Mother.

(b) Child distributes $2,000 cash to Uncle in redemption of his 25 shares. One week later, it adopts a plan of complete liquidation and distributes its remaining assets to Mother pursuant to the plan. What are Mother and Child trying to accomplish through this reunion?

3. Parent Corporation ("P") owns all the stock of Subsidiary Corporation ("S"). P has a $1,000 basis in its S stock and also holds S bonds with a basis and face amount of $1,000. S has the following assets:

Asset	Adjusted Basis	Fair Market Value
Inventory	$10,000	$ 1,000
Land	200	10,000
	$10,200	$11,000

P intends to liquidate S, but before adopting a formal plan S distributes the inventory in satisfaction of its outstanding $1,000 debt to P. On the next day, S liquidates, distributing the land to P. Why did P and S structure the transactions in this manner? Will they achieve their tax objectives?

CHAPTER 8

Taxable Corporate Acquisitions

A. Introduction

There are many ways to structure a corporate acquisition. In the preceding chapter, we previewed one method: a sale by the target corporation[1] of all its assets followed by a distribution of the proceeds of sale to the shareholders in complete liquidation of the target.[2] An alternative is a sale by the shareholders of their stock in the target corporation. In either case, the business can be acquired in exchange for cash, notes, stock or bonds of the acquiring corporation, other property, or any combination of consideration. In an asset acquisition, the acquiring corporation may purchase the assets directly, drop them down to a controlled subsidiary or cause a subsidiary to make the acquisition. In a stock acquisition, the target may stay alive as a subsidiary of the acquiring corporation or liquidate. Variations abound on these basic formats.

Although we quickly will turn our attention to the tax consequences of corporate acquisitions, it may be useful at the outset to consider a few nontax factors that may influence the form of a transaction. Stock acquisitions are usually simpler to execute than asset acquisitions. To sell its assets, the target must prepare conveyance documents for many different items of property, give notice to creditors in compliance with local bulk sales laws, and incur sales or other local transfer taxes. In a stock acquisition, however, it is unnecessary to transfer any of the target's assets; instead, the acquiring corporation simply buys the target's stock directly from the T shareholders. A stock purchase thus may be desirable (or even essential) if the target holds certain nonassignable assets, such as a favorable lease or employment contract, or has valuable rights under state law that might be jeopardized if the corporation were dissolved. On the

---

1. In discussing acquisitions in this and later chapters, the acquired corporation generally will be called the "target," or "T," and the corporate purchaser will be called the "acquiring corporation," or "P." By using the term "target," we do not necessarily mean to suggest that the acquisition is a hostile takeover.

2. A target corporation that sells all or most of its assets usually will liquidate and

distribute the proceeds to its shareholders. Alternatively, T could stay alive as an investment company after the sale. If T is closely held, staying alive likely would cause it to be classified as a personal holding company. For the perils of personal holding company status, see Chapter 14D, infra. For the possibility of a sale of assets by a C corporation followed by a conversion to S corporation status, see Chapter 15F, infra.

other hand, a stock acquisition may expose the buyer to liabilities of the target that may be unknown or contingent at the time of the transaction. This threat normally can be minimized by warranties and indemnity provisions in the stock purchase agreement. But some buyers still prefer to avoid the risk altogether by buying the assets and not assuming any burdens that might be connected with the corporate entity. The presence of unwanted assets, the unwillingness of minority shareholders of the target to sell their stock, and the requirements of regulatory agencies and local corporate and securities law are additional nontax factors that may influence the choice of form.

The principal tax issues raised on a corporate acquisition are best introduced by revisiting the simple example from the preceding chapter. Recall that A is the sole shareholder of Target Corporation ("T") and has a $100,000 basis in her T stock. T's only asset is a parcel of undeveloped land ("Gainacre") with a fair market value of $400,000 and a zero adjusted basis. Purchaser, Inc. ("P") wishes to acquire the land for $400,000 cash. Consider three simple methods of structuring the acquisition:

(1) *Liquidation of T Followed by Shareholder Sale of Assets.* T distributes Gainacre to A in complete liquidation and then A sells Gainacre to P for $400,000.

(2) *Sale of T Assets Followed by Liquidation.* T sells Gainacre to P for $400,000 and then liquidates, distributing the after-tax proceeds of sale to A.

(3) *Sale of T Stock.* A sells her T stock to P for $400,000 and P either keeps T alive as a wholly owned subsidiary or causes T to liquidate and distribute Gainacre to P.

Under any of these methods, one would expect A to recognize gain equal to the difference between her amount realized on the liquidation or sale of stock and the $100,000 adjusted basis in her T stock. In addition, T has $400,000 of corporate-level gain inherent in Gainacre. Should that gain also be recognized and, if so, should P (directly or indirectly through its ownership of T stock) take Gainacre with a $400,000 fair market value basis? If T does recognize gain, who bears the economic burden of the corporate-level tax? Alternatively, can the transaction be structured so that T's gain is deferred through a zero transferred basis in the land? Or, perish the thought, might T's gain be permanently forgiven, with P (or T, if it is still alive), taking Gainacre with a $400,000 cost basis? To what extent do (or should) the answers to these questions depend on the form of the transaction? And how are they affected if the seller is not an individual but a corporation that owns 100 percent of the T stock?

The after-tax economic outcome of these transactions may differ radically depending on the structure selected by the parties. The remainder of this chapter fills in the details, first considering asset acquisitions and then stock acquisitions.

B.   ASSET ACQUISITIONS

1.   TAX CONSEQUENCES TO THE PARTIES

A taxable asset acquisition occurs when a purchaser ("P"), which may be an individual or a business entity such as a corporation or partnership, acquires the assets of a target corporation ("T") in exchange for cash, notes, other property, or a mix of such consideration, and the acquisition does not qualify as a tax-free reorganization under Section 368.[1] Following the sale of its assets, T normally liquidates and distributes the sales proceeds to its shareholders, but the shareholders may choose to keep T alive and cause it to reinvest the proceeds. Under the corporate laws of most states, an asset acquisition also may be accomplished more efficiently by a cash merger of T into P (or a subsidiary of P). On the merger, T's shareholders receive cash or notes (or a combination) from P, and T's assets and liabilities automatically transfer to P (or its subsidiary). The Service views such a "cash merger" as if T sold its assets to P and then completely liquidated.[2]

To illustrate the tax consequences of the most basic asset acquisition methods, return again to the example of A, the sole shareholder (stock basis—$100,000) of T, whose only asset is appreciated Gainacre (basis—zero; fair market value—$400,000). Assume that C corporations and individuals are taxed at a flat 35 percent rate, with a 15 percent preferential rate for capital gains recognized by individual taxpayers.[3]

Liquidation of T Followed by Shareholder Sale of T Assets. If T distributes Gainacre to A in complete liquidation, it recognizes $400,000 gain under Section 336(a) and incurs a tax liability of $140,000 (35% × $400,000). A bears the economic burden of the tax and is obligated to pay it because T has no assets after it liquidates. A recognizes $160,000 gain on the liquidation ($400,000 distribution less $140,000 corporate-level tax less $100,000 basis in T stock) and incurs a shareholder-level capital gains tax of $24,000 (15% × $160,000). A takes Gainacre with a $400,000 basis under Section 334(a) and recognizes no further gain on a sale of Gainacre to P for its fair market value. When the smoke clears, the total corporate and shareholder-level tax on the liquidation and sale is $164,000, leaving A with $236,000. P takes Gainacre with a $400,000 cost basis and, if P is a corporation, it does not succeed to the tax attributes (e.g., earnings and profits, net operating losses, etc.) of T.

Sale of T Assets Followed by Liquidation. The result is identical if T sells Gainacre to P and then liquidates. T recognizes $400,000 gain on the sale, pays a corporate-level tax of $140,000, distributes the $260,000 net

---

1. See Chapter 9B, infra.

2. Rev.Rul. 69–6, 1969–1 C.B. 104.

3. These assumptions approximate the actual rates in effect as this edition went to press in early 2012 and ignore the impact of any state taxes.

proceeds to A in complete liquidation, and A again recognizes $160,000 gain under Section 331(a) and incurs a $24,000 capital gains tax. P takes Gainacre with a $400,000 cost basis and does not succeed to any of T's tax attributes.

Sale of T Assets Not Followed by Liquidation. If T does not liquidate after selling Gainacre to P, T once again recognizes $400,000 gain and incurs $140,000 in corporate-level tax, but A does not recognize gain if T retains and reinvests the $260,000 net proceeds. Keeping T alive defers and may permanently eliminate any tax at the shareholder level. For example, if A holds the T stock until her death, A's heirs will take a stepped-up basis in the stock under Section 1014 and then may liquidate the corporation without paying a shareholder-level tax. This "no liquidation" strategy may have some appeal if A is elderly and her estate is on the verge of obtaining a stepped-up basis in the T stock, but it is rarely desirable if the liquidation will be postponed for many years. First, the double tax on corporate earnings must be navigated if A wants access to T's earnings.[4] Moreover, if T no longer conducts an ongoing business, it likely will be classified as a "personal holding company."[5] As such, it will be required to distribute its net investment income annually to A or face a penalty tax equal to 15 percent of any undistributed income.[6] In many situations, keeping T alive may be more expensive than liquidating, although not as expensive as it was before the tax rate on qualified dividends was reduced to 15 percent.

Conversion to S Corporation. If T chooses to stay alive, it could avoid some of the problems just described by becoming an S corporation. For example, T's income would pass through to its shareholders and be subject to only one level of tax, albeit at slightly higher marginal rates for some high-income individual shareholders. But as an S corporation, T would face other obstacles. To name just two, an S corporation that was once a C corporation may lose its S status or be subject to a special corporate-level tax if it has Subchapter C earnings and profits and significant passive investment income.[7]

2.   ALLOCATION OF PURCHASE PRICE

Code: § 1060. Skim § 197.

Regulations: §§ 1.338–6(a), (b), (c)(1); 1.1060–1(a)(1).

Background. The parties to an asset acquisition typically negotiate and agree upon a purchase price based on the value of the target corporation as

---

4. Dividends received by T, however, would qualify for the 70 percent dividends received deduction under Section 243(a), and corporate-level *regular* tax could be avoided altogether by investing the sales proceeds in tax-exempt municipal bonds. But unless it qualifies for the small corporation exception, T still may be subject to the corporate alternative minimum tax even if it is able to shelter its investment income from the regular tax. See, e.g., I.R.C. § 56(g) and Chapter 1B2, supra.

5. See §§ 541 et seq. and Chapter 14C, infra.

6. I.R.C. § 541.

7. See I.R.C. §§ 1362(d)(3); 1375; Chapter 15B and 15F, infra.

a going concern. For tax purposes, however, a sale of the assets of a going business for a lump sum is treated as a sale of each individual asset rather than of a single capital asset.[1] This fragmentation approach requires the parties to allocate the purchase price among the various tangible and intangible assets that have been sold. The allocation is used to determine the amount and character of the seller's gain or loss, and the buyer's cost basis in each asset for purposes of computing depreciation and amortization deductions and gain or loss on a subsequent disposition.

The parties historically had adverse interests when it came to allocating the purchase price among the assets. Buyers wished to allocate as much as possible to inventory, depreciable property and amortizable intangibles with the shortest recovery periods, and they resisted allocations to land and nondepreciable goodwill. Sellers, by contrast, benefitted by allocating a larger portion of the purchase price to assets yielding a capital gain and less to ordinary income assets. If the seller is a C corporation, these conflicts have diminished with the elimination of a corporate capital gains rate preference. But buyers are still motivated to allocate basis to assets that provide depreciation or amortization deductions over the shortest possible recovery period, and corporate sellers with unused capital losses still prefer capital gains over ordinary income.

The parties may include a negotiated purchase price allocation in their written agreement. Because buyers and sellers historically had adverse interests, negotiated allocations usually were respected by the Service. Indeed, the Service and some courts generally did not permit a party to take a tax reporting position inconsistent with an agreed allocation unless the contract was unenforceable because of mistake, undue influence, fraud or duress.[2] More often than not, however, agreements of sale do not contain any purchase price allocation, allowing the parties to go their separate ways and possibly "whipsaw" the government in the process by taking inconsistent positions. A typical controversy involved the tension between a covenant not to compete and goodwill. Amounts paid by the buyer that are attributable to a covenant by the seller not to compete with the buyer for a stated period of time result in ordinary income to the seller and, before enactment of Section 197, the payments were amortizable by the buyer over the life of the covenant. Payments for goodwill, on the other hand, could not be depreciated or amortized by the buyer before Section 197 was added to the Code, and gain on the sale of goodwill was capital gain to the seller. Thus, sellers preferred allocations to goodwill, while buyers, craving deductions, preferred allocations to a covenant not to compete.

Even without a covenant not to compete, some of the most contentious allocation controversies have involved the amount properly attributable to goodwill and the going concern value of an acquired business. The alloca-

---

1. Williams v. McGowan, 152 F.2d 570 (2d Cir.1945).

2. Commissioner v. Danielson, 378 F.2d 771 (3d Cir.1967), cert. denied, 389 U.S. 858, 88 S.Ct. 94 (1967). Other courts, using a more lenient standard, permitted a party to override a contractual allocation by a showing of "strong proof" that the agreement should not be respected. See, e.g., Ullman v. Commissioner, 264 F.2d 305 (2d Cir.1959).

tion is critical to a buyer who pays a premium—i.e., an amount that exceeds the fair market value of the target's identifiable tangible and intangible assets. At one time, the Service permitted the "proportionate" method of allocation, under which the value of each acquired asset (including intangibles such as goodwill) was determined, and then the aggregate purchase price was allocated in proportion to the relative fair market value of each asset. The proportionate method often had the effect of shifting any premium paid for the business toward depreciable and amortizable assets and away from nondepreciable goodwill. The future tax benefits that resulted from this buyer-friendly allocation method were a stimulus to the corporate takeover mania of the 1980's.

Under another valuation approach, known as the residual method, each tangible and intangible asset (excluding goodwill and going concern value) is valued first. If the overall price paid for the business exceeds the aggregate fair market value of these assets, the excess ("residue") is allocated to goodwill and going concern value. The impact of the residual method is to allocate more of the total purchase price to goodwill and going concern value as compared to the proportionate method. In the case of a "bargain purchase," where the price paid for the business is less than the fair market value of T's assets, nothing is allocated to goodwill and the amount allocated to the identifiable assets (other than cash, cash equivalents and marketable securities) is proportionately reduced.

Congress first moved to regulate purchase price allocations in connection with stock purchases that are treated as asset acquisitions under Section 338 by directing the Treasury to prescribe regulations governing allocation of basis among the target's assets.[3] Not unexpectedly, the regulations mandated use of the residual method. Eventually, Congress extended this approach to asset acquisitions by enacting Section 1060, which includes reporting requirements to protect the Service from being whipsawed. Congress took another step toward certainty with the enactment of Section 197, which requires the cost of most acquired intangible assets, including a covenant not to compete, to be amortized over 15 years. Because a buyer's ability to amortize intangible assets and the timing of that amortization affects the economic stakes of a purchase price allocation, an overview of Section 197 is useful before turning to the specific requirements of Section 1060.

Amortization of Intangibles: Section 197. Section 197 permits taxpayers to amortize many intangible assets ratably over a 15–year period, regardless of their actual "useful life" or recovery period under prior law. Amortizable "Section 197 intangibles" include information bases, customer and subscription lists, patient files, know-how, licenses, franchises, trade names and, notably, goodwill, going concern value and covenants not to compete entered into in connection with an acquisition of all or a substantial part of a trade or business.[4] Some of these assets, such as goodwill and

---

3. I.R.C. § 338(b)(5). See Section C2 of this chapter, infra.

4. I.R.C. § 197(c)(1), (d).

going concern value, were not amortizable at all under prior law, while others were being written off over periods considerably shorter than 15 years. Amortization under Section 197 is available, however, only for acquired intangibles; it is generally not permitted for assets that are created by the taxpayer.[5]

Section 197 puts to rest many of the most contested tax issues in the area of business acquisitions. Litigated disputes abounded under prior law, including one case in which the Supreme Court held that "customer-based" intangibles (primarily subscriber lists) acquired by a publisher on the purchase of a newspaper were amortizable if they had an ascertainable value and a determinable useful life.[6] Rejecting the Service's argument that such intangibles were "nondepreciable per se," the Court concluded that eligibility for amortization turned on whether the asset was capable of being valued and whether that value diminished over time.[7] The Court's approach, and the factual controversies that it necessarily engendered, are now largely moot with the enactment of Section 197.

Allocation of Purchase Price Under Section 1060. The ability of the parties to make strategical purchase price allocations has been reduced with the enactment of Section 197 and the Section 1060 basis allocation rules. Section 1060 applies to any "applicable asset acquisition," defined as any transfer (direct or indirect) of assets which constitute a "trade or business" in the hands of either the buyer or the seller, and the purchaser's basis in the purchased assets is determined wholly by reference to the consideration paid for the assets.[8] This broad definition goes well beyond the typical corporate asset acquisition, extending to sales of sole proprietorships and partnership interests.

Section 1060 requires the buyer and seller to allocate the total consideration received or paid for a business among the various transferred assets using the residual method previewed above.[9] For this purpose, "consideration received" is the seller's aggregate amount realized from the sale of its assets determined under general tax principles, and "consideration paid" is the buyer's aggregate cost of purchasing the assets that is properly taken into account in determining basis.[10] Thus, liabilities assumed by the buyer or to which the transferred property is subject generally are included in total consideration. Aggregate consideration is then allocated among the assets using a refined version of the residual method that places all "acquisition date assets" into one of seven classes and allocates the consideration among those classes in priority order.[11] In general, the amount allocated to an asset (except for the last "residual" category) may

---

5. I.R.C. § 197(c)(2).

6. Newark Morning Ledger Co. v. United States, 507 U.S. 546, 113 S.Ct. 1670 (1993).

7. Id. at 565–570, 113 S.Ct. at 1680–83.

8. I.R.C. § 1060(c); Reg. § 1.1060–1(b)(1).

9. Reg. § 1.1060–1(a)(1).

10. Reg. § 1.1060–1(c)(1).

11. Reg. § 1.1060–1(c)(2). The Section 1060 regulations incorporate by reference the residual method used under Reg. § 1.338–6 for certain stock acquisitions that are treated as asset acquisitions under Section 338. Id.

not exceed its fair market value.[12] Specifically, total consideration is first reduced by cash and cash equivalents (known as "Class I acquisition date assets") transferred by the seller.[13] The remaining consideration is then allocated first to highly liquid assets such as actively traded personal property (e.g., marketable securities), foreign currencies, and certificates of deposit (Class II assets) in proportion to their fair market values, then to accounts receivable, mortgages, and credit card receivables (Class III), then to inventory and other dealer-type property (Class IV), then to all assets other than those in the other classes (Class V—a broad category that includes most tangible assets, such as equipment and real estate), and finally to all Section 197 intangibles except goodwill and going concern value (Class VI). Any remaining consideration, such as in acquisitions where the purchase price includes a "premium" that exceeds the liquidation value of the tangible and intangible assets acquired, is allocated to Class VII, a category limited to goodwill and going concern value.[14]

Effect of Agreement Between the Parties. As first enacted, Section 1060 did not address the question of whether the parties to a transaction should be bound by any written agreement they reach regarding allocation of the purchase price. Concerned that taxpayers might continue to take reporting positions that were inconsistent with their agreements, Congress amended Section 1060 to provide that a written agreement governing the allocation of consideration in an applicable asset acquisition shall be binding on both parties unless the Treasury determines that the allocation (or fair market value) is not appropriate.[15] The regulations provide that a party may refute an agreed allocation or valuation only by proving that the agreement was unenforceable due to mistake, undue influence, fraud or duress.[16] This is the standard long advanced by the Service and applied by the Third Circuit in the *Danielson* case.[17] In holding the parties to their agreement, however, Congress made it clear that it did not intend to restrict the Service's ability to challenge the taxpayers' allocation to any asset by any appropriate appraisal method, particularly where there is a lack of adverse tax interests between the parties.[18] For example, an allocation that departs from the mandated residual method will not be respected even if it is part of a negotiated agreement and it would be reasonable for the Service to make an independent showing of the value of goodwill in order to challenge the taxpayer's valuation of other assets.[19]

Reporting Requirements. The parties to an applicable asset acquisition must attach a statement (Form 8594) to their tax returns, reporting

---

12. Reg. § 1.338–6(c)(1).

13. Reg. § 1.338–6(b)(1). In the unusual case where the total consideration to be allocated is less than the amount of Class I assets, then the purchaser must immediately recognize ordinary income to that extent. Id.

14. Reg. § 1.338–6(b)(2).

15. I.R.C. § 1060(a), last sentence.

16. Reg. § 1.1060–1(c)(4).

17. Commissioner v. Danielson, supra note 2.

18. H.Rep. No. 101–964, 101st Cong., 2d Sess. 1096 (1990). See Reg. § 1.1060–1(c)(4).

19. See generally Staff of the Joint Committee on Taxation, General Explanation of the Tax Reform Act of 1986, 100th Cong., 1st Sess. 355–360 (1987).

information concerning the amount of the total sales price and how it was allocated among the various asset classes.[20] The purchaser also must report any collateral agreements related to an acquisition, such as covenants not to compete, employment agreements, licenses, leases and the like.[21]

C. STOCK ACQUISITIONS

1. BACKGROUND

In a taxable stock acquisition, the purchaser ("P") buys the stock of a target corporation ("T") from T's shareholders for cash or a combination of cash, notes and other consideration. A taxable stock acquisition may be structured as a reverse triangular merger, in which P forms a wholly owned transitory subsidiary ("S"), and S merges into T under state law, with T's shareholders receiving cash and debt obligations of P. When the dust settles, T is a wholly owned subsidiary of P.

Acquisitions of public companies are almost always stock acquisitions. They are sometimes launched when P begins acquiring T stock in the open market.[1] The next step may be a cash tender offer to T's shareholders or a friendly merger negotiated with T's management. If P succeeds in acquiring control of T, the final step is usually a "back-end" merger where recalcitrant minority shareholders are squeezed out of the picture, sometimes for the same price originally offered to tendering shareholders or perhaps on less attractive terms.[2]

Whether the transaction is structured as a direct stock purchase or a reverse triangular cash merger,[3] T's shareholders recognize gain or loss on the sale of their stock, measured by the difference between their amount realized and stock basis, and P takes a cost basis in the T stock it acquires. T shareholders who receive notes generally may report their gain on the installment method if the T stock is not publicly traded.[4] The more difficult conceptual questions relate to the tax consequences to T and the impact of

---

20. I.R.C. § 1060(b). See Reg. § 1.1060–1(e).

21. Reg. § 1.1060–1(e).

1. P may purchase up to five percent of T's stock without any requirement for public disclosure under the federal securities laws. Securities Exchange Act of 1934, § 13(d), 15 U.S.C.A. § 78m(d)(1981).

2. Squeeze outs are facilitated by the modern corporate laws of Delaware and other states where many public companies are incorporated. See, e.g., Del.Corp.Law § 251. For a good basic description of the mechanics, dynamics and economics of corporate takeovers, see Hamilton & Booth, Business Basics for Law Students, ch. 13 (4th ed. 2006).

3. A reverse triangular cash merger is treated for tax purposes as if P purchased T stock directly from the shareholders. Transitory "S" is disregarded. See Rev.Rul. 73–427, 1973–2 C.B. 301; Rev.Rul. 79–273, 1979–2 C.B. 125.

4. I.R.C. § 453(k)(2). Installment sales of very large blocks of stock may be affected by Section 453A, which imposes what amounts to an annual interest charge on a seller's tax liability that has been deferred by the installment method. In general, this provision applies only if the face amount of the seller's installment receivables during the taxable year exceed $5 million.

a stock acquisition on the basis of T's assets and T's other tax attributes. Should a stock acquisition be treated as if it were a taxable asset acquisition coupled with a liquidation of T, or should the form of the transaction control? Should the parties be permitted to select which treatment they would prefer?

Not surprisingly, Congress has exhibited considerable hyperactivity in answering these questions. The *Kimbell–Diamond* case, which follows, is the best place to begin describing the evolution of the current tax treatment of stock acquisitions.

Kimbell–Diamond Milling Co. v. Commissioner

Tax Court of the United States, 1950.
14 T.C. 74.

■ BLACK, JUDGE.

[In August, 1942, taxpayer's milling plant was destroyed by fire and two months later the taxpayer collected insurance as a reimbursement for its loss. It then purchased for approximately $210,000 cash all the stock of Whaley Mill & Elevator Co. in order to use Whaley's plant and equipment to replace its own destroyed facilities. The purchase price consisted of $120,000 of insurance proceeds and $90,000 of additional funds. The taxpayer's sole intention in purchasing Whaley's stock was to acquire the assets of the company through a prompt liquidation.

Taxpayer liquidated Whaley three days after acquiring the stock. In a prior proceeding, reported at 10 T.C. 7, the Tax Court held that the acquisition of Whaley came within the 1939 Code predecessor of § 1033 so that the taxpayer's gain on the involuntary conversion was not recognized. Since the taxpayer's acquisition of the Whaley stock qualified under § 1033, its basis was $110,000 (the sum of the $20,000 adjusted basis of the destroyed assets and the $90,000 of additional funds that were paid in addition to the insurance proceeds). The assets of Whaley acquired by the taxpayer in the liquidation had an adjusted basis to Whaley of more than $300,000; the depreciable assets represented about $140,000 of this total.

The central dispute in the case was over the taxpayer's basis for depreciation in the assets acquired in the Whaley liquidation. After addressing a procedural issue, the Court proceeded to discuss the merits. Note that this case arose under the 1939 Code, which did not contain former § 334(b)(2) or present § 338. Ed.]

* * *

OPINION

Having decided the issue of *res judicata* against petitioner, we must now determine the question of petitioner's basis in Whaley's assets on the merits. Petitioner argues that the acquisition of Whaley's assets and the subsequent liquidation of Whaley brings petitioner within the provisions of [the predecessor of § 332] and, therefore, by reason of [the predecessor of

§ 334(b)(1)], petitioner's basis in these assets is the same as the basis in Whaley's hands. In so contending, petitioner asks that we treat the acquisition of Whaley's stock and the subsequent liquidation of Whaley as separate transactions. It is well settled that the incidence of taxation depends upon the substance of a transaction. Commissioner v. Court Holding Co., 324 U.S. 331. It is inescapable from petitioner's minutes set out above and from the "Agreement and Program of Complete Liquidation" entered into between petitioner and Whaley, that the only intention petitioner ever had was to acquire Whaley's assets.

We think that this proceeding is governed by the principles of Commissioner v. Ashland Oil & Refining Co., 99 Fed. (2d) 588, certiorari denied, 306 U.S. 661. In that case the stock was retained for almost a year before liquidation. Ruling on the question of whether the stock or the assets of the corporation were purchased, the court stated:

The question remains, however, whether if the entire transaction, whatever its form, was essentially in intent, purpose and result, a purchase by Swiss of property, its several steps may be treated separately and each be given an effect for tax purposes as though each constituted a distinct transaction. * * * And without regard to whether the result is imposition or relief from taxation, the courts have recognized that where the essential nature of a transaction is the acquisition of property, it will be viewed as a whole, and closely related steps will not be separated either at the instance of the taxpayer or the taxing authority. Prairie Oil & Gas Co. v. Motter, 10 Cir., 66 F.2d 309; Tulsa Tribune Co. v. Commissioner, 10 Cir., 58 F.2d 937, 940; Ahles Realty Corp. v. Commissioner, 2 Cir., 71 F.2d 150; Helvering v. Security Savings Bank, 4 Cir., 72 F.2d 874. * * *

See also *Koppers Coal Co.,* 6 T.C. 1209 and cases there cited.

We hold that the purchase of Whaley's stock and its subsequent liquidation must be considered as one transaction, namely, the purchase of Whaley's assets which was petitioner's sole intention. This was not a reorganization within section 112(b)(6), and petitioner's basis in these assets, both depreciable and nondepreciable, is, therefore, its cost, or $110,721.74 ($18,921.90, the basis of petitioner's assets destroyed by fire, plus $91,799.84, the amount expended over the insurance proceeds). Since petitioner does not controvert respondent's allocation of cost to the individual assets acquired from Whaley, both depreciable and nondepreciable, respondent's allocation is sustained.

* * *

NOTE

If the stock purchase and subsequent liquidation of the target-subsidiary in *Kimbell–Diamond* had been treated as separate transactions, the buyer would have taken a (higher) transferred basis in the target's assets under Section 334(b)(1). The court looked to the buyer's intent, however, in holding that the stock purchase was merely a transitory step in a transaction that was properly characterized as a purchase of assets. Under this application of the step transaction doctrine, the liquidation was disregarded, and the buyer took a cost basis in the assets.

In the 1954 Code, Congress replaced the elusive intent standard of *Kimbell–Diamond* with a more objective test.[1] If a corporation purchased a controlling (80 percent or more) stock interest in the target corporation and then liquidated the target within a specific period of time, the acquiring corporation was treated as if it had purchased the target's assets. In general, the acquiring corporation took a cost basis in the assets equal to what it paid for the stock rather than the usual transferred basis that results from the liquidation of a controlled subsidiary. Although more "objective" than *Kimbell–Diamond,* the 1954 Code rules were laden with timetables, control and "purchase" requirements and a host of adjustments for cash distributions, liabilities assumed and transactions occurring after the acquisition but prior to the liquidation. Additional problems were created by the requirement that the buyer liquidate the newly acquired target in order to secure a *Kimbell–Diamond* cost basis in the target's assets.[2]

Congress responded to these deficiencies by enacting Section 338, which refines the *Kimbell–Diamond* concept by allowing the acquiring corporation to elect to treat certain stock purchases as asset purchases. Unlike *Kimbell–Diamond* and the prior statutory scheme, Section 338 does not require a corporate buyer of stock to liquidate the target to get a cost basis in its assets. This is convenient when the buyer wishes to keep the target alive as a subsidiary. Under current law, a corporation that acquires control (i.e., at least 80 percent) of a target corporation in a transaction that is taxable to the selling shareholders is thus presented with four basic choices. It may: (1) not make the Section 338 election and keep T alive, leaving T's bases in its assets and other tax attributes unaffected; (2) not elect under Section 338, liquidate T tax-free under Section 332 and inherit its asset bases and other tax attributes;[3] (3) make the Section 338 election and treat the transaction as an asset acquisition under which "new T" takes a cost basis in its assets and is purged of all of its prior tax attributes; or (4) make the election and then liquidate T, inheriting the cost basis in the assets but not any of "old T's" tax attributes.[4]

Before proceeding further, it is important to keep in mind that *Kimbell–Diamond* and Section 338 originated in the *General Utilities* era, when liquidating distributions and sales generally did not trigger a corporate-

---

1. I.R.C. § 334(b)(2) (pre–1982).

2. For historians and masochists, see Bittker & Eustice, Federal Income Taxation of Corporations and Shareholders ¶ 11.45 (5th ed. 1987).

3. Note that the tax treatment of this method is contrary to *Kimbell–Diamond,* which would have treated a stock purchase followed by a prompt intended liquidation of the target as an asset acquisition, giving P a cost basis in T's assets rather than a transferred basis and, under current law, causing T to recognize gain or loss on the sale.

4. T or P's ability to utilize T's net operating losses in the first two situations may be limited. See I.R.C. §§ 269(b); 382; and Chapter 12, infra.

level tax. The principal question then confronting a corporate buyer of stock was whether to take a cost basis or a transferred basis in the target's assets. If T's assets were appreciated, a well advised corporate buyer would make the Section 338 election in order to obtain a stepped-up cost basis in the target's assets at little or no corporate-level tax cost. The stakes are vastly different today, where liquidating sales and distributions generally are taxable events. If a stock purchase is treated as an asset acquisition, the target must recognize gain or loss, and one of the parties (buyer or seller, or both) must bear the economic burden of the corporate tax imposed on any gain. Accordingly, the Section 338 election is undesirable in virtually all cases where the target's assets are appreciated because it rarely makes economic sense to elect to pay tax currently in order to step up the basis of assets and avoid tax later. Section 338 nonetheless survives in the 1986 Code, along with reams of intricate regulations, and it remains an attractive option in a few situations that are discussed below.

2. OPERATION OF SECTION 338

Code: §§ 338(a), (b)(omit (b)(3)), (d), (e)(1), (2)(A) and (D), (g), (h)(1), (2), (3)(A), (4)(A), (5), (6)(A), (9), (11).

Regulations: §§ 1.338–4(a), (b)(1) & (2), (c), (d)(1), (e), –5(a), (b)(1) & (2), (c), (d)(1), (e)(1)–(3).

Overview of Section 338. Section 338 is a complex statutory mechanism that seeks to equate for tax purposes the purchase of an 80 percent or more interest in the stock of the target corporation with a purchase of the target's assets. In general, the goals are to: (1) ensure that the target and its shareholders bear the same tax burden on a sale of the target's stock that they would have incurred on a sale of its assets followed by a complete liquidation; (2) provide the buyer with a cost basis in the assets of the target; and (3) terminate the tax attributes of the target and start afresh, without regard to whether or not the target is actually liquidated.

To achieve these goals, Section 338 provides that if a purchasing corporation ("P") purchases 80 percent or more of the stock of a target corporation ("T") within 12 months or less, it may elect to treat T as having sold all of its assets for their fair market value in a single transaction.[1] T must recognize gain or loss on the hypothetical asset sale, after which it returns as a virgin corporation ("new T") with a cost basis in its assets and none of its former tax attributes.[2] If T is liquidated, this cost basis simply carries over to the parent under the rules governing liquidations of a subsidiary.[3]

The contours of Section 338 are easier to explain than its details. The section is littered with anti-avoidance provisions, many of which are aimed at maneuvers that are beyond the scope of this book. Understanding Section 338 is eased by focusing on its fundamentals.

---

1. I.R.C. § 338(a).

2. I.R.C. § 338(b).

3. I.R.C. §§ 332; 334(b)(1). See Chapter 7C2, supra.

Qualification for Section 338. The Section 338 election is available only to a "purchasing corporation," which is defined as "any corporation which makes a qualified purchase of stock of another corporation."[4] A "qualified stock purchase" is a transaction or series of transactions in which one corporation acquires by "purchase" an 80 percent controlling interest in another corporation during a 12–month "acquisition period."[5] Roughly translated, all of this means that P must buy at least 80 percent of the stock of T within a 12–month period in transactions that are taxable to the selling shareholders.[6]

The Election. If a corporation makes a qualified stock purchase and desires to make the Section 338 election, it must do so no later than the fifteenth day of the ninth month beginning after the month in which the "acquisition date" occurs.[7] The acquisition date is the day within the 12–month acquisition period on which the 80 percent purchase requirement is satisfied.[8] Once made, a Section 338 election is irrevocable.[9] There is no turning back, even with the Commissioner's permission, if the results prove to be undesirable.

Effect of Election: Deemed Sale of Target Assets and Termination of Old Target's Existence. If P makes a qualified stock purchase and follows up with a timely Section 338 election, T is treated as having sold all of its assets at the close of the acquisition date for their "fair market value" in a single transaction and is treated as a new corporation which purchased all of its assets as of the beginning of the day after the acquisition date.[10] As a result, T recognizes gain or loss on this hypothetical sale, just as if it actually had sold its assets.[11] For purposes of this deemed sale, Section 338 provides that T is not treated as a member of an affiliated group if it otherwise might have been.[12] Although the income realized on the deemed asset sale may not be combined with the income of P or its affiliates for tax purposes, the economic burden of the tax liability resulting from the deemed sale is indirectly borne by P, which will factor it into the price to be

---

4. I.R.C. § 338(d)(1).

5. I.R.C. §§ 338(d)(3); 338(h)(1). The requisite stock interest is defined in Section 338(d)(3) by reference to Section 1504(a)(2), which defines "control" as possession of at least 80 percent of the total voting power and 80 percent of the total value of a corporation's stock.

6. "Purchase" is defined to exclude transactions that would not have resulted in the full recognition of gain or loss to the seller (i.e., reorganizations, gifts, bequests, Section 351 transfers) and acquisitions from certain "related persons" within the attribution rules of Section 318. I.R.C. § 318(h)(3).

7. I.R.C. § 338(g)(1).

8. I.R.C. § 338(h)(2).

9. I.R.C. § 338(g)(3).

10. I.R.C. § 338(a).

11. See Section B1 of this chapter, supra.

12. I.R.C. § 338(h)(9). This means that losses of P or any P affiliate or losses of a corporate parent or affiliate of T may not be used to shelter gains resulting from T's deemed asset sale, but T may deduct its own net operating losses against the gains from the deemed sale. See Reg. § 1.338–1(f)(3)(iv). A "consolidated deemed sale return" may be filed, however, by all target corporations acquired by a purchasing corporation on the same acquisition date if the targets were members of the same selling consolidated group. I.R.C. § 338(h)(15). Cf. I.R.C. § 338(h)(10) and Section C3 of this chapter, infra.

paid for the stock. On the day after the deemed sale, T is reincarnated. It returns as a new corporation with no earnings and profits or other tax attributes from its pre-deemed sale era and with a cost basis in the assets that it hypothetically purchased from its former self.[13] If all this talk about deemed transactions seems mysterious, keep in mind that it is simply the mechanism used by the Code to equate purchases of assets and stock when a Section 338 election is made.

Aggregate Deemed Sale Price. In the hypothetical asset sale triggered by a Section 338 election, T is treated as selling its assets for their "aggregate deemed sale price" ("ADSP").[14] This is easy to determine if 100 percent of T's stock is purchased in one transaction and not as easy if the stock purchases do not occur within 12 months or P does not acquire all of T's stock. In general, ADSP is the sum: of (1) the grossed-up amount realized on the sale to P of P's recently purchased T stock, and (2) the liabilities of old T, including tax liabilities from the deemed sale.[15] "Recently purchased stock" is T stock purchased by P during the 12–month acquisition period and held by P at the time of the qualified stock purchase.[16] Thus, if P purchased all of T's stock during the 12–month acquisition period, the ADSP is the total amount realized by the selling T shareholders plus old T's liabilities.

If P purchased less than 100 percent of T's outstanding shares during the 12–month acquisition period, then the concept of "grossed-up" amount realized comes into play. The grossed-up amount realized is an amount equal to the amount realized on the sale to P of P's recently purchased T stock without regard to costs of sale, divided by the percentage of T stock (by value) attributable to that recently purchased stock, less any selling costs (such as brokerage commissions) incurred by the selling T shareholders in connection with their sale of recently purchased stock that reduce their amount realized.[17] The function of this complex formula in situations where P does not acquire 100 percent of T stock is to approximate the total amount that would have been realized on the sale of T stock if P had purchased all the shares at the same average price that P paid for the shares actually purchased during the acquisition period. To illustrate, if during the 12–month acquisition period P purchased 80 percent of T's outstanding stock for $800,000, the grossed-up amount realized on the sale to P of P's recently purchased T stock would be $800,000/.80, or $1,000,000.

Remember that the theory underlying Section 338 is to replicate the tax consequences of an asset acquisition. If P were to purchase all of T's assets, the purchase price would reflect any T liabilities assumed or property transferred subject to liabilities as part of the transaction. Under the principles of the *Crane* case, T's amount realized in such an asset sale would include the amount of those liabilities. In a stock purchase, the

---

13. I.R.C. § 338(a)(2).

14. Reg. § 1.338–4(a).

15. Reg. § 1.338–4(b)(1), (d).

16. I.R.C. § 338(b)(6)(A).

17. Reg. § 1.338–4(c)(1).

amount paid by P for T's stock similarly will take into account the debts and liabilities on T's balance sheet as of the "acquisition date." To properly determine the deemed sale price of T's assets under Section 338, the ADSP is increased by liabilities of old T, including tax liabilities, that properly would be taken into account as amount realized on a disposition by T of its assets to an unrelated purchaser who assumed the liabilities or took assets subject to a liabilities of old T.[18]

Determination of Asset Basis After Deemed Purchase. New T's basis in its assets has been described as a *Kimbell–Diamond* type cost basis, but the actual approach used to determine the aggregate basis and allocate it among T's assets is not quite that simple. The regulations label new T's basis as the "adjusted grossed-up basis" ("AGUB").[19] The AGUB generally is the sum of: (1) the grossed-up basis in P's recently purchased T stock, (2) P's basis in nonrecently purchased T stock (e.g., T stock owned by P before the 12–month acquisition period), and (3) liabilities of new T, including any tax liabilities triggered by the deemed sale.[20] AGUB is similar but not necessarily identical to ADSP. If P holds only recently purchased stock in T and T has no contingent liabilities, the two calculations usually produce the same result.

To illustrate, assume again that during the 12–month acquisition period P purchased 80 percent of T's outstanding stock for $800,000 and assume P does not own any other T stock. In computing ADSP and AGUB, the grossed-up amount realized and the adjusted grossed-up basis are both $1,000,000.[21] But if P owns nonrecently purchased T stock with a per-share basis different than P's basis in its recently purchased stock, the calculation of the ADSP for old T's assets and the AGUB for new T's assets will produce different results.[22] The difference is attributable to the fact that the ADSP formula treats P's nonrecently purchased stock the same as stock that is held by T shareholders other than P, while the AGUB formula uses P's actual basis in its nonrecently purchased T stock. P can make an election to recognize gain on its nonrecently purchased T stock.[23] If such an election is made, the sum of the grossed-up basis in P's recently purchased T stock and P's basis in any nonrecently purchased stock will equal the

---

18. Reg. § 1.338–4(d)(1). General tax principles control the time that liabilities are taken into account. See Reg. § 1.338–4(d)(2). Since determination of the ADSP may depend, in part, on the tax liability triggered by the deemed sale, and old T's tax liability depends on the ADSP, the calculation is potentially circular. The regulations recognize that the determination of ADSP may require trial and error computations. Reg. § 1.338–4(e). They also include examples of a formula to resolve this mathematical teaser. To revisit high school algebra, see Reg. § 1.338–4(g) Examples.

19. Reg. § 1.338–5(a).

20. Reg. § 1.338–5(b)(1).

21. For ADSP, see Reg. § 1.338–4(c); for AGUB, see Reg. § 1.338–5(b), (c).

22. Contingent liabilities that are taken into account in determining a seller's amount realized but are not yet properly included in a purchaser's basis also may be the source of an initial disparity that usually will be corrected by later adjustments. See, e.g., Reg. § 1.338–5(b)(2)(ii).

23. I.R.C. 338(h)(3). Losses on nonrecently purchased stock are not allowed. Reg. § 1.338–5(d)(3)(iii).

ADSP.[24] The election, however, requires P to currently recognize gain on its nonrecently purchased T stock, and so it usually is not desirable from a tax standpoint.

Allocation of Adjusted Grossed–Up Basis Among Target Assets. If P makes a Section 338 election, new T's aggregate AGUB is allocated among its assets under regulations promulgated under Section 338(b)(5). These regulations utilize the same seven-class system and reporting requirements previously discussed with respect to basis allocations in asset acquisitions.[25]

Consistency Rules. Section 338 allows a purchasing corporation to take a transferred basis in T's assets (by not making the election) or, at the cost of a tax on any gain (or deducting any loss) inherent in the target's assets, to take essentially a fair market value basis in those assets. When Section 338 was enacted, the consistency requirement was designed to ensure that P was put to a choice: it could select one or the other, but not both (or some of each) of these options. To achieve that objective, Section 338(e) was intended to prevent P from acquiring some assets from T or an affiliate of T with a cost basis and other assets with a transferred basis during a "consistency period" that begins one year before the start of the acquisition period and extends to one year after the acquisition date.[26] Under Section 338(e), if P acquired such an asset from T during the consistency period, it was deemed to make a Section 338 election with respect to the purchase of T's stock, unless T sold the asset in the ordinary course of its business (e.g., a routine sale of inventory) or P took a transferred basis in the asset.[27] Section 338(f) was designed to ensure that if P makes a qualified stock purchase with respect to T and one or more affiliates (e.g., a wholly owned subsidiary) of T during any consistency period, then all such qualified stock purchases must be treated consistently under Section 338; an election with respect to the first applies to all later qualified stock purchases and if no election is made for the first purchase, none may be made for later ones.

In the final Section 338 regulations, the Treasury significantly narrowed the reach of the consistency period rules because they were designed to patrol against exploitation of the long ago repealed *General Utilities* doctrine. Under the regulations, the asset consistency rules of Section 338(e) generally apply only if P acquires an asset directly from T during the consistency period and T is a subsidiary of another corporation ("S") in a consolidated group.[28] Under the regulations, the stock consistency rules of Section 338(f) are now limited by the regulations to preventing avoidance of the asset consistency rules.[29]

Understanding the limited application of the asset consistency period rules requires a very basic knowledge of the consolidated return regula-

24. See Reg. § 1.338–5(d)(3).

25. See Section C4 of this chapter, supra; Reg. § 1.338–6.

26. I.R.C. § 338(h)(4)(A).

27. I.R.C. § 338(e)(2)(A) and (B).

28. Reg. § 1.338–8(a)(2). The rules are also extended to a few other limited abuse cases that are well beyond the coverage of this text. See Reg. § 1.338–8(a)(3),(4).

29. Reg. § 1.338–8(a)(6).

tions, which generally permit a parent corporation in a consolidated group to increase the basis for its stock in a subsidiary when the subsidiary recognizes a taxable gain on the sale of one of its assets.[30] The relationship of this rule to Section 338 is best illustrated by the following example provided by the Treasury where P is the purchasing corporation, T is the target and S is T's parent:[31]

> The proposed regulations apply the consistency rules in the context of consolidated groups to prevent acquisitions from being structured to take advantage of the investment adjustment rules. If the consistency rules did not apply in such a case, P could acquire assets from T with a stepped-up basis in the assets, and then acquire the T stock at no additional cost to the S group.

> Example. S and T file a consolidated return. S has a $100x basis in the T stock, which has a fair market value of $200x. On January 1, 1993, T sells an asset to P and recognizes $100x of gain. Under § 1.1502–32 [of the consolidated return regulations], S's basis in the T stock is increased from $100x to $200x. On March 1, 1993, S sells the T stock to P for $200x and recognizes no gain or loss.

> The consistency rules of the proposed regulations apply to the transaction because T's gain on the asset sale is reflected under § 1.1502–32 in S's basis in the T stock. However, under the proposed regulations, the District Director no longer has the discretion to impose a deemed section 338 election for T. Instead, under proposed [regulation] § 1.338–4(d), P takes a carryover basis in any asset acquired from T. (This is referred to as the carryover basis rule).

Section 338 Election Coupled With Liquidation of T. If P purchases 80 percent or more of T stock, makes a Section 338 election, and then promptly liquidates T, the stock purchase and subsequent liquidation of T are accorded independent significance for tax purposes—i.e., they are not stepped together and treated as an integrated transaction. P is treated as having made a qualified stock purchase rather than a direct acquisition of assets under the *Kimbell–Diamond* doctrine.[32] On the liquidation, P recognizes no gain or loss under Section 332, and T recognizes no gain or loss on the distribution of its assets to P under Section 337. In any event, neither P nor T would have any significant realized gain or loss because at least 80 percent of the T stock would have been recently purchased, and any built-in gain on T's assets was recognized as a result of the Section 338 deemed asset sale. After the liquidation, P succeeds to T's fair market value basis in its assets.

30. See Reg. § 1.1502–32 and Chapter 13, infra.

31. See Preamble, Prop. Reg. §§ 1.338–4, –5 (CO–111–90), issued Jan. 14, 1992 (1992–1 C.B. 1000).

32. Reg. § 1.338–3(c)(1)(i). See also Rev.Rul. 90–95, 1990–2 C.B. 67 (stating that "Section 338 replaced the *Kimbell–Diamond* doctrine").

Stock Acquisitions Without Section 338 Election. The tax consequences of an acquisition of 80 percent or more of T's stock with no Section 338 election are less complicated. T's shareholders, as always, recognize gain or loss on the sale of their stock. T becomes a subsidiary of P and retains its tax attributes, including the historic basis in its assets, earnings and profits, and the like. If P subsequently liquidates T, or T merges into P or another P subsidiary, neither P nor T recognizes gain or loss, and T's asset bases and other tax attributes carry over to the transferee.[33] Significantly, the initial qualified stock purchase and subsequent liquidation of T (or merger of T into P or a P affiliate) are not treated as an integrated transaction (e.g., as a direct purchase of T's assets by P) even if all the steps were planned from the outset. If the transactions were integrated, T would recognize gain or loss on its assets, a result which is fundamentally inconsistent with P's decision not to make a Section 338 election. The extent to which T (if it stays alive) or P (if it liquidates T) may utilize T's net operating losses after the acquisition is likely to be limited by Section 382, which is examined in a later chapter.[34]

3. ACQUISITION OF STOCK OF A SUBSIDIARY

Section 338(h)(10) Election. The previous discussion assumed that T was not a subsidiary of another corporation. Consider, however, the situation where T is a wholly owned subsidiary of Seller, Inc. ("S"), and P wishes to acquire T. Assume that the value of T's stock (and also its underlying assets) is $400,000; S has a $100,000 basis in its T stock; and T has a $100,000 aggregate basis in its assets. T could sell its assets directly to P for $400,000 in a taxable transaction and then distribute the sales proceeds to S in a tax-free liquidation under Section 332, with the net result being $300,000 of taxable gain to T on the asset sale. Alternatively, T could distribute the assets to S in a tax-free liquidation. S would take the assets with a $100,000 transferred basis under Section 334(b) and recognize $300,000 gain on a sale to P. In either case, S does not recognize gain or loss on its T stock, and P acquires the assets with a $400,000 cost basis. If the disappearance of S's $300,000 gain on its T stock seems inconsistent with the double tax regime, remember that no assets have yet been distributed out of corporate solution to the shareholders of S, the real people who own the enterprise. The policy is to avoid three levels of tax on what may be a single economic gain.

Now assume that for nontax reasons P must acquire T's stock. Under general tax principles, S would recognize gain or loss on the sale of its T stock and P would take the stock with a cost basis. If P makes a Section 338 election, T also is treated as having sold its assets in a taxable transaction. If P does not elect, the bases of T's assets are unchanged and any built-in gain or loss is preserved. Either way, the result is double

---

33. Rev. Rul. 90–95, supra note 32. See also Reg. § 1.338–2(c)(3)(i), discussed in Chapter 9B1, infra.

34. See Chapter 12, infra, and I.R.C. § 269(b).

corporate-level gain, with the potential of a third round of taxation when S distributes the sales proceeds to its shareholders.

Section 338(h)(10) offers relief from this potential triple tax by permitting the parties to ignore S's sale of its T stock and treat the transaction as if it were a sale of T's assets.[1] If a Section 338(h)(10) election is made,[2] the transaction is treated as if old T sold its assets to an unrelated person (new T) while a member of the S consolidated group, and T then distributed its assets (i.e., the proceeds of sale) to S and ceased to exist. In most cases, the final step of the various hypothetical transactions is treated as a tax-free liquidation of T under Sections 332 and 337.[3] The tax consequences of the election are: (1) S recognizes no gain or loss on the sale of its T stock; (2) S inherits T's tax attributes (e.g., earnings and profits);[4] (3) T is treated as having sold its assets for their fair market value in a taxable transaction,[5] and any gain or loss is included on the consolidated return filed by S and its affiliates; and (4) "new T," a subsidiary of P, is treated as having acquired old T's assets for an amount equal to their adjusted grossed-up basis.[6] Two levels of corporate-level gain are thus avoided, and the tax burden of the sale remains with the seller.

Returning to the example, if the parties make a Section 338(h)(10) election, S's $300,000 gain on the sale of its T stock is ignored, and the $300,000 gain on the deemed sale of T's assets[7] is included on the consolidated tax return filed by S and its affiliates. P takes a $400,000 cost basis in the T stock and "new T" takes a $400,000 basis in its assets.

Although the Section 338(h)(10) election is generally desirable because it eliminates two levels of corporate-level gain, it has particular allure when S has a large "outside" gain on its T stock relative to minimal "inside" gain on T's assets. In that scenario, P may purchase T's stock at little or no tax cost to S if the parties make a Section 338(h)(10) election. Of course, the same result could have been achieved if S first liquidated T under

---

1. In general, before the transaction T must be a member of "the selling consolidated group." I.R.C. § 338(h)(10)(A). A "selling consolidated group" is any group of corporations which, for the taxable period which includes the transaction, includes T and files a consolidated tax return. I.R.C. § 338(h)(10)(B). A qualified seller also may be any "affiliated group" of corporations (within the meaning of Section 1504) which includes T, whether or not the group files a consolidated return. See generally Reg. § 1.338(h)(10)–1(b)(3).

2. The election must be made jointly by the S group and P. See Reg. § 1.338(h)(10)–1(c)(2).

3. See Reg. § 1.338(h)(10)–1(d).

4. These inherited tax attributes generally are reduced in proportion to the percent-

age of old T stock held by minority shareholders. Cf. Reg. § 1.381(c)(2)–1(c)(2).

5. The deemed sale price is determined under a formula prescribed by the regulations, which refers to the actual purchase price paid by P for the T stock and is adjusted for liabilities of T. See Reg. §§ 1.338(h)(10)–1(d)(3)(i); 1.338–4.

6. I.R.C. § 338(b). The adjusted grossed-up basis for new T's assets is determined under Reg. § 1.338–5 and is allocated among the assets under the approach discussed earlier in this chapter. Reg. § 1.338(h)(10)–1(d)(2).

7. We have assumed for convenience that the deemed sale price equals the $400,000 fair market value of T's assets.

Section 332 and sold the assets to P, but this method might not be feasible if P needs to keep T alive as a corporate entity for nontax reasons.

The election also is attractive when S's consolidated group has losses that can be applied to offset any gain recognized by T on the deemed sale of its assets. If Section 338 were elected without an accompanying Section 338(h)(10) election, T must file a separate one day return reporting the income from the deemed sale and it could not offset its gain with any losses from S's other operations. If a Section 338(h)(10) election is made, however, the gain on the deemed sale is reported on S's consolidated return and may be offset by losses of S and its other affiliates.

The regulations extend the availability of the Section 338(h)(10) election to two additional situations. First, they permit the election when T and S are affiliated corporations even if T is not a member of the S consolidated group if S sells stock representing at least 80 percent of the voting power and value of T to P on the "acquisition date."[8] Second, a Section 338(h)(10) election is permitted if T is an S corporation immediately before the acquisition date.[9] If T is an S corporation, the gain on the deemed sale of T's assets is reported on old T's final S corporation return and passes through to T's shareholders, who may make appropriate adjustments to the basis of their T stock.[10] These adjustments will affect the gain or loss recognized by these shareholders on the deemed liquidation of old T, and no additional gain or loss is recognized on the actual stock sale. The taxation of S corporations and their shareholders is examined in Chapter 20.

4. Section 336(e)

Section 336(e) is a close but obscure relative of Section 338(h)(10). In some cases, it is an identical twin. Section 336(e) provides that, upon the promulgation of regulations, a corporation that owns at least 80 percent of the voting power and value of the stock of another corporation may elect to treat a sale, exchange or distribution of that subsidiary's stock as if it were a disposition of the subsidiary's assets. If a Section 336(e) election is made, the parent does not recognize gain or loss on the disposition of the subsidiary's stock. The legislative history of Section 336(e) states that "principles similar to those of Section 338(h)(10)" will be used in determining the operation of the Section 336(e) election.[1]

The overlap between Sections 336(e) and 338(h)(10) is apparent when a parent sells the stock of a controlled subsidiary to a corporate purchaser. Section 336(e) is potentially broader, however, and could apply even if the buyer were an individual or entity (such as a partnership) that is not qualified to make a Section 338 election. Moreover, Section 336(e) is not

---

8. Reg. §§ 1.338(h)(10)–1(c)(1), –1(b)(3), –1(d)(4).

9. Reg. §§ 1.338(h)(10)–1(c)(1), –1(b)(4), –1(d)(4).

10. Reg. § 1.338(h)(10)–1(d)(5)(i).

1. H.R.Rep. No. 841, 99th Cong., 2d Sess. II–204.

confined to sales. It potentially encompasses both liquidating and perhaps even nonliquidating distributions of the stock of a subsidiary.

Section 336(e) remains an empty shell without the further details that Congress left to the Treasury to develop through regulations. In 2008, a mere 22 years after Section 336(e) was enacted, the Treasury launched that process by issuing proposed regulations.[2] When finalized, they will permit a corporation with "control" of another corporation ("T") to make an election under Section 336(e) to treat certain sales, exchanges, and distributions of T stock as taxable sales of T's assets. The proposed regulations provide useful guidance on the scope of Section 336(e) and its relationship to Section 338(h)(10), and the requirements for and mechanics of a Section 336(e) election.

For most purposes, the proposed regulations utilize principles established under Section 338(h)(10) except certain familiar definitions have been modified to reflect the greater breadth of Section 336(e). For example, the regulations use the term "disposition" rather than "acquisition" or "purchase" and the terms "sale, exchange or distribution" instead of just "sale." Thus, a "qualified stock purchase" under Section 338 is a "qualified stock disposition" under Section 336(e). The regulations use the term "aggregate deemed disposition price" instead of "aggregate deemed sales price" but retain the much beloved "adjusted grossed up basis." The new term "nonrecently disposed stock" has a meaning similar to "nonrecently purchased stock" in Section 338.[3] To avoid overlap, the regulations make it clear that a transaction satisfying the definition of "qualified stock purchase" in Section 338(d)(3) is governed exclusively by Section 338 and does not qualify for a Section 336(e) election.[4]

To qualify to make a Section 336(e) election, the seller must own stock in a domestic C corporation meeting the requirements of Section 1504(a)(2) (generally, 80 percent of voting power and value) and must sell, exchange, or distribute (including combinations thereof) all of such stock meeting the control requirement during a 12–month disposition period. Thus, some portion of T stock may be retained by the seller or a member of the seller's consolidated group. Any stock disposed of to a "related party" does not count for purposes of determining whether there has been a qualified stock disposition. The seller may unilaterally make a Section 336(e) election, unlike Section 338(h)(10), which requires a joint election by the seller and target corporations.[5]

In the case of a sale or exchange of T stock where a Section 336(e) election is made, the proposed regulations treat Old T as if it sold all its assets to an unrelated corporation (New T) at the close of the disposition date in exchange for the aggregate deemed disposition price (generally, the amount realized on the sale of the stock, adjusted for liabilities). Old T is

2. REG–143544–04, 2008–2 C.B. 947.

3. See generally Prop. Reg. § 1.336–1(b).

4. Prop. Reg. § 1.336–1(b)(5)(ii).

5. See generally Prop. Reg. § 1.336–1, –2(a).

then treated as having completely liquidated into New T.[6] If T stock is distributed as part of a qualified stock disposition, the transaction is treated as a sale of Old T's assets to New T, followed by a liquidation of Old T and a deemed purchase of New T stock by the seller followed by a tax-free distribution of that stock to the seller's shareholders.[7]

To be consistent with the loss limitation rule in Section 311(a) for actual nonliquidating distributions of loss property by a corporation, the regulations limit the recognition of losses on Section 336(e) deemed asset dispositions. This complicated rule effectively limits recognition of realized losses insofar as the deemed disposition of T assets is actually a distribution (rather than a sale or exchange) of T stock.[8]

With this fascinating survey completed, the question remains—so what?—or, put differently, what value does Section 336(e) add as a planning tool and does it include any traps? Here are some answers. Section 336(e) applies to *distributions* of T stock as well as sales and to a combination of sales, exchanges and distributions, and a Section 336(e) election is available even if the purchaser is not a corporation. By contrast, Section 338 does not apply to distributions or when T stock is acquired by a noncorporate purchaser. As noted above, Section 338(h)(10) requires both parties to the transaction to join in an election, while the proposed regulations permit the seller to make a Section 336(e) election unilaterally. In situations where T has NOLs or built-in losses on some assets, a Section 336(e) election will wipe out these tax attributes that otherwise would still have been available to T (subject to some limitations), and thus beneficial to the buyer, if the transaction had been treated for tax purposes as a stock sale. Buyers acquiring stock of a corporate subsidiary in a transaction that is not within Section 338(h)(10) are well advised to be aware of the tax consequences and related economic stakes of a unilateral Section 336(e) election, if it is available to the seller, and to address the issue in the acquisition agreement.

The Section 336(e) regulations are only proposed and the IRS is in no rush to make them final. Representatives of the IRS Chief Counsel's office have informally revealed that they may "rethink" aspects of these regulations and it "may take a little while" (one hopes not as long as the 22 years it took to issue the proposed regulations). No Section 336(e) elections are permitted until final regulations are issued.

PROBLEM

X Corp. owns 98 of the 100 outstanding shares of T Corp. common stock (the only class outstanding). The other 2 shares are owned by unrelated shareholders. T has some assets with built-in losses. In Year 1, X engages in the following transactions. On March 1, it sells 30 shares of T

---

6. Prop. Reg. § 1.336–2(b)(1)(i)(A), –2(b)(1)(ii), –2(b)(1)(iii).

7. Prop. Reg. § 1.336–2(b)(1)(iv).

8. See Prop. Reg. § 1.336–2(b)(1)(i)(B)(2) & (3).

stock to unrelated A for cash; on April 1, it sells 10 shares of T stock to R, a related individual; on July 1, it distributes 50 shares of T stock to X Corp.'s unrelated shareholders; and on December 1, it sells 5 shares of T stock to unrelated B. The value of T stock on July 1 is $100 per share.

(a) If the proposed § 336(e) regulations are made final, may a § 336(e) election be made and, if so, by whom?

(b) Assuming that a § 336(e) election may be made, what are the tax consequences to all relevant parties?

D.   Comparison of Acquisition Methods

A typical student's reaction to this chapter (or indeed the entire course up to now) might be something like this: "After considerable effort, I understand the workings of most Code sections as they are studied, but the course is becoming a conglomeration of random detail." The lament might continue with these questions about taxable corporate acquisitions: "How does it all fit together? Does it matter whether P buys T's assets or stock? What rational buyer ever would make the Section 338 election? Does substance control over form—or form over substance? When does the step transaction doctrine apply?" In short, the understandable plea is—"Give me some perspective!" This section attempts to respond by comparing taxable acquisition methods in a tax planning context, and by providing a comprehensive taxable acquisitions problem.

The repeal of the *General Utilities* doctrine greatly altered the tax economics of corporate acquisitions. Prior to that time, the tax consequences of an asset purchase followed by a complete liquidation, or a stock purchase coupled with a Section 338 election, were essentially the same. T's shareholders recognized a capital gain on their investment; T did not recognize gain or loss on the actual or deemed transfer of its assets except for recapture of depreciation and a few other items; and P (or "new T") obtained a fair market value basis in T's assets. In short, taxable acquisitions involved only a single, shareholder-level tax, which could be deferred if P used installment notes as partial consideration for the purchase.

After *General Utilities* repeal, an asset acquisition is much more expensive. It requires both T and its shareholders to recognize gain unless T does not liquidate. A stock purchase coupled with a Section 338 election is no better because the deemed asset sale results in full recognition of corporate-level gain. In either case, P obtains a fair market value basis in T's assets—but at the price of an immediate corporate-level tax. Corporate-level tax is avoided, however, if P purchases T's stock and does not elect under Section 338. It is perhaps ironic that, after years of effort to equate the tax treatment of different corporate acquisition methods, we are left with an asymmetrical system under which asset acquisitions require two levels of tax with no opportunity for T to defer tax through a transferred basis, while a stock acquisition without a Section 338 election requires only a shareholder-level tax, albeit with the trade-off of a transferred basis in T's assets.[1]

It follows that the preferred alternative for most taxable acquisitions is a stock purchase with no Section 338 election. It is rarely desirable to pay a front-end corporate tax on the gain inherent in T's assets in order to achieve tax savings later from the additional depreciation, amortization and other deductions that would flow from the stepped-up basis in T's assets. The two principal exceptions are: (1) where T has large net operating loss carryovers that would be available to offset the gain recognized on the deemed asset sale;[2] and (2) where T is a subsidiary of another corporation.[3]

The prospect of a two-tier tax also may tilt the method of choice in corporate acquisitions more towards tax-free reorganizations, where neither T nor its shareholders currently recognize gain or loss, but tax attributes at both the corporate and shareholder levels are preserved through transferred and exchanged bases. Acquisitive reorganizations are examined in Chapter 9.

PROBLEMS

1. Target Corporation ("T") is a "C" corporation. T's 1,000 shares of common stock (its only class) are owned by three unrelated individual shareholders as follows:

Shareholder	No. Shs.	Adj. Basis	F.M.V.
A	500	$ 50,000	$ 500,000
B	400	40,000	400,000
C	100	140,000	100,000
	1,000	$230,000	$1,000,000

A and B are in their late 70's and have held their T stock since the company was founded many years ago. C recently inherited her stock.

T has $400,000 of accumulated earnings and profits and the following assets (all held long-term) and liabilities:

Assets	Adj. Basis	F.M.V.
Cash	$200,000	$ 200,000
Inventory	50,000	100,000
Equipment ($100,000 § 1245 recapture)	100,000	200,000
Building (no recapture)	50,000	300,000

---

1. These lingering discontinuities are discussed in Zolt, "The *General Utilities* Doctrine: Examining the Scope of Repeal," 65 Taxes 819 (1987); Yin, "A Carryover Basis Regime? A Few Words of Caution," 37 Tax Notes 415 (1987); and Lewis, "A Proposal for a Corporate Level Tax on Major Stock Sales," 37 Tax Notes 1041 (1987).

2. These losses are available without limitation to offset the gain on T's deemed asset sale. If P acquired T and did not elect under Section 338, T's NOLs would not be purged but they likely would be limited in the future under Section 382. See Chapter 12, infra.

3. See I.R.C. § 338(h)(10) and Section C3 of this chapter, supra.

Securities	400,000	300,000
Goodwill	0	200,000
	$800,000	$1,300,000
Liabilities		
Bank loan		300,000
		$ 300,000

T and its shareholders are considering a sale of the business. Purchaser Corporation ("P") is interested in acquiring T. If specific computations are required by your instructor, assume (for computational convenience) that C corporations are taxed on all their income at a flat corporate rate of 35 percent and individuals are taxed at a flat 35 percent rate on ordinary income and a 15 percent rate on long-term capital gains.

What are the tax consequences of the following alternative acquisition methods to T, T's shareholders, and P?

(a) T adopts a plan of complete liquidation, sells all of its assets (except the cash but subject to the bank loan) to P for $800,000 cash, and distributes the after-tax proceeds to its shareholders in proportion to their stock holdings.

(b) T adopts a plan of complete liquidation, distributes all of its assets (subject to the liability) to its shareholders in proportion to their stock holdings, and the shareholders then sell the assets (less any cash but subject to the bank loan) to P for $800,000.

(c) In general, how would the result in (a), above, change if P paid T $200,000 in cash and $600,000 in notes, with market rate interest payable annually and the entire principal payable in five years?

(d) T sells all of its assets (except for the cash but subject to the bank loan) to P as in (a), above, except that T does not liquidate and instead invests the after-tax sales proceeds in a portfolio of publicly traded securities.

(e) P purchases all the stock of T for $800 per share and makes a § 338 election. (Why didn't P pay $1,000 per share for the T stock?)

(f) P purchases all the stock of T for cash but does not make the § 338 election. (Consider generally what P should pay for the T stock.)

(g) Assuming P and T are indifferent to the form of the transaction, would you recommend the acquisition method in (a) (purchase of assets), (e) (purchase of stock with § 338 election) or (f) (purchase of stock without § 338 election), above?

(h) Would your recommendation in (g), above, change if T had $600,000 in net operating loss carryovers?

(i) Assume that T is a wholly-owned subsidiary of S, Inc., and S has a $200,000 adjusted basis in its T stock. What result if T distributes all of its assets (subject to the liability) to S in complete liquidation, and S then sells the assets to P?

(j) Same as (i), above, except P insists that the transaction must be structured as an acquisition of T stock.

2. Should Congress enact legislation that treats taxable asset and stock acquisitions consistently for tax purposes? If so, what are its options and which would you support?

E. TAX TREATMENT OF ACQUISITION EXPENSES

The expenses incurred in connection with a corporate acquisition may be substantial. Both the purchaser ("P") and the target ("T") ordinarily must pay fees to lawyers, accountants and investment bankers. P may incur additional expenses to obtain debt and equity financing, and T may be obligated to secure an opinion stating that the proposed acquisition is "fair" to T and its shareholders. In virtually all cases, the central tax question becomes whether the expenses are currently deductible, amortizable, capitalized and added to the basis of a particular tangible or intangible asset, or treated as a permanent nondepreciable capital expenditure.

The tax treatment of P's expenses are relatively settled. Costs of obtaining debt financing (such as fees for negotiating the loan and drafting loan documents, up-front commitment fees and other fees paid to the lender) generally must be amortized over the term of the loan to which the expenses relate.[1] Likewise, expenses of obtaining equity financing (e.g., to register newly issued stock, prepare offering documents, etc.) are treated as permanent capital expenditures that are neither currently deductible nor amortizable.[2] Costs attributable to the acquisition of particular T assets or T stock (e.g., legal expenses for drafting an acquisition agreement, closing costs, finder's fees) also are capital expenditures and must be added to the basis of the acquired property.[3] If P forms a new subsidiary to carry out the acquisition, the organizational expenses are currently deductible (up to $5,000, but reduced as total expenses exceed $50,000), with any excess over the deductible amount amortizable over 15 years if P elects to apply Section 248. In addition, P may attempt to classify certain expenses related to an acquisition as normal business expenses. Examples would include expenses related to employment agreements, executive compensation and retirement planning, tax planning, and the annual retainer paid to an investment banker that may have helped arrange the acquisition.

The tax treatment of T's expenses has been more controversial. Assume for example that the target in a friendly corporate takeover incurs legal, investment banking and other fees, including the cost of obtaining an opinion that the terms of the acquisition are fair to T and its shareholders.

---

1. Rev.Rul. 70–359, 1970–2 C.B. 103; Rev.Rul. 70–360, 1970–2 C.B. 103.

2. Rev.Rul. 69–330, 1969–1 C.B. 51.

3. If P acquires T's stock and makes a Section 338 election, these capital expenditures become part of new T's adjusted grossed-up basis and may be allocated among T's assets in accordance with the rules in Sections 338(b)(5) and 1060. See Reg. § 1.338(b)–1(g)(1).

Are these expenses currently deductible by T as ordinary and necessary businesses expenses under Section 162 or must they be capitalized? In INDOPCO, Inc. v. Commissioner,[4] the Supreme Court held that investment banking fees and other expenses incurred by a target corporation in a friendly takeover were nondeductible capital expenditures because they produced significant long-term benefits, such as the availability of the acquiring corporation's resources, the opportunity for synergy, and the benefits resulting from the target's transformation from a public company to a wholly owned subsidiary. In ruling for the government, the Court held that the creation or enhancement of a separate or distinct asset was not controlling in resolving capital expenditure classification questions. In so doing, it rejected the taxpayer's reliance on a line of appellate decisions that had interpreted the Court's opinion in Commissioner v. Lincoln Savings & Loan Association[5] as adopting a test under which creation or enhancement of an asset is a prerequisite to capitalization. The Court clarified its earlier decision in *Lincoln Savings*, stating that the creation of a separate and distinct asset may be a sufficient reason for capitalizing an expense but not an essential prerequisite. It noted further that *Lincoln Savings* did not prohibit reliance on "future benefit" as a test for distinguishing an ordinary business expense from a capital expenditure. However, the Court conceded that an "incidental future benefit" may not require capitalization but that the taxpayer's realization of benefits beyond the year in which the expenditure was incurred is an important factor in distinguishing ordinary business expenses from capital expenditures.

Soon after it was decided, commentators began to focus on the potential ripple effect of the Supreme Court's *INDOPCO* decision—specifically whether the Court's reasoning would be imported to deny deductibility of various other expenses. The Service has calmed most of these nerves, first in a series of rulings confirming the current deductibility of many expenditures[6] and more recently in extensive taxpayer-friendly regulations.[7]

INDOPCO involved a friendly takeover. Should expenses incurred to resist a hostile takeover be treated differently? The contexts in which this issue arises include both defending against a hostile takeover by a corporate raider and arranging for a taxable acquisition by a more friendly "White Knight" buyer. The cases so far indicate that the tax treatment of such expenditures may depend on the eventual outcome of the transaction. In United States v. Federated Department Stores, Inc.,[8] a corporate taxpayer, faced with a hostile offer, arranged a White Knight transaction and

---

4. 503 U.S. 79, 112 S.Ct. 1039 (1992).

5. 403 U.S. 345, 91 S.Ct. 1893 (1971).

6. See, e.g., Rev. Rul. 95–32, 1995–16 I.R.B. 5 (expenditures by a public utility for the implementation and operation of energy conservation and load management programs are deductible under Section 162); Rev. Rul. 94–77, 1994–2 C.B. 19 (severance payments to employees are generally deductible under Section 162); Rev. Rul. 94–38, 1994–1 C.B. 35 (costs to clean up land and treat groundwater contaminated by taxpayer are deductible under Section 162); Rev. Rul. 94–12, 1994–1 C.B. 36 (incidental repair costs are deductible under Section 162); Rev. Rul. 92–80, 1992–2 C.B. 57 (advertising costs are generally deductible under Section 162).

7. See generally Reg. § 1.263(a)–4, –5.

8. 171 B.R. 603 (S.D.Ohio 1994).

agreed to pay "break-up" fees to the White Knight if their merger fell through. Eventually, the hostile bidder was successful and the break-up fees were paid to the White Knight. The Court held that the fees were currently deductible under either Section 162 or Section 165 (as costs incurred in an abandoned transaction). Distinguishing *INDOPCO*, the court found that the fees were incurred to defend the business against attack and not to restructure the corporation in hopes of some future benefit.

In A.E. Staley Manufacturing Co. v. Commissioner,[9] the Tax Court considered a situation where a corporation incurred $23 million in investment bankers' fees and printing costs to respond to a series of hostile tender offers for its stock. The company's board of directors declined two offers but eventually accepted a third bid. Rejecting the taxpayer's argument that *INDOPCO* was distinguishable because the takeover in *Staley* was hostile, the Tax Court held that the fees and costs were nondeductible because they were incurred in connection with a change in the ownership of the taxpayer that "portended strategic changes * * * with long-term consequences" and were capital in nature.[10] The Tax Court also distinguished *Federated Department Stores* because (1) there was no White Knight transaction that could be treated as abandoned and eligible for a loss deduction, and (2) the taxpayer received significant future benefits as a result of the acquisition.[11] Thus, according to the Tax Court the critical question is not whether the transaction is "friendly" or "hostile" but whether an identifiable loss has been sustained and the costs were incurred to realize future benefits.[12]

On appeal, however, the Seventh Circuit reversed and permitted the target corporation to deduct most of the expenses it incurred in resisting a hostile takeover.[13] The court reasoned that *INDOPCO* did not change the law with respect to costs incurred to defend a business because those expenses were to preserve the status quo, not to produce future benefits. It concluded that most of the expenses incurred by the taxpayer in *A.E. Staley* were related to the defense of its business and corporate policy and thus were currently deductible under Section 162(a). Costs properly allocable to unsuccessful efforts to engage in an alternate transaction to prevent the acquisition, such as a financial restructuring, recapitalization, or joint venture, were held to be deductible losses under Section 165. The court also held that fees paid to evaluate the taxpayer's stock and to facilitate the eventual merger were nondeductible capital expenditures.

---

9. 105 T.C. 166 (1995).

10. Id. at 200.

11. Id. at 199.

12. The Service also does not seem to base the tax consequences of the expenditure on whether the takeover was hostile. In Tech. Adv. Memo. 9144042 (July 1, 1991), a target corporation was required to capitalize expenses incurred to thwart a hostile tender

offer. On the facts presented (the target incurred expenses in repurchasing its own stock from a corporate raider), the Service reasoned that the taxpayer failed to prove that the expenditure did not confer a long-term benefit.

13. A.E. Staley Manufacturing Co. v. Commissioner, 119 F.3d 482 (7th Cir.1997).

If either P or T incurs costs in investigating or attempting to consummate an acquisition that ultimately fails, the transactional costs generally are currently deductible as losses under Section 165.[14]

The Service has issued lengthy regulations under Section 263 relating to the tax treatment of amounts incurred to acquire, create, or enhance various kinds of intangible assets.[15] The regulations specify, in extraordinary detail, various categories of rights, privileges and future benefits for which capital expenditure treatment is required. Particular goals of this regulations project were to bring greater clarity to (some would say "erode" or "discard") the "significant future benefit" standard enunciated by the Supreme Court in Indopco, Inc. v. Commissioner, and to resurrect the more taxpayer-friendly "separate and distinct asset" approach of the Court's earlier *Lincoln Savings* decision. The effect of this new liberalized regime is to presume that outlays related to intangible assets are currently deductible unless these or subsequently issued regulations specifically require capitalization.

The regulations include specific rules on an acquisition of a trade or business, a change in the capital structure of a business entity, and certain other transactions such as Section 351 exchanges.[16] Costs that "facilitate" such transactions must be capitalized.[17] This standard is consistent with the previously discussed case law on the purchaser's acquisition expenses. Transaction costs incurred to defend against a hostile takeover are not viewed as facilitating the acquisition. As a result, they may be currently deducted rather than capitalized.[18] This rule follows the Seventh Circuit's decision in *A.E. Staley*. If an initially hostile acquisition becomes friendly, the taxpayer must bifurcate the costs between those incurred to defend against the hostile takeover and those incurred to facilitate the friendly acquisition, using a "facts and circumstances" standard to draw the line.[19] Costs incurred to thwart a hostile acquisition, such as by merging with a White Knight, must be capitalized even if the taxpayer's overall purpose was to defend against a hostile acquisition.[20] But legal fees paid to seek an injunction against a hostile takeover and investment banking fees to locate a potential White Knight acquirer may be currently deducted.[21] And there's much more, including simplifying conventions (e.g., compensation to employees are treated as amounts that do not facilitate a transaction and thus are currently deductible),[22] de minimis exceptions (transaction costs of $5,000 or less generally do not have to be capitalized),[23] and timing rules.[24]

---

14. Rev.Rul. 73–580, 1973–2 C.B. 86.

15. Reg. § 1.263(a)–4, –5, T.D. 9107, 69 Fed. Reg. 436 (Jan. 5, 2004).

16. See Reg. § 1.263(a)–5(a). For accounting rules for debt issuance costs that must be capitalized, see Reg. § 1.446–5.

17. Id. Costs that facilitate the acquisition of an intangible generally must be capitalized under Reg. § 1.263(a)–4(b)(1)(v), (e).

18. Reg. § 1.263(a)–5(l) Example 11.

19. Id. See also Reg. § 1.263(a)–5(l) Example 12.

20. Reg. § 1.263(a)–5(l) Example 11.

21. Id.

22. Reg. § 1.263(a)–5(d)(2).

23. Reg. § 1.263(a)–5(d)(3).

24. Reg. § 1.263(a)–5(e).

F.   POLICY ISSUES: CORPORATE ACQUISITIONS AND THE PROBLEM OF EXCESSIVE DEBT

The tax bias in favor of debt financing and the difficulties in distinguishing between debt and equity were previewed in Chapter 3 principally in the context of the capital structure of a closely held C corporation. The wave of corporate restructurings of public companies that began in the 1980s raised the stakes on this vexing issue. Transactions such as corporate takeovers, redemptions of stock, debt-for-equity swaps and extraordinary distributions resulted in a reduction of $313.3 billion in corporate equity while new net corporate borrowing increased by $613.3 billion. The ratio of debt to equity of nonfinancial corporations increased from 30.3 percent in 1981 to 46 percent in 1987.[1] Although these developments undoubtedly were motivated by many factors other than the interest deduction allowed to corporate borrowers, the preferred tax treatment of debt has become a powerful influence on corporate financing behavior.

In early 1989, the Congressional tax-writing committees held hearings to examine the federal income tax aspects of corporate financial structures and to consider the problem of debt-financed acquisitions. In the wake of the $25 billion leveraged buyout of RJR Nabisco, Inc., a few influential legislators proposed to disallow interest deductions on any debt used to finance a corporate acquisition.[2] The Treasury attempted to change the subject by noting that if the corporate and individual income taxes were integrated, the problems of excessive debt would disappear.[3]

Some illustrative transactions and the policy issues they raise are addressed in the excerpts below from a study prepared by the Joint Committee on Taxation in connection with the 1989 hearings. The Note following the excerpt discusses the narrowly targeted Congressional response to these concerns. Keep in mind that this discussion occurred before the introduction in 2003 of a temporary (at least through 2012) preferential rate on qualified dividends, which reduces but does not eliminate the tax bias favoring debt over equity.

1. Joint Committee on Taxation, Federal Income Aspects of Corporate Financial Structures, 101st Cong., 1st Sess. 2 (JCS 1–89, 1989).

2. For a survey of the "Stamp Out LBOs movement," see Mentz, Carlisle & Nevas, "Leveraged Buyouts: A Washington Perspective of 1989 Legislation and Prospects for 1990," 46 Tax Notes 1047 (Feb. 26, 1990).

3. Id., at 1049, quoting testimony by Secretary of the Treasury Nicholas Brady before the Senate Finance Committee, Jan. 24, 1989. For an overview of the integration issue, see Chapter 1B5, supra.

Excerpt From Joint Committee on Taxation, Federal Income Tax Aspects of Corporate Financial Structures

101st Cong., 1st Sess. (JCS 1–89, Jan. 18, 1989).

III. EXAMPLES OF TRANSACTIONS THAT INCREASE DEBT OR REDUCE EQUITY, AND TAX CONSEQUENCES

There are various transactions which can increase the debt of a corporation or reduce its equity. The discussion below describes broad categories of these transactions and uses examples to illustrate their tax consequences. The examples assume that no restrictions on interest deductions or other tax benefits stemming from interest expenses apply. In many cases, however, such limitations are applicable. * * *

Although there are significant tax reasons which may lead a corporation to engage in these transactions, such transactions may also be motivated by reasons apart from Federal income tax considerations. For example, such transactions may be undertaken to increase the value of a corporation's stock, to enhance earnings per share calculations, to concentrate common stock holdings, to create treasury stock, as a defensive maneuver to ward off a takeover, or for other reasons.

* * *

B. Stock Repurchases

Description

A stock repurchase refers to a corporation redeeming (or buying back) its own shares from stockholders. A corporation may make a tender offer for a certain percentage of its shares at an announced price or a corporation may simply purchase its shares on the market. A corporation may fund a stock repurchase out of cash the corporation has on hand or it may borrow the funds.[67]

Tax consequences

A stock repurchase, whether financed out of cash the corporation has on hand or by borrowing, is generally a taxable transaction with respect to the redeeming shareholders. Taxable shareholders having their stock redeemed recognize any gain (i.e., the excess of the amount received over basis) or loss on the redemption of their shares.[68] There are no immediate tax consequences of a stock repurchase to the redeeming corporation.

A stock repurchase has further tax consequences to the redeeming corporation and to investors in the redeeming corporation over time. If a

---

67. As an alternative to borrowing funds from an outside lender and using the proceeds to repurchase the stock of shareholders, a corporation may repurchase stock by issuing debt directly to redeeming shareholders. This is sometimes called a "debt-for-equity swap."

68. Of course, there will be no tax imposed on those shareholders that are not subject to U.S. income tax on this income, i.e., certain foreign investors and tax-exempt investors such as pension funds.

stock repurchase is financed with cash, the primary tax consequence is that the corporate assets of the redeeming corporation have been reduced. Corporate assets paid out to redeem shareholders' stock no longer produce earnings which are subject to the corporate income tax.[69] If the stock repurchase is financed through borrowing, the effect of the transaction is to replace the equity of the corporation with debt. Earnings of the corporation once available to be paid to shareholders as non-deductible dividends are instead paid to debtholders as deductible interest.[70] Thus, a stock redemption using borrowed funds enables the redeeming corporation to reduce its taxable income, or perhaps eliminate it (or even generate current tax losses which it could carry back to obtain tax refunds).[71]

As indicated by the following example, the resulting reduction in Federal income taxes pays for increased returns to investors. To the extent increased investor returns are paid to taxable shareholders or debtholders, there may be an increase in investor-level taxes paid.

Example III–B

Consider the same facts as in Example III–A above [The facts were: Corporation M has $1.5 million annual income, 99,000 shares of stock outstanding and no debt. M's federal income tax is $510,000 ($1.5 million times 34 percent), resulting in after-tax income of $990,000 and earnings per share of $10. M's stock trades at $80 per share, or 8 times earnings. Ed.] except that Company M announces it will repurchase up to $11 million of its shares at a redemption price of $120 per share, 50 percent more than the price at which the stock has been trading on the market. Taxable redeeming shareholders recognize gain or loss on the redemption of their shares.

At $120 per share, $11 million will purchase approximately 93 percent of Company M's outstanding shares. To finance the share repurchase, Company M issues bonds for $11 million paying 12 percent interest. Approximately 93 percent of Company M's outstanding shares are redeemed.

The distribution of the operating income of Company M before and after the stock repurchase is as follows:

69. This is also the result when the earnings of the distributing corporation are distributed to noncorporate shareholders in circumstances other than in connection with a stock repurchase.

70. A leveraged stock repurchase has exactly the same tax consequences as a leveraged distribution made by a corporation with respect to its stock.

71. A reduction in the redeeming corporation's Federal income tax liability could also increase its cash flow significantly. That increased cash flow might be sufficient to enable the redeeming corporation to cover most of its debt service obligations with respect to the borrowed funds and retire much of the debt over a period of years (although the redeeming company might also have to sell some of its assets to raise cash to assist it in paying off the loan).

	Before	**After**
Redeeming shareholders	$ 920,700	0
Bondholders	0	$1,320,000
Continuing shareholders	69,300	118,800
Corporate income taxes	510,000	61,200
Total operating income	1,500,000	1,500,000
Earnings per share	10	16.20

The leveraged stock redemption has redistributed the income stream of Company M in the same way that the leveraged distribution with respect to stock redistributed the income stream, except that the continuing shareholders of Company M, rather than all the shareholders of Company M, receive the profit of $118,800. The redeeming shareholders of Company M who used to get $920,700 a year in dividends before the redemption receive no part of the income stream after the redemption. New bondholders receive interest of 12 percent a year on $11 million, or $1.32 million. This is one-third more than the entire amount of Company M's after-tax income before the stock repurchases even though the operating income of Company M is unchanged. Continuing shareholders of Company M receive the profit of $118,800 (the remainder of Company M's income after taxes and interest expense).

The taxable income of Company M has been reduced from $1.5 million to $180,000 ($1.5 million minus $1.32 million) because most of the earnings of Company M are now paid out as deductible interest payments. The resulting reduction of corporate Federal income taxes from $510,000 to $61,200 exactly pays for the increased returns to the new bondholders and the continuing shareholders. Depending on whether the increased returns are paid to taxable bondholders and shareholders, there may be an increase in investor-level Federal income taxes paid.

Note also that the earnings per share of Company M have gone up from $10 per share ($990,000 divided by 99,000 shares outstanding) before the leveraged buyout to $16.20 per share ($118,800 divided by 7,333 shares outstanding) after the leveraged buyout. If the stock will still sell for 8 times its earnings on the market after the leveraged buyout, the stock price would rise from $80 to $129.60 ($16.20 times 8).

Taxpayers have also sought similar tax results in connection with so-called "unbundled stock units." On December 5, 1988, four publicly traded companies—American Express Co., Dow Chemical Co., Pfizer Inc. and Sara Lee Corp.announced offers to their shareholders to exchange a certain portion of their outstanding common stock for unbundled stock units comprised of three separate securities:

(1) a 30–year deep-discount bond which will pay quarterly interest in an amount equal to the current dividend of the common stock exchanged;

(2) a share of preferred stock which will yield dividends equal to any increase in the dividend yield of the company's common stock; and

(3) an "equity appreciation certificate" which entitles the holder to acquire one share of common stock for an amount equal to the redemption value of the 30–year bond plus a share of the preferred stock. The new

bond in effect would convert what had been nondeductible ordinary dividends into deductible interest payments, in addition to providing corporate
deductions for an element of original issue discount.[72]

Actual transactions

Stock repurchases have become common corporate transactions. A list
of the largest stock repurchases during 1988 published by The Wall Street
Journal indicated that the largest 21 stock buy-back announcements of
1988 were intended to retire almost 500 million shares of stock worth
approximately $23.8 billion. Ten transactions were listed with a value in
excess of $1 billion. The largest transactions listed were the following: (1)
UAL Corporation buying back 35.5 million common shares with a value of
$2.84 billion; (2) International Business Machines Corporation buying back
17.8 million common shares with a value of $2 billion; (3) CSX Corp.
buying back 60 million shares with a value of $1.86 billion; and (4) Sears
Roebuck buying back 40 million common shares with a value of $1.75
billion.

C. Acquisitions Including Leveraged Buyouts

The acquisition of one corporation by another corporation may be
structured in many different ways. An acquiring corporation may acquire
control of the "target" corporation or it may acquire a small interest in the
stock of another corporation as an investment. The acquiring corporation
may finance the acquisition with debt (either by a new borrowing of the
necessary funds or by keeping an old borrowing outstanding), or with its
own retained earnings, or with funds contributed as new equity capital by
investors.

An acquisition of the control of a target company may be a hostile or
friendly transaction. It may be structured as an acquisition of the stock of
the target company or an acquisition of the assets of the target company.
The target company may continue to operate as an independent company
in the same manner as before it was acquired, or it may be absorbed into
the acquiring company or other companies owned by the acquiring company, or it may cease operations entirely and its assets be divided and sold.

1. Stock acquisitions out of retained earnings

A corporation may finance the acquisition of the stock of another
corporation with internally generated funds (i.e., its retained earnings).
The purchase of the stock has no tax consequences to the shareholders of
the purchasing corporation. Likewise, there are no tax consequences to the

---

72. The four companies currently plan
to replace between 6.5 and 20 percent of their
outstanding common stock with unbundled
stock units. It has been estimated that the
four corporations issuing unbundled stock
units could save, in the aggregate, up to $5.9
billion in Federal income taxes over the 20–
year life of the bonds. Aggregate tax savings
in the first year after the exchange may be as
much as $85 million, with annual tax savings
steadily rising through the 30–year bond
term. New York Times, December 7, 1988, p.
D1. The Internal Revenue Service has not
ruled on the tax treatment of unbundled
stock units.

acquired corporation as a result of the acquisition. The taxable shareholders of the acquired corporation recognize any gain or loss on the sale of their shares.

There are generally no immediate tax consequences to the purchasing corporation as a result of the transaction. However, the total amount of funds in corporate solution, the earnings of which are subject to a corporate-level tax, may be reduced by the amount spent for the acquisition to the extent that shares are acquired by the acquiring corporation from noncorporate shareholders. Moreover, no compensating additional corporate tax may arise when earnings of the acquired corporation are distributed to the acquiring corporation. This is because earnings of the target company which are distributed to the acquiring corporation as dividends will either be nontaxable under the consolidated return rules, or, if the corporations do not file a consolidated return, will be eligible for the dividends received deduction.

2.   Debt-financed stock acquisitions including leveraged buyouts

A corporation may finance the acquisition of another corporation's stock by borrowing. The acquiring corporation may borrow using its own assets as security for the loan or it may borrow using the assets of the target company as security for the loan. In either case, debt has been substituted for equity at the corporate level. When the debt is secured by the acquired corporation's assets, the transaction is more likely to be called a "leveraged buyout."

Description

A leveraged buyout refers to a particular type of debt-financed acquisition of a "target" corporation.[74] The purchasers borrow most of the purchase price of the target company, using the assets of the target company as security for the loan. After the acquisition, the target corporation may be able to service the debt obligation out of its cash flow from operations or the purchaser may sell the assets of the target company and use the proceeds to retire the debt.

A leveraged buyout may occur in many different contexts and may be used by many different types of purchasers. The leveraged buyout, also sometimes called a bootstrap acquisition, has long been used to acquire private (i.e., closely held) corporations. More recently, leveraged buyouts have been used to acquire large public companies. A public company may be "taken private" through a leveraged buyout if the purchasers of the target public corporation are a relatively small group of investors. If the purchasers of the target corporation in a leveraged buyout include the current management of the target company, the transaction is sometimes called a "management buyout." A division or a subsidiary of a company also may be purchased through a leveraged buyout.

---

74. In what is called a "reverse leveraged buyout," public companies which had been converted to private companies in a leveraged buyout become public companies again, with their shares being sold in a public offering to shareholders.

A leveraged buyout of a target company is usually accomplished by a debt-financed tender offer by the existing corporation for its outstanding publicly held stock, or, alternatively, by a tender offer for the target corporation's stock by a largely debt-financed shell corporation established for this purpose. The target corporation will repurchase its stock from its shareholders or the shell corporation will buy all the stock of the target corporation.[76] If a shell corporation is used, the target corporation and the shell corporation will typically merge immediately after the acquisition.

As mentioned above, most of the funds for a leveraged buyout transaction are borrowed, with the purchasers contributing only a small amount of their own funds as equity. Lenders for these transactions have been banks, investment banks, insurance companies, pension funds, and pools of investors. Debt terms reflect the degree of leverage and the loan security involved. Some of the debt incurred frequently is below investment grade, i.e., so-called "junk" bonds.

Tax consequences

A leveraged buyout is generally a taxable transaction with respect to the shareholders of the target corporation.[77] Taxable shareholders selling their stock recognize gain or loss on the sale of their shares.[78] There are no immediate tax consequences of a leveraged buyout at the corporate level since generally neither the repurchase by the target corporation of its own shares nor the purchase of the target corporation's shares by a shell corporation followed by the merger of the target and shell corporation is a taxable transaction.

The primary tax consequences of a leveraged buyout to the target corporation arise from the fact that the equity of the corporation has been replaced by debt. Income of the target corporation once paid to investors as nondeductible dividends on stock is instead paid to creditors as tax-deductible interest on debt.[79] As a result of the interest deductions generated by the borrowing in a leveraged buyout, the target corporation may have little, if any, taxable income in the years following a leveraged buyout and may claim loss carrybacks producing a refund of taxes paid prior to the acquisition.[80] Because the target corporation pays little, if any, of its operating income as Federal income taxes, the portion of the target corporation's income that was once being paid to the Federal government as Federal income taxes may instead be redirected to increase investor

---

76. Shareholders of the target company typically receive a premium for their stock above the price at which the stock has been trading on the market.

77. Of course, there will be no tax imposed on those shareholders that are not subject to U.S. income tax on their income, i.e., certain foreign investors and tax-exempt investors such as pension funds.

78. Taxable shareholders will generally recognize gain (i.e., the excess of the amount received over their basis in the stock) because acquirors typically pay a substantial premium for stock in a leveraged buyout transaction.

79. A leveraged buyout has exactly the same tax effect as a leveraged distribution made by a corporation with respect to its stock and a leveraged stock redemption.

80. Indeed, the target corporation may be able to service its debt obligations out of a cash flow and reduced * * * taxes.

returns. However, to the extent increased investor returns are paid to taxable shareholders or holders of debt, there may be an increase in investor-level Federal income taxes paid.

Example III–C

Consider the same facts as in Example III–A [See p. 403, supra. Ed.] Rather than the management of Company M announcing a distribution with respect to its stock, Company M is acquired in a leveraged buyout. The acquirors pay $120 per share of stock, or 50 percent more than the price at which the stock has been trading on the market, for a total price of $11.88 million. Taxable selling shareholders recognize gain or loss on the sale of their shares.

The acquirors put up $880,000 of their own funds and raise the remaining $11 million of the purchase price by issuing notes paying 12 percent interest to be secured by the assets of Company M. The annual income of Company M after the leveraged buyout is unchanged.

The distribution of the operating income of Company M before and after the leveraged buyout is as follows:

	Before	After
Company M shareholders	$ 990,000	0
Bondholders	0	$1,320,000
Acquirors.	0	118,800
Corporate income taxes	510,000	61,200
Total operating income	1,500,000	1,500,000

The leveraged buyout has redistributed the income stream of Company M in the same way that the leveraged distribution with respect to stock, and the leveraged stock redemption, redistributed the income stream of Company M. However, the acquirors of Company M, rather than all the shareholders (in the case of a distribution with respect to stock) or the continuing shareholders of Company M (in the case of a stock redemption) receive the profit of $118,800. Company M shareholders who before the transaction received $990,000 a year in dividends now receive no distributions. New bondholders receive interest of 12 percent on $11 million, or $1.32 million. This is one third more than the entire amount of Company M's after-tax income before the leveraged buyout, even though the operating income of Company M is the same before and after the leveraged buyout.

The taxable income of Company M has, however, been reduced from $1.5 million to $180,000 ($1.5 million minus $1.32 million) because most of the income of the company is paid out to investors as interest rather than dividends. Federal income taxes are thereby reduced from $510,000 to $61,200. Acquirors make an after-tax profit of $118,800 (pre-tax profit of $180,000 reduced by Federal income tax of $61,200), a 13.4 percent return on their $880,000 equity investment. The income tax reduction of $448,800 exactly pays for the increased returns to investors (bondholders and the acquirors) as a result of the leveraged buyout. Depending on whether the increased investor returns are paid to taxable shareholders or holders of debt, there may be an increase in investor-level Federal income taxes paid.

Actual transactions

Leveraged buyouts of public companies have greatly increased in recent years, and the amounts involved in such transactions have risen dramatically. * * * The largest leveraged buyout transaction to date is the proposed acquisition of RJR Nabisco by the investment firm of Kohlberg Kravis Roberts & Co. ("KKR") for nearly $25 billion. It is expected that this acquisition will be completed by February 1989. Other large leveraged buyout transactions include the acquisition of Beatrice Companies by KKR for $6.25 billion in April 1986, and the management buyout of R.H. Macy & Co., Inc. for $3.5 billion in July 1986.

Newspaper reports indicate that out of the approximately $25 billion needed for the RJR Nabisco acquisition, more than $22.5 billion will be borrowed. Secured bank debt will account for approximately $17.5 billion of the borrowing, with most of the remainder being provided by investment banking firms. A pool of investors organized by KKR will put up $1.5 billion as an equity investment. It has been reported that KKR will contribute approximately $15 million of its own funds as equity. RJR Nabisco shareholders will be paid $109 for each share of common stock. This is almost twice the price at which the stock was trading immediately prior to the announcement of the possible sale of the company. It has been reported that due to increased interest deductions, RJR Nabisco could save up to $682 million annually in Federal and state income taxes and be able to seek the refund of additional amounts of taxes paid in prior years due to the carryback of net operating losses. Other reports have projected the annual savings at $370 million.

In the Beatrice transaction, each common shareholder received $50 per share ($40 in cash). This price of $50 per share was 45 percent higher than the market value of the stock one month prior to the announcement date of the first offer. Financing for the Beatrice leveraged buyout included $6.5 billion in debt and $1.35 billion in equity capital. Four billion dollars of the debt was lent by banks and $2.5 billion came from a new issue of high yield bonds. The equity came from two sources. Six hundred million came from a buyout fund organized by KKR and subscribed to by institutional investors and $750 million came from converting existing common stock to a new issue of preferred stock.

In the Macy transaction, each common share of stock outstanding received $68 in cash. This price of $68 per share was 55 percent higher than the market value of the stock one month prior to the announcement date of the first offer. On completion of the Macy leveraged buyout, the management group held 20 percent of the new company stock and an additional 20 percent was held by General Electric Co.'s credit union. Financing for the Macy leveraged buyout totalled approximately $3.7 billion. Out of this amount, almost $3.2 billion was debt: $770 million was lent from banks, $1.625 billion came from new issues of high yield bonds, and $800 million came from notes secured by mortgages. The remaining $500 million of the financing consisted of $200 million of excess cash of Macy's and $300 million was equity capital contributed by the acquirors.

* * *

NOTE

When Congress first held hearings on the problems of excessive debt, proposals were floated to limit the deductibility of interest used to finance certain "major" and "hostile" acquisitions. Some securities analysts believed that the breadth of these proposals contributed to the stock market crash of October, 1987. A cautious Congress, perhaps squeamish at the prospect of another chilly reception from Wall Street, failed to achieve a consensus on a comprehensive response when it revisited the excessive debt problem in 1989. Instead, the final product was typical of much recent tax legislation: a narrowly targeted set of limitations aimed at particular perceived abuses, accompanied by a delegation to the Treasury to elaborate through regulations. This legislation curbs some of the more egregious uses of "junk bonds," which are high-yield unsecured debt instruments used to finance corporate acquisitions. Other provisions were aimed at the excessive net operating losses generated by debt-financed corporate acquisitions and at corporations paying significant amounts of interest to related tax-exempt entities.

Applicable High–Yield Discount Obligations. The first victim of the 1989 legislation was a type of high-yield debt instrument that does not currently pay interest in cash to the lender. This type of junk bond is usually structured as a zero-coupon instrument with an issue price that is significantly lower than the stated redemption price at maturity.[1] The "spread" between the issue and redemption price is "original issue discount" ("OID"). In general, the issuer of an OID bond accrues and deducts the "spread" as interest over the life of the bond even though the interest is not actually paid until maturity, and the lender (even if a cash basis taxpayer) includes OID in income over the life of the bond.[2] A related device is the "payment-in-kind" ("PIK") bond, which purports to make interest payments in the form of other debt or stock of the corporate issuer rather than in cash. OID and PIK bonds were attractive financing paper for acquisitions because the issuer received a current interest deduction without a corresponding cash expenditure.

One sensible proposal was to treat high-yield zero coupon and PIK bonds as preferred stock on the theory that their high level of risk and dependence on the profitability of the business causes them to more resemble equity than debt. The legislation ultimately enacted[3] did not go that far. Instead, Congress decided to defer (and in some cases disallow) the

---

1. A zero coupon bond is a debt instrument that pays no interest and is sold at a significant discount from its face value.

2. See I.R.C. §§ 1272–1273.

3. See I.R.C. §§ 163(e)(5), (i).

issuer's deduction until interest is actually paid in cash but continue to require the lender to recognize interest income as it accrues. This approach represents a new Congressional willingness to bifurcate certain hybrid securities into debt and equity components. The theory is that a portion of the return on certain junk bonds represents a distribution of corporate earnings with respect to an equity interest in the corporation and should be treated as such for tax purposes. In 2009, Congress temporarily suspended the rule deferring or denying interest deductions to issuers of high-yield debt obligations issued in certain types of exchanges after August 31, 2008 and before January 1, 2010. The IRS extended the suspension to include similar instruments issued during 2010.[4] The purpose of this suspension was to provide tax relief for corporations forced to refinance or modify debt in a depressed credit market.

The restrictions in Section 163(e)(5) apply to an "applicable high-yield discount obligation," which is defined in Section 163(i) as an instrument with: (1) a more than five-year maturity, (2) a yield to maturity that is five percentage points or more than the applicable federal rate in effect for the month in which the obligation is issued, and (3) "significant original issue discount."[5] The OID amount on these bonds is divided between an interest element that is deductible but only when interest is actually paid,[6] and a return of equity element ("the disqualified portion") for which no interest deduction is allowed but which may be eligible for the dividends received deduction in the case of a corporate lender.[7] This approach is a compromise between deferral and total disallowance of the issuer's interest deduction. An instrument generally will have a "disqualified portion" of OID and thus face disallowance of part of the interest deduction if it has significant OID and the yield on the instrument is more than six percentage points over the applicable federal rate.[8]

Limitation on Net Operating Losses Created by Debt–Financed Transactions. Congress also was concerned that corporations were financing leveraged buyouts and similar transactions in part through the tax refunds that were generated by net operating loss carrybacks resulting from the payment of interest expense on acquisition debt. In general, a corporation that has a net operating loss ("NOL") may carry the excess deductions back for three taxable years and forward for fifteen years.[9] If a corporation with NOLs had taxable income in the three prior taxable years, the carryback will result in a refund of federal income taxes paid in those years. The interest deductions resulting from debt-financed acquisitions and other

---

4. I.R.S. Notice 2010–11, 2010–1 C.B. 326.

5. A virtually incomprehensible definition of "significant original issue discount" appears in Section 163(i)(2). Oversimplifying considerably, OID is "significant" if the OID income that accrues in periods ending more than five years after the bond is issued exceeds interest actually paid on the bond.

6. "Payments" for this purpose are limited to actual payments of cash or property other than the stock or debt of the issuer. I.R.C. § 163(i)(3)(B).

7. I.R.C. § 163(e)(5)(A), (B).

8. I.R.C. § 163(e)(5)(C).

9. See I.R.C. § 172 and Chapter 12, infra.

corporate restructurings often were large enough to offset not only the corporation's current operating income but also to generate an NOL carryback. Reasoning that NOL carrybacks are intended as an averaging device to smooth out swings in taxable income caused by business cycle variations and unexpected financial losses, Congress concluded that the interest expense triggered by a takeover was not sufficiently related to business operations in prior taxable periods to justify a carryback of NOLs attributable to acquisition interest.[10]

Section 172(h) addresses this concern by limiting the ability of a corporation to carry back NOLs where the losses are created by interest deductions attributable to leveraged buyouts and other debt-financed transactions, such as corporate repurchases of stock (collectively referred to as "corporate equity reduction transactions" or "CERTs").[11] A CERT is either a "major stock acquisition" (a planned acquisition by one corporation of 50 percent or more of the voting power or value of the stock in another corporation[12]) or an "excess distribution" (generally, unusually large distributions relative to the corporation's prior distribution history or net worth[13]). Interest attributable to a CERT is generally defined as interest allocable to debt that would not have been incurred but for the CERT.[14] A de minimis rule provides that the limitation applies only if the amount of interest expense at issue exceeds $1 million.[15]

Earnings Stripping. A third practice that was limited in 1989 is known as "earnings stripping"—i.e., the payment of deductible interest by a corporate borrower to an economically related lender that is effectively exempt from United States taxation. Deducting a payment to a tax-exempt entity whose economic interests coincide with the payor is a particularly attractive form of tax arbitrage. Earnings stripping payments, which are not necessarily related to acquisitions, are made primarily in the international setting (e.g., a payment from a U.S. subsidiary to a related foreign parent) or, domestically, where a taxable U.S. corporation is related to one or more tax-exempt charitable organizations.

The particulars of the Congressional response are well beyond the scope of this overview. It is sufficient to note that Section 163(j) defers the deduction for any interest paid or accrued by a corporation to certain related persons who are exempt from U.S. tax.[16] The limitation applies only if: (1) the payor corporation's debt-equity ratio exceeds 1.5 to 1,[17] and (2)

---

10. See H.R. Rep. No. 101–247, 101st Cong., 1st Sess. (1989).

11. It is important to note that Section 172(h) does not disallow the interest deduction or limit NOL carryforwards but merely restricts a corporation from carrying back the losses generated by certain debt-financed transactions.

12. I.R.C. § 172(h)(3)(B). A major stock acquisition does not include a qualified stock purchase where the buyer makes a Section 338 election. I.R.C. § 172(h)(3)(B)(ii). A

CERT may include the acquisition of a subsidiary of another corporation.

13. I.R.C. § 172(h)(3)(C).

14. I.R.C. § 172(h)(2).

15. I.R.C. § 172(h)(2)(D).

16. The definition of "related" for this purpose is borrowed from Sections 267 and 707(b). I.R.C. § 163(j)(4).

17. See I.R.C. § 163(j)(2)(A). Section 163(j)(2)(C) generally defines "ratio of debt to equity" as "the ratio which the total in-the payor has "excess interest expense," which generally is any interest expense for the taxable year in excess of 50 percent of the corporation's taxable income without regard to net interest expense (i.e., interest expense less interest income) or net operating losses.[18] The corporation may carry forward any deduction deferred by Section 163(j) and treat it as interest paid to the related party in future years when it may be deductible if the corporation's debt-equity ratio has improved or if it does not have excess interest expense.[19]

debtedness of the corporation bears to the sum of its money and all other assets less such total indebtedness." For this purpose, assets are taken into account at their adjusted basis for determining gain. Id.

18. I.R.C. § 163(j)(2)(B).

19. I.R.C. § 163(j)(1)(B).

CHAPTER 9

ACQUISITIVE REORGANIZATIONS

A. INTRODUCTION

1. HISTORICAL BACKGROUND

Some of the major litigation arising under the early federal income tax laws involved a variety of transactions loosely described as corporate reorganizations. Long before they became distracted by tax considerations, corporate lawyers and investment bankers were busy devising transactions ranging from complicated mergers, acquisitions and recapitalizations to routine changes in the state of incorporation. With the arrival of the income tax, the courts were required to determine whether and to what extent these fundamental changes in the structure of a corporate entity were taxable events.

Working with a pristine statute and an unsophisticated perspective, the Supreme Court became one of the first protectors of the comprehensive tax base. In a series of cases, the Court concluded that even minor changes in the form of a corporate business enterprise (e.g., changing the state of incorporation from New Jersey to Delaware) caused the shareholders to realize gain.[1] While these cases were pending, however, Congress quickly came to the rescue by enacting one of the earliest nonrecognition provisions. Preceding even the forerunner of Section 351, Section 202(b) of the Revenue Act of 1918 provided that no gain or loss would be recognized on the "reorganization, merger or consolidation of a corporation" where a person received "in place of stock or securities owned by him new stock or securities of no greater aggregate par face value."[2]

The rationale for the reorganization provisions reflects the broader policies of nonrecognition. Congress concluded that the tax collector should not impede these diverse transactions because they are mere readjustments of a continuing interest in property, albeit in modified corporate form,[3] and the new property received is "substantially a continuation of the old investment still unliquidated."[4] But to the extent that a shareholder

---

1. Marr v. United States, 268 U.S. 536, 45 S.Ct. 575 (1925). See also United States v. Phellis, 257 U.S. 156, 42 S.Ct. 63 (1921); Rockefeller v. United States, 257 U.S. 176, 42 S.Ct. 68 (1921).

2. Pub.L. No. 254, 40 Stat. 1057 (1919).

3. Reg. § 1.368–1(b). See also S.Rep. No. 275, 67th Cong., 1st Sess. (1921), reprinted in 1939–1 (Part 2) C.B. 181, 188–189,

where the Senate Finance Committee justified the principal forerunners of the modern nonrecognition provisions on the ground that they would permit businesses to proceed with necessary adjustments and remove "a source of grave uncertainty" in the law.

4. Reg. § 1.1002–1(c).

liquidates a corporate investment, recognition of gain or loss *is* appropriate. The 1921 predecessor of the present reorganization regime thus provided that shareholders must recognize their realized gain, if any, to the extent of the "boot" (money and other property) received.[5] Congress soon refined the statutory scheme by making clear what it had suggested in earlier versions: nonrecognition really means deferral rather than total forgiveness of gain or loss. The Revenue Act of 1928 introduced rules for carryover and substituted bases in order to preserve the unrecognized gain or loss for recognition at the time that the shareholder liquidated his investment.[6]

What began as a relatively simple concept has evolved into a vast and challenging body of law that governs some of the most financially significant transactions in the business world. It is important to recognize at the outset that the system you are about to study is not necessarily sensible. Functionally different transactions are lumped together and labelled "reorganizations." At the same time, economically equivalent acquisition methods are tested for reorganization status under sharply different criteria that often place a great premium on the form chosen by the parties. Moreover, determining the tax consequences of a corporate combination or readjustment requires an application of both precise statutory provisions and judicially created "common law" principles of uncertain scope. Analysis is further complicated by the possibility of an overlap between the reorganization provisions and other parts of Subchapter C.

In view of these defects in the reorganization scheme, it is not surprising that commentators long ago called for a complete overhaul of the current system.[7] Some modest reforms have come from the Service through recently issued regulations and rulings that ease the path to qualifying as a tax-free acquisition. Those pronouncements harmonize some of the requirements of Section 368 and in so doing increase flexibility in structuring tax-free acquisitions. But Congress has not yet fully embraced the simplification movement, and so we must turn to a more detailed examination of provisions that Professors Bittker and Eustice have described as "extraordinarily complex, even for the [Internal Revenue] Code."[8]

2.   OVERVIEW OF REORGANIZATIONS

Code: Skim §§ 336(c); 354; 355; 356; 358; 361; 362(b); 368(a)(1), (b), (c); 381(a); 1032.

Regulations: § 1.368–1(a), (b), (c).

The term "reorganization" generally is associated with the rehabilitation of a bankrupt company. Under the Internal Revenue Code, however,

---

5. Revenue Act of 1921, § 202, Pub.L. No. 98, 42 Stat. 227.

6. Revenue Act of 1928, § 113(a)(6)–(9), Pub.L. No. 562, 45 Stat. 791.

7. See generally Federal Income Tax Project, Subchapter C, American Law Institute (1982); Staff of the Senate Finance Committee, The Subchapter C Revision Act of

1985: A Final Report Prepared by the Staff, 99th Cong., 1st Sess. 50–58 (S.Prt. 99–47, 1985). See Section D of this chapter, infra.

8. Bittker & Eustice, Federal Income Taxation of Corporations and Shareholders ¶ 12.01[4].

"reorganization" is a term of art[1] used to describe corporate combinations or readjustments that fall into the following three broad categories:

(1) *Acquisitive reorganizations,* which are considered in this chapter, are transactions in which one corporation (the "acquiring corporation") acquires the assets or stock of another corporation (the "acquired" or "target" corporation). Included in this category are statutory mergers or consolidations ("A" reorganizations); acquisitions of stock of the target for voting stock of the acquiring corporation ("B" reorganizations); acquisitions of assets of the target for voting stock of the acquiring corporation ("C" reorganizations, sometimes called "practical mergers" because of their similarity to statutory mergers); and several other more complex acquisition techniques involving the use of a subsidiary or multiple steps.

(2) *Divisive reorganizations,* which result in the division of a single corporation into two or more separate entities and which often are preceded by a "D" reorganization. Corporate divisions are considered in Chapter 10.

(3) *Nonacquisitive, nondivisive reorganizations,* which involve adjustments to the corporate structure of a single, continuing corporate enterprise. This residual category includes recapitalizations ("E" reorganizations); changes in identity, form or place of incorporation ("F" reorganizations); certain transfers of substantially all of the assets from one corporation to another, followed by a liquidation of the first corporation (nondivisive "D" reorganizations); and transfers of a corporation's assets to another corporation pursuant to a bankruptcy reorganization plan ("G" reorganizations). These transactions are considered in Chapter 11.

A common organizational thread weaves its way through these diverse categories. First, definitional provisions set forth requirements ranging from the general and very flexible test to qualify as a Type A reorganization to the complex criteria imposed by Section 355 for corporate divisions. To qualify as a reorganization, a transaction also must pass muster under "common law" doctrines developed by the courts to reinforce the rationale for nonrecognition. The principal judicial doctrines affecting acquisitive reorganizations are continuity of shareholder proprietary interest, continuity of business enterprise and business purpose. In general, the continuity of interest doctrine requires that a substantial part of the value of the proprietary (i.e., equity) interests in the target corporation must be preserved in the reorganization through an exchange of target stock or assets for stock in the acquiring corporation.[2] For some transactions, the continuity of interest doctrine has been incorporated into the statutory definition of "reorganization." For example, the only permissible consideration in a B

---

1.   See I.R.C. § 368(a)(1); Reg. § 1.368–1(c).

2.   Reg. § 1.368–1(e)(1).

reorganization is voting stock of the acquiring corporation.[3] The doctrine assumes far more importance if the statute is imprecise, as with Type A reorganizations, where the Code merely requires a "statutory merger or consolidation" without any elaboration on the permissible consideration.[4] We therefore examine continuity of interest questions primarily in connection with Type A reorganizations—the context in which that doctrine most frequently arises.

The continuity of business enterprise doctrine, as its name implies, focuses on the continuing business operations of the target. This requirement has been incorporated in the regulations[5] and also is considered with "A" reorganizations. Because the business purpose doctrine was first applied and has the greatest importance in the context of a corporate division, it is discussed in Chapter 10. In general, all these requirements must be satisfied in order for a transaction to qualify as a reorganization.[6] To further complicate matters, the Service sometimes applies the step transaction doctrine to corporate reorganizations to convert what in form may be separate nontaxable steps into what in substance is a taxable transaction, or vice versa.[7]

If all these statutory and judicial requirements are met, they unlock the doors to the "operative provisions"—sections of the Code that provide for nonrecognition of gain or loss and that govern collateral matters such as the treatment of liabilities, basis, holding period and carryover of tax attributes.[8] For example, Sections 354 and 356 grant total or partial nonrecognition of gain to the shareholders of the target corporation in an acquisitive reorganization. Section 358, which we encountered earlier in connection with tax-free incorporations, provides a formula for determining the substituted basis of the stock or securities received by these shareholders in a reorganization. At the corporate level, Section 361(a) generally provides for nonrecognition when a corporation transfers its assets in a reorganization and distributes property in a liquidation pursuant to a reorganization plan,[9] and Section 357 generally ensures that the assumption of the target's liabilities is not treated as boot for this purpose. The acquiring corporation is accorded nonrecognition under Section 1032 with respect to stock used to make the acquisition and takes a transferred basis in the target's assets or stock under Section 362(b). In keeping with the continuity of investment principle, the tax attributes of the target corporation (e.g., earnings and profits and net operating losses) generally carry

---

3. I.R.C. § 368(a)(1)(B).

4. I.R.C. § 368(a)(1)(A).

5. Reg. § 1.368–1(d).

6. Reg. §§ 1.368–1(b); 1.368–2(g). However, because the "E" reorganization involves only a single corporation, there is neither a continuity of interest nor a continuity of business enterprise requirement. Microdot, Inc. v. United States, 728 F.2d 593 (2d Cir. 1984); Golden Nugget, Inc. v. Commissioner,

83 T.C. 28(1984); Rev.Rul. 82–34, 1982–1 C.B. 59. In addition, the legislative history of the "G" reorganization indicates that both doctrines will be leniently applied in an insolvency situation. See Chapter 11D, infra.

7. See, e.g., Rev.Rul. 79–250, 1979–2 C.B. 156.

8. See Section C of this chapter, infra.

9. See also I.R.C. § 336(c).

over to the acquiring corporation under Section 381, subject to various limitations to patrol abuse.[10]

If a transaction does not qualify as a reorganization, these operative provisions do not apply and the tax consequences of the transaction must be determined under other parts of Subchapter C. For example, an asset acquisition that fails as a Type A or C reorganization ordinarily would be a taxable transaction to the shareholders under the rules considered in Chapters 7 and 8. But it is the rare reorganization that fails. Because of the high stakes involved, taxpayers historically were reluctant to proceed with reorganization transactions without first obtaining the Internal Revenue Service's blessing in the form of an advance ruling or, when time was of the essence, a reliable opinion letter from private counsel.[11] More recently, the Service has declined to grant "comfort rulings" on straightforward acquisitions,[12] but it will rule on transactions presenting a "significant issue."[13] As a result, the Service's administrative guidelines are often tantamount to the law in this area, and taxpayers who disagree with the government's viewpoint must proceed with a transaction at their substantial risk.

B. TYPES OF ACQUISITIVE REORGANIZATIONS

1. TYPE A: STATUTORY MERGERS AND CONSOLIDATIONS

Code: § 368(a)(1)(A). Skim §§ 354(a); 356(a); 357; 358(a); 361; 362(b); 368(a)(2)(C), (b); 381(a)(2); 1032.

Regulations: §§ 1.368–1(d)(1)–(3) & (5) Examples 1–5; –1(e)(1); –1(e)(2)(i) & (v) Example 1; –1(e)(8) Example 1; –2(a), (b)(1)(i), (ii), (iii) Examples 1, 2 & 6, (g).

a. THE MERGER OR CONSOLIDATION REQUIREMENT

In General. The Type A reorganization is defined in the Code as a statutory merger or consolidation. For this purpose, "statutory" refers to a merger or consolidation pursuant to local (usually corporate) law.[1] Under a typical state merger statute, the assets and liabilities of the target corporation are transferred to the acquiring corporation without the need for deeds

---

10. See Chapter 12, infra.

11. For the Service's administrative guidelines in evaluating reorganizations, see Rev.Proc. 77–37, 1977–2 C.B. 568.

12. Rev. Proc. 90–56, 1990–2 C.B. 639.

13. See Rev. Proc. 2012–3, § 3.01(39), 2012–1 I.R.B. 116. A "significant issue" is one that meets three tests: (1) it is not clearly and adequately addressed by a statute, regulation, judicial decision, tax treaty, or administrative authority; (2) its resolution is not essentially free from doubt; and (3) it is legally significant and germane to determining

the major tax consequences of the transaction. Id. If there is a significant issue, the Service will rule on the entire transaction. Id.

1. Russell v. Commissioner, 40 T.C. 810 (1963), affirmed, 345 F.2d 534 (5th Cir.1965). The regulations provide that a transaction may qualify as a "statutory" merger or consolidation without requiring it to be effected under a domestic statute, thus permitting foreign corporations to be parties to a Type A reorganization. Reg. § 1.368–2(b)(iii) Examples 13 & 14.

or bills of sale, and the target dissolves by operation of law.[2] The consideration received by the target's shareholders is specified in a formal agreement of merger between the two companies. The shareholders may receive stock or debt instruments of the acquiring corporation, cash or a combination of all three. A consolidation involves a similar transfer of the assets and liabilities of two corporations to a newly created entity followed by the dissolution of the transferor corporations, and the shareholders of the transferors become shareholders of the new entity by operation of law. Either transaction may require approval by a simple majority or two-thirds vote of the shareholders of both corporations,[3] and under state corporate law dissenting shareholders may be granted the right to sell their target stock at a price determined in an appraisal proceeding.[4]

"Divisive" Mergers. To qualify as a Type A reorganization, a merger must be an acquisitive rather than a divisive transaction. To be "acquisitive," the result of the transaction must be that one corporation acquires the assets of another (target) corporation by operation of law, and the target must cease to exist. By contrast, a "divisive" transaction is one in which a corporation's assets are divided among two or more corporations. In Revenue Ruling 2000–5,[5] the Service relied on this distinction in ruling that a transaction in which T "merged" under state law into P, transferring only some of its assets and liabilities, and T remained in existence, was not a Type A reorganization.[6] Similarly, a transaction where T transferred some of its assets and liabilities to each of two acquiring corporations and then T dissolved, with each T shareholder receiving stock in both acquiring corporations, was not a Type A reorganization even though it was a merger under state corporate law.[7] Although both transactions were called "mergers" under state law, they were divisive rather than acquisitive because T's assets were divided between two corporations, and T's shareholders wound up with stock in two separate companies.[8]

Revenue Ruling 2000–5 was the Service's response to a new form of corporate merger statute enacted by the Texas legislature to permit divisive

---

2. See, e.g., Cal. Corp. Code § 1107.

3. Id. As a general rule, most state corporate laws give voting rights to shareholders of the purchasing ("P") and target ("T") corporations. But where the amount of P stock used in the acquisition is less than 20 percent of its outstanding shares, P shareholders usually do not have the right to vote. In an acquisition initiated by a tender offer, there is no formal shareholder vote because T shareholders individually may decide whether or not to sell. Some states, such as Delaware, also do not give P shareholders the right to vote on asset acquisitions not structured as a merger, triangular mergers where a P subsidiary makes the acquisition, stock acquisitions, or certain acquisitions for cash or cash

equivalents. See generally Oesterle, Mergers and Acquisitions in a Nutshell (2d ed. 2007).

4. Under Delaware law, for example, dissenting target shareholders have appraisal rights in statutory mergers (even if they do not have voting rights) but not in asset acquisitions. 8 Del. Code §§ 262, 271.

5. 2000–1 C.B. 436 (Situation 1).

6. Id. See also Reg. § 1.368–2(b)(1)(iii) Example 1.

7. Rev. Rul. 2000–5, 2000–1 C.B. 436 (Situation 2).

8. Some divisive transactions also may be tax-free but they must satisfy the requirements of Section 355. See Chapter 10, infra.

mergers.[9] The understandable concern was that permitting such mergers to qualify as Type A reorganizations would be inconsistent with the policy of Section 368 and undermine Section 355, which imposes strict and detailed requirements for corporate divisions to qualify for tax-free treatment.[10] The ruling serves as a reminder that simple compliance with a state corporate merger law does not ensure that a transaction will qualify as a Type A reorganization.

Mergers Involving Disregarded Entities. In a similar response to emerging acquisition techniques, the Service issued regulations addressing mergers between corporations and disregarded entities (such as a single-member limited liability company).[11] The regulations take a common sense approach to the two most typical transactional forms: (1) the merger of a single-member limited liability company ("LLC") with a corporate owner ("X") into an acquiring corporation ("P"), and (2) the merger of a target corporation ("T") into a single-member LLC in exchange for stock of LLC's corporate owner ("P"). In both situations, the LLC is a disregarded entity and thus is treated for tax purposes as a division of its corporate owner unless it elects to be taxed as a separate corporation. The first transaction does not qualify as a Type A reorganization because X's assets and liabilities are divided between X and P as a result of the merger.[12] But a merger of T into a single-member LLC in exchange for stock of the LLC's corporate owner ("P") may qualify as a Type A reorganization if the other requirements (e.g., the continuity of interest doctrine, discussed below) are met and the separate legal existence of T terminates.[13] This favorable result is consistent with the treatment of a disregarded entity as a division of its owner. It is as if T merged directly into P. Permitting statutory mergers into disregarded entities to qualify as Type A reorganizations offers more flexibility by eliminating the need for these transactions to pass muster under the stricter requirements applicable to Type C stock-for-assets acquisitions.[14]

Shareholder and Business Enterprise Continuity Requirements. The Code is strangely silent as to the permissible consideration in a Type A reorganization and the degree to which the target's historic business must be conducted by the acquiring corporation. To fill these gaps and preserve the integrity of the nonrecognition scheme, the courts developed the

---

9.   For an analysis and critique of Revenue Ruling 2000–5, see Bank, "Taxing Divisive and Disregarded Mergers," 34 Geo. L. Rev. 1523 (2000).

10.   See Chapter 10, infra.

11.   See Reg. § 301.7701–2(a) and Chapter 1D2, supra, for a discussion of disregarded entities—familiarly known as "tax nothings." Certain real estate investment trusts and S corporation subsidiaries also may be treated as disregarded entities for tax purposes.

12.   Reg. § 1.368–2(b)(1)(iv) Example 6.

13.   Reg. § 1.368–2(b)(1)(iii) Example 2.

14.   For example, Type C reorganizations require the acquiring corporation to acquire substantially all of the target's properties and to use mostly voting stock and only a limited amount of boot in making the acquisition. See Section B3 of this chapter, infra.

continuity of proprietary interest and continuity of business enterprise requirements.[15] Both doctrines are examined in the materials that follow.

b.   CONTINUITY OF PROPRIETARY INTEREST: QUANTITY AND QUALITY

Southwest Natural Gas Co. v. Commissioner

United States Court of Appeals, Fifth Circuit, 1951.
189 F.2d 332.

■ RUSSELL, CIRCUIT JUDGE.

The correctness of asserted deficiencies for corporate income tax for the year 1941 and of declared value excess profits tax and excess profits tax for 1942 due by Southwest Natural Gas Company depends upon whether a merger of Peoples Gas & Fuel Corporation with the taxpayer, effected in accordance with the laws of Delaware, was a sale, as asserted by the Commissioner, or a "reorganization" within the terms of Section 112(g) [the predecessor of Section 368] of the Internal Revenue Code, as contended by the taxpayer. The parties so stipulated the issue in the Tax Court. That Court upheld the Commissioner's determination. Southwest Natural Gas Company has petitioned this Court for review.

The facts found by the Tax Court (which, as facts, are not challenged) and the grounds for its judgment in law thereon are fully set forth in its published opinion. In substance that Court held that literal compliance with the provisions of a state law authorizing a merger would not in itself effect a "reorganization" within the terms applicable under Internal Revenue Statutes; that the test of continuity of interest was nevertheless applicable; and that the transaction in question did not meet this test. This ruling is assigned as error upon grounds which, while variously stated, require for their maintenance establishment of at least one of the propositions that: if the literal language of the statute is complied with, that is if there is a "statutory merger" duly effected in accordance with state law, the statute requires it be treated as a reorganization; or, at least where such merger has been effected the Tax Court must hold the transaction a reorganization in the absence of a finding that it was not in truth and in substance a merger; or, even if this be not correct, that the facts of this case disclose sufficient "continuity of interest." It is insisted in either view the Tax Court was required to hold under the facts found by it that the transaction in question was in truth a "statutory merger" and hence a "reorganization."

Consideration of the underlying purposes of the terms and provisions of Section 112 of the Internal Revenue Code in its entirety and of this Section (g)(1)(A) as involved here, in particular, as being enacted "to free from the imposition of an income tax purely 'paper profits or losses' wherein there is no realization of gain or loss in the business sense but

---

15. The earliest continuity of interest cases involved Type C reorganizations but the doctrine now applies primarily to statutory mergers and consolidations.

merely the recasting of the same interests in a different form, the tax being postponed to a future date when a more tangible gain or loss is realized." Commissioner of Internal Revenue v. Gilmore's Estate, 3 Cir., 130 F.2d 791, 794, and thus applicable to transactions which effect only the "readjustment of continuing interest in property under modified corporate forms," clearly discloses, we think, that the accomplishment of a statutory merger does not *ipso facto* constitute a "reorganization" within the terms of the statute here involved. This has been expressly held by the Court of Appeals for the Third Circuit in a well considered opinion, supported by numerous authorities cited. Roebling v. Commissioner, 143 F.2d 810. There is no occasion for elaboration or reiteration of the reasoning and authorities set forth in that opinion. In Bazley v. Commissioner, 331 U.S. 737, 67 S.Ct. 1489, 1491, 91 L.Ed. 1782, the Supreme Court enforced a similar construction with reference to the "re-capitalization" provision of the section. The authorities are clearly to the effect that the terms expressed in the statute are not to be given merely a literal interpretation but are to be considered and applied in accordance with the purpose of Section 112. Thus the benefits of the reorganization provision have been withheld "in situations which might have satisfied provisions of the section treated as inert language, because they were not reorganizations of the kind with which § 112, in its purpose and particulars concerns itself. * * * "

It is thus clear that the test of "continuity of interest" announced and applied by these cited authorities, supra, must be met before a statutory merger may properly be held a reorganization within the terms of Section 112(g)(1)(A), supra. Each case must in its final analysis be controlled by its own peculiar facts. While no precise formula has been expressed for determining whether there has been retention of the requisite interest, it seems clear that the requirement of continuity of interest consistent with the statutory intent is not fulfilled in the absence of a showing: (1) that the transferor corporation or its shareholders retained a substantial proprietary stake in the enterprise represented by a material interest in the affairs of the transferee corporation, and, (2) that such retained interest represents a substantial part of the value of the property transferred.

Among other facts, the Tax Court found that under the merger all of Peoples' assets were acquired by the petitioner in exchange for specified amounts of stock, bonds, cash and the assumption of debts. There was a total of 18,875 shares common stock of Peoples' entitled to participate under the agreement of merger. The stockholders were offered Option A and Option B. The holders of 7,690 of such shares exercised Option B of that agreement and received $30.00 in cash for each share, or a total of $230,700.00. In respect to the stock now involved, the stockholders who exercised Option A, the holders of 59.2 percent of the common stock received in exchange 16.4 per cent of petitioner's outstanding common stock plus $340,350.00 principal amount of six per cent mortgage bonds (of the market value of 90 per cent of principal), which had been assumed by petitioner in a prior merger and $17,779.59 cash. The 16.4 per cent of the common stock referred to was represented by 111,850 shares having a market value of $5,592.50, or five cents per share, and represented the continuing proprietary interest of the participating stockholders in the enterprise. This was less than one per cent of the consideration paid by the taxpayers.

We think it clear that these and other facts found by the Tax Court find substantial support in the evidence, and the conclusion of the Tax Court that they failed to evidence sufficient continuity of interest to bring the transaction within the requirements of the applicable statute is correct.

The decision of the Tax Court is affirmed.

[The dissenting opinion of Chief Judge Hutcheson has been omitted. Ed.]

Revenue Ruling 66–224
1966–2 Cum.Bull. 114.

Corporation *X* was merged under state law into corporation *Y*. Corporation *X* had four stockholders (*A, B, C, D*), each of whom owned 25 percent of its stock. Corporation *Y* paid *A* and *B* each $50,000 in cash for their stock of corporation *X*, and *C* and *D* each received corporation *Y* stock with a value of $50,000 in exchange for their stock of corporation *X*. There are no other facts present that should be taken into account in determining whether the continuity of interest requirement of section 1.368–1(b) of the Income Tax Regulations has been satisfied, such as sales, redemptions or other dispositions of stock prior to or subsequent to the exchange which were part of the plan of reorganization.

Held, the continuity of interest requirement of section 1.368–1(b) of the regulations has been satisfied. It would also be satisfied if the facts were the same except corporation *Y* paid each stockholder $25,000 in cash and each stockholder received corporation *Y* stock with a value of $25,000.

NOTE

Measuring Continuity of Interest. The continuity of interest doctrine historically required the shareholders of the target corporation to receive a sufficient proprietary interest in the acquiring corporation to justify treating the transaction as a wholly or partially tax-free reorganization rather than a taxable sale.[1] The early cases focused on both the quality of the consideration received by the target's shareholders and the percentage of equity consideration (relative to total consideration) received by those shareholders as a group. For example, in one of the first cases to apply the doctrine, the Supreme Court held that a transaction literally satisfying the definition of a reorganization nonetheless was a taxable sale because the T shareholders received only short-term notes of the acquiring corporation.[2]

1. See generally Bittker & Eustice, Federal Income Taxation of Corporations and Shareholders ¶ 12.21.

2. Pinellas Ice & Cold Storage Co. v. Commissioner, 287 U.S. 462, 53 S.Ct. 257 (1933). See also Helvering v. Minnesota Tea Co., 296 U.S. 378, 56 S.Ct. 269 (1935).

In a later case, the Court held that there was sufficient continuity of interest where the T shareholders received 38 percent nonvoting preferred stock of the acquiring corporation and 62 percent cash.[3]

In evaluating continuity of interest, it is the overall continuity preserved in the transaction that controls, not the continuity of any individual shareholder.[4] All classes of stock, whether voting or nonvoting, provide the requisite continuity while any other consideration (cash, short-term notes, bonds, assumption of liabilities) will fail to meet the test.[5] The lines with respect to the percentage of stock that must be received are not so easily drawn if one refers to the case law,[6] but the Service provided a practical benchmark by declaring that it would rule favorably on a Type A reorganization if P uses at least 50 percent equity consideration in making the acquisition,[7] and an example in the regulations confirms the Service's view that 40 percent continuity is sufficient[8]—a position long advocated by experienced tax advisers and supported by case law.[9] Keep in mind that this "percentage" is the proportion of equity consideration relative to total consideration used by P to acquire T, not the percentage of P stock owned by former T shareholders after the P's acquisition of T. Moreover, overall qualification as a reorganization under this liberal standard does not mean that all T shareholders will be able to defer recognition of their gain. Those receiving nonequity consideration must recognize gain, if any, perhaps as ordinary income, to the extent they receive boot.[10] But if the entire transaction fails to qualify as a reorganization, all the parties (including T), not merely those receiving nonequity consideration, must recognize gain or loss.

These venerable principles have not been altered by the enactment in 1997 of Section 356(e), which treats certain debt-like preferred stock, defined in Section 351(g) as "nonqualified preferred stock," as other property (i.e. boot) for purposes of recognition of gain or loss by the T shareholders in a reorganization. In treating nonqualified preferred stock as boot for gain recognition purposes, Congress was responding to concerns about acquisitive transactions in which T shareholders received a relatively secure instrument labelled as "stock" but bearing many of the characteristics of debt in exchange for a riskier equity investment. In those circumstances, Congress believed it was appropriate to view the new debt-like preferred stock as taxable consideration because the T shareholder was obtaining a more secure form of investment. Congress indicated, however, that nonqualified preferred stock would continue to be treated as equity

---

3. John A. Nelson Co. v. Helvering, 296 U.S. 374, 56 S.Ct. 273 (1935).

4. See Rev.Rul. 66–224 at p. 401, supra; Reg. § 1.368–1(e)(1)(i).

5. See, e.g., John A. Nelson Co. v. Helvering, supra note 3.

6. See, e.g., John A. Nelson Co. v. Helvering, supra note 3 (38% redeemable nonvoting preferred sufficient for continuity);

Miller v. Commissioner, 84 F.2d 415 (6th Cir.1936) (25% stock sufficient).

7. Rev.Proc. 77–37, 1977–2 C.B. 568. See also Rev. Proc. 86–42, 1986–2 C.B. 722.

8. Reg. § 1.368–1(e)(2)(v) Example 1.

9. See Ginsburg & Levin, Mergers, Acquisitions and Buyouts ¶ 610.2.

10. See Section B5 of this chapter, infra.

under other provisions of the Code, such as Sections 351 and 368, at least until prospective regulations provide otherwise.[11]

Remote Continuity. The continuity of interest test was once interpreted as requiring the T stock or assets acquired in a reorganization to be held directly by the corporation that issues its stock to T shareholders.[12] This "remote continuity" doctrine focused on the requisite link between the former T shareholders and the T business assets after the reorganization. Subsequent amendments to the Code provided more flexibility—for example, by permitting "drop-down" transfers to subsidiaries of the acquiring corporation[13] or allowing a controlled subsidiary to use its parent's stock as consideration in a merger.[14] The regulations go further by permitting successive transfers of T stock or assets among various members of an affiliated group of corporations or, in some cases, to a controlled partnership.[15] In general, these regulations provide that continuity is not broken by a transfer or successive transfer of the acquired T stock or assets to lower-tier subsidiaries provided that the transferor continues to "control" (using the 80 percent tests in Section 368(c)) each transferee[16] and the continuity of business enterprise requirement is satisfied.[17]

When to Measure Continuity of Interest. In determining whether the requisite proprietary interest in the target corporation has been preserved for continuity of interest purposes, the regulations provide that the appropriate measuring date is the last business day before the first date that the contract is a "binding contract" if the merger agreement provides for "fixed consideration."[18] A "binding contract" is an instrument enforceable under applicable law against the parties to it.[19] The presence of conditions outside the parties' control (such as the need for regulatory approval) or the fact that insubstantial terms remain to be negotiated or customary conditions satisfied will not prevent a contract from being "binding."[20] Consideration is "fixed" if the contract recites the number of shares of P stock and the amount of nonstock consideration to be received by T's shareholders,[21] provided the contract does not include contingent adjustments that prevent T's shareholders from being subject to the economic benefits and burdens of ownership of P as of the signing date (e.g., when T shareholders are entitled to receive additional consideration if the price of P stock declines by specified amounts during the interval between the signing and deal closing dates). Without this pro-taxpayer signing date rule,

11. Staff of the Joint Committee on Taxation, General Explanation of Tax Legislation Enacted in 1997, 105th Cong., 1st Sess. 212–213 (1997). The Obama administration has proposed to repeal the nonqualified preferred stock rule. See Chapter 3B3, supra.

12. See, e.g., Groman v. Commissioner, 302 U.S. 82, 58 S.Ct. 108 (1937); Helvering v. Bashford, 302 U.S. 454, 58 S.Ct. 307 (1938).

13. I.R.C. § 368(a)(2)(C).

14. I.R.C. § 368(a)(2)(D). See Section B4 of this chapter, infra.

15. See, e.g., Reg. §§ 1.368–2(f), –2(k)(1), –2(k)(2) Examples 1–3.

16. Reg. § 1.368–1(k)(1).

17. Reg. § 1.368–1(d)(4), (5).

18. Reg. § 1.368–1(e)(2)(i).

19. Reg. § 1.368–1(e)(2)(ii)(A).

20. Reg. 1.368–1(e)(2)(ii)(B).

21. Reg. § 1.368–1(e)(2)(iii)(A).

a decline in the value of the acquiring corporation's stock between the date that the merger agreement was signed and the date the transaction was consummated could cause the transaction to fall below the continuity threshold. Under the rule, value fluctuations will not jeopardize qualification as a reorganization and convert the transaction into a taxable asset sale. The policy for the signing date rule is that, if a contract provides for fixed consideration, the T shareholders are properly viewed as being subject to the "economic fortunes" of P as of the date the contract becomes binding.[22]

The regulations elaborate on the basic rule, detailing how continuity of interest is measured if the deal terms are modified before the closing date, how tender offers are handled, and how the rules are applied when an agreement provides for shareholder elections, contingent adjustments, and escrowed stock arrangements.[23]

c.   CONTINUITY BY HISTORIC TARGET SHAREHOLDERS

J.E. Seagram Corp. v. Commissioner

United States Tax Court, 1995.
104 T.C. 75.

OPINION

■ NIMS, JUDGE:

[This case arose out of a 1981 takeover contest for Conoco, Inc. After an unsuccessful attempt to negotiate a friendly takeover, J.E. Seagram Corporation ("Seagram") commenced a cash tender offer for Conoco stock. Two weeks later, E.I DuPont de Nemours and Co. ("DuPont") and Conoco entered into an agreement for a two-step acquisition, under which a DuPont subsidiary ("DuPont Tenderor") commenced a competing tender offer to acquire all of Conoco's stock in exchange for a combination of cash and DuPont stock, to be followed by a merger of Conoco into a DuPont subsidiary. The agreement was subject to several conditions, including the requirement that at least 51 percent of Conoco's stock must be tendered.

When the smoke cleared after the various tender offers expired, Seagram had acquired 32 percent of Conoco stock for cash, and DuPont had acquired 46 percent of Conoco stock for cash. DuPont subsequently acquired the Conoco shares it did not own (including Seagram's holding) in exchange for DuPont stock as part of the tender offer and the merger of Conoco into DuPont Tenderor. When the smoke cleared, approximately 78 percent of the Conoco stock had changed hands for cash in the DuPont and Seagram tender offers, but 54 percent of the Conoco stock (including Seagram's stake) was exchanged for DuPont shares.

---

22.   Reg. § 1.368–1(e)(2)(i).

23.   See Reg. § 1.368–1(e)(1)(ii)–(iv). Regulations proposed in 2011 would provide more flexibility to measure consideration on a date between the signing and closing dates in appropriate situations. Prop. Reg. § 1.368–1(e)(2)(vi).

Seagram claimed a loss on its exchange of Conoco stock for DuPont stock. The Service disallowed the loss on the grounds that the transaction constituted a tax-free reorganization. Seagram argued that the exchange of its Conoco stock for DuPont stock was not carried out in pursuance of a reorganization plan, as required by Section 368.

In the first part of its lengthy opinion, the Tax Court held that because DuPont was contractually committed to undertake the merger once it completed its tender offer, the "carefully integrated transactions together constituted a plan of reorganization * * *."

Seagram's second argument was that DuPont's tender offer and merger did not constitute a reorganization because they failed the continuity of interest requirement. The Tax Court's resolution of that issue is set forth below. Ed.]

On the date of the Conoco/DuPont Agreement, July 6, 1981, there were approximately 85,991,896 Conoco shares outstanding. Petitioner is essentially arguing that because it acquired approximately 32 percent of these shares for cash pursuant to its own tender offer, and DuPont acquired approximately 46 percent of these shares for cash pursuant to its tender offer, the combined 78 percent of Conoco shares acquired for cash after the date of the Agreement destroyed the continuity of interest requisite for a valid reorganization. We think petitioner's argument, and the logic that supports it, miss the mark.

* * *

The parties stipulated that petitioner and DuPont, through their wholly owned subsidiaries, were acting independently of one another and pursuant to competing tender offers. Furthermore, there is of course nothing in the record to suggest any prearranged understanding between petitioner and DuPont that petitioner would tender the Conoco stock purchased for cash if petitioner by means of its own tender offer failed to achieve control of Conoco. Consequently, it cannot be argued that petitioner, although not a party to the reorganization, was somehow acting in concert with DuPont, which was a party to the reorganization. If such had been the case, the reorganization would fail because petitioner's cash purchases of Conoco stock could be attributed to DuPont, thereby destroying continuity.

* * *

Respondent points out, correctly we believe, that the concept of continuity of interest advocated by petitioner would go far toward eliminating the possibility of a tax-free reorganization of any corporation whose stock is actively traded. Because it would be impossible to track the large volume of third party transactions in the target's stock, all completed transactions would be suspect. Sales of target stock for cash after the date of the announcement of an acquisition can neither be predicted nor controlled by publicly held parties to a reorganization. A requirement that the identity of the acquired corporation's shareholders be tracked to assume a sufficient number of "historic" shareholders to satisfy some arbitrary minimal percentage receiving the acquiring corporation's stock would be completely unrealistic.

Such a mandate to look only to historic shareholder identity to determine continuity was rejected by the Supreme Court in Helvering v. Alabama Asphaltic Limestone Co., 315 U.S. 179 (1942). In *Alabama Asphaltic*, unsecured noteholders of an insolvent corporation commenced a bankruptcy proceeding against the corporation. The noteholders bought the corporate assets from the trustee and transferred them to a newly formed corporation in exchange for its stock. In discussing these facts, the Supreme Court stated:

> When the equity owners are excluded and the old creditors become the stockholders of the new corporation, it conforms to realities to date their equity ownership from the time when they invoked the processes of the law to enforce their rights of full priority. At that time they stepped into the shoes of the old stockholders. The sale "did nothing but recognize officially what had before been true in fact." * * *

* * *

Some contention, however, is made that this transaction did not meet the statutory standard because the properties acquired by the new corporation belonged at that time to the committee and not to the old corporation. That is true. Yet, the separate steps were integrated parts of a single scheme. Transitory phases of an arrangement frequently are disregarded under these sections of the revenue acts where they add nothing of substance to the completed affair. Gregory v. Helvering, 293 U.S. 465; Helvering v. Bashford, 302 U.S. 454. Here they were no more than intermediate procedural devices utilized to enable the new corporation to acquire all the assets of the old one pursuant to a single reorganization plan. * * *

In reaching this conclusion, the Supreme Court upheld the finding of a valid "A" reorganization by this Court. * * *

In the "integrated" transaction before us petitioner, not DuPont, "stepped into the shoes" of 32 percent of the Conoco shareholders when petitioner acquired their stock for cash via the JES competing tender offer, held the 32 percent transitorily, and immediately tendered it in exchange for DuPont stock. For present purposes, there is no material distinction between petitioner's tender of the Conoco stock and a direct tender by the "old" Conoco shareholders themselves. Thus, the requirement of continuity of interest has been met.

* * *

For the reasons stated in this Opinion, we hold that a loss cannot be recognized by petitioner on its exchange of Conoco stock for DuPont stock, made pursuant to the DuPont–Conoco plan of reorganization. * * *

NOTE

The Historic Shareholder Concept After Seagram. The *Seagram* decision raises several questions about the role of the historic shareholder doctrine in applying the continuity of interest doctrine. In an earlier case,[1] the Tax Court concluded that continuity of interest "must be measured by looking to all the pre-tender offer shareholders' and held that the sale for cash by more than 80 percent of those shareholders was sufficient to prevent the merger of T into P from meeting the quantitative test" of continuity of interest. Isn't that the very same argument that Seagram made to support recognition of its loss? Wasn't Seagram arguing that the DuPont–Conoco merger failed as a reorganization because 78 percent of the historic Conoco shareholders received cash for their stock?

Perhaps the cases can be reconciled by remembering that the attempts by Seagram and DuPont to acquire Conoco were independent of one another. Would it be reasonable to conclude that Seagram's purchase of Conoco stock was "old and cold" for purposes of the DuPont–Conoco merger, so that it was an "historic" shareholder for purposes of that transaction? Is that what the court meant when it said Seagram "stepped into the shoes" of the Conoco shareholders that it bought out?

Or was the Tax Court concerned with the practical effects of its decision in *Seagram* on the world of corporate acquisitions? It noted the difficulty of tracking third-party transactions and the absence of any control by publicly held corporations over their shareholders as practical considerations supporting its decision. The decision offers tax practitioners some interesting planning options. For example, assume Target Corporation ("T") is owned 60 percent by shareholder A and 40 percent by shareholder B, and Acquiring Corporation ("P") wishes to acquire T in a tax-free merger. Before *Seagram*, it was thought that P could not achieve its goal if A wished to cash out of T. Under *Seagram*, however, if A can find an independent third-party purchaser who is willing to buy A's T stock for cash and who eventually becomes a P shareholder after the merger, each of the party's business and tax objectives may be satisfied with careful planning.

The Historic Shareholder Concept: In Memoriam? The Tax Court's decision in *Seagram* represented a significant erosion of the historic shareholder concept. Regulations issued in 1998 appear to go even further by eliminating the relevance of historic T shareholders except in limited situations. Following *Seagram*, the regulations provide that a "mere disposition" of T stock prior to a potential reorganization to buyers unrelated to T or P will be disregarded in applying the continuity of interest doctrine.[2] To illustrate, assume that A, an individual, owns 100 percent of the stock of T, Inc. (value-$100), and T plans to merge into P, Inc. Shortly before the merger is consummated, B, who is unrelated to T or P, purchases all of A's T stock for $100 cash, and then B exchanges her T stock for $50 of P stock

---

1. Kass v. Commissioner, 60 T.C. 218 (1973).   **2.** Reg. § 1.368–1(e)(1)(i).

and $50 cash furnished by P. Under the regulations, A's sale is disregarded and the continuity of interest requirement is met because B's T stock was exchanged for a sufficient amount of P stock (50 percent of total consideration) to preserve a substantial part of the value of the proprietary interest in T.[3]

Relationship of Continuity of Interest Doctrine to Taxable Stock Acquisitions. The tax-free reorganization rules often overlap with other provisions in Subchapter C. One potential jurisdictional conflict is between the treatment of a qualified stock purchase (e.g., P's purchase of 80 percent or more of T stock) as defined in Section 338 and an acquisitive reorganization. The Service has issued regulations addressing the tax consequences of the transfer of T's assets to P or an affiliate of P following a qualified stock purchase where P does not make a Section 338 election.[4] They provide that the T stock acquired by P in the qualified stock purchase will count for continuity of interest purposes if T later transfers its assets to a P subsidiary ("S"), enabling the second step of the transaction to qualify as a tax-free acquisitive reorganization.[5] As a result, T does not recognize gain on the transfer of its assets, which will take a transferred basis in S's hands.[6]

These regulations reverse the holding in Yoc Heating v. Commissioner,[7] a much discussed old Tax Court case where P bought 85 percent of T's stock for cash and notes and, as part of the same transaction, T subsequently transferred its assets to S, a newly formed P subsidiary and then dissolved. P received additional S stock in exchange for its T stock, and the T minority shareholders received cash in exchange for their T stock. The Tax Court viewed P's purchase of T stock and the subsequent T asset transfer to S as an integrated transaction in which P acquired all of T's assets for cash and notes. Consequently, it held that there was insufficient continuity of interest to qualify the asset transfer as a Section 368 reorganization because the historic shareholders of T did not receive any P stock. The upshot was that S received a cost basis in the T assets rather than the transferred basis it would have taken if the acquisition had qualified as a reorganization. Because the *General Utilities* doctrine was still alive at the time of this transaction, T did not recognize any corporate-level gain or loss as a result of the court's decision.

The Section 338 regulations take the position that the result in *Yoc Heating* is inconsistent with the policy of Section 338, which was intended

---

3. Reg. § 1.368–1(e)(8) Example 1(ii). Continuity may not be preserved, however, when the consideration received by A prior to or in connection with the reorganization is in a cash redemption of A's T stock (this usually is a problem only when P furnishes the cash) or if B cashes out the P stock received in the merger in a redemption. See Reg. § 1.368–1(e)(1)(ii), –1(e)(8) Example (5) & (9).

4. Reg. § 1.338–3(d)(1). See Chapter 8C2, supra.

5. Reg. § 1.338–3(d)(2). Similarly, P is treated as a historic T shareholder for purposes of determining whether, immediately after the transfer of T assets, a T shareholder is in "control" of the corporation to which the assets are transferred for purposes of Section 368(a)(1)(D). Reg. § 1.338–3(d)(3). See Chapter 11B, infra.

6. Reg. § 1.338–3(d)(5) Example (iii).

7. 61 T.C. 168 (1973).

to preempt the subjective *Kimbell–Diamond* doctrine.[8] The regulations also provide that the operative reorganization provisions applicable to shareholders of the target corporation in an acquisitive reorganization do not apply to minority shareholders of T unless the transfer of T assets is pursuant to a reorganization under generally applicable tax rules without regard to the regulations.[9] To illustrate, assume P buys 85 percent of the stock of T for cash from shareholder A and does not make a Section 338 election. The remaining 15 percent of T is owned by Mrs. K. Shortly thereafter, as part of the same plan, T merges into S, a 100 percent subsidiary of P, and Mrs. K receives P (or S) stock in exchange for her T stock. Under the regulations, the continuity of interest requirement is not met in determining the tax consequences to Mrs. K, who thus recognizes gain or loss with respect to the exchange of her T stock.[10] Why? How can a transaction qualify as a reorganization for some purposes (T's transfer of its assets) but not for others (Mrs. K's exchange of her T stock)?

d. POST–ACQUISITION CONTINUITY

Another aspect of the continuity of interest doctrine relates to the length of time that the target shareholders must hold their stock in the acquiring corporation. For example, assume T merges into P in a tax-free reorganization in which the only consideration is P stock, but shareholders who hold 80 percent of the T stock are legally committed at the time of the merger to sell their P stock to a third party. Does the prearranged sale disqualify the merger as a Type A reorganization because the continuity of interest test is not met. The selling T shareholders will be taxed in either event, of course, although the timing of their gain may be affected if the merger and subsequent stock sale occur in different taxable years, but what about the 20 percent who retain their P stock? And what are the appropriate tax consequences to the target and acquiring corporations?

The Service has never required T's shareholders to maintain continuity of interest in P for any particular period of time after an acquisitive reorganization. But in determining if the continuity of interest requirement has been satisfied, the Service for many years considered sales and other dispositions of stock occurring subsequent to a merger which are part of the same overall "plan."[11] The courts disagreed over whether a pre-merger intent to sell (without any binding commitment) would defeat continuity of interest.[12]

8. See Chapter 8C1, supra.

9. Reg. § 1.338–3(d)(5) Example (v). See also Kass v. Commissioner, supra note 1.

10. Id. See also Reg. § 1.368–1(e)(8) Example 4(ii).

11. Rev. Proc. 77–37, 1977–2 C.B. 568.

12. See, e.g., McDonald's Restaurants of Illinois, Inc. v. Commissioner, 688 F.2d 520 (7th Cir.1982), rev'g 76 T.C. 972 (1981), where the Tax Court treated a post-merger sale of P stock by former T shareholders as a separate transaction because the shareholders were not contractually bound to sell, but the Seventh Circuit found that a pre-merger intent to sell was sufficient to invoke the step transaction doctrine and cause the merger to lack continuity of interest. See also Penrod v. Commissioner, 88 T.C. 1415 (1987) (no binding commitment or pre-merger intent to sell; continuity of interest test satisfied).

The regulations resolve the issue by providing that subsequent dispositions of P stock received in a potential reorganization by former T shareholders generally will be disregarded in determining whether the continuity of shareholder interest requirement is met, even if the dispositions were pursuant to a preexisting binding contract.[13] This is consistent with the Service's current position that the continuity of interest requirement is satisfied if a substantial part of the value of the proprietary interest in T is preserved through an exchange for a proprietary interest (i.e., stock) of P. But if the facts demonstrate that T shareholders have sold their P stock for cash to P or a related party (e.g., a P subsidiary) before or after the acquisition, the continuity of interest requirement may not be satisfied.[14] For example, if P reacquired stock that it issued in the reorganization from T shareholders in exchange for cash, the reacquisition would be considered in determining if the continuity of interest requirement was satisfied. But sales of P stock by former T shareholders to outsiders would be ignored, even if the sales were pursuant to a binding commitment entered into prior to the reorganization.[15]

Revenue Ruling 99–58, which follows, is another illustration of the Service's tolerance toward post-acquisition continuity issues.

Revenue Ruling 99–58

1999–2 Cum. Bull. 701.

ISSUE

What is the effect on continuity of interest when a potential reorganization is followed by an open market reacquisition of P's stock?

FACTS

T merges into P, a corporation whose stock is widely held, and is publicly and actively traded. P has one class of common stock authorized and outstanding. In the merger, T shareholders receive 50 percent common stock of P and 50 percent cash. Viewed in isolation, the exchange would satisfy the continuity of interest requirement of § 1.368–1(e) of the Income Tax Regulations. However, in an effort to prevent dilution resulting from the issuance of P shares in the merger, P's preexisting stock repurchase program is modified to enable P to reacquire a number of its shares equal to the number issued in the acquisition of T. The number of shares repurchased will not exceed the total number of P shares issued and outstanding prior to the merger. The repurchases are made following the merger, on the open market, through a broker for the prevailing market price. P's intention to repurchase shares was announced prior to the T merger, but the repurchase program was not a matter negotiated with T or the T shareholders. There was not an understanding between the T shareholders and P that the T shareholders' ownership of P stock would be transitory. Because of the mechanics of an open market purchase, P does

---

13. Reg. § 1.368–1(e)(1)(i), –1(e)(8) Example 1(i).

14. Reg. § 1.368–1(e)(1)(ii), –1(c)(2).

15. See Reg. § 1.368–1(e)(8) Example (4)(i).

not know the identity of a seller of P stock, nor does a former T shareholder who receives P stock in the merger and subsequently sells it know whether P is the buyer. Without regard to the repurchase program, a market exists for the newly-issued P stock held by the former T shareholders. During the time P undertakes its repurchase program, there are sales of P stock on the open market, which may include sales of P shares by former T shareholders.

LAW AND ANALYSIS

Requisite to a reorganization under the Internal Revenue Code is a continuity of interest as described in § 1.368–1(e). Section 1.368–1(b). The general purpose of the continuity of interest requirement is "to prevent transactions that resemble sales from qualifying for nonrecognition of gain or loss available to corporate reorganizations." Section 1.368–1(e)(1)(i). To achieve this purpose, the regulation provides that a proprietary interest in the target corporation is not preserved to the extent that, "in connection with the potential reorganization, . . . stock of the issuing corporation furnished in exchange for a proprietary interest in the target corporation in the potential reorganization is redeemed." Id. However, for purposes of the continuity requirement, "a mere disposition of stock of the issuing corporation received in the potential reorganization to persons not related . . . to the issuing corporation is disregarded." Id. The regulation provides that all facts and circumstances will be considered in determining whether, in substance, a proprietary interest in the target corporation is preserved.

Under the facts set forth above, continuity of interest is satisfied. There was not an understanding between the T shareholders and P that the T shareholders' ownership of the P shares would be transitory. Further, because of the mechanics of an open market repurchase, the repurchase program does not favor participation by the former T shareholders. Therefore, even if it could be established that P has repurchased P shares from former T shareholders in the repurchase program, any such purchase would be coincidental. The merger and the stock repurchase together in substance would not resemble a sale of T stock to P by the former T shareholders and, thus, the repurchase would not be treated as "in connection with" the merger. Under the facts presented, a sale of P stock on the open market by a former T shareholder during the repurchase program will have the same effect on continuity of interest as a mere disposition to persons not related to P.

HOLDING

Under the facts presented, the open market repurchase of shares through a broker has no effect on continuity of interest in the potential reorganization.

e.   CONTINUITY OF BUSINESS ENTERPRISE

Bentsen v. Phinney

United States District Court, Southern District of Texas, 1961.
199 F.Supp. 363.

■ GARZA, DISTRICT JUDGE.

[Rio Development Company was a Texas corporation engaged in the land development business along with two other corporations. All three corporations were controlled by the Bentsen family. The three corporations transferred all their assets, subject to liabilities, to a newly formed life insurance company. The transferor corporations then liquidated, and their shareholders became shareholders of the new insurance company. The parties stipulated that there was a business purpose for the transaction.

After failing to obtain an advance ruling from the Service that their exchange of stock in the land development companies for stock in the insurance company was a tax-free transaction, the taxpayers reported a taxable gain and then took the necessary procedural steps to file a refund suit in federal district court. The taxpayers contended that the transaction qualified as a reorganization, while the Service argued that it failed to meet the requirements of Section 368 because of a lack of continuity of business enterprise. Ed.]

The question for the Court to decide is: Was such corporate transaction a corporate "reorganization", as the term "reorganization" is defined in Section 368(a)(1), Internal Revenue Code of 1954, 26 U.S.C.A. § 368(a)(1), even though Rio Development Company engaged in the land development business and thereafter the new Insurance Company engaged in the insurance business?

The plaintiff taxpayers contend there was a corporate reorganization. The Government, Defendant in this cause, maintains that there was not a corporate reorganization under Section 368(a)(1) of the Internal Revenue Code of 1954, because there was not a continuity of business enterprise before and after the reorganization; and that this is a prerequisite as set out in the Treasury Regulations.

This case is governed by the Internal Revenue Code of 1954, 26 U.S.C., the applicable sections of which provide [the quoted excerpts from Sections 368 and 354 have been omitted. Ed.].

* * *

It is conceded that the 1939 Internal Revenue Code was the same in this respect as the 1954 Code, and that the corresponding Treasury Regulations issued under the 1939 Code are similar to the corresponding Treasury Regulations issued under the 1954 Code.

The Treasury Regulation states: "Requisite to a reorganization under the Code, are a continuity of business enterprise under the modified corporate form."

The Government contends that since there was a lack of "continuity of the business enterprise", there was not a reorganization as contemplated under the statutes.

The question for this Court to decide is the meaning of "continuity of business enterprise", and whether or not it exists in this case.

The Government takes the position that "continuity of business enterprise" means that the new corporation must engage in the same identical or similar business. Stated in another manner, the Government maintains it is necessary that there must be an identity of type of business before and after the reorganization.

The plaintiff taxpayers have cited to the Court the case of Becher v. Commissioner, 221 F.2d 252 (2d Cir.1955) affirming 22 T.C. 932 (1954), which the Government has tried to distinguish. In this case the taxpayer owned all the stock in a corporation engaged in the sponge rubber and canvass-product manufacturing business. The new corporation engaged in the business of manufacturing upholstered furniture. In that case, the Government took the position that there had been a reorganization and that a cash distribution to the shareholders of the old corporation was taxable as "boot" and was ordinary income to the shareholders. The Government prevailed in that case, and the Court, at 221 F.2d 252, 253, said:

> " * * * but the Tax Court here correctly held that a business purpose does not require an identity of business before and after the reorganization. * * * "

Other cases cited are Pebble Springs Distilling Co. v. Commissioner, 231 F.2d 288 (7th Cir.1956), cert. denied 352 U.S. 836, 77 S.Ct. 56, 1 L.Ed.2d 55 affirming 23 T.C. 196 (1954). There the old corporation had the power to carry on both a whiskey distilling business and a real estate business, but it engaged solely in the real estate business.

Another case cited to the Court is Morley Cypress Trust v. Commissioner, 3 T.C. 84 (1944). In that case the old corporation owned land held for timber and the land was conveyed to a new corporation engaged in the oil business.

The Government tries to distinguish these last two cases by saying that in the Pebble Springs Distilling Co. case the new corporation could engage in the whiskey distilling business if it had wanted to, and that in the Morley Cypress Trust case, after the problem of continuity of business enterprise had been presented, the required continuity could have been found because both the old and the new corporations were actively engaged in exploiting the natural resources of the same land.

The Government also contends that under Texas law an insurance company cannot engage in any business other than that of insurance.

The Morley Cypress Trust case cited above, this Court believes, is the case most like the case before the Court. In the Morley Cypress Trust case the land was held for timber. In this case it was held for development. In the Morley case land was conveyed to a new oil corporation for use in the oil business. In this case, land (plus proceeds from the sale of land) was conveyed to a new corporation to furnish the means to capitalize a new insurance business.

The Government contends that the corresponding Treasury Regulation issued under the 1939 Code was in existence when the 1954 Code was enacted and Congress did not see fit to make any changes; that Treasury Regulations have the force of law when the Code section which they interpret is reenacted after they have once been promulgated, and cites Roberts v. Commissioner, 9 Cir., 176 F.2d 221, 10 A.L.R.2d 186.

The Government has been unable to present the Court with any decision in which the meaning of "continuity of business enterprise" as used in the Treasury Regulations, has been interpreted. Since no Court had upheld the contention made by the Government as to the interpretation to be given said words in the Regulations, it is unfair to say that Congress had an opportunity to make a change in passing the 1954 Code. Congress was not apprised of the meaning that the Government wishes to give to said language in the Regulations, and therefore the rule expressed in Roberts v. Commissioner, supra, is not controlling here.

This Court finds that no court has passed on the question of whether "continuity of business enterprise", as used in the Regulations, means that the new corporation must engage in the identical type of business or a similar business; and it is, therefore, held that this Court is not bound by any Treasury Regulation since it is the province of the Court to decide whether the Treasury Regulation means what the Government contends it means; and whether or not if it means what the Government contends, said Regulation is one that could be promulgated under the appropriate sections of the Internal Revenue Code.

This Court finds that "continuity of business enterprise", as used in the Regulations, does not mean that the new corporation must engage in either the same type of business as the old or a similar business, for if this be the requirement, then said Regulation is without authority.

To qualify as a "reorganization" under the applicable statutes, the new corporation does not have to engage in an identical or similar type of business. All that is required is that there must be continuity of the business activity.

This Court therefore finds that there was a reorganization under the applicable sections of the Internal Revenue Code.

Under the facts stipulated in this case, it is found that there was a continuity of the business activity and all requisites having been complied with, the plaintiff taxpayers have a right to a refund of the income taxes paid on the exchange of stock. The amounts to be refunded by the Government are to be those as stated in the Stipulation.

The Clerk will notify Counsel for the plaintiffs to submit an appropriate order and judgment.

Revenue Ruling 81–25

1981–1 Cum.Bull. 132.

ISSUE

For a transaction to qualify as a reorganization under section 368(a)(1) of the Internal Revenue Code of 1954, does the continuity of business enterprise requirement apply to the business or business assets of the acquiring (transferee) corporation prior to the reorganization?

LAW AND ANALYSIS

Section 1.368–1(b) of the Income Tax Regulations states that in order for a reorganization to qualify under section 368(a)(1) of the Code there must be continuity of the business enterprise under the modified corporate form.

Rev.Rul. 63–29, 1963–1 C.B. 77, holds that the continuity of business enterprise requirement of section 1.368–1(b) of the regulations was satisfied where a transferee corporation sold its assets and discontinued its business, then acquired the assets of another corporation in exchange for its voting stock, and used the sales proceeds realized from the sale of its assets to expand the business formerly conducted by the acquired corporation. The holding of Rev.Rul. 63–29 is now reflected in the recent amendment to section 1.368–1 (1.368–1(d)) of the regulations, which looks only to the transferor's historic business or historic business assets for determining if the continuity of business enterprise requirement is satisfied.

HOLDING

In a section 368(a)(1) reorganization the continuity of business enterprise requirement does not apply to the business or business assets of the transferee corporation prior to the reorganization.

* * *

NOTE

The continuity of business enterprise doctrine requires P either to continue T's historic business or to use a significant portion of T's historic business assets in a business.[1] This determination is based on all the facts and circumstances, applying the permissive regulations. For example, the continuity of business enterprise doctrine is satisfied in the acquisitive reorganization setting even if P transfers the acquired T assets or stock to controlled P subsidiaries, or in certain cases even to a partnership that is controlled by the P corporate group.[2] Numerous examples in the regulations illustrate how the doctrine is applied to various transactional structures.[3]

f. EXCHANGE OF NET VALUE REQUIREMENT

To prevent transactions resembling sales from qualifying as tax-free reorganizations, regulations proposed in 2005 but not yet final as of early

----

1. Reg. § 1.368–1(d)(1).

2. Reg. § 1.368–1(d)(4) & (5).

3. Reg. § 1.368–1(d)(5). For a rare case in which a transaction was found to fail the continuity of business enterprise require-

ment, see Honbarrier v. Commissioner, 115 T.C. 300 (2000), where the acquiring corporation did not continue the target's historic business or use a significant portion of its historic business assets in a business.

2012 add an "exchange of net value" requirement, which primarily affects transactions in which the target corporation is insolvent. As applied to acquisitive reorganizations, these regulations require both a surrender and a receipt of "net value" by the parties to the transaction.[1] In an asset acquisition, such as a merger or Type C stock-for-assets reorganization, the target corporation ("T") surrenders net value only if the fair market value of the assets it transfers to the "issuing" (i.e., acquiring) corporation ("P") exceeds the sum of the amount of T liabilities assumed by P and the boot (cash and fair market value of other property) received by T.[2] The purpose of this rule is to ensure that T transfers assets in exchange for at least some stock. T (or its shareholders in a stock-for-stock exchange) receives net value if the fair market value of P's assets exceed the amount of P's liabilities immediately after the exchange.[3] This prong of the net value requirement ensures that the P shares received in the reorganization have some economic value.

2.   TYPE B: ACQUISITIONS OF STOCK SOLELY FOR VOTING STOCK

Code: §§ 368(a)(1)(B), (c). Skim §§ 354(a); 358; 362(b); 368(a)(2)(C), (b); 1032(a).

Regulations: § 1.368–2(c).

In its simplest form, a Type B reorganization is P's acquisition of T stock solely in exchange for P voting stock (or the voting stock of P's parent) provided that P emerges from the transaction with "control" of T.[1] For this purpose, "control" is defined as ownership of 80 percent or more of T's voting power and 80 percent or more of the total number of shares of each class of T's nonvoting stock.[2] When the smoke clears, T remains as a controlled subsidiary of P. A transaction that otherwise qualifies as a B reorganization is not disqualified if P transfers all or part of the T stock it acquires to a controlled subsidiary of P.[3]

Solely for Voting Stock Requirement. P "voting stock" is the only permissible consideration in a Type B reorganization. With a few minor exceptions discussed below, the use of even an insignificant amount of nonvoting stock, debt, or cash will disqualify the transaction. As the courts have consistently held, albeit with considerably more verbiage,[4] that there can be "no boot in a B." But the nagging policy question remains: why should the requirements for a stock-for-stock acquisition be so strict when

---

1. Prop. Reg. § 1.368–1(b)(1), (f)(1).

2. Prop. Reg. § 1.368–1(f)(2)(i).

3. Prop. Reg. § 1.368–1(f)(2)(ii).

1. I.R.C. § 368(a)(1)(B).

2. I.R.C. § 368(c).

3. I.R.C. § 368(a)(2)(C).

4. See, e.g., Chapman v. Commissioner, 618 F.2d 856 (1st Cir. 1980) and Heverly v.

Commissioner, 621 F.2d 1227 (3d Cir. 1980), each rev'g Reeves v. Commissioner, 71 T.C. 727 (1979). In *Reeves*, a decision that proved to be an aberration, the Tax Court had held that there could be some boot in a B reorganization as long as P acquired at least 80 percent of T stock for P voting stock in one transaction.

the acquiring corporation in some other types of acquisitive reorganization has the leeway to use from 20 to 60 percent nonequity consideration?

The rigid requirements for a B reorganization have placed considerable pressure on the definition of "voting stock." Although the term is not specifically defined in the Code, "voting stock" has been interpreted to require an unconditional right to vote on regular corporate decisions (election of directors, shareholder proposals, etc.) and not merely extraordinary events such as mergers or liquidations.[5] The class of stock transferred is immaterial provided that it has voting rights. Although the Supreme Court has long held that hybrid equity securities, such as warrants to purchase additional voting stock, do not constitute voting stock, contractual rights to receive additional voting stock may qualify.[6]

The Service has allowed the parties to a B reorganization some flexibility despite the stringency of the voting stock requirement. For example, the "solely" requirement is not violated if the acquiring corporation issues cash in lieu of fractional shares.[7] The acquiring corporation also may pay the target corporation's expenses (e.g., registration fees, legal and accounting fees and other administrative costs) related to the reorganization, but payment of legal, accounting or other expenses of the target's shareholders will constitute forbidden boot.[8] Certain preferred stock with debt-like characteristics, labelled by Section 351(g) as "nonqualified preferred stock,"[9] is treated as boot for gain recognition purposes but remains "stock" for all other purposes until the regulations are modified and provide to the contrary. Thus, the receipt by target shareholders of nonqualified preferred stock with voting rights (an unlikely occurrence) should not disqualify a transaction as a Type B reorganization, but T shareholders would recognize realized gain to the extent of the value of any nonqualified preferred stock received in exchange for their T stock.[10]

Buying Out Dissenting Shareholders. A particular challenge in planning a B reorganization involves shareholders of the target who insist on receiving cash. If the acquiring corporation pays cash directly to these dissenters, the transaction will violate the solely for voting stock requirement and all the target's shareholders must recognize gain. But the Service permits the target to redeem the shares of dissenters prior to a valid B reorganization provided that the cash does not emanate from the acquiring corporation and continuity of interest requirements are satisfied.[11] Another possible approach might be for the transaction to proceed as a stock-for-stock exchange, followed by a later redemption of the acquiring corporation

---

5. Cf. Reg. § 1.302–3(a).

6. Helvering v. Southwest Consolidated Corp., 315 U.S. 194, 62 S.Ct. 546 (1942); Rev. Rul. 66–112, 1966–1 C.B. 68.

7. Mills v. Commissioner, 39 T.C. 393 (1962), affirmed on other grounds, 331 F.2d 321 (5th Cir.1964); Rev.Rul. 66–365, 1966–2 C.B. 116.

8. Rev.Rul. 73–54, 1973–1 C.B. 187.

9. See Chapter 2B3, supra.

10. I.R.C. § 356(e).

11. Rev.Rul. 55–440, 1955–2 C.B. 226. See also Rev.Rul. 68–285, 1968–1 C.B. 147.

stock held by the dissenters.[12] If they were truly dissenters, however, one would assume they would have sought some assurance, albeit informal, that the later redemption would occur. In that event, the redemption likely would be part of the original reorganization plan and, if so, the entire transaction would fail.

Creeping Acquisitions. The acquiring corporation is not required to *acquire* "control" of T in a Type B reorganization. It simply must emerge from the reorganization with control, as measured by the 80 percent benchmarks in Section 368(c). It thus is possible for a Type B reorganization to be the culmination of a series of acquisitions of T stock provided, of course, that only voting stock is used as consideration and any earlier acquisitions of T stock for cash, notes or other consideration were "old and cold"—i.e., unrelated to the final stock-for-stock exchange. Whether or not an earlier cash acquisition is unrelated is essentially a factual "step transaction" question. The regulations assume that acquisitions are related if they occur over a short time span (e.g., 12 months) but not if they are separated by very long interval (e.g., 16 years).[13] This leaves a vast middle ground of uncertainty.

Contingent Payments and Escrowed Stock Arrangements. During the negotiations over an acquisitive reorganization, the parties may disagree over the price to be paid for the target corporation. The acquiring corporation may contend that the target's earnings are unpredictable or that the value of the business is clouded by contingent liabilities. The target may counter by producing optimistic earnings projections. A common method of breaking this type of stalemate is through a contingent consideration agreement. The acquiring corporation may issue a specified amount of stock or securities and agree to issue additional shares under specified contingencies. For example, additional shares may be issued to the former target shareholders if the earnings of the target attain certain levels during a specified time period after the acquisition.

There are a variety of methods to handle the payment of contingent consideration. The parties simply may agree that additional shares will be issued on the happening of specified events. The acquiring corporation may issue negotiable certificates of contingent interest. Or the parties may take the formal step of transferring the additional shares to an escrow agent with instructions to issue the shares if certain future events occur.

At one time, the Service contended that contingent rights to acquire additional stock violated the "solely for voting stock" requirement for a Type B (and Type C) reorganization. This position was not sustained by the courts, however, and the Service now concedes that contingent consideration will not disqualify an acquisitive reorganization if certain conditions are met.[14] The Service has issued guidelines for approval of contingent and

12. See Rev.Rul. 56–345, 1956–2 C.B. 206; Rev.Rul. 57–114, 1957–1 C.B. 122.

13. Reg. § 1.368–2(c).

14. See, e.g., Hamrick v. Commissioner, 43 T.C. 21 (1964), acq.; Carlberg v. United States, 281 F.2d 507 (8th Cir.1960). The Service now agrees that contingent consideration escrowed stock arrangements. The more important requirements for contingent consideration agreements are:[15] (1) to ensure compliance with the continuity of interest doctrine, only additional stock can be received; (2) the acquiring corporation must issue the stock within five years after the reorganization; (3) the arrangement must be based on a valid business reason, such as a valuation dispute; (4) there is a maximum number of contingent shares that can be issued; (5) at least 50 percent of the maximum number of shares of each class of stock must be issued in the initial distribution; (6) the contingent rights may be neither assignable nor readily marketable; and (7) the events triggering the issuance of additional stock are not within the control of the shareholders. Similar requirements are imposed where the acquiring corporation goes beyond merely promising to issue more stock and actually places the shares in escrow with an independent agent. In addition, escrowed stock must be shown as issued and outstanding on the acquiring corporation's financial statements, and the target shareholders must be entitled to any dividends paid on the stock and voting rights if, as is required in a Type B reorganization, the escrowed stock has voting rights.[16]

3.   Type C: Acquisitions of Assets for Voting Stock

Code: § 368(a)(1)(C), (a)(2)(B), (a)(2)(G); Skim §§ 336(c); 354(a); 356(a); 357; 358(a); 361; 362(b); 368(a)(2)(C), (b); 381(a)(2); 1032(a).

Regulations: § 1.368–2(d).

General Requirements. Type C reorganizations are known as "practical mergers" because their end result is generally the same as a merger. The only difference may be the form of the transaction under local corporate law. In a statutory merger, all the assets and liabilities of the target are absorbed by the acquiring corporation automatically, while an asset acquisition technically requires a "transfer" of assets and liabilities under a negotiated agreement and does not necessarily require the target to sell all of its assets or to liquidate.[1]

Despite their similarities in form, it is far more difficult to qualify as a Type C stock-for-assets exchange than as a Type A statutory merger because of the more stringent consideration requirements. Section 368(a)(1)(C) requires the target to transfer "substantially all" of its properties *solely* in exchange for voting stock of the acquiring corporation. Although "voting stock" has the same meaning for both B and C reorganizations, the term "solely" in Section 368(a)(1)(C) is subject to two important exceptions. First, the assumption of liabilities by the acquiring corpo-

---

is not boot but only if the contingent rights to additional shares are not negotiable. See Rev.Rul. 66–112, 1966–1 C.B. 68.

15. See Rev.Proc. 77–37, 1977–2 C.B. 568, amplified by Rev.Proc. 84–42, 1984–1 C.B. 521.

16. Rev.Proc. 84–42, supra note 15.

1. See, e.g., Cal.Corp.Code § 1100; Del. Code Ann. title 8, § 251 (1979). A liquidation of the target is required in a Type C reorganization, however, unless the Commissioner waives the requirement. I.R.C. § 368(a)(2)(G)(ii).

ration (or the taking of property subject to liabilities) is not treated as disqualifying boot.[2] Second, a "boot relaxation rule" permits the acquiring corporation to use up to 20 percent boot, but for this purpose the transferred liabilities are considered as cash consideration.[3] A transaction thus can qualify as a Type C reorganization when the consideration consists of a substantial amount of debt relief as long as no other boot is used and sufficient voting stock is transferred to maintain continuity of interest. But a combination of debt relief and other boot likely will spell doom for the transaction.

To illustrate the operation of these rules, assume that Target ("T") has gross assets of $120,000 and liabilities of $30,000. Acquiring Corporation ("A") proposes to acquire all of T's assets in exchange for the assumption of $30,000 of liabilities and $90,000 of A voting stock. The transaction qualifies as a C reorganization because the liabilities are not treated as boot. But if A assumes the $30,000 of liabilities and transfers $80,000 of voting stock and $10,000 of cash, the transaction does not qualify. The liabilities are treated as "money paid" for purposes of the boot relaxation rule, and thus A has acquired only 66⅔ percent of the $120,000 gross assets of T for voting stock. On these facts, A must use at least $96,000 of voting stock (80 percent of $120,000) in order for the transaction to qualify as a Type C reorganization under the boot relaxation rule. This example illustrates that in the normal situation where T's liabilities exceed 20 percent of the value of its gross assets, no boot may be used.

Substantially All of the Properties. The target also must transfer "substantially all" of its properties. The Service's longstanding administrative benchmark requires a transfer of "assets representing at least 90 percent of the fair market value of the net assets and at least 70 percent of the fair market value of the gross assets held by the target corporation immediately preceding the transfer."[4] These guidelines further provide that "all payments to dissenters and all redemptions and distributions (except for regular, normal distributions) made by the corporation immediately preceding the transfer and which are part of the plan of reorganization will be considered as assets held by the corporation immediately prior to the transfer."[5] Other authorities are not as stringent in defining "substantially all," and it is possible that a complete transfer of *operating* assets may qualify even if the Service's percentage tests are not met.[6] Moreover, the Service has ruled that the "substantially all" test is met when the target corporation sells 50 percent of its historic assets to unrelated parties for cash and then transfers all of its assets, including the sales proceeds, to the acquiring corporation.[7] The key to this favorable ruling is that the overall

---

2. I.R.C. § 368(a)(1)(C).

3. I.R.C. § 368(a)(2)(B).

4. Rev.Proc. 77–37, § 3.01 1977–2 C.B. 568, 569.

5. Id.

6. See, e.g., Rev.Rul. 57–518, 1957–2 C.B. 253; Commissioner v. First National Bank of Altoona, 104 F.2d 865 (3d Cir.1939) (86% of net worth is "substantially all").

7. Rev. Rul. 88–48, 1988–1 C.B. 117.

transaction is not "divisive" because the cash proceeds from the asset sale were not retained by the target or its shareholders.

Liquidation Requirement. At one time, the target corporation in a C reorganization was not required to distribute its assets (which ordinarily will consist primarily of voting stock of the acquiring corporation) in complete liquidation. Some targets chose to stay alive as a holding company with a fresh set of tax attributes.[8] Others opted to distribute the voting stock acquired in the reorganization while retaining other assets that might trigger adverse tax consequences (e.g., a dividend) if distributed to the shareholders.[9] To prevent these and other perceived abuses, Congress added a new rule requiring the target to distribute all of its assets pursuant to the plan of reorganization unless the Service, pursuant to regulations that it has yet to issue, agrees to waive the distribution requirement.[10] In the event of a waiver, however, the legislative history states that the retained assets must be treated as if they had been distributed to the T shareholders and recontributed to the capital of a new corporation.[11]

Creeping Acquisitions. A final issue is the treatment of a transaction where the acquiring corporation has previously purchased some stock of the target and now seeks to assume complete control by acquiring all of T's assets through a liquidation of T. We have seen that a creeping acquisition will not necessarily poison the final stock-for-stock exchange in a B reorganization, at least if the stock previously acquired for cash is "old and cold"—i.e., acquired in an unrelated transaction. For many years, creeping C reorganizations were impeded by the Service's wooden interpretation of the "solely for voting stock" requirement.[12] This longstanding position has been reversed by regulations providing that P's prior ownership of a portion of T stock will not by itself prevent the "solely for voting stock" requirement from being met.[13] The Service finally came to its senses and concluded that a transaction in which P converts an indirect interest in T's assets to a direct interest in those assets does not necessarily resemble a taxable sale by T of those properties.

To enforce the statutory continuity of interest rules, the regulations provide that where the Section 368(a)(2)(B) boot relaxation rule applies to the final step of a creeping Type C reorganization, the sum of: (1) the

---

8. The tax attributes (e.g., earnings and profits) of the target automatically pass to the acquiring corporation on a Type C reorganization. I.R.C. § 381(a)(2).

9. See Rev.Rul. 73–552, 1973–2 C.B. 116.

10. I.R.C. § 368(a)(2)(G). See Rev.Proc. 89–50, 1989–2 C.B. 631, for representations which ordinarily must be included in a request for the Service to waive the liquidation requirement.

11. H.R.Rep. No. 98–861, 98th Cong., 2d Sess. 846 (1984).

12. Rev. Rul. 54–396, 1954–2 C.B. 147 (P, which owned 79 percent of S as result of

prior unrelated cash purchase, acquired T's assets in exchange for P voting stock, after which T liquidated and distributed P stock to minority shareholders. The transaction was ruled not to qualify as a Type C reorganization because P acquired only 21 percent of T's assets for voting stock and the remaining 79 percent as a liquidating distribution in exchange for previously held T stock). The Service's position was sustained in Bausch & Lomb Optical Co. v. Commissioner, 267 F.2d 75 (2d Cir.1959).

13. Reg. § 1.368–2(d)(4)(i).

money or other boot distributed to T shareholders other than P and to T's creditors, and (2) the liabilities of T assumed by P, may not exceed 20 percent of the value of all of T's properties.[14] But if P acquires T stock from a shareholder of T or T itself for cash or boot as part of the acquisition, such consideration is counted as boot in applying the boot relaxation rule.[15] To illustrate, assume that in an unrelated transaction P acquired 60 percent of the stock of T for cash. T's assets have a value of $110, and it has $10 of liabilities. Assume T transfers all its assets to P and, in exchange, P assumes the liabilities and transfers to T $30 of P voting stock and $10 of cash, and then T distributes the P voting stock and cash to its shareholders (other than P) and liquidates. This transaction will qualify as a Type C reorganization because the sum of cash paid and liabilities assumed ($20) does not exceed 20 percent of the value of T's assets.[16] If, however, P's cash acquisition of 60 percent of T was not "old and cold"— i.e., was related to the subsequent asset acquisition—the transaction would not qualify as tax-free because only 30 percent of the consideration used by P was voting stock.[17]

Step Transaction Issues. Assume T Corporation is acquired by P Corporation in a stock-for-stock exchange that qualifies as a Type B reorganization but, as part of an overall acquisition plan, T promptly liquidates, distributing its assets to P. Should the overall transaction be treated as a Type C reorganization and tested accordingly or should the two steps be considered independently in determining the tax consequences? When would it make any difference? The IRS's view on the application of the step transaction to this fact pattern is revealed in Revenue Ruling 67–274, below.

Revenue Ruling 67–274

1967–2 Cum.Bull. 141.

Advice has been requested whether the transaction described below qualifies as a reorganization within the meaning of section 368(a)(1)(B) of the Internal Revenue Code of 1954.

Pursuant to a plan of reorganization, corporation Y acquired all of the outstanding stock of corporation X from the X shareholders in exchange solely for voting stock of Y. Thereafter X was completely liquidated as part of the same plan and all of its assets were transferred to Y which assumed all of the liabilities of X. Y continued to conduct the business previously conducted by X. The former shareholders of X continued to hold 16 percent of the fair market value of all the outstanding stock of Y.

Section 368(a)(1)(B) of the Code provides in part that a reorganization is the acquisition by one corporation, in exchange solely for all or a part of its voting stock, of stock of another corporation if, immediately after the

---

14. Id.

15. Id.

16. Reg. § 1.368–2(d)(4)(ii) Example 1.

17. Reg. § 1.368–2(d)(4)(ii) Example 2.

acquisition, the acquiring corporation has control (as defined in section 368(c) of the Code) of such other corporation. Section 368(a)(1)(C) of the Code provides in part that a reorganization is the acquisition by one corporation, in exchange solely for all or a part of its voting stock, of substantially all of the properties of another corporation, but in determining whether the exchange is solely for stock the assumption by the acquiring corporation of a liability of the other, or the fact that property acquired is subject to a liability, is disregarded.

Under the circumstances of this case the acquisition of X stock by Y and the liquidation of X by Y are part of the overall plan of reorganization and the two steps may not be considered independently of each other for Federal income tax purposes. See Revenue Ruling 54–96, 1954–1 C.B. 111, as modified by Revenue Ruling 56–100, 1956–1C.B. 624. The substance of the transaction is an acquisition of assets to which section 368(a)(1)(B) of the Code does not apply.

Accordingly, the acquisition by Y of the outstanding stock of X will not constitute a reorganization within the meaning of section 368(a)(1)(B) of the Code but will be considered an acquisition of the assets of X which in this case is a reorganization described in section 368(a)(1)(C) of the Code. * * *.

4. TRIANGULAR REORGANIZATIONS

Code: § 368(a)(1)(B) (first parenthetical) and (C) (first parenthetical), (a)(2)(C), (D) and (E), (b).

Regulations: § 1.368–2(b)(2), (f), (j)(1), (3)–(6).

Background. The three basic types of reorganizations offer limited flexibility if the acquiring corporation desires to operate the target as a wholly owned subsidiary. Assume, for example, that P, Inc. wishes to acquire T, Inc. and keep T's business in a separate corporation for nontax reasons. Although this objective could be met by a Type B reorganization, the stringent "solely for voting stock" requirement might be an insurmountable obstacle if P desired to use nonvoting stock as consideration or if a large number of T shareholders were unwilling to accept any class of P stock. Even the flexible A reorganization may not be feasible from a nontax standpoint. P may not wish to incur the risk of T's unknown or contingent liabilities which would remain P's responsibility even if T's assets were dropped down to a subsidiary. P also may be reluctant to bear the expense and delay of seeking formal approval of its shareholders or unwilling to provide T shareholders with the appraisal rights to which they would be entitled under state law on a direct merger.

To maneuver around these problems, corporate lawyers developed other acquisition methods involving the use of a subsidiary. One approach is for P to acquire T's assets in a qualifying Type A or C reorganization and immediately drop down the acquired assets to a newly created subsidiary. This technique does not solve the hidden liability problem, however, and it may not obviate the need for shareholder approval and appraisal rights.[1] An alternative is for P to transfer its stock to a new subsidiary ("S"), and then cause T to merge directly into S, with the T shareholders receiving P stock and, perhaps, other consideration in exchange for their T stock. Or P could form S and have S acquire substantially all of the assets of T in exchange for P voting stock.

The tax consequences of these and other triangular acquisition techniques have been a major subplot within the reorganization drama. In two early cases, the Supreme Court constructed several large roadblocks by holding that transactions similar to those described above failed to satisfy the continuity of interest doctrine if: (1) T merges into S but T shareholders receive P stock in a triangular reorganization, or (2) P makes the acquisition using P stock but drops T or its assets down to a subsidiary.[2]

Over the years, Congress gradually came to recognize that there was no reason to deny tax-free status to "drop downs" or triangular reorganizations that were economically equivalent to the simpler acquisition methods authorized by Section 368. In the 1954 Code, it added Section 368(a)(2)(C), which provides that an otherwise qualifying Type A or C reorganization will not lose its tax-free status merely because the acquiring corporation drops down the acquired assets to a subsidiary and it later added a similar rule for Type B reorganizations. Congress also permitted the acquiring corporation in a B or C reorganization to use voting stock of its parent to make the acquisition. For both drop downs and triangular reorganizations, Section 368(b) now makes it clear that the controlling parent will be a "party" to the reorganization. But the Service persisted in ruling that a merger of the target into a controlled subsidiary of the acquiring corporation was not tax-free when the target shareholders received stock of the parent because the parent was not a "party" to the reorganization and the T shareholder lacked continuity of interest.[3] Once again, Congress responded by adding two new categories of tax-free reorganizations: the Section 368(a)(2)(D) forward triangular merger and the Section 368(a)(2)(E) reverse triangular merger.

Forward Triangular Mergers: Section 368(a)(2)(D). From the time it was authorized as a tax-free reorganization in 1969, the forward triangular merger has become one of the most widely used acquisition techniques. Section 368(a)(2)(D) permits S to acquire T in a statutory merger, using P stock as consideration, provided that: (1) S acquires "substantially all" of the properties of T; (2) no stock of S is used in the transaction; and (3) the transaction would have qualified as a Type A reorganization if T had

---

1. "Drop downs" also are inconvenient because they usually require an inordinate amount of paperwork (e.g., deeds and other documents of transfer, with accompanying recording fees and transfer taxes) as the assets pass from the parent to the subsidiary.

2. Groman v. Commissioner, 302 U.S. 82, 58 S.Ct. 108 (1937); Helvering v. Bash-

ford, 302 U.S. 454, 58 S.Ct. 307 (1938). These cases also suggested that in no event could the T shareholders receive stock in both S and P because the receipt of stock in two separate corporations violated continuity of interest requirements.

3. Rev.Rul. 67–448, 1967–2 C.B. 144.

merged directly into P. In typically perverse fashion, Congress—without expressly articulating its rationale—reached into its bag of requirements and borrowed one from the Type C model ("substantially all of the properties") and another from the Type A model (the tests for permissible consideration). Although the legislative history is obscure, it is now clear that the "could have merged with parent" test merely requires the transaction to pass muster under the continuity of interest doctrine.[4] As a result, T shareholders only must receive at least 50 percent P stock (voting or nonvoting) under the Service's continuity guidelines, allowing the parties the freedom to use up to 50 percent cash and other nonequity consideration. Of course, the T shareholders who receive boot must recognize their realized gain to that extent, but those who receive solely stock will enjoy nonrecognition if the overall transaction qualifies under these liberal standards.

Reverse Triangular Mergers: Section 368(a)(2)(E). Before examining the tax consequences of a reverse triangular merger, the transaction itself must be explained. Suppose P desires to acquire the stock of T in a tax-free reorganization and keep T alive as a subsidiary, but P is unable (or unwilling) to structure the deal as a Type B reorganization because of the "solely for voting stock" requirement. Neither a merger nor an asset acquisition is feasible because T, as a corporate entity, has a number of intangible assets (e.g., grandfather rights under state law; franchises or leases; favorable loan agreements) that would be jeopardized if T were dissolved or it would simply take longer or involve cumbersome regulatory hoops to structure the deal as a merger. One ingenious solution to this dilemma is for P to create S, contributing to it P voting stock, and then for S to merge into T under an agreement providing that T shareholders will receive P stock (and, possibly, other consideration) in exchange for their T stock. A variation on the theme, albeit a rare one, would be to use an existing subsidiary with ongoing business activities. In that event, the reverse merger would result in T's business being augmented by S's, all conducted under the same corporate roof. In either case, when the smoke clears P will own all the stock of T and S will disappear as a result of the merger.

Section 368(a)(2)(E) provides that this type of reverse merger will qualify as a tax-free reorganization if: (1) the surviving corporation (T) holds substantially all of the properties formerly held by both corporations (T and S), and (2) the former T shareholders exchange stock constituting "control" (measured by the 80 percent tests in Section 368(c)(1)) for P voting stock.[5] Once again, Congress borrowed from its bag of requirements and combined tests from Type A (merger), Type B (control) and Type C (substantially all of the properties) reorganizations. The reverse merger is thus less flexible for tax purposes than the forward triangular merger, perhaps reflecting its Type B origins. But there *can* be boot in an "(a)(2)(E)" reorganization; only 80 percent of the T stock must be acquired

---

4. Reg. § 1.368–2(b)(2).

5. I.R.C. § 368(a)(2)(E)(ii). See Reg. § 1.368–2(j)(3)(ii).

for P voting stock, and the rest may be obtained for cash or other property—or simply not acquired at all if P is willing to put up with minority shareholders.

Although Congress deserves applause for abandoning the formalisms of the old case law, its piecemeal approach to triangular reorganizations is yet another example of the major flaw in the reorganization scheme. In enacting Sections 368(a)(2)(D) and (E), each with its own distinct requirements, Congress added further embroidery to what already had become a crazy quilt. As the Senate Finance Committee staff lamented in its preliminary report on the reform and simplification of Subchapter C, many of the arcane distinctions in Section 368 "defy rationalization" and "[n]o discernible public policy would so sharply distinguish among the forms of an acquisition that are economically so similar."[6] Congress would be well advised to move toward a system that would impose consistent requirements on economically equivalent acquisition techniques.[7]

5. MULTI-STEP ACQUISITIONS

Regulations: § 1.338(h)(10)–1(c)(2).

We have seen that choosing the optimal structure for a corporate acquisition involves a wide range of legal and strategical considerations. From the buyer's perspective, important factors include determining the price to be paid for the target corporation and the mix of consideration to be used. Apart from taxes, other factors driving deal structure are the accounting treatment, regulatory hurdles, stock exchange rules, treatment of employer stock options, and timing, to name just a few.

For all these reasons, it is often desirable for the parties to an acquisition to employ a multi-step structure. For example, acquisitions of public companies may proceed at a quicker pace if the first step does not require regulatory clearance, consents from lenders or others with a contractual relationship to P or T, or actions that could impede the momentum of the deal. A good example of a two-step acquisition is when P makes a tender offer for T's stock at an attractive price and acquires sufficient stock to achieve control (but not 100 percent ownership) of T, enabling P to orchestrate a merger of T into P (or more likely into a P subsidiary), squeezing out the minority shareholders. The non-tax aspects of this and other deal structures are complex and beyond the scope of this text. Our concern here is to what extent the federal tax laws have accommodated the multi-step acquisition phenomenon.

---

6. See Staff of the Senate Finance Committee, Preliminary Report on the Reform and Simplification of the Income Taxation of Corporations, 98th Cong., 1st Sess., 26–27, 55–66 (Comm.Print S. 98–95, 1983).

7. See Staff of the Senate Finance Committee: The Subchapter C Revision Act of 1985, A Final Report Prepared by the Staff, 99th Cong., 1st Sess. (S.Prt. 99–47, 1985); Posin, "Taxing Corporate Reorganizations: Purging Penelope's Web," 133 U.Penn.L.Rev. 1335 (1985).

The rulings below are a reflection of the Service's willingness to apply the step transaction doctrine to facilitate multi-step acquisitions.[1] This often results in qualifying the integrated transaction as a tax-free reorganization where the separate steps, if viewed in isolation, would not qualify.

Revenue Ruling 2001–26

2001–1 Cum.Bull. 1297.

ISSUE

On the facts described below, is the control-for-voting-stock requirement of § 368(a)(2)(E) of the Internal Revenue Code satisfied, so that a series of integrated steps constitutes a tax-free reorganization under §§ 368(a)(1)(A) and 368(a)(2)(E) and § 354 or § 356 applies to each exchanging shareholder?

FACTS

Situation 1. Corporation P and Corporation T are widely held, manufacturing corporations organized under the laws of state A. T has only voting common stock outstanding, none of which is owned by P. P seeks to acquire all of the outstanding stock of T. For valid business reasons, the acquisition will be effected by a tender offer for at least 51 percent of the stock of T, to be acquired solely for P voting stock, followed by a merger of a subsidiary of P into T. P initiates a tender offer for T stock conditioned on the tender of at least 51 percent of the T shares. Pursuant to the tender offer, P acquires 51 percent of the T stock from T's shareholders for P voting stock. P forms S and S merges into T under the merger laws of state A. In the statutory merger, P's S stock is converted into T stock and each of the T shareholders holding the remaining 49 percent of the outstanding T stock exchanges its shares of T stock for a combination of consideration, two-thirds of which is P voting stock and one-third of which is cash. Assume that under general principles of tax law, including the step transaction doctrine, the tender offer and the statutory merger are treated as an integrated acquisition by P of all of the T stock. Also assume that all nonstatutory requirements for a reorganization under §§ 368(a)(1)(A) and 368(a)(2)(E) and all statutory requirements of § 368(a)(2)(E), other than the requirement under § 368(a)(2)(E)(ii) that P acquire control of T in exchange for its voting stock in the transaction, are satisfied.

Situation 2. The facts are the same as in Situation 1, except that S initiates the tender offer for T stock and, in the tender offer, acquires 51 percent of the T stock for P stock provided by P.

LAW AND ANALYSIS

1. See also Rev. Rul. 2001–24, 2001–1 C.B. 1290 (following a forward triangular merger of T into S, a P subsidiary, P may drop down the S stock to another of its controlled subsidiaries); Rev. Rul. 2001–25, 2001–1 C.B. 1291 (following a reverse triangular merger of S, a transitory subsidiary of P, into T, T may sell 50 percent of its operating assets to an unrelated buyer without violating the "substantially all of its properties" requirement of Section 368(a)(2)(E) if it retains the sales proceeds).

Section 368(a)(1)(A) states that the term "reorganization" means a statutory merger or consolidation. Section 368(a)(2)(E) provides that a transaction otherwise qualifying under § 368(a)(1)(A) will not be disqualified by reason of the fact that stock of a corporation (the "controlling corporation") that before the merger was in control of the merged corporation is used in the transaction, if (1) after the transaction, the corporation surviving the merger holds substantially all of its properties and of the properties of the merged corporation (other than stock of the controlling corporation distributed in the transaction), and (2) in the transaction, former shareholders of the surviving corporation exchanged, for an amount of voting stock of the controlling corporation, an amount of stock in the surviving corporation that constitutes control of such corporation (the "control-for-voting-stock requirement"). For this purpose, control is defined in § 368(c).

In King Enterprises, Inc. v. United States, 418 F.2d 511 (Ct.Cl.1969), as part of an integrated plan, a corporation acquired all of the stock of a target corporation from the target corporation's shareholders for consideration, in excess of 50 percent of which was acquiring corporation stock, and subsequently merged the target corporation into the acquiring corporation. The court held that, because the merger was the intended result of the stock acquisition, the acquiring corporation's acquisition of the target corporation qualified as a reorganization under § 368(a)(1)(A).

* * *

Section 1.368–1(c) of the Income Tax Regulations provides that a plan of reorganization must contemplate the bona fide execution of one of the transactions specifically described as a reorganization in § 368(a) and the bona fide consummation of each of the requisite acts under which nonrecognition of gain is claimed. Section 1.368–2(g) provides that the term plan of reorganization is not to be construed as broadening the definition of reorganization as set forth in § 368(a), but is to be taken as limiting the nonrecognition of gain or loss to such exchanges or distributions as are directly a part of the transaction specifically described as a reorganization in § 368(a).

As assumed in the facts, under general principles of tax law, including the step transaction doctrine, the tender offer and the statutory merger in both Situations 1 and 2 are treated as an integrated acquisition by P of all of the T stock. The principles of King Enterprises support the conclusion that, because the tender offer is integrated with the statutory merger in both Situations 1 and 2, the tender offer exchange is treated as part of the statutory merger (hereinafter the "Transaction") for purposes of the reorganization provisions. Cf. J.E. Seagram Corp. v. Commissioner, 104 T.C. 75 (1995) (treating a tender offer that was an integrated step in a plan that included a forward triangular merger as part of the merger transaction). Consequently, the integrated steps, which result in P acquiring all of the stock of T, must be examined together to determine whether the requirements of § 368(a)(2)(E) are satisfied. Cf. § 1.368–2(j)(3)(i); § 1.368–2(j)(6), Ex. 3 (suggesting that, absent a special exception, steps that are prior to the merger, but are part of the transaction intended to qualify as a reorganization under §§ 368(a)(1)(A) and 368(a)(2)(E), should be considered for purposes of determining whether the control-for-voting-stock requirement is satisfied).

In both situations, in the Transaction, the shareholders of T exchange, for P voting stock, an amount of T stock constituting in excess of 80 percent of the voting stock of T. Therefore, the control-for-voting-stock requirement is satisfied. Accordingly, in both Situations 1 and 2, the Transaction qualifies as a reorganization under §§ 368(a)(1)(A) and 368(a)(2)(E).

Under §§ 1.368–1(c) and 1.368–2(g), all of the T shareholders that exchange their T stock for P stock in the Transaction will be treated as exchanging their T stock for P stock in pursuance of a plan of reorganization. Therefore, T shareholders that exchange their T stock only for P stock in the Transaction will recognize no gain or loss under § 354. T shareholders that exchange their T stock for P stock and cash in the Transaction will recognize gain to the extent provided in § 356. In both Situations 1 and 2, none of P, S, or T will recognize any gain or loss in the Transaction, and P's basis in the T stock will be determined under § 1.358–6(c)(2) by treating P as acquiring all of the T stock in the Transaction and not acquiring any of the T stock before the Transaction.

HOLDING

On the facts set forth in Situations 1 and 2, the control-for-voting-stock requirement is satisfied in the Transaction, the Transaction constitutes a tax-free reorganization under §§ 368(a)(1)(A) and 368(a)(2)(E), and § 354 or § 356 applies to each exchanging shareholder.

Revenue Ruling 2008–25

2008–1 Cum. Bull. 986.

ISSUE

What is the proper Federal income tax treatment of the transaction described below?

FACTS

T is a corporation all of the stock of which is owned by individual A. T has 150x dollars worth of assets and 50x dollars of liabilities. P is a corporation that is unrelated to A and T. The value of P's assets, net of liabilities, is 410x dollars. P forms corporation X, a wholly owned subsidiary, for the sole purpose of acquiring all of the stock of T by causing X to merge into T in a statutory merger (the "Acquisition Merger"). In the Acquisition Merger, P acquires all of the stock of T, and A exchanges the T stock for 10x dollars in cash and P voting stock worth 90x dollars. Following the Acquisition Merger and as part of an integrated plan that included the Acquisition Merger, T completely liquidates into P (the "Liquidation"). In the Liquidation, T transfers all of its assets to P and P assumes all of T's liabilities. The Liquidation is not accomplished through a statutory merger. After the Liquidation, P continues to conduct the business previously conducted by T.

LAW

Section 368(a)(1)(A) of the Internal Revenue Code provides that the term "reorganization" means a statutory merger or consolidation. Section 368(a)(2)(E) provides that a transaction otherwise qualifying under § 368(a)(1)(A) shall not be disqualified by reason of the fact that stock of a corporation in control of the merged corporation is used in the transaction, if (i) after the transaction, the corporation surviving the merger holds substantially all of its properties and of the properties of the merged corporation (other than stock of the controlling corporation distributed in the transaction), and (ii) in the transaction, former shareholders of the surviving corporation exchanged, for an amount of voting stock of the controlling corporation, an amount of stock in the surviving corporation which constitutes control of the surviving corporation. Further, § 1.368–2(j)(3)(iii) of the Income Tax Regulations provides that "[i]n applying the 'substantially all' test to the merged corporation, assets transferred from the controlling corporation to the merged corporation in pursuance of the plan of reorganization are not taken into account."

Section 368(a)(1)(C) provides in part that a reorganization is the acquisition by one corporation, in exchange solely for all or part of its voting stock, of substantially all of the properties of another corporation, but in determining whether the exchange is solely for stock, the assumption by the acquiring corporation of a liability of the other shall be disregarded. Section 368(a)(2)(B) provides that if one corporation acquires substantially all of the properties of another corporation, the acquisition would qualify under § 368(a)(1)(C) but for the fact that the acquiring corporation exchanges money or other property in addition to voting stock, and the acquiring corporation acquires, solely for voting stock described in § 368(a)(1)(C), property of the other corporation having a fair market value which is at least 80 percent of the fair market value of all of the property of the other corporation, then such acquisition shall (subject to § 368(a)(2)(A)) be treated as qualifying under § 368(a)(1)(C). Section 368(a)(2)(B) further provides that solely for purposes of determining whether its requirements are satisfied, the amount of any liabilities assumed by the acquiring corporation shall be treated as money paid for the property.

Section 1.368–1(a) generally provides that in determining whether a transaction qualifies as a reorganization under § 368(a), the transaction must be evaluated under relevant provisions of law, including the step transaction doctrine.

Section 1.368–2(k) provides, in part, that a transaction otherwise qualifying as a reorganization under § 368(a) shall not be disqualified or recharacterized as a result of one or more distributions to shareholders (including distribution(s) that involve the assumption of liabilities) if the requirements of § 1.368–1(d) are satisfied, the property distributed consists of assets of the surviving corporation, and the aggregate of such distributions does not consist of an amount of assets of the surviving corporation (disregarding assets of the merged corporation) that would result in a liquidation of such corporation for Federal income tax purposes.

Rev. Rul. 67–274, 1967–2 C.B. 141, holds that an acquiring corporation's acquisition of all of the stock of a target corporation solely in exchange for voting stock of the acquiring corporation, followed by the liquidation of the target corporation as part of the same plan, will be treated as an acquisition by the acquiring corporation of substantially all of the target corporation's assets in a reorganization described in § 368(a)(1)(C). The ruling explains that, under these circumstances, the stock acquisition and the liquidation are part of the overall plan of reorganization and the two steps may not be considered independently of each other for Federal income tax purposes. See also, Rev. Rul. 72–405, 1972–2 C.B. 217.

Rev. Rul. 2001–46, 2001–2 C.B. 321, holds that, where a newly formed wholly owned subsidiary of an acquiring corporation merged into a target corporation, followed by the merger of the target corporation into the acquiring corporation, the step transaction doctrine is applied to integrate the steps and treat the transaction as a single statutory merger of the target corporation into the acquiring corporation. Noting that the rejection of step integration in Rev. Rul. 90–95, 1990–2 C.B. 67, and § 1.338–3(d) is based on Congressional intent that § 338 replace any nonstatutory treatment of a stock purchase as an asset purchase under the Kimbell–Diamond doctrine, the Service found that the policy underlying § 338 is not violated by treating the steps as a single statutory merger of the target into the acquiring corporation because such treatment results in a transaction that qualifies as a reorganization in which the acquiring corporation acquires the assets of the target corporation with a carryover basis under § 362, rather than receiving a cost basis in those assets under § 1012. (In *Kimbell–Diamond Milling Co. v. Commissioner*, 14 T.C. 74, *aff'd per curiam*, 187 F.2d 718 (1951), *cert. denied*, 342 U.S. 827 (1951), the court held that the purchase of the stock of a target corporation for the purpose of obtaining its assets through a prompt liquidation should be treated by the purchaser as a purchase of the target corporation's assets with the purchaser receiving a cost basis in the assets.)

Section 338(a) provides that if a corporation makes a qualified stock purchase and makes an election under that section, then the target corporation (i) shall be treated as having sold all of its assets at the close of the acquisition date at fair market value and (ii) shall be treated as a new corporation which purchased all of its assets as of the beginning of the day after the acquisition date. Section 338(d)(3) defines a qualified stock purchase as any transaction or series of transactions in which stock (meeting the requirements of § 1504(a)(2)) of one corporation is acquired by another corporation by purchase during a 12–month acquisition period. Section 338(h)(3) defines a purchase generally as any acquisition of stock, but excludes acquisitions of stock in exchanges to which § 351, § 354, § 355, or § 356 applies.

Section 338 was enacted in 1982 and was "intended to replace any nonstatutory treatment of a stock purchase as an asset purchase under the Kimbell–Diamond doctrine." H.R. Conf. Rep. No. 760, 97th Cong, 2d Sess. 536 (1982), 1982–2 C.B. 600, 632. Stock purchase or asset purchase treatment generally turns on whether the purchasing corporation makes or is deemed to make a § 338 election. If the election is made or deemed made, asset purchase treatment results and the basis of the target assets is adjusted to reflect the stock purchase price and other relevant items. If an election is not made or deemed made, the stock purchase treatment generally results. In such a case, the basis of the target assets is not adjusted to reflect the stock purchase price and other relevant items.

Rev. Rul. 90–95 (Situation 2), holds that the merger of a newly formed wholly owned domestic subsidiary into a target corporation with the target corporation shareholders receiving solely cash in exchange for their stock, immediately followed by the merger of the target corporation into the domestic parent of the merged subsidiary, will be treated as a qualified stock purchase of the target corporation followed by a § 332 liquidation of the target corporation. As a result, the parent's basis in the target corporation's assets will be the same as the basis of the assets in the target corporation's hands. The ruling explains that even though "the step-transaction doctrine is properly applied to disregard the existence of the [merged subsidiary]," so that the first step is treated as a stock purchase, the acquisition of the target corporation's stock is accorded independent significance from the subsequent liquidation of the target corporation and, therefore, is treated as a qualified stock purchase regardless of whether a § 338 election is made. Thus, in that case, the step transaction doctrine was not applied to treat the transaction as a direct acquisition by the domestic parent of the assets of the target corporation because such an application would have resulted in treating a stock purchase as an asset purchase, which would be inconsistent with the repeal of the Kimbell–Diamond doctrine and § 338.

Section 1.338–3(d) incorporates the approach of Rev. Rul. 90–95 into the regulations by requiring the purchasing corporation (or a member of its affiliated group) to treat certain asset transfers following a qualified stock purchase (where no § 338 election is made) independently of the qualified stock purchase. In the example in § 1.338–3(d)(5), the purchase for cash of 85 percent of the stock of a target corporation, followed by the merger of the target corporation into a wholly owned subsidiary of the purchasing corporation, is treated (other than by certain minority shareholders) as a qualified stock purchase of the stock of the target corporation followed by a § 368 reorganization of the target corporation into the subsidiary. As a result, the subsidiary's basis in the target corporation's assets is the same as the basis of the assets in the target corporation's hands.

ANALYSIS

If the Acquisition Merger and the Liquidation were treated as separate from each other, the Acquisition Merger would be treated as a stock acquisition that qualifies as a reorganization under § 368(a)(1)(A) by reason of § 368(a)(2)(E), and the Liquidation would qualify under § 332. However, as provided in § 1.368–1(a), in determining whether a transaction qualifies as a reorganization under § 368(a), the transaction must be evaluated under relevant provisions of law, including the step transaction doctrine. In this case, because T was completely liquidated, the § 1.368–2(k) safe harbor exception from the application of the step transaction doctrine does not apply. Accordingly, the Acquisition Merger and the Liquidation may not be considered independently of each other for purposes of determining whether the transaction satisfies the statutory requirements of a reorganization described in § 368(a)(1)(A) by reason of § 368(a)(2)(E). As such, this transaction does not qualify as a reorganization described in § 368(a)(1)(A) by reason of § 368(a)(2)(E) because, after the transaction, T does not hold substantially all of its properties and the properties of the merged corporation.

In determining whether the transaction is a reorganization, the approach reflected in Rev. Rul. 67–274 and Rev. Rul. 2001—46 is applied to ignore P's acquisition of the T stock in the Acquisition Merger and to treat the transaction as a direct acquisition by P of T's assets in exchange for 10x dollars in cash, 90x dollars worth of P voting stock, and the assumption of T's liabilities.

However, unlike the transactions considered in Revenue Rulings 67–274, 72–405 and 2001–46, a direct acquisition by P of T's assets in this case does not qualify as a reorganization under § 368(a). P's acquisition of T's assets is not a reorganization described in § 368(a)(1)(C) because the consideration exchanged is not solely P voting stock and the requirements of § 368(a)(2)(B) are not satisfied. Section 368(a)(2)(B) would treat P as acquiring 40 percent of T's assets for consideration other than P voting stock (liabilities assumed of 50x dollars, plus 10x dollars cash). See Rev. Rul. 73–102, 1973–1 C.B. 186 (analyzing the application of § 368(a)(2)(B)). P's acquisition of T's assets is not a reorganization described in § 368(a)(1)(D) because neither T nor A (nor a combination thereof) was in control of P (within the meaning of § 368(a)(2)(H)(i)) immediately after the transfer. Additionally, the transaction is not a reorganization under § 368(a)(1)(A) because T did not merge into P. Accordingly, the overall transaction is not a reorganization under § 368(a).

Additionally, P's acquisition of the T stock in the Acquisition Merger is not a transaction to which § 351 applies because A does not control P (within the meaning of § 368(c)) immediately after the exchange.

Rev. Rul. 90–95 and § 1.338–3(d) reject the step integration approach reflected in Rev. Rul. 67–274 where the application of that approach would treat the purchase of a target corporation's stock without a § 338 election followed by the liquidation or merger of the target corporation as the purchase of the target corporation's assets resulting in a cost basis in the assets under § 1012. Rev. Rul. 90–95 and § 1.338–3(d) treat the acquisition of the stock of the target corporation as a qualified stock purchase followed by a separate carryover basis transaction in order to preclude any nonstatutory treatment of the steps as an integrated asset purchase.

In this case, further application of the approach reflected in Rev. Rul. 67–274, integrating the acquisition of T stock with the liquidation of T, would result in treating the acquisition of T stock as a taxable purchase of T's assets. Such treatment would violate the policy underlying § 338 that a cost basis in acquired assets should not be obtained through the purchase of stock where no § 338 election is made. Accordingly, consistent with the analysis set forth in Rev. Rul. 90–95, the acquisition of the stock of T is treated as a qualified stock purchase by P followed by the liquidation of T into P under § 332.

HOLDING

The transaction is not a reorganization under § 368(a). The Acquisition Merger is a qualified stock purchase by P of the stock of T under § 338(d)(3). The Liquidation is a complete liquidation of a controlled subsidiary under § 332.

NOTE

Experienced tax professionals have come to understand that "the step-transaction doctrine generally applies ... except when it doesn't."[1] What factors in the rulings above supported application of the doctrine? Was it because the first step was conditioned on the second occurring? Does Revenue Ruling 2001–26 offer any guiding principle for application of the doctrine, or does it simply assume for purposes of analysis that the tender offer and merger should be integrated?

A critical point made in the most recent multi-step acquisition rulings is that application of the step transaction doctrine is permissible when it does not violate the policy of Section 338. What policy? Does that suggest that the step transaction doctrine should not be applied to the prototype *Kimbell–Diamond* transaction where P purchases 80 percent or more of T's stock and promptly liquidates T, winding up with direct ownership of its assets? If the step transaction doctrine did apply to that fact pattern, P would take a cost basis in T's assets even though no Section 338 election was made—a result clearly at variance with the policy of Section 338.

What if the first step is a qualified stock purchase under Section 338, and P and S (T's corporate parent) jointly make a Section 338(h)(10) election? In that situation, should the first step be viewed in isolation for tax purposes or should step transaction principles be applied, resulting in reorganization treatment and nullification of the Section 338 election?

---

1. See Stratton, "Step–Transaction Doctrine Tested Under Corporate Rulings," 93 Tax Notes 332 (Oct. 15, 2001), quoting an I.R.S. official who was quoting an unnamed law professor.

What if T is not a subsidiary and P unilaterally makes a Section 338 election?

The Service has issued regulations answering some of these questions. They provide that the step transaction doctrine will not apply to a multi-step acquisition if the first step is a qualified stock purchase under Section 338 and the parties to the transaction make a joint Section 338(h)(10) election with respect to that step, whether or not the overall transaction would have qualified as a reorganization.[2] To illustrate, assume that P, Inc. owns all the stock of Y, Inc., a newly formed subsidiary, and S, Inc. owns all the stock of T, Inc. As the first step in P's acquisition of T's assets, Y, Inc. merges into T, with T surviving, and S (T's only shareholder) receives 50 percent P voting stock and 50 percent cash. This step, viewed independently, does not qualify as a reorganization and does constitute a qualified stock purchase. T then merges into P. If P and S do not make a Section 338(h)(10) election, the step transaction doctrine would be applied, and the overall acquisition would be treated as a Section 368 reorganization. But if P and S jointly make a Section 338(h)(10) election, the regulations "turn off" the step transaction doctrine and treat P's acquisition of the T stock in the reverse merger as a qualified stock purchase, causing "old T" to recognize gain or loss on the deemed sale of its assets and "new T"—and then P, after the merger into P—to take a cost basis in its assets.[3] If, however, the first step does not constitute a qualified stock purchase under Section 338(d)(3)—such where the first step, viewed independently, was a Section 368 reorganization—then no Section 338(h)(10) election can be made and the overall acquisition will be treated as a reorganization.[4] The regulations do not address a situation where a unilateral Section 338 election is made by the acquiring corporation with respect to the first step.

Revenue Ruling 2008–25 is unique insofar as it "turns on" the step transaction doctrine for purposes of concluding that P's acquisition of T's assets and assumption of its liabilities fail to qualify as a Type C reorganization but then "turns off" the doctrine in determining the ultimate tax consequences of the failed reorganization. The reason for this seeming inconsistency is the Service's obsession with protecting the policy of Section 338. The upshot is that because P's acquisition of T stock (Step 1) did not qualify as a reorganization, it is treated as a Section 338 qualified stock purchase followed by a tax-free liquidation of T under Section 332. The bad news is that T's sole shareholder, A, who could reasonably have expected to limit his gain to the $10x cash received in the initial reverse merger, must recognize his entire gain just as if he sold his stock for all cash. Since P did not make a Section 338 election, T does not recognize gain on its assets, and P takes those assets with a carryover rather than cost basis.

Would the result have been the same if the second step in Revenue Ruling 2008–25 had been an upstream merger of T into P rather than a liquidation?

---

2. Reg. § 1.338(h)(10)–1(c)(2).

3. Reg. § 1.338(h)(10)–1(e) Examples 11 and 12.

4. Reg. § 1.338(h)(10)–1(e) Example 14.

PROBLEMS

1. Publishing Company, Inc. ("P") is a publicly traded C corporation engaged in the publication of professional textbooks. P has 5 million shares of voting common stock outstanding. The stock is currently trading at $10 per share.

P wishes to acquire control of Target Press, Inc. ("T"), a closely held corporation that is the leading publisher of student study aids for law students. T has 4,000 shares of common stock (its only class) outstanding, held by 10 shareholders each of whom owns 400 shares. T's assets and liabilities are as follows:

Asset	Adj. Basis	Fair Mkt. Value
Cash	$ 600,000	$ 600,000
Inventory	200,000	1,000,000
Equipment	800,000	1,400,000
Goodwill	0	2,000,000
	$1,600,000	$5,000,000

Liabilities		
Bank Loan		$1,000,000
		$1,000,000

Both P and T have substantial accumulated earnings and profits.

T's board of directors has agreed to sell the business for $4 million. Four of T's shareholders have a very low adjusted basis in their stock and wish to minimize their taxable gain on a sale. One shareholder, Dee Minimis, recently inherited her stock and would not have any significant realized gain. The other shareholders are interested in diversifying their investments and less concerned about the tax liability on a sale.

P does not wish to dilute the interests of its current shareholders by issuing too much voting common stock to acquire T, but P is willing to use a mix of consideration (including newly issued preferred stock) and to assume T's $1,000,000 bank loan. For business reasons, P ultimately wishes to operate T's business through a wholly-owned subsidiary and would prefer to avoid exposure to any unknown T liabilities. Assume that any preferred stock used by P to make the acquisition is not "nonqualified preferred stock" within the meaning of Section 351(g).

Various plans are under consideration to complete the acquisition. Consider generally the tax consequences of each of the alternative plans described below, focusing on whether the acquisition will qualify as a tax-free reorganization. Then propose one or more desirable alternatives that are compatible with the objectives of the parties. Unless otherwise indicated, assume in all cases that the consideration to be exchanged for stock or assets of T is valued as of the date that the contract was legally binding.

(a) T merges directly into P, and each T shareholder receives $300,000 of P nonvoting preferred stock and $100,000 of P five-year notes.

(b) Same as (a), above, except four T shareholders (holding 40% of the T stock) each receives $400,000 of P voting common stock and the other six T shareholders each receives $400,000 cash.

(c) Same as (b), above, except that the value of the P stock declined between the time the merger agreement was signed and four months later, when the merger was finalized and, as a result, the four T shareholders holding 40% of the T stock receive only $250,000 of P voting stock.

(d) T merges directly into P, and each T shareholder receives $400,000 of P voting common stock. Pursuant to a binding commitment entered into prior to the merger, six of the former T shareholders (who held 60% of the T stock) sell their new P stock for cash to a third party three weeks after the merger.

(e) Same as (a), above, except shortly after the merger and as part of its original plan, P sells T's assets to an unrelated party at a nice profit and uses the sales proceeds to expand its professional text-book business.

(f) In exchange for their respective 400 shares of T stock, P transfers to each T shareholder $360,000 of P voting preferred stock and $40,000 cash.

(g) P purchases 400 shares of T stock from Dee Minimis for $400,000 cash. Three months later, P transfers $400,000 of P voting pre-ferred stock to each of the nine remaining T shareholders in exchange for their respective 400 shares of T stock.

(h) P acquires all the T assets, and assumes the $1,000,000 liability, in exchange for $3.6 million of P voting common stock (360,000 shares) and $400,000 in P five-year notes. Immediately thereafter, T completely liquidates, distributing the P shares and notes pro rata to its shareholders. P drops down the assets it acquires to S, a newly created subsidiary.

(i) Same as (h), above, except that T retains $400,000 of its cash, P acquires the balance of T's assets, and assumes the liability, for $3.6 million of P voting common stock, and T distributes the P shares and cash pro rata to its shareholders in complete liquidation.

(j) P acquires all the T stock in a reverse triangular merger in which Y–1, a transitory subsidiary of P, merges into T. In the merger, four T shareholders (holding 40% of the T stock) each receive $400,000 cash and the other six T shareholders each receive $400,000 of P nonvoting preferred stock. T then merges upstream into P.

(k) Same as (j), above, except the second step in the transaction is a merger of T into Y–2, a subsidiary of P.

(l) Same as (j), above, except the second step is the complete liquidation of T into P in a transaction that is not a statutory merger
under state law.

(m) Same as (j) above, except T is a wholly owned subsidiary of S, Inc.
Y–1 merges into T and, in the merger, S, Inc. receives $500,000
cash and $500,000 of P nonvoting stock. P and S jointly make an
election under § 338(h)(10).

2. Assume the same basic facts as in Problem 1, above, except that P
purchased 10% of T's stock five years ago for cash, and purchased an
additional 50% of T's stock one year ago for cash. P now wishes to acquire
the remaining 40% of T's stock for P voting stock or, if possible, P
nonvoting preferred stock. The T minority shareholders are willing to
engage in the transaction if they can avoid recognition of taxable gain.
Advise the parties on the best method for structuring the acquisition as a
tax-free reorganization.

3. Are the results reached in Problems 1–2, above, rational as a matter of
tax policy? Would it be preferable to have uniform tax rules governing all
corporate acquisitions?

C. TREATMENT OF THE PARTIES TO AN ACQUISITIVE REORGANIZATION

Up to this point, we have been concentrating on the definition of a
reorganization in Section 368. Compliance with those statutory requirements and the judicial doctrines unlocks the gate to the operative provisions, which govern the tax treatment of the target shareholders and
corporations that are "a party to a reorganization" and provide for transferred and exchanged bases, tacked holding periods and the carryover of
corporate tax attributes such as earnings and profits and net operating
losses. Section 368(b) broadly defines "a party to a reorganization" to
include any corporation resulting from a qualifying reorganization (e.g., the
surviving corporation in a consolidation), the acquiring and target corporations in a straight acquisitive reorganization and the parent corporation in
a "drop down" or triangular reorganization.

This section summarizes the operative provisions, beginning with the
tax consequences to the target's shareholders and security holders and then
turning to the treatment of the target and acquiring corporations.

1. CONSEQUENCES TO SHAREHOLDERS AND SECURITY HOLDERS

Code: §§ 354(a); 356(a), (c), (d), (e); 358(a), (b), (d), (f); 368(b). Skim
§§ 351(g).

Regulations: §§ 1.354–1(a), (b); 1.356–1, –3, –4; 1.358–1(a), –2(a)(1),
(a)(2)(i), (a)(2)(vii), (b), (c) Example 1.

Proposed Regulations: §§ 1.354–1(d)(1), (2); 1.356–1(d) Examples 3 & 4.

Recognition of Gain or Loss. One of the principal benefits of reorganization status is the nonrecognition granted to the shareholders and security holders of the target corporation under Section 354(a). Shareholders are entitled to complete nonrecognition only when they receive solely stock or securities of the acquiring corporation.[1] This invariably occurs in a Type B reorganization, but the target shareholders in a Type A, C or any form of triangular reorganization may receive some boot. In that event, the shareholder must recognize any realized gain to the extent of the money plus the fair market value of any other boot received.[2] For this purpose, boot includes any property other than stock or securities of a party to the reorganization. To prevent avoidance of this rule through the use of debt "securities,"[3] Section 356(d) provides that if the principal amount of securities received exceeds the principal amount of securities surrendered or if securities are received but none are surrendered, the fair market value of the excess is treated as boot.[4] Consequently, a shareholder holding no securities who receives bonds in connection with a reorganization is treated as having "cashed out" his investment to the extent of the bonds—an appropriate result under the continuity of interest principle. But security holders who change their investment to an equity interest or exchange securities for the same or lesser principal amount have not significantly changed the form of their investment and therefore are entitled to nonrecognition treatment. As might be expected, however, a shareholder or security holder who receives boot may not recognize any realized loss.[5]

Characterization of Gain. Section 356(a)(2) provides that any recognized gain is treated as a dividend to a target shareholder if the exchange "has the effect of the distribution of a dividend." In that event, each T shareholder must treat as a dividend the amount of his recognized gain that is not in excess of that shareholder's ratable share of the corporation's accumulated earnings and profits.[6] Any remaining gain is treated as gain from the sale or exchange of the target stock or securities transferred.

The "boot dividend" issue historically was one of the most difficult questions arising under the operative provisions. The Service once contended that dividend treatment was automatic if boot were received,[7] but it later conceded that dividend equivalence should be determined by using the tests ignore applicable to stock redemptions in Section 302(b),[8] treating the boot as if it were received as a distribution in redemption of the *target*

---

1. I.R.C. § 354(a)(1).

2. I.R.C. § 356(a)(1).

3. "Securities" are generally defined to encompass relatively long-term corporate debt instruments but not short-term notes, stock rights or warrants.

4. See I.R.C. § 354(a)(2)(A).

5. I.R.C. § 356(c).

6. Note that the gain is not automatically characterized as ordinary income but, if it has the effect of a dividend, it is treated as

a Section 301 distribution subject to the Section 243 dividends received deduction. In addition, the earnings and profits of the target corporation are reduced under Section 312(a).

7. See Commissioner v. Bedford's Estate, 325 U.S. 283, 65 S.Ct. 1157 (1945).

8. In applying Section 302(b) principles, the Section 318 attribution rules are applicable. I.R.C. § 356(a)(2). Rev.Rul. 74–515, 1974–2 C.B. 118. See also Wright v. United States, 482 F.2d 600 (8th Cir.1973).

corporation's stock immediately prior to the reorganization exchange.[9] Taxpayers argued, however, that dividend equivalence should be determined by examining the effect of the reorganization exchange as a whole, an approach that ultimately was adopted by the Supreme Court in Clark v. Commissioner.[10] Under the *Clark* test, each T shareholder is treated as initially receiving only P stock instead of the combination of P stock and boot actually received, and then P is treated as having distributed the boot in a hypothetical redemption of the portion of P stock not actually received by the T shareholder. If this redemption meets one of the tests for exchange treatment in Section 302(b), the receipt of boot does not have the effect of a dividend, and the shareholder recognizes capital gain or loss. Otherwise, as previewed above, the recognized gain is a dividend (likely a qualified dividend taxable at long-term capital gains rates at least through 2012) to the extent of the shareholder's ratable share of "the corporation's"[11] accumulated earnings and profits, and any remaining gain is capital gain.

Whenever there is a meaningful rate preference for long-term capital gains and dividends are taxed as ordinary income at the highest marginal rates, individual taxpayers will benefit from the Supreme Court's holding in *Clark*.[12] Corporate shareholders, however, ordinarily will prefer dividend classification in order to qualify for the dividends received deduction under Section 243.[13] Dividend treatment also may be preferable to the acquiring corporation because it reduces the earnings and profits that are inherited under Section 381 as a result of the reorganization. Finally, dividend classification may be undesirable where shareholders receiving notes from the acquiring corporation wish to report their gain on the installment method. Unless the target stock exchanged by the shareholder is publicly traded,[14] installment sale treatment generally is available if the transaction is treated as a sale but not if the receipt of installment boot is treated as a dividend under Section 356(a)(2).[15]

The boot dividend issue rarely is important to individual shareholders, however, as long as dividends and long-term capital gains are taxed at the same preferential rate. Since any amount characterized as a dividend under Section 356(a)(2) may not exceed the shareholder's recognized gain, the shareholder is always entitled to recovery of basis. If the dividend is "qualified," the rate is the same unless the capital gain is short-term (or the stock is not a capital asset), in which case dividend treatment is preferable. For transactions involving U.S. corporations, corporate share-

---

9. See, e.g., Shimberg v. United States, 577 F.2d 283 (5th Cir. 1978), cert. denied, 439 U.S. 1115, 99 S.Ct. 1019 (1979).

10. 489 U.S. 726, 109 S.Ct. 1455 (1989). See also Rev. Rul. 93–61, 1993–2 C.B. 118.

11. The statute is unclear, but the majority view appears to be that the dividend determination should be based on the target corporation's earnings and profits.

12. The Service, as it must, has announced that it will apply the *Clark* approach to an acquisitive reorganization. See Rev. Rul. 93–61, 1993–2 C.B. 118.

13. But see I.R.C. § 1059(e)(1)(B), which treats any amount treated as a dividend on a non pro rata redemption of a corporate shareholder's stock as an "extraordinary dividend." See Chapter 4F3, supra.

14. See I.R.C. § 453(k)(2).

15. See I.R.C. § 453(f)(6); Prop. Reg. § 1.453–1(f)(2).

holders will continue to prefer dividend classification because of the dividends received deduction, and dividend treatment is preferable to the acquiring corporation because it reduces earnings and profits inherited from the target corporation on the reorganization.

Allocation of Consideration Issues. The IRS has provided guidance for T shareholders who receive a mix of consideration or surrender different blocks or classes of stock or securities in a Section 368 reorganization exchange. Consider, for example, the tax consequences to a T shareholder who receives both P stock and boot in exchange for two blocks of the same class of T stock, acquired at different times and with different bases. The regulations adopt a default rule that is similar to the strict pro rata allocation of consideration approach used for other transactions governed by Subchapter C. But in a rare taxpayer-friendly gesture, they give the parties considerable flexibility to specify how the consideration received should be allocated as long as the specification is "economically reasonable."[16] Under this permissive approach, a shareholder with multiple blocks or different classes of stock with different bases can minimize her recognized gain by allocating boot to the blocks or classes with the highest per-share basis if the receipt of boot does not have the effect of a dividend. In those now rare cases where the receipt of boot does have the effect of a dividend, the regulations allow T shareholders who hold different classes of T stock some flexibility to specify the class of stock to which the dividend-generating boot should be allocated, but a pro rata allocation must be made among shares of the same class.[17]

To illustrate, assume shareholder A owns two 10–share blocks of T stock each of which has a fair market value of $100. A's basis for Block 1 is $30 ($3 per share) and her basis for Block 2 is $90 ($9 per share). P acquires T in a statutory merger that qualifies as a Type A reorganization. A surrenders her T stock and receives in exchange 10 shares of P stock worth $100 and $100 cash, and the receipt of cash does not have the effect of a distribution of a dividend. A's *realized* gain is thus $70 on Block 1 and $10 on Block 2, for a total of $80 realized gain on the transaction. If the terms of the merger do not specify that the P shares and cash are received in exchange for particular shares of T stock, the default rule requires that a pro rata portion of the cash is treated as received in exchange for each share of T stock based on the fair market value of the surrendered shares. Under this approach, A would recognize $50 of her $70 realized gain on Block 1 and all $10 of her realized gain on Block 2.[18] But if the terms of the merger specify that A receives 10 shares of P stock in exchange for A's Block 1 shares and $100 cash in exchange for his Block 2 shares, A is not required to recognize any of her $70 realized gain on Block 1 (because none of the boot was allocated to that block) and recognizes $10 of gain on Block 2.[19]

---

16. Reg. § 1.356–1(b); Prop. Reg. § 1.354–1(d)(1).

17. Prop. Reg. § 1.354–1(d)(1).

18. Prop. Reg. § 1.356–1(d) Example 3.

19. Prop. Reg. § 1.356–1(d) Example 4.

Dividend Within Gain Approach: Policy Aspects. Section 356(a)(2) limits the amount of any boot dividend to the shareholder's recognized gain. Over 25 years ago, this approach was criticized as a "curious mixing of dividend and sale or exchange concepts" which "permits shareholders with a high basis in their stock * * * to withdraw corporate earnings in a reorganization without dividend consequences."[20] Allowing taxpayers to recover their basis even when a transaction is equivalent to a dividend is inconsistent with the rules applicable to stock redemptions in Section 302 and is difficult to justify. In what has become an annual ritual, the Obama administration has proposed to repeal the "dividend within gain" rule, arguing that "[t]here is not a significant policy reason to vary the treatment of a distribution that otherwise qualifies as a dividend by reference to whether it is received in the normal course of a corporation's operations or is instead received as part of a reorganization exchange."[21] The proposal is among the many on the cluttered pending legislation shelf.

Basis and Holding Period. Target shareholders determine the basis of nonrecognition property (i.e., the stock or nonboot securities received in the exchange) under Section 358 by reference to their basis in the stock that they relinquished, increased by any gain recognized and reduced by any boot received and liabilities assumed. Any boot (other than cash) received takes a fair market value basis under Section 358(a)(2). This is the same formula used many chapters ago in determining the basis of stock received in a Section 351 exchange. If different types of nonrecognition property are received (e.g., two classes of stock or stock and bonds), the aggregate exchanged basis is allocated among those properties in proportion to their relative fair market values under rules provided in the regulations.[22] The nonrecognition property generally takes a tacked holding period under Section 1223(1) and the holding period of the boot commences on the date of its acquisition.

The general basis rule in Section 358 is simple enough to apply when a target shareholder acquired all of her T stock at the same time. But it is not uncommon for a shareholder to have acquired T stock at different times, for different prices. When these multiple "tax lots" of T stock are exchanged in a tax-free reorganization for stock of the acquiring corporation, can T shareholders use the average basis in their T shares to determine the basis for all their new P stock or must they use an approach under which the basis of the P stock received is traced to the basis of the different blocks of T stock surrendered? And does it matter how the shares are held—e.g., in certificates that can be physically identified, or a broker-

---

20. Staff of the Senate Committee on Finance, The Subchapter C Revision Act of 1985: A Final Report Prepared by the Staff, 99th Cong., 1st Sess. 45 (S.Prt. 99–47, 1985).

21. General Explanation of the Administration's Fiscal Year 2013 Revenue Proposals 133 (Dept. of the Treasury, Feb. 2012).

22. I.R.C. § 358(b)(1); Reg. § 1.358–2(a)(2)(i).

age account where separate lots may be more difficult or impossible to track?[23]

From the standpoint of simplicity and administrative convenience, the average basis method has much to offer even when separate lots are easily identifiable. But to prevent potential tax avoidance and also allow taxpayers some flexibility, the Service has concluded that tracing is the preferable approach.[24] Under the regulations, the basis of the stock received in a reorganization transaction, to the greatest extent possible, must be an allocable portion of the basis of each block of stock surrendered.[25] For example, if a T shareholder exchanges more than one block of a single class of T stock acquired on different dates with different bases, the regulations require the basis of the shares surrendered to be allocated to the shares received in a manner that reflects, to the greatest extent possible, that a share of stock received is in respect of (i.e., traceable to) shares of stock acquired on the same date and at the same price.[26] T shareholders who are unable to identify and trace the shares surrendered and received may designate which shares of of P stock are received in exchange for each block of T stock provided the designation is consistent with the terms of the transaction.[27]

The regulations illustrate the tracing approach with this example of a Type A statutory merger where Corporation X is the target and Corporation Y is the acquiring corporation:[28]

> J, an individual, acquired 20 shares of Corporation X stock on Date 1 for $3 each and 10 shares of Corporation X stock on Date 2 for $6 each. On Date 3, Corporation Y acquires the assets of Corporation X in a reorganization under Section 368(a)(1)(A). Pursuant to the terms of the plan of reorganization, J receives 2

23. Even without a reorganization, similar issues are raised when shares are sold by a taxpayer who acquired lots of that stock on different dates or at different prices. See, e.g., Reg. § 1.1012–1(c), providing that if the shares sold cannot be adequately identified, the earliest of the lots acquired is deemed to be sold first. In the reorganization setting, the cases are inconsistent. Compare, e.g., Arrott v. Commissioner, 136 F.2d 449 (3d Cir. 1943) (average basis) and Bloch v. Commissioner, 148 F.2d 452 (9th Cir. 1945) (tracing permissible).

24. See generally Reg. § 1.358–2.

25. Reg. § 1.358–2(a)(2)(i). For simplicity, the discussion in the text is limited to exchanges of stock in acquisitive reorganizations. The regulations use a similar approach for reorganization exchanges of debt securities. If more than one class of stock or security of the target corporation is exchanged for multiple classes of the acquiring corporation,

an additional layer of allocation is required. See, e.g., Reg. § 1.358–2(c) Example 3.

26. Reg. § 1.358–2(a)(2)(i). These regulations also address the more complex situation where stock and securities (e.g., bonds) are received.

27. Reg. § 1.358–2(a)(2)(vii). The designation must be made on or before the date when it is first relevant (e.g., at the time of a sale of the P stock received by the selling shareholder). If no designation is made at the time of a sale or transfer, the taxpayer is treated as selling or transferring the P shares received in respect of the earliest T shares purchased or acquired. Id.

28. Reg. § 1.358–2(c) Example 1. More complex fact patterns are analyzed in thirteen other increasingly mind-numbing examples but, not to worry—somewhere, a reputable company has designed portfolio management software to handle all these basis computations.

shares of Corporation Y stock for each share of Corporation X stock. Therefore, J receives 60 shares of Corporation Y stock. Pursuant to Section 354, J recognizes no gain or loss on the exchange. J is not able to identify which shares of Corporation Y stock are received for each share of Corporation X stock.

J has 40 shares of Corporation Y each of which has a basis of $1.50 and is treated as having been acquired on Date 1 and 20 shares of Corporation Y each of which has a basis of $3 and is treated as having been acquired on Date 2. On or before the date on which the basis of a share of Corporation Y stock received becomes relevant, J may designate which of the shares of Corporation Y stock have a basis of $1.50 and which have a basis of $3.

In reorganizations where T shareholders receive shares of stock or securities of more than one class, or boot is received in addition to stock or securities, and the terms of the exchange specify which shares of P stock or securities are received in exchange for a particular share (or class) of T stock or securities, the specification controls for basis purposes if the terms are "economically reasonable."[29] If there is no specification, a pro rata portion of the P stock and securities is treated as received in exchange for each share of T stock and securities surrendered, based on the fair market value of surrendered stock and securities.[30] This approach is consistent with the allocation of consideration rules discussed above.[31]

2.   CONSEQUENCES TO THE TARGET CORPORATION

Code: §§ 336(c); 357(a), (b), (c)(1); 358(a), (b)(1), (f); 361.

Regulations: § 1.357–1(a).

Treatment of the Reorganization Exchange. Without a nonrecognition provision, the target corporation in an acquisitive reorganization would recognize gain or loss on the transfer of its assets and the assumption of its liabilities by the acquiring corporation. If the acquisition qualifies as a reorganization, however, Section 361(a) comes to the rescue by providing that the target recognizes no gain or loss if it exchanges property, pursuant to the reorganization plan, solely for stock or securities in a corporation which also is a party to the reorganization. Section 357(a) offers similar protection by providing that the assumption of the target's liabilities in a reorganization exchange will not be treated as boot nor prevent the exchange from being tax-free under Section 361(a).[1] These rules apply primarily to Type A and C reorganizations and forward triangular mergers. In a Type B stock-for-stock exchange or a reverse triangular merger, no

---

29. Reg. § 1.358–2(a)(2)(ii).

30. Id.

31. See p. 441, infra.

1. As in the Section 351 incorporation area, the general nonrecognition rule in Section 357(a) is subject to an exception in Section 357(b) if the liability assumption is motivated by tax avoidance or lacks a bona fide business purpose. The Section 357(c) exception for liabilities assumed in excess of the basis of the transferred assets only applies to a Type D reorganization. See Chapters 11 and 12, infra.

assets are transferred because the target corporation remains intact as a controlled subsidiary of the acquiring corporation.

The target in a Type C reorganization may receive a limited amount of boot without disqualifying the transaction under Section 368.[2] In that event, the target must recognize any realized gain (but may not recognize loss) on the reorganization exchange to the extent of the cash and the fair market value of the boot that the target does not distribute pursuant to the plan of reorganization.[3] Any transfer by the target of cash or other boot received in the exchange to creditors in connection with the reorganization is treated as a "distribution" pursuant to the reorganization plan.[4] Since the target in a Type C reorganization is generally required to distribute all of its properties pursuant to the plan,[5] gain or loss rarely will be recognized on the exchange.[6]

Section 361(a) only applies to the *receipt* of boot by the target pursuant to a reorganization plan. An acquiring corporation that transfers appreciated boot property to the target as partial consideration for the target's assets must recognize gain under Section 1001 because, to that extent, the transaction is considered to be a taxable exchange.[7] In that event, the target takes the boot property with a fair market value basis.[8]

Treatment of Distributions. Section 361(c) generally provides that a corporation does not recognize gain or loss on the distribution of "qualified property" to its shareholders pursuant to a reorganization plan. "Qualified property" is: (1) stock (or rights to acquire stock) in, or obligations (e.g., bonds and notes) of the distributing corporation, or (2) stock (or rights to acquire stock) in, or obligations of, another party to the reorganization which were received by the distributing corporation in the exchange. Thus, any stock, securities or even short-term notes of the acquiring corporation received by the target in the exchange and then distributed to its shareholders would constitute "qualified property." Section 361(c)(3) makes it clear that a transfer of "qualified property" by a target to its creditors in satisfaction of corporate liabilities is treated as a "distribution" pursuant to the reorganization plan.

If the target distributes an asset other than qualified property, it must recognize gain (but may not recognize loss) in the same manner as if the property had been sold to the distributee at its fair market value.[9] For example, the target would recognize gain on the distribution of an appreci-

---

2. I.R.C. § 368(a)(2)(B). Boot in a Type C reorganization would include any property other than voting stock of the acquiring corporation (or its parent). See Section B3 of this Chapter, infra.

3. I.R.C. § 361(b)(1), (2).

4. I.R.C. § 361(b)(3). The Service may prescribe regulations as necessary to prevent tax avoidance through abuse of this rule. Id.

5. I.R.C. § 368(a)(2)(G).

6. A rare situation where gain might be recognized is where liabilities of the target are assumed in a transaction to which Section 357(b) or (c) applies.

7. Section 361(a) does not apply in this situation because it only provides nonrecognition to the *recipient* of distributed boot.

8. I.R.C. § 358(a)(2). See also I.R.C. § 358(f).

9. I.R.C. § 361(c)(1), (2).

ated retained asset (i.e., an asset not acquired in the reorganization) or boot (other than notes of the acquiring corporation) which appreciated between the time it was received and the distribution to shareholders.[10]

Sales Prior to Liquidation. Before liquidating, the target corporation in a Type C reorganization may sell some of the stock or securities received from the acquiring corporation in order to raise money to pay off creditors. Prior to the Tax Reform Act of 1986, the courts were divided over whether these sales were entitled to nonrecognition treatment.[11] The current version of Section 361 settles the debate by providing that only transfers of "qualified property" (i.e., stock or obligations of the acquiring corporation) or boot directly to creditors will qualify for nonrecognition because they are treated as "distributions" to the shareholders pursuant to the reorganization plan.[12] Sales of property to third parties are thus fully taxable events even if they were necessary to raise money to pay off creditors.

Basis and Holding Period. If the target corporation retains property received from the acquiring corporation, which only could occur in a Type C reorganization where the Commissioner waives the Section 368(a)(2)(G) distribution requirement, it is deemed to have distributed that property to its shareholders, who then are treated as having recontributed the property to a "new" corporation as a contribution to capital.[13] The basis and the holding period of the property in the hands of the "new" corporation depend upon the consequences to the shareholders. If the property is boot to the shareholders, it receives a fair market value basis and no tacked holding period in the hands of either the shareholders or the "new" corporation to which it is constructively recontributed.[14] If the property is nonrecognition property (e.g., stock or securities of the acquiring corporation) to the shareholders, then their exchanged bases and tacked holding periods transfer to the "new" corporation.[15] These rules are irrelevant in the typical Type C reorganization where the target liquidates and distributes the stock, securities and boot received in the transaction, along with any retained assets, to its shareholders. In that event, basis and holding period are determined under the operative provisions governing shareholders and security holders.

3.   Consequences to the Acquiring Corporation

Code: §§ 362(b); 368(b); 1032.

Regulations: § 1.1032–1.

---

10. Since the target takes a fair market value basis in the boot under Section 358(a)(2) at the time of the exchange, it would recognize only post-acquisition appreciation on a later distribution of the boot.

11. Compare General Housewares Corp. v. United States, 615 F.2d 1056 (5th Cir.1980) (allowing nonrecognition under former Section 337) with FEC Liquidating Corp. v. United States, 548 F.2d 924 (Ct.Cl.1977) (taxing such gains on the ground that former

Section 337 and the reorganization provisions were conceptually incompatible).

12. I.R.C. § 361(b)(3), (c)(3).

13. H.R. Rep. No. 98–861, 98th Cong., 2d Sess. 845–846 (1984).

14. I.R.C. §§ 358(a)(2); 362(a).

15. I.R.C. §§ 358(a)(1); 362(a); 1223(1) and (2).

Recognition of Gain or Loss. The acquiring corporation does not recognize gain or loss on the issuance of its stock or the stock of its parent in an acquisitive reorganization or, for that matter, in any other transaction.[1] To the extent that it may issue securities as consideration for the acquired property, the acquiring corporation recognizes no gain because the acquisition is a "purchase." If the acquiring corporation transfers other "boot" property to make the acquisition, however, it recognizes any realized gain or loss under general tax principles.[2]

Basis and Holding Period: In General. Under Section 362(b), the target assets acquired in a Type A, Type C or forward triangular reorganization take a transferred basis, increased by any gain recognized by the target on the transfer. Since Section 361(a) generally provides that the target does not recognize gain or loss on any exchange of property pursuant to the plan of reorganization, an upward basis adjustment for gain recognized by the target will occur only in the rare Type C reorganization where the target receives boot and does not distribute it to its shareholders or creditors. In the case of a Type B or reverse triangular reorganization, however, the property acquired is corporate stock whose transferred basis is determined by its basis in the hands of the target shareholders. In either case, the property acquired is allowed a tacked holding period under Section 1223(2).

The acquiring corporation in a Type B stock-for-stock exchange or reverse triangular merger often faces some logistical challenges in determining its exchanged basis in the T stock, especially when T is a publicly traded company. Assume, for example, that P acquires all the stock of publicly traded T in a Type B reorganization. P's basis in its newly acquired T stock is the same as the aggregate basis of the former T shareholders, but how is P supposed to acquire this information? For many years, the IRS's position was that P should use its best efforts to "survey" the surrendering T shareholders and, where that was impractical, P could use statistical sampling and estimates.[3] The IRS came to recognize that its procedures had not kept pace with changes in the securities markets (e.g., most stocks are held by brokers and custodians in street name). Revenue Procedure 2011–35[4] is the culmination of several years of study on this arcane but practically important issue. In 35 mind-numbing pages, the IRS sets forth four methodologies that basically provide more modern survey, statistical sampling and estimating techniques for corporations that acquire stock in transferred basis transactions. The most reliable approach is to survey all T shareholders but, when that is impractical, the revenue

---

1. I.R.C. § 1032(a). It was once feared that Section 1032 would not apply where a controlled subsidiary acquired property in exchange for its *parent's* stock. The Service has ruled, however, that the subsidiary does not recognize gain or loss in this situation, presumably because such an acquisition is economically indistinguishable from a direct acquisition by the parent followed by a drop down of the assets to the subsidiary. See Rev.Rul. 57–278, 1957–1 C.B. 124. Reg. § 1.1032–2(b).

2. See Rev.Rul. 72–327, 1972–2 C.B. 197.

3. Rev. Proc. 81–70, 1981–2 C.B. 729.

4. 2011–25 I.R.B. 890.

procedure explains how to use statistical sampling and other fallback techniques and permits the use of one or more of the prescribed methodologies in any combination.

Limit on Importation of Built-in Losses. The effect of the Section 362(b) transferred basis rule is to preserve not only built-in gains but also built-in losses when P acquires T's assets in a tax-free reorganization. This rule made it possible for U.S. corporations to engage in what became known as "basis shift" transactions with U.S. tax-indifferent parties, such as foreign corporations. The primary goal was to shift unrealized economic losses from foreign to U.S. taxpayers, who could then realize the losses and shelter their taxable income.

Section 362(e)(1) attempts to block basis-shift shelters by providing that if a net built-in loss is "imported" in a tax-free reorganization, the basis of such loss property in the hands of the transferee corporation is limited to its fair market value immediately after the transaction.[5] A net built-in loss is imported into the United States if the aggregate adjusted basis of the properties received by a domestic transferee corporation from a person not subject to U.S. tax exceeds the fair market value of the transferred properties.[6]

Basis of Target Stock Received in Triangular Reorganizations. Determining the acquiring parent corporation's basis in the stock of a subsidiary acquired in a reverse triangular reorganization raises a tantalizing technical question. Under Section 368(a)(2)(E), the acquiring corporation either may form a "phantom" subsidiary or use a preexisting operating subsidiary to merge into the target corporation. It ordinarily will transfer voting stock and possibly some boot to the subsidiary which then transfers that property to the target shareholders as the consideration for the acquisition.

In a straight Type B reorganization, the parent determines its basis in the target stock under Section 362(b) by reference to the stock bases of the former target shareholders. In the case of a reverse subsidiary merger, however, Section 358 would appear to require the acquiring corporation to take an exchanged basis—i.e., its basis in the target stock acquired would be the same as its basis in the stock of the disappearing subsidiary. That basis likely would be zero if a phantom subsidiary were used to effect the merger. A similar issue arises in the case of forward triangular merger, where the target merges into a subsidiary formed by the acquiring corporation immediately prior to the reorganization. Since the parent normally forms the subsidiary by transferring its own stock, in which it presumably has a zero basis, it would appear that the parent would retain a zero basis in the stock of the subsidiary even after it absorbs the target.

The Treasury has issued regulations that address the zero basis problem. Those regulations seek to conform the tax consequences of a

---

5. I.R.C. § 362(e)(2)(A). For a similar rule limiting the transfer of built-in losses in Section 351 transactions, see I.R.C. § 362(e)(2), discussed in Chapter 3A, infra.

6. I.R.C. § 362(e)(1)(B), (C).

triangular reorganization with those of a "drop down" transaction in which P acquires T's assets or stock directly and then drops them down to a subsidiary ("S") in a tax-free transaction. To illustrate the operation of the regulations in a forward triangular merger in which T merges into S, a newly formed P subsidiary, the regulations permit P to increase its basis in its S stock by the net basis (assets less liabilities) of T's assets.[7] In a simple transaction where P had no prior basis in its S stock, the net effect is that P's basis in its S stock and S's basis in the acquired T assets will be the same.

In a simple reverse triangular merger where newly formed S merges into T, which survives as a P subsidiary, P's basis in its T stock is adjusted by assuming that T had merged into S in a forward triangular merger, applying the rules discussed above.[8] Thus, in a wholly tax-free reverse merger where 100 percent of the T stock is acquired, P's basis in its T stock would equal T's net basis in its assets plus any preexisting basis that P had in its S stock.

PROBLEMS

1. Acquiring Corporation ("P") has 500,000 shares of voting common stock outstanding (value—$10 per share) and $500,000 of accumulated earnings and profits. Target Corporation ("T") has assets with an aggregate adjusted basis of $300,000 and an aggregate fair market value of $500,000, and $100,000 of accumulated earnings and profits. Except as otherwise indicated below, assume that T has no liabilities. T's ten equal shareholders each owns 100 shares of T voting common stock with an adjusted basis of $20,000 and a fair market value of $50,000. Discuss the tax consequences to P, T and T's shareholders of each of the following alternative transactions:

(a) T merges into P in a qualified Type A reorganization. Each T shareholder receives 4,000 shares of P voting common stock (value—$40,000) and P nonvoting preferred stock (not "nonqualified preferred stock") worth $10,000. What if the P nonvoting preferred were nonqualified preferred stock?

(b) Same as (a), above, but instead of the preferred stock each T shareholder receives 20–year market rate interest bearing B notes with a principal amount and fair market value of $10,000.

(c) Same as (b), above, except that two of the shareholders receive all the notes (with a principal amount and fair market value of $100,000), and the remaining eight shareholders each receives P voting common stock worth $50,000.

---

7. Reg. § 1.358–6(c)(1).

8. Reg. § 1.358–6(c)(2). Additional rules are provided for more specialized situations, such as where S was a preexisting subsidiary, the consideration is mixed, or less than all of T's stock is acquired in a reverse merger. See Reg. § 1.358–6(c)(2)(i)(C), –6(c)(4).

(d) Same as (b), above, except that T had $50,000 of accumulated earnings and profits.

(e) Assume for the remainder of the problem that T has assets with an aggregate fair market value of $600,000, an aggregate adjusted basis of $300,000, and a $100,000 liability. P acquires all T's assets in a qualified Type C reorganization in exchange for P voting stock worth $500,000 and P's assumption of T's $100,000 liability. T immediately distributes the P stock to its shareholders in complete liquidation.

(f) Same as (e), above, except P transfers $500,000 of P voting stock and $100,000 cash to T, which uses the cash to pay off its liability and then distributes the stock to its shareholders in complete liquidation.

(g) Same as (e), above, except P transfers to T $500,000 of P voting stock and investment securities with a basis of $40,000 and a fair market value of $100,000. T sells the securities for $100,000, using the proceeds to pay off its liability, and then liquidates and distributes the P stock to its shareholders.

(h) Same as (e), above, except P transfers $600,000 of its voting stock to T in exchange for all of T's assets and does not assume T's liability. T then sells $100,000 of P voting stock and uses the proceeds to pay off the liability. T then distributes the remaining P stock to its shareholders in complete liquidation.

(i) Same as (h), above, except T transfers $100,000 of P voting stock directly to its creditor in payment of the liability and then distributes the remaining P stock to its shareholders in complete liquidation.

2. Parent Corporation ("P") creates Subsidiary Corporation ("S") by transferring P stock as a preliminary step to acquiring the assets of Target Corporation ("T") in a separate subsidiary. T's shareholders own stock worth $200,000 with a basis of $50,000. T has assets worth $200,000 with a basis of $100,000.

(a) Assuming a valid § 368(a)(2)(D) forward triangular merger, what are the tax consequences to P, S, T and T's shareholders?

(b) Assuming a valid § 368(a)(2)(E) reverse triangular merger, what are the tax consequences to P, S, T and T's shareholders?

(c) What results in (a), above, if the transaction fails to qualify as a reorganization?

(d) What results in (b), above, if the transaction fails to qualify as a reorganization?

D. TAX POLICY ISSUES

Congress has been tinkering with Subchapter C since the enactment of the 1954 Code, but except for enactment of Section 338 in 1982 most revisions have been aimed at narrow technical problems. In the early 1980s, the Senate Finance Committee began a comprehensive study of Subchapter C. The staff reviewed recommendations of prominent bar and accounting groups and relied heavily on the Subchapter C project of the American Law Institute. In September, 1983, it issued its preliminary report—a controversial document that proposed revisions both large and small. Some of the staff's narrower recommendations were incorporated in the Tax Reform Act of 1984.

The Finance Committee staff followed up with its "final report"—the Subchapter C Revision Act of 1985. Some of its recommendations, most notably complete repeal of the *General Utilities* doctrine and a revised approach to limiting net operating loss carryforwards, were incorporated in the Tax Reform Act of 1986. But even the 1986 Act left for another day the centerpiece of both the ALI and the Senate Finance Committee projects— the adoption of an entirely new scheme governing corporate acquisitions, including the replacement of the tax-free reorganization provisions with an essentially elective system that would permit nonrecognition under consistent standards for any corporate acquisition at the price of a carryover basis in the assets of the target corporation. The following excerpt provides a summary of these acquisition proposals, which are still sitting on the "pending" shelf.

Excerpt from Joint Committee on Taxation, Present Law and Background Relating to Selected Business Tax Issues

(JCX–41–06), September 19, 2006.

C. Issues Relating to Mergers and Acquisitions

In general

The different rules permitting particular corporate transactions to receive tax-free treatment are varied and frequently inconsistent. In some cases, more than one rule could apply to the form of a particular corporate transaction. The statute and the administrative pronouncements of the IRS over the years have attempted to resolve overlap situations and to provide guidance regarding other interpretive issues.

The structure of present law is in part a result of the historical development and aggregation of provisions. The structure also reflects reactions to judicial decisions interpreting particular provisions, and reflects legislative developments establishing new rules and accompanying concern that existing provisions, if not limited, might conflict with or undermine the new rules.

The different, and often overlapping, variations within the merger and acquisition rules can be viewed as a significant source of complexity. On the other hand, these rules, as they have been interpreted and clarified over the years through administrative pronouncements, provide a large amount of taxpayer selectivity and certainty. Taxpayers are relatively assured of obtaining a specific tax result so long as the transaction satisfies the formalistic requirements of the chosen merger and acquisition provision. Moreover, comprehensive reform of these rules and the imposition of consistency could not generally be accomplished without recommending fundamental changes in the tax policy reflected by one or another of the provisions.

Discussion of certain proposals

Elective carryover basis for "qualified acquisitions"

An approach that has been suggested by a number of commentators in the past would generally permit a corporation to dispose of a business for any type of consideration, including cash, and elect to pay no corporate level tax, provided the consideration received is distributed to shareholders and that they pay tax (if they are taxable shareholders) on any cash or other consideration that is not a qualified continuing stock interest. The acquiring corporation would not obtain a stepped-up fair market value basis in the acquired corporate assets if the election were made not to pay corporate level tax. Only certain transactions that involved the acquisition of a significant amount of the stock of another corporation or the assets of a corporate business would qualify for this election.

Such a proposal was included in a 1985 report prepared by the Staff of the Senate Committee on Finance.[77] That proposal also included other conforming changes in its attempt to substitute a single approach for the present law varied rules affecting tax-free acquisitions. For example, the proposal would have conformed the various definitions of "control" under present law to the definition for filing a consolidated return.

Another version of such a proposal was presented at, and appears in the report of, an invitational conference addressing subchapter C issues sponsored by the American Bar Association and New York State Bar Association Tax Sections in 1987.[78] An earlier proposal of this type was made by the American Law Institute.[79]

This type of proposal involves a specific policy choice to abandon the existing statutory requirements for continuity of shareholder interest. The proposal would exempt a corporation from tax on a sale of its assets, even if the corporation receives cash consideration for the transfer of a business, so long as the cash is distributed to shareholders and the assets transferred retain a carryover basis.

---

77. The Subchapter C Revision Act of 1985, A Final Report Prepared by the Staff, Committee on Finance, United States Senate, S. Prt. 99–47 (May, 1985).

78. Ginsburg, Levin, Canellos, and Eustice, "Reexamining Subchapter C: An Overview and some Modest Proposals to Stimulate Debate" (copyright 1987 by Martin D. Ginsburg); reprinted in Corporate Tax Reform, A Report of the Invitational Conference on Sub-

chapter C; American Bar Association Section of Taxation, New York State Bar Association Tax Section (1988) pp. 39–80; see, e.g., Proposals VII–VIIC and IX–XI.

79. "Proposals on Corporate Acquisitions and Dispositions" adopted by the American Law Institute June 13, 1980, published in American Law Institute, Federal Income Tax Project Subchapter C (1982).

Several policy arguments can be made in favor of such a change. First, as long as assets do not obtain a stepped up basis, there is corporate level tax in the future as the recipient corporation earns income and retains the low basis assets. Second, as long as shareholders pay tax on any cash that is received, this single tax is sufficient as a current tax. Third, the corporate reorganization provisions are complex and can be manipulated; and an explicit election would simplify corporate tax planning.

Several policy arguments can also be made against such a change. When assets are transferred from one corporation to another for cash, the transferring corporation is generally taxed on gain at the time of the transaction or when the cash is received. Payment of tax in the future, if the recipient corporation pays more because of a carryover basis, is not the economic equivalent of payment of tax at the time of the transaction, but is significantly less due to the time value of money. Questions may arise where to draw the line that would allow certain transfers of corporate assets, such as a transfer of a "business," to be exempt from corporate level tax while other transfers, such as sales in the ordinary course of business, would not be so exempt. Interpretations of the line so drawn would be required. In addition, proposals for such restructuring have often involved new sets of rules such as rules regarding the definition of control or other issues. New rules could also involve further interpretation and could lead to new uncertainty and complexity.

Provide one set of consideration and continuity rules for acquisitive reorganizations

There have been a number of proposals to conform the consideration rules for acquisitive reorganizations to require a specified percentage of stock consideration (*e.g.*, 50 percent) and to conform the rules as to whether the stock must be voting stock.[80]

One policy issue related to such recommendations is the determination what type of stock is counted in determining continuity and for purposes of determining whether shareholders are taxed. For example, one version of such a proposal suggested that all stock would count (thus eliminating a voting stock requirement) but made an exception for certain preferred stock that is redeemable within five years.[81]

The recommendations are typically made only for the reorganization rules contained in section 368. Frequently, no change is recommended to the non-reorganization rules relating to transfers to controlled corporations under section 351.[82] Under this type of proposal, if the rules for non-

---

80. See, e.g., American Bar Association recommendation 1981–5, 107 ABA Repts. 559, 34 Tax. L. Rev. 1386 (1981).

81. American Bar Association recommendation 1981–5, supra.

82. The American Law Institute Proposals that included a provision for elective carryover basis, described above, did include a provision overriding section 351 for certain qualified acquisitions. However, since the basic proposal for qualified acquisitions abandoned a shareholder continuity of interest requirement for qualified acquisitions, the impact of overriding section 351 in those cases was confined to a much narrower range of issues.

reorganization transfers to controlled corporations under section 351 are not modified, then many of the same planning choices that exist under present law would continue to be available. Unless the rules of section 351 are tightened to conform to the new 368 rules in cases that resemble acquisitive reorganizations, it is arguable that little general consistency would be accomplished.[83] On the other hand, such a modification that limited the application of section 351 could be viewed as a policy decision to tighten the rules relating to acquisitive transactions.

83.　Partnership rules also could continue to offer different planning approaches to combining businesses and assets in some circumstances.

CHAPTER 10

CORPORATE DIVISIONS

A. INTRODUCTION

1. TYPES OF CORPORATE DIVISIONS

Code: Skim §§ 355; 368(a)(1)(D), (c).

The preceding chapter examined acquisitive and nondivisive single-party reorganizations. We now turn to a variety of transactions in which a single corporate enterprise is divided into two or more separate corporations. Section 355 allows a corporation to make a tax-free distribution to its shareholders of stock and securities in one or more controlled subsidiaries. If an intricate set of statutory and judicial requirements are met, neither the distributing corporation nor its shareholders recognize gain or loss on the distribution. Section 355 also unlocks the gate to other provisions which govern the treatment and characterization of boot, and collateral matters such as basis, holding period and carryover of tax attributes.[1] The rationale for nonrecognition is that the division of a business conducted under one corporate umbrella into separate corporations is not an appropriate taxable event when no significant assets leave corporate solution and the historic shareholders continue to control all the resulting corporations.

The three types of corporate divisions are commonly known as spin-offs, split-offs and split-ups. To illustrate the elements of these transactions, assume that Alex and Bertha each own 50 percent of the stock of Diverse Corporation ("D"), which for many years has operated a winery and a chicken ranch as separate divisions. For reasons to be elaborated below, the shareholders wish to divide the businesses into two separate corporations on a tax-free basis. The division method they choose will be influenced by their nontax goals. The possibilities are:

1. *Spin-off.* Assume that to comply with a new state regulation, D is required to operate the chicken ranch and winery as separate corporations. To accomplish the division, D forms a new corporation, Poultry, Inc., contributing the assets of the chicken ranch. It then distributes the stock of Poultry pro rata to Alex and Bertha, who emerge as equal shareholders in each corporation. Because a spin-off involves a distribution of property to shareholders without the surrender of any stock, it resembles a dividend.

---

1. See, e.g., I.R.C. §§ 356; 357; 358; 361; 362; 381; 1223(1) and Section D of this chapter, infra.

2. *Split-off.* Alex and Bertha desire to part company, with Alex operating the winery and Bertha the chicken ranch. To help them go their separate ways, D again forms a new corporation, Poultry, Inc., contributing the assets of the chicken ranch. D then distributes the stock of Poultry to Bertha in complete redemption of her D stock. Alex becomes the sole shareholder of D, which now owns only the winery, and Bertha is the sole owner of the chicken ranch. If Alex and Bertha did not want to part company, D could have made a pro rata distribution of Poultry stock in redemption of an appropriate amount of D stock. In either situation, a split-off resembles a redemption because the shareholders have surrendered stock of D.

3. *Split-up.* To comply with a new state regulation, D is required to terminate its corporate existence and divide up its two businesses. The fission is accomplished by D forming Vineyard, Inc. and Poultry, Inc., contributing the winery assets to Vineyard and the chicken ranch assets to Poultry. D then distributes the stock of the two new corporations pro rata to Alex and Bertha in exchange for all their D stock. Because D has distributed all of its assets and dissolved, this transaction resembles a complete liquidation. If the objectives of the parties had been different (e.g., Alex and Bertha wanted to sever their relationship), the transaction could have been effected by distributing the Vineyard stock to Alex and the Poultry stock to Bertha.

As these examples demonstrate, spin-offs, split-offs and split-ups can be classified for tax purposes in two different ways: as a tax-free corporate division or as the taxable transaction that each method resembles. In order to qualify as tax free to the shareholders, the division must satisfy the requirements of Section 355 and its accompanying judicial doctrines. In general, Section 355 allows a corporation with one or more businesses that have been actively conducted for five years or more to make a tax-free distribution of the stock of a controlled subsidiary (or subsidiaries) provided that the transaction is being carried out for a legitimate business purpose and is not being used principally as a device to bail out earnings and profits. In the absence of Section 355, a spin-off likely would be treated as a dividend under Section 301; a split-off would be tested for dividend equivalency under the redemption rules in Section 302; and a split-up would be treated as a complete liquidation under Section 331.

There is one more piece to this introduction to the puzzle. In each of the examples above, Diverse Corporation was required to engage in a preliminary step in order to accomplish its division. Because its two businesses were operated as divisions under one corporate roof rather than as separately incorporated subsidiaries, D had to drop one or more of those businesses into a separate corporate shell before proceeding with the distribution to its shareholders. If that distribution satisfies the tests in Section 355, the initial transfer of assets by D to its new subsidiary (or subsidiaries) will constitute a divisive Type D reorganization.[2] As such, the transfer of assets will be tax free to D under Section 361(a), the assumption of liabilities will be governed by Section 357 and the basis of the transferred assets will carry over to the new subsidiary under Section 362(b).[3] Creation of a new subsidiary, however, is not a condition to qualifying for nonrecognition of gain under Section 355. If its requirements are met, Section 355 applies to distributions of stock of preexisting corporations as well as to new subsidiaries created solely to carry out the division.[4]

2.   NON-TAX MOTIVES FOR CORPORATE DIVISIONS

Many different strategic and economic considerations can lead a company to the decision that its business should be divided. Some of the more routine motives include resolution of shareholder disputes, insulation of one business from the risks and creditors of another, and compliance with a regulatory decree.

In the world of publicly traded companies, one of the most common motives for a division is the desire to separate the distributing and controlled corporations so they each can devote their attention to a single line of business. In the parlance of Wall Street, focusing the old and new corporations on a single business allows investors to have a "pure play" on a particular industry. For example, a corporation engaged in the transportation, energy and real estate businesses might transfer the latter two businesses to newly formed corporations and then distribute all shares of the new entities to the distributing corporation's shareholders to create three companies, each with a single focus. The theory underlying this maneuver is that a more narrowly focused company will have greater success than a conglomerate by virtue of its ability to devote more energy and attention to the single enterprise. This renewed vigor, so the theory goes, will be derived in part from an increased incentive for corporate managers to perform. Because their performance (or at least the perception of their performance) will be reflected more directly in the stock value of a narrowly focused company than in the stock value of a conglomerate, the managers will be more accountable to shareholders. In addition, proponents of corporate divisions expect the resulting streamlined companies to benefit from the freedom of corporate managers to pursue growth opportunities that they otherwise would feel constrained to pursue.

Another common motive for a corporate division is the desire to increase market recognition of the value of a particular business. Executives of a corporation engaged in several lines of business often believe that stock market analysts fail to appreciate the collective value of the corporation's businesses. To overcome this problem, corporate managers often decide to place a particular business in an independent company in the

---

2. The initial transaction also would qualify for nonrecognition under Section 351, but Section 368(a)(1)(D) and its accompanying operative provisions take precedence if the transfer of assets is followed by a Section 355 distribution.

3. See Section D of this chapter, infra.

4. I.R.C. § 355(a)(2)(C).

hope that "the market" will recognize the value of that business (and perhaps also the value of the distributing corporation's remaining businesses) more clearly. Increased recognition of value, it is hoped, will attract more capital for both the old and new corporations and increase returns to shareholders. There is evidence to support the view that a corporate division will lead to increased recognition of shareholder value. Certain studies of corporate divisions have concluded that, following an initial period of investor uncertainty, the stocks of both distributing and controlled corporations that have engaged in a spin-off generally outperform the market.[1] This increase in stock value may be attributable in part to the fact that, following a spin-off, distributing and controlled corporations frequently are seen as attractive candidates for a corporate acquisition.

Yet another agenda driving corporate divisions may be an acquiring corporation's need to pay down debt incurred in making an acquisition by selling off some of the target's businesses or, conversely, for a potential target to better position itself for an acquisition by shedding businesses that depress its value. Congress's desire to curb deferral of corporate-level tax in connection with these break-up acquisition strategies has contributed to much of the complexity of Section 355.

Alternatives exist to achieve many of the goals of a corporate division. For example, a corporation simply could sell the assets of an unwanted business. Similarly, if the business is conducted through a subsidiary, the parent could sell the subsidiary's stock. Because the selling corporation generally is taxed on the sale and its shareholders are taxed a second time when the sale proceeds are distributed, however, a sale often is not tax efficient. In contrast, the parties to a properly structured spin-off incur no current tax and the distributing corporation might even recoup its investment in a pre-existing subsidiary at far less of a tax cost than in a sale. Before the controlled corporation's shares are distributed, the controlled corporation can declare and pay a large dividend that likely will be eligible for the dividends received deduction provided by Section 243.[2]

Another alternative is for a corporation to issue tracking stock (sometimes referred to as alphabet or letter stock). The issuer pays dividends on tracking stock based on the performance of a particular division or subsidiary. The stock is listed and traded separately from the issuer's other shares, giving the illusion that there are shares outstanding in two distinct corporations. In theory, tracking stock allows for market recognition of the value of a business and provides incentives for corporate managers in the same way as a spin-off, but it allows the issuing corporation to retain control of the business in question. Issuing tracking stock also does not involve the tax cost of a sale of the business. Tracking stock does not offer

---

1.   See, e.g., P. Cusatis, J. Miles and R. Woolridge, Restructuring Through Spinoffs: The Stock Market Evidence, 33 J. Financial Economics 293 (1993).

2.   See Chapter 4A, supra. The distributing corporation's dividends received deduc-

tion will be disallowed if the distributing corporation does not hold the controlled corporation's stock for a sufficient period of time. See I.R.C. § 246(c); Chapter 4F2, supra.

all the advantages of a spin-off, however, such as the ability to insulate one business from potential liabilities associated with another. It also may give rise to undesirable administrative and political issues, such as the necessity of satisfying two distinct groups of shareholders.

3.   HISTORICAL BACKGROUND OF SECTION 355

To better understand the technical requirements for a tax-free corporate division, it is helpful to look back at the historical background of Section 355. The early income tax provisions governing spin-offs were elegantly simple but dangerously naive. Interpreted literally, they permitted a corporation to transfer all or part of its assets to a newly formed subsidiary and then to make a tax-free distribution of the stock of that subsidiary to its shareholders as part of a plan of reorganization.[1] The tax avoidance potential of this blanket exemption from the dividend rules was enormous, and the judiciary swiftly responded by curtailing the use of a spin-off as a bailout device. In Gregory v. Helvering, which follows, the Supreme Court made one of its earliest contributions to the common law of taxation[2] and paved the way toward the enactment of a comprehensive statutory solution to the problem of corporate divisions.

Gregory v. Helvering

Supreme Court of the United States, 1935.
293 U.S. 465, 55 S.Ct. 266.

■ MR. JUSTICE SUTHERLAND delivered the opinion of the Court.

Petitioner in 1928 was the owner of all the stock of United Mortgage Corporation. That corporation held among its assets 1,000 shares of the Monitor Securities Corporation. For the sole purpose of procuring a transfer of these shares to herself in order to sell them for her individual profit, and, at the same time, diminish the amount of income tax which would result from a direct transfer by way of dividend, she sought to bring about a "reorganization" under § 112(g) of the Revenue Act of 1928, c. 852, 45 Stat. 791, 818, set forth later in this opinion. To that end, she caused the Averill Corporation to be organized under the laws of Delaware on September 18, 1928. Three days later, the United Mortgage Corporation transferred to the Averill Corporation the 1,000 shares of Monitor stock, for which all the shares of the Averill Corporation were issued to the petitioner. On September 24, the Averill Corporation was dissolved, and liquidated by distributing all its assets, namely, the Monitor shares, to the petitioner. No other business was ever transacted, or intended to be transacted, by that company. Petitioner immediately sold the Monitor shares for $133,333.33. She returned for taxation as capital net gain the sum of

---

1. See, e.g., Revenue Act of 1924, P.L. No. 176, § 203(c), 43 Stat. 253, 256.

2. See Blum, "Motive, Intent, and Purpose in Federal Income Taxation," 34 U.Chi. L.Rev. 485 (1967); Chirelstein, "Learned Hand's Contribution to the Law of Tax Avoidance," 77 Yale L.J. 440 (1968).

$76,007.88, based upon an apportioned cost of $57,325.45. Further details are unnecessary. It is not disputed that if the interposition of the so-called reorganization was ineffective, petitioner became liable for a much larger tax as a result of the transaction.

The Commissioner of Internal Revenue, being of opinion that the reorganization attempted was without substance and must be disregarded, held that petitioner was liable for a tax as though the United corporation had paid her a dividend consisting of the amount realized from the sale of the Monitor shares. In a proceeding before the Board of Tax Appeals, that body rejected the commissioner's view and upheld that of petitioner. 27 B.T.A. 223. Upon a review of the latter decision, the circuit court of appeals sustained the commissioner and reversed the board, holding that there had been no "reorganization" within the meaning of the statute. 69 F. (2d) 809. Petitioner applied to this court for a writ of certiorari, which the government, considering the question one of importance, did not oppose. We granted the writ.

Section 112 of the Revenue Act of 1928 deals with the subject of gain or loss resulting from the sale or exchange of property. Such gain or loss is to be recognized in computing the tax, except as provided in that section. The provisions of the section, so far as they are pertinent to the question here presented, follow:

"Sec. 112. (g) *Distribution of stock on reorganization.*—If there is distributed, in pursuance of a plan of reorganization, to a shareholder in a corporation a party to the reorganization, stock or securities in such corporation or in another corporation a party to the reorganization, without the surrender by such shareholder of stock or securities in such a corporation, no gain to the distributee from the receipt of such stock or securities shall be recognized * * *.

"(i) *Definition of reorganization.*—As used in this section * * *.

"(1) The term 'reorganization' means * * * (B) a transfer by a corporation of all or a part of its assets to another corporation if immediately after the transfer the transferor or its stockholders or both are in control of the corporation to which the assets are transferred, * * *."

It is earnestly contended on behalf of the taxpayer that since every element required by the foregoing subdivision (B) is to be found in what was done, a statutory reorganization was effected; and that the motive of the taxpayer thereby to escape payment of a tax will not alter the result or make unlawful what the statute allows. It is quite true that if a reorganization in reality was effected within the meaning of subdivision (B), the ulterior purpose mentioned will be disregarded. The legal right of a taxpayer to decrease the amount of what otherwise would be his taxes, or altogether avoid them, by means which the law permits, cannot be doubted. * * * But the question for determination is whether what was done, apart from the tax motive, was the thing which the statute intended. The reasoning of the court below in justification of a negative answer leaves little to be said.

When subdivision (B) speaks of a transfer of assets by one corporation to another, it means a transfer made "in pursuance of a plan of reorganization" [§ 112(g)] of corporate business; and not a transfer of assets by one corporation to another in pursuance of a plan having no relation to the business of either, as plainly is the case here. Putting aside, then, the question of motive in respect of taxation altogether, and fixing the character of the proceeding by what actually occurred, what do we find? Simply an operation having no business or corporate purpose—a mere device which put on the form of a corporate reorganization as a disguise for concealing its real character, and the sole object and accomplishment of which was the consummation of a preconceived plan, not to reorganize a business or any part of a business, but to transfer a parcel of corporate shares to the petitioner. No doubt, a new and valid corporation was created. But that corporation was nothing more than a contrivance to the end last described. It was brought into existence for no other purpose; it performed, as it was intended from the beginning it should perform, no other function. When that limited function had been exercised, it immediately was put to death.

In these circumstances, the facts speak for themselves and are susceptible of but one interpretation. The whole undertaking, though conducted according to the terms of subdivision (B), was in fact an elaborate and devious form of conveyance masquerading as a corporate reorganization, and nothing else. The rule which excludes from consideration the motive of tax avoidance is not pertinent to the situation, because the transaction upon its face lies outside the plain intent of the statute. To hold otherwise would be to exalt artifice above reality and to deprive the statutory provision in question of all serious purpose.

Judgment affirmed.

NOTE

The Board of Tax Appeals was more tolerant in its evaluation of Mrs. Gregory's maneuver. Adopting a strict constructionist approach, the Board reasoned that "[a] statute so meticulously drafted must be interpreted as a literal expression of the taxing policy, and leaves only the small interstices for judicial consideration."[1] On appeal to the Second Circuit, Judge Learned Hand—in one of his most famous pronouncements on tax avoidance—agreed that "[a]ny one may so arrange his affairs that his taxes shall be as low as possible; he is not bound to choose that pattern which will best pay the Treasury; there is not even a patriotic duty to increase one's taxes."[2] But he quickly eschewed literalism in favor of the big picture, reasoning that "the meaning of a sentence may be more than that of the separate words, as a melody is more than the notes, and no degree of particularity can ever obviate recourse to the setting in which all appear,

1. Gregory v. Commissioner, 27 B.T.A. 223, 225 (1932).

2. Helvering v. Gregory, 69 F.2d 809, 810 (2d Cir.1934).

and which all collectively create."[3] The Supreme Court's opinion was a less stylish but equally forceful reaffirmation that the language of the Code must be interpreted in light of its purpose.

Gregory v. Helvering has ramifications that go far beyond corporate divisions. It is one of the earliest articulations of the substance over form and step transaction doctrines and paved the way to the related economic substance doctrine that is now "codified" and accompanied by a steep penalty.[4] However amorphous they may be, those doctrines serve as a brooding omnipresence in the responsible tax advisor's conscience. When the system works properly (not always the reality), they also thwart the schemes of aggressive tax avoiders who rely on a literal interpretation of the Code to wreak havoc with its intended purpose. As we will see later in the chapter, the narrower business purpose doctrine emanating from *Gregory* also survives as one of the major requirements for qualification as a tax-free corporate division.[5]

While *Gregory* was pending, Congress saw the light and repealed the tax-free spin-off provision involved in that case. Curiously, split-ups (and, for a time, split-offs) continued to qualify for nonrecognition if they did not run afoul of the limitations in *Gregory*.[6] Congress ultimately realized, however, that not every spin-off is a bailout device, and in 1951 it enacted the statutory forerunner of Section 355 to remove any impediment to corporate divisions "undertaken for legitimate business purposes."[7] In general, the new statute granted nonrecognition to spin-offs that were pursuant to a plan of reorganization unless one of the corporate parties to the reorganization did not intend "to continue the active conduct of a trade or business" or "the corporation whose stock is distributed was used principally as a device for the distribution of earnings and profits * * *."[8] The contours of the present Section 355 thus were being shaped: to qualify as tax free, a spin-off had to be motivated by a genuine business purpose and consist of the separation of one or more active trades or businesses in a transaction that was not being used principally as a bailout device.

With the enactment of Section 355 in the 1954 Code, Congress finally provided a comprehensive statutory scheme governing all three types of corporate divisions.[9] At the same time, the business purpose and continuity of interest doctrines were preserved as independent nonstatutory requirements.

3. Id.

4. See I.R.C § 7701(*o*); 6662(a), (b)(6) & (i); and Chapter 14B, infra.

5. See Section C1 of this chapter, infra.

6. For the history of corporate divisions before the 1954 Code, see Bittker & Eustice, Federal Income Taxation of Corporations and Shareholders ¶ 11.01.

7. S.Rep. No. 781, 82d Cong., 1st Sess. (1951), reprinted in 1951–2 C.B. 458, 499.

8. Revenue Act of 1951, ch. 521, § 317(a), 65 Stat. 493, amending Internal Revenue Code of 1939, § 112(b)(11).

9. The statute does not explicitly refer to spin-offs, split-offs and split-ups, but Section 355(a)(2) makes it clear that Section 355 applies to all three forms of corporate divisions. The different forms continue to be significant if the transaction fails the Section 355 tests.

4.   OVERVIEW OF SECTION 355

Code: §§ 355(a), (b), (c); 368(c).

Regulations: § 1.355–1(b).

Before becoming immersed in technical details, it is important to recall the purpose of Section 355. Congress intended to provide tax-free status to corporate divisions serving legitimate business needs. At the same time, it included safeguards to patrol against the bailout of earnings and profits. A more recent Congressional concern has been to prevent taxpayers from using divisions to avoid corporate-level gain on transactions that are more akin to sales than mere changes in form. Most of the statutory and judicial requirements are directed at these broad objectives. But their precise meaning and scope are not always clear, and the waters have been muddied further by piecemeal changes made over the years to address real and perceived abuses.

a.   STATUTORY AND JUDICIAL REQUIREMENTS

A corporate division will qualify as tax free to the shareholders and the distributing corporation if it satisfies the requirements discussed below.

Control. One corporation (the "distributing corporation," or "D") must distribute to its shareholders (with respect to their stock) or to security holders (in exchange for their securities) the stock or securities of a corporation that D "controls" immediately before the distribution (the "controlled corporation," or "C").[1] For this purpose, "control" is defined by Section 368(c), which requires ownership of 80 percent of the total combined voting power and 80 percent of the total number of shares of all other classes of stock.

Distribution of All Stock or Securities. D must distribute all the stock or securities of C that it holds or, alternatively, an amount of stock sufficient to constitute "control" within the meaning of Section 368(c).[2] If any stock or securities of C are retained, D also must establish to the satisfaction of the Service that the retention is not pursuant to a plan having tax avoidance as one of its principal purposes.[3]

Active Trade or Business Requirement. Immediately after the distribution, both D and C—or in a split-up, both controlled corporations—must be engaged in, or treated as engaged (through a subsidiary) in, a trade or business that has been actively conducted throughout the five-year period ending on the date of the distribution.[4] That business must not have been acquired within the five-year predistribution period in a transaction in which gain or loss was recognized in whole or in part (e.g., a sale of assets taxable to the seller).[5] Moreover, the distributing corporation must not

---

1.   I.R.C. § 355(a)(1)(A).

2.   I.R.C. § 355(a)(1)(D).

3.   I.R.C. § 355(a)(1)(D)(ii); Rev. Proc. 96–30, 1996–1 C.B. 696. See also Rev.Rul. 75–

469, 1975–2 C.B. 126; Rev.Rul. 75–321, 1975–2 C.B. 123.

4.   I.R.C. § 355(a)(1)(C); (b).

5.   I.R.C. § 355(b)(2)(C).

have purchased a controlling stock interest in a corporation conducting the business in a taxable transaction during the five-year predistribution period.[6] In applying these rules, all members of D's and C's "separated affiliated group" (generally, subsidiaries in which the parent owns 80 percent of the voting power and total value) are treated as one corporation.[7]

Not A "Device." The division must not be used "principally as a device for the distribution" of the earnings and profits of either D or C. The "mere fact" that stock or securities of either corporation are sold after the distribution is not to be considered as evidence of a device unless the sales were pursuant to a prearranged plan.[8]

Judicial Limitations: Business Purpose and Continuity of Interest. In addition to the statutory tests, the regulations incorporate three judicially created limitations. Nonrecognition is available only if the distribution is carried out for an independent corporate business purpose[9] and the shareholders prior to the division maintain adequate continuity of interest in D and C, and continuity of business enterprise is maintained after the distribution.[10]

All these requirements are applied without regard to the form the parties choose to accomplish the division. Thus, a distribution may qualify as tax-free under Section 355 irrespective of whether it is pro rata and whether or not the distributee shareholder surrenders stock in the distributing corporation or the distribution is preceded by the formation of a new controlled corporation in a Type D reorganization.[11]

This list of basic Section 355 requirements do not tell the entire story. Several other specialized provisions may cause D to recognize gain on its distribution of C stock even though D's shareholders qualify for tax-free treatment.[12]

b.   TAXATION OF THE PARTIES

Section 355 provides total shareholder-level nonrecognition only where the distributing corporation distributes stock or securities of a controlled corporation.[13] Stock rights or warrants are not treated as "stock or securities" for this purpose and thus constitute taxable boot under Section 356.[14] In the case of a distribution of securities (e.g., long-term notes, bonds,

---

6. I.R.C. § 355(b)(2)(D). The active trade or business test also will be violated if the distributee shareholder is a corporation that acquired control of the distributing corporation within the five-year predistribution period. Id.

7. I.R.C. § 355(b)(3). This rule applies to distributions made after May 17, 2006. See Section B of this chapter, infra, for the details and ramifications.

8. I.R.C. § 355(a)(1)(B).

9. Reg. § 1.355–2(b).

10. Reg. § 1.355–2(c), –1(b).

11. I.R.C. § 355(a)(2).

12. See Section E of this chapter, infra.

13. I.R.C. § 355(a)(1). For this purpose, "nonqualified preferred stock," as defined in section 351(g)(2), received in a distribution with respect to stock other than nonqualified preferred stock is not treated as "stock or securities"—i.e., it will be boot. I.R.C. § 355(a)(3)(D).

14. Reg. § 1.355–1(b).

debentures), if the principal amount of securities of the controlled corporation received by the distributee exceeds the principal amount of the distributing corporation's securities surrendered in connection with the distribution, the value of the excess is treated as boot.[15] If securities of the controlled corporation are received and no securities of the parent are surrendered, the entire value of the securities received is treated as boot.[16] In addition, any stock of a controlled corporation acquired in a taxable transaction within the five years preceding the distribution—which we will come to know as "hot stock"—constitutes boot.[17] The distribution of boot does not necessarily disqualify a transaction under Section 355, but it will cause the distributee shareholder to recognize any realized gain, usually as a qualified dividend taxable at preferential capital gains rates, to the extent of the boot received.[18] At the corporate level, the distributing corporation generally does not recognize gain on the distribution of stock or securities of its subsidiary but may recognize gain on the distribution of appreciated boot or in certain situations where a divisive transaction is used to facilitate the sale of a subsidiary.[19]

The principal hurdles to achieving nonrecognition under Section 355 are the active trade or business and business purpose requirements and the "device" limitation. The government's interpretation of these tests has evolved over the years and currently is reflected in extensive regulations, which have largely supplanted the case law and are a principal focus of this chapter.

B.   THE ACTIVE TRADE OR BUSINESS REQUIREMENT

Code: § 355(a)(1)(C), (b)(1), (2), (3)(A) & (B).

Regulations: § 1.355–3(a)(1)(i), (b)(1), (2), (3).

Lockwood's Estate v. Commissioner

United States Court of Appeals, Eighth Circuit, 1965.
350 F.2d 712.

■ VOGEL, CIRCUIT JUDGE.

The single question involved in this review of an unreported decision of the Tax Court of the United States, entered August 26, 1964, is whether the "spin-off" of part of the business conducted by the Lockwood Grader Corporation of Gering, Nebraska, (hereinafter Lockwood) through the

---

15.   I.R.C. §§ 355(a)(3)(A)(i); 356(d)(2)(C).

16.   I.R.C. §§ 355(a)(3)(A)(ii); 356(d)(2)(C).

17.   I.R.C.   § 355(a)(3)(B).   See   Edna Louise Dunn Trust v. Commissioner, 86 T.C. 745 (1986).

18.   I.R.C. §§ 355(a)(4)(A); 356. See Section C of this Chapter, infra, for a more detailed explanation of the treatment of boot and the other operative provisions that accompany Section 355.

19.   I.R.C. § 355(c), (d).

organization of a new corporation, Lockwood Graders of Maine, Inc. (hereinafter Maine, Inc.) was tax-free to petitioners, recipients of the stock of Maine, Inc., under 26 U.S.C.A. § 355 (Int.Rev.Code). The government contended that the spin-off was not tax-free since the requirements of § 355(b)(2)(B) relating to the conducting of an active business for five years prior to the date of distribution had not been met. The government apparently conceded and the Tax Court found that the petitioners had met all other requirements to qualify under § 355 for tax-free treatment. The Tax Court upheld the government's contention and petitioners appeal.

The now deceased Thorval J. Lockwood, * * * and his wife Margaret were the sole stockholders of Lockwood and had been so since its incorporation under Nebraska law in 1946. Lockwood's predecessor, Lockwood Graders, was a partnership formed in 1935 for the purpose of producing and selling a portable potato sorting machine invented by the decedent. Starting in the early spring of each year Thorval and Margaret drove to Alabama and worked their way north through Missouri to North Dakota for the purpose of selling Lockwood products. The equipment was sold in "all of the potato growing areas of the United States" but primarily in the biggest growing areas such as North Dakota, Idaho and Colorado.

From 1946 to 1951, inclusive, Lockwood operated its business of manufacturing and selling wash lines, potato machinery, parts and supplies to potato shippers in the potato growing areas. Though Lockwood continued to have its principal place of business at Gering, Nebraska, branches were opened, as the business expanded, in Grand Forks, North Dakota; Antigo, Wisconsin; Monte Vista, Colorado; and Rupert, Idaho. These branches performed both manufacturing and sales functions. In 1952, under a reorganization plan, these branches were separately incorporated to promote greater efficiency and to properly provide for expansion. Assets of Lockwood were exchanged for all of the stock of each new corporation and the stock so exchanged was passed without consideration to Thorval and Margaret as sole stockholders of Lockwood. The reorganization plan, among other things, was specifically designed to make use of the tax-free provisions of what is now § 355.

In the early 1950's Lockwood and the other controlled corporations changed the nature of their business somewhat by selling to individual farmers as well as to potato suppliers. Lockwood had previously dealt primarily in grading equipment but at this time it began to manufacture and sell field equipment such as harvesting pieces, bin holders and vine beaters as well.

Beginning as early as 1947 Lockwood began to make some sporadic and relatively inconsequential sales in the northeastern part of the United States. From 1949 to 1955 the primary sales of products and parts in that part of the country were made to Gould & Smith, Inc., a retailer of farming and industrial equipment, of Presque Isle, Maine (although there are no records of sales made to them in 1952). Such sales were found to be of a relatively small volume by the Tax Court. On November 15, 1954, Lockwood established a branch office in Presque Isle, Maine, from which to handle Lockwood products. On March 1, 1956, pursuant to the 1951 plan for reorganization, the Maine branch office was incorporated under the laws of Maine with its principal place of business at Presque Isle, Maine. Maine, Inc., was a wholly owned subsidiary of Lockwood. On incorporating, Lockwood transferred to Maine, Inc., $23,500 in assets consisting of petty cash totalling $150.00, accounts receivable totalling $4,686.67, automobiles and trucks worth $1,100, shop equipment worth $295.00, office furniture and fixtures worth $81.60, and inventory worth $17,186.73. In return for these assets Maine, Inc., issued all of its stock, 235 shares at $100.00 par value, to Lockwood. On March 31, 1956, Lockwood distributed 162 of these shares of Maine, Inc., to Thorval and 73 of them to Margaret. This distribution gave rise to the controversy here involved.

The Tax Court held this distribution to be outside of § 355. According to the Tax Court there was:

> " * * * the absence of evidence that the *Maine business* was actively conducted during the months between March 31, 1951, and August 1953—a span of time totaling over 40 per cent of the requisite five-year period [required by § 355(b)(2)(B).]" (Emphasis supplied.)

The Tax Court found that the Maine business was not actively and continuously conducted until August 1953, at which time a Lockwood salesman traveled to Maine and personally solicited orders from farmers and businessmen other than Gould & Smith. We do not disagree with the factual finding of the Tax Court as to the active conduct of Lockwood's business in Maine prior to the incorporation of Maine, Inc. However, the Tax Court, for reasons set out below, erred in looking only at the business performed by Lockwood in Maine to determine if the five-year active business requirement had been met prior to the incorporation of Maine, Inc. Nothing in the language of § 355 suggests that prior business activity is only to be measured by looking at the business performed in a geographical area where the controlled corporation is eventually formed. In this case, when the entire Lockwood market is viewed, it can be seen that Lockwood was engaged in active business as required by § 355 for the five years prior to the incorporation of Maine, Inc. Since its incorporation Maine, Inc., has carried on the same kind of manufacturing and selling business previously and concurrently performed by Lockwood. Thus all § 355 prerequisites are met and the Tax Court erred in determining this was not a tax-free transfer.

At this point it would be helpful to look at the evolvement of what is now § 355. Prior to 1924 a distribution to stockholders pursuant to a spin-off was taxed as a dividend. From 1924 to 1932, however, the revenue acts changed position and provided spin-offs could be tax-free. From 1934 to 1950 tax-free spin-offs were again abolished since this device was being used as a method for distributing earnings and profits, which would otherwise be taxable dividends, through the issuance of stock in the controlled corporation. Such stock could be disposed of at the more favorable capital gain rates. Because of the usefulness of the spin-off device in the achievement of corporate growth and flexibility, Congress again accorded it tax-free status in 1951. At that time certain conditions were imposed to prevent any abuse from using this device. In 1954 the tax-free spin-off was continued as § 355 of the Code with additional tax avoidance safeguards which included the five-year active business requirement involved in this case.

As stated by the Second Circuit in Bonsall v. Commissioner, 2 Cir., 1963, 317 F.2d 61, at page 65:

> " * * * Only long application may completely clarify the difficult terminology of section 355."

With this we agree. However, certain things have become clear since the enactment of § 355 in 1954. After much controversy it has been determined that tax-free treatment will not be denied to a transaction under § 355 merely because it represents an attempt to divide a single trade or business. See United States v. Marett, 5 Cir., 1963, 325 F.2d 28; Coady v. Commissioner, 33 T.C. 771, affirmed per curiam, 6 Cir., 1961, 289 F.2d 490. The Commissioner has acceded to the holdings of Marett and Coady in Rev.Rule 64–147, 1964–1, Cum.Bull. 136, even though the Commissioner had previously insisted, in § 1.355–1(a) of the Income Tax Regulations, that two or more existing businesses had to be actively operated the five years prior to distribution.

* * *

Respondent in the instant case, although claiming to accept the single business interpretation, points to the language of § 355(b)(1) and argues, as did the government in Coady, that the word *"and"* in that section means that, in determining whether or not the active business requirement was met, one has to look at both the business done by the distributing corporation (Lockwood) *and* the business done as such by the controlled corporation (Maine, Inc.) and its predecessors in Maine. Contrary to the government's position, once it has been ascertained that two or more trades or businesses are not required for § 355 to apply, the crucial question becomes whether or not the two corporations existing after distribution are doing the same type of work and using the same type of assets previously done and used by the prior *single* existing business. § 355(b)(1) has no relevance to respondent's point once it has been determined that only a single business is required.

Here the five years of prior activity we are concerned with involve the prior overall activity of Lockwood. Previous to 1956 Lockwood had carried on *in toto* what Maine, Inc., would later carry on in part in the northeast. We are not concerned with the prior activity of Lockwood in the northeast only, for Congress has never intimated that such a geographical test should be applied and we are not about to apply such a test now. A perusal of the House and Senate Reports indicates conclusively that at no time did the House or the Senate contemplate any kind of geographic test in applying the five-year active business requirement. The facts clearly show that

Lockwood, in fact, was actively conducting the trade or business involved five years prior to the distribution period.

One case, Patricia W. Burke v. Commissioner, 1964, 42 T.C. 1021, did discuss the past business of a controlled corporation as performed in a limited geographical area in finding the prerequisites of § 355 had been met. That case did not, however, hold that there was in fact a geographical test. Further, at page 1028 that court set out what we believe to be the test:

> " * * * as long as the business which is divided has been actively conducted for 5 years before the distribution and the resulting businesses are actively conducted after the division, the active business requirements of the statute are met. Cf. also H. Grady Lester, 40 T.C. 947 (1963)."

Since there is no Congressional intent evidenced to the contrary, the test, restated, is not whether active business had been carried out in the geographic area later served by the controlled corporation but, simply, whether the distributing corporation, for five years prior to distribution, had been actively conducting the type of business now performed by the controlled corporation without reference to the geographic area. In the instant case the facts are abundantly clear that Lockwood had been actively engaged in the type of business later carried on by Maine, Inc., if one refers to a national rather than just the northeastern market.

It was mentioned earlier in this opinion that beginning in 1950 Lockwood began to sell field equipment as well as grading equipment. The respondent apparently does not contend, nor do we find, that Lockwood so changed its business as to be engaged in a new business that had been active for only two years prior to the incorporation of Maine, Inc. Lockwood meets the requirements of an existing five-year active business as set out by the Conference Committee in Conference Report No. 2543 at page 5298 of 3 U.S.C.Cong. & Adm.News, 1954:

> "It is the understanding of the managers on the part of the House, in agreeing to the active business requirements of section 355 and of section 346 (defining partial liquidations), that a trade or business which has been actively conducted throughout the 5–year period described in such sections will meet the requirements of such sections, even though such trade or business underwent change during such 5–year period, for example, *by the addition of new,* or the dropping of old, *products,* changes in production capacity, and the like, provided the changes are not of such a character as to constitute the acquisition of a new or different business." (Emphasis supplied.)

In § 1.355–4(b)(3) of the Income Tax Regulations the Commissioner specifically adopts the above-quoted portion of the Committee Report.

The respondent contends:

> "If the taxpayers' argument prevails, then any corporation with a five-year history could distribute any of its assets regardless

of when they were acquired and regardless of what kind of business they are in after the division, as long as the distributing corporation is in an active business. In other words, taxpayer argues that the five-year history rule requires that only the business of the distributing corporation have a five-year history. For instance, suppose a large manufacturing corporation with a ten-year life acquired some data processing machines in order to better control its inventory and work-in-process flow. If taxpayers' argument is correct, a year later this corporation could transfer all the data processing equipment to a new corporation in exchange for its stock, spin off the stock and claim a tax-free distribution under Section 355 since the manufacturing corporation had more than a five-year life and the data processing business, once an integral part of the original business, was being actively conducted after the spin-off. Moreover, the same logic would allow the spin-off of real estate owned by the manufacturing corporation and used in its business.''

The fears of the government are unfounded. The example of the manufacturing company is more closely akin to the Bonsall case, supra, and is factually distinguishable from the instant case. Here Lockwood had not just recently acquired that part or segment of its business that was spun off. Rather, what was spun off was a part of the business Lockwood had always performed in the past and which it has continued to perform since the distribution. If Lockwood had, just before distribution, acquired or opened up a new or entirely different aspect of its business unrelated to prior activities and had spun this off to the controlled corporation, a different result might ensue. In *Bonsall* the distributing company, a dealer in floor covering materials, attempted to assert a tax-free spin-off occurred when a rental business of *de minimis* proportions was transferred to a subsidiary with the stock of the subsidiary being distributed to the distributor's shareholders. * * * [I]t is clear that in respondent's example and in *Bonsall* the business sought to be spun off was not actively engaged in for five years prior to distribution, which is not the situation in the instant case. Here, what was spun off was merely an integral part of what had been Lockwood's primary and only business from its inception.

Further, it should be remembered that even if the five-year active business requirement is met, there is further protection in § 355 against spin-offs being used for mere tax avoidance, which would be contrary to Congressional intent. § 355(a)(1)(B) will only allow a tax-free spin-off transaction where " * * * the transaction was not used principally as a device for the distribution of the earnings and profits of the distributing corporation or the controlled corporation or both * * *." Under this section, the government and the courts have great latitude in preventing the abuses which the respondent fears will happen by finding for petitioners in this case. Cf. Gregory v. Helvering, 1935, 293 U.S. 465, 55 S.Ct. 266, 79 L.Ed. 596. Herein the respondent does not contend that the purpose of the spin off was designed primarily for tax avoidance. No earnings and profits were in fact distributed to Thorval and Margaret. The Tax Court stated that:

> " * * * we do not view the distribution as running afoul of the congressional purpose behind section 355, * * *."

This being so, and since petitioners otherwise complied with § 355, the decision of the Tax Court will be reversed. The transaction herein involved cannot be treated as a taxable distribution of dividends.

Revenue Ruling 2003–38

2003–1 Cum. Bull. 811.

ISSUE

Whether the creation by a corporation engaged in the retail shoe store business of an Internet web site on which the corporation will sell shoes at retail constitutes an expansion of the corporation's business rather than the acquisition of a new or different business under § 1.355–3(b)(3)(ii) of the Income Tax Regulations.

FACTS

Corporation D has operated a retail shoe store business, under the name "D," since Year 1 in a manner that meets the requirements of § 355(b) of the Internal Revenue Code. D's sales are made exclusively to customers who frequent its retail stores in shopping malls and other locations. D's business enjoys favorable name recognition, customer loyalty, and other elements of goodwill in the retail shoe market. In Year 8, D creates an Internet web site and begins selling shoes at retail on the web site. To a significant extent, the operation of the web site draws upon D's experience and know-how. The web site is named "D.com" to take advantage of the name recognition, customer loyalty, and other elements of goodwill associated with D and the D name and to enhance the web site's chances for success in its initial stages. In Year 10, D transfers all of the web site's assets and liabilities to corporation C, a newly formed, wholly owned subsidiary of D, and distributes the stock of C pro rata to D's shareholders. Apart from the issue of whether the web site is considered an expansion of D's business and therefore entitled to share the business's five-year history at the time of the distribution in Year 10, the distribution meets all the requirements of § 355.

LAW

Section 355(a) provides that a corporation may distribute stock and securities in a controlled corporation to its shareholders and security holders in a transaction that will not cause the distributees to recognize gain or loss, provided that, among other requirements, (i) each of the distributing corporation and controlled corporation is engaged, immediately after the distribution, in the active conduct of a trade or business, (ii) each trade or business has been actively conducted throughout the five-year period ending on the date of the distribution, and (iii) neither trade or business was acquired in a transaction in which gain or loss was recognized, in whole or in part, within the five-year period. Sections 355(b)(1)(A), 355(b)(2)(B), and 355(b)(2)(C).

In determining whether an active trade or business has been conducted by a corporation throughout the five-year period preceding the distribution, the fact that a trade or business underwent change during the five-year period (for example, by the addition of new or the dropping of old products, changes in production capacity, and the like) shall be disregarded, provided that the changes are not of such a character as to constitute the acquisition of a new or different business. Section 1.355–3(b)(3)(ii). In particular, if a corporation engaged in the active conduct of one trade or business during that five-year period purchased, created, or otherwise acquired another trade or business in the same line of business, then the acquisition of that other business is ordinarily treated as an expansion of the original business, all of which is treated as having been actively conducted during that five-year period, unless that purchase, creation, or other acquisition effects a change of such character as to constitute the acquisition of a new or different business. Id.

In Example (7) of § 1.355–3(c), corporation X had owned and operated a department store in the downtown area of the City of G for six years before acquiring a parcel of land in a suburban area of G and constructing a new department store. Three years after the construction, X transferred the suburban store and related business assets to new subsidiary Y and distributed the Y stock to X's shareholders. Citing § 1.355–3(b)(3)(i) and (ii), the example concludes that X and Y both satisfy the requirements of § 355(b).

In Example (8) of § 1.355–3(c), corporation X had owned and operated hardware stores in several states for four years before purchasing the assets of a hardware store in State M where X had not previously conducted business. Two years after the purchase, X transferred the State M store and related business assets to new subsidiary Y and distributed the Y stock to X's shareholders. Citing § 1.355–3(b)(3)(i) and (ii), the example concludes that X and Y both satisfy the requirements of § 355(b).

Rev. Rul. 2003–18, 2003–7 I.R.B. 467, concludes that the acquisition by a dealer engaged in the sale and service of brand X automobiles of a franchise (and the assets needed) to sell and service brand Y automobiles is an expansion of the brand X business and does not constitute the acquisition of a new or different business under § 1.355–3(b)(3)(ii) because (i) the product of the brand X automobile dealership is similar to the product of the brand Y automobile dealership, (ii) the business activities associated with the operation of the brand X automobile dealership (i.e., sales and service) are the same as the business activities associated with the operation of the brand Y automobile dealership, and (iii) the operation of the brand Y automobile dealership involves the use of the experience and know-how that the dealer developed in the operation of the brand X automobile dealership.

ANALYSIS

The product of the retail shoe store business and the product of the web site are the same (shoes), and the principal business activities of the retail shoe store business are the same as those of the web site (purchasing shoes at wholesale and reselling them at retail). Selling shoes on a web site requires some know-how not associated with operating a retail store, such as familiarity with different marketing approaches, distribution chains, and technical operations issues. Nevertheless, the web site's operation does draw to a significant extent on D's existing experience and know-how, and the web site's success will depend in large measure on the goodwill associated with D and the D name. Accordingly, the creation by D of the Internet web site does not constitute the acquisition of a new or different business under § 1.355–3(b)(3)(ii). Instead, it is an expansion of D's retail shoe store business. Therefore, each of D and C is engaged in the active conduct of a five-year active trade or business immediately after the distribution. See Rev. Rul. 2003–18 and § 1.355–3(c), Examples (7) and (8).

HOLDING

The creation by a corporation engaged in the retail shoe store business of an Internet web site that sells shoes at retail constitutes an expansion of the retail shoe store business rather than the acquisition of a new or different business under § 1.355–3(b)(3)(ii).

Revenue Ruling 2007–42

2007–2 Cum. Bull. 44.

ISSUE(S)

Under the facts described below, is a corporation (D) that owns a membership interest in a limited liability company (LLC) classified as a partnership for Federal tax purposes engaged in the active conduct of a trade or business for purposes of § 355(b) of the Internal Revenue Code?

FACTS

Situation 1.

LLC is a domestic limited liability company that has been classified as a partnership for Federal tax purposes since its date of organization. For more than five years, LLC has owned several commercial office buildings that are leased to unrelated third parties. LLC has one class of membership interests outstanding. For more than five years, D has owned a 33 1/3–percent membership interest in LLC, and has owned all the stock of a subsidiary (C), a corporation that has been engaged for more than five years in the active conduct of a trade or business that is unrelated to D's activities.

LLC continuously seeks additional properties to expand its rental business. When a property is located, LLC negotiates its purchase and financing and determines whether renovations or alterations are necessary to make the building suitable for rental. LLC periodically repaints and refurbishes its existing properties.

Pursuant to the terms of its leases, LLC provides day-to-day upkeep and maintenance services for its office buildings. These services include trash collection, ground maintenance, electrical and plumbing repair, and insect control. Additionally, LLC advertises for new tenants, verifies information contained in lease applications, negotiates leases, handles tenant complaints, prepares eviction notices and warnings for delinquent tenants, collects rent, and pays all expenses, including gas, water, sewage, electricity and insurance for the office buildings. LLC also maintains financial and accounting records to reflect income and expenses relating to each of its rental properties as well as LLC's general expenses.

The above described activities of LLC have been conducted for more than five years. The employees of LLC perform all management and operational functions with respect to LLC's rental business. Neither D nor any other member of LLC performs services with respect to LLC's business.

For a valid business purpose, D proposes to distribute all its C stock pro rata to D's shareholders in a transaction intended to satisfy the requirements of § 355.

Except for the issue of whether D is engaged in the active conduct of a trade or business under § 355(b), the transaction will otherwise meet all the requirements of § 355.

Situation 2.

The facts are the same as Situation 1 except that D owns a 20–percent membership interest in LLC.

LAW AND ANALYSIS

Section 355(a) provides that, under certain circumstances, a corporation may distribute stock or securities in a corporation it controls to its shareholders or security holders in a transaction that is nontaxable to such shareholders or security holders. Sections 355(a)(1)(C) and 355(b) require that both the distributing and controlled corporations be engaged, immediately after the distribution, in the active conduct of a trade or business that has been actively conducted throughout the five-year period ending on the date of distribution.

Section 1.355–3(b)(2)(ii) of the Income Tax Regulations, in defining trade or business for purposes of § 355, provides that a corporation is treated as engaged in a trade or business immediately after the distribution if a specific group of activities are being carried on by the corporation for the purpose of earning income or profit, and the activities included in such group include every operation that forms a part of, or a step in, the process of earning income or profit. Such group of activities ordinarily must include the collection of income and the payment of expenses.

Section 1.355–3(b)(2)(iii) provides that the determination whether a trade or business is actively conducted will be made from all the facts and circumstances. Generally, for a trade or business to be actively conducted, the corporation is required itself to perform active and substantial management and operational functions. Generally, activities performed by the corporation itself do not include activities performed by persons outside the corporation, including independent contractors. A corporation may, however, satisfy the active trade or business test through the activities that it performs itself, even though some of its activities are performed by others.

Under § 1.355–3(b)(2)(iv), the active conduct of a trade or business does not include the holding of property for investment purposes. It also does not include the ownership and operation (including leasing) of property used in a trade or business, unless the owner performs significant services with respect to the operation and management of the property.

The fact that a partnership engages in activities that would constitute the active conduct of a trade or business if conducted by a corporation does not necessarily mean that each partner in the partnership is considered to be engaged in the active conduct of a trade or business for purposes of § 355(b). In such a case, the determination of whether a partner is considered to be engaged in the active conduct of a trade or business must be based on the requirements of § 355 and the regulations thereunder taking into account the activities of the partner (if any), the partner's interest in the partnership, and the activities of the partnership.

Rev. Rul. 92–17, 1992–1 C.B. 142, considers whether D, a corporate general partner in a limited partnership, is engaged in the active conduct of a trade or business within the meaning of § 355(b). For more than five years, D owned a 20–percent interest in LP, a limited partnership that owned several commercial office buildings leased to unrelated third parties. D's officers performed active and substantial management functions with respect to LP, including the significant business decision-making of the partnership, and regularly participated in the overall supervision, direction, and control of LP's employees in operating LP's rental business. concludes that D is engaged in the active conduct of a trade or business within the meaning of § 355(b). Rev. Rul. 2002–49, 2002–2 C.B. 288, reaches a similar conclusion where D and another corporation (X) each own a 20–percent interest in a member-managed LLC that is classified as a partnership for Federal tax purposes and D and X jointly manage the LLC's business.

By comparison, § 1.368–1(d)(4)(iii)(B), regarding the continuity of business enterprise requirement applicable to corporate reorganizations, provides that the issuing corporation will be treated as conducting a business of a partnership if members of the qualified group, in the aggregate, own an interest in the partnership representing a significant interest in that partnership business. Those regulations indicate that a one-third interest in the partnership represents a significant interest in the partnership business, and a corporation that owns such interest but does not perform active and substantial management functions for the business of the partnership is nevertheless treated as conducting the business of the partnership.

In Situation 1, D is engaged in the active conduct of LLC's rental business for purposes of § 355(b) because D owns a significant interest in

LLC and LLC performs the required activities that constitute an active trade or business under the regulations.

In Situation 2, D is not engaged in the active conduct of LLC's rental business for purposes of § 355(b) because D neither owns a significant interest in LLC nor performs active and substantial management functions for LLC.

HOLDING

In Situation 1, D is engaged in the active conduct of a trade or business for purposes of § 355(b).

In Situation 2, D is not engaged in the active conduct of a trade or business for purposes of § 355(b).

EFFECT ON OTHER REVENUE RULINGS

Rev. Rul. 92–17 is modified to the extent it indicated that a partner must perform management functions in order for the partner to be treated as engaged in the active conduct of the trade or business of the partnership.

NOTE

Although the anti-bailout objective of the active business requirement is clear enough, this multifaceted test has engendered many controversies. The *Lockwood* case is typical of the Commissioner's unsuccessful early efforts to apply the test strictly. The Service has since retreated on many previously contentious issues and most of these changes of heart are reflected in the regulations and in comprehensive proposed regulations that, although not yet final, are already influencing the interpretation of the active trade or business requirement.[1] The proposed regulations were issued in response to the enactment of Section 355(b)(3), which substantially revised the active trade or business requirement for corporations that utilize complex structures such as subsidiaries and partnerships to conduct their activities. They also incorporate and "upgrade" several decades of rulings and cases. This Note surveys the settled and lingering questions, incorporating selectively the proposed regulations.

Trade or Business: In General. Both the distributing and the controlled corporation (or the controlled corporations in the case of a split-up) must be engaged immediately after the distribution in a trade or business with a five-year history. The regulations treat a corporation as being engaged in a trade or business if:[2]

> * * * a specific group of activities are being carried on by the corporation for the purpose of earning income or profit, and the activities included in such group include every operation that forms a part of, or a step in, the process of earning income or

---

1. See REG–123365–03, 2007–1 C.B. 1357.

2. Reg. § 1.355–3(b)(2)(ii).

profit. Such group of activities ordinarily must include the collection of income and the payment of expenses.

The regulations go on to create a dichotomy between the active conduct of a trade or business and passive investment activities. Although the determination of whether a trade or business is "actively conducted" is a factual question turning on all the facts and circumstances, active business status generally requires the corporation to itself perform active and substantial management and operational functions.[3] For this purpose, the activities performed by persons outside the corporation, such as independent contractors, generally are not taken into account.[4] To preclude a tax-free separation of passive investment assets, "active conduct" does not include the holding of property for investment (e.g., raw land or portfolio securities) or the ownership and operation (including leasing) of real or personal property used in the owner's trade or business unless the owner performs significant management services with respect to the property.[5]

Treatment of Affiliated Groups. A corporation historically was treated as actively conducting a trade or business if it did so directly (e.g., through a division) or if "substantially all"[6] of its assets consisted of the stock or securities of one or more "controlled"[7] corporations each of which was engaged in the active conduct of a trade or business.[8] As a result, a holding company that did not directly conduct any business activities still could satisfy the active trade or business test if substantially all of its assets consisted of stock or securities of a controlled corporation that itself conducted an active trade or business. In some situations, however, the holding company was forced to orchestrate cumbersome predistribution maneuvers by relocating active businesses within the corporate group in order to satisfy the "substantially all" requirement and qualify a distribution under Section 355.[9]

To simplify corporate division planning for affiliated groups, Congress added Section 355(b)(3), which eliminates the "substantially all" test and provides that, for purposes of determining whether a corporation is engaged in the active conduct of a trade or business, all members of that corporation's separate affiliated group ("SAG") are treated as one corpora-

---

3. Reg. § 1.355–3(b)(2)(iii). Under the proposed regulations, some of the corporation's activities, however, can be performed by others, such as employees, shareholders, affiliated corporations, and partnerships in which the corporation is a partner. Prop. Reg. § 1.355–3(b)(2)(iii).

4. Reg. § 1.355–3(b)(2)(iii). Activities performed by independent contractors, however, are considered if the corporation itself performs a sufficient quantity of active management and operational functions. See Rev. Rul. 73–234, 1973–1 C.B. 180; Prop. Reg. § 1.355–3(b)(2)(iii).

5. Reg. § 1.355–3(b)(2)(iv).

6. For advance ruling purposes, "substantially all" was 90 percent of the fair market value of a corporation's gross assets. See Rev. Proc. 96–30, § 4.03(5), 1996–1 C.B. 696; Rev. Proc. 77–37, § 3.04, 1977–2 C.B. 68.

7. "Control" for this purpose was measured by the 80 percent tests for voting power and total shares of all other classes of stock in Section 368(c).

8. I.R.C. § 355(b)(2)(A) (pre–2008).

9. See, e.g., Rev. Rul. 74–79, 1974–1 C.B. 81.

tion.[10] A corporation's SAG is the affiliated group determined under the rules used for consolidated tax returns in Section 1504(a) as if such corporation were the "common parent."[11] Roughly translated, this means that the distributing or controlled corporation will be treated as meeting the active trade or business test if any lower-tier affiliate in its SAG is so engaged. This rule simplifies planning for corporations with complex structures but, as discussed below, it also has a ripple effect on other aspects of the Section 355 regime.

Vertical Divisions of a Single Integrated Business. Suppose a corporation wishes to divide a single trade or business that has been operated for more than five years? Does Section 355 require two separate predistribution trades or businesses, each with its own five-year history, or may one existing business be divided in two? After several defeats,[12] the Service acknowledged that Section 355 can apply to the separation of a single business. Thus, assuming the other statutory and judicial requirements are met, a corporation engaged in an integrated business at one location may transfer half of its assets to a new subsidiary and distribute the stock of the subsidiary to a 50 percent shareholder in a tax-free split-off.[13] Similarly, as illustrated by the *Lockwood* case, a separation of activities in the same line of business conducted at different locations can be accomplished tax-free if one of the locations does not have a five-year history. The current regulations look to the character of the activity and commonality of functions in determining whether geographically dispersed operations constitute a single integrated business.[14]

Horizontal Divisions. The treatment of horizontal (sometimes called "functional") divisions—i.e., separations of certain distinct functions of a single business enterprise—was once uncertain, but they are now authorized by the active trade or business regulations. To illustrate the issue,

---

10. I.R.C. § 355(b)(3)(A). This amendment generally applies to distributions occurring after May 27, 2006. The proposed regulations apply this single-entity approach in testing for active trade or business status immediately after a distribution and also throughout the five-year predistribution period. Prop. Reg. § 1.355–3(b)(3).

11. Under Section 1504(a), an affiliated group is one or more chains of "includible corporations" connected through stock ownership with a "common parent." At least 80 percent of the total voting power and 80 percent of the total value of the stock of each of the includible corporations (other than the common parent) must be owned by one or more of the other corporations, and the common parent must satisfy the 80 percent tests with respect to at least one of the other includible corporations. For purposes of the SAG definition in Section 355(b)(3), the rule in Section 1504(b) that disregards "noninclu-

dible" corporations (e.g., a foreign corporation or an insurance company, among others) does not apply. I.R.C. § 355(b)(3)(A).

12. See Coady v. Commissioner, 33 T.C. 771 (1960), affirmed per curiam 289 F.2d 490 (6th Cir.1961) (single construction business divided into two businesses to resolve shareholder dispute); United States v. Marett, 325 F.2d 28 (5th Cir.1963) (food manufacturer operating at three factories spun off one factory opened eight months before the distribution).

13. See, e.g., Reg. § 1.355–3(c) Examples (4) & (5); Prop. Reg. § 1.355–3(d) Examples 14 & 15.

14. See Reg. § 1.355–3(c) Example 7, which permits a nine-year old department store to spin off a suburban branch constructed three years ago where, after the distribution, each store has its own manager and is operated independently.

assume that a manufacturer of high technology equipment wishes to spin off its research and development function for valid business reasons. The Service once maintained that such support activities did not constitute a separate trade or business because they did not independently produce income.[15] The regulations now sanction some types of horizontal divisions, as illustrated in the following example:[16]

> For the past eight years, corporation X has engaged in the manufacture and sale of household products. Throughout this period, X has maintained a research department for use in connection with its manufacturing activities. The research department has 30 employees actively engaged in the development of new products. X transfers the research department to new subsidiary Y and distributes the stock of Y to X's shareholders. After the distribution, Y continues its research operations on a contractual basis with several corporations, including X. X and Y both satisfy the requirements of section 355(b). * * * The result in this example is the same if, after the distribution, Y continues its research operations but furnishes its services only to X. * * *

Similarly, if a company that has processed and sold meat products for more than five years separates the sale and processing functions, the active business test is satisfied.[17]

The regulations make it clear that the functional separation in the example above satisfies the active business test whether the research department subsequently provides services only to the business from which it was separated or also to other customers. The example reflects the Service's abandonment of any requirement that an active business must "independently" produce income. But even if the active business test is met, tax-free treatment for a functional division is still not assured. The transaction also must have a corporate business purpose, and it must not run afoul of the "device" limitation. As we will discover shortly, the regulations provide that the same functional separations that pass muster under the active business test may present "evidence" of a prohibited bailout device.[18]

Expansion of a Trade or Business. To satisfy the active business test, both the distributing and distributed (i.e., controlled) corporations—or both distributed corporations in a split-up—must have actively conducted businesses for the five years prior to the distribution.[19] In addition, those businesses must not have been acquired within the five-year predistribution period in a transaction in which gain or loss was recognized by the seller, and must not have been conducted by a corporation the control (i.e., 80 percent) of which was acquired by the distributing or any distributee

---

15. Reg. § 1.355–1(c)(3) (pre–1989).

16. Reg. § 1.355–3(c) Example (9). See also Prop. Reg. § 1.355–3(d) Example 16, which reaches the same conclusion provided the research department has significant assets and goodwill.

17. Reg. § 1.355–3(c) Example (10). See also Prop. Reg. § 1.355–3(d) Example 17.

18. See Reg. § 1.355–2(d)(2)(iv)(C).

19. I.R.C. § 355(b)(2)(B).

corporation in a taxable transaction during that five-year period.[20] A purpose of these requirements is to prevent a corporation from using Section 355 to avoid the dividend provisions of Subchapter C by temporarily investing its earnings in a business that it plans to spin off to its shareholders.

The five-year rules have spawned controversies over whether a particular activity is a separate business requiring its own five-year history or simply part of an integrated business which has been active for more than five years. For example, a recently opened suburban branch store may be treated as an integral part of an ongoing department store business with a more than five-year history.[21] On the other hand, businesses with clearly distinct products or services (e.g., a chicken ranch and a winery) are considered to be separate.[22] As *Lockwood* and Revenue Ruling 2003–38 illustrate, similar issues arise in the case of a diversification or expansion of a business within the five-year predistribution period. In rulings and regulations, the Service has offered helpful guidance on this question, suggesting that a new activity in the same line of business will be treated as an expansion of the original business unless the "purchase, creation, or other acquisition effects a change of such a character as to constitute the acquisition of a new or different business."[23] This interpretation permits a corporation to accumulate funds and use them to create or purchase the assets of a business, or buy the stock of a corporation conducting the business, and promptly spin off that business to its shareholders provided the "new" activity is in the same line of business that the distributing corporation historically conducted.[24]

Real Estate. The Service has consistently maintained that the holding of vacant investment land does not constitute an actively conducted business and that separation of owner-occupied real estate will be subject to "careful scrutiny."[25] Real estate qualifies as an active business only if the owner performs "significant services with respect to the operation and

---

20. I.R.C. § 355(b)(2)(C)–(D); Reg. § 1.355–3(b)(1)–(5). For this purpose, a "taxable transaction" is one in which gain or loss was recognized in whole or in part by the seller. If a business is acquired in a tax-free reorganization, its previous history carries over (along with its tax attributes) for purposes of the five-year rule.

21. Reg. § 1.355–3(c) Example (7).

22. See, e.g., Rev.Rul. 56–655, 1956–2 C.B. 214 (retail appliance branch and retail furniture branch considered separate businesses); Rev.Rul. 56–451, 1956–2 C.B. 208 (metal industry magazine separate from magazine to serve electrical industry).

23. Reg. § 1.355–3(b)(3)(ii). See also Rev. Rul. 2002–49, 2002–2 C.B. 288, where a corporation that actively conducted a commercial real estate business in conjunction with another unrelated corporation through a limited liability company in which each corporation held a 20 percent interest continued to engage in the same trade or business (and did not acquire a new or different business) after it acquired the remaining 80 percent of the LLC in a taxable transaction.

24. The proposed regulations endorse this approach and make it clear that a corporation can expand an existing active trade or business by acquiring not only assets but also enough stock (at least 80 percent of the voting power and value) in another corporation in the same line of business to qualify the new subsidiary as a member of the acquiring corporation's "separate affiliated group." Prop. Reg. § 1.355–3(b)(3)(ii), –3(d)(2) Examples 18 & 20.

25. Reg. § 1.355–3(b)(2)(iv).

management of the property."[26] Thus, the Service will not approve the spin-off of vacant land or mineral rights on ranch land, even if development activities are imminent.[27] But it will sanction the separation of an office building substantially leased (10 of 11 floors) to outsiders and actively managed by the lessor.[28] More recently, the Service has ruled that a real estate investment trust's rental activities can constitute an active trade or business if, for example, the REIT provides significant services to its tenants.[29] Even if the active business hurdle is surmounted, however, separations of real estate may be vulnerable under the "device" and business purpose tests.[30]

Limit on Taxable Acquisitions Within Five–Year Predistribution Period. A trade or business does not qualify for purposes of the predistribution business history requirement if it was acquired within the five years preceding the distribution in a transaction in which gain or loss was recognized in whole or in part.[31] Although the statute is not crystal clear, it obviously means gain or loss recognized by seller—e.g., a taxable acquisition in which the buyer takes a cost rather than a carryover basis.[32] Tax-free acquisitions, such as liquidations of a controlled subsidiary, do not disqualify the acquired trade or business nor do acquisitive reorganizations even if the target shareholders recognize some gain because they receive boot.[33] The active trade or business requirement also is not met if within the five-year predistribution period the distributing corporation acquires control, measured by the 80 percent tests in Section 368(c), of a corporation conducting the trade or business in a taxable transaction.[34] The proposed regulations, however, treat stock acquisitions that result in the acquired corporation becoming a member of a separate affiliated group as if they were asset acquisitions because, once the acquisition occurs, the corporations are treated as a single corporation.[35]

26. Id.

27. Reg. § 1.355–3(c) Examples (2) and (3). See also Prop. Reg. § 1.355–3(d) Example 13.

28. Reg. § 1.355–3(c) Example (12). Compare Reg. § 1.355–3(c) Example (13), where the separation of a two-story office building did not qualify where the distributing corporation occupied the ground floor and half of the second floor in the conduct of its banking business and rented the remaining area as storage space. See also Prop. Reg. § 1.355–3(d) Examples 11 & 12.

29. Rev. Rul. 2001–29, 2001–1 C.B. 1348.

30. See, e.g., Reg. § 1.355–2(d)(2)(iv)(C).

31. I.R.C. § 355(b)(2)(C).

32. See Bittker & Eustice, Federal Income Taxation of Corporations and Shareholders ¶ 11.05[2][a]. The proposed regula-tions elaborate in great detail. See Prop. Reg. § 1.355–3(b)(4).

33. Bittker & Eustice, supra note 32.

34. I.R.C. § 355(b)(2)(D)(ii). In addi-tion, if control of a corporation conducting the trade or business is acquired by a corpo-rate distributee shareholder within the five-year period preceding the distribution in a transaction in which gain or loss is recog-nized, the active trade or business require-ment is not met. I.R.C. § 355(b)(2)(D)(i). For an explanation of this cryptic rule and related roadblocks to using corporate divisions to avoid corporate-level gain on the sale of a business, see Section E1 of this chapter, in-fra.

35. Prop. Reg. § 1.355–3(b)(4)(iv)(F). If this regulation becomes final, the applicabili-ty of Section 355(b)(2)(D) will be limited to situations where D acquires stock constitut-ing "control" of C as measured by the Sec-

Activities Conducted by a Partnership or LLC. With the issuance of Revenue Ruling 2007–42,[36] the Service has clarified when a corporate partner is considered to be engaged in the active conduct of a trade or business by attributing to it the activities performed by a partnership in which it holds an interest. Prior rulings held that a corporate partner could be treated as engaged in the active conduct of a trade or business of the partnership if the corporation itself or through its officers performed active and substantial functions for the partnership's business,[37] even if another partner also performed active and substantial management functions. Revenue Ruling 2007–42 goes further and attributes to a member that owns a "significant interest" (at least one-third) in an LLC's capital and profits the trade or business of the LLC even if the corporate member does not itself directly conduct any activities relating to the LLC's business.[38]

PROBLEMS

1. Lemon Corporation has been engaged in the manufacture and sale of personal computer hardware equipment for ten years at two plants, one in Boston, Massachusetts and the other in San Jose, California. During this same period, Lemon also has operated at each location a separate research and development division, each of which had significant assets and goodwill. Lemon's common stock, the only class outstanding, is owned equally by Ms. Micro and Mr. Chips. In each of the following alternative transactions, consider whether the active trade or business requirement has been satisfied:

(a) As a result of a shareholder dispute, Ms. Micro wishes to say goodbye to Mr. Chips. To enable the shareholders to part company but continue in the computer business, Lemon contributes the assets and research division of the Boston facility to a new corporation, Peach, Inc., and distributes all the Peach, Inc. stock to Mr. Chips in redemption of his Lemon stock. Ms. Micro remains as the sole shareholder of Lemon.

(b) Same as (a), above, except that the Boston facility was opened only three years ago.

(c) Same as (b), above, except that three years ago Lemon acquired all the stock of Peach, Inc., which operated the Boston facility, for cash.

(d) Same as (c), above, except Peach had two classes of stock and Lemon acquired enough stock to constitute control under Section

tion 368(c) tests (voting power and other classes of stock) but not the type of control measured by Section 1504(a) (voting power and value) that would cause C to become part of D's separate affiliated group.

36. Supra p. 473.

37. Rev. Rul. 92–17, 1992–1 C.B. 142; Rev. Rul. 2002–49, 2002–2 C.B. 288. See also

Prop. Reg. § 1.355–3(b)(2)(v)(C), which requires the corporate partner to own a "meaningful" interest (at least 20 percent is meaningful based on prior rulings) in the partnership.

38. See also Prop. Reg. § 1.355–3(b)(2)(v)(B), –3(d)(2) Example 23.

368(c) but not enough to make Peach a member of Lemon's separated affiliated group under Section 1504(a)(2). (How could this happen?).

(e) To comply with a divestiture order, Lemon transfers the assets of the research divisions to a new corporation, Research, Inc. and distributes all the Research stock pro rata to the shareholders. After the distribution, Research, Inc. continues to perform services solely for Lemon.

(f) In addition to the operations described above, assume that three years ago Lemon purchased all the stock of Floppy Disk, Inc., a computer software manufacturer, in a taxable transaction. To comply with a regulatory decree, Lemon distributes the stock of Floppy Disk pro rata to its shareholders.

(g) Same as (f), above, except that Floppy Disk merged into Lemon three years ago in a Type A reorganization. The consideration for that acquisition consisted of Lemon nonvoting preferred stock (80%) and Lemon short-term notes (20%).

2.   DC Enterprises ("DC") is a large manufacturing company which owns the 10 story building in which it conducts its business. For the past 15 years, it has used six floors for its own operations and rented the other four floors to unrelated tenants. Six years ago, DC formed a wholly owned subsidiary, Properties, Inc., which leases two other commercial buildings previously owned by DC on a long-term net lease basis, under which the tenants are responsible for property taxes, insurance and maintenance. Consider whether the following alternative transactions satisfy the active trade or business requirement:

(a) On the advice of a management consultant, DC transfers its 10 story office building to a new corporation, Rental, Inc., and distributes the Rental stock pro rata to its shareholders. After the distribution, DC leases from Rental the six floors that it occupies; and Rental continues to rent the other four floors to unrelated tenants. Rental employees actively manage the building and perform repair and maintenance services.

(b) Same as (a), above, except that DC only occupies one floor and the remaining space is leased to unrelated tenants.

(c) Same as (b), above, except the nine floors are rented to outsiders under a long-term net lease.

(d) DC distributes all the stock of Properties, Inc. pro rata to the DC shareholders. After the distribution, Properties continues its rental activities.

C.   Judicial and Statutory Limitations

1.   Business Purpose

Regulations: § 1.355–2(b).

Background. The business purpose doctrine originated in Gregory v. Helvering[1] and rapidly assumed its role as one of the first "common law" principles of federal taxation. The doctrine has become an increasingly important limitation under Section 355 even though it is never mentioned in the Code. The business purpose and device limitations are conceptually linked, each focusing on the taxpayer's motivation for the transaction. It is appropriate to consider the business purpose requirement first because the strength or weakness of a corporate business purpose is evidence in determining whether a transaction was used principally as a device for distributing earnings and profits.[2] Moreover, the regulations have long provided that the "business purpose requirement is independent of the other requirements under section 355."[3] Thus, a corporate division lacking a business purpose can not be accomplished tax free even if it is not used principally as a device to bail out earnings and profits.[4]

Business Purpose Regulations. The regulations define a corporate business purpose as "a real and substantial non Federal tax purpose germane to the business of the distributing corporation, the controlled corporation or the affiliated group to which the distributing corporation belongs."[5] Valid business purposes include compliance with antitrust and other regulatory decrees, resolution of shareholder disputes, or even amicable partings to permit shareholders to pursue separate business interests.[6] Among other business purposes approved by the courts and the Service over the years are: facilitating a merger of the distributing or controlled corporation;[7] increasing access to credit or new equity investment (such as by enabling either the controlled or distributing corporations to raise capital on more favorable terms through a public offering);[8] resolving labor problems;[9] providing an equity interest to a newly-hired key employee;[10] and warding off a hostile takeover.[11]

A pure shareholder purpose, such as personal estate planning, does not suffice under the regulations,[12] but the transaction may pass muster if a

---

1. See p. 459, supra.

2. Reg. § 1.355–2(b)(4), (d)(3)(ii).

3. Reg. § 1.355–2(b)(1).

4. Reg. § 1.355–2(b)(1).

5. Reg. § 1.355–2(b)(2). See also Rev. Proc. 96–30, App. A, 1996–1 C.B. 696, which provided detailed guidelines to be used for ruling purposes in evaluating whether a distribution satisfies the business purpose requirement. But in Rev. Proc. 2003–48, 2003–2 C.B. 86, the Service announced a "no ruling" policy on business purposes issues and deleted the guidelines, which still offer planning guidance. The "no ruling" policy is a pilot program and may be reevaluated by the Service in 2005.

6. Reg. § 1.355–2(b)(5) Examples (1) and (2).

7. Commissioner v. Morris Trust, 367 F.2d 794 (4th Cir.1966); Rev. Proc. 96–30, supra note 5, App. A, §§ 2.07–.08. But see I.R.C. § 355(e) and Section E2 of this chapter, infra.

8. See, e.g., Rev.Rul. 77–22, 1977–1 C.B. 91; Rev.Rul. 85–122, 1985–2 C.B. 118; Rev. Proc. 96–30, supra note 5, App. A, §§ 2.02–.03.

9. Olson v. Commissioner, 48 T.C. 855 (1967).

10. Rev. Rul. 88–34, 1988–1 C.B. 115.

11. See Priv. Ltr. Rul. 8819075 (May 13, 1988).

12. Reg. § 1.355–2(b)(2). But see Estate of Parshelsky v. Commissioner, 303 F.2d 14 (2d Cir.1962), where the court held that a shareholder business purpose justified a spin-

shareholder purpose is "so nearly coextensive with a corporate business purpose as to preclude any distinction between them."[13] For example, in Revenue Ruling 2003–52,[14] the Service ruled that the division of a family farm business into two separate corporations, one to grow grain and the other to raise livestock, satisfied the business purpose requirement. The division was motivated by a desire to permit the two principal shareholders (a brother and sister who disagreed over the future direction of the family business) to go their separate ways and devote their undivided attention to the businesses in which they were most involved, and also to promote family harmony and further the estate planning goals of their parents, who also were shareholders. The Service concluded that since the principal motivation for the transaction was to benefit both businesses, the fact that it also facilitated personal estate planning of the shareholders and promoted family harmony was not fatal.

Similarly, the Service found nearly co-extensive corporate and shareholder purposes on a separation of two lines of business of a public company that was motivated by a desire to increase the aggregate trading price of the stock of both businesses after they became separate corporations.[15] In addition to the obvious shareholder benefit, the higher stock prices were found to benefit the distributing corporation in two alternative situations: (1) by enhancing an equity-based employee compensation plan without diluting the interests of existing shareholders by issuing more stock, and (2) by allowing the corporation to use its own (more valuable) stock as partial consideration for future acquisitions with significantly less dilution of existing shareholder interests.[16]

The Service has ruled that the reduction of state and local taxes can be a corporate business purpose.[17] But the regulations make it clear that the reduction of "non Federal" taxes is not an independent corporate business purpose if: (1) the transaction will result in a reduction in both Federal and non Federal taxes because of similarities in the respective laws, and (2) the reduction of Federal taxes is greater than or substantially coextensive with the reduction of non Federal taxes.[18] For example, a spin-off of a subsidiary to enable one or both of the resulting corporations to elect S corporation status is not a business purpose[19] even though the transaction may bear little resemblance to the original bailout evil of Gregory v. Helvering.

A business purpose for a distribution also does not exist if the same corporate objectives can be met through a nontaxable transaction that does not require a distribution of stock of a controlled corporation and which is neither impractical nor unduly expensive.[20] For example, assume that a corporation manufactures both toys and candy through divisions which are

off even in the absence of a corporate business purpose.

13. Reg. § 1.355–2(b)(2).
14. 2003–1 C.B. 960.
15. Rev. Rul. 2004–23, 2004–1 C.B. 585.
16. Id.

17. Rev.Rul. 76–187, 1976–1 C.B. 97.
18. Reg. § 1.355–2(b)(2).
19. Reg. § 1.355–2(d)(5) Example (6); see Rev. Proc. 96–30, supra note 5, App. C.
20. Reg. § 1.355–2(b)(3).

not separately incorporated, and the shareholders wish to insulate the candy business from the risks of the toy business. If that goal can be achieved by dropping down the assets of one of the businesses to a new subsidiary, a subsequent distribution of the subsidiary's stock to the parent's shareholders is not carried out for a corporate business purpose.[21]

The fact that Section 355 permits a distributing corporation to avoid corporate-level gain on the distribution of stock of a controlled corporation is not considered by the Service to present such a potential for avoidance of federal taxes that it overrides an otherwise valid corporate business purpose.[22] The Service also has ruled that as long as a distribution is motivated in whole or substantial part by a corporate business purpose at the time it is made, the corporation's later failure to succeed in meeting that purpose will not prevent the distribution from satisfying the business purpose requirement.[23] In addition, continuing relationships for a limited period of time between the distributing and spun-off companies do not necessarily jeopardize the distribution from qualifying under Section 355.[24]

A notable recent addition to the list of acceptable business purposes is known as "fit and focus." The Service has ruled[25] that a software company's spin-off of a paper products business satisfied the business purpose requirement because the distribution was motivated by a desire to allow senior management of the distributing corporation "to concentrate its efforts on the software business, which it believes presents better opportunities for growth and allow the management of the paper products business to secure for that business the management resources needed for its full development." The ruling also states that the existence of common directors of the distributing and spun-off companies does not necessarily preclude reliance on a "fit and focus" business purpose.

Advance Rulings. In Revenue Procedure 96–30,[26] the Service set forth in great detail the type of information taxpayers must submit in order to obtain an advance ruling in a Section 355 transaction and provided new insight on the Service's approach to the business purpose requirement. The

---

21. Reg. §§ 1.355–2(b)(3), 1.355–2(b)(5) Example (3). See also Reg. § 1.355–2(b)(5) Examples (4) and (5).

22. Rev. Rul. 2003–110, 2003–2 C.B. 1083 (corporation used Section 355 to separate its baby food and pesticide businesses to improve a market perception problem arising from the baby food company's affiliation with a pesticide business).

23. Rev. Rul. 2003–55, 2003–1 C.B. 961, where the business purpose for a corporate separation was to facilitate the raising of capital through an initial public offering of the stock of what previously was a wholly owned subsidiary of the distributing corporation. Even though market conditions unexpectedly deteriorated and the public offering

was postponed indefinitely, there was a valid business purpose at the time the distribution was made.

24. See Rev. Rul. 2003–75, 2003–2 C.B. 79, where a distribution was made to resolve issues relating to the competition for capital between two businesses (pharmaceuticals and cosmetics) and, after the spin-off, the two companies entered into "transitional" agreements (two years, after which the agreements were to be renegotiated at arm's length for a limited period) relating to information technology, benefits administration, and accounting and tax matters.

25. Rev. Rul. 2003–74, 2003–2 C.B. 77.

26. See supra note 5.

revenue procedure also provided guidelines to be used by the Service in evaluating whether a distribution satisfies the corporate business purpose requirement and a nonexclusive list of valid business purposes. But in 2003, the Service announced a "pilot program" under which it would no longer issue advance rulings on the business purpose requirement and the device limitation.[27] In lieu of guidelines, the Service is releasing more published rulings (many are discussed in the text above) approving a business purpose in a variety of factual contexts.

2.   CONTINUITY OF INTEREST

Regulations: § 1.355–2(c).

The regulations require that those persons who historically owned an interest in the enterprise prior to a corporate division must own, in the aggregate, an amount of stock establishing a continuity of interest in each of the modified corporate forms in which the enterprise is conducted after the distribution.[1] This means that one or more of the shareholders of the distributing corporation must emerge from the transaction (in the aggregate) with at least a 50 percent equity interest in each of the corporations that conduct the enterprise after the division.[2] The continuity of interest test overlaps considerably with the device limitation, which patrols against prearranged postdistribution sales as part of its anti-bailout mission. The regulations nonetheless emphasize that continuity of interest is an independent test that must be met in addition to the other Section 355 requirements.[3]

A common divisive transaction involves the breakup of a corporate enterprise to allow feuding shareholders to part company, with each taking a share of the business in the form of stock in separate corporations. The regulations acknowledge that this type of transaction, whether structured as a split-off or split-up, satisfies the continuity of interest requirement because the prior owners of the integrated enterprise emerge in the aggregate with all the stock of two corporations that survive the separation. Assume, however, that A and B each own 50 percent of the stock of P, Inc., which is engaged in one business, and P owns all the stock of S, Inc., which is engaged in a different business. If new and unrelated shareholder C purchases all of A's stock in P and P then distributes all the stock of S to B

---

27. Rev. Proc. 2003–48, 2003–2 C.B. 86.

1. Reg. § 1.355–2(c)(1).

2. Without explicitly saying so, several examples in the regulations indicate that a 50 percent equity interest, the safe harbor benchmark for Type A reorganizations, is what is needed to "maintain" continuity of interest. See, e.g., Reg. § 1.355–2(c)(2) Example (2); Rev.Proc. 96–30, § 4.06, 1996–19 I.R.B. 8, 18. Although 50 percent continuity historically was required to obtain an advance ruling from the Service, the case law

supports a lower percentage, and the regulations on acquisitive reorganizations now confirm that the Service will accept 40 percent continuity for mergers. Reg. § 1.368–1(e)(2)(iv) Example 1. It follows that 40 percent also should be sufficient for corporate divisions. See Ginsburg & Levin, Mergers, Acquisitions & Buyouts, § 610.2.

3. Reg. § 1.355–2(c)(1). For a rare published ruling on the application of the continuity of interest doctrine to a spin-off, see Rev.Rul. 79–273, 1979–2 C.B. 125.

in redemption of B's P stock, the transaction fails the continuity of interest test because the owners of P prior to the distribution (A and B) do not, in the aggregate, own an amount of stock establishing continuity of interest in both P and S after the distribution.[4] Only the historic shareholders of P (i.e., A and B) may be counted for continuity of interest purposes, and the smoking pistol is present if none of those shareholders owns any stock of P after the distribution. As for who qualifies as an historic shareholder, it appears that a shareholder who acquires P stock prior to the time that P decides to engage in a division should qualify even if the acquisition occurred shortly before the distribution.[5] Apparently, even a person who acquired P stock in contemplation of a distribution of S stock will be treated as an historic shareholder if the acquisition was more than two years prior to the distribution.[6]

The shareholders of the distributing corporation also must maintain continuity of interest after the distribution.[7] A post-distribution continuity issue might arise, for example, if shareholders sold more than 50 percent of the stock of either the distributing or controlled corporations shortly after the distribution. Shareholders who committed themselves to sell prior to the distribution or who had a fixed intention to do so are not likely to have maintained continuity of interest, but an unanticipated sale should not be a problem.

3.　The "Device" Limitation

Code: § 355(a)(1)(B).

Regulations: § 1.355–2(d).

a.　IN GENERAL

Section 355(a)(1)(B) provides that a corporate division may not be "used principally as a device for the distribution of the earnings and profits" of the distributing corporation or the controlled subsidiary. The historic mission of this requirement has been to prevent the conversion of ordinary dividend income into preferentially taxed capital gain through a bailout masquerading as a corporate division.[1] This goal is reaffirmed in the regulations, which provide:[2]

4.　Reg. § 1.355–2(c)(2) Example (3).

5.　See Kaden & Wolfe, "Spin-offs, Split-offs, and Split-ups: A Detailed Analysis of Section 355," 44 Tax Notes 565, 588–589 (July 31, 1989).

6.　Id. at 589. Cf. Rev.Rul. 74–5, 1974–1 C.B. 82, declared obsolete on other grounds by Rev.Rul. 89–37, 1989–1 C.B. 107.

7.　This is similar to the recently abandoned post-acquisition continuity requirement for acquisitive reorganizations. See Chapter 9B1, supra. It remains to be seen

whether the Service will modify its post-distribution continuity rules in the corporate divisions context. For an extensive discussion of the Section 355 version of the continuity of interest doctrine, see Shores, "Reexamining Continuity of Shareholder Interest in Corporate Divisions," 18 Va. Tax Rev. 473 (1999).

1.　See, e.g., Rev.Rul. 71–383, 1971–2 C.B. 180.

2.　Reg. § 1.355–2(d)(1).

* * * a tax-free distribution of the stock of a controlled corporation presents a potential for tax avoidance by facilitating the avoidance of the dividend provisions of the Code through the subsequent sale or exchange of stock of one corporation and the retention of the stock of another corporation. A device can include a transaction that effects a recovery of basis.

Ever since the device limitation was added to the Code, its meaning and scope have been mired in obscurity. The regulations initially fail to burn off the fog, declaring that "generally, the determination of whether a transaction was used principally as a device will be made from all of the facts and circumstances."[3] They go on to offer some guidance by identifying certain "device" and "nondevice" factors which are "evidence" of the presence or absence of a device, but the strength of this "evidence" still depends on "the facts and circumstances."[4]

The role of the device limitation is diminished but not eliminated as long as dividends and long-term capital gains of noncorporate taxpayers are taxed at the same preferential rate. A "device" still may include a transaction that effects a recovery of a shareholder's stock basis. In situations where shareholders have a nominal basis and are indifferent to dividend vs. capital gain treatment, the question remains whether the Service might invoke the device limitation to tax the distributing corporation, which would be required to recognize gain on the distribution if the transaction does not qualify under Section 355, or whether it is sufficient to rely on more targeted corporate-level statutory watchdogs, such as Sections 355(d) and 355(e), which are discussed later in this chapter.[5]

Transactions Ordinarily Not a Device. Notwithstanding the presence or absence of the "device factors" to be discussed below, three transactions "ordinarily" are not considered a tax avoidance device. Distributions are presumed innocent if:

(1) the distributing and controlled corporations have neither accumulated nor current earnings and profits as of the date of the distribution, taking into account the possibility that a distribution of appreciated property by the distributing corporation as part of a divisive transaction would create earnings and profits if Section 355 did not apply;[6]

(2) in the absence of Section 355, the distribution would qualify as a redemption to pay death taxes under Section 303;[7] and

(3) in the absence of Section 355, the distribution would qualify, with respect to each distributee shareholder, as an exchange redemption under Section 302(a).[8]

---

3. Reg. § 1.355–2(d)(1).

4. Reg. § 1.355–2(d)(2)(i), (3)(i).

5. See Section E of this chapter, infra.

6. Reg. § 1.355–2(d)(5)(ii).

7. Reg. § 1.355–2(d)(5)(iii). See Chapter 5H, supra.

8. Reg. § 1.355–2(d)(5)(iv). For this purpose, the waiver of family attribution rules apply without regard to the ten year

Section 303 and Section 302(a)-type redemptions lose the benefit of the presumption, however, if they involve the distribution of stock of more than one controlled corporation and facilitate the avoidance of the dividend provisions of the Code through the subsequent sale or exchange of stock of one corporation and the retention of the stock of another corporation.[9]

Device and Nondevice Factors: In General. The regulations specify three factors that are "evidence" of a device ("device factors") and three factors that are evidence of a nondevice ("nondevice factors"). The device factors are: (1) a pro rata distribution; (2) a subsequent sale or exchange of stock of either the distributing or controlled corporation; and (3) the nature and use of the assets of the distributing and controlled corporations immediately after the transaction.[10] The three nondevice factors are: (1) the corporate business purpose for the transaction; (2) the fact that the distributing corporation is publicly traded and widely held; and (3) the fact that the stock of the controlled corporation is distributed to one or more domestic corporations which would be entitled to a dividends received deduction under Section 243 if Section 355 does not apply to the transaction.[11] The presence of one or more of these factors is not controlling, however, and the "strength" of the evidence depends on the facts and circumstances.[12]

b. DEVICE FACTORS

Pro Rata Distribution. A pro rata distribution—for example, a spin-off—is considered to present the greatest potential for avoidance of the dividend provisions of Subchapter C and thus is more likely to be used principally as a device. As a result, the regulations provide that a pro rata or substantially pro rata distribution is evidence of a device.[13]

Subsequent Sale or Exchange of Stock. A parenthetical clause in Section 355(a)(1)(B) cryptically provides that the "mere fact" that stock or securities of either the distributing or controlled corporations are sold by all or some of the shareholders is not to be construed to mean that the transaction was used principally as a device. But the Service has long contended that a sale of stock of the distributing or controlled corporation shortly after a corporate division is evidence that the transaction was used as a bailout device. The "strength" of the evidence depends upon the percentage of stock disposed of after the distribution, the length of time between the distribution and the subsequent sale and the extent to which the subsequent sale was prearranged.[14]

look forward rule and the requirement to file a waiver agreement in Sections 302(c)(2)(A)(ii) and (iii). See Chapter 5C, supra.

9. Reg. § 1.355–2(d)(5)(i). For an example, see Reg. § 1.355–2(d)(5)(v) Example (2).

10. Reg. § 1.355–2(d)(2).

11. Reg. § 1.355–2(d)(3).

12. Reg. § 1.355–2(d)(2)(i); –2(d)(3)(i).

13. Reg. § 1.355–2(d)(2)(ii).

14. Reg. § 1.355–2(d)(2)(iii)(A).

A subsequent sale or exchange negotiated or agreed upon before the distribution is "substantial evidence" of a device.[15] A sale is always prearranged if it was "pursuant to an arrangement negotiated or agreed upon before the distribution if enforceable rights to buy or sell existed before the distribution."[16] The regulations are more equivocal if a sale was merely discussed by the parties but was "reasonably to be anticipated." In that event, it "ordinarily" will be considered to be previously negotiated or agreed upon.[17] Seemingly ignoring the express language of Section 355(a)(1)(B), the regulations also provide that even in the absence of prior negotiations or agreement, a subsequent sale nonetheless is "evidence of a device."[18] Presumably, the evidence would be fairly weak if the decision to sell were not made until after the distribution.

The perceived bailout abuse of a subsequent sale normally is present only when the selling shareholders cash out their investment. The regulations logically provide that if the shareholders dispose of stock in a subsequent tax-free reorganization in which no more than an "insubstantial" amount of gain is recognized, the transaction will not be treated as a subsequent sale or exchange. Rather, because the shareholders maintain an interest in the continuing enterprise, the stock received in the exchange is treated as equivalent to the stock surrendered.[19] But any sale of the new stock received will be subject to the "subsequent sale" rules and could be evidence of a device.[20]

The Service's reliance on subsequent stock sales (whether or not prearranged) as substantial evidence of a device has always been questionable. To return to the earlier introductory example, assume that Diverse Corporation has actively conducted profitable winery and chicken ranch businesses for more than five years. If Diverse wished to spin off the chicken ranch as Poultry, Inc., it would have no difficulty satisfying the active business test. But what if the spin-off were the prelude to a prearranged sale of the Poultry, Inc. stock by the controlling shareholders? If gain on that sale were taxable to the shareholders at capital gains rates, or even if it merely effected a recovery of part of the shareholders' basis in their Diverse Corp. stock, should the spin-off be viewed principally as a device to bail out Diverse's earnings and profits?

In considering these questions, keep in mind the alternatives available to Diverse. If the corporation simply had sold the chicken ranch assets and distributed the proceeds to its noncorporate shareholders, the distribution likely would have qualified as a partial liquidation, entitling noncorporate shareholders to exchange (and thus capital gains) treatment.[21] The same result would have occurred if the chicken ranch assets were distributed pro

---

15. Reg. § 1.355–2(d)(2)(iii)(B).

16. Reg. § 1.355–2(d)(2)(iii)(D).

17. Id.

18. Reg. § 1.355–2(d)(2)(iii)(C).

19. Reg. § 1.355–2(d)(2)(iii)(E).

20. Id.

21. See I.R.C. § 302(b)(4), (e). But see Rev.Rul. 75–223, 1975–1 C.B. 109, discussed at p. 239, supra, in which the Service ruled that a distribution of stock of a subsidiary may not qualify as a partial liquidation. See also Morgenstern v. Commissioner, 56 T.C. 44 (1971).

rata to the shareholders and sold shortly thereafter. To be sure, a sale or distribution of the chicken ranch assets by the corporation would have triggered gain at the corporate and shareholder levels.[22] But, historically at least, the principal concern in Section 355 was not with the double taxation of corporate earnings but rather the tax treatment of a distribution to the shareholders. If an economically equivalent transaction (i.e., a partial liquidation) would have qualified for capital gain treatment, it seems anomalous to classify a spin-off followed by a prearranged sale of the same business as a device to convert ordinary dividend income to capital gain. In the last analysis, the correct answer from a policy perspective may be to treat partial liquidation distributions as dividends to noncorporate shareholders. Moreover, even if it is not a device, a distribution followed by a taxable sale is unlikely to satisfy the business purpose test and, if the sale closely follows the distribution but somehow escapes the device limitation, the transaction also may fail the continuity of interest requirement. And, of course, much of this discussion is less important as long as dividends and capital gains of noncorporate taxpayers are taxed at the same preferential rate.

Nature and Use of the Assets. The regulations also enforce the device limitation by taking into account the "nature, kind, amount, and use of the assets of the distributing and the controlled corporations (and corporations controlled by them) immediately after the transaction."[23] Thus, the existence of assets that are not used in an active trade or business, such as cash and other liquid assets that are not related to the reasonable needs of the active business, is evidence of a device.[24] To illustrate, assume that Corporation P spins off Corporation S in order to comply with certain regulatory requirements under state law. As part of the separation, P transfers excess cash (not related to the reasonable needs of P's or S's business) to S and then distributes the S stock pro rata to P's shareholders. The result of this infusion of cash into S is that the percentage of liquid assets not related to the trade or business is substantially greater for S than for P. The regulations view this as suspect, providing in an example that the transfer of cash by P to S is "relatively strong evidence of device."[25] When coupled with the pro rata nature of the distribution, the transaction is considered to have been used principally as a device notwithstanding the "strong business purpose" because there was no business purpose for the infusion of cash into S.[26]

The regulations also consider the relationship between the distributing and controlled corporations and the effect of a sale of one of the businesses on the overall enterprise. Evidence of a device is presented if the distribut-

22. See Chapters 7 and 8, supra.

23. Reg. § 1.355–2(d)(2)(iv).

24. Reg. § 1.355–2(d)(2)(iv)(A), (B).

25. Reg. § 1.355–2(d)(4) Example (3).

26. Reg. § 1.355–2(d)(2)(iv)(B); 1.355–2(d)(4) Example (3). Compare Reg. § 1.355–2(d)(4) Example (2), where the transfer of cash and liquid securities from the distributing to the controlled corporation was "relatively weak evidence of device" because after the transfer the two corporations held liquid assets in amounts proportional to the values of their businesses.

ing or controlled corporation is a business that principally serves the business of the other corporation (a "secondary business") and it can be sold without adversely affecting the business that it serves.[27] Thus, the spin-off of a captive coal mine from a steel manufacturer, a transaction which satisfied the active business test,[28] nonetheless presents evidence of a device if the principal function of the coal mine is to satisfy the requirements of the steel business and the coal mine could be sold without adversely affecting the steel business.[29] The apparent concern here is not so much with the potential for tax avoidance through non-arm's length intercorporate transactions between the separated corporations. That type of abuse is adequately policed by Section 482, which authorizes the Commissioner to allocate income or deductions between or among commonly controlled trades or businesses.[30] What appears to be bothering the Service is the likelihood for avoidance of the dividend provisions of the Code when the "related function" is not truly integral to the business from which it has been separated.

c. NONDEVICE FACTORS

Acknowledging that the corporate business purposes for a transaction may be sufficiently compelling to outweigh any evidence of a device, the regulations provide that the corporate business purpose for a transaction is evidence of nondevice.[31] In keeping with the "sliding scale" approach that pervades the device regulations, the stronger the evidence of device, then the stronger is the business purpose required to prevent determination that the transaction was used principally as a device.[32] The strength of a corporate business purpose, of course, is based on all the facts and circumstances, including but not limited to the importance of achieving the purpose to the success of the business, the extent to which the transaction is prompted by a person not having a proprietary interest in either corporation or by other outside factors beyond the control of the distributing corporation, and the "immediacy of the conditions" prompting the transaction.[33]

The fact that the distributing corporation is publicly traded and widely held, having no shareholder who directly or indirectly owns more than five percent of any class of stock, also is evidence of nondevice.[34]

Finally, the fact that the stock of the controlled corporation is distributed to a domestic corporate distributee which, without Section 355, would

---

27. Reg. § 1.355–2(d)(2)(iv)(C).

28. See Reg. § 1.355–3(c) Example (11).

29. Reg. § 1.355–2(d)(2)(iv)(C). Likewise, the separation of the sales and manufacturing functions will constitute evidence of a device if the principal function of the sales operation after the separation is to sell the output from the manufacturing operation and the sales operation could be sold without adversely affecting the manufacturing operation.

30. See Chapter 13A, infra.

31. Reg. § 1.355–2(d)(3)(ii).

32. Id.

33. Id.

34. Reg. § 1.355–2(d)(3)(iii).

be entitled to the Section 243 dividends received deduction, is evidence of a nondevice.[35]

4.   Disqualified Investment Corporations

Section 355(g) was added to the Code to prevent transactions known as "cash-rich split-offs" from qualifying for nonrecognition treatment. The abuse at which Section 355(g) is directed is best illustrated by a simple example. Assume that for more than five years Investor Corp. ("I") has owned a highly appreciated 30 percent interest in Distributing Corp. ("D"). I wishes to accomplish what would appear to be impossible: a sale of its D stock for cash without paying any current tax. D wishes to buy back some of its stock and is willing to assist I plan a tax-efficient disposition. To accomplish these objectives, D transfers a small five-year active trade or business to C Corp. ("C"), a newly formed subsidiary, along with a large amount of cash (or other liquid assets) in exchange for all the C stock. D then redeems I's D stock by distributing its C stock to I in exchange for I's entire holding in D. I then promptly liquidates C (its new cash-rich subsidiary), treating the transaction as a tax-free liquidation under Section 332.[1]

Prior to the enactment of Section 355(g), the transaction described above was likely to qualify as tax-free. The active trade or business test did not require the active business of the controlled corporation to constitute any particular percentage of the overall value of C, and the device test was not violated because the distributee shareholder (I, in the example above) completely terminated its interest in D. This "too good to be true" strategy was employed by several public companies in significant transactions, prompting the Treasury to seek corrective legislation.[2]

Section 355(g) provides that a distribution does not qualify as tax-free if: (1) either the distributing or controlled corporation is, immediately after the transaction, a "disqualified investment corporation," and (2) any person holds, immediately after the transaction, a 50–percent or greater interest (measured by voting power and value) in any disqualified investment corporation but only if such person did not hold such an interest in the corporation immediately before the transaction.[3] D or C is a disqualified investment corporation if the fair market value of its "investment assets" is two-thirds or more of the fair market value of all its assets.[4] Investment assets include cash; corporate stock or securities; partnership interests; debt instruments or other evidences of indebtedness; any option, forward, or futures contract, notional principal contract, or derivative; foreign cur-

---

35.   Reg. § 1.355–2(d)(3)(iv).

1.   For a good discussion of the cash-rich split-off strategy, see Willens, "Dividends, Capital Gains, and Spin-offs Affected by Increase, Prevention and Reconciliation Act," 104 J. Tax'n 327 (2006).

2.   In one reported transaction, Clorox distributed $2.1 billion in cash and a business worth $740 million to a U.S. subsidiary of a German company in redemption of that subsidiary's 29 percent interest in Clorox.

3.   I.R.C. § 355(g)(1). The provision applies to distributions after May 17, 2006, with certain specialized exceptions.

4.   I.R.C. § 355(g)(2)(A)(i).

rency; or any similar asset.[5] Various exceptions and special rules apply to determine a corporation's investment assets and to measure whether a person has a 50–percent-or-greater interest.[6]

If Section 355(g) applies, the transaction is fully taxable at the corporate and shareholder levels, but cash-rich (albeit not as rich) split-offs are still a viable strategy if tainted liquid assets fall below the two-thirds threshold. Indeed, in an ironic twist, Section 355(g) often sanctions the very transaction that it was trying to curtail for those who are able to navigate its rather liberal requirements. An example of a successful navigator was Liberty Media Corporation, which shed its major stake in Time–Warner in a tax-free split-off exchange for the Atlanta Braves baseball team (an active and often successful trade or business) and $1.38 billion in cash. Liberty Media engaged in a similar deal when it exchanged its stake in News Corp. for $465 million in cash and News Corp.'s holdings in satellite provider DirectTV. The cash-rich split-off thus remains an attractive way for corporations with diversified holdings to monetize a highly appreciated asset without paying any tax. In yet another example, as this book went to press in early 2012, Yahoo was considering a split-off of its 40 percent stake in Alibaba Group, a Chinese e-commerce company, in exchange for stock of an Alibaba subsidiary holding $17 billion in cash and operating assets.[7] If the operating assets satisfy the active trade or business test, the cash is less than two-thirds of the value transferred to Yahoo, and Yahoo can establish a business purpose, the transaction could qualify as tax-free notwithstanding Section 355(g).

PROBLEM

Assume that Lemon Corporation from Problem 1 at page 482, operates a computer manufacturing business at only one location where it also conducts research and development through a separate division. Lemon also owns all the stock of Floppy Disk, Inc., a computer software manufacturer that Lemon purchased six years ago in a taxable transaction. The net worths of the computer and software businesses are approximately the same, and both corporations have substantial accumulated earnings and profits. The common stock of Lemon is owned equally by Ms. Micro and Mr. Chips. In each of the following alternatives, assume that the active trade or business requirement is met and consider whether the transactions described satisfy the other requirements of Section 355.

(a) To resolve a shareholder dispute, Lemon distributes all the stock of Floppy Disk, Inc. to Mr. Chips in complete redemption of his stock in Lemon.

5. I.R.C. § 355(g)(2)(B)(i).

6. I.R.C. § 355(g)(2)(B)(ii)–(iv); 355(g)(3)–(5).

7. Das & Monga, "Yahoo Puzzles Over $4 Billion Tax Break," Wall St. Journal, Jan. 6, 2012. After gaining momentum, the deal stalled amidst a major change in management at Yahoo later in 2012.

(b) Same as (a), above, except that Ms. Micro and Mr. Chips are mother and son.

(c) Same as (a), above, except that shortly before the distribution of Floppy Disk stock to Mr. Chips, Ms. Micro sold all of her Lemon stock to Mr. Modem, who wished to acquire the hardware business but not the software company.

(d) To enable the computer manufacturing business to maintain different retirement plans for its manufacturing and research employees, Lemon transfers the assets of the research division to a new corporation, Research, Inc., and distributes all the Research stock pro rata to Ms. Micro and Mr. Chips. After the distribution, Research, Inc. continues to perform services solely for Lemon.

(e) Same as (d), above, except that the purpose of the spin-off is to comply with a regulatory decree. (Compare your answer to Problem 1(e) at page 483.)

(f) To comply with a state law providing that computer hardware and software businesses may not be conducted by parent and subsidiary corporations, Lemon must spin off or sell its Floppy Disk, Inc. subsidiary. In anticipation of the new law, Lemon's board of directors informally negotiated a sale of Floppy Disk to Suitor, Inc. Before the agreement is reduced to an enforceable writing, Lemon distributes the Floppy Disk stock to Ms. Micro and Mr. Chips. Two months later, the shareholders sell the Floppy Disk to Suitor on the same terms negotiated by the Lemon board of directors.

(g) Same as (f), above, except that the Lemon board rejects Suitor's offer and instead distributes the Floppy Disk stock pro rata to the shareholders. Four months later, the shareholders sell their Floppy Disk stock to White Knight, Inc.

(h) Same as (g), above, except the sale by the shareholders is made to Suitor, Inc. on essentially the same terms that had been rejected by the Lemon board of directors.

D. TAX TREATMENT OF THE PARTIES TO A CORPORATE DIVISION

Code: §§ 311(a), (b)(1) & (2); 312(a), (b), (h); 336(c); 355(a)(1)(A), (3), (c); 356; 358(a)–(c); 361; 362(b), (e)(1); 1032. Skim §§ 301; 302; 355(d); 381(a); 1223(1) & (2).

Regulations: §§ 1.312–10; 1.358–2.

1.   INTRODUCTION

If the requirements of Section 355 and the accompanying judicial doctrines are satisfied, other provisions come into play to govern the specific tax consequences (e.g., total or partial nonrecognition of gain, basis, holding period, etc.) to the parties. In this section, we consider the tax consequences if a corporate division is preceded by the formation of one or more new corporations in a Type D reorganization, the consequences of the division itself, and the results if the division fails to satisfy the statutory and judicial requirements.

If one or more corporations are formed as a preparatory step to a qualifying corporate division, the formation of the new subsidiary is a Type D reorganization.[1] The parent (distributing) corporation does not recognize gain or loss on the transfer of assets to the controlled corporation,[2] and it takes an exchanged basis in the new stock that it receives[3] and may tack the holding period of any capital assets or Section 1231 property that it exchanges for the stock.[4] The newly formed controlled corporation does not recognize gain on the issuance of its stock[5] and it takes the assets with a transferred basis and a tacked holding period.[6] The earnings and profits of the parent corporation are apportioned between the parent and controlled corporations according to rules provided in the regulations.[7] Section 381, providing for carryover of corporate attributes in certain corporate acquisitions, does not apply to divisive reorganizations and thus the parent corporation retains its tax attributes other than the earnings and profits which are allocated to the controlled corporation.

2. CONSEQUENCES TO SHAREHOLDERS AND SECURITY HOLDERS

No Boot Received. If the requirements of Section 355 are met, the shareholders or security holders of the distributing corporation generally do not recognize gain or loss on the distribution of stock or securities of the controlled corporation.[1] The aggregate basis of the stock or securities in the distributing corporation held by the shareholder is allocated among the stock and securities of both the distributing and controlled corporations in proportion to their relative fair market values,[2] and the shareholder's holding period in the stock or securities of the controlled corporation

---

1. I.R.C. § 368(a)(1)(D). A "divisive" D reorganization involves a transfer by one corporation of part of its assets to another corporation if, immediately after the transfer, the transferor "controls" the transferee and, pursuant to the same plan, stock or securities of the controlled corporation are distributed to the shareholders of the transferor corporation in a transaction that qualifies under Section 355. Id. For this purpose, the fact that the shareholders of the distributing corporation dispose of part or all of their distributed stock, or that the distributing corporation issues additional stock, is not taken into account. I.R.C. § 368(a)(2)(H).

2. I.R.C. § 361(a).

3. I.R.C. § 358(a).

4. I.R.C. § 1223(1).

5. I.R.C. § 1032(a).

6. I.R.C. §§ 362(b); 1223(2).

7. I.R.C. § 312(h); Reg. § 1.312–10(a), (c). In the case of a newly created corporation, this allocation generally is made in proportion to the relative fair market values of the assets retained by the parent corporation and the assets transferred to the controlled corporation. Reg. § 1.312–10(a). In a "proper case," the regulations provide that this allocation should be made in proportion to the "net basis" (after reduction for liabilities) of the transferred and retained assets. Id.

1. I.R.C. § 355(a)(1).

2. I.R.C. § 358(b), (c).

received in the distribution includes the holding period of the stock or securities of the distributing corporation.[3]

Treatment of Boot. As with most other types of reorganizations, the receipt of boot in an otherwise qualifying corporate division does not necessarily spell doom for the transaction but results in the recognition of gain to the shareholder receiving the boot. For this purpose, boot includes: (1) cash, (2) any property other than stock or securities of the controlled corporation (e.g., short-term debt obligations, stock rights or warrants), (3) securities of the controlled corporation to the extent that their principal amount exceeds the principal amount of any securities surrendered, (4) any stock of the controlled corporation that was acquired by the distributing corporation in a transaction in which gain or loss was recognized within the five-year period prior to the distribution (known as "hot stock"), and (5) nonqualified preferred stock received in a distribution with respect to stock other than nonqualified preferred stock.[4]

The rule treating "hot stock" as boot does not apply, however, to any acquisition of stock of a controlled corporation that becomes a member of the separate affiliated group of the distributing corporation at any time after the stock is acquired and before it is distributed in the Section 355 transaction under scrutiny.[5] This modification was made by regulations that reflect a policy decision to avoid conflicts between the boot rules and the treatment of separate affiliated groups under the active trade or business test discussed earlier in this chapter.[6] For example, if the distributing corporation had acquired all of the controlled corporation's stock in a taxable transaction that qualified as an expansion of the distributing corporation's existing trade or business and later distributed all of that stock within five years of the acquisition in an unrelated transaction, the distribution would satisfy the active trade or business requirement.[7] But without the relief provided by the regulations, it would be fully taxable hot stock. The IRS concluded that such a result was inconsistent with Congressional intent.

The tax treatment of boot depends on the form of the division. In the case of a spin-off, the receipt of boot is treated as a distribution to which Section 301 applies (without regard to the shareholder's realized gain) and is thus a dividend to the extent of the distributing corporation's current and accumulated earnings and profits and a return of capital to the extent

---

3. I.R.C. § 1223(1).

4. I.R.C. §§ 355(a)(3), (4); 356(a), (b), (d)(2)(C) & (D). For the definition of nonqualified preferred stock, see I.R.C. § 351(g)(2) and Chapter 2B3, supra.

5. Reg. § 1.355–2(g)(2)(i). The regulations also provide relief from the hot stock rule for transfers of controlled corporation stock among members of the distributing corporation's affiliated group. Id. For some basic examples of the hot stock relief rule, see Reg. § 1.355–2(g)(5) Examples 1 and 2.

6. See Section B of this chapter, supra. To better understand the hot stock relief rule, it may be helpful to recall that Section 355(b)(3)(A) provides that, for purposes of determining whether a corporation is engaged in the active conduct of a trade or business, all members of that corporation's separate affiliated group are treated as one corporation. Prop. Reg. § 1.355–3(b)(3)(ii).

7. Prop. Reg. § 1.355–3(d)(2) Examples 18 & 20.

of any balance.[8] In the case of a split-off or split-up, both of which involve an exchange rather than a distribution, Section 356(a)(1) requires the shareholder to recognize any realized gain to the extent of the boot received in the distribution. The characterization of that gain is more problematic. Section 356(a)(2) adopts the same rule used for acquisitive reorganizations by providing that if the exchange has "the effect of the distribution of a dividend," the gain recognized is treated as a dividend to the extent of the shareholder's ratable share of accumulated earnings and profits of the distributing corporation.[9] The balance of any recognized gain is treated as gain from the exchange of property.[10] As explained in Revenue Ruling 93–62, which follows this Note, dividend equivalence is tested by applying the "before" and "after" ownership principles of Section 302 (i.e., meaningful reduction of the shareholder's proportionate interest) using an assumption that the shareholder had retained the distributing corporation stock that actually was exchanged for controlled corporation stock and then had received the boot in exchange for distributing corporation stock equal in value to the boot.[11] Whether or not this hypothetical redemption results in a dividend is tested by comparing the shareholder's percentage ownership in the distributing corporation before the transaction with the interest the shareholder would have retained in the distributing corporation if he surrendered only the stock exchanged for the boot. Any loss realized by a shareholder in a Section 355 exchange may not be recognized.[12]

Basis and Holding Period. Section 358 again governs the basis of the boot and nonrecognition property received in the distribution. The boot takes a fair market value basis and its holding period commences as of the date of the distribution.[13] The aggregate basis of the nonrecognition property (i.e., stock and securities) is the same as the basis of the stock or securities of the distributing corporation plus any gain recognized and less any cash and the fair market value of any boot property received in the exchange.[14] That aggregate basis is then allocated among the old and new stock or securities (or the new stock or securities, in the case of a split-up) in proportion to their relative fair market values.[15] Similar to the approach

---

8.   I.R.C. § 356(b). For noncorporate shareholders, virtually all such dividends will be "qualified" and thus taxable at the 15 percent maximum rate at least through 2012.

9.   In one of the many curiosities in the world of reorganizations, neither Section 356(a)(2) nor the applicable regulations refer to *current* earnings and profits.

10.   See Reg. § 1.356–1(b)(2).

11.   Rev.Rul. 93–62, infra p. 500. See also Commissioner v. Clark, 489 U.S. 726, 109 S.Ct. 1455 (1989), which uses a similar approach in testing for dividend equivalence in acquisitive reorganizations where T shareholders receive boot. For discussion of the Service's approach, see Steinberg, "Selected Issues in the Taxation of Section 355 Trans-

actions," 52 Tax Lawyer 7, 11–16 (1997). The author suggests that Revenue Ruling 93–62, while purporting to follow the Supreme Court's approach to dividend equivalence in *Clark*, actually is inconsistent with *Clark's* "post-reorganization" approach insofar as the ruling treats the boot as having been received in a hypothetical redemption occurring *prior* to the split-off.

12.   I.R.C. § 356(c).

13.   I.R.C. § 358(a)(2).

14.   I.R.C. § 358(a)(1).

15.   I.R.C. § 358(b)(2), (c); Reg. § 1.358–2. The Service has never provided any guidance as to the precise date to be used in valuing the corporations for purposes of used for acquisitive reorganizations, if the "old stock" was acquired at different times or for different prices, the distributee shareholders generally must trace their bases in the various blocks of old stock (rather than using an average basis) in determining the basis of the new stock under Section 358. If tracing is impossible, the taxpayer may designate how the Section 358 basis is to be allocated to the new stock received in a manner that minimizes the disparity in holding periods of the surrendered shares to any particular share of stock received.[16] The nonrecognition property ordinarily is eligible for a tacked holding period.[17]

Revenue Ruling 93–62

1993–2 Cum. Bull. 118.

ISSUE

Whether gain recognized on the receipt of cash in an exchange of stock that otherwise qualifies under section 355 of the Internal Revenue Code is treated as a dividend distribution under section 356(a)(2).

FACTS

Distributing is a corporation with 1,000 shares of a single class of stock outstanding. Each share has a fair market value of $lx. A, one of five unrelated individual shareholders, owns 400 shares of Distributing stock. Distributing owns all of the outstanding stock of a subsidiary corporation, Controlled. The Controlled stock has a fair market value of $200x.

Distributing distributes all the stock of Controlled plus $200x cash to A in exchange for all of A's Distributing stock. The exchange satisfies the requirements of section 355 but for the receipt of the cash.

LAW AND ANALYSIS

Section 355(a)(1) of the code provides, in general, that the shareholders of a distributing corporation will not recognize gain or loss on the exchange of the distributing corporation's stock or securities solely for stock or securities of a controlled subsidiary if the requirements of section 355 are satisfied.

---

this allocation. In the case of publicly held companies, the date selected ordinarily is the first day that the stock of the controlled corporation was traded on a listed exchange. For other possibilities, see Bittker & Eustice, Federal Income Taxation of Corporations and Shareholders ¶ 11.12[1].

16. See Reg. § 1.358–2(a)(2)(i), (iv), – 2(c) Example 12. See also Prop. Reg. § 1.358– 2(b), (c), (i) Examples 11 & 12. The proposed regulations also provide guidance on how to allocate consideration in Section 355 transactions involving both stock and boot or multiple blocks or classes of stock and securities. In general, like the rules for acquisitive reorganizations, they require a pro rata, share-by-share allocation as a default rule, but the parties may specify the consideration received in exchange for a particular share or class of stock surrendered if the specification is consistent with the terms of the distribution and is economically reasonable.

17. I.R.C. § 1223(1).

Section 356(a)(1) of the Code provides for recognition of gain on exchanges in which gain would otherwise not be recognized under section 354 (relating to tax-free acquisitive reorganizations) or section 355 if the property received in the exchange consists of property permitted to be received without gain recognition and other property or money ("boot"). The amount of gain recognized is limited to the sum of the money and the fair market value of the other property.

Under section 356(a)(2) of the Code, gain recognized in an exchange described in section 356(a)(1) that "has the effect of the distribution of a dividend" is treated as a dividend to the extent of the distributee's ratable share of the undistributed earnings and profits accumulated after February 28, 1913. Any remaining gain is treated as gain from the exchange of property.

Determinations of whether the receipt of boot has the effect of a dividend are made by applying the principles of section 302 of the Code. Commissioner v. Clark, 489 U.S. 726 (1989), 1989–2 C.B. 68. Section 302 contains rules for determining whether payments in redemption of stock are treated as payments in exchange for the stock or as distributions to which section 301 applies.

Under section 302(a) of the Code, a redemption will be treated as an exchange if it satisfies one of the tests of section 302(b). Section 302(b)(2) provides exchange treatment for substantially disproportionate redemptions of stock. A distribution is substantially disproportionate if (1) the shareholder's voting stock interest and common stock interest in the corporation immediately after the redemption are each less than 80 percent of those interests immediately before the redemption, and (2) the shareholder owns less than 50 percent of the voting power of all classes of stock immediately after the redemption.

In *Clark*, the Supreme Court determined whether gain recognized under section 356 of the Code on the receipt of boot in an acquisitive reorganization under section 368(a)(1)(A) and (a)(2)(D) should be treated as a dividend distribution. In that case, the sole shareholder of the target corporation exchanged his target stock for stock of the acquiring corporation and cash. In applying section 302 to determine whether the boot payment had the effect of a dividend distribution, the Court considered whether section 302 should be applied to the boot payment as if it were made (i) by the target corporation in a pre-reorganization hypothetical redemption of a portion of the shareholder's target stock, or (ii) by the acquiring corporation in a post-reorganization hypothetical redemption of the acquiring corporation stock that the shareholder would have received in the reorganization exchange if there had been no boot distribution.

The Supreme Court stated that the treatment of boot under section 356(a)(2) of the Code should be determined "by examining the effect of the exchange as a whole," and concluded that treating the boot as received in a redemption of target stock would improperly isolate the boot payment from the overall reorganization by disregarding the effect of the subsequent merger. Consequently, the Court tested whether the boot payment had the effect of a dividend distribution by comparing the interest the taxpayer actually received in the acquiring corporation with the interest the taxpayer would have had if solely stock in the acquiring corporation had been received in the reorganization exchange.

Prior to the decision in *Clark*, the Service considered the facts and issue presented in this revenue ruling in Rev. Rul. 74–516, 1974–2 C.B. 121. The determination of whether the exchange of Distributing stock for Controlled stock and boot under section 355 of the Code had the effect of a dividend distribution under section 356(a)(2) was made by comparing A's interest in Distributing prior to the exchange with the interest A would have retained if A had not received Controlled stock and had only surrendered the Distributing stock equal in value to the boot. The Court's decision in *Clark* does not change the conclusion in Rev. Rul. 74–516, because, like Clark, the ruling determined whether the exchange in question had the effect of a dividend distribution based on an analysis of the overall transaction.

The exchange of A's Distributing stock for stock of Controlled qualifies for non-recognition treatment under section 355 of the Code in part because the overall effect of the exchange is an adjustment of A's continuing interest in Distributing in a modified corporate form. See section 1.355–2(c) of the Income Tax Regulations. The Controlled stock received by A represents a continuing interest in a portion of Distributing's assets that were formerly held by A as an indirect equity interest. The boot payment has reduced A's proportionate interest in the overall corporate enterprise that includes both Distributing and Controlled. Thus, the boot is treated as received in redemption of A's Distributing stock, and A's interest in Distributing immediately before the exchange is compared to the interest A would have retained if A had surrendered only the Distributing shares equal in value to the boot.

Under the facts presented here, before the exchange, A owned 400 of the 1,000 shares, or 40 percent, of the outstanding Distributing stock. If A had surrendered only the 200 shares for which A received boot, A would still hold 200 of the 800 shares, or 25 percent, of the Distributing stock outstanding after the exchange. This 25 percent stock interest would represent 62.5 percent of A's pre-exchange stock interest in Distributing. Therefore, the deemed redemption would be treated as an exchange because it qualifies as substantially disproportionate under section 302(b)(2) of the Code.

HOLDING

In an exchange of stock that otherwise qualifies under section 355 of the Code, whether the payment of boot is treated as a dividend distribution under section 356(a)(2) is determined prior to the exchange. This determination is made by treating the recipient shareholder as if the shareholder had retained the distributing corporation stock actually exchanged for controlled corporation stock and received the boot in exchange for distributing corporation stock equal in value to the boot.

EFFECT ON OTHER RULINGS

Rev. Rul. 74–516 is superseded.

3. CONSEQUENCES TO THE DISTRIBUTING AND CONTROLLED CORPORATIONS

Nonrecognition of Gain or Loss: General Rules. The tax consequences to the distributing corporation in a Section 355 transaction initially are determined by Section 361(c) if the distribution is preceded by a Type D reorganization and by Section 355(c) if it is not. In either case, the results generally are the same. If a Section 355 transaction occurs in conjunction with certain changes in shareholder ownership, the distributing corporation also may be required to recognize gain under Section 355(d).[1]

If a Section 355 distribution is part of a reorganization plan—i.e., where the distributing corporation first transfers property to the controlled corporation—no gain or loss is recognized if the property is contributed solely in exchange for stock or securities of the controlled corporation.[2] The distributing corporation recognizes gain, however, if the liabilities assumed by the controlled corporation exceed the aggregate adjusted basis of the transferred property or if it otherwise receives boot that is not distributed to shareholders or creditors as part of the reorganization plan.[3]

The distributing corporation also does not recognize gain on the distribution to its shareholders of "qualified property"—i.e., stock or debt obligations of the controlled corporation.[4] Thus, in the typical spin-off or split-off, where the distributing corporation's basis in the stock of the controlled corporation is less than its fair market value, no corporate-level gain is recognized on the distribution. Section 311(b), which otherwise might have required gain recognition, is not applicable because it only applies to distributions under Subpart A of Subchapter C (Sections 301–307), and Section 355 is not within that portion of the Code.[5] The same result occurs on a split-up. Section 336, which otherwise might have required the recognition of corporate-level gain on a liquidating distribution, does not apply to distributions that are part of a reorganization.[6] Gain is recognized, however, in the rare case where appreciated boot is distributed in a Section 355 transaction that is part of a reorganization.[7]

If the distribution is not preceded by a Type D reorganization—e.g., where the controlled corporation is not a newly formed subsidiary—Section 355(c) takes over for all forms of divisions,[8] providing generally that the

---

1. See Section E1 of this chapter, infra.

2. I.R.C. §§ 368(a)(1)(D); 361(a).

3. I.R.C. § 361(b). The amount of cash and property that a distributing corporation may distribute to creditors without gain recognition is limited to the aggregate adjusted basis of the assets contributed to the controlled corporation in the Type D reorganization. I.R.C. § 361(b)(3).

4. I.R.C. § 361(c)(1), (2).

5. See also I.R.C. § 361(c)(4).

6. I.R.C. § 361(c)(4); see also § 336(c).

7. I.R.C. § 361(c)(2).

8. Section 355(c)(3) makes it clear that Sections 311 (relating to nonliquidating distributions) and 336 (relating to liquidating distributing corporation recognizes no gain or loss on any distribution to which Section 355 applies.[9] Gain must be recognized, however, on a distribution of appreciated property other than "qualified property,"—i.e., other than stock or securities in the controlled corporation.[10] Thus, no gain will be recognized on a distribution of stock or securities of the controlled corporation in a qualifying corporate division even if the recipient share-holder is taxed,[11] but gain is recognized on a distribution of any other appreciated boot.[12]

Recognition of Gain on Certain Disqualified Distributions. The general nonrecognition rule in Section 355(c) does not apply if the distributing corporation makes a "disqualified distribution" of "disqualified stock" within the meaning of Section 355(d). In general, a disqualified distribution is any distribution of stock or securities of a controlled subsidiary ("S") if, immediately after the distribution, any person holds a 50 percent or greater interest in either the distributing corporation or the controlled subsidiary and that interest consists of "disqualified stock," which is defined generally as any stock acquired by "purchase" within the five-year period preceding the distribution.[13] This rule, which is designed to prevent the use of Section 355 to facilitate the tax-free sale of part of a business following a takeover (and in related transactions), is discussed later in the chapter,[14] as is Section 355(e), which taxes the distributing corporation on distributions of controlled corporation stock in certain situations where as part of a "plan" a 50–percent or greater interest in either the distributing or controlled corporations was acquired within two years before or after the distribution.[15]

Carryover of Tax Attributes. The method of allocating the earnings and profits of the various parties to a corporate division depends on the form of the transaction. If a division is preceded by a Type D reorganization, the earnings and profits of the distributing corporation are allocated between the distributing and controlled corporations in proportion to the relative fair market values of the assets retained by each corporation.[16] If the division is not preceded by a Type D reorganization—e.g., where the stock of a preexisting subsidiary or subsidiaries is distributed—the regulations provide methods for determining the decrease in the distributing corpora-

---

distributions) do not apply to a distribution governed by Section 355.

9. I.R.C. § 355(c)(1).

10. I.R.C. § 355(c)(2). The definition of "qualified property" in Section 355(c)(2)(B) is somewhat narrower than the one used to define the same term in Section 361(c)(2)(B), where "qualified property" includes both rights to acquire stock and nonsecurity debt obligations.

11. The recipient would be taxed, for example, if the principal amount of securities received exceeds the principal amount of any securities surrendered. I.R.C. § 355(a)(3)(A).

12. I.R.C. § 355(c)(2)(A).

13. I.R.C. § 355(d)(2)–(5).

14. See Section E1 of this chapter, infra.

15. See Section E2 of this chapter, infra.

16. I.R.C. § 312(h); Reg. § 1.312–10(a). The regulations also state that in a "proper case" the allocation should be made in proportion to the net bases of the transferred and retained assets.

tion's earnings and profits.[17] In no event may any deficit of the distributing corporation be allocated to the controlled corporation.[18]

Earnings and profits are the only tax attributes affected by a corporate division. The carryover rules of Section 381 relating to other tax attributes are not applicable to divisive reorganizations, and thus the tax history of the distributing corporation will remain intact in a spin-off or a split-off. Since a split-up involves the liquidation of the distributing corporation, its tax attributes will disappear as a result of the transaction.[19]

4.   CONSEQUENCES OF FAILED DIVISIONS

If a corporate division fails to qualify under Section 355, the tax consequences depend on the form of the transaction. If the defective division is preceded by the formation of a new corporation, that formation still qualifies for nonrecognition—but under Section 351 rather than Section 368(a)(1)(D).[1]

As for the division itself, the distribution of stock or securities in a nonqualifying spin-off is treated as an ordinary distribution to which Section 301 applies. That means it will be a dividend to the extent of current and accumulated earnings and profits and a return of capital to the extent of any balance. If the distribution takes the form of a split-off, it is tested under the stock redemption rules of Section 302. To avoid being subject to Section 301, the redemption thus must come within one of the Section 302(b) tests for exchange treatment.[2] If the failed division is a split-up, the transaction logically should be governed by the complete liquidation rules, allowing the shareholders to recognize capital gain or loss under Section 331(a).[3]

At the corporate level, the distributing corporation will be required to recognize gain on a distribution of appreciated property in a failed spin-off or split-off under Section 311(b). Section 311(a)(2), however, denies recognition of loss on a distribution of property that has declined in value. In a split-up, the distributing corporation will be required to recognize gain or

---

17.   Reg. § 1.312–10(b).

18.   Reg. § 1.312–10(c).

19.   See Rev.Rul. 56–373, 1956–2 C.B. 217.

1.   Although the formation of the new corporation still qualifies for nonrecognition, different operative provisions come into play to govern the transaction. See I.R.C. §§ 351; 358; 362(a); 1032. See Reg. § 1.312–11(a) for the allocation of earnings and profits in these circumstances.

2.   If the distribution is pro rata, dividend treatment is thus assured. The distribution of stock in a failed split-off would not qualify for partial liquidation treatment un-

der Section 302(b)(4). See Morgenstern v. Commissioner, 56 T.C. 44 (1971); Rev.Rul. 75–223, 1975–1 C.B. 109.

3.   It is possible, however, that certain split-ups will be treated as a reorganization coupled with a dividend. This might occur on a split-up involving a failed division of an operating business from liquid assets in preparation for a sale of the liquid assets. See Bittker & Eustice, Federal Income Taxation of Corporations and Shareholders ¶ 11.15[3]. But it may not matter when dividends and long-term capital gains are taxed at the same rate.

loss under Section 336(a), subject to the limitations on recognition of loss in Section 336(b).

PROBLEM

Father is the sole shareholder of an incorporated department store which he has owned for 25 years. He has a basis of $200,000 in his Store Corporation stock, which is currently worth $2 million. Store has $400,000 of accumulated earnings and profits. Three years ago, Store acquired land in Suburb, where it constructed and then opened a new branch store. The branch has been quite successful and represents $500,000 of the $2 million net worth of Store Corporation. The assets of the branch have a $100,000 basis.

Father recently celebrated his 75th birthday and is exploring some estate planning alternatives. His attorney has suggested that he should have Store Corporation transfer the Suburb store to newly created Branch Corporation in exchange for Branch stock worth $400,000 and Branch securities worth $100,000. Store Corporation, which would be worth $1.5 million after this transaction, then would distribute the Branch stock and securities to Father who in turn would give the Branch stock to his children.

Discuss all the income tax consequences of the above transactions to Father, Store Corporation and Branch Corporation, assuming first that the corporate division totally or partially qualifies under Section 355 and then that it fails to qualify.

E.   USE OF SECTION 355 IN CORPORATE ACQUISITIONS

1.   LIMITATIONS ON USE OF SECTION 355 IN TAXABLE ACQUISITIONS

a.   INTRODUCTION

The repeal of the *General Utilities* doctrine required tax advisors to search for new techniques to avoid corporate-level gain on the sale of all or part of a business. In one common transactional pattern, a corporate buyer of a controlling stock interest in a target corporation may seek to dispose of unwanted pieces of the target, perhaps to help finance the acquisition or maximize overall shareholder value. The tax goal is to consummate those sales without recognizing gain. After Congress blocked several other promising techniques, taxpayers turned to Section 355 to facilitate tax-free sales of unwanted assets in corporate solution. Congress reacted by curtailing the benefits of nonrecognition for certain transactions that previously would have qualified as tax-free divisions. These anti-avoidance limitations, which were previewed earlier in this chapter, are best explained in the context of the transactions at which they were directed.

b. DISPOSITIONS OF RECENTLY ACQUIRED BUSINESSES

Code: § 355(a)(2)(D).

Congress's first line of attack was to amend the active trade or business requirement in Section 355(b)(2)(D) in order to prevent a purchasing corporation ("P") that had recently acquired a controlling stock interest in a target corporation ("T") from disposing of a target subsidiary ("S") without paying a corporate-level tax. To illustrate the prototype transaction at which this rule is aimed, assume that P purchases all the stock of T, which has engaged directly in the active conduct of a trade or business for more than five years. T owns the stock of S, which also has engaged in the active conduct of a trade or business for the requisite five-year period. Both T and S have highly appreciated assets. P does not make a Section 338 election when it purchases T's stock and, as a result, T and S retain their historic asset bases. P intends to dispose of S shortly after the takeover of T.

At one time, the parties could have used a two-step transaction to sell S without recognizing gain. T would first distribute the S stock to P in a tax-free distribution under Section 355.[1] The Service ruled that such a distribution qualified as tax-free and did not violate the active trade or business requirement unless P attempted a bailout by distributing the S stock to its shareholders.[2] P would allocate the cost basis in its T stock under Section 358 between the T stock and the S stock it received in the distribution, obtaining essentially a fair market value basis in the stock of both corporations.[3] After a respectable interval, P then would sell the S stock without recognition of any corporate-level gain by S. Although the new buyer would take a cost basis in the S stock, S would retain its historic lower asset bases. This is noteworthy because the gain inherent in S's assets was not avoided by this technique; it merely was deferred. Moreover, that gain did not accrue while P owned T (and thus indirectly S), and any economic gain that did accrue during P's ownership would be taxed on P's sale of the S stock.[4]

---

1. To avoid problems under the continuity of interest doctrine, P needed to hold the T stock for a respectable period of time (two years was considered safest) to become a "historic" shareholder of T. See Section C2 of this chapter, supra.

2. Rev.Rul. 74–5, 1974–1 C.B. 82. The key to the ruling was that T (the distributing corporation) and S (the controlled corporation) both had been engaged in the active conduct of a trade or business for five years. It did not matter that P (the distributee shareholder of T) had acquired a controlling interest in T in a taxable transaction within the five-year period preceding the distribution.

3. P thus obtained a basis in the S stock that usually was significantly higher

than T's basis in the S stock. T's basis would disappear if the spin-off qualified under Section 355. Cf. I.R.C. §§ 332; 336(e); 338(h)(10).

4. Of course, T could not have sold its S stock without recognizing at least one level of gain. Query whether P should be able to avoid gain on a sale of a piece of T's business when T could not have done so. On the other hand, no corporate-level gain was recognized when T's shareholders sold all their T stock to P and no Section 338 election was made. Query why T or P should not be able to sell S without corporate-level gain provided that gain is preserved through transferred asset bases.

Section 355(b)(2)(D) forecloses this strategy by providing that the active trade or business requirement is not met if control (as measured by the 80 percent tests in Section 368(c)) of the distributing corporation (T) was acquired by a corporate distributee (P) within the five-year period preceding the distribution of stock in the controlled corporation (S). The limitation does not apply, however, if P acquired T in a wholly tax-free transaction, such as an acquisitive reorganization.[5] Distributee corporations that are members of the same affiliated group (as defined in Section 1504(a)) are treated as a single corporate distributee for this purpose.[6]

The principal sanction from denying Section 355 treatment to the above fact pattern is that T must recognize gain on the distribution of its S stock to P. In addition, assuming that T has ample earnings and profits, P has a dividend on receipt of the S stock, but as a corporate parent of T, P likely would be entitled to a 100 percent dividends received deduction.[7] P would obtain a fair market value basis in the distributed S stock[8] and thus recognize no further gain on the subsequent sale. But in the likely event that the buyer of the S stock does not make a Section 338 election, the gain inherent in S's assets is preserved through their transferred bases, raising the specter of yet another corporate-level tax.[9]

PROBLEM

T Corporation ("T") and its wholly owned subsidiary, S Corporation ("S") each have actively conducted a trade or business for more than five years. P Corporation ("P") wishes to acquire T but is not interested in owning the business conducted by S. The assets of T (including its S stock) and S are highly appreciated, and the businesses operated by T and S are equal in value. Consider generally the tax consequences of the following alternative transactions:

(a) T sells its S stock to Buyer Corporation. T's shareholders then sell their T stock to P.

(b) In 2005, P purchases all of T's stock from T's shareholders for cash and does not make a Section 338 election. In 2007, for a valid

---

5. I.R.C. § 355(b)(2)(D)(ii); see also Rev. Rul. 89–37, 1989–1 C.B. 107.

6. Thus, if in the example P had two existing wholly owned subsidiaries (X and Y) and each acquired 50 percent of the T stock for cash, a distribution by T of its S stock within five years after the acquisition would not qualify under Section 355 because X and Y, as members of the same affiliated group, are treated as a single corporation that acquired a controlling stock interest in T within five years preceding the distribution.

7. I.R.C. § 243(a)(3), (b). If P, T and S were members of a consolidated group, the dividend would be deferred and P's basis in its T stock would be reduced by the amount

of the distribution. Reg. §§ 1.1502–14(a)(1), 1.1502–32(b)(2).

8. I.R.C. § 301(d).

9. This double *corporate*-level tax could be avoided if T sold its S stock directly to the new buyer, and the parties jointly made an election under Section 338(h)(10). In that event, T could ignore the gain on the sale of its S stock but S would recognize gain on a deemed sale of its assets, and "new S" would obtain a stepped-up basis in those assets. See Chapter 8C3, supra. Query why the result is worse in a comparable transaction caught by the Section 355(b)(2)(D) trap?

business purpose, T distributes its S stock to P and nine months later P sells the S stock to Buyer Corporation.

(c) Same as (b), above, except that P is an individual.

(d) Same as (b), above, except that P acquired all the stock of T in a tax-free Type B reorganization.

(e) In 2005, P purchases 50% of the T stock from T's shareholders and Buyer Corporation ("B") purchases the remaining 50%. In 2007, T distributes all of its S stock to B in exchange for all the T stock held by B.

c. DIVISIVE TRANSACTIONS IN CONNECTION WITH CERTAIN CHANGES OF OWNERSHIP

Code: § 355(c), (d).

The active business requirement may disqualify a divisive transaction if P acquires a controlling stock interest in T within the five years preceding the distribution of S stock.[10] The requirement does not apply, however, in some other situations that offer promising avenues of escape from corporate-level tax in ostensibly divisive transactions that are really sales. For example, if P did not acquire a controlling stock interest in T, the active business limitation would not preclude essentially the same transaction described in the example above. This opportunity may be illustrated through a simple fact pattern in which four unrelated corporations (A, B, C and D) each purchase a portion of the stock of T with the ultimate objective of winding up with different pieces of T's business that are conducted through separate T subsidiaries. After waiting two years to establish their status as historic shareholders for continuity of interest purposes, A, B and C could exchange their T stock for stock of the desired T subsidiary in a split-off that would qualify under Section 355.[11] All of this could be accomplished without waiting five years after the acquisition of T because no single corporate distributee acquired a controlling stock interest in T. The five-year holding period requirement also does not apply to acquisitions of a controlling interest in T through a partnership or by any other noncorporate purchaser. A variety of other avoidance techniques quickly revealed that Congress had not successfully curtailed the use of Section 355 to avoid corporate-level gain on essentially acquisitive transactions.

The Treasury might have attacked a Section 355 transaction that was inconsistent with *General Utilities* repeal by exercising its authority to issue regulations under Section 337(d).[12] Instead, it returned to Congress for a more comprehensive solution. The result is Section 355(d), which

10. I.R.C. § 355(b)(2)(D).

11. For this purpose, it is assumed that all relevant business of T have a five-year history; the business purpose requirement can be satisfied; and the parties could structure the transaction to avoid the step transaction doctrine.

12. Section 337(d) grants the Service authority to promulgate regulations to prevent circumvention of the purposes of certain amendments made by The Tax Reform Act of 1986 (i.e., repeal of the *General Utilities* doctrine) through the use of any provision of the Code or regulations.

imposes a corporate-level tax on divisive transactions in connection with certain changes of ownership. The House Ways and Means Committee explained the reasons for the change:[13]

> Some corporate taxpayers may attempt, under present-law rules governing divisive transactions, to dispose of subsidiaries in transactions that resemble sales, or to obtain a fair market value stepped-up basis for any future dispositions, without incurring corporate-level tax. The avoidance of corporate-level tax is inconsistent with the repeal of the *General Utilities* doctrine as part of the Tax Reform Act of 1986.

> Under the present-law rules, individual purchasers, or corporate purchasers of less than 80 percent, of the stock of a parent corporation may attempt to utilize section 355 to acquire a subsidiary (or a division incorporated for this purpose) from the parent without the parent incurring any corporate-level tax. The purchaser may acquire stock of the parent equal in value to the value of the desired subsidiary or division, and later surrender that stock for stock of the subsidiary, in a transaction intended to qualify as a non-pro-rata tax-free divisive transaction. Alternatively, the transaction might be structured as a surrender of the parent stock by all shareholders other than the acquiror, in exchange for a distribution (intended to be tax-free) of all subsidiaries or activities other than those the acquiror desires.

> In addition, a non-corporate purchaser, or a corporate purchaser of less than 80 percent of the stock of another corporation, may attempt to utilize section 355 to obtain a stepped up fair market value basis in a subsidiary of an acquired corporation, enabling a subsequent disposition of that subsidiary without a corporate-level tax.

> The provisions for tax-free divisive transactions under section 355 were a limited exception to the repeal of the *General Utilities* doctrine, intended to permit historic shareholders to continue to carry on their historic corporate businesses in separate corporations. It is believed that the benefit of tax-free treatment should not apply where the divisive transaction, combined with a stock purchase resulting in a change of ownership, in effect results in the disposition of a significant part of the historic shareholders' interests in one or more of the divided corporations.

> The present-law provisions granting tax-free treatment at the corporate level are particularly troublesome because they may offer taxpayers an opportunity to avoid the general rule that corporate-level gain is recognized when an asset (including the stock of a subsidiary) is disposed of. There is special concern about the possibility for the distributing corporation to avoid corporate-

13. House Ways and Means Committee, Explanation of the Revenue Provisions to 1991 Budget Reconciliation Bill (Oct. 16, 1990), 101st Cong., 2d Sess. 90–92 (1990).

level tax on the transfer of a subsidiary. Therefore, although the provision does not affect shareholder treatment if section 355 is otherwise available, it does impose tax at the corporate level, in light of the potential avoidance of corporate tax on what is in effect a sale of a subsidiary.

The bill is not intended to limit in any way the continuing Treasury Department authority to issue regulations to prevent the avoidance of the repeal of the *General Utilities* doctrine through any provision of law or regulations, including Section 355.

Because Section 355(d) attempts to reach such a wide range of transactions, its operation is complex. Very generally, Section 355(d) requires recognition of gain by the distributing corporation (but not the distributee shareholders) on a "disqualified distribution" of stock or securities of a controlled corporation regardless of whether the distribution is part of a reorganization.[14] A "disqualified distribution" is any Section 355 distribution if, immediately after the distribution, any person holds "disqualified stock" in either the distributing corporation or any distributed controlled corporation constituting a 50 percent or greater interest (measured by total combined voting power or value) in such corporation.[15] "Disqualified stock" includes: (1) any stock in either the distributing corporation or any controlled corporation acquired after October 9, 1990 by purchase during the five-year period before the distribution, and (2) any stock in any controlled corporation received in a distribution attributable to stock in the distributing corporation described in (1).[16]

In effect, Section 355(d) creates a five-year statutory predistribution continuity of interest test. If violated, the test requires the distributing corporation to recognize gain on the distribution of stock or securities of a subsidiary to a person who ends up with 50 percent or more of the stock of the subsidiary. Some typical examples of the application of Section 355(d) are illustrated by the following excerpt from the legislative history:[17]

> Example 1.   Assume that after the effective date, individual A acquires by purchase a 20–percent interest in the stock of corporation P and a 10–percent interest in the stock of its subsidiary, S, and 40 percent or more of the stock of S is distributed to A within 5 years in exchange for his 20–percent interest in P. (The remainder of the S stock distributed in the section 355 distribution is distributed to other shareholders). Under the provision P must recognize gain with respect to the distributed stock of S because all 50 percent of the stock of S held by A is disqualified stock.

---

14. This is technically accomplished by removing the stock or securities of the controlled corporation from the category of "qualified property" under Sections 361(c)(2) and 355(c)(2). I.R.C. § 355(d)(1). As a result, the distributing corporation must recognize gain as if the stock and securities were appreciated boot.

15. I.R.C. § 355(d)(2).

16. I.R.C. § 355(d)(3). See I.R.C. § 355(d)(5)(B) for the details on the "purchase" requirement.

17. H. Rep. No. 101–964, 101st Cong., 2d Sess. 85 (1990).

Example 2. Assume that after the effective date individual A acquires by purchase a 20–percent interest in corporation P and P redeems stock of other shareholders so that A's interest in P increases to a 30 percent interest. Within 5 years of A's purchase, P distributes 50 percent of the stock of its subsidiary, S, to A in exchange for his 30 percent interest in P (the remainder of the stock of S distributed in the section 355 transaction is distributed to the other shareholders). P recognizes gain on the distribution of the stock of S because all 50 percent of the stock of S held by A is disqualified stock.

For purposes of the definition of disqualified stock, stock or securities generally are considered acquired by "purchase" if they do not have either a transferred basis or a Section 1014 date-of-death basis, and were not acquired in an exchange to which Section 351 or the corporate reorganization provisions apply.[18] An acquisition of property in a Section 351 exchange, however, is considered a purchase to the extent such property is acquired for cash or a cash item, marketable stock or securities, or any debt of the transferor.[19] In the case of carryover basis property which was purchased by the transferor, the acquirer of the property is treated as having purchased the property on the date it was purchased by the transferor.[20] This tacking rule may enable a distributing corporation to achieve purchase status and a five-year holding period, thus avoiding the gain triggered on a disqualified distribution.

To prevent easy avoidance of the 50 percent or more ownership test, an array of aggregation and attribution rules are applied to test shareholder ownership after a distribution. First, a shareholder and all persons related to the shareholder under Sections 267(b) or 707(b) are treated as one person.[21] If two or more otherwise unrelated persons act pursuant to a plan or arrangement with respect to acquisitions of distributing corporation or controlled corporation stock or securities, they are treated as a single person for purposes of Section 355(d).[22] Special rules also apply to attribution of stock from a corporation to its shareholders. The Section 318(a)(2) attribution rules apply to both stock and securities with the threshold for attribution from a corporation reduced to 10 percent.[23] In addition, if a person acquires by purchase an interest in an entity through which stock or securities are attributed, such stock or securities are deemed purchased

18. I.R.C. § 355(d)(5)(A). The legislative history states that there will be an exception for reorganization exchanges in which gain is recognized on receipt of boot. H.Rep. No. 101–964, supra note 17, at 90.

19. I.R.C. § 355(d)(5)(B). The legislative history states that it is expected that regulations will provide an exception for Section 351 exchanges in which such items are transferred as part of an active trade or business (including debts incurred in the ordi-

nary course of the trade or business) and do not exceed the reasonable needs of the business. H.Rep. No. 101–964, supra note 17, at 91.

20. I.R.C. § 355(d)(5)(C).

21. I.R.C. § 355(d)(7)(A).

22. I.R.C. § 355(d)(7)(B).

23. I.R.C. § 355(d)(8)(A).

on the later of the date of the purchase of the interest in the entity or the date the stock or securities are acquired by purchase by the entity.[24]

In yet another anti-avoidance provision, the running of the five-year predistribution period for holding stock or securities is suspended during any period in which the holder's risk of loss with respect to the stock or securities or any portion of the corporation's activities is substantially diminished. Such a reduction in risk can be accomplished by an option in favor of the holder, a short sale, a special class of stock or any other device or transaction.[25] The Service also is granted broad power to prescribe regulations which modify the definition of "purchase" and prevent avoidance of Section 355(d) through the use of related persons, intermediaries, pass-thru entities, options or other arrangements.

2. DISPOSITIONS OF UNWANTED ASSETS IN CONJUNCTION WITH TAX–FREE REORGANIZATIONS

As discussed earlier in this chapter, a corporate division may be used as the vehicle for a tax-free spin-off of unwanted assets in preparation for an acquisition of the rest of the target corporation's business. Consider a typical scenario. An attractive takeover candidate ("T"), engaged in two different businesses, is approached by a motivated buyer ("P") whose interest is limited to only one of those businesses. To facilitate the transaction and maximize shareholder value, T spins off the unwanted business to its shareholders and then is acquired by P in a tax-free acquisitive reorganization. Should the spin-off qualify under Section 355? What if T spins off the wanted business ("Newco") to its shareholders, who then exchange their Newco stock for P stock? Should the form of the transaction make any difference? These and other scenarios present a challenge to the target corporation's tax advisor and provide the student of Subchapter C with an opportunity to relate the requirements for a tax-free corporate division to the acquisitive reorganization concepts encountered in the previous chapter.

In Commissioner v. Morris Trust,[1] the Fourth Circuit held that a spin-off of an unwanted business followed by a prearranged merger of the parent "distributing" corporation with an unrelated acquiring corporation qualified as tax-free—specifically, a Type D reorganization coupled with a Section 355 corporate division, and a Section 368 Type A acquisitive reorganization. The Service ultimately blessed the *Morris Trust* form of transaction[2] and even acknowledged that a spin-off to prepare for an acquisition of a separate business was a valid Section 355 business purpose,[3] but it was less receptive to other transactional patterns despite their economic similarity. For example, a spin off of unwanted assets followed by

24. I.R.C. § 355(d)(8)(B).

25. I.R.C. § 355(d)(6).

1. 367 F.2d 794 (4th Cir.1966).

2. Rev. Rul. 68–603, 1968–2 C.B. 148. See also Rev. Rul. 70–434, 1970–2 C.B. 83

(Type B reorganization followed spin-off of unwanted business).

3. Rev. Proc. 96–30, 1996–1 C.B. 696.

a Type C reorganization or a forward triangular merger was likely to be treated as an integrated transaction, with the unfortunate result that the unwanted assets would be considered in determining whether P transferred substantially all of its properties in the subsequent reorganization. If the unwanted assets were a substantial part of P's overall business, the acquisition would not qualify as a reorganization, and the spin-off also was unlikely to qualify under Section 355.[4]

Other transactional forms also were vulnerable to challenge under the step transaction doctrine. For example, if P contributed the assets of a *wanted* business with a five-year history to newly created S, retained another (unwanted) business, distributed the S stock to its shareholders, and then S was acquired by an unrelated corporation ("X") in an attempted tax-free reorganization, the Service took the position that neither the spin-off nor the reorganization qualified for tax-free treatment. If the steps were prearranged, S was disregarded and P was treated as having made a taxable sale of the wanted assets to X and having distributed the consideration received from X to P's shareholders as a dividend.[5] If P was publicly traded and S was an "old and cold" (i.e., not newly formed) subsidiary, however, the Service ruled that a spin-off of S stock followed by X's acquisition of S in a Type A or Type B reorganization did qualify as tax-free if no formal negotiations with respect to the subsequent acquisition took place prior to the spin-off.[6]

After repeal of the *General Utilities* doctrine, Congress became concerned (some might say paranoid) that Section 355 was being used to avoid corporate-level gain on the sale of a business. Section 355(d), discussed earlier in this chapter, was an early response. Congress followed up by enacting Section 355(e), which virtually eliminates the time-tested *Morris Trust* technique.[7] The legislative history explains that where new shareholders acquire ownership of a business in connection with a spin-off, the transaction more closely resembles a taxable corporate-level disposition of the portion of the business that is acquired rather than a tax-free division among existing shareholders.[8]

Section 355(e) is a typically complex anti-avoidance provision and this discussion is limited to an overview. It requires the distributing (parent) corporation to recognize gain as if it had sold the stock of the distributed controlled subsidiary for its fair market value on the date of the distribution if, as part of a "plan" or series of related transactions, one or more persons acquire[9] (directly or indirectly) a 50–percent or greater interest in

---

4. See, e.g., Helvering v. Elkhorn Coal Co., 95 F.2d 732 (4th Cir.1937), cert. denied, 305 U.S. 605, 59 S.Ct. 65 (1938). But see Rev. Rul. 2003–79, 2003–2 C.B. 80.

5. Rev. Rul. 70–225, 1970–1 C.B. 80.

6. Rev. Rul. 96–30, 1996–1 C.B. 36.

7. See also I.R.C. § 355(f), which disqualifies a transaction in its entirety under Section 355 when one member of an affiliated

corporate group makes a distribution to another member if the distribution is part of a plan or series of related transactions to which Section 355(e) applies.

8. S.Rept. No. 105–33, 105th Cong., 1st Sess. 139–140 (1997).

9. Acquisitions, for this purpose, are not limited to cost basis purchase transactions but also can include tax-free acquisieither the distributing or controlled corporation within two years before or after the distribution.[10] Put differently (and, one hopes, more coherently), the distributing corporation (but not its shareholders) must recognize corporate-level gain on an otherwise tax-free spin-off if "pursuant to a plan" stock of either the distributing or controlled corporation is acquired and the historic shareholders of the distributing corporation do not retain more than 50 percent (by vote and value) of both corporations. Significantly (and inexplicably), neither the distributing nor controlled corporations may adjust the basis of their assets or stock to reflect this recognition of Section 355(e) gain.

Section 355(e) applies only if the transaction is part of a "plan" (or a series of related transactions) to acquire the requisite 50 percent or greater interest in the target. For this purpose, if one or more persons directly or indirectly acquire a 50–percent or greater interest in the distributing corporation or any controlled corporation during the four-year period beginning two years before the distribution, the acquisition is presumed to be pursuant to a plan unless the taxpayer establishes that such a plan did not exist.[11] Whether or not a prohibited "plan" exists is based on all the facts and circumstances.[12]

The regulations have gone through several iterations, and the final version provides considerable flexibility in making this factual determination.[13] In the case of acquisitions (other than public offerings) of the distributing or controlled corporation after a distribution, the distribution and acquisition will be considered as part of a plan only if there was an agreement, understanding, arrangement, or substantial negotiations regarding the acquisition or a similar acquisition (collectively referred to below as "Talks") at some time during the two year period preceding the distribution.[14] Although not labelled as a safe harbor, this "two year lookback rule" operates as a security blanket in many situations, especially in light of the narrow definitions of several critical terms. An "agreement, understanding or arrangement," for example, is generally considered to exist only if the parties have reached a common understanding on most of the significant terms of the transaction.[15] "Substantial negotiations" exist only if the significant economic terms of the acquisition have been discussed at the highest levels (directors, officers, shareholders, or their representatives).[16] In short, for a plan to exist, the dealings must have reached a fairly advanced stage.

---

tions. Certain acquisitions that do not involve a shift in control are disregarded. I.R.C. § 355(e)(3)(A). If the assets rather than the stock of either corporation are acquired, the shareholders of the acquiring corporation are deemed to have acquired the target stock for purposes of determining whether the gain-triggering shift of control has occurred. I.R.C. § 355(e)(3)(B).

10. I.R.C. § 355(e)(1), (2). Technically, this result occurs because the stock or securities in the controlled corporation is not treat-

ed as "qualified property" for purposes of Section 355(c)(2) or Section 361(c)(2), and thus gain is recognized on the distribution under Section 311(b).

11. I.R.C. § 355(e)(2)(B).

12. Reg. § 1.355–7(b)(1).

13. See generally Reg. § 1.355–7.

14. Reg. § 1.355–7(b)(2).

15. Reg. § 1.355–7(h)(1)(i).

16. Reg. § 1.355–7(h)(1)(iv).

The regulations go on to provide that, even though the existence of Talks between the parties within the two years preceding the distribution "tend to show" that the distribution and acquisition are part of a plan, all the facts and circumstances still must be considered, and the existence of a corporate business purpose (apart from facilitating the acquisition) will help the taxpayer rebut the statutory presumption.[17] Further comfort is available from seven safe harbors.[18] A key factor under most of these safe harbors is whether there were bilateral Talks during a specified time period. For example, if the acquisition occurred more than six months after the distribution and there were no Talks during the period commencing one year before and ending six months after the distribution, the transactions are not considered part of a plan if the distribution was motivated by a substantial business purpose other than facilitating the acquisition.[19] If a transaction does not fit within any of the safe harbors, the regulations include a list of "plan" and "nonplan" factors to consider in determining whether a plan exists.[20]

In summary, Section 355(e) obliterates many typical "planned" *Morris Trust* transactions but leaves open the possibility that a spin-off followed by an acquisition will continue to qualify under Section 355 if there was a valid business purpose and Talks with potential acquirers did not occur prior to the distribution and within six months thereafter. On the other hand, the existence of an agreement, understanding or negotiations to sell either the distributing or controlled corporations at the time of the spin-off likely will doom the transaction. In an ironic twist, Section 355(e) would not have changed the tax-free treatment in the actual *Morris Trust* transaction, because the distributing corporation's shareholders received 54 percent of the equity of the acquiring corporation as part of the transaction and thus the "control shift" required to trigger Section 355(e) would not have occurred. As a practical matter, Section 355(e) does not apply when the equity value of the distributing corporation after the spin-off exceeds that of the acquiring corporation.

PROBLEM

Leisure, Inc. is a publicly held corporation that operates a chain of motels and manufactures leisure apparel. Each business has roughly the same net worth and has been operated by Leisure for over five years. Denim Corporation wishes to acquire the apparel business but is not interested in the motels. Leisure would like to dispose of the apparel business, preferably in a tax-free reorganization, and it will continue to operate the motel business for the indefinite future. Consider the tax consequences of the following alternative plans for carrying out the objectives of the parties:

17. Reg. § 1.355–7(b)(2).

18. Reg. § 1.355–7(d).

19. Reg. § 1.355–7(d)(1).

20. Reg. § 1.355–7(b)(3) & (4).

(a) Leisure will transfer the motel assets to a newly formed subsidiary, Motel, Inc., and distribute the Motel stock pro rata to the Leisure shareholders. Leisure then will transfer the assets and liabilities of the apparel business to Denim in exchange for Denim voting stock (representing less than 50 percent of the total outstanding voting stock of Denim after the acquisition), and then Leisure will liquidate, distributing the Denim stock pro rata to its shareholders.

(b) Same as (a), above, except that after the spin-off, Leisure merges into Denim. Under the terms of the merger, Leisure shareholders receive Denim nonvoting preferred stock.

(c) What result if Leisure transfers the apparel business to a new corporation, Cords, Inc., and then distributes the Cords stock pro rata to the Leisure shareholders. Leisure continues to operate the motel business, but Cords, Inc. merges into Denim, Inc., and the Cords shareholders receive Denim voting stock.

(d) Same as (c), above, except that after the merger, the Denim voting stock received by Cords shareholders represents more than 50 percent of the total outstanding stock of Denim.

(e) Same as (b), above, except that the merger of Leisure into Denim occurred one year after the spin-off. What factors are relevant in determining whether the transaction was part of a "plan" to acquire Leisure?

(f) Same as (b), above, except that the business purpose for the spin-off was unrelated to any acquisition of the apparel business, and the merger of Leisure into Denim occurred three years after the spin-off.

(g) Is § 355(e) necessary? How did the typical *Morris Trust* transaction violate the policy of Subchapter C?

CHAPTER 11

NONACQUISITIVE, NONDIVISIVE REORGANIZATIONS

A. TYPE E: RECAPITALIZATIONS

1. INTRODUCTION

Code: §§ 368(a)(1)(E); 354; 356; 358; 1032; 1036; 1223(1). Skim §§ 305; 306.

Regulations: §§ 1.301–1(*l*); 1.305–7(c); 1.368–2(e).

A tax-free reorganization sometimes involves only a single corporation undergoing a readjustment to its capital structure. The most common form of nonacquisitive, nondivisive reorganization is the recapitalization, which qualifies as a Type E reorganization if certain requirements are met. Recapitalizations traditionally have been used for a variety of business and tax objectives. A corporation may reshuffle its capital structure by exchanging stock for bonds in order to improve its debt/equity ratio and calm the nerves of creditors or as a condition to borrowing additional funds. Alternatively, it may exchange debt instruments for stock in order to lessen the sting of the double tax by withdrawing earnings in the form of deductible interest rather than nondeductible dividends. For closely held corporations, recapitalizations may be used as a device to shift control among the shareholders.

Because a recapitalization is a nonacquisitive transaction involving only a single corporation, neither continuity of proprietary interest nor continuity of business enterprise is required to qualify as a Type E reorganization.[1] To be tax free, however, a recapitalization must serve a corporate business purpose.[2] The courts have been tolerant in this area, and the business objectives set forth in the preceding paragraph generally are acceptable. In analogous situations, the courts have recognized that it may be unrealistic and impractical to distinguish corporate from shareholder purposes in a closely held corporation.[3] Thus, shareholder objectives

---

[1]. Rev. Rul. 77–415, 1977–2 C.B. 311; Rev. Rul. 82–34, 1982–1 C.B. 59.

[2]. Rev. Proc. 81–60, § 4.04, 1981–2 C.B. 680.

[3]. Lewis v. Commissioner, 176 F.2d 646 (1st Cir.1949); Estate of Parshelsky v. Com-missioner, 303 F.2d 14 (2d Cir.1962). But see Reg. § 1.355–2(b)(2), requiring a corporate business purpose in a tax-free division under Section 355.

germane to the corporation's business have been sufficient to satisfy the business purpose requirement.[4]

2.   TYPES OF RECAPITALIZATIONS

Recapitalizations fall into four broad categories depending upon the consideration exchanged. These categories raise different issues and are best studied separately.

a.   BONDS EXCHANGED FOR STOCK

If a corporation discharges outstanding bonds by issuing preferred or common stock to the bondholders, the transaction qualifies as a Type E reorganization.[1] Under Section 354(a), the bondholders generally will recognize no gain or loss on the exchange of their debt instruments solely for stock. Section 354(a)(2)(B) creates an exception to nonrecognition to the extent stock received is attributable to accrued and untaxed interest on the bonds. This interest component will be taxed as ordinary income under Section 61.[2] The basis of the stock received in a bonds-for-stock recapitalization will be determined under the familiar rules of Section 358, and the new shareholder will be entitled to a tacked holding period on the stock under Section 1223(1).

On the corporate side, matters are fairly routine. Since the corporation is issuing its stock, it initially will be excused from recognizing gain or loss by Section 1032. However, a debtor corporation that transfers its stock in satisfaction of its debt is treated as if it satisfied the debt with an amount of money equal to the fair market value of the transferred stock.[3] Only an insolvent or bankrupt corporation may exclude any resulting discharge of indebtedness income under Section 108 and must make a corresponding reduction in its tax attributes.[4] Thus, a bonds-for-stock recapitalization may result in gross income for the corporation.

b.   BONDS FOR BONDS

After initially contesting the issue,[5] the Service now concedes that if a creditor exchanges outstanding bonds for newly issued bonds in the same corporation, the transaction qualifies as a Type E reorganization.[6] The

---

4. Cf. Rafferty v. Commissioner, 452 F.2d 767 (1st Cir.1971), cert. denied, 408 U.S. 922, 92 S.Ct. 2489 (1972).

1. Reg. § 1.368–2(e)(1). A recapitalization should be distinguished from conversion of a bond into stock pursuant to a conversion privilege in the bond. The Service has held that the latter situation does not constitute a taxable event as long as the bond is converted into stock of the same corporation. Rev.Rul. 72–265, 1972–1 C.B. 222; Rev.Rul. 79–155, 1979–1 C.B. 153.

2. I.R.C. § 354(a)(3)(B).

3. I.R.C. § 108(e)(8).

4. See I.R.C. § 108(a)(1)(A), (a)(1)(B), (b).

5. See I.T. 2035, III–1 C.B. 55 (1924); Commissioner v. Neustadt's Trust, 131 F.2d 528, 530 (2d Cir.1942), affirming 43 B.T.A. 848 (1941), nonacq. 1941–1 C.B. 17, nonacq. withdrawn, acq. 1951–1 C.B. 2.

6. See I.T. 4081, 1952–1 C.B. 65; Rev. Rul. 77–415, 1977–2 C.B. 311.

bondholder in a bonds-for-bonds exchange generally does not recognize gain or loss unless the bonds received are attributable to accrued and untaxed interest[7] or the principal amount of the bonds received in the exchange exceeds the principal amount of the bonds surrendered.[8] Income attributable to interest will be ordinary in character while gain recognized as a result of receipt of excess bonds generally will be either short-or long-term capital gain.[9] The bondholder's basis in the new bonds will be determined under Section 358 and the new bonds will take a tacked holding period under Section 1223(1).

On the corporate side, the primary concern in a bonds-for-bonds recapitalization will be the discharge of indebtedness rules in Section 108.[10] In addition, a bonds-for-bonds recapitalization may subject the corporation and bondholders to the intricate original issue discount provisions.[11]

c. STOCK FOR STOCK

The regulations provide three examples of stock-for-stock exchanges which qualify as reorganizations. Two examples involve exchanges of outstanding preferred stock for common stock and the third involves an exchange of outstanding common for preferred.[12] Thus, virtually all equity-for-equity exchanges will qualify as Type E reorganizations.[13] In addition, exchanges of common stock in a corporation for common stock in the same corporation or preferred stock for preferred stock will qualify for nonrecognition under Section 1036.[14]

Sections 354 and 356 govern the shareholder level tax consequences of a stock-for-stock recapitalization. The shareholders will recognize gain to the extent they receive boot in the exchange, and the gain will be characterized as gain from the exchange of the stock unless the transaction has "the effect of the distribution of a dividend."[15] The shareholders' basis in the stock received in the exchange will be determined under Section 358 and will take a tacked holding period under Section 1223(1). The corporation

---

7. I.R.C. § 354(a)(2)(B). Cf. I.R.C. § 354(a)(3)(B).

8. I.R.C. §§ 354(a)(2)(A), 356(a)(1), (d).

9. I.R.C. §§ 354(a)(3)(A), 356(a)(1). See Rev.Rul. 71–427, 1971–2 C.B. 183.

10. See I.R.C. § 108(e)(10).

11. In particular, see I.R.C. §§ 163(e), 1272–1275. See Bittker & Eustice, Federal Income Taxation of Corporations and Shareholders ¶ 12.27[4][c].

12. Reg. § 1.368–2(e)(2)–(4).

13. It is unlikely that a conversion of preferred stock into common stock in the same corporation, or vice versa, pursuant to a conversion privilege in the stock would be a taxable event under the theory of Rev.Rul. 72–265, 1972–1 C.B. 222, which deals with

convertible debt instruments. Rev.Rul. 77–238, 1977–2 C.B. 115, however, holds that conversion of stock in furtherance of a corporate business purpose pursuant to a privilege contained in the corporation's certificate of incorporation is a recapitalization under Section 368(a)(1)(E).

14. Section 1036 also applies to exchanges between two individual stockholders. Reg. § 1.1036–1(a). For this purpose, boot generally includes "debt-like" nonqualified preferred stock within the meaning of Section 351(g) unless such preferred stock is exchanged for comparable preferred of the same or lesser value, or in certain recapitalizations of "family-owned" corporations. I.R.C. § 354(a)(1)(C).

15. I.R.C. § 356(a)(2). See Rev.Rul. 84–114, below.

will be entitled to nonrecognition under Section 1032 on the exchange of its stock.

Sections 305 and 306 also may come into play in a stock-for-stock recapitalization. The regulations provide that a recapitalization will be deemed to result in a distribution to which Section 305(c) applies if it is (1) pursuant to a plan to periodically increase a shareholder's proportionate interest in the assets or earnings and profits of the corporation or (2) with respect to preferred stock with dividend arrearages and the preferred shareholder increases his proportionate interest in the corporation as a result of the exchange.[16] The second alternative essentially precludes recapitalizations designed to remedy preferred stock dividend arrearages by taxing them under Sections 305(c) and (b)(4).[17]

Stock received in a recapitalization constitutes "Section 306 stock" under Section 306(c)(1)(B) if: (1) it is not common stock, (2) it was received pursuant to a plan of reorganization, (3) on its receipt gain or loss was not recognized to any extent under Sections 354 and 356, and (4) the effect of the transaction was substantially the same as the receipt of a stock dividend or the stock was received in exchange for Section 306 stock. The regulations provide a cash substitute test for determining whether the transaction has the effect of a dividend.[18] If cash received in lieu of the stock obtained in the recapitalization would have been a dividend under Section 356(a)(2), the transaction has substantially the same effect as a dividend. Thus, if the shareholders exchange common stock for common stock and a proportionate amount of preferred stock, the preferred shares will be Section 306 stock.

Revenue Ruling 84–114

1984–2 Cum.Bull. 90.

ISSUE

When nonvoting preferred stock and cash are received in an integrated transaction by a shareholder in exchange for voting common stock in a recapitalization described in section 368(a)(1)(E) of the Internal Revenue Code, does the receipt of cash have the effect of the distribution of a dividend within the meaning of section 356(a)(2)?

FACTS

Corporation X had outstanding 420 shares of voting common stock of which A owned 120 shares and B, C and D each owned 100 shares. A, B, C

---

16. Reg. § 1.305–7(c). A preferred shareholder's proportionate interest increases if the greater of the fair market value or liquidation preference of the stock received in the exchange exceeds the issue price of the preferred stock surrendered. In such an exchange, the amount considered distributed to the preferred shareholder under Section 305(c) is the lesser of (1) the greater of the fair market value or liquidation preference of the preferred stock received over the issue price of the preferred stock surrendered or (2) the amount of the dividend arrearages.

17. Reg. § 1.305–5(d) Example (1). See also Reg. § 1.305–3(e) Example (12); Reg. § 1.305–5(d) Examples (2), (3) and (6).

18. Reg. § 1.306–3(d).

and D were not related within the meaning of section 318(a) of the Code. X adopted a plan of recapitalization that permitted a shareholder to exchange each of 30 shares of voting common stock for either one share of nonvoting preferred stock or cash. Pursuant to the plan, A first exchanged 15 shares of voting common stock for cash and then exchanged 15 shares of voting common stock for 15 shares of nonvoting preferred stock. The facts and circumstances surrounding these exchanges were such that the exchanges constituted two steps in a single integrated transaction for purposes of sections 368(a)(1)(E) and 356(a)(2). The nonvoting preferred stock had no conversion features. In addition, the dividend and liquidation rights payable to A on 15 shares of nonvoting preferred stock were substantially less than the dividend and liquidation rights payable to A on 30 shares of voting common stock. B, C, and D did not participate in the exchange and will retain all their voting common stock in X. X had a substantial amount of post–1913 earnings and profits.

The exchange by A of voting common stock for nonvoting preferred stock and cash qualified as a recapitalization within the meaning of section 368(a)(1)(E) of the Code.

LAW AND ANALYSIS

Section 354(a)(1) of the Code provides that no gain or loss will be recognized if stock or securities in a corporation a party to a reorganization are, in pursuance of the plan of reorganization, exchanged solely for stock or securities in such corporation or in another corporation a party to the reorganization.

Section 356(a)(1) of the Code provides that if section 354 would apply to an exchange but for the fact that the property received in the exchange consists not only of property permitted by section 354 to be received without the recognition of gain but also of other property or money, then the gain, if any, will be recognized, but in an amount not in excess of the sum of the money and fair market value of the other property. Section 356(a)(2) provides that if such exchange has the effect of the distribution of a dividend (determined with the application of section 318(a)), then there will be treated as a dividend to each distributee such an amount of the gain recognized under section 356(a)(1) as is not in excess of each distributee's ratable share of the undistributed earnings and profits of the corporation accumulated after February 28, 1913.

Under section 302(b)(1) and section 302(a) of the Code a redemption will be treated as a distribution in part or full payment in exchange for stock if it is not essentially equivalent to a dividend to the shareholder.

Rev.Rul. 74–515, 1974–2 C.B. 118, and Rev.Rul. 74–516, 1974–2 C.B. 121, state that whether a reorganization distribution to which section 356 of the Code applies has the effect of a dividend must be determined by examining the facts and circumstances surrounding the distribution and looking to the principles for determining dividend equivalency developed under section 356(a)(2) and other provisions of the Code. See Ross v. United States, 173 F.Supp. 793 (Ct.Cl.1959), cert. denied, 361 U.S. 875

(1959). Rev.Rul. 74–516 indicates that in making a dividend equivalency determination under section 356(a)(2), it is proper to analogize to section 302 in appropriate cases. In Shimberg v. United States, 577 F.2d 283 (5th Cir.1978), cert. denied, 439 U.S. 1115 (1979), the courts indicated that in making a dividend equivalency determination under section 356(a)(2), an analogy to section 302 may be appropriate in cases involving single entity reorganizations.

In United States v. Davis, 397 U.S. 301 (1970), rehearing denied, 397 U.S. 1071 (1970), 1970–1 C.B. 62, the Supreme Court of the United States held that a redemption must result in a meaningful reduction of the shareholder's proportionate interest in the corporation in order not to be essentially equivalent to a dividend under section 302(b)(1) of the Code.

Rev.Rul. 75–502, 1975–2 C.B. 111, sets forth factors to be considered in determining whether a reduction in a shareholder's proportionate interest in a corporation is meaningful within the meaning of Davis. The factors considered are a shareholder's right to vote and exercise control, to participate in current earnings and accumulated surplus, and to share in net assets on liquidation. The reduction in the right to vote is of particular significance when a redemption causes a redeemed shareholder to lose the potential for controlling the redeeming corporation by acting in concert with only one other shareholder. See Rev.Rul. 76–364, 1976–2 C.B. 91.

The specific issue is whether, in determining dividend equivalency under section 356(a)(2) of the Code, it is proper to look solely at the change in A's proportionate interest in X that resulted from A's exchange of voting common stock for cash, or instead, whether consideration should be given to the total change in A's proportionate interest in X that resulted from the exchange of voting common stock for both cash and nonvoting preferred stock.

In Rev.Rul. 55–745, 1955–2 C.B. 223, the Internal Revenue Service announced that for purposes of section 302(b)(3) of the Code, it would follow the decision in Zenz v. Quinlivan, 213 F.2d 914 (6th Cir.1954), that a complete termination of shareholder interest may be achieved when a shareholder's entire stock interest in a corporation is disposed of partly through redemption and partly through sale. See also Rev.Rul. 75–447, 1975–2 C.B. 113, in which the Zenz rationale was applied to section 302(b)(2).

Since the exchange of voting common stock for cash and the exchange of voting common stock for nonvoting preferred stock constitute an integrated transaction, in this situation involving a single corporation, it is proper to apply the Zenz rationale so that both exchanges are taken into consideration in determining whether there has been a meaningful reduction of A's proportionate interest in X within the meaning of Davis. Compare Rev.Rul. 75–83, 1975–1 C.B. 112, which holds that a distribution in connection with a transaction qualifying under section 368(a)(1)(A) of the Code will be viewed as having been made by the acquired or transferor corporation and not by the acquiring or transferee corporation for purposes of making a dividend equivalency determination under section 356(a)(2).

If the exchange of voting common stock for preferred stock and cash in this situation had been tested under section 302 of the Code as a redemption, it would not have qualified under section 302(b)(2) or (3) because there was neither an adequate reduction in A's voting stock interest nor a complete termination of that interest. In determining whether this situation is analogous to a redemption meeting the requirements of section 302(b)(1), it is significant that A's interest in the voting common stock of X was reduced from 28.57 percent ($^{120}/_{420}$) to 23.08 percent ($^{90}/_{390}$) so that A went from a position of holding a number of shares of voting common stock that afforded A control of X if A acted in concert with only one other shareholder, to a position where such action was not possible. Moreover, it is significant that A no longer holds the largest voting stock interest in X. In addition, although A received dividend and liquidation rights from the 15 shares of nonvoting preferred stock, these were substantially less than the dividend and liquidation rights of the 30 shares of voting common stock A surrendered. Accordingly, the requirements of section 302(b)(1) would have been met if the transaction had been tested under section 302, and, therefore, the cash received by A did not have the effect of the distribution of a dividend within the meaning of section 356(a)(2).

HOLDING

When A received cash and nonvoting preferred stock of X in an integrated transaction in exchange for voting common stock of X in a recapitalization described in section 368(a)(1)(E) of the Code, the receipt of cash did not have the effect of the distribution of a dividend within the meaning of section 356(a)(2).

d.   STOCK EXCHANGED FOR BONDS

Bazley v. Commissioner

Supreme Court of the United States, 1947.
331 U.S. 737, 67 S.Ct. 1489.

■ MR. JUSTICE FRANKFURTER delivered the opinion of the Court.

* * *

In the *Bazley* case, No. 287, the Commissioner of Internal Revenue assessed an income tax deficiency against the taxpayer for the year 1939. Its validity depends on the legal significance of the recapitalization in that year of a family corporation in which the taxpayer and his wife owned all but one of the Company's one thousand shares. These had a par value of $100. Under the plan of reorganization the taxpayer, his wife, and the holder of the additional share were to turn in their old shares and receive in exchange for each old share five new shares of no par value, but of a stated value of $60, and new debenture bonds, having a total face value of $400,000, payable in ten years but callable at any time. Accordingly, the taxpayer received 3,990 shares of the new stock for the 798 shares of his old holding and debentures in the amount of $319,200. At the time of these transactions the earned surplus of the corporation was $855,783.82.

The Commissioner charged to the taxpayer as income the full value of the debentures. The Tax Court affirmed the Commissioner's determination, against the taxpayer's contention that as a "recapitalization" the transaction was a tax-free "reorganization" and that the debentures were "securities in a corporation a party to a reorganization," "exchanged solely for stock or securities in such corporation" "in pursuance of the plan of reorganization," and as such no gain is recognized for income tax purposes. Internal Revenue Code, §§ 112(g)(1)(E) [the predecessor of § 368(a)(1)(E)] and 112(b)(3). The Tax Court found that the recapitalization had "no legitimate corporate business purpose" and was therefore not a "reorganization" within the statute. The distribution of debentures, it concluded, was a disguised dividend, taxable as earned income under §§ [61(a) and 301]. 4 T.C. 897. The Circuit Court of Appeals for the Third Circuit, sitting en banc, affirmed, two judges dissenting. 155 F.2d 237.

Unless a transaction is a reorganization contemplated by § [368], any exchange of "stock or securities" in connection with such transaction, cannot be "in pursuance of the plan of reorganization." While § [368(a)] informs us that "reorganization" means, among other things, "a recapitalization," it does not inform us what "recapitalization" means. "Recapitalization" in connection with the income tax has been part of the revenue laws since 1921. 42 Stat. 227, 230, § 202(c)(2). Congress has never defined it and the Treasury Regulations shed only limited light. Treas.Reg. 103, § 19.112(g). One thing is certain. Congress did not incorporate some technical concept, whether that of accountants or of other specialists, into § [368(a)], assuming that there is agreement among specialists as to the meaning of recapitalization. And so, recapitalization as used in § [368(a)] must draw its meaning from its function in that section. It is one of the forms of reorganization which obtains the privileges afforded by § [368(a)]. Therefore, "recapitalization" must be construed with reference to the presuppositions and purpose of § [368(a)]. It was not the purpose of the reorganization provision to exempt from payment of a tax what as a practical matter is realized gain. Normally, a distribution by a corporation, whatever form it takes, is a definite and rather unambiguous event. It furnishes the proper occasion for the determination and taxation of gain. But there are circumstances where a formal distribution, directly or through exchange of securities, represents merely a new form of the previous participation in an enterprise, involving no change of substance in the rights and relations of the interested parties one to another or to the corporate assets. As to these, Congress has said that they are not to be deemed significant occasions for determining taxable gain.

These considerations underlie § [368(a)] and they should dominate the scope to be given to the various sections, all of which converge toward a common purpose. Application of the language of such a revenue provision is not an exercise in framing abstract definitions. In a series of cases this Court has withheld the benefits of the reorganization provision in situations which might have satisfied provisions of the section treated as inert language, because they were not reorganizations of the kind with which § [368], in its purpose and particulars, concerns itself. See Pinellas Ice & Cold Storage Co. v. Commissioner, 287 U.S. 462; Gregory v. Helvering, 293 U.S. 465; LeTulle v. Scofield, 308 U.S. 415.

Congress has not attempted a definition of what is recapitalization and we shall follow its example. The search for relevant meaning is often satisfied not by a futile attempt at abstract definition but by pricking a line through concrete applications. Meaning frequently is built up by assured recognition of what does not come within a concept the content of which is in controversy. Since a recapitalization within the scope of § [368] is an aspect of reorganization, nothing can be a recapitalization for this purpose unless it partakes of those characteristics of a reorganization which underlie the purpose of Congress in postponing the tax liability.

No doubt there was a recapitalization of the Bazley corporation in the sense that the symbols that represented its capital were changed, so that the fiscal basis of its operations would appear very differently on its books. But the form of a transaction as reflected by correct corporate accounting opens questions as to the proper application of a taxing statute; it does not close them. Corporate accounting may represent that correspondence between change in the form of capital structure and essential identity in fact which is of the essence of a transaction relieved from taxation as a reorganization. What is controlling is that a new arrangement intrinsically partake of the elements of reorganization which underlie the Congressional exemption and not merely give the appearance of it to accomplish a distribution of earnings. In the case of a corporation which has undistributed earnings, the creation of new corporate obligations which are transferred to stockholders in relation to their former holdings, so as to produce, for all practical purposes, the same result as a distribution of cash earnings of equivalent value, cannot obtain tax immunity because cast in the form of a recapitalization-reorganization. The governing legal rule can hardly be stated more narrowly. To attempt to do so would only challenge astuteness in evading it. And so it is hard to escape the conclusion that whether in a particular case a paper recapitalization is no more than an admissible attempt to avoid the consequences of an outright distribution of earnings turns on details of corporate affairs, judgment on which must be left to the Tax Court. See Dobson v. Commissioner, 320 U.S. 489.

What have we here? No doubt, if the Bazley corporation had issued the debentures to Bazley and his wife without any recapitalization, it would have made a taxable distribution. Instead, these debentures were issued as part of a family arrangement, the only additional ingredient being an unrelated modification of the capital account. The debentures were found to be worth at least their principal amount, and they were virtually cash because they were callable at the will of the corporation which in this case was the will of the taxpayer. One does not have to pursue the motives behind actions, even in the more ascertainable forms of purpose, to find, as did the Tax Court, that the whole arrangement took this form instead of an outright distribution of cash or debentures, because the latter would undoubtedly have been taxable income whereas what was done could, with a show of reason, claim the shelter of the immunity of a recapitalization-reorganization.

The Commissioner, the Tax Court and the Circuit Court of Appeals agree that nothing was accomplished that would not have been accomplished by an outright debenture dividend. And since we find no misconception of law on the part of the Tax Court and the Circuit Court of Appeals, whatever may have been their choice of phrasing, their application of the law to the facts of this case must stand. A "reorganization" which is merely a vehicle, however elaborate or elegant, for conveying earnings from accumulations to the stockholders is not a reorganization under § [368]. This disposes of the case as a matter of law, since the facts as found by the Tax Court bring them within it. And even if this transaction were deemed a reorganization, the facts would equally sustain the imposition of the tax on the debentures under § [354 and 356]. Commissioner v. Estate of Bedford, 325 U.S. 283.

In the *Adams* case, the taxpayer owned all but a few of the 5914 shares of stock outstanding out of an authorized 6000, par value $100. By a plan of reorganization, the authorized capital was reduced by half, to $295,700, divided into 5914 shares of no par value but having a stated value of $50 per share. The 5914 old shares were cancelled and the corporation issued in exchange therefor 5914 shares of the new no-par common stock and 6 per cent 20 year debenture bonds in the principal amount of $295,700. The exchange was made on the basis of one new share of stock and one $50 bond for each old share. The old capital account was debited in the sum of $591,400, a new no-par capital account was credited with $295,700, and the balance of $295,700 was credited to a "Debenture Payable" account. The corporation at this time had accumulated earnings available for distribution in a sum not less than $164,514.82, and this account was left unchanged. At the time of the exchange, the debentures had a value not less than $164,208.82.

The Commissioner determined an income tax deficiency by treating the debenture bonds as a distribution of the corporation's accumulated earnings. The Tax Court sustained the Commissioner's determination, 5 T.C. 351, and the Circuit Court of Appeals affirmed. 155 F.2d 246. The case is governed by our treatment of the *Bazley* case. The finding by the Tax Court that the reorganization had no purpose other than to achieve the distribution of the earnings, is unaffected by the bookkeeping detail of leaving the surplus account unaffected. * * *

Other claims raised have been considered but their rejection does not call for discussion.

Judgments affirmed.

■ MR. JUSTICE DOUGLAS and MR. JUSTICE BURTON dissent in both cases for the reasons stated in the joint dissent of JUDGES MARIS and GOODRICH in the court below. Bazley v. Commissioner, 3 Cir., 155 F.2d 237, 244.

NOTE

The *Bazley* case involved a pro rata exchange of common stock for common stock and bonds. For noncorporate shareholders, its significance diminishes whenever most dividends and long-term capital gains are taxed at the same preferential rate. Later cases have offered some hope for qualifying a stock-for-stock-and-bonds exchange under Section 368(a)(1)(E) if the exchange is not pro rata.[1] Several tax problems remain for an exchanging shareholder even if the transaction constitutes a Type E reorganization. The rules in Section 356(a)(2) and (d) will likely result in characterization of gain as a dividend to the extent of the fair market value of bonds received and the corporation's earnings and profits. Even if the shareholder does not realize a gain on the exchange, the regulations suggest that a stock-for-stock-and-bonds recapitalization may be separately analyzed with the receipt of bonds being treated simply as a Section 301 distribution.[2] Stock-for-bonds exchanges also may give rise to original issue discount.[3]

PROBLEMS

1. Recap Corporation has $100,000 of accumulated earnings and profits and makes a pro rata distribution to each of its ten shareholders of new common voting stock worth $20,000 and new callable preferred stock worth $10,000 in exchange for each shareholder's old common voting stock worth $30,000. Assume that the new Recap preferred stock is not nonqualified preferred stock.

    (a) What result to the shareholders on the exchange?

    (b) What result when Recap calls the preferred stock?

    (c) What result if a shareholder sells his preferred stock?

    (d) What result if Recap had a deficit in its earnings and profits account at the time of the distribution but it foresaw future potential profits?

2. The ten equal shareholders of Shuffle Corporation each have a $10,000 basis in their Shuffle common voting stock which has a $50,000 fair market value. Shuffle has $250,000 of earnings and profits. What result if the ten shareholders each transfer all their common voting stock in return for common voting stock worth $25,000 and bonds worth $25,000.

3. Leverage Corporation has 8% interest bonds outstanding with a face amount of $1,000,000 and a fair market value of $800,000. It redeems these

---

1. See Seide v. Commissioner, 18 T.C. 502 (1952).

2. Reg. § 1.301–1(*l*). Reg. § 1.354–1(d) Example (3) provides that if a shareholder surrenders all of his stock solely for bonds, the tax consequences of the exchange are determined under Section 302 whether or not the transaction is a recapitalization under Section 368(a)(1)(E).

3. See I.R.C. §§ 163(e), 1272–1275. See generally Bittker & Eustice, Federal Income Taxation of Corporations and Shareholders ¶ 12.27[5][d].

bonds and issues new 12% interest bonds with a fair market value and a face amount of $800,000.

(a) Will the transaction qualify as a reorganization?

(b) What result in (a), above, if 12% interest bearing bonds with a face amount of $800,000 are redeemed for 8% interest bonds with a face amount of $1,000,000 and both sets of bonds have the same fair market value of $800,000?

4. Does an exchange of bonds for stock qualify as an ''E'' reorganization? Why would a corporation engage in such an exchange?

B. NONDIVISIVE TYPE D REORGANIZATIONS

Code: §§ 368(a)(1)(D), (a)(2)(H); 354(b); 381(a)(2). Skim §§ 331; 336; 354(a); 356(a); 358; 361; 1032.

Regulations: § 1.368–2(*l*)(1), (2), (3) Example 1.

Type D reorganizations come in two basic forms. The ''divisive D'' involves a transfer by one corporation of some of its assets to a newly formed controlled subsidiary followed by a distribution of the stock of the subsidiary in a corporate division that qualifies under Section 355. This transaction has been examined in Chapter 10 along with the other aspects of corporate divisions. The second form of Type D reorganization is ''nondivisive.'' It involves the transfer by one corporation of all or part of its assets to a corporation controlled immediately after the transfer by the transferor or its shareholders (or any combination) provided that the stock or securities of the controlled corporation are distributed in a transaction that qualifies under Section 354. For this purpose, ''control'' means ownership of at least 50 percent of the voting power or value of the transferee corporation.[1] Section 354(b) requires the transferor corporation to transfer ''substantially all'' of its assets to the controlled corporation and the stock, securities and other properties that it receives must be distributed, along with its other properties, to its shareholders pursuant to a plan of reorganization.

The ''nondivisive'' D reorganization has always been an odd character in the reorganization alphabet. As illustrated by the *Smothers* case, which follows, it historically was invoked by the Service as a weapon to attack the liquidation-reincorporation transaction, a technique utilized by taxpayers in the days when the *General Utilities* doctrine and a capital gains preference worked in tandem to encourage bailouts of corporate earnings at capital gains rates without any corporate-level tax on distributions in liquidation or sales of assets pursuant to a liquidation plan. To appreciate why, consider a gambit that might have been used in the ''good old days'' by Profit Corp., a family company with $800,000 of accumulated earnings and profits and a $2 million net worth, consisting of $1.5 million of

---

1.   I.R.C. § 368(a)(2)(H)(i).

operating assets and $500,000 of investment securities. Assume the shareholders wish to extract the securities from corporate solution without the sting of a dividend (then taxable at higher ordinary income rates) but to otherwise continue operating their business in a new corporation with fresh tax attributes (e.g., no earnings and profits) and no immediate exposure to the accumulated earnings tax.

One classic plan to accomplish these objectives was for the Profit Corp. shareholders to liquidate the corporation, retain the investment securities and, after an appropriate interval, reincorporate the operating assets under Section 351. Alternatively, Profit Corp. might transfer its operating assets to a new subsidiary in exchange for its stock and then liquidate, distributing the new stock and the investment securities to the shareholders. Whatever the format, the basic objective was to achieve what were then the tax benefits of a liquidation: capital gains at the shareholder level, nonrecognition at the corporate level, a step-up in basis of the assets in the reincorporated enterprise, and a fresh start for the earnings and profits account. The Service countered by arguing, with limited success, that the transaction was a reorganization coupled with the receipt of boot that should be taxed as a dividend.[2]

A liquidation-reincorporation rarely makes sense under current law if its form is respected for tax purposes. Liquidating sales of assets for cash are fully taxable and distributions of appreciated property in complete liquidation will trigger corporate-level gain under Section 336 and significantly raise the tax cost of the strategy. Indeed, if the classic liquidation-reincorporation were carried out, it is now *taxpayers* who may prefer to characterize the transactions as a reorganization. Although they would recognize dividend income to the extent of the boot received, the good news is that noncorporate shareholders likely will qualify for the preferential qualified dividend rate, and the transferor corporation would avoid recognizing gain on its assets under Section 361 because the asset bases would carry over to the transferee. The liquidation-reincorporation strategy may retain its vitality, however, in a few limited situations, such as when the corporation has losses to shelter the gains resulting from the distribution of appreciated assets, where the appreciation in the corporation's assets is negligible, or where the corporation has losses that it is trying to accelerate without removing the loss assets from corporate solution.

Smothers v. United States

United States Court of Appeals, Fifth Circuit, 1981.
642 F.2d 894.

■ Wisdom, Circuit Judge:

J.E. and Doris Smothers filed this civil action to obtain a refund of federal income taxes they paid under protest. This dispute arises from the

---

2. See, e.g., Davant v. Commissioner, 366 F.2d 874 (5th Cir.1966), cert. denied, 386 U.S. 1022, 87 S.Ct. 1370 (1967).

dissolution of one of their wholly-owned business corporations. The taxpayers contend that the assets distributed to them by that corporation should be taxed at the capital gain rate applicable to liquidating distributions. The Internal Revenue Service (IRS) counters by characterizing the dissolution as part of a reorganization, thereby rendering the taxpayers' receipt of the distributed assets taxable at ordinary income rates. The district court viewed the transaction as a reorganization and ruled for the IRS. We affirm.

I.

The facts were stipulated. J.E. and Doris Smothers are married and reside in Corpus Christi, Texas. In 1956, they and an unrelated third party organized Texas Industrial Laundries of San Antonio, Inc. (TIL). The Smothers' owned all of its outstanding stock from 1956 through the tax year in issue, 1969. TIL engaged in the business of renting industrial uniforms and other industrial cleaning equipment, such as wiping cloths, dust control devices, and continuous toweling. It owned its own laundry equipment as well.

Shortly after the incorporation of TIL, the taxpayers organized another corporation, Industrial Uniform Services, Inc. (IUS), specifically to oppose a particular competitor in the San Antonio industrial laundry market. The taxpayers owned all of the stock of IUS from the time of its organization until its dissolution. Unlike TIL, IUS did not own laundry equipment; it had to contract with an unrelated company to launder the uniforms it rented to customers. J.E. Smothers personally managed IUS, as well as TIL, but chose not to pay himself a salary from IUS in any of the years of its existence.[1]

IUS evidently succeeded in drawing business away from competing firms, for TIL purchased its main competitor in 1965. IUS continued in business, however, until 1969. On the advice of their accountant, the taxpayers then decided to dissolve IUS and sell all of its non-liquid assets to TIL. On November 1, 1969, IUS adopted a plan of liquidation in compliance with [former Section 337, which generally provided that a corporation did not recognize gain or loss on the sale of its assets pursuant to a plan of complete liquidation, Ed.], and on November 30, it sold the following assets to TIL for cash at their fair market value (stipulated to be the same as their book value):

---

1. Although the record does not specifically so indicate, and although it is unnecessary to our resolution of this case, we think it instructive to note that IUS apparently did not pay any dividends during its existence, either. We deduce that from the following facts of record: (1) the Smothers' cost basis in their IUS stock was $1000.00; (2) IUS had "approximately $148,162.35" in accumulated earnings and profits at the time of its dissolution; (3) IUS's book value at the time of its dissolution was $149,162.35.

Assets	Amount
Noncompetitive covenant	$ 3,894.60
Fixed assets	491.25
Rental property	18,000.00
Prepaid insurance	240.21
Water deposit	7.50
Total	$22,637.56

The noncompetitive covenant constituted part of the consideration received by IUS from its purchase of a small competitor. The fixed assets consisted of incidental equipment (baskets, shelves, and a sewing machine), two depreciated delivery vehicles, and IUS's part interest in an airplane. The rental property was an old apartment building in Corpus Christi on land with business potential. These assets collectively represented about 15% of IUS's net value. The parties stipulated that none of these assets were necessary to carry out IUS's business.

After this sale, IUS promptly distributed its remaining assets to its shareholders, the taxpayers, and then dissolved under Texas law:

Assets	Amount
Cash (received from TIL)	$ 22,637.56
Cash (of IUS)	2,003.05
Notes receivable	138,000.00
Accrued interest receivable	35.42
Claim against the State of Texas	889.67
Liabilities assumed	(14,403.35)
Total	$149,162.35

TIL hired all three of IUS's employees immediately after the dissolution, and TIL continued to serve most of IUS's customers.

In computing their federal income tax liability for 1969, the taxpayers treated this distribution by IUS as a distribution in complete liquidation within § 331(a)(1). Accordingly, they reported the difference between the value of the assets they received in that distribution, $149,162.35, and the basis of their IUS stock, $1,000, as long-term capital gain. Upon audit, the IRS recharacterized the transaction between TIL and IUS as a reorganization within § 368(a)(1)(D), and therefore treated the distribution to the taxpayers as equivalent to a dividend under 356(a)(2). Because IUS had sufficient earnings and profits to cover that distribution, the entire distribution was therefore taxable to the Smothers' at ordinary income rates. The IRS timely assessed a $71,840.84 deficiency against the Smothers'. They paid that amount and filed this suit for a refund.

The district court held that the transaction constituted a reorganization and rendered judgment for the IRS. * * *

II.

Subchapter C of the Internal Revenue Code broadly contemplates that the retained earnings of a continuing business carried on in corporate form can be placed in the hands of its shareholders only after they pay a tax on those earnings at ordinary income rates. That general rule is, of course, primarily a consequence of § 301, which taxes dividend distributions as ordinary income. The Code provides for capital gain treatment of corporate distributions in a few limited circumstances, but only when there is either a significant change in relative ownership of the corporation, as in certain redemption transactions, or when the shareholders no longer conduct the business themselves in corporate form, as in true liquidation transactions. The history of Subchapter C in large part has been the story of how Congress, the courts, and the IRS have been called upon to foil attempts by taxpayers to abuse these exceptional provisions. Ingenious taxpayers have repeatedly devised transactions which formally come within these provisions, yet which have the effect of permitting shareholders to withdraw profits at capital gain rates while carrying on a continuing business enterprise in corporate form without substantial change in ownership. This is just such a case.

The transaction in issue here is of the genus known as liquidation-reincorporation, or reincorporation. The common denominator of such transactions is their use of the liquidation provisions of the Code, which permit liquidating distributions to be received at capital gain rates, as a device through which the dividend provisions may be circumvented. Reincorporations come in two basic patterns. In one, the corporation is dissolved and its assets are distributed to its shareholders in liquidation. The shareholders then promptly reincorporate all the assets necessary to the operation of the business, while retaining accumulated cash or other surplus assets. The transaction in this case is of the alternate form. In it, the corporation transfers the assets necessary to its business to another corporation owned by the same shareholders in exchange for securities or, as here, for cash, and then liquidates. If the minimal technical requirements of § [former § 337] are met, as they indisputably were here, the exchange at the corporate level will not result in the recognition of gain by the transferor corporation. If formal compliance with the liquidation provisions were the only necessity, both patterns would enable shareholders to withdraw profits from a continuing corporate business enterprise at capital gain rates by paper-shuffling. Unchecked, these reincorporation techniques would eviscerate the dividend provisions of the Code.

That result can be avoided by recharacterizing such transactions, in accordance with their true nature, as reorganizations. A reorganization is, in essence, a transaction between corporations that results merely in "a continuance of the proprietary interests in the continuing enterprise under modified corporate form"—a phrase that precisely describes the effect of a reincorporation. Lewis v. Commissioner, 1 Cir.1949, 176 F.2d 646, 648. Congress specifically recognized that the throw-off of surplus assets to shareholders in the course of a reorganization can be equivalent to a dividend, and if so, should be taxed as such. §§ 356(a)(1)–(2). The reincorporation transactions described above result in a dividend payment to the shareholders in every meaningful financial sense. The assets retained by the shareholders therefore should be taxed as dividends as long as the transaction can be fitted within the technical requirements of one of the six classes of reorganizations recognized by § 368(a)(1).

In general, reincorporation transactions are most easily assimilated into § 368(a)(1)(D) ("D reorganization"), as the IRS attempted to do in this case.[9] A transaction qualifies as a D reorganization only if it meets six statutory requirements:

(1) There must be a transfer by a corporation (§ 368(a)(1)(D));

(2) of substantially all of its assets (§ 354(b)(1)(A));

(3) to a corporation controlled by the shareholders of the transferor corporation, or by the transferor corporation itself (§ 368(a)(1)(D));

(4) in exchange for stock or securities of the transferee corporation (§ 354(a)(1));

(5) followed by a distribution of the stock or securities of the transferee corporation to the transferor's shareholders (§ 354(b)(1)(B));

(6) pursuant to a plan of reorganization (§ 368(a)(1)(D)).

On this appeal, the taxpayers concede that the transaction in issue meets every technical prerequisite for characterization as a D reorganization, except for one. They argue that since the assets sold by IUS to TIL amounted to only 15% of IUS's net worth, TIL did not acquire "substantially all of the assets" of IUS within the meaning of § 354(b)(1)(A).

We hold to the contrary. The words "substantially all assets" are not self-defining. What proportion of a corporation's assets is "substantially all" in this context, and less obviously, what "assets" are to be counted in making this determination, cannot be answered without reference to the structure of Subchapter C. To maintain the integrity of the dividend provisions of the Code, "substantially all assets" in this context must be interpreted as an inartistic way of expressing the concept of "transfer of a continuing business". As this Court implied in Reef Corp. v. Commissioner, 5 Cir.1966, 368 F.2d 125, 132, cert. denied, 1967, 386 U.S. 1018, 87 S.Ct. 1371, 18 L.Ed.2d 454, it is in a sense simply a limited codification of the general nonstatutory "continuity of business enterprise" requirement applicable to all reorganizations.

This interpretation finds support in the history of § 368(a)(1)(D) and § 354(b)(1)(A). The Internal Revenue Code of 1939 had no provision equivalent to the "substantially all assets" requirement, and courts almost uniformly approved attempts by the IRS to treat reincorporation transactions as reorganizations within the predecessor of § 368(a)(1)(D) in the 1939 Code. The "substantially all assets" requirement of § 354(b)(1)(A)

---

9. Reincorporations may also fit within § 368(a)(1)(F)("[a] mere change in identity, form or place of organization, however effected"). * * * The government did not press that theory on appeal. Doubtless that owes to its general reluctance to extend the scope of § 368(a)(1)(F) to acquisitive reorganizations, which derives from the fact that net operating losses may be carried back after an F reorganization. § 381(b)(3). See generally Cohen, The "New F" Reorganization, 36 N.Y.U.Inst.Fed.Tax. 833 (1978). The IRS has in the past occasionally advanced more exotic arguments against reincorporations—e.g., the theory that no real "liquidation" occurs in such transactions, and the theory that even if a liquidation does occur, the distribution of surplus assets is a dividend functionally unrelated to the liquidation—but it did not so argue here. * * *

and the amendment of § 368(a)(1)(D) incorporating that requirement were added during the 1954 recodification as part of a package of amendments aimed at plugging a different loophole—the bail-out of corporate earnings and profits at capital gains rates through divisive reorganizations. There is no indication that Congress wished to relax the application of the reorganization provisions to reincorporation transactions. Indeed, the committee reports indicate the contrary. The Senate report accompanying the bill that contained the "substantially all assets" requirement of § 354(b)(1)(A) and the parallel amendment to § 368(a)(1)(D) stated that the purpose of those changes was only "to insure that the tax consequences of the distribution of stocks or securities to shareholders or security holders in connection with divisive reorganizations will be governed by the requirements of section 355". The report expressly noted that except with respect to divisive reorganizations, the reorganization provisions "are the same as under existing law and are stated in substantially the same form". Even more significantly, the original House version of the 1954 Code contained a provision specifically dealing with reincorporation transactions. That provision was dropped in conference because the conferees felt that such transactions "can appropriately be disposed of by judicial decision or by regulation within the framework of the other provisions of the bill". As the court said in Pridemark, Inc. v. Commissioner, 4 Cir.1965, 345 F.2d 35, 40, this response shows that "the committee was aware of the problem and thought the present statutory scheme adequate to deal with it". By implication, this passage approved the IRS's use of the predecessor of § 368(a)(1)(D) to meet the problem, and shows that the "substantially all assets" amendment was not thought to restrict its use.

Courts have almost unanimously so interpreted the "substantially all assets" language. Moreover, they have also interpreted the other technical conditions for a D reorganization in ways that accomplish the congressional intent to reach reincorporation transactions. For example, the literal language of § 368(a)(1)(D) and §§ 354(a), 354(b)(1)(B) requires that the transferee corporation "exchange" some of its "stock or securities" for the assets of the transferor, and that those items be "distributed" to the shareholders of the transferor, before a D reorganization can be found. Yet both of those requirements have uniformly been ignored as "meaningless gestures" in the reincorporation context, in which the same shareholders own all the stock of both corporations.[14] Smothers does not even challenge the applicability of that principle here.

Properly interpreted, therefore, the assets looked to when making the "substantially all assets" determination should be all the assets, and only the assets, necessary to operate the corporate business—whether or not those assets would appear on a corporate balance sheet constructed according to generally accepted accounting principles. Two errors in particular should be avoided. Inclusion of assets unnecessary to the operation of the

14. The "meaningless gesture" language is from James Armour, Inc., 1964, 43 T.C. 295, 307. * * *

business in the "substantially all assets" assessment would open the way for the shareholders of any enterprise to turn dividends into capital gain at will. For example, if we assume that "substantially all" means greater than 90%, then a corporation need only cease declaring dividends and accumulate surplus liquid assets until their value exceeds 10% of the total value of all corporate assets. The shareholders could then transfer the assets actively used in the business to a second corporation owned by them and liquidate the old corporation. Such a liquidating distribution would be a dividend in any meaningful sense, but an interpretation of "substantially all assets" that took surplus assets into account would permit the shareholders to treat it as capital gain. Indeed, such an interpretation would perversely treat a merely nominal distribution of retained earnings as a dividend, but would permit substantial distributions to be made at capital gain rates. Courts therefore have invariably ignored all surplus assets and have focused on the operating assets of the business—the tangible assets actively used in the business—when making the "substantially all assets" assessment.[15]

Second, exclusion of assets not shown on a balance sheet constructed according to generally accepted accounting principles from the "substantially all assets" assessment would offer an unjustified windfall to the owners of service businesses conducted in corporate form. The most important assets of such a business may be its reputation and the availability of skilled management and trained employees, none of which show up on a standard balance sheet. Other courts have correctly recognized that in appropriate cases those intangible assets alone may constitute substantially all of the corporate assets. Otherwise, for example, a sole legal practitioner who owns nothing but a desk and chair could incorporate himself, accumulate earnings, and then set up a new corporation and liquidate the old at capital gain rates—as long as he is careful to buy a new desk and chair for the new corporation, rather than transferring the old.

When these principles are applied to this case, it is plain that "substantially all of the assets" of IUS were transferred to TIL, and that the transaction as a whole constituted a reorganization. TIL and IUS were both managed and wholly owned by Smothers. By the nature of its business, IUS was wholly a service enterprise; indeed, the parties stipulated that none of the tangible assets of IUS were necessary to the operation of its business. The extent to which those tangible assets were transferred to TIL is therefore entirely irrelevant. IUS's most important assets—its reputation, sales staff, and the managerial services of Smothers—were all transferred to TIL. TIL rehired all three of IUS's employees immediately after IUS's liquidation, and continued to serve IUS's old customers. The same business enterprise was conducted by the same people under the same ownership, and the only assets removed from corporate solution were accumulated liquid assets unnecessary to the operation of the business. To treat this

---

15. Note that liquid assets are "necessary" to the extent they represent working capital. See Swanson v. United States, 9th Cir.1973, 479 F.2d 539, 545–46; Ross Michael Simon Trust v. United States, Ct.Cl. 1968, 402 F.2d 272, 280.

transaction as other than a reorganization would deny economic reality; to permit Smothers to extract the retained earnings of IUS at capital gain rates would make a mockery of the dividend provisions of the Internal Revenue Code.

We do not perceive ordinary income treatment here to be particularly harsh, or a "tax trap for the unwary". It places the Smothers' only in the position they would have been in if they had extracted the retained earnings of IUS as the Code contemplates they should have—by periodically declaring dividends.

Affirmed.

■ GARZA, CIRCUIT JUDGE, dissenting:

After carefully reading the majority's opinion, I find that I must respectfully dissent. Unlike my Brothers, who apparently feel that it is their duty to "plug loopholes", I would remain content in applying the tax law as it reads leaving the United States Congress to deal with the consequences of the tax law as it has been drafted. The only issue before this Court on appeal is whether or not IUS transferred "substantially all of its assets" to TIL. Instead of dealing with this straightforward question, the majority has made a case of evil against liquidation-reincorporation abuses and, in an attempt to remedy every such perceived abuse, they have relieved the Congress of its burden to change the law heretofore requiring that "substantially all" of a corporation's assets be transferred to now read that "only those assets necessary to operate the corporate business" be transferred in order to meet the "D reorganization" requirements. Essentially, the majority has changed the definition of "substantially all assets" to mean only "necessary operating assets." I believe if Congress had meant "necessary operating assets" it would have said so instead of specifically requiring that "substantially all" of the assets be transferred. In my mind "substantially all" plainly means all of the assets except for an insubstantial amount. Under such a definition, the sale of 15% of IUS's assets to TIL could hardly be defined as "substantially all" of IUS's assets.

However, even after having redefined "substantially all" to mean "necessary operating assets", the IUS liquidation still falls short of the "D reorganization" requirements because the stipulated facts are that absolutely none of the assets sold from IUS to TIL were necessary operating assets for either corporation. Faced with an absence of a proper factual setting, the majority goes on to define necessary operating assets as including a corporation's intangible assets. Now while a sale of intangible assets might be an appropriate consideration in determining whether or not "substantially all" assets of a corporation have been transferred, such a consideration simply has no bearing in this case. All of the assets transferred to TIL were depreciated tangible objects sold at book value after which IUS completely ceased all business operations. There simply was no other transfer of IUS's intangible assets as a continuing business.

* * *

Although the Internal Revenue Service has never questioned the bona fides of IUS's liquidation, the majority has gone beyond the stipulated facts by characterizing the liquidation as a tax avoidance scam. I simply cannot agree. After starting from scratch, Mr. Smothers worked for over a dozen years refraining from drawing salary in order that IUS could pay its taxes, employees and other operating expenses and in order for IUS to become a successful self-sustaining business enterprise. Mr. Smothers was successful but, now that he no longer could devote his service to IUS, his years of labor are now labeled by the majority as a mere "paper shuffle." I do not share the majority's attitude.

The reasons for my position can be more easily understood by a simple review of the bottom-line facts. After IUS began showing a profit and started accumulating a cash surplus, instead of immediately investing in a building or in other equipment for its operations, it continued its operations as before. Now, if IUS had purchased real property or depreciable personal property for its operations (instead of leasing as it had been) and had sold these properties pursuant to its plan of liquidation, certainly no argument would be made that the money initially invested in those properties should have been declared by IUS as dividends. However, instead of investing its accumulations, IUS simply put them in its bank account as the tax laws allow and presumably faced any tax consequences posed by such an accumulation.

After IUS ceased operations, was liquidated, and its assets distributed to its stockholders in exchange for their stock, the I.R.S. issued a deficiency, not because IUS was reorganized within the meaning of 26 U.S.C. § 368(a)(1)(D), but rather because the I.R.S. felt the accumulated earnings of IUS coupled with long-term capital gains rates applicable to the stock exchange provided an undesirable windfall to IUS's stockholders. In essence, the I.R.S. sought to expand the "D reorganization" provisions, lessen the availability of long-term capital gains treatment to corporate stockholders, and totally ignore the purpose of the tax upon improperly accumulated surplus as provided in 26 U.S.C. § 531. The majority seeks to do equity for the I.R.S. position by "treating" the IUS liquidation as a "D reorganization." I do not believe the taxpayers or the tax laws are served by upholding an I.R.S. deficiency for the sole purpose of "plugging loopholes." The lesson to be learned from the majority's opinion is clear—future corporations faced with similar circumstances need only invest their otherwise accumulated surplus in some method other than savings. In the process of liquidation they need sell whatever assets exist to third parties unrelated to their stockholders and their stockholders should make no effort to find future employment for the corporation's employees.

It seems to me that in its attempt to "plug" a perceived "loophole," the majority is giving this Court's imprimatur to a variation of the same so-called "mockery" of the tax laws sought to be prevented by its opinion.

For these reasons, I respectfully dissent.

NOTE

The IRS has been rethinking its approach to nondivisive Type D reorganizations. It recently has focused its attention on the "all-cash" D reorganization, in which one corporation purchases substantially all the assets of another corporation solely for cash (or debt) and without issuing any stock. All-cash D reorganizations are used in a variety of situations involving commonly controlled corporations that wish to rearrange and simplify their corporate structure for valid business reasons. They also occur in the international setting, or between corporations filing a consolidated return, where the transaction raises additional issues that are well beyond the scope of our coverage here. From the taxpayer's perspective, the consequences of having this type of asset acquisition characterized as a reorganization rather than a taxable sale can be either good or bad depending on the context and planning agenda.

At first glance, the concept of a tax-free reorganization where the target corporation receives entirely cash consideration in exchange for assets of equal value is counter-intuitive. But the IRS has taken the position that reorganization treatment is appropriate in light of the history of nondivisive Type D reorganizations, interpretations by the courts, and the need for a neutral rule to provide certainty in planning. This result is consistent with the underlying policy of the reorganization scheme, which provides for nonrecognition of gain or loss for transactions that represent a mere change in the form of an investment, which in this case are the assets that remain in corporate solution. This is particularly appropriate when both parties to the transaction are controlled by the same shareholders.

The IRS position evolved from a much discussed private ruling[1] in which it considered a transaction where a corporation owned equally by two unrelated corporate shareholders (A and B) sold all its assets for installment notes with in an amount equal to the fair market value of the assets to a new corporation (Newco) owned 90 percent by B and 10 percent by a corporation unrelated to A and B. In holding that Newco took a cost basis in the acquired assets (which is what it wanted for purposes of determining Section 197 amortization deductions on acquired goodwill), the ruling inferred that the transaction was *not* a D reorganization despite the presence of substantial (but not identical) overlapping ownership of the two corporations. If Newco had issued some stock as consideration for the assets, the literal statutory requirements for a D reorganization would have been satisfied, however, and Newco would have been required to take a lower transferred basis in the acquired assets. By simply not issuing any stock, the taxpayer avoided this undesired result, leading to the possibility that taxpayers could elect the outcome they desired depending on whether or not any stock was issued.

The ruling created a commotion in the mergers and acquisitions tax bar over the issue of whether the issuance of stock is an essential prerequisite for a nondivisive D reorganization. Some commentators argued that a

---

1. P.L.R. 20551018 (Dec. 23, 2005).

transaction could qualify as a D reorganization even though Newco issued no stock or securities because, in similar cases of overlapping ownership, the Service and the courts had held that issuance of stock was unnecessary under what is known as the "meaningless gesture" doctrine.[2] Others contended that the statutory language could not permit such a result if no stock or securities were issued.[3]

Regulations issued in 2010[4] begin to address this esoteric issue. They provide that an acquisition can qualify as a Type D reorganization even where no stock of the transferee corporation is issued and distributed in the transaction when the same person or persons own, directly and indirectly, all of the stock of the transferor and transferee corporations in "identical proportions."[5] For this purpose, an individual and all members of his family having a relationship described in Section 318(a)(1) are treated as one individual.[6] In addition, the distribution requirement under Sections 368(a)(1)(D) and 354(b)(1)(B) is treated as satisfied in the absence of any issuance of stock or securities where there is a de minimis variation in shareholder identity or proportionality of ownership in the transferor and transferee corporations.[7] In these all-cash D reorganizations, the transferee is treated as having issued a nominal share of stock in addition to the actual consideration exchanged, and the transferor corporation is deemed to have distributed that share to its shareholders and, as appropriate, to have further transferred it to the extent necessary to reflect the actual ownership of the two corporations.[8]

The regulations are taxpayer-friendly insofar as they facilitate legitimate restructurings involving asset transfers within a commonly controlled corporate group. Reorganization treatment ensures that a transfer of assets between commonly controlled corporations is not a taxable event whether or not actual stock is issued by the acquiring corporation but, as a trade-off, the transferee takes a transferred basis in the assets it acquires. But what about the transferor's shareholders? Recall that, after selling its assets, the transferor corporation will liquidate and distribute the cash consideration and the nominal share of stock it received in the transaction to its shareholders. Does it matter if the shareholders are individuals or corpora-

---

2.   See James Armour, Inc. v. Commissioner, 43 T.C. 295 (1964); Wilson v. Commissioner, 46 T.C. 334 (1966); Rev. Rul. 70–240, 1970–1 C.B. 81.

3.   See, e.g., "Attorneys Question Ruling That Transaction Wasn't a D Reorganization," 111 Tax Notes 241 (April 10, 2006); Schler, Letter to the Editor, "More on the 'All Cash D' Reorganization," 111 Tax Notes 383 (April 17, 2006). See also Ginsburg & Levin, Mergers, Acquisitions, and Buyouts ¶ 406.1.1.

4.   T.D. 9475, 2010 I.R.B. 304.

5.   Reg. § 1.368–2(l)(2)(i). The regulations thus would not change the result in

P.L.R. 20551018, supra note 1, because ownership in the two corporations was not identical.

6.   Reg. § 1.368–2(l)(2)(ii).

7.   Reg. § 1.368–2(l)(3)(iii).

8.   Reg. § 1.368–2(l)(2)(i). The regulations also clarify the tax consequences if no consideration is received for the target's assets, or if the value of the consideration received is less than the fair market value of the target's assets. Id. For the basis consequences to the target corporation's shareholders, see Reg. § 1.358–2T(a)(2)(iii).

tions? Problem 2, below, provides an opportunity to consider these share-holder-level consequences, which are not directly addressed in the all-cash D reorganization regulations.

PROBLEMS

1.   Brother and Sister Corporation are owned by the same shareholders in the same proportionate amounts. The shareholders have a $200,000 basis in their Brother stock and Brother Corporation has operating assets with a value of $500,000 and basis of $150,000 as well as $200,000 of cash and $250,000 of earnings and profits. Sister Corporation, which has $300,000 of earnings and profits, purchases the operating assets for $500,000 cash and Brother Corporation immediately liquidates.

    (a) What are the consequences of these transactions to the shareholders and to both corporations?

    (b) Will the arguments of the taxpayers and the Service concerning the transactions differ from those advanced in the Smothers case?

    (c) Is there any simpler way for the taxpayers to achieve their objectives?

2.   A, an individual, owns all the stock of T, Inc. and B, T's son, owns all the stock of S, Inc. A has a $200,000 adjusted basis in his T stock. T sells all its assets, in which it has a $100,000 aggregate adjusted basis, to S for $1,000,000 cash and then liquidates, distributing the cash to A. What are the tax consequences of the transaction to all relevant parties?

C.   TYPE F: MERE CHANGE IN IDENTITY, FORM, OR PLACE OF ORGANIZATION

Code: §§ 368(a)(1)(F); 381(b). Skim §§ 331; 351; 354(a); 356(a); 358; 361; 1032.

A Type F reorganization is defined by the Code as "a mere change in identity, form, or place of organization of one corporation, however effected." An example would be a merger of a closely held New York corporation into a newly formed Delaware corporation with the same shareholders in order to take advantage of Delaware corporate law in anticipation of a public offering of the company's stock.[1] Over fifty years ago a noted commentator stated that the Type F reorganization "is so little relied upon by taxpayers that this part of the statute has indeed perished through lack of use."[2] It has survived calls for repeal, however, and experienced a brief

---

    1.   See, e.g., Rev. Rul. 96–29, 1996–1 C.B. 50.

    2.   Paul, Studies in Federal Taxation 82 (3d Ed. 1940). But see Pugh, "The F Reorga-nization: Reveille for a Sleeping Giant?" 24 Tax L.Rev. 437 (1969).

renaissance before resuming its historical role as a relatively dead letter in the tax-free reorganization alphabet.[3]

The resurgence of interest in the Type F reorganization was the result of attempts by taxpayers to carry back the post-acquisition losses of corporations which previously had been operated as an affiliated corporate group to pre-acquisition years of an acquired corporation. Since Section 381(b) only permits such a carryback of net operating losses in an F reorganization, the shareholders argued that the fusion of affiliated corporations qualified as an F reorganization. Although the language of the applicable statute implied that an F reorganization was limited to structural changes in a single corporation, the Commissioner, in his attempt to combat the liquidation-reincorporation bailout device, bolstered the argument that the F reorganization also applied to the merger of two or more active corporations. In the *Davant* case, the Commissioner asserted and the Court accepted the argument that an F reorganization could involve two operating corporations.[4] The Commissioner's argument, together with a ruling in which the Service acknowledged that a reorganization meeting the definition of an F reorganization and some other type of reorganization would be treated as an F reorganization for purposes of Section 381(b),[5] opened the floodgates. The only remaining question was how far shareholders could push combinations of operating corporations into the F reorganization category.[6] In the 1970s, the Service conceded that a combination of active corporations under common control could qualify as an F reorganization if there was a complete continuity of shareholder and proprietary interests.[7] But Congress later slammed the door shut by limiting F reorganization status to a single operating corporation through the addition of the words "of one corporation" to Section 368(a)(1)(F). The Type F reorganization thus once again was relegated to its prior role as a minor provision governing reincorporations in another state and other merely formal changes. The following legislative history explains that amendment:[8]

3. F reorganization issues occasionally resurface, usually in specialized situations. See, e.g., Rev. Rul. 2003–19, 2003–1 C.B. 468 (involving the conversion of a mutual insurance company to a stock insurance company). See also Prop. Reg. § 1.368–2(m), which specifies the F reorganization qualification requirements and provides that continuity of business enterprise and continuity of proprietary interest are not required for a transaction to qualify as an F reorganization.

4. Davant v. Commissioner, 366 F.2d 874 (5th Cir.1966), cert. denied 386 U.S. 1022, 87 S.Ct. 1370 (1967). Actually the Commissioner made the argument at the trial court level, 43 T.C. 540 (1965), and it was adopted by the appellate court in its opinion.

5. Rev.Rul. 57–276, 1957–1 C.B. 126.

6. Compare Movielab, Inc. v. United States, 204 Ct.Cl. 6, 494 F.2d 693 (1974), and Stauffer's Estate v. Commissioner, 403 F.2d 611 (9th Cir.1968), with Berger Machine Products, Inc. v. Commissioner, 68 T.C. 358 (1977), and Romy Hammes, Inc. v. Commissioner, 68 T.C. 900 (1977).

7. See Rev.Rul. 75–561, 1975–2 C.B. 129.

8. H.R.Rep. No. 97–760, 97th Cong., 2d Sess. 540–41 (1982), reprinted in 1982–2 C.B. 634–35.

Present law

A reorganization includes "a mere change in identity, form, or place of organization" (an F reorganization). Generally, present law requires a transferor corporation's taxable year to be closed on the date of a reorganization transfer and precludes a post-reorganization loss from being carried back to a taxable year of the transferor. However, F reorganizations are excluded from these limitations in recognition of the intended scope of such reorganizations as embracing only formal changes in a single operating corporation.

* * *

Conference agreement

The conference agreement limits the F reorganization definition to a change in identity, form, or place of organization of a single operating corporation.

This limitation does not preclude the use of more than one entity to consummate the transaction provided only one operating company is involved. The reincorporation of an operating company in a different State, for example, is an F reorganization that requires that more than one corporation be involved.

Revenue Ruling 96–29

1996–1 Cum. Bull. 50.

ISSUE

Do the transactions described below qualify as reorganizations under § 368(a)(1)(F) of the Internal Revenue Code?

FACTS

Situation 1. Q is a manufacturing corporation all of the common stock of which is owned by twelve individuals. One class of nonvoting preferred stock, representing 40 percent of the aggregate value of Q, is held by a variety of corporate and noncorporate shareholders. Q is incorporated in state M. Pursuant to a plan to raise immediate additional capital and to enhance its ability to raise capital in the future by issuing additional stock, Q proposes to make a public offering of newly issued stock and to cause its stock to become publicly traded. Q entered into an underwriting agreement providing for the public offering and a change in its state of incorporation. The change in the state of incorporation was undertaken, in part, to enable the corporation to avail itself of the advantages that the corporate laws of state N afford to public companies and their officers and directors. In the absence of the public offering, Q would not have changed its state of incorporation. Pursuant to the underwriting agreement, Q changed its place of incorporation by merging with and into R, a newly organized corporation incorporated in state N. The shares of Q stock were converted into the right to receive an identical number of shares of R stock. Immediately thereafter, R sold additional shares of its stock to the public and redeemed all of the outstanding shares of nonvoting preferred stock. The number of new shares sold was equal to 60 percent of all the outstanding R stock following the sale and redemption.

Situation 2. W, a state M corporation, is a manufacturing corporation all of the stock of which is owned by two individuals. W conducted its business through several wholly owned subsidiaries. The management of W determined that it would be in the best interest of W to acquire the business of Z, an unrelated corporation, and combine it with the business of Y, one of its subsidiaries, and to change the state of incorporation of W. In order to accomplish these objectives, and pursuant to an overall plan, W entered into a plan and agreement of merger with Y and Z. In accordance with the agreement, Z merged with and into Y pursuant to the law of state M, with the former Z shareholders receiving shares of newly issued W preferred stock in exchange for their shares of Z stock. Immediately following the acquisition of Z, W changed its place of organization by merging with and into N, a newly organized corporation incorporated in state R. Upon W's change of place of organization, the holders of W common and preferred stock surrendered their W stock in exchange for identical N common and preferred stock, respectively.

LAW AND ANALYSIS

Section 368(a)(1)(F) provides that a reorganization includes a mere change in identity, form, or place of organization of one corporation, however effected. This provision was amended * * * in order to limit its application to one corporation. Certain limitations contained in § 381(b), including those precluding the corporation acquiring property in a reorganization from carrying back a net operating loss or a net capital loss for a taxable year ending after the date of transfer to a taxable year of the transferor, do not apply to reorganizations described in § 368(a)(1)(F) "in recognition of the intended scope of such reorganizations as embracing only formal changes in a single operating corporation." H.R.Rep. No. 760, 97th Cong., 2d Sess. 540, 541 (1982). Although a change in the place of organization usually must be effected through the merger of one corporation into another, such a transaction qualifies as a reorganization under § 368(a)(1)(F) because it involves only one operating corporation. The 1982 amendment of § 368(a)(1)(F) thus overruled several cases in which a merger of two or more operating corporations could be treated as a reorganization under § 368(a)(1)(F). See, e.g., Estate of Stauffer v. Commissioner, 403 F.2d 611 (9th Cir.1968); Associated Machine, Inc. v. Commissioner, 403 F.2d 622 (9th Cir.1968); and Davant v. Commissioner, 366 F.2d 874 (5th Cir.1966).

A transaction does not qualify as a reorganization under § 368(a)(1)(F) unless there is no change in existing shareholders or in the assets of the corporation. However, a transaction will not fail to qualify as a reorganization under § 368(a)(1)(F) if dissenters owning fewer than 1 percent of the outstanding shares of the corporation fail to participate in the transaction. Rev. Rul. 66–284, 1966–2 C.B. 115.

The rules applicable to corporate reorganizations as well as other provisions recognize the unique characteristics of reorganizations qualifying under § 368(a)(1)(F). In contrast to other types of reorganizations, which can involve two or more operating corporations, a reorganization of a corporation under § 368(a)(1)(F) is treated for most purposes of the Code as if there had been no change in the corporation and, thus, as if the reorganized corporation is the same entity as the corporation that was in existence prior to the reorganization. See § 381(b); § 1.381(b)–1(a)(2); see also Rev. Rul. 87–110, 1987–2 C.B. 159; Rev. Rul. 80–168, 1980–1 C.B. 178; Rev. Rul. 73–526, 1973–2 C.B. 404; Rev. Rul. 64–250, 1964–2 C.B. 333.

In Rev. Rul. 69–516, 1969–2 C.B. 56, the Internal Revenue Service treated as two separate transactions a reorganization under § 368(a)(1)(F) and a reorganization under § 368(a)(1)(C) undertaken as part of the same plan. Specifically, a corporation changed its place of organization by merging into a corporation formed under the laws of another state and immediately thereafter, it transferred substantially all of its assets in exchange for stock of an unrelated corporation. The ruling holds that the change in place of organization qualified as a reorganization under § 368(a)(1)(F).

Accordingly, in Situation 1, the reincorporation by Q in state N qualifies as a reorganization under § 368(a)(1)(F) even though it was a step in the transaction in which Q was issuing common stock in a public offering and redeeming stock having a value of 40 percent of the aggregate value of its outstanding stock prior to the offering.

In Situation 2, the reincorporation by W in state N qualifies as a reorganization under § 368(a)(1)(F) even though it was a step in the transaction in which W acquired the business of Z.

HOLDING

On the facts set forth in this ruling, in each of Situations 1 and 2, the reincorporation transaction qualifies as a reorganization under § 368(a)(1)(F), notwithstanding the other transactions effected pursuant to the same plan.

* * *

PROBLEM

Golden State Corporation is incorporated in California. It forms a new corporation in Arizona, Cactus Corporation, transferring all of its assets to Cactus Corporation in exchange for all of the Cactus stock. Golden State Corporation is then liquidated. What tax consequences to the Golden State shareholders?

D. TYPE G: INSOLVENCY REORGANIZATIONS

Code: §§ 368(a)(1)(G); 354(b). Skim §§ 354; 355; 356.

Excerpt From Report of Senate Finance Committee on Bankruptcy Tax Bill of 1980*

S.Rep. No. 96–1035, 96th Cong., 2d Sess. 34–38, reprinted in 1980–2 Cum.Bull. 620, 637.

Present Law

Definition of reorganization

A transfer of all or part of a corporation's assets, pursuant to a court order in a proceeding under chapter X of the Bankruptcy Act (or in a receivership, foreclosure, or similar proceeding), to another corporation organized or utilized to effectuate a court-approved plan may qualify for tax-free reorganization treatment under special rules relating to "insolvency reorganizations" (secs. 371–374 of the Internal Revenue Code).

These special rules for insolvency reorganizations generally allow less flexibility in structuring tax-free transactions than the rules applicable to corporate reorganizations as defined in section 368 of the Code. Also, the special rules for insolvency reorganizations do not permit carryover of tax attributes to the transferee corporation, and otherwise differ in important respects from the general reorganization rules.[1] While some reorganizations under chapter X of the Bankruptcy Act may be able to qualify for nonrecognition treatment under Code section 368, other chapter X reorganizations may be able to qualify only under the special rules of sections 371–374 and not under the general reorganization rules of section 368.

Triangular reorganizations

In the case of an insolvency reorganization which can qualify for nonrecognition treatment only under the special rules of Code sections 371–374, the stock or securities used to acquire the assets of the corporation in bankruptcy must be the acquiring corporation's own stock or securities. This limitation generally precludes corporations in bankruptcy from engaging in so-called triangular reorganizations, where the acquired corporation is acquired for stock of the parent of the acquiring corporation. By contrast, tax-free triangular reorganizations generally are permitted under the general rules of Code section 368.

---

* Some footnotes omitted.

1. Under present law, it is not clear to what extent creditors of an insolvent corporation who receive stock in exchange for their claims may be considered to have "stepped into the shoes" of former shareholders for purposes of satisfying the nonstatutory "continuity of interest" rule, under which the owners of the acquired corporation must continue to have a proprietary interest in the acquiring corporation. Generally, the courts have found the "continuity of interest" test satisfied if the creditors' interests were transformed into proprietary interests prior to the reorganization (e.g., Helvering v. Alabama Asphaltic Limestone Co., 315 U.S. 179 (1942); Treas.Reg. § 1.371–1(a)(4)). It is unclear whether affirmative steps by the creditors are required or whether mere receipt of stock is sufficient.

Transfer to controlled subsidiary

In the case of an insolvency reorganization which can qualify for nonrecognition treatment only under the special rules of Code sections 371–374, it is not clear under present law whether and to what extent the acquiring corporation may transfer assets received into a controlled subsidiary. In the case of other corporate reorganizations, the statute expressly defines the situations where transfers to subsidiaries are permitted (Code sec. 368(a)(2)(C)).

Carryover of tax attributes

In the case of an insolvency reorganization which can qualify for nonrecognition treatment only under the special rules of Code sections 371–374, court cases have held that attributes (such as net operating losses) of the corporation in bankruptcy do not carry over to the new corporation. In the case of other corporate reorganizations, however, specific statutory rules permit carryover of tax attributes to the surviving corporation (Code sec. 381).

Reasons for change

The committee believes that the provisions of existing Federal income tax law which are generally applicable to tax-free corporate reorganizations should also apply to reorganizations of corporations in bankruptcy or similar proceedings, in order to facilitate the rehabilitation of financially troubled businesses.

Also, the committee believes that a creditor who exchanges securities in a corporate reorganization (including an insolvency reorganization) should be treated as receiving interest income on the exchange to the extent the creditor receives new securities, stock, or any other property for accrued but unpaid interest on the securities surrendered.

Explanation of provisions

Section 4 of the bill generally conforms the tax rules governing insolvency reorganizations with the existing rules applicable to other corporate reorganizations. These provisions are the same as section 4 of the House bill.

Definition of reorganization

In general

The bill adds a new category—"G" reorganizations—to the general Code definition of tax-free reorganizations (sec. 368(a)(1)). The new category includes certain transfers of assets pursuant to a court-approved reorganization plan in a bankruptcy case under new title 11 of the U.S. Code, or in a receivership, foreclosure, or similar proceeding in a Federal or State court.

* * *

In order to facilitate the rehabilitation of corporate debtors in bankruptcy, etc., these provisions are designed to eliminate many requirements which have effectively precluded financially troubled companies from utilizing the generally applicable tax-free reorganization provisions of present law. To achieve this purpose, the new "G" reorganization provision does not require compliance with State merger laws (as in category "A" reorganizations), does not require that the financially distressed corporation receive solely stock of the acquiring corporation in exchange for its assets (category "C"), and does not require that the former shareholders of the financially distressed corporation control the corporation which receives the assets (category "D").

The "G" reorganization provision added by the bill requires the transfer of assets by a corporation in a bankruptcy or similar case, and the distribution (in pursuance of the court-approved reorganization plan) of stock or securities of the acquiring corporation in a transaction which qualifies under sections 354, 355, or 356 of the Code. This distribution requirement is designed to assure that either substantially all of the assets of the financially troubled corporation, or assets which consist of an active business under the tests of section 355, are transferred to the acquiring corporation.

"Substantially all" test

The "substantially all" test in the "G" reorganization provision is to be interpreted in light of the underlying intent in adding the new "G" category, namely, to facilitate the reorganization of companies in bankruptcy or similar cases for rehabilitative purposes. Accordingly, it is intended that facts and circumstances relevant to this intent, such as the insolvent corporation's need to pay off creditors or to sell assets or divisions to raise cash, are to be taken into account in determining whether a transaction qualifies as a "G" reorganization. For example, a transaction is not precluded from satisfying the "substantially all" test for purposes of the new "G" category merely because, prior to a transfer to the acquiring corporation, payments to creditors and asset sales were made in order to leave the debtor with more manageable operating assets to continue in business.[5]

Relation to other provisions

A transaction which qualifies as a "G" reorganization is not to be treated as also qualifying as a liquidation under section 332, an incorporation under section 351, or a reorganization under another category of section 368(a)(1) of the Code.[6]

---

5. Because the stated intent for adding the new "G" category is not relevant to interpreting the "substantially all" test in the case of other reorganization categories, the comments in the text as to the appropriate interpretation of the "substantially all" test in the context of a "G" reorganization are not intended to apply to, or in any way to affect interpretations under present law of, the "substantially all" test for other reorganization categories.

6. However, if a transfer qualifying as a "G" reorganization also meets the requirements of section 351 or qualifies as a reorganization under section 368(a)(1)(D) of the Code, the "excess liability" rule of section 357(c) applies if any former shareholder of the transferor corporation receives consideration for his stock, but does not apply if no former shareholder of the transferor corporation receives any consideration for his stock (i.e., if the corporation is insolvent). This rule

A transaction in a bankruptcy or similar case which does not satisfy the requirements of new category "G" is not thereby precluded from qualifying as a tax-free reorganization under one of the other categories of section 368(a)(1). For example, an acquisition of the stock of a company in bankruptcy, or a recapitalization of such a company, which transactions are not covered by the new "G" category, can qualify for nonrecognition treatment under sections 368(a)(1)(B) or (E), respectively.

Continuity of interest rules

The "continuity of interest" requirement which the courts and the Treasury have long imposed as a prerequisite for nonrecognition treatment for a corporate reorganization must be met in order to satisfy the requirements of new category "G". Only reorganizations—as distinguished from liquidations in bankruptcy and sales of property to either new or old interests supplying new capital and discharging the obligations of the debtor corporation—can qualify for tax-free treatment.

It is expected that the courts and the Treasury will apply to "G" reorganizations continuity-of-interest rules which take into account the modification by P.L. 95–598 of the "absolute priority" rule. As a result of that modification, shareholders or junior creditors, who might previously have been excluded, may now retain an interest in the reorganized corporation.

For example, if an insolvent corporation's assets are transferred to a second corporation in a bankruptcy case, the most senior class of creditor to receive stock, together with all equal and junior classes (including shareholders who receive any consideration for their stock), should generally be considered the proprietors of the insolvent corporation for "continuity" purposes. However, if the shareholders receive consideration other than stock of the acquiring corporation, the transaction should be examined to determine if it represents a purchase rather than a reorganization.

Thus, short-term creditors who receive stock for their claims may be counted toward satisfying the continuity of interest rule, although any gain or loss realized by such creditors will be recognized for income tax purposes. [For regulations regarding the treatment of creditors' claims as proprietary interests, see Reg. §1.368–1(e)(6). Ed.]

Triangular reorganizations

The bill permits a corporation to acquire a debtor corporation in a "G" reorganization in exchange for stock of the parent of the acquiring corporation rather than for its own stock.

In addition, the bill permits an acquisition in the form of a "reverse merger" of an insolvent corporation (i.e., where no former shareholder of the surviving corporation receives any consideration for his stock) in a bankruptcy or similar case if the former creditors of the surviving corpora-

---

parallels present law, under which insolvency reorganizations under sections 371 or 374 are excluded from the application of section 357(c).

tion exchange their claims for voting stock of the controlling corporation which has a value equal to at least 80 percent of the value of the debt of the surviving corporation.

Transfer to controlled subsidiary

The bill permits a corporation which acquires substantially all the assets of a debtor corporation in a "G" reorganization to transfer the acquired assets to a controlled subsidiary without endangering the tax-free status of the reorganization. This provision places "G" reorganizations on a similar footing with other categories of reorganizations.

Carryover of tax attributes

Under the bill, the statutory rule generally governing carryover of tax attributes in corporate reorganizations (Code sec. 381) also applies in the case of a "G" reorganization. This eliminates the so-called "clean slate" doctrine.

"Principal amount" rule; "boot" test

Under the bill, "G" reorganizations are subject to the rules governing the tax treatment of exchanging shareholders and security holders which apply to other corporate reorganizations.

Accordingly, an exchanging shareholder or security holder of the debtor company who receives securities with a principal amount exceeding the principal amount of securities surrendered is taxable on the excess, and an exchanging shareholder or security holder who surrenders no securities is taxed on the principal amount of any securities received. Also, any "boot" received is subject to the general dividend-equivalence test of Code section 356.

Treatment of accrued interest

Under the bill, a creditor exchanging securities in any corporate reorganization described in section 368 of the Code (including a "G" reorganization) is treated as receiving interest income on the exchange to the extent the security holder receives new securities, stock, or any other property attributable to accrued but unpaid interest (including accrued original issue discount) on the securities surrendered. This provision, which reverses the so-called *Carman* rule, applies whether or not the exchanging security holder realizes gain on the exchange overall. Under this provision, a security holder which had previously accrued the interest (including original issue discount) as income recognizes a loss to the extent the interest is not paid in the exchange.

Example

The reorganization provisions of the bill are illustrated in part by the following example.

Assume that Corporation A is in a bankruptcy case commenced after December 31, 1980. Immediately prior to a transfer under a plan of reorganization, A's assets have an adjusted basis of $75,000 and a fair market value of $100,000. A has a net operating loss carryover of $200,000. A has outstanding bonds of $100,000 (on which there is no accrued but unpaid interest) and trade debts of $100,000.

Under the plan of reorganization, A is to transfer all its assets to Corporation B in exchange for $100,000 of B stock. Corporation A will distribute the stock, in exchange for their claims against A, one-half to the security holders and one-half to the trade creditors. A's shareholders will receive nothing.

The transaction qualifies as a reorganization under new section 368(a)(1)(G) of the Code, since all the creditors are here treated as proprietors for continuity of interest purposes. Thus, A recognizes no gain or loss on the transfer of its assets to B (Code sec. 361). B's basis in the assets is $75,000 (sec. 362), and B succeeds to A's net operating loss carryover (sec. 381).

Under the bill, the pro-rata distribution of B stock to A's creditors does not result in income from discharge of indebtedness [But see I.R.C. § 108(e)(8), which now makes stock-for-debt exchanges subject to Section 108. Ed.]

Assume the same facts as above except that B also transfers $10,000 in cash, which is distributed by A to its creditors. Although A would otherwise recognize gain on the receipt of boot in an exchange involving appreciated property, the distribution by A of the $10,000 cash to those creditors having a proprietary interest in the corporation's assets for continuity of interest purposes prevents A from recognizing any gain (Code sec. 361(b)(1)(A)).[10]

PROBLEM

Debtor Corporation is in bankruptcy. Debtor's assets have an adjusted basis of $75,000 and a value of $100,000, and the corporation has a net operating loss of $200,000, bonds outstanding (with no accrued unpaid interest) of $100,000 and trade debts of $100,000. Debtor transfers all of its assets to Relief Corporation in return for $100,000 of Relief stock which will pass half to the security holders and half to trade creditors. Debtor's shareholders will receive nothing. What are the tax consequences to the parties?

---

10. See Code sec. 371(a)(2)(A) and Treas.Reg. § 1.371–1(b) for a similar rule relating to distribution of boot to creditors in law.an insolvency reorganization under present

CHAPTER 12

CARRYOVERS OF CORPORATE TAX ATTRIBUTES

A. INTRODUCTION

Code: § 381(a). Skim § 381(c).

The Internal Revenue Code contains a comprehensive statutory scheme governing the carryover of various corporate "tax attributes" (such as earnings and profits, net operating losses, and capital loss carryforwards) on corporate acquisitions and other major transactions involving a change of ownership of a corporation. As always, some brief historical background helps to put the current law into perspective.

Prior to 1954, the Code contained few rules regulating the carryover of corporate tax attributes. The Supreme Court merely followed the lead of lower courts[1] in holding that a corporation's earnings and profits could not be eliminated by means of a reorganization but instead the acquiring corporation inherited the target's earnings and profits along with its assets.[2] Because any other approach would have allowed a profitable corporation to use a reorganization to sweep its earnings and profits account clean and diminish future dividends, the Court's decision was no more surprising than the reaction of the tax bar to the proposition that corporate attributes could survive a reorganization. They assumed, or at least hoped, that an acquiring corporation could inherit negative as well as positive tax attributes in a tax-free reorganization or liquidation. If that assumption proved true, profitable corporations could acquire the assets of their unprofitable brethren solely to succeed to the target's earnings and profits deficit and net operating losses (NOLs). The acquiring corporation thus could assure itself that future distributions would be sheltered by the newly acquired earnings and profits deficit and that future income would be effectively exempt from tax because of the newly acquired NOLs.

The Supreme Court responded by holding that earnings and profits deficits did *not* survive a reorganization[3] and that NOLs could be used only by the corporate entity that incurred them.[4] But tax advisors were not to be

---

1. See, e.g., Commissioner v. Sansome, 60 F.2d 931 (2d Cir.1932), cert. denied, 287 U.S. 667, 53 S.Ct. 291 (1932).

2. Commissioner v. Munter, 331 U.S. 210, 67 S.Ct. 1175 (1947).

3. Commissioner v. Phipps, 336 U.S. 410, 69 S.Ct. 616 (1949).

4. New Colonial Ice Co. v. Helvering, 292 U.S. 435, 54 S.Ct. 788 (1934). But see Helvering v. Metropolitan Edison, 306 U.S. 522, 59 S.Ct. 634 (1939), where the Court outdone. Shortly after these decisions, several reorganizations which followed a similar pattern appeared on the scene. Loss Corp., a corporation with NOLs but no current income to absorb them, would acquire the assets of Profit Corp., a successful company, in a tax-free reorganization. In the process, the Profit Corp. shareholders would receive more than enough Loss Corp. stock to control the continuing and expanded Loss Corp. Since Loss Corp. technically was the surviving entity, it retained its NOLs, which then were used to offset the gains generated by the new business. Once again, the Supreme Court was forced to respond to a device involving trafficking in tax attributes. In Libson Shops, Inc. v. Koehler,[5] the Court decided that even if a loss corporation survives a reorganization, NOLs incurred prior to the transaction only could be used to offset post-acquisition gains if they were generated by substantially the same *business* as well as the same entity which had incurred the losses.

With the arrival of the 1954 Internal Revenue Code, the case law regulating the carryover of tax attributes was replaced by a comprehensive statutory scheme.[6] The principal provisions are: (1) Section 381, which generally provides that a target corporation's tax attributes follow its assets in tax-free reorganizations (other than B and E reorganizations) and tax-free liquidations of a subsidiary; (2) Sections 382 and 383, which restrict the carryforward of net operating losses and certain other losses and credits following a substantial change of ownership; (3) Section 384, which limits the use of loss carryforwards to offset certain gains following a corporate acquisition; and (4) Section 269, which allows the Secretary to disallow deductions, credits or other allowances in certain situations where one corporation's stock or assets were acquired for the principal purpose of obtaining the specific deductions, credits or allowances in question. This chapter first considers the general carryover rules and limitations in Section 381 and then turns to the more specialized limitations on loss carryforwards.

B.   SECTION 381 CARRYOVER RULES

Code: § 381(a), (b). Skim § 381(c).

General Carryover Rules. Section 381(a) provides that in a tax-free liquidation of a subsidiary or a reorganization (other than a Type B or E reorganization), the acquiring corporation shall "succeed to and take into account" some 26 specified attributes of the target,[1] including earnings and profits, NOLs, accounting and depreciation methods and capital loss, in-

---

held that these attributes did follow the target's assets in certain mergers.

5. 353 U.S. 382, 77 S.Ct. 990 (1957).

6. Some commentators and courts have suggested that the *Libson Shops* doctrine survived the 1954 Code, but Congress intended specifically not to incorporate the doctrine into the new statutory scheme governing limitations on net operating loss carryforwards. H.R.Rep. No. 99–841, 99th Cong., 2d Sess. II–194 (1986).

1. I.R.C. § 381(c)(1)–(26).

vestment credit and charitable contribution carryovers.[2] In Type B stock-for-stock acquisition and Type E recapitalization, the acquired or recapitalized corporation remains intact after the transaction and thus no carryover mechanism is necessary. In a triangular reorganization where substantially all of the target's assets are transferred to a subsidiary of the issuing corporation, the subsidiary is the "acquiring corporation" and succeeds to the target's attributes.[3]

Earnings and Profits Deficits. Left unchecked, Section 381 would subject the revenue to some of the same abuses already discussed. As we have seen, one promising tax avoidance strategy is presented where Profit Corp. acquires Loss Corp.'s assets in a reorganization and inherits its earnings and profits deficit and NOL carryovers. To some extent, this abuse is limited by Section 381 itself. Section 381(c)(2) restricts Profit Corp.'s ability to rid itself of its own current or accumulated earnings and profits through a simple acquisition of Loss Corp. by providing that an earnings and profits deficit inherited from Loss Corp. may not be applied against any earnings and profits of Profit Corp. that existed prior to the acquisition. Loss Corp.'s deficit therefore only can be used to offset post-acquisition accumulated earnings and profits. If a distribution is made in a post-acquisition year in which there are current earnings and profits, any offsetting accumulated deficit acquired from Loss Corp. is irrelevant in any event, since the distribution will be deemed to come from the current earnings and profits of the taxable year and then from Profit Corp.'s own pre-acquisition accumulated earnings and profits.[4]

Net Operating Losses. Even though Profit Corp. receives little benefit from Loss Corp.'s earnings and profits deficit, Loss's NOL carryovers still might be used to eliminate Profit's own tax liability. Section 381(c)(1) provides complex rules governing the carryover of NOLs, but it does not prevent them from being misused by Profit Corp. Instead, Section 382, which is discussed later in this chapter, is the designated policing agent in this situation.

Rather than Profit Corp. acquiring the assets and tax attributes of Loss Corp., Loss might acquire Profit's assets in a Type A or C reorganization, maintaining Loss's earnings and profits deficit and NOLs without assistance from Section 381, and then might use those negative tax attributes to offset Profit's past and future income. If Profit's shareholders receive sufficient Loss Corp. stock to control the combined company, the transaction in substance is identical to the acquisition of Loss Corp. by Profit. The benefits of this transaction also are limited by both Sections 381(b) and 382. Section 381(b)(3) generally provides that an acquiring

---

2. Cf. I.R.C. § 312(h)(2), which requires a "proper allocation" of earnings and profits between the acquiring corporation and the target if less than 100 percent of the assets are acquired in a Type C or Type D reorganization.

3. Reg. § 1.381(a)–1(b)(2).

4. I.R.C. § 381(c)(2)(B). See Chapter 4, supra. Thus, an acquired earnings and profits deficit will do no more than prevent undistributed current earnings and profits from becoming accumulated earnings and profits in a subsequent year.

corporation may not carry back an NOL incurred after the acquisition to a taxable year of a profitable target corporation.[5] In one of the few cases interpreting the NOL limitation, the Ninth Circuit has held that Section 381(b)(3) does not limit the carryback of an NOL to a pre-acquisition year of a target corporation which merges into a newly formed subsidiary of the acquiring corporation in a forward triangular reorganization.[6] The court concluded that to deny a carryback in this situation would exalt form over substance and would not present the complex accounting problem that motivated Congress to enact the Section 381(b)(3) NOL carryback limitation.

PROBLEMS

1. Acquiring Corporation ("P") acquires the assets of Target Corporation ("T") in a valid Type C reorganization. Both corporations are calendar year taxpayers and the transactions are completed on December 31, 2010.

(a) If P has accumulated earnings and profits of $30,000 and T has an earnings and profits deficit of $50,000, what result to the P shareholders in 2010 if during that year P has $20,000 of current earnings and profits, T breaks even and P distributes $20,000 cash?

(b) What result in (a), above, if P breaks even in 2010 and makes no distributions during that year but distributes $20,000 in 2011, a year when P also breaks even?

(c) What result in (b), above, if in 2010, P has a $10,000 current earnings and profits deficit?

(d) What result in (b), above, if in addition in 2012 P has a $10,000 current earnings and profits deficit and makes a $20,000 cash distribution?

(e) What result in (d), above, if in addition in 2013, P has $20,000 of current earnings and profits and makes a $20,000 cash distribution?

(f) What result in (e), above, if P makes no distribution in 2013, but distributes $40,000 in 2014, a year in which A breaks even.

2. T Corporation merges into P Corporation two-thirds of the way through P's year. What are the results in the following situations:

(a) P has $30,000 of deficit earnings and profits for the entire year of the acquisition and T has $30,000 of accumulated earnings and profits at the date of the acquisition. The combined corporation makes a distribution of $20,000 in the succeeding year when it breaks even.

5. Because these allocation problems do not exist in a Section 332 liquidation of a subsidiary or a Type E or Type F reorganization, the Section 381(b)(3) limitation does not apply to those transactions.

6. Bercy Industries, Inc. v. Commissioner, 640 F.2d 1058 (9th Cir.1981).

(b) Same as (a), above, except that P Corporation has $30,000 of current earnings and profits for the year and T has a $30,000 earnings and profits deficit at the time of the acquisition. The combined corporation again makes a distribution of $20,000 in the succeeding year, when it breaks even.

(c) Same as (b), above, except that the combined corporation makes a distribution of $30,000 on the last day of the year of acquisition.

3. T Corporation merges into P Corporation in a tax-free Type A reorganization in which T shareholders receive 51 percent of the outstanding P stock. Both corporations are calendar year, accrual method taxpayers and the merger occurs on December 31, 2010. Both corporations have been in existence for two years, with T sustaining a $20,000 loss in each of those years and P earning a profit of $30,000 in each year.

(a) May the combined corporation carry back T's losses and apply them against P's profits for 2008 and 2009?

(b) Assuming that the loss and income patterns continue, determine the combined corporation's net income for the years 2011 through 2015.

(c) What results in (b), above, if T were a profitable corporation with net income of $20,000 in each of the prior and current years but P sustained a $100,000 loss in 2011 followed by a return to the regular gain pattern in 2012?

(d) What result in (c), above, if T and P consolidated into C Corporation and C sustained the $100,000 loss in 2011 followed by $50,000 in gains in the succeeding years?

4. Consider the following questions concerning the carryover of net operating losses:

(a) May a Type F reorganization be preferable to a Type A reorganization?

(b) Is there ever an overlap between a Type F and a Type A reorganization?

C. Limitations on Net Operating Loss Carryforwards: Section 382

1. Introduction

Code: Skim § 382(a), (b)(1), (g)(1), (i)(1)

Before examining the Section 382 limitations on carryovers of corporate NOLs, it is helpful to review the concept of a net operating loss. In general, a net operating loss, often identified by its "NOL" monogram, is the excess of business deductions allowed by the Code over the taxpayer's gross income in a single taxable period.[1] A net operating loss ordinarily may be carried back to the two taxable years preceding the loss year and may be carried forward to the 20 following years.[2] An NOL carryback reduces the taxpayer's taxable income in the earlier year and typically results in a refund. Carryforwards serve as deductions in the subsequent years to which they are carried and reduce the tax due for those periods. NOLs first must be carried to the earliest available year and, to the extent not used, are then carried forward to the next available taxable periods.[3] Net operating losses thus stand as an exception to the annual taxable year concept. The purpose of the carryover scheme is to serve as an averaging device that ameliorates the harsh consequences that would result for a business taxpayer with a fluctuating economic track record. As the Supreme Court has described NOL carryovers, "[t]hey were designed to permit a taxpayer to set off its lean years against its lush years, and to strike something like an average taxable income computed over a period longer than one year."[4] All of this works smoothly in the corporate setting if the owners of the entity are unchanged during the 23–year carryover period. Section 382 addresses the problems that arise if the ownership of a loss corporation changes at a time that the company has unexpired net operating losses.

A profitable company seeking tax savings may be tempted to acquire a corporation with NOL carryovers to use those deductions to shelter its taxable income. To illustrate, assume that Mr. Loser forms Loss Co. to engage in the manufacture and sale of passing fads. The company is initially capitalized with $1,000,000, all represented by Mr. Loser's equity investment. Despite Loser's high hopes, Loss Co. incurs $999,999 in deductible expenses in the first two years of its operation and never earns a cent. At the end of two years, the company has nothing left except $1 in its checking account and a $999,999 NOL deduction that is useless because Loss Co. has no income to offset. At that point, the company is worth $1 plus the value, if any, of its deductions. If Loss Co. is liquidated, the sad story ends. If Loser infuses new property or cash into the corporation to keep the business afloat, then Loss Co. may deduct its loss carryforwards against any future income as long as Loser continues to own a controlling interest in the company.

But what if Profit Co., shopping around for tax deductions, learns of Loss Co.'s difficulties? If Profit wishes to acquire Loss, it has many options. It could: (1) acquire all of Loss Co.'s assets (i.e., $1) in exchange for Profit Co. stock in an acquisitive Type A or C tax-free reorganization, as a result of which Profit Co. would inherit all of Loss Co.'s tax attributes (i.e., its

---

1. See generally I.R.C. § 172.

2. I.R.C. § 172(b)(1)(A). The carryback period is sometimes extended to provide relief to taxpayers who have suffered economic hardship. For example, economic stimulus legislation extended the carryback period for certain 2008 and 2009 losses to up to five years for certain electing small businesses.

Similar extensions have been granted for taxpayers with losses from Federally declared disasters, such as hurricanes and floods.

3. I.R.C. § 172(b).

4. United States v. Foster Lumber Co., 429 U.S. 32, 97 S.Ct. 204 (1976).

$999,999 NOL deduction);[1] (2) acquire the stock of Loss Co. in either a taxable purchase, a tax-free Type B reorganization, or reverse triangular merger, and later liquidate Loss Co. under Section 332, thereby inheriting its NOL carryforwards;[2] (3) acquire Loss Co.'s stock and then transfer its own assets into Loss Co. in a Section 351 exchange; in that case Loss Co., now a wholly owned subsidiary of Profit Co., can operate the Profit business while retaining its own NOLs; or (4) Loss Co. can acquire the assets of Profit Co. in an acquisitive tax-free reorganization by exchanging enough Loss Co. stock to give the Profit Co. shareholders virtually 100 percent ownership of Loss Co. The Profit Co. shareholders then will own Loss Co., which will own all of old Profit Co.'s assets plus a $999,999 NOL carryforward.

Is something wrong here? If Loss Co. lost money, should its NOLs be available to offset Profit's future income or should the use of those NOLs be limited to offsetting later income earned by Loss? Should Profit be able to avoid tax on $999,999 of its future income by acquiring (or being acquired by) the corporate shell of an unsuccessful business?

After pondering these questions for many years, Congress enacted ineffective legislation in the 1954 Code aimed at limiting the use of NOL carryforwards in the corporate acquisitions setting. Amendments followed in 1976, but they were so unappealing that their effective date was delayed four times until 1986, when they were discarded completely in favor of a new Section 382.[3] The current statutory scheme is the outgrowth of decades of study, most notably the Subchapter C Project of the American Law Institute and the Senate Finance Committee staff's Subchapter C study.[4]

When applicable, Section 382 limits the use of a loss corporation's NOL carryforwards when there is a change of ownership of more than 50 percent of the stock of that company over a period of three years or less.[5] Stating this general rule in the language of the Code, the loss limitations are triggered only after an "ownership change,"[6] which is either an "owner shift involving a 5–percent shareholder", or an "equity structure shift,"[7] coupled with a more than 50 percent increase in the stock ownership of "5–

1. I.R.C. § 381(a)(2).

2. I.R.C. § 381(a)(1). If the liquidation occurs immediately after a Type B reorganization, it would be treated as a Type C reorganization. See Rev.Rul. 67–274, 1967–2 C.B. 141; Chapter 9B3, supra. In addition, if Profit Co. acquires the Loss Co. stock and files a consolidated return, the availability of Loss Co.'s losses will be limited by the consolidated return regulations. See Section D3 of this chapter, infra.

3. See generally Jacobs, "Tax Treatment of Corporate Net Operating Losses and Other Tax Attribute Carryovers," 5 Va. Tax Rev. 701 (1986).

4. See American Law Institute, Federal Income Tax Project, Subchapter C (1986); Staff of the Senate Finance Committee, The Subchapter C Revision Act of 1985: A Final Report Prepared by the Staff, 99th Cong., 1st Sess. 32–35, 55–56, 68–71 (S.Prt. 99–47, 1985); Eustice, "Alternatives for Limiting Loss Carryovers," 22 San Diego L.Rev. 149 (1985).

5. I.R.C. § 382(g)(1), (i).

6. I.R.C. § 382(a), (g), (k)(3).

7. I.R.C. § 382(g), (k)(7).

percent shareholders" which occurs during a three-year "testing period".[8] If Section 382 is triggered, it limits the use by a "new loss corporation" of any NOLs of an "old loss corporation" for any "post-change year" (i.e., any year after the ownership change).[9] In general, the taxable income of a new loss corporation that may be offset by preacquisition NOLs is limited to the value of the old loss corporation's stock on the date of the ownership change multiplied by a prescribed "long-term tax-exempt rate."[10] These and many other statutory terms will be explained in detail later in the chapter.

The rationale of Section 382 is to allow a loss company's NOLs to offset only the future income generated by that company's business. If the section is triggered by an ownership change, its limitations apply in two different ways. First, if the Loss Co. business is not continued (or substantially all of its assets are not used) for at least two years after the change of ownership, all of its NOLs are disallowed.[11] Second, if the Loss Co. business is continued or if its assets are used for at least two years, the losses are allowable only to the extent of the income generated from the old Loss Co.'s assets. Because the transactions that trigger Section 382 may involve the combining of a loss company with a profitable company, it may be impossible to determine exactly what part of the combined company's income is generated by the Loss Co.'s business or assets. Section 382 solves this problem by adopting a method to approximate Loss Co.'s income. It irrebuttably assumes that the return on Loss Co.'s equity will be the rate of return payable on long-term tax-exempt bonds. Thus, in any year, Loss Co.'s NOLs can be used by the combined company only to the extent of the value of old Loss Co. multiplied by an assumed return on equity known as the long-term tax-exempt rate.[12] These basic rules are augmented by attribution rules, technical adjustments and a swarm of anti-avoidance provisions that give new dimension to Congressional paranoia.

Our study of Section 382 begins with an examination of the ownership change requirement and then turns to the effect of such a change on the ability to use Loss Co.'s NOL carryforwards.

2.   THE OWNERSHIP CHANGE REQUIREMENTS

Code: § 382(g), (i), (k), (l)(3) & (4). See § 318.

In General. Since the economic burden of corporate losses falls on the individuals who were shareholders when the corporation was losing money, the Section 382 limitations do not intercede as long as those individuals continue as shareholders. After all, they suffered through the losses, so it is only fair to give them the benefit of the accompanying tax deductions.

---

8.   I.R.C. § 382(g), (i), (k)(7).

9.   I.R.C. § 382(a), (d)(2). The "new loss corporation" is the successor to Loss Co. in a merger or asset acquisition; it is Loss Co. itself in a stock acquisition. See I.R.C. § 382(k)(3). The "old loss corporation" is Loss Co. prior to the ownership change. I.R.C. § 382(k)(2).

10.   I.R.C. § 382(b)(1).

11.   I.R.C. § 382(c).

12.   I.R.C. § 382(b)(1).

Consequently, Section 382 applies only if there is an "ownership change," which occurs if the percentage of Loss Co. stock owned by one or more "5–percent shareholders" increases by more than 50 percentage points[1] during the three-year "testing period."[2] Thus, if Profit Co. purchases 51 percent or more of Loss Co.'s stock within a three-year period, or if Loss Co. is acquired in a corporate reorganization and its ownership changes by more than 50 percent, the loss limitations will apply. Similarly, if ten unrelated individuals each purchase six percent of the Loss Co. stock, Section 382 applies.

These various types of ownership changes are divided by the statute into two categories: an "owner shift involving a 5–percent shareholder" and an "equity structure shift."[3] An "owner shift" generally occurs upon any change in the stock ownership (either an increase or a decrease) of any 5–percent or more shareholder (e.g., the taxable purchases illustrated above).[4] An "equity structure shift" includes tax-free reorganizations, certain public offerings and reorganization-type transactions such as cash mergers.[5]

Owner Shift Involving 5–Percent Shareholder. An owner shift involving a 5–percent shareholder is any change in stock ownership (increase or decrease) that affects the percentage of stock owned by any person who is a 5–percent shareholder before or after the change.[6] Most owner shifts are purchases. Thus, if Profit Co. purchases 10 percent of Loss Co. stock from one shareholder, an owner shift has occurred. Apart from purchases, owner shifts can occur as a result of Section 351 exchanges, redemptions, issuances of stock, or recapitalizations.[7] However, the statute specifically excludes owner shifts as a result of a gift, death or divorce transfer.[8] Changes in proportionate ownership attributable solely to fluctuations in the market value of different classes of stock also are disregarded, except to the extent provided in regulations.[9]

Keep in mind that a single "owner shift" is not enough to trigger Section 382; there also must be a more than 50 percent change in ownership of Loss Co.[10] And while a more than 50 percentage point change in ownership is an essential ingredient in the Section 382 recipe, it is not the only one. Here is where the "5–percent shareholder" concept enters the scene. Consider, for example, the consequences of a simple 50 percent change in ownership rule to a publicly traded company that has loss carryforwards. Those NOLs might be limited as a result of random public trading if more than 50 percent of the company's shares happened to

---

1. I.R.C. § 382(g)(1).

2. Id. I.R.C. § 382(i)(1).

3. I.R.C. § 382(g)(2), (3).

4. I.R.C. § 382(g)(2).

5. I.R.C. § 382(g)(3). Regulations designating taxable reorganization-type transactions as equity structure shifts have not yet been issued. See Reg. § 1.382–2T(e)(2)(ii).

6. I.R.C. § 382(g)(2). A 5–percent shareholder is defined as any person holding 5 percent or more of the stock of the loss corporation at any time during the three year testing period. I.R.C. § 382(k)(7).

7. Reg. § 1.382–2T(e)(1).

8. I.R.C. § 382(l)(3)(B).

9. I.R.C. § 382(l)(3)(C).

10. I.R.C. § 382(g)(1).

change hands during a three-year period. To preclude such a result, the type of "owner shift" required to trigger Section 382 occurs only if the percentage of stock of Loss Co. owned by one or more "5–percent shareholders" increases by the requisite 50 percent.[11]

A rule that only counted the increased ownership of 5–percent shareholders might be easily circumvented. For example, a shareholder who held Loss Co. stock while the losses were incurred might sell four percent interests to 25 equal purchasers rather than to a single individual. In so doing, the owner would avoid selling any of his stock to a 5–percent shareholder despite an obvious sale and purchase of tax benefits. To assure that the loss limitations apply in these circumstances, Section 382 generally treats all less than 5–percent shareholders as a single 5–percent shareholder.[12] Thus, the sales to 25 four percent shareholders in the example are treated as sales to a single 5–percent shareholder, and the Section 382 limits apply because that 5–percent shareholder's ownership shifts from zero percent to 100 percent. But in the earlier publicly traded example, the group of less than 5–percent shareholders always would have held 100 percent both before and after the transfers, and thus Section 382 would not apply. Unfortunately, not all "owner shifts" are the result of such simple purchases. The problems at the end of this section explore some of these additional complications.

Equity Structure Shifts. Recall that Section 382 first must be triggered by either an "owner shift involving a 5–percent shareholder" or an "equity structure shift,"[13] either of which must result in an "ownership change." An "equity structure shift" is defined to include tax-free reorganizations[14] and certain taxable "reorganization-type" transactions, public offerings and similar transactions.[15] Consequently, if there is a shift in the ownership of Loss Co. stock in a reorganization, which when combined with any other stock transfers within the three-year period results in a more than 50 percent change of ownership, such an equity structure shift will bring the Section 382 limitations into play.[16]

Special Rules for Determining Change in Ownership. In determining whether a change in ownership has occurred, reorganizations involve some special complications. In a Type A or C reorganization, the acquiring company that inherits the loss is probably an entirely different company from Loss Co. In that event, what ownership is tested under Section 382? This question is answered indirectly by Section 382(k), which defines the "loss corporation" affected by Section 382 as the corporation entitled to use

---

11. I.R.C. § 382(g)(1)(A).

12. I.R.C. § 382(g)(4)(A).

13. I.R.C. § 382(g)(1).

14. I.R.C. § 382(g)(3)(A). Some reorganizations are excluded from the definition of "equity structure shift." Section 382(g)(3)(A) excludes a Type D or G reorganization, unless the requirements of Section 354(b)(1) are met, and a Type F reorganization.

15. I.R.C. § 382(g)(3)(B). The regulations have not yet identified the reorganization-type transactions covered by this rule. See Reg. § 1.382–2T(e)(2)(ii).

16. The regulations acknowledge that any equity structure shift affecting a 5–percent shareholder is also an owner shift. Reg. § 1.382–2T(e)(2)(iii).

the loss after the ownership change. Thus, in a Type A statutory merger or a Type C stock-for-assets reorganization involving a loss corporation and another corporation, the limits apply to the survivor. In order to determine the extent of ownership change that has occurred, the ownership of the surviving corporation must be compared to the pre-reorganization ownership of the old Loss Co. In effect, the statute looks at the pre-and post-reorganization ownership of whatever company possesses the losses—whether this is the acquiring corporation or the target. For example, if Loss Co. is merged into Profit Co., Section 382 requires a comparison of the ownership of pre-merger Loss Co. and post-merger Profit Co. If the pre-merger Loss Co. shareholders own at least 50 percent of the post-merger Profit Co. (defined as "new loss corporation")[17] an ownership change within the meaning of Section 382(g) will not have occurred. On the other hand, if Loss Co. acquires the stock (in a Type B reorganization or reverse triangular merger) or assets (in a Type A or C reorganization, or a forward triangular merger) of Profit Co. in exchange for Loss Co. stock, Section 382 will apply unless at least 50 percent of the post-reorganization Loss Co. stock continues to be owned by the pre-reorganization Loss Co. shareholders.

In order to assure proper results in the context of the fusion of two corporations, one more special rule is required. All shareholders who own less than five percent of a company's stock generally are treated as a single 5–percent shareholder[18]. In a reorganization (an "equity structure shift" for Section 382 purposes), there may be at least two groups of less than 5–percent shareholders—in our examples, the shareholders of Loss Co. and those of Profit Co. If these two groups were treated as a single shareholder, virtually all reorganizations of publicly held companies would escape Section 382. For example, assume that Loss Co. and Profit Co. are both public companies, with no shareholder owning stock of both and no individual owning (directly or indirectly) five percent of either company. If Profit Co. acquires the Loss Co. assets in a merger pursuant to which the old Loss Co. shareholders receive enough Profit Co. stock to become, as a group, 15 percent shareholders of Profit Co., it would appear that Section 382 should apply because the Profit Co. shareholders went from zero to 85 percent ownership of the "new loss corporation." But if all less-than–5–percent shareholders of Loss Co. and Profit Co. are treated as a single shareholder, 100 percent ownership of Loss Co. has remained within the exclusive ownership of that "single" shareholder—i.e., the group of less than 5–percent shareholders owned all of Loss Co. and all of Profit Co. and still owns all of Profit Co. In order to assure that Section 382 will apply in this and similar situations, the statute segregates public shareholders by providing that the group of less than 5–percent shareholders of Profit Co. and the group of less than 5–percent shareholders of Loss Co. are treated as separate shareholders.[19] In the example, ownership of Loss Co. by the

17. I.R.C. § 382(k)(3).

18. I.R.C. § 382(g)(4)(A).

19. I.R.C. § 382(g)(4)(B)(i).

Profit Co. shareholders will have increased from zero to 85 percent and Section 382 therefore will apply.

Attribution Rules. The rules outlined above are buttressed by a set of attribution rules that borrows from and expands upon the attribution regime of Section 318.[20] In general, they treat all stock as owned by individuals, and only actual or constructive ownership by individuals is relevant in testing whether an ownership change has taken place under Section 382. As illustrated by the *Garber Industries* case, which follows, the attribution rules can raise challenging issues of statutory interpretation even in the simplest family settings.

Garber Industries Holding Co. v. Commissioner

United States Tax Court, 2005.
124 T.C. 1.

■ HALPERN, J.

By notice of deficiency dated June 21, 2001, respondent determined deficiencies in petitioner's Federal income taxes for petitioner's 1997 and 1998 taxable (calendar) years in the amounts of $4,916 and $301,835, respectively. The parties have settled all issues save one, leaving for our decision only the question of whether a 1998 stock sale between siblings that increased one sibling's percentage ownership of petitioner by more than 50 percentage points resulted in an ownership change for purposes of section 382, triggering that section's limitation on net operating loss (NOL) carryovers. That issue turns on the interpretation of section 382(l)(3)(A)(i), a matter of first impression for this Court.

Unless otherwise indicated, all section references are to the Internal Revenue Code in effect for 1998, and all Rule references are to the Tax Court Rules of Practice and Procedure. For the sake of convenience, all percentages are rounded to the nearest full percent.

FINDINGS OF FACT

* * *

At the time of petitioner's incorporation in December 1982, Charles M. Garber, Sr. (Charles), and his brother, Kenneth R. Garber, Sr. (Kenneth) (collectively, sometimes, the Garber brothers), owned 68 percent and 26 percent, respectively, of petitioner's common stock. The spouses, children, and other siblings of the Garber brothers owned the remaining shares of such stock. The Garber brothers' parents, who are deceased, never owned any of petitioner's stock.

On or about July 10, 1996, petitioner underwent a reorganization described in section 368(a)(1)(D) (the reorganization). Pursuant to the reorganization, petitioner canceled Charles's original stock certificate for 3,492.85 shares and issued a new certificate to him for 386 shares. As a

---

20. I.R.C. § 382(l)(3).

result, Charles's percentage ownership of petitioner decreased from 68 percent to 19 percent, and Kenneth's percentage ownership of petitioner increased from 26 percent to 65 percent.

On April 1, 1998, Kenneth sold all of his shares in petitioner to Charles (the 1998 transaction). As a result of the 1998 transaction, Charles's percentage ownership of petitioner increased from 19 percent to 84 percent.

On its 1998 consolidated Federal income tax return, petitioner claimed an NOL deduction in the amount of $808,935 for regular tax purposes and $728,041 for alternative minimum tax (AMT) purposes. As one of the adjustments giving rise to the deficiencies here in question, respondent adjusted the amount of petitioner's 1998 NOL deduction, for both regular tax and AMT purposes, to $121,258 pursuant to section 382(b). Petitioner assigns error to that adjustment.

OPINION

I.   Substantive Law

A.   Overview of Section 382

Section 382(a) limits the amount of "pre-change losses" that a corporation (referred to as a loss corporation) may use to offset taxable income in the taxable years or periods following an ownership change. "Pre-change losses" include NOL carryovers to the taxable year in which the ownership change occurs and any NOL incurred during that taxable year to the extent such NOL is allocable to the portion of the year ending on the date of the ownership change. Sec. 382(d)(1). An ownership change is deemed to have occurred if, on a required measurement date (a testing date), the aggregate percentage ownership interest of one or more 5–percent shareholders of the loss corporation is more than 50 percentage points greater than the lowest percentage ownership interest of such shareholder(s) during the (generally) 3–year period immediately preceding such testing date (the testing period). Sec. 382(g)(1) and (2), (i); sec. 1.382–2(a)(4), Income Tax Regs.

B.   Determining Stock Ownership for Purposes of Section 382

Section 382(l)(3)(A) provides that, with certain exceptions, the constructive ownership rules of section 318 apply in determining stock ownership. Under the first of those exceptions, set forth in section 382(l)(3)(A)(i), the family attribution rules of section 318(a)(1) and (5)(B) do not apply; instead, an individual and all members of his family described in section 318(a)(1) (spouse, children, grandchildren, and parents) are treated as one individual.

C.   Regulations

The family aggregation rule of section 382(l)(3)(A)(i) is further addressed in section 1.382–2T(h)(6), Temporary Income Tax Regs., 52 Fed. Reg. 29686 (Aug. 11, 1987). Paragraph (h)(6)(ii) of that section repeats the general rule that, for purposes of section 382, an individual and all members of his family described in section 318(a)(1) are treated as one individual.[6] Paragraph (h)(6)(iv) provides further that, if an individual may be treated as a member of more than one family under paragraph (h)(6)(ii), such individual will be treated as a member of the family with the smallest increase in percentage ownership (to the exclusion of all other families).

II.   Arguments of the Parties

A.   Petitioner's Argument

Petitioner argues that, although siblings are not family members described in section 318(a)(1), Charles and Kenneth are nonetheless members of the same family when such determination is made by reference to their parents and grandparents. That is, as sons, they are both members of each family consisting of a parent and that parent's family members described in section 318(a)(1). Similarly, as grandsons, they are both members of each family consisting of a grandparent and that grandparent's family members described in section 318(a)(1). Accordingly, petitioner argues, Charles and Kenneth are treated as one individual under section 382(*l*)(3)(A)(i), with the result that transactions between them are disregarded for purposes of section 382.

B.   Respondent's Argument

Respondent maintains that the family aggregation rule applies solely with reference to living individuals. Under that view, inasmuch as none of the parents and grandparents of the Garber brothers was alive at the commencement of the 3–year testing period immediately preceding the 1998 transaction, from that point forward there was no individual, within the meaning of section 382(*l*)(3)(A)(i), whose family members (as described in section 318(a)(1)) included both Charles and Kenneth. It follows, respondent argues, that Charles and Kenneth are not treated as one individual for purposes of section 382 and that the 1998 transaction resulted in an ownership change with respect to petitioner under section 382.

III.   Analysis

A.   General Principles of Statutory Construction

As a general matter, if the language of a statute is unambiguous on its face, we apply the statute in accordance with its terms, without resort to extrinsic interpretive aids such as legislative history. * * * Accordingly, our initial inquiry is whether the language of section 382(*l*)(3)(A)(i) is so plain as to permit only one reasonable interpretation insofar as the question presented in this case is concerned. * * *. That threshold determination must be made with reference to the context in which such language appears. Id.

---

6.   The family aggregation rule does not apply, however, to any family member who, without regard to aggregation, would not be a 5–percent shareholder. Sec. 1.382–2T(h)(6)(iii), Temporary Income Tax Regs., 52 Fed.Reg. 29686 (Aug. 11, 1987). That exception in turn does not apply if the loss corporation has actual knowledge of such family member's stock ownership. *Id.;* sec. 1.382–2T(k)(2), Temporary Income Tax Regs., *supra* at 29694.

B.   Language of Section 382(*l*)(3)(A)(I)

Section 382(*l*)(3)(A)(i) provides as follows:

> (A) Constructive ownership.—Section 318 (relating to constructive ownership of stock) shall apply in determining ownership of stock, except that–
>
>> (i) paragraphs (1) and (5)(B) of section 318(a) shall not apply and an individual and all members of his family described in paragraph (1) of section 318(a) shall be treated as 1 individual for purposes of applying this section * * *

Respondent apparently would limit our textual analysis to a single word. According to respondent, Charles and Kenneth are not common members of any individual's family under section 382(*l*)(3)(A)(i) "[b]ecause the commonly used meaning of the term 'individual' does not include a deceased parent". We believe respondent's focus is too narrow. As stated by the Court of Appeals for the Fifth Circuit:

> However, even apparently plain words, divorced from the context in which they arise and in which their creators intended them to function, may not accurately convey the meaning the creators intended to impart. It is only, therefore, within a context that a word, any word, can communicate an idea.

Leach v. FDIC, 860 F.2d 1266, 1270 (5th Cir.1988). In our view, the question is not whether the noun "individual", standing alone, typically denotes a living person–typically it does. The question, rather, is whether the language of section 382(*l*)(3)(A)(i) as a whole definitively establishes, one way or the other, that the identification of a (living) individual whose family members are aggregated thereunder must be made, as respondent maintains (or need not be made, as petitioner maintains), coincident with the determination of stock ownership under section 382 (i.e., on a testing date or at any point during a testing period). Stated negatively, is the language of section 382(*l*)(3)(A)(i) so plain as to preclude either party's position, as so identified?

We are satisfied that the language of section 382(*l*)(3)(A)(i) can variably (and reasonably) be interpreted as being consistent with each party's position in this case. That is, there is nothing in the language of the statute that would make either party's position patently untenable. While a rule attributing stock owned by an individual on a measurement date to members of his family presupposes that the individual is alive, the same need not be said of a rule (such as that contained in section 382(*l*)(3)(A)(i)) that identifies (by reference to an individual) the members of a family that, on some measurement date, are to be treated as a single shareholder. By the same token, the language of section 382(*l*)(3)(A)(i) certainly does not *compel* the conclusion that the individual whose family members are so aggregated need not be alive on that measurement date. Because the answer to our inquiry is not apparent from the face of the statute, we may look beyond the language of section 382(*l*)(3)(A)(i) for interpretive guidance.

C. Legislative History of Section 382(*l*)(3)(A)(I)

Congress enacted the family aggregation rule of section 382(*l*)(3)(A)(i) as part of its overhaul of section 382 included in the Tax Reform Act of 1986, * * * The rule first appeared in the conference committee bill. The conference committee report that accompanied that bill (the 1986 conference report) does not address the temporal aspect of family aggregation identified above: "The family attribution rules of sections 318(a)(1) and 318(a)(5)(B) do not apply, but an individual, his spouse, his parents, his children, and his grandparents are treated as a single shareholder." H. Conf. Rept. 99–841 (Vol.II), at II–182 (1986), 1986–3 C.B. (Vol.4) 1, 182.[10]

D. Other Considerations

1. Family Aggregation Under Pre–1986 Act Section 382

a. General Structure of the Statute

Prior to the amendment of section 382 by the 1986 Act, section 382 contained separate rules for ownership changes resulting from purchases and redemptions, see former sec. 382(a), and those resulting from corporate reorganizations, see former sec. 382(b). Under the "purchase" rules of former section 382(a), ownership changes were ascertained by reference to the holdings of the 10 largest shareholders at the end of the corporation's taxable year (as compared to their holdings at the beginning of such taxable year or the preceding taxable year). Former sec. 382(a)(1) and (2).

b. Family Attribution and Aggregation

Intrafamily sales were excluded from the operation of former section 382(a) by means of stock attribution (as opposed to shareholder aggregation) rules. Specifically, purchases of stock from persons whose stock ownership would be attributed to the purchaser under the family attribution rules of section 318 were ignored for purposes of determining whether an ownership change by "purchase" had occurred. See former sec. 382(a)(3) and (4). Although family members were potentially subject to aggregation for purposes of determining the 10 largest shareholders at year-end, that rule applied only if loss corporation stock owned by one was attributed to the other under the family attribution rules of section 318. Former sec. 382(a)(2) and (3). For that reason, the aggregation rule of former section 382(a)(2), unlike the aggregation rule of section 382(*l*)(3)(A)(i), necessarily applied as of the date on which stock ownership was measured (in the case of former section 382(a)(2), at year end). Accordingly, no inference can be drawn from former section 382(a)(2) as to whether, as respondent maintains, the identification of the individuals whose family members are aggregated under section 382(*l*)(3)(A)(i) occurs as of the date on which stock ownership is measured.

---

10. As noted *supra* part I.B., the members of an individual's family described in sec. 318(a)(1) (to which sec. 382(*l*)(3)(A)(i) refers) are his spouse, children, grandchildren, and parents. Regarding the possible significance of the conferees' reference to "grandparents" in lieu of "grandchildren", see *infra* part III.E.4.

2. Practical Consequences of Each Party's Interpretation of Section 382(l)(3)(A)(I)

a. Petitioner's Interpretation

Under petitioner's interpretation of section 382(l)(3)(A)(i), an individual would be aggregated with (and therefore could, without any section 382 consequences, sell loss corporation shares to) not only his spouse, children, grandchildren, and parents, but also his siblings, nephews, nieces, grandparents, in-laws, great-grandchildren, aunts, uncles, first cousins, and great-grandparents.[12] It is difficult to believe that Congress intended to expand the scope of exempted intrafamily sales so significantly (as compared to both the then-existing version of section 382, see *supra* part III.D.1.b., and the House and Senate versions of revised section 382, see *supra* note 9) with nary a mention of that objective in the 27 pages devoted to section 382 in the 1986 conference report.

b. Respondent's Interpretation

Respondent's interpretation of section 382(l)(3)(A)(i) is perhaps even more troubling than petitioner's. First, it has the potential for being just as expansive as petitioner's interpretation.[13] More importantly, respondent's interpretation leads to arbitrary distinctions. As relevant to this case, respondent would have us believe that the ability of siblings to sell loss corporation shares among themselves without any section 382 consequences is wholly dependent on the continued good health of their parents. We see no rational basis for Congress's having drawn a distinction in this context between siblings whose parents happen to be living and those whose parents happen to be deceased; the former are no more related than the latter.

E. A Third Interpretation

1. Introduction

Our own analysis of the legislative evolution of section 382(l)(3)(A)(i) leads us to believe that both parties have erroneously interpreted that provision. For the reasons discussed below, we conclude that Congress most likely intended the aggregation rule of section 382(l)(3)(A)(i) to apply solely

---

12. As a member of each parent's family (i.e., in his capacity as a child of those parents), an individual would be aggregated with his parents' children (his siblings), grandchildren (his nephews and nieces), and parents (his grandparents). As a member of his spouse's family (i.e., in his capacity as her spouse), an individual would be aggregated with his spouse's parents (his mother-and father-in-law). As a member of each child's family (i.e., in his capacity as a parent of those children), an individual would be aggregated with each child's spouse (his sons-and daughters-in-law) and grandchildren (his great-grandchildren). As a member of each grandparent's family (i.e., in his capacity as a grandchild of those grandparents), an individual would be aggregated with his grandparents' children (his aunts and uncles), grandchildren (his first cousins), and parents (his great-grandparents). See secs. 382(l)(3)(A)(i), 318(a)(1).

13. Respondent's interpretation of the statute differs from petitioner's in that respondent would require that the relevant parent, spouse, child, or grandparent of the individual in question be living when stock ownership is measured. See *supra* note 12.

from the perspective of individuals who are shareholders (as determined under the *attribution* rules of section 382(*l*)(3)(A)) of the loss corporation.[14] In practical terms, our conclusion dictates that we sustain respondent's determination in this case, even though we disagree with his interpretation of the statute.

2.   1986 Act Revisions to Section 382

a.   Relevant Fundamental Changes to the Statute

Among other things, section 621(a) of the 1986 Act replaced the "purchase" rules of former section 382(a) with the concept of the "owner shift", defined broadly to include any change in the respective ownership of the stock of a corporation. Sec. 382(g)(2)(A). The occurrence of an owner shift involving a 5–percent shareholder, see sec. 382(g)(2)(B), (k)(7), is one of two occasions for opening the corporation's stock transfer books to determine whether the aggregate percentage ownership interest of one or more such shareholders has increased by more than 50 percentage points within the relevant "lookback" (testing) period.[15] See sec. 382(g)(1), (i). While the owner shift "trigger" presupposes some type of transaction in the stock of the loss corporation, see H. Conf. Rept. 99–841 (Vol.II), supra at II–174, 1986–3 C.B. (Vol.4) at 174, the requisite increase in stock ownership within the resulting testing period need not be attributable to a purchase, redemption, or, indeed, any transaction in which shares actually change hands, see sec. 382(g)(1)(A) and (B).

b.   Consequences for Family Attribution: Changes in Family Status

Under a system in which an increase in one's percentage ownership of a corporation need not be associated with a transaction in which shares actually change hands, a straightforward application of the family attribution rules of section 318(a) could produce "artificial" ownership increases; i.e., ownership increases solely attributable to changes in family status. For instance, under the attribution rules, the ownership percentage of an individual who marries the sole shareholder of a loss corporation would thereby increase from zero to 100 percent. If the wedding occurred during a testing period (which could be triggered, for instance, by the subsequent issuance of a relatively small number of additional shares to a key employee), then the increase in the nonshareholder spouse's deemed ownership percentage would result in an ownership change. A similar result presumably would occur if the shareholder legally adopted someone during a testing period. See sec. 318(a)(1)(B).

c.   House Bill Provision Regarding Changes in Family Status

The House version of revised section 382 provided that the family attribution rule of section 318(a)(1) would apply "by assuming that the

---

14. In other words, composite shareholders are to be constructed only around individuals who directly or indirectly (through an entity or by means of an option) own shares of the loss corporation.

15. The other such occasion is the occurrence of an equity structure shift (in general, most corporate reorganizations). See sec. 382(g)(1), (3).

family status as of the close of the testing period was the same as the family status as of the beginning of the testing period". H.R. 3838, 99th Cong., 1st Sess. sec. 321(a) (1985) (provision designated as sec. 382(n)(3)(A)). Although the report of the Committee on Ways and Means accompanying the House bill provides no additional insight, see H. Rept. 99–426, at 266 (1985), 1986–3 C.B. (Vol.2) 1, 266, the practical effect of that provision would have been to eliminate the possibility that a change in family status during a testing period could, in and of itself, contribute to an ownership change.[17] The conference committee, in addition to substituting family aggregation for family attribution, dropped the provision in the House bill regarding changes in family status.[18]

d.   Observations

In the context of the parties' arguments in this case, the conference committee's excision of the House bill provision regarding changes in family status is somewhat puzzling. Specifically, under each party's interpretation of section 382(l)(3)(A)(i), the family aggregation rule adopted by the conferees would produce the same "artificial" ownership increases that the House bill provision eliminated in the context of attribution. In terms of our marriage hypothetical, the addition of the shareholder spouse to the nonshareholder spouse's family unit during the testing period would increase the ownership percentage of that family unit by 100 percentage points during that period. If, however, the family aggregation rule applies solely from the perspective of shareholders of the loss corporation, there would be no separate family unit headed by the nonshareholder spouse in our hypothetical and, consequently, (1) no increase in ownership attributable to the marriage, and (2) no need for the remedial provision contained in the House bill. Under that interpretation of the family aggregation rule, the conference committee's excision of the House bill's family status provision makes perfect sense.

3.   Revisiting the Language of the Statute

That our interpretation of section 382(l)(3)(A)(i) provides a cogent explanation for the conference committee's action is of no consequence if a plain reading of the statute does not permit that interpretation. See *supra* part III.A. The use of the term "individual" in section 382(l)(3)(A)(i), however, does not preclude a contextual interpretation pursuant to which the set of individuals contemplated by Congress (i.e., individuals who own shares of the loss corporation) is smaller than the universe of all possible

17. Returning to our marriage hypothetical, under the House bill's provision, the couple's relationship on the testing date would have been deemed to be the same as it was at the beginning of the testing period (i.e., not married), with the result that the nonshareholder spouse's ownership percentage would have been deemed to be zero throughout the testing period.

18. The Senate version of the bill contained no such provision, providing instead for the application of the family attribution rules of sec. 318 without modification. H.R. 3838, 99th Cong., 2d Sess. sec. 621(a) (1986) (provision designated as sec. 382(k)(3)(A)).

individuals (i.e., all living beings). More importantly, we are satisfied that our interpretation proceeds from an entirely natural reading of the statute. Given a stock ownership rule that operates by reference to an individual and other persons who are defined in terms of their relationship to that individual, it is hardly a stretch to surmise that the rule presupposes the shareholder status of the referenced individual.

4. Revisiting the 1986 Conference Report

Having concluded that our interpretation of section 382(*l*)(3)(A)(i) does not do violence to the plain language of the statute, we return to the legislative history to determine whether it is any more supportive of our view than it is of the views of the parties. As indicated above, see *supra* part III.C. and note 10, the 1986 conference report contradicts the statutory language by including an individual's grandparents (rather than his grandchildren) among the family members who are aggregated for purposes of section 382. If that disconnect were attributable to a simple typographical error, one might reasonably expect that the subsequently issued report of the Joint Committee on Taxation explaining the 1986 Act (the so-called Blue Book) would point out the error. See, e.g., Staff of Joint Comm. on Taxation, General Explanation of Tax Legislation Enacted in the 104th Congress at 81 n.59 (J. Comm. Print 1996), (noting that the conference report accompanying H.R. 3448, the bill eventually enacted as the Small Business Job Protection Act of 1996, mistakenly refers to the lessee rather than the lessor in the context of new section 168(i)(8)). The Blue Book for the 1986 Act, however, retains the reference in the 1986 conference report to "grandparents" in the context of section 382(*l*)(3)(A)(i). Staff of Joint Comm. on Taxation, General Explanation of the Tax Reform Act of 1986 at 311 (J. Comm. Print 1987).

As is the case with the conference committee's excision of the family status provision of the House bill, see *supra* part III.E.2.d., the substitution of "grandparents" for "grandchildren" in the 1986 conference report makes perfect sense if the family aggregation rule applies solely from the perspective of individuals who are shareholders of the loss corporation. Section 318(a)(1) (to which section 382(*l*)(3)(A)(i) refers) is phrased in terms of the family members (spouse, children, grandchildren, and parents) *from whom* shares are attributed. The converse of that rule is that shares owned by an individual are attributed *to* that individual's spouse, parents, grandparents, and children. The substitution of "grandparents" for "grandchildren" in the 1986 conference report (reiterated in the 1986 Blue Book) therefore suggests that Congress intended individuals to be aggregated with the same family members to whom their shares would otherwise be attributed under section 318(a)(1), which in turn suggests that Congress intended the family aggregation rule to apply from the perspective of individuals who are shareholders of the loss corporation.[20]

20. We do not mean to suggest that sec. 382(*l*)(3)(A)(i) should be interpreted as incorporating a modified version of sec. 318(a)(1) (i.e., one that substitutes grandparents for grandchildren); such an interpretation pre-

5. Revisiting the Regulations

Having concluded that our interpretation of the family aggregation rule (1) does not violate the plain meaning rule, and (2) arguably finds support in the legislative history of section 382(*l*)(3)(A)(i), we would nonetheless be hard pressed to adopt that interpretation if it were inconsistent with respondent's 17–year–old "legislative" regulations. See, e.g., Chevron, U.S.A., Inc. v. Natural Res. Def. Council, Inc., 467 U.S. 837, 843–844, 104 S.Ct. 2778, 81 L.Ed.2d 694 (1984); see also sec. 382(m) (directing the Secretary to "prescribe such regulations as may be necessary or appropriate to carry out the purposes of this section"). As is the case with the statute, see *supra* part III.E.3., the language of the relevant regulation presents no such obstacle. See sec. 1.382–2T(h)(6), Temporary Income Tax Regs, *supra* at 29686.

Nor does our interpretation of the statute render superfluous the "tiebreaker" rule of paragraph (h)(6)(iv) of the above-cited regulation. See *supra* note 19. To the contrary, that rule serves the useful purpose of precluding purely "vicarious" ownership increases that could otherwise occur under our interpretation of the statute (as well as those of the parties). For instance, if a husband and wife each own shares of a loss corporation, and the husband purchases additional shares from his mother, the ownership percentage of the family unit centered on the wife would increase as a result of the otherwise exempt transaction.[21] The tiebreaker rule precludes that result by treating the wife as a member of the family unit centered on her husband rather than a member of the family unit centered on her, since such inclusion would result in the smallest increase (zero) in percentage ownership.[22] See *supra* part I.C.; *supra* note 21.

IV.   Conclusion

We hold that the family aggregation rule of section 382(*l*)(3)(A)(i) applies solely from the perspective of individuals who are shareholders (as determined under the attribution rules of section 382(*l*)(3)(A)) of the loss corporation. Inasmuch as an individual shareholder's family consists solely of his spouse, children, grandchildren, and parents for these purposes, sibling shareholders are not aggregated under section 382(*l*)(3)(A)(i) if none of their parents and grandparents is a shareholder of the loss corporation.[23] Since Kenneth and Charles were not children or grandchil-

---

sumably would violate the plain meaning rule. See *supra* part III.A.

21.   Since the purchased shares would be included in the holdings of the family unit centered on the husband both before and after the sale, the percentage ownership of the husband-centric family unit would remain unchanged. However, since the purchased shares would not be included in the holdings of the family unit centered on the wife until after the sale, the percentage ownership of the wife-centric family unit would

increase as a result of the sale. A similar result would occur if the purchaser's child (rather than his wife) were a shareholder.

22.   As is the case with changes in family status, see *supra* note 16, this problem did not arise under former sec. 382(a), since the "vicarious" ownership increase would not have been attributable to a purchase by the wife. See former sec. 382(a)(1)(B)(i).

23.   We recognize that our interpretation of the statute suggests a distinction between siblings who are the children or granddren of an individual shareholder of petitioner at any relevant time, they are not aggregated for purposes of applying section 382 to the facts of this case. It follows that Charles's purchase of shares from Kenneth in 1998 resulted in an ownership change with respect to petitioner as contemplated in section 382(g).

PROBLEMS

1. Loss Co. has 100 shares of common stock outstanding and is owned equally by Shareholders 1 through 25, who are not related to one another. Loss Co. has assets worth $1,000,000 and net operating loss carryovers of $8,000,000. Will the Section 382 loss limitations apply in the following situations?

(a) All shareholders sell their stock to Ms. Julie ("J")?

(b) Shareholders 1 through 13 sell their stock to J?

(c) Shareholders 1 through 12 sell their stock to J?

(d) What result in (c), above, if Loss Co. redeems the stock of Shareholders 13 and 14 two years later?

(e) What result in (c), above, if Shareholder 13 sells his stock to New Shareholder 26?

(f) What result in (e), above, if Shareholder 14 also sells her stock to New Shareholder 26?

(g) What result if Shareholders 1 through 25 sell their stock to New Shareholders 26 through 50?

2. Loss Co. is owned 40 percent by Bill and 60 percent by the general public. Loss Co.'s stock is worth $10,000,000. Loss Co. acquires all the assets of Gain Co. (net worth—$10,500,000) in a Type C reorganization in exchange for $10,500,000 worth of Loss Co. voting stock. If no shareholders of Gain Co. owned any Loss Co. stock prior to the transaction, has there been an ownership change?

3. Whale Co. and Minnow Co. (which has loss carryovers) are both publicly held companies, neither of which has any 5–percent shareholder. Whale Co. purchases all the stock of Minnow Co. for cash. Does § 382 apply?

children of a shareholder and those who are not, a distinction that is arguably just as arbitrary as the distinctions resulting from respondent's interpretation of the statute. See *supra* part III.D.2.b. That problem would not arise if the tiebreaker rule of sec. 1.382–2T(h)(6)(iv), Temporary Income Tax Regs., *supra* at 29686, were inapplicable in any instance in which such application would have the effect of exempting a transaction (such as a sale between siblings) that otherwise would have increased the percentage ownership of the purchaser's family unit. Cf. sec. 1.382–4(d)(6)(i), Income Tax Regs. (rules treating an option as exercised do not apply if a principal purpose of the option is to avoid an ownership change by having it treated as exercised); T.D. 9063, 2003–2 C.B. 510, 511 (discussing the need for additional regulations dealing with changes in family composition in the context of sec. 382).

3.   RESULTS OF AN OWNERSHIP CHANGE

Code: § 382(a)–(f), (h), (*l*)(1) & (4).

In General. If an ownership change occurs, the Section 382 loss limitations then must be applied. Before considering any further details, the function of the limitations must be examined. We have seen that Congress designed Section 382 to prevent taxpayers from selling and purchasing tax deductions. If that were the only relevant consideration, the rest would be easy—whenever there is an ownership change, simply eliminate all loss carryforwards. But our study of Subchapter C has revealed one other salient factor—a corporation is treated as a separate entity for tax purposes. Although the individual shareholder may bear the ultimate burden or reap the ultimate benefit of a corporation's losses or profits, it is the corporation itself that is the focus of the corporate income tax.

In Section 382, Congress has adopted a principle of "neutrality" toward a loss company. While the Section 382 limitations restrict trafficking in deductions, they permit the purchaser of a loss corporation to use that corporation's net operating losses to offset the old loss corporation's own subsequent income. What Section 382 seeks to prevent is the use of a corporation's losses to offset another taxpayer's income after an ownership change. It is from this policy that the two limitations in Section 382 directly flow.

Continuity of Business Enterprise Limit. The first limit is found in Section 382(c),[1] which incorporates the continuity of business enterprise doctrine[2] by disallowing all net operating loss carryovers if the old loss corporation business is not continued for at least two years after the ownership change.[3] As described in the reorganization regulations, continuity of business enterprise requires either that the historic business of the loss corporation be continued for at least two years or that a significant portion of its assets are used in some other business carried on by the new loss corporation.[4] As a result, a corporation that runs afoul of this first limit in the second year following an ownership change may be required to amend its tax return for the earlier year and remove any inherited NOL deductions that had been applied against taxable income.

The Section 382 Limitation. A second, more complex limitation is "the Section 382 limitation," under which losses can be used in any "post-change year" only to the extent of the value of the old loss corporation multiplied by the "long-term tax-exempt rate."[5] To illustrate, assume Loss

---

1.   This limitation is inapplicable to the extent of any built-in gains or gains resulting from a Section 338 election as well as any Section 382(b)(2) carryovers related to such gains. See I.R.C. § 382(c)(2) and pp. 578–579, infra.

2.   See Chapter 9B1d, supra.

3.   I.R.C. § 382(c)(1).

4.   Reg. § 1.368–1(d).

5.   I.R.C. § 382(b)(1), (f). "Post-change year" is any taxable year ending after the "change date"—i.e., in the case of an owner shift, the date on which the shift occurs and, in the case of an equity structure shift, the date of the reorganization. I.R.C. § 382(d)(2), (j).

Co. has a value of $200,000 and has losses of $800,000 at a time when the long-term tax-exempt rate is 6 percent. After an ownership change, New Loss Co. may use its loss carryforwards only to the extent of $200,000 multiplied by 6 percent, or $12,000 per year.

The theory of this limit is to allow the loss carryforwards to offset any income earned by the old loss business. But since many of the acquisitions that will trigger the limit involve combining a loss business with some other more profitable enterprise, it is impossible to determine exactly how much income will be generated by the old company. To solve this problem, Section 382 irrebuttably presumes that the old loss business will generate income on its assets at a predetermined rate—the long-term tax-exempt rate. Because the amount of available loss carryforwards depends on the value of the old loss company, the greater the value (and cost) of that company, the more loss carryforwards may be used each year. Although the object of this limit is to defer the use of loss carryforwards by limiting the amount that can be used in any one year, the deferral will turn into a complete disallowance if the losses cannot be used before their expiration under Section 172.

Carryforwards of Unused Limitation. The Section 382 limitation results in some further complexity if it exceeds a corporation's taxable income in a given post-change year. To illustrate, if Loss Co. in the example above, with a value of $200,000, had at least $12,000 of taxable income (disregarding its NOL carryover), the full $12,000 of NOLs that were available in each year after the change of ownership would be used. But if the combined taxable income of the new loss company were only $4,000, the full amount available under the Section 382(b)(1) limitation would not be utilized. In that situation, the $8,000 of available but unused NOLs may be carried forward and the limitation in the following year would be $20,000 (the sum of the regular $12,000 limitation plus the $8,000 carry-over).[6]

Mid–Year Ownership Change. Another special rule applies if the "change date"[7] occurs on a date other than the last day of a year. In that event, the Section 382 limitation for the portion of the year after the change is a prorated amount derived by applying a ratio of the remaining days in the year to the total days in the year.[8] Thus, if the change occurs two-thirds of the way through the year, the limitation for that year is one-third of what otherwise would be available—i.e., $12,000 × ⅓, or $4,000 in the example above.[9]

The Long–Term Tax–Exempt Rate. Returning to the basic Section 382 limitation, recall that it is the value of the old loss corporation multiplied by the long-term tax-exempt rate. The use of this measure to predict the expected return on Loss Co.'s assets is the product of substantial Congres-

---

6. I.R.C. § 382(b)(2).

7. I.R.C. § 382(j).

8. I.R.C. § 382(b)(3)(B).

9. In addition, the limitation is inapplicable to the days of the year prior to the change date. I.R.C. § 382(b)(3)(A).

sional debate.[10] Loss Co. presumably can generate earnings on its assets at a rate at least equal to the higher federal long-term taxable rate. Indeed, if it could not do so some other way, Loss Co. simply could sell its assets and invest the proceeds in long-term federal obligations. Use of the lower tax-exempt rate to predict Loss Co.'s earnings is intended to offset the fact that the amount against which this rate is applied will exceed the real value of Loss Co.'s income-generating assets. How so? Because under Section 382(e)(1), the value of Loss Co. is the value of its stock immediately before the ownership change. Since Loss Co. has loss carryforwards to offset any income it earns in the near future, that income will be essentially tax-free. Loss Co.'s after-tax return will equal its before-tax profit, and the value of its stock will reflect not only the value of its income-generating assets but also the fact that the income which is generated will be tax free.

The Value of the Company. The second component of the Section 382 limitation is the value of the stock of the old loss corporation immediately preceding the ownership change.[11] Congress included several special rules to guard against predictable efforts to abuse this rule by inflating the value of the loss company.

One obvious technique to increase the available NOLs after an ownership change would be for the shareholders to increase the value of the loss company just prior to the change by contributing cash or other property to the corporation. Congress attacked this maneuver with an "anti-stuffing" rule, under which the value of any pre-change capital contribution received by the loss company as part of a plan to increase the Section 382 limitation is disregarded.[12] Any contribution received within two years before an ownership change is generally treated as part of such a plan.[13]

Even without "stuffing" in anticipation of a planned ownership change, shareholders of a loss company may be tempted to transfer cash or income-producing investments to the company. If there is a later ownership change, the allowable losses then would be greater; and if there is not a change, the investment income could be accumulated tax-free at the corporate level because it would be offset by the loss carryforwards. If the shareholders do not wish to transfer portfolio investments to the loss company, they at least might be tempted to prevent the company's profits (assuming it later becomes profitable) from being taken out of the company

10. The long-term tax-exempt rate is defined by Section 382(f) as the highest federal long-term rate determined under Section 1274(d) in effect for the three-month period ending with the month of the ownership change, adjusted to reflect differences between returns on long-term taxable and tax-exempt obligations.

11. I.R.C. § 382(b)(1), (e)(1). For purposes of determining the value of the loss corporation, all stock is counted, even preferred stock that would be ignored in determining whether an ownership change has

occurred. I.R.C. §§ 382(e)(1), (k)(6)(A); 1504(a)(4).

12. I.R.C. § 382(*l*)(1).

13. I.R.C. § 382(*l*)(1)(B). Exempted from this presumption are any contributions to be specified in regulations. The Conference Report instructs the Treasury that the regulations should generally exempt contributions only if they occurred prior to the accrual of the losses or if they were contributions of necessary operating capital. H.R.Rep. No. 99–841, 99th Cong., 2d Sess. II–182.

in order to reinvest these profits in portfolio investments which can accumulate tax-free at the corporate level and be available to increase the Section 382 limit in the event of a subsequent ownership change.

These possibilities did not go unnoticed by an ever suspicious Congress. If at least one-third of a loss corporation's assets consist of nonbusiness (i.e., investment) assets, the value of the corporation for purposes of Section 382 includes only the percentage of its actual net value that represents the percentage of its gross assets which are business assets.[14] To illustrate, if Loss Co. has $2,000,000 of investment assets, $3,000,000 of business assets and $1,000,000 of debt, it has a net value of $4,000,000, but only 60 percent of that value is taken into account for purposes of the Section 382 limitation because only 60 percent of its gross assets are business assets.[15]

If taxpayers are unable to increase useable NOLs by inflating the value of the loss corporation prior to an ownership change, they might be tempted to at least enable a profitable corporation to more easily avail itself of these losses by decreasing the value of the loss corporation after an ownership change. To illustrate, assume Loss Co. has a value of $1,000,000 and loss carryforwards of $1,000,000 and the tax-exempt rate is 6 percent. Profit Co. could acquire Loss Co. for $1,000,000 and use loss carryforwards at the rate of $60,000 per year, which probably would be enough only to offset Loss Co.'s own income. But what if Profit Co. pays $510,000 for 51 percent of Loss Co., and then Loss Co. redeems the remaining 49 percent of its outstanding shares? Loss Co.'s value has decreased by 49 percent (the amount paid to redeem its stock), and its revenues presumably will decrease by the same 49 percent. Profit Co. will have paid only $510,000, but the smaller New Loss Co. may deduct its loss carryovers to the extent of 6 percent times $1,000,000, or $60,000 per year. Once again, Congress cuts off a promising strategy at the pass. Section 382(e)(2) provides that if a redemption or other corporate contraction occurs in connection with an ownership change, the value of the loss corporation is determined only after taking the redemption or contraction into account.[16]

Limit on Built-in Losses. Finally, a corporation generally is subject to the Section 382 limitations only if it has loss carryforwards. A prospective buyer of deductions might be tempted to avoid the section by simply acquiring an asset that did not have the carryforwards themselves but rather the ability to produce them. Specifically, instead of acquiring a corporation that had loss carryforwards, a taxpayer could acquire a corpo-

---

14.   I.R.C. § 382(*l*)(4).

15.   When it applies, Section 382(*l*)(4) specifically requires that the value of the loss corporation shall be reduced by the excess of the value of its nonbusiness assets over an amount of the corporation's debt which bears the same ratio to all the company's debt which the nonbusiness assets bear to all the company's assets. I.R.C. § 382(*l*)(4)(A). See

§ 382(*l*)(4)(D). The net result is as described in the text above.

16.   The legislative history suggests that the "in connection with" standard should be broadly construed to include any redemption that is contemplated at the time of the ownership change. See H.R.Rep. No. 99–841, supra note 13, at II–187.

ration that had substantial unrealized losses and other deductions built into its assets. Assuming a buyer is in the market for deductions, a company with assets having an aggregate basis of $1,000,000 and a value of $100,000 may be as attractive as a company with a $900,000 loss carryforward. Once the company is acquired, the profitable company could sell those assets and use the losses against its own profits.

In its eternal race to stay one step ahead of the taxpayer, Congress has extended the limitations in Section 382 to certain built-in unrealized losses and deductions that economically accrue prior to an ownership change but are not recognized until after the change.[17] If a corporation has assets whose aggregate bases exceed their total value—i.e., a "net unrealized built-in loss"[18]—then any built-in losses which are recognized within five years[19] of an ownership change are treated as loss carryforwards of the old loss corporation and are subject to the Section 382 deduction limits.[20] Depreciation, amortization or depletion deductions during the five-year recognition period are treated as recognized built-in losses for purposes of this rule unless the corporation establishes that such amounts are not attributable to the excess of the adjusted basis over the fair market value of the asset on the change date.[21] To the extent that the new loss corporation establishes that a loss recognized during the five-year period accrued after the ownership change, the loss may be deducted without limitation.[22] Even if the new loss company is unable to establish when any particular loss was accrued, the total amount of loss subject to this rule may not exceed the net unrealized loss built into the old loss corporation's assets.[23] A special de minimis rule provides that a corporation's net unrealized built-in loss is considered to be zero if it does not exceed the lesser of (1) 15 percent of the fair market value of the assets of the corporation, or (2) $10 million.[24]

Special Rules for Built-in Gains. On occasion, Congress is as eager to be fair as it is to be vigilant. In that spirit, the Section 382 limitation is increased to reflect built-in gains and other income items that accrued prior to the ownership change but are recognized within five years after the change. If on the change date the aggregate fair market value of a loss corporation's assets exceeds the aggregate adjusted basis of those assets—i.e., the corporation has a "net unrealized built-in gain"[25]—the Section 382 limitation is increased by any built-in gain (up to total net unrealized built-in gain) which is recognized during the five-year "recognition period"

---

17. I.R.C. § 382(h)(1)(B).

18. I.R.C. § 382(h)(3)(A).

19. This is known as the "recognition period." I.R.C. § 382(h)(7).

20. I.R.C. § 382(h)(1)(B).

21. I.R.C. § 382(h)(2)(B). For example, depreciation deductions attributable to capital improvements made with respect to an asset after the change date would not be subject to the limitation.

22. I.R.C. § 382(h)(2)(B)(i).

23. I.R.C. § 382(h)(1)(B)(ii).

24. I.R.C. § 382(h)(3)(B)(i). For purposes of this test, cash, cash equivalents and marketable securities with a value not substantially different from their bases generally are disregarded. § 382(h)(3)(B)(ii).

25. I.R.C. § 382(h)(3)(A).

following an ownership change.[26] As a result, the new loss company can use its loss carryforwards (in addition to otherwise allowable post-change losses) to offset any built-in gains which it recognizes either on a disposition of an asset of the old loss corporation[27] or because of a Section 338 election made with respect to the loss corporation.[28] The corporation must be able to prove that the built-in gains accrued prior to the change date;[29] and the total increase in the Section 382 limitation may not exceed the net unrealized built-in gain as of the change date.[30] Once again, a de minimis rule provides that net unrealized built-in gains do not increase the Section 382 limitation if they do not exceed the lesser of (1) 15 percent of the fair market value of the corporation's assets, or (2) $10 million.[31]

4.   SECTION 382 RELIEF FOR DISTRESSED BUSINESSES

In response to the severe economic downturn that began in 2008, Congress and the IRS provided valuable "tax holidays" from the Section 382 loss carryover limitation for certain distressed corporate taxpayers. These actions were intended to preserve tax losses for companies that experienced major changes of ownership as a result of various extraordinary federal bailout measures.

A good case study is General Motors, which declared bankruptcy in June 2009. In the bankruptcy proceeding, "old GM" sold its assets to "new GM," a shell corporation. Old GM's shareholders got nothing. Its creditors, which included the U.S. Treasury, automotive labor unions, and the Canadian government, exchanged their debt claims for stock in new GM. The Treasury emerged with 61 percent of new GM and later sold much of its stock to the public.

The first phase of the GM bailout—the Government-imposed restructuring plan, including the exchange of debt claims for stock—was protected by Section 382(n), an obscurely worded provision buried in the American Recovery and Reinvestment Act of 2009. It provided that the Section 382 limitations on use of NOLs and built-in losses would not apply in the case of certain ownership changes occurring after February 17, 2009 pursuant to restructuring plans required under loan agreements with the Treasury

---

26.   I.R.C. § 382(h)(1).

27.   Id. If a taxpayer sells a built-in gain asset prior to or during the recognition period in an installment sale under Section 453, the provisions of Section 382(h) continue to apply to gain recognized from the sale (including a disposition of the installment obligations) after the recognition period. I.R.S. Notice 90–27, 1990–1 C.B. 336.

28.   I.R.C. § 382(h)(1)(C). If an ownership change and Section 338 qualified stock purchase occur simultaneously, the target is treated as selling its assets to itself ("new T") at the close of the acquisition date. I.R.C. § 338(a). In that situation, the Section 382

limit does not apply to the Section 338 deemed sale gain because the losses do not carry over to a "post-change year." I.R.C. § 382(a), (d)(2). When an ownership change takes place prior to a qualified stock purchase (i.e., a creeping qualified stock purchase), Section 382(h)(1)(C) provides special rules when the Section 382(h)(3)(B) de minimis threshold is not satisfied and the corporation's built-in gains are considered to be zero.

29.   I.R.C. § 382(h)(2)(A).

30.   I.R.C. § 382(h)(1)(A)(ii).

31.   I.R.C. § 382(h)(3)(B).

Department under the Emergency Economic Stabilization Act of 2009 when the plan "is intended to result in a rationalization of the costs, capitalization and capacity" of the taxpayer's manufacturing workforce and supplier. This language was custom tailored to ensure that General Motors would not be subject to the Section 382 limitations as a result of its government-imposed restructuring. And later, to ensure that a change of ownership was not triggered when the Treasury sold the bulk of its stock to the public, the IRS came to the rescue with a series of notices declaring that the Section 382 limitation would not apply to government-owned shares of GM and other affected companies even if more than 50 percent changed hands.[1] It was reported that these actions would preserve for new GM as much as $45 billion in NOLs to shelter future profits from federal tax.[2]

In Notice 2008–83, the IRS also administratively relaxed the Section 382 limitations to permit a greater utilization of losses on loans and bad debts of financially distressed banks to facilitate acquisitions at the end of 2008. Shortly after Notice 2008–83 was issued, Wells Fargo Bank agreed to acquire Wachovia Bank for $15 billion. This generous relaxation of the Section 382 limitation preserved approximately $74 billion in Wachovia's bad mortgage loan debts, far more than what would have been available if Section 382 had applied to the transaction.[3] The IRS's unilateral action was widely criticized as exceeding its regulatory authority.[4] Congress eventually agreed by revoking this new type of bank holiday for ownership changes occurring after January 16, 2009 but allowed it to apply with respect to changes occurring on or before that date, including the Wachovia Bank acquisition.[5]

PROBLEMS

1. Loss Co. has net operating loss carryforwards of $10,000,000. It has assets worth $10,000,000 and liabilities of $2,000,000. Profit Co. is a publicly held company worth $100,000,000.

  (a) On January 1, 2011, Profit Co. acquires all of the Loss Co. assets in a merger of Loss Co. into Profit Co. where Loss Co. shareholders receive Profit Co. stock worth $8,500,000. The long-term tax-exempt rate at that time is 5 percent. Assuming the Loss Co. business is continued, to what extent can Profit Co. deduct Loss Co.'s loss carryforwards in 2011?

  (b) What result in (a), above, if Profit Co. instead purchases all of the Loss Co. stock for $8,500,000?

---

1. See, e.g., IRS Notice 2010–2, 2010–2 I.R.B. 251.

2. Smith & Terlep, "GM to Get Tax Break Worth Billions," Wall St. J., Nov. 3, 2010, at B1.

3. 2008–2 C.B. 905.

4. See, e.g., Zelenak, "Can Obama's IRS Retroactively Revoke Massive Bank Giveaway," 122 Tax Notes 889 (Feb. 16, 2009).

5. American Recovery and Reinvestment Act of 2009, § 1261.

   (c) What result in (a), above, if Profit Co.'s taxable income, disregarding any loss carryforward, is $300,000 in 2011?

   (d) What result in (a), above, if Profit Co. discontinues the Loss Co. business and disposes of its assets in 2011?

   (e) What result in (a), above, if the merger occurs on June 30, 2011? Assume the date is halfway through each corporation's taxable year.

2. Loss Co. has loss carryforwards of $10,000,000. It has the following assets, all of which have been held for more than two years unless otherwise indicated:

Asset	Adj. Basis	F.M.V.
Equipment	$2,000,000	$4,500,000
Land	6,000,000	3,000,000
IBM stock	2,000,000	2,000,000
Cash	500,000	500,000

Loss Co. has liabilities of $2,000,000. Profit Co. is a publicly held company worth $100,000,000. On January 1, 2011, Profit Co. acquires all of the Loss Co. assets in exchange for Profit Co. stock worth $8,500,000. The long-term tax-exempt rate is 5 percent.

   (a) Assuming that the business conducted by Loss Co. is continued, to what extent can Profit Co. deduct Loss Co.'s loss carryforwards in 2011?

   (b) What result in (a), above, if the stock and cash had been contributed to the capital of Loss Co. in November, 2010?

   (c) What result in (a), above, if the IBM stock had a value and basis of $5,000,000?

   (d) What result in (c), above, if IBM were a wholly owned subsidiary of Loss Co.?

   (e) What result in (a), above, if Profit Co. acquires 70 percent of the Loss Co. stock for Profit Co. stock on January 1 and the IBM stock and the cash are distributed to Joe, a 30 percent shareholder of Loss Co., on March 1 in redemption of all of his stock?

   (f) Will the result in (a), above, change if Profit Co. sells the equipment in February? Would the answer be different if the land had a basis of zero?

   (g) Assume in (a), above, that the land had a basis of $8,000,000 and that Profit Co. sells the land for $3,000,000 two years later. Is the loss deductible? What if Profit Co. sells the land for $2,700,000?

D.   LIMITATIONS ON OTHER TAX ATTRIBUTES: SECTION 383

Code: § 383.

   Section 383 is a brief section that is easily mastered if one understands the operation of Section 382. It essentially calls for the Treasury to issue regulations that will adopt the principles of Section 382 (i.e., the continuity of business enterprise requirement and ownership change rules coupled with limitations) to limit corporate attributes other than loss carryforwards. Section 383 applies to the Section 39 carryforward of the general business credit,[1] the Section 53 carryforward of the alternative minimum tax credit,[2] and the Section 904(c) carryforward of the foreign tax credit.[3] Section 383 also calls for regulations to employ Section 382 principles to limit capital loss carryforwards of a loss company.[4] In addition, the regulations must provide that any permitted use of a capital loss carryforward in any year will reduce the Section 382 limitation on loss carryforwards for that year.[5]

E.   OTHER LOSS LIMITATIONS

1.   ACQUISITIONS MADE TO EVADE TAX: SECTION 269

Code: § 269.

If a corporation surmounts the hurdles of Section 382, it still may find its losses limited by Section 269. The subjective approach of Section 269 is fundamentally different from the objective tests of Section 382. Section 269 applies to a transaction only if the principal purpose of the acquisition was "evasion or avoidance of Federal income tax by acquiring the benefit of a deduction, credit, or other allowance" which the taxpayer otherwise might not enjoy. Section 269(a) potentially applies to Type A and C reorganizations and forward triangular mergers and to Type B reorganizations or stock purchases where the acquiring corporation previously owned less than 50 percent of the target.[1] Section 269(b) applies to liquidations which occur within two years after a corporation makes a stock purchase which would have qualified for a Section 338 election but only if no such election was made.[2]

If Section 269 applies, the Commissioner has the power to deny any "deduction, credit or allowance." In theory, Section 269 thus has a potentially broader reach than Section 382. Although Congress has indicated that Section 269 should not be applied to a transaction where carryovers were limited by the prior versions of Section 382,[3] the proposed regulations make it clear that current Sections 382 and 383 do not limit the Service's ability to invoke Section 269.[4] Thus, if a tax avoidance device or scheme is

---

1. I.R.C. § 383(a)(2)(A).

2. I.R.C. § 383(a)(2)(B).

3. I.R.C. § 383(c).

4. I.R.C. § 383(b).

5. I.R.C. § 383(b). For regulations implementing Section 383, see Reg. § 1.383–1.

1. I.R.C. § 269(a)(2).

2. See Chapter 8C2, supra.

3. See, e.g., S.Rep. No. 94–938, 94th Cong., 2d Sess. 206 (1976), reprinted in 1976–3 C.B. (Part 1) 244; S.Rep. No. 1622, 83d Cong., 2d Sess. 284 (1954).

4. Reg. § 1.269–7 provides that Section 269 may be applied to disallow a deduction, credit or other allowance when the item is detected, Section 269 can deny even those NOLs that otherwise slip by the limits of Section 382. It is expected, however, that Section 269 will be applied more sparingly now that the objective limits on loss carryovers have been strengthened.

2. LIMITATIONS ON USE OF PREACQUISITION LOSSES TO OFFSET BUILT-IN GAINS: SECTION 384

Code § 384.

Section 384 restricts an acquiring corporation from using its preacquisition losses to offset built-in gains of an acquired corporation. The policy and operation of Section 384 can best be illustrated by an example. Assume that Loss Corporation ("L") has $100,000 of net operating loss carryforwards. At the beginning of the current year, profitable Target Corporation ("T") merges into L in a tax-free Type A reorganization. L and T are owned by unrelated individual shareholders, and the merger does not result in a Section 382 ownership change to L. T's only asset, Gainacre, has a value of $200,000 and an adjusted basis of $125,000 which will transfer to L under Section 362(b). Assume that L sells Gainacre for $200,000 shortly after the merger, realizing a $75,000 gain.

Unless Section 269 or Section 382 applied, L could apply its preacquisition losses to shelter any gains recognized on the disposition of the assets acquired from T. Thus, L could use its net operating loss carryforwards to offset the $75,000 gain on the sale of Gainacre. Because it was not clear that Section 269 would effectively deter this strategy, Congress became concerned that loss corporations would become vehicles for "laundering" the built-in gains of profitable target companies. Section 384—yet another attack on the real and perceived abuses flowing from corporate acquisitions—is the legislative response. Its purpose is to preclude a corporation from using its preacquisition losses to shelter built-in gains of another (usually, a target) corporation which are recognized within five years of an acquisition of the gain corporation's assets or stock. In the example above, L would be prevented from using its preacquisition net operating loss as a deduction against the $75,000 "recognized built-in gain" on the disposition of Gainacre.

Section 384 is triggered in two situations: (1) stock acquisitions, where one corporation acquires "control" (defined by reference to the 80–percent-of-vote-and-value benchmark in Section 1504(a)(2)) of another corporation, and (2) asset acquisitions in an acquisitive Type A, C or D reorganization, if either corporation is a "gain corporation"—i.e., a corporation having built-in gains.[1] As originally enacted, Section 384 applied only when a loss

---

limited or reduced under Section 382 or 383. The fact that an item is limited under Section 382(a) or 383 is relevant to the determination of whether the principal purpose of the acquisition is evasion or avoidance of federal tax.

1. I.R.C. § 384(a), (c)(4) and (5). Section 384 does not displace any of the other Code provisions limiting loss carryovers—e.g., Sections 269, 382, and certain provisions in the consolidated return regulations. Congress has indicated that the limitations of corporation acquired the stock or assets of a gain corporation, but Congress later expanded the provision to apply regardless of which corporation acquired the other. If applicable, Section 384(a) provides that the corporation's income, to the extent attributable to "recognized built-in gains," shall not be offset by any "preacquisition loss" other than a preacquisition loss of the gain corporation. This punishment occurs during any "recognition period taxable year," which is any taxable year within the five-year period beginning on the "acquisition date."[2]

Understanding the operation of Section 384 requires a mastery of its glossary, much of which is borrowed from Section 382. The essential terms are as follows:

(1) The "acquisition date" is the date on which control is acquired, in the case of a stock acquisition, or the date of the transfer, in the case of an asset acquisition.[3]

(2) A "preacquisition loss" is any net operating loss carryforward to the taxable year in which the acquisition date occurs and the portion of any net operating loss for the taxable year of the acquisition to the extent the loss is allocable to the period before the acquisition date.[4]

(3) A "recognized built-in gain" is any gain recognized on the disposition of any asset during the five-year recognition period except to the extent that the gain corporation (in the case of an acquisition of control) or the acquiring corporation (in the case of an asset acquisition) establishes that the asset was not held by the gain corporation on the acquisition date, or that the gain accrued after the acquisition date.[5] Income items recognized after the acquisition date but attributable to prior periods are also treated as recognized built-in gain.[6] This definition should be familiar; it is similar to the definition of the same term in Section 382(h)(2)(A) except that the burden of proof is different. Under Section 382, the burden is on the taxpayer to establish that the asset was held by the old loss corporation before the change date and the recognized gain does not exceed the appreciation in the asset on that date. Under Section 384, it is presumed that a gain recognized during the recognition period is a built-in gain unless the corporation establishes that the asset was not held on the acquisition date or that

---

Section 384 apply independently of and in addition to the limitations of Section 382. Staff of the Joint Committee on Taxation, Description of the Technical Corrections Bill of 1988, 100th Cong., 2d Sess. 421 (1988). In contrast to Section 269, the application of Section 384 is not dependent on the subjective intent of the acquiring corporation.

2. See I.R.C. §§ 384(c)(8); 382(h)(7). The Section 384 limitation also applies to any "successor" corporation to the same extent it applied to its predecessor. I.R.C. § 384(c)(7).

3. I.R.C. § 384(c)(2).

4. I.R.C. § 384(c)(3)(A). In the case of a corporation with a net unrealized built-in loss, as defined by Section 382(h)(1)(B), the term "preacquisition loss" also includes any built-in loss recognized during the five-year recognition period. I.R.C. § 384(c)(3)(B).

5. I.R.C. § 384(c)(1)(A).

6. I.R.C. § 384(c)(1)(B).

the recognized gain exceeds the built-in gain at the time of the acquisition.

(4) The amount of recognized built-in gain for any taxable year is limited to the "net unrealized built-in gain" reduced by recognized built-in gains for prior years in the recognition period which, but for Section 384, would have been offset by preacquisition losses.[7] For this purpose, the definition of "net unrealized built-in gain" is borrowed from Section 382(h)(3), substituting the acquisition date for the ownership "change date."[8] Thus, it is the excess of the aggregate fair market value of the assets of the "gain corporation" over the aggregate adjusted bases of those assets, except that the net unrealized built-in gain will be deemed to be zero unless it is greater than the lesser of (1) 15 percent of the fair market value of the corporation's assets other than cash and certain marketable securities or (2) $10 million.[9]

The limitations in Section 384(a) do not apply to the preacquisition loss of any corporation that was a member of the same "controlled group" that included the gain corporation at all times during the five-year period ending on the acquisition date. For this purpose, the definition of controlled group is borrowed from Section 1563 (as modified to generally require more than 50 percent common ownership of both voting power and value).[10]

As if the foregoing rules were not enough, Section 384(f) authorizes the Treasury to promulgate regulations as may be necessary to carry out the anti-abuse mission of the section.[11]

PROBLEM

Gain Corp., which is wholly owned by individual A, has the following assets and no liabilities:

Asset	Adj. Basis	F.M.V.
Inventory	$150,000	$300,000
Machinery	300,000	200,000
Gainacre	100,000	350,000

Loss Corp., which is wholly owned by unrelated individual B, has $500,000 in net operating loss carryforwards.

Unless otherwise indicated below, assume that Loss Corp. acquired all the assets of Gain Corp. in a tax-free Type A reorganization on January 1, 2010. After the acquisition, B owned 80% and A owned 20% of the Loss Corp. stock. To what extent, if any, may Loss Corp. use its preacquisition

---

7. I.R.C. § 384(c)(1)(C).

8. I.R.C. § 384(c)(8).

9. I.R.C. §§ 384(c)(8); 382(h)(3)(B).

10. I.R.C. § 384(b). The common control testing period would be shortened if the gain corporation was not in existence for the full five-year preacquisition date period by substituting its period of existence. I.R.C. § 384(b)(3).

11. As of early 2012, no regulations had been issued.

net operating loss carryforwards against the gains recognized in the following alternative transactions?:

(a) Loss Corp. sells Gainacre for $500,000 in 2011.

(b) Same as (a), above, except that Loss Corp. acquired all of Gain Corp.'s stock from A for cash (not making a § 338 election) on January 1, 2010, after which it liquidated Gain Corp. under § 332.

(c) Same as (a), above, except Loss Corp. also sells the inventory for $400,000 in 2011.

(d) Instead of (a)–(c), above, Loss Corp. sells Gainacre for $900,000 in 2016.

(e) Same as (a), above, except that Loss Corp. has no net operating loss carryforwards at the time of the acquisition but its only asset is Lossacre, which had a fair market value of $300,000 and an adjusted basis of $500,000. In 2011, Loss Corp. sells Lossacre for $200,000 at the same time that it sells Gainacre for $500,000.

3.   CONSOLIDATED RETURN RULES

C corporations generally determine their taxable income and tax liability without regard to the income and losses of other affiliated entities. The consolidated return rules are an exception to this separate entity principle. Section 1501 permits an "affiliated group of corporations" to elect to file a consolidated tax return in which their separate taxable income and losses are aggregated.[1] An "affiliated group" is defined as a chain of corporations linked by specific levels of stock ownership. The common parent of the group must own at least 80 percent of the total voting power and value of at least one corporation in the chain, and every corporation in the chain must be 80 percent owned (based on voting power and value) by other members of the group.[2]

When computing the consolidated taxable income or loss of an affiliated group of corporations, each member of the group first determines its separate taxable income or loss.[3] The separate taxable income or loss figures of the members of the group are then combined, and the Section 11 tax rates are applied to the aggregate figure to arrive at the group's tax liability.

Because the consolidated return rules permit aggregation of the separate taxable income and loss of the members, the potential exists for one member of the group to offset its taxable income with the losses of another member. For example, without a specific limitation, a profitable corporation could acquire the requisite ownership of a corporation with a large net

---

1. See generally Chapter 1B3, supra, and Chapter 13, infra.

2. I.R.C. § 1504(a)(1), (2). In general, preferred stock is not counted for purposes of the ownership tests and certain corporations subject to special tax regimes, such as tax-

exempt and foreign corporations, are not permitted to be part of an affiliated group. I.R.C. § 1504(a)(4), (b).

3. Reg. §§ 1.1502–2, 1.1502–11(a)(1), 1.1502–12.

operating loss, the two corporations could elect to file a consolidated return, and the joint tax liability of the corporate family would be reduced as the net operating losses of one member are deducted against the income of the other. A multi-layer of statutes and regulations limit the use of net operating losses by corporations filing a consolidated return. First, all of the statutory limitations on the use of NOLs studied earlier in this chapter (i.e., Sections 382, 383, 384 and 269) potentially apply to a consolidated group.[4] If any loss somehow should survive these statutory gatekeepers, the consolidated return regulations contain an additional rule to patrol abuse: the "separate return limitation year" ("SRLY") limitation.[5] The operation of these rules should be familiar because they reflect many of the same policies embodied in the generally applicable statutory limitations.

The SRLY limitation is designed to prevent the use by an affiliated group of net operating losses arising in a separate return limitation year of a member of the group. A separate return limitation year is a taxable year in which the member filed either its own separate tax return or filed as part of another affiliated group.[6] In general, the aggregate net operating losses of a member of an affiliated group arising in separate return years only may be carried over and used to offset the aggregate consolidated income attributable to that member.[7] Thus, if a profitable corporation ("P") acquires a target corporation ("T") with large net operating losses, and the two corporations file a consolidated tax return, preacquisition losses and built-in losses of T may not be used to reduce the post-acquisition tax liability on consolidated taxable income attributable to P.

The regulations include an important exception that restricts the application of the SRLY limitation. Generally, the SRLY limitation does not apply in any case where a corporation becomes a member of a consolidated group (where the limitation otherwise would apply) within six months of the change date of a Section 382(g) change of ownership.[8] As a result, in many acquisitions the SRLY limitation relinquishes jurisdiction over NOLs to Section 382.[9]

---

4. See Reg. § 1.1502–90 through Reg. § 1.1502–99, which apply Section 382 to a consolidated group of corporations.

5. The regulations also include limitations on the use of built-in losses and capital loss carryovers and carrybacks. See Reg. §§ 1.1502–15; 1.1502–22(c), (d). These items are also subject to the SRLY limitation.

6. Reg. § 1.1502–1(e), (f).

7. Reg. § 1.1502–21(c).

8. Reg. § 1.1502–21(g)(1) & (2).

9. A similar rules applies in the case of recognized built-in losses. See Reg. § 1.1502–15(g).

CHAPTER 13

AFFILIATED CORPORATIONS

A. RESTRICTIONS ON AFFILIATED CORPORATIONS

1. INTRODUCTION

For a variety of reasons, business owners often conduct their activities through multiple corporations. For example, to protect a low-risk existing business from potential tort liability, the shareholders of a closely held corporation might form a separate corporation to conduct a new, high-risk activity. Similarly, a holding company with an operating subsidiary might determine that the regulatory requirements of a particular state or country are sufficiently stringent that a planned expansion into that jurisdiction should take place through a new subsidiary. Should these business decisions about the corporate structure affect the manner in which the enterprises are treated for tax purposes?

A corporation, like an individual, generally is treated as a separate taxable entity. If this rule were unqualified, however, business owners would have an incentive in many circumstances to create separate corporations solely to obtain tax benefits. Recognizing this incentive, the Code treats related corporations for many purposes as a single economic unit. There may also be an incentive for related corporations to reduce their tax liability through transactions where they deal with each other on terms which unrelated parties operating at arm's length would not agree. Congress again recognized this incentive and provided tax administrators with a powerful weapon to counteract it. This section of the chapter explores the Code's rules to address these and other concerns about the taxation of affiliated corporations.

2. LIMITATIONS ON MULTIPLE TAX BENEFITS

Code: § 1561(a). Skim §§ 11(b)(1); 535(c); 1551; 1563.

Section 1561. The basic purpose of Section 1561 is to prevent business owners from obtaining multiple tax benefits by subdividing their business among multiple corporations. In its current form, Section 1561 targets four specific benefits: (1) the progressive tax rate structure provided by Section 11(b), (2) the "accumulated earnings credit" provided by Section 535(c),[1] (3) the $40,000 exemption amount used by corporations in calculating their

---

1. The accumulated earnings credit reduces the tax liability of corporations subject to the special tax on accumulated earnings imposed by Section 531. See I.R.C. §§ 531, 532 and 535 and Chapter 14C, infra.

alternative minimum taxable income,[2] and (4) the $2 million exemption amount used by corporations in calculating their liability for the environmental tax imposed by Section 59A.

A simple example illustrates the abuse that Section 1561 is designed to prevent. Suppose that individual A is the sole shareholder of a corporation that both operates an automobile repair shop and sells automobile parts at retail. The parts are sold at a window in the back of the repair shop by employees who also serve as mechanics in the repair operations. Assume that the corporation has total taxable income of $100,000, of which $75,000 is from its repair operations and $25,000 is from its sales of parts. Under the tax rates imposed by § 11(b), the corporation's income tax liability would be:

Income	Tax Rate	Tax
$ 50,000	15%	$ 7,500
25,000	25%	6,250
25,000	34%	8,500
$100,000		$22,250

If A instead divides the corporation's business operations between two separate corporations, Parts, Inc. and Services, Inc., the total tax liability of the businesses would be reduced because more income would be taxed at the lowest 15 percent rate.

Parts				Services		
Income	Tax Rate	Tax		Income	Tax Rate	Tax
$25,000	15%	$3,750		$50,000	15%	$ 7,500
				25,000	25%	6,250
$25,000		$3,750		$75,000		$13,750

Combined Tax Liability

Parts:	$ 3,750
Services:	13,750
Total:	$17,500

Without a rule that takes into account the relationship between Parts and Services, A could obtain a corporate-level tax savings of $4,750 ($22,250—$17,500) simply by creating an additional corporation.

Section 1561 prevents this result (and similar results in the case of the other tax benefits listed above) by providing that the benefit received by certain related groups of corporations cannot exceed the benefit that the group would receive if it were a single corporation. With the exception of the accumulated earnings credit, the benefits targeted by Section 1561 must be divided equally among the group's members unless the members formally agree to a different allocation.[3] Thus, if Parts and Services do not

---

2. See I.R.C. §§ 55(b)(1)(B)(i), (d)(2). **3.** I.R.C. § 1561(a).

enter into a formal allocation plan, the amounts of income in each taxable income bracket in Section 11(b) will be divided equally between them (to the extent that each corporation has taxable income), resulting in the same aggregate tax liability that they would have if they were a single corporation:

Income	Parts Tax Rate	Tax	Income	Services Tax Rate	Tax
$25,000	15%	$3,750	$25,000	15%	$ 3,750
			25,000	25%	6,250
			25,000	34%	8,500
$25,000		$3,750	$75,000		$18,500

Combined Tax Liability

Parts:	$ 3,750
Services:	18,500
Total:	$22,250

Component Members of a Controlled Group of Corporations. Section 1561 applies only to the "component members of a controlled group of corporations." The terms "component members" and "controlled group of corporations" are defined in Section 1563. Although simple in concept, these terms are defined in the Code and regulations with an extraordinary degree of complexity and specificity. Only a brief overview of those rules is provided here.

Section 1563 generally defines three principal types of controlled groups of corporations: a parent-subsidiary controlled group, a brother-sister controlled group, and a combined group.[4] A parent-subsidiary controlled group generally is defined as one or more chains of corporations connected through stock ownership to a common parent, if (1) stock possessing at least 80 percent of the total combined voting power or total value of all classes of stock of each corporation (other than the parent) is owned by one or more of the other corporations, and (2) the parent owns stock possessing at least 80 percent of the total combined voting power or total value of all classes of stock of at least one of the other corporations.[5] Thus, if corporation X owns 80 percent of the total combined voting power of corporations Y and Z, then X, Y and Z are members of a parent-subsidiary controlled group.[6] The definition of a brother-sister controlled group is two or more corporations where five or fewer shareholders who are individuals, estates, or trusts own stock possessing more than 50 percent of the total combined voting power or more than 50 percent of the total value of each corporation, taking into account the stock ownership of each person only to the extent such ownership is identical with respect to each such

---

4. I.R.C. § 1563(a).

5. I.R.C. § 1563(a)(1).

6. See Reg. § 1.1563–1(a)(2)(ii) Example 1.

corporation.[7] For example, assume shareholder A owns 25 percent of X Corporation's common stock and 35 percent of Y Corporation's common stock. Assume further that shareholder B owns 30 percent of X's common stock and 40 percent of Y's common stock. A's and B's identical ownership in X and Y is 25 percent and 30 percent, respectively. Since A's and B's identical ownership of common stock totals more than 50 percent of each corporation, X and Y are members of a brother-sister controlled group. A combined group is a group of three or more corporations, if (1) each corporation is a member of either a parent-subsidiary controlled group or a brother-sister controlled group, and (2) at least one of the corporations is the common parent of a parent-subsidiary controlled group and also is a member of a brother-sister controlled group.[8] For example, if an individual owns 80 percent of the total combined voting power of corporations X and Y, and Y owns 80 percent of the total combined voting power of corporation Z, then X, Y and Z are members of a combined group.[9] Several special rules apply in determining whether a controlled group of corporations exists, including limitations on what constitutes "stock" and an elaborate set of attribution rules similar to those under Section 318.[10]

A corporation generally qualifies as a "component member" of a controlled group of corporations for a taxable year if it is a member on the December 31 that falls within that taxable year.[11] If a corporation is not a member on December 31, it still can be treated as a member for its taxable year if it was a member at some point during the calendar year and was a member for at least one-half of the number of days during its taxable year that preceded December 31.[12] Certain corporations, referred to as "excluded corporations," cannot be component members. Among the excluded corporations are certain corporations that are exempt from tax under Section 501(a) and foreign corporations that are not engaged in a trade or business in the United States.[13] In some cases, a corporation may qualify as a component member of more than one controlled group. Section 1563(b)(4) makes clear that a corporation in this situation can be a member of only one controlled group, and the regulations provide rules for determining to which group it belongs.[14]

Broader Significance of a Controlled Group of Corporations. Section 1561 is one of many provisions in the Code that make use of Section 1563(a)'s definition of a "controlled group of corporations."[15] The definition thus has significance that extends beyond dividing up the four specific tax benefits targeted by Section 1561. Some of these provisions are similar to Section 1561 in that they limit the aggregate amount of a specific tax benefit available to a controlled group of corporations. For example, a

---

7. I.R.C. § 1563(a)(2).

8. I.R.C. § 1563(a)(3).

9. Reg. § 1.1563–1(a)(4)(ii) Example 1.

10. I.R.C. §§ 1563(c), (e).

11. I.R.C. § 1563(b)(1)(A).

12. I.R.C. § 1563(b)(1)(B), (b)(3).

13. I.R.C. § 1563(b)(1)(A), (b)(2).

14. Reg. § 1.1563–1(c).

15. Section 1563 has a modified definition of a brother-sister controlled group that generally applies to other Code provisions. See I.R.C. § 1563(f)(5).

controlled group is limited to one $25,000 amount for purposes of computing the general business credit limitation under Section 38.[16] Similarly, the component members of a controlled group are treated as one taxpayer for purposes of deducting the cost of Section 179 property.[17] In other cases, provisions of the Code use Section 1563(a)'s definition for a slightly different purpose and with a different ownership threshold. For example, Section 267 provides that, in the case of property transferred from one member of a controlled group to another member, any loss realized on the transfer cannot be recognized until the property is transferred outside the controlled group.[18] For this purpose, Section 1563(a) is applied with a "more than 50 percent" rather than an "at least 80 percent" ownership threshold.[19]

3. Section 482

Code: § 482.

Regulations: §§ 1.482–1(a), (b), (c)(1).

a. INTRODUCTION

If a novice in the field of taxation were asked to peruse the Code and select several provisions that he or she thought were of most significance, Section 482 might seem an unlikely candidate. Weighing in at slightly more than 125 words, it could easily be perceived as innocuous. Nothing could be further from the truth. The sparse language of Section 482 is the statutory tip of a large and complex iceberg on which many a taxpayer has run aground.

Section 482 represents a broad Congressional grant of power to the Service to reallocate income, deductions and other tax items among certain commonly controlled taxpayers when the reallocation is necessary to prevent evasion of taxes or clearly to reflect income. Although originally designed to apply principally in the domestic context, Section 482 is of most significance today in international transactions, such as sales of goods by a foreign parent to its U.S. subsidiary or vice versa, and to the use of intangible property. As one might expect of such a broad grant of authority, Section 482 has become one of the Service's principal weapons in its fight against devices used by taxpayers to reduce their tax liability and has spawned a large body of administrative guidance and judicial decisions.

b. STATUTORY ELEMENTS

Section 482 permits the Service to reallocate tax items when three basic elements are present: (1) there are two or more organizations, trades or businesses, (2) that are owned or controlled by the same interests, and

---

16. I.R.C. § 38(c)(6)(B).

17. I.R.C. § 179(d)(6), (7).

18. I.R.C. § 267(a)(1), (b)(3), (f).

19. I.R.C. § 267(f)(1)(A).

(3) the reallocation is necessary to prevent evasion of taxes or clearly to reflect the income of any of the organizations, trades or businesses.

Much of the power conferred by Section 482 derives from the broad meanings of the terms "organization" and "trade or business."[1] This first element is satisfied regardless of whether the taxpayers in question are incorporated, are domestic or foreign, or are affiliated.[2] Sole proprietorships, partnerships, trusts and estates (as well as corporations) all are subject to Section 482.[3] In several contexts, taxpayers have challenged Section 482 adjustments on the ground that the transaction in question did not involve two or more organizations, trades or businesses.[4] In the typical case, however, there is little dispute concerning this first element. When the Service proposes to reallocate income to a U.S. subsidiary from its foreign parent, for example, it generally is clear that two or more business entities are involved.

The second element similarly has received an expansive interpretation and typically is not the subject of most current disputes under Section 482 between taxpayers and the Service. According to the statute, ownership or control can be direct or indirect. The regulations elaborate on this by providing that "controlled" means any kind of control, whether or not legally enforceable, and that "[i]t is the reality of the control that is decisive, not its form or the mode of its exercise."[5] Control thus might exist as a result of a common interest between two otherwise unrelated taxpayers. For example in B. Forman Co. v. Commissioner,[6] two unrelated corporations operating competing department stores formed a new corporation to construct and operate an enclosed shopping mall and office complex, with each shareholder receiving 50 percent of the new corporation's stock and equal representation on its board. Finding that the common control requirement was satisfied, the court upheld the Service's authority to impose an arm's length interest rate on interest-free loans that the shareholders made to the new corporation.

The third element generally is "where the action is" in Section 482 disputes. Because Section 482 itself provides no standard regarding when it is necessary to make allocations to prevent tax evasion or clearly to reflect

---

1. Prior to 1934, the predecessor of Section 482 referred only to trades or businesses. In that year, Congress added the reference to organizations "to remove any doubt as to the application of this section to all kinds of business activity." H.R. Rep. No. 704, 73d Cong., 2d Sess. (1934), reprinted in 1939–1 (Part 2) C.B. 554, 572.

2. I.R.C. § 482.

3. Reg. § 1.482–1(i)(1).

4. See, e.g., Foglesong v. Commissioner, 691 F.2d 848 (7th Cir.1982) (individual and personal service corporation for which taxpayer performs services on an exclusive basis do not constitute two or more organizations, trades or businesses), nonacq., Rev. Rul. 88–38, 1988–1 C.B. 246; Asiatic Petroleum Co. v. Commissioner, 79 F.2d 234, 237 (2d Cir.) (holding company's sole activity of holding stock constitutes a business), cert. denied, 296 U.S. 645, 56 S.Ct. 248 (1935).

5. Reg. § 1.482–1(i)(4). If income or deductions are arbitrarily shifted between organizations or trades or businesses, a presumption of control arises. Id.

6. 453 F.2d 1144 (2d Cir.), cert. denied, 407 U.S. 934, 92 S.Ct. 2458 (1972).

income, the extensive interpretive regulations, administrative rulings, and judicial decisions are the main sources of guidance.

c. ALLOCATION STANDARD AND METHODS

The standard that the Service applies in examining transactions between commonly controlled taxpayers is that of uncontrolled taxpayers dealing with each other at arm's length.[7] That is, the Service compares the results of a transaction between commonly controlled taxpayers with those of a comparable transaction under comparable circumstances between uncontrolled taxpayers.[8] If the results of the two transactions are consistent, then the controlled transaction satisfies the arm's length standard.

For example, suppose that FP, a French manufacturer of perfume, distributes its finished products in the United States by selling them for resale to two U.S. corporations: Company A, a wholly owned subsidiary of FP, and Company B, a corporation not under common ownership or control with either FP or Company A. If the products that FP sells to Companies A and B are identical and the transactions between FP and Company A and FP and Company B are the same in all material respects (e.g., volume of sales and point of delivery), then the Service likely would determine whether the FP–Company A transactions satisfy the arm's length standard by comparing them with FP–Company B transactions. Thus, if FP sells the same product to Company A for $45 per bottle and to Company B for $20 per bottle, then, absent some factor that accounts for this difference, the Service likely would reallocate income from FP to Company A to ensure that the taxpayers do not use pricing to keep artificially low the income earned by the FP–Company A group that is subject to U.S. tax. The reallocation would be from FP to Company A because, by raising the price charged to Company A, FP effectively allocates a larger portion of income to its own taxing jurisdiction. That is, if Companies A and B both sell the same bottle of perfume in the U.S. for $50, Company B will realize a profit of $30 that is subject to U.S. tax. Absent a reallocation of income, Company A will realize a profit of only $5. In this simple example, the Service would reallocate $25 of income to Company A and thereby render that additional income subject to U.S. tax.

In determining whether an "uncontrolled" transaction is a comparable transaction under comparable circumstances, a variety of factors must be considered, such as the contractual terms of the controlled and uncontrolled transactions (e.g., volume of sales or purchases) and the degree of financial and other risks that the parties in each transaction assume.[9] Further, the regulations promulgated under Section 482 provide several methods for determining whether the results of a controlled transaction are at arm's length and, if they are not, for determining the appropriate arm's length result.[10] These methods often are referred to as "transfer pricing

---

7. Reg. § 1.482–1(b)(1).

8. Id.; Reg. § 1.482–1(d)(1).

9. Reg. § 1.482–1(d)(1).

10. See Reg. §§ 1.482–2 through 1.482–9.

methodologies." The particular method that applies will depend in part on the type of transaction at issue. For example, the methods prescribed for a transfer of tangible property differ from those prescribed for a transfer of intangible property.[11] In choosing among the available methods, the "best method rule" dictates that the arm's length result of a controlled transaction be determined under the method that "provides the most reliable measure of an arm's length result."[12]

d. COLLATERAL ADJUSTMENTS

When the Service makes an adjustment under Section 482 with respect to one commonly controlled taxpayer, it also makes collateral adjustments to any other commonly controlled taxpayers involved.[13] The other taxpayer must reflect the collateral adjustment in the documents that it maintains for U.S. tax purposes.[14] A collateral adjustment might have an immediate effect, a deferred effect, or no effect at all (e.g., if the other taxpayer is not subject to U.S. tax and the collateral adjustment has no effect on intercorporate transfers). For example, if the Service uses Section 482 to impute interest income to a U.S. parent with respect to an interest-free loan that the parent makes to its foreign subsidiary, the foreign subsidiary must reflect imputed interest payments in the books that it maintains for U.S. tax purposes. The likely effect would be a decrease in the subsidiary's earnings and profits, which in turn would affect the tax treatment of dividends that the subsidiary pays to the U.S. parent.[15]

e. COMMON TRANSACTIONS

Although the Service has the authority to apply Section 482 to virtually any type of transaction between commonly controlled taxpayers, the regulations set forth five categories of transactions that are most likely to trigger adjustments. These are: (1) loans and advances,[16] (2) the performance of services,[17] (3) the use of tangible property (such as a lease of business premises),[18] (4) sales of tangible property,[19] and (5) the sale or use of intangible property.[20] In each case, the regulations provide guidelines—with varying degrees of specificity—for determining an arm's length result.

Transfers of intangible property such as copyrights, trademarks and patents historically have distinguished themselves as particularly difficult transactions to analyze under the arm's length standard, in part because of the common lack of comparable uncontrolled transactions. To assist the

---

11. Compare Reg. § 1.482–3(a) with Reg. § 1.482–4.

12. Reg. § 1.482–1(c)(1); see also Reg. § 1.482–8.

13. Reg. § 1.482–1(g)(1) & (2).

14. Reg. § 1.482–1(g)(2)(ii).

15. Reg. § 1.482–1(g)(2)(iv) Example 3.

16. Reg. § 1.482–2(a). The application of Section 482 to loans with below-market interest rates has been superseded to a large extent by Section 7872.

17. Reg. § 1.482–2(b); see Reg. § 1.482–9.

18. Reg. § 1.482–2(c).

19. Reg. § 1.482–3.

20. Reg. § 1.482–4.

IRS, Congress amended Section 482 by adding a second sentence, commonly referred to as the "super-royalty" provision, which requires that the income derived from a transfer of intangible property "be commensurate with the income attributable to the intangible." The provision was enacted in part as a result of concern that U.S. taxpayers were developing intangible property in the U.S.—often with the assistance of tax benefits designed to encourage such development—and then insulating the income generated by the intangible from U.S. tax by transferring the intangible to a foreign affiliate at a bargain price.[21] The super-royalty provision addresses this concern by directing that the adequacy of the consideration received by the transferor of an intangible (whether received in a lump sum or periodically) be determined by comparing the consideration with the income derived from the intangible by the transferee.[22] The "commensurate with income" standard generally must be satisfied not only in the year when the intangible is first transferred but also in all subsequent years that the arrangement between the controlled taxpayers is in effect.[23]

f. OTHER ISSUES

Advance Pricing Agreements. Disputes regarding the proper application of Section 482 to a transaction can be extraordinarily time consuming and expensive for everyone involved, particularly if the dispute leads to litigation.[24] In an effort to avoid such disputes, the Service has implemented a procedure under which taxpayers can secure an "advance pricing agreement" with the Service on how Section 482 will apply to one or more transactions between a taxpayer and other parties under common control.[25] The taxpayer initiates the process by proposing transfer pricing methodologies and data to show that the suggested methodologies are the best method for determining arm's length results between the taxpayer and specified affiliates.[26] The Service evaluates the taxpayer's request and if, after discussion, the proposal is acceptable, the parties execute an advance pricing agreement covering the proposed methodologies.[27] Although seeking an advance pricing agreement is by no means a small undertaking, the process can be significantly less burdensome than the alternative of an audit, administrative appeals and litigation.

Penalties and Reporting Requirements. One difficulty for the Treasury in administering Section 482 is its lack of access to taxpayer information.

---

21. H.R. Rep. No. 426, 99th Cong., 1st Sess. 423–425 (1986), reprinted in 1986–3 (vol. 2) C.B. 1, 423–425.

22. See generally Reg. § 1.482–4.

23. Reg. § 1.482–4(f)(2)(i). If the transferor receives consideration in a lump sum, the lump sum is treated as an advance payment of a stream of royalties payable over the shorter of the useful life of the intangible and the duration of the agreement between the parties. Reg. § 1.482–4(f)(6).

24. See, e.g., Ciba–Geigy Corp. v. Commissioner, 85 T.C. 172 (1985) (IRS challenge to royalties paid by U.S. subsidiary to Swiss parent in tax years 1965 through 1969 decided in 1985).

25. Rev. Proc. 2006–9, § 2, 2006–1 C.B. 278; amplified by Rev. Proc. 2006–54, 2006–2 C.B. 1035; modified by Rev. Proc. 2008–31, 2008–1 C.B. 1133.

26. Rev. Proc. 2006–9, supra note 25, at § 2.

27. Id.

To assist the government, Congress has strengthened the applicable penalty and reporting requirements that apply to taxpayers.

In general, a taxpayer faces a 20 percent (and, in some cases, 40 percent) penalty if either (1) the taxpayer files a return that overstates or understates the price paid for property or services by more than a specified percentage of the amount determined to be correct under Section 482,[28] or (2) the Service makes Section 482 allocations that result in a net increase in the taxpayer's taxable income that exceeds a threshold amount.[29] Taxpayers can avoid the penalty in the second situation by reasonably using a method specified in the regulations for determining transfer prices (or, in some circumstances, another appropriate method), maintaining adequate contemporaneous documentation of the method used, and providing this documentation to the government within thirty days of the government's request.[30] A taxpayer desiring to minimize the risk of penalties resulting from a Section 482 adjustment thus may have to devote substantial time and resources at the time of a transaction to documenting the manner in which intercompany prices are determined. A taxpayer desirous of more certainty that penalties will not apply might consider seeking an advance pricing agreement.

As a result of the same concerns that prompted the penalty provisions discussed above, certain taxpayers are required to report to the government (and maintain adequate records with respect to) transactions with related parties. Generally, both U.S. corporations that are 25 percent foreign-owned and foreign corporations engaged in a trade or business in the U.S. are subject to this requirement.[31] Failure to comply can result in substantial penalties.[32]

Proposed Changes to Section 482. Despite Section 482's broad grant of power to the Executive Branch, some tax policymakers have expressed the belief that certain taxpayers, particularly foreign-owned corporations, continue to use transactions with related parties to shift large amounts of income from the U.S. to foreign jurisdictions.[33] A 1992 proposal[34] would

---

28. I.R.C. §§ 6662(a), (e)(1)(B)(i), (h)(1), (2)(A)(ii).

29. Taxpayers are subject to the 20 percent accuracy-related penalty for a substantial valuation misstatement if the net increase in taxable income resulting from a Section 482 adjustment exceeds the lesser of $5 million or 10 percent of the taxpayer's gross receipts, or a 40 percent gross valuation misstatement penalty if the net increase in taxable income exceeds the lesser of $20 million or 20 percent of gross receipts. I.R.C. § 6662(e)(1)(B)(ii), (h)(2)(A)(iii).

30. I.R.C. § 6662(e)(3)(B).

31. I.R.C. §§ 6038A; 6038C.

32. I.R.C. §§ 6038A(d); 6038C(c). In comparison with Section 6038A, Section 6038C authorizes the Treasury Department to require corporations subject to the statute to maintain a broader range of records and to report a broader range of information. I.R.C. § 6038C(a)(2), (b)(2).

33. See, e.g., Hearings Before the Subcomm. on Oversight of the House Comm. on Ways and Means, 102d Cong., 2d Sess. (1992) (statement of the Honorable J.J. Pickle, Chairman of the Subcomm. on Oversight) ("The fact of the matter is that, in our society, a teacher or factory worker can pay more in Federal income tax than a major multinational corporation with billions in annual U.S. sales."); Hearings Before the Subcomm. on Oversight of the House Comm. on Ways and Means, 101st Cong., 2d Sess. (1990) (statement of Fred T. Goldberg, Jr., have amended Section 482 by requiring certain foreign corporations doing business in the U.S. and foreign-owned U.S. corporations to recognize a minimum amount of U.S. taxable income if they have more than a threshold level of transactions with foreign related parties. In general, the minimum U.S. taxable income for an affected corporation was a percentage of the corporation's gross receipts. The percentage was to be established by reference to data derived from domestic corporations in the same industry. Thus, the proposed legislation was designed to ensure that foreign and foreign-owned corporations report a level of income commensurate with that reported by a similarly-situated purely domestic corporation.

This proposal received harsh criticism on a number of grounds, including the soundness of its assumption that foreign-owned corporations with incomes below the industry average are shifting income and the possibility that the proposal violates provisions of tax treaties to which the U.S. is a party.[35] Although the proposal never became law, Congress's constant search for new revenue makes it quite possible that this or a similar provision could be resurrected.

B.   CONSOLIDATED RETURNS

Code §§ 1501; 1502; 1503(a); 1504(a) & (b); 1552. Skim § 243(a)(3), (b)(1) & (2)(A).

1.   INTRODUCTION

Earlier in this chapter, we saw that the Code limits certain tax benefits available to affiliated corporations by treating the corporations, for purposes of determining their entitlement to the benefits, as a single taxpayer.[1] In this section, we explore a related concept: certain closely affiliated corporations are permitted to calculate and report their federal tax liability as if they were a single taxpaying unit.

As a general rule, every corporation subject to the federal income tax must report its tax liability on a separate return.[2] Section 1501 is an exception to this rule. Section 1501 permits an affiliated group of corporations to elect to report its tax liability on a single, consolidated return. The Code, however, provides little guidance on the manner in which an affiliat-

Commissioner of Internal Revenue) ("[T]he aggregate data, and our own examination activities, suggest that foreign controlled companies have adopted transfer pricing and other practices that may significantly understate their U.S. income tax liabilities.").

34. H.R. 5270 (1992), entitled the Foreign Income Tax Rationalization and Simplification Act of 1992, designating the current statutory language as Section 482(a) and adding a new Section 482(b).

35. The proposal was described as being "strongly opposed by the Treasury and, for that matter, by virtually everyone else." Bittker & Eustice, Federal Income Taxation of Corporations and Shareholders ¶ 13.20[4][i].

1. See Section A2 of this chapter, supra.

2. I.R.C. § 6012(a)(2); Reg. § 1.6012–2(a).

ed group must prepare a consolidated return. Congress has delegated that task to the Secretary of the Treasury, who is directed by Section 1502 to issue regulations. Rising to the occasion, the Treasury Department has issued extensive, detailed regulations that are the primary source of guidance on consolidated returns.

In reading the material that follows, consider the extent to which the consolidated return rules truly treat an affiliated group of corporations as a single entity. As you will discover, certain rules fully reflect a single entity model. Others continue to recognize the separate existence of each corporation in the group (a "separate entity" model). This conflict in the regulations is the source of much of their complexity.

2.   ELIGIBILITY AND ELECTION TO FILE A CONSOLIDATED RETURN

a.   ELIGIBILITY

Section 1501 grants the privilege of filing a consolidated return only to an "affiliated group of corporations." The term "affiliated group" is defined in Section 1504(a) as one or more chains of "includible corporations" connected through stock ownership to a common parent that is an includible corporation, if (1) the common parent owns directly stock possessing at least 80 percent of the total voting power and total value of the stock of at least one of the other includible corporations, and (2) stock possessing at least 80 percent of the total voting power and total value of the stock of each includible corporation (other than the common parent) is owned directly by one or more of the other includible corporations. Thus, if corporation X owns stock possessing 80 percent of the total voting power and total value of corporations Y and Z, and if X, Y and Z all are includible corporations, then X, Y and Z are members of an affiliated group of corporations. The result would be the same if Z were an 80 percent-owned subsidiary of Y (i.e., if Z were a second-tier subsidiary of X).

The term "includible corporation" is defined in Section 1504(b) as any corporation, with seven specific exceptions. Among the corporations excluded from the definition are corporations exempt from tax under Section 501, insurance companies subject to tax under Section 801, and all foreign corporations.[1] Historically, S corporations by definition could not be a member of an affiliated group because they were not permitted to have subsidiaries. Under current law, however, S corporations may have both C and S corporation subsidiaries, but they are not allowed to join in the filing of a consolidated return with their C corporation affiliates.[2]

In determining whether an affiliated group of corporations exists, Section 1504(a)(4) provides that nonvoting, nonconvertible stock which is limited and preferred as to dividends and has redemption and liquidation

---

1.   I.R.C. § 1504(b). Several special rules modify the definition of "includible corporation." See I.R.C. § 1504(c)–(f).

2.   I.R.C. § 1504(b)(8). The C corporation affiliates still may file as a consolidated group, but without including their S corporation parent. See Chapter 15B, infra.

rights which do not exceed the stock's issue price, except for a reasonable premium, is disregarded. The features described in Section 1504(a)(4) are those commonly associated with preferred stock. Merely because stock is labelled as preferred stock, however, does not mean that it is ignored in applying the stock ownership requirements of Section 1504(a); only stock that has each of the features listed in Section 1504(a)(4) is ignored. This provision generally is favorable to taxpayers in that it permits a corporation to raise capital by issuing stock described in Section 1504(a)(4) without making the corporation ineligible to join in the filing of a consolidated return.[3]

If a corporation is included (or required to be included) in a consolidated return filed by an affiliated group and subsequently ceases to be a member of the group, the corporation cannot be included in a consolidated return filed by the group (or certain related groups) during the succeeding five years.[4] This is an anti-abuse rule intended to foreclose the temporary elimination of a member from an affiliated group in order to improve the group's or the member's tax results. The Secretary of the Treasury has authority to waive this five-year waiting period under conditions that the Secretary prescribes.[5]

b. ELECTION AND RELATED MATTERS

Even if two or more corporations constitute an affiliated group, the corporations must file separate returns unless they affirmatively elect to exercise their privilege of filing a consolidated return. An affiliated group exercises this privilege by filing a consolidated return not later than the last day prescribed by law (including extensions) for filing the common parent's return.[6] As one might expect in such a regime, a consolidated return must be filed on the basis of the common parent's taxable year, and each subsidiary in the group must adopt the common parent's taxable year beginning with the first consolidated return year[7] for which the subsidiary's income is includible in the consolidated return.[8] In contrast, the method of accounting that each member of the group must use is determined without regard to the method used by the common parent.[9]

3. Sections 1504(a)(5)(A) and (B) similarly address what constitutes "stock" by directing the Secretary of the Treasury to issue regulations that treat (1) warrants, obligations convertible into stock and other similar interests as stock and stock as not stock, and (2) options to acquire or sell stock as having been exercised. See Reg. § 1.1504–4.

4. I.R.C. § 1504(a)(3)(A). More precisely, the corporation cannot again be included in a consolidated return filed by the group before the sixty-first month beginning after the corporation's first taxable year in which it ceased to be a member of the group. Id.

5. I.R.C. § 1504(a)(3)(B). The general circumstances under which a waiver will be granted are set forth in Rev. Proc. 2002–32, 2002–1 C.B. 959, modified by Rev. Proc. 2006–21, 2006–1 C.B. 1050.

6. Reg. § 1.1502–75(a)(1).

7. A consolidated return year is a taxable year for which a consolidated return is filed or required to be filed. Reg. § 1.1502–1(d).

8. Reg. § 1.1502–76(a)(1).

9. Reg. § 1.1502–17(a).

As a condition to the privilege of filing a consolidated return, Section 1501 requires that all corporations that were members of the affiliated group at any time during the taxable year consent to all of the regulations prescribed under Section 1502 that are in existence on the last day prescribed by law for filing the return. This requirement presumably is designed to minimize taxpayer challenges to the regulations.[10] In general, a corporation consents to the regulations by joining in the making of a consolidated return.[11]

The decision to file a consolidated return is a significant one, in part because an affiliated group that does so generally must continue to file on a consolidated basis for all succeeding tax years unless the group no longer remains in existence or the Secretary grants permission to discontinue filing for "good cause."[12] In general, an affiliated group no longer remains in existence if the common parent no longer remains as the common parent (e.g., if the parent sells the stock of all of its subsidiaries to one or more third parties).[13] The Service generally grants permission to discontinue filing for good cause only when there are certain changes in the Code or regulations that have a substantial adverse effect on the group's consolidated tax liability relative to the aggregate tax liability the members would incur if they filed separate returns, or when certain other factors demonstrate that there exists good cause for the discontinuance.[14] In short, the decision to file a consolidated return is one with which an affiliated group likely will have to live for an extended period of time.

3. COMPUTATION OF CONSOLIDATED TAXABLE INCOME

a. OVERVIEW

An affiliated group of corporations that files (or is required to file) a consolidated return is referred to in the regulations as a "consolidated group."[1] A consolidated group is subject to federal income tax on its consolidated taxable income.[2]

The first step in determining a group's consolidated taxable income is to determine the separate taxable income (or loss) of each member.[3] Each member's separate taxable income must be determined by making several adjustments, the most significant of which are (1) the adjustments that take into account transactions between members of the group (so-called "intercompany transactions") and transactions that relate to the stock,

---

10. Not all taxpayers are so easily dissuaded. See American Standard, Inc. v. United States, 602 F.2d 256 (Ct.Cl.1979) (successful challenge to regulations).

11. I.R.C. § 1501; Reg. § 1.1502–75(b)(1).

12. Reg. § 1.1502–75(a)(2), (c)(1), (d)(1).

13. Reg. § 1.1502–75(d)(1).

14. Reg. § 1.1502–75(c)(1)(ii), (c)(1)(iii).

1. Reg. § 1.1502–1(a), (h).

2. Reg. § 1.1502–2(a). A consolidated group also is subject to other federal taxes, including the personal holding company tax, the accumulated earnings tax, and the alternative minimum tax. See Reg. § 1.1502–2; Prop. Reg. § 1.1502–2.

3. Reg. § 1.1502–11(a)(1).

bonds and other obligations of the members (such as intercompany distributions), and (2) the omission of certain items of income and deduction that must be determined on a consolidated basis.[4] After these adjustments, the separate taxable incomes of the members are combined. Next, the items of income and deduction that must be determined on a consolidated basis are calculated in accordance with the regulations and then added to or subtracted from the combined separate taxable incomes. The resulting amount is the group's consolidated taxable income, which is subject to tax at the rates specified in Section 11. Subject to certain restrictions, the consolidated group is allowed credits against this tax (and the other federal taxes to which it is subject), including the general business and foreign tax credits.[5] For purposes of determining each member's earnings and profits, the group's consolidated tax liability also must be allocated among the members.[6]

b.   COMPUTATION OF SEPARATE TAXABLE INCOME

Intercompany Transactions. As the first step in determining a consolidated group's consolidated taxable income, each member's separate taxable income (or loss) must be determined as if the member were a separate corporation, with certain modifications.[7] One modification is that "intercompany transactions" must be taken into account in accordance with the detailed rules set forth in the regulations. An intercompany transaction is a transaction between corporations that are members of the same consolidated group immediately after the transaction.[8] Examples include sales or rentals of property, the performance of services, the licensing of technology (such as a patent), and the lending of money.[9]

The essence of the rules governing intercompany transactions can best be understood by first considering the effect of a transaction between two divisions of a single corporation. For example, assume that corporation X has two divisions, S and B, and that division S transfers land with a fair market value of $100 and a basis of $70 to division B in exchange for $100 cash. No taxable event occurs as a result of the transfers because corporation X continues to hold both the land and the cash. Corporation X would retain a $70 basis in the land and the transaction would have no effect on X's taxable income. If, three years later, division B sells the land to an unrelated third party for $110, then corporation X would realize and recognize $40 of income at that time. The character and other tax attributes of this income generally would depend on the activities of divisions S and B with respect to the land.[10] Similarly, if division S leases office space

---

4. See Reg. § 1.1502–12(a), –12(b) through (r).

5. Reg. §§ 1.1502–2; 1.1502–3; 1.1502–4.

6. I.R.C. § 1552.

7. Reg. § 1.1502–11(a)(1), –12

8. Reg. § 1.1502–13(b)(1)(i).

9. Id.

10. For example, the character of the income as capital gain, Section 1231 gain, or ordinary income generally would depend on whether corporation X held the land for investment, for use in its trade or business, or for sale to customers in the ordinary course of its business. Determining the purpose for to division B in exchange for an annual rental payment of $100, corporation X's taxable income would be unaffected because the arrangement would constitute a mere shifting of assets within one taxable entity.

The regulations governing intercompany transactions contain a "matching rule" and an "acceleration rule" that generally attempt to approximate the results of a transaction between divisions of a single corporation. Before illustrating this point, the rather complex terminology employed by the regulations deserves some mention. The regulations refer to the selling member in a transaction as "S" and to the buying member as "B." S's items of income, gain, deduction and loss from an intercompany transaction are referred to as its "intercompany items."[11] B's tax items arising from an intercompany transaction (or property acquired in an intercompany transaction) are referred to as "corresponding items."[12] A "recomputed corresponding item" is the corresponding item that B would take into account if S and B were divisions in a single corporation and the intercompany transaction were between those divisions.[13]

To return to the illustrations set forth above in the context of a consolidated return, assume that corporations S and B are at all relevant times members of a consolidated group and that, in year 1, S sells land with a fair market value of $100 and a basis of $70 to B for $100 cash. In year 3, B sells the land to an unrelated third party for $110. The sale from S to B is an intercompany transaction, and the $30 gain realized by S is S's intercompany item. Under the matching rule prescribed by the regulations, S takes its intercompany gain into account in computing its separate taxable income only when B takes into account its corresponding item.[14] B has no corresponding item in year 1, and therefore S's $30 gain is deferred. In year 3, B realizes a gain of $10 ($110 amount realized less $100 basis in the land),[15] which is B's corresponding item. B must take this $10 into account in accordance with its method of accounting.[16] Assume that under B's method of accounting B takes the $10 gain into account in year 3 in computing its separate taxable income. Under the matching rule, S takes its $30 intercompany gain into account to reflect the difference between B's corresponding item ($10) and the recomputed corresponding item, i.e., the gain that B would have taken into account in year 3 if S and B were divisions of a single corporation. If S and B were divisions, B would have received the land from S with a $70 basis and therefore would have realized on the sale in year 3 a $40 gain, which is the recomputed corresponding item. Thus, S would take into account in year 3 the difference between this recomputed corresponding item ($40) and B's corresponding item ($10), or $30.

which X held the land would require an evaluation of the purposes for which divisions S and B held the land.

11.   Reg. § 1.1502–13(b)(2)(i).

12.   Reg. § 1.1502–13(b)(3)(i).

13.   Reg. § 1.1502–13(b)(4).

14.   Reg. § 1.1502–13(c)(2)(ii).

15.   B obtained a $100 cost basis in the land under Section 1012 when it purchased the land from S. Reg. § 1.1502–13(a)(2).

16.   Reg. § 1.1502–13(c)(2)(i).

The result in this example is similar to the illustration above when S and B were divisions of a single corporation. There, as here, no gain with respect to the land was taken into account in determining taxable income until the land was transferred to a third party. In this respect, the regulations treat S and B as parts of a single taxpaying entity. The regulations similarly adopt a single entity approach with respect to the tax attributes of the $40 gain realized by the group, such as the gain's character: the character of S's $30 intercompany gain and B's $10 corresponding gain will depend upon the combined activities of S and B with respect to the land.[17] In other respects, the regulations adopt a separate entity approach. For example, the total $40 gain realized is allocated partly to S and partly to B, each of whom takes its portion of the gain into account in determining its separate taxable income. In general, no similar allocation would take place for tax purposes if S and B were divisions of a single corporation.

The matching rule also would apply to any other intercompany transactions between S and B, such as a lease of office space from S to B in exchange for an annual rental payment of $100. Assuming that B's payments of rent are currently deductible under B's method of accounting, S would take into account as current income the difference between B's $100 rental deduction and the recomputed rental deduction (zero), or $100.[18] Although S and B would take the income and deduction into account in computing their separate taxable incomes, the items effectively would offset each other when the separate taxable incomes are combined, so that the transaction generally would have no net effect on the group's consolidated taxable income.

The second cornerstone of the intercompany transaction regulations, the acceleration rule, guards against situations in which S's intercompany items and B's corresponding items cannot be taken into account under the matching rule to produce the effect of treating S and B as divisions of a single corporation.[19] In that case, B continues to take its corresponding items into account in accordance with its method of accounting, but S's intercompany items are taken into account immediately before it first becomes impossible to achieve the effect of treating S and B as divisions, i.e., S's intercompany items are accelerated.[20] To illustrate, assume that immediately after S sells the land to B in year 1 in the example above, the common parent sells all the stock of B to an unrelated third party. Because B no longer is a member of the consolidated group that includes S, the effect of treating S and B as divisions cannot be achieved. The acceleration rule therefore requires S to take its $30 of intercompany gain into account in year 1.[21] B would take any gain or loss on a subsequent sale of the land

---

17. Reg. § 1.1502–13(c)(1)(i).

18. Reg. § 1.1502–13(c)(7)(ii) Example 8. The recomputed rental deduction is zero because B's payments to S would not generate tax deductions if S and B were divisions of a single corporation.

19. Reg. § 1.1502–13(d).

20. Reg. § 1.1502–13(d)(1)(i), (d)(2)(ii).

21. See Reg. § 1.1502–13(d)(3) Example 1(e).

to a third party into account in accordance with B's method of accounting, and this gain or loss would be reported either on B's separate return or, if B is a member of another consolidated group, on that group's consolidated return.

Even if an item is taken into account under the intercompany transaction rules described above, the item can be deferred or disallowed under another provision. For example, Sections 267(f) (deferral of certain losses), 269 (acquisitions to evade or avoid tax), and 482 (allocations among commonly controlled taxpayers) all potentially may apply.[22]

Intercompany Distributions. The regulations also require adjustments to the separate taxable incomes of group members for certain transactions with respect to a member's stock and other obligations. This discussion will be confined to an overview of the treatment of distributions to which Section 301 applies.[23]

An "intercompany distribution" is an intercompany transaction to which § 301 applies.[24] Thus, an ordinary cash distribution made by corporation S to its parent, corporation P, both of whom are members of the same affiliated group immediately after the distribution, is an intercompany distribution.

Intercompany distributions generally are excluded from the gross income of the distributee member.[25] This exclusion from income is available, however, only to the extent that there is a corresponding negative adjustment in the distributee member's basis in the stock of the distributing member.[26] This negative adjustment is made pursuant to the basis adjustment rules set forth in the regulations.[27] Under the basis adjustment rules, a distribution (and certain other tax items) effectively can reduce the distributee member's basis below zero.[28] This negative amount is referred to as the distributee member's "excess loss account."[29] Thus, provided that the distributee member reduces its basis in the distributing member's stock, the distributee does not recognize gain on an intercompany distribution, even if the distribution exceeds the distributee member's basis.[30] A subsequent disposition of the distributing member's stock, however, will cause the amount of the excess loss account to be included in the distributee member's gross income.

A corporation that distributes appreciated property to its shareholders generally recognizes gain, but not loss.[31] These rules are modified in the context of a consolidated return. From the distributing member's perspective, intercompany distributions of property in effect are treated in the

22. Reg. § 1.1502–13(a)(4).

23. See Chapter 4, supra.

24. Reg. § 1.1502–13(f)(2)(i).

25. Reg. § 1.1502–13(f)(2)(ii).

26. Id.

27. See Reg. § 1.1502–32. The stock basis adjustment rules are discussed in more detail in Section B4 of this chapter, infra.

28. Reg. § 1.1502–32(a)(3)(ii).

29. Id.

30. This rule, of course, is contrary to the general rule of Section 301(c)(3)(A).

31. I.R.C. § 311(a), (b).

same manner as the intercompany sales of property examined earlier. Thus, if in year 1 distributing member S distributes appreciated property to its parent, member P, and P sells the property to an unrelated third party in year 3, S would not take its gain into account in computing its separate taxable income until year 3.[32] If instead S realizes a loss on the distribution, then the tax consequences to S depend on P's actions with respect to the property. If P sells the property in year 3 to an unrelated third party, and under P's method of accounting P takes into account in that year its gain or loss on the sale, then S would take its loss into account in year 3.[33] In contrast, if P distributes the property to its shareholders and realizes no further gain or loss, then S's loss is disallowed and never taken into account.[34] The general effect of these rules is to treat P and S as divisions of a single corporation: both gain and loss are taken into account if the property is sold outside the group but, in accordance with the general rules of Sections 311(a) and (b), only gain is taken into account if the property is transferred outside the group in a distribution to a shareholder.

c.   CONSOLIDATED ITEMS

In calculating consolidated taxable income, certain items of income and deduction are taken into account on a consolidated basis. That is, these items generally are omitted in calculating the separate taxable income of each consolidated group member and aggregated with like items from the other members. The net amount of each item is added to or subtracted from the sum of the members' separate taxable incomes (as determined by omitting the consolidated items).[35] The items that must be taken into account on a consolidated basis include capital gain or loss, gain or loss with respect to Section 1231 property, the charitable and dividends received deductions, and the deduction for net operating losses.[36] The regulations provide detailed rules on the manner in which the consolidated amounts of these items must be determined.[37]

Consolidated items may be affected by the intercompany transaction rules. For example, if one member of a consolidated group realizes a capital gain from the sale of property to another member, the selling member's gain may be deferred until a later year. If so, then the gain would not be taken into account in determining the group's consolidated capital gain or loss.[38]

---

32.   Reg. § 1.1502–13(f)(2)(iii), –13(f)(7) Example 1.

33.   See Reg. § 1.1502–13(c)(6)(i), –13(f)(7) Example 1(d). If S distributed the property to a shareholder who is not a member of the affiliated group, however, then S would not recognize its loss under the general rule of Section 311(a). Reg. § 1.1502–13(f)(2)(iii).

34.   See Reg. § 1.1502–13(c)(6)(i), –13(f)(7) Example 1(d).

35.   Reg. § 1.1502–11(a).

36.   Id. See Chapter 12C3 for the limitations on the use of a member's net operating loss carryovers.

37.   See Reg. §§ 1.1502–21 (net operating losses); 1.1502–22 (capital gain or loss); 1.1502–23 (Section 1231 property); 1.1502–24 (charitable contributions); 1.1502–26 (dividends received deduction).

38.   See Section B3b of this chapter, infra.

d. ALLOCATION OF TAX LIABILITY

Once the total tax liability of a consolidated group is determined, the liability must be allocated among the members for purposes of determining each member's earnings and profits.[39] A corporation's federal income tax liability during the year generally reduces its earnings and profits.[40] Among other effects, this reduction in earnings and profits may affect the characterization under Section 301 of distributions made by the members.

Section 1552 provides three methods pursuant to which an affiliated group can make this allocation and also permits the group to select any other allocation method with the approval of the Secretary of the Treasury.[41] Under the first method, the group's tax liability generally is allocated based on the ratio of each member's separate taxable income to the sum of the separate taxable incomes of all members.[42] For this purpose, a member's separate taxable income generally is calculated under the rules discussed earlier (e.g., by applying the intercompany transaction rules) and then adjusted for certain items specified in the regulations.[43] Under the second method, the group's tax liability similarly also is allocated using a ratio, but in this case each member's separately computed tax liability is compared to the sum of the members' separately computed tax liabilities.[44] Again, certain adjustments are required in computing the separate tax liability of each member.[45] The third method generally involves comparing each member's tax liability determined on both a consolidated basis (under the first method) and a separate basis (under the second method) and reallocating any increases in tax liability resulting from consolidation (i.e., any excess of the amount allocated to a member under the first method over the amount allocated under the second method) to those members who experience decreases in tax liability due to the consolidation.[46]

The regulations issued under Section 1502 that address adjustments to earnings and profits for members of a consolidated group provide certain additional allocation methods.[47]

4. STOCK BASIS ADJUSTMENTS

Consistent with the general purpose of the consolidated return rules to treat members of an affiliated group as a single taxpaying unit, a member's basis in the stock of another member is adjusted upward or downward to reflect the subsidiary member's distributions and its items of income, gain, deduction and loss.[1] This rolling basis mechanism prevents the shareholder-member ("P") from incurring a second round of corporate level tax, or

39. I.R.C. § 1552.

40. See Chapter 4B, supra.

41. I.R.C. § 1552(a).

42. I.R.C. § 1552(a)(1); Reg. § 1.1552–1(a)(1).

43. Reg. § 1.1552–1(a)(1)(ii).

44. I.R.C. § 1552(a)(2); Reg. § 1.1552–1(a)(2).

45. Reg. § 1.1552–1(a)(2)(ii).

46. I.R.C. § 1552(a)(3); Reg. § 1.1552–1(a)(3).

47. Reg. § 1.1502–33(d).

1. Reg. § 1.1502–32(a)(1).

enjoying a double deduction, with respect to its investment in S when S's income or loss already has been reflected in the group's consolidated return.

In general, P's stock basis is increased by S's taxable and tax-exempt income, and is decreased by S's taxable loss, any noncapital, nondeductible expenses of S, and any distributions that S makes with respect to its stock.[2] The regulations contain a host of special rules for computing each of these items. Contrary to the Code's conventional wisdom that a negative basis is impermissible, the consolidated return rules allow the effective equivalent of a negative basis. When the items that decrease basis reduce P's basis to zero, any further reductions create an "excess loss account."[3] In general, P must take into account as income or gain the amount of its excess loss account when it is treated as having disposed of the S stock.[4]

For example, assume that the S stock held by P has a fair market value of $100 and an adjusted basis of zero, and that during the taxable year S has $10 of tax-exempt income and also makes a $20 distribution to P. The $10 of tax-exempt income would increase P's basis by $10. The $20 distribution would reduce P's basis to zero and also would create a $10 excess loss account. If P then sells the S stock for $100, P will have a $110 gain ($100 excess of amount realized over adjusted basis plus $10 excess loss account).

5. ADVANTAGES AND DISADVANTAGES OF FILING A CONSOLIDATED RETURN

Given the highly complex rules confronting filers of consolidated returns, one might well ask whether the ordeal is really a "privilege." The answer is that filing a consolidated return is not always advantageous. An affiliated group, with the aid of its accountants and tax counsel, must carefully assess the potential pros and cons. To a large extent, this assessment involves predicting the future direction that the group will take in its business and the likely performance and tax position of each member.

The advantages of filing a consolidated return include the ability to offset income of one member with the losses of another, the exclusion of dividends from the distributee member's gross income, and the ability to defer recognition of gain on intercompany transactions. Disadvantages include compliance with a complex set of regulations, and the permanent nature of the election to file a consolidated return (i.e., the group generally must continue to file a consolidated return even if doing so turns out to be disadvantageous relative to filing separate returns). Thus, an assessment of the desirability of filing a consolidated return involves considering issues such as the extent to which each member will have taxable income or loss, whether any limitations exist on the ability to use losses of one member

2. Reg. § 1.1502–32(b)(2).

3. Reg. § 1.1502–32(a)(3)(ii); 1.1502–19(a)(2).

4. Reg. § 1.1502–19(b)(1), (c).

against income of another, the extent to which the members will engage in intercompany transactions and the effect of the intercompany transaction rules on those transactions, and the likelihood of current members leaving or new members entering the group.

PROBLEMS

1. Corporation P owns 90% of Corporations A and B. Corporations A and B each own 40% of Corporation C. Corporation C owns 80% of Corporation D. Corporation D owns 100% of Corporation E, a tax-exempt organization. Corporation E owns 100% of Corporation F which owns 100% of Corporation G. All of the indicated percentages reflect total voting power and total value owned by the shareholder.

(a) To what extent do the above corporations constitute an "affiliated group"?

(b) What result in (a), above, if Corporation B sells 10% of its stock in Corporation C?

2. P, Inc. owns all of the only class of S, Inc. stock, and P and S are in a consolidated group. During year 1, P performs services for S in exchange for $10,000, and P incurs $8,000 of expenses in performing those services. Assume that S must capitalize its $10,000 cost for the services and takes into account $1,000 of cost recovery deductions in each of years 2 through 11. How will the P–S consolidated group be taxed on this transaction?

CHAPTER 14

ANTI–AVOIDANCE RULES

A. INTRODUCTION

The preceding chapters have demonstrated the many ways that C corporations and their shareholders have sought to lessen the impact of the double tax on corporate profits, avoid the higher marginal individual tax rates on ordinary income, convert ordinary income to capital gain and use tax shelters to reduce income taxes at the corporate and shareholder levels. Congress has responded with a host of anti-avoidance rules, many targeting discrete problems and others seeking a more global solution to errant taxpayer behavior.

This chapter begins with a closer look at the economic substance doctrine, whose common law roots were previewed in Chapter 1. Congress codified this venerable doctrine in 2010 and sharpened its bite with a strict liability penalty that gives the IRS a powerful new weapon in its battle against corporate tax shelters and other tax-avoidance motivated transactions.

The chapter continues by examining two anti-avoidance provisions that historically were major roadblocks to taxpayer exploitation of Subchapter C: the accumulated earnings tax and the personal holding company tax. These penalty taxes were designed to prevent taxpayers from escaping the higher individual tax rates by accumulating operating income of a business in a more lightly taxed C corporation or using the corporation as a vehicle to reduce the tax burden on personal service and investment income. The complex penalty regimes remain intact in the Code, but their importance is diminished whenever the top corporate and individual rates are the same and long-term capital gains and dividends received by noncorporate shareholders are taxed at the same preferential rate. For the benefit of corporate tax historians and others with a need to know, this chapter provides an overview of the two penalty taxes by exploring their contours without becoming distracted by too many details.

B. THE ECONOMIC SUBSTANCE DOCTRINE

1. BACKGROUND: CORPORATE TAX SHELTERS

The economic substance doctrine evolved as a weapon used by the IRS and applied by the courts to deny tax benefits arising from transactions that complied with the literal language of the Internal Revenue Code but lacked an independent business purpose or did not result in any meaningful change in a taxpayer's economic position apart from the reduction of federal taxes. The most prevalent recent application of the economic substance doctrine has been in connection with corporate tax shelters, which are transactions designed and marketed for the purpose of substantially reducing the tax liability of profitable corporations and their wealthy executives and shareholders.[1] Corporate tax shelters are typified by these characteristics: (1) realization of tax losses without corresponding economic loss through transactions having questionable economic substance apart from the desire to reduce United States income taxes; (2) realization of income by "tax-indifferent" facilitators, such as foreign affiliates, domestic corporations with soon-to-expire loss carryovers, and tax-exempt organizations; (3) reliance on the literal language or ambiguities in the Internal Revenue Code to support a result that may be technically defensible but is inconsistent with the spirit of the law and well-accepted tax principles; (4) marketing of transactions under a veil of secrecy by entrepreneurial accounting firms and investment banks in exchange for enormous fees; (5) inconsistent treatment for financial accounting and tax purposes of items resulting from the same transaction; and (6) the willingness of corporate managers and their advisors, emboldened by "reasoned" opinions of tax counsel[2] and the knowledge that IRS audits have been reduced, to play "audit roulette" by taking questionable tax return reporting positions with the hope (and expectation?) that they will never be scrutinized. A crisper and perhaps more informative definition has been proposed by Professor Michael Graetz, who has characterized a tax shelter as "a deal done by very smart people that, absent tax considerations, would be very stupid."[3]

An attack on corporate tax shelters has been proceeding for many years on multiple fronts. Developments have included piecemeal legislation, changes to the rules governing tax practice before the Internal Revenue Service, a sprinkling of test cases involving high profile taxpayers and, as discussed below, codification of the economic substance doctrine and a strict no fault penalty for taxpayers who violate it. Key components of this campaign have been: (1) disallowance of tax benefits derived in certain types of "listed" tax avoidance transactions;[4] (2) disclosure rules that require taxpayers to put the Service on notice if they have engaged in "reportable" transactions and require promoters and tax advisors to "register" corporate tax shelters before the transaction occurs;[5] (3) enhanced

---

1. See, e.g., Joint Committee on Taxation, Background and Present Law Relating to Tax Shelters (JCX–19–02), March 19, 2002; Symposium on Corporate Tax Shelters, Part I, 55 Tax L.Rev. No. 2 (Winter 2002); Part II, 55 Tax L.Rev. No. 3 (Spring 2002).

2. An opinion of counsel assuring a taxpayer that a transaction is "more likely than not" to achieve its intended purpose, ordinarily insulates the taxpayers from various civil penalties. See, e.g., I.R.C. § 6662(a), (d); Reg. § 1.6662–4.

3. See, e.g., Tom Herman, "Tax Report," Wall St. J. at A–1 (Feb. 10, 1999).

4. A "listed" transaction is one that the Service formally determines to have a potential for tax avoidance or evasion. The "list" continues to grow, mostly through published notices and other guidance. See, e.g., Notice 2001–17, 2001–9 I.R.B. 730, identifying a contingent liability shelter as a listed transaction.

5. See, e.g., I.R.C. §§ 6011 (taxpayer must disclose reportable transaction); 6111 (organizers and promoters must register posubstantial understatement penalties for items attributable to corporate tax shelters;[6] (4) stiff no-fault penalties for failure to comply with the tax shelter disclosure requirements;[7] and (5) heightened regulation of the conduct of professional advisors who provide opinion letters and participate in the marketing of corporate tax shelters.[8] To bolster the assault, some commentators have gone so far as to propose that public companies be required to compute their taxable income by reference to the income reported for financial accounting purposes, with only limited deviations permitted for valid tax policy reasons.[9]

The Service's early track record in the test cases was mixed but it markedly improved as more courts became persuaded to apply the established common law doctrines to disallow intended tax benefits from tax-motivated transactions. Not surprisingly, the Tax Court was somewhat more inclined to apply these venerable doctrines than the generalist judges of the courts of appeals.[10] The *United Parcel* case, which follows, was a rare taxpayer victory. It offers an example of how the courts apply the common law economic substance doctrine in a corporate tax shelter case involving a familiar company.

United Parcel Service of America, Inc. v. Commissioner

United States Court of Appeals, Eleventh Circuit, 2001.
254 F.3d 1014.

■ Cox, Circuit Judge:

The tax court held United Parcel Service of America, Inc. (UPS) liable for additional taxes and penalties for the tax year 1984. UPS appeals, and we reverse and remand.

I.   Background

UPS, whose main business is shipping packages, had a practice in the early 1980s of reimbursing customers for lost or damaged parcels up to

---

tentially illegal shelters with the IRS); 6112 (promoters must maintain lists of clients who purchase potentially illegal tax shelters and, on request, must disclose these client lists to the IRS); and Reg. §§ 1.6011–4; 301.6711–1.

6. I.R.C. §§ 6662(d)(1)(B); 6662A.

7. I.R.C. §§ 6707; 6707A; 6708.

8. See, e.g., 31 U.S. § 330(b), (d) and various implementing changes to Circular 230, which regulates professionals who practice before the Treasury Department (including the IRS).

9. See, e.g., Yin, "Getting Serious About Corporate Tax Shelters: Taking a Lesson from History," 54 SMU L. Rev. 209 (2001).

10. For some of the major recent tax shelter cases, most of which involve mind boggling fact patterns, see, e.g., Coltec Industries, Inc. v. United States, 62 Fed. Cl. 716 (Ct. Fed. Cl. 2004); Black & Decker v. United States, 340 F. Supp. 2d 621 (D. Md. 2004); Compaq v. Commissioner, 277 F.3d 778 (5th Cir.2001), rev'g, 113 T.C. 214 (1999); Wells Fargo v. United States, 641 F.3d 1319 (Fed. Cir. 2011); and TIFD III–E, Inc. v. United States, 666 F.3d 836 (2d Cir. 2012). One of the Service's greatest successes to date was in a federal district court. See Long–Term Capital Holdings v. United States, 330 F.Supp.2d 122 (D. Conn. 2004).

$100 in declared value.[1] Above that level, UPS would assume liability up to the parcel's declared value if the customer paid 25per additional $100 in declared value, the "excess-value charge." If a parcel were lost or damaged, UPS would process and pay the resulting claim. UPS turned a large profit on excess-value charges because it never came close to paying as much in claims as it collected in charges, in part because of efforts it made to safeguard and track excess-value shipments. This profit was taxed; UPS declared its revenue from excess-value charges as income on its 1983 return, and it deducted as expenses the claims paid on damaged or lost excess-value parcels.

UPS's insurance broker suggested that UPS could avoid paying taxes on the lucrative excess-value business if it restructured the program as insurance provided by an overseas affiliate. UPS implemented this plan in 1983 by first forming and capitalizing a Bermuda subsidiary, Overseas Partners, Ltd. (OPL), almost all of whose shares were distributed as a taxable dividend to UPS shareholders (most of whom were employees; UPS stock was not publicly traded). UPS then purchased an insurance policy, for the benefit of UPS customers, from National Union Fire Insurance Company. By this policy, National Union assumed the risk of damage to or loss of excess-value shipments. The premiums for the policy were the excess-value charges that UPS collected. UPS, not National Union, was responsible for administering claims brought under the policy. National Union in turn entered a reinsurance treaty with OPL. Under the treaty, OPL assumed risk commensurate with National Union's, in exchange for premiums that equal the excess-value payments National Union got from UPS, less commissions, fees, and excise taxes.

Under this plan, UPS thus continued to collect 25per $100 of excess value from its customers, process and pay claims, and take special measures to safeguard valuable packages. But UPS now remitted monthly the excess-value payments, less claims paid, to National Union as premiums on the policy. National Union then collected its commission, excise taxes, and fees from the charges before sending the rest on to OPL as payments under the reinsurance contract. UPS reported neither revenue from excess-value charges nor claim expenses on its 1984 return, although it did deduct the fees and commissions that National Union charged.

The IRS determined a deficiency in the amount of the excess-value charges collected in 1984, concluding that the excess-value payment remitted ultimately to OPL had to be treated as gross income to UPS. UPS petitioned for a redetermination. Following a hearing, the tax court agreed with the IRS.

It is not perfectly clear on what judicial doctrine the holding rests. The court started its analysis by expounding on the assignment-of-income doctrine, a source rule that ensures that income is attributed to the person who earned it regardless of efforts to deflect it elsewhere. * * * The court

---

1. These facts synopsize the high points of the tax court's long opinion, which is published at 78 T.C.M. (CCH) 262, 1999 WL 592696.

did not, however, discuss at all the touchstone of an ineffective assignment of income, which would be UPS's control over the excess-value charges once UPS had turned them over as premiums to National Union. * * * The court's analysis proceeded rather under the substantive-sham or economic-substance doctrines, the assignment-of-income doctrine's kissing cousins. * * * The conclusion was that UPS's redesign of its excess-value business warranted no respect. Three core reasons support this result, according to the court: the plan had no defensible business purpose, as the business realities were identical before and after; the premiums paid for the National Union policy were well above industry norms; and contemporary memoranda and documents show that UPS's sole motivation was tax avoidance. The revenue from the excess-value program was thus properly deemed to be income to UPS rather than to OPL or National Union. The court also imposed penalties.

UPS now appeals, attacking the tax court's economic-substance analysis and its imposition of penalties. The refrain of UPS's lead argument is that the excess-value plan had economic substance, and thus was not a sham, because it comprised genuine exchanges of reciprocal obligations among real, independent entities. The IRS answers with a before-and-after analysis, pointing out that whatever the reality and enforceability of the contracts that composed the excess-value plan, UPS's postplan practice equated to its preplan, in that it collected excess-value charges, administered claims, and generated substantial profits. The issue presented to this court, therefore, is whether the excess-value plan had the kind of economic substance that removes it from "shamhood," even if the business continued as it had before. The question of the effect of a transaction on tax liability, to the extent it does not concern the accuracy of the tax court's fact-finding, is subject to de novo review. * * * We agree with UPS that this was not a sham transaction, and we therefore do not reach UPS's challenges to the tax penalties.

II. Discussion

I.R.C. §§ 11, 61, and 63 together provide the Code's foundation by identifying income as the basis of taxation. Even apart from the narrower assignment-of-income doctrine—which we do not address here—these sections come with the gloss, analogous to that on other Code sections, that economic substance determines what is income to a taxpayer and what is not. * * * This economic-substance doctrine, also called the sham-transaction doctrine, provides that a transaction ceases to merit tax respect when it has no "economic effects other than the creation of tax benefits." * * *[2] Even if the transaction has economic effects, it must be disregarded if it has no business purpose and its motive is tax avoidance. * * *

---

2. *Kirchman,* which is binding in this circuit, differs in this respect from the oft-used statement of the doctrine derived from Rice's Toyota World, Inc. v. Comm'r, 752 F.2d 89, 91–92 (4th Cir.1985). *Rice's Toyota* *World,* unlike *Kirchman,* requires a tax-avoidance purpose as well as a lack of substance; *Kirchman* explicitly refuses to examine subjective intent if the transaction lacks economic effects.

The kind of "economic effects" required to entitle a transaction to respect in taxation include the creation of genuine obligations enforceable by an unrelated party. * * * The restructuring of UPS's excess-value business generated just such obligations. There was a real insurance policy between UPS and National Union that gave National Union the right to receive the excess-value charges that UPS collected. And even if the odds of losing money on the policy were slim, National Union had assumed liability for the losses of UPS's excess-value shippers, again a genuine obligation. A history of not losing money on a policy is no guarantee of such a future. Insurance companies indeed do not make a habit of issuing policies whose premiums do not exceed the claims anticipated, but that fact does not imply that insurance companies do not bear risk. Nor did the reinsurance treaty with OPL, while certainly reducing the odds of loss, completely foreclose the risk of loss because reinsurance treaties, like all agreements, are susceptible to default.

The tax court dismissed these obligations because National Union, given the reinsurance treaty, was no more than a "front" in what was a transfer of revenue from UPS to OPL. As we have said, that conclusion ignores the real risk that National Union assumed. But even if we overlook the reality of the risk and treat National Union as a conduit for transmission of the excess-value payments from UPS to OPL, there remains the fact that OPL is an independently taxable entity that is not under UPS's control. UPS really did lose the stream of income it had earlier reaped from excess-value charges. UPS genuinely could not apply that money to any use other than paying a premium to National Union; the money could not be used for other purposes, such as capital improvement, salaries, dividends, or investment. These circumstances distinguish UPS's case from the paradigmatic sham transfers of income, in which the taxpayer retains the benefits of the income it has ostensibly forgone. * * * Here that benefit ended up with OPL. There were, therefore, real economic effects from this transaction on all of its parties.

The conclusion that UPS's excess-value plan had real economic effects means, under this circuit's rule in *Kirchman,* that it is not per se a sham. But it could still be one if tax avoidance displaced any business purpose. The tax court saw no business purpose here because the excess-value business continued to operate after its reconfiguration much as before. This lack of change in how the business operated at the retail level, according to the court, betrayed the restructuring as pointless.

It may be true that there was little change over time in how the excess-value program appeared to customers. But the tax court's narrow notion of "business purpose"—which is admittedly implied by the phrase's plain language—stretches the economic-substance doctrine farther than it has been stretched. A "business purpose" does not mean a reason for a transaction that is free of tax considerations. Rather, a transaction has a "business purpose," when we are talking about a going concern like UPS, as long as it figures in a bona fide, profit-seeking business. * * * This concept of "business purpose" is a necessary corollary to the venerable axiom that tax-planning is permissible. See Gregory v. Helvering, 293 U.S. 465, 469, 55 S.Ct. 266, 267, 79 L.Ed. 596 (1935) ("The legal right of a taxpayer to decrease the amount of what otherwise would be his taxes, or altogether avoid them, by means which the law permits, cannot be doubted."). The Code treats lots of categories of economically similar behavior differently. For instance, two ways to infuse capital into a corporation, borrowing and sale of equity, have different tax consequences; interest is usually deductible and distributions to equityholders are not. There may be no tax-independent reason for a taxpayer to choose between these different ways of financing the business, but it does not mean that the taxpayer lacks a "business purpose." To conclude otherwise would prohibit tax-planning.

The caselaw, too, bears out this broader notion of "business purpose." Many of the cases where no business purpose appears are about individual income tax returns, when the individual meant to evade taxes on income probably destined for personal consumption; obviously, it is difficult in such a case to articulate any *business* purpose to the transaction. * * * Other no-business-purpose cases concern tax-shelter transactions or investments by a business or investor that would not have occurred, *in any form,* but for tax-avoidance reasons. * * * By contrast, the few cases that accept a transaction as genuine involve a bona fide business that—perhaps even by design—generates tax benefits. * * *

The transaction under challenge here simply altered the form of an existing, bona fide business, and this case therefore falls in with those that find an adequate business purpose to neutralize any tax-avoidance motive. True, UPS's restructuring was more sophisticated and complex than the usual tax-influenced form-of-business election or a choice of debt over equity financing. But its sophistication does not change the fact that there was a real business that served the genuine need for customers to enjoy loss coverage and for UPS to lower its liability exposure.

We therefore conclude that UPS's restructuring of its excess-value business had both real economic effects and a business purpose, and it therefore under our precedent had sufficient economic substance to merit respect in taxation. It follows that the tax court improperly imposed penalties and enhanced interest on UPS for engaging in a sham transaction. The tax court did not, however, reach the IRS's alternative arguments in support of its determination of deficiency, the reallocation provisions of I.R.C. §§ 482 and 845(a). The holding here does not dispose of those arguments, and we therefore must remand for the tax court to address them in the first instance.

III. Conclusion

For the foregoing reasons, we reverse the judgment against UPS and remand the action to the tax court for it to address in the first instance the IRS's contentions under §§ 482 and 845(a).

REVERSED AND REMANDED.

■ RYSKAMP, DISTRICT JUDGE, dissenting:

I respectfully dissent. Although I agree with the majority's recitation of the facts as well as its interpretation of the applicable legal standard, I find that its reversal of the tax court is contrary to the great weight of the evidence that was before the lower court. The majority, as well as the tax court below, correctly finds that the question before the Court is whether UPS's insurance arrangements with NUF and OPL are valid under the sham-transaction doctrine. Under the sham-transaction doctrine, UPS's transaction ceases to merit tax respect when it has no "economic effects other than the creation of tax benefits," * * *, or has no business purpose and its sole motive is tax avoidance. * * * Thus the question before the Court is not strictly whether UPS had a tax avoidance motive when it formulated the scheme in question, but rather whether there was some legitimate, substantive business reason for the transaction as well. There clearly was not.

As the tax court articulated in great detail in its well-reasoned 114–page opinion, the evidence in this case overwhelmingly demonstrates that UPS's reinsurance arrangement with NUF and OPL had no economic significance or business purpose outside of UPS's desire to avoid federal income tax, and was therefore a sham transaction. First, the tax court based its decision upon evidence that the scheme in question was subjectively motivated by tax avoidance. For example, the evidence showed that tax avoidance was the initial and sole reason for the scheme in question, that UPS held off on the plan for some time to analyze tax legislation on the floor of the United States House of Representatives, and that a letter sent to AIG Insurance from UPS detailing the scheme claimed that AIG would serve in merely a "fronting" capacity and would bear little or no actual risk. The evidence thus showed that this scheme was hatched with only tax avoidance in mind.

Second, the tax court based its decision on overwhelming evidence that UPS's scheme had no real economic or business purpose outside of tax avoidance. For example, the evidence showed that NUF's exposure to loss under the plan (except in the very unlikely event of *extreme* catastrophe) was infinitesimal, and that UPS nevertheless continued to fully bear the administrative costs of the EVC program. NUF was only liable for losses not covered by another insurance policy held by UPS, yet UPS still collected the EVC's and deposited the money into UPS bank accounts, still processed EVC claims, and continued to pay all EVC claims out of UPS bank accounts (while collecting the accrued interest for itself). All NUF really did in the scheme was collect over $1 million in fees and expenses before passing the EVC income on to OPL, which was of course wholly owned by UPS shareholders. In essence, NUF received an enormous fee from UPS in exchange for nothing.

Moreover, the tax court systematically rejected every explanation of the scheme put forth by UPS. UPS claimed that the scheme was meant to avoid violation of state insurance laws, yet the evidence showed no real concern for such laws and that in fact UPS was well aware that federal preemption of these state laws likely made its old EVC plan legal. UPS claimed that it intended OPL to become a full-line insurer someday, yet the evidence showed that it was nevertheless unnecessary to specifically use *EVC income* for such a capital investment. UPS claimed that elimination of the EVC income allowed it to increase its rates, yet one of its own board members testified that this explanation was untrue. I also note that UPS's claim that OPL was a legitimate insurance company fails in light of the fact that OPL was charging a substantially inflated rate for EVCs. Evidence in the tax court showed that in an arms-length transaction with a legitimate insurance company, EVC rates would have been approximately half those charged by UPS (and in turn passed on to OPL), providing further evidence that the transaction was a sham. In sum, UPS failed to show any legitimate business reason for giving up nearly $100 million in EVC income in 1984.

For these reasons, I would affirm the holding of the tax court and find that UPS's arrangement with NUF and OPL was a sham transaction subject to federal tax liability.

NOTE

Corporate tax shelters have not disappeared, but the most aggressive transactions are less prevalent as a result of the IRS's enforcement efforts and its success in several high profile cases. The new disclosure and penalty rules, which affect taxpayers and their advisors, have sent a clear message that overly aggressive behavior may result in serious economic consequences going well beyond disallowance of the claimed tax benefits. Even before the economic substance doctrine was codified, well advised taxpayers were put on notice that if a tax savings strategy seems to good to be true, it should be viewed with appropriate skepticism.

2.   Common Law Roots

The proliferation of corporate tax shelters breathed new life into the economic substance doctrine. The excerpt below elaborates on the common law roots of the doctrine and its varying interpretations by the courts.

Excerpt From Joint Committee on Taxation, General Explanation of Tax Legislation Enacted in the 111th Congress

(JCS–2–11) 369–372 (March 2011).

In general

The Code provides detailed rules specifying the computation of taxable income, including the amount, timing, source, and character of items of income, gain, loss, and deduction. These rules permit both taxpayers and the government to compute taxable income with reasonable accuracy and predictability. Taxpayers generally may plan their transactions in reliance on these rules to determine the Federal income tax consequences arising from the transactions.

In addition to the statutory provisions, courts have developed several doctrines that can be applied to deny the tax benefits of a tax-motivated transaction, notwithstanding that the transaction may satisfy the literal requirements of a specific tax provision. These common-law doctrines are not entirely distinguishable, and their application to a given set of facts is often blurred by the courts, the IRS, and litigants. Although these doctrines serve an important role in the administration of the tax system, they can be seen as at odds with an objective, "rule-based" system of taxation.

One common-law doctrine applied over the years is the "economic substance" doctrine. In general, this doctrine denies tax benefits arising from transactions that do not result in a meaningful change to the taxpayer's economic position other than a purported reduction in Federal income tax.[990]

Economic substance doctrine

Courts generally deny claimed tax benefits if the transaction that gives rise to those benefits lacks economic substance independent of U.S. Federal income tax considerations—notwithstanding that the purported activity actually occurred. The Tax Court has described the doctrine as follows:

> The tax law ... requires that the intended transactions have economic substance separate and distinct from economic benefit achieved solely by tax reduction. The doctrine of economic substance becomes applicable, and a judicial remedy is warranted, where a taxpayer seeks to claim tax benefits, unintended by Congress, by means of transactions that serve no economic purpose other than tax savings.[991]

Business purpose doctrine

A common law doctrine that often is considered together with the economic substance doctrine is the business purpose doctrine. The business purpose doctrine involves an inquiry into the subjective motives of the taxpayer—that is, whether the taxpayer intended the transaction to serve some useful non-tax purpose. In making this determination, some courts have bifurcated a transaction in which activities with non-tax objectives

---

990. * * * Closely related doctrines also applied by the courts (sometimes interchangeable with the economic substance doctrine) include the "sham transaction doctrine" and the "business purpose doctrine." * * * Certain "substance over form" cases involving tax-indifferent parties, in which courts have found that the substance of the transaction does not comfort with the form asserted by the taxpayer, have also involved examination of whether the change in economic position that occurred, if any, was consistent with the form asserted, and whether the claimed business purpose supported the particular tax benefits that were claimed. * * *

991. ACM Partnership v. Commissioner, 73 T.C.M. at 2215.

have been combined with unrelated activities having only tax-avoidance objectives, in order to disallow the tax benefits of the overall transaction.[992]

Application by the courts

Elements of the doctrine

There is a lack of uniformity regarding the proper application of the economic substance doctrine.[993] Some courts apply a conjunctive test that requires a taxpayer to establish the presence of both economic substance (i.e, the objective component) and business purpose (i.e., the subjective component) in order for the transaction to survive judicial scrutiny.[994] A narrower approach used by some courts is to conclude that either a business purpose or economic substance is sufficient to respect the transaction.[995] A third approach regards economic substance and business purpose as "simply more precise factors to consider" in determining whether a transaction has any practical economic effects other than the creation of tax benefits.[996]

One decision by the Court of Federal Claims questioned the continuing viability of the doctrine. That court also stated that "the use of the 'economic substance' doctrine to trump 'mere compliance with the Code' would violate the separation of powers" though that court also found that the particular transaction at issue in the case did not lack economic substance. The Court of Appeals for the Federal Circuit ("Federal Circuit Court") overruled the Court of Federal Claims decision, reiterating the viability of the economic substance doctrine and concluding that the transaction in question violated that doctrine.[997] The Federal Circuit Court stated that "[w]hile the doctrine may well also apply if the transaction has economic substance, a lack of economic substance is sufficient to disqualify the transaction without proof that the taxpayer's sole motive is tax avoidance." [998]

Nontax economic benefits

There also is a lack of uniformity regarding the type of non-tax economic benefit a taxpayer must establish in order to demonstrate that a

---

992. See ACM Partnership v. Commissioner, 157 F.3d at 256 n. 48.

993. "The casebooks are glutted with economic substance tests. Many such tests proliferate because they give the comforting illusion of consistency and precision. They often obscure rather than clarify." Collins v. Commissioner, 857 F.2d 1383, 1386 (9th Cir. 1988).

994. See, e.g., Pasternak v. Commissioner, 990 F.2d 893, 898 (6th Cir. 1993). * * *

995. See, e.g., Rice's Toyota World v. Commissioner, 752 F.2d 89, 91–92 (4th Cir. 1985). * * * As noted earlier, the economic

substance doctrine and the sham transaction doctrine are similar and sometimes are applied interchangeably. * * *

996. See, e.g., ACM Partnership v. Commissioner, 157 F.3d at 247. * * *

997. Coltec Industries, Inc. v. United States, 62 Fed. Cl. 716 (2004) (slip opinion at 123–124, 128), vacated and remanded, 454 F.3d 1340 (Fed. Cir. 2006), cert. denied, 127 S.Ct. 1261 (Mem.) (2007).

998. The Federal Circuit Court stated that "when the taxpayer claims a deduction, it is the taxpayer who bears the burden of proving that the transaction has economic substance." * * *

transaction has economic substance. Some courts have denied tax benefits on the ground that a stated business benefit of a particular structure was not in fact obtained by that structure.[999] Several courts have denied tax benefits on the grounds that the subject transactions lacked profit potential.[1000] In addition, some courts have applied the economic substance doctrine to disallow tax benefits in transactions in which a taxpayer was exposed to risk and the transaction had a profit potential, but the court concluded that the economic risks and profit potential were insignificant when compared to the tax benefits.[1001] Under this analysis, the taxpayer's profit potential must be more than nominal. Conversely, other courts view the application of the economic substance doctrine as requiring an objective determination of whether a "reasonable possibility of profit" from the transaction existed apart from the tax benefits.[1002] In these cases, in assessing whether a reasonable possibility of profit exists, it may be sufficient if there is a nominal amount of pre-tax profit as measured against expected tax benefits.

Financial accounting benefits

In determining whether a taxpayer had a valid business purpose for entering into a transaction, at least two courts have concluded that financial accounting benefits arising from tax savings do not qualify as a non-tax business purpose. However, based on court decisions that recognize the importance of financial accounting treatment, taxpayers have asserted that financial accounting benefits arising from tax savings can satisfy the business purpose test.

Tax-indifferent parties

A number of cases have involved transactions structured to allocate income for Federal tax purposes to a tax-indifferent party, with a corresponding deduction, or favorable basis result, to a taxable person. The income allocated to the tax-indifferent party for tax purposes was structured to exceed any actual economic income to be received by the tax indifferent party from the transaction. Courts have sometimes concluded that this particular type of transaction did not satisfy the economic substance doctrine. In other cases, courts have indicated that the substance of

---

999. See, e.g., Coltec Industries v. United States, 454 F.3d 1340 (Fed. Cir. 2006). * * *

1000. See, e.g., Knetsch, 364 U.S. at 361; Goldstein v. Commissioner, 364 F.2d 734 (2d Cir. 1966) (holding that an unprofitable, leveraged acquisition of Treasury bills, and accompanying prepaid interest deduction, lacked economic substance.

1001. See, e.g., Goldstein v. Commissioner, 364 F.2d 734 (2d Cir. 1966) (disallowing deduction even though taxpayer had a possibility of small gain or loss by owning Treasury bills); Sheldon v. Commissioner, 94 T.C. 738, 768 (1990) (stating that "potential for gain . . . is infinitesimally nominal and vastly insignificant when considered in comparison with the claimed deductions").

1002. See, e.g., Rice's Toyota World v. Commissioner, 752 F.2d 89, 94 (4th Cir. 1985) (the economic substance inquiry requires an objective determination of whether a reasonable possibility of profit from the transaction existed apart from tax benefits); Compaq Computer v. Commissioner, 277 F.3d 778, 781 (5th Cir. 2001) (applied the same test, citing Rice's Toyota World) * * *.

a transaction did not support the form of income allocations asserted by the taxpayer and have questioned whether asserted business purpose or other standards were met.

3. CODIFICATION

Internal Revenue Code: §§ 7701(o); 6662(a), (b)(6) & (i); 6664(a), (c)(1) & (2).

After many years of consideration and controversy, Congress finally codified the economic substance doctrine and added a new strict liability penalty in the Health Care and Education Reconciliation Act of 2010. Section 7701(o) moves the economic substance doctrine from a well recognized but murky judicial principle into the Internal Revenue Code, where its reach is still far from clear. The final successful push for codification was fueled by the urgent need to include revenue-raising provisions in a health care and tax bill that contained spending measures and some tax breaks. The Joint Committee on Taxation estimated that it would generate $100 million in 2010 and $4.3 billion over ten years.[1] The projected additional revenue, however, was not mentioned in this explanation by the Joint Committee of the reasons for codification:[2]

> Tax avoidance transactions have relied upon the interaction of highly technical tax law provisions to produce tax consequences not contemplated by Congress. When successful, taxpayers who engage in these transactions enlarge the tax gap by gaining unintended tax relief and by undermining the overall integrity of the tax system.

> A strictly rule-based tax system cannot efficiently prescribe the appropriate outcome of every conceivable transaction that might be devised and is, as a result, incapable of preventing all unintended consequences. Thus, many courts have long recognized the need to supplement tax rules with anti-tax-avoidance standards, such as the economic substance doctrine, in order to assure the Congressional purpose is achieved. The Congress recognizes that the IRS has achieved a number of recent successes in litigation. The Congress believes it is still desirable to provide greater clarity and uniformity in the application of the economic substance doctrine in order to improve its effectiveness at deterring unintended consequences.

> The Congress believes that a stronger penalty under section 6662 should be imposed on understatements attributable to non-economic substance and similar transactions, to improve compliance by deterring taxpayers from entering such transactions. The

---

1. Joint Committee on Taxation, Estimated Revenue Effects of the Amendment in the Nature of a Substitute to H.R. 4872 (JCX–17–10), March 20, 2010.

2. Joint Committee on Taxation, General Explanation of Tax Legislation Enacted in the 111th Congress 378 (hereinafter "Joint Committee General Explanation"), JCS–2–11 (March 2011).

Congress is concerned that under present law there is a potential to avoid penalties in such cases (based for example on certain levels of tax advice), and that the potential that a taxpayer in such cases may pay only the tax due plus interest is not a sufficient deterrent. The Congress therefore believes it is appropriate to impose a new strict liability penalty in such cases.

Titled "clarification of economic substance doctrine," Section 7701(*o*) provides that any transaction to which the economic substance doctrine is "relevant" shall be treated as having economic substance only if the transaction changes the taxpayer's economic position in a meaningful way (apart from the effect of federal income taxes) and the taxpayer has a substantial purpose (apart from federal income taxes) for entering into the transaction.[3] This is the more rigorous conjunctive test applied by some courts of appeals. It requires an inquiry of both the objective effects of the transaction on the taxpayer's economic position and the taxpayer's subjective motives for engaging in the transaction. Failure to meet either one of the two prongs of the test will cause the transaction under scrutiny to lack economic substance. The legislative history notes that "[t]he provision provides a uniform definition of economic substance, but does not alter the flexibility of the courts in other respects."[4] In the case of individual taxpayers, Section 7701(*o*) only applies to transactions entered into in connection with a trade or business or investment activity; personal transactions are excepted.[5]

In clarifying and enhancing the doctrine, Congress was mindful of its common law roots. To that end, "economic substance doctrine" is defined as the "common law doctrine" under which the income tax benefits with respect to a transaction are not allowable if the transaction does not have economic substance or lacks a business purpose.[6] The determination of whether the economic substance doctrine is "relevant" to a transaction is to be made in the same manner as if the provision had never been enacted.[7] This presumably means that, despite all the hoopla and projected additional revenue to be collected from codification, the law has not fundamentally changed. Or has it? Time and experience may tell. For now, codification has clarified a few important points on which the courts disagreed but also raised new questions of statutory interpretation. For example, the statute requires a taxpayer's non-Federal-income-tax purpose for entering into a transaction to be "substantial" in order to satisfy the second prong of the test. What does it take for a purpose to be "substantial?" Common law precedents, such as those under the Section 355 business purpose test,[8] may offer guidance on this question. One point is resolved by the statute: a purpose of achieving a favorable accounting treatment for financial report-

---

3. I.R.C. § 7701(*o*)(1).

4. Joint Committee General Explanation, supra note 2, at 378.

5. I.R.C. § 7701(*o*)(5)(B). Codification and its accompanying penalty regime are ef-

fective for transactions entered into after March 30, 2010.

6. I.R.C. § 7701(*o*)(5)(A).

7. I.R.C. § 7701(*o*)(5)(C).

8. See Chapter 10C1, supra.

ing purposes may not be taken into account as a non-Federal-income-tax purpose if the origin of the financial accounting benefit is a reduction of Federal income tax.[9]

The Joint Committee's explanation of Section 7701(*o*) states that a taxpayer may rely on factors other than profit potential in meeting either prong of the conjunctive test.[10] But if a taxpayer does rely on profit potential, the statute does not require or establish a minimum return that will satisfy the test, only that the present value of the reasonably expected pre-tax profit must be substantial in relation to the present value of the expected net tax benefits that would be allowed if the transaction were respected.[11] It is expected that the Treasury will provide more guidance on the operation of these new rules. The statute also makes it clear that fees, other transaction expenses, and (possibly, subject to IRS regulations) foreign taxes should be taken into account as expenses in determining pre-tax profit.[12]

A major concern of those who opposed codification was that it might be interpreted to extend to well-accepted tax planning techniques that have never been viewed as targets of the common law judicial doctrines. The Joint Committee on Taxation's technical explanation responds to this concern with what has become known as an ''angel list'' of nonexclusive transactions that Congress does not believe should be invalidated by a strict application of the economic substance doctrine. Examples include: (1) the choice between debt and equity financing; (2) the choice between using a domestic or foreign entity; (3) the choice to enter into a transaction or series of transactions that constitute a corporate organization or reorganization; and (4) related party transactions that do not run afoul of Section 482. This unofficial legislative history (there are no committee reports) also states that Section 7701(*o*) should not be used to disallow tax benefits from tax-motivated transactions that Congress intended to encourage through provisions such as the low-income housing, rehabilitation, new markets and energy tax credits.[13]

To get taxpayers' attention and strengthen enforcement, Congress buttressed codification of the economic substance doctrine with a new strict liability penalty for any underpayment attributable to any disallowance of claimed tax benefits by reason of a transaction lacking economic substance under Section 7701(*o*) or failing to meet the requirements of any similar rule of law.[14] The penalty is 20 percent of the amount of the underpayment, increased to 40 percent if the taxpayer does not adequately disclose the relevant facts affecting the tax treatment in its original tax return (amended returns are too late to meet the disclosure requirement if filed after the taxpayer has been contacted for audit).[15] Unlike most other civil penalties,

---

9. I.R.C. §§ 7701(*o*)(1)(B), (*o*)(4).

10. Joint Committee General Explanation, supra note 2, at 381.

11. I.R.C. § 7701(*o*)(2)(A).

12. I.R.C. § 7701(*o*)(2)(B).

13. Joint Committee General Explanation, supra note 2, at 379.

14. I.R.C. § 6662(b)(6).

15. I.R.C. § 6662(i).

taxpayers may not rely on a reasonable cause or good faith exception, with the result that outside opinions of counsel will not be a defense to imposition of the penalty if it is determined that a transaction lacks economic substance.[16]

Within moments after the economic substance doctrine was codified, anxious practitioners urged the IRS to provide guidance to resolve what they believed to be ambiguities in the statute. In Notice 2010–62,[17] the IRS issued "interim guidance" but it failed to calm the nerves of tax advisors in their search for tidy solutions. In the Notice, the IRS said it would continue to rely on "relevant case law" in applying the conjunctive statutory test; it would not issue rulings on whether or not the economic substance doctrine was "relevant" to a transaction or, if it is relevant, whether the transaction complies with the regulations of Section 7701(*o*); and, contrary to hopes and expectations, it would not issue an angel list of safe transactions. The only meaningful guidance in Notice 2010–62 relates to the adequate disclosure procedures, which are satisfied on a timely filed original tax return or certain amended returns. For this purpose, "adequacy" is achieved by completing IRS forms (e.g., Forms 8275 or 8275–R) that are also used for purposes of the more general accuracy-related penalty regime in Section 6662.

In declining to provide more specific guidance, the IRS appears to have concluded that codification of the economic substance doctrine would have more clout if its contours were as fuzzy as the common law doctrines that preceded it so that only the most adventuresome (or ignorant) tax planners would risk the heightened penalty exposure. Time will tell with more experience, and that will take a while.[18]

PROBLEM

A owns 100 percent of the stock of T Corporation. The stock has a fair market value of $200,000 and A's adjusted basis is $1,000,000. P Corporation wishes to acquire 100 percent of the T stock from A in exchange solely for P voting stock, but A wishes to recognize the built-in loss on the stock so it can be used to offset a large capital gain from another transaction. Knowing that a stock-for-stock exchange would qualify as a Type B reorganization and preclude A from recognizing his loss, A's tax advisor suggests that P acquire the T stock for $199,000 of P voting stock and $1,000 cash. The only reason for using cash is to defeat qualification of the transaction as a tax-free reorganization and allow A to recognize his $800,000 loss. P Corporation agrees to proceed with the transaction as proposed by A's tax advisor.

(a) Is the economic substance doctrine "relevant" to the transaction?

---

16. I.R.C. § 6664(c)(2).

17. 2010–40 I.R.B. 411,

18. For an academic perspective that a lack of comprehensive regulations is a good thing because regulations only would create

their own ambiguities, uncertainties and loopholes, see McMahon, "Living With the Codified Economic Substance Doctrine," 128 Tax Notes 731 (Aug. 16, 2010).

(b) Assuming the answer to (a) is yes, is the conjunctive test in Section 7701(*o*) satisfied?

C.   The Accumulated Earnings Tax

1.   Introduction

For most of our income tax history, the graduated rates applicable to individuals greatly exceeded the relatively flat corporate rates. During the 1950's, the top corporate rate was roughly 50 percent while individuals were taxed at rates ranging up to 88 percent. This rate gap provided an incentive for taxpayers to accumulate business profits or investment income in a corporation. As Professors Bittker and Eustice once said, "use of a corporation as a temporary or permanent refuge from individual income tax rates has been one of the principal landmarks of our tax landscape."[1]

To illustrate a typical accumulation plan that would have invited the tax collector's scrutiny, consider the goals of Accumulator ("A"), a sole proprietor with a profitable business in the days of the 70 percent individual marginal rates. Tempted by the allure of the lower corporate tax rate, A incorporates his business with a healthy (but permissible) dose of debt and pays himself a hefty (but reasonable) salary. His personal consumption needs are fully satisfied by the salary, the interest payments on the debt, and as many nontaxable fringe benefits as the corporation can legally provide. Any additional profits from the business are left to accumulate in the corporation, where they work to increase the value of A's stock. If A needs more funds or later wishes to retire, he can "cash in" on his accumulated profits by selling some stock or liquidating the company, in either case reporting those profits as favored long-term capital gain. An even more attractive alternative would be to avoid entirely the individual income tax by holding the stock until death, when A's heirs would be entitled to a stepped-up basis under Section 1014. Or A might dispose of the business in a tax-free reorganization, emerging with publicly traded stock, albeit with a low substituted basis, which could be sold or held until A's death.[2]

The accumulated earnings tax was enacted to prevent the use of a C corporation to escape the individual income tax by an unreasonable accumulation of earnings. Although not part of its original design, it also serves the broader purpose of inducing corporations to pay dividends and subject their earnings to the double tax when those profits are not required for the reasonable needs of the business.[3]

1. Bittker & Eustice, Federal Income Taxation of Corporations and Shareholders ¶ 1.02 (5th ed. 1987).

2. See I.R.C. §§ 354; 358; 368.

3. See Staff of Senate Finance Committee, Preliminary Report on the Reform and Simplification of the Income Taxation of Corporations, 98th Cong., 1st Sess. 23 (Comm. Print S. 98–95, 1983).

For a brief time between 1987 and 1992, the corporate income tax rates exceeded the individual rates—an inversion from the historic norm that caused some commentators to propose repeal of the accumulated earnings tax on the ground that it was no longer necessary.[4] Under current law, the top individual and corporate rates are the same.[5] This rate parity, along with the introduction of a preferential rate on dividends received by noncorporate shareholders, has reduced the incentive to organize a business as a C corporation. As a result, the accumulated earnings tax is less influential, but its lurking presence still may act as an enforcer of the double tax regime by encouraging profitable companies to distribute some of their earnings as dividends.

2.   THE PROSCRIBED TAX AVOIDANCE PURPOSE

Code: §§ 531; 532.

The accumulated earnings tax is a penalty imposed on a corporation "formed or availed of for the purpose of avoiding the income tax with respect to its shareholders * * * by permitting earnings and profits to accumulate instead of being divided or distributed."[1] The tax is levied at 15 percent on a C corporation's "accumulated taxable income," which is generally defined as taxable income with certain adjustments (e.g., subtracting taxes and dividends paid and adding back the dividends received deduction) to reflect the true dividend paying capacity of the corporation.[2] Most corporations, regardless of motives, are given an accumulated earnings credit that in effect permits an accumulation of up to $250,000.[3] Although closely held corporations are the principal target of the tax, Section 532(c) provides that its application is to be determined "without regard to the number of shareholders," and the Tax Court has held that in theory the tax can apply to a publicly traded corporation even where ownership is not concentrated in a small group of shareholders.[4] As a practical matter, however, publicly traded companies are rarely threatened because of the difficulty of proving that they were formed for the proscribed tax avoidance purpose.[5] In addition, Section 532(b) provides specific excep-

---

4. See, e.g., Wolfman, "Subchapter C and the 100th Congress," 33 Tax Notes 669, 674 (Nov. 17, 1986).

5. Unless Congress extends the Bush tax cuts, however, the top individual marginal rate will increase to 39.6 percent in 2013 and once again will exceed the highest corporate rate.

1. I.R.C. § 532(a).

2. I.R.C. §§ 531; 535. The rate will increase to 39.6 percent in 2013 unless Congress extends the Bush tax cuts or makes them permanent.

3. I.R.C. § 535(a), (c). A corporation is only permitted a $150,000 credit if its principal function is the performance of services in the field of health, law engineering, architecture, accounting, actuarial science, performing arts or consulting. I.R.C. § 535(c)(2)(B).

4. Technalysis Corp. v. Commissioner, 101 T.C. 397 (1993).

5. See, e.g., the legislative history of Section 532(c), which states that "it may be difficult to establish [a tax avoidance purpose] in the case of a widely-held operating company where no individual or small group of individuals has legal or effective control of the company." S.Rep. No. 98–169, 98th Cong., 2d Sess. 187 (1984); H.R.Rep. No. 98–861, 98th Cong., 2d Sess. 829 (1984).

tions from the tax for personal holding companies, foreign personal holding companies, tax-exempt organizations and passive foreign investment companies.

The central issue under the accumulated earnings tax is whether the corporation has been formed or availed of for the proscribed tax avoidance purpose. The statutory standard is met if tax avoidance is one of several factors motivating corporate accumulations.[6] Two statutory presumptions assist in determining the presence of a tax avoidance purpose. First, the fact that corporate earnings and profits are permitted to accumulate "beyond the reasonable needs of the business" is determinative of a tax avoidance purpose unless the corporation proves to the contrary by a "preponderance of the evidence."[7] In addition, the fact that the corporation is "a mere holding or investment company" is prima facie evidence of a tax avoidance purpose.[8]

The regulations generally provide that the presence of the proscribed tax avoidance purpose is determined by all the circumstances of the particular case, including:[9]

1. Dealings between the corporation and its shareholders, such as shareholder loans or corporate expenditures benefitting the shareholders personally;

2. The presence of corporate investments having no reasonable connection with the corporation's business; and

3. The extent to which the corporation has made dividend distributions.

These factors are not conclusive, but the presence of shareholder loans, unrelated corporate investments and a poor dividend history tend to poison the atmosphere on the question of the proscribed tax avoidance purpose. Application of the accumulated earnings tax thus ultimately depends on the corporation's purpose. In United States v. Donruss,[10] a decision that significantly strengthened the tax, the Supreme Court held that the statutory standard was satisfied if tax avoidance is merely one of the purposes for the accumulation even if it is not the corporation's dominant or principal purpose. After reviewing the legislative history, the Court acknowledged the difficulties in applying such a subjective standard and expressed its preference for more objective criteria:[11]

> Two conclusions can be drawn from Congress' efforts. First, Congress recognized the tremendous difficulty of ascertaining the purpose of corporate accumulations. Second, it saw that accumulation was often necessary for legitimate and reasonable business purposes. It appears clear to us that the congressional response to

---

6. United States v. Donruss, 393 U.S. 297, 89 S.Ct. 501 (1969).

7. I.R.C. § 533(a).

8. I.R.C. § 533(b).

9. Reg. § 1.533–1(a)(2).

10. 393 U.S. 297, 89 S.Ct. 501 (1969).

11. 393 U.S. at 307–08, 89 S.Ct. at 506–07.

these facts has been to emphasize unreasonable accumulation as the most significant factor in the incidence of the tax. The reasonableness of an accumulation, while subject to honest difference of opinion, is a much more objective inquiry, and is susceptible of more effective scrutiny, than are the vagaries of corporate motive.

Respondent would have us adopt a test that requires that tax avoidance purpose need be dominant, impelling or controlling. It seems to us that such a test would exacerbate the problems that Congress was trying to avoid. Rarely is there one motive, or even one dominant motive, for corporate decisions. Numerous factors contribute to the action ultimately decided upon. Respondent's test would allow taxpayers to escape the tax when it is proved that at least one other motive was equal to tax avoidance. We doubt that such a determination can be made with any accuracy, and it is certainly one which will depend almost exclusively on the interested testimony of corporate management. Respondent's test would thus go a long way toward destroying the presumption that Congress created to meet this very problem. As Judge Learned Hand said of the much weaker presumption contained in the Revenue Act of 1921 * * *, "[a] statute which stands on the footing of the participants' state of mind may need the support of presumption, indeed be practically unenforceable without it * * *." * * * And, "[t]he utility of * * * [that] presumption * * * is well nigh destroyed if * * * [it] is saddled with requirement of proof of the primary or dominant purpose of the accumulation." Barrow Manufacturing Co. v. Commissioner, 294 F.2d 79, 82 (C.A. 5th Cir.1961), cert. denied 369 U.S. 817, 82 S.Ct. 827 (1962).

After *Donruss*, it became clear that the critical inquiry is the reasonableness of the accumulation. As previewed above, Congress came to the aid of the fact finder by creating a statutory presumption under which an accumulation beyond the reasonable needs of the corporation's business is determinative of the proscribed tax avoidance purpose unless the corporation proves to the contrary by a preponderance of the evidence.[12] This procedural device eases the Government's burden of proof and immunizes a growing corporation that accumulates profits for purposes such as bona fide expansion, potential acquisitions, working capital needs and other valid business objectives.

The presumption is rebuttable, and in theory a corporation that accumulates earnings beyond its reasonable needs can avoid the tax by proving that the accumulation was not motivated by a tax avoidance purpose. As the Supreme Court stated in Donruss:[13]

> [W]e cannot subscribe to respondent's suggestion that our holding would make purpose totally irrelevant. It still serves to isolate those cases in which tax avoidance motives did not contribute to the decision to accumulate. Obviously in such a case

---

12. I.R.C. § 533(a).   **13.** 393 U.S. at 309.

imposition of the tax would be futile. In addition, "purpose" means more than mere knowledge, undoubtedly present in nearly every case. It is still open for the taxpayer to show that even though knowledge of the tax consequences was present, that knowledge did not contribute to the decision to accumulate earnings.

Few corporations, however, are able to make the requisite showing once it is determined that accumulations are unreasonable.[14] Conversely, even if an accumulation is found to be reasonable, the government theoretically might attempt to show the existence of the proscribed purpose.[15] In practice, however, the reasonable business needs standard is almost always the main event, and it therefore will be the focus of our coverage.

3. THE REASONABLE NEEDS OF THE BUSINESS

Code: §§ 533(a); 534(a)–(c); 537(a), (b)(1).

Regulations: §§ 1.537–1(a), (b), (c), –2, –3.

Myron's Enterprises v. United States

United States Court of Appeals, Ninth Circuit, 1977.
548 F.2d 331.

■ SNEED, CIRCUIT JUDGE:

Taxpayer-corporations sued in district court below for a refund of accumulated earnings taxes imposed by the Commissioner. The Commissioner had based the tax on his determination that for taxpayers' fiscal years 1966 through 1968 the reasonable needs of the business stemmed entirely from working capital needs and never exceeded $21,272. The taxpayers contended that their retained earnings for the years in question of $316,000, $374,316, and $415,766 respectively were needed to cover both working capital requirements of $100,000 and the planned purchase and remodeling of the ballroom operated by taxpayers, at an estimated cost of $375,000.

The district court, in Myron's Ballroom v. United States, 382 F.Supp. 582 (C.D.Cal.1974), held that taxpayers had accumulated earnings in excess of the reasonable needs of their business, but not to the extent claimed by the Commissioner. The court also found that the taxpayers had been

---

14. For one isolated example, see T.C. Heyward & Co. v. United States, 66–2 U.S.T.C. ¶ 9667 (W.D.N.C.1966), where a federal district judge held that the corporation's accumulations were so large that it never could have intended to avoid the shareholder tax because no one would be so obvious. Such cases are aberrational. In the future, however, it is still conceivable that a publicly held corporation that is found to have made an unreasonable accumulation might contend that it lacked the proscribed purpose because it is not controlled by any single shareholder or insider group.

15. Such a showing ultimately would be futile, however, in light of Section 535(c)(1), which provides a credit against the accumulated earnings tax in an amount equal to those earnings which have been accumulated for the reasonable needs of the business.

availed of for the purpose of avoiding income taxes. Thus, the court upheld the surtax, but required a partial refund in light of the Commissioner's underestimation of taxpayers' reasonable business needs.

The taxpayers argue on appeal that they are entitled to a full refund (i) because all of the retained earnings in the years in question were required to meet the reasonable needs of their business, and (ii) because they proved by the preponderance of the evidence that they were not availed of to avoid taxes, despite the contrary finding by the district court. The Government argues, in response, that taxpayers were not even entitled to a partial refund—that the Commissioner's initial determination of the reasonable needs of the business was correct and that taxpayers failed to prove lack of tax-avoidance motivation. We conclude that the taxpayers are entitled to the full refund they seek. Therefore, we reverse and remand for such necessary proceedings as are consistent with this opinion.

I.

Taxpayer-corporations operate a ballroom and adjoining cocktail lounge. At all times since taxpayers were formed, they have leased their operating premises from Miss Pearl Rose, an elderly lady who has owned the property for approximately 30 years. The taxpayers began inquiring into the possibilities of purchasing the property in 1957, in part because they did not wish to make needed improvements unless they owned the building. Taxpayers made offers to Miss Rose of $100,000 and $150,000 for the property in the late 1950s—early 1960s, neither of which was accepted. However, at the time of the second offer, Miss Rose told taxpayers that they would have "first choice" if and when she decided to sell the ballroom.

In 1963, taxpayers learned that Russ Morgan, a former orchestra leader at the ballroom, had offered Miss Rose $300,000 cash for the property, in an attempt apparently to take over the ballroom operation. The price offered by Morgan probably reflected the goodwill that taxpayers had built up in their operations and therefore was considerably higher than the value of the ballroom property by itself. Morgan's actions convinced taxpayers that their business could be involuntarily "acquired" by someone purchasing the ballroom from Miss Rose;[3] taxpayers, therefore, promptly offered Miss Rose the identical sum of $300,000. This offer was renewed in 1964, 1965, 1966, 1967, 1968 and 1970. While Miss Rose never objected to the terms of the offers, she never sold and still owned the ballroom at the time of trial.

As the Government points out, Miss Rose was never particularly clear as to when and if she would sell her building. Nevertheless, the district court found (a) that taxpayers "expected at any time during the years 1966,

---

3. While taxpayers had a lease and an option to renew on the ballroom property at the time Morgan made his $300,000 offer to Miss Rose, there was always the possibility that the lease could be broken or evaded. According to Mrs. Myron, Morgan had asked his attorney and Miss Rose's agent "to review [the lease] line by line to see if there was some way or some word—something that could break the lease." R.T. at 73. This possibility of a loophole in the lease left the door open for an involuntary "acquisition."

1967 and 1968 that [they] would be able to purchase the ballroom property from Pearl Rose for a price of $300,000 cash, no less than that amount, and maybe more," 382 F.Supp. at 587, and moreover (b) that the "expectation that the ballroom property would be acquired at any time during the years in issue was a reasonable expectation," id. at 588. Thus,

> "During the years in issue, the acquisition of the ballroom property and the planned improvements and repairs were reasonably anticipated business needs of [taxpayers], and said needs were directly connected with the businesses of the corporations." Id.

The district court further concluded that "[c]onsidering the reasonably anticipated business need of the corporations to purchase the ballroom property * * * the corporations combined required at least $375,000, in addition to their combined working capital needs of $100,000." Id. However, the court went on to hold that in light of taxpayers' sole-shareholder Mrs. Myrna Myron's willingness to loan up to $200,000 to her corporations for purchase of the ballroom "if the corporations did not have sufficient funds to consummate the transactions, * * * a reasonable accumulation [for the purchase] would be $250,000, with Mrs. Myron loaning the balance of funds required," id., thus leading to an excess accumulation in 1967 and 1968.

II.

Section 537 of the Internal Revenue Code provides that the reasonable needs of a business, for purposes of determining whether there has been an excess accumulation of earnings, include "the reasonably anticipated needs of the business." Treas.Reg. § 1.537–1(b)(1) provides that to justify an accumulation of earnings on grounds of reasonably anticipated business needs, a corporation must have "specific, definite, and feasible plans for the use of such accumulation" and must not postpone execution of the plan "indefinitely."[4]

The Government contends that the district court erred in concluding that the taxpayers had a "specific, definite, and feasible plan" to acquire and remodel the ballroom. The Government notes that Miss Rose never agreed to sell the ballroom and argues that taxpayers could not have reasonably expected Miss Rose to so agree within the taxable years in question after nearly a decade of unsuccessful negotiations.

---

4. "In order for a corporation to justify an accumulation of earnings and profits for reasonably anticipated future needs, there must be an indication that the future needs of the business require such accumulation, and the corporation must have specific, definite, and feasible plans for the use of such accumulation. Such an accumulation need not be used immediately, nor must the plans for its use be consummated within a short period after the close of the taxable year, provided that such accumulation will be used within a reasonable time depending upon all the facts and circumstances relating to the future needs of the business. Where the future needs of the business are uncertain or vague, where the plans for the future use of an accumulation are not specific, definite, and feasible, or where the execution of such a plan is postponed indefinitely, an accumulation cannot be justified on the grounds of reasonably anticipated needs of the business." Treas. Reg. § 1.537–1(b)(1).

We agree with other circuits that a determination by the trial court of the reasonably anticipated business needs of a corporation is a finding of fact which must be sustained unless clearly erroneous. * * * A court should be particularly wary of overturning a finding of a trial court supporting the taxpayer's determination of its anticipated business needs, since, in the first instance, the "reasonableness of the needs is necessarily for determination by those concerned with the management of the particular enterprise. This determination must prevail unless the facts show clearly the accumulations were for prohibited purposes." * * * We conclude that the district court was not clearly erroneous in finding that taxpayers' expected purchase and remodeling of the ballroom for $375,000 was a "reasonably anticipated need of the business."

The Government argues that if the instant plan to purchase the ballroom is held to be a reasonably anticipated business need,

> "any individual could organize a one-man corporation, lease a building and discuss with the lessor the purchase of the building at some future time, and then assert that in the meantime business needs required accumulation of corporate earnings." I.A. Dress Co. v. Commissioner of Internal Revenue, 273 F.2d 543, 544 (2d Cir.), cert. denied, 362 U.S. 976, 80 S.Ct. 1060, 4 L.Ed.2d 1011 (1960).

Such fears of artificially constructed needs were well-founded in the quoted case of I.A. Dress Co.; there, the owner of the building that the taxpayer sought to purchase "was willing to sell but at a price some $300,000 more than the taxpayer was willing to pay." Id. The offer of the taxpayer lacked substance and could easily have been a facade. In the instant case, however, the taxpayers were extremely diligent in their attempts to purchase the ballroom; the taxpayers agreed to all of Miss Rose's stated terms—including payment in all cash; the price offered, far from being criticized by Miss Rose as too low, was apparently in excess of the property's fair market value.[5]

Neither do we have a situation where taxpayers' planned purchase of the ballroom was clearly infeasible. See Colonial Amusement Corp., 1948 Tax.Ct.Mem.Dec. (P–H) 48,149 (building restrictions and priorities prevented carrying out of expansion plans). Here, as in Universal Steel Co., 5 T.C. 627 (1945) (war priority restrictions temporarily blocked purchase of pickling plant), the taxpayers "had a right to hope, if not expect," id. at 638,

---

5. The Government argues that in addition to these steps the taxpayers also should have investigated purchasing other property in the general area, once Miss Rose did not prove totally disposing. Cf. Magic Mart, Inc., 51 T.C. 775 (1969), acq., 1969 2 C.B. xxiv. We agree that the failure of a taxpayer to look into the possibility of purchasing alternative properties generally will be a relevant factor in determining whether the taxpayer actually had a reasonably anticipated business need to purchase the sought-after property. However, other factors also must be considered, including the uniqueness of the sought property. Here, as was testified to at trial, a substantial amount of good will was tied up in the ballroom occupied by taxpayers; given that this value would have been lost if taxpayer had moved to another location, we do not believe that taxpayers' failure to pursue other possible properties (if other ballrooms even existed) calls for reversing the finding of the district court.

that Miss Rose would sell to them in the near future. Miss Rose never foreclosed the possibility of sale on the terms offered by taxpayers; she merely wanted to "think it over some more." As expressed by Miss Rose's agent at one point during the negotiations, Miss Rose "was an elderly lady and had a very definite mind"; her answers, according to the agent, would differ depending on how she felt on getting up in the morning. Taxpayers were encouraged at several points in the negotiations; in 1965, Miss Rose's agent had told taxpayers, "Be prepared and ready to go." In light of the reasonable possibility that Miss Rose might have decided to accept the offer at any time during the taxable years in issue, calling for quick collection of $375,000 in cash, it would have been unreasonable to force taxpayers to pay out all of their earnings in dividends. Section 537 allows taxpayers to provide for "reasonably anticipated needs," not merely for certainties.

The district court's finding is supported by several tax court cases. In *Magic Mart, Inc.*, 51 T.C. 775 (1969), acq., 1969–2 C.B. xxiv, the Tax Court held that the taxpayer's accumulation of earnings for 1959 through 1962 was reasonable in light of taxpayer's plan to acquire enlarged and expanded facilities, even though it had tried unsuccessfully to buy larger facilities since 1957 and was not able to close a deal until 1967, five years after the taxable years in question. In *Breitfeller Sales, Inc.*, 28 T.C. 1164 (1957), acq., 1958–2 C.B. 4, the Tax Court held that a General Motors dealership's accumulation of earnings was justified, inter alia, by "the continuing possibility that it might [to avoid harmful competition] be required to finance a new dealership in [a neighboring community]." Id. at 1168 (emphasis added). See also *Universal Steel Co.*, supra.

III.

The Government rests its entire case upon the argued lack of a specific, definite, and feasible plan. No attempt is made to support the trial court's use of Mrs. Myrna Myron's capacity to loan to the taxpayers to reduce the amount of the reasonable accumulation. The Government thus agrees with taxpayers that, assuming a feasible plan, the district court, in determining whether taxpayers unreasonably accumulated earnings, erred in subtracting from the cash needed to purchase the ballroom an amount that Mrs. Myron stated that she would be willing to loan to the taxpayers if necessary. We also agree. Having found that the reasonably anticipated business need of the taxpayers to purchase the ballroom property required at least $375,000 in cash, the district court erred in concluding that a reasonable accumulation was any less.[6]

---

6. That the reasonableness of accumulations should be judged without regard to the borrowing capabilities of the corporation-taxpayer is well established by the case law. See, e.g., *General Smelting Co.*, 4 T.C. 313, 323 (1944), acq., 1945 C.B. 3; B. Bittker & J. Eustice, Federal Income Taxation of Corporations and Shareholders 8–20 to 8–21 & n. 42 (3rd ed. 1971). In computing "accumulat-ed taxable income," which forms the base for the accumulated earnings tax, I.R.C. § 535 provides that a credit will be provided for the amount "retained for the reasonable needs of the business." There is no authority for reducing the credit to reflect the lending capacity of taxpayer's shareholders. If the reasonable business needs of taxpayer equal or outstrip the retained earnings, no surtax

Having determined that the reasonable business needs of taxpayers, within the meaning of section 535, equalled or exceeded the accumulated earnings of taxpayers for the taxable years in question, it is unnecessary for us to consider whether the district court was correct in holding that taxpayers had been availed of to avoid taxes within the meaning of section 531. Taxpayers are entitled to a full refund. The case is remanded to the district court for such necessary proceedings as are consistent with this opinion.

Reversed and remanded.

NOTE

The *Myron's Enterprises* case illustrates the essentially factual nature of the "reasonable business needs" issue. By the time a case reaches the courts, the corporation normally has compiled a laundry list of reasonable business needs to justify the accumulation, and triers of fact typically are reluctant to second guess the business judgment of corporate management in the absence of a clear pattern of abuse. This note and the materials that follow it survey the principal factors taken into account by the Service and the courts in evaluating the reasonableness of a corporation's accumulation.

Reasonable and Unreasonable Needs: In General. After a general reminder that the reasonableness of a particular accumulation of earnings and profits is dependent "upon the particular circumstances of the case,"[1] the regulations provide guidance on what constitutes reasonable and unreasonable accumulations. If supported by the facts, the following grounds "may indicate" that accumulations are being made for the reasonable needs of the business:[2]

1.   To provide for bona fide expansion of the business or replacement of plant;

2.   To acquire a business enterprise through a stock or asset purchase;

---

can be imposed, even though the needs could be financed by borrowing from outside—such financing decisions are for the taxpayer, not the courts to make.

The district court's logic could conceivably be extended to the point of totally nullifying Congress' expressed policy of allowing corporate taxpayers to accumulate earnings necessary for reasonable business needs. A sole shareholder can always loan back any cash distributed by his corporation in dividends if the corporation later needs the money (minus, of course, any income taxes paid). Therefore, to take into account the ability of a shareholder to loan money to the corporation could be construed as virtual authority "for denying all sole stockholder corporations

the right ever to maintain accumulations even for reasonable needs. The test expressed by the statute would then be completely abandoned." Smoot Sand & Gravel Corp. v. Commissioner of Internal Revenue, 241 F.2d 197, 206 (4th Cir.), cert. denied, 354 U.S. 922, 77 S.Ct. 1383, 1 L.Ed.2d 1437 (1957).

1. Reg. § 1.537–2(a). The Supreme Court has held that in ascertaining the reasonable needs of a business, "readily marketable portfolio securities" are to be taken into account at their "net realizable value" rather than cost. Ivan Allen Co. v. United States, 422 U.S. 617, 95 S.Ct. 2501 (1975).

2. Reg. § 1.537–2(b).

3. To provide for retirement of bona fide indebtedness incurred in the trade or business;

4. To provide necessary working capital for the business; or

5. To provide for investments or loans to suppliers or customers in order to maintain the corporation's business.

The following nonexclusive list of purposes "may indicate" that the accumulations are beyond the reasonable needs of the business:[3]

1. Loans to shareholders or expenditures for the personal benefit of the shareholders;

2. Loans having no reasonable relation to the conduct of the business made to relatives or friends of shareholders or other persons;

3. Loans to another corporation in a different business if the two corporations are controlled, directly or indirectly, by the same shareholders;

4. Investments unrelated to the corporation's business; or

5. Retention of earnings and profits to provide against unrealistic hazards.

Anticipated Needs. Section 537(a) defines the "reasonable needs of the business" as including the reasonably anticipated needs. To justify an accumulation as being for a reasonably anticipated need, a corporation must have a business need for the accumulation and must have plans for the use of the funds which are "specific, definite and feasible."[4] The accumulation does not have to be used immediately or even within a short period of time as long as it is used within a "reasonable period," taking into account all the facts and circumstances.[5] The corporation's reasonably anticipated needs are determined based on facts present at the close of the taxable year; subsequent events may not be used to show that the accumulation was unreasonable. Subsequent events, however, can be considered to determine whether the corporation actually intended to consummate its plans for the accumulation.[6] Moreover, if the future plans are not completed, the presence of the accumulation is considered in determining the reasonableness of future accumulations.[7]

The "Business." The regulations expansively define the "business" of a corporation. The "business" includes not only the one in which the corporation has previously engaged but also "any line of business which it may undertake."[8] This definition should provide ample protection for accumulations intended for expansion into activities related to the corporation's existing businesses, and possibly may permit accumulations to finance any line of business permitted by the corporation's charter.[9] If a

---

3. Reg. § 1.537–2(c).

4. Reg. § 1.537–1(b)(1).

5. Id.

6. Reg. § 1.537–1(b)(2).

7. Id.

8. Reg. § 1.537–3(a).

9. See Bittker & Eustice, Federal Income Taxation of Corporations and Shareholders ¶ 7.06.

corporation owns and, in effect, operates a subsidiary, the subsidiary's business may be considered to be the business of the parent for purposes of evaluating the parent's reasonable business needs.[10] The regulations further provide that a subsidiary will be considered a "mere instrumentality" of its parent if the parent owns at least 80 percent of the subsidiary's voting stock.[11] Below the 80 percent figure, the question of attributing the subsidiary's business to the parent is determined by the particular circumstances of the case.[12]

Working Capital. The regulations recognize the need to accumulate earnings to provide "necessary working capital for the business." Working capital needs vary from industry to industry and among enterprises within the same industry, and the courts have struggled to develop standards to ascertain the working capital requirements of any particular business.[13] The judiciary's efforts have evolved into the so-called *Bardahl* formula, named for a 1965 Tax Court case which first employed the approach.[14] The formula, which is a mathematician's delight, attempts to identify a corporation's working capital needs by reference to its "operating cycle"—a concept that remains unsettled.[15] The *Bardahl* formula is viewed as a guidepost rather than a controlling legal principle,[16] and the following excerpt provides some insight into its nature and purpose:[17]

> The formula represents a procedure for arriving at working capital needs by calculating the requirements of capital funds for one "operating cycle" of a business entity. One operating cycle is the length of time (usually expressed as a percentage of a year) it takes to purchase raw materials inventory, process those raw materials into finished goods, sell the finished product, and turn any accounts receivable into cash so that the process may be repeated. Hence, the ultimate percentage which represents this cycle must speak to the turnover time of raw materials, accounts receivable, and any credit cycle. The time it takes to turn over inventory can be computed by dividing either the highest or the average inventory for the year by the costs of the goods sold in that year. This results in a percentage of a year. In similar fashion, the time it takes to turn over a receivable account is computed by dividing the highest receivables for the year by the sales for that year. This likewise is expressed as a percentage of a year. Adding inventory cycle to receivables cycle, one arrives at a theoretical

10. Reg. § 1.537–3(b).

11. Id.

12. Id.

13. See Cunningham, "More Than You Ever Wanted to Know About the Accumulated Earnings Tax," 6 J. Corp. Tax'n 187, 209 (1979).

14. Bardahl Manufacturing Corp. v. Commissioner, 24 T.C.M. 1030 (1965).

15. See Cunningham, supra note 13, at 212.

16. See generally Thompson Engineering Co. v. Commissioner, 80 T.C. 672 (1983); Atlantic Commerce & Shipping Co. v. Commissioner, 32 T.C.M. 473 (1973), affirmed, 500 F.2d 937 (2d Cir.1974).

17. Grob, Inc. v. United States, 565 F.Supp. 391, 395 (E.D.Wis.1983).

time period, again expressed as a percentage of a year, that is required for the total productive process.

The *Bardahl International* case took the additional step of recognizing that those who supply raw materials and labor are not paid immediately. An appropriate credit period, usually 15 or 30 days, is stated as a percentage of a year (divided by 365 days per year), and this is subtracted from the total of the inventory and receivables percentages. When this ultimate percentage rate is applied to the net operating expenses for the year, the result represents the expenses for one business operating cycle * * *. To this are added reasonably anticipated extraordinary expenses during the tax year in question * * *. The sum represents the total requirements of the firm for liquid assets * * *. This is contrasted against the sum of liquid assets such as cash and equivalents * * * and investments which can be converted into cash readily if necessary * * * in order to ascertain whether there is an excess or shortage of available capital * * *. Cognizance must also be taken of any loans unrelated to the business * * *.

The result of this whole process is a figure * * * indicating how much the subject firm has accumulated beyond its reasonable needs. This, in conjunction with its findings on the intent of the parties, should permit a factfinder to ascertain whether or not the corporate entity has been availed of for the purpose of avoiding income tax by one or more of the shareholders. * * *

Stock Redemptions. Corporations sometimes contend that an accumulation of earnings is necessary to create a fund for a later redemption of stock. In response to conflicting results in the courts, Congress has specifically provided that the term "reasonable needs of the business" encompasses accumulations in the year of a shareholder's death or in any subsequent year to the extent they are necessary to make a stock redemption to pay death taxes under Section 303.[18]

The cases are inconsistent as to other types of future redemptions. Some courts have found accumulations to redeem dissenting minority or 50 percent shareholders to be a reasonable need of the business.[19] But corporations have encountered more difficulty when they have attempted to justify an accumulation on the ground that reasonable business needs include accumulating earnings to redeem either a friendly minority shareholder[20] or a majority shareholder.[21] In each case, the question is whether the redemption satisfies a corporate (e.g., preventing continuous deadlocks in

---

18. I.R.C. § 537(a)(2); 537(b)(1). Similarly, reasonable needs are considered to include amounts necessary to redeem stock held by a private foundation that is required to shed its excess business holdings. I.R.C. §§ 537(a)(3); 537(b)(2). See I.R.C. § 4943.

19. See, e.g., Wilcox Manufacturing Co. v. Commissioner, 38 T.C.M. 378 (1979);

Mountain State Steel Foundries, Inc. v. Commissioner, 284 F.2d 737 (4th Cir.1960).

20. See John B. Lambert & Associates v. United States, 212 Ct.Cl. 71 (1976).

21. See Lamark Shipping Agency, Inc. v. Commissioner, 42 T.C.M. 38 (1981); Pelton Steel Casting Co. v. Commissioner, 251 F.2d 278 (7th Cir.1958).

the boardroom) as opposed to a shareholder (e.g., funding a redemption of a retiring shareholder under a buy-sell agreement) purpose.[22] The *Gazette Publishing* case, which follows, illustrates how a redemption can be characterized as a valid response to a threat to the corporation's existence.

Gazette Publishing Co. v. Self

United States District Court, Eastern District of Arkansas, 1952.
103 F.Supp. 779.

■ TRIMBLE, CHIEF JUDGE.

This is an action by the plaintiff, Gazette Publishing Company, a corporation, against the acting collector of Internal Revenue for this district for the recovery of a Section 102, [Now Section 531. Ed.] 26 U.S.C.A. § 102, assessment made for the calendar years, 1946 and 1947.

Plaintiff was incorporated under the laws of Arkansas on June 5, 1889, for the purpose of publishing a newspaper, The Arkansas Gazette, and conducting related business enterprises, and has carried on such business since its incorporation. * * *

* * *

During the years, 1946 and 1947, Mr. J.N. Heiskell was president of the corporation, and Mr. Fred Allsopp was secretary-treasurer and general manager until his death in March, 1946. Upon his death, his son, W.C. Allsopp, who had been assistant business manager, succeeded to the positions held by his father. This situation had existed for many years. The business was run by informal conferences between these men, and no formal meetings of the Board of Directors or stockholders were held in which minutes were kept between March 24, 1944, and November, 1948. Formal meetings were only held when it was necessary to approve or ratify some action of the officers. * * *

* * *

The plaintiff corporation had a long history of paying generous dividends. For the twenty years ending with 1945, the year immediately preceding the questioned years, the corporation had net earnings after taxes of $2,288,000 and paid out $2,167,000 in dividends, retaining in the business for this period no more than $120,000 of the earnings. A study of the record discloses that the dividends paid in 1946 and 1947 were above the Corporation's average dividend in amount over the preceding ten year period. The 1947 dividend of $107,000 was the highest dividend paid since 1936. The record also discloses that more than half of the substantial increase in retained earnings during the period in question over prior years was due to the repeal of World War II excess profits tax. This gave to the officers of the Corporation an opportunity to begin to accumulate funds to

---

22. See generally Rudolph, "Stock Redemptions and the Accumulated Earnings Tax—an Update," 4 J.Corp. Tax'n 101 (1977).

meet the reasonable needs of the business, and without the necessity of reducing dividends.

The sale of the Allsopp stock, in 1948, was not the purpose for which the funds were accumulated during 1946 and 1947. The uncontroverted evidence in this case is that the proposed sale of the stock first came up in a flare of temper between Mr. Patterson and W.C. Allsopp in 1948, and that when the sale was proposed in 1948 it was a complete surprise to the president and the board of directors of the corporation. * * *

* * *

Defendant contends that the price of $1,000,000 paid for the Allsopp stock in 1948 was so far in excess of the true market value of that stock, that it is evident that there was in fact no reasonable need for the accumulation of the funds in 1946 and 1947.

It is in evidence that certain special interests have for many years sought to purchase or acquire stock in the corporation, and an interest in the publication of the Arkansas Gazette, the newspaper published by the corporation. The officers testified that the management has always watched the matter closely, fearing that if some group of special interests should acquire stock in the corporation, however minor it might be, such group of special interests would endeavor to break up the harmony existing in the management, and change the editorial and business policy of the corporation, which had conducted the business of the corporation so successfully so many years. When the Allsopp stock was offered for sale at $1,000,000, all the officers and directors of the plaintiff corporation knew this was in excess of its true market value. They were informed by the attorney for the Allsopp stockholders that the stock could be sold to an outsider for that amount of money. They recognized this as a business crisis. Knowing that their failure to acquire this stock for the corporation might in the future affect the interest of the corporation and its stockholders adversely, it was decided to make the acquisition and promote and keep intact the harmony of management and editorial policy of the corporation.

Defendant does not seem to recognize that this business is subject to changes in circumstances and conditions, and that good business judgment upon the part of management requires changes in plans to meet these changes of circumstances. This is true with this plaintiff as with all other business enterprises, and the courts have recognized that this is so. All business needs are relative. The most pressing needs today may not be the most pressing at a later date, because even more pressing needs may arise because of changed circumstances, and courts have frequently refused to sustain Section 102 Assessments where the funds accumulated for reasonable needs and owing to change in circumstances the funds were used only partially or not at all as originally planned.

In Dill Manufacturing Co., 39 B.T.A. 1023, it was the purchase of the minority stock which forced the postponement of plans for a new plant, and the Board of Tax Appeals, in reversing a Section 102 Assessment by the Commissioner, held the purchase of the minority stock was a reasonable business need of the company. The Board of Tax Appeals, said in that case: "The issue of preferred stock with the obligation to retire it within five years evidenced a debt, (cases cited). And this record, at most, does not establish that the liquidation of the syndicate stock by the partial use of that preferred stock, under the circumstances here, was not required as a reasonable business necessity. Cf. Sauk Investment Co., 34 B.T.A. 732; Mellbank Corporation, 38 B.T.A. 1108."

See also National Yarn Corporation, 9 TCM 603; General Smelting Co., 4 T.C. 313; The Wean Engineering Co., Inc., 2 TCM 510; Emeloid Co., Inc. v. Commissioner of Internal Revenue, 3 Cir., 189 F.2d 230. In the case of Fred F. Fisher, 6 TCM 520, the Tax Court held that the promotion of harmony in the conduct of the business is a proper business purpose. There, taxpayer's sister, a minority stockholder, had been constantly complaining about the conduct of the business. To put an end to the dissension, the company purchased the sister's stock at a price considerably in excess of its fair market value. The Commissioner, contending that the stock purchase was prompted by reasons personal to the stockholders and not in furtherance of any corporate purpose, assessed a deficiency on the other stockholders on the theory that the excessive portion of the purchase price constituted a constructive dividend. But the Tax Court held that the Company's purchase of the sister's stock was in furtherance of corporate purposes. The Tax Court pointed out that "there is no foundation for an assumption that a corporation would never, in its own interests, pay more than the fair market value of its stock in order to rid itself of a complaining minority stockholder," and that the excessive price paid for the stock "was not unreasonable for the purpose of promoting harmony in the conduct of the business and securing it from annoying interference and threats of legal proceedings." The Court said, "regardless of whether * * * complaints were justified, they had a nuisance value sufficient to warrant the action of the corporation in purchasing her stock."

The Arkansas Gazette, published by the plaintiff, is said to be the oldest daily paper west of the Mississippi River. It has enjoyed a long, honorable and successful career under able and eminent editors, among them the present President of the Corporation. It has a well established policy, standing firmly and stoutly for all the great moral issues arising from time to time, has had a great part in the development of the whole state, and has at all times supported worthy public causes and men in public life with telling effect. It has consistently over a long term of years refused to accept advertisements for alcoholic liquors of any kind. It also has had and still has strong editorial policies on many issues which special interests might and would oppose. For this Allsopp stock to have fallen into the hands of some special interest antagonistic to the present and the general policy of the paper, could and probably would have been most disruptive of the harmony of the corporation, even though it constituted a minority of all the stock. The purchase of this stock, even at the advanced price paid, was a reasonable need of the corporation, and was a change in circumstances which fully justified a change in the use of funds accumulated for other needs, and justified the borrowing of the $600,000 in addition to using the funds on hand.

* * *

The Court finds from all the evidence in the case, and giving such weight to the statutory presumptions as the law requires, that the earnings and profits were not accumulated in 1946 and 1947 beyond the reasonable needs of the corporation. Nor were such earnings accumulated for the purpose of preventing the imposition of a surtax upon the stockholders.

NOTE

Sections 533 and 534 work together to provide an unusual procedure for regulating the burden of proof if an accumulated earnings tax controversy is litigated in the Tax Court. As we have seen, an accumulation beyond the reasonable needs of the business is determinative of the forbidden purpose unless the corporation proves otherwise by a preponderance of the evidence.[1] The regulations provide that this presumption adds "still more weight" to the usual presumption of correctness that accompanies the Service's determinations of tax liability.[2] The Commissioner nonetheless will bear the burden of proof on the question of unreasonable accumulations unless it has informed the taxpayer, prior to sending a formal notice of deficiency, that the proposed notice includes an accumulated earnings tax deficiency.[3] Even in the likely case where the Commissioner provides notice, the taxpayer can shift the burden of proof back to the Commissioner by submitting a statement setting forth the grounds on which it relies to establish that all or part of its earnings and profits have not been permitted to accumulate beyond the reasonable needs of the business.[4] The statement must be filed within 30 days of the Commissioner's notification under Section 534(b).[5] To shift the burden of proof, the taxpayer's statement may not consist merely of vague generalities. It must set forth with specificity and clarity the grounds on which it will rely to prove that its accumulations were reasonable.[6]

4.   CALCULATION OF ACCUMULATED TAXABLE INCOME

Code: 535(a), (b), (c); 561; 562(a), (b), (c); 563(a), (d); 565(a)–(d), (f).

The base for the accumulated earnings tax is accumulated taxable income, which Section 535(a) defines as taxable income of the corporation, adjusted under Section 535(b), less the sum of the dividends paid deduction and the accumulated earnings credit.

Adjustments to Taxable Income. The base figure for computing accumulated taxable income is the current year's taxable income. The accumu-

1. I.R.C. § 533(a).

2. Reg. § 1.533–1(b).

3. I.R.C. § 534(a), (b).

4. I.R.C. § 534(c); Reg. § 1.534–2(a), (b).

5. I.R.C. § 534(c).

6. Reg. § 1.534–2(d).

lated earnings tax, however, is directed at real retained economic profits because they are a more accurate measure of the corporation's capacity to pay dividends. As a result, taxable income is adjusted in a manner somewhat similar to that used to adjust taxable income to determine earnings and profits. For example, to arrive at accumulated taxable income, taxable income is reduced by certain nondeductible taxes[1] and charitable contributions in excess of the percentage limitations.[2] These items do not affect taxable income but nonetheless result in a decrease in the corporation's wealth. On the other hand, certain deductions allowed for income tax purposes that do not currently reduce the corporation's real wealth are disallowed in computing accumulated taxable income. These include the dividends received deduction[3] and the net operating loss deduction.[4]

Section 535(b) contains special rules governing the treatment of net capital gains and losses for purposes of determining accumulated taxable income.[5] Section 535(b)(6) permits a corporation to reduce taxable income by its net capital gain for the year less attributable taxes. But for purposes of determining net capital gain prior net capital losses are treated as short-term capital losses in succeeding taxable years.[6] Under Section 535(b)(5)(A) and (B), a corporation can deduct the amount of a net capital loss reduced by the lesser of its "nonrecaptured capital gains deductions" or its earnings and profits as of the close of the preceding year. "Nonrecaptured capital gains deductions" are generally defined by Section 535(b)(5)(C) as the excess of the aggregate amount allowable as a deduction in prior years for net capital gains over the aggregate reductions to capital losses for prior years.

Dividends Paid Deduction. Section 535(a) logically permits a corporation to reduce accumulated taxable income by dividends paid during the taxable year. Section 561(a) defines the "dividends paid" to include dividends[7] paid during the taxable year and certain "consent dividends." Generally, distributions must be pro rata in order to qualify for the dividends paid deduction.[8] Liquidating distributions and redemptions also may produce a deduction for dividends paid.[9] Because a corporation frequently may not have the facts available to determine its liability for the accumulated earnings tax, Section 563(a) provides that dividends paid on or before the 15th day of the third month following the close of a taxable year are considered paid in the earlier year.

1. I.R.C. § 535(b)(1).

2. I.R.C. § 535(b)(2).

3. I.R.C. § 535(b)(3).

4. I.R.C. § 535(b)(4).

5. A separate set of rules applies to a "mere holding or investment company." I.R.C. § 535(b)(8).

6. I.R.C. § 535(b)(6), (7).

7. Section 562(a) generally employs the Section 316 definition of "dividend" for purposes of determining the dividends paid deduction. Reg. § 1.562–1(a) provides that if a dividend is paid in property (other than money) the amount of the dividends paid deduction is the corporation's adjusted basis in the property. The regulation was upheld in Fulman v. United States, 434 U.S. 528, 98 S.Ct. 841 (1978).

8. I.R.C. § 562(c). Differences in dividend rights among classes of stock not attributable to shareholder waivers are permitted.

9. I.R.C. § 562(b)(1).

Consent Dividends. Section 565 permits shareholders to file a consent with the corporation's tax return to include in income as dividends amounts which were not in fact distributed. Consent dividends are treated as if they were distributed in cash to the shareholders and then contributed back to the corporation on the last day of the corporation's taxable year.[10]

Accumulated Earnings Credit. To the extent that a corporation's earnings are retained for the reasonable needs of the business, they are not within the ambit of the accumulated earnings tax. To remove these earnings from the grasp of the tax, a corporation is permitted a deduction for the accumulated earnings credit in determining accumulated taxable income. The accumulated earnings credit is equal to the amount of current earnings and profits (less the dividends paid deduction) retained for the reasonable needs of the business minus the deduction permitted for net capital gains.[11] Section 535(c)(2) provides that the credit shall in no case be less than the amount by which $250,000 ($150,000 in the case of certain service corporations) exceeds accumulated earnings and profits at the close of the preceding taxable year.[12] This has the effect of enabling a corporation to accumulate a minimum of $250,000 regardless of its business needs.

PROBLEMS

1. Which of the following accumulations are likely to be for the reasonable needs of the business?

(a) A corporation retains $200,000 of earnings and profits per year for five years to finance a $1,000,000 expansion of its manufacturing plant. Should it matter if the corporation could have borrowed 80% of the expansion costs?

(b) A corporation which manufactures computer chips accumulates $2,000,000 in order to acquire an office building which is rented to an insurance company under a net lease.

(c) Assume Parent Corporation owns all of the outstanding stock of Brother and Sister Corporations. Can Parent accumulate earnings and profits for Brother? Brother for Parent? Brother for Sister? See Reg. §§ 1.537–2(c)(3), –3(b).

(d) A corporation accumulates earnings and profits for potential § 531 tax liability.

(e) A corporation accumulates earnings and profits in order to redeem a class of limited and preferred stock.

10. I.R.C. § 565(c).

11. I.R.C. § 535(c)(1). Net capital gains are excluded from accumulated taxable income by Section 535(b)(6) but they are part of earnings and profits. If a net capital gain was not excluded from the accumulated earnings credit it would reduce accumulated tax-able income twice: once under Section 535(b)(6) and again under Section 535(c).

12. Accumulated earnings and profits at the close of the preceding year are reduced by dividends treated as paid in such year under Section 563(a). I.R.C. § 535(c)(4).

2. T Corporation (a shoe manufacturer) is a calendar year, accrual method corporation which is not a personal holding company and which has accumulated earnings and profits at the end of year one of $200,000. T is a closely held corporation with three shareholders. In year two T has taxable income (all of which is ordinary income) of $60,000. T also has taxable income of $60,000 in both years three and four. There are no distributions to shareholders in any year.

    (a) What tax results to T under §§ 11 and 531, assuming current § 11 rates on all income in years two, three, and four?

    (b) What possible defenses may T have to the application of § 531?

    (c) What effect will § 534 have on these facts?

D.   THE PERSONAL HOLDING COMPANY TAX

1.   INTRODUCTION

Code: §§ 541, 542(a).

The accumulated earnings tax was not an entirely effective vehicle to prevent the use of a corporation to avoid the individual tax rates (when they were higher than the corporate rates) because it is not imposed unless a corporation has accumulations that are motivated at least in part by tax avoidance. Moreover, the accumulated earnings credit may shelter substantial accumulations from the Section 531 tax. Partially in response to these shortcomings and in order to prevent certain other tax avoidance devices, Congress enacted the personal holding company tax.[1]

The original purpose of the personal holding company tax was to prevent taxpayers from avoiding the higher graduated individual tax rates by using devices known as "incorporated pocketbooks," "incorporated talents" and "incorporated properties." These schemes were structured as follows:

    1. *Incorporated Pocketbooks*. A high bracket individual would transfer passive investments (e.g., stocks, bonds, rental property) to a corporation in exchange for its stock. The corporation then could take advantage of the lower corporate rates and the dividends received deduction for any dividends that it received. The income could be realized at a later date at capital gain rates through a liquidation of the company or, ideally, the stock could be held until the taxpayer's death when his heirs would take a stepped-up basis.

    2. *Incorporated Talents*. A highly compensated individual, such as a movie star, would form a wholly owned corporation and agree to work for the corporation at a small salary. The corporation then would contract out the services of its owner-employee for a sub-

---

1. H.Rep. No. 704, 73rd Cong., 2d Sess. (1934), reprinted in 1939–1 C.B. 554, 562.

stantial sum, and the great bulk of the income would be taxed at the lower corporate rates.[2]

3. *Incorporated Properties*. A taxpayer would transfer both investment property and property which did not generate income, such as a yacht or home, to a corporation. The shareholder then would lease back the property for a nominal amount, and the corporation would attempt to shelter both the rental income and its other income by claiming deductions for depreciation and maintenance on the property.[3]

To combat these plans, Section 541 imposes a penalty tax of 15 percent (scheduled to increase to 39.6 percent in 2013) on the "undistributed personal holding company income" of every "personal holding company." The personal holding company tax is imposed in addition to a corporation's regular income tax. To avoid overlap, personal holding companies are not subject to the accumulated earnings tax.[4] The remaining sections of this chapter consider the details and operation of the personal holding company tax, first examining the definition of a personal holding company and then turning to the determination of the tax.

2. Definition of a Personal Holding Company

Code: § 542(a). Skim § 542(c).

A personal holding company is a corporation which satisfies a stock ownership requirement and an adjusted ordinary gross income test. Unlike the accumulated earnings tax, the determination of whether a corporation is a personal holding company is an objective inquiry that does not depend on whether there is a tax avoidance motive.

a. STOCK OWNERSHIP REQUIREMENT

Code: §§ 542(a)(2); 544.

The first leg of the definition of a personal holding company looks to whether the corporation is closely held. The stock ownership requirement in Section 542(a)(2) is satisfied if at any time during the last half of the taxable year more than 50 percent in value of the corporation's outstanding stock is owned, directly or indirectly, by or for not more than five individuals. Not surprisingly, this test is accompanied by special attribution rules in Section 544(a), under which stock owned by a corporation, partnership, estate or trust is considered owned proportionately by its shareholders, partners or beneficiaries.[1] An individual is considered to own stock owned by his family (brothers, sisters, spouse, ancestors and lineal descendants) or

---

2. See Commissioner v. Laughton, 113 F.2d 103 (9th Cir.1940).

3. Bittker & Eustice, Federal Income Taxation of Corporations and Shareholders ¶ 7.20.

4. I.R.C. § 532(b)(1).

1. I.R.C. § 544(a)(1).

partners,[2] as well as stock held under an option to purchase.[3] Section 544(b)(1) provides that securities convertible into stock are considered stock for purposes of Section 542(a)(2) if the effect of their inclusion is to make the corporation a personal holding company.

b. INCOME TEST

Code: §§ 542(a)(1); 543.

The income test seeks to identify corporations with a significant amount of passive investment income or income attributable to the personal services of a major shareholder. Under Section 542(a)(1), at least 60 percent of a corporation's "adjusted ordinary gross income" (AOGI) must be "personal holding company income" before the corporation will be classified as a personal holding company. To apply this test, one must master some special terminology.

Adjusted Ordinary Gross Income. The function of AOGI is to provide an accurate measuring rod against which to compare a corporation's passive investment and personal service income. Its computation begins with the corporation's gross income, which is then reduced by capital and Section 1231 gains to arrive at ordinary gross income (OGI).[4] These gains are excluded from gross income in order to prevent corporations from timing gains (and inflating their income) to avoid the income test.[5]

Next, a series of adjustments must be made to OGI to determine AOGI. These adjustments also are designed to prevent easy avoidance of the income test by manipulation of the corporation's gross income. For example, gross income includes the full amount of receipts from the rental of property or royalties from mineral exploration. Absent some adjustment mechanism, corporations could generate enough gross income from leveraged investments in these properties to inflate AOGI and escape the personal holding company tax. In order to prevent this technique, AOGI includes not all gross ordinary income but only the corporation's adjusted income from rents and royalties.[6] This amount includes income from rents and mineral, oil and gas royalties only to the extent that the gross income from these activities exceeds the amount deductible for depreciation or depletion, property taxes, interest and rent.[7] Since copyright royalties, royalties from films produced by the corporation and royalties from computer software produced by the corporation generally require more active participation than mineral or oil and gas royalties, the gross amount of royalties from copyrights, produced films or qualifying computer software businesses is included in AOGI.[8] Interest earned by dealers on obligations

---

2. I.R.C. § 544(a)(2).

3. I.R.C. § 544(a)(3).

4. I.R.C. § 543(b)(1)(A), (B).

5. S.Rep. No. 830, 88th Cong., 2d Sess. (1964), reprinted in 1964–1 (pt. 2) C.B. 505, 611.

6. S.Rep. No. 830, 88th Cong., 2d Sess. (1964), reprinted in 1964–1 (pt. 2) C.B. 505, 610.

7. I.R.C. § 543(b)(2)(A), (B).

8. I.R.C. § 543(b)(1), (3).

of the United States and interest on condemnation awards, judgments and tax refunds also is excluded from AOGI.[9]

Personal Holding Company Income. Students of the Internal Revenue Code have come to expect a large degree of complexity when Congress seeks to prevent tax avoidance. Congress must anticipate new efforts to avoid its corrective legislation while not penalizing taxpayers engaged in legitimate business or investment activities. These dual and often competing goals contribute to a web of special rules and exceptions. And so it is that the definition of personal holding company income in Section 543(a) is one of the Code's most diabolical provisions. Before turning to the necessary details, a few generalizations are in order. Incorporated pocketbooks and incorporated talents were Congress's prime targets when it first enacted and expanded the personal holding company tax. Consistent with that purpose, passive investment income and certain income from personal service contracts are the principal components of personal holding company income. But it is possible for rents, royalties, and other forms of income that appear to be passive to result from a corporation's legitimate active business pursuits. Section 543 attempts to identify the purely passive income and the types of personal service income targeted by the personal holding company provisions through the use of various mechanical tests, some of which are examined in more detail below.

Passive Investment Income Items: In General. Passive investment income items are the principal target of the personal holding company tax. Personal holding company income thus includes dividends, interest, annuities, royalties and rents.[10] Capital gains and Section 1231 gains are excluded because they historically have enjoyed preferential rates at both the corporate and individual levels. Dividends are defined by reference to Section 316 and are not reduced by the dividends received deduction. Interest includes imputed interest under provisions such as Sections 483 and 7872, but the types of interest excluded from AOGI (e.g., interest on condemnation awards, judgments or tax refunds) do not constitute personal holding company income. The inclusion of most forms of interest income may create unexpected difficulties for an otherwise active corporation which has sold a substantial portion of its assets on credit in a year when other receipts are minimal.[11] Royalties include income from licenses to use various types of intangible property (e.g., patents, trademarks, technical know-how)[12] a broad definition that may threaten a high technology company, such as a computer software manufacturer, that chooses to license its technology rather than market it directly. Royalties from natural resources, films, copyrights and computer software are treated separately and are discussed below.

Rents. One of the major sources of complexity in Section 543 results from its attempt to draw objective lines between passive investment income

---

9. I.R.C. § 543(b)(2)(C).

10. I.R.C. § 543(a)(1).

11. See, e.g., O'Sullivan Rubber Co. v. Commissioner, 120 F.2d 845 (2d Cir.1941).

12. Reg. § 1.543–1(b)(3).

and profits from an active operating business. Nowhere is this better illustrated than in the area of rents. The treatment of rents was overhauled as part of substantial revisions to the personal holding company tax enacted in 1964. The following excerpt from the legislative history describes the Congressional solution:[13]

> *(c)(v) Rental income.*Under present law rental income is classified as personal holding company income only if it represents less than 50 percent of total gross income. This is based on the concept that where rental income represents the major activity, the activity involved is more likely to be of an active rather than passive character. The House bill retains this 50–percent test (applying it, however, to adjusted income from rents and to adjusted ordinary gross income) but adds a second test providing that rental income may be characterized as passive, or personal holding company income even where it represents 50 percent or more of the adjusted ordinary gross income if, apart from the rental income, more than 10 percent of the ordinary gross income (gross income excluding capital gains) of the company is personal holding company income. For this purpose, income derived from the use of corporate property by shareholders is not viewed as personal holding company income, but income from copyright royalties and the adjusted income from mineral, oil, and gas royalties is included for this purpose as personal holding company income.
>
> Your committee has accepted the House changes in the 50–percent test with one modification. Your committee has made an amendment to this test with regard to rentals of tangible personal property retained by the lessee for three years or less. Under the amendment, in the case of such property, the income is not to be reduced by depreciation attributable to it for purposes of the 50–percent test and also for purposes of computing ordinary gross income. However, in the case of the provision in the House bill that the personal holding company income (apart from rent) may not exceed 10 percent of the ordinary gross income, your committee's amendments provide that the personal holding company income for this purpose may be reduced by dividends paid during the year, by dividends paid in the next year which are treated as if paid in the year in question, and by consent dividends. Your committee believes that this prevents the 10–percent rule from working harshly where the personal holding company income other than rents may exceed 10 percent of ordinary gross income, perhaps by only a small amount but under the House bill, nevertheless, result in the entire amount of rental income being classified as personal holding company income. Your committee's amendment in effect permits taxpayers to meet the 10–percent

---

13. S.Rep. No. 830, 88th Cong., 2d Sess.   611–613.
(1964), reprinted in 1964–1 (pt. 2) C.B. 505,

test after dividend payments (or amounts treated as paid in dividends). At the same time it gives assurance that the personal holding company income (apart from rent) sheltered in the company may not exceed 10 percent of its ordinary gross income.

The fact that rental income, both in applying the 60–percent test and also in applying the 50–percent provision to the rental income itself, is determined on the basis of reducing rental income by depreciation, amortization, property taxes, interest, and rents paid has already been noted above. However, as previously indicated, tangible personal property rented for three years or less is not reduced by depreciation attributable to it for purposes of these tests, under your committee's amendments.

Mineral, Oil and Gas Royalties. Income from mineral, oil and gas royalties also are singled out for special treatment. The "adjusted income" from these royalties constitutes personal holding company income unless: (1) such adjusted income constitutes 50 percent or more of the corporation's AOGI, (2) certain other forms of the corporation's personal holding company income do not exceed 10 percent of its OGI, and (3) the corporation's trade or business deductions, other than salaries and deductions specifically allowed by sections other than Section 162 (e.g., depreciation, interest, state taxes) exceed 15 percent of AOGI.[14]

Copyright Royalties. Under rules similar to those applicable to mineral royalties, copyright royalties are personal holding company income unless: (1) they constitute 50 percent or more of the corporation's OGI, (2) other personal holding company income after certain adjustments, does not exceed 10 percent of the corporation's OGI, and (3) Section 162 business deductions allocable to the copyright royalties, other than salaries, deductions for royalties paid and deductions specifically allowed by sections other than Section 162, equal or exceed 25 percent of OGI reduced by royalties paid and depreciation deductions attributable to the copyrights.[15]

Produced Film Rents. "Produced film rents" are personal holding company income unless they constitute 50 percent or more of OGI. Active motion picture companies thus have nothing to fear from this provision. The purpose and scope of Section 543(a)(5) are explained in the following excerpt from the 1964 legislative history:[16]

> *(c)(viii) Produced film rents.*Under present law payments received from the distribution and exhibition of motion picture films are treated as rentals. As a result, under present law, a corporation may be formed by an individual who owns a motion picture negative and have its earnings treated as rents for purposes of the personal holding company tax. Since in such a case more than 50 percent of its gross income would be considered to be from rents,

---

14. I.R.C. § 543(a)(3).

15. I.R.C. § 543(a)(4).

16. S.Rep. No. 830, 88th Cong., 2d Sess. (1964), reprinted in 1964–1 (pt. 2) C.B. 505, 612–13.

there would be no personal holding company tax payable in this case.

To meet this problem, the bill provides that payments received from the use of, or the right to use, films generally will be characterized as copyright royalty income. Thus, such income will be classified as personal holding company income unless 50 percent or more of the company's ordinary income is from this source, not more than 10 percent of the company's ordinary gross income is personal holding company income, and the deductions properly allocable to this film income represent 25 percent or more of the gross income from this source reduced by royalties paid and depreciation taken.

The bill, however, retains what is essentially the treatment of present law for "produced film rents." Produced film rents are rents arising from an interest in a film acquired before the production of the film was substantially complete. It was thought that less severe tests should be applied in such cases because the participation in the production of the film in itself indicates an active business enterprise in this case. For produced film rent to escape characterization as personal holding company income, as under present law, these rents need constitute only 50 percent or more of the ordinary gross income of the company.

Computer Software Royalties. Prior to 1987, a closely held company that manufactured computer software was confronted with the personal holding company tax if it licensed its technology instead of marketing it directly.[17] Despite the fact that the company was an active operating business, the payments received under the licensing agreements likely constituted personal holding company income under Section 543, which includes both "royalties" and certain "copyright royalties" in the definition of personal holding company income.[18] Congress responded to this problem by providing that computer software royalties do not constitute personal holding company income if they are "active business computer software royalties."[19] That term is defined in Section 543(d)(1) as royalties, received by a corporation in connection with the licensing of computer software, which satisfy four requirements that generally are designed to restrict the exception to corporations earning a substantial portion of their income and incurring significant expenses in the active conduct of the trade or business of developing, manufacturing, or producing computer software.[20]

Personal Service Income. The final major category of personal holding company income is aimed at the incorporated talent. Income from contracts to furnish personal services, including income from the sale or other

---

17. See generally Morgan, "The Domestic Technology Base Company: The Dilemma of an Operating Company Which Might Be a Personal Holding Company," 33 Tax L.Rev. 233 (1978).

18. I.R.C. § 543(a)(1), (4).

19. I.R.C.§ 543(a)(1)(C), (a)(4) (last sentence).

20. I.R.C. § 543(d)(2)–(5).

disposition of such contracts, is tainted if: (1) the individual who is to perform the services is designated by name or description in the contract or can be designated by some person other than the corporation, and (2) the designated individual owns (directly or through attribution) 25 percent or more of the value of the corporation's stock at any time during the year.[21]

Other Items. Personal holding company income also includes rents for the use of tangible property received from a 25 percent shareholder under certain conditions[22] and income derived by the corporation in its capacity as a beneficiary of an estate or trust.[23]

Revenue Ruling 75–67

1975–1 Cum.Bull. 169.

Advice has been requested whether, under the circumstances described below, a corporation will be considered to have received personal holding company income within the meaning of section 543(a)(7) of the Internal Revenue Code of 1954.

B, a doctor specializing in a certain area of medical services, owns 80 percent of the outstanding stock of L, a domestic professional service corporation. B is the only officer of L who is active in the production of income for L, and he is the only medical doctor presently employed by L. B performs medical services under an employment contract with L. L furnishes office quarters and equipment, and employs a receptionist to assist B. P, a patient, solicited the services of and was treated by B.

Section 543(a)(7) of the Code provides, in part, that the term personal holding company income includes amounts received under a contract whereby a corporation is to furnish personal services if some person other than the corporation has the right to designate, by name or description, the individual who is to perform the services, or if the individual who is to perform the services is designated, by name or description, in the contract.

In dealing with a professional service corporation providing medical services, an individual will customarily solicit and expect to receive the services of a particular physician, and he will usually be treated by the physician sought.

A physician-patient relationship arises from such a general agreement of treatment. Either party may terminate the relationship at will, although the physician must give the patient reasonable notice of his withdrawal and may not abandon the patient until a replacement, if necessary, can be obtained. C. Morris & A. Mortiz, Doctor and Patient and the Law 135 (5th ed. 1971). Moreover, if a physician who has entered into a general agreement of treatment is unable to treat the patient when his services are

---

21. I.R.C. § 543(a)(7). For detailed examples of the operation of this provision, see Reg. § 1.543–1(b)(8).

22. I.R.C. § 543(a)(6).

23. I.R.C. § 543(a)(8).

needed, he may provide a qualified and competent substitute physician to render the services. C. Morris & A. Moritz, supra, at 138, 374–75.

Thus, when an individual solicits, and expects, the services of a particular physician and that physician accepts the individual as a patient and treats him, the relationship of physician-patient established in this manner does not constitute a designation of the individual who is to perform the services under a contract for personal services within the meaning of section 543(a)(7) of the Code.

If, however, the physician or the professional service corporation contracts with the patient that the physician personally will perform particular services for the patient, and he has no right to substitute another physician to perform such services, there is a designation of that physician as the individual to perform services under a contract for personal services within the meaning of section 543(a)(7) of the Code.

The designation of a physician as an individual to perform services can be accomplished by either an oral or written contract. See Rev.Rul. 69–299, 1969–1 C.B. 165.

Moreover, if L agreed to perform the type of services that are so unique as to preclude substitution of another physician to perform such services, there is also a designation.

Accordingly, since in the instant case there is no indication that L has contracted that B will personally perform the services or that the services are so unique as to preclude substitution, it is held that income earned by L from providing medical service contracts will not be considered income from personal service contracts within the meaning of section 543(a)(7) of the Code.

Revenue Ruling 84–137

1984–2 Cum.Bull. 116.

ISSUE

Is rental income received by a corporate lessor from a corporate lessee, which [sic] both corporations are owned by the same individual shareholder, compensation for the use of or right to use corporate property by a shareholder under section 543(a)(6) of the Internal Revenue Code for purposes of the personal holding company tax provisions?

FACTS

A, an individual, owns all of the shares of two corporations, X and Y. X's primary business activity is the leasing of realty and tangible personal property to its sister corporation Y for a fair market rental value. A makes no personal use of X's leased assets, which are used solely in Y's manufacturing business. In 1983, X received 100x dollars of rental income from Y and 12x dollars of interest income from its various bank deposits. The 12x dollars of interest income is personal holding company income as defined in section 543(a)(1) of the Code.

LAW AND ANALYSIS

Section 543(a)(6)(A) of the Code provides that amounts received as compensation for the use of, or the right to use, tangible property of the corporation in any case where at any time during the taxable year, 25 percent or more in value of the outstanding stock of the corporation is owned, directly or indirectly, by or for an individual entitled to the use of the property (whether such right is obtained directly from the corporation or by means of a sublease or other arrangement) is personal holding company income.

Section 543(a)(6)(B) of the Code provides that section 543(a)(6)(A) of the Code will apply only to a corporation which has other personal holding company income (as determined under section 543(a)(6)(C)) in excess of 10 percent of its ordinary gross income.

Rev.Rul. 65–259, 1965–2 C.B. 174, states that where rental income is derived from a corporate lessee, any one of whose shareholders also directly or indirectly owns 25 percent or more in value of the outstanding stock of the lessor corporation, the shareholder of the lessee corporation indirectly has the right to use the leased property and such indirect right is obtained by means of an "other arrangement". See 320 East 47th Street Corporation v. Commissioner, 243 F.2d 894 (2d Cir.1957), rev'g in part, 26 T.C. 545 (1956). Thus, Rev.Rul. 65–259 holds that the rental income is personal holding company income under section 543(a)(6) of the Code.

The Tax Court in Allied Industrial Cartage Co. v. Commissioner, 72 T.C. 515 (1979), aff'd, 647 F.2d 713 (6th Cir.1981), and Silverman and Sons Realty Trust v. Commissioner, T.C.M. 1979–404, aff'd, 620 F.2d 314 (1st Cir.1980), disagreed with the holding in 320 East 47th Street Corp. These cases hold that, as between brother and sister corporations, unless a corporate lessee is shown to be a vehicle for facilitating the individual or personal use of leased property by its shareholders, its separate status should not be disregarded so as to impose the personal holding company tax upon the lessor corporation. See also New Colonial Ice v. Helvering, 292 U.S. 435 (1934) XIII–2 C.B. 194; Minnesota Mortuaries, Inc. v. Commissioner, 4 T.C. 280 (1944); acq., 1945 C.B. 5, nonacq., 1965–2 C.B. 7, acq. page 5, this Bulletin.

HOLDING

If rental income is received by a corporate lessor from a corporate lessee, when both corporations are wholly owned by the same individual shareholder and the rented property is used solely in the trade or business of the lessee corporation and not for the individual or personal benefit of the shareholder, then such rental income is not compensation for the use of or right to use corporate property by a shareholder under section 543(a)(6) of the Code for purpose of the personal holding company tax provisions.

* * *

3.   TAXATION OF PERSONAL HOLDING COMPANIES

Code: §§ 541; 545(a).

Personal holding companies are subject to a tax of 15 percent (scheduled to increase to 39.6 percent in 2013) of their undistributed personal holding company income.[1] The key to understanding the computation of the personal holding company tax is the concept of undistributed personal holding company income (UPHCI). The definition of UPHCI bears no relationship to the definition of personal holding company income. As defined in Section 545(a), UPHCI is essentially the corporation's after-tax profits less a dividends paid deduction.

a.   ADJUSTMENTS TO TAXABLE INCOME

Code: § 545(b).

The personal holding company tax is imposed on the corporation's real after-tax profits rather than its taxable income. Accordingly, in determining the tax base, certain adjustments are made to the corporation's taxable income so that it more nearly resembles the corporation's true economic income. Deductions are allowed for payments, such as federal taxes[2] and certain excess charitable contributions, which reduce the corporation's real wealth but are not allowable in computing taxable income.[3] Conversely, certain deductions which are allowable in determining taxable income but which do not decrease the corporation's real earnings for the year are not allowed in determining UPHCI. An example is the Section 243 dividends received deduction.[4] Net operating losses also receive special treatment.[5] Finally, in order to exempt long-term capital gains from the personal holding company tax, corporations may eliminate net capital gains less attributable taxes in determining UPHCI.[6]

Another Section 545(b) adjustment relates to a specific tax avoidance scheme mentioned earlier. Individuals cannot depreciate their homes, yachts, vacation homes or other property held for personal use. In order to obtain the benefits of depreciation, individuals would transfer these assets to a corporation with other income and then lease them back in an attempt to convert the assets to income-producing status in the hands of the corporation. We have already seen that the resulting rental income will likely be personal holding company income. Section 545(b)(6) attacks this same scheme from a different angle. For purposes of determining UPHCI, if the corporation leases its property, the allocable business and depreciation deductions are limited to the rental income from the property unless the corporation can establish that: (1) the rent received for the property was the highest obtainable, (2) the property was held by the corporation in

---

1. I.R.C. § 541.

2. I.R.C. § 545(b)(1).

3. I.R.C. § 545(b)(2). A special mixture of individual and corporate rules apply to determine the amount of the adjustment.

4. I.R.C. § 545(b)(3).

5. I.R.C. § 545(b)(4).

6. I.R.C. § 545(b)(5).

the course of a business for profit, and (3) there either was a reasonable expectation of profit from the property or the property was necessary to the conduct of the business.

b. DIVIDENDS PAID DEDUCTION

Code: §§ 561, 316(b), 562(a), (b), (c), 563, 564, 565. Skim § 547.

The purpose of the personal holding company tax is to force personal holding companies to distribute earnings to their individual shareholders. It follows that to the extent a personal holding company distributes its earnings, the Section 541 tax should not apply. To qualify for the dividends paid deduction, distributions generally must be pro rata.[7] Under Section 561(a), the dividends paid deduction equals the sum of the dividends paid during the taxable year, consent dividends, and the dividend carryover under Section 564. The combination of these provisions make it highly unlikely that any well informed personal holding company ever will be subject to the penalty tax.

Dividends Paid During the Year. Dividends paid during the year are determined by reference to the definition of a dividend in Section 316. For purposes of the dividends paid deduction, the regulations provide that a dividend in kind of appreciated property may only be deducted to the extent of the corporation's basis in the distributed property.[8] This rule is at variance with the treatment of such dividends to shareholders, for whom the "amount" of the distribution is the full fair market value of the distributed property under Section 301(b)(1)(A). But the regulation was upheld by the Supreme Court on the general ground that Treasury Regulations should be sustained by the courts whenever they have a "reasonable basis."[9] Query whether the same approach should be used for distributions of property that has declined in value?

Distributions and redemptions treated as Section 301 distributions are, of course, taxable as dividends to the shareholders to the extent of the corporation's available earnings and profits. If a corporation is a personal holding company, however, distributions may be taxed as dividends even if there are no available earnings and profits. Under Section 316(b)(2), if a personal holding company makes distributions in excess of the available earnings and profits, the distributions are nonetheless treated as dividends for all purposes to the extent of the corporation's UPHCI. This rule also applies if a corporation is considered to make a distribution under Section 563(b) (dividends paid after the year) or Section 547 (deficiency dividends) in a year in which it is a personal holding company.

Section 563(b) Election. If a corporation elects under Section 563(b), dividends paid or on before the 15th day of the third month following the close of a taxable year will be treated as having been paid during the prior year. The amount allowed as a dividend under Section 563(b) can not

---

7. I.R.C. § 562(c).

8. Reg. § 1.562–1(a).

9. Fulman v. United States, 434 U.S. 528, 98 S.Ct. 841 (1978).

exceed either the corporation's UPHCI for the prior taxable year or 20 percent of the actual dividends paid during the prior year.[10]

Consent Dividends. If a corporation does not make actual distributions during the relevant period, it still can qualify for a dividends paid deduction to the extent that its shareholders consent to be taxed as if they had received pro rata distributions during the year and had immediately made capital contributions of the same amount.[11] Consent dividends are deductible only to the extent that all the shareholders consent to be taxed on a pro rata basis[12] and only to the extent that actual distributions would be dividends under Section 316(a) or 316(b).

Dividend Carryover. Even if a corporation pays no actual or consent dividends, it is entitled to a current dividend deduction if it has paid sufficient dividends in either or both of the two preceding years. Under Section 564 the amount of this deduction is the greater of the excess of the dividends paid deduction (without carryovers) over taxable income, as adjusted in Section 545, for the preceding year, or the excess of the combined dividends paid deduction (without carryovers) for the preceding two years over the total taxable income (again adjusted under Section 545) for the same two years. Roughly translated, this means that a corporation that over distributes in prior years may distribute less in the current year in determining its exposure to the tax.

Liquidating Distributions. If a corporation is liquidating, it still may be a personal holding company. Indeed, an operating company may become a personal holding company during the process of liquidating if it ceases its operations in a taxable year prior to its final liquidating distribution and has only passive investment income in that terminal year. In order to avoid penalizing liquidating corporations by denying them a dividends paid deduction for actual liquidating distributions, Section 562(b)(2) provides that if the corporation liquidates within 24 months of adopting a plan of liquidation, liquidating distributions to corporate shareholders are treated as dividends for purposes of the dividends paid deduction to the extent of the shareholder's proportionate share of UPHCI for the year of the distribution. At the corporation's election, liquidating distributions to noncorporate shareholders also may be treated as dividends under Section 316(b)(2)(B) to the extent of the shareholders' proportionate share of UPHCI. If they are so treated, the corporation is entitled to take the dividends paid deduction. Unlike corporate shareholders, however, noncorporate shareholders must treat such liquidating distributions as dividend income under Section 316(b) rather than capital gain under Section 331.

Deficiency Dividends. If a corporation is determined to be a personal holding company for a particular year, Section 547 permits the corporation to reduce its personal holding company tax base (but not interest or penalties) by the amount of its "deficiency dividends." Deficiency dividends

---

10. The timing of the shareholder's income is not affected by the Section 563(b) election.

11. I.R.C. § 565(c).

12. I.R.C. § 565(b)(1).

are defined as amounts paid within 90 days of the determination of personal holding company tax liability which would have been eligible for the dividends paid deduction if distributed in the year in which Section 541 tax liability exists.[13] A deficiency dividend is allowed as of the date a claim for dividend is filed.[14]

PROBLEMS

1. X Corporation is wholly owned by A. Determine whether X is a personal holding company under each of the following alternatives:

    (a) X manufactures umbrellas. In year one, X has $2,000,000 gross receipts from sales, and its cost of goods sold is $800,000. It has no other income or expenses and makes no distributions.

    (b) X's business hits a dry spell in year two. Its gross receipts from sales are $900,000, and its cost of goods sold is $890,000. X also receives $30,000 interest on its $200,000 profit from year one, which it deposited in a savings account.

    (c) What result in (b), above, if X also had $30,000 of § 1231 gains in year two? What about $10,000 of § 1231 gains and $20,000 of § 1245 gain?

2. Consider whether the following corporations are personal holding companies:

    (a) Basketball Corporation is wholly owned by Dr. K, who plays professional basketball. Dr. K contracts to work for the corporation for $150,000 per year. Basketball Corporation then contracts with Team to provide Dr. K's services to Team for $300,000 per year.

    (b) What result in (a), above, if Basketball purchases a movie theater by paying $20,000 down and taking the theater subject to a $180,000 mortgage. During the year, the theater has receipts of $300,000 and deductible expenses (depreciation interest, salaries and film rents) of $300,000?

    (c) Attorney forms Professional Corporation and incorporates his private practice. During the year the corporation earns fees of $300,000 and pays Attorney a salary of $150,000.

    (d) Aside from the personal holding company tax, what other challenges might the Service assert in parts (a)–(c)?

3. Iris Securities Company is wholly owned by Investor. Determine whether Iris is a personal holding company, and if so, the amount of the § 541 tax, under the following circumstances:

    (a) Iris earns a total of $30,000 of interest and dividends in year one. Iris also owns an apartment complex. During the past year, it

---

13. I.R.C. § 547(d)(1).

14. I.R.C. § 547(b)(1). A claim must be filed within 120 days after the determination

of personal holding company tax liability. I.R.C. § 547(e).

collected rents of $100,000. Iris's only deductions were depreciation of $35,000, mortgage interest of $30,000, and property taxes of $5,000. Iris makes no distributions during the year.

(b) Assume that Investor comes to you for tax advice on December 15 of year one. If Iris uses the calendar year as its taxable year, can it avoid personal holding company status? What if Investor comes to you in January of year two?

4.   Operating Company is owned equally by Ms. Active and by X Corporation. Operating Company has been engaged in the retail sales business. In June of year one, Operating Company adopts a plan to liquidate. In December of year one, it sells all its assets for $1,000,000, which it deposits in a short-term savings account. In June of year two, after having earned $50,000 interest during the year, Operating Company liquidates by distributing $525,000 to each shareholder.

(a) What are the tax consequences to Operating and its shareholders?

(b) What alternatives are available?

PART THREE

Taxation of S Corporations

CHAPTER 15

S Corporations*

A. Introduction

We have seen that a C corporation's net income is subject to tax at rates ranging from 15 to 35 percent,[1] and those earnings are taxed again when distributed as dividends to noncorporate shareholders.[2] Although many techniques have been devised to avoid the double tax, it nonetheless remains the principal feature distinguishing the taxation of incorporated and unincorporated businesses. We also have seen that partnerships and limited liability companies are treated for tax purposes as conduits whose income and deductions pass through to the partners or members as they are realized, with the various items retaining their original character in the process.[3] Because income is taxed at the partner level, partnership distributions of cash and property generally do not produce any additional tax liability.[4]

Taxpayers have long sought to obtain the state law benefits of the corporate form (limited liability, centralized management, etc.) without the sting of the double tax. Congress attempted to accommodate this desire in 1958 when it enacted Subchapter S, which then permitted the shareholders of a "small business corporation" to elect to avoid a corporate level tax in most situations. The stated purpose of Subchapter S was to permit a business to select its legal form "without the necessity of taking into account major differences in tax consequence."[5]

As originally adopted, Subchapter S was a modified corporate scheme of taxation rather than a partnership-like pass-through regime. This early version was a strange hybrid of corporate and partnership concepts, laden with complexity. In these formative years, an electing small business necessarily depended on skilled lawyers and accountants to avoid Subchapter S's many technical traps. Calls for reform began with a 1969 Treasury Department study, which in general proposed a liberalization of the eligibility requirements and the adoption of a conduit approach more closely conforming to the tax treatment of partnerships.[6] Congress gradually

---

* See generally Eustice and Kuntz, Federal Income Taxation of Subchapter S Corporations.

1. I.R.C. § 11.

2. I.R.C. §§ 61(a)(7), 301.

3. I.R.C. § 702(a), (b). Most limited liability companies are treated as partnerships for tax purposes. See Chapter 1C2a, supra,

and Schwarz & Lathrope, Fundamentals of Partnership Taxation (8th ed. 2012).

4. I.R.C. § 731(a).

5. S.Rep. No. 1983, 85th Cong., 2d Sess. § 68 (1958), reprinted in 1958–3 C.B. 922.

6. See U.S. Treasury Department, Technical Explanation of Treasury Tax Reform Proposals: Hearings Before the House

relaxed the eligibility requirements through piecemeal legislation, most notably the Subchapter S Revision Act of 1982.[7] The 1982 Act greatly reduced the tax disparities between Subchapter S corporations and partnerships by replacing the modified corporate structure of Subchapter S with a statutory scheme which is similar but not identical to the tax treatment of partnerships and partners under Subchapter K. The Act also introduced the terminology now used in the Code. Electing small business corporations are called "S corporations" while other corporations are known as "C corporations."[8]

Subsequent legislation further liberalized the Subchapter S eligibility requirements and eliminated technical traps for corporations seeking to elect and maintain S corporation status. As a result of these reforms, the tax differences between partnerships and S corporations have narrowed, making operation as an S corporation a viable, albeit less flexible, alternative for some closely held businesses. But significant differences in tax treatment remain between S corporations and unincorporated businesses. For example, Subchapter S status is available only for corporations that satisfy the statutory definition of "small business corporation" in Section 1361(b). This definition restricts eligibility to corporations with 100 or fewer shareholders; prohibits more than one class of stock; and limits the types of permissible shareholders. Moreover, partners' bases in their partnership interests are increased by their share of partnership liabilities,[9] while debts incurred by an S corporation have no effect on the bases of the corporation's shareholders in their stock. This difference may have an impact upon the ability of investors to utilize losses generated by the enterprise and the treatment of distributions.[10] Subchapter K also offers partners more flexibility in determining their individual tax results from partnership operations. Partnership allocations of specific items of income or deduction to a particular partner will be respected as long as the allocation has substantial economic effect, while shareholders of an S corporation are required to report a pro rata share of each corporate item.[11]

For a brief time, the inverted rate structure introduced by the Tax Reform Act of 1986 expanded the role of S corporations by reducing the top individual rate below the maximum rate for C corporations and broadening the corporate tax base. As a result, many closely held businesses requiring the corporate form and able to meet the eligibility requirements chose to operate as S corporations. The maximum individual rate on ordinary income in 2012 equals the top corporate rate, but in 2013 the top individual rate on ordinary income is scheduled to increase to 39.6 percent. More importantly, the emergence of the limited liability company, with its far greater flexibility, and the Service's willingness to allow any unincorporat-

Comm. on Ways and Means, 91st Cong., 1st Sess. 5228–5275 (April 22, 1969).

7. Pub.L. No. 97–354 (1982), reprinted in 1982–2 C.B. 702.

8. I.R.C. § 1361(a).

9. I.R.C. § 752(a).

10. See also I.R.C. § 469, limiting the current deductibility of losses from certain passive activities.

11. Compare I.R.C. § 704(b)(2) with I.R.C. §§ 1366(a) & 1377(a).

ed business entity to elect partnership status for tax purposes, have profoundly influenced the choice of entity decision.[12] At least for newly formed businesses, many predicted that these developments would threaten to send S corporations to the sidelines, despite the more liberal eligibility requirements introduced by Congress. Many existing S corporations remain on the scene, however, and the S corporation tax regime and governance structure are relatively simple and familiar. In fact, S corporations became the most common corporate entity type in 1997 and, for the taxable year 2008, the latest for which data is available, 69 percent of all corporations filing tax returns were S corporations.[13] Thus, S corporations continue to be an important option for many operating businesses and a study of the fundamentals of Subchapter S is essential for a comprehensive understanding of business enterprise taxation. It also is instructive to compare the provisions of Subchapters S and K and to consider which of these pass-through taxation models is preferable from a policy standpoint.[14]

B.   ELIGIBILITY FOR S CORPORATION STATUS

Code: § 1361.

Eligibility to make a Subchapter S election is limited to a "small business corporation," defined in Section 1361(b) as a domestic corporation[1] which is not an "ineligible corporation" and which has: (1) no more than 100 shareholders, (2) only shareholders who are individuals, estates, and certain types of trusts and tax-exempt organizations, (3) no nonresident alien shareholders, and (4) not more than one class of stock. The 100–shareholder limit disqualifies publicly traded corporations from S status, and the one-class-of-stock rule shuts the door to corporations with complex capital structures. Significantly, however, a "small business corporation" need not be small when measured by income or value as a going concern, and some very large enterprises operate as S corporations.

Some remaining aspects of the S corporation eligibility requirements are summarized below.

Ineligible Corporations and Subsidiaries. An "ineligible corporation" may not qualify as a "small business corporation."[2] Certain types of corporations, such as banks and insurance companies, are "ineligible" because they are governed by other specialized tax regimes.[3] At one time, any corporation that was a member of an "affiliated group" also was ineligible to be an S corporation—a rule that effectively precluded S corporations from owning 80 percent or more of the stock of another C or S

---

12. See Chapter 1C2a, supra.

13. See IRS Statistics of Income Integrated Business Data (Table 1: Selected Financial Data on Businesses 1980–2008).

14. See Section H of this chapter, infra.

1. I.R.C. § 1361(b)(1). A domestic corporation is defined as a corporation created or organized in the United States or under the laws of the United States or of any state or territory. Reg. §§ 1.1361–1(c); 301.7701–5.

2. I.R.C. § 1361(b)(1).

3. I.R.C. § 1361(b)(2).

corporation.[4] Under current law, S corporations may hold subsidiaries under certain conditions. C corporation subsidiaries generally are permitted,[5] and a parent-subsidiary relationship between two S corporations also is allowed if the parent elects to treat its offspring as a "qualified subchapter S subsidiary" ("QSSS"), which generally is defined as a 100 percent owned domestic corporation that is not an "ineligible corporation" and otherwise would qualify for S status if all of its stock were held by the shareholders of its parent.[6] If this QSSS election is made, the subsidiary is disregarded for tax purposes, and all of its assets, liabilities, income, deductions, and credits are treated as belonging to its S parent.[7] The regulations provide detailed procedures to govern revocation and other terminations of a QSSS election. In general, they treat a terminating event as a deemed incorporation of a new subsidiary that is governed by general tax principles.[8]

Number of Shareholders. Congress has made S corporations more widely available by gradually increasing the number of permissible shareholders. The current 100–shareholder limit[9] is nearly triple an earlier 35–shareholder cap. For purposes of this limit, a husband and wife (and their estates) are counted as one shareholder regardless of their form of ownership.[10] If stock is jointly owned (e.g., as tenants in common or joint tenants) by other than a husband and wife, each joint owner is considered a separate shareholder.[11] In the case of a nominee, guardian, custodian, or agent holding stock in a representative capacity, the beneficial owners of the stock are counted toward the 100–shareholder limit.[12]

In addition to the special rule for a husband and wife, all the members of a "family" (and their estates) are treated as a single shareholder for purposes of the 100–shareholder limit.[13] A family is defined as the lineal descendants (and their spouses and former spouses) of a common ancestor who is no more than six generations removed from the youngest generation shareholder as of the later of the date the S election is made, the earliest date that a family member holds stock in the corporation, or October 22, 2004.[14]

---

4. I.R.C. § 1361(b)(2)(A) (pre–1997).

5. The S parent, however, may not join in a consolidated return with the C corporation. I.R.C. § 1504(b)(8). See Chapter 13B for a discussion of consolidated returns.

6. I.R.C. § 1361(b)(3)(B). For election procedures, see Reg. § 1.1361–3(a).

7. I.R.C. § 1361(b)(3)(A). See Reg. § 1.1361–4(a)(1). If a subsidiary was in existence and had a prior tax history, the QSSS election triggers a deemed liquidation of the subsidiary under Sections 332 and 337 as of the day before the election is effective. Reg. § 1.1361–4(a)(2).

8. See Reg. § 1.1361–5(b).

9. I.R.C. § 1361(b)(1)(A).

10. I.R.C. § 1361(c)(1)(A)(i); Reg. § 1.1361–1(e)(2).

11. I.R.C. § 1.1361–1(e)(1).

12. Id.

13. I.R.C. § 1361(c)(1)(A)(ii). If a husband and wife are part of a family they are counted as part of a family. I.R.C. § 1361(c)(1)(B)(i).

14. I.R.C. § 1361(c)(1)(B). Adopted children and foster children are treated as children by blood. I.R.C. § 1361(c)(1)(C). A spouse is considered to be of the same generation as the individual to whom the spouse is married. I.R.C. § 1361(c)(1)(B)(ii).

Eligible Shareholders. Congress also has gradually expanded the eligible S corporation shareholder pool. Once limited to individuals who were U.S. citizens or resident aliens, the permissible shareholder list now also includes decedent's and bankruptcy estates,[15] certain types of trusts discussed in more detail below,[16] qualified pension trusts, and charitable organizations that are exempt from tax under Section 501(c)(3).[17] A corporation still may not make an S election if any of its shareholders are C corporations, partnerships, ineligible trusts, or nonresident aliens.[18]

When Subchapter S was first enacted, trusts were not eligible shareholders, primarily because of Congress's desire for a relatively simple one-tier corporate tax regime where all beneficial owners were clearly identifiable. In response to the pleas of tax advisors to closely held businesses, Congress gradually relented by permitting various widely used types of trusts to be S corporation shareholders if certain conditions are met. Under current law, the trusts that are permissible shareholders include:

(1) Voting trusts, in which case each beneficial owner is treated as a separate shareholder;[19]

(2) Grantor trusts—i.e., domestic trusts treated for tax purposes as owned by their grantor—provided the grantor is an individual who is a U.S. citizen or resident.[20] An example would be the commonly used revocable living trust created to provide for continuity of asset management in the event of the grantor's disability and to avoid probate administration on death. For purposes of the 100–shareholder limit, the deemed owner of the trust is treated as the shareholder.[21]

(3) Former grantor trusts that continue as testamentary trusts, but only for the two-year period following the grantor's death.[22] The former deemed owner's estate is treated as the S corporation shareholder.[23]

(4) Testamentary trusts that receive S corporation stock under the terms of a will, but again only for the two-year period after the date of transfer of the stock to the trust.[24] The testator's estate continues to be treated as the S corporation shareholder.[25]

(5) Qualified Subchapter S trusts ("QSSTs"), defined generally as trusts all of the income of which is actually distributed or must be

---

15. I.R.C. §§ 1361(b)(1)(B), (c)(3).

16. See infra text accompanying notes 19–34.

17. I.R.C. §§ 1361(b)(1)(B), (c)(6). The trade-off for tax-exempt pension trusts and Section 501(c)(3) organizations is that their interest in the S corporation is treated as an interest in an "unrelated trade or business," and any net income is generally taxable at the trust or corporate rates. I.R.C. § 512(e)(1).

18. I.R.C. § 1361(b)(1)(B).

19. I.R.C. § 1361(c)(2)(A)(iv), (B)(iv).

20. I.R.C. § 1361(c)(2)(A)(i). Foreign grantor trusts are not eligible shareholders. I.R.C. § 1361(c)(2)(A), flush language.

21. I.R.C. § 1361(c)(2)(B)(i).

22. I.R.C. § 1361(c)(2)(A)(ii).

23. I.R.C. § 1361(c)(2)(B)(ii).

24. I.R.C. § 1361(c)(2)(A)(iii).

25. I.R.C. § 1361(c)(2)(B)(iii).

distributed currently to one individual who is a U.S. citizen or resident.[26] A QSST may only have one current income beneficiary, who must elect QSST status and, as a result, is treated as the owner for tax purposes of the portion of the trust consisting of the S corporation stock with respect to which the election was made.[27] Among other things, the QSST definition permits a Qualified Terminable Interest Property ("QTIP") Trust,[28] the most widely used type of estate tax marital deduction trust created for the benefit of a surviving spouse, to hold S corporation stock.

(6) Electing small business trusts ("ESBTs"), a statutory creation that potentially expands the usefulness of S corporations in estate planning for a family business. All the beneficiaries of an ESBT must be individuals or estates who are eligible S corporation shareholders, or charitable organizations holding contingent remainder interests.[29] The beneficial interests in an ESBT must have been acquired by gift or bequest, not purchase,[30] and the trust must elect ESBT status to qualify as an S corporation shareholder.[31] Each potential current beneficiary of the trust is treated as a shareholder for purposes of the 100–shareholder limit,[32] but the trust's pro rata share of S corporation income is taxable to the trust at the highest individual marginal rates under rules specially designed for this purpose.[33] The significance of the ESBT category is that it permits inter vivos and testamentary trusts with more than one beneficiary—e.g., a "sprinkling" trust where the trustee has discretion to determine whether and how much income or corpus to distribute among several beneficiaries—to qualify as an S corporation shareholder.

The regulation treating a family as one shareholder for the 100–shareholder limit explains that the rule applies to family members who own stock directly as well as those who are shareholders because they are beneficiaries of a QSST or ESBT.[34]

One–Class-of-Stock Requirement. An S corporation may issue both stock and debt, but it may not have more than one class of stock.[35] The purpose of this rule is to simplify the allocation of income and deductions among an S corporation's shareholders and prevent "special allocations" and their potential for income shifting. The one-class-of-stock requirement

---

26. I.R.C. § 1361(d).

27. Id.

28. See I.R.C. § 2056(b)(7).

29. I.R.C. § 1361(e)(1)(A)(i). Charitable remainder trusts, however, may not be S corporation shareholders. I.R.C. § 1361(e)(1)(B)(iii). See also Rev. Rul. 92–48, 1992–1 C.B. 301.

30. I.R.C. § 1361(e)(1)(A)(ii).

31. I.R.C. § 1361(e)(1)(A)(iii). Trusts that already have made a QSST election or are wholly exempt from tax do not qualify as ESBTs. I.R.C. § 1361(e)(1)(B).

32. I.R.C. § 1361(c)(2)(B)(v). If there are no potential current income beneficiaries, then the trust is treated as the shareholder for that period. Id.

33. I.R.C. § 641(d).

34. Reg. § 1.1361–1(e)(3)(ii).

35. I.R.C. § 1361(b)(1)(D).

has spawned many controversies over its history, but the issuance of final regulations has resolved the most contentious issues.

An S corporation generally is treated as having one class of stock if all of its outstanding shares confer identical rights to distributions and liquidation proceeds.[36] Significantly, differences in voting rights among classes of common stock are disregarded, permitting an S corporation to issue both voting and nonvoting common stock.[37] In determining whether outstanding stock confers identical rights to distribution and liquidation proceeds, the regulations look to the corporate charter, articles of incorporation, bylaws, applicable state law, and binding shareholders' agreements.[38]

Commercial contractual arrangements, such as leases, employment agreements, or loan agreements, are disregarded in determining whether a second class of stock is present unless a principal purpose of the agreement is to circumvent the one class of stock requirement.[39] For example, differences in salary or fringe benefits paid to employee-shareholders under compensation agreements will not result in a second class of stock if the agreements are not designed to circumvent the requirement.[40] Bona fide agreements to redeem or purchase stock at the time of death, divorce, disability or termination of employment also are disregarded in determining whether an S corporation has a second class of stock.[41] Other shareholder buy-sell, stock transfer and redemption agreements are disregarded in determining whether a corporation's outstanding shares confer identical distribution and liquidation rights unless: (1) a principal purpose of the agreement is to circumvent the one-class-of-stock requirement, and (2) the purchase price under the agreement is significantly in excess of or below the fair market value of the stock. Agreements that provide for a purchase or redemption of stock at book value or at a price between book value and fair market value satisfy the purchase price standard.[42]

Unless the straight debt safe harbor applies,[43] any instrument, obligation or arrangement issued by a corporation (other than outstanding stock) is treated as a second class of stock if: (1) it constitutes equity under general tax principles, and (2) a principal purpose of issuing or entering

---

36. Reg. § 1.1361–1(*l*)(1). "Outstanding stock" generally does not include stock that is subject to a substantial risk of forfeiture under Section 83 unless the holder has made the Section 83(b) election. Reg. § 1.1361–1(*l*)(3).

37. I.R.C. § 1361(c)(4); Reg. § 1.1361–1(*l*)(1).

38. Reg. § 1.1361–1(*l*)(2)(i).

39. Reg. § 1.1361–1(*l*)(2)(i).

40. Reg. § 1.1361–1(*l*)(2)(vi) Examples (3) & (4). Any distributions (actual, constructive or deemed) that differ in timing or amount are given appropriate tax treatment. For example, even though an employment agreement does not result in a second class of stock, excessive compensation paid under the agreement is not deductible. Reg. § 1.1361–1(*l*)(2)(i), (vi) Example (3).

41. Reg. § 1.1361–1(*l*)(2)(iii)(B).

42. Reg. § 1.1361–1(*l*)(2)(iii)(A). A good faith determination of fair market value is respected unless it is substantially in error and was not determined with reasonable diligence. Id. A determination of book value is respected if it is determined in accordance with generally accepted accounting principles or used for any substantial nontax purpose. Reg. § 1.1361–1(*l*)(2)(iii)(C).

43. See I.R.C. § 1361(c)(5) and notes 47–54, infra, and accompanying text.

into the instrument, obligation or arrangement is to circumvent the distribution and liquidation rights of outstanding shares or the limitation on eligible shareholders.[44] Safe harbors from reclassification are provided for short-term unwritten advances to the corporation that do not exceed $10,000 and obligations held proportionately among the shareholders.[45] The existence of various corporate instruments that give holders the right to acquire stock (e.g., call options or warrants) also may create a second class of stock depending upon whether the right is substantially certain to be exercised by the holder.[46]

Straight Debt Safe Harbor. The interaction of the one-class-of-stock limitation with the debt vs. equity classification issues encountered under Subchapter C[47] historically presented some knotty problems for S corporations with outstanding debt. In the formative years of Subchapter S, the Service adopted a practice of reclassifying nominal S corporation debt owed to shareholders as a second class of stock, causing the corporation to lose its S status.[48] This threat has diminished considerably by a safe harbor provision in Section 1361(c)(5) under which "straight debt" is not treated as a disqualifying second class of stock. "Straight debt" is defined as any written unconditional promise to pay on demand or on a specified date a sum certain in money if: (1) the interest rate and payment dates are not contingent on profits, the borrower's discretion or similar factors; (2) the instrument is not convertible (directly or indirectly) into stock; and (3) the creditor is an individual (other than a nonresident alien), an estate or trust that would be a qualifying shareholder in an S corporation, or a person that is actively and regularly engaged in the business of lending money.[49] The fact that an obligation is subordinated to other debt of the corporation does not prevent it from qualifying as straight debt.[50]

Obligations that qualify as straight debt are not classified as a second class of stock even if they would be considered equity under general tax principles and they generally are treated as debt for other purposes of the Code.[51] Thus, interest paid or accrued on straight debt is treated as such by the corporation and the recipient and does not constitute a distribution governed by Section 1368.[52] But if a straight debt instrument bears an unreasonably high rate of interest, the regulations provide than an "appropriate" portion may be recharacterized and treated as a payment that is

---

44. Reg. § 1.1361–1(*l*)(4)(ii)(A).

45. Reg. § 1.1361–1(*l*)(4)(ii)(B).

46. Reg. § 1.1361–1(*l*)(4)(iii). Exceptions are provided for certain call options in connection with loans or to employees and independent contractors. If the strike price of a call option is at least 90 percent of its fair market value at its issuance, it is not substantially certain to be exercised. Reg. § 1.1361–1(*l*)(4)(iii)(B)–(C).

47. See generally I.R.C. § 385 and Chapter 3B, infra.

48. The courts, however, usually were not receptive to this argument. See, e.g., Portage Plastics Co. v. United States, 486 F.2d 632 (7th Cir.1973).

49. I.R.C. § 1361(c)(5)(B).

50. Reg. § 1.1361–1(*l*)(5)(ii).

51. I.R.C. § 1361(c)(5)(A); Reg. § 1.1361–1(*l*)(5)(iv).

52. Id.

not interest.[53] If a C corporation has outstanding debt obligations that satisfy the straight debt definition but may be classified as equity under general tax principles, the safe harbor ensures that the obligation will not be treated as a second class of stock if the C corporation elects to convert to S status. The conversion and change of status also is not treated as an exchange of the debt instrument for stock.[54]

PROBLEM

Unless otherwise indicated, Z Corporation ("Z") is a domestic corporation which has 120 shares of voting common stock outstanding. In each of the following alternative situations, determine whether Z is eligible to elect S corporation status:

(a) Z has 99 unrelated individual shareholders, each of whom owns one share of Z stock. The remaining 21 shares are owned by A and his brother, B, as joint tenants with right of survivorship.

(b) Same as (a), above, except that A and B are married and own 11 of the 21 shares as community property. The remaining 10 shares are owned 5 by A as her separate property and 5 by B as his separate property.

(c) In (b), above, assume that the shareholders of Z elected S corporation status. What will be the effect on Z's election if one year later A dies and bequeaths her interest in Z stock to F, her long-time friend?

(d) Same as (a), above, except that the remaining 21 shares are held by a voting trust which has three beneficial owners.

(e) Same as (a), above, except that the remaining 21 shares are owned by a revocable living trust created by an individual, the income of which is taxed to the grantor under § 671.

(f) Same as (a), above, except that the remaining 21 shares are owned by a testamentary trust under which the surviving spouse has the right to income for her life, with the remainder passing to her children. The trust is a "qualified terminable interest trust" (see § 2056(b)(7)).

(g) Assume Z has 100 individual shareholders and forms a partnership with two other S corporations, each of which also have 100 individual shareholders, for the purposes of jointly operating a business. Z's one-third interest in this partnership is its only asset.

(h) Z has 100 shares of Class A voting common stock and 50 shares of Class B nonvoting common stock outstanding. Apart from the differences in voting rights, the two classes of common stock have equal rights with regard to dividends and liquidation distributions. Z also has an authorized but unissued class of nonvoting stock

53. Id. Such a reclassification does not result in a second class of stock.

54. Reg. § 1.1361–1(*l*)(5)(v).

which would be limited and preferred as to dividends. The Class A common stock is owned by four individuals and the Class B common stock is owned by E and F (a married couple) as tenants-in-common.

(i) Same as (h), above, except that Z enters into a binding agreement with its shareholders to make larger annual distributions to shareholders who bear heavier state income tax burdens. The amount of the distributions is based on a formula that will give the shareholders equal after-tax distributions.

(j) Z has four individual shareholders each of whom own 100 shares of Z common stock for which each paid $10 per share. Each shareholder also owns $25,000 of 15–year Z bonds. The bonds bear interest at 3% above the prime lending rate established by the Chase Manhattan Bank, adjusted quarterly, and are subordinated to general creditors of Z.

C.   Election, Revocation and Termination

Code: §§ 1362 (omit (e)(5)–(6)); 1378. Skim §§ 444(a), (b), (c)(1), (e); 7519(a), (b), (d)(1), (e)(4).

Electing S Corporation Status. An otherwise eligible corporation may elect S corporation status under Section 1362 if all the shareholders consent.[1] Once made, an election remains effective until it is terminated under Section 1362(d).[2] An election is effective as of the beginning of a taxable year if it is made either during the preceding taxable year or on or before the fifteenth day of the third month of the current taxable year.[3] If the election is made during the first 2½ months of the year, the S corporation eligibility requirements must have been met for the portion of the taxable year prior to the election, and all shareholders at any time during the pre-election portion of the year must consent to the election.[4] If the eligibility requirements are not met during the pre-election period or if any shareholder who held stock during that period does not consent, the election does not become effective until the following taxable year.[5] In some cases, however, such as where an election is technically invalid because of the corporation's inadvertence or failure to obtain all the requisite share-

---

1. I.R.C. § 1362(a). For rules and procedures on shareholders' consent to an S election, see Reg. § 1.1362–6.

2. I.R.C. § 1362(c). See generally Reg. § 1.1362–2.

3. I.R.C. § 1362(b)(1). Elections made not later than 2 months and 15 days after the first day of the taxable year are deemed made during the year even if the year is shorter than 2 months and 15 days. I.R.C. § 1362(b)(4). For rules on how to count months and days for this purpose, see Reg. § 1.1362–6(a)(2)(ii). For the Service's authority to treat a late election as timely if there was reasonable cause for the tardiness, see I.R.C. § 1362(b)(5). See Rev. Proc. 2004–48, 2004–2 C.B. 172, supplemented by Rev. Proc. 2007–62, 2007–41 I.R.B. 786, for the procedures to obtain relief for a late election.

4. I.R.C. § 1362(b)(2).

5. I.R.C. § 1362(b)(2)(B).

holder consents on time, the Service may grant dispensation and waive the defect if there is reasonable cause.[6]

Revocation of Election. An S corporation election may be revoked if shareholders holding more than one-half of the corporation's shares (including nonvoting shares) consent to the revocation.[7] The revocation may specify a prospective effective date.[8] If a prospective effective date is not specified, a revocation made on or before the fifteenth day of the third month of the taxable year is effective on the first day of the taxable year and a revocation made after that date is effective on the first day of the following taxable year.[9]

Termination of Election. Apart from revocation, an S corporation election may be terminated if the corporation ceases to satisfy the definition of a small business corporation or, in certain circumstances, if the corporation earns an excessive amount of passive investment income.[10] The first ground for termination is easily illustrated. Terminating events include: (1) exceeding 100 shareholders; (2) issuance of a second class of stock; or (3) transfer of stock to an ineligible shareholder. In all those cases, the corporation will cease to be a small business corporation and its S corporation election will terminate on the day after the disqualifying event.[11] To prevent or cure transfers that may jeopardize a corporation's S corporation status, the shareholders will be well advised at the outset to enter into an agreement restricting stock transfers.

The limitation on passive investment income is more complex. Under Section 1362(d)(3), an election to be an S corporation will terminate if for three consecutive taxable years the corporation's "passive investment income" exceeds 25 percent of its gross receipts and the corporation has Subchapter C earnings and profits.[12] A termination triggered by excess passive investment income is effective beginning on the first day of the taxable year following the three year testing period.[13] It is important to note that the Subchapter C earnings and profits requirement has the effect of rendering this limitation inapplicable to a corporation that has always been an S corporation or which has been purged of its earnings and profits.[14] Passive investment income generally is defined as gross receipts

---

6. I.R.C. § 1362(f). An ineffective election to treat (1) a subsidiary as a qualified subchapter S subsidiary or (2) a family as one shareholder may also be salvaged under Section 1362(f).

7. I.R.C. § 1362(d)(1)(B). See Reg. § 1.1362–2(a).

8. I.R.C. § 1362(d)(1)(D).

9. I.R.C. § 1362(d)(1)(C). If the revocation is effective on a day other than the first day of a taxable year (e.g., because a prospective date is selected in the middle of the year), the taxable year will be an "S termination year," and the corporation will be taxed pursuant to rules in Section 1362(e).

See Reg. § 1.1362–3 and infra text accompanying notes 19–21.

10. I.R.C. § 1362(d)(2), (3).

11. I.R.C. §§ 1361(b)(1)(A)–(D); 1362(d)(2)(B).

12. See Reg. § 1.1362–2(c). Prior years in which the corporation was not an S corporation are not considered for purposes of the passive investment income component of this test. I.R.C. § 1362(d)(3)(A)(iii)(II).

13. I.R.C. § 1362(d)(3)(A)(ii).

14. An S corporation, however, may acquire earnings and profits under Section 381 in a corporate acquisition.

from royalties, rents, dividends, interest, and annuities,[15] but it does not include gains on the disposition of property, or dividends received by an S corporation from a C corporation subsidiary to the extent they are attributable to earnings and profits of the subsidiary that are derived from the active conduct of a trade or business.[16] For purposes of the overall gross receipts definition, gross receipts from sales or exchanges of stock or securities are considered only to the extent of gains.[17] Gross receipts on the disposition of capital assets other than stock or securities are taken into account only to the extent of the excess of capital gains over capital losses from such dispositions.[18]

When an S corporation election terminates during the S corporation's taxable year, the corporation experiences an "S termination year," which is divided into two short years: an S short year and a C short year.[19] Income, gains, losses, deductions and credits for an S termination year generally may be allocated between the two short years on a pro rata basis or the corporation may elect to make the allocation under its normal accounting rules.[20] The corporation's tax liability for the short taxable year as a C corporation is then computed on an annualized basis.[21]

Inadvertent Terminations. If an S corporation election is terminated, the corporation generally is not eligible to make another election for five taxable years unless the Treasury consents to an earlier election.[22] Section 1362(f) provides relief if a termination is caused by the corporation ceasing to be a small business corporation or by excessive passive investment income. The corporation will be treated as continuing as an S corporation and the terminating event will be disregarded if: (1) the Service determines that the termination was inadvertent, (2) the corporation takes steps within a reasonable time to rectify the problem, and (3) the corporation and its shareholders agree to make whatever adjustments are required by the Service.[23] The corporation has the burden of establishing that under the relevant facts and circumstances the Commissioner should determine that the termination was inadvertent. Under the regulations, inadvertence may be established by showing that the terminating event was not reasonably within the control of the corporation and was not part of a plan to terminate the election, or that the event took place without the knowledge of the corporation notwithstanding its due diligence to prevent the termi-

---

15. I.R.C. § 1362(d)(3)(C)(i). The statute also contains rules for certain specialized items. See I.R.C. § 1362(d)(3)(C)(ii)–(v).

16. I.R.C. § 1362(d)(3)(C)(iv).

17. I.R.C. § 1362(d)(3)(B)(ii).

18. I.R.C. § 1362(d)(3)(B)(i).

19. I.R.C. § 1362(e)(1). The C short year begins on the first day the termination is effective. I.R.C. § 1362(e)(1)(B).

20. See Reg. § 1.1362–3. To use normal accounting rules, an election must be filed by all persons who are shareholders during the S short year and all persons who are share-

holders on the first day of the C short year. I.R.C. § 1362(e)(3). The pro rata allocation method may not be used in an S termination year if there is a sale or exchange of 50 percent or more of the stock in the corporation during the year. I.R.C. § 1362(e)(6)(D). For more rules on taxing an S termination year, see I.R.C. § 1362(e)(6).

21. I.R.C. § 1362(e)(5)(A).

22. I.R.C. § 1362(g).

23. I.R.C. § 1362(f).

nation.[24] For example, if a corporation in good faith determines that it has no Subchapter C earnings and profits but the Service later determines on audit that the corporation's S election terminated because it had excessive passive investment income for three consecutive years while it also had accumulated earnings and profits, it may be appropriate for the Service to find that the termination was inadvertent.

Taxable Year of an S Corporation. To preclude S corporations from using fiscal years to achieve a deferral of the shareholders' tax liability, S corporations must use a "permitted year," which is defined as either a calendar year or an accounting period for which the taxpayer establishes a business purpose.[25] The Service has ruled that the business purpose requirement may be satisfied if the desired tax accounting period coincides with a "natural business year"[26] and has quantified the concept with the same 25–percent test applicable to partnerships seeking to use a natural business fiscal year.[27] Under this test, a natural business year exists if 25 percent or more of the S corporation's gross receipts for the selected 12–month period are earned in the last two months. This 25–percent test must be met in each of the preceding three 12–month periods that correspond to the requested fiscal year.[28]

Section 1378 makes it clear that tax deferral for shareholders does not constitute a business purpose for a fiscal year. The legislative history also identifies several factors which generally do not support a claim of business purpose:[29]

> The conferees intend that (1) the use of a particular year for regulatory or financial accounting purposes; (2) the hiring patterns of a particular business, e.g., the fact that a firm typically hires staff during certain times of the year; (3) the use of a particular year for administrative purposes, such as the admission or retirement of partners or shareholders, promotion of staff, and compensation or retirement arrangements with staff, partners, or shareholders; and (4) the fact that a particular business involves the use of price lists, model year, or other items that change on an annual basis ordinarily will not be sufficient to establish that the business purpose requirement for a particular taxable year has been met.

Fiscal Year Election. Congress has modified these strict taxable year requirements by allowing S corporations to elect to adopt, retain or change to a fiscal year under certain conditions, including the payment of an entity-level tax designed to represent the value of any tax deferral to the shareholders that would result from the use of the fiscal year. The rules

---

24. Reg. § 1.1362–4(b).

25. I.R.C. § 1378(b). See Reg. § 1.1378–1.

26. Rev.Proc. 2006–46, 2006–2 C.B. 859.

27. Id. at §§ 2.02, 2.06, 5.07.

28. If the taxpayer does not have the required period of gross receipts, it cannot establish a natural business year under the revenue procedure. Rev. Proc. 2006–46, supra note 27.

29. H.R.Rep. No. 99–841, 99th Cong., 2d Sess. II–319 (1986).

governing the fiscal year election and the required entity-level payment are found in Sections 444 and 7519.

Section 444 permits a newly formed S corporation to elect to use a taxable year other than the calendar year required by Section 1378 provided that the year elected results in no more than a three-month deferral of income to the shareholders.[30] An election and the Section 7519 payment is not required, however, for any S corporation that has established a business purpose for a fiscal year under Section 1378(b)(2).[31]

The trade-off for a Section 444 fiscal year election is that the corporation must make a "required payment" under Section 7519 for any taxable year for which the election is in effect. The mechanics of the required payment are annoyingly complex, but the concept is clear. An electing S corporation must pay and keep "on deposit" an amount roughly approximating the value of the tax deferral that the shareholders would have achieved from the use of a fiscal year. Thus, if an S corporation whose shareholders all used calendar years elected a fiscal year ending September 30, the corporation would be required to pay a tax that supposedly equalled the tax benefit from the three months deferral received by the shareholders.[32] Under a de minimis rule, no payment is required if the amount due is less than $500,[33] and a payment made in one year generates a balance "on deposit" that may be used in subsequent years.[34]

PROBLEM

Snowshoe, Inc. ("Snowshoe"), a ski resort located in Colorado, was organized by its four individual shareholders (A, B, C and D) and began operations on October 3 of the current year. A owns 300 shares of Snowshoe voting common stock and B, C and D each own 100 shares of Snowshoe nonvoting common stock. Each share of common stock has equal rights with respect to dividends and liquidation distributions. Consider the following questions in connection with the election and termination of Snowshoe's S corporation status:

(a) If the shareholders wish to elect S corporation status for Snowshoe's first taxable year, who must consent to the election? What difference would it make if, prior to the election, B sold her stock to her brother, G? What difference would it make if B is a partnership which, prior to the election, sold its stock to H, an individual?

(b) What is the last day an effective Subchapter S election for Snowshoe's first taxable year is permitted?

---

30. I.R.C. § 444(a), (b)(1).

31. See I.R.S. Notice 88–10, 1988–1 C.B. 478.

32. We say "supposedly" because the Section 7519 "required payment" is determined mechanically, without regard to amounts actually deferred by the shareholders. See I.R.C. §§ 7519(b), (c) and (d) for the details.

33. I.R.C. § 7519(a)(2).

34. I.R.C. § 7519(b)(2), (e)(4).

(c) If the shareholders elect S corporation status, what taxable year will Snowshoe be allowed to select?

In the following parts of the problem, assume that Snowshoe elected S corporation status during its first taxable year.

(d) Can A revoke Snowshoe's Subchapter S election without the consent of B, C or D?

(e) If C sold all of his stock to Olga, a citizen of Sweden living in Stockholm, what effect would the sale have on Snowshoe's status as an S corporation?

(f) Same as (e), above, except that C only sold five shares to Olga and had no idea that the sale might adversely affect Snowshoe's S corporation status.

(g) Would it matter if Snowshoe's business is diversified and 45% of its gross receipts come from real estate rentals, dividends and interest?

D.   Treatment of the Shareholders

Code: §§ 1363(b), (c); 1366(a)–(e); 1367. Skim §§ 1366(f); 1371(b); 1377.

1.   Pass-Through of Income and Losses: Basic Rules

Entity Treatment. Although an S corporation is generally exempt from tax,[1] it nonetheless must determine its gross income,[2] deductions and other tax items in order to establish the amounts which pass through to the shareholders. Like a partnership, an S corporation computes its "taxable income" in the same manner as an individual except that certain deductions unique to individuals (e.g., personal exemptions, alimony, medical and moving expenses) are not allowed.[3] In addition, deductions normally available only to corporations, such as the dividends received deduction, are not allowed,[4] but an S corporation may elect to deduct and amortize its organizational expenses under Section 248.[5] Finally, a wide variety of items, ranging from charitable contributions and capital gains to depletion, must be separately computed in order to preserve their special tax character for purposes of the pass-through to the shareholders.[6] Thus, an S corporation is not entitled to any charitable deduction, but corporate charitable gifts may pass through to the shareholders without regard to the normal 10 percent limit on corporate contributions.

1. For the few limited exceptions, see Section F of this chapter, infra.

2. Section 1366(c) provides that a shareholder's pro rata share of the S corporation's gross income is used to determine the shareholder's gross income.

3. I.R.C. § 1363(b)(2).

4. S.Rep. No. 97–640, 97th Cong., 2d Sess. 15 (1982), reprinted in 1982–2 C.B. 718, 724.

5. I.R.C. § 1363(b)(3).

6. I.R.C. §§ 1363(b)(1); 1366(a)(1)(A).

Although an S corporation is not a *taxable* entity, it is treated as an entity for various purposes. For example, tax elections affecting the computation of items derived from an S corporation (e.g., to defer recognition of gain on an involuntary conversion under Section 1033) generally are made at the corporate level.[7] Likewise, limitations on deductions (e.g., the dollar limitation under Section 179 on expensing the cost of certain recovery property) apply at the corporate level and often at the shareholder level as well.[8] And like a partnership, an S corporation is treated as an entity for filing tax returns and other procedural purposes.[9]

Pass–Through of Income and Deductions. Once the S corporation's tax items have been identified, the next step is to determine the manner in which they pass through to the shareholders. The pass-through scheme applicable to S corporations will have a familiar ring to a student who has endured the rigors of Subchapter K. First, income and deductions are characterized at the corporate level.[10] Section 1366(a)(1)(A) provides that items which may have potentially varying tax consequences to the individual shareholders must be separately reported. The most common separately stated items are capital and Section 1231 gains and losses, dividends taxed as net capital gain, interest and other types of "portfolio income" under the Section 469 passive loss limitations, tax-exempt interest, charitable contributions, investment interest, foreign taxes, intangible drilling expenses and depletion on oil and gas properties.[11] Thus, Section 1231 gains and losses do not fall into any corporate hotchpot; rather, they pass through and are aggregated with each shareholder's other Section 1231 gains and losses in order to determine their ultimate character. All the nonseparately stated items are aggregated and the resulting lump sum passes through as ordinary income or loss.

The timing of the shareholders' income and the allocation of pass-through items also is virtually a mirror image of the partnership rules. The shareholders of an S corporation take into account their respective pro rata shares of income, deductions and other separately stated items on a pro rata, per share daily basis.[12] These items are reported in the shareholder's taxable year in which the corporation's taxable year ends.[13] For example, if an S corporation with a natural business year uses a fiscal year ending January 31, 2013, the shareholders will report the respective pass-through items on their 2013 calendar year tax returns, thus achieving a healthy

7.   I.R.C. § 1363(c)(1).

8.   See, e.g., I.R.C. § 179(d)(8).

9.   I.R.C. § 6037. Cf. I.R.C. §§ 6221–6255.

10.   I.R.C. § 1366(b). See Reg. § 1.1366–1(b). If shareholders are utilizing an S corporation for the principal purpose of converting ordinary income to capital gain or capital loss into ordinary loss on the sale or exchange of property, the regulations generally provide for the character of the gain or loss to be determined at the shareholder level. Reg. § 1.1366–1(b)(2), (3).

11.   See generally Reg. § 1.1366–1(a)(2). See also Rev.Rul. 84–131, 1984–2 C.B. 37, where the Service ruled that a shareholder's share of an S corporation's investment interest is a separately stated item.

12.   I.R.C. § 1366(a)(1). See § 1377(a)(1) for the method of determining each shareholder's "pro rata share."

13.   I.R.C. § 1366(a)(1).

deferral of any gains or an unfortunate delay in recognizing any losses. A deceased shareholder's Subchapter S items are allocated on a daily basis between the shareholder's final income tax return and the initial return of the decedent's estate.[14]

Basis Adjustments. Section 1367 requires S corporation shareholders to increase the basis of their stock by their respective shares of income items (including tax-exempt income) and to reduce basis (but not below zero) by losses, deductions, and non-deductible expenses which do not constitute capital expenditures, and by tax-free distributions under Section 1368. Under the Code's ordering rules, basis is first increased by current income items, then decreased by distributions, and finally decreased (to the extent permitted) by any losses for the year.[15] Any additional losses in excess of a shareholder's stock basis must be applied to reduce the shareholder's basis (again, not below zero) in any corporate indebtedness to the shareholder.[16] If the basis of both stock and debt is reduced, any subsequent upward adjustments must first be applied to restore the basis in the indebtedness to the extent that it was previously reduced before increasing the basis of the stock.[17] These basis adjustments are generally made as of the close of the S corporation's taxable year unless a shareholder disposes of stock during the year, in which case the adjustments with respect to the transferred stock are made immediately prior to the disposition.[18]

2.   LOSS LIMITATIONS

a.   IN GENERAL

Section 1366(d) limits the amount of losses or deductions that may pass through to a shareholder to the sum of the shareholder's adjusted basis in the stock plus his adjusted basis in any indebtedness of the corporation to the shareholder. Losses disallowed because of an inadequate basis may be carried forward indefinitely and treated as a loss in any subsequent year in which the shareholder has a basis in either stock or debt.[1] A special rule also provides that if a shareholder's stock is transferred under Section 1041 to a spouse or former spouse incident to a divorce, any suspended loss or deduction may be carried forward indefinitely by the transferee-spouse.[2] As illustrated by the *Harris* case, which follows this Note, one of the most litigated issues to arise under Subchapter S has involved the determination of a shareholder's basis in S corporation stock and debt for purposes of applying the general loss limitation rules in Section 1366(d).

Losses that pass through to a shareholder of an S corporation also may be restricted by the at-risk limitations in Section 465 and the passive

---

14. Id. See also Reg. § 1.1366–1(a)(1).

15. I.R.C. §§ 1366(d)(1)(A); 1368(d), last sentence. For other details on stock and debt basis adjustments, see Reg. § 1.1367–1, –2.

16. I.R.C. § 1367(b)(2)(A).

17. I.R.C. § 1367(b)(2)(B).

18. Reg. § 1.1367–1(d)(1).

1. I.R.C. §§ 1366(d)(2)(A), 1366(a)(1).

2. I.R.C. § 1366(d)(2)(B).

activity loss limitations in Section 469.[3] The at-risk rules are applied on an activity-by-activity basis, except that activities constituting a trade or business generally are aggregated if the taxpayer actively participates in the management of the trade or business and at least 65 percent of the losses are allocable to persons actively engaged in the management of the trade or business.[4] The passive activity loss limitations cast a wider net and may delay an investor's ability to deduct legitimate start-up losses passing through from a new business operating as an S corporation unless the investor also materially participates in the activity.[5]

Harris v. United States

United States Court of Appeals, Fifth Circuit, 1990.
902 F.2d 439.

■ GARWOOD, CIRCUIT JUDGE:

Facts and Proceedings Below

In June 1982, Taxpayers contracted with Trans–Lux New Orleans Corporation to purchase for $665,585 cash a New Orleans pornographic theater that they intended to convert into a wedding hall. The Taxpayers' obligations under the contract were conditioned on their being able to secure from a third party a loan for not less than $600,000 repayable in fifteen to twenty years.[1] Shortly before this time, Taxpayers had contacted John Smith (Smith), a real estate loan officer with Hibernia National Bank (Hibernia), to discuss the possibility of obtaining financing for the impending acquisition. Smith orally committed to lend Taxpayers $700,000.[2]

Subsequently, to shield themselves from the potential adverse publicity that could follow from the purchase of the pornographic theater, as well as to limit their personal liability and enhance their chances of qualifying for industrial revenue bonds to finance the theater's renovation, in July 1982 Taxpayers formed Harmar (Harmar), a Louisiana corporation, which elected to be taxed pursuant to Subchapter S of the Internal Revenue Code, to purchase and operate the subject property. Harris and Martin each initially contributed $1,000 to the corporation, receiving its stock in return, and each also loaned Harmar $47,500 to satisfy operating expenses. Harris and Martin were the sole shareholders of Harmar, each owning half of its stock.

The purchase of the theater closed on November 1, 1982, and the theater was conveyed to Harmar on that date. Hibernia furnished the

---

3. These limitations apply on a share-holder-by-shareholder basis rather than at the corporate level. I.R.C. §§ 465(a)(1)(A); 469(a)(2)(A).

4. I.R.C. § 465(c)(3)(B).

5. I.R.C. § 469(c)(1).

1. As part of the contract, Taxpayers deposited with the seller $32,500, all of which was to be applied to the purchase price. In the event Taxpayers were unable to procure the loan, the purchase contract called for their deposit to be refunded.

2. Smith asserted in his deposition that he did not know the purpose of the borrowed funds in excess of the purchase price, but he surmised that the money was intended for improvements to the theater. No written loan commitment was ever issued.

$700,000 necessary to close the transaction. In borrowing the funds necessary to acquire the subject property, Harmar executed two promissory notes payable to Hibernia for $350,000 each, each dated November 1, 1982. One of these notes was secured by a $50,322.09 Hibernia certificate of deposit in Harris' name and another $304,972.49 certificate of deposit in the name of his wholly-owned corporation, Harris Mortgage Corporation. Harmar secured the other note, in accordance with its collateral pledge agreement, by its $3,000,000 note (which was unfunded apart from the $700,000) and its collateral mortgage on the theater, each executed by Harmar in favor of Hibernia and dated November 1, 1982. Under the terms of the collateral pledge agreement executed by Harmar in reference to the $3,000,000 note and mortgage, the mortgage secured "not only" Harmar's $350,000 note to Hibernia, "but also any and every other debts, liabilities and obligations" (other than consumer credit debt) of Harmar to Hibernia whether "due or to become due, or whether such debts, liabilities and obligations" of Harmar "are now existing or will arise in the future." Thus, the collateral mortgage secured the full $700,000 loan from Hibernia. Additionally, Taxpayers each executed personal continuing guarantees of Harmar indebtedness in the amount of $700,000 in favor of Hibernia. Smith testified in his deposition that the transaction was structured so that half the loan, as represented by one of the $350,000 notes, would be primarily secured by the certificates of deposit and the other half, represented by the other $350,000 note, primarily by the mortgage on the property purchased, with the entire amount also secured by Taxpayers' individual guarantees.

On its income tax return for the year ending December 31, 1982, Harmar reported a net operating loss of $104,013. Pursuant to [the predecessor of Section 1366], Taxpayers each claimed half of the loss as a deduction on their 1982 individual returns,[5] concluding that their bases in Harmar were in fact greater than Harmar's net operating loss for that year and that they therefore were entitled to deduct the entire loss on their personal returns. On audit, the Internal Revenue Service (IRS) found to the contrary and determined that Harris and Martin each had a basis of $1,000 in his Harmar stock and an adjusted basis in Harmar's indebtedness to each of them as shareholders of $47,500. Pursuant to I.R.C. [§ 1366(d)], the IRS limited Taxpayers' deductions of the net operating loss to what it considered to be their bases in Harmar, $48,500 each. The IRS's disallowance of a portion of the deductions claimed by Taxpayers[6] resulted in additional tax liability, including interest, for Martin of $3,150.58 and for Harris of $1,280. Taxpayers paid the tax in dispute and now appeal the district court's summary judgment dismissing their suit for refund.

Discussion

Taxpayers contend on appeal that in determining the deduction allowable for Harmar's net operating loss, the IRS should have included in

---

5. Harris and Martin claimed deductions for Harmar's loss of $52,006 and $52,007, respectively.

6. The IRS disallowed $4,506 of Harris' deduction and $4,507 of Martin's.

Taxpayers' bases in their Harmar stock the full value of the $700,000 Hibernia loan they guaranteed. I.R.C. [§ 1366] permits a Subchapter S shareholder to deduct from his personal return a proportionate share of his corporation's net operating loss to the extent that the loss does not exceed the sum of the adjusted basis of his Subchapter S corporation stock and any corporate indebtedness to him. See section [1366(d)(1)]. To arrive at their basis figure, Taxpayers seek to recast the transaction in question. They in essence urge that we disregard the form of the Hibernia loan—one from Hibernia to Harmar—in favor of what Taxpayers consider as the substance of the transaction—a $700,000 loan from Hibernia to them, the $700,000 proceeds of which they then equally contributed to Harmar's capital account. As evidence of their view of the substance of the transaction, Taxpayers point to the deposition testimony of Smith indicating that Hibernia looked primarily to Taxpayers, rather than to Harmar, for repayment of the loan, and they call attention to the $700,000 guarantees they each provided Hibernia as well as the $355,294.58 in certificates of deposit that Harris pledged to Hibernia as part of the November 1, 1982 loan transaction.

In its summary judgment memorandum, the district court declared that Brown v. Commissioner, 706 F.2d 755 (6th Cir.1983), was "on all fours" with the instant case and therefore resolved it. In *Brown,* the Sixth Circuit rejected shareholders' substance over form argument in ruling that the shareholders' guarantees of loans to their Subchapter S corporation could not increase their bases in their stock in the corporation unless the shareholders made an economic outlay by satisfying at least a portion of the guaranteed debt. Id. at 757. Without such an outlay, the *Brown* court concluded that " 'the substance matched the form' " of the transaction before it. Id. at 756. The reasoning of *Brown* was followed by the Fourth Circuit in Estate of Leavitt v. Commissioner, 875 F.2d 420 (4th Cir.1989), *aff'g,* 90 T.C. 206 (1988). There, the court, affirming the en banc Tax Court, held that shareholder guarantees of a loan to a Subchapter S corporation did not increase shareholders' stock basis because such guarantees had not "cost" shareholders anything and thus did not constitute an economic outlay. *Leavitt,* 875 F.2d at 422 & n. 9.[7] In reaching this conclusion, the Fourth Circuit affirmed as not clearly erroneous a finding of the Tax Court that the loan, in form as well as in substance, was made to the corporation rather than to the shareholders.[8] Id. at 424. The court

---

7. In reasoning that the shareholders had not increased their stock bases as a result of their guarantees, the court turned to I.R.C. § 1012, which defines basis of property as its cost. Id. at 422 n. 9. Cost of property, in turn, is defined in the Treasury Regulations as the "amount paid for such property in cash or other property." 26 C.F.R. § 1.1012–1(a).

8. The court noted that the loan in question had been made by the bank directly

to the corporation, the loan payments were made by the corporation directly to the bank, and neither the corporation nor the shareholders reported the payments as constructive dividends. Id.

Under *Leavitt,* the presumption is that the form will control and that presumption will not be surmounted absent the shareholder's satisfying the higher standard applicable to a taxpayer's seeking to disavow the form he selected and recast a transaction. See rejected appellants' suggestion that it employ the debt/equity principles espoused in Plantation Patterns, Inc. v. Commissioner, 462 F.2d 712 (5th Cir.1972), in determining whether the shareholders had actually made an economic outlay,[9] instead choosing to employ a debt/equity analysis only after making a finding that an economic outlay had occurred. *Leavitt,* 875 F.2d at 427. The *Leavitt* court reasoned that the legislative history of section [1366] limiting the basis of a Subchapter S shareholder to his corporate investment or outlay could not be circumvented through the use of debt/equity principles. Id. at 426 & n. 16. See generally Bogdanski, Shareholder Guarantees, Interest Deductions, and S Corporation Stock Basis: The Problems with Putnam, 13 J.Corp.Tax'n 264, 268–89 (1986).

Taxpayers press this Court to follow the contrary holding of Selfe v. United States, 778 F.2d 769 (11th Cir.1985). There, the Eleventh Circuit ruled that a shareholder's guaranty of a Subchapter S corporation loan could result in an increase in equity or debt basis even though the shareholder had not satisfied any portion of the obligation. *Selfe,* 778 F.2d at 775. The court remanded the case to the district court for it to employ debt/equity principles in determining if the loan in question was in substance one to the shareholder rather than to the corporation. Id.

The courts have uniformly ruled that a shareholder must make an economic outlay to increase his Subchapter S corporation stock basis. Taxpayers assert that if we look beyond the form of the transaction at what they contend is its substance—a loan from Hibernia to them, which in turn they contributed to Harmar as capital—we must find that a $700,000 outlay occurred and that their stock bases therefore correspondingly increased. They contend that use of debt/equity principles will lead us to such a conclusion.

Ordinarily, taxpayers are bound by the form of the transaction they have chosen; taxpayers may not in hindsight recast the transaction as one that they might have made in order to obtain tax advantages. * * * The IRS, however, often may disregard form and recharacterize a transaction by looking to its substance. Higgins v. Smith, 308 U.S. 473, 60 S.Ct. 355, 357, 84 L.Ed. 406 (1940). The Tax Court has recognized an exception to the rule that a taxpayer may not question a transaction's form in cases such as this one in which the shareholder argues that guaranteed corporate debt should be recast as an equity investment on the shareholder's part. Blum v. Commissioner, 59 T.C. 436, 440 (1972).

In this case we find that the transaction as structured did not lack adequate substance or reality and that an economic outlay justifying the basis claimed by Taxpayers never occurred.

Bowers, Building Up an S Shareholder's Basis through Loans and Acquisitions, J. Tax'n S Corp., Fall 1989, at 22, 29.

9. In *Plantation Patterns,* this Court considered whether a Subchapter C corporation could deduct interest payments made on its debt and whether its shareholders had resulting dividend income. The Court, using a debt/equity analysis, affirmed a Tax Court finding that a corporation's interest payments on debentures were constructive dividends and could not be deducted as interest payments. Id. at 723–24. * * *

The summary judgment evidence reflects that the parties to this transaction intended that the Hibernia loan be one to the corporation. Each of the two $350,000 promissory notes was executed by and only in the name of Harmar. The notes have been renewed and remain in the same form, namely notes payable to Hibernia in which the sole maker is Harmar. Hibernia, an independent party, in substance earmarked the loan proceeds for use in purchasing the subject property to which Harmar took title, Harmar contemporaneously giving Hibernia a mortgage to secure Harmar's debt to Hibernia. The bank sent interest due notices to Harmar, and all note payments were made by checks to Hibernia drawn on Harmar's corporate account. Harmar's books and records for all years through the year ended December 31, 1985, prepared by its certified public accountant, reflect the $700,000 loan simply as an indebtedness of Harmar to Hibernia. They do not in any way account for or reflect any of the $700,000 as a capital contribution or loan by Taxpayers to Harmar, although they do reflect the $1,000 capital contribution each Taxpayer made and Harmar's indebtedness to Taxpayers for the various cash advances Taxpayers made to it. The Harmar financial statements for the year ended December 31, 1986, are the first to show any contributed capital attributable to the Hibernia loan. Further, Hibernia's records showed Harmar as the "borrower" in respect to the $700,000 loan and the renewals of it. Harmar's 1982 tax return, which covered August 15 through December 31, 1982, indicates that Harmar deducted $12,506 in interest expenses. Because only the Hibernia loan generated such expenses for that period, it is reasonably inferable that the deduction corresponded to that loan. The 1982 Harmar return showed no distribution to Taxpayers, as it should have if the $700,000 Hibernia loan on which Harmar paid interest was a loan to the Taxpayers. Further, the return shows the only capital contributed as $2,000 and the only loan from stockholders as $68,000, but shows other indebtedness of $675,000. In short, Harmar's 1982 income tax return is flatly inconsistent with Taxpayers' present position. Moreover, there is no indication that Taxpayers treated the loan as a personal one on their individual returns by reporting Harmar's interest payments to Hibernia as constructive dividend income. In sum, the parties' treatment of the transaction, from the time it was entered into and for years thereafter, has been wholly consistent with its unambiguous documentation and inconsistent with the way in which Taxpayers now seek to recast it. Hibernia was clearly an independent third party, and the real and bona fide, separate existence of Harmar is not challenged. The parties did what they intended to do, and the transaction as structured did not lack adequate reality or substance.

Moreover, if the transaction is to be "recast," it is by no means clear that it should be recast in the form sought by Taxpayers, namely as a cash loan to them from Hibernia followed by their payment of the cash to Harmar as a contribution to its capital, and Harmar's then using the cash to purchase the building. Such recasting does not account for Hibernia's mortgage on the building. In any event, if the transaction is to be recast, why should it not be recast as a loan by Hibernia to Taxpayers, with the

Taxpayers using the funds to themselves purchase the building, giving Hibernia a mortgage on the building to secure their debt to it, and then transferring the building, subject to the mortgage, to Harmar as a contribution to capital? Presumably in that situation Taxpayers' bases in their Harmar stock would be reduced by the amount of the debt secured by the mortgage under I.R.C. § 358(d). See Wiebusch v. Commissioner, 59 T.C. 777, aff'd per curiam "on the basis of the opinion of the Tax Court," Wiebusch v. Commissioner, 487 F.2d 515 (8th Cir.1973).[15] While section 358(d) likely does not affect stockholder basis in the debt of the Subchapter S corporation to the stockholder, Taxpayers have not sought to recast the transaction as a loan by Hibernia to them followed by their loan of the proceeds to Harmar; indeed even after Harmar's books were rearranged starting with the year ending December 31, 1986, the books do not show any indebtedness in this respect of Harmar to Taxpayers and do continue to show Harmar as owing the money in question to Hibernia. There is simply no evidence of Harmar indebtedness to Taxpayers in respect to these funds.

Taxpayers' guarantees and Harris' pledge of certificates of deposit do not undermine the intent of the parties that Harmar be the borrower in this transaction. It certainly is not difficult to fathom that a careful lender to a new, small, closely held corporation such as Harmar would seek personal guarantees from all of its shareholders. See Bogdanski, supra, at 269. Moreover, the wholly unperformed guarantees do not satisfy the requirement that an economic outlay be made before a corresponding increase in basis can occur. See generally *Underwood*, 535 F.2d at 312. In the same light, Harris' pledge to Hibernia of some $355,000 in certificates of deposit of his (and Harris Mortgage Corporation) does not provide such an outlay.[16]

We conclude that the transaction must be treated as it purports to be and as the parties treated it—namely as a loan by Hibernia to Harmar, all payments on which through the relevant time have been made by Harmar to Hibernia. For any funds or other assets Taxpayers have actually provided to Harmar as loans or contributions, Taxpayers are, of course, entitled to basis additions as of the time such contributions or loans were furnished by them to Harmar, but they are not entitled to a 1982 basis addition for Hibernia's 1982 $700,000 loan to Harmar, notwithstanding that it was also secured by Taxpayers' execution of guarantees and Harris' pledge to

---

15. See also Megaard, No Stock Basis for Shareholder Guarantee of S Corporation Debt, 15 J.Corp.Tax'n 340 (1989). Megaard explains that "[u]nder Section 358(d), the assumption by a corporation of its shareholder's debt is treated as money received which reduces the shareholder's basis in the stock." Id. at 349. Cf. id. at 350 ("Having the corporation's assets encumbered by the shareholder's personal debt runs the risk of a basis reduction under Section 358 should the Service argue that the transaction was a purchase by the shareholder of the * * * assets followed by a contribution of the assets to the corporation subject to the debt.").

16. Taxpayers would have us, in effect, convert this pledge to Hibernia into a $700,000 cash contribution made to Harmar by Taxpayers equally. But that did not happen. Taxpayers do not contend that the certificates of deposit were contributed to Harmar's capital.

Hibernia of his and Harris Mortgage Corporation's certificates of deposit in the total face amount of some $355,000.

Conclusion

There was no genuine dispute as to any material fact necessary to sustain the Government's summary judgment motion. The district court's judgment is correct and it is therefore

Affirmed.

NOTE

In *Harris*, the Fifth Circuit joined several other circuits[1] and the Tax Court[2] in holding that the guarantee of an S corporation's loan by its shareholders may not be treated as an additional investment in the corporation which will increase the shareholders' bases for purposes of the loss limitation rule in Section 1366(d). In conflict with this line of authority is the Eleventh Circuit's decision in Selfe v. United States.[3] In *Selfe*, the court reasoned that debt-equity principles under Subchapter C were applicable in determining whether a shareholder-guaranteed debt should be characterized as a capital contribution. In remanding the case for a determination of whether the shareholder's guarantee amounted to either an equity investment or a shareholder loan to the corporation, the court directed the district court to apply the principles of *Plantation Patterns*, a Subchapter C case discussed in *Harris*.

Despite the seeming conflict among the circuits, the Supreme Court has declined to add this fascinating tax issue to its docket.[4]

b. SUBCHAPTER S LOSSES AND SECTION 362(e)(2)

Code: § 362(e)(2)

The rules for allocating and characterizing gains and losses that are inherent in property contributed to a partnership ("precontribution gains and losses") are one of the principal features of the Subchapter K partnership tax regime. Under Section 704(c)(1)(A), precontribution gains and losses generally must be taxed to the contributing partner, and Section 724 prevents partners from gaining a tax advantage by converting precontribution ordinary income into capital gain and precontribution capital loss into ordinary loss. Other provisions buttress these rules by preventing shifting

---

1. See, e.g., Brown v. Commissioner, 706 F.2d 755 (6th Cir.1983); Estate of Leavitt v. Commissioner, 875 F.2d 420 (4th Cir. 1989), cert. denied, 493 U.S. 958, 110 S.Ct. 376 (1989); Uri v. Commissioner, 949 F.2d 371 (10th Cir.1991); Sleiman v. Commissioner, 187 F.3d 1352 (11th Cir. 1999); Grojean v. Commissioner, 248 F.3d 572 (7th Cir. 2001); Maloof v. Commissioner, 456 F.3d 645 (6th Cir. 2006).

2. See, e.g., Estate of Leavitt v. Commissioner, 90 T.C. 206 (1988); Hitchins v. Commissioner, 103 T.C. 711 (1994).

3. 778 F.2d 769 (11th Cir.1985).

4. The Court denied the taxpayer's petition for certiorari in the *Estate of Leavitt* case, supra note 1.

of precontribution gains and losses through partnership distributions and dispositions of partnership interests.[1] In short, Subchapter K has an array of provisions designed to ensure that a partner who contributes property with a precontribution gain will be taxed on that gain and that precontribution losses may not be shifted to other partners.[2]

Subchapter S is relatively primitive compared to its Subchapter K cousin in the treatment of precontribution gains and losses. Under Section 1377, precontribution gains and losses are taxed like any other gain or loss under a per-share, per-day allocation method.[3] Precontribution gains and losses in an S corporation are thus routinely shifted to other shareholders.

Congress decided to attack various schemes by taxpayers to duplicate losses by way of transactions involving corporations. Section 362(e)(2) was one of the provisions enacted to curb those abuses. That section provides that if a shareholder transfers property with an aggregate built-in loss to a corporation in a Section 351 transaction, the corporation's basis in the property must be reduced to the fair market value of such property.[4] If more than one asset is contributed, the basis reduction is allocated among the property in proportion to their respective built-in losses immediately before the transaction.[5] As an alternative to reducing the property's basis, the shareholder and the corporation may elect to reduce the basis of the stock that was received for the property to the stock's fair market value immediately after the transfer.[6]

Section 362(e)(2) potentially will defer or limit precontribution losses in an S corporation, sometimes in a very unusual way. For example, assume that an individual decides to form an S corporation by contributing property with a $20,000 basis and $12,000 fair market value for all of the corporation's stock in a Section 351 exchange. Under Section 362(e)(2), the property's basis will be reduced to $12,000 and the precontribution loss in the property will disappear. If the corporation were to sell the property for $12,000, there would be no gain or loss recognized by the corporation. The shareholder's basis in the stock, however, would still be $20,000 so the loss would remain in the shares. The timing of the loss, however, would be deferred until the shareholder either liquidates the corporation or sells the stock. Alternatively, assume that the shareholder and the corporation elect to reduce the basis of the shareholder's stock to $12,000. In that case, the basis of the property in the corporation would remain at $20,000. If the corporation were to sell the property, it would recognize its $8,000 loss, which would pass through to the shareholder. The shareholder's stock basis would then be reduced by the loss down to $4,000, putting the shareholder in a position where a sale of the stock for its $12,000 fair market value would result in an $8,000 gain. Over time, the shareholder would report an

---

1. I.R.C. §§ 704(c)(1)(B); 737; 751(a).

2. Section 704(c)(1)(C) prevents a shift of precontribution losses to other partners, even a transferee partner.

3. The regulations hold out the possibility of attacking plans to alter the character

of precontribution gains and losses in an S corporation. See Reg. § 1.1366–1(b)(2) & (3).

4. I.R.C. § 362(e)(2)(A).

5. I.R.C. § 362(e)(2)(B).

6. I.R.C. § 362(e)(2)(C).

$8,000 loss and an $8,000 gain, the net result being that the loss essentially disappeared. Finally, assume that the shareholder also contributed property with a $10,000 built-in gain to the S corporation at the same time as the transfer of the property with the built-in loss. In that case, no reduction in the basis of the loss property or the stock would be required under Section 362(e)(2) because the two properties that were transferred did not have an aggregate built-in loss.

It is hard to believe that Congress considered the effects on Subchapter S when it enacted Section 362(e)(2). That section now lurks as a trap for those who either receive poor advice or are not initiated in the ways of Subchapters C and S. Until Congress fixes this problem, taxpayers planning a new venture involving property with a built-in loss will be well advised to consider structuring the venture as a limited liability company or partnership governed by Subchapter K. Alternatively, another strategy for preserving a built-in loss in property would be to offer to make the property available to an S corporation through a leasing arrangement.

3.   SALE OF S CORPORATION STOCK

Code: § 1(h).

The tax consequences of a sale of S corporation stock are determined by regulations promulgated under the "look-through" rules of Section 1(h). In general, S corporation stock is treated as a capital asset that gives rise to capital gain or loss on sale. Unlike the more complex approach taken by Subchapter K to the sale of a partnership interest, Subchapter S historically has not required selling shareholders to characterize a portion of their gain or loss on a stock sale by reference to the types of assets (e.g., ordinary income property) held by the corporation at the time of the sale. When Congress enacted the Section 1(h) capital gains rate regime, however, it authorized the Service to prescribe appropriate regulations to apply the various maximum capital gains rates to the sale of interests in pass-through entities.[1]

The Section 1(h) regulations apply a partial capital gains "look-through" rule for sales and exchanges of interests in an S corporation.[2] Shareholders who sell S corporation stock held for more than one year may recognize collectibles gain (taxable at a maximum rate of 28 percent) and residual capital gain, which is generally taxable at a maximum rate of 15 percent (at least through 2012, possibly at a higher rate thereafter).[3] The selling shareholder's share of collectibles gain is defined as the amount of the net collectibles gain (but not net collectibles loss) that would be allocated to that shareholder if the S corporation transferred all of its collectibles in a fully taxable transaction immediately before the transfer of

---

1. I.R.C. § 1(h)(9).

2. Reg. § 1.1(h)–1.

3. Reg. § 1.1(h)–1(a). In limited situations (e.g., where a transaction is governed by provisions of Subchapter C that treat gain on a sale or redemption of stock as ordinary income), shareholders also may recognize ordinary income on a sale of their S corporation stock. See, e.g., I.R.C. §§ 304, 306.

the stock.[4] The selling shareholder's residual capital gain is the amount of long-term capital gain or loss that the shareholder would recognize on the sale of the stock ("pre-look-through capital gain or loss") minus the shareholder's share of collectibles gain.[5] The look-through rules do not extend to other corporate assets, such as inventory or depreciable real estate, that would generate ordinary income, or to real estate that would produce unrecaptured (i.e., 25–percent) Section 1250 gain on a corporate-level sale. What is the policy justification for this "pick and choose" look-through approach for S corporations?

The regulations illustrate these rules with the following example.[6] Assume that X, Inc., which always has been an S corporation and is owned equally by individuals A, B, and C, invests in antiques. After they were purchased, the antiques appreciated in value by $300. A owned one-third of the X stock and has held the stock for more than one year. A's adjusted basis in the X stock is $100. If A were to sell all of the X stock to T for $150, A would recognize $50 of pre-look-through long-term capital gain. If X were to sell all of the antiques in a fully taxable transaction immediately before the transfer to T, A would be allocated $100 of collectibles gain on account of the sale. Therefore, A will recognize $100 of collectibles gain on account of the collectibles held by X. The difference between A's pre-look-through capital gain or loss ($50) and the collectibles gain ($100) is A's residual long-term capital gain or loss on the sale of the X stock. Thus, A will recognize $100 of collectibles gain and $50 of residual long-term capital loss on the sale of A's X stock.

PROBLEMS

1. S Corporation is a calendar year taxpayer which elected S corporation status in its first year of operation. S's common stock is owned by A (200 shares with a $12,000 basis) and B (100 shares with a $6,000 basis). During the current year, S will have the following income and expenses:

Business income	$ 92,000
Tax-exempt interest	1,000
Salary expense	44,000
Depreciation	8,000
Property taxes	7,000
Supplies	4,000
Interest expense paid on a margin account maintained with S Corp.'s stock broker	6,000
Gain from the sale of equipment:	
§ 1245 gain	7,000
§ 1231 gain	12,000

4. Reg. § 1.1(h)–1(b)(2)(ii). A shareholder's share of collectibles gain is limited to the amount attributable to the portion of the stock transferred that was held for more than one year.

5. Reg. § 1.1(h)–1(c).

6. Reg. § 1.1(h)–1(f) Example 4.

STCG from the sale of AT&T stock	7,500
LTCG from the sale of Chrysler stock held for two years	15,000
LTCL from the sale of investment real estate held for two years	9,000
Bribe of government official	6,000
Recovery of a bad debt previously deducted	4,500

(a) How will S Corporation, A and B report these events? Compare § 704(b)(2) and (c).

(b) What is A's basis in his S stock at the end of the current year?

(c) Whose accounting method will control the timing of income and deductions?

(d) If S realizes a gain upon an involuntary conversion, who makes the election under § 1033 to limit recognition of gain?

(e) Would it matter if the equipment would have been property described in § 1221(a)(1) if held by A?

2. D, E and F each own one-third of the outstanding stock of R Corporation (an S corporation). During the current year, R will have $120,000 of net income from business operations. The net income is realized at a rate of $10,000 per month. Additionally, in January of this year R sold § 1231 property and recognized a $60,000 loss.

(a) Assume D's basis in her R stock at the beginning of the year is $10,000. If D sells one-half of her stock to G midway through the year for $25,000, what will be the tax results to D and G?

(b) What difference would it make in (a), above, if D sold all of her stock to G for $50,000?

3. The Ace Sporting Goods Store (an S corporation) is owned by Dick and Harry. Dick and Harry each own one-half of Ace's stock and have a $2,000 basis in their respective shares. At incorporation, Dick loaned $4,000 to Ace and received a five year, 12% note from the corporation.

(a) If Ace has an $8,000 loss from business operations this year, what will be the results to Dick and Harry? Do you have any suggestions for Harry? Would it matter if on December 15 Ace borrowed $4,000 from its bank on a full recourse basis? What if Dick and Harry personally guaranteed the loan? Compare §§ 752(a) and 722.

(b) If Ace has $6,000 of net income from business operations next year, what will be the results to Dick and Harry?

(c) What difference would it make in (a), above, if the $8,000 loss was made up of $2,000 of losses from business operation and a $6,000 long-term capital loss? See Reg. § 1.704–1(d)(2).

(d) What would be the effect in (a), above, if Ace's S corporation status was terminated at the end of the current year?

4. Allied Technologies, an S corporation, is owned by Betty (25%), Chuck (35%) and Diana (40%). Betty and Chuck also each own one-half of the stock of the Portland Exporting Corporation, also an S corporation.

    (a) If Allied sells investment real estate which it purchased two years ago for $40,000 to Portland for $20,000, what will be the result to Allied? See § 267.

    (b) What difference would it make in (a), above, if Portland were a C corporation?

    (c) Assume Allied is an accrual method taxpayer and owes $1,500 to Betty (a cash method taxpayer) for her December salary. If Allied pays the salary on January 15 of the following year, what will be the tax results to Allied and Betty (assuming both are calendar year taxpayers?) See § 267(e).

E.   DISTRIBUTIONS TO SHAREHOLDERS

Code: §§ 311(b); 1368; 1371(a)(1), (c), (e); Skim § 301(a), (b) and (d).

S Corporations Without Earnings and Profits. If an S corporation has no accumulated earnings and profits, distributions to shareholders are treated as a tax-free return of capital which is first applied to reduce the shareholder's stock basis.[1] Any distribution in excess of basis is treated as gain from the sale or exchange of property—capital gain if the stock is a capital asset.[2] Virtually all S corporations formed after 1982 do not generate earnings and profits[3] and are governed by this simple regime. This basic taxing pattern for distributions by S corporations also governs any distribution of property to which Section 301(c) would apply.[4] Thus, the tax consequences of transactions characterized as Section 301 distributions by other Code provisions, such as Sections 302 (redemptions) and 305 (stock dividends), are determined under Section 1368.

S Corporations With Earnings and Profits. S corporations with earnings and profits present more challenging problems because of the need to harmonize the Subchapter S rules with the corporation's prior C history. Distributions by a C corporation to its shareholders are taxable as dividends to the extent of the corporation's current and accumulated earnings and profits.[5] Some S corporations may have accumulated earnings and profits attributable to prior years when they were governed by Subchapter C. In addition, an S corporation may have inherited the earnings and profits of another company in a corporate acquisition subject to Section 381. In all these cases, the undistributed earnings have not been taxed at

---

1. I.R.C. § 1368(b)(1).

2. I.R.C. § 1368(b)(2).

3. I.R.C. § 1371(c)(1). An S corporation formed after 1982 may generate earnings and profits for any year in which it is not an S corporation and may acquire earnings and

profits under Section 381 in a corporate acquisition. See Chapter 9D, supra.

4. I.R.C. § 1368(c). See Section G of this chapter, infra.

5. I.R.C. §§ 301(c)(1), 316.

the shareholder level and represent an irresistible temptation for a tax-free bailout. There is no free lunch, however, and it thus becomes necessary to identify those distributions which should be taxed at the shareholder level because they are made out of accumulated earnings and profits.

Congress devised a new tax concept—the "accumulated adjustments account" ("AAA")—to serve as the reference point for determining the source of distributions by an S corporation with accumulated earnings and profits. The AAA represents the post–1982 undistributed net income of the corporation. It begins at zero and is increased and decreased annually in a manner similar to the adjustment of the basis in a shareholder's stock.[6] Any distribution by an S corporation with accumulated earnings and profits is treated as a tax-free return of capital to the extent it does not exceed the AAA.[7] A distribution in excess of the AAA is treated as a dividend to the extent of accumulated earnings and profits,[8] and any portion of the distribution still remaining after both the AAA and accumulated earnings and profits are exhausted is treated first as a recovery of basis and then as gain from the sale of property.[9]

One might reasonably ask at this point: what is the purpose of this statutory scheme? The answer is more straightforward than it first appears. The function of the AAA is to identify the source of distributions by those few S corporations with accumulated earnings and profits. It permits the corporation to make a tax-free distribution of the net income recognized during its S corporation era which already was taxed at the shareholder level. Only after these previously taxed earnings are exhausted will a distribution be considered as emanating from accumulated earnings and profits.[10]

Distributions of Appreciated Property. At the shareholder level, the Section 1368 distribution rules make no distinction between distributions of cash and other property. At the corporate level, however, an S corporation that distributes appreciated property (other than its own obligations)

---

6. I.R.C. § 1368(e)(1)(A); Reg. § 1.1368–2. Unlike a shareholder's basis, however, the AAA is not increased by tax-exempt income items and is not decreased for expenses related to tax-exempt income. The adjustments also may result in a negative AAA. Reg. § 1.1368–2(a)(3)(ii). In addition, no adjustment is made for federal taxes attributable to any taxable year in which the corporation was a C corporation. Id.

7. I.R.C. § 1368(c)(1). Except to the extent provided in regulations, the AAA is allocated proportionately among distributions if the distributions exceed the AAA. See Reg. § 1.1368–2(b), (c).

8. I.R.C. § 1368(c)(2).

9. I.R.C. § 1368(c)(2), (3). For lots of details about the AAA, see Reg. § 1.1368–2.

10. In lieu of these rules, an S corporation may elect, with the consent of all shareholders who have received distributions during the year, to treat distributions as a dividend to the extent of accumulated earnings and profits. I.R.C. § 1368(e)(3); Reg. § 1.1368–1(f)(2). There normally is little incentive to make this election. One possible motivation would be to enable the corporation to sweep its Subchapter C earnings and profits account clean and thus avoid the corporate level tax and possible termination of S corporation status that would result from the co-existence of Subchapter C earnings and profits and excessive passive investment income. See I.R.C. § 1375. A similar election is provided during a post-termination transition period. I.R.C. § 1371(e)(2).

recognizes gain in the same manner as if the property had been sold to the shareholder at its fair market value.[11] This familiar rule, borrowed from Subchapter C, applies to liquidating and nonliquidating distributions of property by an S corporation.[12] The gain is not taxed to the corporation but, like other corporate-level income, it passes through to the distributee shareholder, who takes a fair market value basis in the distributed property.[13] The shareholder's basis in his S corporation stock is reduced by the fair market value (not the adjusted basis) of the distributed property.[14] These rules are required to prevent the appreciation from escaping tax through a distribution which is tax-free at both the corporate and shareholder levels followed by a tax-free sale by the shareholder, who would take the property with a fair market value basis.

PROBLEMS

1. Ajax Corporation is a calendar year taxpayer which was organized two years ago and elected S corporation status for its first taxable year. Ajax's stock is owned one-third by Dewey and two-thirds by Milt. At the beginning of the current year, Dewey's basis in his Ajax shares was $3,000 and Milt's basis in his shares was $5,000. During the year, Ajax will earn $9,000 of net income from operations and have a $3,000 long-term capital gain on the sale of 100 shares of Exxon stock. What results to Dewey, Milt and Ajax in the following alternative situations?

   (a) On October 15, Ajax distributes $5,000 to Dewey and $10,000 to Milt.

   (b) On October 15, Ajax distributes $8,000 to Dewey and $16,000 to Milt.

   (c) Ajax redeems all of Dewey's stock on the last day of the year for $20,000. What result to Dewey?

   (d) On October 15, Ajax redeems one-fourth of Dewey's stock for $5,000 and one-fourth of Milt's stock for $10,000.

   (e) Ajax distributes a parcel of land with a basis of $9,000 and a fair market value of $8,000 to Dewey and a different parcel with a basis of $13,000 and fair market value of $16,000 to Milt.

   (f) On October 15, Ajax distributes its own notes to Dewey and Milt. Dewey receives an Ajax five year, 12% note with a face amount and fair market value of $8,000 and Milt receives an Ajax five year, 12% note with a face amount and fair market value of $16,000.

---

11. I.R.C. § 311(b). An S corporation may not recognize loss, however, on a distribution of property that has declined in value. I.R.C. § 311(a).

12. See I.R.C. § 1371(a), which provides that, except as otherwise provided in Subchapter S, the provisions of Subchapter C

apply to S corporations and their shareholders. For more on the coordination of Subchapters S and C, see Section G of this chapter, infra.

13. I.R.C. § 301(d)(1).

14. I.R.C. §§ 1367(a)(2)(A), 1368.

2. P Corporation was formed in 1981 by its two equal shareholders, Nancy and Opal, and elected S corporation status at the beginning of the current year. On January 1, Nancy had a $1,000 basis in her P stock and Opal had a $5,000 basis in her stock. P has $6,000 of accumulated earnings and profits from its prior C corporation operations and has the following results from operations this year:

Gross Income	$32,000
Long-term capital gain	4,000
Salary Expense	18,000
Depreciation	8,000

What are the tax consequences to Nancy, Opal and P Corporation in the following alternative situations.

(a) On November 1, P distributes $5,000 to Nancy and $5,000 to Opal.

(b) Same as (a), above, except that P distributes $10,000 to Nancy and $10,000 to Opal.

(c) What difference would it make in (a), above, if P also received $4,000 of tax-exempt interest during the year and distributed $2,000 of the interest to Nancy and $2,000 to Opal?

(d) During the current year P makes no distributions. On January 1 of next year Nancy sells her P stock to Rose for $6,000. If P breaks even on its operations next year, what will be the result to Rose if P distributes $6,000 to each of its shareholders next February 15?

(e) During the current year P makes no distributions. Nancy and Opal revoke P's Subchapter S election effective January 1 of next year. Assume P Co. has $5,000 of earnings and profits next year. What results to Nancy and Opal if P distributes $7,000 to each of them on August 1 of next year?

F.   TAXATION OF THE S CORPORATION

Code: §§ 1363; 1374; 1375.

The major benefit of a Subchapter S election is the elimination of tax at the corporate level. But this immunity from tax is not absolute. As part of its continuing mission to patrol abuse, Congress has provided that in certain limited situations an S corporation may be subject to tax under Section 1374 on certain built-in gains inherent in corporate property and under Section 1375 on a portion of its passive investment income.

Tax on Certain Built-in Gains: Section 1374. When Congress repealed the *General Utilities* doctrine, it recognized that the shareholders of a C corporation might elect S corporation status in order to avoid the corporate-level tax imposed under the new statutory scheme.[1] For example, assume Liquidating Co. is a C corporation, holds highly appreciated assets,

---

1.   See Chapters 4D, 5E and 7B2, supra.

and is owned by shareholders A and B, who also would realize large taxable gains if they sell their stock or liquidate the company. If A and B cause Liquidating Co. to sell its assets and liquidate, or to distribute its assets in complete liquidation, Liquidating Co. will be taxed on its gains and A and B also will be taxed on their stock gains.[2] If Liquidating Co. qualified as a "small business corporation," A and B could elect S corporation status in order to reduce the double-tax burden on the sale or liquidation. The company then could sell its assets and the gains would pass through to A and B, whose stock bases would be correspondingly increased. The effect of the S corporation/liquidation strategy would be to avoid the full impact of the double tax.

Section 1374 blocks this opportunity by taxing an S corporation that has a "net recognized built-in gain" at any time within ten years of the effective date of its S corporation election.[3] At the outset, two important limitations on this tax should be noted. First, Section 1374 applies only if the corporation's S election was made after December 31, 1986.[4] Second, it does not apply to a corporation that always has been subject to Subchapter S.[5]

In general, Section 1374 is designed to tax an S corporation on the net gain that accrued while it was subject to Subchapter C if that gain is subsequently recognized on sales, distributions and other dispositions of property within a ten-year "recognition period" beginning with the first taxable year in which the corporation was an S corporation. For this purpose, any gain recognized during the recognition period, including income from "ripe" items such as cash-basis accounts receivable or Section 453 installment obligations, is a "recognized built-in gain" unless the corporation establishes either that it did not hold the asset at the beginning of its first S taxable year or the recognized gain exceeds the gain inherent in the asset at that time.[6] Conversely, any loss recognized during the recognition period, including deductible items attributable to the corporation's pre-S life, is a "recognized built-in loss" to the extent that the S corporation establishes that it held the asset at the beginning of its first S year and the loss does not exceed the loss inherent in the asset at that time.[7] Since the taxpayer has the burden of proof under these definitions, a C corporation making an S election should obtain an independent appraisal of its assets to establish their value on the relevant date in order to avoid

---

2. See I.R.C. §§ 331; 336; 1001(a).

3. I.R.C. § 1374(a), (d)(7)(A). The "recognition period" was reduced from ten to seven years in 2009 and 2010 and to five years in 2011. I.R.C. § 1374(d)(7)(B). The reduced time periods apply separately to any asset transferred from a C to an S corporation where the S corporation takes a carryover basis, such as in a tax-free reorganization. Id. See I.R.C. § 1374(d)(8).

4. Tax Reform Act of 1986, P.L. No. 99–514, 99th Cong., 2d Sess. § 633(b) (1986).

5. I.R.C. § 1374(c)(1). This exemption may not apply, however, if the S corporation had a "predecessor" that was a C corporation. Id. This could occur, for example, where a C corporation was acquired by the S corporation in a tax-free reorganization.

6. I.R.C. § 1374(d)(3), (5)(A).

7. I.R.C. § 1374(d)(4), (5)(B).

being taxed on gain arising under the S regime and to benefit from the losses that accrued during the corporation's C years.

The Section 1374 tax is computed by applying the highest rate applicable to C corporations (currently 35 percent) to the S corporation's "net recognized built-in gain," which is defined as the corporation's taxable income computed by taking into account only recognized built-in gains and losses but limited to the corporation's taxable income computed generally as if it were a C corporation.[8] The purpose of the taxable income limitation is to ensure that Section 1374 does not tax the corporation on more income than it actually realizes during the taxable year. To prevent taxpayers from avoiding the tax by manipulating the timing of post-conversion losses, Section 1374(d)(2)(B) provides that any net recognized built-in gains not taxed because of the taxable income limitation are carried forward and treated as recognized built-in gain in succeeding years in the recognition period.[9] Finally, the amount of net recognized built-in gain taken into account for any taxable year may not exceed the net unrealized built-in gain at the time the corporation became an S corporation reduced by any net recognized built-in gains which were subject to Section 1374 in prior taxable years.[10]

The Section 1374 tax easily could be avoided if it applied only to built-in gains recognized on the disposition of assets that were held by the S corporation at the beginning of its first S taxable year. For example, assume that a C corporation converting to S status holds an asset (Oldacre) with a built-in gain which it subsequently exchanges for property of like kind (Newacre) in a Section 1031 nonrecognition transaction. The gain inherent in Oldacre is preserved in Newacre's exchanged basis under Section 1031(d). If the corporation disposes of Newacre within ten years after switching to S status, the Section 1374 tax should apply to the built-in "C gain" even though Newacre was not held on the first day that the corporation was subject to Subchapter S. Section 1374(d)(6) ensures this result by providing that an asset taking an exchanged basis from another asset held by the corporation at the time it converted to S status shall be treated as having been held as of the beginning of the corporation's first S year. In the above example, the built-in gain inherent in Oldacre on the conversion from C to S status is recognized under Section 1374 if the corporation disposes of Newacre at a gain during the recognition period.

Section 1374(d)(8) is another testament to Congress's protective attitude toward the double tax. It ensures that built-in gain in assets acquired by an S corporation from a C corporation in a tax-free reorganization does not escape a corporate level tax. For this purpose, the recognition period

---

8.   I.R.C. § 1374(b)(1), (d)(2). Taxable income, as defined in Section 63(a), is modified by disregarding certain deductions (e.g., the dividends received deduction) and net operating losses. I.R.C. §§ 1374(d)(2)(A)(ii); 1375(b)(1)(B). Net operating loss and capital loss carryforwards from prior years as a C corporation are taken into account in com-puting the amount subject to tax under Section 1374. I.R.C. § 1374(b)(2).

9.   The carryover rule applies only to corporations that elected S status on or after March 31, 1988. I.R.C. § 1374(d)(2)(B).

10.   I.R.C. § 1374(c)(2), (d)(1).

commences as of the date the asset is acquired rather than on the beginning of the first taxable year for which the corporation was an S corporation.[11]

Tax advisors began to plot strategies to reduce the impact of Section 1374 soon after it was enacted. For example, it was suggested that the tax might be avoided if an S corporation sold an asset with built-in gain during the 10–year recognition period on the installment method but delayed receipt of any payments (and thus any recognized gain) until after the recognition period had expired.[12] Not surprisingly, the Service has expressed its displeasure with this gambit. The regulations provide that the built-in gain rules will continue to apply to income recognized under the installment method during taxable years ending after the expiration of the recognition period. The gain, when recognized, will be subject to tax under Section 1374.[13]

Tax on Passive Investment Income. When it widened the gates to Subchapter S, Congress became concerned that a C corporation with earnings and profits might make an S election and redeploy substantial amounts in liquid assets yielding passive investment income such as dividends and interest. Left unchecked, this strategy would enable a profitable C corporation to move to the single-tax regime of Subchapter S and pass through the investment income to its shareholders, who might delay, perhaps forever, paying any shareholder-level tax on the Subchapter C earnings and profits. This plan had particular allure when a C corporation sold all of its operating assets and was seeking an alternative to the shareholder-level tax that would be imposed under Section 331 on a distribution of the proceeds in complete liquidation.[14]

The Code includes two weapons to foil the Subchapter S/passive income ploy. As discussed earlier, an S corporation with accumulated earnings and profits from its prior life as a C corporation will lose its S status if it has passive investment income that exceeds 25 percent of its gross receipts for three consecutive taxable years.[15] In addition, even before its S status is terminated, the corporation will be subject to a corporate-level tax under Section 1375. The tax, which equals 35 percent of the corporation's "excess net passive income," is imposed if an S corporation has earnings and profits from a taxable year prior to its S election and more than 25 percent of the corporation's gross receipts for the taxable year consist of "passive investment income."

For purposes of the Section 1375 tax, "passive investment income" is defined as gross receipts from royalties, rents, dividends, interest, and

---

11. I.R.C. § 1374(d)(8). See Section G of this chapter, infra, for an overview of the tax consequences when an S corporation is the acquiring or target corporation in a tax-free reorganization.

12. See, e.g., Taggart, "Emerging Tax Issues in Corporate Acquisitions," 44 Tax L.Rev. 459, 481 (1989).

13. Reg. § 1.1374–4(h)(1). For the relationship of this rule to other aspects of Section 1374, see Reg. § 1.1374–4(h)(2)–(5).

14. See Chapter 8B1, supra.

15. I.R.C. § 1362(d)(3). See Section C of this chapter, supra.

annuities.[16] Gains on the disposition of property, interest earned on obligations acquired from the sale of inventory, the gross receipts of certain lending and finance institutions, and dividends received from a C corporation subsidiary that are derived from the active conduct of a trade or business, are not passive investment income.[17] To prevent easy manipulation of the gross receipts test, only the excess of gains over losses from dispositions of capital assets (other than stock and securities) is included in overall gross receipts, and gross receipts from the sales or exchanges of stock or securities are taken into account only to the extent of gains.[18] The term "stock or securities" is interpreted expansively and includes stock rights, warrants, debentures, partnership interests, and "certificates of interest" in profit-sharing arrangements.[19]

The computation of the Section 1375 tax is a technician's dream (and a student's nightmare?). The base for the Section 1375 tax, "excess net passive income," is a percentage of the corporation's "net passive income," which is generally equal to passive investment income less deductions directly connected with the production of such income.[20] To arrive at excess net passive income, net passive income is multiplied by a ratio, which has a numerator equal to the excess of passive investment income over 25 percent of gross receipts for the year, and a denominator equal to passive investment income for the year.[21] There is one final caveat: excess net passive income cannot exceed the corporation's taxable income for the year computed with the special changes described in Section 1374(d)(4).[22]

An example may help control the pollution. Assume that X Corporation made a Subchapter S election last year and will have accumulated earnings and profits from prior C corporation operations at the end of its current taxable year, in which X has $50,000 of income from its regular business operations and $35,000 of business deductions. X also receives $15,000 of interest income and $10,000 of dividends and incurs $5,000 of expenses directly related to the production of the investment income.

Is X subject to the Section 1375 tax? The corporation will have Subchapter C earnings and profits at the close of its taxable year and more than 25 percent of its gross receipts are passive investment income ($25,000 out of $75,000 of gross receipts), so the tax is potentially applicable. X's net passive income is $20,000 ($25,000 of passive investment income less directly connected expenses), and it will have $5,000 of excess net passive income ($20,000 of net passive income multiplied by a ratio having $6,250 as the numerator ($25,000 of passive investment income reduced by 25 percent of gross receipts) and $25,000 as the denominator (passive investment income)). Since excess net passive income does not exceed X's taxable

16. I.R.C. §§ 1375(b)(3); 1362(d)(3)(C)(i).

17. I.R.C. § 1362(d)(3)(C)(ii)–(iv).

18. I.R.C. §§ 1375(b)(3); 1362(d)(3)(B); 1222(9).

19. See Reg. § 1.1362–2(c)(4)(ii)(B)(3).

20. I.R.C. § 1375(b)(2).

21. I.R.C. § 1375(b)(1)(A).

22. I.R.C. § 1375(b)(1)(B).

income as determined under Section 1374(d)(4), the corporation's tax liability will be $1,750 ($5,000 × 35 percent).

Section 1375(d) offers one avenue for relief from the Section 1375 tax. The tax may be waived if the S corporation establishes to the satisfaction of the Service that it determined, in good faith, that it had no earnings and profits at the close of a taxable year and, within a reasonable period after discovering earnings and profits, they were distributed. The addition of an "anti-blunder" provision to this complex area is a welcome sign and one hopes the Service is merciful in its administration of Section 1375(d).

Congress also considered the interaction of Sections 1374 and 1375 with the provisions taxing the shareholders of an S corporation. Any Section 1374 tax is treated as a loss (characterized according to the built-in gain subject to tax) sustained by the S corporation which will pass through to the shareholders, and each item of passive investment income is reduced by its proportionate share of the Section 1375 tax.[23]

It is important to keep the application of Sections 1374 and 1375 in perspective. A new corporation making a Subchapter S election generally does not have to be concerned with either provision. Section 1374(c)(1) will protect the corporation from the Section 1374 tax and, since the corporation's activities will not generate earnings and profits,[24] Section 1375 cannot apply to the corporation. Therefore, Sections 1374 and 1375 normally will not play a role in deciding whether to utilize a partnership or an S corporation for a new venture.

Additional considerations come into play if a C corporation is considering a move to a single tax regime. An operating C corporation must consider the impact of Sections 1374 and 1375 on a possible Subchapter S election. Weighed against these penalty provisions is the fact that a shift from C corporation status to partnership status requires a liquidation of the corporation, which may result in significant current corporate and shareholder tax liability.[25] The immediate tax cost of moving to a partnership format may be significant enough to tip the balance in favor of a Subchapter S election and force an accommodation with Sections 1374 and 1375, if planning cannot successfully eliminate their impact.

PROBLEMS

1. Built-in Corporation ("B") was formed in 2000 as a C corporation. The shareholders of B elected S corporation status effective as of January 1, 2004, when it had no Subchapter C earnings and profits and the following assets:

Asset	Adj. Basis	F.M.V.
Land	$30,000	$20,000
Building	10,000	35,000
Machinery	15,000	30,000

23. I.R.C. § 1366(f)(2), (3).

24. I.R.C. § 1371(c)(1).

25. See I.R.C. §§ 331, 336, 1001.

For purposes of this problem, disregard any cost recovery deductions that may be available to B. Consider the shareholder and corporate level tax consequences of the following alternative transactions:

(a) B sells the building for $50,000 in 2005; its taxable income for 2005 if it were not an S corporation would be $75,000.

(b) Same as (a), above, except that B's taxable income for 2005 if it were not an S corporation would be $20,000.

(c) Same as (a), above, except that B also sells the machinery for $40,000 in 2006, when it would have substantial taxable income if it were not an S corporation.

(d) B trades the building for an apartment building in a tax-free § 1031 exchange and then sells the apartment building for $50,000 in 2005, when it would have substantial taxable income if it were not an S corporation.

(e) B sells the building for $90,000 in 2014.

2. S Corporation elected S corporation status beginning in 2010 and will have Subchapter C earnings and profits at the close of the current taxable year. This year, S expects that its business operations and investments will produce the following tax results:

Gross income from operations	$75,000
Business deductions	60,000
Tax-exempt interest	23,000
Dividends	12,000
Long-term capital gain from the sale of investment real property	35,000

(a) Is S Corporation subject to the § 1375 tax on passive investment income? If so, compute the amount of tax.

(b) Same as (a), above, except that S receives an additional $5,000 of tax-exempt interest.

3. The San Diego Bay Boat Storage and Marina Corporation ("Bay") was formed in 2009 as a C corporation and has substantial accumulated earnings and profits. Bay's business consists of three primary activities. About one-third of Bay's gross receipts are derived from marine service and repair work conducted by its two mechanics. Another one-third of Bay's total receipts come from the rental of berths to boat owners. Berthing fees vary depending upon the size of the particular boat. A boat owner renting a berth from Bay must pay a separate charge to have Bay's employees launch or haul out his boat. However, if given advance notice, Bay employees will fuel an owner's boat, charging only for the fuel. The remainder of bay's receipts come from dry storage of boats. Owners pay $200 per month for dry storage in Bay's warehouse where a Bay employee is on duty 24 hours a day. For this fee, Bay employees will launch, fuel (with a charge for fuel) and haul out the boat whenever requested by the owner. Bay's mechanics also will perform a free engine analysis every other year for owners of power boats in dry storage.

Bay is considering the possibility of making a Subchapter S election and has requested your advice concerning any problems which it may have. What difference would it make if Bay were a newly formed corporation?

G.   COORDINATION WITH SUBCHAPTER C

Code: §§ 1371; 1372.

It is important to remember that an S corporation is still a corporation for many tax purposes. It is organized in the same manner as other corporations, and it may engage in most of the transactions and experience the corporate adjustments encountered throughout this text. After incorporating or escaping from Subchapter C, S corporations may make nonliquidating distributions of property or stock, engage in redemptions, or acquire other businesses in either taxable or tax-free transactions. They may sell their assets and liquidate, be acquired by another corporation, or divide up into two or more separate corporations. The tax consequences of these and other events in an S corporation's life cycle are determined by a patchwork quilt of Code sections pieced together from Subchapters C and S. The resulting product provides a challenging opportunity to study the uneasy relationship between a double tax regime and a pass-through scheme.

Section 1371(a) begins the statutory snake dance with the deceptively simple general rule that the provisions of Subchapter C apply to an S corporation and its shareholders. This broad admonition is subject to two related exceptions. First, any provision in the Code specifically applicable to S corporations naturally will apply. Second, if the provisions of Subchapter C are "inconsistent with" Subchapter S, the S rules are controlling. Reliable authority is sparse on precisely how Congress intended to harmonize the rules, but the Service gradually has offered guidance. The details are best raised in the context of specific transactions.

Formation of a Corporation. All the basic rules studied in connection with the formation of a C corporation apply to newly formed S corporations.[1] Shareholders who comprise the founding 80 percent or more "control" group do not recognize gain or loss on the transfer of property to the corporation if the requirements of Section 351(a) are met, but realized gain is recognized to the extent the shareholder receives boot[2] or if the transferred liabilities exceed the shareholder's basis for the transferred property.[3] Shareholders determine their basis in stock, debt obligations and other boot received under Section 358. The corporation takes a transferred basis in any contributed assets under Section 362(a). Organizational expenditures may be deducted and amortized if the corporation elects to do so under Section 248, and the benefit of the deductions passes through to the shareholders.

---

1.   See generally Chapter 2, supra.   **3.**   I.R.C. § 357(c).
2.   I.R.C. § 351(b).

Several other formation issues, most relating to the "small business corporation requirements," are unique to S corporations. To qualify for the S election, the corporation must be mindful of the 100–shareholder limit and the prohibition against certain types of shareholders (e.g., nonresident aliens, partnerships). As for capital structure, an S corporation is limited to one class of stock and thus may not issue preferred stock, but it is free to issue debt, preferably in a form that qualifies for the straight debt safe harbor.[4] Unlike a corporation facing the double tax, an S corporation has no particular incentive to issue pro rata debt to its shareholders.[5]

S Corporations as Shareholders. At one time, an S corporation in its capacity as a shareholder of another corporation was treated as an individual for purposes of Subchapter C. The purpose of this rule was to ensure that an S corporation would not qualify for the Section 243 dividends received deduction, which is designed to prevent double taxation at the corporate level and thus should not be available to a pass-through entity.[6] As drafted, however, the rule had a ripple effect on other transactions, leading Congress to repeal it and clarify the tax consequences of many of the transactions discussed below. The legislative history includes a reminder that S corporations, like individuals, may not claim a dividends received deduction or treat any item of income or deduction in a manner inconsistent with the treatment accorded to individual taxpayers.[7]

Distributions and Liquidating Sales. As discussed earlier,[8] Subchapter S generally preempts Subchapter C in determining the tax consequences of nonliquidating distributions. Section 1368 specifically provides that it shall apply to any distribution to which Section 301(c) otherwise would apply. This means that Section 1368 is the reference point not only for routine nonliquidating distributions but also other transactions, such as dividend-equivalent redemptions and taxable stock distributions, which are classified under Subchapter C as distributions to which Section 301 applies.[9] We have seen that an S corporation recognizes gain under Section 311(b) on a distribution of appreciated property but, unless Section 1374 applies, that gain is not taxed at the corporate level. Instead, the gain passes through to the shareholders, who may increase their stock basis by their respective shares of the gain.

In the case of liquidating distributions and sales, Subchapter C reassumes center stage. Liquidating distributions generally trigger recognition of gain or loss to an S corporation under Section 336 in the same manner as if the corporation were subject to Subchapter C. Sales of assets pursuant to a plan of complete liquidation also are taxable. In either case, however,

---

4. I.R.C. § 1361(c)(5).

5. For the advantages and disadvantages of issuing debt in the S corporation setting, see Eustice & Kuntz, Federal Income Taxation of S Corporations ¶ 6.03[1].

6. See, e.g., S.Rep. No. 640, 97th Cong., 2d Sess. 15, reprinted in 1982–2 C.B. 718, 724–725.

7. See H.R. Rep. 104–737, 104th Cong., 2d Sess. 56 (1996).

8. See Section E of this chapter, supra.

9. See, e.g., I.R.C. §§ 302(d); 305(b). Section 306 is unlikely to apply in the S setting, however, because an S corporation may not issue preferred stock.

these gains will pass through to the shareholders and be subject to a single shareholder-level tax unless Section 1374 intercedes. An S corporation also may make a liquidating sale on the installment method. Under certain conditions, these installment obligations may be distributed without triggering corporate-level gain (unless Section 1374 applies), and the shareholders may use the installment method to report the gain.[10] The *character* of the shareholder's gain in this situation is not determined by reference to their stock, which ordinarily would be a capital asset, but rather "in accordance with the principles of Section 1366(d)"[11]—i.e., as if the corporate-level gain on the sale of the asset had been passed through to the shareholders.[12]

Subchapter C also governs the shareholder-level consequences of a complete liquidation. An S corporation shareholder treats distributions in complete liquidation as in full payment in exchange for the stock under Section 331. Although liquidating distributions and sales result in only one level of tax to an S corporation and its shareholders,[13] variations between the shareholder's stock basis and the corporation's basis in its assets may have an impact on the character of the shareholder's gain or loss. For example, assume A owns all of the stock of S, Inc. (an S corporation with no prior C history) and has a $2,000 basis in her S stock. Assume S owns one ordinary income asset which has a $10,000 fair market value and a $1,000 adjusted basis. If S sells the asset, it will recognize $9,000 of ordinary income. The gain passes through to A, and her stock basis is increased by $9,000, to $11,000, under Section 1367. When S liquidates and distributes $10,000 cash to A, she recognizes a $1,000 long-term capital loss. Alternatively, if the ordinary income asset had a $2,000 basis, S would recognize $8,000 of ordinary income on its sale which would pass through to A, increasing her stock basis to $10,000. When S liquidates and distributes $10,000 cash to A, she would recognize no additional gain or loss.

Taxable Acquisitions of S Corporations. An acquisition of an S corporation may be structured as either a purchase of stock from the shareholders or a purchase of assets from the corporation. The method chosen affects not only the amount, character and timing of gain but also may have an impact on the tax status of the S corporation and perhaps even the acquiring party if it also is an S corporation.

An asset acquisition often is preferable because the purchaser will obtain a cost basis in the S corporation's assets at the cost of only a

---

10. See I.R.C. § 453B(h). To qualify for corporate-level nonrecognition, the S corporation must distribute the obligation in complete liquidation. In addition, the obligations must result from sales of assets (other than nonbulk sales of inventory) during the 12-month period following the adoption of the liquidation plan. See I.R.C. § 453(h).

11. I.R.C. § 453B(h).

12. Thus, if the installment sale would have given rise to ordinary income, that character will pass through to the shareholders when they collect the installment obligations.

13. This is because the corporate-level gain on a liquidating distribution or sale results in upward basis adjustments to the shareholder's stock under Section 1367. A double tax would be imposed, however, if Section 1374 applies.

shareholder-level tax.[14] For example, assume P, Inc. wishes to acquire T, Inc. (an S corporation with no prior C history). If P purchases T's assets, any gain or loss recognized by T on the sale will pass through to its shareholders, and P will obtain a cost basis in the assets. T's shareholders will increase their stock basis by any gain recognized on the sale under Section 1367, thus avoiding a second tax on the same economic gain when T liquidates.

If P is a C corporation and purchases a controlling interest in the T stock, the T shareholders recognize gain or loss on the sale, and P takes a cost basis in the stock it acquires. T's S election will terminate, however, because an S corporation may not have any C corporation shareholders.[15] If P does not make a Section 338 election, T retains its historic bases in its assets, and as a new C corporation it will face the prospect of a corporate-level tax on any built-in gain. If P makes a Section 338 election to obtain a cost basis in T's assets, T—which loses its S status on the acquisition—must pay a corporate-level tax as a result of the deemed asset sale.[16] If P and T make a joint Section 338(h)(10) election, the regulations provide that old T (still considered an S corporation at this point) recognizes gain or loss on the deemed sale of its assets and then is deemed to have distributed those assets in complete liquidation. The gain or loss on the deemed asset sale passes through to T's shareholders, with resulting basis adjustments to their T stock. Those adjustments then may be taken into account in determining the shareholders' gain or loss under Section 331 on the deemed complete liquidation of old T.[17]

Taxable Acquisitions by S Corporations. When the purchasing corporation ("P") is an S corporation, the primary concern usually is the preservation of P's S status. If P purchases the assets of T, the mix of consideration used in the transaction must be tailored to the S corporation eligibility requirements. P thus should avoid using its own stock or hybrid debt in order to avoid running afoul of the 100–shareholder limit or the prohibition against having more than one class of stock.[18]

When an S corporation acquires the stock of T, the acquisition will not necessarily result in a loss of the acquiring corporation's S status because S corporations may have controlled C corporation subsidiaries. In addition, an acquiring S corporation is eligible to make a Section 338 election, which

14. Once again, this assumes that the corporation has no built-in gains that would be taxed under Section 1374. In contrast, an acquisition of assets from a C corporation generates tax at both the corporate and shareholder levels if the target liquidates. See Chapter 8B, supra.

15. I.R.C. §§ 1362(d)(2); 1361(b)(1)(B). After 1996, two or more S corporations may have a parent-subsidiary relationship in which case they are treated as one S corporation for tax purposes. I.R.C. § 1361(b)(3).

16. T's S election terminates when P acquires T's stock, and its short C year includes the day of the terminating event. Thus, the gain on the deemed asset sale must be reported on a one-day return for old T's "short C year." See I.R.C. §§ 1362(e)(1)(B); 338(a)(1). The economic burden of the corporate-level tax is borne by P unless it is reflected in the price paid for the stock.

17. See Reg. § 1.338(h)(10)–1(d)(3)(i), –1(d)(4)(i).

18. See generally I.R.C. § 1361(b).

will trigger immediate recognition of all T's gains and losses. Finally, if an S corporation acquires 80 percent or more of T's stock and liquidates T, the liquidation will be tax free to both corporations under Sections 332 and 337. Following that liquidation, however, any of T's built-in gains while it was a C corporation may later be subject to tax under Section 1374 upon a subsequent disposition.[19]

Tax–Free Reorganizations. An S corporation may be either the target or the acquiring corporation in a tax-free acquisitive reorganization. Looking first to situations where an S corporation is the target, it will lose its S status if it remains in existence as an 80 percent or more subsidiary following a tax-free acquisition of its stock by a C corporation in a Type B reorganization or reverse triangular merger. If an S corporation-target's assets are acquired in a merger or Type C reorganization, the transaction may proceed on a tax-free basis, and the target will terminate its existence as a result of the merger or the liquidation that necessary must follow a Type C reorganization.

If an S corporation is the acquiring corporation in a tax-free reorganization, it necessarily must issue new stock to the target shareholders. Whatever form of acquisition is used, care must be exercised to avoid termination of the election by exceeding the 100–shareholder limit or inheriting an ineligible shareholder. Now that S corporations may have subsidiaries, a Type B stock-for-stock acquisition, once impossible without losing S status, is now a feasible alternative. Similarly, acquisition of the assets of a C corporation in a Type A or C reorganization should not adversely affect the acquirer's S election, but the earnings and profits from the target's C years could jeopardize the acquiring corporation's S status or subject it to the Section 1375 tax if it has substantial passive investment income.[20] Moreover, an S corporation that is the acquiring corporation in a Type A or C reorganization or a forward triangular merger will inherit the target's tax attributes, including its earnings and profits, under Section 381, and its accumulated adjustments account if the target is an S corporation with a prior C history.[21] Finally, any assets acquired from a C corporation in a tax-free reorganization trigger a new ten-year recognition period for purposes of the Section 1374 tax on built-in gains.[22]

Corporate Divisions. An S corporation may divide itself into separate corporations in a transaction that is tax-free at both the corporate and shareholder levels if all the requirements of Section 355 are met. Even when S corporations were not permitted to have subsidiaries, the Service was tolerant in this area, ignoring the transitory nature of a subsidiary formed in preparation for a division.[23] After the division, the new corpora-

---

19. As to built-in gains, see I.R.C. § 1374(d)(8); Reg. § 1.1374–8.

20. I.R.C. § 1362(b)(3); 1375.

21. For rules on AAA carryovers, see Reg. § 1.1368–2(d)(2).

22. I.R.C. § 1374(d)(8).

23. See, e.g., G.C.M. 39678 (1987).

tion (or corporations, in the case of a split-up) may immediately make an S election.[24]

PROBLEMS

1. Hi–Flying Co. is an aggressive growth company which was formed as a C corporation many years ago to develop new innovative technology. Hi–Flying has been successful and expects to receive inquiries concerning possible taxable and tax-free takeovers in the next few years. Can Hi–Flying's shareholders improve their tax situation in a future takeover by making an S election? In general, if Hi–Flying makes an S election, would you advise a potential corporate purchaser desiring a cost basis in Hi–Flying's assets to structure its acquisition as a purchase of stock or assets?

2. Target Corporation ("T") is a C corporation which has substantially appreciated assets and is a takeover candidate being pursued by several suitors. Purchasing Corporation ("P") has a Subchapter S election in effect and is considering making a bid for T. Consider the tax consequences of the following acquisition offers by P:

(a) P will offer to purchase T's stock for cash or a combination of cash and P notes.

(b) P will acquire T in a Type C reorganization.

H.   COMPENSATION ISSUES

S corporation shareholders commonly serve as officers, directors and employees of their corporation. Individuals with this multiple status may have a choice as to whether to withdraw cash as compensation or as a shareholder distribution. Payments of salary are deductible by the corporation as a business expense (with the benefit of the deduction passing through to the shareholders), and are includible in the employee's gross income. Employee wages also are subject to various federal and state employment taxes imposed on both the employer and the employee (e.g., federal social security and Medicare taxes).[1] Distributions, by contrast, generally may be received tax-free by shareholders to the extent of their stock basis, but they do not give rise to a deduction at the corporate level.

Because the payment of salaries to shareholders usually results in a tax "wash" in the case of a profitable corporation (the compensation deduction reduces the operating income that passes through to the shareholders), the

---

24. For other issues, such as how to divide up the accumulated adjustments account, see Eustice & Kuntz, supra note 5, at ¶ 12.10.

1. In general, both the employer and employee must pay social security tax of 6.2 percent on the employee's wages up to the applicable wage base (indexed annually). For 2011 and 2012 the employee's rate was reduced to 4.2 percent. I.R.C. §§ 3101; 3111; 3121. An additional Medicare tax of 1.45 percent, payable by both the employer and employee, is imposed on all of an employee's wages. I.R.C. § 3121(b).

income tax consequences of salaries and distributions may be identical.[2] The escalating employment tax base has influenced many S corporation shareholders who are also service providers to avoid this additional federal levy by foregoing salaries in lieu of larger shareholder distributions. This strategy became known as the "John Edwards loophole" after it was revealed during the 2004 Presidential election campaign that Vice Presidential candidate and former Senator John Edwards had conducted his lucrative law practice as an S corporation. In 1996, the S corporation paid Mr. Edwards $600,000 in wages, and the remaining $5 million of net profits from the law practice was treated as net income from the S corporation and thus not subject to the 2.9 percent Medicare tax, saving him $145,000. The *Radtke* case, below, is one court's hostile reaction to this maneuver.

Joseph Radtke, S.C. v. United States

United States District Court, Eastern District of Wisconsin, 1989.
712 F.Supp. 143, affirmed 895 F.2d 1196 (7th Cir.1990).

ORDER

■ Terence T. Evans, District Judge.

* * *

FACTS

None of the facts are disputed.

Joseph Radtke received his law degree from Marquette University in 1978. The Radtke corporation was incorporated in 1979 to provide legal services in Milwaukee. Mr. Radtke is the firm's sole incorporator, director, and shareholder. In 1982, he also served as the unpaid president and treasurer of the corporation, while his wife Joyce was the unpaid and nominal vice-president and secretary. The corporation is an electing small business corporation, otherwise known as a subchapter S corporation. This means that it is not taxed at the corporate level. All corporate income is taxed to the shareholder, whether or not the income is distributed.

In 1982, Mr. Radtke was the only full-time employee of the corporation, though it employed a few other persons on a piece-meal and part-time basis. Under an employment contract executed between Mr. Radtke and his corporation in 1980, he received "an annual base salary, to be determined by its board of directors, but in no event shall such annual salary be less than $0 per year * * *. Employee's original annual base salary shall be $0." This base salary of $0 continued through 1982, a year in which Mr. Radtke devoted all of his working time to representing the corporation's clients.

2. The tax results are more complex, however, if the S corporation has losses for the taxable year. See Eustice & Kuntz, Federal Income Taxation of S Corporations ¶ 11.02[2].

Mr. Radtke received $18,225 in dividends from the corporation in 1982. Whenever he needed money, and whenever the corporation was showing a profit—that is, when there was money in its bank account—he would do what was necessary under Wisconsin corporate law to have the board declare a dividend, and he would write a corporate check to himself.

Mr. Radtke paid personal income tax on the dividends in 1982. The Radtke corporation also declared the $18,225 on its form 1120S, the small business corporation income tax return. But the corporation did not file a federal employment tax form (Form 941) or a federal unemployment tax form (Form 940). In other words, it did not deduct a portion of the $18,225 for Social Security (FICA) and unemployment compensation (FUTA). The IRS subsequently assessed deficiencies as well as interest and penalties. The Radtke corporation paid the full amount that IRS demanded under FUTA—$366.44—and it also paid $593.75 toward the assessed FICA taxes, interest, and penalties. Then the corporation sued here after a fruitless claim for refunds.

DISCUSSION

* * *

The Radtke corporation acknowledges that wages are subject to FICA and FUTA taxes, but it argues that the Internal Revenue Code nowhere treats a shareholder-employee's dividends as wages for the purpose of employment taxes. The government, on the other hand, contends that "since Joseph Radtke performed substantial services for Joseph Radtke, S.C., and did not receive reasonable compensation for such services other than 'dividends', the 'dividends' constitute 'wages' subject to federal employment taxes." The government does not allege that the Radtke corporation is a fiction that somehow failed to comply with Wisconsin statutes governing corporations.

The Federal Insurance Contributions Act defines "wages" as "all remuneration for employment," with various exceptions that are not relevant to this dispute. 26 U.S.C. § 3121(a). Similarly, the Federal Unemployment Tax Act defines "wages" as "all remuneration for employment," with certain exceptions that are not relevant. 26 U.S.C. § 3306(b). (Dividends are not specifically excepted in either act, and "remuneration" is not defined.) Mr. Radtke was clearly an "employee" of the Radtke corporation, as the plaintiff concedes. *See* 26 U.S.C. §§ 3121(d) and 3306(i). Likewise, his work for the enterprise was obviously "employment." *See* 26 U.S.C. §§ 3121(b) and 3306(c).

According to the Radtke corporation, not all "income" can be characterized as "wages." I agree. See Royster Company v. United States, 479 F.2d 387, 390 (4th Cir.1973) (free lunches did not constitute "wages" subject to FICA and FUTA); Central Illinois Public Service Co. v. United States, 435 U.S. 21, 25, 98 S.Ct. 917, 919, 55 L.Ed.2d 82 (1978) (reimbursement for lunches not "wages" subject to withholding tax; Court says in dicta that dividends are not wages).

At the same time, however, I am not moved by the Radtke corporation's connected argument that "dividends" cannot be "wages." Courts reviewing tax questions are obligated to look at the substance, not the form, of the transactions at issue. Transactions between a closely held corporation and its principals, who may have multiple relationships with the corporation, are subject to particularly careful scrutiny. Whether dividends represent a distribution of profits or instead are compensation for employment is a matter to be determined in view of all the evidence.

In the circumstances of this case—where the corporation's only director had the corporation pay himself, the only significant employee, *no* salary for substantial services—I believe that Mr. Radtke's "dividends" were in fact "wages" subject to FICA and FUTA taxation. His "dividends" functioned as remuneration for employment.

It seems only logical that a corporation is required to pay employment taxes when it employs an employee. See Automated Typesetting, Inc. v. United States, 527 F.Supp. 515, 519 (E.D.Wis.1981) (corporation liable for employment taxes on payments to officers who performed more than nominal services for corporation); C.D. Ulrich, Ltd. v. United States, 692 F.Supp. 1053, 1055 (D.Minn.1988) (discussing case law defining who is an "employee"; court refuses to enjoin IRS from collecting employment taxes from S corporation that paid dividends but no salary to sole shareholder and director, a certified public accountant who worked for the firm). See also Rev.Rul. 73–361, 1973–2 C.B. 331 (stockholder-officer who performed substantial services for S corporation is "employee," and his salary is subject to FICA and FUTA tax); Rev.Rul. 71–86, 1971–1 C.B. 285 (president and sole stockholder of corporation is "employee" whose salary is subject to employment taxes, even though he alone fixes his salary and determines his duties).

An employer should not be permitted to evade FICA and FUTA by characterizing *all* of an employee's remuneration as something other than "wages." Cf. Greenlee v. United States, 87–1 U.S.T.C. Para. 9306 (corporation's interest-free loans to sole shareholder constituted "wages" for FICA and FUTA where loans were made at shareholder's discretion and he performed substantial services for corporation). This is simply the flip side of those instances in which corporations attempt to disguise profit distributions as salaries for whatever tax benefits that may produce. See, e.g., Miles–Conley Co. v. Commissioner, 173 F.2d 958, 960–61 (4th Cir.1949) (corporation could not deduct from its gross income excessive salary paid to president and sole stockholder).

Accordingly, the plaintiff's motion for summary judgment is DENIED, and the defendant's motion for summary judgment is GRANTED. The plaintiff is ORDERED to pay the remaining deficiency on its 1982 FICA taxes along with the assessed interest, penalties, and fees.

NOTE

Subsequent Developments. In accord with *Radtke* are Fred R. Esser, P.C. v. United States,[1] Dunn & Clark, P.A. v. Commissioner,[2] Spicer Accounting Inc. v. United States,[3] Veterinary Surgical Consultants, P.C. v. Commissioner,[4] and David E. Watson, P.C. v. United States.[5] A contrary result was reached in Davis v. United States,[6] where the court declined to recharacterize S corporation distributions as taxable wages. *Davis* is distinguishable, however, because the shareholders performed only minor services on behalf of the S corporation. Legislative attacks on the strategy employed in *Radtke* have not been able to pass in Congress.

Medicare Tax Increases. Beginning in 2013, an additional 0.9 percent Medicare tax is imposed on combined wages and self-employment income in excess of $250,000 for married filing jointly taxpayers ($125,000 for married filing separately) and $200,000 for single taxpayers.[7] As a result, the Medicare tax rate for these "high-income" taxpayers, including employee-shareholders of S corporations, increases from 2.9 to 3.8 percent for amounts over the thresholds. Also beginning in 2013, a 3.8 percent unearned income Medicare contributions tax is imposed on the lesser of a taxpayer's "net investment income" or adjusted gross income (with some modifications not material to our coverage) in excess of the same high-income thresholds.[8] "Net investment income" consists generally of interest, dividends, annuities, royalties, and income from trades or businesses that are Section 469 passive activities with respect to the taxpayer and from certain financial instrument and commodity trading activities[9] but does not include income derived from an active trade or business conducted by a sole proprietor, partnership or S corporation.[10] These new taxes may provide an additional incentive for high-income service providers to conduct their business through an S corporation.

Fringe Benefits. Fringe benefits paid by an S corporation to its shareholder-employees also are subject to special treatment. Section 1372 provides that an S corporation shall be treated as a partnership for purposes of employee fringe benefits, and any shareholder owning either more than two percent of the corporation's outstanding stock or more than two percent of the total voting power of all stock will be treated as a partner. As a result, an S corporation seldom can provide benefits, such as a medical reimbursement plan or group-term life insurance, which are deductible by the corporation and excludable from gross income of its shareholder-employees.[11]

1.   750 F.Supp. 421 (D.Ariz.1990).

2.   57 F.3d 1076 (9th Cir.1995).

3.   918 F.2d 90 (9th Cir.1990).

4.   117 T.C. 141 (2001).

5.   757 F.Supp.2d 877 (S.D. Iowa 2010), aff'd, 668 F.3d 1008 (8th Cir. 2012).

6.   74 AFTR 2d 5618 (D.Colo.1994).

7.   I.R.C. § 3101(b)(2).

8.   I.R.C. § 1411.

9.   I.R.C. § 1411(c)(1) & (2).

10.   I.R.C. § 1411(c)(4) & (5).

11.   For special rules relating to health insurance, see I.R.C. § 162(*l*)(1), (5), and Rev. Rul. 91–26, 1991–1 C.B. 184.

I.   Tax Policy Issues: Subchapter K vs. Subchapter S*

The check-the-box elective classification regime discussed in Chapter 1 has made it easier for virtually any closely held business to obtain pass-through taxation treatment. This has resurrected the longstanding debate on the most desirable structure for a pass-through system. The excerpt below, from a study by the Joint Committee on Taxation, compares the tax treatment of partnerships and S corporations and surveys the competing views on the need to retain two different pass-through regimes.

Excerpt From Review of Selected Entity Classification and Partnership Tax Issues

Staff of Joint Committee on Taxation (JCS–6–97) 23–25 (April 8, 1997).

Need for multiple sets of rules for pass-through entities

[The issuance of final check-the-box classification regulations raises a set of issues regarding] whether there is a continuing need in the tax law for parallel pass-through systems for general business activities.[42] Although S corporations (and their shareholders) generally are treated similarly to partnerships (and their partners), significant differences exist, some of which favor S corporations while others favor partnerships.

For example, the items of income, gain, loss, deduction or credit of a partnership generally are taken into account by a partner pursuant to the partnership agreement (or in accordance with the partners' interest in the partnership if the agreement does not provide for an allocation) so long as such allocation has substantial economic effect.[43] Because of the one-class-of-stock rule for S corporations (sec. 1361(b)(1)(D)), the items of income, gain, loss, deduction or credit of an S corporation cannot be separately allocated to a particular shareholder, but are taken into account by all the shareholders on a per-share, per-day basis. Thus, partnerships generally are considered to be a more flexible vehicle for purposes of allocating particular entity-level items to investors.

Another important difference making partnerships more flexible than S corporations is the treatment of entity-level debt, for purposes of the owner's basis in his interest. A partner includes partnership-level debt in the basis of his interest (sec. 752), whereas an S corporation shareholder

---

* See generally Eustice, "Subchapter S Corporations and Partnerships: A Search for the Pass Through Paradigm (Some Preliminary Proposals)," 39 Tax L.Rev. 345 (1984); Schwidetzky, "Integrating Subchapters K and S—Just Do It," 62 Tax Lawyer 749 (2009).

42. Eliminating the two-tier corporate tax system, perhaps through some form of corporate integration, could also minimize the need for multiple sets of rules for pass-through entities, but is beyond the scope of this discussion.

43. Sections 704(a) and (b). The determination of whether an allocation has substantial economic effect is complex (Treas. Reg. sec. 1.704–1(b)(2)).

does not (sec. 1367). The amount of the partner's or S corporation shareholder's basis in his interest serves as a limit on the amount of losses that can be passed through (secs. 704(d), 1366(d)), which makes increases in basis for entity-level debt important.

The sale of stock in an S corporation generally results in capital gain or loss to the selling shareholder. The sale of an interest in a partnership also generally gives rise to capital gain or loss, but gives rise to ordinary income to the selling partner to the extent attributable to unrealized receivables and certain inventory items (sec. 751).

The distribution of appreciated property by an S corporation to a shareholder (as a dividend, in redemption of shares, or in liquidation) is treated as a taxable sale of such property. Any gain is allocated to all the shareholders on a per-share, per day basis and increases the shareholder's adjusted bases in their shares. The distributee shareholder then reduces his basis by the amount of the distribution (i.e., fair market value of the distributed property) and takes a fair market value basis in the property. By contrast, the distribution of appreciated property by a partnership to a partner generally is not treated as a taxable sale of the property (sec. 731).

An existing C corporation may elect to be treated as an S corporation on a tax-free basis, subject to certain special rules. Converting C corporations are subject to corporate-level tax on the recapture of LIFO benefits,[44] on certain built-in gains recognized within a 10–year period after conversion,[45] and on certain passive investment income earned while the corporation retains its former C corporate earnings and profits.[46] The conversion of a C corporation to a partnership (or sole proprietorship) is treated as a liquidation of the entity, taxable to both the corporation and its shareholders.

The rules of subchapter C generally apply to an S corporation and its shareholders. Thus, for example, an S corporation may merge into a C corporation (or vice versa) on a tax-free basis. Similar rules do not apply to combinations of C corporations and partnerships.

Individual partners treated as general partners generally are subject to self-employment tax on their distributive shares of partnership income. Shareholders of an S corporation are not subject to self-employment tax on

---

44. Sec. 1363(d).

45. Section 1374. For a discussion of how section 1374 allows the conversion of a C corporation to S corporation to be treated more favorably than the liquidation of a C corporation into a sole proprietorship or a partnership, despite the economic equivalence of the transactions, see, letter to Chairman Dan Rostenkowski from Ronald A. Pearlman, Chief of Staff of the Joint Committee on Taxation, recommending several simplification proposals, reprinted in Committee on Ways and Means, Written Proposals on Tax Simplification (WMCP 101–27), May 25,

1990, p. 24. In his 1995 and 1997 budget messages to the Congress, President Clinton recommended that section 1374 be repealed for C corporations above a certain size. [Later proposals made by the Clinton administration would have repealed Section 1374 for C-to-S conversions of corporations with a value of more than $5 million at the time of conversion and treated the transaction as a taxable liquidation of the C corporation followed by a contribution of the assets to an S corporation by the recipient shareholders. Ed.]

46. Section 1375.

S corporation earnings, but are subject to payroll tax to the extent they receive salaries or wages from the corporation.

Partnerships, LLCs treated as partnerships, and S corporations may be treated differently for State income or franchise tax purposes.

Continuing utility of S corporations

If an LLC can provide limited liability to all owners and achieve pass-through status as a partnership under the check-the-box regulations (or under the Service's prior revenue rulings on LLCs), the need for S corporations could be questioned. Particularly in light of the growing use of LLCs, it could be argued that the great flexibility of the partnership tax rules outweigh the principal advantage of S corporations: relative simplicity. Thus, it is argued that the rules for S corporations could be repealed without detriment to taxpayers.[47]

Others say the continued existence of subchapter S is worthwhile. A corporate charter is a prerequisite imposed by regulators for some trades or businesses (e.g., for depository institutions or to hold certain licenses), and LLCs may not meet such regulatory requirements. Moreover, the corporate form is a familiar, time-tested format, while the LLC form is new and unfamiliar (particularly where a business undertakes interstate commerce). Subchapter S supporters further point out that the rules of subchapter S are much simpler than the rules of subchapter K.[48] Others point to specific advantages of subchapter S over the partnership tax rules (primarily the ability to convert from C to S corporation status generally without current corporate tax on appreciation, and the availability of tax-free reorganization rules for business combinations and reorganizations). At least until LLC interests are as easily issued in capital markets as traditional corporate stock, the S corporation may continue to be an attractive vehicle in which to start a business, if it is anticipated that it will later go public. Finally, any repeal of subchapter S would require rules providing for the treatment of existing S corporations.[49]

Whether or not it is advisable to retain both the partnership rules and the S corporation rules, some argue that the complexity of either regime is excessive for small businesses, and a new, much simpler pass-through system should be provided for small businesses that would be consistent with the new simplicity for choice of entity under the check-the-box

47. W. Schwidetzky, "Is It Time to Give the S Corporation a Proper Burial?" 15 Virginia Tax Review 591 (1996).

48. However, it must be pointed out that partners of a partnership may opt for a simple, subchapter-S like structure if they so desire. It could be said that the check-the-box regulations expand the appeal of subchapter S, because prior to those regulations, only entities structured as corporations for State law purposes could elect S corporation status, whereas now, a State-law partnership or LLC

can be classified as a corporation for tax purposes and elect S status (provided applicable requirements are met).

49. See, for example, the letter of July 25, 1995, from Leslie B. Samuels, Assistant Treasury Secretary (Tax Policy) to Senator Orin Hatch, suggesting possible legislative proposals to allow S corporations to elect partnership status or to apply the check-the-box regulations to S corporations.

regulations.[50] A significant question, under such an approach, is the definition of a small business, which could depend on the number of owners, the value of the entity's assets, the amount of its gross or net income (if any), or some combination of these or other factors. Related questions involve the treatment of businesses that grow (or fluctuate in size), crossing the definitional line, and the treatment of tax attributes imported from a more complex tax regime. Weighing of simplicity against accuracy of income measurement and allocation would be a factor in designing a simpler regime.

Others would argue that there is nothing inherently complex in the application of the partnership tax rules to most small business transactions. Small businesses today can achieve the effect of a simplified partnership regime for most common business arrangements. Mandating the use of specific rules for small business would deny them the flexibility of present law partnership rules and, it could be argued, would represent a competitive disadvantage relative to larger businesses.

---

50. American Law Institute, Federal Income Tax Project—Taxation of Pass–Through Entities, Memorandum No. 2 96–105 (Sept. 2, 1996) (G. Yin and D. Shakow, reporters).

INDEX

References are to Pages